INTRODUCTION TO LAW IN CANADA

Ontario Edition
(As of Fall 2011)

INTRODUCTION TO LAW
IN CANADA

Laurence M. Olivo
B.A., M.A., LL.B of the Ontario Bar

Captus Press

INTRODUCTION TO LAW IN CANADA
Laurence M. Olivo

ISBN 978-1-55322-246-0

The publisher and the editor gratefully acknowledge the authors, publishers and organizations for their permission to reproduce their work in this book. Care has been taken to trace ownership of copyright material contained in this book. The publisher will gladly take any information that will enable the rectification of any reference or credit in subsequent editions and apologizes for any errors or omissions.

Captus Press Inc.
Mail: Units 14 & 15
       1600 Steeles Avenue West
       Concord, Ontario
       Canada L4K 4M2
Telephone: (416) 736–5537
Fax: (416) 736–5793
Email: info@captus.com
Internet: http://www.captus.com

Canada We acknowledge the financial support of the Government of Canada through the Book Publishing Industry Development Program (BPIDP) for our publishing activities.

0 9 8 7 6 5 4 3 2 1
Printed in Canada

Contents

Preface

In 1994, after a variety of experiments, I realized that if I was going to meet the needs of my college students for introductory legal materials, I was going to have to dragoon my colleagues to join me in writing the necessary text material. That effort produced our first 5-module edition. Since then, the number and variety of college programs across Canada have increased, as has the demand for a text that presents legal subject matter on a variety of topics that are informative and interesting. We have responded to this challenge over the years by constantly updating and improving modules, and adding modules on a variety of subjects, including some that are quite specialized.

This new edition continues and builds on our previous efforts. Existing modules have been updated with additional review questions, references, and websites. New ones have been added — environmental law, the law of sport, and intellectual property, are but some examples. We have also added a variety of province specific versions of some modules.

Once again, I wish to thank all of our authors, some of whom have been with us for over a decade and some of whom are joining us for the first time, for promptly getting their material to us. Getting a new edition out is always a challenge, and as always, Pauline Lai and her crew at Captus met the challenge — making order out of chaos and producing as usual, a high quality text, on time.

L.M. Olivo
Toronto, Ontario
August 2008

Introduction to Legal Studies —Law as a Concept and System

Laurence M. Olivo
SENECA COLLEGE

Learning Objectives

After reading this chapter, the reader should be able to:

➢ appreciate that law is more than simply a set of rules
➢ understand that law is a flexible concept that varies in accordance with the social needs it must meet
➢ understand the various explanations about why we obey rules
➢ understand the limits of law
➢ understand the arguments in favour of different schools of legal interpretation
➢ understand the dynamics of the relationship between law and morality
➢ understand issues involving law and social change
➢ understand the societal functions performed by a legal system
➢ identify the characteristics of a valid legal system in a democratic society

TABLE OF CONTENTS

INTRODUCTION

In this chapter, we will first discuss the concept of law in general, and then examine it as a component of a democratic society. While there are certain basic elements that are common to all legal systems, we will see that there are a number of perennial, "open" questions about law to which there is no one "right" answer on which everyone can or does agree. Instead we will see that the answers to questions about law depend in part on the nature of a particular society, and in part on the values and expectations of members of that society. We will see that there are various reasons given for why we obey laws, how we should interpret them, whether they should reflect morality and what the limits of law are. We won't necessarily tell you the "right" answer because there is not necessarily a right answer to all of these questions. There is often simply a range of answers that depend on legitimate, but different, points of view. We hope you will gain an appreciation for the complexity and flexibility of law as a concept and as a system and you will feel that you are equipped to intelligently weigh and judge competing points of view. This is not simply an abstract, academic exercise — in a democratic society it is a necessary one. As a responsible citizen, you have to consider points of view, examine your own values and assumptions, analyze, and decide. We hope that this chapter will help you to do that and help you to appreciate the social context that lies behind the specific areas of law that are discussed in subsequent chapters of this text.

THE CONCEPT OF LAW

What Is Law?

Consider the various definitions of law set out in Exhibit 1.1.

These definitions of law are not all the same; some leave out aspects that seem to be important in others. The first definition focuses on law as having a function of regulating behaviour, and instilling tolerance and forbearance. It says nothing about where law comes from, or about what happens if you do

---

EXHIBIT 1.1

Definitions of Law

"[A] set of rules that enable people to live together and respect each other's rights."[1]

"[A] body of rules for the guidance of human conduct which are imposed upon and enforced among the members of a given state."[2]

"[A] statement of circumstances in which the public force will be brought to bear through the courts"[3]

"That which is laid down, ordained or established."[4]

Notes
1. Statement by Irwin Dorfman, President, Canadian Bar Association, 1975, cited in John A. Willes, *Contemporary Canadian Business Law*, 4th ed. (Toronto: McGraw-Hill Ryerson, 1994) at 3.
2. William Blackstone, *Commentaries on the Laws of England*, cited in Willes, *ibid.* at 3.
3. Oliver Wendell Holmes, cited in Willes, *supra* note 1, at 3.
4. *Black's Law Dictionary*, Revised 4th ed. (St. Paul, MN: West Publishing Company, 1968).

not obey it. The second definition also refers to ordering behaviour but introduces the further idea of legal rules as being imposed externally, applying within a state and being enforced if disobeyed. The third definition merely says that in some situations, you will be compelled by state force to obey the law, but the definition does not identify the situations in which obedience will be compelled. The fourth definition also focuses on regulating and ordering behaviour, and again talks about imposing rules externally and enforcing them against those who disobey.

Several themes emerge:

- Laws are rules imposed on us by an external body.
- Laws enable us to live together by controlling conflict.
- Laws teach us to tolerate and respect others (and perhaps the rules themselves — telling us what is "right" or "moral").
- Laws compel us to behave in certain ways because sanctions are applied if we behave improperly.
- Laws indicate when the force of the state will be used to compel you to behave in certain ways.

While these definitions help us to define what law is as a social structure, they leave us with a variety of questions about law and how it functions. The answers to these questions, as we will see, depend in part on the political, philosophical, religious and social views of the individuals asking the questions.

What Is a Legal Rule?

It should be clear from the definitions at the head of this section that not all rules are legal rules. So, how do we distinguish legal from non-legal rules? Consider the following rules of conduct:

- If someone opens a door for you, you say, "Thank you."
- You may not kill another person.

If someone opens a door for you and you walk through it and say nothing, you have broken a rule by being rude, but all would recognize that the rule you have violated is a social **norm**, based on a social value (courteousness). People may avoid you or shun you or say unpleasant things about you because your behaviour is unpleasant to them. But no one will arrest you, find you guilty of an offence, or bring down state-supported sanctions on you. If you kill another person, however, you may also be violating a norm based on the high value placed on human life, but all would recognize that the negative reactions would include detention, a formal determination that a legal rule had been broken, followed by legal punishment.

What makes some societal rules "legal" rules and others not? The short answer is that we can identify legal rules because they have certain features other rules do not: they are backed or enforced by the authority and power of the state. But why are some rules singled out for this kind of treatment and not others? Legal rules are those that are deemed to be very important in preventing a society from becoming dysfunctional and breaking down into anarchy and chaos. In most societies legal rules help to create order and certainty and control the use of force and fraud by individuals to get what they want. For example, most societies will have rules about ownership of property, exchange of property rights, and methods to resolve conflicts and disputes. These rules are so central that all in a society must agree to be bound by them and accept the consequences of not obeying those rules.

How Do Individuals Recognize Some Rules as "Legal" Rules?

In every society, there are clues or indicators to tell members of the society that some rules are legal and must be obeyed. One commentator refers to such clues or indicators as the "rule of recognition",[1] and they will vary from society to society. In traditional societies the rule of recognition will often involve magic, either alone or mixed with religion, to identify certain basic rules. Supernatural origins for rules go a long way towards getting people's attention.

Consider the Ten Commandments. These are 10 basic rules to govern a simple, tribal society. To get everyone's attention, they are revealed by Moses, a recognized leader, in a dramatic way as a revelation directly from God. It must have been quite clear to all but the most dense that these rules were a serious business; this was not just risking others' displeasure for not holding open a door. Look at the nature of the rules: they are not trivial — honouring parents and the deity, no murdering, no stealing, no lying, and so on.

In our society, appeals to magic or the supernatural are not entirely absent. Consider the formal court procedures, the judges' robes, and the ritual recitation for the opening of courts calling upon the deity to protect the sovereign, and the use of oaths to ensure that witnesses tell the truth.

In Canada, we have a variety of rules of recognition, based on our political and social values. We recognize sanctions for rule breaking backed by the force of the state as identifying legal rules, and we recognize certain acts — the passage of rules by a legislature, or the pronouncements of judges — as ways of creating legal rules. We also have some rules about rule making and enforcement — constitutional law — that define valid law and valid legal procedure and tell us whether a rule is a valid legal rule or something else.

Why Do We Obey Legal Rules?

The first reaction of many would be to say that we obey because we fear we will be punished if we do not. While this is probably true in part, it is not a wholly satisfactory explanation. If fear of punishment were the only reason for obedience, we would need to have, as one English Court of Appeal Judge said, "a policeman at everyone's elbow". But clearly, most of us obey most legal rules most of the time, even when the threat of enforcement is not immediate. Most people do not use force and fraud to get their way. Why is this?

There are a number of reasons: one legal commentator, H.L.A. Hart, has said that we obey in part because we have "a habit of obedience".[2] What Hart means here is that through a **socialization** process we learn and internalize norms and values that help us to recognize legal institutions, laws and the requirement of obeying them. Think of how children are socialized in our society. From birth, children are taught to follow rules; schools and other institutions further enforce this. Often, we discover there are negative and unpleasant consequences for not following rules. A desire to be accepted, "to fit in", may also contribute to following rules. So may the fact that there are positive benefits for those who obey.

While Hart's approach explains *how* people learn to obey, it does not explain their motivation for doing so. Explaining motivation requires an examination of human nature. There are two generally competing views on the relationship between human nature and obedience to law. They are associated

---

[1] H.L.A. Hart, *The Concept of Law* (Oxford: Clarendon Press, 1961) chs. 1 and 2.
[2] *Ibid.*

with two English political writers. The more pessimistic view of human nature is that of the 16th-century clergyman and academic, Thomas Hobbes. The more optimistic view is that of the 17th-century writer, John Locke.

The Hobbesian View of Human Nature

Hobbes sees human beings as selfish, violent, and predisposed to use force and fraud to get what they want.[3] The society in which they lived was anarchic, where life was, as Hobbes described it, "nasty, brutish and short". It was only when individuals realized that they could improve their lives by entering into civil society that they were prepared to give up their freedom to resort to force and fraud, which they had while in the state of nature. Hobbes described individuals as entering into a covenant with a sovereign, in which they gave up their individual rights to act as they wished, by permitting the sovereign to have a monopoly on law making and enforcement and the use of force. A covenant without the sovereign having the power to compel obedience would be worthless: as Hobbes put it, "a covenant without the sword is but words." A just and fair sovereign would ensure that individuals lived according to the rule of law and would punish those who did not. But there was no assumption that individuals would behave co-operatively just because it was to their material advantage. Nor was there any notion that individuals had any input into the law, or that their consent to its continued operation was required. The threat of state violence beyond their control was still needed to keep individuals in line and to give them a sense of security. In the end, for Hobbes, we obey the sovereign's rules because we fear the disorder that will arise if we do not and because we will certainly be punished if we do not.

The Lockean View

Locke, writing in the late 17th century, took quite a different view of human nature and of individuals in the state of nature. His view was that in the state of nature individuals were given to living peacefully with each other and co-operating to assist one another. They were not automatically disposed to engaging in force and fraud. And their lives were not seen as being "nasty, brutish and short". To make their lives easier yet, Locke argued that individuals consented to enter into a civil society by way of a compact, where a ruler ruled and made laws only with the consent of the governed, and where the ruler respected certain basic individual rights: chief among them, the right to own property. For Locke, the purpose of law was not to suppress a violent human nature, but to regulate human activity in the interest of preserving and enhancing property and individual rights. For Locke, individuals obeyed law only so long as they consented to rule by the sovereign, and only so long as the sovereign kept his part of the deal by respecting their political and legal rights, and their right to property. Individuals did not obey out of fear of either the sovereign or each other. Rather, they obeyed because they saw the law as serving their interests and because they had consented to its creation — it was "their" law: they had some control over what the rules were and how they were enforced.

Locke's approach underlies the view of law we have in a democratic state: we obey, only so long as a majority of us consent to the law-making process and to the laws made under that process. Mere fear of disorder and of punishment for breaking the law is no longer the only reason for obedience.

---

[3] The work in which this viewpoint was first set out by Hobbes was in his principal work, *The Leviathan*. For a summary of his work, see G. Sabine, *A History of Political Thought*, 3d ed. (New York: Holt Rinehart and Winston, 1965) at 455–76.

What Are the Limits of Law?

The legal system can bring order and certainty to the law, and control force and fraud, but only so long as the whole of the society is prepared to be governed by the **rule of law**. We cannot have a situation in a democratic society where the law applies only to some but not to others. Another way of putting this is to say that no one is above the law. If we are all subject to the law equally, we are more likely to accept our obligations under law, knowing that we have lots of company.

Living under the rule of law has another important consequence. Those elected to govern us must obey the same law that we do, and not use their power to ignore laws they don't like. It also means that they must follow the rules for governing and running the state. For example, in Canada political power is exercised by elected representatives. If an army general, unhappy with the civil government, decides to call out his troops and seize power by a **coup d'état**, there is no question that he is putting himself above the law. Here, we have rule by physical force rather than by law. At this point, the most elegant and inspiring national constitution is no more than wastepaper.

If the law fails to deal with or contemplate situations of serious evil, we may have to recognize that the law will not assist us in dealing with evil. We cannot expect law to solve every problem, and some matters may have to be left to non-legal means. For example, after World War II, leading Nazis were tried for crimes against humanity that did not exist when the offences were committed. Crimes against humanity were not part of international law until after the war, and they were not acts contrary to the valid law of the German state. In such a situation, there may be solutions, but they may not come from the law.[4] To deal with these issues in the legal system, we would have to do a number of things that would violate fundamental principles about how the rule of law should operate. For example, we would punish people for offences that were not known legal offences at the time they were committed.

The law is also limited in its reach when it simply is not respected or accepted by a majority or large minority of the population. The laws about the consumption of alcohol and drugs furnish very clear examples. The attempt to outlaw the sale of alcohol in the United States in the early 20th century was largely judged to be a failure. Prohibition simply did not have any support in urban areas or among those parts of the population who did not see alcohol as the devil's mousetrap but, instead, saw it as part of the expression of their culture. No matter what the law said and no matter how much effort the government made to enforce it, the law was simply ineffective because large numbers of people were prepared to disobey it. In the end, the law was repealed.

The same can be said for the various attempts to prevent the use of controlled drugs, especially cannabis. Some police departments, and even the Canadian Senate, have suggested that the time and effort and money spent in trying to control cannabis use are largely wasted. In the United States, a "war on drugs" has been raging since the 1980s with little to indicate that the "war" is being won. Again, many people simply do not accept the idea that using some types of drugs does any significant social harm that requires the law's intervention.

---

[4] This is taken up in Discussion Question #2 at the end of this chapter.

When individuals decide that the law is wrong, or evil, or even silly, they may engage in civil disobedience, either as an individual act or together with others in a group. The early challenges by Blacks in the 1950s and 1960s to state laws requiring segregation on the basis of race were active forms of civil disobedience. They differed from the type of disobedience seen with respect to drug and alcohol consumption laws. The civil rights protesters were not just breaking laws they did not like; they were also making a political statement when they disobeyed segregation laws.

Should Law Reflect Morality? Whose Morality?

Civil rights protesters decided to disobey the law because they believed the law to be wrong and immoral. The perception that law reflects morality, or that it *should* reflect morality, has deep roots in our minds and in our history, going back to Roman law. Today, this view is expressed in a theory of law called **natural law**, which has its origins in Roman law and the religious law of the Middle Ages. Those who favour this approach argue three things:

- Either through a religious or secular perspective, it is possible, through the use of reason, to discover the true morality that the law should reflect. Divine or natural law is superior to human law, and human law should mirror natural or divine law.

- Human law that does not reflect the moral content of natural or divine law is not valid law.

- Last, law that is not valid need not be obeyed.

Thus, civil rights protesters could argue that segregation laws were immoral because they were contrary to natural law principles and, therefore, need not be obeyed.

This works as long as we all agree on what is morally right. The problem arises when we ask the question, "By whose morality do we decide what we should or should not obey?" This problem is illustrated by the polarized positions on the right of a woman to obtain an abortion. On the one hand, those who believe that life begins at the moment of conception regard abortion as unlawful killing. On the other hand, those who believe that a pregnant woman has a paramount right to control her own body regard abortion as a right that should be available to every woman without having strangers dictate what happens to her. At present, the Supreme Court of Canada has ruled that the last attempt by Parliament to regulate abortion as part of the criminal law violated the *Charter of Rights and Freedoms* and was, therefore, unlawful. This left Canada with no law at all regulating abortion, a condition that has prevailed for nearly two decades, as Parliament has been disinclined to tackle this difficult and divisive issue again, in part because there are polarized views as to which moral principles apply.

The abortion debate illustrates the problems with respect to the relationship between law and morals. It is simply not possible to "prove" that one side or the other is morally correct in the way that scientific truths are proved. When you ask a scientist how she knows she is correct, she can point to her experiment and observations, which others can repeat. If others obtain the same result, we then know a scientific finding is valid or true. If you ask a natural law theorist how he knows he is right, in the end his answer depends on "right reason" or "divine revelation". But his assumptions cannot be tested or proven to be true. For those who require empirical evidence, the natural law theorist can provide none.

An answer to this problem of morality and law has been proposed in another legal theory called **legal positivism**. The positivists say that natural law is "nonsense on stilts",[5] and argue that it is ridiculous to suppose that morality is anything more than the assumptions, beliefs and prejudices of those that hold them. This is not to say that moral views are not important or that the law should not reflect them. But it is nonsense to say that we can know for certain which of several competing moral views might be correct and, on that basis, decide what law is valid and what law is not. The positivist answer is to say the following:

- The law is no more than the language that expresses it.

- The law should accurately express the intent of the lawmakers, and that we should accurately interpret the language of the law without distorting the meaning of the language used.

- We should not be concerned with the moral content of the law as a test for validity.

For the positivist, the law simply is: it may be morally obnoxious, but the answer is not to deny that it is law but to recognize it as law that needs to be altered. In the meantime, the duty of the positivist is to apply the law as he or she finds it.

The positivist is also concerned with procedure. Once you have determined what the proper procedure is for making, interpreting, administering and enforcing the law, the positivist is content if the law meets those procedural requirements. Behind this lies the positivist concern that the law is made according to the rules for rule making in a given society, and operates with order, certainty and regularity — if it does, then the law is valid. If it does not, then it is not valid. But its validity will not turn on whether its content is morally correct.

Judicial Realism

Positivism and natural law identify two opposed philosophical positions on the role of law as a social institution, and on how legal rules should be interpreted. But they do not explain how individuals in the legal system actually engage in judicial decision making. The school of **judicial realism** that developed in the 1920s and 1930s claims to provide this explanation. This is a behavioural theory that holds the psycho-social makeup of judges as the most important factor in understanding how they interpret and apply law. Judicial realism provides a way of predicting and explaining judicial behaviour that realists claim more accurately describes the interpretative process than simply trying to determine if a judge is a positivist or natural law adherent. Realism goes further by trying to explain why a particular judge might take a positivist or natural law position, and why a particular judge might be a positivist on some issues and a naturalist on others. From this view came the idea that judicial theories or legal reasons given in case decisions aren't the "real" reasons for judicial decisions, but merely a smokescreen for the real reasons, which are a judge's political, social or moral values, or personality type.

For example, realists argued in the 1930s that the U.S. Supreme Court, in opposing the Roosevelt New Deal legislation, wasn't just applying the common law to strike down these statutes, but was using it as a cover for its conservative social and economic values. Similarly, a realist might argue today that the Supreme Court of Canada, in striking down Parliament's attempts to legislate on abortion, was not just applying the rules in the *Charter of Rights*

---

[5] The English 19th century legal positivist, Jeremy Bentham, first used the phrase.

and Freedoms, but was using its own values to decide the outcome. Realism does have its detractors, some of whom refer to it as the "what the judge had for breakfast" school of jurisprudence. By this they mean that to focus on a judge's personality and values as the source of a judicial decision overstates the case and ignores the extent to which judicial values of objectivity, rationality and fairness may minimize the role of a judge's personal views.

What Is Justice?

We can sum up the argument about law and morality by asking the question, "What is justice?" A natural law advocate would argue that justice is providing a morally acceptable outcome. A positivist would argue that justice is applying legal rules literally, without injecting morality or values, so that like cases are treated alike. A realist might argue that asking what justice is is the wrong question. Instead, justice is a legal outcome dependent on the psycho-social makeup of those who decide and interpret the law.

Does Law Lead or Follow Social Change?

The rule maker, be it a king, dictator, legislature or judge, may make rules that may change societal institutions and forms of conduct or behaviour. For example, when Parliament passed the first Canada-wide *Divorce Act* in 1968, it made no-fault divorce possible for the first time, and a divorce, in general, became easier and less expensive to obtain. While attitudes towards divorce were changing anyway, the law brought about an increase in the number of divorces in the country, with various cultural and social changes following the change in the law. Suddenly, there were more single-parent families, divorce was not seen as a social stigma or disgrace, and a new phenomenon — the "combined family" — made its appearance, composed of two remarried spouses, and the children of both their previous marriages.

On the other hand, when the rule maker makes or changes law to accommodate changes already occurring in society, then the law is responding to social change that has already occurred in society. When, for example, the first legislation giving trade unions the right to bargain collectively was passed in Canada in the late 19th century, the law was merely regulating economic and social changes in labour relations that were already well underway.

These examples are fairly straightforward, but the reality is a bit more complex. In many cases it is hard to say whether the law is bringing about social change or social change is transforming the law. The process of law making is a dynamic one. Lawmakers may be responding to the perceived views of the electorate on some issues, to inputs and ideas from the civil service on others, or to inputs from interest groups and lobbyists. These inputs may represent views and values that are already held by individuals and groups. To the extent that these views become reflected in the law, they, in turn, may bring about further social change.

Consider the complex relationship between legal and social change. In 1990, the Ontario government attempted to change the laws governing employment benefits by extending the definition of who qualified for these benefits. The definition had included married or unmarried spouses of heterosexual employees. It was now proposed to extend these benefits to "same-sex" spouses. The initial impetus was a lawsuit by a government employee who argued that denial of benefits to his same-sex spouse amounted to discrimination on the basis of sex and sexual orientation. But there were also inputs — pros and cons — from various lobby groups, and a lengthy public consultation process, indicating same-sex family benefits had some support in society but also opposition. At that time, the law was not changed by the legislature. The legislation was introduced but failed to pass. However, the law did change as the result of a series of court decisions, taken over a 10-year period, where judges held that denial of benefits to same-sex spouses was a violation of the equality rights under section 15 of the *Charter of Rights and Freedoms*. The change in the law then attracted little attention as it came incrementally. In the same period, the government had quietly extended such benefits to its employees, as had a number of private employers.

How one views the relationship between law and social change depends on what it is one expects of the law. If law is seen as a means of regulating and controlling individual behaviour, creating order and certainty, and resolving conflicts, then law's purpose may be to conserve the status quo, not introduce social change. On the other hand, law may be seen as a way of bringing about significant social change. Laws eliminating the consumption of alcohol were designed to make the world a kinder, gentler place. Increasing penalties for drunk driving have brought about a huge change in public attitude and behaviour concerning the use of alcohol and motor vehicles. In these cases, law is seen as an agent for a transformation of society, not just for regulating existing patterns of behaviour.

"Vehicles Are Not Allowed in the Park": How Should We Interpret Legal Rules?

As you can now appreciate, how one approaches the law can determine how one will interpret it. By way of a summary of our discussion of concepts of law, consider how the natural law adherents, positivists, and realists might approach the problem in Exhibit 1.2.

How might different approaches to the purpose of law determine the outcome? A positivist might say that interpretation means finding and applying the meaning of ordinary English, and interpreting the law according to the meaning of the language used, without going beyond that to draw on external sources as aids to interpretation. This might result in an interpretation that finds the word "vehicle" modified by the word "toy", so as to take the object out of the reach of the law. It might equally well find that a vehicle is a vehicle, and the law has been broken. In either case, the answer is a technical analysis of language rather than content. It may result in an absurdity, but it is for judges to interpret and apply the law, not question the purpose or intent of the lawmakers. If the law is absurd, then it is up to the democratically elected legislature, not judges, to make the necessary changes Here, the law is seen as limited to what it says — the interpretation is limited to the actual language, is narrow, and somewhat mechanical. But following this approach, we get the same answer every time — the "right" answer, in the

---

Interpreting Legal Rules: A Discussion

EXHIBIT 1.2

A three-year-old child is walking with his parents into a park, along the path. The child is pulling a toy car behind him on a string. At the entrance to the park there is a sign that says, "Vehicles are not allowed in the park." A police officer sees the family and issues a ticket to the parents for permitting their child, under their control, to bring a vehicle, albeit a toy, into the park where this is prohibited by law. The parents argue that this is ridiculous. The officer's reply is that it is her job to enforce the law, not to question its wisdom.

Source: The example is developed from one used by H.L.A. Hart in *The Concept of Law* (Oxford: Clarendon Press, 1961). See chs. 1–2.

sense that we maintain order, certainty and predictability in the law, so we can all easily know the consequences. Like cases are treated alike.

A "natural" lawyer might see this differently. She would note the absurdity of arresting a child with a toy truck, and note that it would be immoral to give the law such effect and purpose. She would draw on principles and values — perhaps on a moral code that supports a child's imaginative play — to give the words a context, rather than interpret them abstractly and without regard for the results. Here, the law would be interpreted according to a morally proper result.

A realist might look at a case like this in terms of his or her own social and political values, and interpret the law to advance particular political principles. What values and principles the judge might choose would come not from an external moral code, but would be influenced by the judge's personality, political or moral views, life experiences and psychological makeup.

This discussion of approaches to interpreting legal rules can seem to be very academic, based on competing legal philosophies. And for this reason one might be tempted to dismiss the importance of these approaches. But in modern legal systems on some issues, judges can be described in practical terms as being on a continuum running from judicial activist to strict constructionist.

Interestingly, some judges may be strict constructionists on some issues and activists on others. A **judicial activist** is one who sees interpretation as a quasi-legislative function where law is interpreted in a way that is consistent with identifiable principles, values and views of society. A **strict constructionist** takes a narrower view, looking to the plain or literal meaning found in the language of the law, and ignoring social policy or values. These approaches are particularly true of, and particularly important in, constitutional law. Political values and principles come to the fore in constitutional law, where courts deal with fundamental issues about rights and the uses of political power. Further, the Constitution now requires the courts to decide how fundamental legal principles in the Constitution and in the *Charter of Rights and Freedoms* are to be interpreted and applied. Judges spend much time trying to fathom the extent of rights identified in the Constitution. For example, section 15 of the Charter sets out certain equality rights by prohibiting discrimination based on a list of grounds, such as race, religion, colour, ethnicity. Activists have said that you must look to the spirit, nature, and purpose of section 15, and be ready to expand the list to include discrimination that is not specifically mentioned but is based on things that are related to items on the list: e.g., not just discrimination on the basis of sex, but also discrimination based on sexual orientation. A strict constructionist, on the other hand, would restrict equality rights to the categories listed, arguing that if the framers of the Constitution wanted to be more expansive, they would have been. They would say that if sexual orientation is not an already protected category explicitly set out in the Charter, it is not the job of judges to put it there — to do so would be to **usurp** the job of the legislature as supreme lawmaker.

Judicial activists are often seen as social engineers trying to implement their own view of the world despite the clear intention of Parliament. In contrast, strict constructionists are often portrayed as narrow and conservative, using narrow interpretations of law to advance a conservative, if not reactionary, agenda. But this probably overstates the case. In reality, most judges bring some activist and some self-restraint approaches to bear on legal interpretation, and their approach may vary depending on the legal issues or questions before them.

CONCLUSION: THE HALLMARKS OF A FUNCTIONAL AND EFFECTIVE LEGAL SYSTEM

So far we have been discussing different concepts of law in terms of the law's function in society. The concern here has been a political one: what is the role of law in a democratic society? What rules are valid legal rules, and what rules are something else? Most commentators agree that in a democratic society the rule of law should prevail — that is, no one should be above the law. But beyond that, are there minimal requirements of a legal system that will be generally accepted in a democratic society? What is necessary to get members of a society to prefer legal solutions to non-legal ones? Lon Fuller, a legal theorist, argues that the reliance on law, rather than on brute force, is a reliance on a rational, consensual approach to problem solving where people defer to norms associated with peaceful conflict resolution.[6] To put it another way, people must have an expectation that the system will work rationally, that like cases will be treated alike and that outcome of conflict resolution, and action in general, will be predictable and certain.

Although Fuller does not say so, the expectation of rationality requires a certain type of society: at a minimum, most members of the society must have access to social and economic resources; they must be free of fear for their own survival and safety. The state apparatus of this society must be seen to be rational and reasonably transparent in its operation, and to have a monopoly over the use of force, which is used with restraint and in accordance with established rules. Examples of political societies that would meet these criteria include Canada, the United States, the European Union countries, and many Asian countries. Examples of states that would not meet these criteria would include Afghanistan and some of the states of sub-Saharan Africa. These latter are sometimes referred to as "failed states": politically unstable, where many societal institutions are in disarray, where the rule of law is not present, and where life is chaotic or, to use Hobbes's phrase, "nasty, brutish and short".

The Characteristics of a Functional Legal System in a Democratic State

Where the rule of law operates, legal systems usually have the following characteristics:

1. Laws Are General in Their Application

Legal rules should exist for most of the requirements and prohibitions in a given society. These rules should also be general in nature, and directed at everyone in a specific situation. For example, the rule prohibiting drivers from exceeding a speed limit applies to all persons driving on a particular section of highway governed by that speed limit. An example of a law that fails to meet this requirement is one actually passed in the English Parliament in the reign of Henry VII: "Richard Rose shall be detained, and boiled in oil." Whoever Rose was, he certainly had powerful enemies: powerful enough to get a law proclaimed just to "get" him. This would be regarded as a perversion of the law.

2. Laws Must Be Promulgated

In a rational system of law, we would expect that if we are to obey laws, they must be proclaimed in such a way that we know what they are.

---

[6] See Lon Fuller, *The Morality of Law* (New Haven: Yale University Press, 1969).

In a society like ours there are specific rules about rule making and rule proclaiming that must be followed, or the rules are deemed to be invalid and of no effect. If the rules for making and proclaiming law are followed, it is presumed that we can all find the law and know what obedience is required. In a society like ours, we are presumed to know the law because it is publicly available. The reality is that the mechanisms for finding the law are so technical that most people will need the help of a lawyer to locate the law and determine how it applies to them. There are some who argue that the legal profession and the judiciary contribute to obscuring the process of finding the law by perpetuating the mystery and complexity that surrounds the law.

It follows from this discussion that "secret" law is no law at all. An example arose some years ago when prison reform activists discovered that prison authorities had, and applied, some internal regulations that they refused to promulgate. Prison reformers succeeded in striking down these "secret" regulations on the grounds that no one could obey or know that they were disobeying a law that was kept a secret. Nor could anyone know if the rules were being applied properly, if only those who made them knew what they were.

Because law making is complicated in Canada, the courts also require laws to be proclaimed according to the proper procedures. For example, a regulation that is drafted, but inadvertently not posted to the official provincial or federal **gazette**, is no law at all. In order for the regulation to be valid and in effect, it must be properly proclaimed, or "gazetted".

3. Law Should Be Prospective Rather Than Retroactive

If a law is passed and proclaimed today, then the expectation is that it takes effect as of today, and governs behaviour from today. Past behaviour should not be made illegal today if, at the time the behaviour occurred, it was legal. Also, no penalty should attach for behaviour that was legal when it occurred. For example, if we pass a law today that says, "All persons who let their cell phone go off in class shall be shot", you would all reach for the button that turns off the ringer on your cell phone. You would know what is expected of you, and you would be able to take the necessary steps to avoid punishment. However, if we pass a law today that says, "As of last Thursday, anyone who let their cell phone ring in class shall be shot", it would be seen as very unfair because persons who let their cell phones ring in class before it was outlawed would be punished for doing something that was perfectly lawful when they did it.

There are some situations where the law may permit retroactive application or impact. Under the **doctrine of foreshadowing**, where a proposed law has had much publicity and been much discussed, it may apply before it is proclaimed. As its content is well known, it is presumed that people would have already taken steps to obey. Similarly, when a budget is passed, it often is deemed to take effect at some time before its passage. For example, a budget passed in March may be given effect as of January 1, as that is the beginning of the taxation year for many taxpayers, although the budget is usually not ready for a month or two later.

There is one other situation where there is retroactive impact. Where a statute is proclaimed in force, we often will not know how the statute is to be interpreted until someone brings a court case challenging the interpretation of language in the statute. It may take the courts months or years to determine the outcome, and the decision will apply back in time to when the dispute first arose for the parties that were involved in the dispute. For others, the decision should take effect only from the time it is made.

4. *Laws Should Be Clear*

This means that the law should not be so obscure or confusing or contradictory that no rational sense can be made of it. It does not mean that the law cannot be complex, or that it cannot be subject to interpretation. The courts have developed various interpretative techniques by which we should be able to clarify and interpret law so that we know what is required.

5. *Laws Should Not Be Contradictory*

A given behaviour or course of conduct should not be legal under one law and illegal under another. In a federal state like Canada, it is possible to have the two levels of government passing contradictory laws. However, the Constitution contains a mechanism that permits the courts to determine which law is valid and should be obeyed, and which is invalid and can be ignored. It does this using constitutional rules to determine which level of government has jurisdiction to enact a particular rule, which in turn resolves the conflict over which law to obey. The problem of contradictory law also looms large in international trade, where in a contract dispute two sets of national laws may apply. Usually these disputes can be resolved by **conflict of laws** rules to determine which of two conflicting rules applies. Similarly, free trade agreements, such as the North American Free Trade Agreement (NAFTA), contain rules for resolving conflicts between domestic rules and rules agreed to by the parties under the trade agreement.

6. *Laws Should Not Make Impossible Demands*

The law should not make rules that are impossible to apply on any rational or logical basis.

7. *Law Should Be Reasonably Constant and Durable*

While the law needs to change to adapt to changing circumstances, it should not be constantly amended and changed so that there is confusion over what law actually is in operation. In order for people to plan complex, long-term undertakings, there must be some assurance that the laws relevant to that undertaking remain certain and predictable.

There are some laws that are amended frequently, however. Tax law is often amended, sometimes annually, in accordance with the requirements of the government's budget.

8. *Law Should Be Capable of Enforcement*

There is an expectation in society that when behavioural requirements have been set out in the law, those requirements will be enforced. Where the rules are breached, sanctions or negative consequences should follow reasonably quickly. This is not only true for criminal law, with its prescribed penalties, but also true for civil disputes where breach of one person's rights by another gives rise to negative consequences for the transgressor in the form of a requirement to pay for the harm done to another.

Without penalties or sanctions, the law would be no more than a statement of principle about what we *ought* to do. It would not be a statement of what we *have* to do. For the most part, the expectation that sanctions will be applied is enough to ensure compliance without having a policeman at everyone's elbow. But as we noted earlier, there may be circumstances where the failure of government to effectively enforce the law may result in increased disregard of the law. For example, if we know the highway speed limits are not going to be enforced because the government decided not to hire more police, we may disregard them because we know we run little risk of being caught and penalized.

But there are other circumstances where vigorous enforcement does not seem to compel obedience. The American "War on Drugs" has gone on for years, with serious penalties for transgressors. But there seems to be little indication that the non-medical use of drugs is subsiding. Similarly, attempts to enforce prohibition and suppress the liquor trade were largely unsuccessful. These examples indicate that where the law is not accepted as legitimate or valid, harsh penalties will not bring about compliance or deter people from breaking said law.

CHAPTER SUMMARY

In this chapter we examined the concept of law, exploring some of its facets and components. We focused particularly on some open questions about what the purpose of law is in a democratic society, and what the minimal requirements are for a valid legal system. We began with a discussion of what law is, distinguishing it from other social institutions, and noted that different commentators focus on different aspects of law as being important. We went on to distinguish legal rules from other kinds of rules, noting that there are different consequences for breaching legal rules and non-legal ones. We also discussed how, in any society, people learn to recognize some rules as legal ones. Having learned to recognize legal rules, we turned to a discussion of why we obey, exploring some contrasting views of human nature that purport to explain why we obey, why we accept the rule of law, and what we expect law to do for us. In this context we also tried to identify law's limitations. Are there things it cannot achieve? Are there circumstances where it will not meet our expectations? We then looked at the relationship between law and morality, asking whether valid law requires a "right" moral content, or whether law should simply promote order and certainty by treating like cases alike. In this context we examined the competing theories of natural law, positivism and judicial realism, and then examined less theoretical approaches to these issues in the context of judicial activism and judicial self-restraint. We next turned to an examination of the relationship between social and legal change, noting the complex interactions that bring about legal change in society. We concluded with a discussion of the characteristics of a legal system in a democratic state by identifying what we think are the minimal requirements that a valid legal system must meet.

GLOSSARY OF NEW TERMS AND KEY CONCEPTS

conflict of laws An area of law concerned with determining which law applies when there is a conflict between the laws of two national systems that could apply to the situation.

coup d'état A French expression used to describe the seizure of state power by force or by the threat of force.

doctrine of foreshadowing Where the requirements of a new law are well known in advance of its final proclamation, in which case, it may be given a retrospective effect.

gazette An official government publication in which official notices are published, such as the promulgation of government regulations or the proclamation that a statute is in force. Publication in a gazette is deemed to be notice to the public of the item published; at that point members of the public are deemed to be aware of the contents of the notice, whether they have read it or not. The government of Canada publishes the

Canada Gazette; provinces publish them as well. Ontario, for example, publishes the *Ontario Gazette*.

judicial activist	One who draws on social value and principles in interpreting law, and who is likely see the law as a way of implanting key principles and policies.
judicial realism	A behavioural theory that holds that the psycho-social makeup of judges directly affects how they interpret and apply law. It provides both a way of predicting and explaining judicial behaviour.
legal positivism	A legal theory that argues that valid law is law that is made in accordance with accepted procedure, and is interpreted by giving accurate meaning to what a law actually says, without trying to fit it to our own moral or value preferences.
natural law	A theory of law that presupposes the existence of a divine or natural law external to and superior to human law. Human law, to be valid, must conform to the moral requirements of natural law, or it is invalid and need not be obeyed.
norm	An identifiable behaviour pattern that is expected and appropriate in a given set of circumstances in a particular society.
rule of law	The idea that no one, including rule makers and enforcers, is above the law or exempt from it.
socialization	A process that describes how we learn the norms and values of our society through interaction in various social institutions: families, schools, and peer groups, for example.
strict constructionist	A judge who interprets the law in terms of what it says literally, and who does not try to change the law by interpreting it to adapt to new principles, values or policies.
usurped	To wrongfully seize control of a legal and political system, and administer it in a way that is contrary to what the law requires.

REVIEW QUESTIONS

1. What are some of the key functions of a legal system?
2. How are legal rules distinguished from other kinds of rules?
3. How do we recognize legal rules so as to differentiate them from others?
4. Why do we obey legal rules?
5. What is Hobbes's explanation for why we obey?
6. How does Locke explain why we obey law?
7. What are some of the things the law cannot be expected to do?
8. How does civil disobedience differ from other forms of disobedience?
9. What does natural law tell us about obedience to law?
10. What does a positivist define as valid law that we must obey?
11. What is judicial realism?
12. Does social change result in legal change?
13. How does a judicial activist differ from a strict constructionist?
14. What are the minimal requirements of a legal system in a democratic system?
15. What is the doctrine of foreshadowing?

[handwritten top margin: LEGISLATION — STATUTE / SUBORDINATE LEGISLATION]

16. In what circumstances might we come across contradictory law in Canada?

17. After 9/11, Canadian anti-terrorism legislation permitted the government to apprehend immigrants as terrorism suspects and hold them indefinitely on security certificates, and deport them if a federal court judge found the evidence used to support the certificate reasonable. The detainee was not allowed to see or question the evidence. What might Fuller have to say about this law?

18. Albert went fishing in the Northern Ontario wilderness. A Game and Fish officer fined him for taking certain fish out of season. Before he left for the trip, Albert had checked to see which fish were in season. As it happened, the regulations were amended and proclaimed after he left home and while he was in the wilderness. Should Albert have been fined?

[handwritten left margin: no principal apply]

[handwritten: It's up to him to check the law]

DISCUSSION QUESTIONS

1. If a general conducts a coup d'état and takes over political power, we have descended into the world of Thomas Hobbes. Discuss.

2. Consider the following facts:

   At the end of World War II, the Allies decided that they needed to punish the leading Nazis for the acts of the German state designed to eliminate whole populations based on ethnic, political or religious grounds. The Allies established a court, sitting in Nuremberg, Germany, with judges from each of the major Allied nations. Leading Nazis were indicted for certain war crimes: genocide (the destruction of an entire ethnic or religious group) and crimes against humanity. They were allowed counsel and the right to present a defence. A number were found guilty of these offences, and were sentenced to hang or to long terms of imprisonment. Many of the accused raised a number of defences. Among them were these:

   (i) They were following orders and obeying laws made in accordance with rules and procedures for making and enforcing law in the state in which those laws were valid and legitimate.
   (ii) The laws creating the offences they were charged with did not exist at the time the offences were committed; the laws are, therefore, retroactive.

   How would natural law and positivism deal with these defences?

3. In the October 5, 2002 edition of the *Globe and Mail*, columnist Doug Saunders reported in his article entitled "What do you do with a problem like Noelle?" that Noelle Bush, the daughter of Florida Governor Jeb Bush (and niece of then President George W. Bush), had been arrested for a drug offence — using a forged prescription to obtain a tranquillizer used by cocaine addicts. She had a long record of drug offences and a serious problem with cocaine, but had been in treatment rather than in jail. Her father had campaigned for governor on a platform that advocated jailing drug offenders and had described drug use as a moral problem requiring stiff jail sentences, asserting that it was not a health problem requiring medical treatment but a criminal offence

requiring jail. When questioned by reporters, Jeb Bush replied, "This is a private issue, as it relates to my daughter and myself and my wife...... The road to recovery is a rocky one for a lot of people who have this kind of problem."

(a) Discuss Jeb Bush's response in the context of the principle that no one is above the law. Does Jeb Bush appear to believe that like cases should be treated alike?

(b) Is Bush's publicly advocated approach to punish drug users likely to succeed?

SUGGESTED READINGS

Finch, J.D. *Introduction to Legal Theory*, 3d ed. (London: Sweet and Maxwell, 1979).

Gall, G.R. *The Canadian Legal System*, 5th ed. (Toronto, Ont.: Carswell, 2004).

Hart, H.L.A. *The Concept of Law* (Oxford: Clarendon Press, 1961).

James, P.S. *Introduction to English Law* (London: Butterworths, 1985).

Lloyd, D. *The Idea of Law*. Reprinted with revisions (Baltimore: Penguin, 1976).

M.D.A. Freeman. *Lloyd's Introduction to Jurisprudence*, 7th ed. (London: Sweet & Maxwell, 2001).

Sabine, G. *A History of Political Theory*, 3d ed. (New York: Holt, Rinehart and Winston, 1961).

VIDEOS AND DVDS

Kramer, Stanley, prod. & dir. *Judgment at Nuremberg*. With Spencer Tracy, Maximilian Schell. 1961. [Video release, 1989; b and w; approximately 190 minutes.] Also available on DVD.

Brook, Peter, dir. *Lord of the Flies*. 1963. [Video release, 1993; colour; approximately 90 minutes.] Also available on DVD.

Lumet, Sidney, dir. & Henry Fonda and Reginald Rose, prod. *12 Angry Men*. [Video release, 1995; b and w; approximately 92 minutes.] Also available on DVD. Remade for TV in colour in 1997 with Ossie Davis, James Gandolfini et al. Available in DVD.

WEBSITE

Access to Justice: <www.acjnet.org/splash/default.aspx>

Canadian Civil Liberties Association: <http://www.ccla.org/index.shtml>

Amnesty International Canada: <http://www.amnesty.ca/>

Systems of Law in Canada

Laurence M. Olivo
SENECA COLLEGE

Learning Objectives

After reading this chapter, the reader should be able to:

➢ identify and understand the distinctive features of the common law system
➢ identify and understand the distinctive features of the civil law system of Quebec
➢ understand how the two legal systems developed
➢ understand the system of legal reasoning used to reach legal decisions in each system
➢ compare and differentiate the key elements in each system
➢ identify the ways in which the two systems have affected each other

TABLE OF CONTENTS

SYSTEMS OF LAW IN CANADA

National Legal Systems

Nation states usually have one legal system. A **legal system** consists of legal rules, principles, institutions, and procedures that operate in a distinctive way. Modern nation states, such as Canada, that are **federal states** may subdivide their legal system into local and national systems, but the two systems usually operate in the same way, according to the same principles. Such systems have simply divided **jurisdictions** on a territorial basis, between local and national political units.

Origins of Canada's Legal Systems

The development of legal systems in Canada has been different from that of most nation states. As a federal state, Canada has divided its legal system into national and local components on a territorial basis: there are provincial and federal laws and courts. There is another division as well: the common law system used at the federal level, including the federal northern territories, and in nine of the provinces, and the civil law system used in the province of Quebec.

This peculiar arrangement is a result of Canada's colonial experience. When France was defeated in the Seven Years' War, sovereignty over Quebec (then called New France) passed from the French to the British in 1760. The British found themselves ruling a colony composed primarily of French-speaking Roman Catholics. The British colonial administrators had to decide how to rule this new colony with its non-British, non-Protestant majority population. British North American colonies up to that time had simply adopted British political institutions and laws when a colony was established. At first, the British followed this policy in Quebec by imposing British political rules and laws on the inhabitants. The latter were unhappy with this arrangement, as social and political institutions were well established, and the intrusion of alien British institutions was disruptive. By the 1770s, as the 13 British colonies on the Atlantic coast inched closer to rebellion, it occurred to subtler minds among British colonial administrators that it might make sense to try to win over the Francophone inhabitants of Quebec by tolerating their religion and accepting their institutions.

Through passage of the *Quebec Act* in 1774, and by some adroit politicking with local elites who were won over and who publicly endorsed British rule, Quebec was given the freedom to practise the Roman Catholic religion and exercise other freedoms. Among these was the right to keep its **private law**, the law governing legal relations, rights, and liabilities between individual persons. This law was based on the laws of France in the late 18th century, as well as on local laws and customs. Laws governing relations between the subject and the state (often referred to as **public law**) were based on British common law.

Subsequently, the Maritime colonies and Upper Canada were established with legal systems based on the British common law, as were all of the later western additions to the Canadian state. In this way, Canada developed with two quite different legal systems: the civil law system in Quebec, governing private law matters, and the common law system everywhere else.

THE COMMON LAW SYSTEM

Legal Rules Based on Previously Decided Cases

In the common law system, decisions in previously decided cases provide the basis for legal rules. Consequently, much of the law in this system is referred to as **case law**. Lawyers also refer to case law as **common law** to distinguish it from **statutory law**, which is law passed by Parliament or a legislature. There are, in fact, different meanings for the term "common law", depending on the context in which the term is used. This is discussed at the end of this chapter.

How Common Law Developed

The Norman Kings Centralize Law Making

The common law legal system had its origins in feudal England. When the Duke of Normandy invaded England and seized the Crown in the 11th century, his successors faced the political task of consolidating their rule over local populations and over the local feudal lords. The Norman kings sought to do this by establishing a strong, effective central government as a counter to the power of local feudal lords.

Judges Develop a Law Common to All England

As part of this strategy, the king travelled about the country dispensing justice personally by resolving disputes that were brought to him. In time, responsibility for dispensing the king's justice fell to the king's advisors, from whose ranks there eventually emerged full-time judges. These judges would travel out from London to major towns in the realm to hear cases. The judges, when travelling, were said to be **on circuit**. To this day, in many common law jurisdictions, judges of some courts still go on circuit to hear cases.

Judges, in the course of solving disputes before them, gradually departed from local custom and developed rules that were common to the realm. These rules, derived from cases and applied as precedents to later disputes, formed the basis for the common law of England. This did not happen quickly or by design. Certain other things had to happen first. Persons who appeared as advocates for disputants began to write down the decisions of judges and, more important, the judges' reasons for these decisions. Once this was done, it was possible to circulate these reasons among judges and advocates (from whose ranks the legal profession later developed). Advocates would then argue that a judge in a previous case had decided the issue in a particular way, and that the decision, being sensible and wise, should then be followed. Of course the advocate for the other party would argue that the facts of the case currently before the court, or the issue before the court, was different from the facts in the previous case, so the previous case was not really a precedent for deciding the present case. Lawyers refer to this latter type of argument as distinguishing a precedent case from the **case at bar** (the case currently before the judge).

Distinguishing cases, and otherwise avoiding the application of an alleged precedent case, are discussed later in this chapter.

Significantly, there was no concerted attempt to attack the common law system of precedent as the basis for developing a system of legal rules. The approach used was practical. Judges saw their role as resolving disputes in a national arena that had little in the way of national law. They developed this law — not consciously or intentionally, but over time — on a case-by-case basis, in reaction to whatever disputes litigants brought before them. It was not elegant; no one sat down and decided to create a body of national law as a conscious, coherent, related whole, as was the case with Roman law and, later, civil law. Instead, the common law evolved, in bits and pieces over time, slowly growing into a body of law covering most of the problems of life in society.

Precedent and *Stare Decisis*

Precedent

As noted in the previous section, the common law system is characterized by a particular process of making rules from the decisions of judges in ordinary lawsuits. This form of rule making is based on the use of **precedent cases**. After a judge has given reasons for judgment in a particular case, another judge hearing a similar case may be persuaded to decide his/her case by applying the reasons for judgment in that earlier and similar case. When this happens, the judge in the second case is said to be using the reasons for the decision in the first case as a **precedent** for the decision of his/her case. The first case is then called a precedent case, and other judges are expected to apply its reasons and to **follow the precedent** when the precedent case has ruled on the legal issues rased in the case before them. In time, a series of cases are decided following the original precedent case. Often the later cases refine and expand the rule (reason for decision) in the original precedent case, and the series of cases will develop a number of related legal rules.

It is useful to note, in discussing precedent, that the precedent value of a case does not lie in the actual decision (who won, who lost), but in the legal reasons for the decision. The reason for decision, formally referred to as the *ratio decidendi* or, more simply, the **ratio** of the case, is where the precedent value of a case lies.

Stare Decisis

A second important feature of the law-making process in the common law system is the doctrine of *stare decisis*. This term is an abbreviation of a longer Latin phrase that means to "stand by decided matters". It reinforces the operation of the doctrine of precedent by compelling judges to follow precedents, in certain circumstances, even where a judge might otherwise not want to.

This idea of a judge being compelled to follow a precedent case is closely tied to the idea of a **hierarchy of courts**. The idea of a hierarchy of courts involves classifying or ranking courts in terms of their power and authority. Courts can be classified as follows:

- **Courts of first instance,** or trial courts, where legal disputes are first heard and decided
- **Appellate courts,** which review the decisions of courts of first instance, and correct errors made by the "lower" courts

Courts can also be classified in terms of the subject matter of cases they can hear and remedies they can grant. The area of activity open to a court to exercise is sometimes referred to as its **jurisdiction**. "Higher" courts have jurisdiction over a broader range of subjects and remedies than "lower" courts do. For example, a "higher" court, the Superior Court of Justice, can hear cases with claims for any amount of money, involving any subject matter. Small Claims Court, which is a "lower court", is limited in the types of claims it can hear and the monetary value of those claims.

The operation of *stare decisis* depends on the hierarchy of courts. Generally, courts higher up in the hierarchy of courts can bind judges in the lower courts in the same geographical jurisdiction so that the latter are bound to follow precedent cases from higher courts. Decisions by courts on a particular level are not binding on courts at the same level, but are considered to be **persuasive**. For example, a decision of a Superior Court of Justice judge is not binding on another Superior Court of Justice judge, but that decision should be treated as persuasive by being accorded respect and by being followed, if possible. Decisions by judges in courts from other jurisdictions are also not binding, but may be considered as persuasive if the decisions come from a higher court in the other jurisdiction, or if the decisions come from judges in another jurisdiction who are highly respected for their legal knowledge and expertise.

EXHIBIT 2.1

Which Decision Is Binding?

¤ A decision of the Supreme Court of Canada binds all courts in the provincial court systems.

¤ A decision of the provincial court of appeal binds all other courts in the provincial court system, and may be considered persuasive by judges in other provinces.

¤ A decision of the superior trial court binds lower trial courts in the province and should be considered persuasive by other judges at the same level in the jurisdiction.

¤ A decision of the lower trial court is not binding on any other court, but may be considered persuasive by other courts at the same level.

The Role of Precedent and *Stare Decisis* in a Common Law System

To summarize, if the doctrine of precedent sets out the idea that a precedent case *ought* to be followed, *stare decisis* sets out the idea that a precedent case *must* be followed in certain circumstances. While there have been some recent developments that lessen the force of *stare decisis* in Canada, making its application less rigid and mechanical, it is considered to be an important feature of a common law legal system.

The common law system differs dramatically from most other kinds of legal systems. Legal rules in this system are not consciously assembled from a series of carefully developed principles laid out and connected in a logical way as is the case in many other legal systems. Instead, judges "made up" the rules as they went along, deciding practical problems that were presented in cases by people with disputes and disagreements. Once a judge made a rule to solve the problem before him, his "solution" would be adopted by other judges with a similar case.

In a sense, legal rules in this system result as a reaction to problems. In other systems, notably the civil law system used in Quebec and in many other parts of the world, rules are often derived from abstract principles, which are organized and codified in a systematic way, ready to be applied to resolve disputes. The latter approach seems simpler, more efficient, less haphazard, and more rational. If this is so, why did the common law not follow this pattern? If we consider the ad hoc way in which the common law developed as an extension of the king's personal power to do individual justice, it is clear that the focus was primarily on the need to make decisions and solve problems, not on developing a systematic and integrated body of law.

A Gloss on the Common Law: The Law of Equity

Origins of the Law of Equity

While common law developed slowly without anyone consciously managing the process, its growth was checked, after a couple of centuries, by the power of the nobility. The local nobles had watched as the king used the development of a centralized legal system, operating out of London, as one of many ways of consolidating royal power. Eventually, the nobles extracted some concessions from the king to check the expansion of royal power and, in particular, the power of the Royal Courts of Justice to interfere with the nobles' management of local affairs. They did this by getting the king to "freeze" the expansion of the common law by prohibiting the creation of any further legal rights to sue, or **causes of action**. The common law was thus left for several hundred years with what came to be called the **ancient forms of action**. This step contributed to the common law becoming unable to use precedent to expand or develop the law further. Instead, the law became frozen.

Avoiding Precedent

EXHIBIT 2.2

Whether a previous case is actually a precedent is not always clear. Lawyers have a variety of techniques they use to find a way around a precedent case, particularly when they wish to avoid, or get around, a precedent that stands in their client's way.

- **Distinguishing a case on its facts:** When faced with an apparent precedent, a lawyer may argue that it is not really a precedent because it is different in its material facts from the **case at bar** (the case that is being argued by the lawyer before the court).

- *Obiter dicta:* There is no simple, objective test for identifying the ratio of a case. Because finding the "true" ratio is a subjective exercise, it is open to argument that the judicial opinion in a case is not the ratio, but mere *obiter dicta*, or more simply, *obiter*. *Obiter dicta* is a judicial opinion set out in a case, but it is not the opinion on which the decision in the case rests. Judicial opinions that are *obiter* are thought to have no precedent value in a case, although they may provide insights for deciding other cases, where the judicial observations may be more relevant. However, note that in recent Canadian case law there is a suggestion that *obiter* in cases from the Supreme Court of Canada may be binding on lower courts, if relevant to cases before them.[1] Previously, *obiter* was thought to be persuasive but not binding.

- *Per incuriam:* A lawyer may argue that a case should not be followed because the judge based her decision and her reasoning on an error of fact or law. For example, the lawyers arguing a case may have inadvertently failed to cite an important precedent case to the judge, or left out important facts by mistake. In either of these situations, the precedent value of the case is arguably weakened, if its true legal or factual base is other than what the judge hearing the case thought it was.

  The *per incuriam* problem illustrates the extent to which a judge in the common law system is dependent on the lawyers presenting a case to define the issues, facts and law to be relied on. When a lawyer makes a mistake and fails to find a relevant case when doing his research, and the other lawyer does not catch the mistake, there is no assurance that a judge, busy with a heavy caseload, will, either. While judges often "check" the cases cited to them, they do not always do so. Further, in the common law system, judges are relatively passive participants in the trial process, reasoning their way to a decision on the basis of legal and evidential information supplied by the lawyers presenting the case.

- **Concurring opinions:** In some proceedings — appeals, for example — the case is heard by a panel of several judges, rather than by one judge sitting alone. When this happens, different judges may come to the same conclusion for different reasons. When two or more judges agree on the result but give different reasons for their decision, their judgments are concurring opinions, but there cannot be said to be a single ratio for the case on which a precedent could be founded. In such a case, the reasons of a particularly eminent judge might carry more weight than the reasons of her colleagues sitting on the same panel, but this does not provide a clear-cut solution to the problem of deciding what the true ratio is.

- **Precedent wrongly decided:** In some cases, it is possible for a lawyer to argue that an earlier case may technically and logically be a precedent but that the reasoning should not be followed because it is wrong. A case may be seen as wrong when, for example, the social situations that gave rise to the reasons no longer exist, so the application of the precedent would give rise to ridiculous results. This approach is not used often, as it constitutes a direct attack on the doctrine of *stare decisis*, which lies at the core of the common law system. Lawyers, being masters of legal subtlety, usually can find a more indirect way of avoiding precedent.

---

[1] *Sellars v. R.*, [1980] 1 S.C.R. 527.

| EXHIBIT 2.3 | An Illustration of the Use of Precedent |

A owns a house with a flat roof. *B* is planning to build a house on the next lot, right next to *A*'s house. *B*'s house is going to be 10 feet higher than *A*'s. *A* discovers that *B*'s house, if built, will create conditions that will increase the snowload on *A*'s house and cause damage to *A*'s roof. *A* tells this to *B* and asks him to redesign his proposed house. *B* refuses.

A wants to stop *B* from building. *A* sues *B* for a tort called nuisance. The tort of nuisance allows one landowner to sue another for damage done to his land as a result of activity by the other on his own land. However, the definition of nuisance, as stated here, is fairly broad, and *A* has to find some cases that show that the definition of nuisance applies to his circumstances.

A finds a case where the court awarded damages to a person whose basement was flooded, when the defendant built a house that diverted rain runoff towards the plaintiff's house and into his basement. At the time the defendant built the house, neither party knew that flooding would result.

A can argue that this case is a precedent:

¤ Its facts on the relevant issue are similar to the case at bar; damage is caused to the plaintiff's property by an act of the defendant on his own property.

¤ Damage was caused by a natural element being channelled by the defendant where otherwise no damage would have resulted. Whether the element was snow or water and whether the damage was to the roof or basement is irrelevant, given that the issue is physical damage caused by the defendant.

B can argue that this case can be distinguished on its facts:

¤ In this case, the defendant had built his house, and the damage to the plaintiff's house had already occurred. Arguably, this case means that you can't sue until damage has occurred. In the case at bar, *B* hadn't built his house, and no damage had occurred to *A*'s house yet.

¤ This case creates liability for water damage. But the case at bar involves snowload. Snow and water behave differently. Therefore, this case cannot, on its facts, support a claim for liability for snowload, where other causal factors may be involved or where the risk may be too remote to impose liability.

¤ This case concerns damage to basements from water. The case at bar is different on its facts, as it concerns snow damage to a roof where other causal factors may be involved or where the risk may be too remote to impose liability.

Meanwhile, as society and social institutions changed and developed, the law did not. As well, because the law was frozen and rigid, the application of its rules could and did cause obvious injustice and unfairness. When the legal result was obviously unfair, a **suitor** would occasionally complain about this to the king who, unlike his judges, was, as the source of justice in the realm, free to fashion personal justice as he saw fit. If the king was persuaded by a suitor, he would issue a decree overruling the judgment of the courts. As more subjects brought these complaints to the king, he referred these matters to his chief administrative officer, the **Chancellor**. The Chancellor would then issue a Chancellor's decree to overrule the court and correct an obvious injustice. Good news travels quickly: in time, the flow of complaints grew so great that the Chancellor had to designate some of his staff to hear these complaints. Gradually the process became institutionalized: the Chancellor's staff became Chancery judges, operating out of the **Court of Chancery**. The decrees of the Chancellor, through the use of the precedent process, evolved into a separate body of law called the **law of equity**. Thus, a second parallel system of courts was established. As the Chancery system became institutionalized, however, the justice delivered became less personal and less flexible. In particular, Chancery judges resorted to judicial reasoning using precedent. This tended to inhibit the expansion of equity law. The result was that the law of equity also became rigid and unresponsive.

Features of the Law of Equity

The common law courts continued to administer the common law while the Court of Chancery administered the law of equity. Initially, the law of equity developed a body of legal rules with two main features:

* rules that would "correct" common law results by granting **equitable remedies**
* preconditions that a suitor had to comply with first in order to invoke the law of equity

As a corrective for the common law, equity was sometimes referred to as "a gloss on the common law". For example, at common law, if one party broke a contractual arrangement, the only remedy the common law recognized was money damages. If the breaking of a contract would cause some injury that could not be compensated for in damages, there was nothing the common law could do. The law of equity, however, could be invoked, and an **injunction** obtained to order a stop to the wrongful behaviour.

Before a suitor could resort to the Court of Chancery and the law of equity, she had to satisfy certain preconditions. Originally, before a suitor could get the Chancellor to interfere with a court decision, the suitor had to show that she had been wronged, that a common law remedy was inadequate or non-existent and that she had behaved properly in her dealings with her opponent. In time, this meant that a suitor in Chancery had to show the court that she had behaved properly in the lawsuit, had not acted underhandedly or oppressively against the other side. If the suitor could not **come into court with clean hands**, Chancery would refuse to hear her or grant the equitable remedies requested.

For example, if a suitor had tried to hide evidence in a case, then it was unlikely that the suitor would meet the preconditions required to invoke the law of equity.

Merger of the Common Law and Equity Jurisdiction

In time, the two parallel court systems and systems of legal rules became cumbersome and rigid. For example:

* It was often difficult for even a highly experienced lawyer to decide whether to start a lawsuit in Chancery or in a common law court. If an error was made, a case would be thrown out and would have to start from the beginning in the other court.

* Decrees from the Chancery Court might conflict with, or be inconsistent with, the orders of the common law courts.

These kinds of problems caused uncertainty in the law, delayed proceedings, and made them more expensive. In the late 19th century, a major court reform movement in the common law world, including Canada, resulted in the merger of the two court systems into one superior court with the power to administer the common law and the law of equity together.

While the separate courts administering the law of equity have passed into history, the law of equity is still relevant today. It continues to be administered by superior court judges who have the power to administer the common law and the law of equity together. Courts today still have available and, where relevant, use powerful equitable remedies, such as injunctions, and orders for specific performance of contracts. These remedies achieve results that cannot otherwise be achieved by traditional common law remedies, which are generally limited to the payment of money for damages sustained.

The Modern Common Law System: Case Law, Equity, and Statutes

The Modern Common Law System as a "Mixed" System of Law

While the common law originated out of a process where the law developed on a case-by-case basis, modern common law systems are more complex and have more sources of legal rules than previously decided precedent cases.[1]

Modern common law systems are mixed systems in terms of the sources of law. In Canada, the principal sources of written law are case law, including both common law rules and equitable rules, and statutory law, which also includes regulations made under the authority of statutes. The development of the law of equity alongside common law has been examined; we now turn to the development of statutory law in the common law system.

How Common Law Developed into a Mixed System of Law

When the common law began to develop, it was the principal source of legal rules. Statutes, which are laws passed by Parliament or a legislature, were not yet a significant factor in legal rule making. In the 11th and 12th centuries, when the common law began to take form, Parliament as we know it did not exist. Over the next several centuries, however, Parliament began to take both the form and function we would recognize today. At first, composed of the Lords (clergy and nobility) and the Commons (representatives of wealthy towns), Parliament was summoned by the king when he needed to raise large sums of money by taxation, usually to finance a war. In time, in exchange for consenting to taxation, Parliament extracted concessions from the king, which resulted in Parliament's increasing its participation in government by passing laws or statutes dealing with matters other than taxation.

Parliamentary Supremacy

As this expansion of parliamentary power represented an erosion of royal power, the king sometimes resisted, and from the 17th century on, there was considerable tension between king and Parliament over the exercise of power by the latter.

All this came to a head, literally, in 1649, when Charles I lost his, when he tried to dismiss Parliament to rule alone. The result was a civil war between the king's adherents and Parliament's, in which the king was beheaded and Parliament ruled alone. What emerged from the English Civil War was a new legal doctrine, **the Doctrine of Parliamentary Supremacy** (also called Parliamentary Sovereignty), under which Parliament was declared to be the supreme lawmaker. This meant that when Parliament passed a law, it negated any other law or rule made outside of Parliament that conflicted with an Act of Parliament. Further, not only did ordinary citizens have to obey the law, but so did royal officials, so that those who governed had to do so according to the law passed by Parliament. Another way of looking at this

---

[1] The sources of law in the common law system are discussed in another chapter, "Sources of Law", offered in the complete edition of this modular textbook. In this chapter, the relationship and development of the main written sources of law are explored.

is to say that no one is above the law. With respect to judge-made law, a statute passed by Parliament would cancel out any conflicting law developed from previously decided cases.

Advantages of Statutory Law over Case Law

Once Parliament had a relatively free hand to legislate, it increased its output of statutes and, from the 17th century onward, it gradually became the source of a growing proportion of legal rules in the common law system. The reason for this growth of statutory law was not simply that Parliament now had the power to act. For example, Parliament could use statutes to respond to particular problems relatively quickly and in a comprehensive way. As society became more complex, statutes provided a more effective way to make rules than the slow and cumbersome common law process of developing judge-made law on a case-by-case basis.

Sorting Out Conflicts between Sources of Law

It is apparent from this chapter that both statutory law and equity developed, at least in part, because of perceived shortcomings of the common law case law precedent system, which was seen as too rigid, too slow and too unresponsive to the needs of a complex society. However, these later additions to the common law system created potential for conflict. If, for example, a rule developed from case law conflicted with a statute, which would prevail? Gradually, over time, the answers to these questions were worked out:

- If there is a conflict between a case law rule and an equitable rule, the equitable rule shall prevail.
- If there is a conflict between a statutory rule and an equitable or common law rule, the statutory rule shall prevail.

While statutory law prevails over case law, note that there is a continuing relationship between statute law and case law. Disputes about the meaning of all or part of a statute are resolved by court cases. Where a case has interpreted part of a statute and expanded or refined previous understandings of what the statute meant, then that case becomes an important determinant of a statute's meaning.

THE CIVIL LAW SYSTEM

In a civil law system, principles and rules of law are found in a set of clearly articulated and connected principles set out in a coherent system of law, in contrast to the common law system, where they are found, if at all, in case law. The system of law usually has a base in a legal theory that has an integrated worldview and that determines the content, focus, and direction of legal rules and principles. For example, modern European (and Quebec) civil law systems owe a great deal to theories of law found in Roman law and in natural law. In addition, the rules and principles are organized in a systematic and logical way. This organizing process, usually called **codification**, results in the codes that are a feature of modern civil law systems.

Key features of a civil law system are

- a coherent, theoretically interrelated system of law, and
- a codified system of law.

In Quebec, private law is based on modern European civil law, organized and codified in the Quebec Civil Code.

The Origins of the Quebec Civil Code

The Law of New France at the Time of the Conquest

When the British took over the governance of New France, now to be called Quebec, they found a French-speaking society that had been established on the shores of the St. Lawrence for over a century. While the colony was governed by French officials, its institutions had evolved in response to local conditions. The legal system in use fit this pattern. It was based originally on the customary law of the Paris region. In its origins, it was a mixture of local custom — some of which was rooted in the feudal system of the Middle Ages — and civil law derived from Roman law. It had been codified before being introduced to New France, and was overhauled afterwards. Thus, the French customary law base, by the time the British arrived, had been further customized to suit local conditions, and had been systematized and codified.

The Impact of British Rule on Quebec's Legal Institutions

As noted, the British experimented with several models of government, as they tried to decide how to treat the French-speaking population of their recently acquired colony. With the *Quebec Act* of 1774, the British opted for leaving the Quebec legal system intact, with respect to the private law. This was not popular with the recently arrived British merchant class, and the Quebec legal institutions did not really become secure until the British, in 1791, separated their colony into Upper Canada (now Ontario), which was primarily English speaking, and Lower Canada (now Quebec), which was primarily French speaking.

In the early British period, the civil law system in Quebec fell into decline. Based as it was on a civil law base, affecting only private law, in an English colony undergoing rapid change, it was not particularly well suited to solving private law problems. It was also not clear how the civil law system could work alongside the rest of the Quebec system of public law, which ran on common law principles. It also did not help that there was no system for legal education in the civil law in Quebec. The civil law system recovered from this decline, however, in part because of a renewal and modernization of civil law in Europe.

The Impact of the Modernization of European Civil Law on Quebec's Legal Institutions

The European systems, while different in substance from each other, shared a systematic codification of legal rules. This was part of a well-established tradition of codification that extended back to codified Roman law. While the influence of Roman law had waned after the collapse of the Roman Empire, it continued to have an impact on European law. The tradition had new life breathed into it during the Renaissance and the **Enlightenment**, with the development of rationally based theories of natural law. Interestingly, none of the intellectual ferment in the civil law reached Britain in any significant way. Civil law had been largely unaffected by Roman law, and the results of changes in the civil law in the early modern period had no effect, either.

In the early 19th century, following political changes brought about by the French Revolution and the reforms to the legal system by Napoleon, law reformers in France and elsewhere in Europe sought to modernize the civil law and to recodify it.

Codification was, and is, more than merely collecting all existing law between the covers of a code book. The process also involves a close review of legal rules and principles, to ensure that they form a consistent, coherent, interrelated system, based on clearly identified principles. In some respects this is a philosophical exercise, in which legal scholars attempt to

---

Avoiding Confusion:
Different Uses of "Common Law" and "Civil Law"

EXHIBIT 2.4

By now it should be apparent that both "common law" and "civil law" can have different meanings depending on the situations where they are used.

Common Law

¤ The body of common custom, or law common to all England, which was an early product of the justice system created by the Norman kings. This usage is now only of historical interest and does not have a contemporary meaning.

¤ The body of case law, from which legal precedents are drawn, is called common law to distinguish it from law from other sources, such as statutory law.

¤ The legal system that developed in England and that features the use of precedent cases as a major source of law is called a common law legal system.

Civil Law

¤ Civil law describes a system of law derived from Roman law and natural law, which is usually codified.

¤ Civil law in the common law system describes private law, consisting primarily of the law of torts and contract.

---

develop a theory of law that underlies and illuminates the rules and principles in a code.

In Quebec, the reformers, influenced by law reforms in France in the 19th century, recodified private law, abandoning the earlier French customary law base and replacing it with a system of principles adapted from the Napoleonic Code, or the French Civil Code. This code covered both substantive private law (similar to the common law of torts and contracts) and civil procedure. Since the mid-19th century when the Quebec Civil Code was formally adopted, Quebec has periodically reviewed and overhauled the code. The latest extensive revisions were completed in 1993. So extensive were these revisions that members of the Quebec Bar were expected to take continuing education courses in the new code if they expected to continue to practise law in Quebec.

Features of a Civil Law Code System in Comparison to a Common Law System

Codified Principles vs. Case Ratios as the Basis for Legal Rules

Codification is a process whereby legal rules and principles are developed and organized into a coherent, interrelated system. The rules or principles, compared to common law rules, are much more general in nature, and are not developed as a narrow answer to a specific case. Instead, the civil law principles are developed as general abstract statements. The general statement of principle or law in the code can then be applied to make a legal decision, with the same principle being applied to many different fact situations.

This is quite different from the common law, where general principles of law are developed as a result of problem solving in specific cases; in other words, judges in the common law system develop legal rules as a result of a search for remedies to practical problems. They reason, **inductively**, from the particular to the general. In the civil law system, judges start with a general principle, clearly identified and defined, and apply it to particular facts in an attempt to define competing rights. They reason, **deductively**, from the general to the particular.

The Function of Precedent in a Civil Code System

In reasoning their way to legal decisions, judges using code systems do not rely on precedent cases. The primary source of law is the code itself, which the judge is expected to interpret and apply without resort to secondary sources, such as cases. Judges are not seen as lawmakers in a code system; they do not make binding rules from cases that can be applied to later cases or used as alternatives to the code itself. It is not necessary for a judge in this system to find a case that supports his position: finding a principle in the code to solve a legal problem is sufficient. More particularly, in contrast to the common law system, in the code system, the doctrine of *stare decisis* is non-existent: a previously decided case can never be binding authority for deciding the case at bar.

At the same time, precedent has some function in the Quebec system. One of the weaknesses of a code system is that the principles and rules in the code are based on philosophical and other assumptions about the way society works or should work. Occasionally, a situation arises that is not specifically covered by an **article** in the code. In such a case, it is generally permissible for a judge in coming to a decision to reason by analogy with a previously decided case that is in some way similar to the case at bar.

Precedent cases may also be used in other, more common situations. First, civil code jurisdictions, like common law jurisdictions, have a hierarchy or ranking of courts, where, for example, trial courts are seen as subordinate to appeal courts. In this context, the decision in an appeal court, on a case similar to the case at bar in a trial court, may be persuasive for the lower court because of the added authority carried by a decision of a higher court. Note, however, that in the civil code system, a higher court does not automatically bind a lower court as it is presumed to do in the common law system. In a code system, the lower court can ignore a similar decision of a higher court. This is not without a potential cost: a judge in a lower court who ignores a decision of a higher court may find her decision reversed by an appeal court. To put it succinctly, precedent may operate, but the doctrine of *stare decisis* does not.

Sources of Law in a Civil Law System

The primary source of law is the Civil Code itself, which contains relatively general rules and principles that are grouped together by subject matter. Another primary source is other statutes. A secondary source is **doctrine**, which is a term that describes commentary by legal scholars on the meaning of various provisions of the code. Note that case law is not a formal source of law in civil code systems. As well, there is no concept of a separate law of equity, as there is in the common law system. The principles in the code are general rather than narrow or rigid so that the circumstances that gave rise to the law of equity in the common law system never arose in the civil code systems. However, illustrating Quebec's ability to borrow from the common law, some equitable remedies, such as injunctions, have found their way into Quebec law.

The System of Law in Quebec: A Mixed Common Law and Civil Law System

We can see that the private law in Quebec is based on the civil law system, using the Quebec Civil Code. To go on from there, to state that Quebec is a civil law and civil code jurisdiction would be to overstate the situation. In fact, the civil law system and the common law system have cohabited in Quebec for over 200 years. As a result of this contact, each has affected the other in a variety of ways. Further, as the result of Quebec's legal system operating in a federal system, large areas of law affecting life in Quebec are based on fed-

	Avoiding Confusion: Key Differences between "Common Law" and "Civil Law"		EXHIBIT 2.5

	COMMON LAW	CIVIL LAW
Use of precedent	yes	rarely
Codified rules	sometimes (statutes)	yes
Defers to higher court	yes	sometimes

eral common law. The effects in Quebec of the mingling of the two systems are as follows:

- The private law, affecting the relations between private citizens in their dealings with each other, is primarily codified civil law.

- Commercial law is based on common law, or on statutes.

- Public law, which governs the relations between the individual and the state (including criminal law), is common law, based on statutes and case law.

- There is a general acknowledgement that Quebec judges tend to resort to precedents more than judges in other civil code jurisdictions. In particular, attention is paid and deference given to the decisions of the Supreme Court of Canada on issues involving the Quebec Civil Code. As well, ignoring decisions of higher courts within the Quebec legal system is unusual, although more frequent than in other provinces. Much of this judicial behaviour can be attributed to the influence of common law and of common law judges in the rest of Canada.

CHAPTER SUMMARY

In this chapter, the reader is introduced to the two systems of law in Canada, the civil law in Quebec and the common law in every other part of Canada. The main characteristics of the common law system are discussed, including the use of previously decided cases as the basis for developing legal rules (the doctrine of precedent), the tendency of precedents to become binding (the doctrine of *stare decisis*), and the development of equity to avoid the rigid application of precedents where unfairness resulted. The chapter also explored a number of analytic devices to avoid the application of precedents. As much modern law is now based on statutes rather than on case law, the relationship between the two sources of law is discussed in terms of the supremacy of the legislature, which results in statute law being able to override case law.

The chapter then identified the main features of the civil law system in Quebec and traced its origins back to French and European law. In contrast to common law, legal rules and principles in the civil law system are found in code books, not cases. One applies the principles in the code to the facts of a case to come to a decision. The chapter concluded by noting that, as a result of Quebec's history in Canada, it is not a "pure" civil law system, as some of the law applied in Quebec is based on English law, and common law methods of legal reasoning have had some influence on legal reasoning in the civil code system.

GLOSSARY OF NEW TERMS AND KEY CONCEPTS

ancient forms of action	During the early development of the common law, by royal order, no new causes of action could be added to the law; this resulted in the existing causes of action becoming frozen and rigid over a long period. These "frozen" causes of action are referred to as ancient forms of action.
appellate court	A court that reviews the decisions of lower courts or courts of first instance for errors of fact or law. *See* "courts of first instance", below.
article	In civil code systems, specific rules or groups of rules.
case at bar	The case currently being tried before the court.
case law	Legal rules derived from decided cases.
causes of action	Facts that give rise to a right to sue based on a legal rule or legal right.
Chancellor	The royal official who originally administered the law of equity. Later, the title was also used by judges appointed to the Court of Chancery, which dealt with equity matters. In England today, the Lord Chancellor is the chief official responsible for the administration of justice in the realm.
codification	A process that results in a coherent, theoretically related and logically consistent system of rules.
Cour of Chancery	The court that administered the law of equity.
"come into court with clean hands"	A principle of the law of equity that requires someone seeking to invoke equitable rules to have conducted himself or herself fairly and honourably in the events leading up to the lawsuit, and in the lawsuit itself.
common law	The Anglo-Canadian system of law that features decided cases as a principal source of law. Also used as a synonym for **case law**, as distinguished from law based on statutes.
court of first instance	The court in which a dispute is first heard and a decision is made. Also called a trial court.
distinguishing cases	Showing how the facts of a case are significantly different from the facts of a case that has been cited as a precedent case.
deductive reasoning	A reasoning process where one draws specific, narrow conclusions based on an analysis of general principles. *See also* inductive reasoning.
doctrine	In civil code systems, secondary sources of law that explain and expand on the articles in the codes that are the primary sources of law.
Doctrine of Parliamentary Supremacy	In a parliamentary system of government like Canada's, the legislative bodies at the federal and provincial levels are free to make whatever laws they wish within their own spheres: the courts cannot overrule them, and are limited to interpreting what the legislature intended. The doctrine has been weakened somewhat by the *Charter of Rights and Freedoms*, which is discussed in another chapter.
Enlightenment, the	An 18th-century European intellectual movement characterized by an interest in rationalism and scientific inquiry.
equitable remedies	A class of remedies that supplement and expand the principal remedies available at common law.
federal state	One in which the power to govern is divided between two or more levels of government. Each level of government usually has supreme governing power within its own sphere; the other level of government cannot interfere with the exercise of jurisdiction.

hierarchy of courts	An idea that in any judicial system the courts can be ranked in terms of their power and jurisdiction.
inductive reasoning	A reasoning process where one makes general conclusions based on an analysis of particular facts. *See also* deductive reasoning.
injunction	A court remedy, developed under the law of equity, where the court can order someone to do something or to refrain from doing it.
jurisdiction	The power or authority of a court to decide matters before it. Often used to refer to the boundary or limits of judicial power, in which case one refers to matters "outside" or "beyond" the court's jurisdiction.
law of equity	Developed in the early common law period as an administrative response to the rigidity and occasional unfairness of the common law courts; the law of equity prevails over the common law, where there is a conflict between the two.
legal system	Includes all of the structures, functions, values, rules, and procedures that are involved in the making and application of legal rules in society.
obiter dicta, obiter	An opinion or principle of law stated in reasons for judgment, which is not the principle that decides the case; for this reason, an *obiter* opinion has little precedent value.
on circuit	A method of administering justice originally used in England to make sure that judges were available in all parts of the realm and not just in the capital. Superior Court judges not only hear cases in the capital city, but also **go on circuit**, hearing cases in county towns on a regular basis. It has also been used in parts of Canada.
persuasive	In the context of *stare decisis*, a case is to be considered persuasive if it should be accorded respect and should be followed, but is not binding.
precedent case, following precedent	An earlier case that is similar in facts to the case at bar so that it can determine the legal result in the case at bar. To **follow the precedent** means that the judge, having found a case to be a precedent, applies the rule from that case to the case at bar.
private law	The law governing legal relationships between individuals.
public law	The law relating to the operation of government, covering relations between the citizen and the state.
ratio, or *ratio decidendi*	The reason for decision, or principle on which the legal outcome of the case can be determined.
stare decisis	A legal doctrine that says that a case determined to be a precedent must be followed, even if a judge does not favour the results that must come from application of the precedent.
statutory law	Law based on a statute; can be contrasted with law derived from cases, called **case law**.
suitor	A person who is suing someone else.

REVIEW QUESTIONS

1. How did Canada come to have two legal systems?

2. What is the doctrine of precedent?

3. What is the difference between the doctrine of precedent and the doctrine of *stare decisis*?

4. (a) What does it mean to "distinguish a case"?
   (b) What is *"obiter dicta"*?
   (c) What is a *"per incuriam"* decision?
   (d) What is the effect of concurring opinions in a case on its value as a precedent?

5. How did the common law method of deciding cases develop?

6. Why did the law of equity develop?

7. What are some of the features that distinguish the law of equity from the common law?

8. What is the relationship between the law of equity and the common law?

9. What is statute law? How is it different from case law?

10. What advantages does statute law have over common law? Common law over statute law?

11. Describe ways in which the civil law system differs significantly from the common law system.

12. Describe the process for making judicial decisions in the civil law system. How does this process differ from the decision-making process in the common law system?

13. In what ways has the common law system had an impact on the civil law system of Quebec?

14. Describe three different meanings of "common law" and two different meanings of "civil law".

15. In what circumstances can you invoke the law of equity?

16. What is the relationship between the law of equity, the common law (case law) and statutes?

17. What role, if any, does precedent play in the civil law system of Quebec?

DISCUSSION QUESTIONS

1. The civil law system in Canada was the result of an experiment in British colonial administration. Discuss and explain.

2. Legal reasoning in the common law system has been described as an ad hoc exercise in solving practical problems. Does this describe the process? How is the legal reasoning process in the common law system different from the legal reasoning process used in the civil law system?

3. In legal argument, one lawyer says that the decision in the case at bar can be determined by referring to the case of *Blogett v. Snogg*, which is a clear precedent. If the other lawyer wishes to avoid this conclusion, what techniques might be used to argue that *Blogett* is not a precedent?

4. All legal systems tend to become rigid and inflexible. Discuss this proposition as it might apply to the common law.

5. If you were a member of the British Colonial authorities in Quebec in 1774, and you were considering letting Quebec keep some of its laws, what areas might you let Quebec keep, and what areas might you want to terminate in favour of British Law?

SUGGESTED READINGS

Baker, J. *An Introduction to English Legal History*, 4th ed. (London: Butterworths, 2002).

David, R. *Major Legal Systems in the World Today: An Introduction to the Comparative Study of Law*, 4th ed., translated and adapted by J.E.C. Brierley (London: Sweet & Maxwell, 1993).

Gall, Gerald L. *The Canadian Legal System*, 5th ed. (Toronto, Ont.: Carswell, 2004).

Glenn, H.P. *Legal Traditions of the World* (Oxford, Ont.: Oxford University Press, 2004).

Keir, D.L. *The Constitutional History of Modern Britain Since 1485*, 9th ed. (Princeton, N.J.: Van Nostrand, 1966).

Kelly, J.M. *A Short History of Western Legal Theory* (Oxford, Ont.: Oxford University Press, 1992).

Kiralfy, A.K.R. *The English Legal System*, 8th ed. (London: Sweet & Maxwell, 1990).

Plucknett, T.F.T. *A Concise History of the Common Law*, 5th ed. (London: Butterworths, 1956).

————. *Studies in English Legal History*. (London: Hambleton, 1983).

Stychin, Carl, & Mulcahy, Linda. *Legal Method and Systems: Text & Materials* (London: Sweet & Maxwell, 2007).

Waddams, S.M. *Introduction to the Study of Law*, 6th ed. (Toronto, Ont.: Carswell, 2004).

Sources of Law

Laurence M. Olivo
SENECA COLLEGE

Learning Objectives

After reading this chapter, the reader should be able to:

➢ understand the concept of legal relevance in determining sources of law
➢ identify the major sources of law in Canada
➢ know how statutory and case law sources are organized and accessed
➢ understand the relationship between statutes and subordinate legislation
➢ become familiar with basic rules of statutory interpretation
➢ understand the relationship between, and the importance of, the various sources of law

TABLE OF CONTENTS

INTRODUCTION: DETERMINING WHAT INFORMATION CONSTITUTES A SOURCE OF LAW

The Concept of a Valid Source of Law

In any legal system, the process of solving a legal dispute involves the reasoned application of "law" to the facts of a dispute. However, how do we know what "law" is? To put it another way, what rules or principles that might solve a dispute are acceptable as legal rules or principles? In answering this question, we are really deciding, by choosing from among the possibilities, what rules or principles are legally relevant and can be accepted by the users of a legal system as a valid source of law.

For example, if you are supposed to clear your sidewalk of snow and ice, and you forget to do it, and someone slips and falls, what is legally relevant to determining whether you are responsible?

- A statute?
- A by-law?
- Case law?
- Moral duty not to cause injury to others?
- Your standing in the community?
- A revelation from God telling you what to do?

In this example, we have to decide which of the above sources of a rule might be legally relevant as the source of a rule in our legal system. Once we have done this, we may describe a source of information that is relevant for inclusion in a legal system as a valid source of law. Then, from among the valid sources of legal rules and principles, we have to choose the rule or principle that is relevant to the problem at hand. In this chapter, we are primarily concerned with the first problem: deciding what are valid sources of law so that we know where to find rules that are legitimate for use in the legal system.

Determining a Valid Source of Law

There is no automatic, objective formula that can be applied to determine what will be considered a valid source of law in a legal system. In each legal system, what is considered a valid source of law depends on many factors, including historical development, customs, and traditions.

For example, because the common law system developed as a means of enhancing royal power, it was important that the king's judges quickly developed some rules that were distinct from local ones and common to the country as a whole. From that need developed the case law system with which we are now familiar and which we accept as a major source of law. In other systems, historical forces led to the government's convening a conference to set up a code of law, as happened in Napoleon's France and in Quebec.

MAJOR SOURCES OF LAW IN CANADA

In Canada, in the common law system, the major sources of law, in the order of their importance to the system, are statute law and case law or common law. There are also some other miscellaneous sources of law that are discussed at the end of this chapter. Another feature discussed here is how the major sources of law are organized so that legal rules can be found, retrieved from their organizational system, and used.[1]

---

[1] This topic will be explored in more detail in another chapter, "Legal Research", which deals with basic legal research skills, offered in the complete edition of this modular textbook.

| EXHIBIT 3.1 | The Statutory Enactment Process |

The process of enacting a statute is fairly cumbersome and time consuming. While on the surface the process looks inefficient, it does provide time and opportunity for members of a legislature to scrutinize and criticize proposed legislation.

Most bills that are introduced are **public bills**, brought in to implement government policy. There are also **private bills,** in which the legislature is asked to implement legislation for some private or purely local purpose. For example, municipalities often request legislation to amend their powers to allow them to exercise some minor power they feel they need. Last, there are **private member's bills**, introduced by individual legislators, which deal with subjects that are not taken up by the government as part of its programs. Because most of a legislature's time is taken up with the government's business, private member's bills are rarely enacted. The enactment process set out below is based on the process in Ontario. Other provinces have similar procedures. For the federal government, note that after passage in the House of Commons, the bill must go through the same process in the Senate before it can receive royal assent.

The Enactment Process

1. **Idea for legislative proposal.** This may come from a minister's initiative, advocacy or lobby group proposal, or other source.

2. **Ministry review of proposal.** Staff advise on proposal, and make recommendations to the minister.

3. **Minister's approval.** A policy submission is prepared by staff and approved by the minister.

4. **Cabinet submission by minister.** A detailed Cabinet submission on the legislative proposal is prepared, reviewed, and commented on by other ministries.

5. **Cabinet submission reviewed by Management Board of Cabinet.** Cabinet reviews amended Cabinet submission and approves, amends, or rejects submission.

6. **Approved Cabinet submission sent to Legislative Drafting Office.** Ministry staff and drafting office staff develop the first draft of the bill. The drafting office will continue to make changes resulting from amendments during the legislative process.

7. **First reading of the bill.** The bill is introduced by the minister, and background information is given to the legislature. The bill is put on the legislative agenda, printed and distributed to legislators and the public, in both a paper version and in an electronic version on the government website.

8. **Second reading.** The bill is debated in general terms. The minister makes opening and closing speeches. All members may speak once on the bill. There are no amendments at this stage. The Speaker calls a vote. If there is unanimous consent, the bill goes directly to third reading; if not, it goes to a standing or select committee of the House, as determined by the minister.

9. **Select or standing committee.** Members of the committee can comment on the bill, hold public hearings, allow public input, and call and question witnesses. The committee then does a clause-by-clause examination, and may amend the bill. The bill is then reported back to the whole House, and, if amended, is reprinted in a second reading version. If there is unanimous consent in the House, the bill may go directly to third reading; otherwise, it is referred to the committee of the whole House.

10. **Committee of the whole House.** Members debate the bill with less formality than is usual in the House; there is no public participation. Members may pass amendments. If so, the bill is reprinted in a third reading version.

11. **Third reading.** The bill is formally debated in general terms; no further amendments are permitted. Any member may move that the final vote be held on the bill.

12. **Royal assent.** If the bill passes, it is presented to the lieutenant governor for his signature or assent to the bill's passage. When the bill receives royal assent, it becomes an Act of the legislature, is given a statute number and reprinted.

13. **Proclamation of Act in force.** A section of the Act itself will determine whether it is proclaimed in force upon receiving royal assent or on a day fixed by the lieutenant governor or on a specified date.

vast - huge

**Major Sources:
Statute Law**

Statutes, or Acts of legislatures ("legislature" as used here includes both provincial legislatures and the federal Parliament), are perhaps the most important sources of law because of the vast quantity of statutory rules, and because they overrule the common law where they conflict with it.

**Statutes in
a Federal System**

In a federal system, the constitution divides the power to govern between the national and provincial governments. The subject matter of a statute determines whether it should be passed by Parliament or by a provincial legislature. To be a valid law, the subject matter of legislation must come within the heads of power granted by section 92 to the provinces or by section 91 to the federal government, under the *Constitution Act, 1867*. If a level of government passes legislation on a subject for which that level has no legislative authority in the *Constitution Act, 1867*, then that legislation is **ultra vires**, or beyond the power of the legislature to enact. In such a situation, the legislation is invalid and need not be obeyed. *↳ törvénybe iktat*

**Relationship
between Statutes
and Case Law**

As noted earlier in this chapter, when a statute is inconsistent with previous case law, the statute overrules the case law. However, it is also important to remember that a large body of case law is case law that interprets statutes, giving depth and meaning to statutory provisions. In some circumstances, case law develops new directions, giving additional meaning to statutory provisions that they may not have had when the statute was originally passed.

Finding Statute Law

On each of the three readings of a bill, a printed version is available through either the clerk of the legislative body or from the government's publication centre or bookstore, or on a private or governmental Internet site. Use of anything other than the third-reading version is not advisable, as the bill is usually amended to some extent between first and third reading.

Bills are numbered sequentially in the order in which they are introduced during a session, and are referenced and accessed by their bill number. Federal bills have the alphabetical prefix "C" before the sequential number, but are otherwise referenced in the same way as provincial bills.[2]

When a bill is passed and becomes a statute, it is referenced by chapter number in the volume of annual statutes for the year it is passed. Numbers are given sequentially to each bill that becomes a statute. The reference to the annual volume of statutes is "S.O.", for Statutes of Ontario, followed by the year and the chapter.

Example: The *Courts of Justice Amendment Act*, S.O. 1991, c. 46

From time to time, at both the provincial and federal level, legislative bodies consolidate all of the statutes and their amendments for the preceding period in a series of volumes called **revised statutes**. These volumes will include all of the public statutes of the legislature in the form they were in at the revision date. The statutes will be set out in alphabetical order and numbered sequentially in the revision volumes, using both the letter of the first word of the Act and a number. The volume in which it appears, the *Revised Statutes of Ontario*, is also cited by its initials, R.S.O., followed by the year of revision and an alphanumeric chapter number.

Example: The *Courts of Justice Act*, R.S.O. 1990, c. C.43

---

[2] See "Suggested Readings" at the end of the chapter for sources of law databases.

EXHIBIT 3.2

The Outline of a Statute

The way a statute is organized will vary with its subject matter. Knowing how a statute is organized, generally, will make it easier for someone reading a particular statute for the first time to find information. The basic organizational scheme for modern statutes is as follows:

1. Long title and chapter number.

2. Preamble. (Usually begins with "whereas" and sets out the main principles and purposes of the Act; the preamble is a useful and legitimate aid to interpreting the statute. Not all statutes have preambles.)

3. Introductory sections containing definitions used in the Act, the scope or application of the Act, powers of officials administering the Act, and other administrative matters.

4. Body of the Act.

5. Housekeeping sections — proclamation date, regulation-making powers, short title of the Act, as required.

Following is a reproduction of an Ontario Act, as it appears in the Ontario government website: e-Laws <http://www.e-laws.gov.on.ca/index.html>.

Absentees Act
R.S.O. 1990, CHAPTER A.3

Last amendment: 2006, c. 19, Sched. C, s. 1(1).

Definition

1. An absentee within the meaning of this Act means a person who, having had his or her usual place of residence or domicile in Ontario, has disappeared, whose whereabouts is unknown and as to whom there is no knowledge as to whether he or she is alive or dead. R.S.O. 1990, c. A.3, s. 1.

Declaration by court

2. (1) The Superior Court of Justice may by order declare a person to be an absentee if it is shown that due and satisfactory inquiry has been made, or may direct such further inquiry to be made and proceedings to be taken as the court considers expedient before making any order. R.S.O. 1990, c. A.3, s. 2 (1); 2006, c. 19, Sched. C, s. 1 (1).

Application, who may make

(2) The application for the order may be made by,
    (a)   the Attorney General;
    (b)   any one or more of the next of kin of the alleged absentee;
    (c)   the person to whom the alleged absentee is married;
    (d)   the person with whom the alleged absentee was living in a conjugal relationship outside marriage immediately before the absentee's disappearance;
    (e)   a creditor; or
    (f)   any other person. R.S.O. 1990, c. A.3, s. 2 (2); 1999, c. 6, s. 1; 2005, c. 5, s. 1.

Appeal

(3) Any person aggrieved or affected by the order has the right to appeal therefrom. R.S.O. 1990, c. A.3, s. 2 (3).

Order declaring person no longer absentee

3. Upon application at any time, the court, if satisfied that such person has ceased to be an absentee, may make an order so declaring and superseding, vacating and setting aside the order declaring the person an absentee for all purposes except as to acts or things done in respect of the estate of the absentee while such order was in force. R.S.O. 1990, c. A.3, s. 3.

Administration of estate

4. The court may make an order for the custody, due care and management of the property of an absentee, and a committee may be appointed for that purpose. R.S.O. 1990, c. A.3, s. 4.

The Outline of a Statute

EXHIBIT 3.2 (continued)

Who may be appointed committee

5. A trust corporation with or without one or more persons may be appointed such committee. R.S.O. 1990, c. A.3, s. 5.

Powers and duties of court and committee

6. Where a committee of the estate of an absentee has been appointed, the powers and duties of the court and committee are the same, with necessary modifications, as the powers and duties of the court and of a guardian of property under the *Substitute Decisions Act*, 1992. 1992, c. 32, s. 1.

Powers of committee to expend money out of estate

7. The committee, subject to the direction of the court, has authority to expend moneys out of the estate of an absentee for the purpose of endeavouring to trace the absentee and in endeavouring to ascertain whether he or she is alive or dead. R.S.O. 1990, c. A.3, s. 7.

Lands in Ontario of foreign absentee

8. Where a person who has had his or her usual place of residence or domicile out of Ontario and who has an interest in land in Ontario has been declared to be an absentee by a court of competent jurisdiction, the Superior Court of Justice may by order, upon being satisfied that the person has disappeared, that his or her whereabouts is unknown and that there is no knowledge as to whether the person is alive or dead, appoint a committee with such authority to manage, sell or otherwise deal with the interest in land as in the opinion of the court is in his or her best interests and those of his or her family. R.S.O. 1990, c. A.3, s. 8; 2006, c. 19, Sched. C, s. 1 (1).

The example of the history of a particular Ontario statute prior to revision in Exhibit 3.3 illustrates the revision process: The legislature first passed the *Courts of Justice Act* in 1984, between the 1980 and 1990 revisions. It was amended on several occasions after 1984, with major amendments in 1989. Amendments are actually in the form of separate Acts. Thus, the *Courts of Justice Amendment Act* appeared as a separate statute in the annual statute volume in the year in which the amendment was passed. In 1990, when all statutes were revised, the revised version of the *Courts of Justice Act* incorporated all of the previous amendments and deleted from the revision anything that had been repealed by an amending Act.

In some respects a statutory revision resembles a reassembly of a statute using scissors and paste, cutting out parts that have been repealed, and pasting in parts that have been added.

However, periodic revisions have become less frequent — the last Ontario revision was in 1990; the last federal one, in 1985. Because statutes are now all available online, when new ones are passed, or existing ones amended, they can easily be edited into the electronic statute database so that they are always in their most up-to-date version. The cumbersome periodic paper revision process may no longer be necessary at all.

Primary and Subordinate Legislation

The legislatures of the 10 provinces, those of the territories, and the federal Parliament all enact legislation by the process described above (with some minor variations). However, the statutes, or **primary legislation**, passed by the legislature may be only the tip of the legislative iceberg on the particular sub-

---

EXHIBIT 3.3   **Finding a Statute: *The Courts of Justice Act*, R.S.O. 1990, c. C.43**

The legislature passes the *Courts of Justice Act*, S.O. 1984, c. 46

S.O.
1984
C.1–83

The legislature amends the Act in 1989 by passing the *Courts of Justice Amendment Act*, S.O. 1989, c. 103

S.O.
1989
C.1–150

The *Courts of Justice Act*, S.O. 1984, and all subsequent amendments are consolidated in the 1990 statutory revision process as the *Courts of Justice Act*, R.S.O. 1990, c. C.43

R.S.O.
1990
v.1
C.A1–A8

R.S.O.
1990
v.2
C.A9–B4

R.S.O.
1990
v.3
C.B5–C6

R.S.O.
1990
v.4
C.C7–82

with respect to iNet

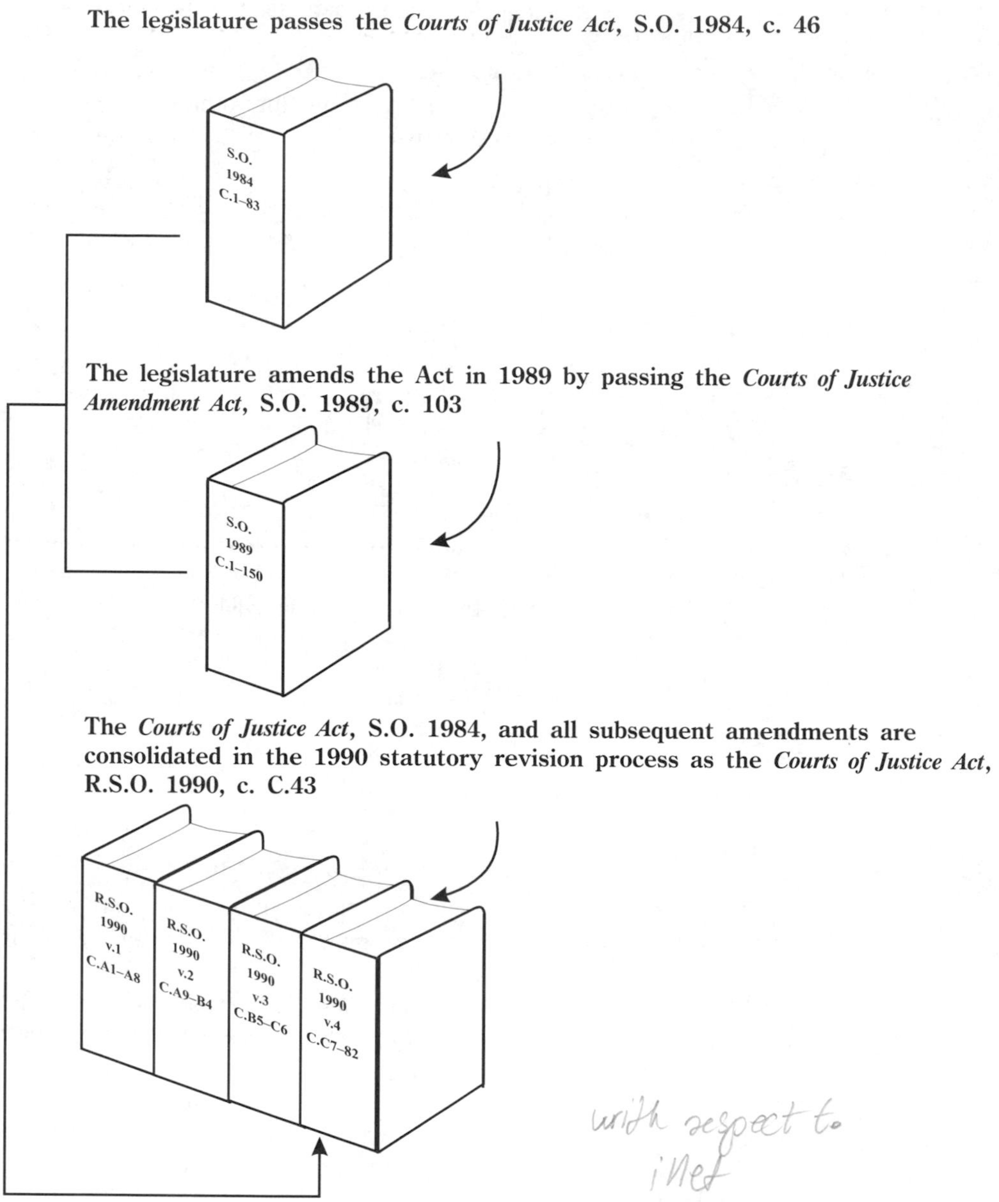

ject covered by the legislation. Many statutes contain provisions, usually found at the end of the statute, in a part dealing with "housekeeping", where either the Cabinet (formally called the lieutenant-governor-in-council for a province and the governor-general-in-council for the federal government) or a minister has the power to make regulations under the Act with respect to subject matter that is set out in the section authorizing the making of regulations. Regulations made by this process are called **subordinate legislation**. In practice, the actual creation and drafting of regulations is left to civil servants in the ministry responsible. The subject matter of regulations usually deals with administrative details and procedures for carrying out the statute's general purposes.

For example, procedural rules used in the courts of Ontario could have been included in the *Courts of Justice Act*. However, if that had been done, the act would have been many times longer than it is now, and the legislature could not have adequately addressed all the technical issues involved in keeping the rules up-to-date. Moreover, as the rules are amended frequently, the legislature would have to be in constant session to deal with the amendments and would have little time for other government business. Instead, the much more responsive and faster regulation-making process is used. In the case of the rules of civil procedure, the regulations establish a rules committee, composed of persons with specialized knowledge who have the power to make the necessary rule amendments by regulation.

Finding Regulations

A torrent of regulations are passed every year. Initially, before they take effect, they must appear in the government's official publication for public notices, called a **gazette** (the *Canada Gazette* is at the federal level, and there are gazettes at the provincial level). When a regulation is gazetted, it is assigned a number in sequence for the year in which it is made. The regulation can then be referenced as, for example, Ontario Regulation 803/88. This means it was the 803rd regulation to be gazetted for 1988. The abbreviation of the citation is: O. Reg. 803/88.

As is the case with statutes, regulations traditionally have gone through a revision process about once a decade in most Canadian jurisdictions. In Ontario, for example, the consolidated regulations then appear in bound volumes called the *Revised Regulations of Ontario* (abbreviated for citation purposes as R.R.O., followed by the year of revision). The plan of the revised regulations is to group the regulations with their authorizing statutes, and set the regulations out in the R.R.O. in numerical sequence, with the regulation number being determined by the alphabetical order in which statutes appear in the R.S.O. For example, as illustrated in Exhibit 3.4, the rules of civil procedure, made by regulation under the *Courts of Justice Act*, have a relatively low number because their governing statute, beginning with a "C", comes early in the alphabetical listing. The regulation for the rules of civil procedure is cited as: R.R.O. 1990, Reg. 194. As with statutes, amendments and additions to the regulations can easily be added to the existing electronic database, making future paper revisions unnecessary.

"The Plain Intention of the Legislature" — Interpreting Statutes

Judges often use the phrase "the plain intention of the legislature" (or one like it) when interpreting statutes. When they use it, they are saying that the meaning of a section of a statute is clear to them. Yet there are few statutes that have not been the subject of litigation, where one lawyer or another has argued that a section of a statute is ambiguous or unclear. This is why case law is sometimes said to give further depth and meaning to statutory rules.

Modern statutes are often very clearly drafted, although the same cannot be said for statutes drafted before 1900. But no statute drafter can foresee every possible situation or contingency that the statute may deal with. Nor does the drafter wish, in every case, to be overly precise, as by so doing, the scope of the statute may become too narrow and inflexible.

The Basic Rule: Determine the Intent of the Legislature

If parliamentary supremacy is to mean anything, it must mean that legislation takes on the meaning that was intended by the members of the legislative body that created the statute. Judges are not free to recreate their own idea of what the statute means.

EXHIBIT 3.4

Finding a Regulation Made under the *Courts of Justice Act*

The *Courts of Justice Act*, pursuant to a regulation, provides for a rules committee that can amend rules of court by regulation. The rules committee in 1985 amended the rules of civil procedure.

The regulation containing the amended rule is gazetted to the *Ontario Gazette* as O. Reg. 803/85.

O. Reg. 803/85, and all other regulations made under the authority of the *Courts of Justice Act*, were consolidated and collected under the Act during the regulation-revision process in 1990. These regulations were given new sequential numbers based on the alphabetical sequence of the Act they are associated with. O. Reg. 803/85 is now Reg. 194, R.R.O. 1990.

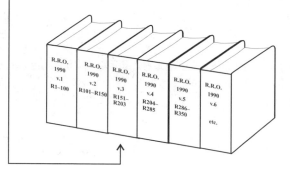

However, the intention of the legislature is really a fiction. Not all the members of the legislature would necessarily agree on the meaning of the statute; even legislators who are members of the governing party might not agree on the meaning or, even, be aware of what the Act is about. But the approach to interpreting an Act begins and ends with finding the legislative intent.

Rules of Construction

A judge begins the search for legislative intent by applying logical and grammatical rules to the language of the statute. Here a judge relies on one or more of the rules of statutory construction. If a judge chooses one rule over another to interpret the language of a specific statute, the result may be very different from what it might have been had another rule been chosen. There is no automatic "right" rule, and some might argue that a judge simply chooses the rule to justify where he or she wants to go, obscuring the real basis for interpretation. Five of the more common interpretative rules are discussed below:

1. **The plain meaning rule**: If the words of the statute are clear and precise in their meaning, then that is the meaning the words are to be given, even if the judge thinks the outcome leads to absurdity or unfairness. If Parliament is supreme, then it may be unfair or absurd if it chooses to be, subject to limits on legislative action imposed by the *Charter of Rights and Freedoms*.[3]

   Example: Consider this excerpt from the *Dog Owners' Liability Act*. "The owner of a dog is liable for damages resulting from a bite or attack by the dog on another person or domestic animal." If the dog bit your pet boa constrictor, a judge, applying the plain meaning rule, might hold that the Act did not apply in this situation because a boa constrictor, though your pet, is a wild animal and not a domestic animal, as domestic animals are considered to be tamed. Here, a plain, obvious and usual meaning is given to the keywords, "domestic animal".

2. **The golden rule**: The words of the statute are to be given their clear meaning unless this would result in an absurdity, in which case it is permissible to examine the ambiguous part of the statute to see if it is inconsistent with the meaning and purpose of the rest of the statute. This rule expands the first rule by inviting a judge to give meaning to ambiguous language in part of the statute by reading it in the context of the whole statute.

   Example: Consider again the statutory language used for the preceding rule. "The owner of a dog is liable for damages resulting from a bite or attack by the dog on another person or domestic animal." If the golden rule is applied, the judge might look for the purpose of the statute and might conclude that it is intended to protect humans and animals with which humans choose to live from being harmed. In this case, the judge might interpret the language more broadly; the judge might reason that because the boa constrictor is a pet, given the Act's purpose, the snake should come within the category of "domestic animal".

3. **The mischief rule**: This rule is restricted in use to statutes that change the common law, rather than codify the common law. With such statutes, the ambiguity might be resolved by asking three questions:
   (i) What was the common law before the Act changed it?
   (ii) What was the mischief or problem that the common law did not adequately address?
   (iii) What remedy did the legislature create to prevent the mischief?

   With the answers to these questions in hand, judges are then supposed to have true insight into the nature and purpose of the Act so that they can interpret the ambiguous language to give effect to the remedy sought and to prevent the mischief from occurring.

   Example: Assuming the section of the *Dog Owners' Liability Act* that is discussed here is not a codification of the common law, a judge might

---

[3] The relationship between the supremacy of the legislature and the Charter is explored in the discussion of the role of the judges and the courts in other chapters — "The Court System", "The Constitution", and "The *Canadian Charter of Rights and Freedoms*" — offered in the complete edition of this modular textbook.

use the mischief rule to determine the true purpose of the statute. Here, the steps for doing that are spelled out. First, the judge asks what the common law was: it might have only afforded protection to humans who were seriously hurt. If so, the judge might ask the second question as to what mischief arose under the common law; here, the judge might find that domestic animals and pets were not protected. Last, the judge would ask what remedy was created by the legislature; the answer was protection for humans and domestic animals and pets, with penalties for dog owners.

4. *Ejusdem generis:* This Latin term means that the meaning of a general word or phrase comes from the more specific words that precede it in a sentence or clause. For example, in the clause "no cats, dogs, or other animals shall be permitted in residences", the word "animals" arguably includes domestic pets, but not barnyard animals or wild animals.

5. *Expressio unius, exclusio alterius:* Under this rule, the specific use of one word or phrase, by logic, implies the exclusion of another word or phrase. Often this means that an ordinary dictionary-defined antonym (a word with an opposite meaning) is excluded. At other times, an appreciation of a particular context is required to use this rule. Where the context itself is ambiguous, the rule may provide more problems than solutions.

   Example: Consider the phrase "domestic animal" in the section of the *Dog Owners' Liability Act* previously referred to. "The owner of a dog is liable for damages resulting from a bite or attack by the dog on another person or domestic animal." Here, if the issue was about a dog attack on a wild animal, the judge might cite the *expressio unius alterius rule*, holding that the qualification of "animal" by the word "domestic" excluded wild animals from the statute's protection.

External Aids to Statutory Interpretation

In addition to the linguistic interpretive rules noted above, there are other sources a judge can use to interpret statutes:

1. **Scholarly and academic writing:** There are a number of articles and texts that deal with major legislation, which judges may cite when interpreting a statute, often as a way of confirming their approach to an issue of interpretation. As well, there are texts, such as *Maxwell on Interpretation of Statutes* or E.A. Driedger's *The Construction of Statutes*, that are virtual encyclopedias for statutory interpretation in Canada.

2. **Interpretation statutes:** These statutes exist at both the federal and provincial levels, and attempt to systematically set out some basic rules of interpretation and construction governing all other statutes in their jurisdiction. Such statutes often contain definition sections that give a meaning for words to be used in all other statutes. An interpretation statute will also set out general canons, or rules of interpretation, to be used in all statutes. An example is the rule that all statutes are remedial and should be given a broad and expansive interpretation.

3. **Legislative history:** In the search for legislative intent, it has long been traditional in Canada and Britain to ignore *Hansard* (the official record of debates in a legislature), committee reports, royal commission reports, ministers' speeches, press releases, and other such documents.

The assumption in Canada has always been that the intent of the legislature is summed up in the words of the statute itself, and one need go
no further than the words of the statute to find the meaning.

The American experience is somewhat different, and much of what
one might call historical documentation from the legislative process
may be used as an aid to interpretation, particularly in constitutional
cases.

However, in *Charter of Rights* cases, there is some indication
that legislative history may have a legitimate interpretive role. There is
a growing use of the technique in constitutional cases as a way of gaining insight into the meaning of legislation under the constitutional
challenge.

4. **Statutory presumptions:** Over time, as a result of custom, convention,
   historical events and interpretative case law, a number of presumptions
   have attached like barnacles to statutes dealing with specific subject
   matter. For example, there is a presumption in criminal law statutes
   that all crimes shall be interpreted strictly and narrowly rather than
   broadly. Another is a presumption that no statute is to be read **retroactively**. This means the statute does not apply to situations that existed
   prior to the statute's enactment but only applies to situations arising
   after its passage.

Major Sources: Common Law

Common Law or Case Law

The use of decided cases as a source of law was a distinctive feature of
the common law system. The importance of cases as a source of law was due
in part to the doctrine of precedent, which requires that cases decided in the
past that are similar to the case at bar be followed. The doctrine of *stare
decisis* took the doctrine of precedent a step further by making precedent
cases of higher courts binding on lower courts within the same jurisdiction.

Case law is not followed if a statute contradicts the ratio of the case, or if
the case can be distinguished. It is noted that when a court considers a precedent to be binding, it needs to first determine whether the court that decided
the precedent is a "higher court".

Also to be considered is whether a precedent, though not binding, should
be seen as **persuasive**. This is determined by a number of possible subjective
factors — the reputation of the judge and the reputation of the court. If the
case comes from a high-level court in another jurisdiction that is respected by
judges in Canada, deference may be given to its decisions. For example, cases
from British superior courts are often deferred to, while cases from American
superior courts often are not. Also, on rare occasions, a judge will reject a
precedent altogether, and take the law from a line of cases in a new direction
entirely. These observations are a reminder that common law can be more
flexible than it at first appears to be.

Finding Case Law

Case law developed as an integral part of the common law system at an
early stage because it was written down so that it was accessible. No one had
to try and remember all of the rules. Its continued importance owes much to
the fact that it continues to be written down and made accessible through **law
reports,** which are published reports of decided cases.

There is no particular system to law report publishing, and much of it is
in private hands. There are "official reports" published by some courts, such
as the *Supreme Court Reports*, which report the decisions of the Supreme
Court of Canada; there are provincial reporting series reporting a medley of

EXHIBIT 3.5

**What Judgments, Reasons for Judgment, and
Reported Reasons for Judgment Look Like**

1. **A judgment or order** is a command from the court; it tells parties what they must do, but not why the judge decided the way he did. Page 1 of a judgment is produced below:

Court file no. 2987/90

SUPERIOR COURT OF JUSTICE

THE HONOURABLE MR. JUSTICE SNORK

TUESDAY, THE 16 DAY OF APRIL 1992

BETWEEN:

HENRY SNOOT

and   Plaintiff

MICHAEL SNIT

Defendant

Judgment

THIS ACTION was heard on the 2nd, 3rd, and 16th day of April, 1992, without a jury at Brampton, in the presence of counsel for both parties,

ON READING THE PLEADINGS AND HEARING THE EVIDENCE and submissions of counsel for the parties,

1. THIS COURT ORDERS AND ADJUDGES that the plaintiff recover from the defendant the sum of $102,000.00.

2. THIS COURT ORDERS AND ADJUDGES that the defendant do pay to the plaintiff his costs of this action, forthwith after assessment.

THIS judgment BEARS INTEREST at the rate of 3 per cent per year, commencing on April 16, 1992.

J.R. Snerg,
Local Registrar

2. A judge's written **reasons for decision** is like an essay, explaining in writing the basis for his decision. Page 1 of a sample reasons for decision is set out below:

SUPERIOR COURT OF JUSTICE

B E T W E E N:		
ANNA ADAMANT	]	J.W. Tough, Esq.
	]	for the Plaintiff
Plaintiff	]	
	]	
and	]	
	]	
	]	
EDWARD ADAMANT	]	Sandra Sharp,
	]	for the Defendant
Defendant	]	
	]	Heard: July 2,3, 1994

What Judgments, Reasons for Judgment, and Reported Reasons for Judgment Look Like

EXHIBIT 3.5 (continued)

TRAINOR, J.

The single issue in this proceeding, is the custody of the child, Adam Adamant, born February 1, 1991.

The resolution of that issue is often one of the most difficult problems that judges encounter. It is particularly so where both parents have demonstrated concern over the welfare of their child. The fact that both parents are well educated, sophisticated, professional people having considered and firm opinions about the proper way in which a child ought to....

3. In a **reported reasons for decision** the typed essay in the preceding example is set out in printed form in a law report, and contains additional information. A sample law report version of Reasons for Decision is set out below.

RE GILL AND REGISTRAR OF MOTOR VEHICLES ET AL. *name of the case*
RE HEFFREN AND REGISTRAR OF MOTOR VEHICLES

Ontario Court of Appeal, Houlden, Goodman and Finlayson JJ.A. *judges of appeal*

Sentence — Driving offences — Provincial suspension of driver's licence — Legislation providing for increased periods of suspension depending on number of convictions for Criminal Code driving offences — Motorist liable for increased period of suspension only where offence for which increased penalty sought occurred after prior conviction — Highway Traffic Act, R.S.O. 1980, c. 198, s. 26. *— key words*

Section 26(1) of the *Highway Traffic Act*, R.S.O. 1980, c. 198, which provides that the driver's licence of a motorist who is convicted of a *Criminal Code* driving offence is thereupon suspended for a period of "(*a*) upon the first conviction, three months; (*b*) upon the first subsequent conviction, six months; and (*c*) upon an additional subsequent conviction, three years" imposes a penalty and should be construed in the same way as criminal legislation which imposes an increased penalty by reason of previous convictions. Accordingly, the rule of statutory interpretation applies that where a statute imposes an increased penalty for a subsequent conviction, the offence for which the increased penalty is sought must have occurred after the prior conviction, before the increased penalty can be imposed. The fact that section 26(1) refers to a "conviction" rather than "offence" is not a significant distinction. An occurrence does not become an offence until there is a conviction but once there is a conviction, the terms "conviction" and "offence" are used interchangeably for the purpose of applying the rule of interpretation. *[lawyer's interpretation]*

Benn v. Registrar of Motor Vehicles et al. (1981), 59 C.C.C. (2d) 421, 10 M.V.R. 214, **overd** *— overruled*

R. v. Cheetham (1980), 53 C.C.C. (2d) 109, 17 C.R. (3d) 1; *R. v. Skolnick*, [1982] 2 S.C.R. 47, 68 C.C.C. (2d) 385, 138 D.L.R. (3d) 193, 29 C.R. (3d) 143, 16 M.V.R. 35, 42 N.R. 460, **apld** *applied*

R. v. Joslin (1981), 59 C.C.C. (2d) 512, 10 M.V.R. 29; *R. v. Negridge* (1980), 54 C.C.C. (2d) 304, 17 C.R. (3d) 14, 6 M.V.R. 14, **consd** *considered* *[parallel citation]*

Other cases referred to

Christie v. Britnell (1895), 21 V.L.R. 71; *Farrington v. Thomson and Bridgeland*, [1959] V.R. 286; *R. v. O'Brien, Ex. p. Chamberlain* (1908), 38 N.B.R. 381; *O'Hara v. Harrington*, [1962] Tas. S.R. 165

Statutes referred to

Criminal Code, ss. 234, 234.1, 235, 236

Highway Traffic Act, R.S.O. 1980, c. 198, s. 26(1) (am. 1983, c. 63, s. 11), (2) (rep. & sub. 1984, c. 61, s. 1)

Rules and regulations referred to

(Ont.) Rules of Civil Procedure (Ont.), rule 21.01
(Ont.) Rules of Practice (Ont.), Rule 124
(Ont.)

APPEALS by the registrar from a judgment of Smith J., 12 C.C.C. (3d) 23, and of McKinley J. on applications pursuant to Rule 124 (Ont.) to determine points of law.

Leslie M. McIntosh, for appellants.
Alan D. Gold, for respondent, Sukhpal-Singh Gill.
Robert J. Upsdell, for respondent, Louis Arnold Heffren.

[handwritten: representatives]

[handwritten: ↑ headnote] The judgment of the court was delivered by

FINLAYSON J.A.:—Both these appeals are by the Registrar of Motor Vehicles (hereinafter Registrar) with respect to licence suspensions under s. 26(1) of the *Highway Traffic Act*, R.S.O. 1980, c. 198, as amended, by reason of convictions by the two respondents for certain automobile related offences under the *Criminal Code....*

Source: "Re Gill and Registrar of Motor Vehicles et al., Ontario Court of Appeal, Houlden, Goodman and Finlayson JJ. A., September 3, 1985" 21 C.C.C. (3d) 1986, pp. 234–35. Reproduced from *Canadian Criminal Cases* with the permission of Canada Law Book, A Division of The Cartwright Group Ltd. (1-800-263-3269, www.canadalawbook.ca).

cases from a particular province; and there are Canada-wide reporting services reporting decisions of note from across the country. There are also reports that focus on specialized areas of law, such as the *Canadian Practice Cases*, that report cases dealing with procedural law. Some cases are reported in only one reporting series, while others may be reported in several. Some, however, are not reported at all. The decision to report is a subjective one, made by the editorial boards of the various law reports.

An unreported case, though not easily accessed, still has precedent value. In recent years, particularly with the establishment of computer case databases, it has become possible to list and summarize easily many of these unreported cases. As well, there are computerized indices of legal issues that allow relatively quick and thorough searches to be done that will identify reported and unreported cases. Because the case reporting process is unco-ordinated and unsystematic, the process of finding an appropriate precedent case can still be a time-consuming exercise, particularly compared to the search for a principle in the civil law system, where an article in the code that provides the answer can be quickly located. But as more lawyers use indexed databases of unreported cases, such as Quicklaw and LexisNexis, the distinction between reported and unreported cases may diminish.[4]

---

[4] The subject of finding law and dealing with basic legal research techniques is explored in another chapter, "Legal Research", offered in the complete edition of this modular textbook.

| How Reasons for Decision Are Set Out in Published Law Reports | **EXHIBIT 3.6** |

Case reports usually follow a generic format, which is set out below:

1. case name
2. court and judge(s)
3. date of decision
4. catch lines — phrases in bold print that can be scanned quickly to identify key facts and issues in the case, and that are also used as index headings and subheadings in the index to the law report series
5. headnote: a summary of the facts, the decision, and the reasons for the decision, including a list of cases, statutes, and other authorities referred to
6. a brief description of the form or purpose of proceeding (Appeal from ... Motion for....)
7. names of lawyers for the parties
8. full text of the judgment
9. final disposition

MISCELLANEOUS SOURCES OF LAW

While statute and case law are the most common and most important sources of law in the common law system, there are other sources of law that crop up occasionally.

Practice and Usage

These two terms loosely describe ways in which things may be done that may achieve legal recognition. These forms of behaviour, which have no formal authorization or sanction, will generally be accepted as a source of law if they go unchallenged, and other conduct or consequences that rest upon them will also be seen as legitimate. However, if a practice is challenged, the fact that it occurs is not sufficient to justify it as a source of law.

Custom and Convention

A practice or usage that has been in existence and in use for long enough (whatever "long enough" may mean), at some point can become enshrined in law as a custom or convention, at which time it is a source of law. Determining when the threshold is reached is a subjective process, with different results in different jurisdictions. There are, however, two key factors:

- The activity has gone on for a long time.
- There has been no interruption or interference with the activity.

In Canada, custom and convention has been a very important source of constitutional law. In 1981, the Supreme Court of Canada decided that the Trudeau government could **repatriate** the Canadian Constitution by taking over control of constitutional change from the Parliament of the United Kingdom. The court's decision turned on a lengthy and detailed analysis of custom and convention with respect to the amount of provincial support required before the federal government could seek an amendment to the Constitution.[5]

---

[5] *Reference re Amendment of the Constitution of Canada*, [1981] 1 S.C.R. 753.

Scholarly Legal Writing

On rare occasions, the musings of legal scholars may be a source of legal rules, where no other authority speaks to an issue. More often, however, such works are commentaries on existing law, useful in interpreting the law, rather than being a source of it.

Morality

Ever the delight of natural law theorists, morality has had a rough ride in modern common law. In the 19th and 20th centuries, where the issue was raised, the court would often deflect it by stating that "the court is not a court of morals." While morality might underlie a particular legal rule or principle, it rarely is the source of law, and operates only when no other source of law provides a solution to a particular legal problem.

The Crown or Royal Prerogative

This describes the power of the sovereign or, in Canada, the sovereign's representative (the Governor General, federally, and the Lieutenant Governor, provincially) to act in certain ways. Historically, the power is derived from the predemocratic era when the King had power to rule personally and use his personal power as a royal right. As the relationship between the King and Parliament evolved, so did the prerogative. Parliaments have steadily taken away parts of the prerogative power by legislating it away; once a prerogative power is lost, by custom and convention, it cannot be revived. Further, the sovereign or his or her representatives rarely exercise a prerogative power without advice from the government.

Some examples of the use of the prerogative are the dissolution of a legislature prior to calling an election and the pardoning of criminals. To the extent that the prerogative can be exercised without having to take or follow advice of elected representatives, the prerogative can be viewed as a source of law.

CHAPTER SUMMARY

This chapter was about the sources of law used for legal problem solving in the common law system. There are two principal sources of law: statute law, including subordinate legislation, and case law. There are also some miscellaneous sources: practice and usage, custom, convention, scholarly legal writing, morality, and the Crown prerogative. The secondary sources are used only when statute and case law do not provide answers. As between statute and case law, where a statute contradicts case law, the statute prevails.

The chapter also went beyond a description of the sources of law: it showed how statutes are made, in terms of how statutes are developed from a policy making and refining process, then formally prepared according to modern drafting conventions, and then formally enacted. The chapter went on to make the point that a statute is like a skeleton, and that it is fleshed out with regulations and with case law interpreting the sections of the Act.

Attention then turned to the interpretation of statutes by the courts. The major interpretive purpose is to discover the intent of the legislature, but the rules for doing this are sufficiently flexible to allow for quite different conclusions to be drawn, in a particular case, as to what the intent was. The chapter then identified other, more technical, rules for interpreting statutes.

The chapter then turned to case law, including a discussion of how one finds appropriate case law.[6]

---

[6] This issue is canvassed in more detail in another chapter, "Legal Research", offered in the complete edition of this modular textbook.

Last, the miscellaneous or secondary sources of law (practice and usage, custom and convention, scholarly legal writing, morality, the Crown prerogative) were identified and discussed in terms of when they can be used and what their range or utility is.

GLOSSARY OF NEW TERMS AND KEY CONCEPTS

bill	What a statute is called when it is introduced in a legislature. If it passes, it is then called an **Act**.
Cabinet submission	A document used to circulate a policy proposal for comment, or other government action, among the various ministries of the government. It then goes, eventually, to Cabinet, where Cabinet ministers decide how to deal with the matter.
committee of the whole House	While a bill is normally scrutinized by a **standing committee** of the legislature that deals with the subject matter covered by the bill, a bill may be considered by a committee consisting of all of the members of the legislature for the clause-by-clause discussion usually done in standing committee.
gazette	The name of a publication issued by governments in Canada on a regular basis, usually weekly, containing official notices and announcements, and in which regulations made under the authority of a statute are first published. A regulation usually takes effect at publication; consequently, the **gazetting** of a regulation is an important step in its becoming enforceable.
judgment or order	A command from the court that mus be followed.
law reports	Cases in which judges give reasons for judgment explaining a legal decision are gathered up and published in case reporting books called **law reports**. Law reports may be officially published by the government, law societies, or private publishers. They are no longer necessarily only in book form, as many law report series are available from online computer services and on CD-ROM.
Legislative Drafting Office	Most legislative bodies have a group of lawyers who are specialists in the art of drafting statutes. This office does not determine the content of legislation but does determine the form that legislation takes.
Management Board of Cabinet	A Cabinet committee that acts as a gatekeeper, determining which matters come before Cabinet.
persuasive	With respect to case law, a case decided by a respected judge from another jurisdiction, which is not binding on the court in the case at bar, is said to be persuasive if it otherwise influences the court.
primary legislation	Statutes are primary legislation; the term is used to distinguish statutes from regulations passed under the authority of statutes. Regulations are sometimes referred to as **subordinate legislation**.
private bill	A bill usually passed at the request of a specific person and that affects a particular person or body. For example, municipalities often ask to have a private bill passed in order to amend that municipality's powers.
private member's bill	A bill introduced by an individual MP or legislator that is not part of the government's legislative program. As the government controls the agenda of a legislature in order to get **government bills** passed, there is rarely time to consider private member's bills, and these usually do not come to a final vote.
proclaim in force	A bill does not come into force automatically when it is passed; it must first be proclaimed in force. This may be on a specific date, or when the government is ready, or upon passage of the bill, if the bill so provides.
public bill	A bill that affects the general law of the jurisdiction and concerns matters of a general or public nature.

repatriate	One repatriates something when one recovers its nationality. Canada repatriated its Constitution when it recovered from the United Kingdom the right as a nation to amend its own Constitution.
reported reasons for decision	A judge's written reasons for making a judgment or an order.
retroactive	A legal rule that takes effect in the period before the rule was created. Law is not supposed to be retroactive, and it is presumed that a law, when passed, takes effect only from and after the time of its passage.
revised statutes	In Canada, the federal government and the provinces consolidate and revise all statutes at regular intervals, deleting parts that have been repealed, and adding amendments since the date of the last revision.
second reading	A stage of the process that results in a bill becoming a law. At this stage, the bill is debated in the legislature at length, the basic principles are discussed, and the bill is defended by the minister responsible for it. A vote to approve at this stage is a vote of approval in principle.
subordinate legislation	A law made by a body subordinate to the Parliament under the authority of a parliamentary statute.
third reading	When the bill comes before the legislature after the committee stage has been completed, it receives its third and final reading and is voted on in its third reading form.
ultra vires	A Latin maxim that describes action that is unlawful because there is no authority to take that action; in a federal system, the maxim describes a statute passed by a legislative body that had no authority to pass the statute. The statute is, therefore, invalid and unlawful.

REVIEW QUESTIONS

1. How do we decide what a "valid source of law" is in a particular society?

2. What are the primary and miscellaneous sources of law in a common law system?

3. What steps have to be taken to make a political policy proposal into law?

4. Suppose the federal government and a provincial government both pass the exact same legislation. Does this create a problem? If so, what rules do we have for resolving the problem?

5. Suppose there is a common law rule that requires you to do something, and a statute that requires you to do the exact opposite. Which law do you obey? Why?

6. If a provincial statute was passed last year, describe the process to be used to locate it so you can read it.

7. You are told to look for a provincial statute called the *Road Servicing Act*. You have no idea whether it is a new statute, an amended statute, an old statute that has not been amended, or a bill. Describe, in sequential order, the sources you would examine to find the statute.

8. What are revised statutes? What problem do they solve? What would happen to our laws if there was no statutory revision process?

9. What is subordinate legislation? Why is it necessary?

10. Suppose you came across a reference to Regulation 543/94. Describe what you would do to find the regulation so you could read it.

11. Describe the following rules of statutory interpretation:
    (a) the plain meaning rule
    (b) the golden rule
    (c) the mischief rule

12. Are there real distinctions between the rules in Question 11, or are they really the same rule?

13. Using examples, explain how the following grammatical interpretive rules operate:
    (a) *ejusdem generis*
    (b) *expressio unius, exclusio alterius*

14. Is it permissible to delve into the history of legislation to determine the meaning of the statute?

15. What are statutory presumptions? Give two examples, and illustrate how the presumptions work.

16. What is an "unreported case"?

17. What is the difference between a "judgment", "reasons for judgment", and "reported reasons for judgment"?

18. A legal practice has been going on for 700 years; it was challenged once in court 10 years ago. Can we rely on the practice and cite it as a source of law?

19. In what circumstances could one cite the writings of a very learned, erudite, and respected legal scholar as a source of law?

20. Suppose a law was passed this year that criminalized a conduct that occurred in 1988, when that conduct was lawful. What do we call this kind of law? Is it a valid law?

21. The last revision of Ontario statutes and regulations took place in 1990. Is it time for another?

DISCUSSION QUESTIONS

1. Anna signed an apartment lease that contained the following clause: "A tenant may keep a dog, cat or other domestic pet on the premises." Anna doesn't own a cat or a dog, but she caught a young aardvark on a trip to Africa, tamed it, and brought it home. The aardvark is an anteater that lives in southern Africa. It is small, quiet, and well-behaved. The landlord found out about the aardvark. He saw it looking out of Anna's window and knew it wasn't a cat or a dog. The landlord argued that Anna is violating the lease by keeping the aardvark. Anna argues that her keeping an aardvark does not violate the lease.

    Using rules of statutory construction, and statutory presumptions, where relevant, argue both Anna's case and the landlord's.

2. If you have access to the Internet, use the free Web search service e-Laws to find a section of an Ontario statute, the *Family Law Act*, that indicates how the Act applies to polygamous marriages. See "Suggested Readings" for the appropriate website address.

SUGGESTED READINGS

Attorney General of Canada v. Attorney General of Manitoba et al., [1981] 1 S.C.R. 72; originally called *A Reference re the Amendment of the Constitution of Canada*, this case contains a discussion of the nature of convention as a source of law.

Driedger, E. *The Interpretation of Statutes*, 4th ed. (Toronto, Ont.: Butterworths, 1983).

Fitzgerald, M.F. *Legal Problem Solving: Reasoning, Research and Writing*, 4th ed. (Toronto, Ont.: Butterworths, 2007).

Kiralfy, A.K.R. *The English Legal System*, 8th ed. (London: Sweet & Maxwell, 1990).

Sullivan, R. *Driedger on the Construction of Statutes*, 4th ed. (Toronto, Ont.: Butterworths, 2003).

Thornton, G.C. *Legislative Drafting*, 4th ed. (London: Butterworths, 1996).

WEBSITES

Federal laws: <http://laws.justice.gc.ca/en/index.html>
    (federal government consolidated statutes and regulations)

e-Laws: <http://www.e-laws.gov.on.ca/index.html>
    (Ontario statutes, regulations and current bills — free access)

Quicklaw: <http://ql.quicklaw.com>
    (all provincial and federal statutes and Canadian case law — private subscription service)

LexisNexis Canada: <http://www.butterworths.ca> for information
    (all U.S., provincial and federal cases and statutes — private subscription service)

Types of Law

Laurence M. Olivo
SENECA COLLEGE

Learning Objectives

After reading this chapter, the reader should be able to:

➢ understand the distinction between public and private law
➢ understand the distinction between substantive and procedural law
➢ know the principles underlying private law
➢ know the principles underlying procedural law
➢ have an overview of the subject areas of public and private law

TABLE OF CONTENTS

INTRODUCTION: A LAW BESTIARY

In the Middle Ages, a bestiary was a book that described the animal kingdom. It was full of fabulous beasts, some of which had not ever been seen by the authors, and some of which, like the unicorn, did not actually exist.

A formal categorization of different types of law could take the form of a "law bestiary", full of distinctions that, while interesting, are not particularly helpful in giving students an idea of the breadth and reach of the law. Instead, this typology will define its organizing principles in terms of the way practising lawyers look at the law, and then define types of law in light of the principles identified.

Principles to Consider in Organizing a Typology of Law

Artificial and Real Distinctions

It is quite possible to build a largely theoretical typology of law that is both logical and elegant. But to be useful, a typology of law must define law in terms of concepts and areas of law that will help a student to understand the operation of the Canadian legal system. For example, to simply define law by subject matter alone is to really do no more than give dictionary definitions. Instead we need to identify important elements of law, and then see how they relate to each other.

Organizing Concepts

In developing a typology, the following concepts are of some importance:

1. **Positive law:** We need to focus on positive law — that is, the law of the state system. One of the features of a positive law system is that legal rules are in the command mode: *A* shall pay *B*, which means that there was implied an element of compulsion with penalties if *A* did not pay *B*. These are essential parts of any state legal system or positive law system. Contrasted to this are other conceptions of law: norms, values, morality, and religious beliefs, in which obedience does not depend on physical force. Some very interesting typologies of law can be built from norms values, etc., but a non-positive law's impact on legal systems in operation in the world is, at best, indirect. Consequently, non-positive law is omitted from our typology.

2. **Domestic and international law:** To some extent, international law has some impact that requires our attention. However, when it has impact, it is usually because it has been incorporated within the domestic system of law of the Canadian state or influenced the content of that law. For example, the *Hague Convention* governing international child abduction is a piece of international law. But its rules might as well be yelled out in a desert for all the importance that law has. What makes the *Hague Convention* important is that it has been incorporated into the Ontario *Children's Law Reform Act* and has become part of Ontario's domestic law and part of the domestic law of other provinces as well. As a result, the distinctive feature it has is that the law is now enforceable. It can command more than lip service, which significantly distinguishes it from much of public international law. Because public international law usually lacks independent enforcement mechanisms and because states often ignore such a law when it suits a state's interests to do so, public international law will be excluded from our typology.

   There is a sphere of international law, however, that is of great practical importance, and that is private international law. Private international law concerns private disputes between individuals that involve more than one national jurisdiction. There are two principal questions that usually have to be considered in the private international law arena:

- In which jurisdiction shall the issues be determined? This involves deciding which court system of which nation has the right to try the matter.
- Under the law, of which jurisdiction shall the issues be determined? This involves deciding which national legal system shall be used as a source of legal rules. Even where one national system is determined to have jurisdiction, the law that is applied to the problem may be the national law of a country other than the one that has jurisdiction to try the matter.

For example, a manufacturer of communication systems in Canada may contract to supply products to a German company making components for a shipbuilding company in Korea. If there are problems with the components and those problems lead to a lawsuit, where would one sue? In Canada? Germany? Korea? Which nation's laws would apply? The international aspects of these transactions make this an international private law problem, but what actually happens is that private international law, in sorting this out, really converts the problem into a domestic legal matter.

This area of law is of growing importance with globalization and the increase in various kinds of transnational commercial and other transactions.

3. **Private and public law:** Within a system of positive domestic law, there are usually significant differences between private law, which regulates the conduct of individuals as between themselves over private matters, and public law. In private law, the focus is on facilitating and regulating interaction rather than punishing it. Public law regulates the operation of the state and the interaction between the citizen and the state. Here the law is more likely to take the form of commands, spelling out rights and obligations and visiting sanctions on those who disobey.

4. **Procedural and substantive law:** Procedural law concerns itself with the process of the law, the route one takes to justice. Substantive law concerns rights, obligations and rules of conduct that regulate activity. If substantive law is about the content of rules, procedural law is about how those rules are to be used.

To summarize, our concern is to explore the divisions and elements of the domestic or national state system of law in Canada in terms of the way that law is organized.

SUBSTANTIVE LAW OF THE CANADIAN LEGAL SYSTEM

Public Law

Generally, public law is law that concerns public matters rather than purely private ones. There are four principal substantive areas of public law:

Criminal Law

While crime often has a private dimension in terms of injuries done to victims, it almost always is seen in terms of its public dimension. The theory is that crime tatters the social fabric and threatens social stability. Originally, in common law, criminal acts were those that were socially disruptive and were seen as a personal affront to the sovereign, who had primary responsibility for maintaining social peace. At the same time, crime was also seen in terms of the harm to individual victims, so criminal law had some private law aspects. For example, until this century, it was possible and, in some common law jurisdictions, common for crimes to be privately prosecuted by the victim rather than by the state. Today, however, criminal law rules and procedures are quite distinct, and the investigation, prosecution, and punishment of crime is a virtual state monopoly.

Constitutional Law

This area of law is concerned about rules by which the state operates. If the functions of the state were a sort of game, constitutional law would describe the rules by which the game is played. Constitutional law usually takes the form of a statutory document but may also consist of custom, convention and practices. For example, in Canada, such law defines what powers each level of government has, determines how the state apparatus is to be operated, and sets out certain areas of individual freedom upon which the state may not trespass. Constitutional law is sometimes described as fundamental law, without which the political and legal system cannot operate. One characteristic of constitutional law is that it is more difficult to repeal or amend than ordinary law. Another is that when there is a conflict between ordinary law and constitutional law, ordinary law is subordinate to constitutional law.

Administrative Law

This is a very broad and pervasive area of law, generally concerned with the regulation of activity, often private activity, where there is a perceived public interest. For example, if you own land in a residential neighbourhood, you cannot build whatever you wish on that land, as the land may be zoned for certain types of buildings. If you seek permission to exceed what the zoning allows, you will have to get permission from an administrative board that balances your private right against the public interest.

Taxation Law

This was one of the earliest areas of public law to develop as the sovereign took a personal interest in collecting public revenue, which, in many respects, was personally the King's money. Over time, the state's interest in revenue raising has not diminished, and neither has the citizen's desire to avoid paying taxes. Part of the public law of taxation is concerned with adjudicating disputes between taxpayers and the state. However, where a taxpayer's conduct amounts to fraud, the matter is dealt with as a criminal law matter.

Private Law

Private law is the law concerned with regulating the interactions between individuals as private persons.

Key Private Law Principles

While private law can be characterized in a variety of ways, there is a collection of principles and rules that provides most of the substantive law for almost all private law. These groups of principles are as follows:

- **Tort law:** This area of law can be described as civil wrongs by one individual against another. It includes intentional harm, harm resulting from carelessness (negligence), and some harmful acts where intention is entirely absent. Many torts — assault, for example — are also crimes. This is not surprising, as criminal law developed from tort law. Where a tort has been committed, the remedy granted is usually money damages to compensate the person harmed for the injury sustained.

- **Contract law:** This area developed from the tort of breaking one's word, to become an independent cause of action based on the idea that promises could not be given and broken at will, but were enforceable. Contract law, then, concerns the enforcement of promises, under various conditions. The remedy for breach of contract is usually monetary compensation. Sometimes, however, the courts will order performance of the contract.

- **Property law:** This area of law is concerned with rules for establishing what is capable of ownership, how things are to be owned, how we are to determine who owns something and the definition of types of property: real property (land) and personal property, both tangible (chattels or things) and intangible (rights).

Subject Matter of Private Law

The subject matter of private law is capable of almost endless division, which would result in an indigestible law bestiary. The areas that are set out below are principal areas of law in the Canadian system. For each of the areas listed, bear in mind that all of them will rely on tort, contract, and property law to some extent, as the source of their rules.

- **Family law:** This area of law was once part of the now vanished ecclesiastical or church law. It was originally seen as involving moral and religious matters. The religious and moral aspects are now largely absent from the law. Today, the law in this area borrows heavily from the contractual concept of partnership, so the law concerns itself largely with the dissolution of marriage partnerships and things incidental to that dissolution: property, support, custody, and divorce. There are other areas that are included in family law: adoption, child welfare (dealing with children whose basic family needs are not being met), and, in some instances, law dealing with the crimes of children.

- **Estates, wills, and trusts:** This area of law is closely related to family law and property law as it concerns itself with the distribution of property, often within a family, on the death of an individual. The law of trusts is closely connected to estate law, as it facilitates a person's (called a trustee) holding and controlling property for the benefit of someone else (called a beneficiary). However, the law of trusts is also a major part of commercial law.

- **Real estate law:** This area of law is concerned with the highly technical area of transferring and otherwise dealing with interests in land. An important subset also concerns itself with the process of land-use planning, although this may properly be considered part of administrative law.

- **Corporate and commercial law:** Sometimes this area is simply called business law. Closely involved with contract law, it is concerned with the various forms of business organization, banking, insurance and financial law and, generally, the law governing commercial operations.

- **Patents and intellectual property:** This growing area of law, similar in its basics to business law, is concerned with the law surrounding the protection and marketing of ideas in various forms, whether the substance is patents on things or processes, or copyrights on ideas.

- **Agency:** This area of law concerns itself with the relations of principals and agents, among themselves, and between themselves and others. The focus is on legal rights and obligations that arise when someone acts on your behalf as an agent. This can also be seen as a proper part of corporate and commercial law, or contract law.

PROCEDURAL LAW

Procedural law is concerned with the legal process by which rights and liabilities are **adjudicated**. Its focus is on the **adversarial** aspect of the law in the context of legal dispute resolution.

Procedural Norms

While we can describe a system of procedural rules as steps to be taken to settle a dispute, procedural law is about more than what steps to take. It is also about attitudes and values concerning how those steps should be taken.

Generally, procedural rules are structured to deal with the three perennial problems of legal systems: fairness, cost and delay. Procedural rules are designed to deliver justice as inexpensively and quickly as possible without sacrificing a just result.

Second, there is also a concern that, whatever procedural rules are, they be uniformly and evenly applied so that similar cases are treated in the same way. Another way of putting this is to say that the rules of the system should be applied objectively and without bias: justice should not only be done, but be seen to be done.

Closely related to consistency in applying procedural rules is the concern that the rules themselves be fair. Procedures that are inherently one-sided or arbitrary, or cause delay, or raise costs might be seen to be inherently unfair.

Law of Procedure

Incorporating the norms discussed in the preceding paragraph, this area of law concerns the process of settling disputes. It is characterized by detailed, complex, and technical rules of civil procedure to govern private law disputes, and rules of criminal procedure that are tailored to the criminal law process.

Law of procedure is also looked to to provide fair and transparent rules for regulating activities and resolving disputes in administrative law.

Law of Evidence

This area of law is often considered in the context of procedural rules, both civil and criminal. It concerns the legal rules that determine what kind of information can be used to prove facts that are in issue. Law of evidence is concerned with reliability, **probative value**, and relevance of information to be considered by the court in deciding a dispute.

CONCLUSION

The purpose of this chapter is to provide a panoramic view of the Canadian legal system in terms of some of its major components. By talking about divisions of law, it is easy to assume that the law operates in clear and distinct divisions, and that the divisions here are the only important ones. It is important to remember that the borders between the divisions are not all that distinct and sharp, and that there can be considerable overlap among them.

CHAPTER SUMMARY

This chapter set out a typology that allows the reader to conceptually organize law into categories. The context for this categorization is the positive law of the Canadian legal system. Positive law is the law actually in use, and is distinguished from morality and from religious law, which are omitted from the typology. Also omitted is public international law, except where it has been incorporated into the Canadian legal system.

The chapter then set out the relevant categories of law: public substantive law, private substantive law, and procedural law. Public substantive law consists of rules of law governing conduct that focus on the relationship between the individual and the state. Private substantive law is focused on the legal relationships between individuals. Procedural law concerns itself with rules and processes within a legal system that facilitate the operation of, and use of, substantive legal rules. Throughout the chapter, the reader was reminded that the categories are more than repositories for lists of rules; the contents of the categories are often determined by overarching principles that are grounded in societal norms and values.

GLOSSARY OF NEW TERMS AND KEY CONCEPTS

adjudicate	The process of hearing and deciding a case.
adversarial system	The trial process in the common law system, where the parties attempt to present their case in the best light possible, and to destroy the case of the opposite party.
domestic and international law	The positive law of a nation state. International law is concerned with the law that governs relations between nations and between individuals in an international context.
positive law	The law of nation states that controls and regulates social interaction.
private and public law	Private law concerns legal relationships between private persons; public law concerns legal relationships between private persons and the state.
probative value	The extent to which specific evidence proves a fact alleged by the party presenting it. Evidence of high probative value is evidence that strongly supports a party's case.
procedural and substantive law	Procedural law concerns rules and procedures under which a legal system operates. Substantive law is concerned with legal rights and remedies.

REVIEW QUESTIONS

1. What principles or concepts are used in organizing the typology of law as discussed in this chapter?

2. What is positive law? Give an example of law which is *not* positive law.

3. What impact does international law have on the positive domestic law system?

4. What are the main characteristics of public law? Of private law?

5. What are the main characteristics of procedural law?

6. How is substantive law distinguished from procedural law?

7. In what way is constitutional law distinct from other forms of public law?

8. From the legal situations set out below, identify the categories of law that are relevant to resolving the issues:

(a) Abraham got into an argument with Isaac in a bar. He punched Isaac in the face and broke several of Isaac's front teeth so that Isaac spent a lot of time and money at his dentist's.

(b) Delbert didn't declare some cash he received for a carpentry job as part of his earned income on his tax return.

(c) Jo Ann promised to sell her car to Linda, but later refused to go through with the deal.

(d) Armgard, in giving testimony in court, started to say what Juan had told her. The judge stoped her testimony.

(e) Beryllium wished to have Tungsten appear at trial to give evidence, and to ensure that Tungsten shows up, she issued a summons to a witness.

(f) Kate copied friends' CDs, which she then downloaded on her iPod.

(g) Graufus was a bloodthirsty tyrant who ruled Doofusonia with an iron hand. He regularly slaughtered opponents.

DISCUSSION QUESTIONS

1. Private substantive law can be seen as being composed of a number of areas of law, but it really all comes down to being aspects of tort, contract, and property law. Discuss this statement.

2. Public international law has sometimes been described as more wishful thinking than law. Discuss.

3. The only reason private international law has real impact is because it is not really international law. Discuss.

4. International law is often described as "not really law" because it lacks an effective enforcement mechanism. But is effective enforcement the only reason the law is obeyed? Discuss.

5. Ox is a car manufacturer in Spain. Many of the components are designed and built elsewhere and then shipped to Ox's assembly plant. McCart, an Australian living in China, bought an Ox. While driving it, the brakes failed. The brakes were designed and manufactured in Argentina. There is evidence that the brakes were defective in design and construction.

   Using your knowledge of types of law, identify issues and problems that might confront McCart in suing for damages.

6. While public international law is said to lack teeth because it does not have enforcement mechanisms, it may not be so much longer. Examine the case of the former president of Serbia, Slobodan Milosevic, who was subjected to international prosecution for crimes against humanity. In examining the issues, you may wish to use websites such as <www.theglobeandmail.com> to find articles on Milosevic and the International War Crimes Tribunal in The Hague. You may also wish to check the websites maintained by those who criticize the process and the prosecution as simply revenge by the winners, or you may conduct conventional library research.

   Does international law have teeth now? Why or why not? Discuss.

SUGGESTED READINGS

David, R. *Major Legal Systems in the World Today: An Introduction to the Comparative Study of Law*, 3rd ed., translated and adapted by J.E.C. Brierley (London: Sweet & Maxwell, 1985).

Derrett, J.D.M. *An Introduction to Legal Systems* (New York: Praeger, 1968).

Gall, Gerald L. *The Canadian Legal System*, 5th ed. (Toronto, Ont.: Carswell, 2004).

Structure of the Canadian Government

Irv Ash
SENECA COLLEGE

Learning Objectives

After reading this chapter, the reader should be able to:

➢ describe and understand the theory of parliamentary democracy and the party system and how it applies to Canada

➢ differentiate between the various levels of government in Canada

➢ understand how the Canadian government operates in each level

➢ understand the concepts of *intra vires* and *ultra vires* as they relate to the validity of a statute passed by a level of government

➢ differentiate between the three branches of government — the executive branch, the legislative (parliamentary) branch, and the judicial branch — recognizing their key components

➢ recognize and apply the theory of parliamentary supremacy in the Canadian context

➢ distinguish between the Canadian theory of parliamentary supremacy and the American theories of separation of powers and checks and balances

➢ recognize how the structure of the Canadian government affects the Canadian legal system

TABLE OF CONTENTS

INTRODUCTION

Constitutional law partly deals with the exercise of power by various parts of government. It explains which parts exercise legislative power (making new laws), executive power (implementing the laws) and judicial power (interpreting the law and deciding disputes). Constitutional law also explains the limitations imposed on those powers. In a federal state, there is constant tension between the levels of government as each level tries to enhance its powers.

This chapter intends to examine basic concepts of the Canadian government in the context of constitutional law. The structure of the Canadian government is based on the Constitution, both written and unwritten, as well as on agreements reached between levels of government. To fully understand the structure, one could initially study the history of the English government since the 13th century, as well as the history of Canadian colonial policies followed by the post-Confederation political practice. Such a historical study is not covered in this chapter. It is appropriate, however, to discuss the following concepts based on both constitutional law and political science as practised in Canada:

- *Parliamentary democracy* as a theory
- Levels of government
- Branches of government
- Parliamentary supremacy

In dealing with these items, we will occasionally discuss how these or similar concepts are practised in the United States in order to highlight what is unique and different about the Canadian government.

PARLIAMENTARY DEMOCRACY

The theory of government by parliamentary democracy involves a number of basic elements. To understand the theory, it is necessary to look at each element separately and then as a whole. This chapter will compare competing elements and theories in use in other countries with those in Canada. Proposals to change the system will also be examined in the process.

Democracy

The first key element is **democracy**. One definition states: "Democracy in itself is simply a technique, a way of making certain decisions by accepting the will of the majority."[1] Another definition, by Jackson and Jackson, elaborates: "An essential characteristic of democracy, therefore, is the reconciliation of the need for order and certainty with a degree of influence for competing political interests."[2] These and other definitions indicate that democracy can be seen as a system of governance whereby the majority rules but with certain restrictions, such as the recognition of minority rights or universal rights and political interests. Almost every state in the world calls itself democratic, but in order to be such, the state must have limitations on the power of the majority to govern. These limitations include a fixed time in power (that is, fixed dates or amount of time in power before elections) and protection of certain rights (usually in constitutional documents or theory).

---

[1] Mark O. Dickerson & Thomas Flanagan, *An Introduction to Government and Politics: A Conceptual Approach*, 5th ed. (Toronto, Ont.: ITP Nelson, 1998) at 217.

[2] Robert, J. Jackson & Doreen Jackson, *An Introduction to Political Science: Comparative and World Politics*, 3d ed. (Scarborough, Ont.: Prentice Hall Allyn and Bacon Canada, 2000) at 92.

Totalitarianism

Contrast the concept of democracy with the concept of **totalitarianism**, which is another common type of governance used in the world today. Jackson and Jackson define the term as "those states in which leaders impose their objectives or goals upon their people to an unlimited degree ... [E]fforts are made to control all aspects of society; to subordinate individuals and groups to the dominant leadership."[3] Some writers[4] have quoted with approval Friedrich and Brzezinski's definition of totalitarianism[5] as including the following elements:

- An official ideology
- A single party typically led by one man
- A terroristic police
- A communications monopoly
- A weapons monopoly
- A centrally directed economy

It could be stated that democracy is the rule of the majority within certain limits whereas totalitarianism is the rule of one or few with no limits. Although minorities in a democracy may see no practical differences between the systems, it could be argued that the minorities in a democracy have protections inherent in their system, even when the majority exercises power not approved by the minority. Note also that the definitions used above describe the extremes. As each system moves closer to the other, it may be difficult to clearly recognize the differences.

The Athenian Model of Direct Democracy

If democracy means rule of the majority within certain limits, what does the "parliamentary" part of the phrase "parliamentary democracy" mean? "Parliamentary" relates to the method used to allow the majority to rule. The first methodology to use democracy was a "**direct democracy**" employed by the Athenians over 2400 years ago. Decisions were made on the basis of one citizen, one vote, where the majority carried the day. Furthermore, leaders of the state were selected by lot for short terms. This type of democracy had many problems. First, in Athens only male citizens could vote, thereby excluding a large majority of the people in Athens, including slaves and women (children were also excluded but they have always been excluded in every system), although such exclusions could be eradicated. Second, there was the practical physical difficulty of assembling more than a few thousand people to hear and participate (although this problem can be alleviated somewhat with current and future technology allowing for teleconferencing and electronic voting). Third, it was difficult to have a calm and fruitful discussion on complex political issues that arise in the modern world (especially when the matter was urgent). Fourth, the leaders were not necessarily experienced or, likely, in office long enough to gain experience. A newer expression of direct democracy has developed in the past 300 years, and it will be discussed next.

Representative Democracy

Since the Athenian model of direct democracy was generally ineffective in most circumstances, the next form of democracy to develop was "**representative democracy**", whereby the citizens of a state elected persons who would govern the citizens through laws. Regular elections would allow the majority to somehow control those elected, who would not be in power for life but,

---

[3] *Ibid.* at 99.

[4] Jackson & Jackson, 2000; Dickerson & Flanagan, 1998.

[5] Carl J. Friedrich & Zbigniew Brzezinski, *Totalitarian Dictatorship and Autocracy*, 2d ed. rev. (Cambridge, MA: Harvard University Press, 1965).

instead, would have to justify their policies and themselves at some intervals. This system remedied problems of getting participants together, engaging in rational discussions based on experience. This became the broad model for democracies in the past three centuries.

Brief History of the English Parliamentary System

The English parliamentary system was the initial model of representative democracy. Here is a quick overview of how it developed. Initially, when England was united in the 11th century, the style of government it had would now be classified as totalitarianism. The king (or queen) was the government and ruled through ministers appointed by and serving at the pleasure of the monarch. The parliament, which was elected by a select group of landowners, first convened in 1295 and was strictly an advisory body. Throughout the centuries, the monarch and parliament argued over power, which led to the English Civil War in the 17th century, with the monarch relinquishing certain powers to parliament. Eventually, the monarch relinquished more power to parliament, leading to the system called a **constitutional monarchy**, where, theoretically, all power resides in parliament. This concept of a monopoly of power being vested in parliament is called parliamentary supremacy, which will be dealt with at the end of the chapter.

The Canadian Parliamentary System versus the U.S. Presidential System

The Canadian parliamentary system versus the U.S. presidential system of representative democracy is a comparison of two main models: the **parliamentary system** (originally and still in use in England, as well as in Canada and in other countries) and the **presidential system** (originally and still American, and in use in many other countries). Comparisons between these two systems can, again, throw light on both and allow for a more detailed discussion of the Canadian system. Both systems depend on three branches of government: the executive branch, which enforces the law; the legislative (parliamentary) branch, which makes the law; and the judicial branch, which interprets and applies the law to settle disputes. However, in the parliamentary system, the theory holds that the legislative (parliamentary) branch is supreme. This means that the laws passed by the legislative branch override what the other two branches do. The presidential system, on the other hand, believes in both "separation of powers" among the three branches and in a concept of "checks and balances" to ensure that no one branch is supreme.

The parliamentary system developed through the election of individuals who were members of parties. Each political party would have a member of its party stand for election in a riding (or district) against members of other parties. Whoever won the election for that riding would be part of the legislative branch representing the people of that riding in Parliament. The leader of the political party who had the majority (or plurality if a minority government) would become the prime minister (or premier) and leader of the executive branch. The leader would appoint individuals from within the elected members of the party to be ministers in the Cabinet, who would be in charge of various ministries, such as health, justice, environment, and so on. The leader and the Cabinet ministers are, therefore, both in the legislative and executive branches in the parliamentary system.

In contrast, the presidential system has an election for a leader called a "presidential election", which is separate from the election for members of the legislative branch (the House of Representatives and the Senate). Remember, in the parliamentary system, the leader of the party stands for election only in a single riding. In contrast, in the presidential system, the president stands for election throughout the country and is elected when he or she receives sufficient votes, even though his or her party does not win the most seats (ridings or districts) in the legislature. This means that the president is not part of the legislative branch. Furthermore, the people the president appoints to Cabinet are also not members of the legislative branch; they are not elected in elections at all and are considered separate from the legislative branch.

Also, in the parliamentary system the executive branch (usually in consultation with other groups) appoints the judiciary. By contrast, in the presidential system some judges can be elected, in some instances, in their districts. Other judges are appointed by the executive branch and, in some cases, confirmed by the legislative branch.

There is both a clearer separation of powers among the three branches, as well as a system of checks and balances of power of government, in the presidential system than in the parliamentary system. These concepts shall be developed later in the section on "Branches of Government". They are mentioned here simply to allow for some comparison between the two systems.

Elections in Both Systems

Election practices are somewhat similar, although different in key components, in the parliamentary system in Canada and the presidential system in the United States. In both countries, members of parties stand for election in ridings or districts or seats against members of another party or parties. Whoever wins the vote, commonly in Canada by a **plurality** (that is, the most votes cast, even if not more than 50 percent), wins the riding, district, or seat. Neither in Canada nor in the United States is the voter required by law to cast a vote. However, there are other countries that do require all voters to vote. Generally speaking, voter turnout has been shrinking in both Canada and the United States in the past few elections. Commentators have suggested reasons for the decrease in voter turnout, especially voters' apathy caused by distrust of most politicians due to perceived corruptions arising from campaign contributions from wealthy persons or by lobbyists. Campaign finance reform and the effect of lobbyists on government are important issues recently discussed in both countries, especially in the United States.

The Party System in Canada

The party system is essential in Canada, even more so than in the United States because the political party that wins the election wins at least a plurality, if not a majority, of the ridings. By winning a plurality or majority of seats, the party retains control of the legislative branch, with its members also in charge of the executive branch. In the United States, however, due to a separate election of the president, who appoints his Cabinet from people who are not part of the legislative branch, the executive and the legislative branches are not as closely connected. Moreover, even if the party of the president controls the Senate and the House of Representatives, the president does not have most of the controls that the leader of the Canadian executive branch has in controlling the legislative branch. In the United States, the president runs for a fixed term of four years; senators, six years; and members of the House of Representatives, two years.

When referring to the "Government of Canada", the term includes both the leader of the party in power and the party itself because of the close relation between the executive branch and the majority of the legislative branch. The members of the government — federal in the House of Commons and provincial in the provincial legislature — are all elected and consist of the following:

- **Leader (prime minister, premier)**
- **Cabinet ministers and secretaries** (members of the legislature who head ministries)

- **Backbenchers** (members of the government in power who vote with the government)
- **Leader of the opposition** (the leader of the party with usually the second most seats after the legislature)
- **Members in opposition to the government** (members of other parties, independent members or members of the ruling party who have been thrown out of the party caucus)

Municipal governments are very different and will be discussed later in this chapter.

In Canada, there is no fixed term for any member of Parliament or provincial legislature. The constitutional restriction requires that an election must occur no later than five years after the previous election. As a matter of convention, there will be an election any time that the government loses a majority vote in the House of Commons or provincial legislature (called "losing confidence"). If the government never loses a majority vote, the government can remain in power up to the five-year limit, but it normally chooses an election date that is favourable for its re-election. It is, therefore, essential to the government in power that it never loses a majority vote. This is achieved by enforcing party discipline. Each party has a **party whip**, who will talk to party members to ensure that they vote according to the party's way. Rebel members are "threatened" with removal from caucus or expulsion from the party. A good example of the kind of issues that arise when party discipline fails is seen in the Canadian Alliance Party's problems in the years 2000 to 2002. Party discipline usually means that all party members vote the way the leader of the party wants; however, sometimes the leader allows party members to vote as they see fit in a **free vote**. The deficiencies, real or perceived, in the current party system in place in Canada have led to calls for possible changes in terms of both direct democracy and in **single-member majoritarian** or even **multi-member proportional representation**.

Modern Model of Direct Democracy

Party discipline forces members to vote according to what the party wants even if the member's constituents want the member to vote differently. Party discipline leads to consistency and order, but it is seen as a barrier to "true" representation of constituents. One response is giving constituents more say in governing through various forms of direct democracy. The Canadian Alliance Party[6] led this movement in the past by advocating such proposals as **referendum (and/or plebiscite)**, **initiative (or proposition)**, and **recall**. Although referenda have been used in the past in Canada to "decide" major issues, such as conscription during World War II, Quebec "separation" in 1980 and 1995 and the Charlottetown Accord in 1992, enthusiasts intend to advocate a binding referendum for many more decisions of the government. It would allow voters more control over many areas normally voted on by the legislators. Arguments against referenda centre on the cost, delays, and the complexity of allowing all voters to vote on issues. On the other hand, referenda are seen as a way of controlling the influence of lobbyists, financial supporters, and other organized special interests on the members.

Initiatives or propositions are mechanisms that allow voters to raise issues themselves to be voted upon, unlike referenda, which are proposed by the politicians. The same arguments in favour of or against referenda apply here.

---

[6] The Canadian Alliance Party dissolved in 2003 after merging with the Progressive Conservative Party to form the Conservative Party.

A recall is proposed to make members of government aware that if they do not "make the constituents happy", their constituents can remove them from office. A recall vote is usually authorized when a certain number of voters sign a recall petition. Critics of recall cite costs as well as pressure on members to curry favour with their constituents and support their impulsive whims, making it difficult to make well-thought-out, hard decisions. Of course, direct democracy flies in the face of the theory of representative democracy, which is based on voters' selecting an experienced and/or wise person to represent their interests and the society as a whole. These calls for direct democracy probably occur because a growing number of people do not believe that members represent voters' interests as they are subject to too much influence by lobbyists or are, even, corrupted by outside sources.

Single-Member Majoritarian and Multi-Member Proportional Representation

During an election in Canada, members of various parties stand for election in a specific riding, and the candidate who gets the most votes, even if not more than 50 percent, wins the seat. Political scientists[7] refer to this as the **single-member-plurality system** because one person gets the plurality of the votes. Using the language of horse racing, it is sometimes referred to as the "first past the post" system. In a strong two-party system, such as in the United States, this system almost invariably produces a winner who gets the majority of the votes. However, in Canada, where there are at least four and sometimes more parties fielding candidates in some ridings, the winner often only has a plurality, sometimes as low as 35 percent of the votes cast. In that case, almost two-thirds of the voters who cast their vote wanted someone other than the winner to represent them. This can lead to voter frustration and disaffection. One suggestion is to use the single-member majoritarian system to have a runoff election a short time after the first election, with only the top two finishers in the previous election standing in the runoff. This would ensure a majority winner. This system is used in major elections in many countries, such as in the French election for president. There are extra costs involved, and the difficulty in doing it in all elections makes it unwieldy, but it may be useful in major elections, such as in the presidential races, where voters want to make a clear choice. Such a system might have prevented certain problems arising from the election of U.S. President George Bush in 2000. Green Party backers of Ralph Nader, a well-known consumer advocate and presidential candidate in 2000, would have seen their candidate eliminated in the first round, and their votes would then likely have gravitated to Al Gore, giving him a clear victory over Bush.

As discussed, this single-member majoritarian system does not address concerns in a parliamentary system, where party members are elected by pluralities, and even the party that wins power may have only a plurality of votes. The general concept proposed to make our parliamentary elections more responsive to the views of voters is **proportional representation**. It is used in other countries to deal with this problem. Such a system is described by Jackson and Jackson as being "designed to ensure that parties, or groups of voters, are represented more fairly and equitably than is often the case under the single-member plurality or majoritarian formulas."[8] Various forms of the system allow for parties to get seats proportionately based on the percentage

---

[7] See Jackson & Jackson, 2000; Dickerson & Flanagan, 1998; and Gregory, S. Mahler, *Comparative Politics: An Institutional and Cross-National Approach*, 3d ed. (Upper Saddle River, N.J.: Prentice Hall, 2000).

[8] Jackson & Jackson, *supra* at 401.

of votes the party receives, as compared to the number of all votes cast. This can be done either on a national vote or on a riding basis. The major argument against proportional representation is based on the likelihood of a weak minority or a coalition government, such as those in Italy and Israel. This can lead to either numerous elections or a diffusion of power to small parties. In this case, small parties could have the votes to prop up or defeat the government, giving them a power far beyond what is warranted by their actual national support. On the other hand, any party who gains a minimum number of votes will have members in the legislature and, therefore, give its voters some say in governing. Although both direct democracy and proportional representation have been proposed in Canada in recent years, the system has not changed, but readers can expect these or other proposals to change the system.

A number of proposals have been made for variations of proportional representation since 2003 and even put before voters in some provinces. The paper "Electoral Reform Initiatives in Canadian Provinces" prepared by James R. Robertson and revised in 2006[9] details the chronology of proposals in British Columbia, New Brunswick, Ontario, Prince Edward Island and Quebec. In British Columbia where the proposed system was put to a vote in 2005, it narrowly lost; more recently in Ontario, in 2007, a referendum proposing the system, known as MMP as noted in the Ontario Referendum site (<http://www.yourbigdecision.ca/en_ca/default.aspx>), lost decisively.[10] Because of the multiplicity of the attempts, the closeness of the vote in British Columbia and the steadily declining popular vote numbers in federal and provincial elections, it is likely that more proportional representation proposals will be made and may even change the structure of some Canadian governments.

FORMS OF GOVERNMENT

Levels of Government in General

A study of the approximately 200 countries in the world shows many forms of government, from the highly centralized to the loosely connected groups within the country. The forms of government depend on the size of the population, the country's traditions in terms of governance and the complexity of issues facing the country. In addition, for other reasons, countries are governed along a continuum, ranging from one unitary, strong, national government to the loosely confederated regions in a country with a relatively weak national government. The various levels of government that can exist have been broadly described by Dickerson and Flanagan:

> Governments can also be classified according to the degree of centralization they exhibit. The two main types applicable to modern circumstances are the **unitary system**, in which a single sovereign government controls all regions of the country, and **federalism**, in which sovereignty is divided between a central government and several regional or provincial governments. Two other types of less practical significance are **devolution** and **confederation**. The former is a variant of the unitary state in which the central government creates regional governments but can override them as it wishes, even to the point of abolishing them. The latter is an inherently unstable arrangement in which sovereign constituent governments create a central government without sovereign power of its own.[11]

---

9   Found at <http://www.parl.gc.ca/information/library/PRBpubs/prb0417-e.htm> as part of the Library of Parliament.

10   See Jeff Gray, "Voters roundly reject MMP", *The Globe and Mail* (October 11, 2007). Available online: <http://www.theglobeandmail.com/servlet/story/RTGAM.20071011.welectrefer11sb/BNStory/ontarioelection2007/home>

11   Dickerson & Flanagan, *supra* at 295.

An example of a unitary system was that of Great Britain before the 1990s. They had a national government and municipal governments with no regional governments. Since the referendum of 1997, however, Great Britain would seem to be an example of devolution: a regional government with certain powers allocated to it by the national government has been established in Scotland.

When Canada was formed in 1867, it was called a confederation. In fact, that was, initially, a misnomer, as the country was really a federation of provinces with a central government with paramount power. It could be argued that, over the years, between court rulings and agreements between the federal and provincial governments, Canada has become more of a confederation, with stronger provincial power and a weaker national government. On the other hand, the United States was created in 1776 as, initially, a federation of the original 13 states with a federal government and a shared sovereignty. The American Civil War, starting in 1861, can be looked upon as a dispute where some of the states (the Confederacy) believed that the country was a confederation, thereby allowing any state to secede at will. The northern states believed that there was really a federation, and that states could not easily leave. The North won, and their viewpoint prevailed to the extent that most political scientists would call the United States a federation.

Other examples of countries whose form of government was changed over time are Czechoslovakia and Yugoslavia. From the 1940s on, both were federations. Decades later, they split into separate new countries based on regions: the former by peaceful means, and the latter by a devastating war.

Levels of Government in Canada

As it currently exists, Canada can be classified as a federation, although there are pressures to make it more of a confederation as defined above. A federation is a sovereignty shared between the central and constituent governments. Here the central government, based in Ottawa, is called federal and the constituent governments are called provincial. Generally, the federal (national) government has **powers** in respect of dealing with other countries (national defence, treaties, income tax, customs, immigration) and with national policies (criminal law, post office, shipping and ports, railways, telecommunication, etc.). The provincial (regional) government is more local in nature (property and civil rights, sales taxes, labour and employment legislation, etc.). Generally, sovereignty is split between the two levels of government on the following bases:

- Enumerated (sovereign) powers (each level is given specific and separate powers, allowing each level to legislate exclusively in certain areas)
- Concurrent powers (both levels can legislate in the same area, but not on the exact same point)
- Overlapping powers (both levels have the same rights to legislate in the same area, and conflicts may arise)
- Paramount powers (one level has the final and ultimate right to legislate, and the other level only has a subordinate right or no right to legislate)

Municipal Government — Not a Level of Government in Canada

Although we discuss municipal governments, there is no legally separate level of government in Canada called municipal. Municipal government is a creation of the province under the Canadian Constitution and has no independent existence. It can be changed or even abolished by the province that created it. Furthermore, the municipal government derives all of its powers from those handed to it by the province and, therefore, has no greater power than what the province itself has and delegates to it. Although there have been recent discussions about giving extra or new powers to provinces by way of Charter status or the granting of certain revenue-raising powers,[12] the current status of municipal government has not changed.

Constitutional Foundations for Levels of Canadian Government

Prior to 1867, there was no national government in what is now Canada. Instead, there were colonies of Great Britain, which were described collectively as British North America in the 1860s. The confederation in 1867 created a national government and turned the colonies into provinces. Under the *British North America Act* (now the *Constitution Act, 1867*) powers were given to both the federal government (s. 91) and to the provinces (s. 92).

Outside the Power: Legislation Ruled to be Invalid

While each level of government has a constitutionally defined area of activity, what happens when one level of government goes outside its own area? The short answer is that if a jurisdictional dispute about the right to legislate in a particular area arises, the courts determine the issue. **Ultra vires** and **intra vires** are terms used by the judicial branch to state that a level of government is either outside (*ultra vires*) or inside (*intra vires*) its power under the Constitution to pass a law; therefore, such law is invalid or valid, respectively.

Mechanics of How Levels Operate

The federal level consists of the House of Commons and Senate, which together comprise the federal legislative branch that makes laws. Members of the House of Commons are elected (with the prime minister and the Cabinet ministers who, with civil servants, form the federal executive branch); senators are appointed by the executive branch. Laws that the federal legislative branch creates are passed pursuant to section 91 of the *Constitution Act, 1867.*

In each province, there is a provincial legislative assembly with all members elected. Also members of the assembly, the premier and the Cabinet ministers, together with civil servants, form the provincial executive branch. Laws that the provincial legislative branch creates are passed pursuant to section 92 of the *Constitution Act, 1867.*

The municipal level usually has a mayor and councillors, all elected with powers given under the *Municipal Act*, a statute passed by each provincial government to allow for the creation of municipalities and to delegate powers to them under section 92 of the *Constitution Act, 1867.*

Municipalities were amalgamated in Ontario and Quebec over the past five years, even though many in those cities objected. Furthermore, regional governments, which used to be interposed between the provincial and municipal governments, seem to be disappearing. Both are examples of the provincial government having a free hand to alter part of itself: that is, its creation, the municipal government.

Recent Modifications to the Levels

Over the past 40 years there have been numerous federal–provincial conferences regarding power-sharing, medicare, funding for education, and so on. These conferences have been attended by the representatives of the executive branches of the federal and provincial governments; the conferences have, to various degrees, successfully exercised power in many areas. It has been

---

[12] Royson James, "A New Deal for Cities" *The Toronto Star* (15 June 2002).

argued by Donald V. Smiley, a well-known writer, that this process is an example of **executive federalism**, which is defined as the "relations between elected and appointed officials of the two orders of government in federal–provincial interactions and among the executive in interprovincial interactions."[13] Smiley suggested that the executive branches, both federal and provincial, were gathering more power than possibly should be allowed, both constitutionally and in practice.

OVERVIEW OF THE CANADIAN GOVERNMENT

In Canada, as in most countries, there are three branches of government: one that enforces the laws (executive branch); one that makes the laws (legislative or parliamentary branch); and one that interprets and applies the laws (judicial branch).

The Three Branches of Government

Below is a summary of each branch of government in Canada in respect of (a) its major and associated functions and (b) the people who are part of each branch. (See also Exhibit 5.1.)

Executive Branch

The major function of the executive branch at both the federal and provincial levels is enforce the laws. Other associated functions the branch is responsible include

- proposes laws, although voted in by the legislative branch
- pass regulations without going through the legislative branch
- appoints judges, who are in the judicial branch
- help operate all three branches (through the civil service)

The executive branch includes the prime minister, the federal Cabinet, and the Governor General as the Queen's representative at the federal level. At the provincial level, the executive branch comprises the premier, the provincial Cabinet, and the Lieutenant Governors as the Queen's representative. Both levels of executive branches are staffed with civil services, including the police forces.

Legislative Branch

For both federal and provincial governments, the major function of the legislative branch is to make or create laws. And through laws, the legislative branch also creates administrative bodies that have some of the powers of all three branches in a limited setting. The federal legislative branch is made up of members of the House of Commons and members of the Senate, while the provincial branches are composed of members of the provincial legislatures.

Judicial Branch

The judicial branch is made up of judges and court officials and associated civil servants. The branch's major function is interpret and apply the laws, as well as adjudicate and resolve disputes. Its associated functions include

- help enforce judgments in civil court
- impose sentences in criminal court

[13] Donald V. Smiley, *Canada in Question: Federalism in the Eighties*, 3d ed. (Toronto, Ont.: McGraw-Hill Ryerson Limited, 1980) at 91.

The Branches of Government

EXHIBIT 5.1

	EXECUTIVE BRANCH	LEGISLATIVE BRANCH	JUDICIAL BRANCH
A1. Major Functions	Enforce the laws	Make or create laws	Interpret and apply the laws, and adjudicate and resolve disputes
A2. Associated Functions	¤ Propose laws, although voted in by the legislative branch ¤ Can pass regulations without going through the legislative branch ¤ Appoint judges, who are in the judicial branch ¤ Through the civil service, help operate all three branches.	Through laws, create administrative bodies that have some of the powers of all three branches in a limited setting	¤ Help enforce judgments in civil court ¤ Impose sentences in criminal court
B. People in Branch	1. Federal level ¤ Prime Minister ¤ Federal Cabinet ¤ The Queen's representative: the Governor General ¤ The federal civil service, including the police services 2. Provincial level ¤ Premier ¤ Provincial Cabinet ¤ The Queen's representative: the Lieutenant Governors ¤ The provincial civil service, including the police services	1. Federal level ¤ The federal House of Commons ¤ The Senate 2. Provincial level ¤ The provincial legislatures	The judges, court officials, and associated civil servants *federal court system* *provincial court system*

Please note that the Prime Minister, the federal Cabinet, the premiers, and the provincial Cabinets in the executive branch are also members of their respective parliaments and, as such, are also part of the legislative branch. Note: the terms "parliament" and "legislature" are interchangeable.

Interactions between Branches

Because members of the executive branch are also part of the legislative branch, the two branches are connected. The executive branch, especially in a majority government, is likely to persuade the legislative branch to pass specific laws. The fact that part of the executive branch appoints judges, who basically are the judicial branch, implies a connection between the executive branch and the judicial branch.

Under the theory of parliamentary supremacy, the laws made by the legislatures *are supposed to* override both the decrees of the executive branch and the decisions of the judicial branch. But judges could make law as a result of case decisions; and in handing out sentences, they also enforce the law. In Canada, judges can somewhat override parliamentary supremacy in three ways set out below. ⤷ *modification*

PARLIAMENTARY SUPREMACY

The Theory of Parliamentary Supremacy

The theory of parliamentary supremacy states that any law passed by parliament overrides any decision of a judge or a decree of the executive branch. Traditionally, this theory is reflected in the statement that statute law overrides the law of equity that overrides common law. For example, once the legislature passes a statute, the executive branch cannot, in theory, change it. Furthermore, a statute can be passed to override a decision of the judicial branch that the legislature does not agree with. An example is the fairly recent case where the Supreme Court of Canada held that extreme drunkenness could possibly be a defence to sexual assault. After that case, the legislature amended the *Criminal Code* to state that extreme drunkenness could not be used as a defence in these circumstances. This theory recognizes the supreme power of the legislature, which was first developed in England where, initially, the Crown possessed political power before ceding it to Parliament. As England at the time was a unitary state, no issue of different levels of government with different areas of power existed.

Parliamentary Supremacy in the Canadian Context

At least one modification to the theory of parliamentary supremacy is necessary since two levels of government exist in Canada. The courts have stated that each level is supreme in its own areas of jurisdiction and that if there is any conflict between the levels, generally the federal level will be supreme. Other modifications based on Canadian reality are noted below, including the concentration of power in the hands of the executive branch, and not in the supremacy of Parliament, under the theory of **responsible government**.

Canadian versus American Theories

In the United States, different theories are subscribed to — namely, the theory of **checks and balances** and the closely associated theory of **separation of powers**. In the American context, the three branches of government discussed above exist, with very specific and separate powers. Following are the branches in the United States:

- The executive branch, which consists of the president and the federal Cabinet, and, at the state level, the governors and the state Cabinet and the civil service
- The legislative branch, which consists of the House of Representatives and the Senate and, in each state, the legislatures

- The judicial branch, made up of the courts at both the state and federal government levels.

Furthermore, each branch has the ability to override what the other two branches do: by way of veto for the first two branches, and by judicial decision for the courts. In this way it is hoped that none of the branches will get too powerful but, rather, will be held in "check" by the other branches. Patrick Monahan, a Canadian constitutional law expert, summarized the two competing variations on how the branches of government use power in the following passages:

> [C]ertain constitutions, most notably the United States constitution, embrace the doctrine of the separation of powers. Under this doctrine, there is a strict separation between the executive, legislative, and judicial branches of government, with no single branch being permitted to encroach on the powers or jurisdiction of the others. Thus in the United States, the president (the head of the executive branch, responsible for enforcing and administrating the laws) cannot be a member of the legislative branch, or Congress. ... The United States constitution proceeds from the premise that concentrating power in particular institutions or individuals is dangerous, since those who granted such powers are likely to abuse them at the expense of individual liberty. The solution is to divide the state into mutually exclusive branches so as to preclude this concentration of power and the abuse that will (it is assumed) necessarily flow from it. ... These checks and balances often make it difficult for a president to implement the political program that may have led to his or her election. They reflect (once again) the American suspicion and mistrust of state power, and the preference for limiting government as the best means to protect individual liberty.
>
> The doctrine of the separation of powers has never been a dominant feature of the Canadian or the United Kingdom constitutions. Indeed, far from dividing power, the Canadian and British approach is to concentrate political power in the hands of the executive. This concentration of power is achieved through the doctrine of responsible government, under which both the legislative and executive branch are subject to the control of the prime minister [or premier]. The prime minister controls the executive, since the governor general (the formal head of the executive branch of government) must exercise all of his or her powers on the basis of the prime minister's advice. At the same time, the prime minister controls Parliament — the legislative branch — since the governor general is obliged to appoint as prime minister the leader of the party controlling the greatest number of seats in the elected House of Commons. Thus a Canadian prime minister with a majority in the House of Commons has far greater scope to implement his or her political program than does the American president.[14]

It appears that the reality of Canadian government is responsible government, which by its nature gives a tremendous concentration of power to the leader of the political party in power. However, certain modifications to parliamentary supremacy allow the judicial branch to limit the power not only of the legislative branch but, also, of the leader of the political party in power.

---

[14] Patrick J. Monahan, *Constitutional Law* (Concord, Ontario: Irwin Law, 1997) at 22–23.

Modifications to Parliamentary Supremacy

Judicial Interpretation

This is a modification that almost every country in the world theoretically recognizes. A statute is passed and, often, needs to be interpreted in court, either through a case that involves the statute or by **reference**. A reference is a method of getting an issue before the court without needing an actual fact situation affecting real persons to occur before the issue can be decided. The judge is given the right to decide the exact meaning of the words, including the possibility that they mean nothing and, therefore, should be null and void. Thus, even though the statute was legally passed by Parliament, it could, in effect, be overridden by the court. Of course, Parliament can pass a new law to override the decision; but that new statute would come before the courts for interpretation, possibly going through the process again.

Sections 91 and 92 and the Concept of Ultra Vires

Sections 91 and 92 of the *Constitution Act, 1867* create a division of powers between the federal and provincial levels that is specific to Canada. Any federal country, including Canada, with two levels of government that have specific powers, gives their courts power to determine if one level of government has inappropriately used power that belongs to the other level of government. Cases have come before the court, either under a fact situation or by reference, where the court must determine whether the level that passed the law operated within its powers or intruded on the other level's powers. If the judge determines that there was an intrusion, it would be decided that the law was ultra vires and, therefore, null and void. Thus, the court could determine if the law was valid and, with some finality, override the law made by parliament.

Infringement of the Rights Set Out in the Charter

As discussed in another chapter, the courts have been given the job of reviewing any law made to determine if that law infringes on anyone's rights or freedoms and, if it does, in certain circumstances to declare the law null and void. There are two exceptions to this right of the court. First, if the court finds that such infringement is "demonstrably justified in a free and democratic society" under section 1 of the Charter, the law is saved and declared valid. Second, the legislature can save some laws under the "notwithstanding" provision of section 33 of the Charter. There are also other exceptions that protect the rights of separate schools and First Nations. Many people have decried the numerous laws thrown out by the judicial branch, citing this judicial activity as evidence of "judicial activism" that has gone too far from the theory of parliamentary supremacy.

Judicial Activism

no modification

The modifications to parliamentary supremacy set out above, especially declaring laws null and void due to infringement of rights set out in the Charter, have given power to the judicial branch. Many critics have suggested that this power has led to judicial activism. They denounce this as transferring power from the elected representatives of the people to a non-elected body — the legislative branch. There are many examples where the Supreme Court of Canada has upheld certain principles, which led to disallowing parts of statutes, such as the *Morgentaler* decision in the 1980s regarding abortion and cases in the 1990s regarding mandatory retirement. On one hand, it can be argued that the majority supports one position but, possibly, the courts' decisions sometimes support the minority position. Thus, protecting the minority is served in a democracy by placing more power in the hands of the judicial branch than having complete, uncontrolled parliamentary democracy.

CONCLUSION

By reviewing the representative democratic government that exists in Canada, we have seen how the federal system works within a modified theory of parliamentary supremacy. After this discussion, it can be argued that the whole exercise can be summed up with one question: who has the power in the legal system in Canada? The legislative, executive, or judicial branch? Although parliamentary supremacy states that all power resides in the legislative (parliamentary) branch, the practicalities of political life in Canada suggest that there is a large concentration of power in the hands of the executive branch. Furthermore, it can also be argued that the Constitution of Canada seems to have given more power to the judicial branch. Or that all three branches can be considered more powerful than the other two branches, depending on which theory you approve of, which practicality you find convincing or which constitutional viewpoint you take.

Although there are no clear answers to the question of which branch has the most power, it is important to recognize each branch and how the structure of the Canadian government operates.

CHAPTER SUMMARY

In this chapter, the reader learned that the structure of Canadian government is based initially on parliamentary democracy as both democracy and Parliament are discussed. Features of the competing system of totalitarianism are also summarized to gain a better understanding of democracy.

A parliamentary structure suggests the need for representatives to be elected to a legislative or parliamentary assembly with certain powers. We contrasted this with direct democracy, which either has no representative or one whose powers are circumscribed by electors by various methods. To further understand the parliamentary process, we compared the Canadian parliamentary system and the U.S. presidential system in terms of where the power is in both systems and how they hold elections. Other alternatives to the current electoral system in use in Canada were also examined and discussed.

After a review of the parliamentary democracy, we described the levels of government and the federation in place in Canada, with both strong federal and provincial governments. Again, comparisons were made with other types of central-local government structures. It is emphasized that there is no legally separate municipal level of government in Canada, and that municipal government is a creation of the provincial level.

Next were the branches of government: executive, legislative and judicial. Each branch's functions, its members, and the interactions among the branches are outlined. The key point to remember relates to the theory behind the Canadian parliamentary system, the interactions of the branches (parliamentary supremacy) as compared to the theories behind the U.S. presidential system and the interaction among the branches (separation of powers and checks and balances). A comparison of the theories allows for a deeper examination of the Canadian theory of parliamentary supremacy and how it works practically, recognizing three modifications from the classical theory, wherein Parliament has all the power. The three modifications have taken some of parliament's power (or too much power, if critical thinking about too much judicial activism is accepted) and given it to the judicial branch.

GLOSSARY OF NEW TERMS AND KEY CONCEPTS

backbenchers	Elected members of the legislative branch of the party of the government in power who are not Cabinet ministers or Cabinet secretaries.
Cabinet ministers and secretaries	Elected members of the legislature who head ministries.
checks and balances	The theory that, in combination with separation of powers, supports the presidential system of government, stating that each of the three branches of government has equal power and ensuring that each branch does not allow the other branches to overstep its own powers.
confederation	A loose type of federalism where the strong local governments have sovereign powers over a weak central government.
constitutional monarchy	The government system in countries (such as England and Canada) where the monarch relinquishes his or her power to Parliament to the extent that, theoretically, all power resides in Parliament, and the monarch is a figurehead.
democracy	A type of government where elections allow for making certain decisions by accepting the will of the majority.
devolution	A system where a central government allows some powers to be given to a localized government, with the ultimate power residing with the central government.
direct democracy	A system that allows the electorate more control than other types of democracy and includes at least two types:
	(i) the **Athenian Model**, where decisions are made on the basis of the one citizen, one vote mechanism, where the majority carried the day and all major decisions were put to a vote of the electorate, and
	(ii) the **Modern Model**, where representatives are elected, but mechanisms are in place to allow at least some control of the representatives to make them "listen" to the electorate.
executive federalism	A system of government where the relations between elected and appointed officials of the two levels of government in federal-provincial interactions and among the executives in interprovincial interactions are part of the power that is concentrated in that branch.
federalism	A system of government where sovereignty is divided between a central government and several regional or provincial governments.
free vote	A type of voting by representatives in a party system of government, where the party in power disregards party discipline and allows the members of the party to vote according to their conscience.
initiative (or proposition)	A mechanism of the modern model of direct democracy, where the voters can require that an issue be put on a ballot for a vote by the electorate that will bind the government.
intra vires	A Latin phrase that means "inside the power of the level of government to pass a law".
leader of the opposition	The leader of the party with, usually, the second most seats after the legislature.
members in opposition to the government	Members of parties other than the one in power, independent members, or members of the ruling party who have been thrown out of the party caucus.
multi-member proportional representation	A mechanism to ensure that all parties who receive a minimum number of votes receive a number of seats based on the proportion of that party's vote to all votes cast.
parliamentary system	Originally and still in use in England as well as in Canada and in other countries, where a legislative branch is elected to make laws and where part of the legislative branch is also part of the executive branch.

party whip	A person who talks to party members to ensure that they vote according to the party's way and may even "threaten" removal from caucus or expulsion from the party if the member wishes to rebel.
plurality	The winner in an election who receives the most votes cast, even if it is not more than 50 percent.
powers (types) of federal and provincial governments	The rights given constitutionally to both levels of government in a federation can include the following:

1. **Enumerated (sovereign) powers**, with each level given specific and separate powers, allowing each level to legislate exclusively in certain areas.
2. **Concurrent powers**, with both levels being able to legislate in the same area but not on the exact same point.
3. **Overlapping powers**, with both levels having the same rights to legislate in the same area, with conflicts possible as a result.
4. **Paramount powers**, with one level having the final and ultimate right to legislate, and the other level having only a subordinate or no right at all to legislate.

premier	The leader of a Canadian provincial party in power as the government.
presidential system	A system, originally and still American, but in use in many other countries, where the legislative branch is separate from the executive branch and where the executive branch is headed by a person who is elected in a country-wide election.
prime minister	The leader of a Canadian federal party in power as the government.
proportional representation	A system designed to provide representatives in multi-member constituencies of a number of minorities by calculating the votes for each party and comparing them to the votes cast in an election.
recall	A mechanism of the modern model of direct democracy where the voters can require that an elected representative lose her or his seat if a minimum number of voters sign a recall petition.
reference	A method of getting an issue before the court without requiring an actual fact situation affecting real persons before the issue can be decided.
referendum (and/or plebiscite)	A mechanism of the modern model of direct democracy where the government can require that an issue be put on a ballot for a vote by the electorate, which will bind the government.
representative democracy	A system where the citizens of a state elect candidates who will run the government by laws.
responsible government	A political concept that indicates the executive (comprised of the elected MPs of one party, who make up the Cabinet) is responsible to all of the elected members of Parliament as a whole.
separation of powers	The theory that, in combination with checks and balances, supports the presidential system of government, stating that each of the three branches of government has separate powers.
single-member-majoritarian system	The situation where the candidate in an election who gets the majority of the votes wins the seat.
single-member-plurality system	The situation where the candidate who gets the plurality of the votes in an election wins the seat.
totalitarianism	A common type of governance used in the world today, where leaders impose their objectives or goals upon their people to an unlimited degree.
ultra vires	A Latin phrase that means "outside the power of the level of government to pass a law".
unitary system	A political system wherein a single sovereign government controls all regions of the country.

REVIEW QUESTIONS

1. Define democracy and its main characteristics.

2. Compare democracy and totalitarianism.

3. Discuss four problems that arise from the Athenian Model of direct democracy.

4. What is the difference between the parliamentary system and the presidential system?

5. How is a government formed after an election in the parliamentary system?

6. Enumerate the members of the legislative branch by title and function.

7. In the parliamentary system involving parties, define party discipline and how it is used to ensure that members of the governing party vote in a certain way.

8. Discuss three methods proposed under the Modern Model of direct democracy that will give individuals voting for representatives more power over their representatives.

9. Describe and explain by examples the four types of centralization of government currently in use.

10. Discuss the levels of government in Canada. Why is the municipal government not a level of government?

11. Discuss how the branches of government are connected in the parliamentary system and the presidential system, respectively, showing their differences.

12. Define the theory of parliamentary supremacy and the three modifications to that theory in the Canadian context.

13. How does the correction of the infringement of rights under the *Charter of Rights and Freedoms* transfer power away from the legislative branch and give it to the judicial branch?

14. Why are elections for a riding in Canada usually won by a plurality, whereas the elections for a seat in the United States are usually won by a majority?

15. Discuss what mechanism has been suggested to make parliamentary elections more responsive to minorities of voters, and how it works.

16. Which provinces have looked at changing their elections system to include some type of proportional representation?

17. What is judicial activism and why is it looked upon suspiciously by one group of politicians and approvingly by another group?

DISCUSSION QUESTIONS

1. Using two issues under the *Charter of Rights and Freedoms*, discuss how the court has exercised too much or appropriate judicial activism to deal with the issue.

2. Based on the need for "effective government, responsive to the needs of all the people", discuss which is better: the parliamentary or presidential system of government.

3. Some of the mechanisms proposed in the Modern Model of direct democracy should be installed in the Canadian system of government. Do you agree with this statement? Why or why not?

SUGGESTED READINGS

Beatty, David. *Constitutional Law in Theory and Practice* (Toronto, Ont.: University of Toronto Press, 1995).

Carmichael, Don, et al. *Democracy, Rights and Well-Being in Canada*, 2d ed. (Toronto, Ont.: Harcourt Brace Canada, 2000).

Dickerson, Mark O., & Thomas Flanagan. *An Introduction to Government and Politics: A Conceptual Approach*, 5th ed. (Toronto, Ont.: ITP Nelson, 1998).

Hogg, Peter W. *Constitutional Law of Canada*, loose-leaf ed. (Toronto, Ont.: Carswell, 1997).

Jackson, Robert J., & Doreen Jackson. *An Introduction to Political Science: Comparative and World Politics*, 3d ed. (Scarborough, Ont.: Prentice Hall Allyn and Bacon Canada, 2000).

Mahler, Gregory S. *Comparative Politics: An Institutional and Cross-National Approach*, 3d ed. (Upper Saddle River, New Jersey: Prentice Hall, 2000).

Monahan, Patrick J. *Constitutional Law* (Concord, Ontario: Irwin Law, 1997).

Morrison, Alan B. *Fundamentals of American Law* (Oxford, U.K.: Oxford University Press, 1996).

Smiley, Donald V. *Canada in Question: Federalism in the Eighties*, 3d ed. (Toronto, Ont.: McGraw-Hill Ryerson Limited, 1980).

VIDEOS

N.F.B. *Our Constitution — The Law of the Land*. 1991. [28 min. video cassette.]

N.F.B. *Our National Parliament — The Inside Story*. 1991. [31 min. video cassette.]

The Constitution

Janet I. Mason
BARRISTER AND SOLICITOR

Stanley Gershman
BARRISTER AND SOLICITOR

Learning Objectives

After reading this chapter, the reader should be able to:

➢ understand that Canada's Constitution is based on a series of British statutes, conventions and common law

➢ identify the three main documents that make up Canada's Constitution

➢ understand the division of powers between the provinces and the federal government, distinguishing between matters of a national and local nature

➢ understand the various formulae for amending the Constitution

➢ identify the various methods that may be used where there is a real or potential conflict between laws made by the legislative bodies and the Constitution

➢ understand from the case study the basis upon which each level of government has the power to enact criminal law

➢ identify the formal requirements for valid criminal law from the case study

TABLE OF CONTENTS

INTRODUCTION

Canada's Constitution has evolved as Canada has evolved from being a British colony to a sovereign nation. To appreciate the significance and importance of our Constitution, we have to understand Canada's roots and the history of its development as an independent country. A constitution is an important and fundamental characteristic of a democratic nation and is composed of the rules and practices that provide "a legitimizing framework for the organization and exercise of governmental power in such nation".[1]

Canada began not as an independent nation but as a colony of Great Britain.[2] Prior to our original Constitution, the nation we call Canada was made up of several colonies or provinces, including Upper Canada (later renamed Ontario), Lower Canada (later renamed Quebec), New Brunswick, Nova Scotia, Prince Edward Island and Newfoundland. These colonies were ruled by governors appointed by, and accountable to, the British government and, to some extent, by elected colonial legislatures. Legislative representatives of all these colonies met in a series of conferences in 1864 in Canada and, finally, in London, England, in 1866, to work out the plans for a new union. These plans were set out as resolutions that were enacted in a statute called the *British North America Act, 1867*,[3] passed by the British parliament on July 1, 1867. This statute was built upon already existing traditions and colonial constitutions. The preamble to the statute states that the new dominion of Canada would have "a constitution similar in principle to that of the United Kingdom [Great Britain]".

This Constitution applied at first only to Ontario, Quebec, New Brunswick and Nova Scotia since Prince Edward Island and Newfoundland refused at this time to join in a new federation.[4] The idea for this union originated from the aspirations of the colonial legislative representatives, who were moved by recent threatening events, such as the bloody American Civil War, the continuing reverberations of the American revolution, the possibility of war between the United States and Great Britain, and the changing feelings of an over-extended England as to its relationship with its colonies, especially on the volatile North American continent. The representatives of the four uniting colonies felt the need to bond together to deal more vigorously with these feared potential threats, and to protect and preserve their strongly dependent relationship with Great Britain. In order to unite, the provinces created a new federal level of government and a **parliament** to deal with matters of interest to the whole country. Provinces with provincial **legislatures** were also established for the four former colonies.

Canada's Constitution serves four main functions:

1. To establish a political and economic union based on federal and democratic principles.

2. To outline a framework for the machinery of government and establish governmental institutions (e.g., Parliament, provincial legislatures, courts).

---

[1] *Canada (Director of Investigation & Research, Combines Investigation Branch) v. Southam*, [1984] 2 S.C.R. 145 at 155.

[2] The terms "Great Britain" "United Kingdom" and "England" are used interchangeably.

[3] (U.K.), 30 & 31 Vict., c. 3 [*BNA Act, 1867*].

[4] Over the course of time, other provinces joined the federation, creating the Canada we know today. Newfoundland was the last to join in 1949.

3. To distribute legislative, or law-making, powers and executive, or decision-making, powers between the provincial and national levels of government, thereby imposing legal limits on what a particular level of government could or could not do in relation to other governments.[5]

4. To solidify and confirm the colonies' desire to continue to be closely associated with Great Britain and its system of governance, and to reject the influence of the United States of America.

Great Britain's governmental structure had evolved over centuries. The country was first governed by an absolute monarchy and then evolved a constitutional monarchy — i.e., rule by the monarchy and an aristocracy of landowners. Eventually it evolved into a type of liberal representative democracy, where most citizens had the right to vote for representatives to Parliament.[6]

England's constitution in 1867 was not found in a single document. It could be found in separate legal documents, such as the Magna Carta of 1215 and the Bill of Rights of 1689. This constitution was composed mainly of political principles and practices or unwritten rules, known as **conventions**, that had arisen during its evolution into a liberal democracy. But in becoming a democracy, Britain had retained certain formal vestiges of the monarchy and aristocracy in its governmental structure. As a result, Canada's Constitution, which was to be similar in principle to that of the United Kingdom, as formulated in the *BNA Act, 1867*, seemed to express the form of Canada's government as a mixture of democratic institutions and a constitutional monarchy that provided a role for the monarchy and a non-elected "aristocracy" (i.e., the Senate). In practice, the Canadian government also functioned in accordance with British conventions that were not expressed in the *BNA Act, 1867*.

Conventions and Practices

The *BNA Act, 1867* is far from complete in describing the structure and function of our government. Many British constitutional conventions and practices not incorporated in the *BNA Act, 1867* became part of the Canadian "unwritten constitution". These included the following:

- the selection and role of the prime minister;
- the composition of the executive of the House of Commons or Cabinet; and
- the existence and role of political parties.

These conventions also included various principles, such as the following:

- the rule of law: the concept that no man, not even the monarch, was above the law;
- the independence of the judiciary: the concept that judges were independent of the government that appointed them; and
- parliamentary sovereignty: the concept that Parliament, as the representative of the people, was supreme in making law.

---

[5] Bernard W. Funston & Eugene Meehan, *Canada's Constitutional Law In a Nutshell*, 2d ed. (Scarborough, Ont.: Carswell, 1998) at 11–12.

[6] In fact, Great Britain did not become a democracy until much later and was what Fareed Zakaria designates as constitutional liberalism. As he points out, in 1867 Great Britain allowed barely 6.4 percent of its population to vote in the parliamentary elections. Fareed Zakaria, *The Future of Freedom: Illiberal Democracy at Home and Abroad* (New York, New York: W.W. Norton & Company, 2003) at 20.

In addition to constitutional conventions and practices, case or common law on some subjects is also part of our Constitution, as a result of a series of **precedent** cases that established some constitutional principles. Aboriginal rights were often established in this way. These interpretations of precedent continue to shape constitutional matters today. However, relying on the common law alone as a central source of constitutional matters can be problematic. Ordinary statutes can be used to easily override the common law. This vulnerability to arbitrary change seems to make precedent a poor choice for the protection of constitutional matters.

The Road to Independence

Even though the former colonies were referred to as a Dominion, Canada in form, if not in practice, remained a colony of Great Britain. Over the years, however, an evolution occurred in which Canada gradually gained independence from Great Britain. An early step in this process was the "Balfour Declaration" of 1926, which gave current and former colonies status equal to Britain.

> [The United Kingdom and the dominions] are autonomous communities within the British Empire, equal in status, in no way subordinate one to another in any aspect of their domestic or external affairs, although united by a common allegiance to the Crown, and freely associated as members of the British Commonwealth of Nations.[7]

The Balfour Declaration was implemented by the passage of the *Statute of Westminster 1931*[8] in December 1931. Now, no law passed by England could apply to a dominion unless the dominion consented: in effect, giving Canada autonomy from the British parliament. The *BNA Act, 1867* was made an exception to the *Statute of Westminster* so that the British parliament remained the only legislative body with the power to amend it, since the *BNA Act, 1867* was a British statute. This exemption prevented any Canadian government from making arbitrary changes to our Constitution. It was to be another 50 years before Canada's legal autonomy was fully achieved by the passage of the *Canada Act 1982*,[9] which brought our Constitution under the authority of our Canadian government.

The Privy Council and Supreme Court of Canada

Until 1949, Canada's final court of appeal was the Privy Council of the United Kingdom. This made the Privy Council, not the Supreme Court of Canada, the final arbiter in the interpretation and application of the *BNA Act, 1867*. On December 23, 1949, a federal bill to abolish the right of appeal to the British Privy Council was proclaimed. For any cases started after that date, the Supreme Court of Canada then became the final arbiter in interpreting the Constitution and also became the final court of appeal.

Canada's Constitutional Independence

The final step to an independent nation and to a constitution that more appropriately reflected the non-colonial liberal democratic nature of our government was taken by Prime Minister Pierre Trudeau in 1982. The prime minister was primarily responsible for promoting the passage by the British parliament of the *Canada Act*. The *Canada Act* enacted the *Constitution Act, 1982*[10] and did away with the exemption of our Constitution to the *Westminster* by indicating

---

[7] M. Ollivier (ed.), *The Colonial and Imperial Conferences from 1887 to 1939*, vol. 3, 137–344 (Ottawa: Edmond Cloutier, Queen's Printer, 1954).

[8] (U.K.), 22 & 23 Geo 5, c. 4 [*Westminster*].

[9] (U.K.), 1982, c. 11 [*Canada Act*].

[10] Being Schedule B of the *Canada Act 1982*, (U.K.), 1982, c. 11, s. 1.

that no Act of the parliament of the United Kingdom henceforth should extend to Canada and by replacing the authority of the British parliament to amend our Constitution with an amending formula allowing for our local government to make such amendments:

> **2.** No Act of the Parliament of the United Kingdom passed after the *Constitution Act, 1982* comes into force shall extend to Canada as part of its law.

The *Constitution Act, 1982* retained the consolidated and amended *BNA Act, 1867* and renamed it the *Constitution Act, 1867*.[11] Most important, the Constitution also included the *Canadian Charter of Rights and Freedoms*.[12] The *Charter* guaranteed certain individual and collective rights and placed limits on the powers of government and legislators to interfere with such rights.

How the Constitution Differs from Statutes

There are two ways in which the Constitution[13] is significant and different from other laws. The first is that the Constitution has **supremacy** over all other laws in Canada. This means that any legislation that contravenes or is inconsistent with the Constitution is invalid and, therefore, of no force or effect (s. 52(1)):

> The Constitution of Canada is the supreme law of Canada, and any law that is inconsistent with the provisions of the Constitution is, to the extent of the inconsistency, of no force or effect.

The second way the Constitution differs from other laws is that it cannot be amended with the relative ease with which other laws are changed (i.e., by repealing or passing new legislation in the traditional manner), but can only be amended in accordance with certain rules and procedures set out in the Constitution itself.

THE DIVISION OF POWERS BETWEEN PARLIAMENT AND THE LEGISLATURE

Interpreting the Constitution

Canada has changed in many ways since the *BNA Act, 1867* was created. For example, the role of government has increased. Publicly funded programs, such as education and health care, have expanded or been introduced, and technological advances have occurred. The drafters of the *BNA Act, 1867* could not have contemplated many of the economic, political and social changes that have occurred. In order to ensure that the Constitution is able to adapt to new events, it is to be interpreted in a flexible manner. Therefore, the heads of powers are not restricted to a narrow definition based on what existed at the time of drafting. For example, the federal power identified as "postal service" is not limited to the postal service available in 1867. To quote Lord Sankey's popular analogy, the Constitution is to be like a "living tree capable of growth and expansion within its natural limits".[14] A progressive understanding of the heads of powers ensures that the Constitution remains relevant and fulfills its function of "provid[ing] the basis for the entire government of a nation over a long period of time".[15]

---

[11] (U.K.), 30 & 31 Vict., c. 3, reprinted in R.S.C. 1985, App. II, No. 5 [*Constitution Act, 1867*].

[12] Part I of the *Constitution Act, 1982*, being Schedule B to the *Canada Act 1982* (U.K.), 1982, c. 11 [*Charter*].

[13] A reference to the Constitution includes the *Constitution Act, 1982* and the *Constitution Act, 1867*.

[14] *Edwards v. Canada (A.G.)*, [1930] AC 124, [1930] 1 D.L.R. 98 (PC).

[15] Peter W. Hogg, *Constitution Law of Canada*, 2002 Student ed. (Scarborough, Ont.: Carswell, 2002) at 398 [*Hogg*].

Federal Powers

The Constitution lists certain matters and allocates them as either federal or provincial responsibilities and leaves any residual power to the federal government. Matters that affect the nation as a whole, such as the military, and those that cross provincial boundaries are referred to as **extraprovincial** matters. For example, railways would be within federal jurisdiction since they extend across provincial borders. Parliament is the legislative body that deals with federal matters, while the legislature of each province has jurisdiction over provincial matters. Jurisdiction under the Constitution empowers Parliament and legislatures to enact laws regarding an area of responsibility. Sections 91 and 92 of the *Constitution Act, 1867* list the specific areas of jurisdiction for each level of government and are reproduced in Exhibits 6.1 and 6.2.

The terms used to describe the heads of power are deliberately broad, and include associated administrative and enforcement functions. For example, "copyright" is an articulated federal head of power that includes the administrative and procedural requirements of registering copyrights within Canada. Parliament would also provide penalties for violations of its statutes.

Peace, Order and Good Government

An exceptional federal power can be found in the "peace, order and good government" ("**POGG**") category. POGG consists of three branches:

1. The gap or residual branch, where power to govern may be found when matters arise that are not specifically allocated in the Constitution to either Parliament or the legislature (this branch is rarely used as the court prefers to fit the activity being conducted to an existing head of power).

2. The emergency branch, whereby laws of a *temporary* nature may be implemented that allow Parliament to intrude into matters of provincial jurisdiction (e.g., the *War Measures Act*).

3. The national concern branch, which gives Parliament the power to control matters that are beyond a local or provincial concern, such as aeronautics or atomic energy, which are of concern to the nation as a whole.

Concurrent Jurisdiction

There are also categories where the federal and provincial governments appear to share responsibility. For example, marriage is one head of federal jurisdiction and involves the power to determine what constitutes a legal marriage in Canada (s. 91(26)). However, the province has the authority and responsibility under section 92(12) for the "solemnization of marriage" (i.e., the procedural aspects of getting married). The Constitution also identifies areas where both Parliament and the legislature have **concurrent jurisdiction**. These areas are old age pensions (s. 94(a)), agriculture and immigration (s. 95). Criminal law also has concurrent jurisdiction, and each level of government can pass such laws. However, provincial criminal laws must be grounded under a head of provincial power. Concurrent criminal jurisdiction is how provinces are able to impose fines and other penalties under the *Highway Traffic Act*, since intra-provincial roads would fall under the legislature's power as "local works and undertakings" (s. 92(10)).

Provincial Powers

Provincial heads of power are contained in section 92 of the *Constitution Act, 1867* and are listed in Exhibit 6.2. These matters concern the individual province and are referred to as matters that are **intra-provincial** and, therefore, of local concern.

91. It shall be lawful for the Queen, by and with the Advice and Consent of the Senate and House of Commons, to make Laws for the Peace, Order, and good Government of Canada, in relation to all Matters not coming within the Classes of Subjects by this Act assigned exclusively to the Legislatures of the Provinces; and for greater Certainty, but not so as to restrict the Generality of the foregoing Terms of this Section, it is hereby declared that (notwithstanding anything in this Act) the exclusive Legislative Authority of the Parliament of Canada extend to all Matter coming within the Classes of Subjects next hereinafter enumerated; that is to say, —

1. Repealed.
1A. The Public Debt and Property.
2. The Regulation of Trade and Commerce.
2A. Unemployment insurance.
3. The raising of Money by any Mode or System of Taxation.
4. The borrowing of Money on the Public Credit.
5. Postal Service.
6. The Census and Statistics.
7. Militia, Military and Naval Service, and Defence.
8. The fixing of and providing for the Salaries and Allowances of Civil and other Officers of the Government of Canada.
9. Beacons, Buoys, Lighthouses, and Sable Island.
10. Navigation and Shipping.
11. Quarantine and the Establishment and Maintenance of Marine Hospitals.
12. Sea Coast and Inland Fisheries.
13. Ferries between a Province and any British or Foreign Country or between Two Provinces.
14. Currency and Coinage.
15. Banking, Incorporation of Banks, and the Issue of Paper Money.
16. Savings Banks.
17. Weights and Measures.
18. Bills of Exchange and Promissory Notes.
19. Interest.
20. Legal Tender.
21. Bankruptcy and Insolvency.
22. Patents of Invention and Discovery.
23. Copyrights.
24. Indians and Lands reserved for the Indians.
25. Naturalization and Aliens.
26. Marriage and Divorce.
27. The Criminal Law, except the Constitution of Courts of Criminal Jurisdiction, but including the Procedure in Criminal Matters.
28. The Establishment, Maintenance, and Management of Penitentiaries.
29. Such Classes of Subjects as are expressly excepted in the Enumeration of the Classes of Subjects by this Act assigned exclusively to the Legislatures of the Provinces.

And any Matter coming within any of the Classes of Subjects enumerated in this Section shall not be deemed to come within the Class of Matters of a local or private Nature comprised in the Enumeration of the Classes of Subjects by this Act assigned exclusively to the Legislatures of the Provinces.

Disallowance

While Canada generally considers itself a federal state, in reality it is quasi-federal. In a truly federal state, each level of government enjoys equal status and autonomy under its head of power. However, the *Constitution Act, 1867*, in sections 55, 56 and 90, in effect gives the federal government a veto power

EXHIBIT 6.2

**Section 92 of the *Constitution Act, 1867*
— Provincial Heads of Power**

92. In each Province the Legislature may exclusively make Laws in relation to Matters coming within the Classes of Subjects next hereinafter enumerated; that is to say, —

1. Repealed.
2. Direct Taxation within the Province in order to the raising of a Revenue for Provincial Purposes.
3. The borrowing of Money on the sole Credit of the Province.
4. The Establishment and Tenure of Provincial Offices and the Appointment and Payment of Provincial Officers.
5. The Management and Sale of the Public Lands belonging to the Province and of the Timber and Wood thereon.
6. The Establishment, Maintenance, and Management of Public and Reformatory Prisons in and for the Province.
7. The Establishment, Maintenance, and Management of Hospitals, Asylums, Charities, and Eleemosynary Institutions in and for the Province, other than Marine Hospitals.
8. Municipal Institutions in the Province.
9. Shop, Saloon, Tavern, Auctioneer, and other Licences in order to the raising of a Revenue for Provincial, Local, or Municipal Purposes.
10. Local Works and Undertakings other than such as are of the following Classes:
    (a) Lines of Steam or other Ships, Railways, Canals, Telegraphs, and other Works and Undertakings connecting the Province with any other or others of the Provinces, or extending beyond the Limits of the Province:
    (b) Lines of Steam Ships between the Province and any British or Foreign Country:
    (c) Such Works as, although wholly situate within the Province, are before or after their Execution declared by the Parliament of Canada to be for the general Advantage of Canada or for the Advantage of Two or more of the Provinces.
11. The Incorporation of Companies with Provincial Objects.
12. The Solemnization of Marriage in the Province.
13. Property and Civil Rights in the Province.
14. The Administration of Justice in the Province, including the Constitution, Maintenance, and Organization of Provincial Courts, both of Civil and of Criminal Justice, and including Procedure in Civil Matters in those Courts.
15. The Imposition of Punishment by Fine, Penalty, or Imprisonment for enforcing any Law of the Province made in relation to any Matter coming within any of the Classes of Subjects enumerated in this Section.
16. Generally all Matters of a merely local or private Nature in the Province.

over provincial laws, referred to as **disallowance**.[16] Disallowance permits the Governor General or Lieutenant-Governor (both positions under federal jurisdiction) the power to set aside objectionable laws. This power is not likely to be exercised often because it tends to undermine the two-tiered approach of our Constitution. The United States, as a point of comparison, is a federal state. Differences include the residual constitutional power being allocated to the individual state and not to the federal government. Only federal powers are articulated in their constitution and receive a broad interpretation.[17] In the United States, the issue of paramountcy does not generally arise because of clearly enunciated powers and the equal status of both levels of government. There is nothing in the U.S. Constitution permitting any level of government to disallow legislation validly enacted.

[16] Hogg, *ibid.* at 117.
[17] Hogg, *ibid.* at 389.

AMENDING THE CONSTITUTION

**Sections 38 and 42:
The General
Amending Formula**

The *Constitution Act, 1982* includes specific formulae for amendment, depending on subject matter, and articulates the requirements for general changes (including the identification of certain provincial matters that must use the general formula), specified categories that require unanimity, and federal and provincial unilateral changes. The general formula (s. 38) requires that seven provinces that make up at least 50 percent of Canada's population agree to the constitutional amendment. Since the population of Ontario and Quebec make up more than 50 percent of Canada's population, at least one of them would have to vote for the amendment for it to be successful.[18] In addition, a province is free to opt out of a proposed change where a majority in the provincial legislature agrees to do so (s. 38(3)).

Section 42 lists matters that must be subject to this formula in order to prevent the federal government from arbitrarily making changes that may affect provincial concerns. These matters include proportionate representation of each province in the House of Commons, powers of the Senate, number of Senators and the establishment of a new province. Any matter not mentioned in sections 41, 43, 44 or 45 must follow the general formula of section 38, as implied in s. 52(3):

> Amendments to the Constitution of Canada shall be made only in accordance with the authority contained in the Constitution of Canada.

**Section 41:
Amendment by
Unanimous Consent;
Section 43:
Amendments
Relating to Some But
Not All Provinces**

A constitutional amendment for certain matters will require the agreement of Parliament, the legislatures of all provinces, the House of Commons and Senate. These matters are listed in section 41 of the Constitution and include proposed changes to the role of the Governor General or Lieutenant-Governor of a province, provincial House of Commons members, and the composition of the Supreme Court of Canada. Alternatively, where a proposed amendment affects only some provinces, those affected by the change are required to agree to it along with federal approval (s. 43).

**Sections 44 and 45:
Federal and
Provincial Unilateral
Amendments**

For matters that fall completely under federal jurisdiction, Parliament can unilaterally (i.e., without consent of the provinces) amend the Constitution. Provinces have a similar unilateral power to amend where the matter does not concern Parliament in any way. For example, a constitutional change on a provincial matter that directly or indirectly affects the position of Lieutenant-Governor (a federal jurisdiction) could not be done under provincial unilateral power. Instead, this type of change would require the unanimity formula found under section 41 of the *Constitution Act, 1982*. The complicated procedure of obtaining consents to amending the Constitution protects it from arbitrary changes by Parliament or the legislatures.

FEDERAL AND PROVINCIAL LEGISLATIVE CONFLICT/INCONSISTENCY

> [F]ederalism was the legal response of the framers of the Constitution to the political and cultural realities that existed at Confederation. It thus represented a legal recognition of the diversity of the original members. The division of powers, one of the basic components of federalism, was designed to uphold this diversity within a single nation. Broad powers were conferred on

---

[18] Hogg, *ibid.* at 75.

provincial legislatures, while at the same time Canada's unity was ensured by reserving to Parliament powers better exercised in relation to the country as a whole. Each head of power was assigned to the level of government best placed to exercise the power. The fundamental objectives of federalism were, and still are, to reconcile unity with diversity, promote democratic participation by reserving meaningful powers to the local or regional level and to foster co-operation among governments and legislatures for the common good.[19]

It is reasonable to expect that there will be occasions in our quasi-federal system where a law made by Parliament will or might conflict with a law made by the legislature. There are a number of legal principles that have been developed to sort out constitutional conflicts and legislative inconsistencies:

- the double aspect doctrine;
- the paramountcy doctrine;
- the colourability doctrine;
- the interjurisdictional immunity doctrine; and
- the necessarily incidental doctrine.

> As the final arbiters of the division of powers, the courts have developed certain constitutional doctrines, which, like the interpretations of the powers to which they apply, are based on the guiding principles of our constitutional order. The constitutional doctrines permit an appropriate balance to be struck in the recognition and management of the inevitable overlaps in rules made at the two levels of legislative power, while recognizing the need to preserve sufficient predictability in the operation of the division of powers. The doctrines must also be designed to reconcile the legitimate diversity of regional experimentation with the need for national unity. Finally, they must include a recognition that the task of maintaining the balance of powers in practice falls primarily to governments, and constitutional doctrine must facilitate, not undermine what this Court has called "co-operative federalism"....[20]

When the constitutionality of legislation is challenged based on the division of powers, the analysis always begins with an examination of the "pith and substance" of the legislation. "This initial analysis consists of an inquiry into the true nature of the law in question for the purpose of identifying the 'matter' to which it essentially relates."[21] The purpose of the enacting body and the legal effect of the law will both be examined. If the dominant purpose and effect of the legislation is within the enacting body's jurisdiction, the legislation will be valid even if there are minor intrusions into the other level of government's jurisdiction. In such cases, the double-aspect doctrine or the necessarily incidental doctrine could apply and lead to a finding of validity. Where the enacting body has transgressed into the jurisdiction of the other, the doctrine of colourability (dealt with during the initial "pith and substance" analysis), paramountcy, or interjurisdictional immunity can apply.

The Double Aspect Doctrine

The **double aspect doctrine** applies where both Parliament and the legislature have authority to enact laws on a matter. These powers may be expressly concurrent, such as the power to regulate immigration under section 95 of the *Constitution Act, 1867*, noted earlier, or they may arise from the exercise of the right to legislate the matter under another heading in the Constitution. Assuming that both laws are valid and of equal importance, and that it is possible for each to operate without conflict or inconsistency, they will be upheld

---

[19] *Canadian Western Bank v. Alberta*, 2007 SCC 22, at para. 23 [*Western Bank*].
[20] *Ibid.* at para. 24.
[21] *Ibid.* at paras. 25, 26.

as a double-aspect matter. Both laws would be a valid exercise of power for each level of government.

For example, Parliament has the power to regulate the creation and structure of federally incorporated companies (a matter for Parliament since these corporations operate nationally, as opposed to operating within a province and are, therefore, a matter of national or extraprovincial concern). However, the legislature has the power under property and civil rights to regulate commercial activity within the province. This means that Parliament will define the rights, liabilities and internal structure of a federally incorporated company, such as a national retail chain. The legislature will have regulations in place regarding the registration of all corporations within the province and related reporting requirements.

The Paramountcy Doctrine

Where the two valid laws conflict, and an individual cannot comply with both, the federal **paramountcy doctrine** is triggered. Paramountcy results in the provincial statute, to the extent of the conflict or inconsistency, being declared inoperative by the court. The test for paramountcy requires that the party submitting the assertion first demonstrate that the federal and provincial laws were validly enacted in relation to the division of powers under the Constitution. If valid, compliance with both laws simultaneously must be shown to be impossible because of either an operational conflict (it is impossible to comply with both laws) or because compliance with the provincial law frustrates the purpose of the federal law.[22]

The paramountcy doctrine will not necessarily invalidate the whole law, and the provincial law may remain in force despite the inoperable section(s). In the event that the federal law is later repealed and no longer in force, the provincial law will fully operate since the conflict or inconsistency no longer exists. There is no express reciprocal provincial power of paramountcy, though a federal statute can be challenged where it appears that Parliament is attempting to regulate a matter under provincial jurisdiction.

The Colourability Doctrine

The **colourability doctrine** is triggered where a law is enacted with a stated purpose that appears to contradict the actual purpose. *R. v. Morgentaler*[23] concerned provincial legislation that led to the prosecution of Dr. Morgentaler for performing an abortion in his private clinic located outside of a Nova Scotia hospital. Dr. Morgentaler was acquitted at trial after the judge decided that the law the doctor was charged with breaking was beyond the jurisdiction of the province to enact. The Supreme Court, in 1988, had ruled that abortion was not to be regulated by the criminal law and that it was not an offence for a woman to obtain an abortion in a clinic.[24] This judgment determined that a province did not have power to enact criminal legislation regarding the provision of abortion at clinics.

The province appealed the decision to the Supreme Court, submitting that the *Medical Services Act* was a valid exercise of its power under hospitals, property and civil rights and matters of a local nature as stated in the Constitution. The stated purpose of the Act was to "prohibit the privatization of the provision of certain medical services in order to maintain a single high-quality

---

[22] *British Columbia (A.G.) v. Lafarge Canada Inc.*, 2007 SCC 23 at para. 77, summarizing *Canadian Western Bank v. Alberta*, 2007 SCC 22 at 75.

[23] [1993] 3 S.C.R. 463, 107 DLR (4th) 537 [*Morgentaler*], aff'g *R. v. Morgentaler* (1991), 83 D.L.R. (4th) 8 (N.S.C.A.) and 99 N.S.R. (2d) 393.

[24] *R. v. Morgentaler*, [1988] 1 S.C.R. 30, 44 D.L.R. (4th) 385 [*Morgentaler 1988*].

EXHIBIT 6.3

Paramountcy Doctrine

Regulations passed under the federal *Food and Drugs* Act, R.S.C. 1970, c. F-27 sought *attempted* to regulate the minimum and maximum alcohol content for the marketing of "light beer". Labatt was selling a light beer that had an alcohol content above the limit listed in the relevant provisions under the Act. Labatt challenged the provisions of the legislation, alleging the matter was under provincial jurisdiction and, therefore, Parliament had no authority to dictate its alcohol content. The federal government responded by claiming that the power to enact the provisions was valid under its trade and commerce power and, additionally, relied on POGG (national concern branch) and criminal law power.

The Supreme Court examined each source of power and its applicability in the circumstances and determined, in a 6–3 decision, that a federal head of power could not be found to support the validity of the challenged provisions. The Court determined that Parliament's trade and commerce power could not provide the necessary basis by which Parliament enacted the provisions. Labatt had breweries in many provinces, and sales were generally of a local nature (i.e., within the province, as opposed to having one central brewery that distributed the product across provincial boundaries). In addition, Parliament's general trade power is concerned with general trade regulations, as opposed to focusing on the process of a single industry, such as breweries. As a matter concerning intra-provincial trade, breweries appeared to be the responsibility of the legislature.

The national concern branch of POGG also failed to uphold the provision since the alcohol content of light beer was not shown to be of national concern. A criminal law basis was also unsuccessful since the provisions did not serve a public purpose. The provisions did not serve a consumer protection purpose, nor did the law appear concerned with compositional changes in food, or false or misleading advertising or labelling. Justice Estey characterized the provisions as being the detailed regulation of the brewing industry, noting that it did not attempt to protect the health of Canadians.

The Supreme Court held that the relevant provisions were a detailed regulation of the brewing industry regarding the production and sale of its product that infringed on provincial jurisdiction. As such, the provisions could not be constitutionally justified. They were, therefore, found to be outside Parliament's power to legislate, and rendered inoperative.

Source: *Labatt Breweries of Canada Ltd. v. Canada (A.G.)*, [1980] 1 S.C.R. 914, 110 D.L.R. (3d) 594.

health-care delivery system for all Nova Scotians". A regulation passed under the Act listed the medical services to which the Act applied and included abortion where it was performed outside a hospital. The Act also denied health insurance coverage for abortions performed in violation of its provisions, which included those performed at an abortion clinic located outside a hospital.

The Supreme Court examined the Act and found that the province had jurisdiction over hospitals and the medical profession under the *Constitution Act, 1867* (ss. 92(7), (13) and (16), noted above). However, the determinative issue involved a consideration of whether or not the Act's purpose was an attempt to legislate the quality and nature of health care delivery, which would have made it a proper exercise of provincial power, or a criminal law enacted for a public purpose that would have made it improper. The structure of the legislation appeared to be criminal (i.e., a prohibition and penalty for a public purpose). While the province is able to enact criminal laws regarding matters under a provincial head of power, the prohibition of abortion had been held to be a federal criminal matter in the 1988 case. Therefore, the Supreme Court considered whether or not the Act was, in effect, an attempt to prohibit abortions outside of a hospital as a method of suppressing or punishing the "socially undesirable conduct of abortion". The Court was concerned that the *stated* purpose of the Act simply disguised the *intended* purpose of the Act.

In its decision, the Supreme Court decided that the Act, as far as the abortion provision was concerned, had the same legal effect as the federal legislation. This legislation had been struck down in Morgentaler's successful 1988 challenge. It appeared that the intended purpose of the Act was to regulate a matter (e.g., abortion) that had been found to be under Parliament's jurisdiction. In addition, an investigation into the events leading up to the passage of the Act and accompanying legislative debates did not support the purpose as stated in the Act. Therefore, the Court held that the Act was **ultra vires** of provincial power by application of the colourability doctrine. The legal effect of the law and accompanying regulations identified a purpose other than that stated in the law.[25]

Interjurisdictional Immunity Doctrine

While a level of overlap is to be expected in our quasi-federal state, the core of the head of power is protected by the **interjurisdictional immunity doctrine**. The core may be understood as a "vital or essential part",[26] and as the "basic, minimal and unassailable content"[27] of a constitutional head of power. To illustrate, Parliament is given authority for federal undertakings under the Constitution. Communication systems that travel across provincial boundaries would be considered a federal undertaking. But federal jurisdiction extends beyond the physical cables and can include associated matters, such as the terms of employment for those employed by the communication provider. Thus, the federal undertaking would be immune from provincial legislation and, for example, minimum wage legislation would not apply to employees. The provincial legislation would not be rendered invalid but may be read down (i.e., interpreted narrowly, thereby reducing applicability) so as to be inoperative regarding the federal undertaking.

> What is "vital" or "essential" is, by definition, not co-extensive with every element of an undertaking incorporated federally or subject to federal regulation. In the case of federal undertakings, ... [there is] a "general rule" that there is *no* interjurisdictional immunity, provided "the application of [the] provincial laws does not bear upon those [federal] subjects in what makes them specifically of federal jurisdiction.[28]

The interjurisdictional immunity doctrine may appear to be similar to the paramountcy doctrine, but there exists an important distinction. Paramountcy is triggered only where there are two valid laws, each properly enacted under a level of government's head of power, that conflict or are inconsistent. Unlike paramountcy, interjurisdictional immunity can be triggered in the absence of any federal law concerning the matter. Where a provincial law intrudes into the core of a federal head of power, despite Parliament's failure to legislate the matter under its relevant head of power, the provincial law would be inapplicable. However, this doctrine is not frequently used and has been a source of debate.[29]

---

[25] *Ibid.*, defining the colourability doctrine.

[26] *Commission du Salaire Minimum v. Bell Telephone Co.*, [1966] S.C.R. 767.

[27] *Bell Canada v. Québec (Commission de la santé et de la sécurité du travail du Québec)*, [1988] 1 S.C.R. 749.

[28] *British Columbia (A.G.) v. Lafarge Canada Inc.*, 2007 SCC 23, [2007] S.C.J. No. 23, para. 42.

[29] See the Supreme Court's review of the doctrine in *Canadian Western Bank v. Alberta*, 2007 SCC 22.

**Necessarily
Incidental Doctrine**

The **necessarily incidental doctrine** allows Parliament or the legislature to infringe on a head of power belonging to the other, provided that it does not go to the power's core. In order to do so, the infringing portion of the legislation must be shown to be "incidental" to the overall purpose and, simply, part of the larger legislative scheme. When applied, the technically invalid part of the legislation is held to be valid because of its close relationship to the larger, valid scheme of the legislation. *General Motors of Canada Ltd. v. City National Leasing*[30] challenged the inclusion of a civil action remedy under the federal legislation. Civil actions (e.g., a tort action) are a provincial head of power, property and civil rights, under the *Constitution Act, 1867.*

The legislation concerned anti-competitive behaviour, and the fact that the option of launching a civil action was under provincial authority was not in dispute. After consideration, the Supreme Court found that the potential civil action infringed on the power of the legislature, and that the remainder was properly enacted under federal jurisdiction. The Court conducted further analysis to see whether the infringement, a relatively minor aspect of the overall valid legislation, could be "constitutionally justified by reason of its connection with valid legislation". The Court held that the provision of the civil action, while encroaching on provincial power, was a remedial one, had been done before and was limited in the Act by restrictions to its application. The option of a civil action was an "integral, well-conceived component" of the legislation, functionally related to the purpose of the Act, and could help the legislation fulfill its objectives. As such, the provision was found to be necessarily incidental to the Act, and constitutionally valid.

DIVISION OF POWER AND CRIMINAL LAW

The criminal law is a concurrent power between Parliament and the legislature. Parliament enjoys a broad power to enact criminal law for the public good, whereas the legislatures must ground their criminal law in an existing head of provincial power. Section 91(27) grants Parliament the broad power to enact criminal legislation, and section 92(15) empowers the legislature to pass criminal laws on matters under their jurisdiction. Parliament's broad power to enact criminal legislation can include economic regulation that includes a criminal penalty and laws to prevent harm. In addition, criminal law must follow a particular structural format.

The *Criminal Code*[31] is federal legislation and applies on a national level. Regardless of where you reside in Canada, theft and murder, for example, are offences punishable under the *Criminal Code*. Municipal by-laws and provincial offences (e.g., traffic offences) are provincial matters and are applicable only within a particular community or province. This is why, for example, highway speed limits may differ from province to province. Since the province is empowered to deal with local undertakings, they can legislate these areas using their criminal law power. However, should the legislature enact criminal law that concerns a matter outside of its jurisdiction — for example, for a **public purpose** (i.e., to punish or prevent objectionable behaviour) — such a law would be ultra vires. Parliament seems to be likewise disallowed from passing criminal legislation that infringes on a head of power of the legislature, such as including a provision in regulatory legislation that provides, as the sole

---

[30] [1989] 1 S.C.R. 641, 58 D.L.R. (4th) 255.
[31] R.S.C. 1985 c. C-46.

penalty, grounds on which to base a civil action. As discussed, grounds for civil actions are a provincial power under property and civil rights.

The federal criminal law power is "plenary in nature" and has been broadly construed:

> A crime is an act which the law, with appropriate penal sanctions, forbids; but as prohibitions are not enacted in a vacuum, we can properly look for some evil or injurious or undesirable effect upon the public against which the law is directed. That effect may be in relation to social, economic or political interests; and the legislature has had in mind to suppress the evil or to safeguard the interest threatened. (*Reference re Validity of Section 5(a) of the Dairy Industry Act*, [1949] S.C.R. 1 [the *"Margarine Reference"*], at p. 49)
>
> ...
>
> For a law to be classified as a criminal law, it must possess three prerequisites: a valid criminal law purpose backed by a prohibition and a penalty (*Reference re Firearms Act (Can.)*, [2000] 1 S.C.R. 783, 2000 SCC 31, at para. 27). The criminal power extends to those laws that are designed to promote public peace, safety, order, health or other legitimate public purpose. In *RJR-MacDonald Inc. v. Canada (Attorney General)*, [1995] 3 S.C.R. 199, it was held that some legitimate public purpose must underlie the prohibition. In *Labatt Breweries* [*of Canada Ltd. v. Attorney General of Canada*, [1980] 1 S.C.R. 914], in holding that a health hazard may ground a criminal prohibition, Estey J. stated the potential purposes of the criminal law rather broadly as including "public peace, order, security, health and morality" (p. 933). Of course Parliament cannot use its authority improperly, e.g. colourably, to invade areas of provincial competence: *Scowby v. Glendinning*, [1986] 2 S.C.R. 226, at p. 237.

In determining whether the purpose of a law constitutes a valid criminal law purpose, courts also look at whether laws of this type have traditionally been held to be criminal law: *Ward v. Canada (Attorney General)*, [2002] 1 S.C.R. 569, 2002 SCC 17, at para. 51; *Reference re Firearms Act (Can.)*, [2000] 1 S.C.R. 783, 2000 SCC 31, at para. 32; *RJR-MacDonald v. Canada (Attorney General)*, [1995] 3 S.C.R. 199, at para. 204; *R. v. Morgentaler*, [1993] 3 S.C.R. 463, at p. 491.[32]

Parliament may use economic regulations to deal with anti-competitive practices in competitive markets where the efficient use of labour, capital and natural resources is required. Competitive markets include industries such as pulp and paper, cattle farming or securities. As these markets frequently cross provincial boundaries, making it difficult for a province to regulate anti-competitive practices, Parliament may impose regulatory schemes. These regulatory schemes must fall under federal jurisdiction, such as trade and commerce, and can include a criminal prohibition with a penalty.

In addition to economic regulations and a general power to enact criminal law for a public purpose, Parliament can pass laws designed for the prevention of harm (e.g., gun control legislation).[33] This preventative legislation is in addition to established *Criminal Code* offences regarding firearms. The *Criminal Code* includes penalties for persons who do not comply with the proper use or possession of firearms. The gun control legislation concerns other requirements, such as licensing and the creation of a national registration system. The gun control legislation was seen to maintain the "peaceful character"

---

[32] *R. v. Demers*, 2004 SCC 46, [2004] S.C.J. No. 43, paras. 16–17.
[33] *Firearms Act*, S.C. 1995, c. 39.

of Canadian society, and to "help the police fight crime and violence".[34] As such, the Supreme Court upheld the preventative legislation as a valid exercise of Parliament's criminal law power.

Proprietary Articles Trade Assn. v. Canada (A.G.)[35] established that all criminal law must follow a structural formula comprising a prohibition with penal consequences. This translates into the following formula: if you commit "x" act, you may receive "y" consequences, which can be a fine or term of imprisonment. However, this formula alone had the potential to allow Parliament to legislate any matter simply by following the formal structure required for criminal legislation. In an effort to limit federal criminal power, the *Margarine Reference*[36] articulated a third requirement for all criminal legislation: it must serve a public purpose. Where criminal legislation is not concerned with the prevention of harm or fails to provide consequences for public harm or wrongs, it will not fulfill the necessary criteria for a valid criminal law. Parliament would not be able to support such a law under its criminal power, as was the case with *Morgentaler 1988*, discussed earlier under the colourability doctrine.

The public purpose requirement, while placing a boundary on the federal power to enact criminal law, continues to allow Parliament a broad ability to enact criminal legislation. A public purpose may concern the physical protection of a person, such as from an assault, and also extends to cover matters of public concern: for instance, environmental pollution. Additionally, the criminal law should adjust and change in response to evolving cultural values and technological developments. Just as the Constitution is to be interpreted in the context of present-day social values, the criminal law power is to be similarly evolutionary. For example, at one time a married woman was considered to be the possession of her husband and, as a result, he could beat her. Societal values no longer echo this view, and a husband who beats his wife today will be charged with assault. In addition, Parliament has authority to identify new offences and is empowered to deal with emerging social harms. The development and use of the Internet, for example, has given rise to a number of concerns, including misleading advertising, fraud or theft. The criminal law is able to respond to these new concerns since its broad power is not frozen in time. As such, the *Criminal Code* contains more than the traditional offences against bodily integrity or theft and includes prohibitions against making, circulating or publishing a false prospectus (s. 400(1)) and forgery of trademarks (s. 406). Thus, as societal values change and technological advances occur, Parliament's power to enact criminal law has the flexibility to deal with concerns about the public good that arise.

CHAPTER SUMMARY

This chapter identified the sources of the Canadian Constitution. The various statutes, conventions and common law developments evolved over time as Canada moved towards autonomy and full independence. The three main documents that make up Canada's Constitution today are the *Constitution Act, 1867*, the *Constitution Act, 1982*, and the *Canadian Charter of Rights and Freedoms*. The Constitution is supreme over all other laws in Canada, and any

---

[34] Joel Bakan et al., *Canadian Constitutional Law*, 3d ed. (Toronto, Ont.: Emond Montgomery, 2003) at 412–13, quoting the Minister of Justice after the *Firearms Act* 3rd reading in the House of Commons.

[35] [1931] A.C. 310.

[36] *Reference re Validity of Section 5(a) of the Dairy Industry Act (Margarine Reference)*, [1949] S.C.R. 1, [1949] 1 D.L.R. 433.

legislation that contravenes or is inconsistent with it is of no force or effect. In order to protect the Constitution from arbitrary change, a special amending formula determined by subject matter is required.

The Constitution identifies specific matters and allocates them as either federal or provincial responsibility. Matters of national concern are legislated by Parliament, and matters of local concern are legislated by the provincial legislatures. The federal legislative body also has a special power to legislate for the peace, order and good government of Canada. In addition, there are identified areas where both levels of government can legislate, known as areas of concurrent jurisdiction. The fact that the federal government continues to have the power to veto provincial laws through disallowance supports the proposition that Canada is a quasi-federal state rather than a "true" federal state.

A variety of methods used to resolve conflict or inconsistency between laws enacted by each level of government was examined. The methods explained included the double-aspect doctrine, paramountcy doctrine, colourability doctrine, interjurisdictional immunity doctrine and necessarily incidental doctrine.

The chapter concluded with a discussion of the powers to enact criminal laws. Criminal law is identified as a concurrent power, and both Parliament and the legislature are empowered to enact valid criminal laws. However, only Parliament can enact criminal laws for the public good, and provincial legislatures are restricted to legislating criminal laws grounded under a provincial head of power. It was noted that the criminal law is able to respond to changes in technology and societal values, empowering Parliament and the legislatures to deal with criminal concerns as they evolve.

GLOSSARY OF NEW TERMS AND KEY CONCEPTS

colourability doctrine	Where a law is enacted for a stated purpose that appears to be different from its actual or intended purpose.
concurrent jurisdiction	Where both legislative bodies have power to legislate on the matter.
convention	Political principles and practices or unwritten rules that have become a part of our constitutional order.
disallowance	A power the federal government has that enables it to veto a provincial law.
double aspect doctrine	Applies where both Parliament and the legislature have power to legislate the same matter.
extraprovincial	Matters that cross provincial boundaries.
interjurisdictional immunity doctrine	Protects the core or essential part of a head of power and prevents the other level of government from intruding upon it.
intra-provincial	Matters that concern only a particular province.
legislature	The provincial or local legislative body.
necessarily incidental doctrine	Allows Parliament or the legislature to infringe upon the other's head of power, provided that it does not go to the core of the other's head of power; must be shown to be only incidental to the overall valid legislation.
paramountcy doctrine	Where each level of government has enacted valid legislation on the same matter that results in conflict or inconsistency, paramountcy dictates that the federal law will override the provincial law to the extent of the conflict or inconsistency.
Parliament	The federal or national legislative body.
POGG	A federal head of power with three branches: the gap branch, national concern branch and emergency branch.

precedent	Relevant to the common law: a decided case that provides a basis for later cases involving similar facts; lower courts are required to follow the decisions, or precedents, of higher courts.
public purpose	In the criminal law context, punishes or prevents objectionable behaviour; includes such things as public peace, order, security, health and morality.
supremacy	The position of having the superior or greatest power or authority; the Constitution has legal superiority over any conflicting or inconsistent law.
ultra vires	Beyond the scope of power allowed or granted to the legislative body, thus rendering the legislation of no force or effect.

REVIEW QUESTIONS

1. Identify the three main documents found in the *Canada Act* that make up the Constitution.

2. What are the two most relevant functions of Canada's Constitution today?

3. Canada's Constitution was not exclusively created by legislation. Aside from statutes, in what other ways did the Constitution evolve?

4. Why can Canada be viewed as a quasi-federal state, as opposed to a federal state?

5. Briefly explain the requirements of the five amending formulas.

6. Identify the five doctrines that can be used where there is a real or potential conflict between valid federal and provincial legislation.

7. At the federal level, the criminal law must follow a particular form. How should the legislation be structured at both a federal and provincial level?

8. Identify the important difference between the doctrines of paramountcy and interjurisdictional immunity. In a competition between a federal and provincial law where the doctrines will not apply, what will happen?

DISCUSSION QUESTIONS

1. The provincial government has noticed that people who wear purple shirts cause a serious allergic reaction in the majority of the population. The legislature has decided to pass a law prohibiting the wearing of purple shirts that, when contravened, will result in a fine or imprisonment. Does the province have authority to pass this law? Would such legislation be valid? Why or why not?

2. It is 1940, and you wish to appeal your wrongful conviction to the highest court available. Identify the court you would appeal to. Would you be able to appeal to this court today? Support your answer.

3. Assume that both Parliament and the legislature have the power to pass laws concerning firearms. Each level of government enacts a valid law on the matter. The federal legislation requires that all firearms be registered in a national directory. The provincial legislation requires only that the firearm owner purchase a licence. There is no requirement to register the firearm. How would this inconsistency be resolved?

4. The federal government has enacted legislation that requires banks to return a portion of their annual profit to each customer. Where the bank fails to return a portion, the customer's only stated recourse is to launch a civil action. Can Parliament enact such a law? Identify the two doctrines that would likely be considered by the court and apply them to the circumstances. Which one is more likely to prevail?

5. A new and potentially valuable mineral has been discovered at the border of a province. Each level of government is claiming a right to legislate regarding the excavation, processing and export of the mineral. Identify and discuss the heads of power under which each level of government can claim authority to legislate the matter. Whom do you think would be more likely to have authority should a court be asked to decide? Why?

6. Banking falls within federal jurisdiction pursuant to section 91(15) of the Constitution. Banks are now permitted to sell insurance for various types of loans and general purposes (life and home insurance, for example). Is the insurance component of a bank exclusively within the jurisdiction of Parliament, or will provincial insurance legislation govern?

SUGGESTED READING

Bakan, Joel, et al. *Canadian Constitutional Law*, 3d ed. (Toronto, Ont.: Emond Montgomery, 2003).

Carcone, Janet, & Stanley Gershman. "The Charter of Rights and Freedoms" in Laurence Olivo, ed., *Introduction to Law in Canada* (Toronto, Ont.: Captus Press, 2003).

Department of Justice Canada. *A Consolidation of The Constitution Acts 1867 to 1982* (Ottawa, Ont.: Canadian Government, 2001).

Funston, Bernard W., & Eugene Meehan. *Canada's Constitutional Law In a Nutshell*, 2d ed. (Scarborough, Ont.: Carswell, 1998).

Hogg, Peter W. *Constitutional Law of Canada*, 2002 Student ed. (Scarborough, Ont.: Carswell, 2002).

MacIver, R.M. *The Web of Government* (New York: The Free Press, 1965).

Zakaria, Fareed. *The Future of Freedom: Illiberal Democracy at Home and Abroad* (New York: W.W. Norton & Company, 2003).

The *Canadian Charter of Rights and Freedoms*

Janet I. Mason
BARRISTER AND SOLICITOR

Stanley Gershman
BARRISTER AND SOLICITOR

Learning Objectives

After reading this chapter, the reader should be able to:

➢ understand that the *Charter* was enacted to protect civil liberties and individual rights
➢ identify the limitations of the *Bill of Rights*
➢ understand how the entrenchment of *Charter* rights and freedoms protects them from arbitrary interference by government
➢ understand that the *Charter* will apply to non-government entities under certain circumstances
➢ distinguish between private and public interest standing
➢ identify the circumstances where government is permitted to infringe on *Charter* rights
➢ comprehend the remedies available for constitutional inconsistency
➢ understand the unique nature of Aboriginal rights under the *Charter*

TABLE OF CONTENTS

INTRODUCTION

Although we live in a representative parliamentary system, the right to elect a legislature to represent us does not fully account for all the positive aspects of our system of governance. Our form of democracy is not characterized simply by governance based on the constitutional exercise of the will of the majority of its citizens. The British political system from which ours is derived has traditionally granted some protections for individual rights against state (i.e., government) interference. These protections evolved through constitutional conventions, practices, and customs. However, the individual rights protected were not guaranteed to be immune from interference. The federal Parliament and provincial legislatures could make laws on any subject matter within their respective constitutional jurisdiction. There was no overarching law that required Parliament or a provincial legislature to take into account individual rights or freedoms when enacting legislation. As a result, elected federal and provincial representatives could enact legislation that took away individual rights and freedoms that had been protected by conventions, practices, and customs. The need thus arose for special legislation that would protect individual rights and freedoms from being arbitrarily infringed upon at the whim of an elected government.

In the latter half of the 20th century, the question for Canadians was whether or not legislative steps should be taken to explicitly define basic individual rights and freedoms. If legislative steps were taken, the next stage would require the implementation of a regime that would protect these rights and freedoms from government interference or from the imposition of the will of the majority on a minority group. This protection would need to have the authority to limit the legislative power of government when the exercise of legislative power infringed on those rights and freedoms. It would also require the power to control inappropriate government actions and systems that negatively affected an individual's rights. Canadians answered the question in the affirmative, and Parliament defined the rights and freedoms to which each citizen is entitled. These rights and freedoms were then protected by their inclusion in the *Constitution Act, 1982* as the *Canadian Charter of Rights and Freedoms*.[1]

While the *Charter* has enjoyed great success and acceptance, a number of policy issues associated with its rights and freedoms have challenged government, the judiciary, and legal theorists:

- Whether or not the rights of an individual (or a minority group) should override the rights of the community (or majority) when the latter rights are also protected by the *Charter*

- Whether or not we should permit unelected judges to override the will of Parliament or provincial legislatures, which are composed of representatives elected by a majority of Canada's citizens

- Whether or not there are circumstances under which the government should be allowed to infringe on a protected right or freedom; and if so, when an infringement is justified

Competing views on rights issues demonstrate the difficulties associated with the balancing of one right or freedom against that of another.

---

[1] Part I of the *Constitution Act, 1982*, being Schedule B to the *Canada Act 1982* (U.K.), 1982, c. 11 [*Charter*].

This chapter begins with a discussion of the *Bill of Rights*[2], which was enacted as standard federal legislation prior to the *Charter*, and identifies its shortcomings. The protection of the rights and freedoms obtained by the *Charter*'s entrenchment in the Constitution is examined. Attention is then directed towards identifying the entities that are governed by the *Charter* as well as those that are beyond its jurisdiction. Proper **standing** is discussed and is a pre-condition to claiming an infringement of a right or freedom (i.e., initiating a *Charter* challenge in the court). The methods by which the government is permitted to infringe upon *Charter* rights and freedoms are considered. The remedies available when a *Charter* challenge establishes an unjustified infringement of an individual's right are identified. This chapter concludes with a discussion of Aboriginal rights under the *Charter* and recognizes their uniqueness under the law.

THE BILL OF RIGHTS

The route to the creation of the *Charter* began in 1960 with Parliament's enactment of the *Canadian Bill of Rights*. This represented Canada's first attempt to enshrine and protect basic individual rights. The *Bill of Rights* contains many of the rights later included in the *Charter* and remains valid legislation today. However, the *Bill of Rights* was unable to protect the enunciated rights from arbitrary government interference for four reasons: (i) the *Bill of Rights* was limited in its application because it only applied to laws made by the federal government; (ii) the provincial legislature was under no duty to comply with its provisions and was free to infringe on the individual's rights; (iii) as ordinary legislation, the *Bill of Rights* could be easily changed by Parliament through the enactment of new legislation that amended or revoked existing provisions; and (iv) Parliament could pass laws that expressly excluded compliance with the recognized rights.

In practice, the courts came to regard the *Bill of Rights* as "quasi-constitutional" in application if not in form.[3] Federal statutes were expected to comply with the *Bill of Rights* requirements. Federal legislation that infringed on the *Bill of Rights* was held to be either invalid or **inoperative**, although legal opinion on this lacked clarity. The difficulty was that one ordinary piece of legislation (i.e., the *Bill of Rights*) was able to override another ordinary piece of legislation without constitutional authority. To put it another way, if Parliament were supreme in its law-making power, could the Parliament that passed the *Bill of Rights* in 1960 bind or limit the legislative power of future Parliaments to pass laws that contradicted the *Bill of Rights*? The answer to this question divided the judiciary and blunted the effect of the *Bill of Rights*.

The *Charter* deliberately excluded two rights that are contained in the *Bill of Rights*. The first is the right to a fair hearing when a determination concerning an individual's rights and obligations is required. A fair hearing under these circumstances would demand that the individual be allowed to be present at, and generally participate in, such hearing. Determining an individual's right or obligation is a serious matter that should not be decided in the absence of the individual affected by the decision. However, the *Charter* principle of fundamental justice under section 7 can require individual participation. The content of that participation may be limited to written submissions.

[2] S.C. 1960, c. 44, reprinted in R.S.C. 1985, Appendix III [*Bill of Rights*].
[3] *Hogan v. The Queen*, [1975] 2 S.C.R. 574.

The second omission concerns the protection of property rights through a "due process" clause. This right has a very narrow application under the *Bill of Rights* because property is generally not dealt with under federal legislation. "Property" is a provincial head of power under the Constitution, and the *Bill of Rights* would not protect an individual from provincial interference with property rights. The exclusion of property rights from the *Charter* means that there is no protection of property rights in the provincial context, under the Constitution.

The exclusion of property rights from the *Charter* may be due to concerns that arose as a result of its inclusion in American legislation. The American *Bill of Rights* includes a guarantee of due process of law where a person is to be deprived of property. When federal legislation was passed prohibiting slavery in various states, the guarantee was invoked to protect the property rights of slave owners. In 1857, the U.S. Supreme Court held that all slaves owned prior to the enactment of legislation prohibiting slavery would remain the property of their owners. The U.S. Supreme Court decided that freeing existing slaves would amount to depriving the owners of their property rights in their slaves. The subsequent passage of constitutional amendments resolved the issue and emancipated the slaves.[4] However, the idea that the property rights of one individual might override the basic freedoms of another lingered in the minds of constitutional theorists.

THE *CANADIAN CHARTER OF RIGHTS AND FREEDOMS*

The shortcomings of the *Bill of Rights* led to the *Charter* being included as part of Canada's "supreme" law, the Constitution. Factors that helped identify the need for more extensive legislation included the limited application of the *Bill of Rights*, its questionable authority to demand compliance, and its ability to be easily overridden. Therefore, the new legislation would have to apply to both the federal Parliament and provincial legislatures. It would also have to be powerful enough to protect the rights and freedoms that it contained by demanding compliance with its provisions. To ensure that these requirements were met, the *Charter* was entrenched as part of Canada's Constitution.

The **entrenchment** of the *Charter* in the Constitution means that the courts have been given a clear role in deciding when a *Charter* right has been violated. The result is that, under certain circumstances, the courts have the power to overrule the decision of an elected Parliament. Since 1982, the courts have developed analytical techniques for deciding *Charter* issues. The courts will conduct an analysis that will first consider whether or not the legislation in question is valid under the division of powers in the Constitution. If the legislation is found to be an invalid exercise of legislative power, such as a province passing a law on a federal matter, the courts will decide the matter on this constitutional, division of power basis. Further *Charter* analysis becomes unnecessary. The right that the individual is alleging was infringed does not even have to be considered in such a case. But if the legislation or government action is a valid exercise of constitutional power, the courts must continue with the analysis. The additional analytical stages are discussed later in the chapter.

---

[4] Peter W. Hogg, *Constitutional Law of Canada*, 2002 Student ed. (Toronto: Carswell, 2002) at 696 [Hogg], discussing *Dred Scott v. Sandford* (1857), 60 U.S. (19 How.) 393.

EXHIBIT 7.1

Canadian Charter of Rights and Freedoms

Whereas Canada is founded upon principles that recognize the supremacy of God and the rule of law:

Guarantee of Rights and Freedoms

Rights and freedoms in Canada
1. The Canadian Charter of Rights and Freedoms guarantees the rights and freedoms set out in it subject only to such reasonable limits prescribed by law as can be demonstrably justified in a free and democratic society.

Fundamental Freedoms

Fundamental freedoms
2. Everyone has the following fundamental freedoms:

(a) freedom of conscience and religion;
(b) freedom of thought, belief, opinion and expression, including freedom of the press and other media of communication;
(c) freedom of peaceful assembly; and
(d) freedom of association.

Democratic Rights

Democratic rights of citizens
3. Every citizen of Canada has the right to vote in an election of members of the House of Commons or of a legislative assembly and to be qualified for membership therein.

Maximum duration of legislative bodies
4.(1) No House of Commons and no legislative assembly shall continue for longer than five years from the date fixed for the return of the writs at a general election of its members.

Continuation in special circumstances
　　(2) In time of real or apprehended war, invasion or insurrection, a House of Commons may be continued by Parliament and a legislative assembly may be continued by the legislature beyond five years if such continuation is not opposed by the votes of more than one-third of the members of the House of Commons or the legislative assembly, as the case may be.

Annual sitting of legislative bodies
5. There shall be a sitting of Parliament and of each legislature at least once every twelve months.

Mobility Rights

Mobility of Citizens
6.(1) Every citizen of Canada has the right to enter, remain in and leave Canada.

Rights to move and gain livelihood
　　(2) Every citizen of Canada and every person who has the status of a permanent resident of Canada has the right

(a) to move and take up residence in any province; and
(b) to pursue the gaining of a livelihood in any province.

Limitation
　　(3) The rights specified in subsection (2) are subject to

(a) any laws or practices of general application in force in a province other than those that discriminate among persons primarily on the basis of a province of present or previous residence; and
(b) any laws providing for reasonable residency requirements as a qualification for the receipt of publicly provided social services.

EXHIBIT 7.1 (continued)

Canadian Charter of Rights and Freedoms

Affirmative action programs

(4) Subsections (2) and (3) do not preclude any law, program or activity that has as its object the amelioration in a province of conditions of individuals in that province who are socially or economically disadvantaged if the rate of employment in that province is below the rate of employment in Canada.

Legal Rights

Life, liberty and security of the person

7. Everyone has the right to life, liberty and security of the person and the right not to be deprived thereof except in accordance with the principles of fundamental justice.

Search or seizure

8. Everyone has the right to be secure against unreasonable search or seizure.

Detention or imprisonment

9. Everyone has the right not to be arbitrarily detained or imprisoned.

Arrest or Detention

10. Everyone has the right on arrest or detention

(a) to be informed promptly of the reasons therefore;

(b) to retain and instruct counsel without delay and to be informed of that right; and

(c) to have the validity of the detention determined by way of habeas corpus and to be released if the detention is not lawful.

Proceedings in criminal and penal matters

11. Any person charged with an offence has the right

(a) to be informed without unreasonable delay of the specific offence;

(b) to be tried within a reasonable time;

(c) not to be compelled to be a witness in proceedings against that person in respect of the offence;

(d) to be presumed innocent until proven guilty according to law in a fair and public hearing by an independent and impartial tribunal;

(e) not to be denied reasonable bail without just cause;

(f) except in the case of an offence under military law tried before a military tribunal, to the benefit of trial by jury where the maximum punishment for the offence is imprisonment for five years or a more severe punishment;

(g) not to be found guilty on account of any act or omission unless, at the time of the act or omission, it constituted an offence under Canadian or international law or was criminal according to the general principles of law recognized by the community of nations;

(h) if finally acquitted of the offence, not to be tried for it again and, if finally found guilty and punished for the offence, not to be tried or punished for it again; and

(i) if found guilty of the offence and if the punishment for the offence has been varied between the time of commission and the time of sentencing, to the benefit of the lesser punishment.

Treatment or punishment

12. Everyone has the right not to be subjected to any cruel and unusual treatment or punishment.

Self-incrimination

13. A witness who testifies in any proceedings has the right not to have any incriminating evidence so given used to incriminate that witness in any other proceedings, except in a prosecution for perjury or for the giving of contradictory evidence.

Interpreter

14. A party of witness in any proceedings who does not understand or speak the language in which the proceedings are conducted or who is deaf has the right to the assistance of an interpreter.

EXHIBIT 7.1 (continued)   *Canadian Charter of Rights and Freedoms*

Equality Rights

Equality before and under law and equal protection and benefit of law
15.(1) Every individual is equal before and under the law and has the right to the equal protection and equal benefit of the law without discrimination and, in particular, without discrimination based on race, national or ethnic origin, religion, sex, age or mental or physical disability.

Affirmative action programs
   (2) Subsection (1) does not preclude any law, program or activity that has as its object the amelioration of conditions of disadvantaged individuals or groups including those that are disadvantaged because of race, national or ethnic origin, colour, religion, sex, age or mental or physical disability.

OVERVIEW OF THE *CHARTER*

Charter rights and freedoms are not absolute. Section 1 permits government to infringe — i.e., limit — a right or freedom where doing so is "demonstrably justified in a free and democratic society". This ability to infringe is restricted to the *Charter*; therefore, other constitutional provisions, such as the entrenchment of specific Aboriginal rights under section 35, cannot be infringed or limited. The reason that infringements are permitted under section 1 is that circumstances may arise where a limitation of a right or freedom permits the achievement of a benefit to society that is seen to be greater than the detriment that would result from the infringement. In determining whether or not to restrict a *Charter* right, the Supreme Court of Canada has developed a strict test that the government must meet if a right is to be infringed. This is discussed later in this chapter.

Section 2 identifies fundamental freedoms that characterize democratic society. Individuals have the freedom to practise their religion, to think and believe what they choose, express themselves, and associate with others. The freedom of expression contained in section 2(b) can be controversial. The Supreme Court of Canada in *Irwin Toy v. Quebec*[5] held that freedom of expression was important for facilitating the search for truth, participation in social and political decision making, and self-fulfillment. This broad freedom is not concerned with the content of the message contained in the expression. The "truth" of the message is not relevant to its protection unless it runs afoul of a valid criminal law. The form of expression is not limited to art, books, or communications by news agencies. Expression may also be found, for instance, in picketing, handing out pamphlets, or other similar types of physical activity. The only clear exclusion from s. 2(b) protection is violence as a form of expression.[6] However, section 1 can be used to limit freedom of expression. In *Irwin Toy* the Court upheld a Quebec law that banned certain types of advertising geared towards children less than 13 years of age, despite the fact that this form of expression is protected by section 2.

---

[5] [1989] 1 S.C.R. 927 at 968–71, 58 D.L.R. (4th) 577 [*Irwin Toy* cited to S.C.R.].
[6] *Ibid.*

Canada enjoys a democratic system of government, and its process should reflect democratic values. This obligation is found in sections 3 to 5. The right is broader than simply a right to vote, mandating the holding of elections every five years (barring "real or apprehended war"), or the minimum time requirement for the sitting of the legislatures. Any procedure or practice that negatively impacts the democratic process may be found unconstitutional under the *Charter*.

Every citizen has "the right to enter, remain in, and leave Canada" under section 6(1). Section 6(2) establishes an individual's right to move across provincial boundaries and to work or gain a livelihood in another province. These mobility rights are derived from the fact that Canada is a federal state. Canadian federalism involves two levels of government authority: the central, or national, federal Parliament; and the regional, i.e., provincial, legislatures.[7] Therefore, a citizen or permanent resident of the national state has the *Charter* right to travel between all provinces. However, that is not to say provinces have no choice about who moves in or out of their jurisdiction. Section 6(3) goes on to state that the mobility right is subject to "any laws or practices of general application in force in a province". In other words, you do not have the right to move to another province and open a business that is not permitted under that province's law. The mobility right should not undermine the autonomy of each provincial authority.

Section 7 contains another broad right: "the right to life, liberty, and security of the person and the right not to be deprived thereof except in accordance with the principles of fundamental justice".[8] While liberty is clearly affected when a person is imprisoned, it can also be infringed outside of the criminal law.[9] For example, laws relating to the involuntary civil commitment of a person with a mental illness also affect a person's liberty because the person is "involuntarily" committed to, and detained in, a psychiatric facility. A s. 7 challenge requires the claimant to prove (i) that there has been or could be a deprivation of a s. 7 right; and (ii) that the deprivation was not, or would not be, in accordance with the principles of **fundamental justice**.[10] If the claimant proves the foregoing, the government bears the burden of justifying the deprivation under section 1.

R. v. Morgentaler (1988)[11] concerned, among other things, the security of the person. Security of the person relates not only to state interference with a person's bodily integrity, it can also include the person's psychological well-being in a criminal context. The *Morgentaler 1988* case concerned criminal legislation that made it a criminal offence for a woman to obtain an abortion when the prescribed procedure was not followed. Where the procedure was complied with, the abortion was legal and the woman obtained the protection of a specific defence contained in the *Criminal Code*. The Court held that the

---

[7] Hogg, *supra* note 4 at 104.

[8] The meaning of the phrase "principles of fundamental justice" has been judicially discussed in *Charter* challenges brought under the heading of life, liberty and security of the person. Though the term has no precise definition, the principles correspond to established common law principles and the basic tenets of our legal system. These would include such things as procedural fairness (the right to notice and the right to be heard), as well as a substantive component (i.e., that the principles would be considered fundamental to cultural views of justice). See e.g. *Morgentaler 1988*, *infra* note 11; *Rodriguez v. British Columbia (A.G.)*, [1993] 3 S.C.R. 519, 107 D.L.R. (4th) 342; *New Brunswick (Minister of Health and Community Services) v. G.(J.)*, [1999] 3 S.C.R. 46, 177 D.L.R. (4th) 124.

[9] *Blencoe v. British Columbia (Human Rights Commission)*, [2000] 2 S.C.R. 307: "'liberty' is engaged where the state imposes compulsions or prohibitions that 'affect important and fundamental life choices' such as not loitering in a particular place or producing documents or testifying" (para. 49).

[10] *Charkaoui v. Canada (Citizenship and Immigration)*, [2007] 1 S.C.R. 350, 2007 SCC 9.

[11] [1988] 1 S.C.R. 30, 44 D.L.R. (4th) 385 [*Morgentaler 1988* cited to S.C.R.].

mandatory requirements of a woman to obtain the approval of a committee at an accredited or approved hospital prior to having an abortion, as well as to have the medical procedure at an accredited or approved hospital, breached the s. 7 right to security of the person. Fulfilling the procedural requirements inevitably resulted in delay. The Court found that

> s. 251 of the *Criminal Code* is *prima facie* a violation of the security of the person of thousands of Canadian women who have made the difficult decision that they do not wish to continue with a pregnancy. ... Not only does the removal of the decision-making power threaten women in a physical sense; the indecision of knowing whether an abortion will be granted inflicts emotional stress. ... Forcing a woman, by threat of criminal sanction, to carry a foetus to term unless she meets certain criteria unrelated to her own priorities and aspirations, is a profound interference with a woman's body and thus a violation of security of the person. ... [T]here is yet another infringement of security of the person. It is clear from the evidence that s. 251 harms the psychological integrity of women seeking abortions ... delays ... greatly [increase] the stress levels of patients....[12]

The next issue was whether the infringement was in accord with fundamental justice. Fundamental justice concerns the administrative structures and procedures, and their fairness. If the procedures are unfair, the right to fundamental justice may be infringed. The Court in *Morgentaler 1988* found that the structure and procedure imposed were unfair in effect. They contained "so many potential barriers to its own operation that the defence it create[d] w[ould] in many circumstances be practically unavailable to women who would *prima facie* qualify for the defence, or at least would force such women to travel great distances at substantial expense and inconvenience in order to benefit from a defence that is held out to be generally available". The law was found to be unconstitutional.

The legal rights contained in sections 8 to 14 include limiting government's power of search and seizure, as well as arbitrary detention or imprisonment; identification of the rights that arise upon arrest or detention and rights that arise upon being charged with an offence; the right to be free from cruel and unusual punishment; the right of witnesses not to incriminate themselves in a proceeding; and the right of a party or witness to have the assistance of an interpreter. These rights apply to the criminal process and related situations. For example, detention can arise outside of the arrest process and trigger the right to counsel. In *R. v. Therens*[13] the Court held that a demand to accompany a police officer to the station to provide a Breathalyzer sample constituted detention under the *Charter* and that the right to counsel arose.

Equality rights are found in section 15. Everyone has the right to be considered equal in the eyes of the law and deserves the protection and benefit of the law without discrimination. This provision relates to enacted or future laws, which must treat all constituents the same. It would similarly apply to government policies that are administered (e.g., a benefit program). The right can be infringed by government action or inaction that explicitly, or by its effect, results in differential treatment. For example, in *Eldridge v. British Columbia (A.G.)*,[14] the Court held that government's failure to provide funding for sign language interpreters in hospitals breached section 15. Communication with health care providers is an indispensable component in the delivery of medical services. The failure to provide an interpreter where

---

[12] *Ibid.* at paras. 23, 24, and 30.

[13] [1985] 1 S.C.R. 613, 18 D.L.R. (4th) 655 [*Therens* cited to S.C.R.].

[14] [1997] 3 S.C.R. 624, 151 D.L.R. (4th) 577 [*Eldridge* cited to S.C.R.].

necessary to a person with an auditory disability constituted government "inaction". This inaction meant that a disadvantaged group (people with an auditory disability) did not benefit equally from the medical services offered to the general public.

The discriminatory grounds identified in the *Charter* are race, ethnicity, colour, religion, sex, age, or disability. This list is not exhaustive. Analogous grounds of discrimination have been identified by the Court. In *Corbiere v. Canada (Minister of Indian and Northern Affairs)*,[15] the majority noted the following about the identification of analogous grounds:

> It seems to us that what these grounds have in common is the fact that they often serve as the basis for stereotypical decisions made not on the basis of merit but on the basis of a personal characteristic that is immutable or changeable only at unacceptable cost to personal identity. ... s. 15 targets the denial of equal treatment on grounds that are actually immutable, like race, or constructively immutable, like religion.[16]

The Court has held that citizenship, sexual orientation, marital status, and Aboriginal residence are analogous grounds.[17] The test applied in a s. 15(1) challenge requires a finding of "(1) different treatment on the basis of a personal characteristic, (2) that is an enumerated or analogous ground, (3) which is discriminating in purpose or effect."[18]

Section 15(2) permits discrimination where the purpose is to ameliorate disadvantages suffered by an identified group. Government can design programs for the benefit of a specific group despite any discriminatory effect to others outside of that group. Such programs or policies are insulated from *Charter* challenge under section 15(1).

Canada's founding nations are considered to have been the British and the French. Section 16 identifies the official languages of Canada as English and French and gives them equal status. The language rights contained in sections 16 to 23 constitute a limited form of bilingualism.[19] The obligation of government to provide bilingual services is limited to the federal sphere unless there is "significant demand" or it is "reasonable" to have communications and services in both languages (s. 20). New Brunswick is specifically included under both provisions as its provincial government, during negotiations over the *Charter*, agreed to this. Minority language education rights are contained in section 23. Regardless of the language of the majority in a province, and where certain requirements are met, people have the right to have their child educated in the minority language of that province.

The remaining *Charter* provisions, sections 24 to 34, deal succinctly with a variety of issues. Section 24(1) provides for enforcement of the *Charter*, and section 24(2) permits the exclusion of evidence obtained in a manner that infringed a right or freedom. The *Charter* is not to be applied or interpreted in a manner that would limit, reduce, or take away from Aboriginal treaty or other rights and freedoms that attach to First Nations (s. 25). The *Charter* is not the sole source of rights and freedoms and will not override those from another source (s. 26). Common law rights would be an example of a right

---

[15] [1999] 2 S.C.R. 203 [*Corbiere*].

[16] *Ibid.* at para. 13.

[17] See respectively, *Andrews v. Law Society of British Columbia*, [1989] 1 S.C.R. 143; *Egan v. Canada*, [1995] 2 S.C.R. 513; *Miron v. Trudel*, [1995] 2 S.C.R. 418; *M. v. H.*, [1999] 2 S.C.R. 3; and *Corbiere*, *supra* note 15. In *Corbiere*, restricting the voting right in a band election to on-reserve residents (Aboriginal residence) was found to be an analogous ground by the Court.

[18] *Canada (A.G.) v. Hislop*, 2007 SCC 10 (CanLII) at para. 36.

[19] Hogg, *supra* note 4 at 1127.

EXHIBIT 7.2

Application of the *Charter*

32(1) This Charter applies

  (a) to the Parliament and government of Canada in respect of all matters within the authority of Parliament ...; and

  (b) to the legislature and government of each province in respect of all matters within the authority of the legislature of each province.

---

from another source. The *Charter* is to be interpreted in a manner that upholds and facilitates Canada's multicultural heritage (s. 27). The application of the *Charter* is guaranteed equally to male and female persons (s. 28). The entrenchment of Aboriginal rights is found outside of the *Charter*, in section 35 of the Constitution.

THE APPLICATION OF THE *CHARTER*

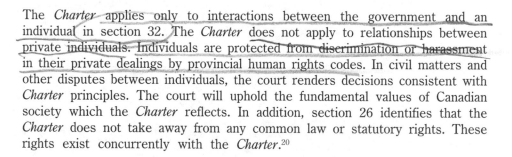

The *Charter* applies only to interactions between the government and an individual in section 32. The *Charter* does not apply to relationships between private individuals. Individuals are protected from discrimination or harassment in their private dealings by provincial human rights codes. In civil matters and other disputes between individuals, the court renders decisions consistent with *Charter* principles. The court will uphold the fundamental values of Canadian society which the *Charter* reflects. In addition, section 26 identifies that the *Charter* does not take away from any common law or statutory rights. These rights exist concurrently with the *Charter*.[20]

GOVERNMENT ACTION AND ACTORS

As discussed, the government must be involved if the *Charter* is to be used to uphold a right or freedom. A challenge to legislation clearly involves the application of the *Charter* since government involvement is evident. However, there are situations where the government may be involved although not initially visible in the matter. The *Charter* extends to individuals and entities exercising governmental responsibility (e.g., ministers and officials) as well as entities controlled by government. The *Charter* will also apply to entities to which government responsibilities have been delegated.[21] Government cannot circumvent *Charter* obligations by privatizing services or delegating responsibility to the private sector. The *Charter* may, therefore, apply in a number of additional circumstances: where an entity is controlled by government; implementing government programs; exercising government functions; deriving its powers from the state; or exercising statutory powers of compulsion. The *Charter* can also apply to government omissions. There may be situations where the government's failure to legislate a matter or to legislate it inadequately can give rise to a *Charter* infringement.

---

[20] *Ibid.* at 728.

[21] Joel Bakan et al., *Canadian Constitutional Law*, 3d ed. (Toronto: Emond Montgomery Publications Limited, 2003) at 787 [Bakan].

Entities Controlled by Government

mandatory retirement

application of the Charter (controlled entity)

For an entity to qualify as being "controlled by government", the government must have significant routine or day-to-day control of the operation of the entity. This appears to be a straightforward criterion, but the Supreme Court of Canada has applied it with seemingly conflicting decisions. In *McKinney*,[22] the mandatory retirement policies of four Ontario universities were challenged. The allegation was that the retirement policies infringed on *Charter* equality rights. First, the Court had to determine whether "government" was present under the circumstances; otherwise, the *Charter* would not apply. The Court found that universities performed an important public service. However, entities performing a public service *alone* will not automatically trigger the application of the *Charter*. The Court then considered the amount of government involvement in the agreements negotiated between the universities and their employees. Evidence showed that the universities negotiated contracts and collective agreements independently and not at the direction of government. Therefore, the universities were not controlled by government when they made the agreements that contained the retirement policies. The Court identified additional factors that supported the independence of the universities. For example, each university had its own governing body, whose duty "[was] not to act at the direction of the government but in the interests of the university ...". While the government was seen to regulate and fund universities, it had no legal power to control them, and the *Charter* did not apply.

Douglas/Swantlen Faculty Association v. Douglas College[23] also concerned a challenge to mandatory retirement policies. However, in this case the Court determined that the college was a government entity and the *Charter* applied. The Court noted that the provincial government appointed the governing body of the college. In addition, the minister was also allowed to "issue directions" to the college and was required to approve all by-laws. The government retained the right, at all times, to direct the operation of the college. The college's lack of autonomy distinguished the situation from that of the universities in *McKinney*.[24] The high level of government involvement in the operation and decision-making process at the college meant that it was controlled by government.

Implementing Government Programs

A similar debate surrounded the applicability of the *Charter* to hospitals. In *Stoffman v. Vancouver General Hospital*,[25] the Supreme Court determined that the day-to-day control of a hospital was outside government power. Like *McKinney*, the *Charter* did not apply to the hospital's mandatory retirement policy. However, a successful *Charter* challenge against a hospital was brought in *Eldridge*.[26] Eldridge alleged discrimination because the hospital failed to provide free sign language interpreters for deaf patients. The failure denied deaf patients the same level of medical treatment as able-hearing patients. In providing medical services, the hospital was carrying out a specific government program. Responsibility for identifying the services to be delivered belonged to the government. When providing the services, the hospital was acting as an agent for the government, and the *Charter* applied.

---

[22] *McKinney v. University of Guelph*, [1990] 3 S.C.R. 229, 76 D.L.R. (4th) 545 [*McKinney* cited to S.C.R.].

[23] [1990] 3 S.C.R. 570, 77 D.L.R. (4th) 94.

[24] *McKinney*, *supra* note 22.

[25] [1990] 3 S.C.R. 451, 77 D.L.R. (4th) 55.

[26] *Supra* note 14.

Exercising Government Functions: Power from the State and Statutory Powers of Compulsion

Entities that have the power to implement law, decide a question of law, or force an individual to comply with its ruling are generally subject to the *Charter*. Municipalities are not a level of government specifically recognized in the Constitution. They are created by provincial governments under the power contained in section 92(8) of the Constitution. However, municipalities enact and enforce by-laws and conduct other activities similar to those of government. Since municipalities perform government functions, the *Charter* will apply to the by-laws they enact and other actions. Similarly, statutorily appointed arbitrators (whose powers are derived from the state) and entities exercising powers of compulsion (such as those of the Human Rights Commission, which can compel compliance to decisions) would also fall within the sphere of the *Charter*.

Omissions

The domain of the *Charter* is expansive enough to include not only what the government or government entity *does*, but also to what it omits to do. An absence of legislation on a matter is unlikely to result in government being forced to legislate on the basis of a *Charter* right. Exceptions do, however, occasionally arise. To illustrate, Alberta's human rights legislation deliberately omitted the grounds of sexual orientation as a basis for discrimination. Therefore, persons discriminated against on the basis of sexual orientation were prevented from filing a human rights complaint. In *Vriend v. Alberta*,[27] the Supreme Court held that sexual orientation was to be included as a ground in the provincial Human Rights Code. Since the Alberta legislature chose to enact a Human Rights Code that was under-inclusive in its application, it was under a positive obligation to ensure that the legislation complied with the *Charter*.

STANDING

Appropriate **standing** is required in order for an individual to bring a *Charter* challenge. Standing can be based on either a private or public interest in the matter. An "individual" includes both a corporation (which is considered to have the same legal rights and responsibilities as a person) and a person. However, a corporation's standing is limited. There is no definitive method of identifying the grounds a corporation may base its challenge on. Each case would be determined by the court in the specific circumstances. Supreme Court decisions have held that corporations can bring a challenge under some s. 2 rights (e.g., freedom of expression in an advertising context[28]), but not others (e.g., freedom of religion has been held inapplicable to corporations, as shown in Exhibit 7.3). The Supreme Court has also limited a corporation's standing in that a corporation cannot bring an "independent civil action" in order to challenge the validity of a law unless it can claim that one of its *Charter* rights has been infringed.[29] A corporation would not have any standing regarding the infringement of rights applicable only to an actual person. For example, a corporation could not complain about a violation of its right not to be arbitrarily detained (s. 9) since that is not physically possible. The type of standing can also affect available remedies.

---

[27] [1998] 1 S.C.R. 493, 156 D.L.R. (4th) 385.

[28] See e.g. *Irwin Toy, supra* note 5; *Rocket v. Royal College of Dental Surgeons*, [1990] 2 S.C.R. 232, 71 D.L.R. (4th) 68; and *RJR MacDonald Inc. v. Canada (A.G.)*, [1995] 3 S.C.R. 199, 127 D.L.R. (4th) 1.

[29] Bakan, *supra* note 21 at 1301.

Private Interest Standing

EXHIBIT 7.3

Big M Drugstore Mart was charged with being open for business on a Sunday in contravention of Alberta's *Lord's Day Act*, R.S.C. 1970, c. L-13 ("*Lord's Day Act*") and brought a challenge asserting that the legislation was unconstitutional. The Attorney General of Alberta claimed that the drugstore was unable to base its challenge on the *Charter* right of freedom of religion since a corporation could not hold religious beliefs. Therefore, Big M Drug Mart Ltd. ("Big M") lacked the required standing by which to bring the challenge. The Court held, however, that any individual charged with a criminal offence could challenge the applicable law on its constitutionality. Big M was asserting that the *Lord's Day Act* was inconsistent with section 2(a) of the *Charter* — i.e., freedom of religion — and, therefore, constitutionally invalid. The drugstore was not asserting that its right to freedom of religion had been infringed.

The Court found that the purpose of the legislation at the time of enactment was to proclaim the "standards of the Christian faith". The standards meant that businesses were closed on Sundays to respect the Christian holy day. As such, it could be seen that the law's purpose was a religious matter that may offend and discriminate against non-Christian Canadians. This would violate section 2(a) of the *Charter*.

> [By this statute] [n]on-Christians are prohibited for religious reasons from carrying out activities which are otherwise lawful, moral and normal. The arm of the state requires all to remember the Lord's Day of the Christians and to keep it holy. The protection of one religion and the concomitant non-protection of others imports disparate impact destructive of the religious freedom of the collectivity.
>
> — Justice Dickson

The Attorney General proposed that the legislation supported a secular day of rest for the benefit of all Canadians. The Court rejected this argument since the legislation's purpose at enactment was clearly religious, and not secular. Legislation should not be construed as having a purpose other than that by which it was enacted. In addition, the *Lord's Day Act* appeared to contradict section 27 of the *Charter*. Section 27 requires that the *Charter* be "interpreted in a manner consistent with the preservation and enhancement of the multicultural heritage of Canadians". The Court held that the Act was constitutionally invalid under section 52(1).

Source: *R. v. Big M Drug Mart Ltd.*, [1985] 1 S.C.R. 295, 18 D.L.R. (4th) 321.

---

solely or separate issue

Private Interest Standing

Private interest standing in a *Charter* challenge may arise in different ways. It can be based solely on a claim of a *Charter* infringement of a right or freedom, or corollary to a proceeding. A challenge can be brought as an independent action that seeks declaratory relief (i.e., the court "declares" that the individual's right or freedom has been infringed) or other remedy. A *Charter* challenge can also be raised as a separate issue in an ongoing criminal or civil proceeding. Where an individual is charged with a criminal offence, standing to bring a *Charter* challenge automatically applies should appropriate circumstances arise. Life, liberty and security of the person, and other legal rights contained in the *Charter* are always relevant to criminal actions.

Public Interest Standing

Where an individual asserts public interest standing, three requirements must be met: (i) the individual must have a genuine interest in the question before the court; (ii) the action must raise a serious legal question; and (iii) there can be no other reasonable or effective way that the issue can be brought before the court.[30] The third requirement is often the most difficult to

---

[30] *Minister of Justice v. Borowski*, [1981] 2 S.C.R. 575, 130 D.L.R. (3d) 588.

fulfill.[31] The case of the *Canadian Council of Churches v. Canada*[32] was based on public interest standing on behalf of refugees. The Council's concern was that people were being denied refugee status in Canada without their presence at a hearing. Decisions regarding refugee status were generally made on the recommendation of immigration staff without an opportunity for the person to be present or speak to the decision maker. The Council easily met the first two requirements for standing. The Council regularly assisted refugees (genuine interest) and the fact that the hearings did not require the presence of the refugee claimant indicated a violation of the principles of fundamental justice (a serious legal question). However, the Council was unable to fulfill the third requirement. The Court found that people claiming refugees status were able to bring their own claim and had done so in the past. Therefore, there existed a reasonable and effective way for the matter to otherwise come before the court. It was unnecessary for the Council to do so on a refugee's behalf, and standing was not granted.

INFRINGING ON *CHARTER* RIGHTS OR FREEDOMS

Charter rights are not absolute, and the government is permitted to infringe upon our civil liberties under certain circumstances. The *Charter* also responds to the special needs of identified groups that have historically been disadvantaged. Ameliorative programs are expressly permitted in the *Charter* (s. 6(4)). These programs aim to protect or improve the position of historically disadvantaged groups, such as Aboriginal peoples or women. Therefore, upholding *Charter* rights may involve balancing competing rights. This balancing can result in one group's rights, such as the more advantaged majority, being infringed by another. Government power to infringe on *Charter* rights can also be found in sections 33 and 1.

Section 33: The "Notwithstanding" Clause

33(1) Parliament or the legislature of a province may expressly declare in an Act of Parliament or of the legislature, as the case may be, that the Act or a provision thereof shall operate notwithstanding a provision included in section 2 or sections 7 to 15 of this Charter.

(2) An Act or a provision of an Act in respect of which a declaration made under this section is in effect shall have such operation as it would have but for the provision of this Charter referred to in the declaration.

(3) A declaration made under subsection (1) shall cease to have effect five years after it comes into force or on such earlier date as may be specified in the declaration.

(4) Parliament or the legislature of a province may re-enact a declaration made under subsection (1).

(5) Subsection (3) applies in respect of a re-enactment made under subsection (4).

Although it is not often used, section 33 permits Parliament or the legislature to pass legislation that infringes on certain *Charter* rights. Section 33 allows the legislative body to declare the legislation valid notwithstanding the *Charter*. The *Charter* rights that can be limited or overridden are those contained in section 2 and sections 7–15.[33] The notwithstanding clause

---

[31] See also *R. v. Banks* (2007), 84 O.R. (3d) 1, 2007 ONCA 19 at para. 24; known as the "squeegee kids" case.

[32] [1992] 1 S.C.R. 236, 88 D.L.R. (4th) 193.

[33] That is, freedom of conscience and religion; freedom of thought, belief, opinion and expression, including freedom of the press and other media of communication; freedom of peaceful assembly; freedom of association; life, liberty

must follow a set format and automatically expires in five years unless the legislative body re-enacts it. There is no identified limit to the number of re-enactments permitted, and each one will run for an additional five-year period.[34]

Parliament and the majority of the provinces have never used the override provision contained in section 33. This reluctance appears to be due to government's principled commitment to the *Charter*. Furthermore, the use of section 33 may be strongly opposed by "opposition parties, the press, the organized bar and civil liberties groups".[35] It is reasonable to believe that Canadians would not look favourably on a democratic process that regularly and arbitrarily overrides entrenched *Charter* rights. At the same time, section 33 can be seen to leave the legislative "last word" with the elected Parliament or legislature. In effect, section 33 prevents the judiciary from interfering with laws that government, the elected representatives of the people, enact to best serve their constituents.

One province that has used the notwithstanding clause is Quebec. Quebec did not assent to the *Constitution Act, 1982* or to the *Charter* — a position that continues today. When the *Constitution Act, 1982* was proclaimed, the Quebec legislature enacted a statute that added notwithstanding clauses to all existing legislation. In effect, the section 33 override meant that the relevant sections of the *Charter* did not apply to Quebec law. This blanket statute was not renewed after the set term expired.

As a matter of form, the legislation must expressly state that it intends to operate despite one or more of the relevant rights or freedoms being overridden. The specific right or freedom being infringed must be clearly identified in the legislation by section number(s) and can include all of the rights contained in the *Charter*.[36] The law must also contain a declaration that "[the] statute is to operate notwithstanding a Charter right".[37] The declaration makes it clear that the legislative body deliberately intended to override the identified right(s).

Section 1 Justification

1. The *Canadian Charter of Rights and Freedoms* guarantees the rights and freedoms set out in it subject only to such reasonable limits prescribed by law as can be demonstrably justified in a free and democratic society.

The arbitrary use of section 33 to override portions of the *Charter* is not the only method by which government can create or uphold legislation that infringes on *Charter* rights. Section 1 of the *Charter* contains a limitation clause that permits government, where it fulfills necessary requirements, to infringe a right or freedom. This method of infringement often occurs where the legislating body is attempting to balance competing rights between individuals or groups. Section 1 allows an infringement where such a balance is desired. While a particular right or freedom may involve additional analytical and contextual processes for s. 1 justification, the requirements outlined below are generally engaged.

The court must first find that the law was validly enacted under the Constitution and that the *Charter* applies in the circumstances. Validity of the law may be undisputed and therefore not considered by the court. (A chal-

---

and security of the person; legal rights (e.g., unreasonable search and seizure and self-incrimination); and equality rights.

[34] Hogg, *supra* note 4 at 815.

[35] *Ibid.* at 819.

[36] *Ford v. Quebec (A.G.)*, [1988] 2 S.C.R. 712.

[37] Hogg, *supra* note 4 at 815.

EXHIBIT 7.4	General *Charter* Analysis

1. Preliminary Considerations:
   (a) Does the *Charter* apply under the circumstances?
   (b) Is the legislation validly enacted under the Constitution?

2. Stage 1 Analysis: Is the limit prescribed by law?
   (a) Does the law have the required standard of clarity?
   (b) Is the law too vague or overbroad?

3. Stage 2 Analysis: Is the limit "reasonable and justified" in a free and democratic society?
   (a) What is the law's objective?
   (b) What is the law's rational connection to achieving this objective?
   (c) Does the law use the least restrictive means required in order to achieve its objective?
   (d) Is the benefit obtained by the law greater than the level of infringement?

---

lenge can be to the application or effect of the law.) The individual alleging the infringement is then required to prove that a *Charter* right has been infringed. Where the infringement is proven, the burden of proof shifts to the government. The government must fulfill two requirements in order for a s. 1 justification to succeed. The first, if disputed, is that the limit must be "**prescribed by law**". The law must be adequately accessible (i.e., published) and must set out the circumstances to which the legal rule applies. Any exceptions to the application of the law must be clearly stated. *Therens*[38] illustrates this point. The accused was required to accompany a police officer and provide a Breathalyzer under [former] section 235 of the *Criminal Code*. However, the Court ruled that Therens's accompaniment of the officer constituted detention. Section 10(b) of the *Charter* states that when detained, the person has the right to be informed of the right to counsel. The officer did not inform Therens of his s. 10(b) right. The Court examined section 235 of the *Criminal Code* and found that the provision did not include an express exemption from the application of section 10(b). Therefore, the officer's failure to inform Therens of his right to counsel was not prescribed by the law and infringed his *Charter* right.

All laws must meet a standard of clarity. They cannot be so vague that individuals cannot understand what is required of them and regulate their conduct accordingly. Additionally, the consequences of non-compliance should be foreseeable to a reasonable degree.[39] The requirements of the first stage of the s. 1 justification are usually fulfilled by government.

The court may also consider, at some point in its analysis, whether the statute suffers from issues of **vagueness** or **overbreadth**. These issues are concerned with the language used in the legislation and whether it is sufficiently detailed so that it can fulfill its objective. The right to freedom of expression may be infringed where a law states that "anyone found with a photograph of a naked child is guilty of possession of child pornography". The objective of such a law would be the protection of children. The protection of children from the harm of child pornography is a pressing and substantial need in our society. However, in an artistic or personal context, there may be material caught by such a broadly worded law that does not put a

---

[38] *Supra* note 13.
[39] Hogg, *supra* note 4 at 774.

child at risk of harm. Consider the parents who take a photograph of their baby lying naked on a bearskin rug. The photograph would be caught by the provision, classified as pornography, and the parents charged. The result would be an unnecessary and unjustified infringement of the person's right to freedom of expression. In such a case, the legislation's overbreadth would likely result in a failure of a s. 1 justification.

The second stage is more demanding of government and requires that the limit be justified in a free and democratic society. The court follows a four-step analytical process that examines (i) the law's objective or purpose; (ii) its rational connection to achieving the objective; (iii) whether or not the legislation employs the least drastic means required to achieve the objective; and (iv) whether the level of benefit is proportionate relative to the level of infringement.[40] The burden of justifying the infringement is on the government. Generally, the more severe the infringement, the higher the level of justification required. Social science and/or expert evidence is often used and provides context.

At the first step of the second stage, the court will identify the legislative objective of the infringing statute. In order to support a s. 1 justification, the objective must be considered to be a "pressing and substantial need" within society. This step may require only the assertion of a theoretical objective.[41] The objective can be found in the preamble to the statute, as in *Big M*,[42] and may be characterized either generally or narrowly at the court's discretion.[43] For example, the law may be generalized as protecting a vulnerable group, such as children, which would qualify as a pressing and substantial social objective in support of the infringement.

Rational Connection

Where the first step is met, the next consideration requires that the infringement is rationally connected to achieving the objective. For example, *Oakes* challenged a reverse onus clause in the *Narcotics Act*. The Act stated that any *unauthorized* people who had a narcotic substance in their possession were presumed to be in possession for the purpose of trafficking. The Act did not identify a minimum amount of narcotic. The reverse onus clause meant that the accused had the burden of proving that they were not intending to traffic in narcotics. This burden violated the accused's *Charter* right to be presumed innocent (s. 10(d)). The government failed to justify the infringement at this stage of the analysis. The Supreme Court held that there was no rational connection between the basic fact of possession and the presumed fact of possession for the purpose of trafficking. In other words, being in possession of *any* narcotic did not unequivocally translate into trafficking. The *Narcotics Act* was amended to include a minimum amount of narcotic before the reverse onus clause applied:

> The rational connection stage of the test requires the Attorney General to "show a causal connection between the infringement and the benefit sought on the basis of reason or logic": see *RJR-MacDonald*, at para. 153, and *Harper*, at para. 104. It is clear that logic and reason may play a large role in establishing such a causal connection. Such a connection is "often a difficult matter to establish by evidence, and the Supreme Court of Canada has not

---

[40] The test was articulated by the Supreme Court of Canada in *R. v. Oakes*, [1986] 1 S.C.R. 103, 26 D.L.R. (4th) 200 [*Oakes* cited to S.C.R.] and further clarified in *Dagenais v. Canadian Broadcasting Corp.*, [1994] 3 S.C.R. 835, 120 D.L.R. (4th) 12.

[41] *R. v. Bryan*, [2007] 1 S.C.R. 527, 2007 SCC 12 at para. 39 [*Bryan* cited to S.C.R.].

[42] *R. v. Big M Drug Mart Ltd.*, [1985] 1 S.C.R. 295, 18 D.L.R. (4th) 321.

[43] Hogg, *supra* note 4 at 783.

always insisted on direct proof of the causal relationship": P.W. Hogg, *Constitutional Law of Canada* (loose-leaf ed.), vol. 2, at pp. 35–31, cited with approval in *Thomson Newspapers*, at para. 39.[44]

Minimal Impairment

The minimal impairment, or least drastic or restrictive means, factor requires the government to show that the selected method of achieving the objective results in minimal impairment of the *Charter* right. This tends to be the most onerous hurdle for s. 1 justification. At this step, alternative and potentially fewer infringing means of achieving the objective will be examined. The court may again consider social science and other expert evidence. The government is required to provide evidence that the infringement is virtually the only effective means of achieving the objective. The court may also consider whether or not to defer to the decision of the legislative body that enacted the legislation. Where it is shown that a balancing of the competing interests of various groups has been done to the best of the legislative body's ability, the court can defer to the legislative body's decision. The court is generally sensitive to the boundaries of judicial review and reluctant to be seen as interfering in the democratic process.

> The standard for this stage of the analysis is still best encapsulated by the well-known passage from *RJR-MacDonald*, at para. 160:
>
>> The impairment must be "minimal", that is, the law must be carefully tailored so that rights are impaired no more than necessary. The tailoring process seldom admits of perfection and the courts must accord some leeway to the legislator. If the law falls within a range of reasonable alternatives, the courts will not find it overbroad merely because they can conceive of an alternative which might better tailor objective to infringement.
>
> Of course, as this Court unanimously recognized in *Harper*, the minimal impairment analysis may be the stage of the *Oakes* test in which context is most important: see paras. 33 and 110.[45]

Balancing

The final analytical step reviews the balance between the level of infringement and objective sought — i.e., the *proportionality* of the law. The court considers the effects of the infringement relative to its contribution in achieving the legislative objective. The question can be seen to ask "whether the *Charter* infringement is too high a price to pay for the benefit of the law".[46] A s. 1 justification would fail where the benefit is determined to be less than the level of infringement on a *Charter* right. For example, freedom of expression is a fundamental value of democracy. If Parliament enacted legislation that prohibited news agencies from reporting on criminal trials, freedom of expression would be infringed. The purpose of the legislation may be pressing and substantial: to ensure a fair trial for the accused. Prohibiting news reports prevents influencing potential jurors, which helps achieve the law's purpose and appears rationally connected. But the fairness of most trials would not be compromised by a news report. As a result, many people would experience a significant infringement of a fundamental right while few would benefit. The degree of infringement would be greatly outweighed by, and disproportionate to, the benefit obtained from the law.

---

[44] *Bryan, supra* note 41 at para. 39.

[45] *Ibid.* at para. 42.

[46] Hogg, *supra* note 4 at 801.

The final stage of the *Oakes* analysis requires a balancing between the salutary and deleterious effects of the legislation. At this stage, it is important to note that it is inappropriate to require a greater standard of proof for the existence of the salutary effects of the legislation than for the deleterious effects.[47]

REMEDIES

Anyone whose *Charter* right has been infringed can file a claim and seek a remedy under section 52(1) or section 24. The availability of a remedy will depend on the relief requested and the claimant's standing. Constitutional and *Charter* remedies seek to correct constitutional inconsistencies. Constitutional inconsistencies may arise in legislation or through the action or inaction of government. Thus, the *Charter* and Constitution can be said to regulate the conduct of government.

There are two provisions that provide a remedy for a *Charter* infringement. Section 52(1) establishes the supremacy of the Constitution and states that laws that are inconsistent with it are without force or effect. There are a number of ways the court may implement such a remedy. The s. 52(1) remedy is available when legislation is challenged on constitutional or *Charter* grounds.

Section 24(2) empowers the court to exclude evidence obtained in an unconstitutional manner from a proceeding. Section 24(1) contains a remedial remedy that empowers the court to award whatever is appropriate and just in the circumstances. Any court with jurisdiction to hear the matter can use these remedies.[48] However, s. 24 remedies generally apply only to *Charter* infringements.

Canada (A.G.) v. Hislop[49] contains a review of constitutional remedies, commencing at para. 81, that includes identifying when a suspension of a declaration of invalidity, and/or the imposition of a retrospective or prospective remedy, is appropriate.

Section 52(1) Remedy

52(1) The Constitution of Canada is the supreme law of Canada, and any law that is inconsistent with the provisions of the Constitution is, to the extent of the inconsistency, of no force or effect.

The applicable remedy for an individual challenging the constitutionality of a law is found in section 52(1). Once the issue of constitutional inconsistency is raised, the analysis shifts from the individual whose right has been infringed to the legislation itself. The issue becomes the constitutionality of the law, rather than a determination of whether or not a *Charter* right has been infringed. When a court renders a remedy under section 52, it is careful to limit its interference with the legislative process. After all, it is the legislating

---

[47] *Bryan, supra* note 41 at para. 48.

[48] The Superior Court of Justice is always a court of competent jurisdiction to hear a *Charter* matter requesting a s. 24 remedy. However, there are exceptional circumstances where a "court of competent jurisdiction" for a s. 24 remedy may include a tribunal or other court. Where the tribunal has been given statutory powers to settle all differences between the parties (Hogg, *supra* note 4 at 847, referring to *Weber v. Ontario Hydro*, [1995] 2 S.C.R. 929) it may be able to effect a s. 24 remedy. In addition, where a *Charter* issue arises during a trial taking place in a venue other than the Superior Court of Justice, the initial court may be in the best position to decide the matter (Hogg, *supra* note 4 at 846, referring to *R. v. Smith*, [1989] 2 S.C.R. 1120, 1129). It may not be necessary to move the *Charter* issue to the Superior Court of Justice.

[49] [2007] 1 S.C.R. 429; 2007 SCC 10.

EXHIBIT 7.5

Application of s. 52(1)

Schachter concerned a challenge to a government benefit program. The challenge was based on constitutional inconsistency because a group had been *excluded* from receiving the benefit. The issue concerned federal employment insurance benefits ("EI") for paternity leave. Only biological mothers were given paid leave under EI, whereas an adoptive mother and father both qualified. A biological father challenged his denial of the benefit as an infringement of his section 15 equality rights. The lower court found that the benefit program did violate the biological father's section 15 equality rights. The court used section 52(1) to extend the benefit program to include EI paid leave for biological fathers. On appeal, the Supreme Court of Canada outlined the additional issues raised by the application of section 52(1).

The application of either section 24 or section 52 requires that the "nature of the violation and the context of the legislation" be considered by the court. The remedies of severance and **reading down** minimize judicial interference with government legislation. **Reading in** allows the law to be "consistent with the basic purposes of the Charter". Severance shows respect for the decision of Parliament or the legislature by only removing the offending provision(s). Severance can remove the offending portion with some precision. However, with reading in, the issue of how far to extend the legislation is not so easily defined. Where it is difficult to define the boundary for reading in, it is the role of the legislating body to fill in any omissions or gaps. Under those circumstances, it is not appropriate for the court to read in.

The legislative objective and the implementation process also must be considered by the court. In cases where the objective is furthered by reading in, budgetary repercussions must be considered. Any addition to the benefit group may result in too much interference in the legislative process. Where the process or objective is unclear, or significant budgetary repercussions arise from judicial interference, the matter should be referred back to the legislating body for amendment. The Court determined that both these issues were relevant to the facts in *Schachter*.

The benefit's lack of a clear legislative objective meant that legislative intent may have been to deliberately exclude biological fathers in response to unique circumstances experienced solely by adoptive parents. Furthermore, by expanding the paid leave, the Court applied the benefit to a group much larger than that which the statute expressly covered. This expansion raised significant budgetary issues that potentially denied another benefit to another group due to lack of funds. As such, the lower court was improper in its reading in of biological fathers. The provision should have been declared invalid and temporarily suspended to allow the legislative body time to amend.

However, this was not necessary as the statute had already been amended prior to the hearing of the appeal. The benefit group had been extended to include paternity leave for biological fathers, but the term for which the benefit applied to both groups was for a shorter period.

Source: *Schachter v. Canada*, [1992] 2 S.C.R. 679, 66 D.L.R. (4th) 635.

---

body, as elected representatives of the people, who draft the law. It is not up to the judiciary to significantly amend or change legislation. Rather, courts limit their interference (i.e., exercise judicial restraint) or order the legislating body to amend.

The court has six options that can be implemented under the s. 52 remedy. The court can strike down, sever, read in, read down, order a constitutional exemption or provide a declaration of invalidity. The remedy chosen will depend on the particular circumstances. After determining that the legislation is inconsistent, the court may **strike down** the offending legislation in its entirety. However, this appears to be an extreme response to a matter that Parliament or the legislature deemed important enough to legislate. Alternatively, the court may choose to **sever** the portion of the law that is inconsistent so long as two requirements are met. First, the remaining legislation must remain coherent and intelligible when the provision(s) is severed.

Second, the court must be of the opinion that the legislative body would have intended to enact the legislation without its unconstitutional component.

Where the law is held to be under-inclusive (as in the Alberta Human Rights Code discussed earlier) by excluding a particular group, the court may **read in** the group and thereby include it in the legislation. This would require the legislation to meet the two requirements of intelligibility and intent to legislate as discussed under severance. If the legislation appears overbroad, the court may **read down** the law so that its application is narrowed to meet constitutional requirements. This remedy may be selected in situations similar to the child pornography example noted prior. On a case-by-case basis, the court may provide a **constitutional exemption**. This means that the law is valid in its application but, under the circumstances, violates a particular claimant's right. The court makes no changes to the law and instead decides that the claimant is entitled to be exempt from the law's application.

The court generally declares a law invalid and then, temporarily, suspends the **declaration of invalidity**. This renders the legislation valid for a limited period of time in order to prevent a more serious outcome. For example, if the theft provisions in the *Criminal Code* were declared to be immediately invalid, theft would not be a crime. This would allow people to loot the local store without consequence. Temporarily suspending the declaration of invalidity avoids such an outcome.

Parliament or the legislature is expected to take the opportunity provided by the suspension to amend the offending legislation. When amending, the enacting legislative body may choose to make the amendment required for constitutional compliance. The legislative body can also choose to exercise a s. 33 exemption (if permitted) or amend to allow for a s. 1 justification. The court will likely intervene in a subsequent challenge to the same legislation where the government has failed to take the opportunity provided to rectify the problem.

Section 24 Remedies

24(1) Anyone whose rights or freedoms, as guaranteed by this Charter, have been infringed or denied may apply to a court of competent jurisdiction to obtain such remedy as the court considers appropriate and just in the circumstances.

(2) Where, in proceedings under subsection (1), a court concludes that evidence was obtained in a manner that infringed or denied any rights or freedoms guaranteed by this Charter, the evidence shall be excluded if it is established that, having regard to all the circumstances, the admission of it in the proceedings would bring the administration of justice into disrepute.

The remedy for a *Charter* infringement on an individual's right may be found in section 24. Claims based on public interest standing cannot use the s. 24 remedies since the claimant has not personally suffered an infringement. The broad power contained in section 24 gives the court full discretion regarding the type of remedy that can be implemented. For example, the court may issue an **injunction** compelling a specific change in the behaviour of the government. If more widespread change is warranted, or there has been a failure of government to meet identified *Charter* requirements, a **structural injunction** may be implemented. Structural injunctions may be used where an institution's process or operations result in the systemic violation of a *Charter* right.[50] For example, a federal law enforcement department may require that all applicants meet a specified fitness standard prior to being hired. The standard chosen is based on a male fitness standard. There is no

---

[50] Bakan, *supra* note 21 at 1299.

infringement for having a physical standard that prospective applicants must meet. However, it is likely that most women could not meet the imposed male standard and, as a result, would not be hired. It is the *process* or *system* itself that, when applied, has the *effect* of infringing women's right to equality under the *Charter*. A structural injunction would force the offending institution to stop the infringing behaviour and revise the unconstitutional process or system. The law enforcement department might be required to implement two different fitness standards based on gender to prevent further infringements.

Damages may be awarded under section 24 but would be rare. Constitutional remedies generally seek to correct, rather than punish, constitutional inconsistencies. The goal is to ensure compliance with the *Charter* rather than punish non-compliance. However, circumstances may arise where an award of damages is appropriate. For example, damages may be awarded if the infringing conduct is found to be a blatant violation of the public official's responsibilities (such as acting maliciously or in bad faith). The usual remedy is a declaration that the individual's rights have been violated. The declaration would likely be suspended to give government the opportunity to correct the constitutional inconsistency.

Section 24(2) empowers the court to render evidence inadmissible where it is found to have been obtained by infringing the *Charter*.

ABORIGINAL RIGHTS

> **35**(1) The existing aboriginal and treaty rights of the aboriginal peoples of Canada are hereby recognized and affirmed.

Aboriginal rights are exceptional under the Constitution. When the first Europeans arrived in Canada, the country was already populated by Aboriginal peoples. Aboriginal peoples lived in organized communities, were self-sufficient, had established cultures and exercised their own form of government. The Aboriginal presence in Canada prior to European arrival provides the basis for their unique or *sui generis* rights and subsequent treatment under the Constitution.[51] Constitutional protection of Aboriginal rights extends to those rights and treaties that existed at the time the *Constitution Act, 1982* was enacted. This protection also extends to any treaties signed after that date.

Aboriginal rights concerning Aboriginal title to land only extend to land exclusively occupied by the Aboriginal group. The right attaches to exclusive occupation that occurred prior to sovereignty and that continues today. But Aboriginal rights include more than a right to historically occupied land. Additional rights have been identified and embrace the practices, cultures and traditions of the particular Aboriginal group. These practices, cultures, and traditions must be considered integral and distinctive to the group asserting the right.[52] For example, if the group has traditionally hunted on (but not exclusively occupied) a particular piece of land and continues to do so today, it may be able to establish a present-day Aboriginal right to use that land for hunting. The practice, culture, and tradition must be shown to have existed prior to the Aboriginal group's first contact with European settlers.

The Constitution allocates authority to govern Indian matters to the federal government (s. 91(24)). However, provincial laws of a general nature may be applicable where they do not affect the core of the federal head of power

---

[51] *R. v. Van der Peet*, [1996] 2 S.C.R. 507.
[52] *Ibid.*

Indian Act, s. 88

EXHIBIT 7.6

Subject to the terms of any treaty and any other Act of Parliament, all laws of general application from time to time in force in any province are applicable to and in respect of Indians in the province, except to the extent that those laws are inconsistent with this Act or the *First Nations Fiscal and Statistical Management Act*, or with any order, rule, regulation or law of a band made under those Acts, and except to the extent that those provincial laws make provision for any matter for which provision is made by or under those Acts.

(i.e., "Indianness").[53] Provincial legislatures are able to legislate because the federal *Indian Act*,[54] a statutory instrument, expressly permits it. In effect, the provincial legislation is transformed by section 88 of the *Indian Act* into federal legislation and rendered valid. This is the authority by which the Ontario *Highway Traffic Act*, for example, governs on Indian land — a matter constitutionally under federal jurisdiction. The provincial Act applies to all highway users and does not single out Indians for different treatment. It is a law of "general application" under section 88. The province is not intruding into federal jurisdiction when exercising its authority to legislate highways. But if the Act contained a provision that required Indians to drive at a different speed limit from other road users, issues would arise. The law would be invalid because it specifically deals with Indians and is therefore an intrusion into the core of a federal head of power. Such a provision would also infringe on *Charter* rights regarding equality.

Provincial laws of general application and Aboriginal rights can intersect in ways that require adjudication and the application of a constitutional doctrine. In *R. v. Morris*,[55] Tsartlip Indian band members were charged under a provincial wildlife law that prohibited hunting at night with an illuminating device and a firearm. In defence, the accused submitted that they had a right to hunt over the unoccupied lands under an 1852 treaty. At trial, the judge had found that the Tsartlip had indeed hunted at night with illumination since "time immemorial". The trial court ultimately decided, however, that night hunting was "inherently unsafe" and the provincial legislation applied, effectively trumping the Aboriginal treaty right.

In a 4–3 decision, the majority of the Supreme Court of Canada found that the Tsartlip right to hunt at night with an illuminating device was protected by treaty. The Court also found that the Aboriginal right did not include a right to hunt in a dangerous manner. The prohibition in the provincial law against unsafe hunting would apply to band members. Sections 27(1)(d) and (e) of the provincial wildlife act, however, were held to be overly broad because the prohibition against night hunting with illumination included both safe and unsafe hunting, which infringed the band members' treaty right. The provisions were overly broad in their application and the law was read down so as not to apply to the Tsartlip band members. The appeal was allowed, the convictions set aside and acquittals entered.

---

[53] "Indianness" is described as "an integral part of primary federal jurisdiction over Indians and lands reserved for the Indians", *Four B Manufacturing v. UGW*, [1980] 1 S.C.R. 1031.

[54] R.S.C. 1985, c. I-5.

[55] [2006] S.C.R. 915, S.C.J. No. 59 [*Morris* cited to S.C.R.].

The Court decided that the first consideration was whether the impugned provisions of the applicable legislation infringed a treaty right. At this step the character, scope and limit of the Aboriginal right must be identified. This step was dispatched by a historical review of the practices of the band and treaty interpretation. The trial judge's finding that the Tsartlip had hunted at night with illuminating devices since "time immemorial" was significant. The treaty permitted the Tsartlip to hunt and fish in unoccupied lands "as formerly", which included the established practice of night hunting. The Court found that the Tsartlip were not limited to night hunting using only ancestral or historical methods, such as bows and arrows. Hunting practices are permitted to evolve without limiting the right and include 21st century tools and equipment, such as guns, spotlights and motor vehicles. The Court decided that the continuation of existing methods of hunting was the intent of the treaty right:

> This evidence reveals that the weapons, means of transportation and illuminating devices used in hunting have become more modern. But changes in method do not change the essential character of the practice, namely, night hunting with illumination. What was preserved by the Treaty and brought within its protection was hunting at night with illuminating devices, not hunting at night with a particular *kind* of weapon and source of illumination. This conclusion is dictated by the common intentions of the parties to the Treaty, as distilled from the context in which the Treaty was entered into. The purpose of the hunting clause was to preserve the traditional Tsartlip way of life, including methods of gathering food. It was, in addition, designed to benefit the settlers, whose interests at the time lay in friendship with the Indian majority on Vancouver Island.[56]

The evidence did not demonstrate that the Tsartlip hunted in a dangerous manner and the accused had been acquitted of this charge at trial. Much of the relevant area of the province was uninhabited save by Aboriginal people who were seen only occasionally:

> Protected methods of hunting cannot, without more, be wholly prohibited simply because in some circumstances they could be dangerous. All hunting, regardless of the time of day, has the potential to be dangerous. ... The blanket prohibition of s. 27(1)(d) and (e) applies ... throughout British Columbia, including the vast regions of the interior. Much of the north of the province is uninhabited except by aboriginal people, and there are areas where even they are seen only occasionally. To conclude that night hunting with illumination is dangerous everywhere in the province does not accord with reality and is not, with respect, a sound basis for limiting the treaty right.[57]

The second consideration examined whether the legislation was valid and applicable under the constitutional division of powers and incorporated under section 88 of the *Indian Act*. There was no dispute regarding provincial authority to enact the law; it concerned property and civil rights, an area under provincial jurisdiction pursuant to section 92(13) of the *Constitution Act, 1982*. Parliament governs Indians and a provincial law that impairs an "integral part of primary federal jurisdiction over Indians and Lands reserved for Indians ... will be inapplicable to the extent of the impairment ... provincial laws of general application are precluded from impairing "Indianness".[58] Treaty rights to hunt are squarely within federal jurisdiction. But those facts alone were insufficient to resolve the issue.

[56] *Ibid.*, para. 33.
[57] *Ibid.*, paras. 39–40.
[58] *Ibid.*, para. 42.

The Court found that meeting this test would not automatically result in the Aboriginal right trumping the provincial legislation, which could nevertheless be incorporated under section 88 of the *Indian Act*. While section 88 is expressly subject to treaty rights, the Supreme Court has qualified the "treaty exception" in prior decisions and under certain circumstances. If the provincial law or regulation's interference with the treaty right is *insignificant*, the provincial law can be applicable by incorporation under section 88. Thus, the Court had previously found that the imposition of a small access fee solely for maintenance purposes on land used in the exercise of a treaty right to hunt was "an insignificant interference with a treaty right, and consequently did not infringe that right". However, a licensing scheme that imposed "hunting method, the kind and numbers of game, the season and the permissible hunting area" had been found to infringe a treaty right to hunt. This second type of infringement was referred to as a *prima facie* infringement. The infringement resulted because the provincial legislation "denie[d] to holders of treaty rights ... the very means of exercising those rights ... and was in direct conflict with the treaty right". A *prima facie* infringement will trigger the express protection of treaty rights in section 88 (and the provincial law will not be applicable to the extent it interferes with the right) but an insignificant infringement will not.

The provincial prohibition against night hunting with illumination was "absolute" and applied province-wide, including

> [the] ... most northern regions where hours of daylight are limited in the winter months and populated areas are few and far between. The legislature has made no attempt to prohibit only those specific aspects or geographic areas of night hunting that are unsafe by, for example, banning hunting within a specified distance from a highway or from residences. The impugned provisions are overbroad, inconsistent with the common intention of the parties to the treaties, and completely eliminate a chosen method of exercising their treaty right.[59]

The majority found that the Tsartlip's hunting practice had never resulted in an accident and that it was possible to identify uninhabited areas where night hunting would not "jeopardize safety": "These facts amply demonstrate how something less than an absolute prohibition on night hunting can address concern for safety." The categorical ban on night hunting with illumination was a *prima facie* infringement of the Tsartlip's treaty right and could not be incorporated under section 88 of the *Indian Act*. The impugned provisions were read down so as not to apply to the Tsartlip band.

Sections 35 and 25 of the Constitution

Aboriginal rights and treaties are protected by section 35 of the *Constitution Act, 1982*. The only reference to Aboriginal rights in the *Charter* is found in section 25. While section 35 does not expressly recognize a right to self-government, any treaties that include such rights, such as a right to make decisions about matters regarding education, would be upheld under this section. The entrenchment of Aboriginal rights outside of the *Charter* means that the s. 33 notwithstanding and the s. 1 justification clauses are not able to support government infringement. In the event that Parliament chooses to infringe on an Aboriginal right, Parliament is required to follow a different process of justification. The process is similar to that already discussed under s. 1 justification. Section 35 also states that where a constitutional amendment is proposed that affects an Aboriginal right, a conference must be held and the matter discussed with Aboriginal representatives.

[59] *Ibid.*, para. 58.

EXHIBIT 7.7

Section 25 of the Charter

The guarantee in this Charter of certain rights and freedoms shall not be construed so as to abrogate or derogate from any aboriginal, treaty or other rights or freedoms that pertain to the aboriginal peoples of Canada including

(a) any rights or freedoms that have been recognized by the Royal Proclamation of October 7, 1763; and

(b) any rights or freedoms that now exist by way of land claims agreements or may be so acquired.

Section 25 of the *Charter* provides clarity regarding the effect of *Charter* provisions on Aboriginal rights (see Exhibit 7.7). The *Charter* establishes and protects the civil liberties that all individuals are entitled to enjoy. Section 25 ensures that Aboriginal rights are not eliminated or reduced by the application of the *Charter*. Therefore, it is unlikely that a non-Aboriginal Canadian can bring a successful claim based on an infringement of his or her equality right (s. 15). This section appears to prevent *Charter* interference with the *sui generis* nature of the rights belonging to Aboriginal peoples. The Constitution makes it clear that Aboriginal rights are matters appropriately dealt with in exceptional ways.

CHAPTER SUMMARY

This chapter began with a discussion of the underlying needs that led to the creation of the *Charter*. The need for legislation to protect civil liberties and limit the behaviour of government was identified. The *Bill of Rights* was an early attempt to limit Parliament's power to interfere with civil liberties. The inclusion of the *Charter* in the *Constitution Act, 1982* entrenched enumerated rights. Entrenchment protects them from arbitrary changes and improper infringements by legislating bodies and government officials.

The *Charter* applies only where government is involved. As discussed, government is not limited to the acts or omissions of Parliament and the legislatures. An entity controlled by government, implementing a government program, exercising government functions, receiving power from the state or statutory powers of compulsion, may be found to qualify as "government" under the specific circumstances. In such cases, the *Charter* will apply. It was seen that the application of the *Charter* may depend on the level of routine control exercised by the government within the entity.

Appropriate standing is required for an individual to bring a *Charter* challenge and can be based on a private or public interest in the matter. The limitations on challenges that can be brought by a corporation were discussed. Public interest standing requires that the individual fulfill three requirements: demonstrate a genuine interest in the matter, raise an important legal question, and demonstrate that there is no other way for the matter to be brought before the court.

It was noted that *Charter* rights and freedoms are not absolute. The implementation of ameliorative programs can mean that, in certain circumstances, government can justify infringing on *Charter* rights. Sections 1 and 33 also allow for government infringement. The steps for s. 1 justification require that the infringement is prescribed by law and "demonstrably justified in a free and democratic society" (s. 1). Alternatively, the government can exercise its right under section 33 to enact legislation despite its infringement on selected sections of the *Charter*.

The discussion of remedies demonstrated that section 52(1) applied to issues concerning the constitutionality of a law. Section 52(1) may apply to any constitutional issue, whether related to the heads of powers under the Constitution, or a *Charter* infringement. Under this section, the court may strike down the offending law in its entirety, sever the offending provision(s), read in an excluded group, read down the legislation and thereby narrow its application, or hold that the matter requires a constitutional exemption. The court can temporarily suspend a declaration of invalidity to give the legislating body the opportunity to amend the law. The remedy available under section 24(1) gives broad discretion to the judiciary to provide any remedy deemed just in the circumstances. However, an award of damages is rare and section 24 is limited to *Charter* infringements. Section 24(2) permits the exclusion at trial of evidence obtained by a *Charter* infringement.

The chapter concludes with a brief discussion on the *sui generis* nature of Aboriginal rights. Aboriginal rights are predicated on the presence of organized societies of Aboriginal peoples prior to the arrival of the first Europeans. The entrenchment of Aboriginal rights occurs outside of the framework of the *Charter*, and the infringement provisions of sections 1 and 33 do not apply. Section 25 of the *Charter* ensures that Aboriginal rights are not compromised by the civil liberties contained therein.

GLOSSARY OF NEW TERMS AND KEY CONCEPTS

constitutional exemption	In the circumstances, the court holds that the law is valid in its general application but does not apply under the circumstances.
damages	A monetary award to compensate for harm suffered.
declaration of invalidity	Where the court renders a decision striking down a legislation or a portion thereof for unconstitutional inconsistency; usually accompanied by a temporary suspension that makes the law valid for a limited period; the legislating body is expected to amend the legislation during that time in order to achieve constitutional compliance.
entrenchment	Included as part of our Constitution, thereby enjoying constitutional supremacy (i.e., the position of having the superior or greatest power or authority); requires a special procedure to amend; the *Charter* has legal superiority over inconsistent laws, acts or actions of government.
fundamental justice	The principles that correspond to established common law principles and the basic tenets of our legal system, including procedural fairness.
injunction	A court order that compels a specific change in behaviour.
inoperative	The law or portion thereof would be without force or effect, as if it did not exist.
overbreadth	Where the law is so broadly written that it infringes upon a *Charter* right unnecessarily.
prescribed by law	The law must be accessible and clear, with consequences of non-compliance reasonably foreseeable.
read down	Where the court holds that the law is overbroad, it may narrow the law's application so as to ensure constitutional compliance.
read in	Where the court determines that the law is under-inclusive, it may read in the omitted group into the legislation.
severance	Where the court renders invalid the constitutionally inconsistent portion of the law.

standing	Required before a *Charter* challenge can be brought; the individual may have to fulfill certain criteria before achieving standing.
strike down	Where the court rules the whole law is constitutionally invalid and renders it without force or effect.
structural injunction	A court order that compels changes more broadly than that of an injunction; considered where a significant part of an institution is operating unconstitutionally.
sui generis	Unique or of its own kind.
vagueness	An uncertain meaning; the law is unclear and, therefore, persons cannot regulate their behaviour in order to comply with it.

REVIEW QUESTIONS

1. The legislative forerunner to the *Charter* was the *Bill of Rights*. What were its limitations? Is the *Bill of Rights* still relevant legislation today?

2. Can the *Charter* apply to the private sector? Under what conditions will it apply?

3. Identify the three requirements for bringing a public interest challenge for an infringement of a *Charter* right.

4. Are there circumstances under which government is allowed to infringe upon a civil liberty? How could such an infringement be done?

5. List the six options the judiciary can implement under a s. 52(1) remedy.

6. What is the significance of section 35 — Aboriginal rights — being situated outside of the *Charter* provisions? Does this mean that government cannot infringe on Aboriginal rights?

DISCUSSION QUESTIONS

1. A corporation has been charged with violating a provision in the *Criminal Code*. Can the corporation claim that a *Charter* right has been infringed?

2. The Supreme Court of Canada has determined that a provision within a piece of legislation infringes upon a *Charter* right. The remaining portion of the legislation is constitutional. What remedies may the court consider in such circumstances?

3. You are interested in joining a recreational program located in British Columbia. The Musqueam Indian Band runs the program and receives funding from the federal government. Unfortunately, the group declines your application, stating that it accepts only members who are Aboriginal people. You feel that this infringes your equality rights under section 15 of the *Charter*. Would a challenge be successful? Why or why not?

4. The provincial legislature has enacted a new law that states that all female students will receive an educational grant of $500.00. Is this legislation constitutional? What might the court determine in such circumstances?

5. Quebec has designed new legislation that requires Canadians to obtain a visa prior to entering the province. Anyone without the visa will

be expelled from the province. Included in the legislation is a s. 33 not-withstanding clause. Can the infringement be upheld as constitutionally valid?

6. Obtain a recent Supreme Court of Canada (<http://scc.lexum.umontreal.ca/en/index.html>) decision on a constitutional or *Charter* issue. Summarize the analysis of the court, provide your opinion on its findings and whether or not you agree.

SUGGESTED READING

Funston, Bernard W., & Eugene Meehan. *Canada's Constitutional Law In a Nutshell*, 2d ed. (Scarborough, Ont.: Carswell, 1998).

Department of Justice Canada. *A Consolidation of The Constitution Acts 1867 to 1982* (Ottawa, Ont.: Canadian Government, 2001).

Zakaria, Fareed. *The Future of Freedom: Illiberal Democracy at Home and Abroad* (New York: W.W. Norton & Company, 2003).

Bakan, Joel, et al. *Canadian Constitutional Law*, 3d ed. (Toronto, Ont.: Emond Montgomery, 2003).

Hogg, Peter W. *Constitutional Law of Canada*, 2002 Student ed. (Scarborough, Ont.: Carswell, 2002).

MacIver, R.M. *The Web of Government* (New York: The Free Press, 1965).

Mason, Janet & Stanley Gershman. "The Constitution" in Laurence Olivo, ed., *Introduction to Law in Canada* (Toronto, Ont.: Captus Press, 2008).

Mason, Janet. "Aboriginal Rights" in Laurence Olivo, ed., *Introduction to Law in Canada* (Toronto, Ont.: Captus Press, 2008).

Legal Research

Mary Ann Kelly
SENECA COLLEGE

Learning Objectives

After reading this chapter, the reader should be able to:

➢ locate, both in paper and online, a federal or provincial statute if given the citation or the name of the statute

➢ locate, both in paper and online, a federal or provincial regulation given the citation or the name of the regulation

➢ update both federal and provincial regulations and statutes

➢ find a case when given the name or citation of the case

➢ find at least one or two cases in point when given a particular legal topic

➢ draft a simple case brief

➢ identify the relevant secondary sources of law, and be able to demonstrate a basic understanding of how they are organized and used

TABLE OF CONTENTS

INTRODUCTION

Legal research is a practical skill and is best learned by carrying out, in a law library, the steps as outlined in this chapter. The books and guides referenced in this chapter will be right at hand, and you will be able to refer to them as you work your way through the chapter. As you read about a skill in this chapter, such as updating a statute, you can practise it with the materials available in the law library. It is difficult to learn much about a practical skill merely by reading about it and imagining the process intellectually. For instance, one can read all about driving a car. The experience, however, does not become real or valuable for the vast majority of people until they have an opportunity to sit behind the wheel of a car and actually set the vehicle in motion.

The chapter is intended to be an introduction to, and an overview of, the process of conducting legal research. Legal research is a complicated skill and requires in-depth study that is beyond the scope of this chapter; but the material here will serve as an introduction to the techniques required to perform some basic research. As with all practical skills, the more opportunity you have to practise, the more familiar you become with the techniques and the more proficient you become in using them.

The ability to find the current law is an essential skill for anyone working in a legal setting. Legal research is conducted to provide answers to legal problems and questions. The identification of the legal issues involved in any given circumstances provides the framework for researching the question or problem presented. Once you have identified the legal issues, you are ready to begin your search for answers by looking at the appropriate research sources.

However, it is important to remember when doing legal research that the law is a moving target. It is changing and developing all the time. When starting to research a topic, one should always assume that the law has changed and needs to be updated. If it is a statute or a regulation, it may have been amended or repealed by the provincial legislature or by the federal Parliament. If it is a case, a decision by a higher court may have overturned a lower court decision; or there may be a newer case, which deals with a fact situation that is more similar to the facts of the case we are researching and may, therefore, be more directly in point. The first principle of all legal research is "update, update, update". That is the only way to ensure that you are not relying on old law.

SOURCES OF LEGAL RESEARCH

There is a distinction in legal research between **primary** and **secondary sources** of law. Primary sources are the actual statutes, regulations or case law decisions. They are referred to as primary sources because they are law, in and of themselves. They have legal force and effect.

Secondary sources are materials that summarize, analyze or explain the primary sources, such as textbooks, legal encyclopedias, articles, law journals, etc. These secondary sources are not, in themselves, legally binding but offer an extremely useful, preliminary method of identifying and defining the legal issue. They provide an excellent starting point for research because they provide us with an overview of an area of law and can help us refine and focus our legal issues and lead us to the most relevant primary sources of law.

HOW TO GET STARTED

Do you know the name and citation of the statute, regulation or case for which you are searching? If you do, then your task is to find the legislation or the case. If you do not know the statute or case name, then your search will be much broader, and you will have to approach it in a different way. For instance, you may want to read some legal textbooks or law journal articles that address the area of law you wish to research. These secondary sources of law can be a great help in finding some case law or legislation to use as a starting point in the research.

The Internet might also prove useful before you head off to the library. There are a number of Internet sites that provide a collection of legal topics and Internet links to other sites that may be useful. Some examples of these sites are *Access to Justice* <http://www.acjnet.org/>, *Canadian Legal Information Institute* <http://www.canlii.org/> and *Legal Line* <http://www.legalline.ca/default.aspx?TabID=8192>. There are many other good sites as well. Most of the law schools in Canada have information about legal research on their websites. You may want to look at some of the following, for example:

- Bora Laskin Law Library, University of Toronto
  <http://www.law-lib.utoronto.ca/resguide/toc.html>

- Osgoode Hall Law School Library, York University
  <http://library.osgoode.yorku.ca>

- University of British Columbia, Faculty of Law,
  Best Guide to Legal Research
  <http://legalresearch.org/>

- University of Montreal, Faculty of Law
  <http://www.lexum.umontreal.ca/index_en.html>

FINDING THE LAW AND CASES WHEN YOU HAVE A GOOD IDEA OF WHAT YOU ARE SEARCHING FOR

Finding Legislation When You know the Statute Name or Topic

Legislation is government-made law. It is important to understand how legislation is made in order to be able to find it when researching.[1] The three types of legislation are statutes, regulations and bills.

Finding Provincial [Ontario] Statutes and Regulations on the Internet

At one time, in order to find provincial statutes, it was necessary to do an extensive search in hard-copy sources in the library in order to locate the up-to-date, consolidated versions of the statutes. Today, however, it is possible to locate the statutes online at <http://www.e-laws.gov.on.ca/index.html>. This site is operated by the Ontario Ministry of the Attorney General. The e-Laws site contains the following:

- Current consolidations of most public statutes and their associated regulations
- Source law — public and private statutes as enacted and regulations as filed — from January 1, 2000

---

[1] An explanation of the legislation-making process is discussed in another chapter, "Sources of Law", offered in the complete edition of this modular textbook.

- Historical versions of consolidated statutes and regulations, available for statutes and regulations that were amended or affected by a coming-into-force-event after January 1, 2004
- Many repealed public statutes
- Many revoked or spent regulations

A consolidated version incorporates all the existing amendments to the statute or regulation.

On the e-Laws site, current consolidated statutes can be located by the first letter of the statute's title. The regulations associated with a particular statute are accessed through clicking the plus sign beside the statute name. By clicking on the letter "H" to the right of the statute name, it is possible to obtain a legislative history of each statute.

If you do not know whether there is a statute that relates to your research issue, the site permits a search by keyword. You key in the relevant word or words and the search engine will list all the Ontario statutes containing those words. The statutes and regulations may be searched together, or each may be searched separately.

The site aims to provide consolidated statutes and regulations within two business days of the enactment of the statute or the filing of the regulation. At the top of each statute there is a notice of e-Laws currency that advises of the currency date of that particular statute.

In addition, you can browse and search for source law from January 1, 2000. There are also a set of legislative tables, a link to current Ontario bills on the Ontario legislature website and a list of all the source law statutes since January 2001. It is also possible to link to the *Ontario Gazette* online, to the legislation sites for other provinces and to the Government of Canada website, which provides access to federal statutes, regulations and bills.

However, the e-Laws website is not yet considered an official copy of the consolidated statutes and from time to time, it may be necessary to do a search in the library in the hard-copy format.

Finding Provincial [Ontario] Statutes in Hard-Copy Format

To search for a provincial statute, the place to start is with the set of volumes entitled the *Revised Statutes of [the Province]*[2] (see Exhibit 8.1). In Ontario, it is the *Revised Statutes of Ontario, 1990* and is usually abbreviated to R.S.O. 1990. Traditionally, the government of Ontario has published a set of these revised statutes every 10 years or so. To date, however, there was no publication for 2000, so the last revised statutes set is the one published in 1990.

This set of dark blue volumes contains the statutes of Ontario with their complete and current legal wording as of December 31, 1990. The statutes have been consolidated. This means that all the amendments that have been made to the statute have been incorporated into the consolidated statute. For instance, the legislature may have enacted a statute in 1982. In 1986 and 1988, parts of the statute were amended. Each statute as it appears in the R.S.O. 1990 contains all the amendments up to the last day of 1990. There is no need, in most legal research, to look back before the last set of *Revised Statutes*.

The statutes are listed alphabetically by title, and each has an alphanumeric chapter number. *Alphanumeric* means that each statute is designated by the first letter of its name, followed by the number of that statute in the

---

[2] It is called the *Re-enacted Statutes* in Manitoba.

| EXHIBIT 8.1 | | Where to Start When Looking for a Legislation |

JURISDICTION	CONSOLIDATED VOLUME OF STATUTES	CONSOLIDATED VOLUME OF REGULATIONS
Canada	Revised Statutes of Canada 1985	Consolidated Regulations of Canada 1978
Alberta	Revised Statutes of Alberta 2000	N/A
British Columbia	Revised Statutes of British Columbia 1996	N/A
Manitoba	Re-enacted Statutes of Manitoba 1988	Re-enacted Regulations of Manitoba 1988
New Brunswick	Revised Statutes of New Brunswick 1973	N/A
Newfoundland & Labrador	Revised Statutes of Newfoundland 1990	N/A
Northwest Territories	Revised Statutes of the Northwest Territories 1988	Revised Regulations of the Northwest Territories 1990
Nova Scotia	Revised Statutes of Nova Scotia 1989	N/A
Nunavut	Consolidated Statutes 1999	N/A
Ontario	Revised Statutes of Ontario 1990	Revised Regulations of Ontario 1990
Prince Edward Island	Revised Statutes of PEI 1988	
Quebec	Revised Statutes of Quebec 1977	1981
Saskatchewan	Revised Statutes of Saskatchewan 1978	1983
Yukon	Revised Statutes of the Yukon 2003	N/A

list of statutes under that letter of the alphabet. For instance, the *Highway Traffic Act*, R.S.O. 1990, c. H.8, has an alphanumeric chapter designation of H.8. When all the statutes beginning with the letter H are listed alphabetically, the *Highway Traffic Act* is the eighth statute on the list.

If you know the name of the statute for which you are searching, you may go directly to the R.S.O. and select the volume alphabetically. If you do not know if there is a statute dealing with the issue you are researching, you can go to the index for the R.S.O. 1990. The subject matter covered by the statutes is broken down into general headings, presented in bold, and sub-headings that list more specific topics under that general heading. Once you have found the issue or subject you are researching, you can then determine the name of the relevant statute or statutes and locate the statute in the appropriate R.S.O. volume. However, locating the statute in the R.S.O. 1990 is only the first step. It is then necessary to update.

Since the statutes in the R.S.O. 1990 are only current up to December 31, 1990, you must determine whether the statute you are looking for was amended after that date. One of the major purposes of the legislature is to make law. Every year since 1990, the Ontario legislature has enacted new statutes and repealed and amended existing ones. For instance, if we looked in the R.S.O. 1990 for a statute relating to residential tenancies, we would find a statute dealing with this topic called the *Landlord and Tenant Act*.

However, there is no longer a statute by this name in Ontario. In 1997, the legislature made significant amendments to this statute and re-enacted it with a new name, The *Tenant Protection Act*. Then, in 2006, the *Tenant Protection Act* was repealed and a new statute, the *Residential Tenancies Act* replaced it. If we did not update our statute from the R.S.O. 1990, we would not know this and would be relying on a seriously outdated piece of legislation that has been replaced by new law.

For each year, starting with 1991, there are annual volumes, the *Statutes of Ontario*, abbreviated as S.O., and followed by the year that the volume covers. These books are bound with red covers and are usually located next to the R.S.O. in the library. To determine whether a statute, relevant to your research topic, has been enacted, amended or repealed since 1990, you must look in the Table of Public Statutes in the blue pages at the back of the most recent annual volume.

Another, and more popular, method to conduct an update of statutes is to use the *Ontario Statute Citator*. The *Citator* is published by a private legal publisher in multi-volume loose-leaf binders.

To update a statute using the *Citator*, you must first consult the white pages at the front of the *Citator*. The statutes are organized alphabetically by title. Any amendments are listed under the name of the statute along with the citation in the relevant volume of the *Statutes of Ontario*. You may then go to the cited volume of the *Statutes of Ontario* to find the amending statute.

You must then refer to the *Weekly Bulletin Service* in the pink pages at the front of the *Citator*. The most recent edition of this weekly service will contain any changes made after the main body of the *Citator* was published.

The final stage in updating is to check for any new bills, just passed by the Legislature, that will affect the statute you are researching. To do this, you must consult each volume of *Canadian Current Law Legislation* since the last update of the *Citator*.

Instead of looking in the *Canadian Current Law Legislation* volumes, you may wish to consult the bills site of the Ontario Legislature at <http://www.ontla.on.ca/web/bills/bills_current.do?locale=en>.

If you cannot locate the statute you are looking for after following this route, you may wish to check to see if, in fact, it is a federal statute rather than a provincial one.

Finding Provincial [Ontario] Regulations in Hard-Copy Format

There are several ways to determine whether the statute you are working with has accompanying regulations. The easiest way is to use the *Ontario Regulations Service*. This is published in several volumes and it reprints the regulations portion of the *Ontario Gazette*. You can look up regulations directly without having to find an actual copy of the Gazette itself.

The green section found at the front of each volume is an annual consolidated index that lists all regulations in force until the end of that calendar year. For instance, to find any regulations under the *Residential Tenancies Act*, consult the list under *Residential Tenancies Act* in the green pages of the Regulations volume for the latest year. The enabling statutes are arranged alphabetically.

The yellow section found in the most recent volume is an index of *recent* amendments and regulations, which is current to within the last month. You can update from this point by checking the issues of the *Ontario Gazette* that have been published since the last volume of the *Ontario Regulations Service*. Refer to the index at the back of each issue and search for any recently issued regulations by enabling statute title.

Finding Federal Statutes and Regulations on the Internet

The federal government website may be found at <http://laws.justice. gc.ca/en/>. It is operated by the federal Department of Justice. This site operates in much the same manner as the Ontario site. It is possible to search for federal statutes by title or by subject matter. When a statute is opened, the related regulations are listed below the index to the statutory provisions. As on the Ontario site, keywords can be used to search the statutes and regulations. The site is generally updated every week. The current — to date — is displayed at the top of every statute or regulation.

The site also gives specific search instructions.

Finding Federal Statutes in Hard-Copy Format

Just as with Ontario, the statutes published on the federal website are not the official versions of the statutes. Therefore, it may be necessary to do a search for the statutes and regulations in the hard-copy format.

The process for finding and updating a federal statute is very similar to the process for finding the Ontario statutes (see above for details).

The starting point is the last set of volumes of the *Revised Statutes of Canada*, the R.S.C. The Government of Canada has not published a set of revised statutes since 1985. These volumes are bound in light blue covers. They contain the consolidated statutes of Canada as of 1985 and must be updated from that time. The statutes are listed in the R.S.C. volumes in an alphanumeric manner that resembles the listing of the Ontario statutes in the R.S.O. They are given a chapter that includes the letter of the alphabet with which the name of that statute commences, and a number that indicates which number that statute has been given under that letter of the alphabet. For instance, in the case of the *Fisheries Act*, R.S.C. 1985, c. F-14, the letter "F" is the first letter of the name of the statute, and the number "14" means that it is the 14th statute listed alphabetically under the letter "F".

There is a set of annual volumes, bound in beige cover, entitled the *Statutes of Canada*, abbreviated as S.C., that contain the changes to the federal statutes as they were in 1985. The first volume of the *Statutes of Canada* is for the year 1986, and there is a volume for each year following. If the statute you are looking for is not in the R.S.C. 1985, then it may have been enacted after 1985, and you will have to turn to the volumes of the *Statutes of Canada* to find it.

Each annual volume of the *Statutes of Canada* contains a Table of Statutes. To find a statute passed after 1985, go to the most recent volume of the S.C., turn to the Table of Public Statutes in that volume and find the name of the statute you are looking for. Under the listing, you will find a reference to the specific volume of the S.C. in which the statute can be located.

However, as with the Ontario statutes, there is another, more popular method to conduct an update of statutes: use the *Canada Statute Citator*. The *Citator* is published by a private legal publisher in multi-volume loose-leaf binders.

Locate your statute in the *Citator*. Then check the green pages in the *Citator*. These pages are called the "Monthly Bulletin", and they will list any amendment to your statute. If the statute is not listed, it has not been amended. If it is listed, the amendments are up-to-date as of the date indicated on the top of the page of the latest bulletin.

The final stage in updating is to check for any new bills just passed by Parliament that will affect the statute you are researching. To do this, you must consult each volume of *Canadian Current Law Legislation* since the last update of the *Citator*.

Instead of looking in the *Canadian Current Law Legislation* volumes, you may wish to consult the bills site of Parliament of Canada at <http://www.parl.gc.ca/common/bills.asp?Language=E&parl=39&Ses=2>.

Finding Federal Regulations in Hard-Copy Format

The *Canada Regulations Index* is a three-volume publication that lists all federal regulations in force to the end of the previous year. The index is arranged by name of statute under which the regulations are issued.

To find the regulations to a statute locate the name of the statute in the white pages of the index, where statute titles are listed alphabetically. Under the name of the statute you will find a list of citations for all the regulations and amendments accompanying that statute.

In order to update the regulation, you must consult the yellow pages at the front of each volume, which are published monthly. Look up the enabling statute title for a list of any recently issued regulations. Then, to ensure that you are totally current, you must look at the bi-weekly issues of the *Canada Gazette Part II* published since the date at the bottom of the first page of the most recent *Canada Regulations Index*. Refer to the table of contents at the back of each issue. You may check for either the regulation name or the enabling statute title.

Finding Case Law When You Know the Name of the Case or the Citation

Not every court case is reported or published. Private legal publishers print case reports and decide which cases they will include in their volumes. Publishers choose the cases on the basis of their legal interests. Very important cases will usually be reported in more than one law-reporting series. These case reports are the judges' reasons for deciding the case in a particular manner. It is important to note that reports are not word-for-word transcriptions of what happened in the courtroom. Those word-for-word documents are called transcripts and are not generally available to anyone other than the parties and their lawyers.

Publishers will often have a number of law reports or reporters that they publish. These reports may cover specific legal areas, such as Canadian Criminal Cases or the Reports on Family Law; or they may cover cases decided by specific courts, such as The Supreme Court Reports. Some reporting series may cover only one province, such as the Ontario Reports, which report only cases decided in Ontario; or they may have national coverage, such as the Dominion Law Reports.

It is the case citation that directs the legal researcher to the proper page, in the correct volume of a specific case-reporting series. Learning how to read a case citation is very important.

Most cases are cited by name of the case, volume number, abbreviation or name of the reporting series and page. For example: *R. v. Pelletier* (1978), 38 C.C.C. (2d) 515 (Ont. C.A.). This citation tells you that the decision of the Ontario Court of Appeal (Ont. C.A.) in the case involving *R. v. Pelletier* can be found in volume 38 of the 2nd series of the *Canadian Criminal Cases* (C.C.C.) at page 515. If the year is in round brackets, it is there for convenience only and is not necessary to locate the case. If the year is in square brackets, it is essential to finding the case. For example *R. v. Khan*, [1990] 2 S.C. R. 531 tells you that the decision of the Supreme Court of Canada, in the case of *R. v. Khan*, can be found in volume 2 of 1990, [1990] 2, of the Supreme Court Reports (S.C.R.) at page 531.

If you are uncertain how to read the citation for the case for which you are searching, the leading style guide is the *Canadian Guide to Uniform Legal Citation* (the "McGill Guide") (6th ed., 2006). This guide can be found in the reference sections of any law library.

If you have been given only the name of a case and not the full citation, you may find the full citation by consulting the *Canadian Abridgment's Consolidated Table of Cases*. The *Canadian Abridgment* is a secondary legal source, published by a private publisher, that provides a number of different components that can help the legal researcher in locating and updating cases. All law libraries and most major libraries will have a set of the *Abridgment* volumes in their reference section.

The *Consolidated Table of Cases* provides an alphabetical list of cases, and the name of either party in the case may be used to find the full case citation. You must then go to the library shelves containing the specific case reporting series — e.g., Canadian Criminal Cases or the Supreme Court Reports — to locate the text of your case.

Each reporting series will also have a cumulative index after a certain number of volumes in the series have been published. This cumulative index will list all the cases that have been published over a number of volumes so that you will not need to open each volume in the series to look in each individual index for your case.

Updating Case Law

Once you have found your case by name or by citation, you now must determine whether or not your case has been overturned on appeal. You will also want to determine how other judges have treated the case. For instance, have other judges followed the case, or not? This process is called updating or noting up a case. In order to do this, you must once again turn to the *Canadian Abridgment*, this time to the volumes called *Canadian Case Citations*.

There are two parts to *Canadian Case Citations*: a set of hardcover volumes dealing with cases decided from 1867 to 1990, and a set of softcover, supplemental volumes that refer to cases decided from 1991 onward.

If you wish to update a case decided prior to 1991, go first to the hardcover and then proceed to the update volume in softcover. For cases decided from 1991 onward, you may refer directly to the softcover, supplemental volumes.

After looking in the supplemental volume, you must then check the quarterly update of *Canadian Case Citations* for your case name, and then the monthly updates up to the latest one available. Your case is now up-to-date as of the date of the latest monthly issue.

The *Case Citations* uses a system of symbols to explain how your case has been dealt with.

F   means that another court has followed the case because it is binding case law.

C   means the case was considered or mentioned in another case.

A   means the case was applied or followed even though it wasn't binding on that court.

D   means the case was distinguished, or not followed, because the facts were found to be different in the other case.

FINDING THE LAW AND CASES FOR A GIVEN TOPIC WITHOUT KNOWING WHAT MAY BE RELEVANT

Finding a specific case or statute by name or citation is relatively easy. A more complicated type of research involves locating all the relevant law to answer a particular legal issue or question. A legal research project may seem daunting at first, particularly if you know little about the area of law you are about to research, but starting with some secondary sources will often be of great assistance in developing a focus. For instance, as we noted above, reading a recent textbook or law journal on a particular legal topic may prove very valuable in locating some preliminary primary sources of law on the issue, such as statutes or cases.

Some additional secondary legal sources will also prove helpful.

The *Canadian Abridgment*: Case Digests

We have already looked at a part of the *Canadian Abridgment, The Consolidated Table of Cases*, that will help us find cases when we know the name of the case for which we are searching. *The Canadian Abridgment: Case Digests* is another part of the *Abridgment* that can assist us to find cases when we are presented with a legal issue, topic or problem and don't know if there is relevant case law in that area.

The Case Digests, a set of red and black, hardcover volumes, contain summaries or digests of reported Canadian cases covering a period of almost 200 years. The volumes are arranged alphabetically by legal subject. The cut-off date for the cases summarized in each volume is noted on the title page. Each of the hardcover volumes is updated by way of a softcover supplement. The softcover supplements are further updated by another set of softcover supplements that are issued biweekly, and contain the most recent reported cases.

The hardcover volumes are identified by the letter "R" that appears on their cover. For instance, "R14" is volume 14 in the hardcover set, and R14 Supplement would be the supplemental softcover volume relating to that hardcover volume.

Each subject in the *Abridgment* is organized according to a system called the Key Classification System. This means that each subject is broken down into many different, smaller parts made up of specific points related to the main subject area. For instance, "Estates" would be a subject area of law. It is, in fact, located alphabetically in hardcover volume R14.

However, there are numerous subheadings in this major area of law, such as what power the court has to deal with wills and estates, what happens if someone dies without a will, and what does the case law say about changing a will, among many, many others. The Key Classification System identifies each of these subject parts and sub-parts by a series of numbers and letters. All cases related to that specific subject part would have the same Key Classification, starting first with a roman numeral, then Arabic numerals, and then letters.

Using the subject area "Estates", as an example, "Requirements for Validity" is a sub-heading, which is further broken down into various parts, such as "Witnesses", which is then broken down again.

ESTATES
IV. Requirements for Validity
    4. Witnesses
       b. In presence of testator

Therefore, ESTATES IV. 4. b. would contain a summary of all the cases relating to whether a witness had to be present when the testator, or maker of the will, was actually drawing up the will. Each of these cases would have its own individual consecutive number, such as 477, 478.

There are several ways to search using the *Case Digests*.

1. You can go directly to the hardcover volume dealing with the area of law you wish to search. For instance, if you were looking for information on parties to a contract, you could locate the volume dealing with contracts, and search through it until you found all the relevant cases.

2. You can use the *Key and Research Guide*, which provides an alphabetical list of all of the legal subjects and their sub-headings covered in the *Case Digests*. This can be a very helpful way for a novice researcher to start his or her search since the *Key and Research Guide* lays the subject out with all its various parts, which will give you an instant overview of a very complex area of law. The *Key* will direct you to the appropriate hardcover volume, in which you will find the relevant cases summarized under the Key Classification System number.

3. You can use the *General Index*, a separate, loose-leaf part of the *Abridgment*. It is organized alphabetically, by keyword, with citations to the corresponding key numbers in the hardcover volume.

4. If you already have one case on point, you can look that case up by name in the *Abridgment, Consolidated Table of Cases*. The case will be followed in the *Consolidated Table* by its volume and case digest number. It is then possible to go to the appropriate volume and digest number to find other, similar cases.

No matter which method you use, once you have found the cases you are looking for in the hardcover volumes, you must then update the cases by referring to the Supplement for the appropriate volume and then checking each of the most recent monthly issues of the *Canadian Current Law: Case Digests*.

The *Canadian Encyclopedic Digest*

The *Canadian Encyclopedic Digest*, or CED as it is commonly known, is a secondary source of law that can provide information about an area of law and will serve as a reference point for finding relevant primary sources. It is a loose-leaf, multi-volume encyclopedia that can be found in all law libraries and in the reference section of many large public libraries. There are two distinct editions of the CED, although many libraries hold only the edition most relevant to their area. The *Ontario* edition is bound in green, and the *Western* edition, covering the four western provinces, in brown.

There are several hundred legal subject titles that correspond to very broad legal topics. The subject titles are arranged alphabetically in loose-leaf volumes so that librarians can easily update them. Each volume has a volume number. The first pages of each volume provide a table of contents that shows a list of the subject titles located in that volume. (See Exhibit 8.2.)

Each subject title is broken down into parts. The parts all have separate names and are designated by a Roman numeral. Each part is broken down into sections, each of which has a name and is designated by a number. Finally, each section is broken down into paragraphs that are designated by the typographical symbol § followed by a number. The paragraph contains a short summary of law on a topic, as well as references to the cases and statutes that are relevant to that topic.

Once you have found the applicable subject title, you should check the table of contents at the beginning of the title to ensure that you find all relevant parts, sections and paragraphs.

The main volumes of the CED are updated through the use of yellow supplementary inserts, which are placed at the beginning of each title. If you are looking in a subject title that has a yellow update inserted at the beginning of the title, you must check to see if the paragraphs you are relying on have been updated. You do this by matching the paragraph numbers in the main body of the title with the paragraph numbers in the yellow inserted supplement. If the paragraph numbers you are looking at are not in the supplement, they are current in the main material and have no update.

EXHIBIT 8.2

The Canadian Encyclopedic Digest

Table of Cases
Table of Statutes
Table of Rules
Table of Regulations

3

July 1994

Source: *Canadian Encyclopedic Digest*, Third Edition — Ontario Volume 8A Title 42 — Western Volume 11 Title 44 — Table of Contents page (Release Line July 1994). Reproduced by permission of Carswell, a division of Thomson Canada.

In addition to the main volumes, the CED has a *Key and Research Guide*. If you are not clear what subject title in the main volume will be most helpful, you may wish to start with the *Index Key*, which is a separate volume of the *Key and Research Guide*. Each subject title in the main volumes contains a subject index related to that title. The *Index Key* combines the individual subject indexes and an extensive system of cross-reference. All phrases or keywords are listed alphabetically. Beside each entry is the volume and title number of the general subject that deals with that keyword or phrase. The volume number appears before the hyphen, and the title number follows the hyphen. For example, 1-1§6 means that the keywords you are looking for are contained in volume 1, title 1, paragraph 6.

Finding Cases on the Internet

While it is possible to do a very thorough search for statutes and regulations on the Internet, the search for case law is much more limited in scope.

The Canadian Legal Information Institute (CanLII) has quite a comprehensive database of case law, with links to many of the major court sites in

Canada. The site can be found at <http://www.canlii.org/>. It is possible to search for cases both by case name and by topic. However, while the CanLII database includes cases from the Supreme Court of Canada and the Ontario Court of Appeal for every year dating back into the 1800s, cases from other courts may go back only 10 or 20 years, and not all years during the period are included. Earlier cases must be searched in the print sources. Therefore, the site is most helpful to those who know the name of the case for which they are searching. If you are trying to search for a case by topic, the site will be much less useful as there is so much law that is not included in the database.

Another site that may prove useful is the Ontario Court site established by the Government of Ontario. It can be found at <http://www.ontariocourts.on.ca/>.

There are also some administrative tribunals that provide free Internet access to their decisions. For instance, both the Canadian and the Ontario Human Rights Commissions have cases online, as does the Ontario Labour Relations Board. To determine whether the administrative tribunal you wish to search has cases online, conduct a search for the tribunal first.

In addition to the free Internet sites, a number of legal publishers offer fee-for-service or subscription sites. Two of these are Lexis-Nexis®Quicklaw™ and WestlaweCARSWELL. Both offer very comprehensive databases for legal research in both case law and legislation.

Several Canadian legal publishers provide access to their online databases for a subscription fee. *The Canadian Abridgment* and the *Canadian Encyclopedic Digest* may both be accessed online through subscriptions with Carswell.

Finally, a number of publishers also produce CD-ROMs that contain legal research tools. For instance, Carswell has *The Canadian Abridgment* and the *Canadian Encyclopedic Digest* in CD-ROM version, available for purchase.

BRIEFING A CASE

One of the ways that legal researchers summarize their work is through a **case brief**. Summarizing the research work is important, as it provides a method for the researcher to compare various cases and analyze them without having to read each case in its entirety each time. Case briefs are also necessary if the researcher is conducting the research for someone else. The case brief provides an effective way for the person reading the research to easily access the contents of the relevant cases.

Drafting a case brief is really a matter of style, although each brief should contain certain essential information, such as a concise statement of the facts of the case, an identification of the issue or issues with which the case deals, a statement of the decision, and a summary of the judge's reason for the decision. The brief should also contain the citation for the case so that it can be easily located in the law reports.

The brief should indicate which level of court made the decision, and should also give the name of the judge or judges. The doctrine of *stare decisis*[3] and the importance of precedents in the common law mean that decisions of higher courts, such as appeal courts, are binding on lower courts that are deciding cases on the same facts. In an appellate court case, it is usual that the court sits with a panel of judges, normally three judges in the

---

[3] Discussed in detail in another chapter, "Sources of Law", offered in the complete edition of this modular textbook.

Ontario Court of Appeal, and five, seven or nine judges in the Supreme Court of Canada. One judge will write the reasons for judgment for all the judges or for the majority. Each of the judges involved in the majority decision should be named. If the case involves concurring or dissenting opinions, the names of the judges writing these opinions should also be noted.

The brief should identify the parties. If there are multiple parties involved in the case or if the roles of the parties changed at the various levels of court, the parties' roles should be described: e.g., Smith is the plaintiff at trial, but the respondent on the appeal.

The facts of the case, as found by the court, should be set out or summarized in narrative form and in chronological order. Often the parties will have varying versions of the facts, but it is the facts that the court finds to be true that are essential to the case brief. It is important to identify the type of proceeding before the court: whether it is an action, an application, or an appeal, etc. The remedy being sought should also be noted.

Identifying the issue being determined in the case is a very important part of the case brief. Sometimes, when judges write the case decisions, they will set out the issue in the decision itself. In these cases it is very easy to determine the issue because the court has clearly identified it. In other cases, however, the issue may not be as clearly set out, and the researcher must analyze the case to locate it. The issue is the legal question that the court was asked to decide. For instance, in a torts case, one of the issues might be whether or not the defendant was negligent. Another issue might be the amount of damages.

The judgment may be stated simply — e.g., "the appeal was dismissed", or "the defendant was found liable in negligence", or "the accused was found guilty". It is not necessary to state the judge's reasons for the decision in this part of the brief.

The next section of the brief should deal with the court's reason for the decision. This is referred to as the *ratio decidendi* of the case. This is often the most challenging part of the brief, distilling a lengthy judgment into a concise summary or recognizing the main points in the reasoning of a case report that may not be clearly written. The researcher must analyze the rationale of the judge or judges in applying the law to the facts of a particular case. If there is more than one issue in the case, each issue must be analyzed and the *ratio* set out for each issue the case deals with.

Ratios or reasons for decision are usually supported by legal authorities — i.e., other cases or statutes. The other cases identified in the case the researcher is briefing should be cited. If a judge has distinguished another case, that should also be noted in the case brief.

Finally, the researcher must present a short statement of the principle of law in the case. This involves identifying the precedent value of the case.

HOW TO CITE LEGAL SOURCES

The citation of cases, statutes, and regulations must follow a precise format. This format tells the researcher exactly where to find the full text of the document. The citation format for each of these legal sources is presented below.

Cases

The names of the parties should be italicized. This is called the style of cause. The names of all the parties in a multiple-party case are not normally included. The editors of the law reports will have shortened the name, and this is referred to as the short style of cause. The *v.* between the party names stands for the word *versus*. When citing a case orally, in Canada we say "and" instead of "versus". For instance, the case of *Smith v. Jones* would be said as "Smith and Jones".

If the law report is organized by year, it will be in square brackets [ ]. The year, when it is in square brackets, is essential to finding a case. A year in round brackets ( ), or parentheses, is presented only for convenience and it can be located in the reports without reference to the year.

The next part of the citation is the abbreviations for the law reporter when the case is located. A particular law reporter might be produced in a number of editions. Not all reporters have more than one edition, but if there is a number in parentheses after the case name, that is the series or edition number. The number before the abbreviated name is the volume number of the reporter series, and the number behind the abbreviated reporter name or the edition number, if there is one, is the page number on which the case can be found. For instance, the case of *Waldron v. Royal Bank*, used in the example above, can be found in volume 78 of the 4th edition of the *Dominion Law Reports*, on page 1.

Statutes

Federal Statutes

Federal statutes may be found in the last consolidated version, the *Revised Statutes of Canada 1985* (R.S.C. 1985), and amendments to the statutes existing in 1985 and new statutes can be found in volumes of *Statutes of Canada* (S.C.) published every year.

An example of a citation of a federal statute, included in the last consolidated version of federal statutes, would be:

Criminal Code, R.S.C. 1985, c. C-46, s. 8

NAME	JURISDICTION	YEAR	CHAPTER	SECTION
Criminal Code	R.S.C.	1985,	c. C-46,	s. 8

The statutes enacted after the last consolidated version in 1985 would be cited as:

Firearms Act, S.C. 1995, c. 39

NAME	JURISDICTION	YEAR	CHAPTER	SECTION
Firearms Act	S.C.	1995,	c. 39	

Provincial Statutes

A provincial statute citation example for a statute included in the last consolidated volume of any province (Ontario statutes) would look like this:

Negligence Act, R.S.O. 1990, c. N.1, s. 100

NAME	JURISDICTION	YEAR	CHAPTER	SECTION
Negligence Act	R.S.O.	1990,	c. N.1,	s. 100

As discussed above, the last hard-copy consolidated volume of the Ontario statutes was published in 1990. The name of the statute should be italicized or underlined in the citation.

A statute passed by the legislature after the last consolidated volume of statutes was printed would be cited as follows:

Nursing Act, 1991, S.O. 1991, c. 32

NAME	JURISDICTION	YEAR	CHAPTER	SECTION
Nursing Act, 1991,	S.O.	1991,	c. 32	

This citation tells the researcher that the statute can be found in the *Statutes of Ontario* volume for the year 1991.

Regulations

Federal Regulations

As with cases and statutes, in order to find a regulation, you must be able to read the citation. A revised federal regulation, included in the last consolidated version of federal regulations, the *Consolidated Regulations of Canada* (C.R.C.) in 1978, would be cited as follows:

Canada Grain Regulations, C.R.C. 1978, c. 889

The vast majority of regulations have been introduced or amended since 1978, so you will find only a few that use the C.R.C. (Consolidated Regulations Canada). Most regulations will, therefore, be cited as not revised, as follows:

Copyright Regulations, SOR/97-457.

Federal Regulations that are not revised are followed by SOR — which stands for Statutory Orders and Regulations — then by a forward slash, the last two digits of the year the regulation was made, and then by the number of the regulation. So the *Copyright Regulation* was made in 1997, and it is number 457 for that year.

Provincial Regulations

Ontario Regulations were last revised and consolidated at the same time as the statutes in 1990. The revised regulations may be found in the *Revised Regulations of Ontario*, R.R.O., 1990. A revised regulation to the *Milk Act*, R.S.O. 1990, c. M.12 is cited as follows:

Cheese Marketing — Exemptions, R.R.O. 1990, Reg. 749

An example of a citation for an Ontario Regulation that has been filed since the last revised version of the regulations is a regulation to the *Family Law Act*, R.S.O. 1990, c. F.3.

Child Support Guidelines, O. Reg. 391/97

An Ontario regulation that has been filed since the last volume of revised regulations in 1990 is identified as O. Reg., which stands for Ontario Regulation, followed by the number of the regulation and then by a backward slash and the last two digits of the year the regulation was made.

CHAPTER SUMMARY

This chapter provided a practical overview of some basic legal research techniques and a summary of some methods of reporting the findings of that research. It reviewed the primary and secondary sources of law and how to find a statute or case law, first in paper format, and then through electronic research, including the Internet.

The fact that legal research is a practical skill was emphasized and students were encouraged to read the chapter in a law library, where they could access the necessary tools and follow along with the text.

GLOSSARY OF NEW TERMS AND KEY CONCEPTS

case brief	A short summary of a case, provided in a specific format, that a legal researcher prepares to report on and provide future reference of the research results for him or herself, or for the person requesting the research.
primary sources	The actual statutes, regulations or case law decisions that are law and have legal force and effect.
ratio decidendi	Latin phrase that refers to the core legal reason for deciding a case.
secondary sources	Materials that summarize, analyze or explain the primary sources of law, such as textbooks, legal encyclopedias, articles, law journals, etc. These sources are not legally binding but offer an extremely useful, preliminary method of identifying and defining the legal issue.

REVIEW QUESTIONS

1. Is a bicycle a vehicle under the Ontario *Highway Traffic Act*? What section of the statute explains this?

2. You have found the case of *Delaney Boat Lines v. Barrie (City)*. It is a case decided by the Ontario Court of Appeal in 1976 and can be found in two different law reports. It is in the Dominion Law Reports on page 389 of the 128th volume of the third series. It is also in the Ontario Reports, second series, volume 15, on page 675. Give the proper, full citation for this case.

3. Is there a federal statute that tells us who is not eligible to be a member of the National Film Board? Name and give the citation for the statute.

4. Our client is going into the hospital for serious surgery. What statute does she have to follow to make a will?

5. Our client's husband has been ordered to pay child support. He has not paid. What statute applies?

6. The client wants to go moose hunting in Northern Ontario. Does he need a licence?

7. Our client is a landlord who wants to evict the tenant in his downstairs apartment for non-payment of rent. What statute applies?

8. The Ontario *Health Care Consent Act* was passed in 1996. It is chapter 2 for that year. From this information, write the citation for the statute.

DISCUSSION QUESTIONS

1. Read and prepare a case brief for the following case:
   Crocker v. Sundance Northwest Resorts Ltd., [1988] 1 S.C.R. 1186

2. Describe the method you used in locating the following statutes:
   (a) The Ontario *Human Rights Code*
   (b) The *Canadian Human Rights Act*

SUGGESTED READINGS

Banks, Cate, & Heather Douglas. *Law on the Internet* (Toronto, Ont.: Irwin Law, 2006).

Banks, Margaret A., & Karen E.H. Foti. *Banks on Using a Law Library: A Canadian Guide to Legal Research*, 6th ed. (Scarborough, Ont.: Carswell, 1994).

Castel, J.R., & O.K. Latchman. *The Practical Guide to Canadian Legal Research*, 2d ed. (Scarborough, Ont.: Carswell, 1996).

Kerr, Margaret, JoAnn Kurtz & Arlene Blatt. *Legal Research: Step by Step*, 2d ed. (Toronto, Ont.: Emond Montgomery, 2006).

McGill Law Journal. *Canadian Guide to Uniform Legal Citation*, 6th ed. (Scarborough, Ont.: Carswell, 2006).

Tjaden, T. *Legal Research and Writing*, 2d ed. (Toronto: Irwin Law, 2004).

Yogis, J.A., M.C. Innis, M.J. Iosipescu & M.E. Deturbide. *Legal Writing and Research Manual*, 6th ed. (Markham, Ont.: Butterworths, 2004).

WEBSITES

Catherine P. Best. *Best Guide to Canadian Legal Research*: <http://www.legalresearch.org>

Canadian Legal Information Institute (CanLII): <http://www.canlii.org>

The Ontario Court System

Mary Ann Kelly
SENECA COLLEGE

Learning Objectives

After reading this chapter, the reader should be able to:

> understand the constitutional framework for the court system in Canada and Ontario

> describe the hierarchy of courts in Canada and Ontario

> understand the impact of court reform in Ontario

> describe the issues related to judicial appointments

> understand the principal steps in civil and criminal proceedings

> identify alternative dispute resolution methods and be aware of the differences

TABLE OF CONTENTS

INTRODUCTION

Generally speaking, the purpose of the court system in Canada is to resolve disputes in a fair and just manner. In the process of examining and resolving the issues put before them, the courts also make law by interpreting and defining and applying both statutes and the common law. Courts, therefore, play a major role in both the structure and operation of government in Canada, as well as affecting Canadian society as a whole.

This chapter will examine the court system in Canada, with particular emphasis on the courts in Ontario.

THE CANADIAN JUDICIAL SYSTEM

Constitutional Framework of the Courts

Canada is a federal state. In a federal state, there is more than one level of government. In Canada, the two major levels of government are the federal government and the provincial government. Each level has its own powers and responsibilities, spelled out in the *Constitution Act, 1867*. Since courts are an integral part of the Canadian governmental system, responsibilities for court administration and operation are set out in the Constitution. The system is quite complicated because no single level of government has sole responsibilities for courts, and both levels of government may be involved at the same time in the operation of a particular court or courts.

Power to Create and Administer Courts

Section 92 of the *Constitution Act, 1867* gives the provinces responsibility for the administration of both civil and criminal courts in the province. Therefore, it is primarily the provincial governments that establish the court structure, and operate and administer the courts. The provinces do this by passing statutes and creating regulations that deal with everything from what the courts will be called to what type of robes the judges will wear.

This does not mean that the federal government has no role in the establishment and operation of courts. On the contrary, the *Constitution Act, 1867* gives the federal government some responsibility for the administration of some courts. Section 101 provides the federal government with the power to establish and operate the Supreme Court of Canada, the Federal Court, the Tax Court and military courts that deal with courts martial of people in the Canadian Armed Forces.

Power to Create Procedural Law

Once courts have been established, there must be procedural rules that dictate how cases will proceed through the court. Each court has its own set of procedural requirements. The Constitution gives the provincial government the power to create procedure for all the civil courts in the province. However, the power to create procedure for the criminal courts is the responsibility of the federal government, since criminal law is a federal responsibility. The federal government also creates the procedural requirements for the courts for which it has created the Supreme Court and the other federally created courts, mentioned above.

Power to Appoint Judges

To further complicate the matter, although the province has the responsibility for administering the courts in the province, they do not have the sole power to appoint the judges who sit in those courts. Section 96 of the *Constitution Act, 1867*, gives the federal government the power to appoint judges in the superior courts of each province. The provincial government has the authority only to appoint judges to the lower level of courts in the province. Of course, the federal government has the sole power to appoint judges to the courts that they have the constitutional power to create. For instance, only the federal government has the authority to appoint judges to the Supreme Court of Canada.

Judges who sit in the courts of a province but who are appointed by the federal government are commonly referred to as **federally appointed judges**. Those appointed by the province are referred to as **provincially appointed judges**. In many areas of law, only a federally appointed judge has the legal authority, or jurisdiction, to hear a particular type of case. For example, only a federally appointed judge can deal with a divorce or certain matters in criminal law.

The Organization of Courts

Each province has a statute, and a number of regulations that prescribe how the courts in that province will be established, how they will operate, and how they will be administered. Although each statute is distinct, there are more similarities among the provincial statutes than there are differences. In

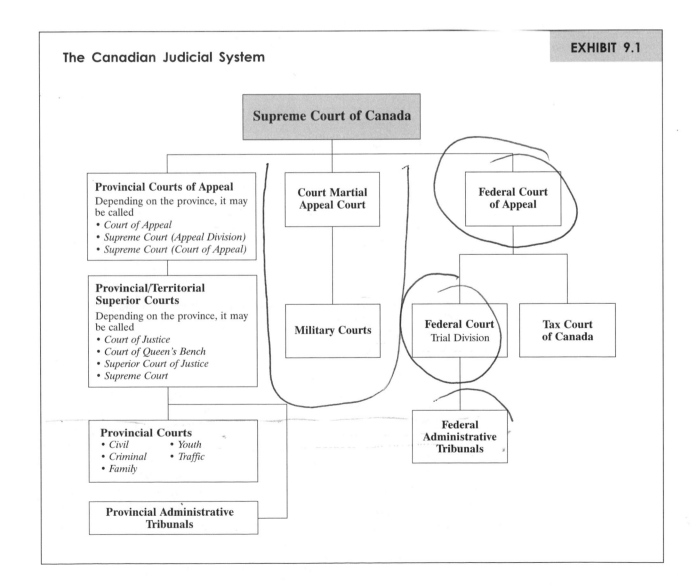

The Canadian Judicial System

EXHIBIT 9.1

- **Supreme Court of Canada**

- **Provincial Courts of Appeal**
  Depending on the province, it may be called
  • *Court of Appeal*
  • *Supreme Court (Appeal Division)*
  • *Supreme Court (Court of Appeal)*

- **Provincial/Territorial Superior Courts**
  Depending on the province, it may be called
  • *Court of Justice*
  • *Court of Queen's Bench*
  • *Superior Court of Justice*
  • *Supreme Court*

- **Provincial Courts**
  • *Civil*   • *Youth*
  • *Criminal*   • *Traffic*
  • *Family*

- **Provincial Administrative Tribunals**

- **Court Martial Appeal Court**

- **Military Courts**

- **Federal Court of Appeal**

- **Federal Court** Trial Division

- **Tax Court of Canada**

- **Federal Administrative Tribunals**

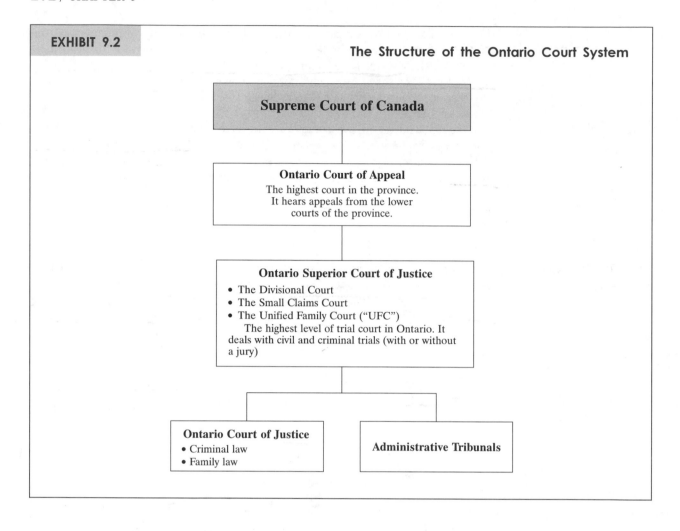

EXHIBIT 9.2

The Structure of the Ontario Court System

Supreme Court of Canada

Ontario Court of Appeal
The highest court in the province.
It hears appeals from the lower
courts of the province.

Ontario Superior Court of Justice
• The Divisional Court
• The Small Claims Court
• The Unified Family Court ("UFC")
   The highest level of trial court in Ontario. It
deals with civil and criminal trials (with or without
a jury)

Ontario Court of Justice
• Criminal law
• Family law

Administrative Tribunals

Ontario, the statute that governs court creation and administration is called the *Courts of Justice Act*.[1]

There are three levels of court in the present Ontario court system:

1. The Ontario Court of Appeal, the highest court in the province

2. The Ontario Superior Court of Justice, comprising a number of branches:
    (a) The Divisional Court
    (b) The Family Court
    (c) The Small Claims Court

3. The Ontario Court of Justice

The judges of the Court of Appeal and the Superior Court are appointed by the federal government, and those of the Ontario Court of Justice are appointed by the provincial government.

Between 1881 and September 1, 1990, the court structure in Ontario remained essentially the same, and the names of the courts did not vary. However, in 1990 the government undertook a major court reform that drastically altered the framework of the court structure and changed all the names

---

[1] R.S.O. 1990, c. C.43.

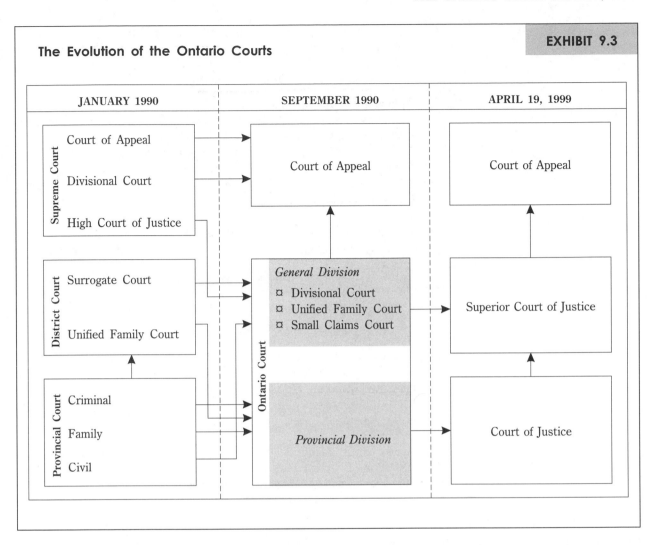

The Evolution of the Ontario Courts

EXHIBIT 9.3

of the courts. Then, on April 19, 1999, the court names were once again changed, although there was no change, at that time, to the actual structure of the court hierarchy.

The court structure outlined above is the one currently in place in Ontario. It was put into place on April 19, 1999. However, it is necessary to understand the court structure and names prior to that time. The name changes in the court system did not alter a particular level of court's authority to set precedent. Therefore, for the purpose of legal research, it is important to be able to determine whether a court decision is, in fact, binding precedent over another court.

Exhibit 9.3 shows the various changes to the Ontario Court Structure. Prior to September 1, 1990, there were three levels of court in Ontario:

1. The Supreme Court of Ontario, which consisted of three courts:
   (a) The Court of Appeal, which was the highest court in the province
   (b) The Divisional Court, which heard some minor appeals and some reviews of the decisions made by administrative tribunals
   (c) The High Court, which heard trials involving higher claims for money or property, divorce matters and more serious criminal offences

2. The District Court, which consisted of three courts:
   (a) The Surrogate Court, dealing with wills and estates
   (b) The Unified Family Court, which was a special pilot project begun in 1976 to hear all family law matters

3. The **Provincial Court**, which had three divisions:
   (a) The Provincial Court (Criminal), which heard bail hearings and less serious criminal matters;
   (b) The Provincial Court (Family), which had the jurisdiction to hear family law matters other than divorce; and
   (c) The Provincial Court (Civil), which comprised the Small Claims Court.

The Supreme Court of Ontario and the District Court were presided over by federally appointed judges, and the Provincial Court by provincially appointed judges.

Between September 1, 1990, and April 18, 1999, there were two levels of court:

1. The Ontario Court of Appeal, the highest court in the province

2. The Ontario Court of Justice, consisting of two branches:
   (a) The Ontario Court (General Division), presided over by federally appointed judges
   (b) The Ontario Court (Provincial Division), presided over by provincially appointed judges

The Ontario Court (General Division) was equivalent in all but name to the present Superior Court of Justice, and the Ontario Court (Provincial Division) was equivalent to the present Ontario Court of Justice.

THE HIERARCHY OF COURTS

The Supreme Court of Canada

The Supreme Court is the highest court in the land, and has been since 1949. Before that, decisions made by the court could be further appealed to the Judicial Committee of the Privy Council in England. (Criminal appeals to the Privy Council were ended in 1935.) Once the Court decides an issue, that decision becomes the law of Canada, applicable across the country.

The Supreme Court of Canada hears **appeals** from the provincial or territorial courts of appeal and from the Federal Court of Appeal. In most instances, there is no absolute right to appeal, and the party must first seek **leave of the court** or permission from the Supreme Court to have its case heard. Most often, only cases that involve new interpretations of the law, serious criminal cases, cases involving constitutional issues and cases involving conflicting decisions from different provincial courts of appeal will be granted leave. However, the federal government may refer an important legal matter to the Court for an opinion, and the government does not need to first seek leave. Likewise, in a criminal case, if a judge of the provincial or territorial court of appeal dissents on a point of law, there is an absolute right to appeal the decision to the Supreme Court.

The Supreme Court of Canada consists of nine judges, all appointed by the federal government. By legislation,[2] the Court must have three judges

---

[2] *Supreme Court of Canada Act*, R.S.C. 1985, c. S-26.

from Quebec. By custom, the balance of the Court is made up of three judges from Ontario, two from the western provinces and one from the Atlantic provinces. The Court sits, whenever possible, as a panel of nine judges. However, if one of the judges is ill, or otherwise unable to hear a case, the panel will be made up of an uneven number in order to avoid a tie decision. The minimum number of judges required to form a panel is five.

The Court of Appeal

The Court of Appeal is the highest court in Ontario. It hears appeals of cases from the Superior Court of Justice. In most instances, the court sits as a panel of three or five judges. An uneven number of judges is required for appeals in order to ensure that there is not a tie decision. There is only one Court of Appeal for the entire province, and it sits at Osgoode Hall in Toronto. If a party wished to appeal a decision that was made somewhere else in Ontario, the party must come to Toronto to have the appeal heard.

Court of Appeal judges are appointed by the federal government.

The Superior Court of Justice

The Superior Court of Justice has "inherent jurisdiction". This means that it can hear any case on any matter except those that are specifically required by statute to be heard in another court. The Superior Court, therefore, hears the most serious criminal matters and the civil cases that involve claims for money or property valued at more than $25,000. Claims for $25,000 and less are heard by the Small Claims Court. The Family Court Branch is discussed in more detail below.

The federal government appoints Superior Court judges. There is a Superior Court in each region of the province.

The Superior Court has the jurisdiction to decide a case on principles of both common law and the law of equity. Lower courts do not have jurisdiction to decide cases on the law of equity. The court has a number of branches: the Divisional Court, the Family Court, and the Small Claims Court.

The Divisional Court

Not all appeals go to the Court of Appeal. Ontario has another court to which some appeals may go: the Divisional Court, which is a branch of the Superior Court of Justice. It hears appeals on cases involving less than $50,000, on interlocutory or temporary orders and on final orders of Masters, who are judicial officials who hear some matters in the Superior Court. Divisional Court is also the court that reviews decisions of administrative tribunal if a party seeks a review.

There are no separate judges appointed to the Divisional Court. It is the Superior Court judges who sit in this court on a rotating basis. In many instances, they hear cases in a panel of three judges, just as does the Court of Appeal, although, in some instances, there is jurisdiction for one judge alone to hear a case.

The Family Court

The Family Court is a branch of the Superior Court, and it is a relative newcomer to the Ontario Court system. The court has jurisdiction to hear all family law matters. Prior to the Family Court's forming a specific branch of the Superior Court, family law matters were heard in much the same way that criminal cases and general civil cases were heard. The Superior Court had exclusive jurisdiction to hear divorce cases and those involving division of matrimonial property, but there were court matters involving the family that this court had no authority to hear, including child protection and adoption cases under the *Child and Family Services Act*. These latter cases were under the exclusive jurisdiction of the Ontario Court of Justice.

There were many family law cases that did not involve a divorce, a division of property or child protection and adoption. Many cases involved only issues of family support and custody and access to children. These cases could be heard in either the Superior Court or the Ontario Court of Justice, depending on where the party or his or her lawyer decided to commence the matter. This meant that there was no consolidated approach to family law litigation. Different levels of court were dealing with family law matters, and, sometimes, a case would have to change from one level of court to another after it was begun.

Family law matters do not lend themselves easily to an **adversarial system**, particularly one where there is a split jurisdiction and the very real possibility of a lack of continuity. To address this situation, in 1977 the Ontario government initiated a pilot project in Hamilton called the Unified Family Court. In 1995, the unified court was extended to four more locations and, in 1998, it was made a branch of the Superior Court of Justice. Since then, the court has expanded into other locations. There is currently a Family Court Branch of the Superior Court in the following locations: Hamilton, Barrie, Napanee, London, Kingston, Ottawa, Newmarket, Oshawa, Peterborough, Lindsay, Cobourg, Bracebridge, St. Catharines, Cornwall, L'Orignal, Brockville and Perth. In all of these locations, only the Superior Court, Family Court, hears family law cases. In all other locations, including Toronto and Brampton, the old system of split jurisdiction remains in place. Some family law matters are heard in the Superior Court, and others in the Ontario Court of Justice.

Small Claims Court

Small Claims Court hears civil cases that involve claims for money or the recovery or possession of property that is valued at no more than $25,000, exclusive of costs and interest. The procedural rules in this court are very simplified, which makes it possible for parties to bring, present and argue their cases without a lawyer. There is an opportunity for paralegals to provide representation in Small Claims Court.

All judges of the Superior Court are judges of the Small Claims Court. However, the *Courts of Justice Act*[3] provides that the senior judge in a region may appoint lawyers as **deputy judges** for a period of three years. In many regions, it is the deputy judges who sit in Small Claims Court, and not the judges of the Superior Court.

Ontario Court of Justice

Unlike the Superior Court, which has inherent jurisdiction to hear all cases, except those specifically required by statute to be held in another court, the Ontario Court of Justice is a "creature of statute" and, therefore, has a much more limited jurisdiction. For instance, judges of this court cannot decide cases involving equitable principles.

The provincial government appoints the judges of this court. They have jurisdiction to hear criminal matters, provincial offences, and in regions where there is no specific Family Court branch of the Superior Court, they may also hear family law matters that do not involve divorce or division of matrimonial property.

Young offenders cases are heard in the Ontario Court of Justice. When people refer to "Youth Court", they are actually referring to a courtroom of the Ontario Court of Justice that deals with young people who have been charged with a criminal offence.

---

3 R.S.O. 1990, c. C.34, s. 32.

Similarly, "Traffic Court" and "Provincial Offences Court" are courtrooms of the Ontario Court of Justice in which proceedings dealing with offences charged under the *Highway Traffic Act* and other provincial statutes are heard.

THE ROLE OF COURTS

Courts play an essential role in the Canadian system of government. Certainly, one of their major functions is to resolve disputes, but they also interpret the law, deal with constitutional issues and have a role in protecting the individual rights and freedoms of Canadians.

Courts and Dispute Resolution

Courts provide a **forum** for resolving disputes between individuals within our society. The dispute will be presented in a formal manner, in which the **litigants** follow prescribed procedural and evidentiary rules. The judge determines the case as a neutral, unbiased figure, after hearing the evidence and the legal submissions of the parties in dispute. The decision will be founded on accepted and established legal principles.

In the event that one or both of the parties are dissatisfied with the result of the court proceeding, they understand that they may be able to pursue their dispute to an **appellate court**. But once the process is complete, there will be an outcome, and the dispute will be resolved.

Courts and Legislative Interpretation

Another role of the court — sometimes in the context of resolving a dispute — is to interpret the terms of a statute or a regulation in a particular fact situation. As discussed in the explanation of the development of case law in another chapter, the drafting of statutes is an art that attempts to take into account all the contingencies and all the situations that are to be governed by that particular piece of legislation. This is not an easy task, and oftentimes there are issues that are unclear when a legal situation develops. Often, the courts are called upon to determine what the legislation really means and how it applies to a specific case. This role of the courts is one of clarifying and finding a just application of the law.

Courts and Constitutional Questions

In much the same way as courts resolve disputes between individuals or between individuals and corporations, our courts resolve disputes between different governments within the Canadian federation. These disputes relate to the distribution of powers between the federal and provincial governments as prescribed by the *Constitution Act*.

In this role, the courts provide a check on legislators who may exceed their constitutional limits by passing a statute that is outside their power for making law. We say that a law that exceeds the constitutional power of a level of government is **ultra vires**. Further, where the constitution permits shared or **concurrent** powers at more than one level of government, the courts resolve the questions as to which government is constitutionally paramount, which legislation will prevail and which will be withdrawn.

Courts and Individual Rights and Freedoms

It is through the courts that Canadians have the power to defend their individual rights against the improper exercise of power by government, governmental bodies and agents. That role has taken on an enhanced importance in the two decades since the enactment of the *Charter of Rights and Freedoms* and the codification of the former common law remedies for administrative law in the judicial review statutes.

V. *Enforcing the Charter of Rights and Freedoms*

It is sometimes said that the Charter is a shield, not a sword. What this means is that the Charter prescribes rights that an individual may use to defend himself or herself against interference or infringement of that right by the government.

We will discuss the Charter in more detail in another chapter. It is important to note that the Constitution gives the courts two remedial provisions if it is found that the government has, in fact, infringed on an individual's Charter rights.

Section 52 of the *Constitution Act* permits the courts to declare a law that is inconsistent with the provisions of the Constitution to be "of no force and effect". The section of the *Criminal Code* dealing with therapeutic abortions, for example, is a law that the courts have ruled to be inoperative and unenforceable under this section of the Constitution.

Section 24 of the Charter permits an individual to apply to the courts where his rights have been infringed "to obtain such remedy as the court considers appropriate and just in the circumstances." That section has been used in numerous criminal cases to overturn convictions or to stay proceedings when police or the prosecution have violated the rights of an **accused**.

VI. *Judicial Review*

In the area of administrative law, courts have the authority, on an application for judicial review, to reexamine the exercise of power by a government board, agency or commission. This means that an individual whose rights and privileges are affected by a decision of one of these bodies, or whose eligibility to receive, or continue to receive, a government benefit has been denied, may ask a court to rule whether the agency, board, or commission has properly exercised its power.

The court may grant relief to the individual by ordering the government to do what it is that it should have done, or not to do what it is proposing to do.[4] In this role, the courts apply what are known as the principles of natural justice to both the merits of the agency/board/commission decision and to the process it used to reach its decision.

THE ROLE OF THE JUDICIARY

An Independent Judiciary

Judges, or as they are referred to collectively, the judiciary, form the judicial branch of government. This branch plays an integral part in the justice system since judges not only make law through the common law system, they also interpret the statute laws made by the legislative branches of government at the federal and provincial levels.

One of the chief characteristics of the judicial branch is that it is to operate independently of the other two governmental branches — the executive branch and the legislative branch — meaning that the judiciary does not answer to the other branches for any decision it makes. This approach is meant to preserve the right of Canadians to have their cases heard by an independent, unbiased court, a court that bases its decisions on the evidence put before it, not on an allegiance to a level of government or to a political party.

However, the fact that judges are not accountable to an elected body is a source of controversy in some circles. Since the entrenchment of the *Charter*

---

[4] See *Judicial Review Procedure Act*, R.S.O. 1990, c. J.1 and *Statutory Powers of Procedure Act*, R.S.O. 1990, c. S.22.

of Rights and Freedoms in the Constitution, there are some who take the view that judges have, to a certain extent, usurped or taken over the role of the legislature in the making of law.

The Appointment of Judges

All judges in the Canadian legal system are appointed by one of the levels of government. The power to appoint judges is laid out in the *Constitution Act*. The federal government appoints judges to the Supreme Court of Canada, the Federal Court and the superior court of each of the provinces. This means that in Ontario, the federal government appoints all the judges of the Court of Appeal and the Superior Court of Justice. The provincial government appoints judges of the Ontario Court of Justice.

The actual process for the appointment of judges has, until relatively recent times, been shrouded in mystery. It was generally accepted, up until a couple of decades ago, that affiliation with and financial donation to a political party could result in a judicial appointment once that party came into power and formed the government. Of course, this process put into question the impartiality of judges and made critics of the system wonder about judges' independence.

In the late 1980s, the federal Minister of Justice created new rules and a new process for the appointment of superior court judges in the provinces. There is now an independent committee — made up of lawyers, judges and lay people — oversees the appointments. Lawyers who have been members of the Bar for a minimum of 10 years may apply to the committee for a consideration for an appointment to the bench. All applications are reviewed, applicants are interviewed, and the committee applies specific criteria in assessing applicants' suitability as judges. The committee then makes recommendations to the minister, and the minister consults further with provincial representatives, judges and people in the community before any appointment takes place. This process has been established with the hope of finding the best candidates — i.e., those who properly reflect the communities they serve rather than the policies of a particular political party.

In Ontario, there is a similar process for the appointment of judges to the Ontario Court of Justice.

Since the advent of the new process, many women and members of various ethnic and cultural groups have been appointed. Slowly, very slowly, the bench is starting to include women and members of minority groups.

Perhaps the most controversial appointment process involves the selection of the nine judges who sit on the Supreme Court of Canada. A vacancy on the court arises due to the death or retirement of a judge. At that point, the protocol for the selection of a new appointment is put in place. Historically, the vast majority of justices of the Supreme Court have been appointed after serving as judges on the Court of Appeal of their province; however, two relatively recent appointments have involved the selection of practising lawyers who have never before served as judges on any court.

A list of candidates is prepared subject to certain limitations. The list of possible candidates will be restricted, first, by geography. As we learned earlier in this chapter, by law three of the nine judges must be appointees who are members of the Bar of the province of Quebec. Also by tradition, three judges are from Ontario, two are from the western provinces, and one is from the Atlantic provinces. If an Ontario judge dies or retires, the list of potential appointees will be made up of only eligible members from Ontario.

It is the Governor General who makes the actual appointment of the Supreme Court judges, but the final selection is made by the prime minister in consultation with relevant people. Parliament does not need to approve the appointment. There are those who would argue that the appointment process for the Supreme Court needs revision to have more public input. For instance, in the United States, the Senate must ratify all potential presidential appointments to the U.S. Supreme Court. However, this model has resulted in much political disagreement and what some might argue is an overly detailed examination of the personal history of some candidates. As a result, in the eyes of many Canadians, the American process may not have much to recommend it.

Despite calls for changes to the appointment process in Canada, the court has made strides in presenting a more representative face to Canadians. The first woman justice was appointed in 1991: Madam Justice Bertha Wilson, who has since retired. Since her appointment, four other women have followed her onto the Court. Presently, there are four women justices sitting on the Court, including the Chief Justice, The Right Honourable Beverley McLachlin.

Minorities are still not very well represented on the court, but part of that may change as more members of immigrant communities are called to the bar and have an opportunity to establish the necessary credentials to be considered for an appointment to the Supreme Court.

Discipline and Discharge

Once appointed, judges are eligible to remain on the bench until the mandatory retirement age of 70 or 75, depending on the jurisdiction.

Judges are supervised in their roles by the chief justice or the senior judge in a region. Such supervision, however, is normally limited to the assignment of cases and other administrative functions related to court operation. The chief justices or senior judges do not discipline or discharge judges should a complaint arise about the conduct of a judge. Judges are permitted to hold office only during "good behaviour". Complaints that a judge has been deficient or neglectful or has otherwise engaged in inappropriate behaviour or misconduct must be heard by the Canadian Judicial Council if the judge has been federally appointed, and by the provincial judicial council if the appointment has been made by the province (e.g., the Ontario Judicial Council). The federal council is made up of the chief justice of the Supreme Court of Canada and the chief justices of each of the provinces and territories. Provincial judicial councils are made up primarily of judges and lawyers, but some do have members who represent the community at large. In Ontario, for example, a number of positions must be filled by non-lawyer members of the community.

These councils investigate all allegations and complaints made against judges, determine the validity of the complaint and, ultimately, make recommendations to the minister for disciplinary actions, including removal from the bench.

COURT PROCEEDINGS

The process followed as a case wends its way through the court system is governed by procedural law. Each step in either a civil or criminal court case is prescribed by a set of rules that dictate the proper procedure to be followed in that court. In addition, there are different rules for criminal matters and civil matters.

The civil law rules of the Superior Court of Justice are called the **Rules of Civil Procedure**. The Small Claims Court of the Superior Court has its own set of specialized rules, as does the Family Court branch. There are also rules for the Court of Appeal. All of these rules are separate regulations to the *Courts of Justice Act*.

Criminal procedure is found, primarily, in the procedural provisions of the *Criminal Code*; and for provincial offences, procedure is found in the Ontario *Provincial Offences Act*. There are, however, some rules relating to provincial offences appeals that are also found in regulations to the *Courts of Justice Act*.

These rules can be very complicated, and they are studied in separate law courses that are specifically related to procedure. For instance, in a course on civil litigation, students would make a very close study of the Rules of Civil Procedure. We will offer only a very brief overview of the major steps in both civil and criminal proceedings.

Civil Proceedings

The Rules of Civil Procedure, used in the Superior Court of Justice, divide a civil lawsuit, or **action**, into four major segments: the pleadings, the pre-trial procedure, the trial and post-trial procedure. These rules govern cases where the claim is in excess of $25,000. Claims for $25,000 or less are heard in the Small Claims Court and governed by separate rules of that court.

Pleadings

In a civil court proceeding, the rules require the parties to exchange certain prescribed documents, setting out the details of the case and their positions in relation to these details. These documents are referred to collectively as **pleadings**.

The parties in a basic action are the plaintiff and the defendant. The plaintiff commences the court proceeding and seeks a particular remedy from the court. The defendant opposes the plaintiff's claim. In an action, there can be multiple plaintiffs and multiple defendants.

The lawyer for the plaintiff files a **statement of claim** with the clerk or registrar of the particular courthouse. The clerk then opens a court file, places a court seal on the original document, signs it on behalf of the registrar, and returns the original to the plaintiff, keeping a copy in the court file. This process is called **issuing**. Once the pleading has been issued, the court proceeding has been officially commenced.

The statement of claim must then be given to the defendant so that he can determine the nature of the claim being made against him. The process of giving the document to the other side is called service. Once the defendant has received a copy of the statement of claim in a manner prescribed by the rules, we say that service has been effected. The defendant then has a specified number of days to answer the claim, should he choose to do so. A defendant is not required to file any document in his defence, but if he elects not to do so, it is almost certain that the court will give the plaintiff the relief she is seeking and deliver a judgment against the defendant.

Should the defendant choose to offer a defence to the claim, the pleading he must serve on the plaintiff and file with the court is known as a **statement of defence**. If the defendant delivers the statement of defence within the required time period, then the plaintiff may deliver a reply to any issues the defendant has raised in the statement of defence. Once a reply has been delivered, pleadings — for purposes of this illustration — have been completed, and the action moves on the pre-trial stage.

Pre-trial Procedure

The primary purpose of this stage of proceedings is to permit each party to gather all the available information from the other. In this way, they may assess the strength of their own case and determine whether or not a **settlement** of the case, without trial, is possible. The two major steps in pre-trial procedure are discovery and pre-trial conference.

In discovery, the parties may seek disclosure of all the documents that the other is relying upon to support his or her case, and they may also cross-examine the other party, under oath, outside the courtroom. Television and movies sometimes present cases that involve the witness being hit with a major surprise during the trial. This may make for a very exciting television show or film, but it doesn't have much to do with real court practice. In real courts, it is not productive to spend time taking a case all the way to trial when there is information available that, if disclosed to the other party, will result in the case being settled with less time and expense for everyone involved.

If the parties have not been able to arrive at settlement after discovery, the action will be placed on the list for trial. It will not be called for trial, however, until there has been a pre-trial conference. This is an informal meeting of the parties, their lawyers and a judge. The purpose of the conference is to have the judge assist the parties in reaching a possible settlement and, where that is not possible, to narrow the issues for trial. In narrowing the issues, the judge will have the parties focus only on the matters over which there is a real issue. Many side facts and legal points in any court case may not be contentious. The parties may agree on these points and will only need to take court time to present the fundamental issues on which they cannot agree.

After the pre-trial conference, if the case is not settled, it will be assigned a trial date.

Trial

The parties must each arrange to have their witnesses served with a subpoena or a summons requiring them to appear in court to give evidence.

The plaintiff and her witnesses present their side of the case first. Each witness will be **examined in chief** by the plaintiff's lawyer. Then the defendant's lawyer will have an opportunity to **cross-examine** those witnesses.

At the conclusion of the plaintiff's case, the defendant's counsel will then call his witnesses and examine them in chief. The plaintiff's counsel will then cross-examine them. All of the evidence is taken down through a court reporting process, which may involve a live court reporter in the courtroom or the use of tape-recording devices.

Then counsel for both parties will present their final arguments in a last attempt to persuade the judge[5] to accept their witnesses' version of the facts rather than the version of the witnesses for the opposing party. Final argument also involves counsel for each party presenting the points of law that support their client's position. The lawyers will then refer the judge to any supporting case law or statutes that may assist him or her in the decision-making process.

The judge will then decide the case. In some instances, the decision will be delivered orally shortly after the conclusion of the final argument, and the judge may or may not provide reasons or an explanation for the judgment. In other cases, the judge will **reserve judgment** and provide written reasons and the decision at a later date.

The judgment may find for the plaintiff for all or part of his claim, or dismiss the action in favour of the defendant. The judgment may also include an award for **costs**.

In most instances, costs are awarded to the successful party in the action. The unsuccessful party is ordered to pay a portion of the successful party's

---

[5] For brevity, this overview does not include a discussion of civil juries.

legal expenses. These costs are awarded on scales that are established and set out in the rules. The most often applied scale for costs will pay only from a third to a half of the winning party's actual costs, so the winning party will still be significantly out of pocket for a major portion of the expenses related to the litigation.

Occasionally, the higher scale for costs may be used; but even then, the costs awarded usually do not compensate them for the true costs involved in taking the matter to trial.

Post-trial Procedure

Enforcement

In the event that the plaintiff is awarded a money judgment at trial, the judgment is only as good as her ability to enforce it against the defendant and obtain the money. Civil proceedings include a process for enforcing a judgment.

Once the plaintiff has been successful in the action and has been awarded the payment of money, she can now be referred to as the **judgment creditor**. The judgment creditor has a number of options available if the defendant does not voluntarily pay the money owed under the judgment. The defendant may now be referred to as the **judgment debtor**.

First of all, she can obtain a **writ of seizure and sale** from the court office. This document can then be filed with the sheriff's office. When the document is filed, the debtor is essentially prohibited from selling his assets or disposing of his property. The writ of seizure and sale acts as a lien against his property.

The plaintiff can direct the sheriff to execute the writ and seize and sell the judgment debtor's property or, if she is unclear what property the debtor actually owns for her to seize, she may conduct an **examination in aid of execution**. The judgment debtor will be required to provide sworn evidence about his finances and his property.

The judgment creditor may also rely on a **garnishment**, which provides another avenue of enforcement. A notice of garnishment is obtained from the court office and delivered to any source of income or holdings of the debtor that can be liquidated: that is, converted to money. Upon receipt of the Notice of Garnishment, the source must withhold from the debtor the amount specified in the notice. In this way, the judgment creditor may take a portion of the debtor's wages or salary, a portion of his investments and bank accounts and any receivables that are payable to him, until the judgment debt is satisfied.

Criminal Proceedings

The term "criminal proceedings" applies to court cases in which a person has been charged with a criminal offence. Most criminal offences are contained in the *Criminal Code*. However, there are other federal statutes that contain criminal law, such as the *Food and Drug Act*, the *Narcotics Control Act*, and the *Youth Criminal Justice Act*. These are all Acts passed by the Parliament of Canada. Under the *Constitution Act*, only the federal government has the authority or jurisdiction to make criminal law.

The provincial governments may, however, create offences under provincial statutes (e.g., speeding or drinking under age). These offences are not criminal in nature, and a conviction for a provincial offence does not ever result in a criminal record.

In Canadian law, crimes are dealt with as wrongs against society as a whole, not simply as a wrong against a particular victim. The court procedure is called a prosecution and is normally brought by government lawyers referred to as **Crown prosecutors** or **Crown attorneys**. The person charged with the offence is referred to as the **accused**.

Process

There are several categories of criminal offence in Canadian law. The most serious criminal offences are referred to as **indictable offences**. They are prosecuted in a very formal and complex manner and carry the gravest penalties or sentences. Murder is an example of an indictable offence.

Minor offences under the *Criminal Code* are categorized as **summary conviction offences**. The word "summary" in this case means quick and simple, and the procedure for prosecuting this type of offence is much more condensed and less complicated than the procedure for prosecuting indictable offences. Summary offences carry relatively light penalties. The maximum punishment for most summary offences is a fine of $2,000 and/or a jail term of up to six months.

In addition, there is a category of offence that is neither a summary offence nor an indictable offence. Offences of this type are referred to as hybrid offences and may be prosecuted as either a summary or indictable offence at the preference of the prosecutor. The prosecutor would make this decision based on factors such as the circumstances surrounding the offence and the accused's prior criminal record.

The police lay most criminal charges, although there is provision for an individual to lay a **charge** against another individual. When the person is charged with an offence, he or she being accused of committing a criminal act. The formal accusation is contained in a formal court document called an **information**. An information must be sworn before a **justice of the peace** or a judge, who must be satisfied that there are reasonable and probable grounds for laying the charge.

It is quite likely that the police will arrest the accused if he is being charged with an indictable criminal offence. An arrest involves the police's taking the accused person into custody. However, if a person is charged with a less serious summary offence, he or she is not to be arrested unless there is a very good reason for doing so. Instead, the police officer may give an **appearance notice** to the accused, requiring him or her to attend court at a particular time on a specified date in order to answer the charge against him or her. An appearance notice is usually given to the accused when the police officer arrives on the scene and finds the accused at the scene of the crime. If the officer uses an appearance notice, he or she must then lay the information later.

Another way to bring the accused before the court without an arrest is to lay the information first before the justice and ask the justice to issue a **summons** to the accused. The summons is a formal order directing the accused to appear in court. The police would use this process when they need time to investigate the situation before charging someone and when, therefore, giving an appearance notice at the scene of the crime would not be appropriate.

An accused who has been arrested may or may not be held in custody until the trial date. Shortly after the arrest, there will be a bail hearing to determine if the accused can be released while awaiting trial. The decision to grant bail will be based on the potential danger to the community and the likelihood that the accused will actually appear for trial if released.

Pre-trial Procedure

If the accused pleads not guilty to the offence, the case will be set for trial. However, before the trial date can be set, there are number of steps that must be completed. These steps vary according to whether or not the accused has been charged with a summary offence or with an indictable offence.

Summary conviction offences are always tried in the Ontario Court of Justice without a jury. Most indictable offences may be tried either in the

Ontario Court or in the Superior Court by a judge alone, or by a judge and jury. The accused has the right to elect the level of court and, if the Superior Court is chosen, to choose whether the trial will take place before a jury. For hybrid offences, the Crown must first elect whether the matter will proceed summarily or by indictment. Once that choice has been made, the case will proceed in the same manner as a purely summary or indictable offence.

Before trial, the accused is entitled to disclosure from the Crown. In the disclosure process, the prosecution is required to advise the accused of all the evidence in the possession of the police that the Crown intends to present at the trial. This gives the accused and his counsel the opportunity to fully understand the nature of the case against the accused and allows for the preparation of any defence that may be available.

In addition, the case must be "pre-tried" before a trial date is set. A conference will be set up involving the Crown, the counsel for the defence and, usually, a judge. A pre-trial is often used for plea negotiations. It is also used to determine which facts are not in dispute, to narrow trial issues and to assess the time that will be required for trial.

If the accused elects to be tried in the Superior Court of Justice, a **preliminary hearing** will normally be conducted. At the preliminary hearing, the Crown is required to present sufficient evidence to a judge of the Ontario Court of Justice in order to satisfy the judge that there is enough evidence against the accused to necessitate a trial. The defence is not required to present any part of its case, but counsel for the accused has an early opportunity to cross-examine some of the witnesses for the Crown. It is rare for a judge to find that there is not enough evidence to continue the prosecution and proceed to trial. However, a preliminary hearing can be invaluable to the defence in testing the Crown witnesses and in obtaining a picture of the strengths and weaknesses in the prosecution's case.

Trial

In a criminal trial, the Crown presents its case first, and must prove the guilt of the accused beyond a reasonable doubt. Witnesses will be called and examined, in chief, by the prosecutor. The lawyer for the accused will then have an opportunity to cross-examine the Crown's witnesses.

When the Crown has presented all its evidence, then the defence may present its case. Since the accused has a constitutional right to be presumed innocent until proven guilty beyond a reasonable doubt, the accused need not call any evidence at all. At the end of the Crown's case, the defence may take the position that the Crown has not met its burden of proof and may ask the trial judge to acquit the accused without the defendant's presenting any evidence or any defence. This is called a **directed verdict**.

However, in most cases, the Crown will have presented enough evidence to warrant the accused's presenting a defence. If a defence is presented, the Crown will have an opportunity to cross-examine the defence witnesses after the accused's counsel has examined them in chief.

Once each side has concluded its case, the prosecutor and the defence counsel present legal argument. If the case is being heard by a judge and jury, it is the role of the jury to determine which version of the facts it believes. The jury is sometimes referred to as the trier of fact. In a trial by jury, the judge must then instruct the jury on the law and how members of the jury are to apply it. This is called the **charge to the jury**. In a trial by judge alone, it is the judge who determines which version of the facts is more credible.

The accused must be acquitted if there is a reasonable doubt as to guilt. If no reasonable doubt is found, the accused will be convicted, and the judge will impose a sentence. The sentence or the range of sentence for each offence can be found in the *Criminal Code*. If there is a range of sentence, which is the case with most offences, the judge will determine which option is the most appropriate for the offender given the circumstances of the offence, the likelihood of rehabilitation and the need to deter both this particular accused and other members of the public who may be tempted to commit a similar offence.

In Canadian law, both the accused and the Crown may appeal the decision in a criminal matter. The level of court that hears the appeal will be determined by the level of court that made the decision being appealed.

ADMINISTRATIVE TRIBUNALS

In addition to the court system, there is another major area in which legal disputes are addressed. Governments regulate a great deal of activity under the statute laws that they create. Many of these statutes establish tribunals to administer disputes between the government and private citizens in relation to the application and interpretation of specific regulations. It is the responsibility of these tribunals to resolve complaints and determine remedies for various issues that arise. The Labour Relations Board, the Ontario Human Rights Commission and the Workplace Safety and Insurance Board are all examples of provincial agencies that have statutorily created tribunals to resolve disputes. The Immigration and Refugee Board, the RCMP Public Complaints Commission and the National Parole Board are examples of federal administrative tribunals.

Administrative tribunals operate within an area of law called, not surprisingly, administrative law. Certain legal principles and rules must be applied by the tribunals in arriving at their decisions. These principles and rules seek to enforce a standard of fairness. For instance, the tribunal must be unbiased, and the person who is asking for a remedy must have an opportunity to be heard.

Usually, if a statute creates an administrative tribunal to deal with a certain issue, a court will not have jurisdiction to consider the dispute. The role of the courts in relation to administrative tribunals is only to determine that the tribunal decision-making process has been made in accordance with the principle of administrative law.

Administrative tribunals are sometimes referred to as quasi-judicial bodies. That means that although they are less formal than courts, they follow a pattern in their process and procedure similar to that of courts. Tribunals each establish their own forms or pleadings and their own practices. Depending on the statute that creates a tribunal, parties may be able to represent themselves at a hearing, or may be represented by a lawyer or an agent.

ALTERNATIVES TO THE COURT SYSTEM

In light of the cost of court proceedings, and the backlog of cases in the court system, more parties and their lawyers are looking for speedier, less adversarial and less costly methods of resolving disputes. As a result, many are relying on approaches to resolving legal conflicts that do not centre on the court system. These methods are collectively referred to as alternate dispute resolution, or ADR.

Alternate dispute resolution has long been used in labour disputes between management and unions. Many business contracts contain provisions for alternate dispute resolution, and it has taken hold in commercial matters.

More recently, ADR approaches are also being used in family law and in general disputes involving individuals and between individuals and businesses. The following comprise the major methods of alternate dispute resolution.

Negotiation

Negotiation is a voluntary process that may be either formal or informal. There is no third person who attempts to resolve the dispute; the parties themselves meet to identify issues of concern, explore options for the resolution of the issues, and search for a mutually acceptable agreement to resolve the issues raised. Lawyers may represent the disputing parties. Any resolution of the dispute is as a result of the parties' agreement between themselves to be bound by the decision that they make together.

Mediation

Mediation is a process where a neutral third person, called a mediator, helps the parties try to resolve the dispute. The parties have the opportunity to describe the issues, discuss their interests, understandings and feelings, provide each other with information, and explore ideas for the resolution of the dispute. The mediator acts as a facilitator assisting the parties in communicating and negotiating more effectively, thereby enhancing their ability to reach a settlement. Parties are not required to come to agreement. The mediator does not have the power to make a decision for the parties but can help the parties find a resolution that is mutually acceptable. The only people who can resolve the dispute in mediation are the parties themselves.

Conciliation

Conciliation and mediation are very much alike in that a neutral third person is involved in attempting to have the parties reach their own resolution to the dispute. There is no universally held view as to what the differences are between mediation and conciliation, but many ADR practitioners in Canada believe that in the process of mediation, the parties meet face-to-face, while in conciliation, each meets only with the conciliator. The conciliator acts as the go-between.

Arbitration

Arbitration is the method of ADR that most resembles a court proceeding. A neutral third person, an arbitrator, is appointed and paid by the parties to make a decision on the dispute. Normally the parties agree that they will be bound by whatever decision is made, although the agreement setting up the arbitration process may provide that the decision may be appealed to a court. The parties also determine the manner in which the issues are presented to the arbitrator. They may decide to present their issues through a formal hearing process, or they may agree to have the arbitrator base the decision on written submissions.

Diversion

This method of ADR is used most often in criminal matters. Diversion removes from the formal criminal justice process people charged with minor offences who do not have serious criminal records. To be eligible for diversion, the accused must admit responsibility for his or her offences and agree to participate in alternative measures programs. This usually entails having to perform acts of contrition or redress, such as writing an essay, writing a letter of apology to the victim, performing community service work, providing restitution or compensation, or making a charitable donation.

Initially, diversion was available only for young persons charged with a criminal offence. Now, however, diversion is more widely available to adults, although it is most often used in Aboriginal communities or in minority communities. The concept involves giving a minor offender the opportunity to

take constructive action to remedy the situation that led him to the court system without imposing a conviction and a criminal record.

CHAPTER SUMMARY

This chapter described the constitutional framework for court administration, in which the responsibility for running the courts and appointing judges is split between the provinces and the federal government. The structure and the hierarchy of the courts in the Ontario system were also described.

The reader was introduced to various roles of the court in resolving disputes, interpreting legislation, resolving constitutional disputes, and protecting the rights of individuals. The procedure for appointing judges was introduced, as was the role of the judiciary as a branch of government.

A brief overview of both civil and criminal court proceedings was presented.

Finally, the specialized forums for resolving disputes outside the court system were described. The creation of administrative tribunals was noted as an auxiliary system for dispute resolution related to regulatory government policies and programs. Further, methods of alternate dispute resolution or ADR were surveyed and defined.

GLOSSARY OF NEW TERMS AND KEY CONCEPTS

accused	The person charged with an offence, and the respondent in court as the party opposed to the Crown.
action	A civil proceeding that is not an application and that includes a proceeding commenced by a claim, notice of action, or statement of claim.
adversarial system	A system by which disputes between opposing parties are resolved.
appeal	A review of a decision made at one level in the judicial process by one or more judges at a higher level.
appearance notice	A form in criminal proceedings that requires that an accused appear in court on a specific date to answer charges against him.
appellate court	A court that exercises jurisdiction to hear appeals.
charge	An accused is charged with a criminal offence when a document called an information is sworn before a justice of the peace, alleging that there are reasonable and probable grounds to believe the accused has committed a specifically named criminal offence.
charge to the jury	The jury is the trier of fact but, before jury members enter deliberations, at the conclusion of the case, the judge will instruct them on the necessary law in relation to determining the facts.
concurrent	In constitutional terms, where two or more governments have jurisdiction over the same subject matter.
costs	The allowable fees and disbursements related to the proceedings in an action, usually awarded to the successful party at trial.
cross-examine	The opposite side's examination of a witness following examination-in-chief, used to weaken the effect of that witness's testimony, discredit the witness and elicit favourable evidence for the cross-examining party.
Crown Prosecutor or Crown Attorney	In Canada, the federal government and each of the provincial governments is called the Crown; in criminal proceedings, it is the term used to describe the government as prosecutor.

deputy judge	In Ontario, a barrister and solicitor may be appointed for a three-year term to sit in Small Claims Court as the presiding judge.
directed verdict	When the Crown has been unable to meet the onus to prove all the elements of a criminal offence, at the end of the presentation of the Crown's case, the defence has no need to call a defence at all and will ask the court to find the accused not guilty.
examination in aid of execution	In the Rules of Procedure in Ontario, a successful party in an action may question or examine the unsuccessful party to determine the unsuccessful party's ability to pay a judgment and/or an order for costs.
examined in chief	When a witness is questioned in a trial by the counsel who summonsed that witness.
federally appointed judges	Judges appointed by the federal government.
forum	The place where legal remedies can be sought, usually a court.
garnishment	A proceeding whereby a judgment creditor may give notice to a third party that monies owing by that party to the judgment debtor must be paid to the relevant sheriff's office to the credit of the judgment creditor.
indictable offence	A criminal offence that is triable by indictment; the more serious category of criminal offences: equivalent to the American felony.
information	The legal document, sworn before a justice of the peace, that alleges that the accused has committed a specific offence. It is the document that formally commences all criminal prosecutions.
issuing	The process by which the court office essentially verifies the start of the civil court proceeding by placing a court seal on some documents, which the registrar signs and then opens a court file.
judgment creditor	The successful party who in an action is owed money by the unsuccessful party, and thereby becomes a creditor for that judgment money.
judgment debtor	The party who owes money as the result of a judgment, and who is subject to certain collection proceedings.
justice of the peace	A judicial official with jurisdiction over minor criminal offences and the initiation of a legal process (e.g., swearing an information).
leave of the court	Some steps in a court proceeding cannot be taken automatically. Permission from the court must first be obtained.
litigants	The parties to the court proceeding.
pleadings	The documents in a civil lawsuit that set out the factual and legal matters at issue in the case, and that the rules require the parties to exchange prior to the court hearing.
preliminary hearing	A hearing conducted by a provincial judge to determine whether there is sufficient evidence to commit an accused for trial, in relation to an indictable offence charge.
provincial courts	Courts that a provincial legislature establishes and maintains to administer justice in the province, under section 92(14) of the *Constitution Act*.
provincially appointed judges	Judges appointed by the provincial government.
reserve judgment	The judge does not give judgment immediately at the end of a trial but, rather, takes time to consider the matter and write reasons for judgment.
rules of procedure	The rules in civil proceedings contained in the relevant regulation passed under the *Courts of Justice Act* for the conduct of civil cases; in criminal proceedings, these are those rules formulated under the authority of the *Criminal Code* for the conduct of criminal prosecutions.
settlement	An agreement by the parties in dispute that resolves the dispute.
statement of claim	The originating process (document) that commences an action and documents the facts relied upon in support of the plaintiff's claim and the remedy or relief sought.

statement of defence	A brief written statement by the defendant that responds to the allegations in a statement of claim.
summary conviction offence	The less serious criminal offences: equivalent to the American misdemeanour.
summons	A legal document, issued by the court, that requires a person to appear in criminal court or suffer certain legal consequences.
ultra vires	Latin, meaning "beyond the powers"; a statute that is determined by the courts to be outside the powers assigned by the Constitution to the legislature that enacted it.
writ of seizure and sale	A document that a judgment creditor obtains from the court office as evidence of an unpaid judgment, and delivers to one or more sheriff's offices in order to enforce the judgment.

REVIEW QUESTIONS

1. What type of cases are heard by the Supreme Court of Canada?

2. Our court system establishes a hierarchy of courts. Name and describe the three major court levels in Ontario.

3. Describe three roles of the courts in our legal system.

4. If a person wishes to sue another in Ontario for non-payment of a loan of $8,000, to which court must the action be brought?

5. What have been some of the challenges facing family law court matters in Ontario?

6. What is the role of diversion in the criminal court system?

7. In what circumstances in a criminal proceeding would a preliminary hearing be held?

8. In what sense does the creation of administrative tribunals unclog the court system in Ontario?

9. What is the primary distinction between arbitration and mediation?

10. What legislation dictates the procedure in a court hearing?

11. What do we mean when we say that the judiciary in Canada is independent?

DISCUSSION QUESTIONS

1. Judges are said to interpret the law, not to make law. However, in a recent decision of the Supreme Court of Canada, the court found that a federal statute was unconstitutional because it discriminated in the administration of a benefit program. The court was afraid that if it relied on section 52 of the Charter, its only remedy was to make the law — and therefore the statutory authority for the benefits — "of no force and effect". That would basically kill the whole program until Parliament could get around to amending the law, which one justice referred to as "equality with a vengeance". So, the court ordered that the law be read so as to include a segment of the population that it appeared to exclude, and make that segment eligible for those benefits. What is your view? Is the court making law?

2. Do you think that judges in Canada should be elected rather than appointed? What are the particular advantages or disadvantages to appointment instead of election?

3. What public interest may there be in trying to resolve court cases before they go to trial?

4. Should we have television cameras in our trial courtrooms in Canada?

5. Where an accused person is acquitted after a trial, should the Crown be ordered to compensate the accused in whole or in part for the costs of his defence?

6. Is voluntary mediation likely to be any more successful than mandatory mediation, in which the rules of the court require that the parties hire an independent mediator to attempt to resolve their dispute before they can set a trial date?

SUGGESTED READING

Boyd, Neil. *Canadian Law, an Introduction*, 3d ed. (Toronto, Ont.: Thompson-Nelson, 2002).

Gall, Gerald L. *The Canadian Legal System*, 4th ed. (Toronto Ont.: Carswell, 1995).

Mewett, Alan W., & Shaun Nakatsuru. *An Introduction to the Criminal Process in Canada*, 4th ed. (Toronto, Ont.: Carswell, 2000).

Olivo, Laurence, & Mary Ann Kelly. *Civil Litigation* (Toronto, Ont.: Emond Montgomery, 2003).

Willes, John A. *Contemporary Canadian Business Law, Principles and Cases*, 6th ed. (Toronto Ont.: McGraw-Hill Ryerson, 2001).

The Legal Profession in Ontario

Laurence M. Olivo
SENECA COLLEGE

Learning Objectives

After reading this chapter, the reader should be able to:

> recognize social, economic, and legal forces that are causing change in the way legal services are offered

> know how lawyers are trained

> know how lawyers are accredited for specialization

> be aware of the general standards of ethics for the legal profession

> be aware of the methods used to control lawyers' professional behaviour

> understand the role of the legal aid plan and how it operates

> appreciate the nature of the lawyer–client relationship, and know the principal responsibilities of both parties in the relationship

> understand the roles of the law clerk and the paralegal in the legal services market

> know the differences between law clerks and paralegals

> be aware of how law clerks and paralegals are trained and regulated

> be aware of current changes and developments for law clerks and paralegal-occupational groups

TABLE OF CONTENTS

INTRODUCTION

At one time, the term "legal profession" was used simply to describe lawyers, implying that these were the only legal workers that needed to be described. However, the legal services area has grown in terms of the number of persons employed doing legal work. It has also become more complex in its organization, and the occupational roles have become more varied.

The Law Office in 1900 and Today — Changes and Trends

The law is often described as a conservative enterprise, one that is resistant to change. While some things have not changed in 100 years, if one walked into a law office today, there would be some significant differences from what one would have found in Canada in 1900.

Size

Most lawyers in 1900 were sole practitioners, or had a handful of associates or partners. Even established firms in large urban centres would not have had much more than a dozen lawyers. The focus of a legal practice would have been local, with services being provided for local populations.

Today, the size and structure of firms has changed. Elite, establishment firms providing legal services for wealthy individuals and corporations often have more than 150 lawyers, although many of them will be younger associates (employees), rather than partners in the firm. Among the larger firms, there has been a trend towards amalgamation so that there are fewer large firms than formerly; but the newly amalgamated firms are quite large indeed, and are sometimes referred to as **mega-firms.** Of these, many will in turn be connected by alliance to other firms in other provinces or countries. Some of these firms have also established branch operations outside their province of origin. This is a great departure from former custom, where law firms, even large ones, were local in nature, offering services within one province only. The organized Bar is, in fact, structured along provincial lines in Canada. Thus, to be admitted to the Bar in Ontario, for example, does not automatically give a lawyer the right to practise in other provinces or countries. The lawyer must still meet the requirements for practice in other jurisdictions, making the organization of interprovincial firms difficult.

There have been changes in the rules for lawyers who practise in more than one jurisdiction. The Federation of Law Societies of Canada has developed new rules for lawyers who are licensed to practise in one province but also practise occasionally or often in another province. When a lawyer is doing occasional work in a province other than her home province, she will continue to be governed by her home province's law society without having to make formal arrangements with the law society in the other province. On the other hand, if a lawyer is working full-time or continually in a province where he is not a member of the Bar, under the new rules, that lawyer will only have to acknowledge that he has familiarized himself with areas of law that are different from those in his home province, using materials provided by the law society of the province where he wishes to practise. He may then be licensed to practise in that province.[1]

Whether an interprovincial firm or not, what would have been a large firm in 1900 (over 20 lawyers) would now be classed as a medium-size firm.

---

[1] The Law Society of Upper Canada, By-Law 4, ss. 9(1) and (2), as amended, January 2011. There are now three classes of lawyer licence: private practitioners, those employed by the Crown, and those who are members of the bars of other provinces who appear occasionally in Ontario. There is also now a licence for paralegals, as a separate branch of the legal profession.

Today, medium-size firms in large centres are often quite specialized in what they do (these are sometimes referred to as "law boutiques"), or offer full services to small-business clients and the general public. Such firms are often found in smaller cities, providing a full range of services.

Firms with fewer than 20 members would, particularly in urban areas, be classed as small firms. Small firms are the ones that have changed the least: they tend to serve non-elite clients (small businesses and ordinary citizens), and offer a general range of legal services. They are more likely to be found outside the downtown core of major cities, in suburban areas or in the outlying parts of the province.

Demographic Makeup

In 1900, the law was the almost-exclusive preserve of white males of the established Anglo-Celtic or Francophone Quebec ethnic groups. There were few practitioners of "other" ethnic or visible minority origin. There were also a mere handful of women practitioners.

Beginning in the 1950s, however, the demographics began to change. With changes in educational policy following World War II, which made post-secondary education and law school more accessible, a growing number of those of non-British and non-French background began entering the legal profession. In the early 1970s, the number of women in the profession began to increase as the women's movement helped to redefine occupational choices for women and to insist on rights of access to educational and economic opportunities. At the same time, visible minorities in the legal profession began to increase in numbers, reflecting greater legal access to institutions and the increasing proportion of some visible minorities in the general population.

The changes in the ethnic and gender makeup of the legal profession have caused lawyers and their professional governing bodies to examine the experiences of women and minorities in the profession, as there is some evidence of **systemic discrimination**, which may or may not be intentional, within the profession. A number of explanations have been advanced for this pattern — chief among them is the notion that the way in which law has been practised, with long hours, is not compatible with major parenting responsibilities assumed disproportionately in Canada by women, whether they have a career or not.[2] There is also some evidence that suggests that "other" ethnics tend to be proportionately under-represented in large firms serving elite clients. The Law Society of Upper Canada has been in the process of examining accessibility issues within the profession, as have other bodies governing the legal profession in other provinces. It is reasonable to expect that these issues will continue to be of concern for some time to come.

Training

While legal education today is often seen as a theoretical, academic enterprise, training in 1900 was practical. Upon graduation from high school, a student in many parts of Canada could become a lawyer by becoming an **articling clerk** or an apprentice in a law office, "learning the law" from a qualified lawyer. At the end of several years of articling, apprentice lawyers would take the Bar exams and, if successful, would be **called to the bar** and become a full-fledged lawyer, ready to set up on their own. In many

---

[2] The phenomenon of women's not advancing in their profession because of assumptions that they will not have the time or resources to focus on professional life is sometimes referred to as "the glass ceiling".

respects, this form of training resembled the training programs for skilled tradespersons, such as plumbers or cabinetmakers.

Over time, the program gradually acquired a more academic component. In Ontario, students articled by day and took formal legal subjects at night. No university degree was required prior to commencing legal training, but many students did complete a university course of study before entering formal legal training.

The governing bodies of the profession still saw the training program as one for acquiring practical skills through "hands-on" techniques and played down an academic and analytic approach to legal training.[3] Eventually, those who favoured a more academic approach to law won out. Now, students must complete at least two years of university prior to applying for entry to one of the Canadian law schools offering a three-year law degree, where law and legal reasoning are studied in an academic and theoretical way. There is little practical training in law at law school, although there is pressure now from the legal profession for law schools to offer more.

Upon successful completion of law school, a student must serve as an articling clerk with a practising lawyer for 12 months. During or following the articling period, the student must also complete the Bar admission course requirement. Students have some leeway in scheduling when, and in what order, they article and take the Bar exam. The Bar admission course has become a self-paced and self-directed course with exams.

After being called to the bar, lawyers are not required to undergo further training unless they cease to use their skills and leave the legal profession for a number of years, and then seek to resume practice. However, it has become common for lawyers to attend continuing education sessions on various legal topics as a means of keeping their knowledge up-to-date. In 1900, there were few opportunities to take continuing education subjects, and lawyers were supposed to keep up with changes in the law as best they could.

Specialization

In 1900, all lawyers were trained as "general practitioners", with an assumption that any lawyer could and would provide a whole range of general legal services. While some lawyers had areas of expertise and could be said to specialize in certain areas of law, there was no certification process or formal recognition of specialization among lawyers that would allow the public to identify a specialist.

The situation has changed since 1900. As the law has grown more complex, there has been increasing specialization; in Ontario, this has been recognized by allowing lawyers with specialized practices to apply for certification as specialists and to advertise their specialty to the public. There is still no formal educational process for training specialists, and, on call to the bar, all lawyers have been trained only as generalists, as was the case in 1900.

The situation for lawyers is also mirrored by office staff. In 1900, the other staff would have consisted of a secretary or clerk, often male. Today,

---

[3] In Ontario in the late 1940s, the debate between advocates of the academic versus trade-school approach to legal education led to a revolt by the academically inclined teachers at Osgoode Hall Law School (then run directly by the Law Society on a "trade-school" model). Led by Cecil Wright and Bora Laskin, the academically inclined teaching staff resigned from Osgoode Hall and trooped up University Avenue to the University of Toronto, where they established the Faculty of Law at the University of Toronto, Canada's first academic law school. The rebels had tried and failed to persuade the Law Society to modernize its educational system, and went to the University of Toronto only when no option was left. For a highly readable account of these events, see C.I. Kyer & Jerome E. Bickenbach, *The Fiercest Debate* (Toronto, Ont.: The Osgoode Society, 1987).

a law office is much more likely to have other staff besides a secretary, with the degree of specialization of staff increasing as the size of the law firm increases. In addition to secretaries, one is likely to find law clerks or paralegals, investigators, patent agents, accounting staff, computer systems staff, and law office managers. Some of these staff run the business end of the law firm, while others perform various professional tasks that need not be performed by lawyers and can be performed under a lawyer's supervision.

Marketing

The idea of marketing and advertising a law firm was unknown in 1900. Indeed, lawyers, as professionals, were forbidden to advertise and market themselves in a formal way until the 1980s, when the rules of professional conduct were relaxed to permit "tasteful" advertising. This was seen to benefit smaller firms seeking to tap into the mass market. Large firms with elite clients were thought not to need to advertise, as they marketed themselves discreetly and informally. However, even large firms now do some marketing, often in the form of "newsletters" to clients, advising them on changes and developments in law that affect them. Specialist and boutique firms also advertise their services to other firms to solicit referrals for their specialized services.

Another aspect of marketing is the use, by some lawyers, of storefront law offices in shopping centres. This approach is designed to be customer friendly so as to capture the part of the market made up of ordinary people who use lawyers infrequently, if at all, and who might feel more comfortable using lawyers who are located in a non-traditional, less formal setting. Storefront law firms are not necessarily less expensive than firms located in downtown office buildings, however, particularly if they are doing work that is more than routine.

Organization of Law Practices

The forms of business organization used by law practices in 1900 were either one lawyer practising as a sole practitioner, perhaps with an employed lawyer as an associate, or several lawyers owning the firm together as partners. The partnership might also employ some lawyers as associates. Lawyers were not permitted to run their businesses as limited liability corporations. The Law Society required lawyers to remain personally liable for professional negligence and defaults. Thus, they could not shelter personal assets by setting up a corporation to insulate themselves from personal liability.

With the growth of firm size and with firms operating in more than one province or country in the 1990s, the Law Society decided to permit lawyers to have limited liability partnerships, thus allowing the law practice to have some of the protections and business efficiencies conferred by the corporate form of business organization. However, lawyers are still held personally liable for negligence arising from the practice of law, even if the firm is a limited liability partnership. A firm using this form of business organization is required[4] to have the letters "LLP" after the firm name.

Also, the Law Society now permits lawyers to form partnerships with other professionals, such as accountants, in order to offer a broader range of services. However, lawyer-partners are required to have control of the firm and to ensure that non-legal professionals do not breach the Law Society's Rules of Professional Conduct.

---

[4] The Law Society of Upper Canada, By-Law 7, as amended, April 2009.

The Law Society permits firms to incorporate as professional corporations, with the lawyer owners taking shares in the company rather than partnership interests. A corporate form of ownership is considered to be attractive to small firms for tax purposes in some instances.[5] Lawyers will, however, still be personally liable for their own negligence.

Characteristics of the Profession

So far we have been describing how the legal profession and the provision of legal services have changed during this century. We now turn to a more detailed examination of the legal profession and the legal services sector generally. In order to better understand the nature of the legal profession, both on its own and in comparison to other legal service occupations, it is useful to distinguish conceptually between professionals and other occupational groups. The distinctions are important because they help to explain the differences between lawyers and other occupations in the legal services area in terms of how they are organized, the norms and values under which they operate, and the status and power that they have or lack.

A profession has the following characteristics:

- A *systematic theory* or *body of knowledge* that is difficult to learn and over which the professional claims a monopoly.

- *Authoritative use of the body of knowledge over which the professional claims a monopoly.* Because the professional has a monopoly over a body of knowledge, the claim is made that the professional is the only one who has authority to use professional knowledge because no one else is equipped to do it or to even determine if a professional is using the knowledge properly.

- *Societal approval of the use of the body of knowledge.* Where professionals have persuaded the rest of us that they are the only ones who should be authorized to use a body of knowledge, then the profession has established itself and its monopoly. At this point, the rest of us cease to control what the professional does, and we leave it to the professionals to control themselves.

- *Ethical codes* are important characteristics of professional groups. Because the members of the group have a monopoly over what they do, the rest of us do not have sufficient knowledge to police their activities and prevent them from abusing the power that comes with a monopoly over knowledge. A solution to this has been to permit professionals to form organizations to govern themselves, and to require them to adhere to rules of professional conduct that determine what kind of behaviour is or is not permitted. Many of the regulations contained in these types of ethical codes prohibit and punish behaviour by professionals that would barely raise an eyebrow if the prohibited acts were done by others. For example, a sexual relationship between an employee and customer does not usually attract punishment by co-workers in the same trade, or prevent the employee from ever working in that field again. However, if a doctor has such a relationship with a patient, it is likely to lead to disciplinary actions from the professional regulatory body, possibly with the doctor's licence and right to practise medicine being revoked.

---

[5] M. Fitz-James, "Convert Your Law Firm Interest into Corporate Securities" *Law Times* (29 April 2002). Also see, the Ontario *Business Corporations Act*, R.S.O. 1990, c. B.16, s. 3.2.

THE LEGAL PROFESSION

Governance of the Legal Profession

The Law Society — Governance in Whose Interest?

As noted earlier, the legal profession is organized on a provincial, rather than national, basis, reflecting its local origins. This is further reflected in the way in which lawyers, as a professional body, govern themselves. Each province and territory has the right to govern the legal profession within its territorial jurisdiction, and each has, by statute, turned that right over to the profession by allowing it to establish and operate an organization to govern the profession. These organizations, called "law societies", are distinguished from voluntary associations such as the Canadian Bar Association; the voluntary organizations have no power to regulate the legal profession. The law society, on the other hand,

- determines who can become a lawyer,
- determines educational requirements that must be met to become a lawyer,
- determines admission requirements, and
- disciplines lawyers with sanctions up to and including removal from the profession by **disbarment**.

In the ensuing discussion of how law societies work, the actual example used will be the Law Society of Upper Canada, the governing body of the legal profession in Ontario.

It should be apparent that the Law Society is a very powerful body. It is given its monopoly of control over the legal profession on the assumption that it will act in the public interest, particularly when the public interest and the interest of lawyers as a profession clash.

The governing body of the Law Society is called **convocation**. It is composed of individual **benchers**, the majority of whom are elected by members of the legal profession itself. The position of bencher is not salaried. Consequently, there is an over-representation of established lawyers from larger firms, whose firms can afford to have them devote considerable time to serving on Law Society committees and otherwise carrying out their duties. Starting in the 1980s, attempts were made to broaden the representative nature of the convocation by ensuring that a certain portion of bencher positions were reserved for lawyers practising outside Toronto. Under proposed paralegal licensing provisions, there will also be two paralegal benchers. Significantly, public representation is limited to a small number of "lay benchers" (i.e., non-lawyers) who are appointed by the attorney general. One may wonder whether the public interest is represented by this arrangement for choosing the governors of the Law Society or whether the arrangement has more in common with the governance of a private club.

Entry to the Profession — Legal Education

An individual who wishes to become a lawyer must first complete at least two years of a university degree as a prerequisite for applying to law school. Most applicants, however, will have a BA degree prior to making application. Law schools consider applicants on the basis of their academic grade-point averages, together with their scores on a standardized test called the LSAT (Law School Admission Test). Many law schools give no weight to letters of reference, instead relying completely on a formula based on grade-point average and LSAT scores. There are some exceptions: mature students who may lack formal educational requirements may still be admitted. In addition, some law schools have educational-equity policies that purport to keep places available for minorities who are under-represented in the legal profession.

Once admitted to a law school, the law student undergoes three years of instruction leading to a bachelor of laws degree (LLB). During this period, the student is taught legal rules and principles in an indirect way. Rather than learning rules by rote through lectures and reading, students learn legal principles by reading case law and extracting the rule from the reasoning of the judge in the case. For example, in a contracts course, the students will learn the basic rules governing contract law from reading contract cases. In this way, students learn techniques of legal reasoning and analysis, not just a collection of legal rules (sometimes called "black-letter" law). This method of learning law is very similar to the approach used by judges and lawyers to resolve legal problems through the application of the doctrine of precedent in the common law legal system. This approach, called the case-study method, was pioneered in the United States in the 19th century at Harvard Law School. It did not become a common teaching technique in Canada until after World War II.

With the case-study method as the dominant method of instruction for three years, students are expected to learn enough about the art of legal reasoning to make tolerably good appellate judges. However, there have been criticisms from the profession that the graduates do not have enough practical skills to function as lawyers. Ontario has responded to this criticism in two ways. First, law schools have introduced more clinical programs, where students can work for a term with a practitioner or in a law clinic under a professor's supervision. Second, the Law Society requires and supervises further practical legal education by requiring students to complete one year of articles and to pass Bar admission exams focused on practice skills. The Law Society also requires students to take the Bar admission course, a series of practical courses with exams that must be passed prior to the call to the bar.

Currently, the Law Society is in the process of getting out of the business of educating law students. Instead, students may have the option of taking distance-learning courses prior to taking the Bar exam, or they may take the Bar exam directly after articling. It appears that the Law Society is attempting to shift away from direct responsibility for legal education prior to the call to the bar, expecting the law schools to take up the responsibility for providing practical training. In this writer's view, this is a vain hope. Since the end of World War II, the university-based law schools have been resisting attempts by law societies to get them to do more than approach law as an intellectual exercise. The law schools show minimal signs that they will take responsibility for producing competent practitioners, so the Law Society is likely to be left with the responsibility for practical legal training for the foreseeable future.

Students who have completed law school and have been awarded an LLB degree must decide in which province they wish to be admitted to the Bar. In Ontario, the Law Society recognizes an LLB from any of the law schools in Canada where the common law system is the basis for instruction, on completing the articling requirement, Bar admission course and testing requirements. Having cleared these last hurdles, the student of law is called to the bar as a **barrister and solicitor**.[6] Once called to the bar, the lawyer may practise in any area of law. As well, following the call to the bar, a lawyer is not subjected to any further evaluation of competence or skill unless there are complaints to the Law Society, or unless the lawyer stops functioning as

---

[6] The term "barrister and solicitor" is borrowed from English legal practice. However, in England, unlike Canada, one is either "barrister" or "solicitor", not both. In England, there are two separate and distinct professions. A barrister is an advocate who argues cases in courts; a solicitor deals with all other legal matters we think of as being

a lawyer for a number of years. A lawyer who wishes to re-enter the profession after some years of absence may have to meet some requalification requirements.

Maintenance of Professional Standards — Specialization and Certification

As noted in the preceding section, once a lawyer has been called to the bar, he or she is loosed upon the public to practise in all areas of law, without further evaluations of competence except in a narrow range of circumstances. However, the Law Society, as well as voluntary organizations such as the Canadian Bar Association, run continuing education programs that many practitioners use in order to keep abreast of changes in the law, and to specialize. Although the Law Society requires members to participate in continuing education programs or activities, there is no proposal currently to test members or to evaluate them. Further, members are expected to voluntarily report their activities, including "self-conducted" continuing education. However, lawyers who do not engage in activity where they practise or use their professional skills may be required to undertake activities to requalify themselves before being allowed to return to practice.

For those lawyers who wish to specialize in a particular area of law, there is a process for becoming certified as a specialist in an area of law, with the right to advertise that fact to the general public. The certification process requires the applicant to have practised in a particular area of law for a reasonable period of time, to take continuing-education courses in the area, and to undergo a **peer review**. There is, however, no requirement that an applicant for certification work under the supervision of a certified specialist or pass examinations, as there is for medical specialists.

Discipline and Ethical Standards

As a self-governing profession, lawyers claim to have the knowledge to decide when a fellow lawyer has fallen below the standards of appropriate professional behaviour, whether it has to do with incompetence or misbehaviour. When a lawyer has been found to have fallen below professional standards, the Law Society also claims the right to remedy the situation. It does so in three ways. First, it can discipline or punish the lawyer for misbehaviour by taking away a lawyer's right to practise, suspending the lawyer from practice, or requiring the lawyer to practise under conditions imposed by the Law Society. Second, the Law Society can compensate clients for incompetent work through its malpractice insurance fund. Third, it can repay part of a client's loss due to a lawyer's dishonesty through a compensation fund, which is separate from the malpractice insurance fund.

The discipline process begins with a complaint about a lawyer's conduct, either by a member of the public or by another lawyer. The Law Society requires a lawyer who is the subject of a complaint to respond to the complaint. If the response is not satisfactory, or if it is otherwise warranted, the Law Society can carry out further investigations. If misconduct has occurred, the Law Society can charge the lawyer with either of two offences:

part of a lawyer's business, except arguing cases in courts. Recently, this split in the English Bar has begun to change, as solicitors have been given the right to argue cases in courts in England. In Ontario and the rest of Canada, we have a unitary Bar — this means that there are no restrictions on the areas in which a lawyer may practise. In Ontario, one is simply a lawyer and is admitted to the legal profession. What is confusing is that we have hung on to English terms that describe forms of professional organization that have not existed in Ontario for more than a century. Now that paralegals are licensed by the Law Society in Ontario, by-laws and the rules of conduct often refer to "licencees" when they affect both lawyers and paralegals.

- **Professional misconduct:** Into this category fall wrongful acts by a lawyer while acting in a lawyer-like capacity. Examples include failing to perform an undertaking given to another lawyer, failing to keep a client's business confidential, and stealing a client's money. Some offences are professional offences only, but some, like stealing a client's money, are criminal acts as well. Interestingly, there are few misconduct proceedings based on mere incompetence. Penalties for professional misconduct range from a reprimand to suspension from practice, to disbarment.

- **Conduct unbecoming to a barrister and solicitor:** This refers to wrongful acts by a lawyer acting outside of her professional capacity that would bring the legal profession into disrepute. An example would include a lawyer who defrauded someone in a non-law-related business transaction, where the victim was led to trust the lawyer because of her professional standing. Penalties are as indicated for professional misconduct.

Any profession that claims to be independent and self-governing must establish publicly accepted high standards of conduct, and enforce those standards rigorously in order to keep its credibility with the public. Specific professional standards of conduct that must be met are set out in Rules of Professional Conduct.[7] (See Exhibit 10.1 for Ontario's Rules of Professional Conduct for lawyers.) The rules prescribe courses of conduct lawyers are

---

Rules of Professional Conduct for Lawyers, The Law Society of Upper Canada

EXHIBIT 10.1

AS AMENDED JULY 2011

The title of each rule with brief comments is set out below. A review of the rules will identify the concerns professional bodies have about their members' behaviour. The rules now generally refer to licencees when they refer to rules affecting both lawyers and licensed paralegals.

RULE 1: CITATION AND INTERPRETATION

This rule defines various terms including "conduct unbecoming a barrister and solicitor", "professional misconduct", and "independent legal advice". Some of these terms had not previously been precisely defined. Commentary is provided to aid in interpretation of key terms. As there are now two branches of the legal profession, the generic term "licencee" is used to describe "legal practitioners" who may be either paralegals or lawyers licensed in Ontario. In some circumstances, legal practitioner will include a lawyer who is a member of the bar of another province.

RULE 2: RELATIONSHIP TO CLIENTS

2.01 COMPETENCE: It is now defined with some specificity, and reflects the Law Society's concern that a lawyer have all-around competence in those areas where he or she offers services to the public. Generally, lawyers should not take on work they are not competent to do. It is not expected that generalists or junior lawyers or, even, specialists will be able to provide competent service in every area of law. Lawyers who give business advice should clearly distinguish it from legal advice given to a client. This is particularly important in a multi-disciplinary practice (a firm composed of lawyers and accountants, for example) where a client may assume a lawyer may be able to give more than legal advice.

---

[7] The Law Society of Upper Canada, *Rules of Professional Conduct*, July 2011, as amended. Other law societies have similar sets of rules. The Canadian Bar Association (CBA) has a code of ethics that is similar in content to the Law Society's rules of professional conduct. However, the CBA code of ethics is not enforceable and consists of merely guidelines. The CBA is a voluntary association of lawyers and has no power over the profession.

2.02   QUALITY OF SERVICE: A lawyer is expected to be honest and objective in his or her advice, and should encourage compromise and settlement where possible; a lawyer should not threaten criminal proceedings in order to obtain an advantage in civil litigation and, in particular, to collect a debt. A lawyer is obliged to not knowingly assist a client in any dishonesty or crime, or instruct the client on how to violate the law. This includes meeting the requirements of the criminal law to report large cash receipts from clients in order to prevent money laundering by those involved in organized crime. In addition, a lawyer must verify a client's identity and understand the objectives of the retainer. A lawyer shall not use his or her trust account for any purpose not related to providing legal services. Where a lawyer has a personal, intimate or sexual relationship with a client, the lawyer must be especially careful to ensure that he or she can deal objectively and dispassionately with the client's business prior to taking on a retainer. If a client suffers from a disability that affects decision making, the lawyer shall treat the client as much as possible as he or she would a client in a normal lawyer–client relationship. If a lawyer receives a medical legal report that the doctor has asked not be shown the client, the report must be returned to the doctor, unless the lawyer has instructions to receive the report on those terms. However, if a report contains information that might cause harm to the client, the lawyer shall attempt to persuade the client not to read the report, and if the client insists, he or she should be persuaded to receive the report at the doctor's office, where its contents can be explained and medical advice given. In real estate transactions, a lawyer should advise the client of the availability of title insurance to protect the client's interest in the property; however, the lawyer should explain that this is one option, and it is not a substitute for the lawyer diligently investigating the title and advising the client. If acting for a large organization, a lawyer who becomes aware of wrongdoing or criminal conduct has a duty to "report up" to the person who instructs him or her, and if that person does not respond, to report to progressively higher officials. In the end, if no responsible employee of the organization acts, the lawyer should withdraw his or her services.

2.03   CONFIDENTIALITY: A lawyer owes a duty of confidentiality to every client, even after the relationship ends, unless disclosure is authorized by law or required by a court, or where the lawyer believes there is imminent risk of harm to others by the client. A lawyer may also make disclosure to defend himself or herself or his or her employees in criminal or civil proceedings. Where a lawyer has a corporate client, and becomes aware of wrongdoing within the corporation, he or she is obliged to draw it to the attention of senior officers of the corporation or members of the board. In the wake of the passage of federal legislation on money laundering, the rule has been amended to require lawyers to keep detailed records when receiving large amounts of cash from a client, and to disclose those records to authorities under certain conditions, notwithstanding that such reporting would otherwise violate confidentiality requirements.

2.04   AVOIDANCE OF CONFLICT OF INTEREST: A lawyer must avoid any involvement in any activity that would likely affect the lawyer's judgment or loyalty to a client. Specifically, a lawyer can only act for one side in a dispute, unless the client, adequately informed, agrees to the lawyer continuing to act. A lawyer may not act against a former client unless the matter is completely unconnected to the former matter. A lawyer's partner or associate may act in a new matter against a former client, where confidential information relevant to the former client is in issue, provided the former client consents and that measures are take to ensure that no disclosure of the confidential information takes place. Where a lawyer is retained by several clients, he or she must ensure there is no conflict between them, and if a conflict arises, he or she must withdraw from representing them. A lawyer may no longer act for a lender and borrower at the same time, except in a narrow range of situations (amount below $50,000 or the lender is a financial institution, or relatives or friends who are not at arm's length). In a real estate transaction, the transferor and transferee must be represented by different lawyers, although the lawyers may be in the same firm, provided they observe general conflict rules. Lawyers who prepare wills for spouses who have a shared and common intention about disposing of their property are jointly retained by both spouses; if one spouse later gives new instructions, that is a new retainer and the lawyer may not notify the other spouse of the request, but must also decline the retainer because it creates a potential conflict of interest. Lawyers who act for corporations and organizations must keep in mind that the interest of the organization or corporation may be different from that of those who direct and control it, and that the organization or corporation is the client that the lawyer is to serve if there is a conflict. The same duty applies if the lawyer is a director of an organization or corporation. There may be an obligation to report wrongdoing of corporate and organizational officers in this context. Where a lawyer is affiliated with others who are not lawyers in offering legal services, as in a multi-disciplinary practice, the lawyer must clearly disclose to clients possible loss of solicitor–client privilege due to (i) involvement of non-lawyers working with the lawyer, and (ii) any financial arrangement between the lawyer and affiliated entity that may affect the lawyer's professional judgment. After making disclosure to the client on all aspects of the affiliation, the lawyer must obtain the client's explicit consent to accept the retainer. The lawyer must also have a system to search for conflict of interest of the affiliation. The lawyer shall take all steps to ensure that non-lawyers in a multi-disciplinary practice observe confidentiality. Generally all law firms are required to have systems set up to prevent disclosure of confidential information. To prevent mortgage fraud, a lawyer is obliged to assure himself or herself of the identity of a client and to take special care when acting on behalf of a borrower and a lender. The Law Society now requires that lawyers and paralegals take specific steps to verify a new client's identity. In certain limited circumstances, a lawyer may act for the transferor and transferee of real property: for examples, when the parties are related, or when the lawyer is providing service in a remote location where there are no other lawyers.

2.05   CONFLICTS FROM TRANSFER BETWEEN LAW FIRMS: When a lawyer leaves a firm that acted for a client, and moves to a firm that is acting against that client, and the transferring lawyer possesses actual knowledge of matters harmful to the client, the firm to which the lawyer has transferred shall cease to act in a matter in which the client's interests may be harmed unless the client consents. This rule also applies to transferring employees, in that lawyers are expected to exercise due diligence and make inquiries of new employees to ensure the rule is not violated. Where a law firm is a multi jurisdiction firm, it is treated as if it is one firm for the purpose of this rule. The rule also applies to transfers to and from corporations, as in-house counsel, and to transfers involving government departments as transferring firm or transferee firm.

2.06   DOING BUSINESS WITH A CLIENT: A lawyer who enters into business transactions with clients put himself or herself in a conflict of interest situation. The lawyer is obliged to disclose and explain the potential conflict, must require independent legal representation in the transaction, and recommend that the client receive independent legal advice. If the client wishes the lawyer to continue to act, then the lawyer must obtain the client's written consent. A lawyer shall not borrow from a client, unless the client is a lending institution or a related person. A lawyer shall not invest in mortgages from which the client is borrowing or lending money, subject to some exceptions. Nor shall a lawyer give a guarantee on a loan transaction where the client is a borrower or lender.

2.07   PRESERVATION OF CLIENT'S PROPERTY: A lawyer shall care for a client's property in a careful and prudent manner and observe all relevant rules in safeguarding the client's property and interests in property.

2.08   FEES AND DISBURSEMENTS: Fees shall be reasonable, and interest on overdue accounts shall be in accordance with the *Solicitors Act*. The lawyer shall not acquire an interest in the subject matter of litigation. Contingency fees may now be charged except in criminal and family law matters. Any contingency agreement must be clear as to how the fee is calculated, and indicate that it may be reviewed by the court. In rendering accounts the lawyer shall separate fees from disbursements, and shall divide fees fairly when acting for several clients. A lawyer who refers a matter to another lawyer or paralegal may accept a referral fee if it is reasonable and the client consents. A paralegal may also refer a matter to a lawyer and accept a referral fee. Where a client consents, fees may be divided between licencees in different firms, provided the fee is divided in proportion to the work done by each licencee. Lawyers shall not split fees with non-licencees or pay a referral fee to anyone who is not a licencee. However, in multi-disciplinary firms, lawyers may split fees with non-licencees in the firm, or share with non-licencees the general revenue and cash flow of a multi-disciplinary firm.

2.09   WITHDRAWAL FROM REPRESENTATION: A lawyer may not withdraw services except where there is a serious loss of confidence between the parties, the lawyer cannot obtain instructions, or the client has not paid fees. In a criminal matter, and in some other situations, the right to withdraw may be subject to court review and supervision. A lawyer must withdraw if fired by the client, if told by the client to do something that conflicts with the lawyer's duty as officer of the court, if the client is engaged in dishonesty in the proceeding, or if the lawyer is not competent to handle the matter. On withdrawal, the lawyer is responsible for minimizing hardship to the client. This includes returning all client property, providing the client with necessary information, accounting for all funds, promptly rendering an account, and co-operating with the lawyer the client retains. When giving reasons to a court for withdrawing, the lawyer must not breach the obligation to the client to maintain confidentiality.

RULE 3: THE PRACTICE OF LAW

3.01   MAKING LEGAL SERVICES AVAILABLE: A lawyer shall make services available to the public in an effective and convenient way; a lawyer may decline to take on a particular client, but the right to do so should be exercised prudently.

3.02 and *3.03*   MARKETING and ADVERTISING: This is permitted if it is "tasteful" and does not compare rates charged by other firms. Fees may be advertised but the advertisement shall contain an accurate statement of amounts, including disbursements and taxes, and service at that price must be made available to all clients. A lawyer may advertise that he or she is a certified specialist if that is true, and a lawyer may advertise that he or she restricts the practice of law to specific areas of law. If the firm is multi-disciplinary (containing accountants, for example) that fact may be advertised. Offering professional services may be done by any means in a reasonable way that does not exploit or take advantage of clients who are vulnerable due to traumatic events that affect their physical or mental state.

3.04   INTERPROVINCIAL LAW FIRMS: A lawyer may agree with other lawyers elsewhere to form an interprovincial law firm, but the firm's members who practise in Ontario shall be governed by the Law Society, and the firm shall not permit members who are not authorized to practise in Ontario to practise law here.

RULE 4: RELATIONSHIP TO THE ADMINISTRATION OF JUSTICE

4.01   THE LAWYER AS ADVOCATE: Generally, the lawyer shall resolutely defend the client's interest, but shall not permit the client to mislead the court or engage in dishonest conduct in connection with the proceeding; nor shall the lawyer behave discourteously to opponents, witnesses or the court. In civil matters, the lawyer shall ensure that the client makes full disclosure on discovery, and that errors and omissions are corrected, and that undertakings to provide information are honoured. The lawyer shall act prudently in arranging and negotiating a plea bargain with a prosecutor in a criminal matter. The lawyer shall scrupulously honour all undertakings given to a party or to the court.

4.02   THE LAWYER AS WITNESS: A lawyer who is appearing as advocate shall not submit his own affidavit in evidence or give oral evidence unless otherwise required by law to do so or the evidence is of a non-controversial nature.

4.03   INTERVIEWING WITNESSES: A lawyer may interview anyone as a witness; however, a lawyer must not approach a person represented by another lawyer or a corporation where there is in-house counsel, except by going through the lawyer for the person or corporation, or where a client is seeking a second opinion of a lawyer or paralegal.

4.04   COMMUNICATING WITH WITNESSES GIVING EVIDENCE: A lawyer may not engage in conversations with a witness, particularly one favourable to his or her cause, where the conversation might influence or direct the witness as to what evidence the witness should give. This rule now specifically identifies the circumstances where a lawyer may or may not discuss a witness's evidence. The rule distinguishes between talking to "friendly" and opposing witnesses, and is generally designed to prevent a lawyer from tampering with a witnesses evidence. When there is any

**Rules of Professional Conduct for Lawyers,
The Law Society of Upper Canada**
AS AMENDED JULY 2011

EXHIBIT 10.1 (continued)

doubt, a lawyer wishing to speak to a witness should get the consent of opposing counsel or of the court.

4.05   COMMUNICATIONS WITH JURORS: A lawyer shall not communicate with anyone he or she knows to be a member of a jury panel.

4.06   THE LAWYER AND THE ADMINISTRATION OF JUSTICE: The lawyer shall encourage public respect for the administration of justice.

4.07   LAWYERS AS MEDIATORS: A lawyer who acts as a mediator shall tell participants that he or she is not acting in his or her capacity as a lawyer, and that the mediation is not protected by solicitor–client privilege.

RULE 5: RELATIONSHIP TO STUDENTS, EMPLOYEES AND OTHERS

5.01   SUPERVISION: The lawyer is responsible for ensuring that diskettes used to access the provincial online land registration system are kept secure and that the lawyer supervises the use of diskettes assigned to non-lawyer employees, and in general assumes complete responsibility for all work on the file. A lawyer shall not permit a non-lawyer to advise a client on title insurance, and a lawyer must take full responsibility for electronically signing documents.

5.02   STUDENTS: Lawyers shall observe procedures of the Law Society in recruiting students, and provide them with a meaningful articling experience. A student shall carry out in good faith all duties required by the articling principal.

5.03   SEXUAL HARASSMENT: Lawyers shall not harass colleagues, staff, students, clients or any other person.

5.04   DISCRIMINATION: Lawyers have special responsibility not to discriminate in providing services and offering employment. A detailed commentary sets out the grounds for discrimination. There is a further provision imposing requirements on lawyers to take steps to ensure that there is no discrimination in employment within a firm, with a particular focus on accommodation of disabilities.

RULE 6: RELATIONSHIP TO THE SOCIETY AND OTHER LAWYERS

6.01   RESPONSIBILITY TO THE PROFESSION GENERALLY: The lawyer shall conduct himself with integrity, and promptly meet financial obligations, including financial obligations incurred on behalf of clients. The lawyer has a duty to report misconduct by other lawyers, including criminal charges, and encourage clients who have claims against dishonest lawyers to report the claims.

6.02   RESPONSIBILITY TO THE LAW SOCIETY: A lawyer shall respond promptly to all communications from the Law Society.

6.03   RESPONSIBILITY TO LAWYERS AND OTHERS: A lawyer is responsible for behaving with courtesy and good faith in his or her professional dealings, and is not to engage in sharp practice. In particular, the lawyer shall not record a conversation with another lawyer, or a client, without giving notice of the intention to do so. A lawyer shall not communicate with a represented person unless that person's legal representative consents. A lawyer, who is not otherwise interested in a matter, may give a second opinion if retained to do so by the client's legal representative. The rule has been refined to indicate certain persons within an organization or entity, such as a corporation, with whom an opposing lawyer may not communicate. It, therefore, follows that other persons within the organization may be approached. The rule tries to strike a balance between protecting privileged information and requiring an entity to produce relevant information.

6.04   OUTSIDE INTERESTS AND THE PRACTICE OF LAW: A lawyer who engages in another business besides his or her law practice shall not allow participation in the other business to jeopardize professional integrity.

6.05   THE LAWYER IN PUBLIC OFFICE: A lawyer in public office shall carry out official duties adhering to standards as high as those that govern him or her professionally. Where a lawyer or an associate is a member of a public body, the lawyer shall not appear before that body unless its rules permit. When a lawyer leaves public office, he or she shall not act for a client in any matter for which the lawyer has responsibility before leaving public office.

6.06   PUBLIC APPEARANCES AND PUBLIC STATEMENT: A lawyer is free to make public statements subject to obligations to clients, the profession and the courts. In particular, the lawyer shall not make statements about a matter before a tribunal that would detrimentally affect the right to a fair hearing.

6.07   PREVENTING UNAUTHORIZED PRACTICE: The lawyer shall assist in preventing the unauthorized practice of law, and shall not associate in his or her practice with anyone who has been disbarred or suspended by the Law Society from the practice of law. Obligations that must be observed by suspended lawyers are set out.

6.08   RETIRED JUDGES RETURNING TO PRACTICE: Appellate judges shall not return to practice without the express consent of Convocation. Judges of lower courts may not appear before their former judicial colleagues or before lower courts for a period of two years. A committee of convocation must know, review, and approve a retired judge's application to be re-admitted as a licencee to practice law.

6.09   ERRORS AND OMISSIONS: Where a lawyer discovers possible errors and omissions in his or her own work for a client, the lawyer must inform the client, advise the client to get separate legal advice, and must advise the insurer. A commentary to this rule now sets out a step-by-step protocol that a lawyer must follow with a client when a possible error or omission has occurred.

6.10   RESPONSIBILITY IN MULTI-DISCIPLINE PRACTICES: A lawyer in a multi-discipline practice must ensure that non-lawyers comply with these rules.

6.11   DISCIPLINE: A lawyer is subject to discipline by the Society no matter where the conduct occurs, and the lawyer can be disciplined for professional misconduct or for conduct unbecoming a lawyer.

expected to follow in certain situations, and describe forms of conduct that are prohibited. In addition, there are also general requirements of integrity and competence to which the practitioner is expected to adhere. There is some variation in ethical rules from province to province. For example, contingency fees, where a lawyer charges the client no fee if he or she loses, and takes a percentage of the judgment if he or she wins, have long been considered improper in Ontario, in most cases, but are generally permissible in Alberta.

In addition to the rules of conduct administered by law societies, the Canadian Bar Association, a voluntary association, also has its own code of ethics. The difference between the CBA code of ethics and the rules of professional conduct of the law societies is that the law societies' rules are binding, while the CBA codes are not. There are other differences in the actual rules as well.

Legal Aid

Before the 1960s, in most provinces, a client wishing to retain a lawyer was free to do so, provided he or she could pay for the lawyer's services. There were some exceptions, particularly in serious criminal cases where the death penalty was a possibility, where the court would appoint counsel, at no charge, to serve a client. In other cases, where there was perceived to be a crying need for justice, a lawyer might serve a deserving client *pro bono publico* and charge no fee because the issue before the court was important. However, for most civil lawsuits and less serious criminal matters, a client could either pay a lawyer or represent herself.

Lawyers often say that "a lawyer who represents himself has a fool for a client." The truth behind this is that even a skilled lawyer will have difficulty exercising his judgment coolly, objectively, and dispassionately when the lawyer is personally involved in the case. One might well ask how a layperson, not trained in the law and lacking dispassionate judgment about her own situation, will do when arguing her own case? The answer is that except in minor and simple matters, the skilled help of a lawyer is necessary if justice is to be done.

The lofty notion of equal justice under law only applied if those seeking justice had the money to pay for it. As a judge once observed, "The law is like the Ritz Hotel. Anyone who can pay for a room is welcome to stay there."

In order to ensure that there was equal access to the judicial process, the provinces, starting in the 1960s, brought in programs to pay for legal services for those who could not afford a lawyer. The Ontario Legal Aid Plan, introduced in 1967, was typical of these plans.

Before 1998, the Ontario Legal Aid Plan was funded in part by the government and in part from interest paid on money held in trust by private law firms for their clients. In this sense, private clients provided a subsidy to legal aid clients. The legal aid plan was administered by the Law Society, not by the government. This gave the legal profession more control over the plan than it otherwise might have. When the plan was first introduced, there was some resistance from the private Bar, where some feared they would lose business to the plan. Administrative control by the Law Society helped allay some of those fears, especially as the government supplied most of the funding for the plan's operation.

In 1998, the Law Society agreed to transfer its control and administration of the Legal Aid Plan to a public corporation set up by the Ontario government. The primary reason for this was the Law Society's disinclination to administer a system over which it had lost control due to government funding cutbacks. The funding cutbacks caused disagreements on how the plan should be run among several factions among the benchers and members. It also appeared that the Law Society might not be able to run the plan in the public interest without alienating many participating members of the Bar or the general public.

The new public corporation is funded primarily by the government, and its activities are much more likely to be affected by government control and fiscal considerations. Some benchers have voiced fears that the Legal Aid Plan will be influenced by political considerations that will override the objective task of providing equal access for clients of modest means to the justice system. There is also a fear that the corporation will abandon the certificate system (see next section) in its search for cheaper, more impersonal, assembly line justice, where client needs come second to operating an inexpensive legal aid system, and where the independent judgment of lawyers in serving their clients will be compromised.

The Certificate System

There are two payment schemes under the Ontario plan. The first scheme requires clients, with a legal problem who cannot afford to hire a lawyer, to prove to the legal aid plan that they qualify for legal aid; upon doing so, the plan will issue them a legal aid certificate. This is like a modified blank cheque — it provides payment for services to any lawyer prepared to accept the person with the certificate.

A client may then take the certificate to any lawyer who will accept their case by accepting the certificate. When a lawyer accepts the certificate, the lawyer agrees to be paid by legal aid at the legal aid rate, which is often much less than the fee paid to that lawyer by a non-legal aid client. The lawyer and client will then have a lawyer–client relationship that is the same as it would be for a non-legal aid client, except that legal aid will pay the legal fees.

The certificate system has some shortcomings. First, the cuts in government funding have caused legal aid to greatly reduce the number of certificates issued. Those involved in civil matters, including some family law matters, and those charged with less serious criminal offences rarely have certificates granted to them. Second, even where a certificate is issued, it arguably provides second-class service to clients on legal aid. There are often limits on what services a private lawyer is allowed to provide to a legally aided client on a certificate. For some legal problems, legal aid pays so far below market rates that many lawyers have refused to take legally aided clients. For example, many lawyers refuse to take family law cases of any complexity on legal aid, which means that many individuals in need of legal services for divorce and other family law matters cannot find adequate legal representation. Last, while many young lawyers do legal aid, as they obtain more experience and fee-paying clients, they cut down or stop taking legal aid cases. The result is that relatively few experienced lawyers provide legal aid service, except in serious criminal matters. There is a sliding scale of legal aid fees based on experience, but the top of the scale is much below what an experienced lawyer would be paid by a private client. Therefore, there is little financial incentive for an experienced lawyer to participate in the legal aid system.

On the other hand, the certificate system virtually created the criminal defence Bar. Prior to legal aid, most of those accused of crimes who could not afford counsel represented themselves, often with dire results. Under legal aid, anyone who could not afford a lawyer when charged with an offence was likely to have a choice of criminal lawyers who would act under a legal aid certificate. Once lawyers were assured that someone would pay on behalf of accused criminals, it became feasible to practise criminal law on a regular basis, with the result that a growing number of lawyers developed expertise in this area. Now, however, the number and range of certificates in criminal matters has been greatly restricted.

The Clinic System

The second scheme under the legal aid plan is the legal aid clinic system. Here, instead of hiring a member of the private Bar at legal aid's expense, the client attends a legal aid clinic and receives legal services from clinic lawyers and staff. The clinics are funded by legal aid, and focus their attention on those whose legal problems or income preclude them from having access to the private Bar. For example, much of the legal activity in the poverty law area (public assistance, government-sponsored benefits, landlord and tenant) has been done by legal aid clinics that specialize in these kinds of legal problems, and often have staff with more expertise than most private law firms. It has been argued, with some justification, that legal aid clinics have done more to advance the legal interests of the poor and less powerful members of society than the private Bar has, simply because the clinics have been mandated to advance the law in this area and have developed the expertise to do it. By contrast, the private Bar has paid little or no attention to poverty law because people with problems in this area did not use lawyers for the obvious reason that they could not afford the services of a lawyer.

As the cost of running the legal aid system increases, it is likely that efforts will be made to increase the use of clinical services at the expense of the certificate system, because clinics are thought to deliver services in a less expensive way. There is a counter-argument, however, that the quality of service may not be as high in the clinics because the caseload may be too high; as a result, clients get a more bureaucratized form of service than they would receive from a private lawyer retained on a certificate. At present, Ontario Legal Aid is examining a number of new clinic pilot projects and expanded use of duty counsel. Duty counsel are present in some courts to give parties general advice and help in representing themselves, but duty counsel cannot act for clients.

The Professional Role of Lawyers

Many people retain and use lawyers without really understanding the nature of the relationship a client has with a professional such as a lawyer. Professional values often make the relationship a client has with a lawyer different from what a relationship would be with those offering other types of goods or services. Some of the important differences are discussed below.

Officer of the Court

Although a lawyer's primary duty is to his client, he also owes a duty to the court as an officer of the court. This means that where the client's interest conflicts with the lawyer's duty to the court, the client's interest must give way.

As an officer of the court, the lawyer has a duty not to deceive or mislead the court, in pursuit of the client's interest, or to otherwise contribute to perverting the course of justice.

So, while a lawyer, as an officer of the court, has a duty to fearlessly raise every issue, advance every argument, and ask every question, no matter how distasteful, a lawyer may not resort to illegal, discourteous, disrespectful, dishonest, or unfair behaviour. For example, a lawyer is expected not to advance evidence that is known to be untrue and that would have the effect of deceiving the court. If a client insists, the lawyer is caught in a peculiar conflict: on the one hand, the lawyer cannot assist the client with the deception; on the other hand, as we will see later in this chapter, the lawyer cannot inform the court the client is going to give false testimony, nor can the lawyer abandon the client. While there is some difference of opinion as to how a lawyer resolves this conflict, the general answer is that the lawyer must stop acting for the client, and then assist the client in finding a new lawyer. Although no longer acting for the client, the lawyer is obliged to keep silent and to not reveal the client's information to anyone.

The Contractual Relationship between a Lawyer and a Client

Lawyers are expected to make themselves available to any member of the public who wishes to retain their services, provided that their skills or competency meet the client's needs and that the client can pay their fees. Once **retained** by a client, lawyers are obliged to complete the work for which they were retained. Lawyers may not "fire" their client, unless the client has asked them to do something improper or illegal or refuses to pay fees or give instructions. No lawyer may refuse to act for a client merely because the client is unsavoury, unpleasant, or disreputable.

The lawyer also owes the client a duty of competence, and is obliged to keep the client informed as to the progress of work being done, answer the client's questions and, generally, provide the client with necessary information.

In general, the rule is that the lawyer advises the client, and the client gives the lawyer instructions after being advised. For example, if a lawyer receives an offer to settle a case, the lawyer is obliged to candidly discuss the offer with the client, even if it is unreasonable and not worthy of serious consideration. If a lawyer is given particular instructions by a client, the lawyer is obliged to carry them out unless it would be unlawful to do so. When a lawyer believes instructions from a client are ill-advised, the lawyer should tell the client so, and obtain the instructions in writing. A lawyer who acts on the instructions of a client, where the client claims no such instructions were given, will be found to have acted without instructions, unless the lawyer can prove otherwise. In this situation, the presumption is that the client's version of events is correct, unless the lawyer has the instructions in writing, in which case the lawyer will be able to rebut the presumption.

Unlike other contracts for service, a client is not obliged to simply pay any bill presented by a lawyer. A lawyer has an obligation to charge fairly for work done, based on the complexity of the work, the importance of the matter to the client, the degree of skill and experience of the lawyer, and the ultimate result for the client. If a client feels he or she has been overcharged, he or she may have his or her bill reviewed by an **assessment officer**. The assessment officer has the power to reduce a bill if there is overcharging. On occasion, the assessment officers have been known to reduce a bill to zero.

Confidentiality and Privilege

At the core of the lawyer–client relationship is the idea that whatever a client tells a lawyer, in the context of a lawyer–client relationship, is confidential and cannot be revealed by the lawyer to anyone without the client's consent. This is sometimes referred to as the **solicitor–client privilege**. We say that information given by a client to a lawyer is privileged. This means that third parties cannot compel either the lawyer or the client to reveal the content of communications between them. It is important to remember that the privilege is the client's, not the lawyer's. It is up to the client to decide if the privilege can be waived. The information a client gives a lawyer is privileged, even where the client admits breaking the law. As noted earlier, while a lawyer cannot assist the authorities by revealing this information, the lawyer also should not continue to act on behalf of the client, knowing the client intends to deceive the court.

Why does lawyer–client communication carry a legal privilege that is not available between doctor and patient, or priest and penitent? While doctors and priests are professionally required to not reveal things told to them in confidence, they can be compelled by a court to reveal what they were told. Lawyers cannot be compelled to reveal what their clients have told them. The usual reason given for lawyer–client privilege is that, in order to have perfect trust between a lawyer and client, and perfect frankness in their dealings, a client must be able to level with his lawyer and tell his lawyer the whole story so that a lawyer can give accurate and useful advice. If a client holds back information, the lawyer is prevented from effectively serving the client. Of course, similar arguments could be made in favour of doctors and priests, but they do not seem to have been taken as seriously by the courts as have the arguments for lawyer–client privilege.

LAW CLERKS

Many of the functions traditionally performed by lawyers can be performed by trained laypersons, working under a lawyer's supervision. Individuals who do this kind of work are called law clerks or legal assistants. Over the past

20 years, the number of persons employed as law clerks has increased dramatically, and this occupation continues to expand, as lawyers in both the private and public sectors discover that their operations can be more cost effective if some of their work is delegated to others.

Nature of the Work

Law clerks are employed in private law firms, government, corporations, banks, and insurance companies. In large firms or specialized operations, law clerks, like lawyers, specialize — a law clerk may do only corporate work, litigation, real estate, or wills and estates. In smaller, general practice firms, they may do a bit of everything. While a law clerk is supervised by lawyers, he or she is expected to use analytic skills, creativity and imagination; to work independently; to be a good problem solver, and to communicate well with other staff and clients, both orally and in writing. Numeracy skills are also important.

There are some changes in the nature of the work indicated by some emerging trends. Where a law firm has a large and complex case, it may hire law clerks, on a contract basis, with some of the work being administrative. Foreign-language skills are also becoming important as law firms go international.

Training and Qualifications

There are two career routes to becoming a law clerk. Some people start as legal secretaries, and advance into a legal assistant's position by learning the skills on the job. In some places, there are part-time courses in the evenings that provide some academic content in support of work experience. The other route to a law clerk's position is to attend a community college program, usually two years in length (full-time), where a student is taught law and procedure. Such programs usually have a work-experience component. Because language is the basic tool of law, law clerks must have excellent language skills, whichever way they train.

Ethics and Licensing

Because a law clerk works under the supervision of a lawyer as a lawyer's agent, the law clerk is bound by many of the ethical rules that bind a lawyer. For example, as a lawyer must keep a client's business confidential, so must that lawyer's law clerk.

While a law clerk is not a licensed occupation, law societies have expressed concerns about the scope of activity allowed to law clerks and other non-lawyers engaged by a lawyer to assist in the provision of legal services. With the licensing of paralegals, the boundaries of permissible activities have been further defined to ensure that non-lawyers are not performing functions that may only be performed by lawyers and licensed paralegals. By-Law

---

A Typical Day for a Law Clerk	EXHIBIT 10.2

A typical day for a generalist law clerk in a small general practice firm might begin at 9:00 a.m. The clerk opens and reviews mail, dictating answers to some letters. Next, the clerk may interview a client to obtain information to draft a statement of claim, and then draft the statement of claim for the lawyer's approval. In the afternoon, the clerk may complete a house purchase using the electronic registration system. The courthouse to file documents and check the trial list, and then meet with the supervising lawyer to discuss matters to be dealt with the next day.

7.1 sets out the rules governing permissible and impermissible conduct (impermissible conduct was formerly set out in the Rules of Professional Conduct for lawyers). In general, By-Law 7.1 requires that lawyers closely supervise the work of their non-lawyer staff. Specifically, law clerks and other non-licencees are prohibited from the following:

- Taking instructions from clients or giving undertakings on behalf of a lawyer, unless the lawyer is closely supervising the work

- Giving legal advice to clients

- Negotiating with third parties without the client's specific approval and without the lawyer's supervising the process

- Signing or sending correspondence, other than on routine or administrative matters, unless it is reviewed by a lawyer

- Using the lawyer's personalized diskette to access the online real property registration system

- Appearing as advocates (the Law Society now requires non-lawyers employed by lawyers who appear before tribunals and lower courts to be licensed paralegals, unless the appearance is limited to routine or administrative matters, such as setting dates for trial in criminal courts)

- Sending collection letters on behalf of a client, unless reviewed by a lawyer

In general, these rules do not so much limit what a law clerk may do as impose a great deal of responsibility on a lawyer to closely oversee and supervise the work done by unlicensed non-lawyer employees.

With paralegals being recognized as a licensed professional group and with the restriction on advocacy work for law clerks, the Institute of Law Clerks, a voluntary association representing the interests of law clerks, has been clamouring for recognition and similar treatment. It is not hard to understand why. Professional standing will likely raise occupational status and income. It might also help to safeguard the scope of permissible activity for law clerks — as noted, the right to appear as advocates in lower courts and tribunals has been curtailed for law clerks in favour of paralegals.

Notwithstanding the limits on the activity of law clerks set out in By-Law 7.1, there is much that law clerks can do, depending on the nature of the law practice.

In a general practice, the work of law clerks will mirror the range of work done by lawyers in general practice. Here, law clerks may do legal research, write legal and factual memoranda for the supervising lawyer, and draft routine court documents, contracts, agreements, wills, and other legal documents in accordance with a lawyer's directions. Clerks may also interview clients and witnesses, attend to routine correspondence, carry out land-title searches and other types of searches using public electronic and paper registration systems. In addition, law clerks may also do some secretarial work, the law firm's bookkeeping and routine collection work for the law firm's unpaid fees.

In large firms or in smaller "law boutiques" where lawyers are specialized, law clerks also tend to be specialized. In a real estate practice, law clerks handle routine matters involving transactions for the purchase and sale of land, prepare transfers and other title documents, search public records to verify the seller's right to sell, and complete purchase and sale transactions.

Corporate and commercial law clerks prepare and draft documents to incorporate businesses, keep corporate records up-to-date, handle routine correspondence, draft contracts and financial documents, and attend to the purchase and sale of businesses.

Law clerks working in the probate and estate law areas are concerned with the administration of the estates of deceased persons. Clerks may collect information, inventory property, prepare estate taxation documents and estate accounts, draft wills from instructions, and generally attend to routine estate administration.

Law clerks working with litigation lawyers collect information from clients, interview witnesses, draft court documents and some correspondence, research legal questions, and sometimes appear in the lower courts on routine or administrative matters.

PARALEGALS

Unlike law clerks, paralegals are non-lawyers who are licensed by the Law Society to offer advocacy services directly to the public without supervision by a lawyer. Historically, paralegals developed as an occupational group to appear in courts where non-lawyer agents could appear. As the number of paralegals increased and their scope of practice expanded, the Law Society tried to restrict paralegal activity. From the 1980s until 2005, there were a series of legal actions, task forces, and commissions examining whether or not paralegals should be given recognition, and if so how they should be regulated.[8]

The Law Society report, which finally accepted the legal existence of paralegals and their regulation by the Law Society, set the stage for government action to license paralegals. In 2005, the government introduced the *Access to Justice Act, 2005*. Schedule C of the Act amends *The Law Society Act* to give the Law Society the power to regulate all aspects of the provision of legal services by paralegals in 2007.

As a result, there are changes to the Law Society's governing structure. Two paralegal benchers will be added to Convocation (consisting of 40 lawyers and 8 non-lawyer benchers), which is the main governing body of the profession. Convocation will also have a permanent standing committee on paralegals that will consist of five paralegals, five lawyer benchers and three lay benchers. The Attorney General will initially appoint the paralegals; the Law Society will appoint the benchers. Once the paralegals become licensed, they will elect their own members to this committee and to Convocation, as lawyers do.

All paralegals will now have to be licensed. Licencees will have to complete an approved college training program, pass a licensing exam, and be of "good character".

Scope of Practice   Paralegals are advocates and may appear in Small Claims Court, the Ontario Court of Justice under the *Provincial Offences Act*, and on summary conviction criminal offences where the maximum term of imprisonment is no more than six months. They may also appear before administrative tribunals, including the Financial Services Commission of Ontario in respect of no-fault auto insurance claims. Federal tribunals may regulate who appears before them and may

---

8   See *R. v. Lawrie and POINTTS* (1987) 59 O.R. (2d) 161 (Ont. C.A.); Ontario Task Force On Paralegals, *Report of the Task Force on Paralegals* prepared for the Ontario Ministry of the Attorney General (Toronto, Ont.: Queen's Printer, 1990) [The Ianni Commission Report]; Hon. P. de C. Cory, "A framework for Regulating Paralegal Practice" (31 May 2000); *A Consultation Document on a Proposed Regulatory Framework*, Law Society Report to Convocation, 25 April 2002.

permit those who are not licensed paralegals to appear. Immigration consultants, for example, who appear on immigration appeal matters, are governed by the Canadian Society of Immigration Consultants and do not have to be licensed paralegals. Further, being a licensed paralegal, by itself, does not guarantee a right to appear before a federal tribunal. A paralegal will still have to meet whatever standard a federal board sets in order to appear before it.

As part of being advocates, paralegals may perform some related functions. They may give legal advice, draft documents and negotiate settlements in connection to any proceeding in any forum where they are entitled to appear. Paralegals may not, however, offer non-advocacy services; they are not permitted to do traditional solicitor's work, such as preparing wills, administering estates, incorporating companies, preparing partnership agreements or separation agreements, or doing uncontested divorces.

Licensing

The Law Society now has the authority to issue paralegal licences and has determined what standards an individual must meet to obtain a licence. Not everyone who offers advocacy services will require a licence. The following fall outside of the provisions of the *Law Society Act* and do not require a licence:

- Persons who represent themselves, or appear occasionally to assist a friend or family member without charge
- Persons who carry on a business where they are governed by an Act of Parliament or the Legislature that specifically regulates their activities
- An employee or volunteer representative of a trade union who appears at labour arbitrations or in proceedings before the labour board

There are also individuals who are exempted by Law Society by-law:

- In-house paralegals employed by a single employer
- Employees of legal aid clinics
- Aboriginal court workers
- Staff of the Worker Advisor and Employer Advisor under the *Workplace Safety and Insurance Board*
- MPP constituency assistants
- Labour union staff representing members in compensation matters or representing retirees who were union members, and those representing families at Coroner's Inquests
- Certain members of regulated professions, such as architects, real property appraisers, and human resources officers who, as part of their duties, appear as advocates from time to time before provincial tribunals

Aside from these exceptions, the Law Society's position appears to be that other professionals who appear in courts and tribunals that are within the scope of a paralegal's permitted area of practice will have to be licensed.[9]

Two Paralegal Licensing Streams

An existing professional group facing licensing for the first time encounters a unique problem. Existing practitioners are already out there doing the work; they have learned the skills in a variety of ways and have varying

---

[9] This is a general description of exempt classes. A more detailed description is in By-Law 4 and on the Law Society website. As there is likely to be further changes in who or who is not exempt in the next few years, it is advisable to refer to the website for a detailed update (<www.lsu.org>; follow the link to "paralegals" and "licensing").

levels of expertise. Licensing them involves verifying their paralegal skills and good character so that the licensing body is satisfied that they are competent to practise as paralegals. After the pre-licensing paralegals have been accounted for, new entrants to the profession without previous professional experience will be subjected to a different licensing regime, one that prescribes a detailed educational program prior to licensing.

Here is how the Law Society's licensing regime works:

- *Grandparented applicants*: Those who had been working as paralegals for at least three years in the last five years at the time the licensing regime was established in May 2007 are considered to be **grandparented**. This means that they are licensed without formal education and training that will be required of later applicants. Grandparented applicants had to apply for a licence by October 31, 2007, and if of "good character" their names were registered as paralegal candidates. They then had to write a qualifying exam before May 2008. If the grandparented applicants completed this process and showed evidence that they were insured for malpractice, they were licensed.

- *Transitional applicants*: Those who at the time of the establishment of the licensing process were not eligible to be grandfathered and who applied between November 1, 2007, and June 30, 2010, were licensed if they graduated from a Ministry of Training, Colleges and Universities-approved paralegal college diploma program within 3 years of making application, met the good character requirements, passed the licensing exam, and showed evidence of having necessary malpractice insurance.

- *Post-transitional applicants:* Those who apply after July 1, 2010, must have graduated from a Law Society certified college paralegal program, provide evidence of good character, pass the licensing exam, and show evidence of having malpractice insurance. Ministry-approved paralegal programs will now have to be certified by the Law Society; Seneca and Algonquin Colleges were the first to be certified in June 2008, and others have since followed.

Once this regime is in place, paralegals will have a regulatory regime much like that for lawyers. This should not be a surprise because the professions are similar, as are the regulatory issues regarding protection of the public and maintenance of professional standards. Paralegals will have to be insured, maintain trust accounts for retainers and client's other funds, restrict themselves to the permitted areas of practice, and, generally, adhere to the Paralegal Rules of Professional Conduct, a summary of which is set out in Exhibit 10.3. You will note how similar these rules are to the professional conduct rules for lawyers in Exhibit 10.1.

COURT ADMINISTRATION STAFF

Nature of the Work   Court administration staff work in courts and administrative tribunals. Their primary duties are to provide services in courtrooms as clerk-recorders, court monitors and court reporters. They also staff court offices, overseeing the management of court files, ensuring procedural steps are properly followed and, in general, managing case files and the pre-trial process. In addition, some staff are employed in institutional maintenance roles, dealing with court employees, budget, physical resources, and planning. Staff must have a detailed knowledge of court or tribunal operations and court or tribunal rules of procedure. In particular, they must be able to understand, interpret and

EXHIBIT 10.3

Paralegal Rules of Conduct,
The Law Society of Upper Canada
AS AMENDED MARCH 2011

RULE 1: CITATION AND INTERPRETATION

1.01 and 1.02   DEFINES TERMS, RECOGNIZES TWO CLASSES OF LICENCES: Lawyers and paralegals. Paralegals recognized as being able to operate as sole proprietorships, partnerships, or limited liability corporations, as lawyers do.

1.03   STANDARDS OF PARALEGALS: Paralegals have a duty to provide legal services to clients and are expected to act honourably and with integrity towards clients, courts and tribunals, the public and other paralegals. Paralegals must recognize the diversity of Ontario's population and act to protect the dignity of individuals and to respect human rights laws. The purpose of the Rules is to express the high standards expected of paralegals and describe how they may be disciplined. Paralegals are expected to respect the rules in spirit as well as to the letter.

RULE 2: PROFESSIONALISM

2.01   INTEGRITY AND CIVILITY: Paralegals shall conduct themselves so as to maintain the integrity of the profession and make legal services available in an efficient and convenient way compatible with the integrity and independence of the profession. This includes acting in good faith and with civility. A paralegal who engages in other activities or holds public office must not allow those activities to compromise or impair the integrity or standards of the profession. A paralegal who acts as a mediator must make clear that he or she cannot act as a representative of either party.

2.02   UNDERTAKINGS: An undertaking is a personal promise from a paralegal; it should be given and confirmed in writing where possible, and must be honoured. Undertakings that cannot be honoured should not be given.

2.03   HARASSMENT AND DISCRIMINATION: The *Human Rights Code* applies to these rules and the profession. A paralegal shall not engage in sexual harassment or harassment under any of the prohibited grounds in the Code with respect to clients, other paralegals, their clients or other members of the public. A paralegal shall not discriminate against others under any of the provisions of the Code with respect to employment or the provision of services to the public.

RULE 3: DUTY TO CLIENTS

3.01   COMPETENCE: A paralegal shall not offer services to the public that he or she is not competent to perform. If a paralegal discovers that work for a client is beyond his or her competence, he or she must inform the client promptly and obtain the client's consent to obtain the advice and assistance of a licencee (another paralegal or a lawyer) who is competent to do the work. A competent paralegal is one who knows general legal principles and the law and procedure in the area where the paralegal provides services. The competent paralegal is able to investigate facts, identify issues, determine client objectives and, on that basis, advise clients as to their options; the competent paralegal implements the client's instructions. In this connection, the paralegal will know how to do legal research, analyze the issues, apply the law to the facts, write and draft appropriate documents, negotiate and know alternate dispute resolution (ADR) techniques, and possess the necessary advocacy skills. In addition, the paralegal is expected to work diligently and in a cost effective way on behalf of the client, meet all deadlines, respond promptly to client questions, manage the practice effectively, and meet changing standards, and changes in the law. In this connection a paralegal is expected to engage in continuing legal education as part of keeping up with the demands of his or her practice.

3.02   ADVISING CLIENTS: A paralegal shall give honest and candid advice and shall not knowingly assist in dishonesty, fraud or crime on behalf of clients, taking care not to become the dupe of a client. If the paralegal discovers an institutional client engaging in dishonesty, fraud, or crime, the paralegal shall draw this to the attention of progressively senior officers of the organization; and if the impropriety is not corrected, the paralegal must withdraw under Rule 3.08.   A paralegal shall not take on work outside the ordinary scope of his or her practice. A paralegal shall try to settle a client's case and not litigate for the sake of litigating and will advise the client of ADR options. If a client has a disability, the paralegal shall provide as normal a paralegal–client relationship as possible. If the client appears to be unable to manage his or her affairs, the paralegal shall take steps to see to the appointment of an appropriate representative. If a paralegal receives a medical-legal report on behalf of a client that contains a provision that it not be shown to a client, it is to be returned and no copy made, unless there are instructions from the client to receive a report on that basis. If a report contains information that might be harmful to the client, the paralegal shall attempt to dissuade the client from seeing the report, but it must be shown to the client if the latter insists, but the paralegal can insist the client attend at the doctor's office to see the report.

In the event the paralegal discovers an error or omission in the provision of legal services to a client, he or she must inform the client, advise the client to seek legal advice with respect to the consequences of the error and immediately inform the errors and omissions insurer. If a client speaks French, he or she must be advised of language rights under the *French Language Services Act*. If a paralegal acts on matters involving statutory automobile insurance benefits, in addition to complying with licence requirements, he or she must also comply with the regulations imposed under the *Insurance Act*.

3.03 CONFIDENTIALITY: The paralegal shall keep strictly confidential anything told to him or her by a client and shall not reveal the information to anyone unless required by law. All client documents shall be kept safe and out of sight of anyone not entitled to see them. If a paralegal has information that indicates there may be serious harm to the health or safety of others, that may justify disclosure. A paralegal is also entitled to disclose client information in some circumstances where he or she is alleged to be criminally or civilly liable or guilty of professional misconduct as a result of a client's affairs or activity. A paralegal may also disclose client information in order to collect a debt for unpaid fees. However, no more information should be disclosed than is necessary in those circumstances.

3.04 CONFLICTS OF INTEREST: Paralegals are not to represent both sides in a dispute and may not act for a client where there is a conflict of interest with the paralegal unless the client is informed and consents. A paralegal may not act against a client a paralegal previously represented, if the paralegal has relevant knowledge from a previous retainer. However, a paralegal's partner may act against a former client of the paralegal, if the party consents, and if there are suitable safeguards to prevent the partner from obtaining information about the client from the other paralegal. Paralegals who act for more than one client on a matter must advise clients that information from one client is shared with all and that there is no confidentiality between the clients and the paralegal. If a paralegal has a continuing relationship with one joint client, the other must be advised of that fact. If a contentious matter arises between joint clients, the paralegal may have to transfer one or both of the clients to avoid a conflict of interest depending on the circumstances, although the rule also allows join client to mediate the dispute without the paralegal having to terminate the retainer. The joint client rule is also more relaxed where the clients are deemed to be sophisticated. If the paralegal is in a multi-disciplinary practice or offers legal and other non-legal services through affiliated enmities, confidentiality rules apply to non-licencees and with respect to affiliated, non-legal services in respect of a client.

3.05 CONFLICTS OF INTEREST — TRANSFERS: If a paralegal transfers from one firm to another, and has information about a former client which creates a conflict with a client in the new firm, the new firm must cease to act for its client, unless the client of the transferring paralegal consents, or unless the new firm can show that adequate safeguards will prevent confidential information about the client of the transferring paralegal reaching the new firm. A transferring paralegal may not disclose confidential information about a former client to the new firm, and no paralegal in the new firm can discuss its client's affairs with the transferring paralegal. If the confidential information is not relevant to a matter the transferring paralegal must give notice to the former client, the new firm's client and swear an affidavit or declaration to that effect.

3.06 DOING BUSINESS WITH A CLIENT: If a paralegal's client enters into a business transaction with a paralegal, the latter has a duty prior to accepting any new retainer to inform the client of any potential or real conflicts of interest, and shall require the client to have independent legal advice, and if the client still wishes to have the paralegal act, the latter shall obtain an informed consent from the client. If a paralegal is unable to disclose a conflicting interest to the client, because of other confidentiality concerns, the paralegal shall decline the retainer. A paralegal shall not borrow from clients unless the client is a financial institution or close relative. Nor shall a paralegal provide guarantees for a client who is a borrower, unless the lender is a financial institution providing a loan to a client who is a relative, or who is in a business venture with the paralegal, and the paralegal has disclosed potential conflicts of interest to the client and the lender, and both have had independent legal advice.

3.07 CLIENT PROPERTY: A paralegal shall exercise care and prudence with a client's property, inform the client of any property (including money) received on the client's behalf, and keep careful records to ensure the client's property is identifiable. A paralegal shall return a client's property on request.

3.08 WITHDRAWAL FROM REPRESENTATION: Having accepted a retainer, a paralegal shall not withdraw services from a client except as provided in these rules. A paralegal may withdraw, subject to a court or tribunal's approval if the client has lost confidence in the paralegal, or refuses to accept the paralegal's advice on an important point. A paralegal must withdraw if fired by the client, the client requires that the paralegal breach his or her duty to the court or tribunal, the client behaves dishonourably in the proceedings, or requires unethical and improper behaviour by the paralegal or the paralegal finds he or she is not competent to deal with the matter. Unless it would do serious harm to the client's interest a paralegal may withdraw if he or she has not been paid. In withdrawing from a case, if the matter is criminal and quasi criminal, the client must have sufficient time to find a new representative, and the paralegal must account for monies received from the client, and notify the court of the withdrawal. If there is not sufficient time between withdrawal and the trial, the paralegal must try to obtain an adjournment and obtain the court's permission to withdraw. On withdrawal the paralegal must take steps not to prejudice the client's interests, must deliver to the client papers and property, provide necessary information, account for funds held and render a final account and co-operate with the successor for an orderly transfer of the case. A successor must also take steps to ensure that the former paralegal has in fact withdrawn.

RULE 4: ADVOCACY

4.01 THE PARALEGAL AS ADVOCATE: The paralegal shall represent the client resolutely and honourably, while treating the tribunal, opposing parties and their representatives with civility. The paralegal shall pursue all lawful claims, remedies and defences unless they have been waived by the client with an informed consent. The paralegal shall discourage the client from resorting to frivolous, vexatious, harassing and improper conduct. The paralegal shall not appear before a judicial officer with whom he or she has a conflict of interest. Nor shall a paralegal abuse the court process by misleading the court, manipulating witnesses or evidence, or harassing witnesses; a paralegal shall not dissuade a witness from giving evidence. Where a client is required to disclose documents before trial, the paralegal shall ensure that full disclosure is made. If a paralegal does or omits to do what is required under this rule, he or she shall promptly disclose the error to the client. Where a charge has been or may be laid against a client, the paralegal may enter into plea bargaining negotiations with the prosecutor unless the client instructs otherwise provided the paralegal fully advises the client on the options available, the client is prepared to admit the charge, and the client voluntarily instructs the paralegal to enter a guilty plea. A paralegal who acts as a prosecutor shall act for the public good and treat the tribunal with candour and respect.

4.02 INTERVIEWING WITNESSES: There being no property in a witness, a paralegal may interview any witness or potential witness whether under subpoena or summons or not. Where a person is represented by a licensee, that person may be questioned or approached only through the licensee who represents him or her, who can consent on behalf of his or her client.

4.03 INTERVIEWING WITNESSES GIVING TESTIMONY: Generally, there are restrictions on discussions a paralegal may have with a favourable witness once the witness has begun to give

Paralegal Rules of Conduct,
The Law Society of Upper Canada
AS AMENDED MARCH 2011

EXHIBIT 10.3 (continued)

evidence. Generally a paralegal may not discuss the witness's evidence with him or her until testimony has been concluded.

4.04   THE PARALEGAL AS WITNESS: A paralegal shall not submit his or her own affidavit in a proceeding where he or she is an advocate, subject to some exceptions. Similarly, the paralegal shall not give oral evidence in a proceeding in which he or she is also an advocate, unless the rules of the tribunal permit.

4.05   DEALING WITH UNREPRESENTED PERSONS: A paralegal should encourage an unrepresented client to obtain legal representation, and should make clear that he or she cannot represent the person's interest, and that he or she must diligently act on behalf of the client who retained him or her.

RULE 5: FEES AND RETAINERS

5.01   FEES AND RETAINERS: Fees and retainers shall be fair and reasonable, reflecting the nature, complexity or difficulty of the work required, the amount involved, the importance of the issues at stake to the client, the results obtained, and the requirements of statutes that limit or control fees that may be charged. No fee paid on behalf of a client by someone else shall be accepted without informing the client. In sending out an account, a paralegal shall clearly set out fees and disbursements separately. Monies held in trust by a paralegal shall not be transferred to a paralegal's personal account unless an account is rendered to the client. A paralegal may enter into a contingency fee arrangement with a client in non-criminal or non–quasi-criminal matters. The client shall be informed of all of the factors determining the fee and when and how it is to be paid if the paralegal is successful. If there is a joint retainer, the fees must be fairly divided. A paralegal may not split fees with a non-licencee, but may split fees with another licencee in a different firm, provided the client consents, and the split is fair and reasonable. A paralegal may give and accept a referral fee from another licencee, provided it does not arise from a withdrawal of service, and further, provided the client gives an informed consent. This rule will permit paralegals and lawyers to split fees and to pay and receive referral fees. Paralegals, as well as lawyers, are now required to verify the identity of new clients.

RULE 6: DUTY TO THE ADMINISTRATION OF JUSTICE

6.01   A paralegal shall foster respect for the administration of justice. If aware of a danger to the court or those in it, he or she shall inform the court of any dangerous situation. Provided it does not result in a conflict of interest or otherwise breach court orders or statutory rules, a paralegal may communicate with the media and make public statements provided the statements do not prejudice a party's right to a fair trial. A paralegal is required to report any unauthorized practice, and may not enter into partnership or other arrangements to offer legal services with any licencee who has been disbarred, struck off, or otherwise is not permitted to offer licensed services.

RULE 7: DUTY TO LICENSEES AND OTHERS

7.01   A paralegal shall not engage in sharp practice; he or she shall agree to reasonable requests for adjournments and waiver of procedural formalities where it does no harm to the client. A paralegal shall not engage in abusive or unprofessional behaviour, and should not engage in negative, disparaging comments about other licencees except in representing a client in a complaint against another licencee. A paralegal shall promptly respond to professional communications from other licencees, and be punctual in fulfilling commitments. A paralegal shall not record conversations with clients or licencees even if lawful, without informing the other person.

RULE 8: PRACTICE MANAGEMENT

8.01   PROFESSIONAL RESPONSIBILITY: A paralegal shall operate his or her practice in a responsible way, in particular, taking responsibility for the practices finances, its professional operations, and for supervising staff, and pay any insurance deductible promptly as required. A paralegal shall supervise staff to whom tasks are delegated. In particular a paralegal may not permit non-licensed staff to provide legal services, to be held out as a licencee, to do things only paralegals may do, or do things paralegals are not permitted to do.

8.02 MAKING LEGAL SERVICES AVAILABLE: A paralegal shall make legal services available to the public in an efficient and convenient way. In offering legal services, a paralegal shall not make false, or misleading claims, use coercion or duress, or take advantage of a vulnerable person or one who has suffered trauma but not had a chance to recover. Nor shall a paralegal attempt to entice away a client from another licencee, unless the client initiates the change of retainer. A paralegal may not engage in communicating services in a way that bring the profession or the administration of justice into disrepute, nor shall he or she advertise services beyond the scope of permissible practice.

8.03 MARKETING: A paralegal may market legal services if the marketing is true, accurate, not misleading or deceptive and is in the best interest of the public, and consistent with the public interest and professional standards. A paralegal may advertise fees if it is precise as to services offered for the fee, discloses any extra charges, and the paralegal sticks to the fee quoted.

8.04 INSURANCE: All paralegals must obtain and maintain errors and omissions insurance as stipulated by the Law Society. Paralegals shall promptly report any claim for negligence, and shall assist the insurer is settling or defending the claim. If the insurer pays the claim, the paralegal must promptly pay the deductible.

RULE 9: RESPONSIBILITY TO THE LAW SOCIETY

9.01 RESPONSIBILITY TO THE LAW SOCIETY: A paralegal shall promptly reply to any communication from the Law Society. The paralegal must report misconduct to the Law Society unless it would breach confidentiality or be unlawful. Reportable events include misappropriation of funds by a licencee, abandonment of a practice, criminal activity related to a licencee's practice, mental instability or other conduct prejudicial to licencee's clients. A paralegal is obliged to encourage a client to report dishonest conduct by another licencee. If the client refuses to report dishonest conduct, the licencee shall obtain the client's written direction not to report, while pursuing the client's other remedies. If the client makes a private deal with a dishonest licencee, the paralegal shall inform the client of the provisions of the criminal law with respect to the concealment of offences, and shall refuse to act for that client. If a paralegal is charged with an offence described in By-Law 8 he or she shall report the charge and its disposition to the Law Society. A paralegal may be disciplined by the Law Society for professional misconduct (conduct which violates the rules and practices governing paralegal practice) and conduct unbecoming a paralegal (conduct in the private life of a paralegal that would bring the profession into disrepute). The rule defines professional misconduct, and conduct unbecoming to a paralegal.

apply procedural rules, and use court forms properly. They must develop language and numeracy skills to do problem solving and to provide advice to lawyers and the public. The work is usually done during normal business hours in court offices and courtrooms across the province. Court staff are a mix of full-time and contract workers, many of whom are part of a unionized civil service. Currently there are no professional or licensing requirements for this profession.

Training and Qualifications

Historically, staff were recruited from civil service applicants and trained on the job. However, some community colleges offer a court and tribunal administration diploma program in which students can acquire a background in law and procedure geared to court and tribunal administration settings, along with some of the generic literacy, numeracy and analytic skills essential to working in this area. Court reporters may also train in office administration programs, where they learn necessary word processing and dictation skills, although court staff operating recording equipment are replacing traditional court reporters. These individuals will only need transcription and word processing skills.

CHAPTER SUMMARY

Although this chapter is about the legal profession, it also examined the emerging legal services industry, in particular the increased role of individuals who are not lawyers but who perform a variety of specialized legal services.

The chapter presented a dynamic view of the legal profession by comparing legal services offered in the 1900s with those offered today. Important changes include the increasing size of law firms, additional specializations, changes in training of lawyers and other legal workers, more aggressive marketing of legal services, and the emergence of independent paralegals.

The legal profession was then examined in the context of the traditional model of professions: a self-regulating monopoly. The law society is the governing body of the profession, controlling who may enter the profession, governing the members' conduct, disciplining the members, and determining appropriate training for them. Detailed attention was paid to the rules governing professional conduct, as these have important implications for public acceptance of the profession's monopoly and for the guidance of others who provide legal services.

Duties and responsibilities of lawyers in their relationship with their own clients and the courts were examined, focusing on the tension that can arise in the face of conflicting duties owed to clients and to the courts.

The legal aid system was discussed in terms of the certificate and clinic systems, with a focus on emerging trends in offering legal aid services, as government and the law societies attempt to contain rising costs of the system.

Finally, three emerging professional groups offering legal services were examined: law clerks/legal assistants, who perform legal services under the supervision of lawyers; specialized court and tribunal staff; and paralegals/independent court agents, who legitimately may offer a limited range of services directly to the public, either in competition with lawyers or in areas of the legal services market unserviced by lawyers.

GLOSSARY OF NEW TERMS AND KEY CONCEPTS

articling clerk	Also called a **clerk under articles** or, more simply, an articling student. This is the title for a law student who has completed law school, and then works in a law firm under supervision for one year to acquire practice skills.
assessment officer	An officer of the court with the power to review a lawyer's bill if it is disputed by the client, and to determine costs payable by one party to another as a result of a court order for costs.
barrister and solicitor	The professional title of lawyers in Canada. For further discussions, see note 6 on page 201.
bencher	A lawyer elected by other lawyers to the **convocation**, the governing body of the law society. There are also a number of *lay benchers*, who are not lawyers but are appointed by the government to represent the interests of the general public.

call to the bar	A ceremony in which a law student, after completing the required legal education, officially becomes a lawyer and a member of the legal profession in a province.
convocation	The governing body of the Law Society of Upper Canada, which is composed of **benchers.**
disbarment	A process whereby a lawyer who has committed a serious infraction of the rules of professional conduct is made to leave the legal profession after a disciplinary hearing.
grandparented	A gender-neutral term referring to a class of persons existing prior to the imposition of a new system of rules, who are permitted to adhere to the system that existed prior to the establishment of the new system of rules.
mega-firm	A colloquial expression used to describe very large, often transprovincial or transnational law firms.
peer review	A system used in the professions to assess the quality of a professional's work by having other skilled professionals review and comment on the quality of that work.
pro bono publico	A Latin expression that means "for the public good". It describes a situation where the client cannot afford to pay fees, so a lawyer takes on a worthy legal cause for no fee in order to see justice done.
retained	A client who has hired a lawyer has *retained* the lawyer's services by paying a deposit for legal services called a **retainer.**
retainer	Has several meanings, depending on the context. It describes the contract between a lawyer and client for services to be performed by the lawyer. Also, it can be used to describe the money deposit made by the client to the lawyer as advance payment on services to be performed by the lawyer. Last, it may refer to a contractual relationship in which the client pays the lawyer a fee for being available to provide whatever services the client requires during a stipulated time period. Here, the lawyer will also charge further amounts for the actual work done while he or she acts as retainer to the client. This kind of retainer is often used by corporate clients that need to have a lawyer on call.
solicitor–client privilege	A privilege, which belongs to the client, that requires that anything said to a lawyer by a client dealing with an issue for which the lawyer has been retained cannot be revealed to anyone without the client's consent.
systemic discrimination	An unintentional inequitable treatment of a minority that arises as a result of the negative impact on a minority of institutions or existing ways of doing things. For example, the requirement of long hours by large firms may give rise to systemic discrimination against women lawyers, who are primarily responsible for child care.

REVIEW QUESTIONS

1. What are the major differences between the law offices in 1900 and those of today with respect to the following:
   - women and minorities in the legal profession?
   - size of law firms?
   - specialization?
   - education and training of lawyers?
   - ways legal services are marketed to the public?

2. Discuss the chief characteristics of a profession.

3. How does the legal profession:
   - govern itself?
   - train its members?
   - determine who may enter the profession?
   - control misbehaviour among its members?

4. How does the legal aid plan deliver legal services to less qualified legal aid clients?

5. How is the legal aid plan funded?

6. What are the criticisms towards the legal aid plan with respect to the quality of legal service provided to clients?

7. What trends appear to emerge with respect to changes in the delivery of legal aid services?

8. Cite an example of the disciplinary offence, "professional misconduct". How is professional misconduct different from the offence of "conduct unbecoming to a barrister and solicitor"?

9. Describe a lawyer's duty as an "officer of the court".

10. What are the characteristics of the contractual relationship between a lawyer and his or her client?

11. How are law clerks regulated?

12. May law clerks employed by and supervised by lawyers appear in lower courts where agents may appear?

13. In what courts and tribunals do licensed paralegals have the right to appear?

14. What requirements will a paralegal have to meet in order to be licensed?

DISCUSSION QUESTIONS

1. In the future, the provision of legal services is likely to be less regulated and more competitive. Discuss.

2. The Law Society has been described by some as well designed to protect the interests of the public; others have described it as the oldest monopoly in the province, protecting only the interests of its members. Discuss.

3. If you are asked to group the rules of professional conduct into categories, what categories would you create? Which rules would you place in each category?

4. As a law clerk working for a lawyer, your firm's client tells you that to make sure she wins in her upcoming court case, she plans to give a version of relevant events that she knows is untrue. What should you do? What action should the lawyer responsible for this case take?

5. You are an independent paralegal. A husband and wife who have agreed to separate approach you. They ask you to draw up a separation agreement for them. Should you do this work? Discuss, assuming that there is no regulation of paralegals.

6. You are investing some money in a business venture with someone who happens to be a lawyer. The relationship you have with him is a business relationship, but it is not a lawyer–client relationship (you have not hired him or her as your lawyer). He asks for some money in cash as part of the venture, and without furnishing a receipt. You are reluctant to do this, but he persuades you, saying, "You can trust me, I'm a lawyer." Later, you discover that he has stolen your money. Is this professional misconduct? Discuss.

7. "The Law Society's regulatory issues for paralegals are virtually the same as they are for lawyers." Examining the Rules of Professional Conduct for both groups of licencees, comment on the accuracy of this statement.

SUGGESTED READINGS

Arthurs, H.W. "Paradoxes of Canadian Legal Education" 3 Dal. L.J. 639.

Eisen, L. *Technology in Practice*, 2d ed. (Toronto, Ont.: Carswell, 1991).

Estrin, C.B. *Everything You Need to Know About Becoming a Legal Assistant* (Albany, N.Y.: Delmar Publishing, 1995).

Gold, N. (ed.) and Centre for Studies in Canadian Legal Education. *Essays on Legal Education* (Toronto, Ont.: Butterworths, 1982).

Graves, D.L. *How to Survive in a Law Firm* (New York: Wiley Law Publisher, 1993).

Law Society of Upper Canada. *Transitions in the Legal Profession* (Toronto, Ont.: The Law Society of Upper Canada, May 1991).

Ministry of the Attorney General (Ontario). *Task Force on Paralegals* (Toronto, Ont.: The Queen's Printer, 1990) [The Ianni Commission Report].

Ontario, Working Group on Paralegals. "A Consultation Document on a Proposed Regulatory Framework" Report to Convocation, Government Relations Committee (25 April 2002).

Oughtred, Wendy. *Going it Alone: A Start Up Guide for the Sole Practitioner* (Toronto, Ont.: Canada Law Book, 1995).

Plant, Albert. *Making Money: the Business of Law* (Toronto, Ont.: Canada Law Book, 1993).

Towler, Patricia. *Articling in Canada: A Survival Guide 1996* (Toronto, Ont.: Carswell, 1995).

Waddams, S.M. *Introduction to the Study of Law*, 5th ed. (Toronto, Ont.: Carswell, 1997).

WEBSITES

Canadian Bar Association: <http://www.cba.org>

Law Society of Upper Canada: <http://www.lsuc.on.ca>

Institute of Law Clerks of Ontario (ILCO): <http://www.ilco.on.ca/>

Paralegal Society of Ontario: <http://www.paralegalsociety.on.ca/flashpage.html>

Criminal Law

Mary Ann Kelly
SENECA COLLEGE

Learning Objectives

After reading this chapter, the reader should be able to:

➢ understand the policy and legal issues in relation to criminal law
➢ understand the different elements of an offence
➢ understand the distinction between complete and incomplete offences
➢ understand who may be party to an offence
➢ understand and describe various criminal offences
➢ understand and describe various criminal defences

TABLE OF CONTENTS

INTRODUCTION

In Canadian law, a crime is not simply an offence committed against the particular victims. It is regarded as a wrong against society as a whole. Crime is seen as a potential breakdown in the social order and the safety and security of all Canadians. It is for this reason that criminal offences are not, for the most part, prosecuted by the actual victim of a particular offence. Rather, they are prosecuted by the state. In Canada, prosecutions are carried out in the name of the Queen, who is still the legal head of the Canadian state. The police investigate the offence, gather evidence and lay charges. Government lawyers, often referred to as Crown prosecutors, or Crown attorneys, prosecute the case before the courts.

Criminal law is an area of public law because it regulates the interaction of persons with the government, as opposed to private law, which regulates persons' relationships with each other. Under the Canadian Constitution, the power to make criminal law is assigned to the federal government.

Criminal law is contained in the *Criminal Code of Canada*, but it is not the only federal statute that deals with criminal offences. The *Controlled Drug and Substances Act*,[1] the *Food and Drugs Act*,[2] the *Income Tax Act*,[3] and the *Youth Criminal Justice Act*[4] all contain criminal offences.

The provinces, while they have no criminal law-making authority under the Constitution, have the power to make laws regulating conduct in areas that fall within provincial law-making jurisdiction. Clearly, it would be very difficult to successfully regulate conduct if there were no consequences for failing to follow the provincial regulation. For instance, the power to regulate speed on highways in the province is a provincial responsibility. If there were no penalties attached to speeding, the provinces would have major difficulties enforcing speed limits. The provinces therefore have the jurisdiction to create provincial offences. Although these offences are sometimes referred to as quasi-criminal offences, they attract no criminal consequences and do not result in a criminal record.

The question of what causes crime has plagued sociologists and criminologists for many years. No one factor has been pinpointed as the primary cause of crime, but it is suggested that a host of biological, psychological and other social factors could predispose an individual to commit a crime. Some of these factors include poverty and the general distribution of wealth in society, heredity, physical defects, mental imbalance, emotional difficulties, lack of education and association with criminals.

Crime is not static but evolves as society evolves. While the nature of a particular act may not change, society's perception of it may. For example, the majority of Canadians have come to view the simple possession of marijuana for personal use as no longer deserving of a criminal penalty. Currently the federal government is looking at an amendment to the criminal law that would **decriminalize** this offence. This does not mean that marijuana possession would then be legal. It would still be illegal but would no longer attract criminal punishment such as a potential jail term. Rather, a conviction would result in a fine and there would be no criminal record for the convicted person. Clearly, this kind of change reflects a change in attitude about what kinds of wrongs are deserving of criminal consequences.

[1] S.C. 1996, c. 19.
[2] R.S.C. 1985, c. F-27.
[3] R.S.C. 1985, c. 1.
[4] S.C. 2002, c. 1.

THE ELEMENTS OF AN OFFENCE

A criminal offence is made up of two separate elements: the **actus reus** and the **mens rea**. The *actus reus* are the elements of the offence that describe the wrongful conduct or actions, and the *mens rea* consists of the mental elements that are required for proving the offence. The Crown must prove every single element of the offence beyond a reasonable doubt, or the accused person will be acquitted of the charge.

Actus Reus

Actus reus is a Latin term that means "an action involving guilt". Before an accused person can be convicted, the Crown must prove that the accused committed the *actus reus* of the offence. The *actus reus* of each offence can be determined by carefully reading the provisions that create the offence. For instance, the elements for the offence of assault are laid out in section 265 of the *Criminal Code*:

(1) A person commits an assault when
    (*a*) without the consent of another person, he applies force intentionally to that other person, directly or indirectly ...

In order to establish the *actus reus* of this offence, the Crown must prove that the accused person applied force, directly or indirectly, to the victim and that the force was applied without the victim's consent. It is not sufficient merely to prove that the accused applied force. The Crown must also prove that the force was applied without the victim's consent. If the victim engaged in some voluntary activity with the accused, such as stepping outside a bar to fight with the accused, that may be enough to imply that the victim was consenting to the force being applied. If that were the case, the Crown would not be successful in proving all the elements beyond a reasonable doubt. In most offences, the accused must actually take some action in order to meet the *actus reus* of the offence. Some offences involve a failure to act, or an omission. However, in order for the *actus reus* of an offence to involve an omission, there must be a positive legal duty upon the accused to take some action so that his failure to do so amounts to a wrongful action. For instance, failure to provide the necessaries of life to a dependant under 16 years old may amount to a guilty action.

Mens Rea

Mens rea is another Latin term that means "a guilty mind". It is not sufficient for someone to merely commit a prohibited act. Generally speaking, at the same time that the accused is committing the wrongful action, he or she must have the necessary intent to accompany the action. In addition to establishing that the accused committed the wrongful action, the Crown must show that the accused had a willing mind and was capable of making a choice to act. For example, if a person falls against another on a crowded bus when the bus stops suddenly, there has been an application of force, but the person applying the force did not mean it to happen and is, therefore, unlikely to be charged with a criminal offence.

In order to determine the particular mental element, or *mens rea* necessary for a specific offence, one must read the statutory provision creating the offence. There are two broad categories of *mens rea*: knowledge or intent, recklessness or wilful blindness.

Knowledge or Intent

"Intent" means that a person intends or means to commit the offence and can (or is presumed to) foresee the wrongful results. Offences that require this level of *mens rea* often contain words like "intentionally", or "knowingly", or "wilfully". The Crown must prove beyond a reasonable doubt that the accused "intentionally", "knowingly" or "wilfully" committed the *actus reus* of the offence.

It is important to distinguish motive from intent. Intention is quite different from motive, but the two are sometimes confused. Motive explains the reason why a person may have acted the way that he or she did. It is often irrelevant to a finding of guilt in a criminal case. If a mother steals a loaf of bread to feed her starving children, she may have an unselfish motive, but she is intentionally stealing the bread. The reason she was stealing the bread is irrelevant in establishing her guilt. However, once she is convicted, the judge may take the reasons for committing the offence into consideration in determining her sentence.

Recklessness or Wilful Blindness

Some offences do not involve intention in the true sense. Instead, the accused deliberately takes an unjustifiable risk, knowing that certain wrongful consequences can flow from that risk-taking. For example, a child who deliberately throws a stone at a neighbour's window is performing an intentional act. The act of a child who is throwing stones in the general area of the neighbour's window and then *accidentally* breaks it, however, is deemed a **reckless** act.

Wilful blindness is closing one's mind to the consequences of one's actions. For example, a convenience store owner buys 100 cartons of cigarettes from someone selling them from the back of his SUV, at a quarter of their regular price. He asks no questions. The cigarettes are stolen goods. The store owner is unlikely to be able to escape criminal responsibility by simply claiming that he did not know the goods were stolen. A reasonable person would be highly suspicious of the circumstances of this purchase, and, if he did not know, it is likely due to the fact that he didn't want to know.

Strict and Absolute Liability Offences

Although it is a general principle of law that offences involve elements of both *actus reus* and *mens rea*, the level of the *mens rea* required for a conviction may differ. On some less serious criminal offences, and on most offences created under provincial statutes for regulating some areas of provincial concern, such as behaviour on the highways and the serving of alcohol, the prosecution does not need to prove any *mens rea* for the offence at all.

According to the Supreme Court of Canada decision in *R. v. Sault Ste. Marie*,[5] offences fall into three categories:

1. Offences, in which *mens rea* or a mental element must be proven by the prosecution. Most criminal offences fall into this category. The prosecution must prove intention, recklessness or wilful blindness, according to whichever wording is contained in the provision that creates the offence.

2. **Strict liability** offences, in which the prosecution is only required to prove the *actus reus* of the offence. There is no requirement to prove a mental element. However, the defendant may raise a defence of due

[5] (1978), 40 C.C.C. (2d) 353.

diligence. Due diligence requires a person to take all reasonable precautions to avoid the offence. If the defendant can establish this on the balance of probabilities, he or she will be acquitted of the charge.

3. **Absolute liability** offences, in which the prosecution need only prove the *actus reus* beyond a reasonable doubt. There is no requirement to establish a mental element to the offence. The defendant may not raise any defence related to *mens rea*. That the defendant took reasonable care to avoid committing the offence is irrelevant. He or she will be convicted if the *actus reus* has been proven and there is no defence established that is related to the commission of the *actus reus*.

[handwritten margin note: need only actus reus but beyond the reasonable doubt]

INCOMPLETE OFFENCES

Generally speaking, Canadian law does not hold people criminally responsible for a guilty mind if there is no accompanying guilty action. However, if there were no exceptions to this principle, it would be possible for people to plan criminal offences and for the police to be unable to intervene to stop the offence and charge the perpetrators before the *actus reus* of the offence was complete. Also, a criminal mastermind could direct the planning of a major offence, send other people in his gang to commit it and avoid criminal responsibility because he did not participate in the *actus reus* of the offence. Clearly, both these scenarios are unacceptable.

Therefore, in criminal law there is the concept of incomplete offences. There are two types of incomplete offences: attempts to commit a criminal offence and conspiracy to commit a criminal offence.

Attempts

The fact that a person was unable to carry out an offence because "something went wrong" does not mean that an offence has not been committed. It is unlawful to **attempt** to commit an offence as stated in section 24(1) of the *Criminal Code*:

> Every one who, having an intent to commit an offence, does or omits to do anything for the purpose of carrying out the intention is guilty of an attempt to commit the offence whether or not it was possible under the circumstances to commit the offence.

The Crown must prove beyond a reasonable doubt that the accused had the intention to commit the offence. It need not, however, prove that the *actus reus* was complete. The accused must only have taken some step towards the commission of the offence and have the necessary intent or *mens rea* to commit the offence in order to be found guilty of an attempt.

[handwritten margin note: no need to be completed]

Conspiracy

Conspiracy is another example of an incomplete offence. A conspiracy is an agreement between two or more people to carry out a criminal offence. In order to prove a conspiracy, the Crown must prove that the people involved had a serious intention to carry out the proposed act. They need not prove that the *actus reus* was carried out by anyone. However, if the *actus reus* was actually completed by some members of the planning group and not others, the planners who took no part in the completion of the *actus reus* can still be convicted of conspiracy. Conspiracy is often used in drug offences and in charges laid against organized crime.

The penalty imposed upon a conviction for conspiracy is the same penalty one would have received if the offence had been fully carried out.

PERSONS WHO MAY BE CHARGED WITH AN OFFENCE

A person who actually commits the offence is the principal offender. In addition, people who assist the principal offender in some way to commit an offence may also be held criminally responsible for the offence and may be liable to the same punishment as the principal offender. The assistance may have been given before, during or after the commission of the main offence. Moreover, the persons who assist the principal offender may be convicted even if the principal offender is not.

[handwritten: aiding - help in carrying out]
[handwritten: abetting - encouraging]

Aiding and Abetting, s. 21

To be found guilty of **aiding** in the commission of an offence, the accused must have offered the principal offender some help in carrying out the offence. **Abetting** is encouraging the principal offender to commit the offence. The Crown must prove that the accused knew that the principal was committing or intended to commit an offence, and that the accused aided or assisted or helped the offender. Merely being present at the scene of a crime is not sufficient for a conviction. The accused must actually have intended to help or encourage the principal offender in some way.

Moreover, if the accused was tricked or duped into helping the offender, he will not be held responsible for aiding or abetting. Rather, he will be regarded as an innocent agent.

[handwritten: advising or get someone]

Counselling, s. 22

A person who advises or gets another person to commit an offence may be found guilty of the offence, even if the offence was committed in a different way than what was suggested. In fact, even if no offence is actually committed by the person who was counselled to commit it, the person who did the counselling may be convicted.

[handwritten: help the offender after]

Accessory after the Fact, s. 23

One may also be held criminally liable for an offence if one knew that an offence has committed and one offered assistance to the offender for the purpose of helping him to escape detention or capture. Providing food, shelter or clothing to the offender after the commission of the offence are all considered sufficient for a conviction as an **accessory after the fact.**

Until recently, a spouse who offered assistance to an offender, even if it was to assist in escaping detection, could not be convicted as an accessory after the fact. However, section 23 of the *Criminal Code* has been amended, and a spouse is no longer excluded from criminal responsibility when acting as an accessory.

SPECIFIC OFFENCES

Violent Offences

[handwritten: murder, manslaughter, infanticide]

Homicide *[handwritten: 3 forms]*

[handwritten: non culpable = can't be held accountable for some's death]

Homicide is considered the most serious violent crime that one person can commit against another because the judicial system cannot provide any remedy for the victims. Under section 222(1) of the *Criminal Code*, homicide is an act that directly or indirectly causes the death of another person. Homicide can be culpable or non-culpable or, in simpler terms, blameworthy or non-blameworthy. Non-culpable homicide is not an offence because the person who causes the death is not held responsible. For example, if a death resulted from a traffic accident where the victim drove through a red light, the offence is not homicide. Culpable homicide is, under the Code, an offence, and the person causing death is held accountable for the death. The Code recognizes three forms of culpable homicide: murder, manslaughter and infanticide.

☐ MURDER

Murder is committed under the following circumstances stated in section 229 of the *Criminal Code*:

- If the person causes the death means to do so.
- If the person causes the death means to cause bodily harm and knows the act is likely to cause death.
- If the person causes the death while committing a criminal act, whether the death is caused accidentally or not.

In other words, for a murder offence, both *actus reus* (the physical act) and *mens rea* (the mental intent) must be present (except under s. 231(4), where the victim is a law enforcement agent — e.g., a police officer).

There are two types of murder under the Code: first-degree and second-degree. Murders that are not first-degree murder are considered second-degree murder. Murder is first-degree when the death is caused on purpose (s. 231(2): "when it is planned and deliberate"). Moreover, if the victim is a police officer or any other law enforcement agent listed in section 231(4), or if the death occurs during the perpetration of, or an attempt to perpetrate, any of the offences listed in section 231(5), including a hijacking of a plane, a sexual assault, or a kidnapping, then the offence is first-degree murder.

Sentencing for murder is mandatory. Murderers in Canada receive life imprisonment. The minimum penalty for first-degree murder is life imprisonment without eligibility for parole for 25 years. For second-degree murder, the minimum time to be served in prison without parole eligibility can vary from 10 up to 25 years. The sentencing principles that judges consider in the length of sentence and parole are laid out in sections 718.2 and 745 of the Code.

☐ MANSLAUGHTER

Manslaughter is a culpable homicide that does not fall under murder or infanticide, and it is further categorized as voluntary manslaughter and involuntary manslaughter.

Manslaughter is considered involuntary manslaughter if the killer lacks the mental intent to cause death. Involuntary manslaughter generally occurs in two situations: first, when the death is caused by criminal negligence, and second, when the death occurs during the commission of another crime, where there is no intent to cause bodily injury or death.

Voluntary manslaughter occurs when the intent exists but only after "adequate provocation" — that is, the accused has been sufficiently provoked to the extent that a "reasonable or ordinary person" would be incited to lose self-control. It should be noted that the time between provocation and the killing should not be enough to allow the passion to cool off.

Anyone who commits manslaughter, whether it is voluntary or involuntary, is guilty of an indictable offence and is liable to life in prison. There is also no minimum punishment or minimum time of ineligibility for parole. As a result, the sentences can vary greatly, depending on the circumstances of the death and the intent. A lesser sentence may be considered if the accused is believed to be too intoxicated to be capable of having had a conscious intent to kill. A longer sentence may be given if the accused has been convicted of other offences.

☐ INFANTICIDE

Infanticide, the final type of culpable homicide, is defined under the *Criminal Code*, section 233. It occurs when a mother, suffering from the side effects of giving birth so that her mind is disturbed, by a wilful act or omission, causes the death of her newborn child. Infanticide is the only culpable homicide that does not have a minimum or maximum sentence of life in prison. Under section 237 of the Code, the sentence for infanticide is imprisonment for a term not exceeding five years.

Property Offences

Offences involving property make up the vast majority of offences listed in the *Criminal Code*. In this section we will focus on theft and break and enter.

Theft

Theft is the most basic property offence. The *actus reus* of the offence requires taking or converting someone else's property. Converting property involves using property for one's own purposes as though one were the true legal owner, thereby depriving the rightful owner of his use of the property. An example of converting, or conversion, would be borrowing a friend's stereo while the friend was away on holiday, setting it up and then refusing to return it to the friend at the end of the loan period.

The *actus reus* must be accompanied by an intention to fraudulently deprive another person of her property. Moreover, the person taking or converting the property to his own use must do so without colour of right. The term **colour of right** refers to a situation in which a person honestly believes that they have a legal right to the property. To be convicted of theft, the Crown must prove the accused knew, or should have known, that he had no legal right to the property in question. For instance, if the accused found an old leather chair on the side of the road, he might believe that the chair had been abandoned and might take it home to use in his family room. He would be acting under "colour of right" if it were reasonable to believe that the chair actually had been abandoned, even if it had not, and that it had, rather, fallen off the back of a moving van and the true owner was searching for it.

The *Criminal Code* provides different penalties and modes of trial, depending on whether the value of the property taken or converted exceeds the value of $5,000. Theft of property valued at over $5,000 is an indictable offence, liable for punishment for a term of up to 10 years. Theft of property valued at less than $5,000 is a hybrid offence, subject to Crown election to be prosecuted as either an indictable offence or a summary conviction offence.

Break and Enter

A break and enter occurs if premises are illegally entered by a person who intends to commit an indictable offence once inside. The illegal entry does not necessarily have to involve the breaking of a window or a lock, or any other type of forced entry. Simply opening an unlocked door and going inside is sufficient to complete the *actus reus* of the offence.

The *mens rea* of the offence is the specific intent to commit an indictable offence inside the premises. The usual indictable offence that the accused intends to commit inside would be theft. The Crown is required to show that the accused entered with the intent of committing an indictable offence. However, evidence that the accused illegally entered the premises will normally be enough, absent evidence to the contrary, that the accused was intending to commit an offence inside.

The penalty for break and enter is quite severe and includes a maximum penalty of life imprisonment where the offence involved a dwelling house, and a maximum of 10 years for any premises other than a dwelling house.

Controversial Offences

Abortion

Abortion is an extremely controversial issue that involves differing religious, moral and social viewpoints. "Pro-choice" groups believe that a decision to have an abortion should be between a woman and her doctor and that the government of Canada and criminal law should not be involved at all. "Pro-life" groups take the anti-abortion position and believe that abortion should result in a criminal conviction.

Until 1988, a legal abortion could only be obtained if the woman received permission from a "therapeutic abortion committee" set up by an "approved hospital". The committee considered the applicant's medical information and the recommendations of her doctor and decided whether an abortion would be performed based on a finding that continuing the pregnancy would endanger the woman's health and well-being. However, not all hospitals had these committees and, in some areas of the country, abortions were unavailable because there was no hospital with a committee.

In 1988, in the case of *R. v Morgentaler, Smoling and Scott*,[6] the Supreme Court of Canada ruled that section 287 of the *Criminal Code* was unconstitutional in that it restricted approval of abortion to these hospital committees. The three accused were medical doctors who were charged with performing abortions in clinics without committee approval. The Supreme Court examined a number of Charter issues and, among other things, determined that "security of the person" within the meaning of section 7 of the Charter must include a right of access to medical treatment for a condition representing a danger to life or health without fear of criminal sanction. The Court then deemed section 287 of the Code to be of no force and effect because of its unconstitutionality.

As a result, although section 287 remains in the *Criminal Code*, it cannot be enforced, and, therefore, there is no enforceable law in Canada that prohibits abortions.

Obscenity

Obscenity is another offence that may generate public concern. Section 2 of the Charter guarantees freedom of expression, including freedom of the press. The issue then becomes, What kind of writing, photographs, films, etc., constitute obscenity, and how does freedom of expression interact with the *Criminal Code* provisions? In other words, just how involved should the criminal law be in prohibiting material, given freedom of expression, and when does material cross the line into "undue exploitation of sex"? Can some material be art in the eyes of some individuals while being obscene in the view of others? These are the questions courts are asked to examine when deliberating on obscenity offences.

Section 163 of the *Criminal Code* states the following:

(1) Every one commits an offence who
   (a) makes, prints, publishes, distributes, circulates, or has in his possession for the purpose of publication, distribution or circulation any obscene written matter, picture, model, phonograph record or other thing whatever ...

(8) For the purposes of this Act, any publication a dominant characteristic of which is the undue exploitation of sex, or of sex and any one or more of the following subjects, namely, crime, horror, cruelty and violence, shall be deemed to be obscene.

---

[6] [1988] 1 S.C.R. 30.

Pursuant to the above section and section 164, a judge may issue a warrant, allowing the police to seize any material deemed to be obscene. The person found with the material will be charged and, if convicted, will be liable for up to two years imprisonment.

The defences that accused persons usually bring forward to such a charge include challenging the allegation that the "dominant characteristic" of the materials is sexual, or that it there is an "undue exploitation of sex". In deciding these issues, the courts will generally look to accepted community standards of tolerance at the time the material was seized.

Prostitution

Prostitution itself is not a criminal offence in Canada. What is an offence is procuring and communicating for the purpose of prostitution. The *Criminal Code* defines "procuring" as an attempt to obtain a female person for sexual intercourse with another person, or living wholly or in part off the avails of prostitution of another person.[7] A prostitute cannot be convicted of living on the money she makes herself, but someone who relies on the prostitute's earnings to support himself may be convicted. This offence is aimed primarily at pimps, who many see as victimizing women and enticing young people into the sex trade. *take advantage*

Communicating involves stopping, or attempting to stop, another person, in a public place, for the purpose of asking them to engage in prostitution. Both the prostitute and/or the client may be charged with this offence. It is a summary conviction offence.

There are many people in the community who believe that prostitution is not being properly controlled by the *Criminal Code*, and that it would be better to set up "red light" districts, where prostitutes are licensed and regulated by the government. Those who take this particular approach say that rounding up prostitutes and taking them to jail overnight does little to stop them, and that the next night they will be out on the same streets again. Instead, some propose that the sex trade be confined to a particular district where residents of neighbourhoods are not exposed to it, and where prostitutes can be protected from pimps through government licensing.

Those opposed to this approach argue that licensing prostitutes is not a proper activity for governments and that prostitution is very closely linked with other offences, such as the drug trade. These people believe that decriminalizing prostitution would create an opportunity for organized crime. In addition, there are concerns about the trafficking in women from poorer countries, who may be enticed into prostitution unwittingly.

Possession of Marijuana for Personal Use

In 2002, the federal government tabled a bill[8] to amend the *Controlled Drugs and Substances Act*.[9] The proposed changes to the statute would result in the decriminalization of the possession of small amounts of marijuana for personal use. As the bill was never passed, possession continues to be an offence. However, conviction for possession for the purposes of trafficking, growing marijuana and other related offences would still result in a criminal record for the offender.

[7] *Criminal Code*, R.S.C., 1985, c. C-46, s. 212.

[8] Bill C-38, *An Act to Amend the Controlled Drugs and Substances Act*, Second Session, Thirty-seventh Parliament, 51-52 Elizabeth II, 2002–2003.

[9] S.C., 1996, c. 19.

People in support of this change to the legislation take the position that the use of marijuana is not addictive and that there is no evidence that it leads to the use of harder drugs. It is recognized that large numbers of people in Canada have used or experimented with marijuana, and it is, to many, unfair that people who are caught with a small amount should be followed throughout their lives by a criminal record.

However, there is another group opposed to decriminalization. This group includes the Canadian Association of Chiefs of Police, which is concerned that marijuana use can lead to involvement with more serious drugs and that decriminalization does not give police a range of escalating options for dealing with the offence. The Association is also concerned about the potential increase in smuggling of marijuana into and out of Canada.

DEFENCES

Canadian criminal law developed from British common law. However, for well over a hundred years Canada has had a criminal law statute. There are no common law offences left in Canada. The only offences of which a person may be charged and convicted are prescribed by the *Criminal Code*. However, the Code specifically preserved common law defences.[10] Therefore, common law defences are still available under Canadian criminal law.

Some defences are raised in relation to whether the accused actually committed the *actus reus* of the offence, and other defences go to the *mens rea* elements.

Defences Going to the *Actus Reus*

In order to meet the requisite elements of the *actus reus* it is essential that the accused person performed the necessary actions voluntarily. If he did not have control over his actions, he may be able to raise a successful defence that negates one or more elements of the *actus reus*.

I. Automatism

Automatism is a common law defence. The term refers to behaviour that a person performs while in a state of impaired consciousness. The most common example of a state of automatism is a person who is sleepwalking.

In order to successfully raise automatism as a defence, the state of automatism must have been caused by something other than a mental disorder or self-induced intoxication. Automatism may be caused by a physical condition that produces impaired consciousness, a blow to the head or, even, by involuntary intoxication, such as unknowingly drinking a spiked beverage.

The defence may be raised in relation to any offence and, if successful, would result in the complete acquittal of the accused. Automatism is, therefore, a complete defence to the charge. However, such a defence is very difficult to establish.

II. Provocation

Provocation can only be used as a defence to a charge of murder; it is not applicable to any other offence. If the defence is accepted, the conviction for murder will be reduced to the lesser and included offence of manslaughter. Provocation is, therefore, only a partial defence, not a complete defence, because the accused is not acquitted.

---

[10] *Criminal Code*, R.S.C. 1985. Chap. C-46, s. 8(3).

Provocation may involve blows, words, or gestures that cause a person to lose the power of self-control. It must be sudden, and the reaction of the accused must be immediate. The accused must not have had any time at all to consider the consequences of his actions.

The standard for establishing provocation is an objective one. The provocation must have been of such magnitude that it would have caused the average person to lose control. If an accused has little self-control and is liable to fly off the handle at minor slights, he will likely have considerable difficulty establishing this defence.

Duress

Duress is a very complicated defence, with both a statutory and a common law aspect.

Section 17 of the *Criminal Code* provides the statutory defence.

> A person who commits an offence under compulsion by threats of immediate death or bodily harm from a person who is present when the offence is committed is excused for committing the offence if the person believes that the threats will be carried out and if the person is not a party to a conspiracy or association whereby the person is subject to compulsion, but this section does not apply where the offence that is committed is high treason or treason, murder, piracy, attempted murder, sexual assault, sexual assault with a weapon, threats to a third party or causing bodily harm, aggravated sexual assault, forcible abduction, hostage taking, robbery, assault with a weapon or causing bodily harm, aggravated assault, unlawfully causing bodily harm, arson or an offence under sections 280 to 283 (abduction and detention of young persons).

The statute requires that, in order for this defence to be established, the accused must act under the threat of imminent bodily harm or death, to herself or members of her family. Second, the person making the threats must be present when the offence is committed; and finally, the defence is not available for the offences excluded by section 17, which includes most of the serious offences, such as murder, assault causing bodily harm, arson, and sexual assault.

In 2001 the Supreme Court of Canada found section 17 to be in violation of section 7 of the Charter to the extent that it allows individuals who acted involuntarily to be found guilty of a criminal offence. The requirement in the section that the person issuing the threat be present at the commission of the offence, coupled with the necessity of the threat being immediate, created the constitutional issue. There are circumstances where the threat may not be immediate from a person present at the scene, and yet the act may still be involuntary in the sense that the person had no realistic choice other than breaking the law to avoid the threat being carried out. Thus section 17 is too restrictive.

The common law defence of duress never included the statutory requirement that the person doing the threatening be present for the commission of the offence or that the threat be immediate. Thus, the Supreme Court found that it created no constitutional violations in that regard. The court restated the elements that must be established for the common law defence to succeed:

1. The accused must have acted solely as a result of threats of death or serious bodily harm to herself or another person.

2. The threats must have been of such gravity or seriousness that the accused believed that the threats would be carried out. However, a threat that is too far in the future may be found not to be a real threat.

3. The threats must have been of such gravity that they might well have caused a reasonable person placed in the same situation as the accused to act in the same manner as she did. To put that another way: Would a person of reasonable firmness, sharing the characteristics of the accused, such as her age and her background, have responded to the threats?

4. Finally, the accused must not have had an obvious safe avenue of escape.

III. *Necessity*

In raising the defence of necessity, the accused is saying that some sort of urgent or exigent circumstances required him or her to commit the offence. In other words, he or she broke the law in order to prevent the infliction of a greater harm. In addition, there must be no other legal alternative available to the accused. If there is a legal alternative available, then the accused must take the legal avenue.

Necessity is a common law defence.

IV. *Self Defence*

Self defence is a statutory defence contained in sections 34 and 35 of the *Criminal Code*. It is a complete defence in that, if successful, it will lead to the acquittal of the accused.

A person is permitted to use reasonable force to protect themselves and those under their protection, from an unprovoked assault by another. However, the defence will only be successful when the force used was not intended to cause death or grievous bodily harm and when the force was no more than what was necessary to repel the attack.

In cases where an accused claiming this defence killed or seriously injured the attacker, the accused must have acted under a reasonable fear of death or serious injury.

Defences Going to Mens Rea

Canadian criminal law does not hold people criminally responsible unless they know or should have known that they were engaged in wrongful conduct. People who are unable to exercise control over their mental functions may not be held criminally liable for their actions.

Mental Disorder

The defence of mental disorder has replaced the defence of insanity in Canadian law. The defence is laid out in section 16 of the *Criminal Code*:

> (1) No person is criminally responsible for an act committed or an omission made while suffering from a mental disorder that rendered the person incapable of appreciating the nature and quality of the act or omission or of knowing that it was wrong.

In order to establish the defence, several elements must be proved. First, an accused must be suffering from a mental disorder. A mental disorder is defined in section 2 of the Code as a "disease of the mind". In determining what constitutes a disease of the mind, courts apply a legal test, not simply a medical test. A psychiatrist or psychologist may give evidence as to the accused's mental health, but it is up to the judge to determine whether the legal definition has been met.

Second, once the disease of the mind has been established, one of two tests must be met. It must be proved that the disease of the mind is such that the accused is incapable,

1. of appreciating the nature or quality of his act, or
2. of knowing it is wrong.

Courts have drawn a distinction between "knowing" and "appreciating". To "know" means to merely be aware of one's physical actions. To "appreciate" involves a higher awareness and understanding of the consequences of one's actions. The courts have interpreted "knowing it is wrong" to mean that in addition to knowing it was legally wrong, the accused must also know his or her actions were morally wrong.

If the accused is found not guilty by reason of mental disorder, the court may order an absolute discharge, which means that the accused may go free without any conditions placed upon him; such a discharge would be rare and would most certainly never be granted for serious offences.

It is more likely that after a finding of not guilty by reason of mental disorder the court would either order the accused be detained in a secure psychiatric hospital for up to 90 days, pending a review by a provincially appointed board that includes at least one psychiatrist, or refer the case immediately to a board, which has 45 days to conduct its review. It is the provincial review board that determines if and when the accused should be released into the community. In making this determination, the board is required to take into account the need to protect the public from dangerous persons, the mental condition of the accused, the likelihood of a successful reintegration of the accused into society, and the other needs of the accused.

Intoxication

Offences in the *Criminal Code* can be divided into specific intent offences and general intent offences. The defence of intoxication is available for specific intent offences only.

For most offences, the Crown must prove only that the accused committed the *actus reus* intentionally, knowingly or recklessly, as the case may be. These offences are general intent offences. The vast majority of offences in the *Criminal Code* are general intent offences, and a defence of intoxication is not available for these offences.

Specific intent offences are sometimes referred to as offences requiring an ulterior intent. In other words, the Crown must prove what amounts to two levels of intent. For example, the offence of break and enter is a specific intent offence. The Crown must prove not only that the accused intended to break and enter the premises but also, and this is the second level of intent, that the accused intended to commit an indictable offence once inside. Other examples of specific intent offences are murder, theft, and assault with a weapon.

The defence of intoxication may be used to establish that the accused was too impaired to form the necessary second level of intent for specific intent offences.

In 1994, in the case of *R. v. Daviault*, the Supreme Court of Canada ruled that intoxication could be a defence to a general intent offence if the level of intoxication was so extreme that it produced a state in the accused akin to a mental disorder or automatism. This case was widely criticized, particularly as it involved a violent sexual assault. In response to the public outcry, the federal government added section 33.1 to the *Criminal Code*. The section statutorily overrides the case law in *Daviault*, and precludes the use of self-induced, voluntary intoxication to a general intent offence involving an element of assault or interference with the bodily integrity of another.

Mistake of Fact

This defence involves the accused establishing that although she committed the *mens rea*, she did so based on an honest belief in a set of facts that made her believe she was not committing an offence — for instance, if the accused truly believed that her husband had perished at sea and she then entered into a marriage with another man even while, unbeknownst to her, her first husband was still alive. Certainly the *actus reus* of the offence of bigamy would be complete. She entered into a marriage with a second husband while the first husband was still alive and while she was still married to him. However, if she could prove that she honestly believed her first husband was dead, she could successfully raise a *mens rea* defence. She did not intend to break the law.[11]

CHAPTER SUMMARY

This chapter provided a brief introduction to substantive criminal law in Canada. Criminal law is a type of public law that involves the Crown as one of the parties. The person accused of the offence is the other party. The purpose of criminal law is to prosecute and punish an accused on behalf of society as a whole, and not necessarily on behalf of the alleged victim of the offence.

In a criminal prosecution, the Crown has the burden of proving each of the elements of the offence, beyond a reasonable doubt. The elements of an offence may be divided into the wrongful act — the *actus reus* — and the wrongful intent — the *mens rea*.

A number of offences were discussed, dealing with both offences against persons and offences against property. A number of controversial offences were presented to illustrate that as Canadian society changes, public opinion about what constitutes criminal behaviour may change. Further, as a barometer of change, the *Charter of Rights and Freedoms* has also been used to test whether criminal law complies with the constitutional rights and freedoms guaranteed to Canadians.

The chapter then reviewed some selected common law and statutory defences that go to the *actus reus* of the offence, and some that go to the *mens rea* of the offence.

GLOSSARY OF NEW TERMS AND KEY CONCEPTS

abet	To encourage, incite, or set another on to commit a crime.
absolute liability offence	A type of offence where the Crown could obtain a conviction by simply proving that the accused committed the prohibited act.
accessory after the fact	Someone who assists or protects another after the other person has committed a crime.
actus reus	This is a Latin term that means "a guilty act". The *actus reus*, along with *mens rea*, is one of the two essential elements of a crime.
aid	To help, assist, or facilitate the commission of a crime.
attempt	Any act done with intent to commit a criminal offence.
automatism	An unconscious, involuntary act where the mind does not go with what is being done.

---

[11] *Tolson*, (1889) 23 Q.B.D. 168.

colour of right	the genuine appearance or presumption that there is an existing legal right when in fact no such right exists.
conspiracy	An agreement between two or more people to carry out a crime.
decriminalize	The act of removing a particular offence from criminal liability while not making the actions legal. Actions that were once regarded as criminal offences remain offences but no longer attract a criminal record.
mens rea	This is a Latin term that means "a guilty mind". *Mens rea*, along with *actus reus*, is one of the two essential elements of a crime.
recklessness	A state of mind that pays no regard to the possible injurious consequences of an act.
strict liability offence	An offence for which the Crown need only prove that the accused committed the actions required to complete the offence. There is no need to prove the intention or *mens rea* of the offence, but the accused may raise the defence of due diligence, meaning that the accused took all due care to try to prevent the commission of the offence.
wilful blindness	A conscious closing of one's mind to the consequences of one's acts.

REVIEW QUESTIONS

1. What is the difference between *actus reus* and *mens rea?*

2. Describe two different levels of intent in criminal law.

3. What is an incomplete crime? Give two examples.

4. Describe three forms of culpable homicide.

5. Give two circumstances where a charge of assault could be successfully defended by the accused.

6. What is the present law in Canada regarding abortion (or procuring a miscarriage)?

7. Why should an accused have more than "tactical defence" reasons for advocating the defence of "not guilty by reason of mental defect"?

8. What elements must be established to effectively raise the defence of necessity?

9. What is the difference between a specific intent offence and a general intent offence? Why is it important to be able to make this distinction in establishing a defence such as drunkenness?

10. Who may be convicted of an offence?

DISCUSSION QUESTIONS

1. Recent political campaigns have stressed the need to focus on crime prevention as a means of making our communities safer and more secure. One argument is that we can prevent crime by addressing the causes of crime. What, in your view, are the causes of crime?

2. Do you think some crimes — for example, prostitution — should be decriminalized and regulated, rather than prohibited? What should be the criteria for determining which of the crimes in the *Criminal Code* could be repealed?

3. *Mens rea* is a necessary component in assessing guilt in a criminal proceeding. If John has taken drugs or consumed alcohol to the point where he is so impaired that he does not know what he is doing, should he be able to successfully argue that he did not have the necessary *mens rea* at the time of the offence?

4. In the *Criminal Code*, compare the sections related to the crimes of impaired driving causing death, criminal negligence causing death, manslaughter, second-degree murder, and first-degree murder.
   (a) Briefly, what are the levels of intent required to convict an accused on each of those charges?
   (b) Briefly, explain the rationale for the differences in punishment.

5. Discuss the following statement: "The defence of not guilty by reason of mental disorder is an easy way to avoid responsibility for criminal liability."

SUGGESTED READING

Barnhorst, Sherrie, & Richard Barnhorst. *Criminal Law and the Canadian Criminal Code*, 4th ed. (Toronto, Ont.: McGraw-Hill Ryerson, 2004).

Greenspan, E., & M. Rosenberg, eds. *Martin's Annual Criminal Code*, Student Edition (Aurora, Ont.: Canada Law Book, 2008).

Mewett, Alan W., & Shaun Nakatsuru. *An Introduction to the Criminal Process in Canada*, 4th ed. (Toronto, Ont.: Carswell, 2000).

Pink, Joel E., Q.C., & David Perrier. *From Crime to Punishment: An Introduction to the Criminal System*, 6th ed. (Toronto, Ont.: Thompson Carswell, 2007).

Verdun-Jones, Simon N. *Criminal Law in Canada, Cases, Questions and the Code*, 4th ed. (Scarborough, Ont.: Thompson-Nelson, 2007).

Criminal Procedure

Mary Ann Kelly
SENECA COLLEGE

Learning Objectives

After reading this chapter, the reader should be able to:

➢ identify the role of criminal procedure in the justice system in general and the criminal law system in particular

➢ understand the various types of jurisdiction involved when dealing with criminal offences

➢ describe the various classifications of criminal offences and the procedure for prosecuting each type of offence

➢ demonstrate an understanding of the procedure for bringing the accused before the court, including powers of arrest and purpose of a bail hearing

➢ describe the various investigatory powers available to the police and the role the *Charter of Rights and Freedoms* plays in relation to police investigatory powers

➢ outline the various steps in a criminal trial

➢ describe the various sentencing principles applied by the court and the sentencing options available to the court in relation to different types of offences

➢ provide an overview of the procedure for dealing with young persons in the criminal justice system

TABLE OF CONTENTS

INTRODUCTION

This chapter will provide an overview of procedural criminal law but not substantive criminal law. The latter deals with the elements involved in criminal offences and the various defences available to those offences. Criminal procedure deals with the power of the police to investigate offences, and the methods of bringing an accused person before the court; the court has jurisdiction over the process of prosecuting an offence and trying the offence charged.

Criminal procedure is more than just a "technicality". Since it is the government or state that is prosecuting the offence, it is essential that proper procedure be followed in order to ensure a fair process. The state has multiple resources available to it: police, to investigate alleged offences; government forensic specialists and laboratories; prosecuting counsel, who are paid by the government. All of these resources are directed at the prosecution of individuals; and, in order that individuals who normally are not able to avail themselves of similar resources have a fair opportunity to defend themselves, the prosecution will be held to strict procedural standards. This has always been the case in Canadian law but is even more crucial since the enactment of the *Charter of Rights and Freedoms.*

CLASSIFICATION OF OFFENCES

The *Criminal Code* classifies all criminal offences into one of three categories. **Indictable offences** are the most serious offences and include such things as murder. **Summary conviction offences** are the least serious forms of criminal offence. Hybrid offences, or "Crown option" offences, are those offences that may be prosecuted as an indictable offence or a summary conviction offence on the election of the Crown.

The classification of an offence determines the procedure to be followed in arresting the accused and in charging him. It also determines which level of court will hear the case and the route to be followed through the court system in the event of an appeal. (See Exhibit 12.1 for an illustration of the process.)

In addition to these offences in the *Criminal Code*, which is a federal statute, there are also offences created by provincial statute. These offences are not criminal offences but are, rather, regulatory offences committed pursuant to a provincial statute, like the offence of speeding created by the *Highway Traffic Act*. In some provinces, including Ontario, these provincial offences are prosecuted under a provincial statute created for that purpose. But, in some provinces, these provincial offences are prosecuted under the procedure for the prosecution of summary conviction. The manner in which these provincial offences are prosecuted may differ, but no matter how they are prosecuted, they do not lead to a criminal record. A discussion of provincial offences is outside the scope of this chapter.

Summary Conviction Offences

These offences are the most minor in the *Criminal Code*. The procedure for dealing with them is contained in Part XXVII of the Code.

Trials for summary conviction offences are held in the provincial court before a judge alone; there is no provision for a jury trial for these offences, and penalties are much lower than for other offences. The maximum fine is $5,000, and the longest term of imprisonment is six months. Both a fine and a jail sentence can be imposed: for instance, an offender may be sentenced to 30 days in jail and a fine of $200.

An Overview of the Criminal Proceedings

EXHIBIT 12.1

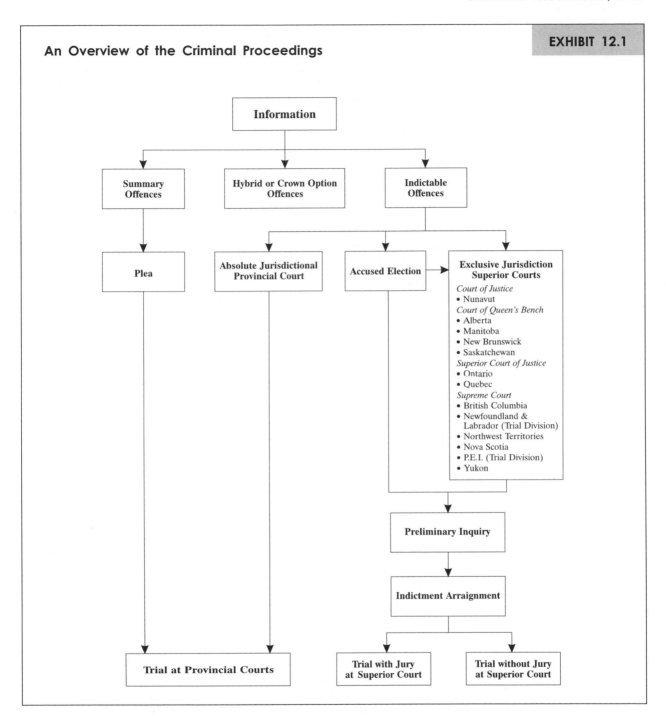

A document called an information contains the charges against the accused and is the legal document upon which the accused is prosecuted. Informations are discussed later in this chapter.

Indictable Offences   These offences are the most serious in the *Criminal Code*. The procedure for prosecution of indictable offences is more complex. Indictable offences are grouped in the Code, according to their seriousness. Each of this group has a different mode of trial.

The first group of offences is listed in section 469 of the Code, and they are the most serious indictable offences. They include murder and treason.

Trials of these matters must be heard before a judge of the superior court and a jury, unless both the Crown and the accused consent to proceed without a jury.

The second category of indictable offences is listed in section 553 of the Code. Generally speaking, these offences are the least serious indictable offences. They are more serious than summary conviction offences but considerably less serious than the offences listed in section 469. This group of offences includes driving while disqualified, keeping a common bawdy house or keeping a gaming and betting house. Trials of these matters must be heard in the provincial court by a judge sitting alone without a jury. There is no provision for trial by jury for offences of this type.

All indictable offences not listed in sections 469 or 553 fall into the final group. When charged with one of these offences, the accused is permitted to choose or elect the mode of trial according to the procedure outlined in section 536. The options are as follows:

- Trial by a provincial court judge without a jury and without preliminary hearing.
- Trial by a superior court judge alone.
- Trial by a superior court judge and a jury.

Failure of the accused to elect one of these options will result in the accused being deemed to have elected a trial by a judge and a jury.

The election as to the mode of trial must be made before a judge of the lower court or court of first instance, such as the provincial court. In Ontario, the accused is given the choice to be tried by a judge alone at the Superior Court of Justice or by a provincial judge in the Ontario Court of Justice. If the accused elects a trial in the superior court and requests a preliminary inquiry, the preliminary inquiry will be held in the provincial court. Preliminary inquires are discussed later in this chapter.

The legal document upon which the accused is prosecuted varies depending upon the level of court in which his trial is held. If he is tried in the provincial court, either because that is his election or because it is an offence listed in section 553, he will be tried on a document called an information. If he is tried before the superior court, he will be tried on the basis of a legal document called an **indictment**. Both of these documents are discussed in detail later in this chapter.

Hybrid or Crown Option Offences

Many offences in the *Criminal Code* are neither summary conviction offences nor indictable offences. They may be tried as either, depending upon the manner in which the Crown wishes to prosecute. These offences are commonly referred to as **hybrid offences**, although that term itself is not used in the Code. Until the Crown elects to proceed by summary conviction, the offence is deemed to be an indictable offence and proceeds in that manner. If the Crown then chooses to prosecute as a summary conviction offence, the summary conviction procedures kick in at that point. The Crown normally makes this election at the time the accused is arraigned.

If the Crown elects to prosecute by indictment, the accused will then be given an election as to the mode of trial: either by a judge in the provincial court or by a judge in the superior court with or without a jury. If the accused elects a superior court trial, there will then be a preliminary inquiry if the Crown or accused requests it; otherwise, it goes straight to trial. It is important to distinguish between the election that the accused makes and the election the Crown makes on how to proceed on a hybrid offence.

If the Crown elects to proceed summarily, the matter will be set over for trial in the provincial court, and the penalties available for a conviction will be those available for any summary conviction offence. The accused will have no election available in the same way as if he were charged from the beginning with a summary conviction offence.

You can determine whether an offence is hybrid by its wording. For instance, section 267, assault with a weapon or causing bodily harm, is a hybrid offence:

> Every one who, in committing an assault,
>
> (*a*) carries, uses or threatens to use a weapon or an imitation thereof, or
> (*b*) causes bodily harm to the complainant,
>
> *is guilty of an indictable offence and liable to imprisonment for a term not exceeding ten years or an offence punishable on summary conviction and liable to imprisonment for a term not exceeding eighteen months.* [italics added]

TRIAL JURISDICTION

When we say that a court has jurisdiction, we mean that it has the power or authority to deal with a matter. A court that has jurisdiction over a criminal matter has the power to try a case. There are two types of jurisdiction. A court must have a general jurisdiction over the offence, which means the power to hear that type of offence. It must also have the territorial jurisdiction or authority in the geographical area in which the offence is alleged to have occurred.

Jurisdiction over the Offence

The *Criminal Code* sets up a relatively complex structure for determining which courts have jurisdiction to hear which offences. If a court has absolute jurisdiction to hear an offence, it is the only court that may deal with that type of offence. The following is a simplified overview of the structure within the Ontario court system:

1. Summary conviction offences are heard in the Ontario Court of Justice.

2. The most serious indictable offences listed in section 469 of the Code, which include murder, treason and piracy, are in the absolute jurisdiction of the Superior Court of Justice.

3. The least serious indictable offences, listed in section 553, are in the absolute jurisdiction of the Ontario Court of Justice.

4. Indictable offences not listed in sections 469 or 553 may be heard by either the Ontario Court of Justice or the Superior Court of Justice, depending on the election of the accused, as discussed above, in relation to indictable offences.

Territorial Jurisdiction

In order for a court to have territorial jurisdiction over an offence — i.e., the power to hear that case — the offence and/or the accused must have some connection with that province. The general rule is that a court in a province cannot deal with a criminal case unless the offence is alleged to have been committed, in whole or in part, in that province. However, if the accused is found, arrested, or is in custody in a province, a court in that province may try him, even though the offence was not committed there.[1] In addition, an accused may plead guilty to an offence in any province.

---

[1] *Criminal Code*, R.S.C. 1985, c. C-46, s. 470.

The courts in Canada normally only have jurisdiction to try criminal matters where the offence was allegedly committed in whole, or in part, in Canada. There are some exceptions to this general common law rule, however. The Code provides that some offences, including piracy, hostage-taking, hijacking, treason and conspiracy, among others, may be tried in Canada if the offence has some connection with Canada, even though it was not committed in Canada. In addition, there are special provisions for the prosecution of offences that occur at sea, in Canadian waters.

Limits upon Jurisdiction

There is generally no time limit for the prosecution of indictable offences. Normally an accused may be tried for an indictable offence at any time and the court never loses jurisdiction to hear the matter. Practically, however, the longer the time between the commission of the offence and the trial, the more difficult it becomes for the Crown to obtain a conviction. With the passage of time, witnesses' memories fade and evidence may become weaker.

In relation to summary conviction offences, or for a hybrid offence where the Crown elects to proceed summarily, the information must be laid within six months of the commission of the offence. After that time, the court will have no jurisdiction to hear the matter.

Section 11(b) of the *Charter of Rights and Freedoms*

One of the legal rights guaranteed by the *Charter of Rights and Freedoms*[2] is the right, under section 11(b), to be tried within a reasonable time. There is, however, no strict definition of what amount of time is "reasonable". In deciding whether the amount of time between the laying of the charge and the trial is reasonable, the court will look at the reason for the delay; any waiver of any time periods by the Crown or the defence; the resulting prejudice to the accused, if any; and the length of the delay. Should the court find that the rights of the accused have been infringed on, the court would grant a stay or a dismissal of proceedings under section 24(1) of the Charter.

INVESTIGATORY POWERS

The role of the police in the criminal justice system is to investigate offences and to charge and, possibly, arrest the people accused of committing them. The *Criminal Code* provides the procedural law regarding search and seizure, questioning of suspects and the powers of arrest.

Because the police powers to search, arrest and question an accused are some of the most intrusive powers available in our legal system, they must be exercised in accordance with the *Charter of Rights and Freedoms*. Failure of police to honour an individual's rights may result in evidence being found to be inadmissible or, even, in a charge being dismissed or stayed.

Search and Seizure

All searches conducted by the police must follow the common law and statutory rules for exercising these powers. The *Criminal Code* and the *Controlled Drug and Substances Act*[3] and the *Food and Drugs Act*[4], among other statutes, all provide procedure for conducting searches. Some powers to search are authorized by the common law in some limited circumstances. An accused

---

[2] Schedule B to the *Constitution Act, 1982*, R.S.C. 1985, Appendix II, No. 44.
[3] S.C. 1996, c. 19.
[4] R.S.C. 1985, c. F-27.

may be searched as part of a lawful arrest or when the police have reasonable grounds for believing the accused is carrying a weapon in contravention of the law.

Charter Issues

Section 8 of the Charter guarantees everyone the right to be "secure against unreasonable search and seizure". The question then becomes whether a search meets the requirement of being "reasonable". In the case of *R. v. Collins*,[5] the Supreme Court of Canada set out the test for determining whether or not a search is reasonable:

- The search must be authorized by either the common law or statute law.
- The law authorizing the search must be reasonable.
- The search itself must be conducted in a reasonable manner.

In addition, to be found reasonable, a search cannot be arbitrary and must be based on reasonable and probable grounds that an offence has been committed and that evidence relating to that offence is likely to be found at the place to be searched. Any evidence gathered as a result of an "unreasonable" search — i.e., one not meeting these criteria — may become inadmissible in court, by virtue of section 24 of the Charter. That section provides that evidence that brings the administration of justice into disrepute shall be excluded.

The Search Warrant

Other than in exceptional circumstances, such as in cases in which a warrant cannot be obtained because it would be impractical to obtain it by reason of urgent or exigent circumstances, the police must obtain a warrant to conduct a search and seizure. A search with a properly obtained warrant is constitutional as long as there is nothing in the manner in which the search is conducted that is unreasonable. Section 487 of the *Criminal Code* provides a justice with the authority to issue a **search warrant**.

In order to obtain a warrant, a police officer must swear an information before a justice of the peace. An information is a legal document similar to an information for laying a charge, which is discussed later in the chapter. The justice must be satisfied that there are reasonable and probable grounds to believe there is physical evidence relevant to an offence that has been committed or is suspected of having been committed to be found in the place to be searched. If so satisfied, the justice may issue a warrant authorizing a search.

The warrant must contain the following:

- Sufficient detail to identify the offence that was committed or is suspected of having been committed — i.e., the section number of the offence, the date and time of the offence, the name of the victim and the manner in which the offence was committed.

- A list of the items to be seized, described sufficiently that they can be identified.

- A clear identification of the place or receptacle to be searched; for instance, if it is a building, the address must be provided.

---

[5] (1987), 33 C.C.C. (3d) 1 (S.C.C.).

Section 487(2.1) and (2.2) provides that the person authorized under the warrant to search for data may use a computer system in the place searched to locate or reproduce data stored on a computer at the premises.

Section 487.05 provides authority to a provincial judge to issue warrant to seize bodily substances for DNA analysis, and section 487.091 provides similar authority to obtain handprints, fingerprints, footprints, teeth impressions, or other bodily impressions.

Although the normal procedure for obtaining a warrant would involve the attendance of the person seeking the warrant before a justice of the peace, the police may also obtain a warrant over the telephone. However, this warrant, called a telewarrant, will be granted only in circumstances where the offence being investigated is an indictable offence and there is no time to obtain a warrant by way of the normal procedure. For instance, if the police had reasonable or probable grounds to believe that the time involved in obtaining warrant through the regular procedure would result in the destruction of evidence, they would seek a telewarrant.

Execution of the Search Warrant

Even if the search is authorized by law, the search must be conducted reasonably. The police officer must normally have the warrant in his or her possession and must present it if asked to do so by the occupants of the premises. Only reasonable force may be used in the execution of the warrant. Unless the police have reasonable grounds for believing that evidence will be destroyed unless they enter the premises without warning, they must make a demand to open before making a forcible entry. Finally, a warrant may be executed only during the day, unless the warrant specifically permits a night execution.

Search and Seizure without a Warrant

In some limited circumstances, the common law permits a police officer to conduct a search without a warrant. The person may be searched as incident to a lawful arrest. This means that when the police arrest a person, they may search him if they have a valid reason, related to the arrest, for conducting the search, such as protecting themselves, protecting the evidence, or discovering evidence. The search must still meet the test of being a reasonable search.

In addition to the common law rules authorizing some limited power to search without a warrant, section 487.11 of the *Criminal Code* provides a police officer the authority to conduct a warrantless search in exigent or urgent circumstances. The circumstances must be such that it would be impracticable for the police to obtain a warrant. For instance, if the police were in hot pursuit of a suspect who ran into his house to escape arrest and to immediately destroy evidence, they may conduct a search without a warrant.

Investigation and Questioning of Suspects

Questioning suspects is another manner in which the police may intrude upon the privacy of individuals and, as such, the law requires that certain limits be placed on the police power of interrogation.

When a Person Is Not Detained

Police may question a person with regard to a criminal offence, but the person is under no obligation to answer the questions. The person may exercise his or her right to remain silent. The police must let a person walk away if the person wishes to remain silent and if the police have no grounds for making an arrest. However, if a person wishes to speak, he or she may not intentionally mislead the police, or he or she may be charged with several offences, such as obstructing a police officer or public mischief. In addition, anything the person does say may be used in court against him or her if the police later decide to charge him or her with an offence.

When a Person Is Detained and Arrested

The power of the police to arrest and detain individuals deprives these individuals of their freedom. Therefore, when a person is put under arrest or detention, additional rights are accorded the arrested person under the *Charter of Rights and Freedoms*, and certain limitations and duties are imposed upon the police.

Upon arrest or detention, section 10 of the Charter requires that the police promptly inform the accused of the reason for his arrest, advise him of his right to retain counsel and his right to retain counsel without delay. The accused must also be given a reasonable opportunity to consult a lawyer if he indicates a wish to do so.

In addition to being advised of his specific rights afforded under section 10 of the Charter, he must be told of his right to remain silent and that, if he chooses to speak, anything he says may be used against him in court. This is commonly referred to as the police obligation to read the person his rights. Failure of the police to do so may prohibit anything the accused says from being admitted into evidence, and this violation of his rights may even result in the entire case against him being dismissed.

In section 10, arrest is distinguished from detention. Clearly, when a person is arrested he is being detained, but if he is detained prior to an arrest, he is entitled to be advised of his rights at that point. Failure of the police to advise the accused is a direct violation of his rights and can result in a stay or dismissal of any charges laid against him.

In the case of *R. v. Therens*,[6] the Supreme Court of Canada ruled that a detention occurs when a person reasonably believes that they must comply with the police and remain under police control. The police need not use any physical restraint or words to detain the person. The test is whether the person believed he was unable to leave.

Once the person indicates a wish to remain silent until he has consulted a lawyer, the police must stop questioning him until he has been given an opportunity to speak to counsel. The police are not permitted to trick him into saying something when he has exercised his right to remain silent. However, if the person is advised of his rights and still elects to talk to the police without consulting a lawyer, the police may continue to question him.

Other Investigative Tests

The police may ask the accused to participate in other investigative procedures in addition to an interrogation.

Lineups

A suspect in a police investigation may be asked to participate in a lineup. There is no obligation upon a person to do so, and the person may refuse. However, if the suspect refuses to participate in person, the police may still use a photo lineup in which the victim or other witnesses will be shown a set of photographs of different people and asked if they recognize anyone. To be admitted as evidence against the accused, the lineup must have involved people of somewhat similar age and physical appearance as the suspect.

---

[6] (1985), 18 C.C.C. (3d) 481 (S.C.C.).

Breath and Sobriety Tests

If a police officer has reasonable grounds to believe that an individual has been driving while impaired by alcohol, section 254 of the *Criminal Code* permits that officer to require the driver to take a Breathalyzer test. The driver must comply with the request, or she will be charged with the criminal offence of failing to comply with a breath demand. This offence carries penalties as serious as the charge of driving while impaired, so there is no advantage to the suspect to refuse to comply.

Polygraph Tests

Polygraph or lie detector tests are not admissible as evidence in any court of law. The technology is not regarded as reliable enough to meet evidentiary requirements. Nevertheless, the police use the test fairly regularly as an investigative tool. A suspect is never obligated to consent to take a test of this kind.

BRINGING THE ACCUSED BEFORE THE COURT

It is the role of the police to investigate crime, gather evidence and lay appropriate charges against particular accused persons. The next step in the process is bringing the accused before the court to be prosecuted, so her guilt can be legally tested according to Canadian law. The way to best ensure that an accused is brought before the court would be for the police to arrest her and detain her until her court date. However, this is neither practical nor feasible. It would mean that we would have many people detained for extremely minor offences, at considerable public expense, while awaiting their day in court. In addition, such a process would be open to constitutional challenge on a number of levels. Therefore, there are a number of procedures available for bringing the accused before the court, some that involve arrest and some that do not.

Process One: Summons or Arrest Warrant

A criminal prosecution formally begins with the laying of a document called an **information**. A person called an informant, who is usually a police officer, appears before a justice of the peace and provides sworn allegations that the accused has committed an offence. The information will not be laid unless the justice of the peace is satisfied that there are reasonable grounds to believe an offence has been committed by the accused.

If the justice is properly satisfied, she may do one of two things:

1. Issue a **summons** requiring the accused to appear before the court on a specified day, at a specified time, to answer the charge. The summons is then delivered personally to the accused. This personal delivery is called service. Failure of the accused to appear as required will result in the accused's being charged with the additional criminal offence of failing to appear. A warrant will be issued for the accused's arrest, and the accused will be detained and brought before the court to answer both the original charge and the additional charges resulting from the accused's initial failure to obey the summons.

2. Issue a warrant for the arrest of the accused. A warrant for arrest is a court order directing the police in a particular location to take the accused into custody and deliver the accused to the court.

There is a positive duty on the justice to issue a summons rather than an arrest warrant, unless the evidence of the informant establishes, on reasonable and probable grounds, that it is in the public interest to arrest the accused. This usually means that an arrest warrant will be issued for more serious offences when there is concern that an accused may destroy evidence or when it appears that the accused may try to escape justice by fleeing the jurisdiction.

Process Two: Appearance Notice or Arrest without a Warrant

Process One is followed when the police have been investigating a crime, and they believe they have found the perpetrator whom they wish to now charge with the offence. However, a great deal of crime comes to the attention of the police before they have an opportunity to lay the information. For instance, the police receive a telephone call to come to the scene of an alleged offence. When they arrive, they conduct an investigation; as a result of their investigation, they have reasonable grounds to charge a person who is present at the scene. Obviously, it is impractical for the police to ask the accused to wait while they head off to find a justice and swear out an information. The *Criminal Code*, therefore, provides another procedure for starting the process to bring the accused before the court prior to the information being laid.

A police officer may arrest a person without a warrant in the following circumstances:

1. The police officer has reasonable grounds to believe the person has committed, or is about to commit, an indictable offence.
2. The police officer finds the person committing an offence, either indictable or summary conviction.
3. The police officer has reasonable grounds to believe there is an executable warrant out for the arrest of the person.[7]

However, the Code prohibits the officer from arresting a person without a warrant for less serious indictable offences, hybrid offences, and summary conviction offences unless the officer has reasonable grounds to believe that it is in the public interest to do so or that the person may not appear in court.

Where the police officer has no reasonable grounds to arrest the accused without a warrant, the office may issue an appearance notice to the accused. The appearance notice is a document requiring the accused to attend in court on a specified day and time to answer the criminal charge. If the accused fails to appear, he faces the same consequences as an accused who fails to honour a summons — i.e., arrest and further criminal charges for failing to appear.

The officer must swear the information before a justice as soon as is practicable after the accused has been arrested without a warrant or issued an appearance notice.

RELEASE OF THE ACCUSED PRIOR TO TRIAL

If the accused has been arrested, either with or without a warrant, it does not automatically mean that the accused will remain incarcerated right up until trial. There are several procedural steps that permit the accused to be released even after an arrest has been made.

---

[7] *Criminal Code*, R.S.C. 1985, c. C-46, s. 495.

Release by the Officer in Charge

When an officer has arrested an accused person without a warrant, the officer in charge has several options. The first is to release the accused on a promise to appear (in court). The officer in charge may also issue a recognizance to the accused. A recognizance is a promise that the accused will pay a certain amount of money, most often $500, if he or she fails to appear in court. The accused will only be released by way of this option on a charge with a minor indictable offence, a hybrid offence or a summary conviction offence.

Judicial Interim Release

The second option the officer in charge may have is to detain the accused, pending a bail hearing. The formal name for bail is judicial interim release. This second option is used when the accused has been charged with a serious indictable offence, has a prior record for failing to appear in court, or the police believe the accused should be released only under rigorous conditions placed upon him or her by a judge or a justice of the peace as a term of the release.

In these situations, the accused must appear in court for a "show cause hearing", often referred to as a bail hearing. Normally, the hearing must take place within 24 hours of the arrest. The purpose of a bail hearing is for a justice of the peace or a judge to determine whether the accused should be released while awaiting trial, and if so, what conditions should be placed upon the accused.

The purposes of the conditions are to ensure, as much as is possible, that the accused appears in court for trial and is not a danger to the public if released. Common conditions to ensure public safety include prohibitions from drinking alcohol, being in the presence of certain persons, possessing firearms and other weapons, or contacting the victim. In addition, the accused may be required to report to the police any change of address or employment and to surrender his passport.

The court may require the accused to enter into a recognizance, with or without sureties. In a recognizance without sureties, the accused will forfeit an amount of money or valuable property should he or she fail to appear for trial or breach any of the conditions placed upon release. In a recognizance with sureties, someone other than the accused promises to pay money or surrender valuables in the event that the accused does not appear at trial or breaches release conditions.

There are three types of bail provided for under the *Criminal Code*:

1. Regular bail situations.
2. Reverse-onus situations.
3. Bail for offences listed in section 469.

Regular Bail Hearings

In regular bail situations, the Crown bears the onus of proving why the accused should not be released on bail while awaiting trial.[8] Generally speaking, the justice of the peace is required to release the accused without conditions, pending trial, unless the Crown is able to prove, on the balance of probabilities, that (i) the accused is unlikely to appear for trial; (ii) the accused poses a risk to public safety if released; or (iii) the accused's detention is necessary in order to maintain confidence in the administration of justice.

If the Crown is able to establish the primary ground — that is, there is a risk that the accused will not appear for trial, there is no need to move on to the second or third ground. However, if the Crown cannot prove the primary

---

[8] *Criminal Code*, R.S.C. 1985, c. C-46, s. 515.

ground, the Crown can then attempt to prove the secondary — that is, there is a risk to public safety if the accused is released.

In evaluating the risk to public safety, the court is required by section 515(10)(b) of the Code to consider "all circumstances", such as the seriousness of the alleged offence, the criminal record of the accused, the strength of the case against the accused, the likelihood of the accused committing a further offence, any danger the accused may pose to witnesses or victims, and the accused's employment and living situation.

Even if the court is satisfied that bail should be denied on the primary or secondary grounds, it must also consider under section 515(10)(c) whether the release of the accused would undermine the public's confidence in the justice system. This tertiary ground for detention is rarely used, and if the accused is to remain in custody awaiting trial, the accused is usually held under the primary or secondary ground, or both.

Reverse-onus Situations

Although in most bail situations the onus is on the Crown to prove, beyond a reasonable doubt, that the accused should not be released on bail, the onus to prove that they should be released awaiting trial shifts to the accused in the following situations:

1. The accused is charged with an indictable offence committed while he or she is out on bail awaiting trial for another indictable offence.

2. The accused is charged with an indictable offence and is not a Canadian resident.

3. The accused is charged with the offence of failing to appear at a court hearing or with a breach of condition of a bail order.

4. The accused is charged with committing an offence under the *Controlled Drug and Substances Act*, which carries a potential sentence of life imprisonment.

5. The accused is charged with an offence involving organized crime, a terrorist offence, or certain offences related to terrorism.

If an accused is successful in showing cause why he or she should be released on bail, the judge or justice of the peace may order his or her released pursuant to a recognizance or other conditions.

Bail for Offences in s. 469

Section 469 contains some of the most serious offences in the *Criminal Code*, including murder and major offences against the state, such as treason. There is no automatic entitlement to a bail hearing for these offences. An accused must apply for release under section 522, and if a bail hearing is granted, it must take place before a judge of the Superior Court.

Bail Review

There is a provision in section 520 of the *Criminal Code* for the accused to challenge a denial of bail or the imposition of specific conditions that the accused believes are unfair or improper. This process is called a bail review. The accused applies to a judge of the superior court. The Crown must be given at least two days notice of the request for a review. At the hearing, the judge will hear any evidence, review the transcripts of the bail hearing, and either dismiss the application or vacate the original bail order and make a new order granting bail or altering the conditions of release. The onus at a bail review hearing is on the accused, not on the Crown.

THE ARRAIGNMENT

The arraignment is the reading of the charge against the accused in open court, and it marks the commencement of the trial process. The court clerk reads out the charges, and the accused is asked how he or she wishes to plead. The arraignment takes place before a provincial court judge.

If the plea is guilty, the accused will be sentenced or the court may ask for a pre-sentence report to assist it in determining the most appropriate punishment for the accused.

If the accused pleads not guilty, what happens next will depend on the charge against the accused. If the charge is a summary conviction offence or one of the less serious indictable offences listed in section 553, or if the accused chooses trial by a provincial court judge, the accused will go to trial in the provincial court (e.g., Ontario Court of Justice). The trial does not normally proceed immediately after the arraignment due to court scheduling problems, but it could take place right away. Usually a future date is set for trial, and the accused must return.

If the offence is an indictable offence that is to be heard in the superior court either because the accused has elected to be tried in that court or because the provincial court has no jurisdiction to hear that type of offence, the accused may request a preliminary hearing.

THE PRELIMINARY INQUIRY

The purpose of the **preliminary inquiry** is for a provincial court judge to determine whether the Crown has sufficient evidence to warrant sending the accused to trial. A preliminary inquiry is available in the following circumstances:

1. The accused has been charged with an offence listed in section 469 of the *Criminal Code* — for example, murder or treason.

2. The accused has been charged with an indictable offence that permits an election of the mode of trial, and the accused has elected trial before a judge of the Superior Court, sitting with or without a jury.

3. A provincial court judge has declined jurisdiction to try the case and has decided to hold a preliminary inquiry instead of a trial.

The accused is not entitled to a preliminary inquiry for a summary conviction offence or for an offence on which the accused has elected to be tried before a provincial court judge and the judge does not decline jurisdiction.

A right to have a preliminary inquiry can be waived by the defence; however, it is normally not waived because the inquiry gives the defence an opportunity to test some of the Crown's witnesses through cross-examination and to assess the strength of the Crown's case. Although the defence is entitled to call evidence at the inquiry, this is rarely, if ever, done. Calling defence evidence would alert the Crown to the defences raised by the accused and give the Crown an opportunity to mend any evidentiary holes in its case.

Under the *Criminal Code*, the Attorney General of the province may send the accused to trial without a preliminary inquiry, even if the accused would normally be entitled to one, based on the three criteria listed above. This is called preferring an indictment. The provincial Attorney General rarely uses this process.[9]

A preliminary inquiry is always held before a provincial court judge. In Ontario, that would be a judge of the Ontario Court of Justice. The Crown must satisfy the judge that there is sufficient evidence that, if believed, would result in a reasonable, properly instructed jury finding the accused guilty. The provincial court judge does not, at this point, assess or weigh the evidence on its credibility. The judge merely determines whether there is enough evidence against the accused to warrant a trial. At the end of the inquiry, the judge will either commit the accused for trial or dismiss the charges. In the vast majority of cases, the accused is committed for trial. It is then up to the trial judge in the Superior Court — and the jury, if there is one — to determine the strength, weight and credibility of the Crown's evidence and to hear and assess the defences raised by the accused.

INFORMATIONS AND INDICTMENTS

Informations and indictments are legal documents prescribed by the *Criminal Code* that contain the charges against an accused. The documents must provide enough detail so that the accused can fully appreciate the charge and be able to prepare a full answer and defence to the charge. The documents form part of the court file related to the prosecution of the offence.

The Information

All criminal prosecutions formally commence with the laying of an information. As discussed above, the informant, who is usually a police officer, must appear before a justice and provide sworn evidence that the accused committed an offence or that the officer believes, on reasonable and probable grounds, that the accused has committed an offence. The justice must be satisfied that there are, indeed, reasonable grounds for believing that the accused committed an offence.

If the accused is tried in the provincial court (e.g., the Ontario Court of Justice), either because the accused has been charged with a summary conviction offence or because the accused has elected trial by a provincial court judge, then the accused will be tried on the basis of the written allegation in the information. The information will be the only written allegation of the offence charged.

The Indictment

If the accused is to be tried in the superior court, then the information that commenced the prosecution will be replaced with an indictment. This replacement takes place after the preliminary inquiry or, if there is no preliminary inquiry, after the accused has been committed to trial on consent or on a **preferred indictment**. The indictment is not a sworn document, but the Crown Attorney signs it. Like an information, it sets out the allegations against the accused.

Rules Respecting the Wording of Counts

The information or the indictment may contain a number of counts against the accused. A count, in this context, means the allegations against the accused. Numerous counts may be included in one information or indictment, but there are rules about how they must be presented.[10]

---

[9] See the Ontario case against Paul Bernardo.
[10] See s. 581 of the *Criminal Code*.

Each count must contain a "single transaction". This means that each count can contain only one alleged offence. If the accused is charged, for instance, with committing a sexual assault against a number of victims, the allegations against the accused, in relation to each victim, must be contained in a separate count in the information or indictment.

In addition, the "single transaction" rule requires that if the accused is charged with more than one type of offence involving the same victim — for instance, fraud and theft — each offence must be contained in a separate count of the information or indictment. If a count contains more than one transaction, it is said to be duplicitous.

Finally, there is a requirement that each count must disclose an "offence known to law". The accused must know with what offence he or she is being charged in order to mount a proper defence.

Informations or indictments that contravene the rules are normally simply amended to comply. However, if the defect causes an injustice or prejudice to the accused, an amendment will not be granted, and the charges against the accused will be quashed.

THE TRIAL

At trial, the onus or burden is upon the Crown to prove each element of the offence beyond a reasonable doubt. Failure of the Crown to meet this burden of proof on any aspect of the charge will result in the acquittal of the accused.

The Crown presents its case first. The prosecution calls all of its witnesses to give evidence, one after another. Witnesses are normally served with a subpoena requiring them to attend at court to give evidence at a certain date and time. Failure of a witness to obey a subpoena has legal consequences, and the witness may even be apprehended and brought to court under a warrant to testify.

The Crown attorney conducts an examination-in-chief or direct examination of each of the witnesses it calls. This means that the Crown asks non-leading questions of the witness, who has taken an oath or affirmation to tell the truth. Non-leading questions are those that do not suggest the answer. For instance, "It was raining that night, was it not?" is a leading question. The question itself implies that it was, indeed, raining. Asking the witness what the weather was that night is a not a leading question. There is no answer suggested by the person asking the question.

After the Crown has examined each of its witnesses, the lawyer for the defence may ask questions. This is called cross-examination. There is no rule in cross-examination that prohibits leading questions, and the cross-examiner may ask all the leading questions he or she likes. The purpose of cross-examination is to test the witnesses — that is, to see if their story holds up under pointed questioning. When the defence has finished its cross-examination of the witness, the Crown may be given a chance to re-examine the witness to clarify answers given by the witness during cross-examination.

When the Crown has called all its witnesses, the defence has to decide if it believes the Crown has met the burden of proving the case beyond a reasonable doubt. If the defence believes that the Crown has not done this, the defence will bring a motion for a directed verdict. This means that the defence lawyer will ask the judge to find the accused not guilty on the basis that the Crown has not proved the case against the accused.

If the motion for a directed verdict is unsuccessful, the Crown and counsel for the defence will then make legal arguments that support their position to the court. These legal arguments are called submissions.

EXHIBIT 12.2

Aspects of Trial Procedure

First Court Appearance

The first date scheduled for a court appearance on the matter is normally not the date on which the case will be heard. This is often referred to as the "set date". The accused often does not have a lawyer at this point and requires an adjournment to retain counsel.

Pre-trial Conference

The major purpose of the pre-trial conference is to ensure the efficient use of court time by narrowing the issues and addressing any pre-trial procedural matters, such as the plea to be entered, which motions will be argued, and whether any Charter issues will be raised. Section 625.1 of the Code provides that pre-trial conferences are mandatory in any Superior Court trial before a judge and a jury, and they may be ordered for a non-jury trial. However, in some Ontario jurisdictions, including Toronto, pre-trials are required by judges in all Superior Court criminal trials. In addition, the procedural rules for the Ontario Court of Justice make pre-trial mandatory in all criminal cases in that court.

Pre-trials are informal meetings that involve a judge and the Crown and the accused. However, the judge hearing the pre-trial will not be the same judge who hears the trial. This is done to ensure that the judge hearing the trial is not influenced by anything said in the informal setting of a pre-trial.

Voire Dires

A *voire dire* is a mini hearing that takes place to determine whether a certain piece of evidence is admissible in a trial. A *voire dire* is often referred to as "a trial within a trial". It may take place either before the trial begins or during a trial if an issue arises about a point or piece of evidence. If the *voire dire* is held during the course of a jury trial, the jury is required to leave the courtroom for the duration of the *voire dire*.

The Arraignment

The arraignment is the reading of the charges to the accused in the courtroom and the request from the court for the accused to enter a plea to the charges. It marks the formal commencement of the trial.

Plea of Guilty

If the accused pleads guilty at the arraignment, the court will either proceed with sentencing or request that a pre-sentence report be prepared to supply the court with further information about the background, character and general circumstances of the accused. The pre-sentence report is prepared by a probation officer, and its purpose is to aid the court in determining which sentence is most appropriate for the accused.

Charge to the Jury

In a jury trial, the judge must prepare the jury to deliberate on the case after counsel have made their closing arguments. This is called the judge's charge to the jury. The purpose of the charge to the jury is for the judge to summarize the Crown and the defence's cases, to draw the jury's attention to any major pieces or points of evidence, and to advise jury members on how the law relates to the offence that the accused has been charged with. Following the charge, the jury is sequestered or closed away to determine the guilt or non-guilt of the accused.

At the end of submissions, if there is a jury, the jury will retire to determine the facts of the case; and if there is no jury, the judge alone will determine whether the accused is guilty or not guilty.

SENTENCING

Principles of Sentencing

For most offences there are a number of options available to the court in imposing a sentence on the accused who has been found guilty at the end of a trial or who has pleaded guilty without a trial. The basic principles of sentencing in Canadian law include denunciation, deterrence and rehabilitation.

Denunciation

The purpose of denunciation is to convey the fact that society condemns the offender's actions. Any sentence imposed must be sufficient to demonstrate this condemnation for breaking the legal rules that govern society. Through the principle of denunciation, society is demonstrating to each of its members that failure to respect the rules and abide by them will result in a proper penalty. This is not about revenge. It is about disapproval.

Deterrence

The purpose of **deterrence** is to discourage continued criminal behaviour. Specific deterrence attempts to ensure that this specific offender will receive a significant enough sentence that he or she will not be prone to committing further offences. It is the principle of specific deterrence that results in more serious sentences for repeat offenders who are not getting the message.

General deterrence works to discourage the general public from committing the offence, since they know that it will attract a particular legal consequence.

When focusing on general deterrence, courts look at the gravity of the offence, the actual harm caused by the offence, and the public attitude towards the offence. If the court, on the other hand, chooses to focus on specific deterrence, greater consideration will be given to the individual, the individual's criminal record and attitude, and the possibility of rehabilitation.

Rehabilitation

Rehabilitation works to address any underlying issues that have contributed to the offender committing the offence, such as addiction, mental disorder, social conditions, lack of education, etc. It is hoped that with sufficient rehabilitation programs the offender, once released, will not be subjected to the same factors and will, therefore, be less likely to re-offend.

Aggravating and Mitigating Factors in Sentencing

Aggravating factors are circumstances that increase the seriousness of the offender's actions, while mitigating factors are circumstances that decrease the seriousness of the offender's actions. Section 718.2 of the Code requires the court to consider these factors in determining an appropriate sentence for the offender.

Aggravating factors include offences committed on the basis of hatred of the victim's race, ethnicity, sexual orientation, etc.; offences involving spousal or child abuse; offences involving breach of trust or authority; offences involving firearms; offences involving terrorism; and offences committed as part of a criminal organization.

Mitigating factors may include the age of the offender; the mental or physical disability of the offender; the fact that the offender eventually cooperated with the authorities and pleaded guilty, thus avoiding forcing the victim to testify and saving the government the cost of a trial; and the fact that the offence is a first offence.

The Sentencing Process

Once the accused has been found guilty at trial, or if the accused pleads guilty, the sentencing process begins. The offender may be sentenced immediately following the finding or the plea, but in many instances, particularly with first offenders, the court may ask for a **pre-sentence report**. This report is prepared by a probation officer, who looks into the background of the accused and provides the court with information as to the accused's character apart from the offence, the accused's residential circumstances and employment, the accused's chances of being rehabilitated, the accused's remorse, etc. The judge will use this report to assist in determining the most appropriate sentence for the offender.

Another type of report that may be presented to the court is a **victim impact statement**. People who have suffered emotional or physical damage as a result of an offence, or the relatives of a deceased victim, may provide a written statement to the court that outlines the effect of the offence on their lives. In addition, during the sentencing process the Crown may wish to call evidence from the victims or other relevant people who will provide the court with information on the impact of the offence on the victim.

Before sentencing, both the Crown and the defence may make submissions to the court on the appropriate sentence. Sometimes, the Crown and the defence will agree beforehand on the appropriate sentence, and this proposed sentence will be presented to the judge. This is called a joint submission. The court is under no obligation to accept such a sentencing recommendation, but normally it does.

Types of Sentences

Once the accused has pleaded guilty or is found guilty at the conclusion of a trial, the judge can impose the following sentencing alternatives as set out in the *Criminal Code*. These sentencing alternatives may be imposed separately, or some of them may be combined. When applying the sentence, the judge will take into consideration a number of factors, including the nature of the offence, any aggravating or mitigating evidence, the circumstances of the accused and the need for public safety.

Absolute or Conditional Discharge

The judge may grant an absolute or conditional **discharge** where the accused is a first-time offender and the offence is minor. The authority to impose these sentences is found in section 730(1) of the *Criminal Code*. These sentences may not be imposed where an accused is convicted of an offence for which a minimum penalty is prescribed by the Code or where a maximum penalty of 14 years or life is prescribed.

With either type of discharge, there is no conviction registered against the accused. This means that the accused will not have a criminal record. An absolute discharge is effective immediately, and the accused will have no further obligation to deal with the criminal justice system in relation to that offence. Courts will use this sentence only in the most unusual of circumstances.

A conditional discharge requires the accused to abide by certain conditions for a specified period of time. For instance, the accused may be required to keep the peace and be of good behaviour, or be required to abstain from alcohol. If the accused abides by the conditions for the requisite period, the accused will have no conviction registered. If the accused fails to obey the conditions, the accused may be charged with the further offence of failure to comply and may be sentenced for the original offence.

Before deciding to grant a discharge, a court must be satisfied that it would be in the best interests of the accused and not contrary to the public interest.

Fines

Section 734 of the Code provides that the court can order the offender to pay money as a penalty. This sentencing option is available only where there is no minimum sentence of imprisonment prescribed for that particular offence. In addition, the court may impose a fine only after it is satisfied that the offender has the ability to pay, or that the offender is eligible for the fine option program established under section 738. The fine option program permits the offender to discharge a fine by performing certain work over a period of two years. These programs have not been established in every jurisdiction.

At the time the fine is imposed, the court will usually provide an alternate jail sentence in the event the fine is not paid. For example, the court may order a fine of $250 or 30 days in jail. If the offender requires more time to pay the fine, the court may grant an extension of the time period for making payment.

Fines will be used for only fairly minor criminal offences and for provincial offences. The maximum fine for a summary conviction offence is $5,000 for individuals and $100,000 for an organization, such as a corporation. There is no maximum fine for an indictable offence.

Restitution

An offender may be required to pay money directly to a victim to help cover the victim's losses or for damage to property caused by the crime. This type of payment is called a restitution order. The purposes of restitution are to provide victims with some financial compensation for the crime committed against them or their property and to promote a sense of responsibility in the offenders and an acknowledgment of the harm they have caused.

Victim Surcharge

Each offence carries with it a victim surcharge, which is an amount of money the offender must pay upon conviction for any offence. The money is paid to the provincial and territorial governments to develop and provide programs, services, and assistance to victims of crime. The amount of the victim surcharge is 15 percent of any fine that is imposed on an offender or, if no fine is imposed, $50 for a summary conviction offence or $100 for an indictable offence.

The surcharge may be increased if the court is satisfied that the offender can pay the higher amount. It may also be waived if the court is satisfied that the surcharge would cause undue hardship to the offender or the offender's family.

Suspended Sentence and Probation

The court may decide to delay or suspend passing a sentence and release the offender on probation for a specified period of time. This sentencing option is provided in section 731 of the Code. Suspended sentences are available only for offences that do not carry a minimum sentence.

An offender on probation with a suspended sentence remains out of custody but is supervised by a probation officer and must follow any conditions included in the probation order. These conditions may require the offender to do certain things or to refrain from certain behaviour. For example, in addition to being required to report to a probation officer at a particular time and place, the offender may be required to perform community service, provide "restitution" to the victim, live in a certain location, and refrain from using alcohol or drugs and from owning firearms. The conditions are normally set in such a way as to fit the particular offence involved and to ensure, as much as possible, that offenders do not find themselves in the same circumstances in which they committed the offence.

If the offender breaches any of the terms of the order, he or she can be charged with the further criminal offence of breach of probation and may face being sentenced for the original offence as well. A probation order may last for up to three years. It is important to remember that even though the offender is not placed in custody if the probation terms are kept, this type of sentence still results in a criminal record.

Conditional Sentence of Imprisonment

If an offender is convicted and the court imposes a sentence of less than two years' imprisonment, section 742.1 of the Code provides that the court may order that the sentence be served in the community, with certain conditions, instead of in jail. The court must be satisfied that serving the sentence in the community will not endanger the safety of the public. The offender must live at a specific location, usually the offender's own home, under very detailed and quite restrictive conditions. If the conditions are not met, the offender may be required to serve the rest of the sentence in jail.

Imprisonment

Imprisonment is the most serious sentence available, and it is used for the more serious offences or for repeat offences. The maximum period of imprisonment available for a summary conviction offence is six months. For indictable offences, the maximum period of imprisonment varies according to the offence, and for some offences it ranges as high as life imprisonment.

An offender who receives a sentence of less than two years serves the sentence in a provincial correctional institution. In most instances, this means that the offender is closer to his or her family and support network while serving the sentence. Maintaining these connections may be very important for the offender's rehabilitation and reintegration into the community at the end of the imprisonment. An offender sentenced to two years or more usually serves the sentence in a federal penitentiary.

If the sentence imposed is 90 days or less, the court may order that the sentence be served intermittently. Offenders serving intermittent sentences are allowed to leave the institution for blocks of time for a specific purpose, such as attending school or work, or caring for a family member who needs help. Usually, they are released during the week but must report back to the institution on weekends until they have served the time set out in the sentence. An intermittent sentence must be accompanied by a probation order, which sets out the conditions the offender must follow while he or she is not in jail. If the offender breaches any condition, the offender can be charged with the additional offence of breach of probation and may face being imprisoned full-time.

Indeterminate Sentence for Dangerous Offenders

Normally, a sentence of imprisonment sets out the specific amount of time that the offender must serve. However, an offender convicted of a violent offence may be declared to be a dangerous offender and sentenced to an *indeterminate* period of detention. *Indeterminate* means that the court does not specify a time period that the offender must serve. The Crown must make a special application to have a person declared a dangerous offender. This type of application is normally made only when an offender has a long series of violent offences. A person declared a dangerous offender is kept in jail with no fixed date for release. The National Parole Board reviews the case after seven years, and every two years after that.

YOUNG PERSONS IN CONFLICT WITH THE LAW ——————————————

Under British common law, the age of criminal responsibility was 7. In Canada, historically, children who committed offences and were 14 years of age or older were tried in adult courts, as were those between 7 and 13 if it could be proven that they had the ability to form a criminal intent. By the latter part of the 19th century, however, Canadian society had begun to recognize that children had special needs and should, therefore, be tried separately from adult offenders. In 1908, the federal government passed the *Juvenile Delinquents Act*. It was amended in 1929. Under this statute, the age of criminal responsibility ranged from 7 to 16 years.

By the early 1980s, the *Juvenile Delinquents Act* had attracted some severe criticism from both legal and social welfare quarters. It was viewed as paternalistic, and the legal rights of children were often ignored in that they were rarely represented by counsel in court, and judges, police and probation officers were given too much control over the offender. In 1984, the *Juvenile Delinquents Act* was repealed, and the *Young Offenders Act* came into force. It raised the age of criminal responsibility to 12 and extended the definition of *youth* to include those up to 18 years of age. However, an application could be made under the statute for any youth over 14 years of age to be tried as an adult. Normally it was the Crown who would make this application for some young people who were charged with serious violent offences, such as murder, manslaughter, or sexual assault.

By the late 1990s, significant problems were identified in the youth justice system. These included the overuse of incarceration as a sentence (Canada has the highest youth incarceration rate in the Western world); the lack of a coherent process to ensure the effective reintegration of the young person being released from custody; the failure to make a distinction between serious, violent offences and less serious offences; the complicated and time-consuming procedure for applying for transfer to adult court; the inconsistency in sentencing; and the insufficient recognition of the concerns of victims.

In an effort to address these issues, Parliament enacted the *Youth Criminal Justice Act* (YCJA).

The *Youth Criminal Justice Act*

The *Youth Criminal Justice Act* came into force on April 1, 2003. The YCJA, like the legislation preceding it, does not create offences; rather, it is a procedural statute setting out the process for young persons to be tried for criminal offences. In order to determine the substantive law — that is, the elements of offences and the various defences available, reference must be made to the *Criminal Code*.

The following are the principles of the YCJA:

- The youth justice system must protect society.

- Youth must be treated separately from adults in the criminal justice system, given their differing needs and maturity levels, and the youth justice system must provide due process to young persons, as well as rehabilitation, and reintegration into society.

- Measures to address youth crime must
  - hold the offender accountable;
  - address the offending behaviour of the youth;
  - reinforce respect for social values;
  - encourage repair of the harm done to victims and the community; respect gender, ethnic, cultural and linguistic differences;

- involve the family, community and other agencies; and
- be responsive to the circumstances of youth with special requirements.

• The parents and victims both have a role in the system and should be encouraged to participate.

In order to achieve these goals, the statute sets up a new procedural framework for dealing with sentencing, publication of records and custody and reintegration into the community.

Sentencing Options

As mentioned, Canada had the highest rate of youth incarceration in the Western world in the late 1990s. The youth incarceration rate was higher than the incarceration rate for adults, and the length of incarceration for young persons was longer than that for adults convicted for similar, less serious offences. There was also no consistency in sentencing from province to province.

The YCJA retained most of the prior options for sentencing and added some new options.

Retained Prior Options

In general, the YCJA retained the sentencing options available under the *Young Offenders Act*. These include incarceration in either a closed or open custody setting, absolute discharge, conditional discharge, a fine of up to a $1,000, probation, a prohibition order, restitution or compensation to the victim, and a community service order. Under a restitution or compensation order, the offender may be sentenced to repay the victim if a payment would be appropriate, or to compensate the victim in some other manner for damage caused. Under a community service order, the accused is required to complete a certain number of hours of unpaid work, up to a maximum of 240, in a community service organization.

In relation to custodial sentences, for most offences, the young person can be incarcerated for up to two years. For offences, other than murder, for which an adult may be sentenced to life imprisonment, a young person may be given a sentence of up to three years. For first-degree murder the sentence is up to 10 years, with no more than six years spent in custody and the balance on conditional supervision. Finally, for second-degree murder, the young offender may be sentenced to up to seven years, with no more than four years in custody and the balance on conditional supervision.

Under the sentencing principles of the YCJA, custody is to be reserved primarily for violent offenders and serious repeat offenders.

One major change to sentencing in the YCJA is that adult sentences are available for any youth over 14 years of age who is convicted of an offence that carries a sentence of more than two years. There is no requirement for an application to transfer the trial to adult court in order for an adult sentence. Rather, once the young person has been found guilty of a serious offence, the youth justice court judge may apply an adult sentence. If an adult sentence were applied, the young person would not be held in an adult prison but in a youth facility, unless it would not be in the best interests of the young person or would endanger the safety of others.

New Options Under the YCJA

• *Reprimand* — a stern lecture or warning from a judge for minor cases in which the court believes the reprimand will be sufficient.

• *Intensive Support and Supervision* — like an intensive probation order that involves very close monitoring and support to assist the young person to change his or her behaviour. The caseload of the probation officer carrying out the supervision would be much smaller than a regular probation caseload, allowing for more contact with the young person.

* *Attendance Order* — requires the young person to attend a specific program at times and under conditions set by the judge.

* *Deferred Custody and Supervision* — allows the young person to serve the sentence in the community under conditions. If the conditions are breached, the young person may be placed in custody. It is not a sentence that is available for serious, violent offences.

* *Intensive Rehabilitative Custody and Supervision Order* — a sentence available for serious, violent offenders. This order is available if
  * the young person has been found guilty of murder, attempted murder, aggravated sexual assault or is a repeat offender of violent offences;
  * the young person is suffering from a mental or psychological disorder or emotional disturbance;
  * a treatment plan has been developed for the young person; and
  * there is an appropriate program available.

Publication and Records

Contrary to what many members of the public believe, records of young persons are not destroyed at age 18. Evidence of prior findings of guilt is often used against adults in court at bail hearings and sentencing. However, a record may be made unavailable under certain circumstances after certain periods of time. Sentences other than alternative measures and discharges will not be purged, however, if there is an intervening offence within the specified time period. Fingerprints of a young person may be kept for an additional period of time.

Under the *Young Offenders Act*, in most circumstances it was an offence to publish the name of a young person, whether it is before or after a finding of guilt, unless the young offender had been transferred to adult court. A special order had to be obtained if the police wished to publish the name and photograph of a young person who was wanted for a specific offence. Such orders were rarely granted. The rationale for this was that the publication of the young person's name would interfere with the person's rehabilitation.

It is still a core principle of the YCJA that the identity of the young person be protected. However, the procedure will permit publication of the names of all youth convicted of a crime who receive an adult sentence. In addition, the names of 14- to 17-year-olds given a youth sentence for murder, attempted murder, manslaughter, aggravated sexual assault, or repeat violent offences may be allowed. Publication would also be allowed if a youth were at large and considered by a judge to be dangerous. The court may decide that publication is not appropriate in a particular case. Finally, the records of youth who receive adult sentences are treated the same as the records of adult offenders.

Custody and Reintegration

One of the general principles of the YCJA is that young persons in conflict with the law are more easily rehabilitated than are adults in similar situations. Therefore, every sentence involving custody must consider the eventual reintegration of the young person into the community with supports to help prevent the young person from re-offending. Every period of custody must be followed by a mandatory period of supervision in the community, and the supervision period must be equal to half the period of custody imposed. This means that if a young person receives a custodial sentence of two years, the young person must be supervised in the community for one year. During this time, the young person is to be monitored and controlled in order to ensure that he or she receives the necessary treatment and programs to return successfully to the community.

All periods of supervision must contain mandatory conditions prescribed by the legislation, such as keeping the peace and reporting to authorities. In addition, specific conditions, tailored to meet a particular young person's circumstances, may be applied, such as attending school, keeping a curfew, and attending designated treatment programs.

If the young person does not abide by any of the conditions while on supervision, the young person may be returned to custody. However, if the breach was minor, the court may apply additional conditions or vary the existing conditions rather than re-incarcerate the young person.

All young persons held in custody must be separated from adult offenders. If the young person is being held past his 18th birthday on a youth justice court sentence, it is presumed under the YCJA that he will be moved to an adult facility upon reaching the age of 20. However, the statute also provides that the young person may be held in a youth facility past his 20th birthday if provincial authorities determine it is appropriate to do so.

Measures outside the Formal Court Process

Almost half the matters brought to youth justice court are minor offences, such a shoplifting, possession of stolen property, failure to appear, and breach of a probation condition. Often these matters may be better dealt with outside the formal court process. The YCJA provides a number of options that may result in the young person never being prosecuted for the offence. The Act requires the police, in every case, to consider all options, including informal alternatives to the court process, before laying charges. In addition, each province may determine whether it is appropriate to require Crown counsel to pre-screen charges before they are laid against a youth. These measures help to ensure that the more expensive and formal court process is reserved for youth crimes that warrant it.

Jurisdiction of the Youth Justice Court

Young persons charged with offences are brought before special courts, separate from adults. These courts are all called youth justice courts. Each province may designate whether it wishes to appoint provincially or federally appointed judges to deal with criminal matters involving young persons. In Ontario, judges of the Ontario Court of Justice who deal with adult criminal matters are the provincially designated judges to sit in youth justice court, which is, very often, simply a separate courtroom in a courthouse dealing with adult criminal prosecutions.

CHAPTER SUMMARY

This chapter provided an outline of procedural law in the Canadian criminal justice system. Procedural law is central to the system in that it provides the crucial balance between the interests and the power of the state in apprehending and prosecuting offenders and the rights of the individual who has been drawn into the system.

The different classifications of criminal offences were examined first as the type of offence charged dictates the procedure to be followed. Whether the offence is a summary conviction offence, an indictable offence, or a hybrid offence will determine the powers of arrest, the appropriate court to which the accused will be brought, and the process the case will take through the court system.

The chapter then examined the jurisdiction of courts to hear criminal cases. There are two bases for jurisdiction: jurisdiction over the offence and territorial jurisdiction. Some cases must be heard in the superior court, and others in the provincial court.

The first step in any criminal case is the police investigation and the laying of the charge. Police powers to investigate were outlined. Police investigatory powers are limited by the rights of the individual under the *Charter of Rights and Freedoms*. An improperly conducted investigation that violates a suspect's rights can result in the case being tossed out of the system. Police must, therefore, follow the rules laid out in the *Criminal Code* for conducting searches and seizures, questioning suspects, and holding lineups and other investigatory tests.

The procedure for bringing the accused before the court was then discussed. It is a principle of our criminal justice system that the accused must not be held in detention awaiting trial unless the Crown can establish on the balance of probabilities that there is sufficient reason for holding the accused in custody. The chapter summarized the various procedural requirements for arrest and detention and the different types of bail hearings that may be conducted, depending upon the offence charged.

We then looked at the different charging documents, informations and indictments, and then followed a criminal case through the court, from the preliminary inquiry through to sentencing. The principles of sentencing were discussed, and then the available sentencing options were examined.

Finally, the chapter presented an overview of the youth criminal justice system that is governed by the federal *Youth Criminal Justice Act*. We discussed the special provisions, policies, and procedures for prosecuting young persons between the ages of 12 and 18 years of age.

GLOSSARY OF NEW TERMS AND KEY CONCEPTS

deterrence
A principle of sentencing directed at discouraging an offender from reoffending or dissuading a member of the public from committing a similar offence.

discharge
A sentence whereby there is no conviction registered against the accused, even though the charge was proved.

hybrid offence
An offence for which the *Criminal Code* permits the Crown to elect whether to proceed by indictment or by way of summary conviction.

indictable offence
The more serious offences in the *Criminal Code*.

information
The sworn legal document that formally starts the prosecution of the accused by alleging that there are reasonable and probable grounds to believe that the accused committed the specific offence charged.

indictment
The legal document setting out the allegations against the accused, which replaces the information when the matter is to be tried in the superior court.

preliminary inquiry
A hearing prior to the trial of an indictable offence, at which the Crown must establish that there is enough evidence against the accused to justify placing the accused on trial.

preferred indictment
The process whereby the Attorney General of a province has the authority under the *Criminal Code*, in certain circumstances, to commit the accused person to trial in the superior court, without a preliminary inquiry.

pre-sentence report
A report prepared by a probation officer with information as to the character, residential circumstances, employment, chances of being rehabilitated, and remorse, etc. of the offender, which a judge will use to assist in determining the most appropriate sentence.

search warrant	A court order that permits the police to enter and search specified premises to look for specified evidence that the police have satisfied the court they have reasonable grounds for believing is located at or in those premises.
summary conviction offence	A less serious criminal offence that is tried in the provincial court or before a provincial court judge.
summons	A court order requiring an accused to appear in court to answer a criminal charge.
victim impact statement	A type of report or written statement presented to the court, outlining the effect of the offence on their lives, by people who have suffered emotional or physical damage as a result of an offence or by the relatives of a deceased victim.

REVIEW QUESTIONS

1. What are the differences between a indictable offence, a summary conviction offence and a hybrid offence?

2. Under what circumstances will an accused be able to elect the level of court at which he or she wishes to be tried?

3. What is jurisdiction, and how does it affect criminal proceedings in Canada?

4. When may the police conduct a search without a warrant?

5. Constable Sharma is a police officer. While on patrol in the police car, he is called into Shepherd's Drug Mart in Wacco Mall. There he finds Bertha, who is being held by the store detectives. She has apparently stolen nail polish valued at $27.00. He decides to charge her with theft. Do you think he should arrest her?

6. Under what circumstances may the police arrest a person without a warrant?

7. What is the difference between a regular bail hearing and a reverse onus bail hearing?

8. What is the difference between specific deterrence and general deterrence?

9. What would you consider to be the major difference in procedure between the adult criminal system and the system under the *Youth Criminal Justice Act*?

10. Describe the three classifications of offences in the *Criminal Code.*

DISCUSSION QUESTIONS

1. In regard to the three principles of sentencing — denunciation, deterrence and rehabilitation — which do you think should be the most important, and why? Based on what you hear or read in the media, discuss whether or not you believe the Canadian criminal courts are appropriately applying the principle that you believe is the most important.

2. "Since the introduction of the *Charter of Rights and Freedoms*, courts have become more concerned with the rights of the criminals than they are with the rights of the victims."

   Discuss this statement in the context of the following:

(a) The right of the police to search and to seize evidence

(b) The power of the police to arrest the accused

(c) The procedure on bail hearings

3. In the following scenarios, discuss the procedural steps that a police officer wishing to charge the accused should follow.

(a) After an investigation, there is sufficient evidence for Martin to be charged with murder in the death of his business partner.

(b) The police officer received a 911 call about an assault and, upon arriving at the club, he found Desmond kicking a smaller man who was down on the ground. The officer is going to charge Desmond with assault under section 265 of the *Criminal Code*. He looks in the *Criminal Code* and determines that this is a hybrid offence.

4. "Youth crime will continue to be a problem in Canada because the *Youth Criminal Justice Act* isn't taken seriously by youth."

Do you think this is a valid statement? Discuss your views.

5. The government of Canada is in the process of amending the *Criminal Code* to provide that reverse-onus bail provisions will apply to persons who are charged with serious gun offences. Do you think these provisions will reduce gun-related offences?

SUGGESTED READINGS

Bala, Nicolas. *Youth Criminal Justice Law* (Toronto, Ont.: Irwin Law, 2002).

Canada, Department of Justice. *The Youth Criminal Justice Act, Summary and Background* (Ottawa: Department of Justice, 2002), online: Department of Justice, Program and Initiatives, Youth Justice Renewal <http://www.justice.gc.ca/eng/pi/yj-jj/ycja-lsjpa/back-hist.html>.

Greenspan, E., & M. Rosenberg, eds. *Martin's Annual Criminal Code, Student Edition* (Aurora, Ont.: Canada Law Book, 2008).

Mewett, Alan W., & Shaun Nakatsuru. *An Introduction to the Criminal Process in Canada*, 4th ed. (Toronto, Ont.: Carswell, 2000).

Pink, Joel E., Q.C., & David Perrier. *From Crime to Punishment: An Introduction to the Criminal System*, 6th ed. (Toronto, Ont.: Thompson Carswell, 2007).

WEBSITE

Law Courts Education Society of B.C.: <www.lces.ca/ycja-youth/>

The Law of Torts

JoAnn Kurtz
SENECA COLLEGE

Learning Objectives

After reading this chapter, the reader should be able to:

➢ identify and understand the elements of a tort
➢ identify and understand the different levels of guilty mentality in the commission of an act
➢ identify and understand variously named intentional torts
➢ identify and understand the main defences to intentional torts
➢ analyze and apply to fact situations the law as it relates to intentional torts and the defences to intentional torts
➢ identify and understand the elements of negligence
➢ analyze and apply to fact situations the elements of negligence
➢ understand the law of occupiers' liability
➢ understand the law as it relates to strict liability torts
➢ identify and understand the different kinds of damages awarded in tort actions

TABLE OF CONTENTS

INTRODUCTION

Torts is the area of law that deals with compensation of individuals for harm done to them by others in a non-contractual relationship. Together with actions for breach of contract, tort law is the basis for the vast majority of civil litigation.

Tort law includes matters as diverse as the following:

- Assault and battery
- Trespass to property
- Medical malpractice
- Nuisance
- Fraud
- Product liability
- Defamation
- Motor vehicle accidents

A discussion of torts is a discussion of civil wrongs, although the conduct involved may or may not also constitute a criminal wrong. In tort law, the victim of the wrongful act sues the wrongdoer for damages, and the major focus is on compensation of the victim. In criminal law, the state prosecutes the wrongdoer, and the major focus is on punishment of the wrongdoer.

What Are Torts?

Tort law dates from the time of the Norman Conquest of England in 1066. The word **tort** means "wrong" and comes from the old Norman-French language, which was used by the English courts until after the Middle Ages.

The law of torts, which has evolved over time, deals with certain types of wrongful and/or harmful conduct that cause certain types of harm or damage to another person. There are three elements in this definition of a tort:

1. Wrongful conduct
2. Harm
3. Cause

Each element must be examined.

What Types of Wrongful Conduct Constitute a Tort?

The answer to this question is rather unsatisfying, at least initially. The types of conduct that constitute a tort are those the courts have, over time, recognized as being redressable by some appropriate legal action. The range of categories has expanded since 1066, and is still growing today.

What Is Meant by Harm?

For there to be a tort, it is not enough to have a wrongful conduct; that wrongful conduct must have harmed the victim, and the type of harm must be one that is recognized by the courts.

Example

John decided to have a party. He invited all of his neighbours to the party except Jane, as a result of which her feelings were terribly hurt.

Unfortunately for Jane, hurt feelings is not a type of harm recognized by the courts.

The kinds of harm recognized by the courts have expanded over the years. In the 19th century, emotional or nervous shock was not a recognized category of harm, but now it is.

What Is Meant by Cause?

As stated earlier, the wrongful conduct must cause harm to the plaintiff. At the simplest level, there must be a physical connection between the act of the wrongdoer and the harm suffered by the victim. However, the legal definition of cause is not limited to simply establishing a causal connection between the wrongful conduct and the harm. Questions of remoteness of harm also arise, as will be discussed later in this chapter.

LEVELS OF GUILTY MENTALITY

Tort law looks at the wrongdoer as well as the victim. In particular, tort law examines the wrongdoer's state of mind while committing the wrongful act or conduct. This examination takes place because for different types of torts, different levels of blameworthiness or guilty mentality are required by the courts before a wrongdoer will be found liable in law to his victim.

Intentional Acts

An act is **intentionally** committed if the person committing the act wishes to produce the results that follow from her act. If a woman swings her fist at a man, wishing to strike that man in the nose and does, in fact, hit him in the nose, she is said to have intentionally hit his nose. The focus here is on the act itself, and not on the consequences of the act. In the situation just described, what is relevant is that the wrongdoer hit the victim's nose intentionally. The fact that she may or may not have intended to break his nose by doing so is irrelevant.

Intentional conduct is considered to carry the highest level of blameworthiness. This chapter will discuss classes of torts that must be intentionally caused to be actionable.

Recklessness

When an act is **recklessly** committed, the person undertaking a course of action has no specific intention or wish to cause harm, but has specific knowledge that the course of action might cause harm, and the course of action is undertaken in any event.

Example

A young man drives his car at high speed through a crowded schoolyard. The driver knows that by doing so he may well strike a child with his car. While he does not intend to hit any particular child in that he does not aim his car at any particular child, he nonetheless hits a young child with his car. In this instance, it would be said that the driver recklessly struck the child with his car. While he had no specific intention to strike the particular child with his car, he did know that he would likely strike some child, and undertook the activity in any event. Note that the focus here is on the striking of the child with the car. That is the act that is said to be recklessly committed.

Reckless conduct carries the next highest level of blameworthiness, and is more relevant to criminal law than to civil law. In tort law, the next level of guilty mentality after intention is negligence, the definition of which is broad enough to encompass reckless conduct.

Negligence

As with recklessness, when an act is **negligently** committed, the person undertaking a course of action has no specific intention or wish to cause harm. However, unlike recklessness, there is no requirement that the wrongdoer have specific knowledge that the course of action might cause harm. It does not matter what the wrongdoer knows or thinks. The test is whether a reasonable person in the position of the wrongdoer would know that harm might occur. If the answer is yes, the wrongdoer is held responsible on the basis that she ought to have known that her course of action would or could cause harm.

Example

Anne is driving her car at an excessive rate of speed. She is a skilled driver who always speeds and is confident that she is capable of handling her car and avoiding any accidents. Suddenly, the car in front of Anne stops, and Anne collides with the stopped car. If she had been driving at the posted speed limit, she would have been able to stop.

In this example, Anne did not intentionally collide with the car. She did not recklessly collide with the car (because she had no specific knowledge that this collision might occur). She was, however, negligent, because a reasonable person would have known that this collision might occur. Accordingly, the law states that Anne ought to have known.

This chapter will discuss classes of torts that must be negligently caused to be actionable.

Strict Liability

In all of the previous categories of guilty mentality, there is some element of blameworthiness on the part of the wrongdoer. What if a person's act causes harm to another, but the act is not intentionally, recklessly or negligently committed; in other words, the person is blameless? Generally, in such circumstances, the person will not be liable in law to the person harmed.

There are, however, some circumstances in which a blameless person causing harm may be held liable to the victim. The circumstances where this occurs are called **strict liability** torts. This category of torts will be discussed later in this chapter.

INTENTIONAL TORTS

It is to be remembered that a tort is comprised of three elements: wrongful conduct + harm + cause. This section discusses those kinds of conduct recognized by the courts to be wrongful when committed intentionally — in other words, when the level of guilty mentality required by the wrongdoer is that of intention.

In examining the definitions of the various intentional torts, it is to be noted that the elements of harm and the causal connection between the wrongful conduct and the harm are included in each definition.

What follows is a brief discussion of the most common intentional torts. There are other torts — such as malicious prosecution, abuse of process, maintenance and champerty, the intentional infliction of mental suffering, deceit and interference with contractual relations — that are not discussed.[1]

---

[1] Readers interested in obtaining more information about these other named torts should consult the torts texts listed under the heading "Suggested Readings".

Battery

Battery is the intentional infliction of a harmful or offensive contact with another person, including something that the person is wearing or carrying. That contact can be made by a part of the wrongdoer's body, by something the wrongdoer is carrying, or by something the wrongdoer has thrown.

The contact does not have to harm the victim to constitute battery; it must merely be offensive or unwanted (e.g., spitting). If the contact is unwanted by the victim, it does not matter that the wrongdoer did not intend it to be offensive (e.g., an unwanted kiss). However, jostling in a crowd or tapping someone on the shoulder to get the person's attention do not constitute battery because a certain amount of unwanted contact is considered by the courts to be inevitable in everyday life.

Contact with a person, if unwanted and offensive to that person, will constitute battery, even if the purpose of the contact is meant to benefit the victim. So, for example, surgery, even if beneficial to a patient, is considered battery if performed without that person's consent.

Unwanted or offensive contact constitutes battery even if the victim is unaware of the contact at the time it is made (e.g., sexual touching of a patient by a dentist when the patient is anaesthetized). The cause of action arises when the victim discovers the wrongdoing.

Assault

In tort law, **assault** is the intentional creation in the victim of a reasonable apprehension of imminent harmful or offensive contact. Keeping in mind that battery is defined as harmful or offensive contact, it can be said that assault is the creation of a reasonable apprehension of imminent battery.

Usually the victim's apprehension of imminent harmful or offensive contact is followed rapidly by that contact, and so battery usually follows quickly upon the heels of assault. But it is possible for each one to occur without the other.

Example 1

Lucy and Ethel are facing each other. Lucy takes a punch at Ethel's head but does not hit Ethel because Ethel ducks.

In this situation, Lucy has intentionally created in Ethel a reasonable fear of being punched in the head — a quite offensive contact. However, the contact does not occur. In other words, Lucy has committed the tort of assault but not battery.

Example 2

Ethel sneaks up behind Lucy, who remains totally unaware of Ethel's presence, and hits her in the head with a fry pan.

In this case, Ethel has committed the tort of battery but not assault. There was a very offensive contact, but because Lucy had no idea it was about to occur, there was no creation of fear of that contact.

Assault includes actions such as shaking a fist at another person or pointing a gun at another person.

The victim must reasonably fear that the offensive contact is imminent. So if a wrongdoer phones a victim from across town and tells the victim the wrongdoer will be coming over in two hours to beat the victim, that conduct, while wrong and perhaps even criminal, does not constitute the tort of assault. If, however, the wrongdoer tells the victim that a bomb has been planted in the victim's apartment that will be detonated by the wrongdoer over the phone, the tort of assault has been committed.

False Imprisonment

False imprisonment occurs when a person intentionally and without lawful justification confines another person within fixed boundaries.

The word "false" means wrongful. The word "imprisonment" does not mean that confinement in a prison is required. A person can be confined anywhere, such as a home, a car, or a boat. The victim must be totally confined within definite boundaries. There is no false imprisonment if there is a reasonable means of escape from the area of confinement. So, for example, there can be no false imprisonment in a room with two doors, if only one is blocked. However, the means of escape must be reasonable — in other words, available to the victim without danger. So, for example, there would be false imprisonment if, in order to escape, the victim would have to jump from a window, out of a moving car or out of a boat into the ocean.

There is no false imprisonment where a person voluntarily submits to confinement — for example, on a bus or plane trip. However, it is false imprisonment if a victim "voluntarily" goes into a confined area to avoid embarrassment, for example, if detained without justification on suspicion of shoplifting.

Trespass to Chattels

Historically, there were three torts to deal with chattels: trespass to chattels, detinue and conversion. While there are differences in both the definition of each tort and the remedy available in each case, they all involve the intentional interference with chattels owned by or in the lawful possession of another person. Because the distinctions among the three torts are quite subtle, for the purpose of this discussion all three will be referred to as **trespass to chattels**.

This tort covers the unjustified touching of chattels owned by or in the lawful possession of another, whether or not damage is caused to the chattel. For example, a teenager who scratches a neighbour's car with his keys has committed the tort of trespass to chattels.

It would also constitute trespass to chattels to take possession of a chattel contrary to the wishes of the person who owns or is in lawful possession of the chattel. For example, a teenager who takes his neighbour's car without permission has committed the tort of trespass to chattels.

Trespass to chattels not only covers the unlawful taking of a chattel but also the unlawful keeping of a chattel that has been obtained lawfully.

Example

George is a mechanic. Jerry gives his car to George to repair and return to him later that day. George does not do the repairs but instead takes the car on a one-week trip to Florida.

George's actions in this situation constitute a trespass to chattels. While George obtained possession of Jerry's car lawfully, the possession became unlawful when the car was used for a different purpose than authorized by Jerry, and also when the car was kept by George longer than authorized by Jerry.

Trespass to Land

Trespass to land involves the intentional interference with land owned by or in the lawful possession of another person. The tort of trespass to land is committed when the wrongdoer enters, without consent, the lands owned by or in the lawful possession of another person. It is also trespass to lands to refuse to leave the property when ordered to do so by the owner or person in lawful possession, even if the initial entry onto the property was lawful.

This action is used primarily as a means of asserting a right of ownership to real property so as to prevent the trespasser from obtaining a possessory title to the property.

Nuisance

Nuisance is interference with a landowner's use and enjoyment of his lands as a result of actions or conduct on neighbouring lands. Put another way, it is the intentional use of land in a way that interferes with a neighbour's use and enjoyment of her land.

This tort must be compared with the tort of trespass to lands, which protects the rights of landowners from interference by the actions of wrongdoers on the landowner's property. The tort of nuisance protects these rights by restricting behaviour on neighbouring land.

The tort of nuisance has been used to try to prevent or obtain damages for such matters as noise, odours, damage by a neighbour's tree roots and pollution from neighbouring factories.

In determining cases involving nuisance, the courts must balance the competing interests of neighbouring landowners: one owner's right to use his land as desired as opposed to the other owner's right not to be disturbed.

Defamation

Defamation is the publication of a statement that a reasonable person would see as damaging to one's reputation; or that holds the person up to contempt, hatred, scorn, or ridicule; or that causes the person to be discredited or shunned.[2]

Defamation is comprised of two torts: slander and libel. Slander involves spoken words or gestures. Libel involves more permanent statements, such as those in writing, in movies or on television.

Defamation law is a very complex area with its own defences, the best known of which is that the statement made is true. A more complete discussion of this area of law is beyond the ambit of this chapter.[3]

Conclusion

All of the intentional torts contain the three elements discussed earlier: wrongful conduct + harm + cause.

All of the intentional torts are examples of conduct that the courts consider to be wrongful when the acts are committed intentionally. The elements of harm and the causal connection between the wrongful conduct and the harm are included in the definition of each tort.

DEFENCES TO THE INTENTIONAL TORTS

A plaintiff may succeed in proving that a defendant has committed an intentional tort. However, if the defendant can successfully establish one of the recognized defences to the intentional torts, the defendant will not be liable to the plaintiff.

What follows is a brief discussion of the most common defences to the intentional torts. There are other defences, such as legal authority and necessity, that are not discussed.[4]

---

[2] *Murphy v. LaMarsh* (1970), 73 W.W.R. 114 (B.C.S.C.).

[3] Readers interested in the subject of defamation should consult the torts texts listed under the heading "Suggested Readings".

[4] Readers interested in these additional defences should consult the torts texts listed under the heading "Suggested Readings".

Consent

If the victim consents to the commission of an act that would otherwise constitute a tort, the wrongdoer is not liable. The consent may be express (i.e., stated) or implied (i.e., by conduct).

Consent is invalid if obtained by fraud, under duress, or from someone who is legally incapable of consenting — for example, under a mental disability.

The defence of consent is especially significant in tort actions arising from medical treatment or sports-related injuries. Where a person voluntarily participates in a sport, that person is taken to have consented to all contact within the rules, and probably to contact not intended to cause injury resulting from common infractions of the rules.

Self-Defence/ Provocation

A person may, without liability, harm another in order to protect himself from an actual or threatened attack. To constitute **self-defence**, the purpose of the action must be to prevent future or continued aggression, not to retaliate for a past attack. The degree of force used must be only that necessary to prevent the attack. For the defence to succeed, the use of force itself must be reasonably necessary, and the amount of force used must be reasonable.

> *Example 1*
>
> Frasier and Niles are having a heated discussion when, all of a sudden, Frasier punches Niles in the jaw. Niles, seeing that Frasier is preparing to punch him a second time, punches Frasier in the stomach to prevent him from doing so.

In this example, Niles can clearly sue Frasier for the torts of assault and battery. Frasier might, however, also sue Niles for assault and battery, in which case Niles could rely on the defence of self-defence.

Self-defence should not be confused with **provocation**, which is not a defence but a mitigating factor. Provocation is conduct on the part of the victim that causes the wrongdoer to lose her power of self-control and occurs at the time of, or shortly before, the wrongdoer's wrongful conduct.

> *Example 2*
>
> Frasier and Niles are having a heated discussion. Niles taunts Frasier by repeatedly insulting Frasier's mother. Frasier finally loses his self-control and punches Niles in the mouth.

In this example, Frasier cannot rely upon the defence of self-defence because he was not seeking to protect himself from physical attack. However, Frasier could rely upon Niles's provocation as a mitigating factor.

If the mitigating factor of provocation is successfully invoked, the damages otherwise payable to the victim will be reduced, but the wrongdoer will not totally avoid liability, as would be the case with the successful invocation of the defence of self-defence.

Defence of Others

This defence would arise where a person harms another person in order to protect a third person. The same principles apply to this defence as to the defence of self-defence. There are very few cases where this defence has been raised.

Defence of Property

A person is permitted to defend his property against wrongful interference by the use of reasonable force.

This defence is most commonly raised where a property owner takes steps to physically eject a trespasser. The force used must be only sufficient to expel the trespasser and must not cause unnecessary injury. If the trespasser initially entered the land lawfully, force cannot be used to eject the trespasser until she has first been asked to leave and has not done so.

NEGLIGENCE

Once again, it is important to remember the three elements of a tort: wrongful conduct + harm + cause. Under the heading "Intentional Torts", it was shown that wrongful conduct includes those acts intentionally committed that fall within the recognized and named intentional tort categories. Those categories cover injury to the person, both emotional and physical (e.g., assault, battery, false imprisonment, and emotional infliction of mental suffering); injury to property (e.g., trespass to lands and trespass to chattels); and economic injury (e.g., deceit).

In examining the law of negligence, the focus is still on the element of wrongful conduct. However, the definition of *wrongful conduct* will now be expanded to include acts committed negligently, as opposed to intentionally. As with intentional torts, the conduct examined causes injury to the person, injury to property or economic injury.

Wrongful Conduct — Duty of Care

The level of guilty mentality called negligence has previously been defined. Harm is said to be negligently caused if the wrongdoer ought to have known that his conduct was likely to cause harm. The question to be asked, then, is, harm to whom?

According to the law of negligence, a person undertaking an act is not required to know about the world at large. In deciding what actions to undertake, people are not required to think about everybody all the time; they are only required to think about some people. The question is, who?

This question is answered through the legal concept of **duty of care**. A person is responsible in law to (that is, ought to know about) those to whom the law says she owes a duty of care. To whom is a duty of care owed? A duty of care is owed to those

> who are so closely and directly affected by my act that I ought reasonably to have them in contemplation as being so affected when I am directing my mind to the acts or omissions ... in question.

This definition of duty of care comes from a decision of the House of Lords called *Donoghue v. Stevenson* (see Exhibit 13.1).

EXHIBIT 13.1

Duty of Care: Definition

The plaintiff's friend bought her a bottle of ginger beer at a store in Scotland. The ginger beer was manufactured by the defendant. The plaintiff could not examine the contents of the glass bottle prior to opening it because the bottle was opaque. After drinking part of the ginger beer, the plaintiff discovered that the bottle had contained the remains of a decomposed snail. This discovery caused the plaintiff to become ill.

The House of Lords held that the defendant manufacturer, in manufacturing its ginger beer, ought to have the ultimate consumers of the product in contemplation, and therefore owed a duty of care to the plaintiff.

Source: *Donoghue v. Stevenson*, [1932] A.C. 562.

| EXHIBIT 13.2 | Is there a Duty of Care Owed? |

The plaintiff was a passenger on a bus. As she was getting off the bus, the defendant, who was on a motorcycle, speeded by the other side of the bus and collided with a car approximately 50 feet past the bus. The defendant was killed in the collision. The plaintiff heard the noise of the impact but saw nothing of the accident other than the blood left on the street after the defendant's body had been taken away. The plaintiff suffered nervous shock in reaction to the event. The plaintiff sued the defendant's estate.

The House of Lords held that the defendant owed the plaintiff no duty of care because he could not reasonably have expected a person in the position of the plaintiff to have been affected by his conduct. The defendant certainly owed a duty of care to the owner of the car with which he collided, but he was not liable to the plaintiff because no duty of care was owed to her.

Source: *Bourhill v. Young*, [1943] A.C. 92.

It should be noted from the definition of *duty of care* that the identity of those to whom a duty of care is owed depends on the activity being undertaken (acts) or the activity being refrained from (omissions). Responsibility can flow both from positive acts and from omissions (refraining from acting).

Before a defendant can be held liable to a particular plaintiff, the plaintiff must demonstrate that the defendant owed a duty of care to him. This principle is illustrated in another decision of the House of Lords, *Bourhill v. Young* (see Exhibit 13.2). As can be seen in this case, it is not enough for a defendant merely to owe and breach a duty of care; the duty of care must be owed to the plaintiff in question.

In determining whether a duty of care is owed, one should ask whether a reasonable person in the position of the defendant could anticipate the possibility of harm occurring to the plaintiff if the defendant acted carelessly in the circumstances. If the answer to the question is yes, a duty of care is owed by the defendant to the plaintiff.

Wrongful Conduct — Breach of Duty of Care/ Standard of Care

Once it is established that a person owes a duty of care to another, it is necessary to ask two questions:

- What standard of care is required of that person?
- Has that person breached that standard?

The standard of care owed by one person to another is a duty to exercise reasonable care and skill towards the other person so as to avoid causing harm to that person. The standard is measured by reference to the reasonable person. A person is required to behave as a reasonable person would have done to prevent harm to the ultimate victim. What is reasonable will vary with the circumstances, so the specific standard of care will vary with the circumstances. But the general rule is always the same.

The circumstances that will affect the specific standard of care include

- the inherent danger of the activity in question, including
  - the likelihood or chance that injury of some kind can occur as a result of the activity in question;
  - the seriousness of the injury that might occur;
- the importance to the community at large of the activity in question; and
- the position, profession, or occupation of the defendant.

Inherent Danger of the Activity

The more inherently dangerous an activity is, the higher the standard of care to which the person undertaking the activity will be held. The courts examine both the likelihood of injury occurring and the seriousness of the injury that might occur. So, for example, a person delivering explosives is held to a higher standard of care than a person delivering groceries, both because it is more likely that some injury can occur as a result of the first activity and because any injury that might result would be far more serious.

Importance to the Community

A person engaged in an activity for personal gain is held to a higher standard of care than a person engaged in an activity that is of importance to the community. So, a person transporting passengers in a taxi would be held to a higher standard of care with respect to his driving than would be the driver of a municipal ambulance transporting an injured person to the hospital.

Profession or Occupation of the Defendant

If the defendant is a member of a profession that involves the employment of particular skills, she is required to behave in accordance with the standards of the reasonable practitioner in that profession. A nurse carrying out an emergency operation at a remote location, therefore, would not be held to as high a standard of care as a surgeon carrying out the same operation in a hospital.

To summarize, wrongful conduct includes acts committed negligently. A defendant is negligent vis-à-vis a particular plaintiff if the defendant owes that plaintiff a duty of care, and the duty of care has been breached.

Harm

For a defendant to be liable to a plaintiff in negligence, in addition to wrongful conduct, there must be actual loss or harm to the plaintiff, and the loss or harm must be to a legally recognized interest.

Example

Murphy is driving her car, and Miles is driving his car directly behind her. They are both travelling quite slowly, but Miles is following Murphy's car too closely. When Murphy stops her car, Miles's car is so close as to strike Murphy's car. However, because of the slow speed at which he was driving, no damage is done to Murphy's car, and she suffers no physical injuries or emotional harm.

In this case, there is wrongful conduct. Miles owed Murphy a duty of care, and he breached that duty of care by driving too closely behind her car. However, Murphy suffered no loss or harm. Accordingly, Murphy would not succeed in an action in negligence against Miles.

Legally recognized interests include the following:

- Damage to person
- Damage to property
- Nervous shock or emotional trauma
- Economic loss
- Damage to reputation

Cause

It is not enough for a plaintiff to prove wrongful conduct on the part of the defendant and harm suffered by the plaintiff. As previously stated, the wrongful conduct of the defendant must have caused the harm to the plaintiff.

At the simplest level, there must be some physical connection between the act of the wrongdoer and the harm suffered by the victim. One way to determine whether or not this physical connection exists is to use the "but for" test. Can you say that the harm to the plaintiff would not have happened but for the conduct of the defendant? If so, it can be said that the defendant's conduct was the cause of the harm to the plaintiff.

Example 1

Alex is standing at the curb with his back to Fred. Fred swings a baseball bat at Alex's head. Alex, totally unaware of Fred's conduct, steps off the curb, walks into the path of an oncoming car and is injured.

In this instance, there is wrongful conduct — Fred's swinging the baseball bat at Alex's head. There is also harm — the injuries suffered by Alex when he is struck by the car. There is, however, no causal connection between the two: Fred's conduct did not cause Alex's injury.

If the facts of Example 1 are changed slightly, the result is different.

Example 2

Alex is standing at the curb with his back to Fred. Fred swings a baseball bat at Alex's head. As Fred is doing so, Alex sees Fred's reflection in a nearby store window and, in attempting to escape Fred's attack, runs into the path of an oncoming car and is injured.

Again, there is wrongful conduct, and there is also harm. This time, however, there is a causal connection: Fred's conduct caused Alex's injury.

These two examples serve to illustrate factual causation, or causation in fact. However, the legal definition of *cause* is not limited to simply establishing a physical, causal connection between the wrongful conduct and the harm. Once that connection is established, the courts will examine the connection to ensure that the connection is **proximate** and not too remote.

While the term "proximate" means close, and the term "remote" means far, the terms do not address issues of physical closeness. Rather, the issue is one of reasonable foreseeability: Was it reasonable to foresee that the harm to the victim was a likely result of the conduct of the wrongdoer?

This issue is well illustrated by the New York State Court of Appeals decision of *Palsgraf v. Long Island Railroad Co.* (see Exhibit 13.3). In this case, there was causation in fact, but not causation in law because the conduct was not the proximate cause of the harm to the plaintiff. Causation in fact is physical causation, while causation in law is proximate causation.

Conclusion

When all three factors — wrongful conduct + harm + causation — are present, the plaintiff will have a cause of action in tort against the defendant. In negligence the element of wrongful conduct is present if the defendant owes a duty of care to the plaintiff and the defendant breaches that duty, and so the required elements may be summarized as follows:

- A duty of care owed by the defendant to the plaintiff
- Breach of that duty by the defendant
- Harm to a legally recognized interest of the plaintiff
- Causation that is proximate

	EXHIBIT 13.3

Negligence and Proximate Cause

The plaintiff was standing at the defendant's railway station platform. As a train bound for another destination began to pull away from the station, two men ran to catch the train. One man reached the train without incident. The second man, who was carrying a package, made it aboard the train but looked as if he were about to fall. A guard on the train reached forward to help him in, while a guard on the platform pushed him from behind, and the package was dislodged and fell onto the tracks. The package, which was quite small and ordinary looking, in fact contained fireworks, which exploded when they fell. The force of the explosion knocked over some scales at the other end of the platform, many feet away, where the plaintiff was standing. The plaintiff was injured. The plaintiff sued the Long Island Railroad Co. for the negligence of its employees.

The court held that, while the conduct of the guards started a chain of events that resulted in the plaintiff's injury, it was not reasonably foreseeable that the conduct of the guards could cause any injury to the plaintiff.

Source: *Palsgraf v. Long Island Railroad Co.* (1928), 248 N.Y. 339; 162 N.E. 99.

EFFECT OF THE CONDUCT OF THE PLAINTIFF IN NEGLIGENCE

Even if all of the elements of a cause of action in negligence are proved, the plaintiff's right to recover damages from the defendant may be limited or eliminated as a result of certain kinds of conduct by him.

Voluntary Assumption of Risk

This defence to a negligence action is very closely related to the defence of consent in intentional torts. When consent is used as a defence to an intentional tort, the argument made is that the plaintiff consented to the commission of the specific act that forms the basis of the tort. The basis of the defence of voluntary assumption of risk, also known by the Latin phrase *volenti non fit injuria*, is not that the plaintiff consented to being injured, but that she consented to accept the risk of being injured by participation in a particular activity.

In order to establish this defence, the defendant must prove that

- the plaintiff had knowledge of the risk of injury involved in the activity; and
- the plaintiff consented to, or assumed, the risk involved.

This agreement to assume the risk may be expressed, or it may be implied from the conduct of the plaintiff.

Because this defence is based on consent, as with the defence of consent, the plaintiff must be legally capable of giving consent for the defence to apply. It will not apply if the plaintiff was incapable of consenting because of, for example, fraud, duress, or mental disability.

This defence has been successfully applied with respect to sports-related injuries, voluntary participation in fights and injuries suffered by willing passengers in cars driven by drunk drivers. The courts have declined to apply the defence, on public policy grounds, to risks of danger assumed by a person rescuing someone from a situation caused by someone else's negligence (e.g., someone running into a burning building to rescue a person trapped there).

Illegality

The defence of illegality is also known by the Latin phrase *ex turpi causa non oritur actio*. This defence, in some cases, prevents a plaintiff who was participating in criminal conduct at the time of his injury from successfully suing the defendant who caused the injury. It is considered contrary to public policy to permit wrongdoers to profit from their wrongdoing. It has also been said that there is no duty of care owed to a person involved in a crime.

Example
Fred and Barney are engaged in the armed robbery of a bank. Fred fires his gun negligently, and Barney is injured.

In this case, Barney would not succeed in an action for damages in negligence against Fred.

PROOF OF NEGLIGENCE

Burden of Proof

In the usual case, the burden of proof is on the plaintiff to prove all of the required elements of negligence — that is, a duty of care owed by the defendant to the plaintiff, a breach of that duty, harm to the plaintiff, and proximate causation. The plaintiff must present evidence that will satisfy the court on the balance of probabilities that all of these elements are present and that the plaintiff's cause of action has, therefore, been established.

Res Ipsa Loquitur

The plaintiff will not be able to provide evidence proving all elements of an action in negligence if he does not know how the accident was caused. In such a case, the plaintiff may be able to rely on the maxim *res ipsa loquitur*, which means, "The thing speaks for itself." *Res ipsa loquitur* is a rule of evidence by which the plaintiff, because he cannot explain how the accident happened, asks the court to make a *prima facie* finding of negligence, which the defendant then has an opportunity to rebut.

Where the maxim applies, once the plaintiff proves that the particular accident occurred, the court presumes, or makes a prima facie finding of, negligence on the part of the defendant. It is then up to the defendant to try to rebut that presumption.

When the Maxim Applies
The maxim will apply only where three conditions are met:

- The thing that caused the damage must have been in the sole control of the defendant.
- The accident was of the kind that would not ordinarily have happened without negligence.
- There must be no explanation as to how the accident happened.

Some examples of cases where the maxim has been applied are as follows:

- A case where a barrel fell out of a window
- Cases of foreign objects found in consumer products
- A case where swabs were left inside a surgical patient
- A case where a glass door shattered after being opened in a normal way

Effect of the Maxim on the Defendant's Case
As stated earlier, where the maxim applies, once the plaintiff proves that the accident occurred, negligence on the part of the defendant is presumed,

and it is up to the defendant to rebut that presumption. In order to do so, the defendant may prove how the accident took place, and that it took place without negligence on her part: in other words, that she, in fact, took reasonable care. Alternatively, the defendant may simply provide a reasonable explanation, consistent with the evidence, as to how the accident might have occurred without negligence on her part.

CONTRIBUTORY NEGLIGENCE

This topic addresses how the courts handle the situation where more than one party is negligent. Perhaps the plaintiff was negligent. Perhaps there are two defendants, whose negligence both contributed to the plaintiff's injury. The term "contributory negligence" applies to both of these situations.

Contributory Negligence of the Plaintiff

What It Is

Where there has been contributory negligence on the part of the plaintiff, it means that the plaintiff has failed to act carefully in protecting his own safety; it does *not* mean that the plaintiff has necessarily breached any duty owed to the defendant.

Example

Burt is running through a crowded corridor. Ernie is reading a book while walking through the corridor in the opposite direction. Burt runs into Ernie. Had Ernie been looking where he was going, he could have gotten out of Burt's way.

In this situation, Ernie did not cause the collision; Burt did. But had Ernie been adequately looking after his own safety, the collision could have been avoided. Ernie is not liable in negligence to Burt for any injuries Burt might have suffered but is contributorily negligent with respect to his own injuries.

Effect of Plaintiff's Contributory Negligence

Historically, any negligence on the part of the plaintiff totally prevented her from recovering any damages from the defendant. Over time, this rule was revised by the courts and was ultimately replaced by statutory provisions that state that the plaintiff will not be totally disentitled to damages; rather, the plaintiff's damages will be reduced proportionally to the extent to which she was at fault. In Ontario, the statute dealing with contributory negligence is the *Negligence Act*.

Damages in tort actions are discussed later in this chapter. It should be noted now, however, that the court will put a dollar value on the plaintiff's injuries and then reduce that amount by the percentage to which the plaintiff was at fault. So, in the example above, if Ernie's damages were assessed initially at $10,000, and Ernie were found to be 15 percent at fault in the accident, Burt would be ordered to pay Ernie only $8,500.

Joint Tortfeasors

The word "tortfeasor" means someone who commits a tort. The term "joint tortfeasors" is used when more than one person is responsible in tort for the injuries caused to a plaintiff. Under the provisions of the Ontario *Negligence Act*, the court determines the extent of responsibility of each of the tortfeasors and then apportions liability for damages accordingly. How this apportionment takes place will depend on the circumstances of the accident.

Example 1

A pedestrian is struck by a car driven by Thelma, as a result of which the pedestrian's leg is broken. The pedestrian is then struck by a car driven by Louise, as a result of which the pedestrian's arm is broken.

In this case, two accidents happen in rapid succession, and while only one plaintiff is involved, each accident results in clearly separate injuries to the plaintiff. In such a case, which is unusual, the court would be able to ascertain the damages appropriate to each injury. Thelma would be responsible for the damages calculated for the broken leg, and Louise would be responsible for the damages calculated for the broken arm.

In the more typical contributory negligence situation, one set of injuries to the plaintiff is caused by the negligence of two or more defendants.

Example 2

The plaintiff is a passenger in Thelma's car. Thelma is speeding. Louise is driving her car in the other direction and makes an improper left hand turn into the path of Thelma's car. As a result, Thelma's car broadsides Louise's car. The plaintiff is injured in the collision.

In this case, the plaintiff has suffered one set of injuries, for which both Thelma and Louise are at fault. The court would first set a monetary value on the plaintiff's injuries. Then the court would determine the degree to which Thelma and Louise were respectively at fault for the accident, and would apportion responsibility for the plaintiff's damages accordingly.

The Ontario legislation states that each of the joint tortfeasors is jointly and severally liable to the plaintiff for the entire amount of the damages awarded, but as between themselves, each is liable to contribute and indemnify each other to the degree to which each is at fault. So, in Example 2, if the plaintiff's damages are $10,000, and Thelma is 40 percent at fault and Louise is 60 percent at fault, the plaintiff can obtain payment of the $10,000 from either of the defendants or from both in any combination (so long as the total amount of the damages collected does not exceed $10,000). However, as between Thelma and Louise, Thelma is only responsible for $4,000 and Louise, for $6,000. If the plaintiff collects more than $4,000 from Thelma, Thelma can force Louise to repay her the amount in excess of $4,000.

Usually, the plaintiff will sue all parties responsible for the accident that causes his injuries. However, if the plaintiff fails to do so, the other tortfeasor can, by a proceeding called a **third party proceeding**, have the omitted tortfeasor made a party to the action.

OCCUPIERS' LIABILITY

This is an area of negligence law dealing with the liability of occupiers of property to those injured on their property. It is an area in which a statute defines the parties who owe a duty of care, the parties to whom the duty of care is owed, and what the standard of care is. A plaintiff would have to establish that a duty of care was owed to her by the defendant, in accordance with the statute, and that the standard of care established by the statute was breached. As with any other tort, the plaintiff would also have to establish harm and causation.

The Common Law

The common law in this area was very confusing. Persons entering onto the property of others were classified into categories according to whether or not they had the permission of the owner and the nature of that permission. Different standards of care were owed by owners of property to each category of entrant.

Legislation

In Ontario, this area of law is now governed by a statute called the *Occupiers' Liability Act*, which replaces the common law. In Ontario, the *Trespass to Property Act* also has some relevance to this area.

Definition of Occupier

An occupier is the person who is in physical possession of the premises or who has responsibility for and control over the condition of the premises, the activities conducted on the premises, or the persons allowed to enter the premises. All occupiers owe a duty of care to those persons specified in the legislation.

If a landlord has a contractual duty to maintain or repair the premises, and is in default of that duty, he is considered to be an occupier and can then be sued by an entrant. In this circumstance, the tenant would be an occupier as well.

To Whom Duty of Care Is Owed

An occupier owes a duty of care to persons entering on the premises.

General Standard of Care

The standard of care required by an occupier is to take reasonable care to see that persons entering the premises and the property they bring with them are reasonably safe while on the premises.

Contract

The general standard of care can be restricted or modified by contract.

Assumption of Risks

The standard of care owed by the occupier is lower where the person entering the premises willingly assumes, expressly or impliedly, the risks of entering the premises. Whether or not the entrant has assumed those risks is determined in the same way as with the doctrine of voluntary assumption of risk elsewhere in negligence law. However, unlike elsewhere in negligence law, if there has been an assumption of risk, it does not act as a complete defence against liability; it merely results in a lower standard of care being applied.

In such cases, the occupier's standard of care is not to create a danger with the deliberate intent of doing harm or damage to the person entering the premises or her property, and not to act with reckless disregard of the presence of that person or her property.

In the Ontario statute, the classes of persons who are deemed to have willingly assumed all risks are stated to include

- those who enter the premises intending to commit criminal acts;

- those who trespass on rural, agricultural premises, vacant premises, wilderness premises, closed golf courses, utility rights of way, unopened road allowances, private roads, and recreational trails, or who enter on such premises for free recreational purposes.

STRICT LIABILITY

Strict liability torts are those where a defendant is held responsible for harm done to the plaintiff even though the conduct involved was neither intentional nor negligent. The circumstances in which a blameless person is held responsible are quite limited. In those limited circumstances, the conduct is considered "wrongful" even though committed without intention or negligence. The additional elements of harm to the plaintiff and causation also have to be proved.

Rylands v. Fletcher

The decision of the House of Lords in *Rylands v. Fletcher*, (1868) L.R. 3 H.L 330, is the basis of strict liability in contemporary tort law. The case relates to the escape of a dangerous substance:

> The defendant built a reservoir on his land to supply water to his mill. There were unused mine shafts under the land that, unknown to the defendant, were connected to the plaintiff's mine. When the reservoir was filled, water flowed through the unused mine shafts and flooded the plaintiff's mine.
>
> The trial judge held the defendant to be liable to the plaintiff even though the harm was neither intentionally nor negligently caused. He stated, "the person who for his own purposes brings on his lands and collects and keeps there anything likely to do mischief if it escapes, must keep it in at his peril, and, if he does not do so, is prima facie answerable for all the damage which is the natural consequence of its escape."
>
> The House of Lords added an additional requirement for liability: that the defendant must have put his land to a non-natural use.

The requirements for liability under the rule in *Rylands v. Fletcher* are as follows:

- The thing that escapes must have been brought onto the land. There is no liability, under this rule, for the escape of things naturally on the land.

- The thing that escapes must be either inherently dangerous or something that, while ordinarily safe, may become dangerous if it escapes.

- The thing must escape from land over which the defendant has control, to a place outside his control.

- The defendant must have put his land to a non-natural use — that is, a use that introduces special dangers to the neighbourhood.

Defences

There are several defences available under *Rylands v. Fletcher*. The defendant is relieved of liability if the escape is the result of an act of God — that is, an extraordinary, natural event that could not be foreseen or protected against. It is also a defence if the escape of the object was the result of the unforeseeable intentional or negligent act of the plaintiff or of a third party. If the act was foreseeable, the defence will not apply on the basis that it should have been protected against. The express or implied consent of the plaintiff to the presence of the dangerous thing is also a defence.

Vicarious Liability

A person's liability is said to be **vicarious** when it is not based on the person's own wrongdoing but on someone else's wrongdoing. Vicarious liability is a form of strict liability in that the level of guilty mentality of the person is irrelevant: a person who is totally blameless can be held liable for damages. The most common example of vicarious liability is that of an employer for torts committed by his employee during the course of employment. If an employee commits a tort in the course of her employment, the employer is vicariously liable, even if totally innocent of any individual wrongdoing. Another example of vicarious liability is the liability of the owner of a motor vehicle for any torts committed by a person who drives the motor vehicle with the owner's consent.

DAMAGES IN TORTS

As stated at the outset of this chapter, the major purpose of tort law is the compensation of victims, rather than the punishment of wrongdoers. Victims of torts are compensated by being awarded an amount of money called *damages*, and the courts are called upon to put a dollar value on the injuries inflicted on them. It must be remembered that no damages will be awarded unless the plaintiff succeeds in establishing all of the required elements of a tort.

Damages awarded for the purpose of compensating the plaintiff are called **compensatory damages**. In addition, in unusual circumstances the court may also award the plaintiff **punitive damages**, the purpose of which is to punish the defendant.

Compensatory Damages

There are two categories of compensatory damages: special damages and general damages.

Special Damages

Special damages, also called specific damages, compensate the plaintiff for actual monetary losses and out-of-pocket expenses incurred prior to judgment (e.g., medical expenses, the cost of repair of damaged property and lost income).

To be awarded special damages, it is necessary to specifically ask for them in the statement of claim. It is also necessary to prove each and every item requested.

General Damages

There are two types of general damages. The first type compensates the plaintiff for items of non-pecuniary loss — that is, loss not easily measurable in dollar terms, such as pain and suffering and loss of enjoyment of life.

In order to be awarded this type of damages, the plaintiff must present evidence in court as to pain she has endured and the impact that the injuries suffered have had on her life. Based on this evidence, the court will assess her damages by placing a dollar value on her loss.

The second type of general damages compensates the plaintiff for anticipated out-of-pocket expenses, such as future medical expenses and future loss of wages. The court will estimate the amount of these expenses.

Punitive Damages

If the court considers the conduct of the defendant to be particularly outrageous, it has the jurisdiction to award *punitive damages*, also called **exemplary damages**. The purpose of these damages is to punish the defendant and, by making an example of him, to deter others from behaving in a similar fashion. This category of damages is not commonly awarded.

LIMITATION PERIODS IN TORT LAW

In all the provinces, there are statutes that limit the period of time in which lawsuits for various causes of action must be commenced. In the area of tort law, there are many different limitation periods, depending on the manner in which the injury arose and the identity of the defendant. So, for example, there are special limitation periods that apply to motor vehicle accident cases, to medical malpractice cases and to actions against government bodies.

CHAPTER SUMMARY

In this chapter, the reader was introduced to the history and nature of torts, and to the three elements required of a cause of action in tort — namely, wrongful conduct + harm + cause. The chapter then discussed the different levels of guilty mentality with which an act may be committed.

The circumstances in which a conduct is considered wrongful when committed with the different levels of guilty mentality were examined. Various specifically named intentional torts and the most common defences to the intentional torts were studied. The chapter also presented the elements of negligence, proof of negligence, defences to negligence and contributory negligence. Specific areas of occupiers' liability and strict liability torts were covered as well. In addition to wrongful conduct, there was a discussion of the requirement of harm to a legally recognized interest of the plaintiff, and a discussion of causation, including the distinction between causation in fact and causation in law.

The chapter concluded with a description of the different types of damages in tort actions and a brief review of limitation periods in tort actions.

GLOSSARY OF NEW TERMS AND KEY CONCEPTS

assault	The intentional creation in the victim of a reasonable apprehension of imminent harmful or offensive conduct.
battery	The intentional infliction of a harmful or offensive contact with another person.
compensatory damages	A monetary award made to a successful plaintiff to compensate the plaintiff for the injuries and losses the plaintiff suffered because of the acts of the defendant.
defamation	The publication of a statement that tends to tarnish a person's reputation in the estimation of right-thinking members of society or holds that person up to hatred, ridicule, or contempt.
duty of care	A duty owed by all persons contemplating an act or omission to all persons who might reasonably be affected by the act or omission.
exemplary damages	See **punitive damages**.
ex turpi causa non oritur actio	A defence that prevents another from making a successful tort claim, on the basis that the claimant was engaged in illegal behaviour.
false imprisonment	When a person intentionally and without lawful justification confines another person within fixed boundaries.
intentional act	An act that is committed with the wish to produce the results that follow from the act.
negligent act	One in which there is no intention to cause harm, or even any knowledge that harm might be caused, but in which a "reasonable person" would know that harm might be caused by the act.

nuisance	Interference with a landowner's use and enjoyment of her lands as a result of action or conduct on neighbouring lands.
provocation	Conduct on the part of a victim that causes the wrongdoer to lose self-control. The conduct by the wrongdoer must be a near-immediate response to the victim's provocative conduct. Provocation is a mitigating factor, but not a defence.
proximate cause	The connection between an act and its effect. An act is a proximate cause of an effect if the effect is reasonably foreseeable by a reasonable person doing the act.
punitive damages	Damages paid to a plaintiff not as compensation for a loss, but to punish exceptionally outrageous or wrongful conduct by a defendant.
reckless act	One acts recklessly when one knows that one's actions might cause harm, even where there is no intention to produce harmful results.
res ipsa loquitur	A situation where negligence is apparent from what has happened and from the surrounding circumstances so that the plaintiff need not prove specifically how the defendant was negligent.
self-defence	Acts that are designed to prevent or stop physical aggression by another, not including revenge or retaliation.
strict liability	Situations where an actor is liable for harm resulting from an act, whether or not the actor is blameworthy.
third party proceeding	A procedure in a lawsuit where, if P sues D and D claims the damage was done by X, D can have X added as a third party in the lawsuit.
tort	A legal wrong for which a person can sue to recover money damages.
trespass to chattels	The wrongful interference with things owned by or in lawful possession of another person.
trespass to land	The intentional interference with rights in land owned or in the lawful possession of another person.
vicarious liability	A situation where one is liable to someone not for one's own acts but for the acts of another for whom one is legally responsible in some way.
volenti non fit injuria	A situation where a person cannot claim against another, where the person agreed to undertake a risky activity that might cause the harm that occurred.

REVIEW QUESTIONS

1. What is the major purpose of tort law?

2. Name three elements of a tort.

3. (a) What is the level of guilty mentality required in an intentional act?
    (b) What is the level of guilty mentality required in a reckless act?
    (c) What is the level of guilty mentality required in a negligent act?
    (d) What is the level of guilty mentality required in a strict liability tort?

4. In what types of actions is the defence of consent especially significant?

5. What must be proved to establish the defence of self-defence?

6. Discuss the major differences between self-defence and provocation.

7. To whom does one owe a duty of care?

8. What factors are taken into account in determining the standard of care owed by one party to another?

9. Give some examples of legally recognized harm.

10. What is the difference between causation in fact and causation in law?

11. What must the defendant prove to establish the defence of *volenti non fit injuria*?

12. Explain the defence of *ex turpi causa non oritur actio*.

13. (a) What is *res ipsa loquitur*?
    (b) In what circumstances does it apply?
    (c) What is its effect?

14. What is the effect on the plaintiff's case if the plaintiff is found to be contributorily negligent?

15. (a) Define "an occupier".
    (b) To whom does an occupier owe a duty of care?
    (c) What is the general standard of care required by an occupier?

16. Provide two examples of strict liability.

17. (a) What are special damages, and how are they calculated?
    (b) What are general damages, and how are they calculated?
    (c) What are punitive damages?

18. Define "joint liability" in tort.

19. If two persons are found to have injured another, how are damages apportioned?

DISCUSSION QUESTIONS

1. Eric and James were friends. Eric lent James his car for a period of one week, to be returned on Monday at 8:00 a.m. James did not return Eric's car until Wednesday at 10:00 a.m. Eric was very angry and told James so. Rather than apologizing, James punched Eric in the nose and then turned around and walked away. Eric was so stunned that he did nothing for several minutes. When James was about 10 feet away, Eric threw his car keys at James, striking him in the back.

   Discuss all possible causes of action between the parties and all possible defences or other mitigating factors.

2. Alfred spilled a cup of coffee on the tiled floor of the corridor outside his office. He went to get some paper towels to clean the spill, but he got into a conversation with a fellow office worker and forgot all about it. Gus was walking down the hall carrying a box of ball bearings. He slipped on the spilled coffee and dropped the box, which broke, causing the ball bearings to roll down the length of the corridor. At the same time, a pizza delivery man was just turning into Harrison's office, at the far end of the corridor from Alfred's office. He slipped on several of the ball bearings and fell into Harrison's office, dropping the pizza box on Harrison. The pizza box opened and the hot cheese from the pizza burned Harrison.

   Discuss whether or not Alfred's conduct caused Harrison's injury in fact and in law.

3. As a result of the facts in Question 2, Harrison suffered very painful injuries that prevented him from working for an entire year. He had no income for that period. Serious burns to Harrison's hands prevented him from participating in two of his favourite activities, bowling and knitting, for a period of one year. In addition, Harrison had medical and other expenses related to his recovery.

If Harrison successfully sued Alfred, what kind(s) of damages might he be awarded, what is the purpose of those damages, and how would they be calculated?

4. Eberhardt was walking through a fairground when someone threw a lit firecracker at him. Instinctively, he grabbed it and pitched it away from himself. The firecracker landed under a car and went off. Unbeknownst to Eberhardt, the car was full of a very sensitive explosive. The shaking of the car from the firecracker caused the explosives in the car to go off, injuring Florinda. If Florinda sued Eberhardt, discuss the defences he might use.

SUGGESTED READINGS

Fridman, G.H.L. *The Law of Torts in Canada*, 2d ed. (Toronto, Ont.: Carswell, 2002).

Kerr, M., J. Kurtz & L.M. Olivo. *Canadian Tort Law in a Nutshell*, 2d ed. (Toronto, Ont.: Carswell, 2005).

Klar, L. *Tort Law*, 3d ed. (Toronto, Ont.: Carswell, 2003).

The Law of Contract

JoAnn Kurtz
SENECA COLLEGE

Learning Objectives

After reading this chapter, the reader should be able to:

➢ describe the nature of a contract and its use and value in society
➢ identify the essential components of a contract
➢ describe the formal requirements necessary to create a valid contract
➢ identify the grounds upon which a contract may be attacked
➢ understand how contracts are interpreted
➢ understand how contracts are discharged
➢ understand how a contract is breached
➢ understand the remedies for breach of contract

TABLE OF CONTENTS

INTRODUCTION

Contracts in Everyday Life

Despite their popular image, **contracts** are not just long, incomprehensible documents with tiny print. Contracts are an everyday part of everyone's life, and can be oral or in writing. Leases, credit cards, the purchase of a car, membership in a health club and the purchase of groceries all involve contracts.

As varied as these examples of contracts are, they all have elements in common.

Elements of a Contract

A contract is an agreement between two or more parties that is enforceable at law.

All contracts contain the following elements:

- The parties must have reached an *agreement*, as evidenced by the fact that there has been *offer* and *acceptance*.
- The parties must *intend to be legally bound*.
- Both parties must have given *valuable consideration*, such as payment or an act, or a promise to pay or act.
- The parties must have the *legal capacity* to contract.
- In some cases, certain *legal formalities* must be complied with (e.g., some contracts must be in writing).

Classification of Contracts

Contracts may be classified in a number of ways:

Deeds are written contracts that have been signed, witnessed, sealed and delivered. As will be seen later in this chapter, the seal takes the place of consideration.

Simple contracts are all contracts that are not deeds. They may be oral or written.

Bilateral contracts are contracts in which a promise by one party is exchanged for a promise by the other party (e.g., the promise to do something in return for a promise of payment).

Unilateral contracts are contracts where one party promises to do something if the other party does something first — for example, a promise to pay a reward if someone finds your lost dog. Only the person promising to pay the reward is bound to do anything by such a contract.

CONTRACT FORMATION: OFFER AND ACCEPTANCE

In order to determine whether or not a contract has been formed, the courts ask whether an agreement has been arrived at. This issue is addressed by asking whether one party, called the **offeror**, has made an offer that has been accepted by the other party, called the **offeree**.

Offer

An **offer** is an expression of willingness to enter into a contract on the terms specified in the offer. It is made with the intention that the offer will become a binding contract if it is accepted.

An offer may be express (i.e., stated) or implied (by conduct), and it may be made to one particular person or to a group of people. It may also be made to the world at large, which is the case when a person offers a reward.

Invitation to Treat

An offer must be distinguished from an *invitation to treat*, which is a request for offers that can then be accepted or rejected.

When a store advertises merchandise for sale, the advertisement is not an offer to sell the goods, but merely a request for shoppers to make an offer to purchase the goods at the advertised price. Likewise, when a store displays merchandise for sale, the store is requesting that shoppers make an offer to purchase the goods at the display price. In both cases, under contract law, the store is not legally bound to actually sell the goods at the advertised price (although it would be poor business not to do so, and contrary to certain consumer protection legislation).

Acceptance

Acceptance is the unconditional agreement to, and acceptance of the terms of, the offer. Acceptance must be communicated to the offeror.

Acceptance must be *unconditional*. There can be no changes made to the terms of the offer. If any changes are made, the result is a *counter-offer*, the effect of which is to end the original offer.

Example 1

Fred offers to sell Barney his car for $2,000. Barney agrees to buy the car but says he will only pay $1,750. Fred says no. Barney then tells Fred that he will pay $2,000.

In this example, Fred is not obligated to sell the car to Barney for $2,000. When Barney changed the price, he made a counter-offer that Fred was free to accept or reject. When Fred rejected the counter-offer, Barney could no longer accept Fred's original offer because his counter-offer had terminated it.

Acceptance must be made in the manner requested in the offer. If no specific manner is stated, it must be made in a reasonable manner. An offer cannot be worded in such a way that if the offeree says nothing it constitutes acceptance — some act of acceptance is required.

Acceptance must be made within the time stated in the offer. If no time limit is set, acceptance must be made within a reasonable time.

Acceptance must be communicated to the offeror. The only exception is for unilateral contracts, where performance constitutes acceptance, and there is no need to notify the offeror in advance of one's intention to accept.

Acceptance is effective when it is communicated to the offeror. When it is reasonable or required that acceptance be made by mail, acceptance becomes effective when it is mailed, even though the offeror is unaware that the offer has been accepted. This rule, called the **postal acceptance rule**, applies even if the letter is delayed, destroyed, or lost.

Example 2

Thelma mails a letter to Louise on September 1, offering to buy Louise's computer for $500. Louise receives the letter on September 7. On September 10, Louise mails a letter to Thelma accepting her offer. The letter is not received by Thelma until September 17. On September 15, Thelma telephones Louise to tell her she no longer wants to buy the computer and so is withdrawing her offer.

In this example, the offer was accepted on September 10, when Louise mailed her letter of acceptance to Thelma. After this date, Thelma could no longer withdraw her offer.

In Ontario, the *Electronic Commerce Act*[1] governs the time of receipt of acceptance by electronic means such as e-mail, fax, voice messaging and interactive websites. If the offeror designates an electronic method of acceptance, acceptance becomes effective when the message enters the designated electronic system and is able to be retrieved.

Termination of Offer

An offer can be terminated in a number of ways. An offer is terminated if the offeree makes a counter-offer, or if the offeree rejects the offer.

An offer can be terminated by **revocation**. An offeror can revoke or withdraw the offer any time before it is accepted by the offeree.

An offer can also terminate by **lapse**. If an offer is stated to be open for acceptance for a fixed period of time, at the expiry of that time period it will lapse. If the offer does not state a period of time, the offer lapses after a reasonable time.

An offer also terminates on the death of the offeror.

CONTRACT FORMATION: INTENTION TO BE LEGALLY BOUND

For there to be a binding contract, the parties must intend to create a legally enforceable agreement. If this intention is lacking, even though all the other elements of a contract are met, no contract will be formed.

In contract law, exaggerated advertising claims are not treated as forming the basis of a binding contract but are considered "mere puff". There is now, however, consumer protection legislation that limits this principle.

No contract will result from an offer made as a joke — for example, if a mother jokingly offers to pay $500 to any woman who will marry her son. In addition, no contract will result from social arrangements.

Example

Elaine invites Jerry over for dinner, and Jerry accepts. Elaine spends a great deal of time and money on the dinner, and then Jerry forgets to show up.

Even though Elaine prepared the dinner on Jerry's promise to show up, it is a well established principle of contract law, as noted by the authors of a leading contracts text, that "to offer a friend a meal is not to invite litigation."[2]

CONTRACT FORMATION: CONSIDERATION

In contracts, no one does anything for nothing. A contract is not enforceable unless something of value is given by each party to the other. That something of value is called **consideration**. Without consideration, there is only a **gratuitous promise**, which the courts will not enforce. Consideration may be an act, a promise to act, or a promise to refrain from acting (**forbearance**).

[1]   S.O. 2000, s. 17.
[2]   G.C. Cheshire, C.H.S. Fifoot & M.P. Furmston, *The Law of Contract* (London, U.K.: Butterworths, 1972).

Rules Relating to Consideration

Past Consideration

In contract law, *past consideration* is no consideration at all. Consideration, to be valid, must be a present or future act. Past consideration is a past act, or services rendered, or a benefit conferred in the past.

Example

Niles, a not-too-bright budding entrepreneur, decides to go into the lawn maintenance business. He arrives at Frasier's home when Frasier is at work. His plan is to mow and fertilize Frasier's lawn and then present him with a bill on his return from work. When Frasier returns from work, Niles proudly shows him the work he has done and presents Frasier with a bill for $50. In order to get Niles to leave, Frasier promises to pay him the $50 the next week. The next day, Frasier delivers a letter to Niles telling him that he won't pay the bill.

Niles cannot enforce Frasier's promise to pay him $50. Frasier's promise was given in exchange for work already completed. This is a promise given in exchange for past consideration, which is no consideration at all. Therefore the promise to pay is considered a gratuitous promise and is unenforceable.

Adequacy of Consideration

Consideration must be valuable — that is, it must have monetary value — but the courts will not generally examine whether or not the value of the consideration is adequate. In the absence of fraud or misrepresentation, it is considered to be up to the parties to negotiate their deal, not the courts.

Performance of an Existing Duty

Performance of an existing duty or a promise to perform an existing duty is not good consideration. The existing duty can be a public duty or a contractual duty. So, for example, a policeman, who has a public duty to protect the public, cannot charge a citizen money to protect her. If the citizen agreed to pay the policeman, the promise would be gratuitous and unenforceable.

Example

Laverne agreed to build a bookcase for Shirley to be completed on June 15. Shirley agreed to pay Laverne $250. On June 10, Laverne told Shirley she would not be able to complete the job on time. Shirley offered her an additional $50 to complete the bookcase by June 15. Laverne agreed, and the bookcase was completed on time.

Laverne cannot enforce Shirley's promise to pay her the extra $50. Laverne was already under a contractual duty to complete the bookcase by June 15. Her renewed promise to do so did not constitute valid consideration, and so Shirley's promise is a gratuitous promise and, therefore, unenforceable.

Part Payment of Debts

The principle that performance of an existing duty does not constitute valid consideration causes a problem for debtors who wish to settle their debts for an amount less than the original amount owing.

Example

George owes Jerry $10,000 but cannot afford to pay him. George approaches Jerry to try to settle the debt for a lesser amount. Jerry agrees to accept $5,000 in full settlement of the debt.

Under the common law of contract, Jerry's agreement to accept $5,000 is not enforceable because George is not giving him any valid consideration; he is already contractually obliged to pay the $5,000.

In Ontario, the common law position has been changed by a statute called the *Mercantile Law Amendment Act*. According to the provisions of that statute, Jerry's acceptance of the lesser sum of $5,000 would act as a full discharge of the debt. If Jerry agrees to accept $5,000, he can change his mind at any point before payment is received by him.

Promissory Estoppel

While a person cannot sue to enforce a gratuitous promise, sometimes a gratuitous promise can be used as a defence against a lawsuit that contradicts the promise. The equitable principle that allows a defendant to do this is called **promissory estoppel**.

Assume in the above example that George told Jerry he had no money of his own to repay the loan but would borrow $5,000 to do so. If he borrowed the money in reliance upon Jerry's promise not to sue for the balance, Jerry would be *estopped* from suing George for the balance. This principle could be used by George in addition to the provisions of the *Mercantile Law Amendment Act*.

There are three elements required before promissory estoppel can be relied upon:

- The other party must make a clear and unambiguous promise not to enforce his legal rights.
- The party seeking to invoke the principle must have acted in reliance on that promise to his detriment.
- It would be inequitable for the other party to go back on his word.

Exceptions to Requirement for Consideration

Deeds — in other words, contracts under seal — do not require consideration to be enforceable. The seal takes the place of consideration. In medieval times, sealing a deed involved impressing a coat of arms into a pool of hot wax poured on the document. Today, the usual practice is to attach a round red sticker on the document.

A gratuitous *promise to make a gift to a charity* will be enforced if

- the charity has made a legal commitment based on the pledge (e.g., the hiring of a contractor or the purchase of materials); or
- other donors have also pledged money; because if one donor fails to pay, it undermines the gift of the others.

CONTRACT FORMATION: CAPACITY

A contract cannot be enforced against a person not mentally competent to enter into it.

Corporations

Corporations are recognized as persons and can enter into contracts. The document by which a particular company is created sets out the corporation's objects. The contract must be within those objects. Most incorporating documents define the corporate objects very broadly.

Mentally Impaired Persons

This topic covers persons impaired by disability, drugs, or drunkenness. Mentally impaired persons are liable for contracts they enter into for **neces-**

saries: that is, essentials of life, such as food, clothing, shelter, medical care, education, tools to earn a living, and transportation to work.

For non-necessaries, the contract is valid unless

- the mentally impaired person was incapable of understanding the nature of the transaction; and
- the other party was aware of the incapacity.

In such a case, the contract is voidable at the option of the mentally impaired person. The impaired person must

- repudiate (i.e., end) the contract as soon as her impairment disappears; and
- be able to return all the benefits she received under the contract.

Minors

Minors are also called infants. In Ontario, both terms refer to persons under the age of 18.

Because minors are considered to need protection from their lack of knowledge and experience, the law provides that most contracts entered into by minors are *voidable* by the minor; in other words, the minor can choose to end the contract. The adult party is bound by the contract even though the minor is not. The result is that, for most contracts, a minor can sue to enforce his rights under a contract, but the adult party cannot.

Whether or not a contract is voidable depends on the subject matter of the contract.

Contracts for Necessaries

If a contract for necessaries (defined above) has been *partly executed* (i.e., partly performed), in that the adult party has sold and delivered the goods to the minor, the minor is bound by the contract and must pay for the goods. The minor is only required, however, to pay a reasonable price.

If a contract for necessaries is *executory* (i.e., both parties have exchanged only promises and no performance has yet taken place), the minor is not bound. An example of an executory contract is one where the minor has ordered books, but they have neither been delivered nor paid for.

If a contract for necessaries is *fully executed* (i.e., fully performed), the contract will not be set aside. A fully executed contract is one where the goods have been delivered and paid for.

If *money is lent* to a minor for the purchase of necessaries, and the money is, in fact, used that way, the minor is contractually bound to repay the money.

A minor is bound by a *beneficial contract of service* — for example, a contract of apprenticeship — if the contract is not exploitative.

Contracts for Non-necessaries

The adult party to a contract with a minor for non-necessaries is bound by the contract; the contract is enforceable against the adult party. The minor may have the contract declared void, but if the minor repudiates the contract, she must, if she is the buyer of goods, return the goods, whatever state they are in; if she is the seller, she must be able to return the money paid to her.

If the contract has been fully executed — that is, the goods sold and fully paid for — the contract will not be set aside, but the court may order the adult party to refund any excessive amount charged to the minor.

If the contract is an ongoing one — for example, a book-of-the-month club — and the minor has received some benefit under the contract, the minor cannot recover money he has paid for benefits already received but can repudiate the contract with respect to future liability.

When the Minor Reaches the Age of Majority

Where the contract in question is for necessaries, the minor's liability to pay continues after he reaches the age of majority.

Where the contract is for non-necessaries and benefits the minor on one occasion only, the minor must ratify the contract in writing after she becomes 18 years old, or the contract automatically ends.

Example

Mark Minor orders a stereo on June 15, to be delivered on June 30. Mark's 18th birthday is June 25.

In this example, Mark must ratify the contract in writing after he becomes 18, or the contract automatically terminates, and any deposit he might have paid would have to be refunded.

Where the contract confers a continuous benefit on the minor, such as a partnership agreement or the purchase of a car on instalments, the minor must repudiate the contract upon becoming 18 in order to end it. If he does nothing or continues to use the item or make payments, he will be bound.

CONTRACT FORMATION: FORMALITIES

Contracts can be oral, written without a seal (a simple contract), or written and under seal (a formal contract or deed). They are all equally valid. There are, however, certain contracts that must be in writing to be enforceable.

The Statute of Frauds

The original *Statute of Frauds* was passed in England in 1677, and there is still a Statute of Frauds in Ontario. By its provisions, contracts dealing with certain subjects are not enforceable unless the agreement, or some note or memorandum of the agreement, is in writing and is signed by the person being sued. These contracts include the following:

- a *promise of an executor* by which the executor agrees to pay the debts of the estate personally;

- *guarantees*. A **guarantee** is a promise by one person to pay the debt of another person if he defaults. A guarantor's liability arises only if the principal debtor defaults. Therefore, the guarantor's liability is said to be a secondary, not primary, liability. An agreement to pay, whether or not the other debtor first defaults, is called an **indemnity** and does not need to be in writing;

- *contracts relating to land*, except for leases of less than three years.

To satisfy the requirement of the statute, the contract itself may be in writing, or there may be some memorandum or note of the agreement in writing. Such things as letters, receipts, telegrams, and notes will satisfy this requirement as long as the documents contain all the essential terms of the agreement. Only the person who is being sued must have signed the document.

The Doctrine of Part Performance

If strictly applied, the requirements of the *Statute of Frauds* could be used to allow a party to avoid responsibility under an otherwise valid contract.

> *Example*
>
> Woody agrees to work for Mia for a period of five years. Mia agrees to transfer a one-half interest in her house to Woody at the end of the five-year period. Woody works for Mia for five years and then asks Mia to transfer the one-half interest in her house to him. Mia says, "Contract? What contract?"

If the provisions of the *Statute of Frauds* were strictly applied, Mia would be able to take advantage of the statute to, in effect, perpetrate a fraud on Woody.

The *doctrine of part performance* was developed to protect against such a situation. According to the doctrine, the *Statute of Frauds* does not apply where

- there has been part performance of the contract alleged;
- the acts that constitute the part performance are clearly referable to the contract being alleged and tend to prove the existence of the contract;
- it would be a fraud to allow the party who is trying to avoid her obligations to take advantage of the fact that the contract is not in writing; and
- except for the requirement of writing, there is a valid and enforceable contract.

Other Statutes

There are other statutes that require that certain formalities be complied with for specific types of contracts. Some examples follow.

> *Sale of Goods Act*
>
> A contract for the sale of goods of a value exceeding $40 must be in writing to be enforceable unless the buyer accepts all or part of the goods, gives something in earnest to bind the contract, or makes partial payment on the contract.

> *Consumer Protection Act*
>
> An executory contract for goods or services of a value exceeding $50 is not binding on the buyer unless the contract is signed by the parties and each party has received a duplicate copy of the original contract.

> *Family Law Act*
>
> Marriage contracts, paternity agreements, cohabitation agreements, and separation agreements are unenforceable unless made in writing, signed by the parties and witnessed.

GROUNDS ON WHICH A CONTRACT MAY BE ATTACKED

Mistake

An implicit element of any contract is that the parties have truly and freely agreed or consented to the terms of the contract. The requirement that the parties have mental capacity to enter into the agreement is one way that this issue of consent is addressed. In addition, a party to a contract can avoid contractual responsibility in some instances where the consent was obtained by *mistake*. It must be kept in mind that the legal meaning of *mistake* is far more restrictive than the ordinary meaning of the word.

Common Mistake

It is possible for both parties to enter into a contract on the basis of a false assumption. If both parties make the same mistake, it is called an identical or **common mistake**.

If the parties enter into a contract and are both mistaken as to the existence of the subject matter of the contract, the contract will be void.

Example 1

Alan and Sandy enter into a contract for the sale of Alan's book collection. Neither of them knows that the warehouse where Alan's books are stored has burned down, thus destroying the books.

Both parties mistakenly believed the subject matter of the contract to exist. The contract would be void.

However, where the parties are both mistaken as to the value or quality of the subject matter, the contract will be valid.

Example 2

Max sells Jacob a painting. They both believe that the painting was painted by a famous artist and is very valuable. It is later discovered that the painting was painted by someone else and is worth a lot less than either of them thought.

This contract will be valid.

Mutual Mistake

This term is used to describe the situation where both parties are mistaken, but the mistakes are different. An example of a **mutual mistake** is the English case of *Raffles v. Wichelhaus* (see Exhibit 14.1). As can be seen, in a case such as this, the position of the defendant is favoured, because the court will not enforce such an ambiguous contract.

Unilateral Mistake

This term is used to describe the situation where only one party is mistaken, and the other party is aware of the mistake. If the mistake relates to the terms of the contract itself, as opposed to a mere error in judgment as to the quality of the subject matter of the contract, the contract will be void.

Mutual Mistake

EXHIBIT 14.1

The defendant agreed to buy cotton from the plaintiff to be shipped from Bombay aboard a ship called *Peerless*. Neither party was aware of the fact that there were two ships by that name scheduled to leave Bombay: one in October and another in December. The plaintiff was referring to the ship leaving in December, while the defendant was referring to the ship leaving in October. The plaintiff's shipment arrived two months later than the defendant had anticipated. As a result of price fluctuations in that period, the defendant refused to accept and pay for the shipment. The plaintiff sued for payment. The defendant pleaded mistake as a defence.

The court held that the contract was totally ambiguous, and a reasonable person could not tell whose interpretation to choose. Accordingly, the plaintiff's claim was dismissed.

Source: *Raffles v. Wichelhaus* (1864), 159 E.R. 375.

Example

Lisa offers to sell to Michael her French landscape painting for $500. Michael agrees, believing it to be the painting hanging in her living room. In fact, Lisa owns two French landscape paintings, and she is offering for sale her less valuable painting that hangs in her den. Lisa is aware of Michael's mistake.

In this case, the contract would be void. However, if Michael knows that Lisa is offering to sell the painting in her den and accepts the offer in the mistaken belief that it is worth more than it actually is, the contract will not be void.

Mistake as to the Identity of One of the Contracting Parties

Where one person is mistaken as to the identity of the other contracting party, the contract will be void if

- the identity of the other party is of crucial importance to the contract;
- the mistaken party had an identifiable person in mind with whom he intended to contract; and
- the other party was aware of the mistake.

Clerical Mistake

If a party can show that the parties were in complete agreement on the terms of their contract, but by an error wrote down these terms incorrectly, the court can correct the error. This remedy is called *rectification*.

Non Est Factum

The general rule is that a person is bound by the contracts she signs, even if the person has not read or understood the document. An exception to this rule is where the person, through no carelessness of her own, is totally mistaken as to the nature and effect of the document signed.

In this case the person would plead ***non est factum***. Generally, the party relying upon this defence is either illiterate or prevented by some disability from reading the document and is, therefore, forced to rely upon someone else's representation as to the nature and effect of the document signed.

Misrepresentation

A **misrepresentation** is a *false statement of fact* that *induces* the other party to enter into the contract. The misrepresentation may be either fraudulently or innocently made.

Where a misrepresentation is made, the other party may be entitled to have the contract terminated.

False Statement of Fact

The false statement must be with respect to a specific existing fact or a past event. Even if false, the following do not constitute misrepresentation in law:

- A statement of future conduct or intention
- A statement of opinion or belief
- A statement as to what the law is

To be a misrepresentation, a statement must exist. Generally, silence or non-disclosure does not constitute misrepresentation.

Meaning of Inducement

The other party must have relied upon the false statement in deciding whether or not to enter into the contract, and the false statement must have been a major factor — although not necessarily the only factor — in her deciding to enter into the contract. There is no inducement if the other party used his own judgment, or if he did not rely on the statement.

Remedies for Misrepresentation

The main remedy for misrepresentation is the equitable remedy of **rescission**. In other words, the innocent party may seek to have the contract set aside, and have the parties put back in the position they would have been in if the contract had never been made. In order to obtain this remedy, the innocent party must act promptly, and it must be possible to substantially restore the parties to their original position.

If the misrepresentation was negligently or fraudulently made, the innocent party may, in addition to rescission, also seek damages in tort for deceit (fraudulent misrepresentation) or for negligent misrepresentation. If the misrepresentation was innocent, there is no right to claim damages.

Undue Influence and Duress

Where a contract is entered into as a result of one party's having exerted improper pressure over the other party, the contract may be set aside.

The term **undue influence** describes a situation where a party enters into a contract as a result of improper pressure being brought to bear on her so as to render her "morally unable" to resist the will of the other party. As a result of this pressure, the party enters into a contract that is not to her advantage but is to the advantage of the other party.

In most cases, the innocent party must prove that undue influence was applied. However, in some relationships the court presumes that some degree of influence exists, such as the influence of parent over child or solicitor over client.

The term **duress** applies to the situation where a party entered into a contract as a result of actual or threatened violence, against him or his family, or as a result of a threat of criminal prosecution or libel. The threat must have been made by the other party to the contract.

Illegality

The courts will not enforce contracts whose purpose is illegal. The purpose of the contract may be illegal because it contravenes the provisions of a statute or because it contravenes public policy. If the purpose of a contract is illegal, the contract will be considered void. In some situations, the contract will also be considered illegal.

Different Treatment of Void and Illegal Contracts

A contract that is considered *void* because of an illegal purpose will be void only in so far as it contravenes the particular statute or public policy. If only a term is considered illegal, the void term may be severed, and the remainder of the contract enforced, if it is possible to do so without substantially altering the contract. If a contract is merely void for illegal purpose, the courts will assist the parties in disengaging from the void contract. Either party may sue to recover any money paid or property transferred pursuant to the contract.

If the contract is not only void but *illegal*, the effect on the parties will depend on whether or not the contract is illegal as formed. Contracts to commit a crime or contracts expressly forbidden by statute are contracts illegal as formed. In these contracts, generally, neither party will be able to sue or acquire rights under the contract, or recover money paid or property transferred under the contract. If the contract was legal as formed, but one party (and not the other) performs or intends to perform the contract in an illegal manner, the "guilty" party cannot sue on the contract for damages or recover money paid or property transferred under the contract, but the innocent party may be able to sue on the contract.

Illegal Contracts

A contract may be illegal by virtue of a provision in a statute, or it may be illegal at common law. A contract is *illegal by statute* if the statute expressly or implicitly forbids the making of the contract. Where a statute requires that a member of a trade or profession be licensed, the failure of the person to have a licence will be a good defence to an action by that person to collect fees for work performed. If, however, the person to whom the services were performed wishes to sue, the unlicensed individual cannot rely on her own lack of a licence as a defence.

The following are examples of contracts considered *illegal at common law*:

- Contracts to commit a crime or a tort
- Contracts encouraging sexual immorality
- Contracts prejudicial to public safety
- Contracts prejudicial to the administration of justice
- Contracts encouraging public corruption

Void Contracts

Contracts may be *void by statute* or *void at common law*. An example is found in the *Workplace Safety and Insurance Act*, which states that any provision in any employment contract that purports to deprive an employee of the protection of the legislation is void. Another example is the *Gaming Control Act* of Ontario. While it is not necessarily illegal to bet, a winner of a bet cannot use the courts to collect on the bet, and a loser of a bet cannot use the courts to recover what he paid.

The most common example of a contract void at common law is a contract in restraint of trade.

Contracts in Restraint of Trade

Contracts to lessen competition are considered contrary to public policy and are void, unless they are reasonable as between the parties and with respect to the public interest. There are three types of contracts in restraint of trade:

- Agreements between manufacturers to fix prices or to limit production
- Agreements between an employer and an employee regarding subsequent employment of the employee
- Agreements between the buyer and seller of a business

Agreements between manufacturers to fix prices or to limit production are void not only at common law, but under the federal *Competition Act*.

Courts look very carefully at contractual provisions by the employer that attempt to restrict the employee's right to work after the employment is terminated. Such provisions are considered to be reasonable only if the employee has knowledge of trade secrets or secret processes or is in a position of influence to entice away customers. Even if the circumstances make it reasonable for restrictions to be placed, the nature of the restrictions must be no wider than reasonably necessary, and they must be reasonable as to geographic area and duration.

Agreements by a seller of a business not to subsequently compete are looked upon more favourably by the courts. Again, however, the person seeking to uphold the restrictions must show that they are reasonable in view of the nature of the business being sold. The restrictions must again be reasonable in scope, duration, and geographic area.

In both employment and business sale situations, if the restrictions as drafted are found to be unreasonable, they will be void in total; the courts will not redraft the provisions for the parties.

INTERPRETATION OF CONTRACTS

The statements, promises, and provisions of a contract are called the **terms of the contract**. It is the terms of the contract that determine the rights and obligations of the parties. A term of a contract may be express or implied. If a term is broken, the importance of the term determines the remedies available to the wronged party.

Before the court can enforce a contract, the court must determine what the term or terms in question mean. In doing so, the court tries to ascertain the true intention of the parties as expressed in the language of the contract. This exercise will involve a balance between interpreting the language of the contract in accordance with its plain meaning and interpreting the contract in the context of the circumstances surrounding it.

The Requirement of Certainty

For a contract to be enforced by the court, its terms must be reasonably certain. If the terms of the contract are too vague, the court will not know what to enforce, and the contract will, therefore, be unenforceable or void.

The Parol Evidence Rule

The *parol evidence rule* is a rule used in the interpretation of written contracts. The rule limits the use of extrinsic evidence, whether written or oral, in interpreting the written language of the contract. Such evidence is not admissible to add to, subtract from, change or contradict the terms of the contract as written. This rule flows from the presumption that, when a contract is reduced to writing, the written document is meant to include all of the terms of the contract. The rule could be used to exclude oral statements, draft contracts, or correspondence.

As with any rule, there are exceptions to the parol evidence rule. The main exceptions are as follows:

- Evidence of the customs of an area or of trade usage of a particular term may be admitted to add to, but not contradict, a written agreement (e.g., a baker's dozen is 13, not 12).

- Evidence is admissible that the contract has not yet come into operation or has ceased to operate.

- The presumption that the written document is meant to include all of the terms of the contract may be rebutted by evidence proving that the contract was partly written and partly oral. The additional oral terms must not vary or contradict the written terms; they may only complete the written terms.

- Evidence is admissible if it relates to the validity of the contract. Accordingly, the court will hear evidence on issues such as mistake, misrepresentation, lack of capacity, or lack of consideration.

- The court will admit evidence of clerical error in recording the terms of the agreement, leading to the remedy of rectification.

- The court will admit extrinsic evidence to explain ambiguous terms in the contract.

- The court will admit evidence as to the existence of a **collateral contract**. In such a case, the argument would be that external evidence is not being offered to contradict the written terms of the contract; instead, it is evidence of a separate and additional contract between the parties, which may contradict the written contract. For such evidence to be admitted, the collateral contract must itself have all of the elements of a valid contract, including separate consideration.

Classification of Terms

Not all terms of a contract are of equal importance. Contract law categorizes terms based on their importance. Breaches of different categories of terms have different effects.

Condition

This expression is used to describe an important term of the contract. Breach of a **condition** entitles the wronged party to sue for damages and to treat the contract as over, relieving her of any obligation to perform under the contract.

Warranty

This expression is used to describe a less important term of the contract. Put another way, any terms that are not conditions are **warranties**. When a warranty is breached, the wronged party has the right to sue for damages, but he cannot treat the contract as over and must still perform his obligations under the contract.

Implied Terms

Certain contract terms may be implied into a contract, even though not expressed by the parties. There are three ways this can occur: by statute, by custom and by the court.

Terms Implied by Statute

There are certain statutes that imply terms into particular types of contracts. For example, the *Residential Tenancies Act* states that certain provisions with respect to the termination of a residential tenancy are included in all residential leases, whether or not expressly stated in the contract between the landlord and the tenant.

Terms Implied by Custom

Where the contract is silent on a particular matter, the court may imply terms based on evidence of local custom or trade usage.

Terms Implied by the Court

The court may imply a term not expressly stated by the parties, where the court's opinion is that the parties must have intended to include the term in order to give effect to the contract. For the court to do so, the term must be so obvious as to go without saying. In implying such terms, the court is attempting to give effect to what must have been the intention of the parties.

Exculpatory Clauses

Exculpatory clauses are clauses by which a party attempts to limit her liability for breach of contract, misrepresentation, or negligence. These clauses are also called disclaimer clauses or exclusion clauses.

Before a court will give effect to such a clause, the court must be satisfied that the clause has been incorporated into — in other words, is part of — the contract and that, as a matter of interpretation, it covers the situation in question.

Incorporation

If the contract containing the exculpatory clause is written and signed, the other party is bound by the clause even if he has not read the document, and whether or not he understands the clause. The clause can, however, be rendered ineffective if there has been a misrepresentation as to its effect. (See Exhibit 14.2.)

If the contract containing the exculpatory clause is not signed, reasonable and sufficient notice of the exclusion clause must be given to the other party. To satisfy this notice requirement, the following must occur:

- The clause must be in a document that the other party would assume to contain contractual terms and not in a document that merely acknowledges payment, such as a receipt.

- The existence of the clause must be brought to the notice of the other party before or at the time the contract is entered into, not after.

Interpretation

Once the court finds that the exculpatory clause is, in fact, part of the agreement, the court must interpret the clause to determine whether or not it covers the situation in question. In doing so, the court interprets the entire contract. The courts have held that liability can be excluded only by clear words.

The court applies certain rules of construction in interpreting exculpatory clauses. The main rules of construction are as follows:

- Under the *contra preferentem rule*, an exculpatory clause is construed strictly against the party who drafted the clause. Any ambiguity in the language of the clause will be construed as narrowly as possible. Especially clear words are required to exclude liability for negligence.

- There is a presumption of construction that an exculpatory clause is not intended to defeat the main purpose of the contract.

An Example of the Effect of Misrepresentation

EXHIBIT 14.2

The plaintiff took a dress to the defendants to be cleaned. She signed a receipt after being told it excluded the defendant's liability for damage to sequins. In fact, the clause excluded the defendants from liability for damage of any kind. The dress was returned with a stain.

The court held that, because the defendants misrepresented to the plaintiff the effect of the clause, the exemption clause would in this instance protect the defendants only for damage done to sequins.

Source: *Curtis v. Chemical Cleaning & Dyeing Co. Ltd.*, [1951] K.B. 805.

- An exculpatory clause can protect the party relying upon the clause against liability for a **fundamental breach** of contract only if the language of the clause specifically and clearly covers the breach in question. A fundamental breach of contract is a serious breach of the contract.

PRIVITY OF CONTRACT AND ASSIGNMENT OF CONTRACT RIGHTS

Privity of Contract

The general rule at common law is that a contract does not confer any rights or impose any obligations on a person who is not a party to the contract. A person who is not a party to a contract is said not to be *privy to the contract* and is called a third party or a *stranger to the contract*. To succeed in an action in contract, the plaintiff must prove **privity of contract** between her and the defendant. In other words, the plaintiff must prove that they were both parties to the same contract.

Example 1

Alice buys a tuna salad sandwich from a takeout delicatessen. The mayonnaise in the tuna salad has gone bad. Alice gives the sandwich to Ralph, who develops food poisoning.

In this example, Ralph would have no cause of action in contract against the delicatessen because he was not a party to the contract with the delicatessen for the purchase of the sandwich. Put another way, there was no privity of contract between Ralph and the delicatessen.

Example 2

Bob owes Carol $200. Bob offers to repair Ted's car if Ted will pay Carol $200. Bob does the repairs on Ted's car. Ted does not pay Carol.

In this example, Carol cannot sue Ted. There is no privity of contract between them. Carol can sue only Bob, and only Bob can sue Ted.

Example 3

The facts are the same as in Example 2, except Carol is also made a party to the contract with Bob and Ted.

Carol is still unable to sue Ted. While there is privity of contract and consideration flowing between Bob and Ted, there is no consideration flowing from Carol to Ted. For a person to be able to sue on a contract, there must be not only privity of contract between the parties but also consideration for the promise given by the person who is suing to enforce the promise.

Example 4

A landlord rents a store to a tenant. Under the contract between them, the landlord agrees to make the store available to the tenant, and the tenant agrees to pay the rent. The tenant in turn sublets the store. The subtenant agrees to pay the rent directly to the landlord. The subtenant fails to pay the rent.

In this example, the landlord would be unable to sue the subtenant directly for the rent. The landlord would have to sue the tenant, with whom she had privity of contract. The tenant in turn can sue the sub-tenant.

Assignment of Contractual Rights and Obligations

This subject is related to privity of contract. Most contracts confer rights and impose obligations on both parties. For example, in a lease, the landlord has the obligation to make the premises available to the tenant and has the right to receive rent; the tenant has the right to occupy the premises and the obligation to pay rent.

Contractual Obligations

A party to a contract cannot assign or transfer his obligations under the contract to a third party without the consent of the promisee (the person to whom the obligation is owed under the contract).

Where the contract involves the provision of a unique service — for example, that of an entertainer or a portrait painter — the obligation must be personally performed.

Where the contract does not involve the provision of a unique service, the **promisor** (the person who owes the obligation under the contract) may arrange for someone else to carry out the obligation on her behalf. However, the promisor remains responsible to the **promisee** for the proper performance of the contract obligation. This is known as *vicarious performance*. The promisor assumes the role of an employer and, in essence, hires someone to do his work for him. However, the contract work is being done on the promisor's behalf and, if it is not done properly, the promisee sues the promisor, not the person who did the work on her behalf.

Example

Burt hires Ernie to wash the windows of his house. Ernie hires Elmo to wash the windows for him. Elmo breaks one of Burt's windows.

In this example, Burt cannot sue Elmo in contract because there is no privity of contract between them. However, Burt can sue Ernie because Burt remains responsible under the contract to see that his contractual obligations are properly performed.

Contractual Rights

A party to a contract may assign his rights under a contract to a third party without the consent of the promisor. The person who assigns contract rights to another is called the **assignor**. The person to whom the contract rights are assigned is called the **assignee**.

Once the contract rights have been assigned, if the promisor does not fulfill her obligation, the assignee may sue the promisor on the original contract without having to join the assignor (who was the original promisee) as a party to the action, provided that the following conditions are met:

- the assignment was absolute — in other words, unconditional and complete;
- the assignment was in writing; and
- the promisor was given notice in writing of the assignment.

Example

Gaugin lends Picasso $12,000. Picasso agrees to repay the loan in instalments of $1,000 per month plus 10 percent interest. Gaugin decides to move to Tahiti and needs the money immediately. He agrees to sell his right to receive the loan payments to Monet. Monet pays him $10,000. Gaugin is willing to accept this lesser amount in return for getting the money immediately. Gaugin and

Monet draft and sign a written agreement in which Gaugin unconditionally assigns to Monet his right to receive the loan payments from Picasso. Gaugin notifies Picasso in writing of the assignment.

Upon receipt of the notice of the assignment, Picasso is obligated to make all future payments to Monet. If Picasso does not make the payments, Monet can sue Picasso directly, without having to add Gaugin as a party, even though there is no privity of contract between Picasso and Monet. If Monet were to sue Picasso, Picasso would be able to rely upon any defences he could have raised against Gaugin.

DISCHARGE OF CONTRACTS

When a contract is discharged, it means that the obligations under the contract are cancelled and that the contract is no longer operative. A contract may be discharged by performance, by agreement, by frustration, by operation of law, or by breach.

Discharge by Performance

When parties enter into a contract, they expect that the obligations under the contract will be performed by both parties and, when performance is completed, that the contract will come to an end. In fact, this is what occurs in the majority of contracts.

Before a contract can be said to be discharged by performance, both parties must have fulfilled their obligations under the contract.

The general rule is that performance under the contract must be exactly in compliance with the contract provisions. There is, however, an exception in the case of *substantial performance*. Where a party has substantially performed his obligations under the contract, he may enforce performance of the other party's obligations. The court may, however, reduce the other party's obligations because of the incomplete performance. (See Exhibit 14.3.)

Tender of Performance

Sometimes a party's attempt to perform her contractual obligation will be refused by the other party. An attempt to perform is called a **tender of performance**.

EXHIBIT 14.3	The Principle of Substantial Performance

The plaintiff and defendant entered into a contract for the plaintiff to carry out repairs to the defendant's house. The work as completed by the plaintiffs differed from the contract in three minor respects that could be corrected at a relatively small cost to the defendants. The defendant refused to pay the plaintiff on the grounds that the contract had not been performed as required.

The court held that the defendant was not relieved of his obligation to pay because of a trivial failure of performance. The defendant was ordered to fulfill his obligation under the contract, which was to pay the contract price, subject to a deduction equal to the cost of correcting the defects in the plaintiff's work.

Source: *Dakin & Co. Ltd. v. Lee*, [1916] 1 K.B. 566.

Example

Alex, who owns a dress shop, agrees to buy 50 dresses from Kim for $75 each. Delivery is to take place on April 1. Prior to the scheduled delivery date, Alex finds similar dresses from another supplier for $60 each, and buys from that supplier instead. When Kim attempts to deliver the dresses on April 1, Alex refuses to accept delivery, thinking that, as a result, he will not have to pay the contract price.

In this case, Kim's tender of performance relieves her of any further obligation under the contract. Her tender of performance is the equivalent of performance, and she can sue Alex for the contract price.

Tender of Payment

A tender of payment is treated somewhat differently than a tender of performance. If a party is under a contractual obligation to pay money, and the other party, for some strange reason, refuses to accept payment, the party is not relieved of his obligation to pay under the contract. However, he will not have to pay any interest on the money or any costs in any subsequent court action to collect the money.

When money is to be paid under a contract, unless the contract provides otherwise, payment is to be made in cash.

Discharge by Agreement

The parties to a contract may, by subsequent agreement, agree that the contract is at an end.

Waiver

A **waiver** is an agreement between parties to an existing contract that the contract is not to be performed. A waiver is itself a contract and must be supported by consideration. If the contract being terminated is one under which neither party has performed, the consideration flowing from each party is a release of the other party's obligation to perform under the contract. If one party has performed under the contract and the other party has not, the waiver must either be supported by its own consideration or be under seal.

Material Alteration of the Contract Terms

Sometimes the parties to an agreement wish to change the terms of the agreement. If the agreed-upon change results in a material alteration of the terms of the original contract, the effect is to discharge the original contract and replace it with a new one.

Accord and Satisfaction

This term describes the situation where a promisor who cannot perform her obligation under the contract offers the promisee money or some other substitute if the promisee will release her from her original obligation.

Example

Elizabeth enters into a contract to buy carpeting from Hugh, to be delivered on June 30. Hugh is unable to obtain the carpeting from his supplier in time for delivery and so offers a different style of carpeting to Elizabeth at a reduced price. Elizabeth accepts.

Discharge by Frustration

Sometimes, without the fault of either party, it becomes impossible to perform under the contract as required. In some of those situations, the doctrine of frustration provides that the contract is discharged.

The following are the situations where the doctrine has been held to apply:

- The doctrine applies where performance becomes *impossible* — for example, a contract to rent a concert hall for a piano recital where the concert hall burns down before the concert date.

- A contract is frustrated where a change in law, while the contract is in effect, renders further performance under the contract *illegal*.

- The contract may be considered frustrated where performance, though possible, would be something radically different than what the parties originally intended. For example, a person rents a hotel room for the express purpose of watching a parade, which is then cancelled.

The doctrine of frustration does not apply in cases where performance of the contractual obligations is possible but will cause hardship. The fact that a party's contractual obligations prove to be more onerous than expected does not constitute sufficient grounds for frustration. The doctrine will also not apply to a situation where a party wilfully disables himself from performing.

In Ontario, the *Frustrated Contracts Act* sets out what happens if a contract is frustrated:

- If a party started to perform her obligations before the contract was frustrated (whether or not the other party has received any benefit from the performance) and that party has received any payments from the other party, the party can keep the money already paid to the extent that she has incurred expenses. Any excess over expenses must be returned.

- If a party started to perform his obligations before the contract was frustrated (whether or not the other party has received any benefit from the performance) and payments were due from the other party but unpaid at the time of frustration, the party can sue to recover his expenses up to the amount of money that was due to be paid.

- If a party started to perform her obligations before the contract was frustrated, and the other party has received benefits under the contract, the party receiving the benefits must pay for the benefits received.

Under these rules, a party who performed part of a contract would have to bear the entire loss if he incurred expenses but the other party received no benefit and was not liable to pay any money at that time. Accordingly, it is prudent when drafting a contract to arrange for payments by instalments sufficient to cover expenses as they are incurred.

Discharge by Operation of Law

When a person who files for, or is petitioned into, bankruptcy is subsequently discharged from bankruptcy, she is discharged from most contractual liabilities.

A person who wishes to sue upon a contract must do so within the time limits specified by the *Statute of Limitations* or other relevant legislation. If no action is taken within the specified time, the cause of action expires.

BREACH OF CONTRACT

A breach of contract occurs when a party does not fulfill his obligations under the contract as promised. Some breaches of contract will relieve the other party of her responsibility under the contract; others will not.

Only breach of a condition (i.e., an essential term) will give the other party the right to treat the contract as being at an end and to sue for damages. A breach of warranty (i.e., a less important term) will give the innocent party the right to sue for damages, but he will still be required to perform his obligations under the contract.

Express Repudiation

A party may breach a contract by **express repudiation**. In such a case, one party tells the other party that she does not intend to perform her contractual obligation as promised. In such a case, the innocent party does not have to sit and wait for the appointed date of performance to come and go before suing for damages. Instead, if the term in question is a condition, the innocent party can treat the contract as being immediately at an end by notifying the promisor of this fact and stating his intention to sue for damages.

Alternatively, the innocent party can choose to insist on performance and wait until non-performance on the appointed date, and then sue for damages. There is a risk, if this option is chosen, that the contract will be frustrated before the date set for performance.

When a contract is expressly repudiated before the time fixed for performance, it is called an **anticipatory breach**. Repudiation can also occur after performance has begun.

Performance Rendered Impossible by One Party

A breach of contract occurs if a party wilfully or negligently renders her performance impossible.

Example

Fred agrees to sell Barney his car for $5,000, with the car to be delivered in two weeks. The next day, Fred is offered $7,500 for the car and sells it to Wilma.

In this example, Fred cannot rely on his inability to perform as a defence, since he made himself unable to perform.

Failure to Perform

This term describes the situation where, without advance warning, a party does not fulfill his contractual obligations. This failure to perform can take the form of a total failure to perform, or significantly inadequate performance, or performance that fails to comply with the contract in a minor way. The extent of the failure affects the remedy available to the other party.

The major question for the innocent party is whether or not the party is relieved of her obligations under the contract. As stated earlier, the innocent party can treat the contract as at an end only where there has been a breach of a significant term (condition) of the contract.

Determining whether or not such a breach has taken place is particularly tricky with respect to contracts intended to be performed in instalments. In such a case, the innocent party will be relieved of his duty to perform only where

- there is good reason to believe that future performance will be equally deficient; or
- the deficiency is significant in relation to the whole performance promised.

Example

Dave owns a flower store. He enters into a contract with Beth to supply him with 10 dozen roses each week for a period of one year. During the first week, Beth supplies Dave with only 2 dozen roses.

In this example, Dave would be free to find himself another supplier. He would not be obliged to continue to accept deliveries from Beth.

As stated previously, where a party substantially performs her obligations under a contract, the other party cannot rely on trivial breaches to relieve him of the obligation to perform. Rather, that party, while entitled to damages for the defective performance, is bound to perform his obligations under the contract.

REMEDIES FOR BREACH OF CONTRACT

Types of Remedies

The remedies available to the innocent party following a breach of contract depend on the nature and seriousness of the breach in question. If the breach is significant enough, the innocent party may be able to *repudiate* the contract. In other words, the innocent party can treat the contract as being at an end, and will be relieved of her obligation to perform under the contract. Both in cases where the breach is significant enough to give rise to the right of repudiation, and in cases of less significant breaches, the innocent party may have the right to sue for *damages*. In some cases, the innocent party may be entitled to the *equitable remedies of rescission* — **specific performance**, *injunction*, or *quantum meruit*.

Damages

Purpose of Damages

Generally, in contract law, the purpose of damages is to place the innocent party in the same position he would have been in if the contract had been performed. However, the plaintiff in an action for breach of contract may not be awarded damages for all of his losses if some of the losses suffered are too *remote* a consequence of the defendant's breach. In other words, the court will not force the defendant to compensate the plaintiff if the losses suffered by the plaintiff are too far removed from, or are not reasonably foreseeable consequences of, the defendant's breach.

Remoteness of Damages

To establish that the plaintiff's damages are not too remote, the plaintiff must be able to prove either of the following:

- The loss in question flows naturally from the breach. In other words, the nature of the loss is such that a reasonable party to the contract would have expected it to result from the breach in question.

- If the loss is special or unusual, it is reasonable to believe, given the circumstances of the particular contract, that at the time the contract was made, the parties would have been aware that the loss in question would be a probable result of the breach. (See Exhibit 14.4.)

Measure of Damages

Once it is determined that a certain type of loss is not too remote, the court must determine how the damages for the loss are to be calculated.

Since the purpose of contract damages is to put the innocent party in the position she would have been in had the contract been performed, the damage

---

The Principles of Remoteness of Damage

EXHIBIT 14.4

These principles are illustrated in the following two English cases.

Hadley v. Baxendale

The plaintiffs, who owned a mill, ordered a new mill shaft from the defendants. They gave the defendants their broken mill shaft to use as a pattern for a new shaft. The defendants promised to deliver the new mill shaft within a day but did not deliver it until a week later. Unknown to the defendants, the plaintiffs did not own a spare mill shaft, and the mill was out of operation for the week. The plaintiffs sued for damages for their loss of profits for the period of the delay.

The court held that the damages were too remote. The damages did not arise naturally from the breach because the plaintiffs might well have owned a spare mill shaft. The damages were not reasonable in contemplation of the parties when the contract was entered into because the defendants did not know that they had been given the plaintiffs' only mill shaft.

Source: *Hadley v. Baxendale* (1854), E.R. 145.

Victoria Laundry (Windsor) Ltd. v. Newman Industries Ltd.

The plaintiffs owned a laundry and dyeing company. They decided to purchase an additional boiler so that they could expand their business. They would also then be in a position to obtain certain profitable dyeing contracts. The plaintiffs contracted with the defendants for the purchase of a boiler. The defendants were aware that the plaintiffs required the boiler immediately. The defendants were five months late in delivering the boiler. The plaintiffs sued the defendants for loss of profits of two kinds: the loss of normal profits from the additional business that could have been handled with the additional boiler; and the loss of profits from the profitable dyeing contracts they were unable to obtain because they did not have the additional boiler.

The court held the defendants liable for the loss of normal profits but not for the loss of profits from the dyeing contracts. The loss of profits from the dyeing contracts did not flow naturally from the breach, and the defendants did not and could not have known about them.

Source: *Victoria Laundry (Windsor) Ltd. v. Newman Industries Ltd.*, [1949] 2 K.B. 528.

---

award will include an amount equal to the profits she might reasonably have expected to make if the contract had been performed. It is not enough to simply compensate the wronged party for her out-of-pocket expenses, which would have the effect of putting her in the position she would have been in if the contract had never been made. Damages for loss of anticipated profits are called **expectation damages**.

Example

Esther owned a swimsuit manufacturing company. She purchased fabric from Ben. The fabric was to be dyed with water-resistant colours. Esther used the fabric to manufacture a line of swimsuits. It was then discovered that the dye used to colour the fabric ran when the fabric was placed in water, and the swimsuits had to be destroyed.

In this example, Esther would be entitled to damages based on the profit she would have made on the sale of the swimsuits to her customers. The damages would not be calculated to simply compensate her for the purchase price of the fabric and the cost of manufacturing the swimsuits because this approach would not provide her with her lost profits.

There are unusual cases in which the courts have held that the more appropriate approach would be to simply compensate the plaintiff for expenses incurred in reliance on the contract, which have been wasted by the defendant's breach. This approach puts the plaintiff in the position he would have been in if the contract had never been made. An example of such a case is the English decision of *Anglia T.V. v. Reed*, [1971] 3 All E.R. 690, summarized below:

> The plaintiff hired the defendant, an actor, to appear in a movie. The plaintiff hired a director and a designer. The defendant then repudiated the contract. It was held that the plaintiff could recover its wasted expenditure on the director and the designer.

Generally, the nature of damages in a contract case is limited to economic damages. There are, however, some unusual cases in which damages have been awarded for *mental anguish* arising out of a breach of contract.

Damages for mental anguish have been awarded in a contract for a vacation that did not turn out as promised. Because there is no loss of profits for the vacationer, damages would otherwise be limited to a return of the money paid.

The courts have also, although rarely, awarded damages for mental anguish in wrongful dismissal cases.

Mitigation of Damages

While a plaintiff is entitled to be compensated by an award of damages for all reasonably foreseeable losses caused by the wrongdoer's breach of contract, the plaintiff is under a duty to take all reasonable steps to **mitigate** her **damages**. In other words, the plaintiff must take all reasonable steps to reduce the amount of loss caused by the breach of contract. The plaintiff will not be awarded damages for any part of the loss that she could have mitigated.

Example

Theresa rents a store from Lawrence for $1,000 per month for a period of one year. After two months, she decides to close down her business. She vacates the premises and stops paying her rent. Lawrence tries to find another tenant, but nobody is willing to pay $1,000 per month for the store. One prospective tenant offers to pay him $800 per month, but he refuses. The store remains vacant for the remaining 10 months of the lease.

In this example, Lawrence will not be able to recover the full 10 months' lost rent of $10,000 from Theresa because he could have reduced his losses by re-renting the store for $800 per month. Had he done so, his losses under the lease would have been only $2,000 instead of $10,000. Lawrence will, therefore, be awarded only $2,000 in damages.

Liquidated Damages and Penalties

Some contracts contain a clause setting out what a party will pay if he breaches the contract. The court will allow the other party to recover this amount from the wrongdoer, without requiring her to prove her actual loss, if the amount specified in the contract represents a genuine attempt to pre-estimate the loss that would be caused by such a breach. This type of provision is called a **liquidated damages clause**. If, on the other hand, the amount is not a pre-estimate of damages but is, instead, designed to be used as a threat to compel performance by the other party, the clause is called a **penalty clause** and will not be enforced. Instead, the innocent party will be able to recover only the damages she can prove.

Equitable Remedies

There are a number of equitable remedies that may be granted in breach of contract cases. These remedies are available only at the discretion of the court where the remedy of damages would be inappropriate or inadequate.

Rescission

Under this remedy, the courts declare that a contract is void. It is as if the contract had never been made, and the parties are put in the position they would have been in if the contract had never been made. The purpose of rescission is totally different from that of damages, which is to put the parties in the position they would have been in if the contract had been performed. Accordingly, a party cannot both seek rescission *and* sue for damages.

This remedy is available, at the option of the wronged party, in cases of misrepresentation, duress, undue influence, and for some kinds of mistake.

Specific Performance

Under this remedy, the breaching party is ordered to perform his obligations under the contract. Specific performance will be ordered only where damages would be an inadequate remedy (e.g., in a contract for the sale of a unique item). This remedy is most commonly granted with respect to contracts for the sale of land because each parcel of land is considered to be unique.

Specific performance will not be ordered with respect to a contract for personal services.

Injunction

Under this remedy, a party to a contract is ordered to refrain from conduct that constitutes a breach of the contract. For example, a manufacturer may have a contract to supply goods to a wholesaler in which she agrees not to sell the goods to any other wholesaler. If the manufacturer were to attempt to sell the goods to someone else, the wholesaler may be able to obtain an injunction to prevent her from doing so.

Quantum Meruit

A claim in quantum meruit is a claim for reasonable remuneration. This remedy is sought where it is found that there is no contract between the parties or where there was a contract but it ends.

Example

Alice hires Robert to renovate her kitchen. Halfway through the job, Alice refuses to let Robert in to complete his work and then refuses to pay him on the basis that the contract provided for payment upon completion, and the contract was not completed.

In this example, the contract does not set out how to calculate payment for a partial job. Robert would be entitled to reasonable compensation for the work done.

CHAPTER SUMMARY

In this chapter, the reader was introduced to the basics of contract law and the fact that all contracts contain the same elements: offer and acceptance; the intention to be legally bound; valuable consideration; legal capacity of the parties to the contract; and, in some cases, compliance with certain legal formalities. The chapter explored these elements in a discussion of the manner in which contracts are formed.

The chapter then analyzed the grounds on which a contract, once formed, may be attacked. Mistake, misrepresentation, undue influence, duress, and illegality were discussed.

There was also a discussion of the way in which contracts are interpreted by the courts, including the approach taken to express terms and implied terms.

The requirement of privity of contract was explored, as was the manner and extent to which contractual rights and responsibilities may be assigned by the parties to a contract.

The chapter proceeded with a discussion of the ways in which a contract can be discharged: by performance, by agreement, by frustration, by operation of law, and by breach. Different forms of breach of contract were identified and discussed.

The chapter concluded with a discussion of the different remedies for breach of contract. Both damages and the equitable remedies of rescission, specific performance, injunction, and *quantum meruit* were explored.

GLOSSARY OF NEW TERMS AND KEY CONCEPTS

anticipatory breach	When a contract is expressly repudiated before the time fixed for performance, it is called an anticipatory breach.
assignee	The assignee is the person to whom the contract rights are assigned.
assignor	A person who assigns her rights under a contract to a third party.
bilateral contracts	Contracts in which a promise by one party is exchanged for a promise by the other party.
collateral contract	A separate, additional contract between parties to a contract in writing. A collateral contract must have all of the elements of a valid contract.
common mistake	It is possible for both parties to enter into a contract on the basis of a false assumption. If both parties make the same mistake, it is called a common or identical mistake.
condition	An important term of the contract.
consideration	Something of value given by each party of a contract to the other.
contract	An agreement between two or more parties that is enforceable at law.
deeds	Contracts that are written, signed, witnessed, sealed, and delivered.
duress	A situation where a party enters into a contract as a result of actual or threatened violence against the party or the party's family, or as a result of a threat of criminal prosecution or libel. The threat must have been made by the other party to the contract.
exculpatory clause	A clause by which a party attempts to limit his liability for breach of contract, misrepresentation, or negligence.
expectation damages	The award of damages in an amount equal to the profits the innocent party might reasonably have expected to make if the contract had been performed.
express repudiation	The situation where one party tells the other party that she does not intend to perform her contractual obligation as promised.

forbearance	Refraining from action; giving up a right.
fundamental breach	A serious breach of the contract.
gratuitous promise	A promise to do something for which no consideration is given and which is, therefore, unenforceable.
guarantee	A promise by one person to pay the debt of another person if that person defaults.
indemnity	A promise by one person to pay the debt of another person, whether or not the other debtor first defaults.
lapse	The expiry of an offer, either at its stated expiry date or, in no stated expiry date, after a reasonable time.
liquidated damages clause	A clause in a contract that states the amount of damages to be paid in the event of a breach of the contract, where the amount specified represents a genuine pre-estimate of the damages that would be caused by such a breach.
misrepresentation	A false statement of fact that induces the other party to enter into the contract.
mitigation of damages	The plaintiff is under a duty to mitigate his damages. In other words, he must take all reasonable steps to reduce the amount of the loss caused by the breach of contract.
mutual mistake	The situation where both parties to a contract are mistaken, but the mistakes are different.
necessaries	Essentials of life, such as food, clothing, shelter, medical care, education, tools to earn a living, and transportation to work.
non est factum	A defence pleaded by a person who, through no fault or carelessness of her own, is mistaken as to the nature and effect of a contract signed.
offer	An expression of willingness to enter into a contract on the specified terms, made with the intention of it becoming a binding contract if accepted.
offeree	The person to whom the offer is made.
offeror	The person who makes an offer.
penalty clause	A clause that specifies the amount of damages to be paid in the event of a breach of contract, where the amount is not a genuine pre-estimate of the damages that would actually be caused by such a breach but is, instead, an amount sufficient to be used as a threat to compel performance of the contract.
postal acceptance rule	When it is reasonable or required that acceptance be made by mail, acceptance becomes effective when it is mailed, even though the offeror is unaware that the offer has been accepted. This rule applies even if the letter is delayed, destroyed, or lost.
privity of contract	The relationship between two persons who are parties to the same contract.
promisee	The person to whom the promise is made; the person to whom the obligation is owed.
promisor	The person who makes a promise under a contract; the person who owes the obligation.
promissory estoppel	An equitable principle that allows a defendant, in some circumstances, to use a gratuitous promise made to him as a defence to a lawsuit that contradicts the promise.
rectification	The equitable remedy whereby a court corrects the clerical mistake made by the parties in reducing their agreement to writing.
rescission	An equitable remedy whereby the court is asked to set aside a contract and restore the parties to the position they would have been in if the contract had never been made.
revocation of offer	The withdrawal of the offer by the offeror. It may be done at any time before acceptance by the offeree.
simple contracts	Any contracts that are not deeds. They may be oral or written.
specific performance	Under this equitable remedy, the breaching party is ordered to perform her obligations under the contract.

tender of performance	An attempt by a party to a contract to perform his obligations under the contract.
terms of the contract	The statements, promises, and provisions of a contract are called the terms of the contract. These terms of the contract determine the rights and obligations of the parties. A term of a contract may be expressed or implied.
undue influence	Where a party enters into a contract as a result of improper pressure being brought to bear on her so as to render her "morally unable" to resist the will of the other party. As a result of this pressure, the party enters into a contract that is not to her advantage but is to the advantage of the other party.
unilateral contracts	One party promises to do something if the other party does something.
waiver	An agreement between parties to an existing contract that the contract is not to be performed.
warranty	A less important term of the contract. Put another way, any terms that are not conditions are warranties.

REVIEW QUESTIONS

1. How is an invitation to treat different from an offer?

2. What is the postal acceptance rule?

3. Name five ways an offer can be terminated.

4. (a) What is past consideration?
   (b) Is it valid consideration?

5. What is promissory estoppel?

6. What are a minor's rights and responsibilities on a contract for necessaries?

7. What are a minor's rights and responsibilities on a contract for non-necessaries?

8. What is the doctrine of part performance?

9. (a) What is a common mistake?
   (b) What is a mutual mistake?
   (c) What is a unilateral mistake?

10. (a) What is a misrepresentation?
    (b) What is the remedy for misrepresentation?

11. What is undue influence?

12. What is duress?

13. How are void contracts and illegal contracts treated differently by the courts?

14. What is the parol evidence rule?

15. (a) What is a condition?
    (b) What is a warranty?

16. Can an exculpatory clause protect a party from liability for fundamental breach of contract and, if so, in what circumstances?

17. What is vicarious performance?

18. (a) What does it mean when a contract is discharged?
    (b) Name five ways a contract may be discharged.

19. (a) What is an anticipatory breach?
    (b) What may the innocent party do in the event of an anticipatory breach?

20. What is the purpose of damages in contract?

21. How can a plaintiff establish that his damages are not too remote?

22. What is meant by the statement that the plaintiff is under a duty to mitigate her damages?

23. What is rescission, and when is it available?

24. What is specific performance, and when is it available?

25. What is an injunction?

26. What is *quantum meruit*?

27. What is the difference between tender by performance and tender by payment?

28. What is a frustrated contract?

DISCUSSION QUESTIONS

1. Larry wrote to Joyce, offering to buy her car for $3,000, and asked for a reply by mail. Joyce received Larry's offer on January 3. At 10:00 a.m. on January 4, Joyce mailed a letter to Larry in which she accepted his offer. Larry did not receive the letter until January 11. On January 5, he saw another car he liked better and telephoned Joyce to revoke his offer. Can he do so? Why or why not? Would the answer be different if Joyce's letter was lost in the mail and never received by Larry? Why or why not?

2. Marlene bought a shirt from Tom Taylor's Shirt Shop and gave it to her husband Robert as a birthday present. When Robert wore the shirt, he developed a terrible skin rash. It was discovered that the shirt fabric had been dipped in an acid-like substance as part of the manufacturing process and that the acid had not been rinsed out. What rights in contract, if any, does Robert have against Tom Taylor's Shirt Shop?

3. Elizabeth owns a factory that manufactures casual shirts and sweatshirts. In January, the heating system of the factory broke down, and she had to shut down the factory. She hired Tony's Plumbing and Heating to repair the heating system. It was a term of the contract that Tony's would finish the repairs within a week. Tony's had some trouble getting supplies, which delayed completion of the work as promised. The repairs took two months and, as a result, Elizabeth lost her regular monthly profits of $1,000 per month. In addition, Elizabeth lost a valuable contract to make sweatshirts for a Rolling Stones concert tour on which she would have made a profit of $10,000. Elizabeth sues Tony's. What is Tony's liability for damages to Elizabeth?

4. Morris wants to sell his ratty old sofa for $100. He walks into a bar and meets his friend Victoria. He offers to buy her a drink or two. She accepts but becomes drunk. When she is drunk, Morris tells her he has a sofa that she could use, and he will sell it to her for only $100. He also tells her that it is a collector's item and worth far more than the

price he is asking. He then hands her what he says is a purchase agreement, but in fact it is a two-month lease of the sofa for $400. She agrees to buy it for the price he is asking. She wakes up the next morning, realizes she bought a sofa she didn't need, calls Morris and tells him she won't pay him and doesn't want the sofa. If Morris sues, what defence(s) can she raise?

SUGGESTED READINGS

Fridman, G.H.L. *The Law of Contract in Canada*, 5th ed. (Toronto, Ont.: Carswell, 2006).

Waddams, S.M. *The Law of Contract*, 5th ed. (Toronto, Ont.: Canada Law Book, 2006).

Real Property Law

Joan Emmans
SENECA COLLEGE

Learning Objectives

After reading this chapter, the reader should be able to:

➢ explain the concept of "holding" land by way of estates
➢ compare different interests in land
➢ differentiate between registry and land titles systems of registration
➢ explain the steps involved in a real estate transaction
➢ demonstrate an understanding of mortgages
➢ identify the classes of tenancies
➢ explain the concept of a tenancy and the roles of the parties to a tenancy

TABLE OF CONTENTS

INTRODUCTION TO REAL PROPERTY LAW

The common law began to develop in England at a time when society was organized along feudal lines. In a feudal society, at least in theory, all land was ultimately owned by the king. The king would grant an interest in land to the nobility, who in turn would grant part of their interest in land to others lower down the social scale. In this kind of society, land ownership was the most important form of wealth. It also confirmed status: One who owned land had a higher status than one who did not, and a landowner had a higher status than those whose wealth took other forms, such as merchants. Further, land ownership also conferred political power in a way that other forms of wealth did not. Given the importance of land ownership, it should not be surprising that a lot of the early common law focused on the development of land law and that the law became relatively complex at an early date.

The law of feudal England was based on the idea that the king *owned* the land and that he *granted* interests or estates in land. An estate in land is therefore an interest in land or real property.

Real property is the air above the surface of land, the land itself and everything that is permanently attached to it, including buildings, trees, flowers, fences, swimming pools, etc. **Chattels**, which are considered to be personal property, become **fixtures** (part of the real property) when they are permanently affixed to a building or to the land itself. For example, a furnace begins its existence as a chattel but once installed in a house becomes a fixture.

Our system is one of *holding* an interest or estate in land, as the Crown technically *owns* it all; and by way of Crown patents, the Crown has granted much of it to individuals who have the right to hold it or to dispose of it as they wish. However, if, upon a landholder's death, the land has not been sold and there are no heirs nor a will leaving the land to someone else, the land will revert to the Crown.

ESTATES IN LAND

Freehold Estates

A **freehold estate** is an interest in land that may last for an unlimited period of time. There are several forms of freehold estate.

Fee Simple

The form with the highest rights and fewest obligations is **fee simple**. Most people who own land in fee simple believe that they have absolute ownership of the property. In fact, it is as close to absolute ownership as one may get, but it is always subject to some restrictions (see Exhibit 15.1). In other words, you cannot do whatever you wish with your property.

There may be other types of restrictions, such as **easements** and **restrictive covenants**, which are created by someone else's interest in the property. These will be discussed later in the chapter.

Life Estate

Another form of freehold estate is the **life estate**, which gives someone (the "life tenant") an interest in land for the duration of a designated person's life, most often the life tenant's. The life tenant has **exclusive right of possession** of the property, for the duration of the designated person's life, and may use it personally or rent it out. Upon the death of the designated person, the property either reverts back to the original grantor (**reversion**), or goes to the

---

Restrictions to Land Ownership Right

EXHIBIT 15.1

The following are examples of the restrictions that land may be subject to:

(a) Municipal by-laws may restrict the size and type of house built, the type of building materials used, the use to which the property is put, etc.

(b) An owner may prevent trespassers to his property but may not refuse admittance to a police officer with a search warrant if a crime is committed, or is suspected of having been committed, on the property.

(c) An owner cannot create a **nuisance** on his property that results in damage to, or loss of enjoyment in, a neighbouring property. Examples of nuisance may include noxious odours, contaminants, loud noise, or dangerous animals.

(d) An owner may not subdivide his property into smaller parcels for sale without prior approval by the planning authorities within the municipality.

(e) An owner of property with a river or stream running through it may not interfere with the quality or quantity of water on properties upstream or downstream from his property. For example, he may not dam the river or alter its course in any way if such a move affects the quality or quantity of the water upstream or downstream.

---

person(s) named to take up the interest in the land upon the death of the designated person (**remainder**).

Example

Reversion — *B* gives property to *A* for life. Upon *A*'s death the property will revert back to *B* or to *B*'s estate if *B* is deceased.

Remainder — *B* gives property to *A* for life then to *C* in fee simple. Upon *A*'s death, the property will go to *C*.

Rights in the Matrimonial Home

Rights in the **matrimonial home** differ from province to province. In Ontario, each spouse has a right to possession of, or a right to occupy but not necessarily own, the matrimonial home. Thus, the sale of any residential property must have the consent of both spouses, regardless of which spouse actually owns the property.

Leasehold Estates

A **leasehold estate** is an interest in property for a specific period of time. Upon agreement of the owner of the property ("landlord") and the person holding the leasehold interest ("tenant"), the length of time of the interest ("rental period") may be extended. A leasehold interest is a lesser estate than freehold, and the holder has fewer rights than those of the holder of a freehold estate. One right that they have in common is the right to exclusive possession of the property.

Leasehold estates are examined later in this chapter.

Condominiums

Condominium ownership combines individual ownership of "units" with shared ownership (together with all other unit owners) of "common elements". In the purchase of a condominium, be it a residential, commercial, or industrial one, the buyer gets a unit that she has the exclusive right to occupy. She also gets to use, along with all other unit owners, certain common areas, such as parking lots or garages, storage areas, lawns, recreation areas, hallways, and elevators. Sometimes, parts of the common areas, such as parking garages contain "exclusive use" portions, each of which is connected to a specific unit. For example, the owners of Unit 64 are given the exclusive right to park their car in space number B6 in the parking garage. When they sell the unit, they will also transfer the right to use space B6.

Each unit owner is required to maintain her own unit. Every month the unit owners must pay their proportional share of common expenses. These payments are applied to expenses such as liability insurance, snow removal, lawn maintenance, possibly utilities, and repairs.

A condominium corporation, made up of all the unit owners, runs the affairs of the condominium. Unlike an ordinary business corporation, a condominium corporation has no share capital, does not have limited liability (all unit owners are liable for the debts of the corporation), and comes into existence upon the registration of the condominium plan.

Ownership of individual units may be financed by way of mortgage, and the units can be bought and sold in the same way that ordinary freehold estates can be transferred.

INTERESTS IN LAND (LESS THAN ESTATES)

Easements

An easement is a right enjoyed over land by someone other than the owner of the land for a specific purpose. For example, the owner of parcel *A* (owner *A*) may have the right to travel over the driveway on adjacent property belonging to owner *B* in order to get to his (owner *A*'s) property.

An easement carries with it certain characteristics. There must be a dominant and a servient tenement. The **dominant tenement** is the land that benefits from the easement, while the **servient tenement** is the land that supplies or is subject to the easement. The dominant and servient tenements cannot be registered in the same name. If so, the easement is said to **merge** (disappear), as there is no longer a need for it (one does not need a right to pass over or use one's own property).

The owner of the servient tenement has no obligation to maintain the easement, but the owner of the dominant tenement has the right to make the easement suitable for its stated use — but not to expand the easement. For instance, the owner of a dominant tenement who uses a neighbouring driveway for access to his property may grade the driveway to ensure his car remains intact. However, he may not widen the driveway and cut down trees to enable him to travel back and forth with his mobile crane. The owner of the dominant tenement may not obstruct the easement but may merely use it for its designated purpose. For example, if the purpose of the easement is to gain access to property, one may use it to pass over but not park on it.

Easements may be created by express grant, in which one owner grants by way of deed an easement or **right-of-way** in favour of an adjoining or nearby owner. Once granted, the easement will last indefinitely, unless extinguished. When property is sold, the easement goes along with it, or **runs with the land**. In other words, a sale of the dominant tenement will include the rights to the easement; the sale of the servient tenement will be subject to the rights of the owner of the dominant tenement to the easement.

An easement may also be created by prescription (a **prescriptive easement**). If one has openly and continuously used property other than one's own for an uninterrupted period of more than 20 years, with the knowledge of the owner of the property but without her consent and without any payment to the owner, one *may* have established an easement over the property. However, if the owner, at any time during the 20-year period, blocks the easement (for example, locks an entry gate), the time period must re-start. In other words, there must be 20 *uninterrupted* years. The easement runs with the land, so it is *not* necessary for ownership of either properties to remain the same over the 20-year period.

If the property is registered in a **land titles** system, it is not possible to create a prescriptive easement.

An **easement by implication** or a **right-of-way of necessity** is created when the only access to a property is over another person's property. For instance, if the owner of Block *A* severs a lot from the back and there is no access to the property, it will be necessary for the owners of the new lot to get access to their property by travelling over Block *A*. Note, however, that access does not necessarily have to be by road — it is possible to have property that is accessible only by water.

Lastly, some easements are created by statute. These do not necessarily meet all the criteria for easements, however, as the dominant tenement may be nowhere near the servient tenement. An example of a statutory easement is one in favour of a telephone company, which permits the company to run cables through a property and then to access the property for the purposes of maintaining and repairing the cables. While this is not technically an easement, it is usually considered one since the effect on the property is the same as that of an easement.

Restrictive Covenants

A restrictive covenant is a restriction on the use of property, which an owner may impose on subsequent owners of the property. For instance, if a person is severing a lot from his land and wishes to control how the property will be used (for example, the size of the house to be built, the type of building, the type of building materials used, the distance from lot lines, and the type of fencing used), the owner may insert these requirements in the Agreement of Purchase and Sale, and the purchaser will either have to agree to those requirements or reject the agreement. Subsequently, these restrictions will either be included in the deed or will be registered by way of a separate document on the title to the property. Thus, they will likely be binding on subsequent purchasers of the property, since most standard form Agreements of Purchase and Sale contain a clause indicating the purchaser will accept title subject to any registered restrictions, provided they are complied with.

In order to be enforceable, restrictive covenants must be negative, not positive in nature. The courts will not force a property owner to *do* something with his property but will *prevent* him from doing something. For example, a restrictive covenant on s property in Pigtown may not say, "The house must be made of bricks"; however, it may say, "The house shall not be made of straw or sticks."

As with an easement, there must be a dominant and servient tenement. In the example of a severed lot, the lot would be the servient tenement, and the remaining land (owned by the person desiring the restrictions) would be the dominant tenement.

The restrictions must be reasonable in nature and cannot be contrary to public interest.

Restrictive covenants are common in new subdivisions and take the form of building schemes, which affect every lot in the subdivision. They provide the builder with a means of maintaining uniformity and standards throughout the subdivision, and they may be enforced by all owners in the subdivision, not just the original grantor or builder.

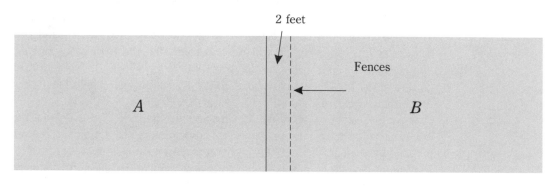

EXHIBIT 15.2

Adverse Possession

Owner A puts up a fence that encroaches onto Owner B's property a distance of two feet for the full length of the property. If Owner A maintains and uses that property without any consent from Owner B or any acknowledgement to Owner B of Owner B's title to the two-foot strip, Owner A may, after the requisite limitation period has elapsed, make a claim to the two-foot strip by virtue of adverse possession, as all criteria have been met.

2 feet

Fences

A

B

Many restrictions that used to form part of restrictive covenants are now covered by municipal by-laws, which deal with matters such as building setbacks, house size and parking restrictions.

Adverse Possession

In jurisdictions without a land titles system of registration, it is possible to obtain an interest in land through **adverse possession**, which in effect extinguishes the title of the registered owner (see Exhibit 15.2). In order to make a claim based on adverse possession, the claimant must have been using the land openly, visibly, exclusively, continuously, and without the consent of the owner for a period of at least 10 years. (The **limitation period** varies from 10 to 20 years, depending on the jurisdiction.) If that possession period is interrupted at all by the owner, its calculation must start again from the time of interruption.

Most often, adverse possession involves pieces of land that are annexed to adjoining properties and treated as theirs by the owners of the adjoining property.

The onus, however, is on the person claiming adverse possession to prove it — **title** does not automatically transfer to the claimant, since the law presumes the registered owner of the land to be in possession of it (either personally or through tenants).

Encroachments

If a part of a person's property extends beyond its own boundary onto another's property, it is said to encroach. For example, if the corner of Mrs. Smith's garage is on Mr. Brown's property, it is an **encroachment**. Similarly, if Mrs. Smith's eaves overhang onto Mr. Brown's property, they encroach. If the property is not in a land titles system and the building has been in place for sufficient time (10 to 20 years, depending on the province), the owner of the land on which the encroachment lies will have lost the right to object to it.

For instance, in Ontario, after 10 years, Mr. Brown could not ask Mrs. Smith to move her garage or her eaves. Written agreements between the two owners (known as encroachment agreements) are often used to permit the encroachment to remain. It should be noted that if the encroachment is on Crown land, the limitation period may be significantly longer than the normal period. However, the Crown has the right to **expropriate** the necessary land in any case.

Mineral Rights/ Timber Rights

The owner of land in fee simple will have the right to extract any minerals from the land, unless the original Crown patent expressly reserved the mineral rights to the Crown, in which case any minerals extracted would be Crown property. Similarly, the Crown sometimes reserved timber rights. In Ontario, all timber rights reserved in Crown patents dated prior to April 2, 1869, are void.

Licence

Sometimes, a person may be given a right or a **licence** to use another person's land, with or without payment for that right. However, a licence may be revoked at any time by the licensor (the property owner). In this way, a licence differs from a lease. A landlord must wait until the lease period has expired before retaking her ownership rights in full.

TITLE TO LAND

Individual

Land can be held by an individual or corporation alone or by more than one person. When ownership is registered in two or more names it is said to be concurrent. Three types of **concurrent ownership** are **tenancy-in-common**, joint tenancy, and partnership.

Tenancy-in-Common

Unless otherwise specified, when more than one person takes title to property, they are deemed to be holding it as tenants-in-common. Each person holds a share of an undivided interest in the property. These shares may or may not be equal. For example, *A* and *B* may each hold a 50 percent share in property as tenants-in-common; or *A* may hold a 65 percent share, and *B*, a 35 percent share as tenants-in-common.

If one party dies, that party's share forms part of her estate, and the heir(s) of the estate will become owners as tenants-in-common with the existing owner(s).

> *Example 1*
>
> *A* and *B* each hold a 50 percent interest in property as tenants-in-common.
>
> *A* dies.
>
> The beneficiary of *A*'s estate will hold a 50 percent interest as tenants-in-common with *B*.

A tenant-in-common may transfer her interest to any third party without the consent of the other owners — the transferee then becomes a tenant-in-common with them.

Example 2

A and *B* each hold a 50 percent interest in property as tenants-in-common.

A sells her interest to C without getting *B*'s consent.

C now holds a 50 percent interest as tenants-in-common with *B*.

Joint Tenancy

If two or more parties wish to hold property as **joint tenants**, it must be expressly stated on the title document. The parties take title at the same time from the same person by the same document, and all have the same quantity of interest. The most notable feature of a joint tenancy is the right of survivorship. If *A* and *B* hold property as joint tenants, and *A* dies, *A*'s interest in the property passes immediately to *B* — it does not become part of *A*'s estate.

If one of the joint tenants transfers or mortgages his share or becomes bankrupt, that joint tenant becomes a tenant-in-common with the other joint tenants, and the joint tenancy with respect to that joint tenant is severed.

Example 1

A, *B* and *C* own Blackacre as joint tenants. *A* mortgages his share of the property to his mother. This severs the joint tenancy. *A* now has a one-third interest as a tenant-in-common with *B* and *C*, who still hold a two-thirds interest as joint tenants.

Family law legislation may prevent the severance of a joint tenancy in a matrimonial home without consent of the spouse of the party making the severance. In Ontario, The *Family Law Act*, 1986, created an exception to the rule that on death, property automatically passes to the surviving joint tenant.

Example 2

A and *B* hold property as joint tenants and the property is a matrimonial home for one of them (that is, they are not married to each other, but *A* is married to *C*, and the property is a matrimonial home for *A* and *C*). If *A* dies, the property does not pass immediately on to *B*. Instead, the joint tenancy is deemed to be severed just before *A*'s death, and *A* and *B* are considered to be tenants-in-common. Thus *A*'s share (50%) forms part of *A*'s estate.

Partnership

Property may also be held concurrently by *partners*. On transfer of the property, it may be necessary to provide documentary evidence that the property was bought and held as partnership property and that the transferors are all the partners within the partnership.

REGISTRATION OF INTEREST IN LAND

Every time ownership or title to a property changes, the change must be recorded in a public registry office. This is a government office usually located in the "county seat" of each regional political division within a province, and it maintains a written record of the ownership of every piece of land within the county. There are generally two systems of registration of land: a **registry** system and a land titles or "Torrens" system.

Registry System

Under the registry system, an abstract book is maintained for each concession lot in a township and for each lot within a registered plan of subdivision. It lists all documents accepted by the registry office that give some form of interest in the particular lot. Since some lots (particularly concession lots) may be divided into several parcels, there may be many pages showing many interests in each lot. Thus, it is a purchaser's responsibility (usually assumed by the purchaser's lawyer) to ascertain which interests apply to the particular parcel within a lot that the purchaser is buying. In Ontario, the lawyer must go back 40 years and look at all relevant documents to establish that the present owner does, in fact, have good title to the land and has the right to transfer title to the purchaser. As registration of a document is no guarantee of its validity, the lawyer (or title searcher) must verify that each document is correct. Since the property may have changed hands many times in 40 years, a registry search could involve looking at hundreds of documents and may take several days to complete. Under the registry system, some interest in land may not be registered. For example, the right of an adverse possessor (mentioned earlier) might exist but might not be registered on title.

Land Titles System

In a land titles system, each parcel of land is recorded in a register as a separate unit of property. Thus, a title searcher does not have to sift through documents to determine whether or not they pertain to a specific property. Each unit of property has its own page(s) in the register, and only *current* interests in the property will be recorded. All others will have been "ruled off". Thus, the need for a 40-year search is eliminated. Unlike the registry system, the government guarantees that the only interests in the land are shown in the register — *there are no others* (such as those of an adverse possessor). If there is an error in the register and someone suffers a loss due to the error, an assurance fund provides compensation for the loss. In Ontario, all land will eventually be in the land titles system.

PROPERTY TRANSFERS

Listing Agreement

When a property owner wishes to sell property, she usually enters into a listing agreement with a registered real estate broker. In exchange for a commission (being a percentage of the sale price), the broker agrees to market the property for the owner.

Agreement of Purchase and Sale

When a prospective buyer wishes to make an offer on the property, he usually asks a real estate salesperson or a lawyer to draft the offer, which he signs. If the offer is acceptable to the seller, the seller signs it, and the actual purchase and sale transaction takes place on a set date, or **closing date**, usually four to six weeks from the date of signing the acceptance.

Purchaser's Responsibilities

During that period, it is the purchaser's or purchaser's lawyer's responsibility to search title to the property, verifying that, in fact, the vendor owns the property and has the right to sell it. As well, the purchaser must make sure that municipal taxes are not in arrears, that the property complies with the local zoning by-laws, that utility accounts are up-to-date and that there are no outstanding judgments against the owner or any prior owners that may act as liens against the property. If there are any problems, the purchaser's lawyer must notify the vendor's lawyer in writing by way of a **requisition letter** prior to the deadline (or **requisition date**) set out in the agreement of purchase and sale. In the requisition letter the lawyer will identify the problem and ask that it be rectified. If the problems can be remedied and they are, then the transaction is completed on the scheduled closing date. If they cannot be solved and they are sufficiently serious, the purchaser may have the right to back out of the agreement.

Vendor's Responsibilities

The vendor's lawyer must prepare all the necessary documentation to be signed by the vendor in order to complete the sale. The lawyer must also make arrangements to pay off, from the proceeds of the sale, any existing mortgages that the purchaser is not taking over from the vendor. (A purchaser's agreement to take over or assume a vendor's obligations under a mortgage is known as an **assumption of the mortgage**.) As well, the vendor's lawyer will attempt to resolve any issue that the purchaser's lawyer has raised in the requisition letter. The vendor must keep the property insured and in good repair up until the transaction closes.

Closing

On the date scheduled for closing, the vendor's lawyer provides the deed to the property (which gets registered) and any other necessary documents, together with keys. The purchaser's lawyer delivers the money required. The actual closing procedure varies from province to province, but upon the successful closing of the transaction, the purchaser becomes the new owner of the property.

New Developments in Real Estate Transactions

Electronic Registration

Ontario has automated its land registration system, and no doubt other jurisdictions will ultimately do the same. Title searches and document registration can be done from a personal computer in the law office, thus reducing the amount of paper required in a real estate transaction and eliminating the need to attend at the registry office.

Title Insurance

As in the United States, title insurance is now an option for Canadians. Traditionally, clients rely on their lawyer's title opinion, which indicates that all the necessary searches have been done and that the clients have a good and marketable title to their property. If the lawyer errs and a subsequent problem with the title arises, the lawyer must take steps to correct the problem or face the possibility of a lawsuit for negligence. If a client chooses title insurance instead of relying on the lawyer's opinion, the insurer protects against possible title problems that could subsequently arise. If such a problem does occur, the insurer must deal with it, not the client. Thus, the expense of negligence lawsuits and the hassle of dealing with subsequent title problems are eliminated for the client. As well, the costs associated with purchasing property may be reduced, as fewer searches may have to be done in the first place. More importantly, title insurance protects the property owner against fraud.

MORTGAGES

Definition

A **mortgage** is simply a means of providing land as security for indebtedness. In the past, when a borrower gave a lender a mortgage on her property in exchange for money, upon registration of the mortgage on title, the property was actually transferred to the lender, on condition that it be transferred back to the borrower upon payment in full of the debt. While that is still true in some jurisdictions, in others a mortgage (or "charge") does not actually transfer an interest in the land; rather, it creates a security interest in — or **encumbrance** on — the land, which is discharged when the debt is paid in full.

Parties

The person borrowing the money and using property as security is the **mortgagor**. The person or institution lending the money is the **mortgagee**. Sometimes, another party who has no interest in the property will be required by the mortgagee to guarantee that if the mortgagor defaults, that party, the **guarantor**, will take responsibility for payment of the mortgage as well as for all other obligations of the mortgagor.

Rights and Obligations

The primary right of the mortgagor is the right to a **discharge** of the mortgage when all principal and interest has been paid back to the mortgagee. Prior to exercising that right, the mortgagor has a number of obligations.

First of all the mortgagor must make all periodic payments according to the terms of the mortgage document. Typically, a blended monthly payment is required that is made up of interest and principal. Each payment thus reduces the amount of principal outstanding. However, this reduction is minimal during the early years of a mortgage, which is gradually reduced or **amortized** over a long period of time. A default in payment usually triggers an acceleration clause, which states that on default, the entire amount of principal and interest becomes due immediately. (There will be more discussion on default later in this section.)

The mortgagor must also keep municipal taxes paid up, since failure to do so enables the municipality to claim a lien on the property, which takes priority over all other encumbrances, including mortgages. This means that the municipality has the first right to be paid out of the money from the sale of the secured property. Some mortgagees require the mortgagor to make payments towards taxes along with the monthly mortgage payment. The mortgagee then pays the taxes directly to the municipality, thus ensuring the mortgagee's top priority as an encumbrancer.

The mortgagor has a duty to keep adequate insurance on the property if it contains a building, in order to protect the mortgagee's security. In the event of damage to the building, proceeds of the insurance would be paid first to the mortgagee to satisfy outstanding principal and interest, and the balance of the proceeds, if any, to the mortgagor. It is the mortgagor's duty to keep premiums paid up-to-date.

Lastly, the mortgagor has an obligation to keep the property in good repair and not to commit **waste** (or reduce the value of the property). These obligations ensure that the mortgagee maintains the value of its equity in the property.

There may be other non-standard duties that a mortgagee requires of the mortgagor (such as provision of post-dated cheques), which will be stated in the mortgage document.

Assignment of Mortgage

A mortgagee may sell or assign the mortgage to a new mortgagee. This may be done when the mortgagee has her own debt and uses her rights under the mortgage as security for that debt. For example, if a mortgagee obtains a bank loan, and the bank requires security, the mortgagee may assign her interest in the mortgage to the bank. A mortgage may be assigned without the mortgagor's consent. However, the **assignment** is ineffective until the mortgagor has knowledge of it. Thus, if the mortgagor continues to pay the original mortgagee, the assignee has no remedy until the mortgagor has been notified. The assignment should be registered and, upon notice to the mortgagor, the mortgagor's rights and obligations, as discussed earlier, continue. This includes the mortgagor's right to a discharge of the mortgage from the assignee upon full payment of the mortgage debt.

Assumption of Mortgage

When a property owner sells property that is subject to a mortgage, the purchaser may insist that the mortgage be discharged (usually by way of payment from the sale proceeds) or may assume the mortgage and take over its rights and obligations. In the latter case, the original mortgagor, unless released by the mortgagee, will remain potentially responsible for the mortgage until its discharge.

Example

Owner *O* sells his property to buyer *B*, who agrees to assume the existing mortgage held by mortgagee *M*. If *B* defaults on the mortgage payments, *M* has rights to the property, which *M* may enforce, or *M* may sue *O* on his original covenant to repay the mortgage debt.

Many unwary sellers wrongly believe that once they have sold their property, they have released all rights and obligations under the mortgage if the purchaser assumes the mortgage. It may be several years later that they are made aware of their error, after the purchaser has defaulted on a payment or payments, and the mortgagee sues the original mortgagor or vendor.

Discharge of Mortgage

When a mortgage debt, including interest, has been fully paid, the mortgagor is entitled to a discharge of the mortgage. Usually, the mortgage document will provide that the mortgagor is responsible for all expenses relating to the preparation and registration of the discharge. Once a discharge is registered, the property is no longer subject to the mortgage, and the mortgagee no longer holds any interest in the property.

Remedies for Default

In the event of default of payment or breach of a covenant by the mortgagor, the mortgagee has several options. The most common step is to commence **power of sale** proceedings. This is done by giving the mortgagor and all subsequent encumbrancers notice that the property will be sold, and giving each of them the opportunity to pay off the arrears and bring the mortgage into good standing, or else pay the full amount outstanding under the mortgage. If the prescribed time elapses without payment, the mortgagee may sell the property. (If the mortgagor is in possession or occupying the premises, it may be necessary for the mortgagee to get a court order for possession prior to selling.) Once sold, the proceeds are used to (a) satisfy the mortgage debt; (b) pay any subsequent encumbrancers and execution creditors; and (c) give any excess to the mortgagor. If there is a shortfall rather than a surplus, the mortgagee may sue the mortgagor for the difference. For that reason, the mortgagee has a duty to obtain the best price possible when selling the property. It is not enough to merely cover the costs of the mortgage, if the value of the property is considerably higher.

Another option for the mortgagee is to commence an action for **foreclosure**. This is a court proceeding in which the mortgagor or any subsequent encumbrancers may request the opportunity to redeem the mortgage (that is, pay it off) or request a sale of the property under court supervision. The time periods involved usually turn foreclosure into a lengthy and expensive procedure. If nobody redeems the mortgage or requests a sale, the mortgagee applies for a final order of foreclosure (F.O.F.), which is then registered on title to the property. At that time, the mortgagor and subsequent encumbrancers lose all rights to the property, and the mortgagee may deal with it as he wishes. However, if the mortgagor obtains the funds necessary to redeem the mortgage after the F.O.F. has been registered, and the property has not been sold, the mortgagor may apply to have the F.O.F. set aside.

Another alternative is for the mortgagee to apply to the court to have the property sold under the supervision of the court. Usually, this is done by way of either tender or public auction, often subject to a **reserve bid**. Once sold, the proceeds are distributed in the same way as for property sold under power of sale. If there is a shortfall, the mortgagee may obtain judgment for the amount of the deficiency as part of the procedure.

Priority of Mortgages

If there is more than one mortgage affecting a property, their priority is based on their order of registration. For example, a mortgage registered on January 6, 1995, takes priority over one registered on January 10, 1995. Similarly, a mortgage registered at 10:00 a.m. on January 6, 1995, takes priority over one registered at 10:05 a.m. on January 6, 1995. For that reason, it is most important that title be checked immediately prior to registration of a mortgage, to ensure that the mortgagee is in its expected priority as first or second or third mortgagee.

LEASEHOLD ESTATES (LANDLORD AND TENANT LAW)

Creation of a Tenancy

As noted earlier, a leasehold interest (or tenancy) is created when a property owner (landlord) gives a tenant a right of exclusive possession of property for a certain length of time. If the right is less than exclusive (for example, if the property is being shared with others), it is more likely a licence or an easement. The period of the tenancy must be determined, or be capable of being determined. In other words, it is for a set period, such as a month, a year, or five years. Some leases may be automatically renewed at the end of the period and then continue until either the landlord or tenant gives the other **notice to quit**. In the absence of a right to renewal, or automatic renewal, when the period of a tenancy ends, the tenant's interest and right to exclusive possession revert back to the landlord.

A tenancy may be based on a written or verbal lease or on express or implied conduct.

Residential Tenancies

Many provinces have established legislation for residential tenancies, most of which give residential tenants additional *security of tenure* and provide *stringent notice requirements* with respect to time to vacate and reasons for requiring vacation of the premises. The remainder of the section on leaseholds deals with general leasehold matters, mainly applicable to commercial tenancies.

Classes of Tenancies

Fixed Term Tenancy

A **fixed term tenancy** expires on a certain date without action by either landlord or tenant, and is most often based on a written lease.

Periodic Tenancy

A **periodic tenancy** comes into effect in one of two ways: (a) either a tenancy of fixed duration renews itself automatically at the end of its term and continues without further agreement between the parties until either party gives notice to quit; or (b) a lease terminates and the tenant continues to occupy the premises and the landlord accepts rent on a periodic (weekly, monthly or yearly) basis.

Tenancy at Will

A **tenancy at will** is not really a leasehold interest, since it is not for a given length of time and the right of possession is not necessarily exclusive. The tenant has possession only until the landlord decides otherwise. There may or may not be rent payable. The most common example of a tenancy at will is when a real estate transaction (purchase/sale) does not close and the vendor allows the purchaser to take possession of the property until it closes. (This type of arrangement must be entered with caution — usually, a written agreement is required, stating that the purchaser will vacate if the transaction is not closed within a certain number of days.)

Tenancy at Sufferance

A **tenancy at sufferance** is not really a tenancy but merely an occupancy of the property. No rent is payable and no consent is given by the landlord to possession of the premises. An example of a tenancy at sufferance is an overholding tenant who refuses to vacate after notice by the landlord. It differs from a tenancy at will, which has the consent of the landlord.

Rights and Obligations

Tenant's Obligations

The main obligation of the tenant is to pay rent when it is due. It is usually in the form of money (often paid by cheque) but may also be in the form of services, such as janitorial or superintendent duties. The payment must be in full without deduction, unless the landlord has expressly authorized deduction (for example, if the tenant has paid for a repair that the landlord authorized, the tenant may deduct the amount paid from the rent). If there is a lease, the amount of rent to be paid is set out in the lease and, unless the lease provides otherwise, cannot be increased until the lease expires, at which time the parties may negotiate a new rent. The law regarding payment of rent in the event of destruction of the premises (for example, by fire) varies from province to province. Thus, it is important to address that issue in a written lease, particularly a commercial lease, as the commercial tenant is otherwise liable for payment of the rent.

Commercial tenants may also, by lease, be obligated to pay municipal taxes and to insure the premises. If these obligations are not set out in the lease, they are the responsibility of the landlord, although insurance is optional (though prudent) unless required by a mortgagee. The tenant should insure contents and carry liability insurance.

The tenant must use the premises in a reasonable manner and return them in the same condition at the end of the lease as they were at the beginning. Responsibility for repairs is usually set out in the lease.

Tenant's Rights

During the term of the lease, provided rent has been paid, the tenant has the right to **quiet possession** or the right to occupy the premises undisturbed by the landlord or any agents of the landlord. For example, the landlord has no right to ask the tenant to leave for three days so that the premises may be painted, unless the tenant consents.

A tenant may **assign** or **sublet** the leased premises, unless the lease provides otherwise. Usually, the landlord will insist that the lease contain a clause requiring the landlord's consent to an assignment or sublet; similarly, the tenant may insist that the clause further state that "the consent may not unreasonably be withheld." (These words are implied by statute in some provinces.) That is, the landlord must have good reason to refuse — he cannot be arbitrarily unco-operative. An assignment is a transfer of the tenant's entire leasehold interest; a sublet is a transfer of part of the leasehold interest (either part of the term or part of the premises). In both cases, the original tenant remains liable to the landlord in the event of the assignee's or sub-tenant's default.

Landlord's Obligations and Rights

Most of the landlord's obligations and rights are the reverse of the tenant's. For example, as described above, the landlord has the obligation of ensuring that the tenant gets quiet possession. Note that the phrase does not refer to peaceable occupancy of the premises but, rather, to the right to no physical interruption of the tenant's possession of the property. The landlord must also make sure that the premises are suitable for the purposes for which the landlord and tenant intended them to be used. (For example, if a tenant rents a warehouse to store crystal, the landlord cannot use the adjoining premises for a jackhammer training school.) As noted earlier, matters of insurance and repairs are usually dealt with in the lease; if not, they are the responsibility of the landlord. In return for providing the premises as indicated, the landlord is entitled to receive rent from the tenant.

Termination of a Tenancy

When commercial tenancies are for a fixed term, unless the lease is renewed or a new lease entered, the tenant must vacate the premises on or before the date of expiry of the lease. If *both* parties agree, the lease may terminate before its expiry, and the tenant vacates on an agreed-upon date. In both situations, the termination of the lease is known as a **surrender**.

A periodic tenancy is brought to an end by either party giving the other a notice to quit. Many leases deal with the length of notice time required. In the absence of such a term in the lease, provincial legislation specifies the time requirements, usually equal to the tenancy period. For instance, in a month-to-month tenancy, the notice to quit would have to be given a full month prior to the effective date of the end of the tenancy; so, if a landlord wanted a tenant out by July 31, notice would have to be given *prior to* July 1. For periodic yearly tenancies, notice requirements vary among provinces from 60 days to six months.

Termination may occur due to a breach of a covenant by one of the parties. If the tenant is in arrears with respect to rent, after the landlord has demanded the rent and a certain amount of time has elapsed, the landlord may exercise the "right of re-entry" (repossess the premises), which effectively terminates the tenancy.

There are other remedies for breach of a covenant that do not terminate the tenancy. For instance, if a tenant is in arrears, the landlord may **distrain** against the tenant's goods. This right of **distress** allows the landlord to keep the goods until the arrears are paid, or sell whatever goods are necessary to cover the arrears. It should be noted that if the landlord re-enters, she loses the right of distress.

Either landlord or tenant may bring an **action on the covenant** if the other is in breach of a covenant. Depending on the type of breach, the type of action and by which party, the court may order (a) correction of the breach; (b) an injunction to restrain further breach; (c) damages; or (d) termination of the lease. Note: None of the above provisions relating to termination apply to residential tenancies.

CHAPTER SUMMARY

This chapter provided the reader with a general overview of the law governing real property. It described the different estates that parties may hold in land, which in lay terms are known as owning or leasing land. It also discussed other interests that parties may have, and in what ways these interests may be limited.

The different ways of holding title to property, either alone or with other parties, were then described, followed by a brief discussion of the types of land registration systems.

The next section gave a short description of what is involved in the sale or purchase of real property, including who does what in a typical transaction.

Mortgages were dealt with in the following section — what a mortgage is; who is involved in a mortgage; what is required of both parties and what happens if there is a default in payment; and, if there is more than one mortgage on a property, how priority is determined.

The last section looked at landlord and tenant law, focusing mainly on commercial tenancies. There was a discussion of the different types of tenancies, how they begin and end, and what responsibilities lie where during the term of the tenancy.

GLOSSARY OF NEW TERMS AND KEY CONCEPTS

action on the covenant	Legal proceeding based on a clause contained in a contract, such as a lease or a mortgage.
adverse possession	Occupation of land inconsistent with the right of the registered owner (i.e., displacing the true owner).
amortization	Payment of a debt by way of a fixed number of payments that gradually results in the principal and interest being reduced or paid off.
assignment of lease	Transfer of a tenant's entire leasehold interest to another tenant.
assignment of mortgage	Transfer of a mortgagee's rights under a mortgage to another mortgagee.
assumption of mortgage	Transfer of a mortgagor's obligations under a mortgage to another mortgagor (usually a purchaser of the property that is subject to the mortgage).
chattel	Personal property that is tangible and moveable.
closing date	Date upon which the transfer of ownership of real property takes place.
concurrent ownership	Ownership by more than one person.
discharge of mortgage	Release by mortgagee of obligations of the mortgagor under the mortgage (usually indicates full payment has been made).
distrain	To seize goods by distress. (See **distress**.)
distress	Right to seize goods in order to satisfy a debt.
dominant tenement	Land that benefits from the service of another property (e.g., from an easement or from a restrictive covenant).
easement	A right enjoyed by the owner of land over the lands of another.
easement by implication	See **right-of-way of necessity**.
encroachment	Extension of property beyond its boundaries onto an adjoining property.
encumbrance	An outstanding claim or lien recorded against a property.
exclusive right of possession	Right to occupy property, to the exclusion of all others.

expropriate	Deprive a property owner of her right in all or part of her property.
fee simple	The most extensive freehold estate possible.
fixed term tenancy	A tenancy for a set period of time.
fixture	Anything permanently attached to real property.
foreclosure	Court action that results in mortgagor losing all interest in property due to his default in payment of a mortgage.
freehold estate	An interest in land that may last for an infinite or an indefinite period of time.
guarantor	Person who agrees to assume all obligations of a mortgagor under a mortgage, in the event of the mortgagor's default.
joint tenants	Two or more persons holding title to land where there is a right of survivorship: that is, death of one joint tenant results in title automatically going to surviving joint tenant(s).
land titles	System of registration of interests in land in which only current interests are shown and the government guarantees that no other interests affect the land.
leasehold estate	An interest in property for a specific period of time.
licence	A right to do something (for example, enter on someone's land), which may be revoked at any time.
life estate	An interest in land for the duration of a designated person's life.
limitation period	Time period during which a proceeding to enforce a right may be commenced.
matrimonial home	Property occupied by a husband and wife.
merger	Loss of a right (for instance, an easement) due to its coinciding with another and greater right in the same person.
mortgage	A means of providing land as security for indebtedness.
mortgagee	The lender whose security is the mortgage.
mortgagor	The borrower, and holder of title to the land that is subject to the mortgage.
notice to quit	Notice by either a landlord or tenant to the other party, indicating an intention to terminate the tenancy.
nuisance	An inconvenience that materially interferes with the enjoyment of one's property.
periodic tenancy	A tenancy that renews itself on a periodic (weekly, monthly, or yearly) basis.
power of sale	Right of a mortgagee to force sale of property in the event of default, without taking court action.
prescriptive easement	Easement obtained by uninterrupted usage for a period of time.
quiet possession	Occupancy without interruption or interference.
registry	System of registration of interests in land in which many interests are recorded (not just current ones), and the title searcher must determine which ones are applicable to the title being searched.
remainder	An interest in land that becomes effective upon the occurrence of a specific event (for example, the death of a life tenant).
requisition date	Date prior to which any problems relating to title must be made known to the vendor of the property or to the vendor's solicitor.
requisition letter	Letter from the purchaser or purchaser's solicitor outlining to the vendor any problems on title that the purchaser requires to be remedied prior to closing.
reserve bid	Lowest acceptable price.
restrictive covenant	A restriction or limitation on the use of property, which an owner may impose on subsequent owners of the property.

reversion	Return of an estate in land to the original owner upon the occurrence of a specific event (for example, the death of a life tenant).
right-of-way	Right to pass over another's land.
right-of-way of necessity	A right to pass over another's land as the only means of access to one's own property.
runs with the land	Extends beyond the original parties and binds subsequent owners of the property.
servient tenement	Land that is subject to a service (e.g., an easement or a restrictive covenant) in favour of another property (being the dominant tenement).
sublet	Transfer of part of a leasehold interest (either part of the term or part of the premises).
surrender of lease	Termination of a fixed-term lease.
tenancy at sufferance	Occupancy of property with no rent payable and no consent given by the landlord to possession of the premises.
tenancy at will	Right of possession is not for a given length of time, and may or may not be exclusive.
tenancy-in-common	Ownership of land by two or more persons; upon the death of one person, that person's share becomes an asset of her estate.
title	Registered ownership of property.
waste	Lasting damage to property (e.g., destruction of a house or allowing it to fall into disrepair).

REVIEW QUESTIONS

1. How does holding land in "fee simple" differ from holding a "life estate" in land?

2. Describe the difference between a "freehold" estate and a "leasehold" estate.

3. Give an example of how an easement may be created.

4. List three requirements of a restrictive covenant.

5. How does an "encroachment" differ from an "easement"?

6. What is one advantage that joint tenancy has over tenancy-in-common?

7. Outline three major differences between a registry and a land titles system of registration.

8. What is the risk involved to a vendor of property when a purchaser assumes the mortgage?

9. Describe two remedies available to a mortgagee if a mortgagor defaults in payment.

10. How does a "tenancy at will" differ from a "tenancy at sufferance"?

DISCUSSION QUESTIONS

The following may be used in a discussion or a debate:

1. Adverse possession should be permissible under all systems.

2. Purchasers and vendors of real estate do not need lawyers to complete their transactions.

3. Darren Developer decided to build what he considered to be the ultimate subdivision. In it were to be one-acre lots with Victorian reproduction houses. In order to keep the subdivision "up to standard", Darren registered restrictive covenants on the title to each of the lots. Included in the restrictions were the following:

    (a) All lawns must be sprayed annually with weed-killing agents.

    (b) No car parked in a place visible to the street (i.e., not in a garage) shall have a "red-book value" of less than $20,000.

    (c) No house shall have a square footage of less than 3,000 square feet.

    Describe any problems Darren may have in enforcing the above restrictions.

4. Roy Miller owned a parcel of land known as Roadsend. Roy died, and in his will he gave a life estate in Roadsend to his life partner, Mary Wasilenki. On Mary's death, Roadsend is to be transferred to Roy's nephew, Barney Miller, in fee simple. Barney convinced Mary to move into an apartment as Roadsend required a lot of maintenance. Now Barney has listed Roadsend for sale. He says he has the right to sell it, since nobody else owns it in fee simple. Mary, he claims, only has a right to live there, and since she has already moved out, he can sell it. Discuss.

5. Andrews, Buchinsky, Caruso and Day (all unmarried) own a lot on Clear Lake as joint tenants. In January of this year, Andrews makes an assignment in bankruptcy. In February, Caruso dies.

    How is the title to the property now held?

6. Tara Tenant signed a five-year lease for office space in a building owned by Larry Landlord. She specifically chose this building because of its view of Lake Ontario. Two years into the lease, Larry commenced construction of a new building on an adjoining lot that he owned. The noise and dust of the heavy equipment interfered greatly with Tara's work, and the new tower effectively blocked her view of the lake. Tara moved out, and Larry sued her for damages for his lost rent. Tara's defence was that Larry had breached his obligation to provide quiet possession, and that the only reason she rented the space was for its lake view, which was no longer there.

    Who would be successful, and why?

SUGGESTED READINGS

Burke, M. *Ontario Real Estate Procedures*, 2d ed. (Toronto, Ont.: Carswell, 1994).

Donahue, D.J., P.D. Quinn, & Danny C. Grandilli. *Real Estate Practice in Ontario*, 6th ed. (Toronto, Ont.: Butterworths, 2003).

Kurtz, J., J. Emmans, & A. Blatt. *Residential Real Estate Transactions*, 2d ed. (Toronto, Ont.: Emond Montgomery Publications, 2005).

Moore, Marguerite. *Title Searching & Conveyancing in Ontario*, 5th ed. (Toronto, Ont.: Butterworths, 2003).

Ontario Real Estate Legislation, Annual ed. (Aurora, Ont.: Canada Law Book).

Topical Law Reports. *Ontario Real Estate Law Guide*, Vols. 1 and 2. (North York, Ont.: CCH Canadian Limited, updated monthly).

Business Organizations

Ginevra M. Saylor

FRASER MILNER CASGRAIN LLP

Learning Objectives

After reading this chapter, the reader should be able to:

➢ understand the main sources of law regulating business organizations in Canada

➢ recognize the main factors to consider when choosing the best way to organize a business and how the method chosen allocates responsibility for the business's liabilities

➢ identify several kinds of business organizations and understand how the three main types are created, owned, operated, and ended

➢ identify the advantages and disadvantages associated with each kind of business organization

➢ recognize the main documents that must be filed and understand the requirements that must be met to operate a corporation

TABLE OF CONTENTS

INTRODUCTION

Imagine you would like to start your own business selling some kind of goods or providing a service. How would you choose to operate the business? Would you want to be in complete control or would you want to share responsibility for making important decisions with others whose skills may complement your own? Where would you get the money to start your business? Would you feel comfortable shouldering all of the risks and knowing that you might be personally liable for all of the debts your business may incur? Would you be willing to meet a number of formal requirements for starting and running the business, some of which might necessitate hiring a lawyer? Every entrepreneur who decides to go into any business — from the most simple, such as offering to clean people's houses, to the most complex, such as manufacturing and selling highly technical medical equipment world-wide — must consider these and a host of other questions when choosing the best way to organize the business enterprise.

There are a number of ways to organize a business, and each carries with it a different set of advantages and disadvantages. In every instance, the relative advantages and disadvantages of each option must be weighed against the backdrop of the relevant market, industry, and economy, as well as the entrepreneur's goals, desires, personality, and appetite for risk.

Business organizations provide substantial benefits that Canadian law recognizes and encourages. They provide structures that allow for orderly, efficient business organizations that benefit both consumers and business owners. Business organizations offer options for financing a commercial venture that allocate both the risk of loss and profit, introducing predictability and order for those who invest in businesses.

SOURCE OF LAW

Both the federal and provincial governments have specific legislation addressing all or some aspects of establishing and operating partnerships and corporations, and many also govern how sole proprietorships, franchises and other business organizations must behave. Much of contract law and torts (the law of injury) are governed by common law, which also establishes many of the remedies available.

Some laws, like corporate, partnership, and contract law, directly regulate commercial activity. Other equally important laws affect only distinct activities or aspects of a business. The latter include, for example, employment standards and labour legislation, securities regulations, and tax law. Combined, these all establish the framework within which modern business organizations operate in Canada.

SOLE PROPRIETORSHIPS

Of the many ways to operate a business, by far the easiest and quickest to start is the **sole proprietorship**. Basically, any time individuals start running a business for their own benefit without forming a corporation, partnership or other kind of organization, they have created a sole proprietorship. Establishing and operating a sole proprietorship involves very few formal requirements. Far less planning and preparation is required apart from that related to the business itself, making the sole proprietorship very attractive to first time business people embarking on a small-scale enterprise.

Starting the Business Depending on the type of business and jurisdiction, the person starting a business may need do no more than begin operating. However, certain businesses in some locations may require a bit more. Some jurisdictions require sole proprietors to register their businesses to ensure that creditors can easily find out information about exactly who owns the businesses with whom they deal. In Ontario, for example, all those operating a business under any name other than their own must register under the *Business Names Act*. Failing to register can result in fines and other significant penalties.

Many provinces regulate certain professions, requiring specific education, degrees and licences, as well as membership in a regulatory body. Common examples include lawyers, doctors, dentists and engineers. Before starting a sole proprietorship delivering any of these services, one would need to have the appropriate provincial licence and membership in the qualifying organization. Additionally, many municipalities require licences to operate certain businesses, such as restaurants and taxi services.

Another requirement sole proprietors need to consider is taxes that might apply to all businesses, regardless of how they are organized. Many Canadian provinces require business people to charge customers and remit to the government tax on goods and services. In some provinces, this requirement kicks in only after the business earns a specified threshold amount of money in a tax year. If the business employs others, additional tax and withholding requirements also may apply.

Who Runs the Show? As sole owner and operator, the sole proprietor has complete control, setting strategy and planning the course the business will take. Any profits the business reaps go to the sole proprietor and, because the business and the owner are the same, the owner may use business profits to satisfy purely personal debts in no way related to the business or its activities. But, the reverse is also true: the fact that the business and owner are the same makes the owner fully responsible for all debts the business incurs. So, the business's creditors are free to collect from not only the business's accounts and assets, but also from the owner's personal bank accounts and property. The owner's house, car, and any other personal assets all are equally at risk as any property associated with or used in the business. Depending on the nature and size of the business, the owner's exposure to potential liability could be quite extensive. In addition to any money the business might owe suppliers, landlords, customers and others, the sole proprietor could also become responsible for unanticipated liabilities, like, for instance, personal injuries someone suffers while at the place of business or injuries employees negligently cause to others while on the job. Although sole proprietors can limit their exposure to some of these potential liabilities by purchasing insurance and carefully negotiating contracts with those they do business with, doing this can quickly become costly and addresses only a portion of the risk.

Employing Others Although sole proprietors must run their business alone, they are free to hire employees to work for them. However, because owners have no separate identity from their business, they may not treat themselves as an employee. Employees may in no way be involved in running the business and making major decisions, or the law at some point may consider the business a partnership, regardless of how the owner and employee see or call their working relationship. Employees are paid wages, vacation, and bonuses, rather than sharing in a portion of the profits. Likewise, employees are not liable for the business's debts.

Growing and Changing

Given that sole proprietors are personally liable for all of their business's debts — putting at risk nearly everything they own — when businesses start to grow, many decide to abandon sole proprietorship for another type of business organization. Taking on a broader clientele, entering into more and more contracts with suppliers and others, and expanding to more locations can expose most to far more risk than they are willing to confront. At some point, the dollar value of the potential personal liability becomes just too great for one person to bear alone. Additionally, as a business becomes larger, it may diversify and become increasingly complex, making it prudent to involve others with different skills and expertise. Finally, a business with potential for huge expansion and growth could require financial backing from one or more additional investors to reach its full potential. All of these reasons could signal the end of the sole proprietorship and the birth of a new business organization.

Closing Shop

Sometimes sole proprietors choose to end their businesses entirely, rather than transforming from one form of business to another. As the only owner and decision maker, the sole proprietor may end the business any time, whether it is failing or succeeding. Of course, the sole proprietor remains personally responsible for paying all of the business's debts, including taxes, and, after doing so, is entitled to any remaining assets.

Advantages and Disadvantages

A great deal can be said for the sole proprietorship, including having complete control over how the business is run. Because so few formalities are required, starting the business can be quick and relatively inexpensive. And, naturally, being able to keep all profits is a substantial reward for the time, money and effort invested in the business. On the other hand, raising all of the money needed to start a business can be extremely difficult, if not impossible, and could require borrowing heavily. Once the business is started, establishing goodwill, name recognition, and steady customers can take more time than some small businesses can afford to stay afloat and compete. Finally, and most significantly, being responsible for all debts and other liabilities the business incurs to the full extent of one's personal assets poses a formidable downside for sole proprietors.

PARTNERSHIPS

We have just learned that the hallmark of sole proprietorships is one person's owning and operating a business alone. For a number of reasons, many people prefer to involve others. Although doing so does mean sharing the profits and giving up some measure of control, it also spreads among others the financial burden and responsibility for future liabilities. Moreover, the business may benefit from the diverse skills, expertise and strengths others bring to the organization.

Partnerships are one form that businesses involving more than one person may take. Basically, a partnership exists whenever two or more people carry on business together with a view to profit. But not all commercial arrangements involving more than one person are partnerships. Because the parties' activities must be taken with a view to profit, a purely charitable or strictly social enterprise probably would not be a partnership. Likewise, passively co-owning property with others might not be a partnership, even if the property generates some income for the co-owners. Even though sharing profits strongly suggests a partnership exists, profit-sharing alone is not conclusive. For instance, under Ontario's *Partnership Act*, a creditor who is repaid fixed amounts from the profits of a debtor's business is not in partnership with the debtor. Similarly, employees taking part in a profit sharing plan at work are not in partnership with their employer.

Governing Law

Although recognized at common law, today partnerships in Canada are governed extensively by statute as all of the provinces have enacted partnership legislation. Generally speaking, these partnership laws serve two functions. First, they provide a set of mandatory rules governing the relationship between partnerships and third parties they deal with, such as customers and suppliers. Second, the laws supply rules for a partnership's internal operations and the partners' relationship. Unlike the former, the latter rules apply only if the partners themselves have entered into no partnership agreement establishing their internal relations.

Starting a Partnership

A partnership exists as soon as two or more individuals start carrying out an activity that brings them within the definition of partnership. In fact, a partnership may exist without the partners' knowledge or intent to operate as a partnership, and people may be deemed to be in partnership where they have entered into no oral or written agreement and even have expressly stated their intention not to be partners. Even so, as with sole proprietorships, partnerships may need to obtain provincial or municipal licences to engage in specific businesses, register their business names in certain jurisdictions and comply with other similar requirements. Although not required, many partners also enter a partnership agreement when forming their business.

Partnership Agreements

Typically, a partnership agreement helps a business operate more harmoniously by addressing in advance such issues as how decisions will be made, who will be responsible for which aspects of the business, how and when profits will be distributed, how the partnership will admit new members, and how it may be dissolved. As observed, in the absence of a partnership agreement, the relevant provincial statute determines these and other issues regarding the partnerships' internal operation. Where the partnership agreement addresses any of these internal issues differently than the applicable statute, the terms of the partnership agreement will prevail. However, if the partnership agreement tries to change the relationship between the partnership and external third parties in a way that contradicts the statute, the statutory requirement prevails.

If no partnership agreement exists, provincial statutes generally provide that partners share equally in partnership profits and losses and that all are entitled to participate in managing the business. While most decisions generally may be made by a majority of the partners, admitting new partners and changing the fundamental nature of the business require all partners' agreement.

Concept of the Firm

As observed, a partnership creates no new legal entity separate from the partners. Commonly called "firms", partnerships may employ others but may not employ the partners themselves. The partnership is not taxed as an entity. Instead, partnership profits are included as income of the partners, who are taxed as individuals. By statute, the partnership's net profit is allocated equally among all partners, unless a partnership agreement provides otherwise. The partnership's losses are allocated to the partners in the same way.

Partners' Rights and Duties

Historically, partnerships are founded on mutual trust and confidence. Partners owe each other a fiduciary duty, meaning they must deal with each other and their business in utmost good faith and never put their personal interest ahead of the partnership's. Developed at common law, partners' fiduciary relationship to each other has been expressly incorporated into some provinces' partnership statutes — British Columbia's, for instance. Other provincial statutes, like Ontario's, make no express reference to the fiduciary duty; however, the duty is evidenced throughout the statutory provisions addressing partners' specific duties to each other. For example, Ontario's *Partnership Act* requires partners to provide the partnership with true accounts and full information regarding the partnership; to disclose all benefits derived from transactions involving the partnership and from using the partnership's name, property or business connections; and to reveal any profits made from competing with the partnership's business. Partners may choose to modify some of these responsibilities to each other through a partnership agreement.

Like sole proprietors, partners directly operate their business. Although provincial partnership statutes give all partners the right to take part in managing the partnership, the particular role each plays often is defined more particularly in a partnership agreement. In this way, partners may allocate responsibility among themselves according to their strengths, expertise, education and interests.

The law considers each partner to be an agent of the partnership, meaning each alone can bind the partnership to contracts and other obligations without the other partners' consent as long as the partner is acting in the ordinary course of the partnership's normal business. This fundamental principle of **agency** means that partners who neither consented to, authorized, nor later ratified another partner's actions may become obligated to perform contracts, be liable for the individual partner's torts, and vicariously liable for employees' acts done in the ordinary course of business. Because the partnership is not bound by a partner's action falling outside the scope of its normal business, what constitutes the partnership's normal business has been the subject of court cases. Exceptions to this principle do exist, however, particularly concerning third parties who contract with the partnership under circumstances that are not quite so innocent. For instance, a partnership might not be bound by a contract one partner entered into with a third party who knew that the partner had no authority to enter into the contract.

Partnership statutes also treat certain property as partnership property, regardless of whether title to the property remains in the name of an individual partner. Ontario's statute includes as partnership property all property each partner contributed to the partnership and all property acquired on the partnership's behalf during its course of business. Additionally, property regularly used in the business may become partnership property even if the partner who individually owned it never formally or expressly gave it to the business. When property becomes partnership property, partners lose their individual rights to it. Again, partners can modify their rights to partnership property through a partnership agreement.

Responsibility for Partnership Liabilities

Given that partnerships have no separate existence from their partners, every partner faces unlimited personal liability for partnership liabilities. This means each partner's personal property is at risk along with the partnership property should the partnership have insufficient assets to cover its debts when due. Partners may try to mitigate this harsh result through their partnership agreement by requiring themselves to reimburse any partner who individually covers partnership debts or allocating more responsibility for partnership debts to certain partners than others. However, these agreements bind only the partners and have no affect on third parties dealing with the partnership. So, regardless of the partnership agreement's terms, an aggrieved third party has recourse against all partners, and a partner who pays out more than specified in the partnership agreement has recourse against only the other partners.

Timing is important in determining a partner's liability for partnership debt as partners generally are liable for only obligations that arose while they were a partner. Note, however, that liability for obligations that arose during a partner's tenure remain after the partner leaves and even dies, with the debt passing to the deceased partner's estate.

Even though partners generally face no liability for obligations arising after they leave the partnership, they must take care to ensure that they do not inadvertently become liable. In most provinces, this involves notifying the public of the partner's retirement and not allowing the firm to give the appearance that the partner remains.

Types of Partnerships

The partnerships discussed so far, where all partners are liable for the partnership's acts and debts, are called **general partnerships**. However, other types of partnerships may be permitted by statute depending on the jurisdiction.

Limited Partnerships

Another type of partnership is the **limited partnership**. Unlike general partnerships, limited partnerships are a creature of statute and come into existence only if those involved take certain steps in compliance with the jurisdiction's governing law. In other words, they are not formed by simply starting to operate as a partnership; rather, a document must be filed and, in some jurisdictions, periodically renewed with the appropriate ministry or department. In many provinces, such as Ontario, limited partnerships are governed by a separate statute, called the *Limited Partnership Act*.

In a limited partnership, one or more general partners are personally liable for the partnership liabilities, while one or more limited partners are liable only to the extent of their individual investment in the limited partnership. In this way, general partners have the opportunity to involve others in the business as somewhat passive investors. The general partners manage and operate the business on their own with little or no input from the limited partners. In fact, a limited partner who takes too active a role in managing the business runs the risk of being deemed to be a general partner and losing the protection of limited liability. In return, the limited partners share in the partnership's profits and have other rights, including, for instance, having their contribution returned, dissolving the partnership, and reviewing the partnership's books and accounts.

Limited Liability Partnerships

The fact that many professions may not incorporate in most jurisdictions throughout Canada has generated another type of special partnership, the **limited liability partnership** (or LLP). In some provinces, professionals, including lawyers and accountants, for example, may form limited liability partnerships to limit individual partners' liability for their employees' and fellow partners' negligence. Although the individual partners' liability is somewhat limited, they remain personally liable for all other partnership liabilities, their own negligence, and the negligence of others that they personally supervise. Additionally, the partnership remains fully responsible for all liabilities, including individual partners' and employees' negligence.

In most jurisdictions, partnerships must meet certain requirements to become a limited liability partnership. For instance, Ontario's *Partnership Act* requires the partners to enter an agreement to operate as a limited liability partnership, be part of a profession whose governing statute permits operating as a limited liability partnership, register under the *Business Names Act*, and include LLP in the partnership's name.

Dissolving the Partnership

Partnerships may voluntarily choose to go out of business or be forced to close shop. Partnerships might involuntarily be stopped from continuing with their business if their activities become illegal or if operating their type of business as a partnership becomes illegal. Sometimes courts have discretion to terminate a partnership, for example, where a partner becomes mentally incompetent or incapacitated.

Provincial statutes typically codify when and how partnerships end. For instance, under Ontario's *Partnership Act*, a partnership ends when, among others, a fixed term for which it was created expires, the single undertaking it was created for is accomplished, any partner dies or becomes insolvent (unable to meet debts as they come due), and any partner notifies the others of an intent to end the partnership. However, partners can change some of the circumstances that will trigger the partnership's end through their partnership agreement.

Whatever the reason, when a partnership dissolves, debts to all third parties are paid first. Next, money the partnership might owe to individual partners is repaid and capital contributed to the partnership is then returned to the partners. Finally, any net assets remaining are divided among the partners equally or according to the partnership agreement.

Advantages and Disadvantages

The main advantages of a partnership are sharing the cost of financing a new business among more than one individual and having the opportunity to involve people with a broader range of skills, expertise, business connections and experience. The possibility of entering into a partnership agreement gives the partners flexibility in structuring their relationship and dividing responsibility for different aspects of the business according to skills and interests.

The major and very serious drawback is the partners' unlimited personal liability for the partnerships' obligations and each others' actions in the ordinary course of business. Additionally, becoming obligated to perform contracts and being liable for other partners' actions without consent presents a serious disadvantage as does the possibility of remaining liable after retiring from the partnership unless certain steps are taken.

CORPORATIONS

The business organizations discussed so far have shared one crucial element: the owners' personal liability for their business's liabilities. Although participants may be able to reduce their exposure or limit the extent of their personal liability, the very real risk of losing more than one's investment in the business generally remains. The risk to one's personal assets exists because fundamentally the business and its owners are as one.

Many people entering business are unwilling to take on such a far-reaching risk that exposes their personal assets and makes no distinction between their business and private life. Many find the risk's scope unreasonable given how many unknowns come with any business and how much of that risk falls completely outside of the owners' control. What is more, as a business succeeds, it often grows and with growth comes even greater exposure to increasingly substantial liability. For these and other reasons, many entrepreneurs choose to incorporate.

Corporation: A Separate Legal Entity

The **corporation**'s appeal as a business organization primarily stems from the legal fiction that grants corporations a separate legal identity. So, unlike partnerships and sole proprietorships, corporations are distinct from their owners. As recognized legal persons in their own right, corporations enjoy many of the Constitutional and other entitlements any other person in Canada enjoys, including the right to own property, enter contracts, take legal action against others, and form partnerships. In fact, even some of the rights under Canada's *Charter of Rights and Freedoms* apply to corporations. But, along with rights, corporations have responsibilities that may subject them to contract, tort, and even criminal liability.

The distinguishing feature of corporations is this separation of ownership from liability. In a corporation, one or more people purchase **shares** in the corporation, with the percentage of shares held equalling the portion of the corporation the shareholder owns. Each shareholder's liability is limited to the amount invested in purchasing the corporation's shares and, absent extraordinary circumstances, the shareholder has no personal liability for the corporation's obligations. Although shareholders may take some part in managing and running the business, in many corporations the day-to-day operations are left entirely to others.

Origin of the Law of Corporations

The law has recognized corporations for hundreds of years, although how they are formed and operated has changed over time. A watershed event in the history of corporations happened in 1897 when the British House of Lords crystallized the concept of the corporation as a separate legal entity in the seminal case, *Salomon v. Salomon & Co.*[1]

In this case, Mr. Salomon had operated for many years as a sole proprietor before incorporating his business. After incorporating, Mr. Salomon held a significant majority of the company's shares and continued to run the business; a half-dozen members of Mr. Salomon's family owned the remaining shares. The company also owed a secured debt to Mr. Salomon. Unfortunately, sometime after incorporation, the business fell on hard times and a liquidator was appointed to settle the company's debts and distribute to the shareholders whatever (if anything) remained. The case arose when the liquidator resisted paying Mr. Salomon the secured debt the company owed him before paying other creditors whose debts were not secured, even though the law requires that secured creditors be paid first.

In ruling in Mr. Salomon's favour, the court fully embraced the notion of separate legal existence, even where a very closely held corporation is, in essence, run by a single majority shareholder. As a secured creditor of the corporation, Mr. Salomon was entitled to recover because he had complied with all legal requirements for incorporation. However, since Salomon, courts have had many opportunities to re-examine this legal fiction and have been willing to "pierce the corporate veil" of limited liability and hold shareholders personally liable, albeit in very rare circumstances involving fraud, a sham company, or other egregious wrongdoing.

Creating a corporation is a far more formal process than starting up a sole proprietorship or partnership. Formal registration, fees, and other require-

---

[1] [1897] A.C. 22, 66 L.J. Ch. 35 (H.L.).

ments must be followed to create, operate, change, sell, and ultimately end a corporation. The law comes from a number of sources.

Modern corporations are governed primarily by statute, with most incorporating either federally or provincially. Generally speaking, businesses incorporate federally if their enterprise falls within a federally regulated sphere, such as telecommunications, or will operate in more than one province. The *Canada Business Corporations Act* (the CBCA) establishes the rules for incorporating and operating a federal corporation. On the other hand, businesses incorporate under the laws of a Canadian province or territory if they intend to operate within one province or territory. In the past several decades, most of the provinces and territories have adopted corporate law statutes similar to the federal CBCA, making the incorporation process fairly uniform across much of the country.

A company incorporated in one province wishing to operate in another province must obtain permission under that province's extra-provincial licensing laws. The requirements for operating extra-provincially vary somewhat across the jurisdictions. Although federal corporations need no extra-provincial licence to operate in any of Canada's provinces or territories, they generally must file information similar to that required for an extra-provincial licence before starting to operate in most provinces.

Federal and Provincial Incorporation by Certificate

Under the federal and most provincial statutes, businesses incorporate by registering with a designated government authority. Once the required documentation is filed along with a fee, a **certificate of incorporation** is issued and the corporation exists. In these jurisdictions, the certificate of incorporation must be issued once all registration requirements have been met if the registration appears to be correct on its face. In fact, a certificate may only be refused for failing to meet the registration requirements and for no other reason.

The registration process is fairly straightforward, streamlined and fast. In fact, businesses that will involve few shareholders and complexities can be incorporated without a lawyer's help as many commercial incorporation packages containing the needed forms and instructions are available for purchase. Even so, a lawyer's advice is prudent for more complex incorporations involving, for example, more than one class of shares with different rights attached or property that will be transferred to the new corporation. Additionally, nearly all new corporations would benefit from a lawyer's tax planning advice.

Incorporation Process

The incorporation process typically involves three steps.

Step One. The first step in incorporating under federal and comparable provincial systems is preparing the **articles of incorporation** for the proposed company. The statute and associated regulations establish the required content and form of the articles. The articles must include the name of the corporation if the business will operate under a corporate name. A corporation instead may decide to operate as a number company, either initially or in the long term. In this case, Corporations Canada (or comparable provincial authority if filed provincially) assigns a number that becomes the corporation's name. (For more information on corporate names, see Exhibit 16.1.) The articles also must name the city or town and province where the corporation will have its head office in Canada; the full address may be provided later on a separate form.

Next, the articles must state a fixed number of **directors** the corporation will maintain on its board of directors or the minimum and maximum

EXHIBIT 16.1

Naming the Corporation

Federal and provincial statutes and their associated regulations require all corporations to have a name and specify restrictions and requirements the name must meet. These requirements are intended to make it easy for the public to distinguish one company from the next, and they ensure that corporations' names in no way mislead or deceive the public. Although requirements vary across jurisdictions, generally corporate names must be unique and distinct from other corporations' names and may not exceed a specified maximum number of characters, or be too general, nondescript, or obscene. The name must include one of the words that designate the legal status as a limited liability corporation, such as Incorporated, Inc., or Limited.

In Ontario, corporations may use a trade name in conjunction with, and in some circumstances instead of, their official name. However, the trade name must be registered under the *Business Names Act* and the proper corporate name must be used on contracts, invoices, negotiable instruments, and orders for goods and services.

Because a corporation's name may not be confusingly similar to other corporations' names, the proposed name should be carefully researched before submitting the articles of incorporation. For example, in Ontario, corporations planning to operate under a name other than a number name must submit evidence that the proposed name most likely is safe to use. The evidence is a report of a search for the name in the computerized name search system, known as NUANS. The report must reveal that the proposed name conflicts with no existing or proposed corporate name. Private search firms perform these searches and provide the reports for a fee.

To avoid the cost and time associated with the NUANS search, some corporations opt for a number name. If the corporation later wants to adopt a proper name, it may obtain a search and change its name by filing amended articles of incorporation.

number of directors the corporation must have at any given time. The articles must also indicate the classes and maximum number of shares the corporation will be authorized to issue. Although corporations are free to impose no restrictions on their shares, if they wish to impose restrictions they must do so in the articles of incorporation. A corporation planning to have two or more classes of shares must specify the rights, privileges, restrictions, and any conditions attached to each class. Similarly, if the corporation will issue shares in series, the articles must give the directors authority to fix the number of shares in each series and determine the rights, privileges, restrictions, and conditions attached to each series.

Corporations may, but need not, restrict the business they may conduct. If they choose to restrict the business, they must do so in the articles. In the absence of business restrictions in the articles of incorporation, the corporation will have the capacity to carry on any business. The articles may also include any other provisions that the applicable statute allows corporations to include in their **by-laws** or a **unanimous shareholder agreement** (both discussed below). If the company will be a private (or **non-offering) corporation**, meaning that its shares will not be sold to the public (as opposed to a public or **offering corporation** whose shares are sold to the public), the articles must restrict the number of shareholders the corporation may have and prohibit offering shares to the public.

Finally, the articles of incorporation must list the names, addresses and signatures of the incorporators. Simply stated, incorporators are the people asking for incorporation. Although the incorporators may be and often are the people actually interested in starting the corporation, they need not be. Frequently, the incorporators signing the articles are the lawyers handling the incorporation.

Step Two. The next step in incorporation is filing the articles of incorporation, filing fee, and completed Initial Registered Office and First Board of Directors form, which states the full address of the head office and lists the names of the corporation's first directors. The first directors will set up the corporation and serve only until the shareholders elect actual directors at their first shareholders meeting. Although the incorporators sometimes take on the role of first directors as well, they need not be the corporation's first directors.

Step Three. In the final step in incorporation, the federal or comparable provincial authority signs and issues the certificate of incorporation. The corporation exists as of the date on the certificate of incorporation.

Other Methods of Incorporation

Throughout Canada, the certificate system outlined above is by far the most common way businesses are incorporated. However, two other methods bear mention: incorporation by **letters patent** and by **memorandum of association**. In the letters patent system, incorporation is a sovereign act, meaning the Crown or province issues a charter to the corporation in the form of letters patent granting the corporation existence. This older system remains for specific types of corporations across the country.

Under the other system, registration by memorandum of association, a corporation comes into existence on registration of a memorandum of association. The main difference between this and the certificate system is that the memorandum of association creates a contractual relationship among a company's members, with their rights and duties emanating from the contract. By contrast, corporations given existence through a certificate of incorporation are statutory constructs, with all rights and duties emanating from the governing statute.

How Corporations Run

As observed, a great deal of activity takes place before a corporation exists. The people involved in setting up the corporation are called **promoters**. The promoters sometimes are the same people who end up preparing, signing and filing the articles of incorporation; often, however, they are not. Commonly, promoters prepare for the corporation's management, perform several initial administrative functions, float securities, and may set up contracts for the corporation. When promoters arrange pre-incorporation contracts, they must take care not to become personally liable on the contracts, which the corporation must ratify on coming into existence to become party to them. Promoters have a fiduciary relationship with the corporation they promote, meaning they must deal fairly and act in the corporation's best interests. Although promoters may choose to, they are required to neither subscribe for the corporation's shares nor become first directors.

After the corporation comes into existence, still more must be done to get the business up and running, and the federal and provincial statutes provide some structure. The first order of business is the first directors meeting, which any incorporator or first director may call. At this organizational meeting, the first directors may adopt the form of the new corporation's shares and corporate records, authorize shares to be issued, appoint **officers**, appoint an auditor to hold office until the first annual shareholders meeting is held, make banking arrangements, make by-laws, and transact any other business.

By-laws are permanent and continuing rules that commonly address the corporation's administration and how it will conduct business and define the members' rights and duties among themselves. Neither the Ontario nor the federal *Business Corporations Act* insists that corporations have any by-laws, while some other jurisdictions require every corporation to pass by-laws or the equivalent. In some provinces, the by-laws also must be publicly filed with the articles of incorporation. Some aspects of a corporation's affairs that by-laws commonly cover include the following:

* How the corporation's shares will be subscribed for, allotted, and recorded
* The books and records the corporation will keep and who will maintain them
* Who has signing authority
* The time, place, notice, procedural, and **quorum** requirements for directors and shareholders meetings
* The appointment, pay, duties, and removal of directors, officers, agents and employees
* Banking arrangements

To be valid, by-laws must be made in good faith, in the corporation's best interests, for a proper purpose and may not be discriminatory, unreasonable, oppressive, illegal or contrary to public policy.

Ownership

Corporations are owned through shareholdings. One or more persons own an interest in the corporation by exchanging property or money for shares of the corporation. So, the amount of shares an individual holds represents that person's capital investment in the corporation.

Historically and under modern statutes, corporations typically have one or both of two major types or classes of shares: common and preferred. The term "common share" generally refers to shares that give the holders the right to participate in the corporation through, for instance, unrestricted rights to periodic payments from the corporation's profits (called **dividends**) and distribution of whatever property remains after all creditors are paid when the company goes out of business. When a corporation establishes only one class of shares with no differentiation among them, the shares are common shares. By contrast, preferred shares generally are special shares with some type of priority or other preferential treatment attached to them. Typical preferences include a priority right to receive dividends, special voting rights, and the right to be repaid one's capital investment if the company dissolves.

Within these two broad classifications of shares exist a number of possibilities, and large companies offering their shares to the public may have several classes and series of shares with different rights, restrictions, and preferences attached to them. In addition to being governed by the federal or provincial business corporations statutes, public — or offering — companies' shares classes and restrictions, as well as dealings with shareholders, are highly regulated by securities legislation and Securities Exchange Commission, which is a regulator body that regulates stock markets.

Some shareholders investing in a corporation wish to retain a certain percentage ownership interest in the corporation. To accomplish this, some corporations will attach pre-emptive rights to certain preferred shares. Pre-emptive rights give the holders of that class of shares the first opportunity to buy a sufficient number of any new shares issued to keep their proportionate ownership interest in the corporation. If these shareholders decline the shares, the corporation is then free to sell to others.

Shareholders acquire their shares in any number of possible ways, with the two most frequent being buying shares from existing holders and subscribing for newly issued shares. "Subscribing" simply means offering to buy shares through a written application to the corporation. Because the subscription is an offer, the corporation is not bound to sell the shares until it accepts the offer.

Shareholder Powers, Rights and Remedies

Particularly in companies with many shareholders and absent special arrangements, shareholders generally take no part in a corporation's day-to-day management and affairs. However, this does not mean shareholders wield no power. In fact, Canadian corporate law statutes grant shareholders specific powers, rights, and remedies.

The first major power shareholders have is to elect and remove the corporation's directors, a power they exercise through annual shareholders meetings. The CBCA requires the directors of new corporations to call the first annual shareholders meeting within 18 months of incorporation and annually from then on. Provincial statutes have similar requirements. At the annual shareholders meeting, shareholders take care of three matters. First, the shareholders elect new directors as needed; because directors' terms often are staggered, the shareholders typically are filling vacancies on the board as individual terms end. Second, they review the corporation's financial statement for the year and the auditor's report. Finally, they either reappoint the auditor or waive appointment. These three are the only business matters conducted at the annual meeting. However, shareholders may also hold special meetings to discuss any other business; should they wish to combine the special with the annual meeting, they may do so in a combined Annual and Special Meeting of the Shareholders.

Under the federal and provincial statutes, a minimum percentage of all shareholders must be present — called a quorum — at the meeting, either in person or by proxy. Attending by proxy means appointing in writing any other person to vote one's shares. In large companies with publicly sold and traded shares, federal and provincial *Securities Acts* apply stringent rules to soliciting proxies.

Unless the corporation's by-law's state otherwise, one share carries one vote, and **resolutions** are passed by a simple majority. However, special resolutions dealing with a fundamental change in the corporation (like amending the by-laws or articles of incorporation or deciding to end the corporation) generally require two-thirds of the shareholders' votes to pass.

Shareholders also have the right to obtain access to certain information and put forward shareholder proposals at their meetings. Additionally, shareholders may augment their powers through a unanimous shareholder agreement. Signed by all shareholders, the agreement reserves some of or all of the powers of directors — essentially the company's management and operations — for the shareholders. When shareholders take on all or part of the directors' powers, they also assume a commensurate degree of responsibility and potential liability associated with being a director. So, instead of their liability being limited to the amount invested in the company, the shareholders may open themselves to greater risk and potential personal liability by entering into a unanimous shareholder agreement.

Federal and provincial legislation governing corporations also gives shareholders a number of remedies when they are dissatisfied with how the corporation is managed or how they are treated. Although a detailed look at the available remedies is beyond this chapter's scope, a few bear mention. The federal and Ontario statutes both provide an **oppression remedy**, which allows shareholders, creditors, directors, or officers to apply to the court for relief if they believe that any actual or threatened act or failure to act by the corporation or any use of the directors' powers is oppressive or unfairly prejudicial.

Another remedy available to shareholders is the **derivative action**, which allows an individual to bring or intervene in (become a party to) a court action in the name, or on behalf, of the corporation. In this class action, the individual acts as a representative for others in asserting or defending the corporation's rights. The court's decision then binds all other shareholders as though they themselves participated. In addition to current and former shareholders, current and former directors and officers and anyone else a court considers proper may bring a derivative action.

Available both federally and in provinces, such as Ontario, is an application for an inspection or investigative order. Here, the shareholder asks the court for an order directing an investigation into the corporation.

Directors

At common law and under Canadian federal and provincial legislation, a corporation's directors manage the corporation's affairs and plan its strategy in line with its articles of incorporation. Although a unanimous shareholders agreement may modify this, most corporations — particularly widely held companies with many shareholders — operate under this model. The CBCA requires directors to be an individual person (not a legal entity like a corporation) 18 years or older, who is of sound mind and not an undischarged bankrupt. The federal and provincial statutes also have Canadian residency requirements for boards of Canadian corporations. For instance, the federal act requires at least 25 percent of the directors on a corporation's board to be Canadian residents. Corporations with four or fewer directors (including those with one director) must have at least one Canadian resident director.

The first directors listed in the articles of incorporation hold power until the first annual shareholders meeting, at which time the shareholders elect the first true board. Directors must consent to be a director and, once elected, remain in office either until their term expires (without re-election), the shareholders remove them, or they die or resign. Each year, the shareholders elect, by a simple majority vote, new directors to fill any vacancies. The legislation the business is incorporated under sets out a code for directors meetings, which must be followed unless the corporation's articles or by-laws provide otherwise. As with shareholder meetings, a quorum of directors, defined by statute or established in the company's articles or by-laws, must be present at any directors meeting to conduct business.

At their meetings, the directors may conduct any of the corporation's business, deciding issues and taking action through resolutions. At a minimum, directors must call an annual shareholders meeting and approve the corporation's financial statements each year. Directors present at any meeting are deemed to consent to any resolution passed unless they require their dissent to be recorded in the minutes, send a written dissent to the board secretary before the meeting is adjourned, or send by registered mail or deliver to the corporate office their dissent immediately after the meeting is adjourned. Directors absent from the meeting are also deemed to consent to all action taken at the meeting unless they send their written dissent or require their dissent to be recorded in the minutes within seven days of learning about a resolution. Each director has one vote, which may not be assigned to a proxy. In one-director corporations, the sole director may act through written resolutions instead of meetings.

Directors' Duties and Liabilities

The directors of any corporation have two broad responsibilities, commonly called the **fiduciary duty** and the duty of care. The fiduciary duty requires directors to act honestly and in good faith with a view to the best interests of the corporation, putting the corporation's interests ahead of their own and avoiding conflicts of interest. Typical conflicts arise when a director holds a personal interest in a material contract with the corporation or gains an opportunity because of information learned in the course of being a director. Directors must disclose all conflicts and refrain from voting on any related resolution. Failure to disclose a conflict may make a director liable for any gain earned from the conflicting interest. Directors also generally are prohibited from taking advantage of a business opportunity the corporation had or sought; personal liability can attach even where the director resigns before taking the opportunity and the corporation suffers no real loss. The second duty requires directors to exercise a minimum standard of care in carrying out their duties, often described as the care, diligence and skill a reasonably prudent person would exercise in similar circumstances.

Holding directors liable for certain actions taken in their corporate capacity helps keep them accountable to shareholders and responsible for the corporation's failure to meet its legal obligations. Traditionally, director obligations extended only to shareholders, but Canadian courts recently have extended directors' duties to employees, creditors, and other stakeholders.

In addition to the two broad duties discussed above, some corporate law statutes impose liability on directors for specific actions, such as voting to issue shares for insufficient value, declaring dividends when the corporation is unable to pay its liabilities, improperly using confidential information, and allowing employee wages and vacation to go unpaid. In addition to fines and even imprisonment in some cases, directors who do not comply with statutory duties may be forced to account for any benefit, reimburse the corporation for improper expenditures, and disgorge their profits. In addition to specific duties that corporate law statutes impose, a number of other federal and provincial statutes impose duties on directors that expose them to potential personal liability. These include liability for failure to withhold and remit certain taxes and pension contributions, environmental offences and damages, and failure to take reasonable measures to ensure employee health and safety.

To fully understand the scope of potential liability, however, one must also look at whom the law considers to be a director or officer. In some cases, directors' liabilities may attach to individuals who have been neither elected nor appointed to office. So individuals who assume some or all of a director's duties or actively and directly guide a corporation's affairs could be deemed to be de facto directors and face personal liability.

Of course, some of the potential liability can be reduced through directors and officers insurance. Additionally, directors may raise several defences that may eliminate or reduce their liability. These defences include that the director exercised reasonable due diligence, skill, and care in taking the action; was not a director at the time an action was taken or liability arose; and reasonably relied on another professional as permitted by statute.

Officers

The board of directors often delegates some of its powers to one or more of their number, designated as the managing director or management committee. Federal and provincial legislation also allows directors to delegate some of their powers to a number of officers that they appoint. Directors may serve as officers and may even hold more than one office in the same corporation. Typical offices include chairman of the board, secretary, treasurer, president, vice-president, chief executive officer, general manager and comptroller. Generally, officers owe the corporation the same duties and face some of the same potential liabilities as directors.

Funding the Corporation

In addition to the money corporations bring in from their business activities, corporations rely on two other main sources of funds: equity and debt capital. The investment owners make in the corporation through buying shares constitutes equity capital. But corporations also are funded through debt. Just like any other legal person, most corporations finance themselves at last in part by borrowing money and buying on credit. In addition to borrowing from financial lending institutions, corporations sometimes borrow

---

EXHIBIT 16.2

Unlimited Liability Corporations

Even though one of incorporation's primary attractions is the limited liability the owners enjoy, a few Canadian provinces — Nova Scotia and Alberta, for instance — provide an alternative option called the **unlimited liability corporation** (ULC). Nova Scotia was the first Canadian province whose law allowed for the formation of ULCs. Under Nova Scotia's statute, a business may incorporate a company whose members have unlimited liability to the corporation's creditors, while in every other respect the corporation is a full corporation, with separate status as a legal person and the associated powers and rights.

Although for many years the option was rarely used, recently the use of ULCs has increased dramatically, mainly as a tax planning strategy in cross-border matters. Differences in how the United States and Canada treat corporations for income tax purposes have triggered the ULC's increased popularity. Under Canadian tax law, parent corporations cannot flow their profits and losses through to their United States subsidiaries, or the reverse, to reduce the taxable amount by offsetting one company's profits with the other's losses. Although this applies equally to ULCs, ULCs do derive the positive tax treatment that corporations receive. Conversely, because of their unlimited liability, ULCs are excluded from the definition of corporation for United States tax purposes. So, United States tax law treats ULCs as flow-through entities, meaning a Canadian parent or subsidiary corporation can apply its United States subsidiary's or parent's losses to offset the related Canadian corporation's profits.

Nova Scotia's law provides some measures for limiting the liability of some members of a ULC. For instance, members generally are liable only for debts that existed up to the time they stopped being a member, and former members are not required to contribute unless the current members cannot satisfy the debts. Liability may also be limited by contract as some creditors are willing to agree to enter into arrangements where only specified members will be held liable to satisfy the debt if unpaid.

---

from their own shareholders and nothing in the law prohibits being an owner and creditor of the same corporation. Corporations frequently issue bonds and debentures in exchange for money lent, with the holders of bonds and debentures repaid the amount loaned with interest.

Corporate Records and Corporate Governance

To ensure accountability, federal and provincial statutes require corporations to keep certain corporate records in a specified form and make them available to specific people involved in the corporation, including shareholders, directors, and creditors. Although the specifics vary among jurisdictions, some common principles prevail. Generally, corporations must keep a register of the articles of incorporation, by-laws and any unanimous shareholder agreement; a register of the corporation's directors; and registers of all minutes and resolutions of every shareholders, directors, and committee meetings. Corporations must also keep a register of all shareholders, including their names, addresses, number of shares held, and the date and details of the shares' issuance and transfer. Finally, corporations must keep accounting records consisting of, for example, documents supporting their financial statements, contracts, invoices and bank statements.

In recent years, large **public corporations** have come under pressure to improve their corporate governance and become more accountable. With several highly publicized scandals on both sides of the border and the stunning collapse of corporate giants, both the government and investors are looking for ways to ensure corporations keep a tighter rein on their management.

The United States' passage of the *Sarbanes Oxley Act*, which imposes tighter regulations on such corporate matters as financial reporting, disclosure, and conflicts, has had an impact on Canadian corporations as well, given the number that issue shares in the United States and have parent or subsidiary corporations there.

Amalgamating Companies

Corporations often decide to join with another business to expand geographically or in size, or both. Under the federal and many provincial statutes, when two or more corporations choose to consolidate into a single new corporation, an **amalgamation** occurs. These statutes provide a specific process that must be followed to amalgamate. The federal statute allows three methods for amalgamating, depending on the relationship the companies involved had going into the process.

The first method is a long-form amalgamation. This method must be followed when neither of the amalgamating companies is a wholly owned subsidiary of the other and both are not wholly owned subsidiaries of the same parent company. If, instead, one of the corporations is a wholly owned subsidiary of the other, the vertical short-form procedure may be followed. Finally, the horizontal short-form procedure applies where both amalgamating companies are wholly owned subsidiaries of the same parent corporation.

In the long-form procedure, an amalgamation agreement is approved by the shareholders of each corporation, **articles of amalgamation** are filed, and a Certificate of Amalgamation is issued. The short-form procedures are the same, except no amalgamation agreement or shareholder approval is needed.

Winding Up and Dissolving a Corporation

Like the other forms of business organizations, corporations sometimes choose or are forced to go out of business. The provincial and federal corporate law statutes provide a procedure for voluntarily and involuntarily settling a corporation's affairs and ending its existence if the corporation is solvent (meaning it is able to meet its debts as they come due). If the corporation is insolvent, it instead falls within the federal *Bankruptcy and Insolvency Act*'s jurisdiction and that Act's procedures apply. In the case of solvent corporations, whether voluntary or involuntary, the process involves two distinct steps.

The first step involves **winding up** the corporation's affairs and liquidating the company. Basically, all of the corporation's property and assets are called in and converted to money to pay the corporation's debts. After the debts are paid and any remaining assets are distributed to the shareholders, the second step is to dissolve the company. A consent to **dissolution** is obtained from the Minister of Finance and the consent and Articles of Dissolution are filed. At this point, a certificate of dissolution is issued and the corporation no longer exists.

Advantages and Disadvantages of Incorporation

The primary and very substantial advantage of incorporation is the limited liability conferred on the owners by virtue of the corporation's separate legal identity. The owners of shares are not personally liable for the debts or wrongful acts of the corporation, which is a separate legal entity from the individual shareholders. At most, shareholders will lose the value of their shares. However, in some cases, a major or controlling shareholder may be held personally liable for a corporation's liabilities if they were the controlling or directing mind of the corporation and used the corporation to engage in fraud or illegal acts, or to benefit the shareholder at the expense of the corporations. In situations like these, the court may invoke the doctrine of the corporate alter ego, "lifting the corporate veil" to fix liability on the individual shareholders who were improperly using and manipulating the corporation.

Additionally, corporations have greater flexibility in financing their operations and raising capital and may involve hundreds and even thousands in owning, managing and operating the business. Other than the formalities that must be followed, incorporation really carries very few disadvantages and has become perhaps the most prevalent way of carrying on even small businesses involving few or even one person.

FRANCHISES

Many people intrigued by the possibility of operating their own business lack the money, know-how, and skills to take on full responsibility for all aspects of establishing and operating a business. Considering all the elements that go into building a profitable business — from scoping out a good location, to developing attractive advertising and marketing, to knowing what to charge customers and pay suppliers — the many hurdles, uncertainties, and risks can be daunting. Enter the **franchise**, which for many first-time entrepreneurs appears to offer a more balanced and secure middle-ground. A franchise agreement is a contract between the owner of an established business (called the franchisor) and another party (called the franchisee), giving the franchisee the right to operate a business using the franchisor's business, name, and approach at an agreed-upon location. The franchise agreement generally indicates that the parties' relationship is neither a partnership nor a joint venture (see below). Perhaps the most prominent examples include fast-food restaurants.

Because these relationships carry a very real potential for abuse, given the imbalance of power that often characterizes them at the outset, many provinces have enacted laws governing franchises, typically requiring such safeguards as obliging the franchisor to deal fairly with and disclose specified information to franchisees and entitling franchisees to withdraw from an agreement within a specified number of days after entering into it.

Franchise Agreements

Although franchise agreements vary significantly depending on the business, parties, and other circumstances, certain terms are common to most. Generally, the agreement gives the franchisee a licence to use the franchisor's trademarks and other intellectual property related to the enterprise. The franchisor often agrees to help find a good location, possibly design or build the business premises, and provide some training in the business approach. The franchisee typically agrees to operate the business under the franchisor's established standards and pay a fee, often related to the volume of business. Sometimes the franchisee also must purchase supplies from only the franchisor and promote the business using only the franchisor's approved advertising.

Advantages and Disadvantages for the Franchisor

Franchising a business allows the owner to move into new locations and grow its name recognition without the burden of financing and running a business at each location. While giving up some control, the owner often retains substantial say over the business's standards, quality, look, promotion and other elements comprising its goodwill and value. Of course, the owner also earns fees from each franchise agreement entered into, often based in part on the volume of sales.

On the other hand, regardless of the standards and other rules the franchise agreement requires of the franchisee, the franchisor loses some measure of control over its name and goodwill, courting the risk that any one of its franchisees may operate the business poorly and tarnish the business's reputation. Additionally, franchisors often find ending the franchise relationship more difficult, stressful and problematic than anticipated.

Advantages and Disadvantages for the Franchisee

For many, the franchise represents an opportunity to start one's own business that might otherwise not exist. Opening a new business under an established name, with business processes known to work well, and with training and other support available greatly enhances the first-time businessperson's likelihood of succeeding. In many cases, the franchisor has already identified good locations for franchises, sells the franchisor the product and other supplies needed to operate, and even supplies promotional items and advertising.

But being tightly associated with the franchisor also has its drawbacks. Many people who decide to go into business for themselves are attracted by the thought of calling the shots and running a business the way they think best. Depending on the franchise agreement's terms, the franchisee may feel very limited by the standards and other rules restricting how the business may be run. Additionally, while being required to purchase supplies from the franchisor often brings the franchisee lower cost on some products, because of the franchisor's bulk purchases at discounted prices, some franchisee's find themselves unable to take advantage of lower local prices and find themselves at the franchisor's mercy when requests for supplies are filled too slowly. Depending on the volume of sales and the agreement made, the franchisee may be disappointed in the amount of profits actually realized at the end of the day.

OTHER FORMS OF BUSINESS ARRANGEMENT

Licences

Licence arrangements also arise purely from contract. Typically, the owner of some type of intellectual property, like a trademark or copyright, gives another permission to use the intellectual property in connection with a business in return for a fee or royalty. Common examples include a major movie company's licensing of clothing manufacturers and toy companies to use its characters and name on their goods.

Distributorships

Distributorships occur under a variety of arrangements where one business agrees to sell another business's products. In some cases, the agreement grants the business the exclusive right to distribute the other's products in a particular location or region. Sometimes the distributor agrees to assume responsibility for warranty services along with distributing the manufacturer's products. In any case, the arrangement brings the manufacturer yet another opportunity to get its product out to more customers.

Joint Ventures

The joint venture is another kind of business organization that can take many forms, including that of partnership or corporation. A joint venture typically refers to any situation where two or more parties — which themselves may be individuals, partnerships or corporations — agree to combine their resources for a common enterprise. **Joint ventures** commonly arise where the stakes and risks are high, the likelihood of success is low, but the anticipated payoff on success is substantial. Common examples include exploration and scientific research.

Strategic Alliances	Similar to the joint venture, a **strategic alliance** generally refers to an arrangement where two or more businesses agree to work together on a specific project or towards a common outcome. Examples include agreements to combine research and development activities or to refer business to one another in the other's jurisdiction.

CHAPTER SUMMARY

In this chapter, we learned to distinguish among the three primary and a few additional methods for organizing and operating a business in Canada. We also examined the major advantages and disadvantages associated with each of these business structures, paying particular attention to the extent to which each shifts the owners' and operators' personal responsibility for the business enterprise's liabilities. Finally, we took a closer look at how corporations are formed, owned, operated, financed, changed and, ultimately, dissolved under both federal and provincial laws.

GLOSSERY OF NEW TERMS AND KEY CONCEPTS

agency	An arrangement where one party, the agent, is given authority to act on behalf of the other party, the principal, and create binding obligations between the principal and third parties.
amalgamation	A process where two or more corporation combine to form a new corporation.
articles of amalgamation	Under federal and some provincial corporate law statutes, the document that sets out the name and structure of a new corporation made up of two combined or amalgamated corporations.
articles of incorporation	Under federal and some provincial corporate law statutes in Canada, the document that sets out a corporation's name and basic structure.
by-laws	The relatively permanent rules establishing how a corporation will be managed and operated.
certificate of incorporation	In many Canadian jurisdictions, the document that signifies the corporation's existence as a separate legal entity and the date on which it came into existence.
corporation	A business entity created by the federal or provincial government.
derivative action	A court action that a representative initiates or intervenes in to assert a right or defence on a corporation's behalf.
director	An individual named in the articles of incorporation or elected by a corporation's shareholders to manage the corporation.
dissolution	The way a corporation's or partnership's business is terminated.
distributorship	An arrangement where one business agrees to sell another business's products and may or may not take on the business's warranty services as well.
dividend	A payment to shareholders from the corporation's profits, representing the shareholder's proportional interest in the profits.
doctrine of the corporate alter ego	A legal doctrine that permits the courts, in cases of fraud or other wrongs that might not be remedied, to ignore the corporate structure and fix liability on individual controlling shareholders of the corporation.

fiduciary duty	A duty one party owes to another to act in utmost good faith and in the other's best interest.
franchise	An arrangement where the owner of an established business contracts with another, giving the other party the right to operate a business using the owner's business's name and process or approach at an agreed-upon location.
general partnership	A form of business where two or more people carry on a business with a view to profit, with each partner acting as agent for the partnership and other partners and having unlimited personal liability.
joint venture	An arrangement where two or more individuals, partnerships, corporations or other entities agree to pool resources for a common enterprise.
letters patent	A sovereign grant of corporate existence from the Crown.
licence	A business arrangement where the owner of some type of intellectual property allows another to use property in connection with another business in return for a fee or royalty.
limited partnership	A partnership made up of one or more general partners with unlimited personal liability and responsibility for running the business, and one or more limited partners whose liability is limited generally to the extent of their investment in the business and who take no part in running it.
limited liability partnership	A form of partnership some jurisdictions permit for certain professionals who may not otherwise limit their liability through incorporation; the limited liability partnership generally limits individual professionals' liability for their employees' and other partners' negligence.
memorandum of association	In some jurisdictions, a document that establishes a corporation's basic structure.
non-offering corporation	A corporation whose shares are not offered to the public; also called a private company or corporation.
offering corporation	A corporation whose shares are offered to the public; also called a public company or corporation.
officer	An individual appointed by the directors of a corporation to perform certain of the directors' duties that are delegated to the officer.
oppression remedy	Relief a court grants to one or more shareholders whom a corporation has treated unfairly or with prejudice.
partnership	A business organization where two or more people carry on business together with a view to profit.
promoter	A person interested in creating a corporation who takes on the preliminary tasks required to file for incorporation and prepare the business for operation as a corporation.
public corporation	A corporation whose shares are offered to the public; also called an offering company or corporation.
quorum	The number of shareholders or directors that must be present at a meeting to conduct business.
repossession	An action by the seller on a conditional sale contract or by the lender on a secured loan, where the seller/lender seizes the property that was sold under a conditional sale contract, or given as collateral for a loan.
resolution	A decision a corporation's directors have made authorizing the corporation to do a specific action or transaction.
shares	The portion of a limited liability corporation that an individual owns.
sole proprietorship	A business owned and operated by a single individual without creating another form of business organization.

strategic alliance	An arrangement where two or more businesses agree to work together on a specific project or towards a common outcome.
unanimous shareholder agreement	An agreement that some or all of a corporation's shareholders enter into, often to preserve some or all power to manage the corporation themselves instead of the officers and directors.
unlimited liability corporation	A special kind of corporation some Canadian provinces permit, where the owners remain personally liable for the corporation's actions and debts; because one of the primary advantages of incorporation is lost, this form of business organization is used for very limited and strategic purposes, typically related to obtaining favourable tax consequences for a number of related companies or transactions.
winding up	The process of calling all of a corporation's property in to be liquidated and first paid to all creditors and then distributed to owners before dissolving the corporation.

REVIEW QUESTIONS

1. In the context of business organizations, what does "limited liability" mean, and why is it important?

2. Describe the main steps involved in incorporating a federal corporation.

3. What is the difference between an incorporator and a promoter of a corporation?

4. What business must be conducted at the annual shareholders meeting?

5. In general, what is the difference between a common share and a preferred share?

6. How does a corporation acquire directors, and what do the directors do?

7. Who appoints officers, and from where do they derive their powers?

8. What is the difference between share capital and debt capital?

9. What is a joint venture, and who may participate in one?

10. What is the difference between a general partnership and a limited partnership?

DISCUSSION QUESTIONS

1. What are the major advantages and disadvantages associated with operating a sole proprietorship?

2. What are the major advantages and disadvantages of operating a partnership?

3. What does "piercing the corporate veil" mean? Do you think the concept is fair? Under what circumstances do you think a court should consider applying this concept?

4. Under what circumstances might the directors of a corporation become personally liable?

5. Describe some of the powers shareholders have and some ways shareholders maintain control over a corporation.

6. Why might a businessperson choose to operate a franchise?

SUGGESTED READINGS

Business Corporations Act (Ontario), R.S.O. 1990, c. B.16.

Canada Business Corporations Act, R.S.C. 1985, c. C-44.

Companies Act (Nova Scotia), R.S.N.S. 1989, c. 81.

Martel, P. *Business Corporations in Canada: Legal and Practical Aspects* (Toronto, Ont.: Thomson Canada Ltd., 2007).

McGuiness, K.P. *Canadian Business Corporations Law*, 2d Ed. (Markham, Ont.: LexisNexis Canada Inc., 2007).

VanDuzer, J.A. *The Law of Partnerships and Corporations*, 2d Ed. (Toronto, Ont.: Irwin Law, 2003).

Debtors' Rights and Creditors' Remedies

Ginevra M. Saylor
FRASER MILNER CASGRAIN LLP

Learning Objectives

After reading this chapter, the reader should be able to:

➤ understand the relationship between debtors and creditors

➤ describe security and the concept of secured transactions

➤ describe the various remedies available to the creditor for the collection of overdue debts

➤ identify the principal steps involved in the litigation of collections actions in court

➤ describe the major methods available for the enforcement of judgments obtained through litigation

➤ understand the purpose, procedure, and effect of bankruptcy proceedings

➤ identify the protection provided to the debtor and explain the role of consumer protection legislation

TABLE OF CONTENTS

INTRODUCTION

> He solemnly conjured me, I remember, to take warning by his fate; and to observe that if a man had twenty pounds a year for his income, and spent nineteen pounds nineteen shillings and six pence, he would be happy, but that if he spent twenty pounds one he would be miserable.
> —*David Copperfield* by Charles Dickens

So goes the advice of Mr. Micawber, a veteran of England's 19th century debtors' prison, to young David Copperfield on approaching the responsibilities of adulthood. The formula seems simple enough: never spend money you do not have. Yet Mr. Micawber, and most members of modern society, do find themselves in debt at one time or another. Many also find themselves unable to meet those debts as they come due. And so begins the relationship of the debtor and creditor and the debt collection process.

Creation of a Debt In the simple commercial transaction, one party offers goods or services for sale, and the other accepts by paying for them. However, in our complex economy, a variety of arrangements permit the consumer to receive the benefit of the transaction before paying.

For example, most people buying a car do not tender in one payment the large sum of money required. Rather, the buyer pays a small portion of the total sale price as a down payment and agrees to pay the remaining balance in the future under terms agreed on by the buyer and seller. The arrangement benefits both parties. Clearly, far fewer would be able to buy an expensive item like a car were such arrangements not available. The seller, in turn, would not sell as many cars and could not command as high a price.

Similarly, people often need a sum of money they do not currently have. Suppose an individual wishes to buy items from one seller who is unwilling to extend the buyer credit. That individual may contact a financial lending institution, such as a bank, to borrow money. The bank may agree to lend an amount of money on the borrower's promise to repay the sum borrowed within a specific time period and in a mutually agreed-upon way. The borrower also agrees to pay an additional sum, in the nature of **interest**, as a fee for using the lender's money. The interest typically is an amount calculated in terms of the sum originally borrowed (the **principal**).

In each of the above examples, one party receives the benefit of the transaction and, in return, promises to fully repay the other at some future date, creating a debt. A **debt** is an amount of money one person owes to another. Our economic system not only encourages but also relies on credit and the creation of debt. It is only when problems arise that the legal system may be called in to intervene. For example, suppose the borrower has agreed to repay the bank a certain amount each month and fails to pay for three months. Or, an automobile buyer claims the car bought was defective and refuses to pay the balance owed. In each case, the person who extended the credit will attempt to recover the unpaid amount.

Types of Debtors Any person who owes money to another is a **debtor**. However, not all debtors — or their debts — are alike. The way a creditor chooses to pursue collection is largely determined by the type of debtor and debt involved.

Consumer debtors are individuals who have acquired debt purchasing goods and services or borrowing money for use in their personal life. Two common examples of consumer debt are credit card purchases and residential mortgages.

People who owe money may fail to honour their debts on time for many reasons. Often, the consumer faces an unexpected and innocent financial setback. Consumers may suddenly be laid off from work or stricken with a debilitating illness that prevents them from earning an income for an extended period of time. Marital breakdown leading up to separation or divorce often causes financial uncertainty as well. Consumer debtors in these circumstances may want to meet their financial obligations but honestly lack the means to do so. In these circumstances, some creditors may be inclined to take a lenient approach to collection and attempt to work with the debtor, operating under the theory that "you cannot get blood from a stone." The amount of leniency the creditor extends often depends on the debtor's own conduct. Debtors who communicate with their creditors and act in good faith are more likely to receive sympathetic treatment.

However, not all debtors fall into their financial difficulties innocently. Some recklessly or irresponsibly manage their affairs, with little regard for whether they will be able to pay their debts when due. Still others intentionally avoid paying their debts, ignoring overdue notices, raising unfounded claims against creditors, and leaving the jurisdiction. In such cases, a creditor may take more aggressive steps to collect the debt. The creditor may seek the assistance of others, such as a **collection agency**, an investigator, or a lawyer. If necessary, the creditor may pursue the matter in court through a civil action against the delinquent debtor.

Another kind of debtor is the commercial debtor. Commercial debt is created when a business owes money for matters incidental to operating the business. This debt may arise from buying materials used to manufacture a product, leasing equipment, hiring services, or acquiring inventory.

As with the consumer debtors, many factors may lead commercial debtors to stop paying their debts on time. A major societal event, such as an economic recession, a crisis in the company's industry, or a political controversy may cause a business to face an unexpected sales or production reduction. A company may experience a protracted strike or lose key management personnel. Or the business may fail because of incompetence or mismanagement. Again, the reason for the debtor's failure to pay and the debtor's behaviour will play a large part in how the creditor decides to pursue the debt.

Debts do not die with the debtor. When people die owing money to others, those debts become their estate's debts. An estate consists of all property and assets the deceased owned at the time of death. An individual or group of individuals appointed by the court or the deceased through a will must administer the deceased's estate. Before distributing the estate's assets to the deceased's heirs or beneficiaries, the estate's personal representative must ensure all proper debts of the deceased are paid. In discharging this duty, the personal representative must advertise for creditors, advising them who to contact to collect their debts. The personal representative's failure to satisfy the estate's debts before final distribution of the assets can result in personal liability for paying the creditors from the representative's own assets.

Secured and General Creditors

As observed, a **creditor** is a person or entity to whom something is owed. Creditors range from individuals who independently sell a friend their computer to major institutional lenders making commercial loans of several million dollars to large corporations. Not all creditors, however, start from the same position when collecting their debts.

Many creditors at the inception of the debtor-creditor relationship take steps to enhance the likelihood that they ultimately will recover the amount owed. Creditors may structure the agreement with the debtor to provide direct recourse against some of the debtor's property. Additionally, such arrangements can provide creditors with priority in collecting their debt before some or all of the debtor's other creditors. Such advantages are obtained by requiring **security**. A creditor who has taken some form of security is called a **secured creditor**.

Security comes in many forms. It may be real estate, personal goods, stocks, bonds, or the equipment used by a business. Security is often referred to as collateral.

A common secured transaction is buying a home with a mortgage. Frequently, the purchaser will obtain the bulk of the money needed to complete the transaction from a bank or other institutional lender through a special type of loan arrangement known as a mortgage or charge. Through the agreement, the lender obtains not only the borrower's promise to repay the debt but also a claim against the land itself. Consequently, should the borrower fail to repay the debt according to the agreement's terms, the lender may enforce its claim against the property by taking possession of and ultimately selling it to satisfy the debt. Assuming all statutory requirements for protecting the secured interest have been met, the lender has access to the property used as collateral before any of the debtor's other creditors, even those whose claims arose before the lender's.

Whatever the form of security, the essential features of secured transactions are that the secured creditor obtains special rights against one or more assets of the debtor, and those rights stand in priority to the claims of the debtor's other creditors. However, to ensure their preferred status over other creditors, secured creditors generally must meet two requirements. First, the agreement or contract creating the secured interest must be in writing and describe the property in sufficient detail to accurately identify it. Second, secured creditors must comply with all statutory requirements for registering a secured interest with the proper public office. For example, a secured interest in land must be registered against title to the land in the appropriate Land Registry Office. Likewise, an interest in personal property must be filed with the designated ministry under provincial *Personal Property Security Acts*.

Not all secured interests arise from a contract between parties. Sometimes a creditor receives a preferred or special interest in a debtor's property by statute or under common law (as discussed in the next section).

By contrast, a creditor who takes no security and obtains no preferred claim over specific assets is called an unsecured or **general creditor**. A general creditor may have no option but to bring a court action against a debtor who does not satisfy a debt. Furthermore, the general creditor will rank behind the debtor's secured creditors for satisfaction of the claim, at least with respect to those assets used as collateral.

METHODS OF COLLECTION

Demand for Payment

In the collection process, the creditor wants to be paid as quickly and inexpensively as possible. At times, creditors may have a further interest in preserving their relationship with a particular debtor so that the two may conduct more business together in the future. This arises where the debtor is the creditor's ongoing commercial client, experiencing a temporary setback in business. Finally, creditors have an underlying concern in preserving their reputation and goodwill.

The collection process typically begins with one or more notices to the debtor, advising that the account is overdue, and demanding payment. The demand will state the total amount due, including interest or late fees, the date when the amount must be fully paid, and the possible consequences of failing to pay or contact the creditor. The creditor may also telephone the debtor to demand payment and find out the debtor's intentions. If the debtor is co-operative and communicative at this point, the creditor may be willing to agree to partial or periodic payments. A creditor may even agree to reduce the debt in exchange for an immediate lump-sum payment. The more reasonable the debtor's behaviour, the more likely early settlement becomes. Creditors are fully aware of the expense and difficulty involved in the collection process and often would rather receive a certain, albeit lesser, amount than face the uncertainties and delay inherent in later stages of the process.

Many creditors involve others in the collection process. Where the debtor cannot be found, the creditor may hire an investigator to locate the debtor. Using information the creditor provides, investigators search public records and other sources to trace debtors.

It is also common for creditors to turn delinquent accounts over to a collection agency. A collection agency is an independent company whose business is obtaining debt repayment for its clients. Given the nature of the service and the potential for abusing and harassing debtors, these agencies are regulated by the government and generally must be registered.

Enforcing a Lien

As noted, creditors may enhance their likelihood of collecting by requiring security in return for an extension of credit. The common law and modern statutes have developed similar rights by operation of law for individuals performing certain kinds of labour and services through the creation of a **lien**. While some liens entitle one person to retain property belonging to another until the property's owner satisfies specific demands, other liens are nonpossessory and operate like a charge.

Consider an individual who takes an automobile to a garage for repairs. The mechanic and the owner agree that certain repairs will be made and a specific amount will be paid when the repairs are completed. If the owner fails to pay when notified that the work is done, the mechanic may keep the car until the owner has fully paid. The mechanic creates a lien on the automobile by improving the property with the owner's permission.

Common Law

At common law, the right to a lien was restricted to those who performed services in the nature of repairs or improvements to goods; to innkeepers over the property of their guests; and to common carriers (those engaged in shipping and transportation) over goods shipped. Some professionals, such as lawyers and bankers, have a common law lien over documents prepared by them or left in their possession. To enforce their rights over the debtor's property, lien claimants must have already performed the services, and payment must be due. At common law, the lien provided only the right to withhold the goods and did not include a right to sell those goods to satisfy the debt.

Extension by Statute

Statutory law extends the protection of the lien to more professions and businesses and adds the right to sell the goods in some circumstances. For example, in most jurisdictions the lien obtained by one who performs work on a chattel (an item of personal property) includes the right to sell the property and use the proceeds to cover the debt after a designated period of time and notice to the debtor. Similarly, under current innkeeper statutes, hoteliers may sell guests' property on the premises, after the bills remain unpaid for a specified period and after providing proper notice to the guest. These laws also extend the entitlement to operators of boarding and lodging

EXHIBIT 17.1

Lien for Storage

Suppose Frank buys furniture from Furno-rama in Ottawa and asks the store to ship the goods to Toronto, where he lives. The store agrees to ship the furniture to a storage facility in Toronto, and Frank agrees to pay the storage fee and arrange for final transport to his residence when notified that the goods have arrived. When the goods arrive, the warehouse notifies Frank, but he makes no arrangement for transport to his home and tenders no payment for storage. After four months, the warehouse decides to sell the furniture.

Under Ontario's statutory scheme, the warehouse must notify both Frank and the furniture store of its intention to sell the goods unless the charges are paid in full by a specific date. The notice must state that the goods will be advertised for sale at a public auction, and must include the proposed sale's time, date and location. The notice must be sent to any other person the warehouse knows to have an interest in the goods.

houses. Notably, however, the right to sale has not been extended to common carriers, although nothing prevents individual common carriers from securing this right by including an express term in their contracts with consumers.

Although the details vary among the provinces, statutes authorizing the right to sale generally require the following:

- A specific number of months to pass after payment comes due
- Advance notice to the owner of the creditor's intent to sell the property if the debt is not paid
- The time, date, and place of the sale be advertised
- Sale by public auction
- The proceeds be used first to cover costs of the sale and next to pay the overdue debt, with any surplus going to the debtor

The statutes provide strict guidelines regarding the sale's advertisement and conduct.

Warehouse and other storage operators are one class of labourers who had no lien at common law but now have a lien by statutes, e.g., Ontario's *Repair and Storage Liens Act*.[1] Under this Act, warehouse operators may hold goods stored at their facility for the amount of the charges due and sell the goods to cover the unpaid debt.

Construction Liens

Another industry that has benefited from the statutory extension of liens is the building and construction trade. Under such provincial legislation, all tradespeople supplying labour or materials to improve a piece of land may obtain a lien, or charge, against the land itself to secure payment for the work or supplies provided. The construction lien gives the lien claimant the right to ultimately sell the land to satisfy the debt if it remains unpaid and the lien is not discharged.

A large-scale construction project involves a series of contracts and sub-contracts. Generally, the owner enters into an agreement with a general contractor, who assumes responsibility for supervising the entire project. The general contractor then engages electricians, carpenters, roofers, plumbers and

---

[1] R.S.O. 1990, c. R-25.

other tradespeople through a series of subcontracts. Each of the subcontractors in turn may enter into subsidiary contracts for goods or services to be supplied at the construction site. Under this scheme, the only individual with a direct contractual relationship with the landowner is the general contractor. To sue in contract under common law, a plaintiff must have privity of contract with the defendant, meaning that the plaintiff and defendant both are parties to the contract. So, at common law, no subcontractor could sue the owner for failing to pay for services rendered, even though the owner has received the benefit of those services. Rather, the subcontractors must commence action against the party with whom they directly dealt.

Legislation, such as Ontario's *Construction Lien Act*,[2] removes the obstruction to recovery that privity of contract imposes. The Act outlines the steps subcontractors must take to generate (preserve) and enforce (perfect) a lien against the land. The Act also establishes a less formal and faster procedure for enforcing the lien and recovering the debt through the courts. Finally, the statute creates a system of holdbacks to amass a fund from which all unpaid contractors on the project could be paid. Each time the owner pays the general contractor or one subcontractor pays another, a certain percentage must be held back to ensure the remaining unpaid contractors are paid.

Landlord's Right to Distraint

Provincial landlord and tenant legislation generally gives landlords a right to seize (*distrain*) a tenant's property located in the leased premises and sell it to satisfy arrears in rental payments. However, the landlord's right to **distraint** is limited. First, the landlord has rights only over property to which the tenant holds title. Second, the right to distrain entirely depends on the existence of a lease. So, if the landlord decides to terminate the lease and evict the tenant, the right to distrain the tenant's property is lost. Finally, should the tenant fall into bankruptcy, the landlord's right to distrain becomes a preferred claim for three months' back and three months' accelerated rent, which ranks ahead of most other creditors, under the *Bankruptcy and Insolvency Act*.

Other Statutory Liens

Various statutes create liens against a landowner's property for arrears in payments related to the land, such as real estate taxes, government loans for improvements to land, and utility services. Statutes create similar rights in employees against their employers for wages, vacation time, and other employee benefits accrued.

Conditional Sales Contracts and Repossession

Many sellers of expensive durable goods use a special form of contract called **conditional sales contracts**. These contracts give sellers a direct remedy against defaulting purchasers through the very goods sold.

In the standard conditional sales contract — say, for the purchase of a car — the buyer makes an initial down payment and agrees to pay the remaining balance with interest in monthly instalments of a specified amount for a specified time. The buyer obtains immediate possession, while the seller retains title until the balance owed is paid in full. The buyer also might agree to insure the car and keep it in good condition. These agreements typically also give sellers the right to repossess and resell the car if the buyer fails to make the monthly payments. The seller may exercise these rights in priority

---

[2] R.S.O. 1990, c. C-30.

to other creditors with claims against the purchaser. In many provinces, however, sellers need to register under a provincial *Personal Property Security Act* (for instance, Ontario's R.S.O. 1990, c. P.10).

The essential feature of conditional sales contracts, like other sales contracts involving credit, is the creation of a debt. As a result, the creditor has available the ordinary contract remedy for breach — namely, the right to sue to recover the debt.

The right to **repossession** and sale is a powerful remedy, with much potential for abuse by the creditor and serious hardship to the debtor. Accordingly, the provinces have instituted legislation to mitigate the harm to the buyer and curtail creditors' reckless use of the right. Although provincial statutes vary, they share some common features.

Most jurisdictions prohibit sellers from using force to regain possession of the goods sold. Although sellers are free to either enlist the services of the local sheriff or repossess the goods themselves, if they choose to do so themselves, they must employ no unlawful or abusive means. If the seller enters the buyer's property without permission or responds to the buyer's resistance with physical force, the buyer may assert claims against the seller for the torts of trespass and assault. The seller's proper response to a buyer's resistance is to obtain a court order authorizing the steps necessary to repossess the car. If the buyer continues to resist after a court order is issued, the buyer risks being held in contempt of court.

As observed, following repossession the seller may resell to a new purchaser. Many statutes protect buyers before the resale. The buyer generally has the right to regain possession if he pays the entire balance due plus any costs the seller incurred repossessing and initiating collection procedures. Notice must be given that the buyer's default in payment accelerates the deadline for full payment of the balance, meaning the buyer must now pay all remaining payments and not just the missed back payments to regain possession. Some provincial legislation defeats the seller's right to repossess after the buyer has completed a substantial portion of the contract, such as paying two-thirds of the contract price. These statutes protect buyers who have made timely payments for an extended period from losing the goods for missing one payment near the end of the contract. Were the law otherwise, the seller would receive a significant windfall for the buyer's minor breach.

Statutes also regulate the required notice, conduct, and distribution of proceeds from the sale. Generally, sellers may first reimburse themselves for the costs incidental to the resale, then apply the proceeds to satisfy the debt. In some jurisdictions, if the proceeds are insufficient to cover the debt, the seller retains the right to sue for the balance. Although rare, the situation may arise where the proceeds of the sale are greater than needed to clear the debt, resulting in a surplus. Under Ontario law, any surplus realized on repossession and resale, beyond that needed to pay the debt and all attendant costs, must be released to the debtor.

Many conditional sales contracts are further complicated by third parties. In practice, merchants often do not finance conditional sales arrangements themselves. Rather, the contract is turned over, or assigned, to a finance company for collection. If the debtor defaults, the seller is liable to the finance company. The finance company taking the contract is called the **assignee**. Under contract law, a contract's assignee takes the contract subject to any personal defences the buyer has against the seller. For example, if the goods are defective, the buyer may raise this as a defence against paying the finance company in the same way the defence could have been raised directly against the seller.

Bank Loans

Bank loans are regulated by the federal government, through the *Bank Act*.[3] One major feature of the Act is the inclusion of more kinds of assets permitted as collateral. The Act also identifies criteria as to who may qualify for a bank loan.

An important section of the Act, section 427, empowers chartered banks to lend to a wide range of businesses and tradespeople, including wholesale and retail purchasers of goods, manufacturers, farmers, and fisherpeople. Under section 427, borrowers may use as collateral the inventory, equipment, or future products of the business or trade. For example, a farmer may borrow money to finance the purchase of farm machinery, seeds, and other material needed to grow crops. In return, the farmer may use future crops that will be grown using the purchases made with the borrowed funds as collateral. Note that banks may take other types of security as well.

Borrowers are expected to use the money they earn through sale of the goods produced to reduce the outstanding loan. Should the borrower fail to do so, the Act provides the bank with a remedy against the goods or equipment used to secure the debt. Thus, the bank may take possession of the goods, sell them and apply the proceeds to reduce the debt and cover any incidental costs. If the sale yields a surplus, it goes to the borrower. If the sale does not raise enough to satisfy the debt, the bank may sue for the deficiency.

Foreclosure and Power of Sale

As noted above, in most transactions involving real property (land), the land itself secures the purchaser's debt. In transactions involving a mortgage, or charge, borrowers deliver a charge of their land to their lender, creating a legal interest in the land. In the event of default, the lender may enforce this interest in the land, using one of two main methods: foreclosure and power of sale.

In the power of sale, creditors have the right to seize and sell the charged property, following non-payment for a set number of months. For instance, under Ontario's *Mortgages Act*,[4] the right to sell arises on three months' default. Creditors must follow statutory requirements for giving all interested parties notice and conducting the sale. In a power of sale, creditors retain the right to sue the debtor for any deficiency but must relinquish any surplus to the debtor. Note that creditors need not first invoke the powers of the court to enforce their interest through a power of sale.

Conversely, foreclosure is a court action. In response to an action in foreclosure, a debtor may choose to file a response and defend against the action or try to cure the default. Creditors who succeed in their action become owners of the property and may do as they please with it. If they decide to sell the property and realize an amount greater than the debt owed, they may keep the surplus. However, if the proceeds of the sale do not fully satisfy the debt, they may not sue the debtor for the deficiency.

Enforcement of Security

Many different types of secured transactions and forms of collateral exist. Even so, key steps generally must be followed whenever creditors choose to enforce a secured interest.

Creditors must demand payment before enforcing their interest against a debtor's assets. The demand must provide the debtor with reasonable notice of the time within which the debtor must pay the amount demanded.

---

[3] S.C. 1991, c. 46.
[4] R.S.O. 1990, c. M-40.

Secured creditors next must choose an appropriate way to take control of the asset either by themselves or with a bailiff's help. Alternatively, where the asset is an operating business, creditors may ask the court to appoint a **receiver** to manage the business and collect the income.

Before the asset may be sold, notice must be given to the debtor and any others who may have an interest in the asset. The law clearly sets out the requirements for the amount, manner, and method of notice to give debtors a full and fair opportunity to cure the default and preserve their asset.

Finally, the law requires that the creditor act in good faith and in a commercially reasonable manner when selling the asset. Creditors who fail to meet the legal standards at any stage of the process could be liable for damages to the debtor or others injured as a consequence.

LITIGATION

Deciding whether to collect a debt through court action is not simple. The basic question that creditors must address is the likelihood of being able to enforce a court judgment if successful. Some debtors simply have no assets or income from which a judgment could be collected. Because we no longer punish individuals who cannot meet their debts, the creditor's judgment may be worthless. An individual with no assets or income is "judgment proof".

Given the expense and time involved in litigation, most creditors would not want to invest in obtaining a judgment that may never pay off. Similarly, creditors may decide that pursuing a court judgment against a business that has gone under due to extreme financial loss is not worth the effort. Before initiating court proceedings, creditors should carefully address the following questions:

- Is collecting this debt crucial to my financial position?
- Does the debtor have assets or income from which enforcement is likely?
- Is pursuing this debt worth possibly damaging my business relationship with this debtor?
- Are less expensive means available for minimizing the impact of not collecting this debt on my business (for example, as a "tax write-off")?

After weighing the costs and benefits, creditors who decide to pursue collection through litigation initiate an action by filing a claim with the appropriate court.

Generally, two levels of court hear these claims, depending on the amount of the debt and kind of relief the creditor seeks. In Ontario, the two courts are the Superior Court of Justice and the Ontario Small Claims Court. Using Ontario as an example, we will look at the major steps involved in the court process.

Small Claims Court

Small Claims Court offers a faster, cheaper, and relatively informal forum to litigate claims falling within its limited jurisdiction. Although the court applies settled principles of law, it operates extensively on good conscience and fairness. Many rules of evidence and trial procedure are relaxed, and the court helps litigants navigate the proceedings.

Small Claims Court jurisdiction is subject to the following restrictions:

- The claim must be to recover property or money.
- The amount of money or value of property must be below a specified amount.

- The action must be commenced in the territorial division where either the matter arose or the debtor lives or conducts business.

Although parties may have lawyers, many claims are successfully litigated in Small Claims Court without a lawyer's help. So, many choose to either represent themselves or be represented by a paralegal.

Before filing a Small Claims action, creditors send debtors a written demand letter, outlining the facts supporting the claim and the exact amount due. Next, creditors complete a pre-printed claim form, obtained from the Small Claims Court clerk. If asked, the clerk may help creditors — now plaintiffs — complete and file the form. The claim states all parties' names and addresses, a concise statement of facts in the case, and the exact amount claimed, including interest. Relevant documents, like invoices, are attached to the claim, which the plaintiff files along with a fee. The document is delivered to serve on the debtor, now the defendant, usually by a court bailiff.

Defendants must complete and file a defence within 20 days of being served with the claim if they wish to contest the matter. Again, defendants may complete the form themselves or have the Small Claims Court clerk help them. The defence form includes a concise statement of the defendant's reasons for disputing the claim. Both the claim and defence are drafted in plain language and focus on the facts.

A defendant with a claim against the plaintiff may raise it in the same action as a **counterclaim**, which is called a defendant's claim in Small Claims Court. If the counterclaim is for an amount exceeding the monetary threshold, a motion may be made to transfer the matter to a higher court. Similarly, if the plaintiff has sued more than one defendant, any defendant may file a **cross-claim** arising from the same transaction against a co-defendant. Finally, the defendant may bring an entirely new party into the matter, by filing a **third-party claim** against an individual also involved in the transaction that gave rise to the original claim. All of these are initiated through a defendant's claim. The plaintiff, and any others against whom claims are filed, may file responses.

At this point, many debtors acknowledge the debt and file no response to the claim. Under such circumstances, the creditor may obtain a **default judgment** against the debtor, by following the procedures set out in the rules of practice. If the claim is for a specific amount, the default judgment is issued administratively with no need for hearing. If an unspecified amount is demanded, the defendant is noted in default; a damage hearing is held, where a judge receives evidence and ascertains the amount of damages.

If the defendant disputes the claim, the parties are assigned a date for trial. Before the trial, the parties may exchange documents related to the case and typically engage in at least one pre-trial conference with a judge to try to settle the dispute and streamline the hearing.

The Small Claims Court trial is far less formal than a regular court proceeding, with judges taking an active role in drawing forth evidence and helping unrepresented parties present their cases. If a judgment is entered against the defendant debtor for an amount beyond a set limit, the debtor may file an appeal. If no appeal is taken, the plaintiff may take steps to enforce the judgment.

Formal Court Proceedings

Debts exceeding the Small Claims Court's monetary limits must be commenced in a formal court of record with strict rules of practice. As a result, most litigants in formal court proceedings are represented by a lawyer.

The plaintiff creditor commences an action by filing a formal **pleading**, called the statement of claim. The claim identifies the parties, states the

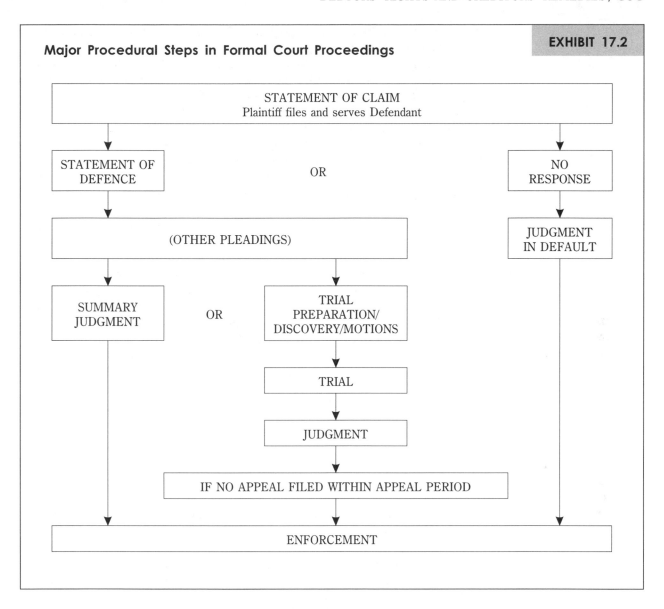

Major Procedural Steps in Formal Court Proceedings   EXHIBIT 17.2

precise relief requested and sets forth all material facts giving rise to the plaintiff's claim. The plaintiff may also request pre- and post-judgment interest, as well as costs of the litigation. The claim is filed along with the mandatory filing fee.

The plaintiff must deliver the statement of claim to the defendant. **Service** must be made on the defendant within six months of filing, although the court may grant an extension of this time if need can be established.

Once served, defendants must file a statement of defence within 20 days if they are within Canada, 40 days if in the United States, and 60 days if in another country. In their defence, defendants must specifically outline all of the plaintiff's allegations that they admit, all those that they deny, and those of which they have no knowledge. Furthermore, they must plead their own version of the facts and clearly assert all defences they have against the claim. Defendants may raise any counterclaim, cross-claim, or third-party claim in addition to their defence. In turn, the plaintiff may file a reply to the defence and a defence to the counterclaim. Parties on a cross-claim or third-party claim may also file responsive pleadings.

Defendants who do not respond to a statement of claim may face serious consequences. First, they are deemed to have admitted to all allegations that the plaintiff made in the statement of claim. Second, the plaintiff may have them noted in default. Finally, the plaintiff may obtain a judgment in default against them, avoiding the need for trial.

After the plaintiff has the registrar of the court note the defendant in default, the plaintiff may obtain the actual default judgment. Where the plaintiff's demand is for a liquidated amount or for property to be returned, the plaintiff's lawyer may file a requisition for the registrar to sign the default judgment. The requisition must include a copy of the statement of claim, proof that the claim was served on the defendant, and a proposed bill of costs of the proceeding.

If, instead, the plaintiff demanded an unliquidated amount, the final judgment cannot be obtained by simply filing a requisition. Rather, the plaintiff's lawyer must file a formal motion before the court. At hearing, the judge will either grant judgment or order that the case proceed to trial.

Whenever a default judgment is awarded, the defendant may file a motion to have the order set aside. To succeed, defendants must establish at a minimum that they received either no or insufficient notice of the claim.

Either the plaintiff or the defendant may obtain a judgment from the court without the need for trial by filing a motion for **summary judgment**. A summary judgment may be obtained only after the statement of claim and defence and any other pleadings in the case have been filed. Summary judgment is available where one party can demonstrate to the court that the case presents no genuine issue for trial. Rather, the case either presents only a question of law or no issue at all, and the party is, therefore, entitled to a judgment as a matter of law. The motion for summary judgment must set forth the grounds for entitlement and must include any affidavits, documents, transcripts or other evidence supporting the request. To counter the motion, the responding party must present evidence that the case does, in fact, raise a triable issue. The judge will then decide whether to grant the moving party summary judgment or send the case on for trial.

In contested matters, parties attempt to settle the matter by mutual agreement throughout the entire process, until a judgment is entered. Before trial, the parties also engage in various forms of **discovery**, or information sharing, including producing all relevant documents and orally questioning parties through examinations for discovery. An important part of the process, discovery helps define the real issues in the case, helps lawyers prepare for court, helps advance settlement, and helps prevent surprises at trial.

If no settlement is reached, the case is listed for trial. At the conclusion of the trial, a judgment is issued. The unsuccessful party has the right to file an appeal within a prescribed period of time. If no appeal is filed, the judgment becomes final. Creditors who have succeeded in obtaining judgment in their favour, from which no appeal is taken, must then begin the process of collecting or enforcing the judgment.

ENFORCEMENT OF ORDERS

Following the entry of an order in court, the debt becomes a judgment debt, and the parties are designated "judgment creditor" and "judgment debtor". At this point, assuming a judgment debtor has the means available, he or she may pay the entire judgment. Instead, the judgment debtor may make arrangements with the judgment creditors or through the court to pay the judgment over time. Some judgment debtors simply do nothing. In the face of no payment or arrangements, some judgment creditors choose to enforce their judgment through one or more available mechanisms.

Protection of the Debtor

Debtor's Rights

All of the enforcement mechanisms impose strict requirements for giving judgment debtors adequate notice of action planned against them. For instance, debtors must have an opportunity to contest the action or to prepare for the hardship that will follow. Notice also gives debtors one more chance to pay and stop the proposed action.

Assets Exempt from Enforcement

At early common law, sheriffs could seize nearly all debtors' assets except the clothes on their back. Both federal and provincial legislation greatly expand the protection afforded judgment debtors, by exempting certain property to ensure that debtors are left with some food, clothing, shelter, and means to earn a living. Even so, some exemptions are not available for debtors owing spousal or child support.

Federal exemptions include federal government benefits, such as Canada Pension Plan benefits, government annuities, and veteran's allowance benefits. The major common law exemption protects damages orders for pain and suffering awarded to the debtors in a lawsuit.

Provincial statutes supplement the federal and common law with a range of exemptions. Depending on the jurisdiction, these may include the following:

- Provincial welfare payments
- Pensions (except to satisfy an order for support and maintenance)
- Worker's compensation benefits
- Necessary and ordinary clothing, up to a certain value
- Household furniture and utensils, up to a certain value
- Tools of trade, livestock, equipment, feed and similar items of values specified in amounts
- A percentage of one's wages

Major Methods of Enforcement

Writ of Seizure and Sale

Under this procedure, the sheriff is empowered to take possession of the debtor's assets and sell them. The money realized is distributed to judgment creditors who have filed writs with the sheriff. To initiate this procedure, creditors obtain a writ from the registrar of the court after filing a requisition stating the date and amount of the judgment, the amount and dates of any payments the debtor made, and the amount remaining.

The creditor files the writ with the sheriff, along with a direction to enforce the writ. The writ remains in effect for six years from the date it is filed and may be renewed for an indefinite number of six-year periods before it expires.

In response to the writ and direction, the sheriff seizes all of the debtor's property within the Sheriff's jurisdiction. Creditors should file a writ in each district where they believe the debtor owns property. Where personal property (as opposed to real estate) is seized, the Sheriff must give the debtor an inventory of the seized items at the debtor's request.

Before selling the debtor's real and personal property, the sheriff must give the debtor notice, by both mail and newspaper publication. Even after a sale is held, courts will void any transaction if the debtor satisfies the debt before purchasers have paid for and received title to the debtor's property.

Finally, proceeds of the sale are distributed to the debtor's creditors, in the way the statute prescribes. Some provincial statutes require sheriffs to distribute the proceeds to all of the debtor's judgment creditors who have filed a writ called execution creditors.

Garnishment

A second enforcement method is income **garnishment**, which allows creditors to collect directly from third parties (garnishees) who owe money to the judgment debtor. For example, subject to the exemption of a certain percentage, the judgment debtor's employer could be required to pay a portion of the debtor's paycheque each pay period to the sheriff for the garnishor's benefit.

The judgment creditor starts the garnishment process by filing a requisition with the court registrar, including a copy of the judgment, an affidavit stating the amount owed, and the names of the proposed garnishees. The notice of garnishment is sent to the named garnishees, to the sheriff of the county where the proceeding began, and to the judgment debtor.

Once notified, the garnishee must pay the specified amount to the sheriff; failing to do so can result in an order against the garnishee and in favour of the garnishor. However, the rules do provide garnishees with a mechanism for contesting a garnishment by disputing the underlying debt to the judgment debtor. To dispute the underlying debt, the garnishee submits a garnishee's statement describing the grounds for dispute to the garnishor, to the judgment debtor, and to the court. The garnishor, the garnishee, the judgment debtor, and any other interested party may file a motion for a garnishment hearing to address any issues.

Examination in Aid of Execution

Many creditors do not ask for a significant amount of information regarding the debtor when entering into commercial relationships. So when collection problems arise, judgment creditors often have insufficient information to make adequate use of the available enforcement measures. Likewise, the judgment debtor's circumstances may change over the course of time required to fully satisfy a debt. The rules entitle judgment creditors to orally question debtors about their assets, liabilities, and resources for paying a judgment in an "examination in aid of execution".

At the examination, the debtors must disclose under oath all such information regarding the nature and location of all non-exempt property they own, all sources of income, any property they disposed of before or since entry of the judgment, and their intentions with regard to satisfying the judgment. In certain circumstances, such as situations involving debtors whose whereabouts are not known or who are entirely unco-operative, the court may permit the creditor to orally examine others with information about the debtors, their income or their assets.

Writs of Possession, Delivery, and Sequestration

Not all judgments are a sum of money. For instance, the judgment may instead permit the plaintiff to recover from the defendant a parcel of land or an item of personal property. Such judgments are enforced through a Writ of possession for land and a writ of delivery for personal property. Each Writ directs the property to be delivered to the judgment holder. If a writ of delivery is ignored, the aggrieved party may file a motion for a writ of sequestration, directing the sheriff to take possession of and hold the property until the party complies with the order.

Other Assistance

The court may provide other help to judgment creditors having difficulty enforcing judgments. Courts may issue contempt orders against judgment

---

	EXHIBIT 17.3
Tracing the Proceeds	

Suppose Joe owes Moe $100,000. Joe owns a cottage, valued at approximately $200,000, which he transfers to his wife, Roe. Roe sells the cottage to Beau for $200,000 and places the proceeds in her own bank account. If Moe obtains a judgment against Joe in court, provincial legislation allows Moe to unravel the transaction and trace the proceeds of the cottage's sale, originally owned by Joe, to Roe's individual bank account to enforce his judgment against Joe.

---

debtors for non-compliance and other obstructive behaviour, such as hiding or transferring property to others to defraud their creditors. Additionally, specific statutes provide creditors with relief from such wilful behaviour.

Other provincial statutes provide remedies for specific behaviour, such as transferring property to another to defeat creditors' rights. These statutes allow creditors to bring suit against the third party the property was transferred to and recover the asset. A common example is where debtors "sell" their property to friends or family for little or no money. Similar relief may permit creditors to trace the proceeds of a fraudulent sale of a debtor's property into the hands of others for recovery. (For an example, see Exhibit 17.3.) Some provincial laws also provide creditors with relief from debtors with insufficient assets to cover their debts who choose to pay some creditors and ignore others.

Finally, courts may appoint one or more individuals, called receivers, to help collect and distribute a debtor's assets. The receiver may, for example, collect rent from the tenants in a building the debtor owns or the income the debtor's business generates.

BANKRUPTCY

Individuals whose income and other assets are not sufficient to pay their financial obligations as they come due are **insolvent**. At some point following their insolvency, debtors may become **bankrupt** by voluntarily entering or being forced into the process governed by the federal *Bankruptcy and Insolvency Act*.[5] The Act provides a uniform procedure throughout Canada to address both creditors' and debtors' rights. The Act performs three essential functions for society:

- Protects creditors through a framework for fairly distributing a debtor's assets to all creditors.
- Gives debtors a chance to clear their debts and begin with a clean slate.
- Helps debtors and creditors compromise by restructuring all of the debts under court supervision.

Commencing the Proceedings

Consumer bankruptcy proceedings are initiated in one of three ways. First, the debtor may file an assignment in bankruptcy. Here, debtors recognizing the poor state of their financial affairs voluntarily assign their assets to a **trustee** for ultimate distribution to their creditors. Basically, the debtor files the assignment and a sworn statement of affairs. Depending on the size of the

---

[5] R.S.C. 1985, c. B-3 as am. by S.C. 1992, c. 27.

debtor's estate, the matter may be eligible for summary administration of the estate.

In the second method, an insolvent debtor starts a proceeding in the hope of avoiding bankruptcy by making a proposal to the creditors. Debtors, through a proposal trustee, offer their creditors a compromise plan for paying their debts. The creditors vote in classes to accept or reject the proposal. If the proposal is accepted by the creditors, it must be approved and supervised by the court. The debtor's later failure to meet the plan's terms may change the matter into a full bankruptcy proceeding. Likewise, the creditors' rejection or the court's disapproval of the plan generally leads to a declaration of bankruptcy.

The third method for commencing consumer bankruptcy proceedings is involuntary. Any of the debtor's creditors with a claim of $1,000 or more, or any group of creditors whose aggregate claims exceed $1,000, may file an application for a bankruptcy order against the debtor. The applicant must demonstrate that the debtor's creditors are not being paid and that the debtor has committed an act of bankruptcy under the Act within the past six months. Acts of bankruptcy cover a wide range of behaviour, including failure to meet liabilities as they come due, attempting to remove or hide property, and defaulting in a proposal to creditors. The debtor is served with notice, and a hearing is scheduled. Debtors wishing to dispute the application may file a response before the hearing date. If the creditors succeed, a bankruptcy order is issued and a trustee takes control of the debtor's assets and administers the bankruptcy.

Administering the Bankruptcy

Whether started voluntarily or forced by creditors, proceedings follow a similar course. Immediately, other proceedings that unsecured creditors have initiated to assert their individual claims against the debtor are frozen (stayed). Instead, creditors must file and prove their claims with the debtor's trustee. Secured creditors, however, generally retain their right to enforce their interest in secured property against the trustee. Debtors immediately lose the capacity to enter into contracts, engage in commercial activity, and deal with their property.

Within a specified number of days, the trustee calls the first meeting of the bankrupt's creditors to address preliminary matters, typically including the creditors' approval of the trustee's appointment, a review of the debtor's sworn statement of assets and liabilities, and the report summarizing the debtor's oral examination, and other matters related to administering the bankrupt's estate. The trustee must collect and sell the debtor's assets, through tender, public auction, or private contract. Strict guidelines mandate how assets are sold. Following disposition of the assets, the trustee distributes the proceeds to the creditors according to a scheme detailed in the Act. Under the scheme, subject to rights of secured creditors, proceeds are distributed in the following order:

1. Cover costs of administering the bankrupt's estate (including any legal fees)
2. Pay preferred creditors, as defined in the Act
3. Pay ordinary unsecured creditors, their *pro rata* shares equally

The underlying principle appears to treat all unsecured creditors equally. Absent bankruptcy, some of the debtor's creditors may be fully compensated, while others receive nothing. Through bankruptcy, all creditors who have proven their claims with the trustee receive a proportionate share of the available assets. Thus, no general creditor receives full payment, but neither is any left completely unpaid.

Discharging the Bankrupt

The final phase of the typical consumer bankruptcy is **discharging the bankrupt**, which gives the bankrupt a chance to start fresh, unencumbered by the burden of insurmountable debt. A discharge releases the debtor from liability for most debts remaining after distribution of the assets. In other words, the debts are treated as though paid in full.

Individuals facing a consumer bankruptcy for the first time are entitled to an automatic discharge from bankruptcy within nine months of the proceeding's start. Where no one objects, the discharge is entered either absolutely or with conditions imposed on the debtor.

Sometimes, one or more creditors or the trustee objects to the discharge. In that case, a hearing regarding the circumstances and the bankrupt's behaviour before and throughout the proceedings is held. Hearings also are required for bankrupts not initially entitled to an automatic discharge.

One circumstance that raises the need for a hearing is where the debtor's assets are too low to pay the creditors at least 50 cents on each dollar of debt. At hearing, bankrupts must satisfy the court that they cannot justly be held responsible for this result. Usually misconduct — such as refusing to co-operate during the process, hiding or transferring assets, or engaging in commercial transactions after insolvency — can jeopardize entitlement to a discharge.

Even absolute discharge does not release a bankrupt from certain debts. For example, family obligations, such as alimony and support arrears, will remain following discharge. Once discharged, the debtor is neither insolvent nor bankrupt, and regains the capacity to enter into contracts and own and deal with property.

CONSUMER PROTECTION LEGISLATION

To satisfy principles of justice and fairness, the law demonstrates an equal concern for the problems and rights of both debtors and creditors. Faced with the frustration inherent in collecting delinquent debts, creditors sometimes are tempted to use means beyond the bounds of what society considers appropriate. When creditors use legitimate methods excessively or use entirely impermissible approaches, both common and statutory law step in to protect debtors.

Creditors who exert undue pressure on debtors through constant harassment, threats of harm, and other offensive behaviour or who publicly malign debtors could find themselves liable under tort or criminal law. Debtors have successfully sued overzealous creditors for torts, including assault, trespass, defamation, and false imprisonment. Creditors have also faced prosecution for such criminal offences as threats, harassment, extortion, and conspiracy. So, even though creditors may at times need to exert some pressure to inspire payment, they must take care to never cross the line into tortious or criminal misconduct.

In addition to debtors' traditional remedies, Canadian provinces have enacted legislation to protect consumers from unfair business practices and unconscionable collection methods. Generally, these laws are designed to

- ensure consumers freely enter into contracts they truly intend to be bound by;
- protect consumers from defective, dangerous, and useless products;
- make consumers fully aware of the total costs of their contracts; and
- stop creditors from harassing, threatening, or injuring consumers in the collection process.

Most consumer protection legislation tries to balance consumers' and entrepreneurs' interests along with society's interest in encouraging the continued commercial activity a thriving economy needs. Although a detailed survey of the varied consumer protection laws Canadian provinces have enacted is beyond this chapter's scope, the following highlights a few key concepts.

Recognizing that many consumers might be induced to enter contracts for goods or services based on sellers' inflated claims only to find that their purchases fall disappointingly short of those claims, consumer protection laws typically prohibit unfair practices. For example, Ontario's *Consumer Protection Act* considers making any false, misleading, deceptive, or unconscionable representation to be an unfair practice. Below are some examples of false, misleading or deceptive representations:

- Representing goods are of a particular standard, quality, grade, style, or model that they are not
- Representing goods are available for a reason that does not exist
- Representing goods will be available or can be delivered at a specific time when it is known or ought to be known that they cannot
- Representing that goods are new or unused if they are not

Representations may be unconscionable when a seller knows or ought to know that, for instance,

- the consumers are not reasonably able to protect themselves because of disability, ignorance, illiteracy or inability to understand the language an agreement is in;
- the price grossly exceeds the price that similar goods and services are available for;
- the transaction is excessively one-sided in favour of the party dealing with the consumer; and
- the consumer is subjected to undue pressure to enter the transaction.

Depending on the jurisdiction, consumers induced to enter a contract as the result of an unfair practice may be able to rescind the contract and pursue any remedy available at law, including monetary damages. If the contract cannot be rescinded under the circumstances, the consumer may be able to recover the amount that the consumer's payment exceeded the true value of the goods or services delivered, the damages, or both.

Consumer protection legislation also typically regulates specific kinds of sales and contracts where consumers could be susceptible to pressure or caught off guard. For this reason, many provincial consumer protection statutes regulate agreements that are entered into over the telephone or Internet, or at locations other than the seller's place of business, or that involve credit or instalment payments. Additionally, statutes like Ontario's consumer protection law regulate what may be charged for repairs (to an automobile, for example) after a mechanic or other service provider has given the consumer an estimate of what the job will cost.

A third area provincial legislation regulates is the registration and practices of collection agencies. As noted above, creditors often hire collection agencies to contact their debtors to arrange or obtain payment. In addition to licensing and registration requirements, these statutes may create a general regulatory scheme, providing for investigations, hearings, sanctions, fines and even imprisonment. These provincial statutes also regulate collection agencies' operations and conduct. The wide range of behaviour these statutes prohibit includes, for instance,

- using threatening, intimidating, coercive or profane language;
- calling debtors on holidays and other specified days or times of day (such as early morning or late night);
- giving false or misleading information to others that might harm the debtor or debtor's family;
- continuing to contact a debtor who has provided the name and contact information of the debtor's lawyer and has asked that the lawyer be contacted instead; and
- contacting the debtor's employer except once to obtain employment information, unless the employer guaranteed the debt, the consumer has given written authorization, or a court order or wage assignment has been entered.

Additionally, these laws often establish how frequently collection agencies may contact debtors.

CHAPTER SUMMARY

In this chapter, the reader was introduced to the concept of debt, significant elements in the relationship between debtors and creditors, and the wide range of methods used to collect debts. The chapter described different ways to secure debt and other ways creditors may obtain an advantage in collecting their debts over other creditors' claims.

The reader was introduced to the procedure involved in litigating a creditor's claim against a debtor and the many devices available for enforcing a judgment obtained in court.

The chapter discussed the purposes and effect of bankruptcy proceedings and how the law of bankruptcy seeks to protect the interests of both creditors and debtors. A survey of the main steps involved in the typical consumer bankruptcy was included.

The discussion concluded with a brief look at legislation designed to protect consumers against unfair business practices and unconscionable collection activities.

GLOSSARY OF NEW TERMS AND KEY CONCEPTS

assignee	A person who has been granted a benefit by someone, usually a person granted contract benefits by one of the original contracting parties.
bankrupt	An insolvent person against whom or by whom bankruptcy proceedings have been instituted under the federal *Bankruptcy and Insolvency Act*.
collection agency	A business engaged in obtaining and arranging the payment of money owed to another.
conditional sales contracts	A contract where purchase obtains delivery of the goods, but does not obtain legal ownership until some or all of the purchase price is paid.
counterclaim	A claim asserted by the defendant against the plaintiff in a legal proceeding.
creditor	A person to whom a debt, or a specified sum of money, is owed.
cross-claim	In a legal proceeding by a plaintiff against two or more defendants, a claim by one defendant against a co-defendant.
debt	A sum of money one person owes to another.
debtor	A person who owes a sum of money to another.

default judgment	An order of court entered against a defendant who has failed to defend or respond to a legal action instituted in court.
discharge (of a bankrupt)	The release of a person from the legal status of bankruptcy. The person regains the legal capacity to enter into contracts and deal with his or her own property. The discharge may include forgiving unpaid debts.
discovery	The process of gathering and exchanging information relevant to a legal proceeding in preparation for trial of the matter. Discovery may include the production of documents and oral questioning of parties.
distraint	A landlord's right to take possession and sell a tenant's property found within the leased premises to compensate the landlord for unpaid rent.
garnishment	The process whereby a creditor may collect money from a third party who owes money to the debtor to enforce a court judgment the creditor has obtained against the debtor.
general creditor	An unsecured creditor who has no priority or special rights; a creditor who has neither taken nor otherwise acquired an interest in the debtors' assets to ensure payment of the debt.
insolvent	In general, one whose income and assets are insufficient to pay her obligations as they become due.
interest	The compensation paid to another for the use of money borrowed.
lien	A right to retain possession of property belonging to another to compel payment of a debt. A legal interest in property titled to another.
pleading	A document filed with the court, setting out a party's claim or defence in a legal proceeding.
principal	With respect to lending money, the amount the borrower originally borrowed and actually received.
receiver	A person appointed by a secured creditor or court to collect and hold income generated by assets owned by a party in a legal proceeding.
secured creditor	A creditor who has required that the debtor give collateral in return for the extension of credit or has otherwise acquired an interest in a debtor's property with respect to a debt.
security	A legal interest in real or personal property that a debtor gives to a creditor to ensure payment of the debt. Also known as collateral, the security gives the creditor access to the property if the debt is not paid and priority over other creditors regarding the asset used as collateral.
service	The delivery of a court document to a party in legal proceedings in the manner specified by the Rules of Civil Practice.
summary judgment	An order of the court in favour of a party who can satisfy the court that the case presents no issue of fact for trial or no issue at all.
third-party claim	In legal proceedings, a claim a defendant makes against a person not already a party to the proceedings, regarding the same event or transaction as the plaintiff's main action.
trustee	The individual responsible for the administration of a bankrupt's estate, including disposition of the bankrupt's assets and distribution of the proceeds to the bankrupt's creditors.

REVIEW QUESTIONS

1. Explain some of the reasons why a creditor might prefer out-of-court collection methods rather than commencing a court action against a debtor.

2. What is the difference between a secured creditor and a general creditor, and how do their rights differ?

3. What is a construction lien? In response to what dilemma was legislation providing for the construction lien passed?

4. Over what claims does a Small Claims Court have jurisdiction? Outline some of the major differences between litigation of a claim in Small Claims Court and in a formal court.

5. Define "garnishment" and identify the garnishor and the garnishee in these proceedings.

6. What are the main forms of protection provided to the debtor by law with respect to a judgment creditor's enforcement of a court judgment against the debtor?

7. Describe the main purposes and functions of the federal *Bankruptcy and Insolvency Act.*

DISCUSSION QUESTIONS

1. Billy Bob sues Buster in court for non-payment of a debt and obtains a judgment of $5,000. After the expiration of the appeal period, Billy Bob decides to enforce the judgment against Buster. Buster owns a fully paid boat, a stereo system, a valuable coin collection, and a cottage, all in the same location. He is currently employed by the Big Bang Balloon Company. How might Billy Bob go about enforcing his judgment?

2. Allard purchases an automobile from Zoey's Autorama for $7,000. He gives Zoey a down payment of $5,000, and agrees to pay the remaining balance in monthly instalments of $100. Allard and Zoey sign a standard conditional sale contract, which includes a clause permitting Zoey to repossess and sell the automobile in the event of Allard's default in payment. With three instalments remaining, Allard misses one monthly payment. In response, Zoey goes to Allard's home at 4:00 a.m. to repossess the automobile, which is parked in Allard's garage. The garage door is open, so Zoey enters. However, Allard, hearing a noise, goes to the garage and shouts, "Stop! Thief!" Zoey shoves him aside, jumps into the car, and drives away. Discuss the issues raised by the above and the likely outcome of those issues.

3. Chet takes his motorcycle to Freda's garage for repairs. Freda makes the needed repairs, then calls Chet to tell him that the motorcycle is ready to be picked up and that he owes her $600. Chet arrives at the shop and says, "I'm here to pick up my bike, but I can't pay you for a couple of months because I just got fired." What may Freda do?

4. Penny rents an apartment from Bill under a one-year lease. Penny fails to pay the rent for four months. Frustrated, Bill notifies Penny that he is terminating the lease and commences the process of evicting Penny. In the meantime, Bill takes possession of the property in Penny's apartment, including a stereo system and table Penny borrowed from her friend Guy. When Penny and Guy ask Bill to return the seized items, Bill states that he will return the property as soon as Penny pays the four months' back rent she owes. Discuss the issues raised by the problem.

5. Given that a secured creditor has far greater rights than a general creditor, why would a creditor ever choose to enter into an unsecured transaction?

SUGGESTED READINGS

Bennett, Frank. *Bennett on Bankruptcy*, 9th ed. (Toronto, Ont.: CCH Canada Ltd. 2006).

Bennett, Frank. *Bennett on Collections*, 4th ed. (Toronto, Ont.: Carswell, 1998).

Canada. *Bankruptcy and Insolvency Act*, R.S.C. 1985, c. B-3, as am. 1985 (1st Supp.), c. 27.

Kenkel, Joseph F. *Small Claims Litigation*, 3d ed. (Toronto, Ont.: Butterworths, 1998).

Olivo, L.M. *Debtor-Creditor Law and Procedure* (Toronto, Ont.: Emond Montgomery Publications, 1999).

Ontario. *Collection Agencies Act*, R.S.O. 1990, c. C-14.

Ontario. *Consumer Protection Act, 2002*, S.O. 2002, c. 30, Sched. A.

Zuker, M. *Ontario Small Claims Court Practice*, Annual ed. (Toronto, Ont.: Carswell).

Employment Law

Michael Mac Neil
CARLETON UNIVERSITY

Learning Objectives

After reading this chapter, the reader should be able to:

➢ identify different legal devices regulating the employer-employee relationship

➢ compare some of the advantages and disadvantages of each of the regulating devices

➢ identify rights of workers and employers in the employment relationship

➢ understand the interaction between contracts, statutes, and collective bargaining in defining employment rights and obligations

➢ know some of the institutions from which a worker can obtain assistance in claiming their rights

TABLE OF CONTENTS

GOVERNING THE WORKPLACE

Every society organizes systems for producing the goods and services it needs. In many non-industrialized societies, individuals or families are responsible for looking after most of their own needs, including the growing or hunting of food, the building of shelter, and the supplying of other necessities. In more complex societies, a division of labour occurs. People specialize in specific tasks, and sell their products or services to others, using either a barter or a money-payment system. This allows the specialists to acquire the necessities or luxury goods that they are not able to produce for themselves. In modern industrial societies, even more specialization occurs, and many goods or services are produced by large corporate or governmental entities, who hire workers to provide their labour for a wage payment and to work under the direction of persons responsible for the management of the workplace. This sale of labour for wages is the central feature of an **employment relationship**, and is the primary means by which most people in our society can expect to provide for their wants and needs.

Given the extent and importance of employment relationships in our society, it is not surprising that they are regulated by law. There are three main sources of regulation: contract, statute, and collective bargaining.

The Contract of Employment

The employment relationship is regarded as a contractual one. No one is forced to work against his will. To do so would be to impose a form of slavery upon him. The law assumes that people voluntarily agree to work for others, and the voluntariness is not undermined by the fact that people have to work to acquire the wages they need to pay for wants and necessities. Thinking of the employment relationship as a contractual one has a number of consequences.

Formalities

In order to determine if there is an employment contract, one must ensure that the formalities for entering a contract have been complied with:

- offer of employment
- acceptance
- **consideration** moving forward from both parties
- sufficient certainty

Contracts in Writing

The contract need not be in writing, unless it is for a period of more than one year. In many employment contracts, no definite period of employment is expressed, and such contracts need not be in writing.

Enforcement of Contracts

The general rules of contract law apply with respect to the interpretation and enforcement of the employment contract. This means, for instance, that a worker who claims that the employer has wrongfully terminated the contract by firing her is not normally entitled to reinstatement as a remedy, but is only entitled to damages for the wrongful dismissal.

Implied Terms

Where the contract is silent on an issue, as informal and even written contracts of employment sometimes are, the court will nevertheless find that certain rights and obligations are implied terms of the contract. For instance, there is an implied duty of loyalty placed on employees, and an implied duty on an employer to give reasonable notice before dismissing an employee, if the contract is of indefinite duration and does not explicitly set out the notice period. However, an express term in the contract will override a term that would otherwise have been implied.

One of the problems with thinking of the employment relationship as contractual is that one tends to lose sight of the fact that the contracting parties are not equal. In many situations, the employee does not bargain about the terms of the employment relationship, but instead takes or leaves the package that the employer offers. Thus, the employer sets the wage rate, and may include a variety of express terms in the contract that may limit the rights that employees might otherwise expect to obtain, such as the length of notice to which they are entitled before being laid off, or restrictions on taking a job with a competitor of the present employer.

Statutes

For many reasons, legislatures have enacted statutes that regulate the employment relationship. One reason is a concern that the inequality of bargaining power that exists between employers and employees often leads to contracts that are unfair. Hence, these statutes set out rights and obligations that apply, despite what a contract may say. These statutory interventions deal with many aspects of the employment relationship, including minimum terms and conditions of employment, occupational health and safety, discrimination in employment, workers' compensation for job-related illnesses and injury, unemployment insurance, and pension plans. More details on many of these statutes are provided in the discussion of employer and employee obligations.

Collective Bargaining

In Canada, **freedom of association** is regarded as a fundamental right. This means, in the context of employment, that employees in most workplaces have the right to form a union, and to demand that the union represent them in bargaining with the employer. Workers often decide to join together in such a fashion, at least in part, because they believe they are more likely to make a better deal with the employer through collective action than by having each worker enter into individual employment contracts. Legislation has been enacted by each province and the federal government that provides a mechanism by which a trade union can obtain **certification** as the bargaining representative of employees.

Once a union has been certified, the employer is required to **bargain in good faith** with the union, and no longer to bargain individually with employees. The legislation protects workers who engage in union activity by prohibiting employers from discriminating against or firing workers because they are engaged in such activity. As well, employers are prohibited from interfering with the activities of the trade union. These **unfair labour practices** give meaning to the concept of freedom of association.

If the union and the employer are successful in making a collective agreement, that agreement is binding for all employees in the bargaining unit, whether they agree with it or not. Some people have described the effect of a collective agreement as being similar to legislation, in that it sets out the rules to which the citizens (i.e., the workers) of the workplace are bound. The collective agreement typically deals with such issues as wages, job classifications, promotions, seniority, fringe benefits, etc. The agreement often contains a union security clause, which ensures financial security for the union, and may even make it a condition of employment that employees be members of the union. The collective agreement also must contain a clause providing that disagreements about the interpretation and application of the collective agreement shall be settled by **grievance or rights arbitration**.

If the parties are not successful in making a collective agreement, then the general approach of labour legislation in Canada, especially in the private sector, is to allow the parties to engage in strikes or lockouts as means of trying to force the other side to capitulate. A variety of conditions must be met before a strike can occur, but once those conditions are met, workers are free to withdraw their labour and to set up picket lines seeking support. The government, however, does seek to help prevent such strikes, or to bring them to an end, by providing conciliation and mediation services. Furthermore, picketing is stringently regulated. For many public-sector workers, although certainly not all, striking is prohibited, and the parties are required to submit their dispute to **interest arbitration**. As well, the government sometimes will decide that a strike, which is permitted by the statutes, is nevertheless causing too much harm to the public interest, and will enact an ad hoc statute requiring the strike to end, and usually providing for binding arbitration.

It is important to understand the interrelationship between collective bargaining and the other modes of regulating the employment relationship. A collective agreement displaces individual contracts of employment so that in a unionized workplace, an individual employee is not entitled to enter into an individual contract of employment. If such an employee is fired, for example, he would not be able to commence an action for wrongful dismissal, but must rely on the grievance/arbitration mechanism set out in the collective agreement to obtain a remedy. However, many statutory provisions regulating the workplace also apply to unionized workers. Hence, individual workers, or the union acting on their behalf, can make complaints that a statute has been violated. Some statutes, such as occupational health and safety laws and employment-equity laws, actually provide a role for the union, where one exists, on committees and in other aspects of the enforcement of the statutes.

THE EMPLOYMENT RELATIONSHIP

Forming the Employment Relationship

Although employment is a dominant means of organizing the performance of work in our society, it is not the only means. There are many people who work as **independent contractors**, selling their services to others. It is often necessary to distinguish between employees and independent contractors because many statutes apply only to employees, not to independent contractors. For instance, an independent contractor is not entitled to minimum protection guaranteed by the *Employment Standards Act*, nor must deductions be made from her pay for unemployment insurance.

At common law, there were a number of terms used to describe the employment relationship. It was once common to call it a master-servant relationship, and even today one can find the use of such language. Another term used to distinguish an employment contract from one made with an independent contractor is to call the former a contract of service, and the latter a contract for services. There is no single test for determining whether a person is an employee or an independent contractor. The most important factor that the courts will examine is the extent to which the employer is able to control the work being done. If the employer can specify the work and how it is to be done, it is more likely that the person performing the work is an employee.

However, the issue of control does not always determine the issue. For example, a doctor may be employed by a hospital or clinic, but when it comes to the treating of patients, very little control would be exerted by the employer. Hence, it is necessary to look at other factors as well, such as who owns the tools, who bears the risk of making a profit or loss, and where the work is being performed. Another way of thinking about it is to ask, "Whose

> | EXHIBIT 18.1 | Who Is an Employee? |

The manager of a convenience store makes a claim under the *Employment Standards Act*. To do so, she must establish that she is an employee for the purposes of the Act. The contract signed by the manager specifically states that the manager is not an employee but, rather, an independent contractor. The evidence establishes the following:

1. All stock handled by the manager remains the property of the company. A daily allowance is made for breakage or pilferage of the inventory, but any shrinkage beyond this amount is the responsibility of the manager. However, if a break-in occurred, the manager would not be responsible for what was stolen.

2. The manager is required to put up a performance bond, and any default in the contract by the manager, including quitting without notice, will allow the store to recover the full amount of the bond as liquidated damages for loss of profits and goodwill.

3. The company maintains ownership of the premises, all fixtures and merchandise. It holds the insurance policy on all assets. It supplies the shirts and aprons worn by the manager and provides laundering at its expense.

4. The manager has discretion to determine hours of work, is free to hire others to assist her, and has discretion in the ordering of goods. However, the manager is required to devote her whole time to the business, and is not permitted to engage in another. Any wages paid to the assistants are made by the company, but are deducted from the amounts otherwise payable to the manager. The company regularly monitors these additional employees, provides them with uniforms, and pays for laundry. The manager can only order inventory from suppliers designated by the company.

5. A clause in the contract allows the contract to be terminated at any time, with or without cause.

On the basis of these factors, an adjudicator concluded that the store manager was, indeed, an employee for the purposes of the *Employment Standards Act*, rather than an independent contractor. Do you agree?

business is it?" Is the person carrying on business for himself, or is he working for somebody else? Another way of attempting to answer the question is to ask whether the worker is part of the employer's business — i.e., whether she is functionally integrated into the employer's operations. Still another test looks at the economic realities of the relationship.

In all of these tests, it is often a matter of weighing conflicting elements in order to determine the outcome. Even where a contract explicitly states that a person is not an employee, when one looks at all the elements of the relationship, it may still be possible to conclude that it really is an employment one.

The issue is becoming more problematic these days because employers are often seeking the greater flexibility and, sometimes, lesser costs that can be achieved by using contractors. With the growing emphasis on knowledge-based jobs, with less need for production-line work, and with the use of computers and modems at home, the issue of what constitutes an employee is a challenging one.

Employers' Obligations

In the individual employment relationship, the obligations owed by the employer to the employee arise from three sources. First are the express contractual provisions. For example, the duty to pay wages for work done is normally a contractual one, although employment standards legislation now typically stipulates that at least a minimum wage must be paid. The second major source of obligations is the various statutes described above. They impose a wide variety of obligations on employers and create rights for employees, as well as creating institutional mechanisms by which those rights can be enforced. A third source of obligations arise from implied terms in the employment contract by courts. These terms are sometimes meant to fill in gaps where the parties have failed to specify necessary terms, and are sometimes a means of incorporating customary practices into the legal framework. A discussion of some of the employer's most important obligations follows.

Payment of Wages

All Canadian provinces impose a minimum-wage requirement. As of May 2008, Ontario has the highest general minimum wage of $8.75 an hour, with this scheduled to rise to $10.25 per hour by March 31, 2010. Six provinces have general minimum wages set between $8.00 and $8.50 per hour. Prince Edward Island has the lowest general minimum wage, as of May 1, 2008, at $7.50 per hour. There are a number of reasons governments have introduced minimum wages: to help combat poverty, prevent exploitation of workers, and further equality goals. However, minimum wages have been criticized as distorting labour markets and causing employers to invest more in labour-saving devices, thus causing higher levels of unemployment. In practice, minimum-wage levels are rarely high enough to ensure that a family would be able to live above the poverty level on the minimum wages of a single-wage earner. As well, minimum-wage schedules often provide for a lower minimum-wage level for youths, and for employees who receive tips, such as waiters and bartenders.

Some employees believe that it is unfair that employers may make deductions from their wages. In Ontario, a regulation pursuant to the *Employment Standards Act* stipulates that no deductions may be made from wages unless required by statute or a court order, or if a written authorization by the employee so permits. Even with a written authorization, the employer may not make deductions for faulty workmanship, loss of property, or cash shortages if another person, other than the employee, has access to the cash or property.

The biggest pay-related problem for workers arises from the fact that the employee is, in effect, a creditor of the employer. An employee does not typically get paid until after the work has been done. For a variety of reasons, an employer may refuse, or be unable to pay, the wages owed. As a creditor, the employee has a number of avenues that can be followed, such as bringing an action in court; but typically, these are unsatisfactory because of the expense and delay involved. For that reason, it is common for employment standards legislation to create special mechanisms for the collection of wages owed. Where the employer has become insolvent or bankrupt, in the absence of statutory protection, workers would merely rank as unsecured creditors. This means that, after all the secured creditors have seized all the assets, they would not be very likely to recover any or a substantial portion of the payments owed to them. Some employment standards Acts seek to alleviate this problem to some extent by treating the claims of employees as if they were secured interests, thereby allowing employees to rank ahead of unsecured creditors. Another means of increasing the likelihood of employees receiving their wages is to make the directors of a company personally liable for wages in the event that the company fails to pay. However, even this protection is not likely to guarantee the payment of all wages owed.

Employment Standards

Employment standards legislation typically covers a wide variety of issues. As already mentioned, it provides for minimum wages and mechanisms for the collection of wages owed. It also provides for minimum standards for such issues as vacations, overtime work and pay, fringe benefits, notice of termination, parental leave, etc. The exact details of these statutory provisions vary from province to province; but normally, these standards are minimums, which means that the parties to the employment contract may negotiate terms that are better for the employee, but may not include contract terms that provide for less than these minimums. Any contractual term that provided for lesser benefits would not be enforced. In some jurisdictions, a union can agree in a collective agreement to provisions that may not be as good as certain statutory standards, and some statutory provisions may not apply at all to any employee covered by a collective agreement.

Not only do the statutes provide substantive rights, they also often create special mechanisms for the enforcement of these rights. Rather than requiring employees to go to court to collect wages owed or to obtain other remedies for violation of the statute, a special process will be established for receiving and dealing with employee complaints. In Ontario, for example, a complaint may be made to the Ministry of Labour. An employment standards officer is typically appointed to investigate the complaint, and if she finds that it is warranted, she may make an order requiring the employer to comply with the Act. An order, or the refusal to make an order, can be reviewed by the Labour Relations Board, whose decision can be reviewed by a court. Employees covered by collective agreements, however, must file a grievance and use the dispute resolution process created by the collective agreement. They are not entitled to file a complaint with the Ministry of Labour.

One of the problems with employment standards legislation is that it often fails to provide swift relief to employees. There may be insufficient resources allocated to the enforcement of the statute, so there may be considerable delays in obtaining any sums that owed.

Healthy and Safe Working Environment

One of the ongoing problems facing workers is the hazards to which they are exposed in the workplace. Every year, thousands of workers are injured on the job, many are affected by illnesses that can be linked to workplace conditions, and many die. The law has a role to play both in attempting to reduce the level of workplace injuries and illnesses, and in providing compensation to those who would otherwise lose income as a result of these illnesses and accidents.

At common law, employers were required to provide workers with safe tools, a safe system of work, and fellow workers who did not carelessly endanger them. However, the common law duty has largely been made irrelevant by the introduction of statutory regimes imposing a wide range of requirements on employers to ensure that workplaces are healthy and safe. As well, workers' compensation statutes provide a means of ensuring income security to injured workers, while simultaneously providing incentives for employers to make investments that will ensure a safer workplace.

Occupational health and safety statutes use a number of devices to protect workers:

1. *General performance standards.* These impose obligations on employers and employees alike, similar to those that existed at common law, to take reasonable steps to ensure the health and safety of the workplace. These provisions are enforced by inspectors, and by the possibility of prosecution, which normally takes place only if a serious accident has occurred.

2. *Set specific standards.* These may include the wearing of protective equipment, the guarding of dangerous equipment, the reduction of toxic

substances in the workplace, etc. These standards can be enforced by inspectors who have the authority to order an employer to comply, failing which fines may be imposed, or the employer's operations shut down until compliance is achieved.

3. *Joint responsibility.* Employers and employees are required to co-operate on committees that investigate and come up with plans for making the workplace safer.

4. *Right to refuse unsafe work.* Employees are given the right to look after their own interests by refusing to perform work that they believe is unsafe. There may be disagreements about whether work is actually unsafe, so processes are normally established by which an inspector can be called in to assess the situation. To make the right effective, an employee who reasonably refuses unsafe work must be protected from discipline or dismissal by the employer.

5. *Providing information.* One means of ensuring that workers act in a safe manner and take steps to protect themselves is to ensure that they are informed about the hazards in the workplace, and the best means of dealing with those hazards. Occupational health and safety statutes now provide for a system called **WHMIS (Workplace Hazardous Materials Information System)**, in which manufacturers of hazardous products are required to label their products and provide information about the hazards. Employers, in turn, are required to train workers in the identification and handling of hazardous products.

None of these measures ensure that workers will not be injured on the job, and they have often been criticized for their inadequacies. For instance, prosecution is often not an effective deterrent, in part because few contraventions of the Act are prosecuted, convictions are difficult to obtain, and the level of fines in the past has not been large enough to be a major deterrent. The inspection system has been criticized because of low levels of staffing, a traditional reluctance of inspectors to be confrontational, and because of the difficulty of having an outsider impose the best solutions on a particular workplace. The setting of standards has been problematic, with standards set at such levels that workers continue to be exposed to risks, and to bear the uncertainties where scientific evidence has not yet established clear causal links between toxic substances and workplace diseases. Internal responsibility systems have not been as effective as they may have been, in part because of the failure to actually establish them as required in some workplaces, as well as the lack of training for committee members, inadequate communication in the workplace, and failure to give the health and safety committee any real powers to make changes in the workplace.

Workers' Compensation

Given that workers continue to be injured, some system must be in place to provide compensation for injured workers. **Workers' compensation** statutes were introduced early in the 20th century in recognition of the inadequacies of the common law system. At common law, an employee had to prove that an employer was negligent in order to establish a claim, and a variety of defences were available to employers that made it difficult for workers to succeed. Under the workers' compensation Acts, the right of workers to sue their employer in court was taken away, in exchange for a guarantee of a right to compensation for a workplace-related illness or accident, without having to prove that the employer was at fault. Over the years, the levels of benefits have changed, but the system has remained relatively stable.

The payments to workers are funded by premiums paid by the employer. These premiums reflect the level of claims made by workers in that particular industry, and may also include a factor that measures the safety record of the individual employer (**experience rating**). The use of individualized experience rating is designed to encourage employers to invest more in safety. The danger is that it may cause an employer to pressure workers not to report compensable injuries.

There are several aspects of workers' compensation schemes worth mentioning:

1. *Not all employees are covered by the legislation.* Typical exclusions include homework, funeral work, taxidermy, veterinary work, education, photography, etc. One must consult the legislation and regulations in each province to determine who is and who is not covered.

2. *No compensation will be paid unless the disease or accident arises out of and in the course of employment.* It will often be difficult to pinpoint the cause of a worker's illness, and there is often considerable litigation about whether a worker's absence is caused by an injury or disease that arose out of, and in the course of, employment. This is particularly problematic with respect to diseases that may have long incubation periods, and the best one can demonstrate is a probability that there is a connection between workplace exposure to a toxic substance and the disease.

3. *The heads and quantum of compensation are determined by the legislation.* There are four main categories of benefits: death, total disability, permanent partial-disability, and temporary. As well, medical expenses and costs of rehabilitation are normally covered. Workers usually obtain only a percentage of lost wages, ranging from 75 to 90 percent, with an upper cap on the wages that will be covered. This is, in part, designed to discourage workers who are able to work from malingering.

4. *A complex administrative system is established to administer workers' compensation statutes.* In Ontario, the Workplace Safety and Insurance Board and its employees make decisions about whether an injury is compensable, the level of compensation, the level of premiums to be levied, etc. There is typically some process by which initial decisions can be appealed.

Anti-Discrimination Legislation

Discrimination in employment is generally prohibited by human rights statutes. This means that employers are generally prohibited from discriminating on named grounds, both in making decisions about whom to employ, and with respect to terms and conditions of employment. The grounds of prohibited discrimination have increased over the years. Ontario, for example, now prohibits discrimination on the following grounds: race, ancestry, place of origin, colour, ethnic origin, citizenship, creed, sex, sexual orientation, age, record of offences, marital status, family status, and handicap.

Human rights norms clearly evolve over time. For example, many jurisdictions commonly defined "age" in their human rights statutes so as to allow employers to engage in a policy of mandatory retirement at the age of 65. The Supreme Court of Canada held that defining "age" in this way did not violate the equality guarantee in section 15 of the *Charter of Rights and Freedoms*, at least as applied to university professors. However, with changing demographics, many governments now wish to encourage workers to work for longer periods, and so many provinces such as Ontario and British Columbia that used to permit mandatory retirement no longer do so.

Another example of emerging human rights norms can be found in relation to the prohibition of discrimination on the basis of family and marital status. Again, because of changing demographics, as well as due to increased participation of women in the workforce, and because of greater commitment of fathers to family responsibilities, employers are being asked to accommodate family responsibilities, especially child care arrangements. Courts, arbitrators and human rights tribunals are struggling to determine the extent of employers' duties in this area.

The prohibition on discrimination means that an employer may not ask certain kinds of questions when hiring people. For instance, questions about race, marital status, ethnic origin, etc. would normally not be permitted, unless the employer can demonstrate that questions relate to a ground of discrimination that is not prohibited by the statute.

Proving that discrimination in hiring has occurred is often very difficult. In the absence of a direct statement made by the employer, the most that the individual can do is show that they applied for the job, were qualified for the job, did not get the job, and either that the job has not been filled or has been filled by someone who is not a member of the same class listed in the statute. In that event, the onus would then be placed on the employer to provide a credible explanation of how the decision was made without any discriminatory intent.

It is not, however, necessary to demonstrate that an employer had the intention to discriminate, if it can be shown that the effect of an employer's policy is to discriminate. For an employer to demonstrate the acceptability of a rule or standard that either directly discriminates or has an adverse impact on a identifiable group, it can show that the rule is a *bona fide* **occupational requirement (b.f.o.r.)**. The Supreme Court of Canada has held that the employer must show: "1) that the employer adopted the standard for a purpose rationally connected to the performance of the job; 2) that the employer adopted the particular standard in an honest and good faith belief that it was necessary for that legitimate work-related purpose; and 3) that the standard is reasonably necessary to the accomplishment of that legitimate work-related purpose." To demonstrate the last point, the employer must show "that it is impossible to accommodate individual employees sharing the characteristic of the employee without imposing undue hardship on the employer" (**reasonable accommodation**).

Another discrimination issue of which both employers and employees should be aware is **harassment**. Harassment can occur on any of the prohibited grounds of discrimination, but the one that has received the most attention is harassment on the basis of sex and race. Harassment can take several forms. One form, sometimes referred to as **poisoned environment** harassment, involves a course of vexatious conduct or comment that is known, or that ought reasonably to be known, to be unwelcome. This might involve sexual or racial slurs, propositioning, etc. A second form, applicable primarily to sexual harassment, is sometimes called **quid pro quo harassment**. It involves a sexual solicitation or advance made by a person in a position to confer or deny a benefit or advancement, where it is known or ought reasonably to be known that the solicitation or advance is unwelcome. It also includes reprisals, or threats of reprisals, where such a solicitation or advance is rejected.

Harassment can be engaged in by managers towards the workers for whom they are responsible or by co-workers, or it can arise between customers and employees. The employer has an affirmative duty to prevent such harassment, and there is a growing trend towards requiring the establishment of sexual harassment policies, through which workers are clearly informed about prohibited conduct, and that provide mechanisms through which com-

---

EXHIBIT 18.2   **Firefighters, Aerobic Capacity and Indirect Discrimination**

In 1994, the government of British Columbia introduced a set of standards to ensure the ability of their employees engaged in fighting forest fires to perform their jobs safely and efficiently. Meiorin, a female, had been hired three years earlier, and had been found to be a satisfactory employee. However, of the four tests she was required to complete, she was unable to meet the standard for one designed to test aerobic capacity. She took 11 minutes, 49.4 seconds to run a designated distance — the standard required that she be able to do it in 11 minutes. As a result of her failure to meet the standard, she was dismissed. Her union filed a grievance on her behalf, arguing that the standard was discriminatory.

The Supreme Court of Canada accepted evidence that, owing to physiological differences, most women have lower aerobic capacity than men, and that most women, even with training, could not increase their aerobic capacity to the level required by the standard. This meant that the standard, on its face, had a discriminatory impact, with the consequence that the employer had to demonstrate that it was a b.f.o.r. The Court accepted that the standard was adopted for a purpose rationally connected to the performance of the job: namely, to ensure safety and efficiency. It also accepted that the standard was adopted in good faith. However, it rejected the claim that the standard was reasonably necessary to ensure safe and efficient performance of the job. Part of the problem was that the employer was not able to show that the process by which the standard was developed took sufficient account of the differing aerobic capacities of men and women and, therefore, was unable to show that the standard did not discriminate unnecessarily on the basis of sex. Furthermore, the employer failed to demonstrate that it could not accommodate Meiorin without undue hardship, given the evidence that she had been performing the job satisfactorily for three years without imposing any safety risks on herself, her colleagues or the general public.

As a result, the employer was ordered to reinstate Meiorin to her position as a firefighter, and to compensate her for her losses flowing from her dismissal.

Source: *British Columbia (Public Service Employee Relations Commission) v. BCGSEU (Meiorin)*, [1999] 3 S.C.R. 3.

---

plaints about such conduct can be adequately investigated and remedied if it is found that there has been harassment.

If a person is unable to obtain a satisfactory resolution of a complaint of discrimination or harassment through the employer, a formal complaint can be made to a human rights commission, which will investigate the complaint. If it finds that there is some basis to the complaint, it will often try to mediate a settlement. If that is not successful, the commission then can refer the complaint to a board of inquiry or adjudication panel, which will conduct a hearing and make a binding decision. The commission will normally represent the complainant at such a hearing, thus relieving the individual of the expense of self-representation; although in practice, complainants sometimes choose to have their own independent representation. An alternative avenue of redress is open to employees covered by a collective agreement. They can file a grievance, and arbitrators in many jurisdictions have been granted the authority to interpret and enforce human rights statutes.

There are many criticisms of the human rights system. In particular, it has been noted that despite the existence of human rights commissions for some time, there is substantial evidence of under-representation of women, visible minorities, and the disabled in many workplaces. As well, there is considerable evidence demonstrating that women's work is under-valued in terms of remuneration. The traditional human rights statutes have not adequately addressed systemic forms of discrimination, and this is now leading, in some jurisdictions, to new forms of legislation that attempt to address problems of pay and employment equity.

Pay Equity

There is considerable evidence to demonstrate that women are under-paid compared to men. There are a number of reasons why this might occur, including lower educational attainment of women, their frequent absences from the workforce because of parental and familial obligations, working shorter hours, etc. However, even when these factors are taken into account, studies show there is a significant portion of the differences in pay that can only be accounted for by discrimination. This discrimination may take the form of segregating women in lower-paying jobs, and under-valuing the worth of their work.

There have been several traditional legal responses to this form of discrimination in employment standards and human rights statutes. The first was to impose a requirement of **equal pay for equal work**. This required that if a man and a woman, working for the same employer, were doing the same job, they should be paid the same. The requirement of equal work meant that the two jobs had to be substantially the same before they could be compared. For instance, a nurse's aide and a nurse's orderly have been held to be performing the same work. A comparison of this kind allows protection against the most overt forms of discrimination, but it does little to deal with the problems of occupational segregation and under-valuing of women's work.

The second response was to require **equal pay for work of equal value**. Under this standard, rather than comparing two jobs, one compares the value of the jobs being performed. Value is normally determined by looking at a composite of skill, effort, responsibility, and the conditions under which the job is being performed. This allows for the comparison of jobs, say that of a gardener and a secretary, even though the two jobs are not the same. However, the mechanisms for the implementation of equal pay for equal value have often been inadequate, relying on individual complaints, which for various reasons are often not made.

Pay equity statutes have been the most recent attempt in some jurisdictions to deal with the problem of pay inequality. The organizing concept continues to be equal pay for work of equal value, but the process by which it is achieved is substantially different. A positive obligation is placed on employers to achieve pay equity by preparing a pay equity plan. To do so, the employer must systematically compare female and male job classes to determine whether pay equity exists. This requires a classification of jobs into male and female classes, an evaluation of the value of those job classes, and a comparison of pay rates for those classes. If this process of evaluation demonstrates that pay inequities exist, the employer is required to rectify the pay inequities within a specified time period. The pay equity statutes in most jurisdictions apply only to public sector workers, except in Ontario where private sector employers with more than 100 employees are required to develop a pay equity plan.

Despite these developments, a number of questions must be asked. One is how one deals with the problem when there is no male job class to which a female job class can be compared. Another is to ask whether one should concentrate on only the wage element of discrimination, or whether one should also focus on the factors that cause occupational segregation. This might involve emphasizing the education of women for jobs that have not been traditionally regarded as women's work, and the use of affirmative action strategies to overcome job segregation.

Employment Equity

It is widely acknowledged that discrimination is sometimes systemic in nature, and many argue that systemic remedies and more proactive strategies are required to eliminate these forms of discrimination. Systemic discrimination is often identified by the under-representation of certain groups of employees in particular workplaces or particular occupations. For example, if there is evidence that five per cent of all job applicants have disabilities, but evidence shows that less than one per cent of workers in a particular workplace have a disability, then one might want to look more closely to determine if this under-representation is the result of systemic forms of discrimination. There have been several human rights cases where employers have been ordered to engage in a thorough review of their hiring and promotion policies in order to identify and eliminate barriers to employment of women and visible minorities. In addition, the federal government has enacted **employment equity** legislation, imposing obligations on federally regulated employers to take steps to achieve more equitable representation of certain designated, traditionally under-represented groups: namely, women, Aboriginal people, visible minorities and disabled workers. Ontario had a similar statute in effect for several years, but it was repealed in 1996. A much more limited statute, applying to public sector employers and confined to removing access barriers for persons with disabilities, was enacted in Ontario in 2001.

Under the federal *Employment Equity Act*, the employer is required to collect workforce data that will enable it to determine the representation of the designated groups in various occupations. The employer is then expected to assess the extent to which designated groups are under-represented in all occupational categories. Next, the employer is expected to review its employment systems to determine what barriers, if any, might be contributing to the under-representation of designated groups. The employer should then, in consultation with employees and any unions representing its employees, develop plans to eliminate these barriers, and to accommodate members of under-represented designated groups. Normally, the employer will be required to establish hiring and promotion targets, as well as representation targets, and to put in place positive programs that will help to achieve these targets.

The *Employment Equity Act* is a controversial statute. While there may be a fairly general consensus about the goal of eliminating discrimination in our society, there is considerable disagreement about the means by which it should be achieved. Proponents of the statute argue that previous attempts to deal with the problem through human rights statutes have failed, as is evidenced by the continuing under-representation of the designated groups in many workplaces, occupational categories and levels. Opponents of the statute claim that the imposition of numerical goals amounts to a form of reverse discrimination and is antithetical to the norms of equality before the law and equal opportunity, which they claim are part of our socio-legal heritage. They argue that more qualified members of non-designated groups will end up not being hired. These people end up being innocent victims who bear the burden of eliminating discriminatory activities in which they did not engage. Proponents, however, argue that while these individuals may not be responsible for the discrimination, they are often the beneficiaries of past discriminatory activities, and that individuals have no claim of right to particular jobs: a society can take measures to distribute employment opportunities in order to alleviate the consequences of past discriminatory conduct and to produce a more just distribution of employment opportunities.

Employees' Obligations

Employee obligations arise from the same three sources as those of employers: express terms, statutory regulation, and implied terms. However, as you may have noted from the analysis of employer obligations, the use of statutory regulation is very important in determining the rights of employees and the obligations of employers. An analysis of employer rights and employee obligations tends to demonstrate, however, that express, and especially implied,

EXHIBIT 18.3

Employees' Obligation — Loyalty and Whistleblowing

Employees are expected to be loyal to their employers. The Supreme Court of Canada has held, for example, in a case involving a federal government employee, that the employee must not engage in a "sustained and highly visible attack on major Government policies" as that displays a lack of loyalty to the employer that is "inconsistent with his duties as an employee": *Fraser v. PSSRB*, [1985] 2 S.C.R. 455. However, there are also situations where there may be a public interest in encouraging employees to act as whistleblowers, to report illegal action or wrongdoing, an obligation that may conflict with the obligation of loyalty. The Supreme Court has indicated that such whistle blowing may be justified where the employer is engaged in illegal acts or policies that jeopardize the life, health, or safety of the employee or of others. Nevertheless, it is clear that the duty of loyalty may act as a limit on the free expression rights of employees, especially government employees. A number of cases have emphasized the especially high loyalty expectations on employees such as police officers, the breach of which can easily justify dismissal.

More recently, various statutes have been enacted designed to protect whistle blowing employees, whether public servants or private sector employees, from discipline or dismissal. The federal Public Servants' Disclosure Protection Act, for example, prohibits reprisals against a public servant who has made a disclosure pursuant to the Act, and provides that a complaint about a reprisal may be made to the Public Sector Integrity Commissioner. The Saskatchewan Labour Standards Act prohibits reprisals against employees who have reported unlawful activities to a lawful authority. The Supreme Court of Canada has held that this provision protects an employee who has reported financial misconduct by her immediate supervisors to supervisors further up the ladder within the employer organization: *Merk v. International Association of Bridge, Structural, Ornamental and Reinforcing Iron Workers, Local 771*, 2005 SCC 70.

contractual terms play a much more important role. This may be a reflection of the power relations that exist between employers and unions, and the tendency of the judiciary to regulate the employment relationship in such a way as to fortify property rights and status concepts.

An employee's express obligations tend to take the form of an agreement to perform the job specified in accordance with the rules and regulations of the employer. There may be details about the hours to be worked, breaks, vacation periods, etc. One problematic issue that sometimes arises is the extent to which an employer is entitled to modify those obligations, for example, by transferring the employee to a new location or by changing job duties. The employer's right to do so may arise as an implied term of the contract or as a result of mutual agreement between the parties. An employee who refuses to accept such changes may be entitled to quit and to bring an action for **constructive dismissal**, arguing that the employer's unilateral attempt to modify the obligations of the employee is a breach of the contract of employment. Constructive dismissals are discussed in more detail later in this chapter.

Another express obligation to which many employees are subject arises from restrictive covenants contained in the contract of employment. A **restrictive covenant** is a promise by the employee not to do certain things that might harm an employer's goodwill, data, trade secrets, or expertise. A restrictive covenant will often limit the right of an employee to go to work for a competitor or to set up a business in competition with that of the employer. The law has traditionally been somewhat suspicious about restrictive covenants, because they limit the rights of individuals to engage in economic activity. Hence, before a court will enforce a restrictive covenant, it must be satisfied that the covenant is reasonable, and needed to protect a legitimate proprietary interest of the employer. Hence, restrictive covenants often specifically refer to a geographical location, a specified time limit, and a precise occupation in which the employee is limited in competing with the employer. An employer is not entitled to merely prevent competition, but is entitled to protect legitimate assets such as goodwill, trade secrets, and confidential information. If employees have been wrongfully dismissed, they would not be bound by the terms of a restrictive covenant.

Most of the important obligations owed by an employee to the employer arise as the result of implied terms. These include obligations to be loyal and work in furtherance of an employer's interest, to obey lawful orders, to avoid misconduct, to work in a competent manner, to serve honestly and faithfully, and to indemnify the employer for economic losses arising from the employee's negligence. Upper-level managerial employees and directors of a company also owe **fiduciary duties** to the employer, in addition to the obligation of fidelity. This, in effect, means that such an employee is not entitled to try and capture for herself a business advantage or opportunity that rightfully belongs to the company.

These obligations have their genesis in the historical master-servant relationship, which depended on notions of status. In other words, they do not arise out of express agreement by the employee, but out of the idea that certain obligations arise from your status in life. The status of servant makes one subject to the rule of the master, and the servant is expected to act in accordance with the master's wishes and interests. While modern courts no longer use the language of master and servant, they have adapted the law so that the employer-employee relationship continues to be one in which the employee is expected to act in ways that further the interests of the employer. The content of these obligations most often arises in the context of a wrongful dismissal suit, in which the employer is claiming that the employee's actions provided cause for dismissal, and the employee is claiming not to have done anything that warranted summary dismissal.

TERMINATION OF EMPLOYMENT

The ending of an employment relationship can have severe consequences for employees. Not only are they left without a source of income, they are left without the opportunity to engage in a meaningful, productive activity. Studies have shown that communities affected by plant closings and high rates of unemployment typically have greater levels of both physical and mental diseases, as well as higher levels of crime. While the impact of job termination on individuals is likely to vary widely, there is no doubt that for many it causes considerable stress. Nevertheless, in a globally based, competitive economy, employers seek to maximize flexibility in the deployment of workers, including the ability to lay off employees with minimal cost.

The legal framework regulating the termination of employees is quite complex. It is influenced by the contractual nature of the employment relationship, as well as by statutory protections, and any additional protection that may be gained by workers through collective bargaining.

The contract of employment may be for a specified period of time, in which case the relationship comes to an end automatically at the time specified.

Retirement

The employment relationship may also come to an end when an employee retires. In many workplaces, there is a mandatory retirement age, unilaterally imposed by the employer or established in a collective agreement. Many argue that this is a form of discrimination on the basis of age and, in some provinces, mandatory retirement is prohibited. In other provinces, however, the human rights statute, while prohibiting discrimination on the basis of age, defines age to cover people only until age 65, thereby permitting mandatory retirement. In the case of *McKinney v. University of Guelph*, the Supreme Court of Canada held that it was not a violation of the Charter of Rights for a university to have a mandatory retirement policy, nor was it a violation for the provincial legislature to enact a statute permitting an employer to impose a mandatory retirement policy.

Firing

The general principle is that a worker may be terminated at any time for cause. An employer has cause for dismissal when an employee has violated the employment contract in a sufficiently serious manner that the employer is justified in terminating it immediately. In most instances, cause is associated with misconduct by an employee. This may take the form of theft, insubordination, or conduct that is detrimental to the employer's interests. Not all forms of misconduct will constitute cause. Courts must determine whether the employee's conduct "gives rise to a breakdown in the employment relationship". Incompetence can be cause for dismissal; however, the employer must demonstrate that the incompetence was serious, and that the employee was warned about it and was given an opportunity to improve performance. Where the employer acts because of economic circumstances, lack of work, or for other reasons not associated with the employee's conduct, there is no cause for dismissal.

In the absence of cause, an employer can end the employment relationship by giving appropriate notice. Employment standards statutes typically provide minimal periods of notice that must be provided in the absence of cause. In Ontario, the minimum period of notice varies between one and eight weeks, depending on the length of the employment relationship. These are only minimums, and an employee may be entitled to more notice as the result of either an express or implied term of the contract.

If the contract provides for notice greater than that of the statute, then that defines the notice that must be given. If the contract is of indefinite duration and is silent with respect to notice, courts typically read into the contract of employment the requirement of reasonable notice. What is reasonable will depend on a variety of factors, with the most important being the length of time served by the employee, as well as age, level of responsibility, and availability of similar employment. The employee is entitled to whichever is the greater, reasonable notice or the minimum notice provided for in the employment standards legislation. In practice, an employer will often make a payment in lieu of notice, rather than expecting an employee to continue working during the notice period.

If the employer dismisses an employee without cause, and without giving reasonable notice or payment in lieu, the employee may commence an action for **wrongful dismissal**. In a wrongful dismissal action, the employer has the onus to show that there was cause for dismissal. If the employer does not show cause, then the employee is entitled to damages measured on the basis of wages and other benefits that would have been received during the period of reasonable notice. The length of notice may be extended to award what are sometimes referred to as *Wallace* damages (after the decision of the Supreme Court of Canada in *Wallace v. United Grain Growers Ltd.*, [1997] 3 S.C.R. 701), where bad faith conduct by the employer in the manner of the dismissal leads to significant medical consequences for the employee. Moreover, a court may award punitive damages where employer conduct is particularly high-handed or outrageous, and merits special sanction, if that conduct constitutes a separate

| EXHIBIT 18.4 | Wrongful Dismissal — Reasonable Notice |

When Edna Cronk was dismissed from her job with Canadian General Insurance Co. at the age of 55, she had been working for the company and its predecessor full-time for a period of 28 years, with a six-year break when she stayed home to look after children. Even then, she worked on a part-time basis for the company. She was terminated as a result of an internal reorganization by the employer. She claimed that she should be entitled to 20 months' notice of dismissal.

The court was required to address two issues. In determining the amount of notice that should be provided where there is no cause for dismissal, it is normal to consider both the length of time the employee has been working for the employer, and the level of responsibility of the job. Employees with longer service and more responsible, especially managerial, positions, are normally entitled to more notice.

The Court decided that Cronk's notice period should be calculated using the full length of time that she had worked for the employer and its predecessor, given that she had left full-time employment to raise a family, continued to work part-time while doing so, and returned to full-time employment at the request of the employer. However, the Court of Appeal reversed the trial judge's ruling that she should be entitled to the same length of notice as a senior managerial employee. The court held that the well-established rule that senior managerial and specialized employees are entitled to a longer period of notice should be followed. It was important to adhere to precedent to promote reasonable certainty and predictability. As a result, the Court of Appeal reduced the notice period from 20 months to 12 months.

Source: *Cronk v. Canadian General Insurance Co.* (1995), 25 O.R. (3d) 505 (C.A.).

actionable harm. Reinstatement is not a remedy that is available in a wrongful dismissal action. However, for employees covered by a collective agreement that prohibits dismissal except for **just cause**, reinstatement is a remedy that is commonly used if the employer is unable to show just cause for dismissal. A unionized employee, rather than bringing an action for wrongful dismissal, would file a grievance that, if not settled between the union and the employer, would go to grievance or rights arbitration. It is the arbitrator, rather than the court, that would decide whether there was cause for dismissal, and whether the employee should be reinstated.

A dismissed employee who is seeking damages may be under an obligation of mitigation in order to reduce the amount of damages arising from the dismissal. The employer is required to demonstrate that the employee has failed to make a reasonable effort to find alternative employment and that such alternate employment was available. A recent Supreme Court of Canada decision has concluded that the dismissed employee may, in some circumstances, be required to mitigate damages by accepting an offer of employment from the employer that has dismissed him or her.

Sometimes an employer, rather than dismissing an employee, will change the working conditions in such a way that the employee will quit. In such circumstances, the employee may still be able to claim that the change in working conditions amounts to a *constructive dismissal* and, therefore, damages should be awarded in the same manner as if a wrongful dismissal had taken place. It is not always easy to know whether changes in working conditions or breaches of the employment contract justify an employee's resignation and treating it as a dismissal. An employer must have some flexibility in being able to modify work assignments. On the other hand, from the employee's perspective, there must be some core of employment conditions that the employer cannot be entitled to unilaterally modify or, at least, not to modify

Wrongful Dismissal — Damages	**EXHIBIT 18.5**

Kevin Keays worked for Honda Canada for fourteen years. After working for several years, he developed Chronic Fatigue Syndrome, which his doctor reported was likely to cause him to be absent from work about four days per month. The employer initially accommodated these absences. However, the employer changed its position, telling Keays that their doctors, in reviewing Keays files, had concluded that he did not have a disability justifying regular absences from work. This was despite clear documentation in Keays' files confirming the Chronic Fatigue Syndrome diagnosis. Honda then demanded that Keays meet with Honda's occupational health specialist. When Keays asked for clarification of the purpose of the meeting, the methodology to be used by the doctor, and the parameters for his assessment, he was told by the employer that no further explanation would be given. As a result, Keays refused to meet with the doctor, and Honda fired him for insubordination.

The Court found that the dismissal was wrongful because the order for Keays to meet with the company doctor was not reasonable, given the refusal to respond to Keays' questions. An employer has no just cause to dismiss an employee for refusing to follow an unreasonable employer order. Moreover, in this case, the court concluded that the employer was acting in bad faith in making the order because it was using the order as a prelude to dismissing Keays so that it would not have to accommodate his disability.

In determining damages, the Court concluded that Keays was entitled to reasonable notice of fifteen months. Moreover, because the employer had acted in bad faith in the manner in which it dismissed Keays, leading to significant medical consequences for him, this notice period, following the decision of the Supreme Court of Canada in *Wallace v. United Grain Growers Ltd.*, [1997] 3 S.C.R. 701, was increased to 24 months. The trial judge also concluded that punitive damages in the amount of $500,000 were warranted, given that Honda' actions were discriminatory, high handed and outrageous. On review at the Court of Appeal, all aspects of the damage award were upheld, except that the amount awarded for punitive damages was reduced from $500,000 to $100,000, with one dissenting judge who agreed with the trial judge's assessment of $500,000. The Supreme Court of Canada heard an appeal in the case in 2007, but as of May 1, 2008 has not yet handed down its decision.

Sources: *Keays v. Honda Canada Inc.* (2006), 82 O.R. (3d) 161 (C.A); aff'g, in part, (2005), 40 C.C.E.L. (3d) 258 (Ont. S.C.J.).

without giving due notice. Hence, courts are called upon to balance the conflicting interests, which they do by determining what the terms of the contract are, whether they have been breached, and whether those breaches are fundamental.

Quitting

Just as there is a duty on an employer to provide reasonable notice in terminating a contract of indefinite duration, there is a corresponding duty on an employee if he wishes to terminate the contract by quitting. Some, but not all, provinces provide for a minimum period of notice in their employment standards legislation. In practice, there have been very few cases in which courts have been asked to provide a remedy to an employer for the failure of an employee to provide reasonable notice of an intention to quit. This is probably because the level of damages likely to be obtained in a successful action is sufficiently low that it does not justify the expenses involved in bringing an action.

Plant Closings

One form of termination that merits special legislative treatment arises where there is a full or partial closing of the employer's operations. Where this results in a large number of employees being let go at one time, there may be special difficulties for the employees in adjusting to the layoffs. For that reason, many provinces specify longer than usual notice periods. For instance, in Ontario, if 50–199 persons are laid off, eight weeks' notice must be given; 200–499 employees, 12 weeks; 500 or more employees, 16 weeks. In addition, an employer can be required to participate in actions to consider alternatives to the terminations and to facilitate the adjustment process by, for example, providing job placement (sometimes called "outplacement") counselling to terminated employees. The government does not actually prevent an employer from laying off employees; it merely seeks to cushion the impact on employees by providing longer notice periods and by seeking ways of helping employees to adjust to the changed circumstances.

Severance Pay

Another measure that has been taken in some jurisdictions, including Ontario, for employees that are governed by the *Canada Labour Code*, is to require an employer to pay **severance pay** when an employee is terminated. In Ontario, an employer is required to pay severance pay where 50 or more employees are terminated as a result of the permanent discontinuance of all or part of the employer's business. As well, if the employer has a payroll of more than $2.5-million per annum, severance pay must be paid even in the case of individual terminations. Only employees who have been employed for five or more years are so entitled. The severance pay is in addition to any amount that the employee may be entitled to as pay in lieu of statutory notice. Several justifications are offered for requiring severance payments. They are an additional cushion to help employees adjust to being laid off. They recognize that even employees who find alternative employment immediately lose tangible benefits such as seniority. As well, it is a way of forcing an employer to internalize some of the costs of a layoff so that in some situations, an employer may decide that the costs of laying off exceed the costs of maintaining employment at the usual level.

CHAPTER SUMMARY

This chapter has described three regimes by which the legal system regulates the rights and obligations of employees. The contract of employment, legislation, and collective bargaining are each used, sometimes in overlapping fashion, to determine the rules by which employees and employers come together in order to engage in productive activity. Legislation and collective bargaining can both be seen as responses to the inadequacy of individual employment contracts to ensure justice in the workplace. Nevertheless, for many workers, individual contracts continue to be a very important determinant of their rights.

The rights under an individual contract are primarily enforced by courts, especially in the context of wrongful dismissal cases. Unionized workers rely primarily on the grievance/arbitration system. Both groups of employees, however, may be able to turn to a number of different statutory agencies to protect rights created by legislation. Human rights commissions, workers' compensation boards, safety inspectors, employment standards officers, and other public officials and institutions are responsible for ensuring that statutory rights are fulfilled.

The law recognizes an expanse of rights and obligations possessed by employers and employees. These range from employee obligations of fidelity and obedience to employer obligations to maintain a workplace that is safe, free from discrimination, and that meets minimum employment standards. However one assesses these forms of regulation, difficult issues of fairness and efficiency inevitably must be taken into account.

GLOSSARY OF NEW TERMS AND KEY CONCEPTS

bargain in good faith (duty to)
A statutory duty placed on unions and employers when negotiating a collective agreement.

bona fide occupational requirement (b.f.o.r.)
A defence available to employers whose rules have an adverse discriminatory impact on particular groups; the employer must show that the rules are necessary and adopted in good faith.

certification
A process by which a union, enjoying the support of the majority of employees in a bargaining unit, obtains the right to bargain exclusively with the employer on behalf of those employees.

consideration
Before a contractual promise is enforceable, the person seeking to enforce it must give something in exchange for the promise: consideration, which can be money payment, provision of goods or services, or a promise to do something in the future.

constructive dismissal
A situation in which an employee who has quit is entitled to bring an action for wrongful dismissal on the basis that the employer has caused the dismissal by breaching the employment contract.

employment equity
A policy that has the goal of eliminating barriers to equality in employment and ensuring the proportional representation of all groups in the workplace.

employment relationship
A legal relationship, based in contract that is sometimes referred to as a contract of service, and that is distinguished from independent contracting or a contract for services.

employment standards
Minimum legislative standards are set out in legislation to which employers and employees are bound, dealing with such issues as minimum wages, vacation pay, holidays, notice of termination, etc.

experience rating
A means by which the premium paid by an employer for workers' compensation reflects that employer's record with respect to compensable injuries.

equal pay for equal work
A principle that requires an employer to pay a man and a woman the same wages if they are doing substantially the same job. (*See also* **equal pay for work of equal value** and **pay equity**.)

equal pay for work of equal value
A principle which requires an employer to pay a man and a woman the same wages if their jobs are of equal value; the jobs themselves may be different. (*See also* **equal pay for equal work** and **pay equity**.)

fiduciary duties
Obligations owed by upper-level managerial employees to place the employer's interest ahead of their own when it comes to business opportunities.

freedom of association
A general principle of international law that is recognized by the Charter of Rights and by collective bargaining statutes, whereby workers are free to join a union and participate in its lawful activities free from employer interference.

grievance or rights arbitration
A process by which grievances under a collective agreement are settled by a neutral third party, whose decision is binding on the union, the employer, and the employees. Grievance, or rights arbitration, differs from interest arbitration in that a rights arbitrator decides what rights have already been created by the collective agreement, while an interest arbitrator actually creates the rights that are then inserted into the collective agreement.

harassment
A form of prohibited discrimination in which a person either seeks to use coercion to solicit sexual favours, or engages in a course of vexatious comment or conduct that the person knows, or ought reasonably to know, is unwelcome.

interest arbitration	A process by which collective bargaining disputes are settled by a neutral third party, rather than through the use of strikes or lockouts. The arbitrator's decision is binding on the union and the employer for the duration of the collective agreement.
just cause	A requirement under collective agreements that prohibits an employer from dismissing an employee unless it can be shown that there is a good, reasonable, or just cause for the dismissal.
mitigation	Obligation on a dismissed employee to seek reasonable alternative employment, in order to reduce the amount of damages arising from a wrongful dismissal. The onus is on the employer to demonstrate that an employee has failed to make reasonable efforts, and to show that if reasonable efforts were made, the employee likely could have obtained reasonable alternate employment.
pay equity	A principle that requires equal pay for work of equal value (see above), and that requires an employer to implement a review of pay practices to determine if such inequities exist, and to take measures to end them.
poisoned environment	A form of harassment in which a person's course of conduct or vexatious comment, especially of a sexual or racial nature, makes it very unpleasant for other workers.
quid pro quo harassment	A form of harassment in which a person who exercises managerial or supervisory control seeks to solicit sexual favours by making threats or promises.
reasonable accommodation	An employer who has a rule that adversely discriminates against members of a group must demonstrate that it has made reasonable efforts to accommodate the needs of that group.
restrictive covenant	An express term of an employment contract in which the employee agrees not to engage in employment, or start a business that would interfere with the employer's proprietary rights, such as goodwill, trade secrets, and confidential information.
severance pay	An entitlement of workers, under some employment standards legislation, to a payment when their jobs are terminated, usually based on a formula that multiplies weekly or daily wages by the number of years worked.
unfair labour practices	Limits, contained in collective-bargaining statutes, on the conduct in which an employer or a union can engage, designed to protect the freedom of association of workers and the autonomy of unions.
WHMIS (Workplace Hazardous Materials Information System)	A system required by occupational health and safety statutes to label toxic substances in the workplace, and to educate workers about how to properly handle such substances.
workers' compensation	An employer-funded statutory scheme by which workers are entitled to be compensated for wages lost as a result of workplace accidents or disease, without having to demonstrate negligence or fault by the employer.
wrongful dismissal	A dismissal in which the employer has violated the contract of employment by firing an employee without cause and without giving reasonable notice.

REVIEW QUESTIONS

1. What are the three major systems for regulating the employment relationship?

2. What is the difference between an employee and an independent contractor?

3. What are three requirements for a valid employment contract?

4. What remedies are available to an employee who has not received wages owed by an employer?

5. Describe some employment standards and how they interact with a collective-bargaining regime.

6. Describe four ways in which occupational health and safety statutes attempt to ensure a safer and healthier workplace.

7. What is the difference between equal pay for equal work, equal pay for work of equal value, and pay equity?

8. Name at least three objectives required by employment equity principles.

9. For employees not covered by collective agreements, name the three primary sources of employee obligations.

10. In a successful wrongful dismissal action, what is the primary remedy given by the courts?

DISCUSSION QUESTIONS

1. When should employees have a right to strike, and when are governments justified in prohibiting employees from striking?

2. In a globalizing world, is it more important for employment standards legislation to provide robust minimum standards, or is it more important to have flexible standards so that employers will be able to compete against companies based in other countries?

3. Canada has relatively high levels of deaths and injuries on the job. How can we improve the legal regulation of occupational health and safety so as to make the workplace safer?

4. What steps, if any, should Canada be taking to ensure pay equity and to deal with underrepresentation of women, minorities and the disable in the workplace?

5. Should there be a law that prohibits employers from firing workers unless they can show that there is just cause for doing so?

SUGGESTED READINGS

Adams, George W. *Canadian Labour Law*, 2d ed. with annual supplements (Aurora, Ont.: Canada Law Book, 1993).

Aggarwal, Arjun, & Madhu M. Gupta. *Sexual Harassment in the Workplace*, 3d ed. (Toronto, Ont.: Butterworths, 2000).

Carter, Donald D., et al. *Labour Law in Canada*, 5th ed. (The Hague: Kluwer Law International, 2002).

Dee, Garth. *Ontario Workplace Safety and Insurance Act and Commentary* (Markham, Ont.: LexisNexis Butterworths, 2004).

Echlin, Randall S., *For Better or Worse: A Practical Guide to Canadian Employment Law* (Aurora, Ont.: Aurora Professional Press, 2003).

England, Geoffrey. *Individual Employment Law* (Toronto, Ont.: Irwin Law).

England, G., *Employment Law in Canada*, 4th ed. (Markham, Ont.: LexisNexis Canada, 2005).

Fudge, Judy, & Patricia McDermott, eds. *Just Wages: A Feminist Assessment of Pay Equity* (Toronto, Ont.: University of Toronto Press, 1991).

Gilbert, Douglas G., & L.A. Liversidge. *Workers Compensation in Ontario, A Guide to the Workplace Safety and Insurance Act*, 3d ed. (Aurora, Ont.: Canada Law Book, 2001).

Grossman, Michael. *The Law of Occupational Health and Safety in Ontario*, 2d ed. (Toronto, Ont.: Butterworths, 1994).

Labour Law Casebook Group, *Labour and Employment Law: Cases, Material and Commentary*, 7th ed. (Toronto, Ont.: Irwin Law, 2004).

Law Society of Upper Canada, *Employment Law* (Toronto, Ont.: Irwin Law, 2007).

Levitt, Howard A., *The Law of Dismissal for Human Resource Professionals* (Aurora, Ont.: Canada Law Book, 2007).

Pay Equity Task Force. *Pay Equity: A New Approach to a Fundamental Right* (Ottawa, Pay Equity Task Force, 2004).

Rayside, David. *Equity, Diversity and Canadian Labour* (Toronto, Ont.: University of Toronto Press, 2007).

Rootham, Christopher. *Labour and Employment Law in the Federal Public Service* (Toronto, Ont.: Irwin Law, 2007).

Sproat, John R. *The Wrongful Dismissal Handbook*, 2d ed. (Toronto, Ont.: Butterworths, 2002).

Weiner, Nan. *Employment Equity: Making It Work* (Toronto, Ont.: Butterworths, 1993).

Weiner, Nan, & Morley Gunderson. *Pay Equity: Issues, Options and Experiences* (Toronto, Ont.: Butterworths, 1990).

Vosko, Leah, ed. *Precarious Employment: Understanding Labour Market Insecurity in Canada* (Montreal, Que.: McGill Queen's University Press, 2006).

Unionized Employment Law

Michael Kanter
ONTARIO MINISTRY OF LABOUR

Melody Crawford
YORK UNIVERSITY

Learning Objectives

At the conclusion of this chapter, the reader should be able to:

➢ describe the various stages in the unionized employment law system and their relationship

➢ explain how the legislation protects the right of employees to join a union and participate in its lawful activities

➢ explain how the legislation regulates the *process* rather than the *content* of collective bargaining

➢ describe how the parties jointly set up the rules of the workplace through the negotiation process

➢ describe how the parties administer those rules through the grievance and arbitration process

➢ explain some of the principles regulating the relationship between the employee and his or her union

TABLE OF CONTENTS

INTRODUCTION

For employees not covered by a collective agreement, wages and working conditions are regulated by the common law contract of employment. The employment contract is one specific type of contract, and the legal principles governing it are similar to those governing contracts in general. The contract of employment, in theory, is a contract entered into by two free and equal parties who meet and bargain over the terms of employment. The reality is otherwise, in that the bargaining power of the employer is generally stronger than that of the employee. Trade unions have their origins in the notion that employees can increase their bargaining power by grouping together to bargain as a collective. But when employees began to do this, the common law courts were uncomfortable with the idea of a union being a party to a contract. Governments in the late 19th century began to create legislation to protect trade unions because the common law did not recognize unions as legal entities. Unionized employment law is the story of government legislation aimed at creating a set of rules that differ substantially from non-union employment law. While the differences between the two systems of law can be exaggerated, there are important distinctions, and most commentators are of the opinion that employees obtain substantial benefits by choosing to unionize.

UNION ORGANIZING

Unfair Labour Practices

Historically, the common law was hostile to trade union activity, viewing such a combination to be restrictive to trade. The main purpose of the early labour relations statutes in both Canada[1] and the United States was to require employers to recognize unions as legitimate entities. Unions are accordingly given statutory protection so that employers cannot, for example, dismiss employees for joining a union, or refuse to bargain with a union. In the broadest sense, an **unfair labour practice** is a conduct that violates the protection provided by labour relations statutes. While unions can also commit unfair labour practices, a major focus of most provincial labour relations Acts is on the prevention of employer activity that undermines the role of unions as representatives of employees. In accordance with this purpose, the *Ontario Labour Relations Act* prohibits employers from intimidating or threatening employees who choose to form a union.[2]

Unfair labour practices can occur at various points, from the organizing of a union to the administration of the collective agreement. For example, it will be noted below that the **duty to bargain in good faith** is an important obligation imposed on both parties. Breach of this duty would be an unfair labour practice. But unfair labour practices perhaps occur most frequently at the time that a union is organizing. An employer might, for example, dismiss an employee who is helping a union to organize. If the employer takes action against such an employee for the purpose of undermining the union, then it is a violation of the Act. Even if the employer can show that there are performance problems with the employee, the employer is not permitted to use the employee's organizational activity as a reason for dismissal. The employer

---

[1] Our focus in this chapter is on Ontario, since most employees are covered by provincial legislation. However, the basic principles of Ontario law are the same as in most of the other provinces. For highlights of labour law reform introduced by the Conservative government as of October 1995, see Exhibit 19.2 in the text.

[2] See ss. 70, 72, 76 of the *Labour Relations Act*, S.O. 1995, c. 1, sch. A.

EXHIBIT 19.1

Unfair Labour Practice: Case Study

Honest Ed's, [1985] OLRB Rep. 1609, illustrates how it is an unfair labour practice for an employer to discharge an employee when the employee's union activity is one of the reasons for the discharge.

In that case Mr. MacNeil had been employed by the company for approximately eight months. He had been warned many times about his attendance, punctuality, appearance and attitude. He was scheduled to be at work one Saturday and, on that day, he called in sick. However, later in the afternoon the supervisor (Mr. Pironcelli) saw MacNeil outside the employer's premises in good health. The supervisor decided on that Saturday to discharge MacNeil for his absence and previous poor punctuality and attendance. However, the supervisor did not inform MacNeil until two working days later (on the Tuesday). The supervisor explained that he waited until the Tuesday to discharge MacNeil because of a supervisors' meeting that was scheduled for that Tuesday. Even though the supervisor had the authority to dismiss MacNeil, he testified that he wished to review the matter with the other supervisors (buyers).

The case involved an unfair labour practice because it also happened that Mr. MacNeil had been active in a trade union's organizing campaign among the employer's employees. The supervisor was aware of Mr. MacNeil's active role in the union. One of the key facts in the case was that Mr. MacNeil had made a pro-union speech in the employer's cafeteria during his supper break on the day before he was terminated.

The issue in the case was whether the employer was able to establish that the discharge was not motivated, either in whole or in part, by the employee's union activity. The Board had to be persuaded that the employee's exercise of rights under the *Labour Relations Act* played no part in the decision to terminate. The Board concluded as follows:

> The respondent [employer] has not persuaded us that Mr. MacNeil's union activities ... and his speech to the employees on Monday were not a significant element in the discussion among the buyers that led to the discharge of Mr. MacNeil. Mr. Pironcelli, who on his own evidence, had decided to dismiss Mr. MacNeil on the Saturday waited until the following Tuesday to do so. The decision to dismiss Mr. MacNeil, if it was Mr. Pironcelli's alone, could have been effected either Saturday or Monday. Waiting one more day to review the matter with his colleagues suggests to us that Mr. Pironcelli was somewhat unsure about dismissing Mr. MacNeil, but was persuaded to do so after the buyers' board meeting. Therefore, having regard to all of the evidence before us, we are not satisfied that the respondent did not act contrary to the Act when it discharged Mr. MacNeil on Tuesday, July 15, 1985. (at pp. 1612–13)

---

would have to show that the dismissal had nothing to do with the organizational activity. Thus it can be seen that the Act is designed to protect employees from being disciplined or dismissed for deciding to associate with a union.

It is worth noting that when a union files a complaint that a person has been disciplined (or discharged) for associating with a union, the employer bears the burden of showing that the employee's union activity did not play a part in the decision to discipline. This means that if the employer is not willing to come forward and offer an explanation as to why it disciplined the employee, then the employer will lose the case. The Labour Board is required to inquire into the motive of the employer, and if it is in doubt as to the motive, it resolves the matter in favour of the union.[3] A reason for shifting the onus is that only the employer knows the true reasons for its actions

---

[3] See, for example, *Honest Ed's*, [1985] OLRB Rep. 1609.

Highlights of Ontario Labour Law Changes   **EXHIBIT 19.2**

In November 1995, the Conservative government passed amendments to the *Labour Relations Act* that repealed the changes made to the Act by the previous NDP government. Several other changes were also made. Highlights of the changes are listed below.

◻ Repealed the ban on replacement workers, which once again (i) allows employers to hire replacement workers during a strike (or lockout), and (ii) allows employees on strike to cross their own picket line and return to work.

◻ Repealed automatic access to first contract arbitration, which once again requires unions to prove to the Labour Board that the bargaining process has been frustrated before they can get access to an arbitrated first contract.

◻ Repealed a new practice of requiring the Board to combine full- and part-time employees into a single bargaining unit. Also repealed the right of unions to apply for a combination of bargaining units involving the same employer.

◻ Collective bargaining rights for professionals in the fields of architecture, dentistry, land surveying, law, and medicine were repealed. Collective bargaining rights for agricultural workers were also repealed.

◻ Repealed the right of unions to gain access to malls (and other quasi-public property) so that they can organize and picket at the entrances and exits of employers located inside these malls.

◻ Requires a certification vote in a workplace prior to certification regardless of how many workers sign membership cards. This abolished the standard practice in existence since 1950 under which unions were certified by having over 55 per cent of the workers sign cards.

◻ Requires unions to hold strike votes within certain times instead of allowing unions to decide whether to have a strike vote and the timing of such a vote.

---

and should be willing to come forward to offer a credible explanation for those actions.

As noted, **collective bargaining** law prohibits employers from interfering in employees' rights to participate in union activity. This sometimes gives rise to conflicts between union rights, on one hand, and employer rights on the other. For example, while the union might like to have the right to enter the employer's property to explain to employees the benefits of joining a union, the employer might argue that this unduly interferes with its right to operate its business efficiently. This becomes a difficult conflict between organizing rights and property rights, a tension that the law needs to resolve on an ongoing basis. Since property rights are older and more established than organizing rights, the question becomes: To what extent is the law willing to change traditional property rights so that organizing is facilitated? If property law is not changed to make this accommodation, then it will be much harder for unions to organize.

Accordingly, Ontario's Act prevents employees from soliciting union membership from other employees during work time but allows it during break time. The current Act does not permit full-time union organizers to enter the employer's property, nor does it allow the union access to malls in order to organize a store inside the mall.

There is also sometimes a conflict between the employee's right to participate in union activity and the employer's right to free speech. An employer is generally permitted to express its view on unionization, but the employer must not cross over into the realm of coercion or intimidation. For example, a threatening, anti-union speech during working time would constitute an unfair labour practice.

A discussion of unfair labour practices is not complete without some reference to remedies. If a breach of the Act occurs, but the innocent party is not able to obtain an effective remedy, then the law is open to criticism. The history of collective bargaining legislation is to some extent a story of the Labour Board being given more and more authority to effectively remedy a wrong. Thus, for example, if the employer commits the unfair labour practice of dismissing employees associated with a union organizing drive, the Board not only can order reinstatement with back pay but can also force the employer to give the union access to its premises for the purpose of union activity.[4]

Also with reference to the issue of remedies, Ontario's Act, as well as the legislation in a number of other Canadian jurisdictions (e.g., B.C., Manitoba, Nova Scotia, New Brunswick), has a provision that allows for the automatic certification of a union where the employer commits such serious unfair labour practices that a vote is unlikely to disclose the wishes of the employees. This unfair labour practice certification provision is intended to deter wrongful employer interference in union organizing campaigns, and to provide an effective remedy where no other remedy can counter the effects of the interference. In other words, as a deterrent to employers, the Act provides for the most effective remedy of all for the trade union, of gaining the right to represent the employees, even where there is no testing of the wishes of those employees.

For example, if an employer acted to swiftly dismiss several key organizers in an organizing drive at a workplace, it is possible that the union would be unable to obtain majority support in that workplace. While the union might not be able to win a vote, this is probably the result of the coercive actions of the employer, which has the result of "poisoning" the workplace. The employer is, in effect, warned by the Act that if it commits serious unfair labour practices it could be faced with certification.[5] This provision is treated by the Ontario Labour Relations Board as an extraordinary remedy, and there are, usually, only a handful of successful cases each year.

However, it is important to note that the Board does not have authority to act as a criminal court. Labour proceedings are not criminal in nature, and the legislation is designed to compensate rather than to punish. Accordingly, the Board does not issue fines and does not imprison persons. At the same time, however, it is expected that a remedy of compensation will have some deterrent effect on an employer. In the rare cases where flagrant violations of the Act occur on a continuing basis, it is open to either party to seek the Board's consent for prosecution in the provincial offences court system.

Certification

Certification refers to the process before the Board where a union acquires the right to bargain on behalf of a defined group of employees. Once a union is certified, the employer is required to recognize it and bargain with it. A prerequisite to certification is an indication that a majority of employees in the

---

[4] See, for example, *Toronto Fabricating Co.*, [1985] OLRB Rep. 1528.

[5] A union was successful in an unfair labour practice certification application at a Windsor Wal-Mart store in February 1997. There has been considerable controversy in this case because the coercive action in that case consisted of the failure of the store management to respond to employee questions about job security in the event of unionization rather than more direct coercive action, such as dismissal of organizers. It is also controversial because a significant number of the employees themselves appear unhappy that the union was certified and seem determined to seek decertification of the union as soon as possible. See *Wal-Mart*, [1997] OLRB Rep. at 141.

defined group wish to be represented by a union. Once a union is certified, no employee in the unit can continue to deal directly with the employer regarding terms and conditions of employment. In other words, even if a particular employee voted against the union (or did not sign a card) and does not wish to be represented by it, that employee will be represented by the union. This follows from giving the union the *exclusive* right to represent employees in the group and also follows from a system that is designed to accommodate the wishes of the majority.

As part of the certification process, the Labour Board determines whether a majority of employees wish to join a union. There are two main methods to determine majority support, with some controversy over which approach is more appropriate. The current law in Ontario requires that there be a vote in every case to determine whether a majority of employees support the idea of unionizing. If a sufficient percentage of employees sign union membership cards (40%), the Labour Board will order a vote. If that threshold is not met, the Board will dismiss the application. This is in marked contrast to the second approach, which relies on the percentage of signed membership cards as the best indication of majority support. Under this approach, if the percentage is high enough (usually 55%), the Board will certify without a vote, on the theory that enough employees have demonstrated support for the union by signing up with it.

Generally speaking, unions prefer to talk to employees, have them sign union cards, and obtain certification without the need for a formal vote. Accordingly, under the second approach, if the union can show the Board that it has signed up over 55 per cent of eligible employees, the Board will certify. However, if the union only signs up between 40 and 55 per cent of the eligible employees, then the Board will order a vote. Finally, if the union goes to the Board with less than 40 per cent of the eligible employees, the Board will dismiss the application. The second approach was the norm in Ontario for over 40 years, until the Conservatives changed the law in 1995.

Certain employees are not eligible to be included in the group sought to be represented by the union. The most important exclusion is managerial employees. The Act assumes that some employees are so closely identified with management that there would be a conflict of interest if they were to be included among the unionized employees. Managerial employees are those who exercise effective control over the terms and conditions of employment of other employees. For example, making decisions about hiring and firing would make an employee managerial and would, thus, exclude them from the union.

Also excluded are employees who have regular access to confidential labour relations information. Thus, for example, an employee who handled information relevant to the negotiation process or the grievance and arbitration process would be excluded. For such employees, the performance of their job functions on behalf of the employer might put them in conflict with their interests as members of the union.

Once the Board has determined which employees are not eligible to be included in collective bargaining, it must resolve any conflicts concerning the "appropriate bargaining unit". This is the defined group of employees within a given company that the union is seeking to represent. This group, referred to in terms of job categories, is called the **bargaining unit**. In other words, when a union seeks bargaining rights, it must tell the Board which employees it seeks to bargain on behalf of. Is it employees in the plant only, or in the plant and the sales office? Is it full- and part-time employees or just one of these groups? Is it employees in one location of the employer, or in all of the locations of that employer?

The main criteria that the Board uses in making this determination is usually referred to as the **"community of interest"** among employees. The

Board is looking to see that the group of employees has a sufficiently common set of interests that it makes sense for them to bargain together. If the interests are too diverse, then it makes more sense to have separate bargaining units. In further refining the concept of community of interest, the Board generally considers such things as the nature of the work, hours of work, work location, and method of payment. While the Board does not want too many small bargaining units that are likely to have very little bargaining power and create administrative inefficiencies, it is possible for one employer to have, at a single location, two or three bargaining units, each representing a group of employees with a different community of interest.

Bargaining Structure

Two or more bargaining units can be combined during collective bargaining in a voluntary arrangement designed to centralize bargaining, as occurs in the construction industry. Or, similarly, a full-time bargaining unit and a part-time unit in a retail store could bargain together, resulting in a single **collective agreement** for both groups. Bargaining structure is a key factor in shaping the outcomes and process of collective bargaining. Bargaining in Canada typically does not take place at a centralized level but occurs on a workplace-by-workplace basis between a single employer and a single bargaining unit in one location. This form of bargaining structure can best be described as highly fragmented and decentralized. One problem is that such small structures can lead to inefficiency and increased industrial conflict. Therefore, some people are in favour of more centralized bargaining structures, such as multi-employer or multi-union bargaining.

THE COLLECTIVE BARGAINING PROCESS

Conciliation and Mediation

It often happens during contract negotiations that the parties reach an impasse or find that they are experiencing difficulties in reaching agreement on the various issues that divide them. In Ontario, conciliation and mediation are two related forms of third party assistance that the parties may use in the hope of reaching an agreement.

Conciliation is compulsory in Ontario, whereas mediation is voluntary. Before either of the disputing parties can engage in any type of job action (namely, a strike or lockout), they are required by law to meet with a conciliation officer. Once a notice to bargain has been given, either side is then free to apply to the Ministry of Labour for conciliation.

A conciliation officer is a neutral third party who is appointed by the Ministry of Labour, and who is both knowledgeable about and experienced in negotiations and dispute resolution. The role of the conciliator is to assist the parties in reaching an agreement on the issues that separate them. The conciliator's job is not to judge or evaluate the parties' positions, but only to help find a solution that will be acceptable to both parties. The conciliator is free to make recommendations to the parties; however, they are not binding on the parties. When a conciliator feels that a settlement cannot be reached, she reports back to the Minister of Labour, who then issues a **"no-board report"**. It is this document that starts the countdown to any job action taken by the parties. A legal strike or lockout may take place 14 days after such a report has been issued.

Conciliation takes place during the course of negotiations in advance of a strike or lockout; **mediation**, on the other hand, usually occurs just prior to, or even during, a strike or lockout. Unlike conciliation, mediation is not compulsory. Either party can request (in writing or by telephone) the services of a mediator. If both parties do not agree to mediation, the Ministry of Labour will not impose it on them.

Both conciliation officers and mediators are neutral third parties appointed by the Ministry of Labour, charged with the task of trying to help the parties find some common ground for agreement. They hold no binding power or authority over the parties, but can and often do suggest proposals or make recommendations in an attempt to find a solution acceptable to the disputing parties. Conciliation is essentially a form of mediation that occurs earlier in the collective bargaining process. Most provinces do not require conciliation.

The Duty to Bargain in Good Faith

Union and management representatives engaged in collective bargaining have a statutory *duty to bargain in good faith*. The *Ontario Labour Relations Act* requires that "the parties ... shall bargain in good faith and make every reasonable effort to make a collective agreement."[6] The purpose of the duty to bargain is to require the parties to follow a process that will lead them to a collective agreement. Labour Boards are reluctant to review the "fairness" of proposals, based on the theory that the parties themselves are best able to determine the content of their agreement.

While this obligation may seem clear at first, the problem lies in the ambiguity of what constitutes bad faith bargaining. There is a very fine line between bad faith bargaining and what is known as "hard bargaining". Hard bargaining, which is legal and involves bargaining to protect one's economic interest, can be contrasted with "surface" bargaining, which is illegal and involves bargaining with no genuine interest in reaching a collective agreement. Behaviour that one labour board may consider bargaining in bad faith may be considered simply hard bargaining by another board, leading to a degree of unpredictability in the caselaw

If either party feels that the other is in breach of its duty to bargain in good faith, they make an application to the Labour Relations Board alleging that an unfair labour practice has been committed. There are some tactics that are generally reflective of bad faith bargaining that include, but are not limited to:

- failing to recognize the bargaining authority of the other party;
- the persistent refusal to meet and bargain;
- failure to disclose pertinent information;
- an unwillingness to discuss an issue;
- attempting to circumvent the bargaining agent and, instead, attempting to negotiate directly with employees; and
- reneging or revoking previous concessions or agreements on a given issue.

When a party is accused of bargaining in bad faith, the Labour Board reviews the party's conduct during the entire period of negotiations. So while a single instance of conduct that appears to be in bad faith might not constitute an unfair labour practice, if the Board sees a pattern of such behaviour emerging, a party may be found in violation of the *Labour Relations Act*.

First Agreement Arbitration

In Ontario, if the parties in a collective bargaining relationship cannot agree on the terms of a first agreement, either of them can apply to have it settled by arbitration. The Labour Board will direct settlement of the first agreement by arbitration only if certain conditions are met. For example, the Board can

---

[6] See s. 17 of the *Ontario Labour Relations Act*, S.O. 1995, c. 1, Sch. A.

order arbitration if the employer has adopted an uncompromising position without reasonable justification. These conditions are imposed because of the government's view that first contract arbitration should not be automatic but, rather, should only be available if one side is frustrating the process to such an extent that a first collective agreement is not being reached. Note that the party applying for first contract arbitration, normally the union, would not have to go as far as having to establish bad faith bargaining on the part of the employer, but would have to establish that the employer was making the process unsuccessful. The rationale for not making first contract arbitration automatic is that the union might rely on it rather than going through the important effort of trying to reach a deal though negotiation with the employer.

An application for first agreement arbitration can be made after the parties have been in a legal strike or lockout position for 30 days. Other than the passage of time, no other grounds need be established. A private board of arbitration will listen to the proposals of both parties on all of the unsettled issues and then make a ruling on them. These issues ruled on by the board of arbitration, together with any issues previously settled by the parties, will constitute the collective agreement.

First contract arbitration is important in ensuring that newly certified unions have the opportunity to secure a collective agreement. During the period surrounding the negotiation of a first contract, both union and management find themselves in a new, unfamiliar and, often, unstable relationship which can make bargaining difficult. In addition, during this period workers frequently find themselves in a "make it or break it" situation in which employers who continue to resist the idea of being unionized conduct themselves in a way that frustrates collective bargaining. The conduct of some employers during the negotiation process can make it difficult for the parties to agree on even the most basic terms and conditions. Without access to first contract arbitration, it can take months or years to reach a collective agreement, or alternatively, the union may end up being decertified before such an agreement can be reached.

INDUSTRIAL CONFLICT

Strikes and Lockouts

The right to resort to economic sanctions forms an integral part of the collective bargaining process. The union's primary economic sanction is the **strike**, and the employer's is the **lockout**. The main purpose of a strike or lockout is to exert (economic) pressure on the parties at the bargaining table to make a concerted effort to cooperate and to present reasonable demands in order to reach a collective agreement. It is usually in the best interests of the parties to avoid such disputes, which are costly to both the union and management. Essentially, a strike is a withdrawal of labour by employees acting in combination, and a lockout is the closing of a place of employment by the employer in an effort to compel employees to agree to terms and conditions of employment.

Once a no-board report has been issued by a conciliation officer, a strike or lockout may legally commence within 14 days. In many jurisdictions, including Ontario, a compulsory strike vote must be held before the union may call a strike. Even when a strike vote is not mandatory, it is commonplace for unions in Canada to hold them, since they usually wish to have the support of their memberships before engaging in any type of job action. Most unions have provisions within their constitution outlining the procedures governing work stoppages, which include strike votes.

In Ontario, during a strike employers are free to operate with the use of replacement workers. Bargaining unit employees are also free to return to work or to refuse to participate in the strike. The previous NDP government had prohibited both of these practices, but the Conservative government repealed the NDP legislation. Regardless of the current law in Ontario, the question of whether employers should be able to operate during a strike, with the use of replacement workers, is a highly contentious issue in industrial relations. When an employer is permitted to use replacement workers, this option may affect the bargaining power between the parties and, generally, tends to increase the tension on the picket line. Quebec is the only Canadian jurisdiction that has had legislation banning replacement workers for many years (since 1977); it is only in the last 10 years that other jurisdictions have begun to experiment with the idea of placing restrictions on the use of replacement workers. Such jurisdictions include British Columbia and the federal jurisdiction. While the issue is quite controversial, it should be noted that some employers, even where they are permitted to use replacement workers, do not do so, either because it is not practical (e.g., skilled replacement workers cannot be found), or because the employer does not want to risk poor relations with the union.

Strikes and lockouts can be caused by a variety of factors, both economic and non-economic. On the economic side, strikes and lockouts are influenced by such factors as wages, unemployment, inflation, profits, and business cycles. Non-economic factors include the size of the bargaining unit (smaller bargaining units seem to be subject to a larger number of work stoppages); conflict within the parties (both union and management); and the relations between the parties — whether, for example, relations are hostile or cooperative, trusting or suspicious. Also important are the knowledge, experience, and skills of the negotiators at the bargaining table, which can influence whether a settlement is reached or a work stoppage occurs.

As specified in the *Ontario Labour Relations Act*, a strike or lockout cannot legally take place during the life of a collective agreement. Strikes that occur while an agreement is in operation are illegal and are known as "**wildcat strikes**". Despite the fact that Canada has a relatively high number of (legal) work stoppages among industrialized countries (second only to Italy), over 95 per cent of all collective agreements are settled without resorting to a work stoppage.[7]

Picketing

A major component of many strikes is picketing. Generally, there are two types of picketing. The first is known as primary picketing. This is picketing that takes place at the site of the employer or of an employer that has allied itself with the struck employer. The second type is termed secondary picketing, which takes place at the site of a neutral, unrelated employer. Typically, a supplier of a struck employer would be a neutral employer. The difference between the two is that primary picketing is legal, while secondary picketing is not. An issue that sometimes arises before a court or labour board is whether the employer being picketed is an allied employer. For example, where the employer being picketed owns the struck employer, rather than a neutral third party.

Picketers sometimes block entrances and exits to the employer's operations, causing delays and hindering the operation of the business (should the employer decide to continue to operate at a reduced level during the dispute). Picketing has sparked debate over concerns for employers' private prop-

---

[7] See Ontario Federation of Labour publication *Labour Law Act Fact #14*, OLRA Workshop, 1991.

erty rights, as well as the employer's right to continue to operate during a work stoppage. To some extent picketing is regulated by laws outside labour legislation, such as the *Trespass to Property Act*, the *Criminal Code*, and rights established at common law. For example, if picketers engaged in criminal activity, such as assault, they could be charged under the *Criminal Code*.

Legislation in Ontario, which was repealed in 1995, tried to strike a different balance between a worker's right to picket and an employer's private property rights. Where the employer is located on third party property, such as a mall or industrial park, the union could picket on the third party property at or near the entrances and exits of the operations. Should there be any conflict between rights for the purpose of picketing under the *Labour Relations Act* and any other rights established at common law or under the *Trespass to Property Act*, the right of access under the *Labour Relations Act* prevailed.

Interest Arbitration

In addition to grievance (or rights) arbitration, which is dealt with in more detail below, arbitrators also deal with a second type of arbitration known as **interest arbitration**. This involves establishing the terms and conditions of a collective agreement that the parties could not settle themselves. Interest arbitration is presided over by a three-person board of arbitration or a single arbitrator whose decision(s) is binding on both parties. Where a three-person board is used, each side chooses a representative, and then the two representatives choose a third person to chair the panel. Where the parties are unable to agree on a single arbitrator or the chair of a board of arbitration, the Minister of Labour will make an appointment.

Depending on the type of arbitration being used, the board can settle the issues in dispute in one of two ways. Most often the parties use **conventional interest arbitration**, where the arbitrators have authority to fashion a settlement that they deem appropriate. The settlement, therefore, can and often does differ from the positions presented by the parties. For example, if the issue in dispute is wages and the union is asking for a four per cent increase, but management is offering zero per cent, the board might decide (as they often do) to "split the difference" and order a settlement of two per cent.

On occasion, however, the parties may decide to use **"final offer" arbitration**, which can be done on a total package or an issue-by-issue basis. This procedure leaves no room for compromise — instead, the board of arbitration is forced to choose the exact position of either the union or management.

Voluntary interest arbitration is permitted under the *Labour Relations Act*, but it is not used very often since both parties must agree to it and, more often than not, neither wishes to relinquish its decision-making powers to a third party. It is important to note that interest arbitration is frequently used in different areas of the public sector, especially for those who work in so-called "essential services" such as police, firefighters, and hospital workers. Many of these workers do not have the right to strike but, rather, must settle any disputes by means of binding arbitration. While conventional interest arbitration may be useful in solving some public sector disputes, its use is not encouraged elsewhere since it tends to produce a "chilling effect" on bargaining; that is, it is alleged that one or both of the parties may withhold concessions during negotiations in the hope of gaining a better settlement if the dispute goes to arbitration. It is also alleged that conventional interest arbitration has a "narcotic effect", in that repeated or heavy reliance on it leads the parties to depend on it during later rounds of bargaining.[8]

---

[8] See, for example, A. Craig & N. Solomon, *The System of Industrial Relations in Canada* at 316.

COLLECTIVE AGREEMENTS

Mandatory Terms

Most current labour legislation in Canada requires that several mandatory provisions be included in any collective agreement. The requirements differ from province to province, but the basic mandatory provisions are as follows:

Recognition Provision

It defines the group of employees who will be governed by the terms and conditions of the collective agreement and are represented by the union. In other words, this article defines the "bargaining unit", which usually corresponds to the description contained in the certification order issued by the Labour Relations Board. However, this provision can be worded in such a way as to allow for additions to, or exclusions from, the bargaining unit in the future, should the parties jointly decide on such changes. Under a recognition provision, the union must be recognized as the exclusive bargaining agent of the employees in the bargaining unit.

No Strikes or Lockouts Provision

This provision specifies that no strike or lockout will take place during the life of the collective agreement. If no such provision is contained in the agreement, the *Ontario Labour Relations Act* deems that one exists.

Grievance and Arbitration Procedure

It outlines the method by which any collective bargaining disputes will be settled by binding arbitration. This provision must outline, as a bare minimum, an arbitration mechanism, a procedure for the selection of an arbitrator, and an acknowledgement that the decision of the arbitrator(s) is firm and binding on the parties to the collective agreement. The statute imposes such a provision on the parties if it is not included in their agreement. Parties usually negotiate something more than the bare minimum, usually a provision that is tailored to suit their needs. This often includes guidelines for a grievance procedure that specifies the various steps through which a grievance must proceed before reaching arbitration. (See section below on Steps in the Grievance Procedure.)

Term Provision

It outlines the term of a collective agreement, including a start date and an expiry date. Collective agreements must have a minimum term of one year. Parties often negotiate other dates into this type of clause to specify when negotiations for the next collective agreement are to take place. The *Ontario Act* provides that either party to an agreement may give notice to bargain a new collective agreement at any time within the last 90 days of the previous agreement.

Rand Formula/Agency Shop Provision

While employees are not required to join the union, both members and non-members are required to pay union dues since the union is legally obligated to represent all persons in the bargaining unit, whether they are members or not. This minimum form of union security provision must be included in a collective agreement at the request of the union.

Other Terms

While the provisions contained in any collective agreement vary greatly, there are several prominent provisions found within most, if not, all agreements. We outline four of them here.

Management's Rights Provision

This provision explicitly recognizes that management has the exclusive right to make decisions pertaining to the management of the company or organization. It is usually based on the idea of "residual rights" — that anything not contained in the collective agreement is deemed automatically to fall within the area of management rights, and that any powers, rights, or privileges that were exercised by the employer prior to unionization continue thereafter, except for those specifically constrained by the collective agreement.

Seniority Provision

It is based on the notion that employees with long service records should be given preferential treatment based on such service. Many provisions require that **seniority** be taken into account in job promotions, layoffs and recalls, the determination of benefits, choice of shifts and vacations, and entitlement to overtime. The relative importance assigned to seniority differs greatly from agreement to agreement.

Discipline Provision

It outlines the right of management to discipline or discharge employees provided that there is "just cause". Discipline provisions are always subject to the employee's right to grieve. The amount of detail in such clauses varies, and sometimes includes specific rules and penalties to which the employees shall be subject.

Union Security Provision

There are three basic types of union security clauses found within collective agreements:

- **Union shop** — requires that all employees join the union within a specified period after being hired, as a condition of employment. It is also possible to have a modified union shop provision, whereby current employees do not have to join the union but all employees hired after the signing of the collective agreement must join.

- **Closed shop** — restricts the employer to hiring and employing those workers who are members of the union in good standing. Usually associated with union hiring halls, it is found most frequently in the construction industry.

- **Rand Formula/Agency shop** — see the earlier discussion of mandatory provisions in collective agreements. The union may request this form of union security, and the employer must agree to it. Alternatively, the union may seek to obtain a stronger form of security in bargaining.

It is important to note that any closed or union shop provisions are subject to certain restrictions under the *Labour Relations Act*. For example, employees with religious objections are permitted to pay an amount equivalent to the union dues to a registered charity.

THE GRIEVANCE AND ARBITRATION PROCESS

Introduction

Once a collective agreement has been negotiated, the parties require some method for resolving disputes that arise during the term of the agreement. It is not unusual for an agreement to last for two years, and so it is clear that dispute resolution is a very important feature of the labour relations system. The method used for resolving disputes is the **grievance and arbitration**

process. The parties themselves try to resolve disputes about the interpretation of the agreement by meeting to discuss the issues and, if they are unable to resolve the differences on their own, they must submit their dispute to arbitration, where a single arbitrator or a three-person board of arbitration makes a binding decision.

This system of binding arbitration is so fundamental to the system that the Act requires the parties to resolve their differences in this manner. This means that, for example, even if a union and employer wished to negotiate a process whereby the union could go on strike or the employer could lock out when a grievance could not be settled, they would be prohibited by the Act from doing so.

These differences or disputes between the parties about how to properly interpret the agreement are generally referred to as **grievances**. Grievances are allegations that the collective agreement has been violated. The principle is that the party alleging violation of the agreement must point to some clause or article in the agreement that has been violated. In other words, a grievance is not a general complaint about workplace issues but, rather, is a specific allegation that a clause in the agreement has been violated.

Sometimes disputes arise where the collective agreement does not appear to address an issue of importance to the parties. For example, an employer may wish to implement technological change that has a major impact on the work in the bargaining unit. In such cases, arbitrators have decided that employers are free to implement such changes because there is no clause in the agreement that prevents the employer from doing so. This is usually referred to as the **residual theory of "management rights"**, according to which employers are free to direct the workplace as they see fit, subject to what has been given up in the agreement (and subject to the duty to exercise management rights fairly). In other words, management retains a general managerial prerogative to direct the workplace, subject to any restrictions on it that are negotiated into the agreement. Management rights give the employer a significant amount of control in the workplace.

Steps in the Grievance Procedure

The following is a typical procedure that would occur if an employee had a grievance. (Management can also file grievances, but the practical reality is that most grievances are initiated by the union, since a collective agreement is designed to provide a series of rights to the employees.) The collective agreement will typically refer to a series of "steps" that culminate in arbitration if the grievance is not resolved.

Step one may involve the employee raising the grievance in a rather informal manner with the immediate supervisor. The matter is discussed, with the supervisor required to reply within a certain number of days following the discussion. The employee will probably have the right to be accompanied by a union representative.

Step two and all of the following steps involve higher degrees of formality and higher levels of authority on both sides. Generally the union notifies the employer that it is moving the grievance to the next step. At each step the parties have a meeting, and within a certain number of days following the meeting the employer replies in writing. The aim is to settle the grievance at one of these levels. As the process unfolds, and arbitration becomes more of a possibility, it is hoped that the parties can find some common ground and avoid the uncertainty associated with arbitration. Arbitration usually involves some risk because it is usually not clear who will prevail in arbitration, due to the inevitable ambiguities of collective agreements.

Step three and, perhaps, a fourth step are the last opportunities before the issue is referred on to **(grievance) arbitration**. If the parties do not settle the issue, and the union does not withdraw the grievance, the parties will choose an arbitrator or a board of arbitration, and a date will be set for a hearing.

It is important to note that most grievances do not move all the way through the system to arbitration. The parties have too great a stake in getting along with each other on an everyday basis, and if a large number of grievances go on to arbitration, it is probably a sign that the parties have a poor working relationship. Arbitration is an adversarial process, and the parties generally prefer to avoid it. In addition, and equally important, it is expensive and time-consuming. The parties share equally the costs of the arbitrator.

The Arbitration Hearing

The arbitration hearing is the final step in the grievance procedure. If a grievance cannot be settled either at one of the steps outlined above or at some later point prior to the hearing, then it will proceed to arbitration. The parties usually set out in their agreement that both parties must agree upon an arbitrator or a board of arbitration. Essentially, the hearing consists of the parties introducing evidence and then making arguments as to why their interpretation of the collective agreement is correct. The arbitrator listens to the arguments much like a judge; and then, some time after the hearing, he will mail a decision to the parties. The decision is final, subject to a very limited basis for review by the courts.

The advantage of using a three-person board is that each side is permitted to choose a nominee to sit on the board. The nominee is someone who is biased in that they represent either the union or employer community. The nominees together choose the neutral chair of the board. The decision of two of the three members of the board will be the majority decision. The disagreeing member may write a "dissent", giving the reasons for disagreeing with the decision. Nominees are useful in that they can help the chair appreciate the point of view of their side. However, while a board might result in a fuller consideration of the case, it also costs more and can result in more delays.

Procedurally, an arbitration hearing is similar to a court hearing, except that the process is more informal. The atmosphere is more casual, and the rules of evidence are not as strict. In discipline and discharge cases, employers are required to proceed first and bear the burden of showing that they had just cause for imposing the discipline. In other cases, the party alleging that the agreement has been violated will have to prove their case. It is important to note that an arbitrator is not bound to follow previous decisions that are similar. However, arbitrators do rely fairly heavily on the parties bringing previous cases to their attention to serve as guidance for the decision.

The main problems with arbitration can be summarized as delays, costs, and increasing legalization of the process. It can take several years from the time an incident occurs to the time an arbitration decision is given to the parties. To address the problem of delay, governments have taken different steps, such as in Ontario, where the government introduced "expedited" arbitration. This allows either party to bypass the provisions in their collective agreement and go directly to the Ministry of Labour for an arbitrator who will hear the case almost immediately. The Ontario government has also taken steps to introduce more arbitrators into the system, so that the parties have more people to choose from. This tends to result in fewer delays and lower costs.

It has been noted that the parties share the cost of arbitration equally. It has become quite expensive, in particular, to use the services of the most popular arbitrators. Most governments do not regulate the fees of arbitrators, though this is an option should fees continue to escalate.

The increasing legalization of the process refers not only to the growing tendency to use lawyers to argue arbitration cases, but also to the increasing use of technical arguments in cases. There is a tension between a simple process that gets to the heart of the issue in a straightforward way and a more complex process that is aimed at procedural fairness. The more complicated the process becomes, the greater the risk that individual employees will lose faith in the system.

UNIONS AND THEIR MEMBERS

The Duty of Fair Representation

One of the most important duties owed by the union to its members is the **duty of fair representation**. Note that the union has the exclusive right to represent everyone in the bargaining unit. Depending on what type of union security clause exists in a workplace, it is possible for some employees in the bargaining unit not to be members of the union, even though the union has the right to represent them. Related to the right to represent everyone in the unit is a corresponding duty to represent them fairly. This would prevent, for example, the union from deciding not to take up a grievance on behalf of a bargaining unit employee who did not join the union.

Employees are not parties to the collective agreement and, hence, have no direct right to enforce it through arbitration. It is the union that is the party to the agreement and, without the duty imposed on it of fair representation, it is possible that it might decide, in a given case, not to enforce the agreement. The duty is important in protecting employees both during the negotiation process and during the administration of the collective agreement.

Most of the problems arise during the administration of the collective agreement. Here the issue is generally whether the union is fairly representing an employee in deciding not to pursue a grievance on the employee's behalf. The Labour Board requires that the union turn its mind to the merits of the grievance and make an honest decision as to whether to pursue the matter. For example, the union does not breach its duty if it researches the matter, concludes that the grievance has little merit and, considering the cost and likelihood of setting a bad precedent, decides not to pursue the grievance. Of course, there may be grey areas, where the union is unclear about the chances of succeeding at arbitration. Where the issue is more serious, such as a discharge case, most unions will err on the side of caution and take the case all the way through to arbitration.

The Right to Belong to and Remain in the Union

Issues arising out of the relationship between the employees and their union are generally dealt with by the courts rather than by the Board. Historically, such internal union matters have been viewed as a matter of contract. The terms of the contract are the constitution and by-laws of the union, and these terms are to be interpreted by the courts. Accordingly, if a union member was expelled by the union and wished to take action against the union, the member would seek redress through the courts. The court would not only interpret the express terms of the contract but, probably, would also imply certain terms into the contract which would ensure that the union was fair to the member.

There are several instances, however, where the Board can become involved because the internal union matter crosses over into the relationship between the union and the employer. One such example is where the union expels a member and then, pursuant to a union shop security clause, asks the employer to discharge the expelled member. The union shop security clause permits this because it requires all employees to join and remain as members of the union. The *Labour Relations Act* protects against the possible abuse of such a security clause by stating that a union cannot ask for the discharge of an employee who has been expelled because of reasonable dissent.

Note that in this example, the *Labour Relations Act* is not involved in the expulsion unless the matter involves the relationship between the union and the employer. A second example is the duty of fair representation. At first glance this appears to be solely a matter between the union and the employee, while in fact the duty of the union pertains to the quality of its representation of employees vis-à-vis the employer.[9]

CHAPTER SUMMARY

In this chapter, we discussed the major features of the law regulating union-management relations. First, it is noted that labour relations legislation, with the *Ontario Labour Relations Act* as an example, provides a statutory framework for the parties in terms of the organizing and collective bargaining process. The Act protects employees from employer intimidation or coercion for choosing to participate in legitimate union activity. It regulates the organizing and certification process, as well as the negotiation process that follows these. Part of the negotiation process involves the right of either party to invoke economic sanctions in the form of the strike or lockout. Breaches of the Act are unfair labour practices.

Once the parties have negotiated their collective agreement, the focus of the chapter shifts away from the Act toward the administration of the agreement through the grievance and arbitration process. In this phase of the union-management system, the parties resolve disputes about the interpretation of the collective agreement. Note that disputes do not go to the Labour Board. Instead, the parties generally choose their own arbitrators, who have the authority to make binding decisions interpreting the agreement. While the collective agreement made by the parties can be described as the private law of the parties, it is also noted that some terms of the agreement are mandatory.

Finally, it is noted that the relationship between the union and its members is only partly regulated by the Board. Insofar as the matter is purely an internal union matter with no impact on the employer, the relationship is regulated by the courts and dealt with as a matter of contract. Insofar as the matter involves the union's relationship with the employer, such as the duty of fair representation, it is dealt with by the Act. Perhaps in the future the Board's powers will be further expanded to deal more completely with internal union matters.

GLOSSARY OF NEW TERMS AND KEY CONCEPTS

bargaining unit	A defined group of employees of a particular employer who are represented by a union.
certification	The process before the Board whereby a union acquires the right to represent a defined group of employees known as the bargaining unit.
closed shop	A union security provision that restricts the employer to hiring and employing only those workers who are members of the union.

---

[9] See, for example, George Adam, *Canadian Labour Law* at 12, 13.

collective agreement	A contract or an agreement in writing between a union and an employer (or between multiple unions and/or multiple employers) that outlines the terms and conditions of employment for the employees covered by such agreement. Also outlines the rights and duties of the union and the employer.
collective bargaining	A procedure whereby employees can deal or negotiate with their employer collectively through a trade union, rather than on an individual basis. Unions and employers negotiate and put into writing agreements that govern such issues as the wages and working conditions for the group of employees the union represents (known as the bargaining unit). The union also represents and acts on behalf of those same employees in matters or disputes that may arise during the term of the collective agreement.
community of interest	The criteria the Labour Board uses in determining the appropriate bargaining unit. It refers to employees who have enough of a common set of interests that it makes sense for them to bargain together. Taken into consideration are such factors as the nature of the work, hours of work, work location, and method of payment.
conciliation	A process whereby a conciliation officer (who is a neutral third party) is appointed by the Ministry to meet with the union and management during contract negotiations in an attempt to find a settlement that is acceptable to both parties. Conciliation is compulsory before the parties can be in a legal strike or lockout position.
duty of fair representation	Under the Act, a trade union has a duty imposed upon it to represent fairly all of the employees in a bargaining unit for which it has bargaining rights, regardless of whether the employees are members of the union. It is a violation of the Ontario *Labour Relations Act* if a union represents employees in a manner that is discriminatory, arbitrary, or in bad faith.
duty to bargain in good faith	Both the union and the employer have a statutory duty placed upon them by the *Labour Relations Act* to bargain in good faith and to make every possible effort to conclude a collective agreement. (While there is no single definition of what constitutes bad faith bargaining, a party will usually be found in violation of the Act if a Labour Board can discern a pattern of behaviour consistent with bad faith bargaining over a given period of time.)
grievance	A specific allegation that a clause or provision in the collective agreement has been violated.
grievance (or rights) arbitration	A compulsory process that settles any disputes concerning the interpretation of a provision of an existing collective agreement, either by a single arbitrator or a three-person board of arbitration whose decision is binding.
interest arbitration	A process whereby the terms and conditions of a collective agreement that the parties could not settle themselves are established by binding arbitration. Usually presided over by a three-person board, interest arbitration can be of the conventional type, whereby arbitrators have the authority to fashion a settlement they deem appropriate, or it can be final-offer, whereby the board must select the exact position of either the union or management either on an issue-by-issue or a total package basis.
lockout	The closing of a place of employment by the employer in an effort to compel employees to agree to terms and conditions of employment.
mediation	A voluntary process available to the parties following conciliation whereby a mediator (also a neutral third party) is appointed and meets with the parties, often more than once, in an effort to settle a dispute. Mediation can take place immediately before a strike or lockout may be about to commence and may continue throughout the work stoppage. However mediators, like conciliators, have no authority over the two parties.
no-board report	The notice sent to the parties by the Minister of Labour informing them that the minister does not find it advisable to appoint a conciliation board. After the notice has been mailed, a legal strike or lockout may commence within 14 days.
rand formula/agency shop	A union security provision that requires that all members of the bargaining unit pay union dues, regardless of whether they are a member of the union.
residual theory of management rights	The idea that management retains a general prerogative to direct the workplace as it sees fit, subject to any restrictions that are negotiated into the collective agreement (and also subject to the duty to exercise management rights fairly).

seniority	A principle based on the idea that employees who have long service records with a company should be given preferential treatment based on such service. Seniority considerations are often prominent in the determination of job promotions, layoffs and recalls, vacation time, work shifts, etc.
strike	The withdrawal of labour by employees acting in combination (usually to compel the employer to agree to terms and conditions of employment, although strikes can take place for other reasons).
unfair labour practice	Conduct by either the employer or the union that violates the *Labour Relations Act*.
union shop	A union security provision that requires that all employees join the union within a specified period of time after being hired.
wildcat strike	A type of strike that occurs during the life of a collective agreement and is illegal.

REVIEW QUESTIONS

1. How does the *Labour Relations Act* attempt to protect the rights of unions and employees seeking representation during organizing? Why is such protection necessary?

2. Under the *Labour Relations Act*, some persons are prevented from seeking union representation.
   (a) What persons are prevented from seeking representation?
   (b) Why are they prevented from doing so?

3. What is a bargaining unit, and how does a labour board determine its appropriate composition?

4. Draw a comparison between conciliation and mediation services.

5. Why is first contract arbitration important?

6. When can a legal strike or lockout take place, and why might one occur?

7. Distinguish between interest arbitration and grievance (or rights) arbitration.

8. What is the difference between conventional interest arbitration and the "final-offer" type?

9. What are the three basic types of union security provisions found in collective agreements, and how do they differ?

10. What are "management rights" under a collective agreement?

11. What is a "grievance" under a collective agreement?

12. Why do most grievances not result in arbitration?

DISCUSSION QUESTIONS

1. Are employees sufficiently protected by the *Labour Relations Act* from actions by the employer designed to prevent them from organizing a union in the workplace?

2. Is it necessary that the Act contain a duty to bargain in good faith? What might happen without it?

3. What is the purpose of imposing a duty of fair representation upon the union? Provide several examples of situations where it might be relevant.

4. Should employers have the right to hire "replacement employees" during a strike? How does it affect the bargaining strength of the parties?

5. Discuss the main problems with the grievance arbitration process. Are there further steps the government might take to address these problems?

6. Which method for permitting certification of a union is more appropriate: card signing, or requiring a vote in every case?

7. Discuss why an employee who is working in a position covered by a collective agreement should or should not be made to join the union.

8. A unionized workplace employs assembly line workers and a smaller group of office staff. How should the bargaining unit be defined?

SUGGESTED READINGS

Adams, George W. *Canadian Labour Law*, 2d ed. with annual supplements (Aurora, Ont.: Canada Law Book, 1993).

Gunderson, J., et al. *Union-Management Relations in Canada*, 4th ed. (Toronto, Ont.: Addison-Wesley, 2002).

Carter, D.D., et al. *Labour Law in Canada*, 5th ed. (Toronto, Ont.: Butterworths, 2001).

Brown, Donald, & Beatty David. *Canadian Labour Arbitration*, 3d ed. with annual supplements (Aurora, Ont.: Canada Law Book, 1991).

Craig, Alton, & N. Solomon. *The System of Industrial Relations in Canada*, 5th ed. (Toronto, Ont.: Prentice Hall, 1996).

WEBSITES

Canada Labour Code: <http://laws.justice.gc.ca/en/l-2/16036.html>

Federal Conciliation and Mediation Service: <http://labour.hrdc-drhc.gc.ca>

Ontario Labour Relations Board: <www.gov.on.ca/LAB/olrb/eng/homeeng.htm>

Ontario Ministry of Labour: <www.gov.on.ca/LAB/english>

Consumer Law

Alan Auerbach
WILFRID LAURIER UNIVERSITY

Learning Objectives

At the conclusion of this chapter, the reader should be able to:

➢ define "consumer" and "consumer law"
➢ appreciate the history of consumer-protection legislation
➢ know the relevance of product standards
➢ differentiate among basic types of laws
➢ recognize consumer responsibilities
➢ know how to locate federal and provincial statutes
➢ understand the main federal ministries and statutes
➢ know the key federal regulations and policies on financial services
➢ be familiar with Ontario's consumer-related ministries and regulations
➢ see Quebec's new *Consumer Protection Act* as a model
➢ integrate and understand the best and worst features of consumer legislation that affect you
➢ understand insurance from a consumer's perspective
➢ know basic consumer aspects of motor vehicles
➢ know the Ontario regulations on private transfers of car ownership

TABLE OF CONTENTS

INTRODUCTION

The Meaning of "Consumer Law"

What, exactly, is **consumer law**? You know that legal practice is divided into various specialty areas such as commercial, criminal, real estate, family, and litigation law. But consumer law is not one of these branches, at least as recognized by the profession. "Consumer law" does not appear in law dictionaries; it is a lay term rather than a legal one because it's hard to define. Nonetheless, we will try.

Consumer is broadly used to mean "ordinary person", and more specifically to mean "purchaser" or "end user". The earliest use of this word in law was by Boston lawyer Louis Brandeis; when he was litigating public interest cases, he argued at an 1897 tariff hearing on behalf of what he termed "the consumer".

In the sense of "end user", most of us are consumers of hundreds of products such as toasters, televisions, and trucks. Certainly we need some form of product protection because a few of these goods are costly and complex, sometimes frustrating and fragile, and at times dangerous or even deadly.

We are also consumers of services, professions, political parties, and even business, religious, and volunteer organizations; here, it is harder to differentiate protection from intrusion. When you buy a television set, of course the law should protect you from being electrocuted by it, or from the seller's demand for more than the ticket price. But as a consumer of the programs and advertisements that you see on the set, it is less clear what level of protection should apply. As another example, maybe the law should protect vulnerable youngsters from being "brainwashed" by "cults", but sociologists have difficulty in defining such terms, and the law needs clear definitions. Similarly, if your neighbour sells you a "natural" product to cure your ills, the law may have problems differentiating among drugs, herbs, and dietary supplements, and in knowing how to treat a home-based business. A final complexity of the word "consumer" is that its common derivative word, "consumerism", has various socio-political meanings.

The Coverage of Consumer Law in This Chapter

This chapter highlights marketplace laws as they apply to lay persons (as opposed to corporations or to lawyers). It omits the laws of real estate, tort, employment, debtors/creditors, and the court system, as each of these topics is available as a chapter in the present series. Given how broadly "consumer" must be defined, other omissions had to be a judgment call. If you spend summers panning for gold and winters getting your muscles massaged, you might deem the statutes on mining, stake-claiming, and precious metals, and those on massage therapists, physiotherapists, and chiropractors all to be "consumer legislation". But space limitations require that we address the more typical consumer.

Most statutes relating to the marketplace are in the hands of Canada's 10 provinces and three territories. The provincial legislation is generally similar (with the exception of Quebec), and there is sporadic coverage of consumer issues in the territories. Despite the prominence of provincial jurisdiction, a few consumer-relevant laws are federal. (In cases where the same laws are covered by different jurisdictions, federal statutes take precedence over provincial ones, which override municipal by-laws.)

Accordingly, this chapter covers, after the introductory topics, the relevant federal legislation, that of Ontario, and of Quebec, with some reference to other provinces. After a short commentary on Canadian consumer law, the chapter ends on two topics that come under both federal and provincial regulation: insurance and motor vehicles.

The History of Consumer Law

The phrase *caveat emptor* sums up the attitude of early lawmakers to protecting the consumer. It is Latin for "let the buyer beware", meaning that purchasers buy at their own risk; the sellers or manufacturers are free of responsibility in the transaction. Until recently there were seven reasons for the absence of consumer laws:

1. Although most charges and prosecutions of violations of consumer law are made by the government agency responsible for the legislation, the law also expects that ordinary people can take legal action against merchants, manufacturers, and corporations. But in past generations, the law was not available to the average person. Back when most people were so impoverished and illiterate that legal action was impractical, there was no thought of drafting laws that would allow a consumer to sue.

2. The first consumer laws protected against defective products, but until recently, so few consumer goods were available that there was little to worry about. Even if you are young, you probably own more varied possessions than your grandparents ever did. (Yes, in past centuries the highest stratum of society did own possessions galore, but these goods were often chosen more for their artistic than their utilitarian merit.)

3. The few goods that were widely available were simple to understand and operate, and easy to adjust or repair. Prior to electricity, food might be kept cool in a cold cellar or ice box, structures that would last virtually forever; the life of today's complex refrigerator is around 15 years, and is likely to need repairs within that period. Similarly, compare a sundial with a watch, a quill pen with a data-communications system, or a bow-and-arrow or spear with an auto-loading firearm.

4. The consequences of failure used to be relatively minor. For instance, contrast the results of a defective steering system on a horse-drawn wagon with that on an automobile or aircraft. A watchdog failing to bark might have meant the loss of the family cooking pot and the next day's food; today's faulty burglar alarm could cost possessions accumulated over a lifetime. Defects in a hot water bottle would be easy to detect, and if missed would result only in a damp bed, but hidden flaws in an electric blanket could expose the sleeper to harmful electric shock or fire.

5. Personal calamities were once common; everyone was affected by losses due to accident or disease. Product failures, like the many other losses, were seen as part of life. If a newly purchased horse died, it was seen as an act of God, so when people bought the first cars and they "died", the owners tended to be fatalistic rather than litigious. But in today's climate of "entitlement to perfection", consumers are less willing to accept lapses in product durability, safety, or efficiency.

6. People have long been conditioned not to challenge authority, whether religious, educational, or professional, so this later spilled over into business and commerce. Thus, after centuries of accepting that the earth was flat because those in power said so, when you bought a pair of "Neverleak" rubbers, you were not likely to complain — despite your wet feet.

7. Finally, organized religion was a dominant influence on most of the cultures that Canadian law derives from. All major religions date from simpler times and do not dwell on material possessions. Thus, it was illegal in Canada to blaspheme long before it was against the law to store guns improperly or to sell unsafe microwave ovens.

When consumer-protection laws arrived, some of the first ones covered medicines. They were needed: back then, some "patent medicines" included opiate drops as baby soothers, alcohol as tonics, and pills containing tapeworms for weight reduction. But other early product-fitness laws were intended not to protect the ordinary consumer but the businessman. For instance, we will cover Ontario's *Sale of Goods Act*,[1] which seems designed to protect the consumer. But this statute was drafted in the late 19th century to ensure that if a merchant or manufacturer bought some business equipment for a declared purpose, as a presumed expert the seller was responsible for ensuring that it was suitable.

Early consumer-protection legislation focused on products only. That's because until recently, services were even more limited than goods were. To be "in service" originally meant that you were a live-in servant, and if your employer were dissatisfied with your work you could be dismissed without warning, justification, holiday pay, or references. Thus, service inadequacy was not considered to be a problem. But today, you can get your lawn, your dog, and your image groomed by professional service providers, and increasingly legislation is designed to protect those who buy services.

This is not to say that today's legislation always reflects today's consumer problems, because laws tend to evolve much more slowly than society and technology change. Most current statutes predate, sometimes by a century, consumer issues such as credit cards, multilevel marketing plans, computers, the Internet, and telemarketers, and they catch up slowly.

Not only do laws change, but so does the interpretation of them as established by **caselaw**. Marketplace issues have undergone staggering transformations recently, so the establishment of caselaw can be more substantial than changes to statutes. For instance, prior to the globalization of industry, an item either was or was not made in Canada. However, a recent charge of misleading advertising in regard to a "Made in Canada" label was dismissed at trial when the Court found that at least 51 per cent of the labour and raw material was Canadian. This case, then, effectively redefined the meaning of "Made in Canada."

Product Standards and the Law

The word "standard" has various meanings; it's employed in government documents to mean legislative criteria, and by policy makers to mean policy criteria. It's also used to ensure that millions of things fit together, from trains on tracks to rear ends on seats. With the globalization of trade, information systems, and financial transactions, universally accepted standards are critical. For instance, the Internet exists only because of international standards that allow you to access the World Wide Web (www) from various types of computers using various browsers.

In this chapter, we are more interested in the world of trade, where "standard" refers to technical aspects that establish safety or performance criteria. It's not a new concept; the Magna Carta included a chapter on standards, and over two centuries ago the United States Constitution dealt with establishing the "standards of weights and measures".

Some products have no legally-mandated standards. Household clocks can vary in accuracy, noise, longevity, or design, and novelty clocks run backward or show a ten-hour day. Some systems have standards that are quite strict and universal but not due to any law; for instance, each of 800,000 firms in almost 100 countries use a distinctive "Universal Product Code" for each of its products — because of bar-code standardization. But every car sold in Can-

---

[1] R.S.O. 1990, c. S.1.

ada *must* conform to a hundred federal standards; dozens of them govern just the lighting system, ensuring, for instance, that all cars' rear lights are of prescribed intensity, hue, and location.

Product standards are not usually created or designed by lawmakers but by a consensus of technical experts, manufacturers, and consumer representatives. However, the standards are often required by governments through reference in legislation. For instance, it may be illegal to install electrical equipment that has not been certified by an organization recognized by the government, or for a child to ride a bicycle without wearing a helmet certified to a "voluntary" standard.

Product liability cases are often trials of product standards, insofar as makers argue that their compliance with the requisite standard shows that they acted properly. Suits are virtually never brought against the standardization organizations themselves, because they take pains to ensure that their procedures for establishing standards are comprehensive, reasonable, and fair. There are many government-recognized standardization organizations in the world; the main one in this country is the **Canadian Standards Association (CSA).** This not-for-profit institution, founded in 1919, has offices throughout Canada and elsewhere. Its headquarters is 178 Rexdale Blvd., Etobicoke ON, M9W 1R3, 416-747-4000; its Web site is <www.csa.ca>. The second most important one, **Underwriters' Laboratories of Canada (ULC),** is concerned only with safety and protection; its site is <www.ulc.ca>. A product that is certified by these agencies bears a stylized CSA or ULC logo; CSA claims that a billion products are so designated.

Most developed countries have their own standards organizations; for instance, the British Standards Institution (BSI) was founded in 1901, the American National Standards Institute (ANSI) in 1918, and ULC in 1894. Standards are still being developed. In 1987, the Geneva-based International Organization for Standards (ISO) published the "ISO 9000" series of standards. Applied to manufacturing, software, service, and internal corporate procedures, these standards have been adopted by the 90 countries that represent 95 per ent of the world's industrial output. The Standards Council of Canada (www.scc.ca) is a federal Crown corporation to promote standardization. Based in Ottawa and reporting to Parliament through the Minister of Industry, it accredits organizations for certification, testing, ISO registration, and standards development.

Levels of Laws

As we will be covering many consumer-related statutes of different types under various headings, the following outline of Canadian laws as they apply to consumer legislation may be helpful.

Common vs. Statutory Law

Many laws are not to be found in the statutes cited in this chapter. **Common law** is the unwritten law of the land based on reason, custom, usage, and **precedents.** Except in Quebec, Canadian common law is largely based on the ancient unwritten law of England, about which Sir Edward Coke (1552–1634) wrote that "the common law is nothing else but reason." The most familiar use of this phrase is "common-law marriage" (a marital partnership not solemnized by a formal religious or civil ceremony or recorded in the jurisdiction's archives).

Common law is contrasted with **statutory laws,** which are formalized by governments that write, label, and print them. Federal statutes are enacted by the Parliament of Canada, provincial statutes are passed by a provincial legislature, and municipal ones are in the hands of a municipal council or equivalent.

Civil vs. Criminal Law

Civil law deals with private rights. Thus, a civil legal suit is between two individuals or corporations (the plaintiff who initiates the action, and the defendant against whom the action is taken). The court hears arguments from the two, and reaches a decision based on precedent and logic.

Criminal statutes deal with violations of public rights as defined and governed by elected officials, and enshrined in the Criminal Code of Canada. The "plaintiff" is the government, the outcome is guilty or not guilty of violating a specific statute, and the penalty-range upon conviction is specified in the statute. If, after parking by a hydrant, you drove at top speed to run down your enemy, you could be charged by the municipality, the province, and the federal criminal justice system. On the parking charge you could settle out of court by paying a fine, for the speeding you might be able to as well, but for the third — attempted murder, manslaughter, or murder, depending on your aim and other factors — you would have to appear in court.

Consumer Duties and Responsibilities

"The customer is always right" was a slogan advanced by a retailer, but it does not represent reality. Buyers should recognize that most products should not be expected to serve them indefinitely; most have a finite "design life". With some items it is the responsibility of consumers to unpack, assemble, and set them up in accordance with directions. With other products, proper maintenance or servicing is their responsibility. Product abuse, whether in storage, servicing, or operating, can void warranties.

It is also the buyer's obligation to know the retailer's return policy before purchase. Many stores are so liberal, accepting goods for refund or exchange for any or no reason and after considerable time, that consumers assume all stores follow this model. In law, when you buy something it becomes your property and your payment becomes the seller's property; you can no more demand a refund than the store can tell you it changed its mind, does not want your money, and demands the product back.

Where to Find Federal and Provincial/Territorial Statutes

This ends the introductory material; we now engage the laws themselves as they relate to Canadian consumers. All the laws of the federal government, as well as of the 10 provincial ones, and those of the territories (Yukon, Northwest Territories, and Nunavut), are available on the Web at <www.ACJNet.org> (the Access to Justice Network). More specific or specialized sources are presented at the end of the sections below.

FEDERAL CONSUMER LEGISLATION

Federal law was created to help consumers in general, by prohibiting all activities that are deemed harmful to society; an example is false or misleading advertising. Whereas provincial law focuses on providing remedies for consumers hurt by unethical or unfair business activities, federal legislation is more concerned with banning certain conduct and punishing those who practise it.

Industry Canada

Industry Canada (formerly Consumer and Corporate Affairs Canada) is mandated to: provide protection from product-related hazards, establish and administer rules and guidelines for business conduct, encourage competition among businesses, enforce standards for trade in commodities, and encourage the disclosure and diffusion of technological information and ensure that information presented to consumers is accurate. Its address is 50 Victoria St., Hull, QC,

K1A 0C9; 819-997-1591/1177 for food and non-food products respectively. Its site called Consumer Connection at <www.strategis.ic.gc.ca> links to every federal statute.

Four statutes are enforced by Industry Canada:

1. The ***Consumer Packaging and Labelling Act***[2], under the Consumer Products Branch, requires that the label on dry goods indicates the product identity or generic name, the quantity if other than one, and the name and place of business for postal delivery of the "dealer" (maker, importer, distributor, or retailer).

2. The ***Textile Labelling Act***[3], which applies mainly to clothing, requires the label to show the name of the fibre and, if more than one, the percentages by weight.

3. The ***Precious Metals Marking Act***[4] governs primarily gold and silver, but also platinum and palladium. It regulates relevant claims and abbreviations or symbols such as "k" for karat. For instance, to be stamped or referred to as "sterling", the item must be 92.5 per cent silver.

4. The ***Competition Act***[5] is the most complex, and is outlined next.

The Competition Act

The *Competition Act* prohibits misleading advertising and deceptive marketing practices in promoting the supply or use of a product or service, or any business interest. The Marketing Practices Branch of the Competition Bureau administers and enforces these provisions under the authority of the Director of Investigation and Research. The Director can resolve matters through prohibition orders or undertakings, or can lay criminal charges.

The *Competition Act* is the only federal statute of general application to all forms of advertising in Canada. It sets the boundaries between what Parliament defines as acceptable business practices and those that it deems to be unlawful. This law applies to all means of making representations, including print, TV and radio ads, and audio-visual illustrations. Its provisions are worded broadly enough to include representations that are generated and distributed electronically. This new "borderless marketplace" presents legal complexities, for instance, when the buyer resides in Canada, the seller is in Colombia, the goods are shipped from Japan, and payment is cleared through a Swiss bank. However, charges were laid in Canada under this law in 1996 against a company that advertised a **multilevel marketing plan** (also called "pyramid selling") on the Internet to prospects both inside and beyond Canada.

In respect to investments and share offerings, most cases of false or misleading representations come under the purview of provincial securities statutes rather than under the *Competition Act*. But there are exceptions; in 1992 the Principal Group was fined $500,000 under this statute for making false representations in its annual report.

The *Competition Act* covers diverse consumer issues such as testimonials and product tests. However, the parts that connect with most consumers are sections 52 to 59, which are related to *misleading advertising and deceptive marketing*. Here is a plain-language outline:

---

[2] R.S.C. 1985, c. C-38.

[3] R.S.C. 1985, c. T-10.

[4] R.S.C. 1985, c. P-19.

[5] R.S.C. 1985, c. C-34; S.C. 1986, c. 26.

- All representations, in any form whatever, that are false or misleading in a material respect are prohibited.

- Any representation in the form of a statement, warranty, or guarantee of the performance, efficacy or length of life of a product, not based on an adequate and proper test, is prohibited; the onus is on the one making the claim to prove that it is based on an adequate and proper test.

- Any representation that purports to be a warranty or guarantee of a product, or a promise to replace, maintain or repair an article or part thereof, is prohibited where their form is materially misleading or where there is no reasonable prospect that the warrantee, guarantee, or promise will be carried out.

- Any materially misleading representation as to the price at which a product is ordinarily sold (in the market area, unless specified to the advertiser's own selling price) is prohibited.

- Where two or more prices are clearly shown on a product, its container, or wrapper, the product must be supplied at the lower price.

- A multilevel marketing plan that features "head hunting" fees, required purchases as a condition of entry into the plan, and inventory loading or the lack of a buy-back guarantee on reasonable commercial terms constitutes a prohibited "scheme of pyramid selling".

- An operator or participant in a multi-level marketing plan cannot make representations relating to compensation unless the representations include disclosure of compensation received by a typical participant.

- Section 57 is commonly termed the "non-availability" provision. Advertising a bargain price product (defined as an article or a service) that the advertiser does not have available for sale in reasonable quantities is prohibited — unless the advertiser establishes that the non-availability of product was due to unavoidable circumstances, or the customer was offered a "rain check" (a promise to supply the product or its equivalent at the advertised price within a reasonable period of time). The Act does not prohibit "upselling" (the promotion of items that are costlier or more profitable than those that attracted the buyer but the cheaper goods must be available in reasonable quantities); in **bait-and-switch** advertising, the offence involves the "bait" rather than the "switch": that is, the cheaper goods are not available in reasonable quantities.

- An "advertisement" includes any representation that can be generally defined as a "public notice", even when addressed to a comparatively small number of people. A purely private communication is not advertising, but a bargain price on a label is. The term "bargain" has been held to connote to the average person a "price that is less than the usual price"; whether the price is actually a bargain is irrelevant. The maximum penalty under this section is a fine of $25,000 and imprisonment of one year; fines have increased substantially in recent years.

- The supply of any product at a price higher than the price currently being advertised is prohibited (unless the price advertised was erroneous and immediately corrected, or where the seller is not engaged in the business of dealing in that product).

- Any contest that does not disclose the number and approximate value of prizes or important information related to the chances of winning, that does not select participants or distribute prizes on the basis of skill or on a random basis, or in which the distribution of prizes is unduly delayed, is prohibited.

* In the early 1990s, the publication *Guiding Principles for Environmental Labelling and Advertising* dealt with the new concern of improper "green" claims. For instance, assertions such as "mercury free", "recycled", and "biodegradable" must (in the absence of qualifiers) mean that the products are totally mercury free, recycled, or biodegradable; and declarations of degradability must be supported by recognized tests.

The Act also forbids certain mergers and monopolies that are deemed to be against the public interest. In 1999 there was an unprecedented number of merger proposals involving petroleum, the media, retailing, and especially banking. The Act also prohibits price fixing that would eliminate normal competition among businesses in the marketplace. One serious form of price-fixing is **bid rigging**. This is an agreement whereby bidders on a contract refrain from submitting bids, or where bidders agree to submit a pre-arranged price, all without making their intentions known to the potential purchaser beforehand. In 1997, four electrical contractors were prosecuted by the Attorney General of Canada and fined a total of $2.55-million; the following year, because another electrical contracting firm pleaded guilty to 10 counts of bid rigging, it was fined only $100,000. The Competition Bureau offers an educational program to assist purchasers in the detection and prevention of bid rigging.

Other examples of prohibited trade practices are (a) conspiracy between parties with the intent of lessening competition, (b) **predatory pricing** (selling at an unreasonably low price to eliminate competition), and (c) **discriminatory allowances** (discounts and rebates that are not offered to competing purchasers).

Violations committed under the Act are criminal offences for which offenders are subject to substantial fines and/or imprisonment terms; for instance, (a), above, carries a penalty of up to a $10-million fine and five years imprisonment. The Act also provides for the recovery of damages to consumers who have been misled or unfairly treated, and the consumer may initiate civil action in any court.

In 1999, five foreign firms comprising what was described as "the world bulk vitamin cartel" confessed to a conspiracy that rigged Canadian prices. They were fined a total of $88-million, the largest criminal fines ever imposed under the *Competition Act*, and the largest in Canadian history. Moreover, the then-vice-president of a sixth firm that conspired with one of the five was sentenced to nine months imprisonment; other executives are also facing jail terms at the time of this writing.

Prosecutions for competition offences are criminal prosecutions, and for this reason, the Crown must prove its case to the criminal law standard of "beyond reasonable doubt". This is a very high standard of proof and explains why there are relatively few federal prosecutions for competition and trade offences.

Under the Program of Advisory Opinions, businesses wishing to avoid coming into conflict with the Act can request an opinion on whether proposed promotions would cause an inquiry to be initiated. The Bureau also has a program by which anyone can, anonymously if wished, bring forward information concerning possible violations of the Act. Pamphlets, videos, and other information are available from: Competition Bureau, Complaints and Public Enquiries Centre, 50 Victoria St., Hull, QC, K1A 0C9, or at 1-800-348-5358. The Web site is <www.competition.ic.gc.ca, where among other information, the Annual Report of the Commissioner of Competition can be found.

Health Canada

Health Canada is an agency concerned with diverse health issues such as fitness, medical devices, and protection from disease and other hazards. It is one of the most up-to-date of the federal agencies, needing to keep up with contemporary additions to the marketplace such as genetically engineered foods, the wildly popular assortment of so-called natural or herbal dietary supplements, and domestic devices that emit various types of radiation. We will look at only two of its many sets of regulations.

The Food and Drugs Act[6]

Canada was a pioneer in grading certain common foods for quality, and in controlling the labelling of canned goods. For instance, as early as 1790, Nova Scotia required that either "prime", "second", or "third" be branded on every barrel of butter; in 1874 a national law forbade the adulteration of food and drugs.

In the early 1900s, some 60,000 brands of "patent medicines" were being sold, some of them containing stimulants, sedatives such as alcohol or cocaine, or dangerous adulterants. In 1920, the first comprehensive federal *Food and Drugs Act* was designed to insure standards of purity in foods, household chemicals, cosmetics, medicines, vitamins, and contraceptives. However, the patent medicine market continued to flourish. Following a 1977 crackdown that required manufacturers to validate their claims and justify their ingredients, all but 1,200 of these "liver pills" and "gout drops" were discontinued.

The Act protects Canadians from possible risk to health, and from fraud and deception in regard to food, drugs, and cosmetics. It outlaws the sale of foods that contain poisonous or harmful substances, and prohibits the sale of food that is unfit for human consumption, and food that has been processed under unsanitary conditions. Furthermore, it regulates the packaging and labelling of food and drugs to ensure that the contents match the label claims.

As examples, the following would violate this Act: cream cheese without a "best-before" date, packaged food with no list of ingredients, and an orange "punch" labelled as "orange juice". The maximum penalty for such violations is $5,000 and/or imprisonment for three years. In addition, government inspectors have the authority to seize a product or commodity.

The Hazardous Products Act[7]

The Hazardous Products Act outlaws dangerous products, and alerts consumers to items that require care when used. The Act divides such products into two categories. The first comprises goods that subject the public to unnecessary and unacceptable hazards. Such products might be poisonous, toxic, explosive, corrosive, or infectious, and cannot be sold in Canada. The second involves items such as household cleaners and detergents, goods that can be imported, advertised, and sold in Canada, but only under the conditions stipulated in the Act.

Financial Services

If you need funds to buy a house, you go to a bank. Where does the bank go to get *its* money? Except in their objective to make a profit for themselves and their shareholders, banks are unlike other business because they can lend money that they get from, in essence, the Government of Canada — meaning you. Conversely, suppose you win the lottery and want to become a lender by opening "The Bank of Jennifer." Sorry, you cannot compete; existing banks

---

[6] R.S.C. 1985, c. F-27.
[7] R.S.C. 1985, c. H-3.

basically have a monopoly, although this may change due to Canada's free trade treaty commitments to permit foreign banks to operate more freely in Canada.

Under the **Bank Act**, which is overseen by The Office of the Superintendent of Financial Institutions, banks have amassed huge assets, significant market control of financial services, and considerable economic power in a country with one of the most highly concentrated banking systems in the world. They have also developed political power that they use to resist attempts by consumer groups and political organizations such as the 1998 *National Liberal Caucus Task Force on the Future of the Financial Services Sector* to make them as accountable and consumer-oriented as their American and British counterparts.

The federal government deals with topics such as credit unions, bank service charges, and whether banks should be allowed to retail insurance policies at their branches. Through the Canada Deposit Insurance Corporation, it insures, consumers' bank deposits. It may also determine if banks can be sold or merged. (In 1999, the Minister of Finance rejected merger proposals by the Bank of Montreal and the Royal Bank of Canada, and by the CIBC and TD Bank, but accepted the purchase of Canada Trust by TD.)

Regulation of interest rates also falls within federal jurisdiction. Bank credit cards originated in 1968, and by 1997 there were over 50 million of them in circulation in Canada (some 30 million of which are Visa or MasterCard). Their users pay an interest rate of around 10 to 12 percentage points higher than the Bank of Canada rate. Retail credit cards are even more costly for users with an unpaid balance; most charge 28.8 per cent. The only federal law that deals with credit-card interest rates is Section 305.1 of the Criminal Code; it defines a criminal interest rate as an effective annual rate that exceeds 60 per cent on the credit advanced under an agreement. Most users are unaware that they are not credited for partial payments in terms of interest, and don't understand the complex formulas used by the credit card firms. By contrast, the U.S. *Fair Credit and Charge Card Disclosure Act* of 1988 is an example of effective disclosure provisions.

Currently, 43 per cent of retailed vehicles are leased rather than purchased. Revisions to the *Bank Act*[8] in 1980 permitted banks to lease vehicles over 21 tonnes, and 1992 legislation extended these powers to federal trust companies and life insurance firms. At the time of this writing, banks are applying for the right to lease light vehicles as well; this is being resisted by the government on the basis that banks' access to confidential client information, plus the possibility of competing with the same car-leasing small businesses to which they provide credit, creates a conflict of interest and may amount to unfair competition under the *Competition Act*.

The federal government also covers **tied selling**. This is the requirement of a consumer to buy one product as a condition of purchasing another one, as when consumers must move their RRSP to a financial institution in order to apply for a line of credit there. (This differs from **cross selling**, also termed **product bundling**, which is the offer of a lower price for a product if the consumer agrees to buy another one, as in the offering of a lower mortgage rate for moving all bank accounts to that institution.) Tied selling with respect to insurance is illegal under the *Competition Act*, the *Bank Act*, and the *Trust and Loan Companies Act*.[9]

---

8 R.S.C. 1985, c. B-1.
9 S.C. 1991, c. 45.

The Web site of the Office of the Superintendent of Financial Institutions is <www.osfi-bsif.gc.ca>. A free complaint resolution process is available through each participating bank's ombudsman (in place for all the major banks), and, if not successful, through the Canadian Banking Ombudsman, <www.bankingombudsman.com>.

This ends the sections on federal legislation and practice. Next, we look at two provinces: Ontario because of its large population and economic importance, and Quebec because it has a recently revised, comprehensive set of consumer laws.

ONTARIO

Ministry of Consumer and Commercial Relations

The Government of Ontario has more statutes, rules, and regulations than any other jurisdiction in Canada; indeed, it has more than the average country. Most of the statutes relating to consumers come under the Ministry of Consumer and Commercial Relations (**MCCR**); it oversees some 60 statutes, more than any other Canadian ministry.

MCCR's regulations affect you throughout your life: your birth and marriage are recorded according to the *Vital Statistics Act* and the *Marriage Act*; your entertainment may be governed by the *Theatres Act*, *Wine Content Act*, and *Liquor Control Act*; your activity under the *Racing Commission Act* may bring you into contact with the *Debt Collectors Act*; and you can expect to eventually be subject to the *Funeral Directors and Establishments Act* and the *Cemeteries Act*.

This massive ministry can be contacted at 1-800-268-1142, from which you can access, for instance, the gas busters hotline; the seniors line; information on loan brokers, credit, and collection agencies; fitness and modelling operations; home repairs; and you can order various brochures. Five administrative bodies were recently established to oversee motor vehicle dealers, real estate agents and brokers, travel agents and brokers, electrical safety, and technical standards and safety businesses (including fuel and elevator safety); but primarily, MCCR is organized into the following three divisions.

The Corporate Services Division deals mainly with alcohol, gaming, and racing; the Registration Division covers property registration and marriage and name-change regulations. The Business Division oversees some 20 statutes of interest to consumers. Those of particular relevance to consumers are described below, but this division is responsible also for the *Business Regulation Reform Act, Collection Agencies Act, Consumer Protection Bureau, Discriminatory Business Practices Act, Funeral Directors and Establishments Act, Loan Brokers Act, Motor Vehicle Dealers Act, Ontario New Home Warranties Plan, Prepaid Services Act, Real Estate and Business Brokers Act, Safety and Consumer Statutes Administration,* and *Travel Industry Act.*

The Business Practices Act[10]

The **Business Practices Act** (sample in Exhibit 27.1) is designed to eliminate abusive selling tactics by defining false and deceptive representations, and by prohibiting business practices such as representing that (a) goods have qualities, benefits, and characteristics that they do not possess; (b) the goods are new when they are not; (c) a service, replacement, or repair is needed when it is not; and (d) a price advantage exists when it does not.

---

[10] R.S.O. 1990, c. B.18.

EXHIBIT 20.1

Unfair Business Practices in Ontario

2. For the purposes of this Act, the following shall be deemed to be unfair practices:

    (1) A false, misleading or deceptive consumer representation including, but without limiting the generality of the foregoing,

    i. a representation that the goods or services have sponsorship, approval, performance characteristics, accessories, uses, ingredients, benefits or quantities they do not have,

    ii. a representation that the person who is to supply the goods or services has sponsorship, approval, status, affiliation or connection the person does not have,

    iii. a representation that the goods are of a particular standard, quality, grade, style or model, if they are not,

    iv. a representation that the goods are new, or unused, if they are not or are reconditioned or reclaimed, provided that the reasonable use of goods to enable the seller to service, prepare, test and deliver the goods for the purpose of sale shall not be deemed to make the goods used for the purposes of this subparagraph,

    v. a representation that the goods have been used to an extent that is materially different from the fact,

    vi. a representation that the goods or services are available for a reason that does not exist,

    vii. a representation that the goods or services have been supplied in accordance with a previous representation, if they have not,

    viii. a representation that the goods or services or any part thereof are available to the consumer when the person making the representation knows or ought to know they will not be supplied,

    ix. a representation that a service, part, replacement or repair is needed, if it is not,

    x. a representation that a specific price advantage exists, if it does not,

    xi. a representation that misrepresents the authority of a salesperson, representative, employee or agent to negotiate the final terms of the proposed transaction,

    xii. a representation that the proposed transaction involves or does not involve rights, remedies or obligations if the representation is false or misleading,

    xiii. a representation using exaggeration, innuendo or ambiguity as to a material fact or failing to state a material fact if such use or failure deceives or tends to deceive,

    xiv. a representation that misrepresents the purpose or intent of any solicitation of or any communication with a consumer.

    (2) An unconscionable consumer representation made in respect of a particular transaction and in determining whether or not a consumer representation is unconscionable there may be taken into account that the person making the representation or the person's employer or principal knows or ought to know,

    i. that the consumer is not reasonably able to protect his or her interests because of physical infirmity, ignorance, illiteracy, inability to understand the language of an agreement or similar factors,

    ii. that the price grossly exceeds the price at which similar goods or services are readily available to like consumers,

    iii. that the consumer is unable to receive a substantial benefit from the subject-matter of the consumer representation,

    iv. that there is no reasonable probability of payment of the obligation in full by the consumer,

    v. that the proposed transaction is excessively one-sided in favour of someone other than the consumer,

    vi. that the terms or conditions of the proposed transaction are so adverse to the consumer as to be inequitable,

    vii. that he or she is making a misleading statement of opinion on which the consumer is likely to rely to his or her detriment,

    viii. that he or she is subjecting the consumer to undue pressure to enter into the transaction.

    (3) Such other consumer representations under paragraph 1 as are prescribed by the regulations made in accordance with section 16.

Source: *Business Practices Act*, R.S.O. 1990, s. 2.

This Act provides consumers with remedies that were unavailable to them under common law. In the case of proven misrepresentation it allows the cancellation of a contract and the total refund of payment. It allows for damages when consumers fall victim to innocent misrepresentation, and outlines available remedies.

The statute requires an element of "reliance"; if a retailer's misrepresentation of an item did not influence the decision to purchase, the Act would not apply. Otherwise, there are three avenues for relief: (a) a request to the seller to cancel the agreement if sought within six months, (b) a request to the Court to cancel it, and (c) a request for mediation by the government.

The Consumer Protection Act[11]

The *Consumer Protection Act* deals mainly with **executory contracts**, those that are to be partially or fully performed in the future. It's designed to protect vulnerable people such as live-alone seniors from aggressive and persistent door-to-door salespeople. It allows a 48-hour (two working days) "cooling off" period on such contracts with a value above $50 if the transaction takes place at a location other than the seller's place of business, and if either the payment is not made in full or if all the goods are not provided at once.

For instance, if you make a time-payment purchase of a vacuum cleaner at home, or a massage chair at a county fair, you may rescind the contract within 48 hours after receiving your copy of the bill. (At the time of this writing, if passed, the *Red Tape Reduction Act, 1999* will increase the "cooling off" period to 10 days, telephone calls excepted.) The cancellation can be registered-mail postmarked within that time, and sent to the name/address required to be shown on the contract (or delivered personally). Any deposit or trade-in must be returned; title of the trade-in does not pass to the seller until the two-day period has expired without **recission**. And you can return the partial goods at the seller's expense. (If the full goods are delivered at once, or if you sign a credit card or cheque for full payment, the 48-hour provision does not apply. You may have other remedies such as suing for misrepresentation, but persistence in the course of selling is legal.)

The Act also protects you from having to pay for, or even having to return, any unsolicited goods. Also, it prohibits a seller from repossessing goods (except as permitted by an Ontario Court judge) after you have paid two-thirds the amount owing. It requires that full disclosure be made on credit transactions, including the amount owed and the cost of borrowing expressed as an annual percentage. **Referral selling**, the rewarding of a buyer for finding other customers, is prohibited by the statute. Finally, there can be an order for immediate cessation of the use of "statements in an advertisement, circular, pamphlet or similar material" if the director "believes on reasonable and probable grounds" that a seller or lender is being false, misleading, or deceptive.

The Consumer Reporting Act[12]

What kind of information is filed on you, for whom, and why? If you apply to rent an apartment, the renter needs to know if you can afford it; if you apply for a job, the employer might need to know if you are bondable; and if you want a loan or credit card, your payment history and character could be in issue. This statute states the kind of data that a consumer reporting agency

[11] R.S.O. 1990, c. C.31.
[12] R.S.O. 1990, c. C.33.

can disclose to an inquirer, stipulates how it can be used, and protects consumers against outdated and inaccurate information.

One type of business covered by the *Consumer Reporting Act* is a **credit reporting agency**. It keeps records of writs and judgments that might affect your ability to pay your bills, and of your credit transactions. The records are usually filed at the nearest credit bureau. The other type is a **personal information reporting agency**. It might collect and store data on your lifestyle (character, reputation, health, mode of living) as well as your credit history. Both kinds of agency sell their information to businesses that need to know about you (not to the public); they must be registered with the MCCR, and must advise you when an inquiry is made.

After seven years there can be no listing of criminal convictions, writs, tax or fine information, and a discharged once-and-only bankruptcy. Also excluded are criminal charges that were dropped, and a notice of claim representing the intention to sue if issued over 12 months before the report date unless there is proof on file that it is still active.

The *Consumer Reporting Act* emphasizes accuracy; for instance, agencies must make a "reasonable effort" to verify any unfavourable information before listing it. You are entitled to an easily readable, plain language copy of all the information in both your credit history and personal information files. If you contest an entry and supply proof of the error upon request, the agency must either support its entry, delete it, or correct the error, and must report any corrections to certain recipients of the incorrect data. See *Credit Report Agencies* in the Yellow Pages. Otherwise, you can complain to the Registrar of Consumer Reporting Agencies.

If a business seems to downgrade your creditworthiness (denying you a benefit or increasing your fee) you can demand to receive, within 60 days, the name and address of the agency or the nature and source of the information that's being acted upon. A conviction of knowingly providing false information or contravening the Act can result in a $2,000 fine and/or a year in prison; the maximum fine for a corporation is $25,000.

The Repair and Storage Liens Act[13]

Centuries before there was much in the way of machinery to fix, common law protected innkeepers from not being paid for lodging and food provided; they could hold onto the guest's luggage or horse as security. This "holding onto" became enshrined in statutory law as a **lien**, which is the entitlement of one person to keep another's property or to put a claim on it until paid the related funds due. (The word comes from the Latin verb *ligare*, to bind, from which we also get terms such as ligature.) The law of liens on personal property, the *Repair and Storage Liens Act (RSLA)*, protects both those who fix or store goods and their owner.[14]

Essentially, if you don't pay me on time for my agreed-upon work or storage, I can retain possession of what I repaired, improved, or stored for you until you do — through a lien on it. After three months awaiting payment and giving proper notice, I can dispose of (sell, keep, or donate) it.

What if I fix some machinery at your factory or farm, or if I let you take your van so you can earn the funds to pay my bill on it? Even without possession of the goods on which I am owed payment, I have **non-possessory lien** rights. I may obtain "a signed acknowledgement of indebtedness" (such as an invoice for the services performed) from you, and register a *Claim for*

---

[13] R.S.O. 1990, c. R.25.
[14] For the law regarding liens on land for improvements to land, see the *Construction Lien Act*, R.S.O. 1990, c. C.30.

Lien in the Personal Property Security Registration (PPSR) system, which is covered next. The RSLA could allow a sheriff to seize the article so that it could be sold to satisfy the lien.

Personal Property Security Registration (PPSR) System

The PPSR system records and reproduces data on (a) consumer and business loans where personal property is used as collateral and (b) repair and storage liens. For instance, to borrow money to buy a car, you can expect to sign a "security agreement" turning over rights to the car if you don't repay the loan.

The "financing statement" sent to the Personal Property Registration Branch is recorded in a computer file and is available for searching by lenders and buyers. Within 30 days of registering the financing statement the lender must give the borrower the registration details. The statement contains the lender's name and business address, the registration period, identification of the collateral, and the amount and maturity date of the loan. It also holds the borrower's name, address, and birth date (the latter for identification, in that there are some five million registrations in the PPSR system). The borrower should check these details for accuracy.

Unlike business loans (which can be registered in perpetuity), consumer loans are limited to a five-year registration period at a time. When repaid, the lender must register a "discharge" within 30 days or be subject to any resulting damages plus up to a $500 payment to the borrower.

Performing a Search

Searches can be performed in Toronto at 375 University Ave. Elsewhere, one of the 55 local land registry offices can inform you of the closest location. Also, it can be done by mail using an enquiry form available at any office that handles PPSR searches, or by telephone at 1-800-267-8847 (325-8847 in Toronto) with an approved credit card.

Many registrations now are of vehicles rather than the horse or luggage of a guest at an inn. But a consumer need not conduct a search when buying from a registered dealer a new car or other item, or a used car worth $15,000 or less. If a search is conducted, it can be performed against a vehicle's **VIN** (vehicle identification number), against a business (by its registered or incorporated name), or against an individual by full name and date of birth.

Other modules are available for this text that provide more detailed information on other aspects of lien rights and obligations and their extension into, for instance, construction liens, repossession in a conditional sales contract, liens for real estate taxes and utility services, the use of liens by professionals such as architects, and liens by employees against their employers for unpaid wages or benefits.

The Motor Vehicle Repair Act

Historically, MCCR received more complaints about car repairs than any other topic. Following the passage of this fairly recent statute, the percentage has dropped from top place. This act balances the protection of consumers from being "held up" for unnecessary repairs or charged for repairs not performed, and of car technicians from giving a best-guess estimate and finding, once the work has started, that further repairs are required.

This statute requires repairers to "post a sign in a conspicuous place clearly visible to prospective customers" stating, for instance, that written estimates are available, how all charges are calculated, that your replaced parts will be returned upon request, and the MCCR complaints phone number. It must also indicate whether any commissions are paid. (If you are told that many parts need replacement and you know that the mechanic receives extra payment for parts you agree to buy, you might want a second opinion.)

If you request a written estimate, it must be free (unless you are first given a written estimate for making the estimate, or if the mechanic cannot get authorization to repair and must assemble or repair the vehicle in order to move it out of the way). The estimate must be detailed, including the type of parts to be used, hourly rate, and number of hours, and cannot be exceeded by more than 10 per cent.

You cannot be charged for repairs undertaken without your authorization in writing or by telephone if the repairer records your name, phone number, date, and time of authorization (an OK by phone allows for slippage, so be careful what you say). The invoice must be detailed; among the 10 requirements are the labour itemization, the warranty, and whether replaced parts are new, used, or reconditioned. If your repaired car becomes inoperable or unsafe because of faulty work, you can, if it is the only reasonable solution, take it to a nearby garage and later demand reimbursement for the new bill from the original repairer.

The *Sale of Goods Act*

Ontario's *Sale of Goods Act*[15] says that goods must be suitable for the declared purpose for which they were bought. "Where the buyer, expressly or by implication, makes known to the seller the particular purpose for which the goods are required, ... there is an implied condition that the goods will be reasonably fit for such purpose...." (Section 15). Thus, if you buy a cell phone without comment and find that it doesn't work where you live, your only recourse is the retailer's return policy. But if you initially inform the seller that you are buying it for use in Hidden Valley, then if you find that this location is a "dead spot", the seller cannot simply maintain that it is your phone now, and that any complaints should go to the manufacturer.

This Act is administered not by MCCR but by the office of the Attorney General (416-326-2220). It is based on an English statute of 1893 that derived in turn from common law. Although revised in 1960, some of the language retains century-old obscurity, for instance, "An implied warranty ... may be annexed by the usage of trade." This 53-section Act also gives the following consumer rights:

Good Title
Each purchaser has the right to receive good title for goods purchased. This gives the new owner the option to resell the item, the full use of the merchandise, and the sole control over it.

Compliance with Description
Purchasers who do not receive the goods at the time of making the contract can demand to inspect the goods before accepting them. Those who choose not to inspect the goods must accept them at their own risk.

Merchantability
Consumers have the right to receive products that are of good quality and that can perform their purpose or task with little difficulty.

---

[15] R.S.O. 1990, c. S.1.

EXHIBIT 20.2

When Will Ontario Catch Up?

Ontario's consumer-protection laws date from simpler times when you handed over cash and the merchant gave you the goods. If they disintegrated on the way out of the store, bad luck. There were no cars to repair, no data-transmission to invade our privacy, and no junk mail, phone calls, or faxes.

Now cashiers juggle high-tech credit cards, bar-codes, and debit cards. Phone hucksters computer-dial you with dubious deals from far-off states, provinces, and countries. You can buy a computer from your TV screen, then buy a TV from your computer screen.

Consumers have also changed: they want a marketplace in which they are informed and protected. Yet, Ontario laws say little about telemarketing, negative-option schemes, refunds and exchanges, third-party warranties, cross-border mail orders, home repairs, or late delivery of pre-paid goods. Though half of all transactions in Ontario now involve services, the law still ignores most services.

Ontario's original consumer legislation hardly changed for 50 years, but starting in the 1960s, the MCCR has been adding to and patching the laws in response to consumer complaints, resulting in a maze of general and specific statutes.

A legislative review to update, consolidate, and simplify these laws occurred in 1986, sparked by MCCR chief Monte Kwinter under Liberal David Peterson. Kwinter's successors William Wrye and Greg Sorbara added further changes based on wide consultations. Before Peterson called the 1990 election, Sorbara tried to ensure that the changes would be continued by the next government; he circulated a draft for public comment, which was supportive. Enter the NDP, and Bob Rae put the MCCR in the hands of Peter Kormos (who left the overhaul on a back burner), and then replaced Kormos with Marilyn Churley.

Churley, the fifth minister to deal with this law reform, renewed the project, added sharper teeth to the measures, and named the statute **The Fair Marketplace Code.** She also replaced its legalisms with plain language, so that "Rescissions pursuant to itinerant hawkers" would become "Cancellations of deals made with in-home sellers." The Code integrates six statutes (including the *Sale of Goods Act*), plus common law, into one that basically says, "If you want to do business in Ontario, whether with goods or services, here are the ground rules that will be fair to both sides."

The Code was welcomed by sellers because it clarifies good business practices (which should reduce disputes and lawsuits), and deters fly-by-nighters from skimming the cream. It specifies not only consumer rights and remedies but responsibilities too; all parties will know where they stand. It would show the world that Ontario's a good place to do business and to be a consumer.

University of Waterloo economist Bob Kerton called it "a framework which encourages honest sellers to succeed, while deterring scam artists." Other consumer advocates said that Ontario consumers need "this clear, generic law stipulating that you can't lie, cheat, or take advantage of a consumer, because at the moment, consumers often don't know where they stand." Another asserted that the code "will make Ontario the best jurisdiction in North America for consumers."

That's not the case at the moment. Ontario has been outdistanced by Quebec and several states and western provinces, for instance, Alberta's *Fair Trades Act*. But the three ministers who have headed the MCCR since the Progressive Conservative Party assumed power in June of 1995 (David Tsubouchi, Norm Sterling, and Bob Runciman) have shelved this comprehensive change, making it the most delayed modern statute in Ontario legislative history.

Financial Services Commission of Ontario

Another government body related to consumer law is the *Financial Services Commission of Ontario*. This new organization combines the former Ontario Insurance Commission, the Pension Commission of Ontario, and the Deposit Institutions Division of the Ministry of Finance. Its phone is 800-668-0128; the Web site is <www.fsco.gov.on.ca>.

Its insurance sector, the Ontario Insurance Commission, regulates all insurers licensed to do business in Ontario (whether for auto, life, or travel), provides a dispute-resolution ombudsman (whose report is not binding on either side), and offers various brochures. Its Web site <www. ontarioinsurance.com> lists all licensed car insurers by type, gives rate information and other consumer advice, and posts a comprehensive car insurer Claims Satisfaction Survey. (General information on insurance is provided in the second-last main section below.)

Accessing Ontario Statutes

The complete texts of all Ontario statutes can be viewed at <www.gov.on.ca> and choosing Language (English or French), Look up Acts and Regulations, Full Text of Ontario's Legislation (acts and regulations), Access to the Statutes and Regulations site, and English or French. The Web postings are not considered official; for that, official copies of statutes can be ordered from the Ontario Government Bookstore (1-800-668-9938 or <www.gov.on.ca/MBS/ english/publications>).

QUEBEC

We now turn to the second major province. Quebec is reviewed here because (a) the *Civil Code of Quebec* was updated recently (January 1, 1994), (b) the Code includes the *Consumer Protection Act*, a comprehensive set of regulations for consumer protection and business regulation, and (c) only Quebec law derives from the Napoleonic Code rather than English common law. The full statutes can be found in a bilingual paperback listed in the suggested readings at the end of this chapter.

In the summary below, the word "Act" will refer to the *Consumer Protection Act* [*Loi sur la protection du consommateur*]. It was drafted in French; where the English translation seems less precise, or where the French version might be helpful, the latter is shown in brackets. In the summary below, the abbreviation "M/M/A" will mean *merchant, manufacturer or advertiser* (a phrase that appears in many of the Act's 365 sections); "s" means section.

The *Consumer Protection Act*

The Act starts, unfortunately, with some hazy definitions. A "consumer" is a "natural person [*personne physique*], except a merchant who obtains goods or services for the purposes of his business." A merchant "includes any person doing business or extending credit in the course of his business." Thus, the Act's consumer protection apparently applies to all people in Quebec other than business people in the context of their work.

Section 22 says that a merchant soliciting a consumer for a "remote-parties" contract (one in which the buyer and seller are not in direct contact) cannot demand total or partial payment prior to the performance of the principal obligation. Thus, if I offer you my shopping service in which I will furnish goods not from my own stock but from other suppliers, I cannot extract your money until I deliver the main items. (If you solicited the transaction with me, I could require advance payment.)

In Chapter III on warranties, "Goods forming the object of a contract must be fit for the purposes of which goods of that kind are ordinarily used ... [and] must be durable in normal use for a reasonable length of time, having regard to their price, the terms of the contract and the conditions of their use." Where the goods "are of a nature that requires maintenance, replacement parts and repair service must be available for a reasonable time after the making of the contract" unless the merchant or manufacturer warns the consumer in writing prior to the contract that these services are not supplied. Moreover, the goods or services must conform to their description in the contract and to the statements or advertisements regarding them made by the merchant or manufacturer.

Itinerant merchants, those doing business elsewhere than "at his address", are covered where the contract exceeds $25. For instance, the contract must be fully detailed, and under section 58 the consumer has the right to cancel it within 10 days; moreover, the merchant must inform the consumer of this entitlement in writing. If the goods are not delivered within the cancellation period, no payment can change hands.

One of the largest parts of Chapter III (over 80 sections in Division III) relates to credit. As examples, the credit rate must be described in a simple and standardized format, the contract must provide for one deferred payment and permit full or partial payment prior to maturity, and the merchant must furnish the consumer a statement at least 21 days prior to the imposition of credit charges. If the consumer defaults on payment after having paid half of the debt, the merchant cannot repossess the goods except with a court order.

Division IV on automobiles (and motorcycles) provides comprehensive protection to the Quebec consumer. When a car under warranty needs towing or breakdown service, the owner does not pay, and all provisions apply equally to subsequent owners of the vehicle; coverage applies to both parts and labour. Under section 237, it is illegal to misleadingly replace a car's odometer reading or alter it.

Used cars offered for sale or long-term lease must bear a label, readable from the exterior, showing the price, full model-identifying details, the distance the vehicle has travelled, any type of commercial service it has undergone, the warranty offered, and all repairs carried out when in possession of the seller. If the label includes defects and a price estimate of repairs, the merchant is bound by that estimate. A certificate of mechanical inspection must be included, and the name and phone number of the previous owner must be provided upon request. The warranty covers between six months or 10,000 kilometres (whichever comes first) down to one month or 1,700 kilometres, depending on the class of vehicle, which is a function of age and distance driven.

Before performing any repairs, the merchant must provide a detailed written estimate that cannot be exceeded without a written waiver from the owner. There are nine items that must be included in the bill, and most replaced parts must be provided upon request. If the owner refuses to pay an amount not in accordance with the requirements, the merchant may not retain possession of the car. Moreover, the consumer entitlements must be conspicuously posted in the shop.

Under Division V, the repair of major household appliances is also subject to a written estimate that cannot be charged for without advance notice, and the bill for repairs must be complete and detailed. Repairs are warranted for three months.

Division VI requires that physical fitness studios (health clubs, or *studios de santé*) provide clients with detailed and complete contracts that cannot exceed one year. Prior to the beginning of the delivery of the services, the merchant cannot receive payment, and the client can cancel the contract. The client can also cancel within the first 10 days of the commencement of services, or during the first 10 per cent of the contract duration; any payment exceeding one-tenth of the contract amount must be returned within 10 days.

In terms of general business practices, there is considerable emphasis on being truthful; under Title II, merchants, manufacturers, and advertisers are prohibited from making any false or misleading representations to consumers. Apart from this general restriction, many specific types of such representations are specified as illegal, such as misrepresenting the quantity of goods on hand, or discrediting goods or services offered by others. This particularly applies to the sale price: section 223 stipulates that it must be indicated clearly and legibly, higher amounts cannot be charged, and any installment payments indicated cannot overshadow the total price.

To give another example, and to illustrate the plain yet specific wording in the Act, here is section 225 verbatim: No M/M/A "may, falsely, by any means whatever, (a) invoke a price reduction; (b) indicate a regular price or another reference price for goods or services; (c) let it be believed that the price of certain goods or services is advantageous." It's evident that this section was sparked by consumer complaints: "No merchant or manufacturer may refuse to perform the warranty granted by him on the pretext that the document evidencing it has not reached him or was not validated." And in case anything was left out, no M/M/A "may fail to mention an important fact in any representation made to a consumer." Thus, if a car for sale had undergone major repairs, this must be disclosed.

The distinction between businesses and consumers is becoming blurred, as non-business people are increasingly being offered commercial opportunities to operate out of their residences. It would violate the Quebec statutes to, "... when soliciting or making a contract, make false representations concerning the profitability or any other aspect of a business opportunity offered to a customer." Nor can a person be charged for goods that were not ordered.

Those who advertise must have a sufficient quantity "to meet public demand" unless the ad indicates to the contrary. Premiums (such as price rebates) cannot be emphasized more than the goods or services themselves. Ads promoting contests for gifts, prizes, or rebates must include all the terms clearly. As for multilevel or **pyramid selling** plans, no benefit can be offered for the consumer signing up other individuals.

No M/M/A can falsely indicate (a) certification, recommendation, sponsorship, approval, affiliation, or association with a third party, (b) the latter's approval, certification, or sponsorship of goods or services, or (c) a particular status or identity. Nor can a M/M/A distort the meaning of any information, opinion, or testimony, or "rely upon data or analyses falsely presented as scientific."

The holding of a permit under the Act does not entitle anyone to imply that it means competence, solvency, recognition, or approval. The holding of a permit or the furnishing of a required security cannot be mentioned in an ad. Every ad must specify that the sponsor is a merchant who must be identified, including the street address. Ads cannot urge consumers to obtain goods or services by credit.

Applications for credit must explicitly state that's what they are. Moreover, credit rates and terms, and the conditions of a long-term lease, must be stated in accordance with the Act.

Commercial advertising cannot be directed to persons under the age of 13 years, in terms of the context, nature, purpose, manner, and time and place of the ad. Nor can ads invite payment by cheques from the government of Quebec, Canada, or a municipality. If such cheques are accepted as payment, no charge can be levied for this service.

A merchant who accepts payment prior to issuing a contract must place those funds in a trust account (until the funds are repaid on demand, or a contract is made). This account must be a single one in an institution recognized under the *Deposit Insurance Act*, the president of the institution must be informed of the account, and the details must be entered in the merchant's books.

Schedule 1 prescribes the forms to be used in consumer matters. These include forms for a loan contract, an installment contract, and cancelling a contract. Another section of the Act, comprising 180 sections, deals with its application. For instance, farm and forestry loans come under a different statute, as do student loans.

The Application of the Act

In the second half of the Act, a number of "Schedules" specify the design and wording of the *forms* prescribed under the Act. For instance, section 58 mentioned above permits a contract with an itinerant merchant to be cancelled within 10 days; Schedule 1 [Annexe 1] gives the applicable forms, namely, the detailed "Statement of Consumer Cancellation Rights", and the forms to be completed by the buyer and seller. It also covers the "Form of Writings", specifying the minimum quality of the paper, and even how the reader is to be informed if the writing is continued on the back. In brief, contracts may be handwritten or printed; if typed, the font, colour, and minimum size are specified.

There are 180 clauses on how the Act is to be applied. These include definitions (e.g., a "mobile home" is "any structure intended to be used all year round as a dwelling and to be connected to public services and capable of being transported on its own frame by towing or by any other means"), and exemptions (for instance, section 22 does not apply to the subscription to a newspaper, periodical, or magazine).

The application section specifies what consumer-protection information must be included in a contract. Such required material comprises specified clauses from the Act, a recommendation that the consumer refer to other relevant clauses, and advice to consult the "Office de la protection du consommateur" (not all the material is provided in English). Contracts requiring such information include those involving itinerant merchants, credit and loans, long-term lease of goods contracts, the lease of services involving sequential performance, and those that contain a provision of forfeiture of benefit of the term. Other contracts requiring such announcements are those involving automobiles, motorcycles, and household appliances. Similar stipulations regard certain types of advertising, such as for credit and long-term lease.

A repairer of cars or motorcycles must "post up, in a conspicuous place of his establishment, a sign giving the following particulars" (the regulations outlined in the paragraph starting "The section on automobiles" above, but in French only). Moreover, the sign must be on "stiff material with a white non-glossy surface"; the minimum size and the font details are also specified. When a car odometer is replaced with one that cannot be reset, a permanent label must be affixed to the inside of the instrument panel window, near the odometer, clearly indicating the reading of the replaced odometer.

Although advertising directed to children is prohibited, the section on applications permits it in limited circumstances such as in some material (primarily magazines) directed at children. It also further restricts it; for instance, ads may not exaggerate product attributes, use superlatives, directly incite a child to buy, or portray "reprehensible social or family lifestyles". Nor can a comic strip be included (except to promote a comic book), nor can an ad suggest that a product "will develop in a child a physical, social or psychological advantage over other children his age."

You may recall that section 223 covers how prices must be indicated; the Applications sections exempts various categories of goods, such as those selling for no more than 40 cents, and those in automatic vending machines. Also excluded from coverage are categories representing a minority of those sold in a given store — if those categories are themselves posted on a clear list and the prices are clearly and legibly shown near where the articles are sold.

The Applications also covers the various permits required of merchants, and the forms they must use to apply for them or for renewals. For instance, an application to be a physical fitness studio operator must include financial records and a security deposit of $15,000.

Commentary on the Quebec Code

In terms of content, Quebec consumers now have the strongest and clearest protection in Canada. Nonetheless, two forms of promotion that could be covered more specifically are telemarketing, and improper claims made or implied by individuals on behalf of a company. Additionally, the restrictions should apply to the government itself. The Advertising Standards Canada (ASC) ruled that a $520,000 series of 1999 Quebec government ads claiming that the province received less money than Ontario in the last federal budget violated national advertising standards in that they were inaccurate and left out key information. (ASC is a voluntary organization funded by 100 media outlets, ad agencies, and corporations; its only power over advertisers is to list bad ones in its biannual report.)

The definition of "consumer" is restrictive, as it only applies to merchants. Consumer-protection laws generally exclude commercial transactions; a railway company would hardly expect government laws or offices to redress its complaint that its new locomotive was delivered scratched. Moreover, a doctor (if considered a "merchant" under the Act) should know how to choose a stethoscope, a psychologist should be able to safely buy a test. But not every "merchant" is a skilled professional or a corporation with its own purchasing agent. Presumably, a butcher would be protected while buying a car or having the house painted, but not in buying a delivery van or having the shop fumigated. So if you buy your first dough-mixer for your new, one-person pizza parlour and it is defective, the best consumer-protection statute in Canada excludes you. Whereas Ontario seems to favour the merchant over the consumer (as in the history of its *Sale of Goods Act*, which primarily created a vehicle for merchants to sue other merchants), Quebec disregards the needs of small business people in its definition of "consumer".

COMMENTARY ON CANADIAN CONSUMER LEGISLATION

Generally, Canadian consumers are reasonably well served by their provincial and federal legislation, although, as one example, Australia has more complete coverage, better provisions for consumer redress, and a much better capacity to address cross-border infractions. Here are some specific ways in which our consumer laws could be improved.

Style Weaknesses

In the past few decades, the use of "plain language" (wording that is clear to most readers) has become a feature of many types of documents such as textbooks, insurance contracts, instruction manuals, and also laws — including the new Quebec statute. It's time to refine and define this aspect with all laws that touch the ordinary person, as is the case with consumer-protection legislation. In some American states such as Florida, the law requires that any written contract must be fully understandable by 60 per cent of the population.

The use of gender-exclusive language has been increasingly considered unacceptable, a departure from the definition of a "person" as male under Canadian law in the early 20th century. When women were included and allowed to vote, most writers (who were generally male) maintained that male nouns and pronouns properly referred to both males and females; the word "man" was supposed to refer to a human being. Today we have to accept the fact that laws rely on precedent and long-established conventions in the meaning of terms. Statutes are gradually being written and revised with non-exclusionary language, but these changes are taking place slowly, and parts of the past are still with us.

Content Weaknesses

A comprehensive way of improving Canadian statutes would be to increase the consistency among the provinces and territories. For instance, as a result of Quebec's requirement that all material facts about a car must be disclosed to the potential buyer, some wrecked Quebec cars that had been written off as total losses by the insurer and then repaired were brought to Ontario for sale to unknowing buyers. Ontario's laxer legislation provided an outlet for cars that in Quebec would be sold for scrap. As other examples, a substance-abuser could have a driver's licence revoked in one province and obtain a new one in another, a bankrupt could leave creditors stranded in one province and obtain new credit in another, and a fraud artist could close down in one jurisdiction and set up in another.

Consistency would help interprovincial trade and commerce. Picture a firm with many successful branches in Ontario that wishes to open another in Manitoba. To do so, it must hire a Manitoba law firm to ensure that it would be in compliance with all of the relevant consumer and business legislation that differ in subtle ways from that of Ontario. That may be just enough to kill the expansion. Similarly, imagine an Asian firm planning to invest in many new branches throughout either England or Canada. It learns that it must learn and conform to either one set of consumer regulations or as many as 14 (federal, 10 provincial, three territorial).

Consistency could also benefit some consumers. Time was, most people were buried within a few blocks of the house in which they were born. Today, many people move a number of times during their lives and careers, often changing provinces. Nowadays you can communicate with, buy from, or sell to someone across the country more easily than the previous generation could have done just across town. In this sense the country is shrinking and thereby calling for uniformity in how business is conducted and consumers are treated.

As society and technology become more complex, and as our demands for safety and security increase, it is understandable that our lives will become increasingly rule-regulated. It's also understandable that past history and current problems differ across areas of Canada. But when a simple, common occupation and tool-of-the-trade such as a taxi and driver are subject to hundreds of regulations and statutes, including federal, provincial/territorial, and municipal/regional ones, surely consistency, currentness, and clarity should be worthy objectives for all of our legislators.

Another area for improvement is the need for currentness; most of the statutes discussed date from the 1960s and 1970s, when the marketplace was different. Legislation is needed that would invite the investigation and prosecution of "scam artists" whose targets are beyond the jurisdiction in question. Authorities in BC were recently unsuccessful when the court refused to prosecute deceptive telemarketers who were phoning Americans, because the relevant statute was worded to protect only British Columbians. We cannot expect other jurisdictions to crack down on those who prey on us if we do not reciprocate.

Finally, the Canadian consumer movement is small, fragmented, and underfunded. Most volunteer organizations have experienced recent funding cuts, and some such as the Consumers' Association of Canada have been particularly hard hit. Investing in volunteerism is practical because the members do not get paid, and legislative support for such organizations would benefit all consumers.

We conclude this chapter with coverage of two special topics that most consumers deal with uncertainly, insurance and motor vehicles. Unlike the other subjects covered, these often-troublesome areas are treated from a general consumer advisement or paralegal perspective as well as from a legal one.

INSURANCE

The principal of insurance is that you (or your parent, spouse, or employer) pay now for protection that you might be entitled to collect on later. Considering what would happen if the insurer were unwilling or unable to fulfill its contractual obligations when the time comes, you can see that the government is obligated to protect policyholders. Recently, more than 100 disabled employees of a venerable department store had been receiving disability benefits while unable to work. When Eaton's prepared a bankruptcy proposal in late 1999, it turned out that it had been "self-insuring" its long-term disability and drug plans, and almost all payments stopped without warning. If the store had bought insurance to protect its employees, the regulators and the insurance industry would have ensured that the carrier itself would never fail to protect those who depended on it.

Although the shared-risk principle of insurance is simple, the legislation and terminology are complex. A firm or individual licensed by the federal government (under the *Insurance Companies Act*) can sell insurance anywhere in Canada; an insurer licensed by a province (as by the *Insurance Act of Ontario*) can conduct business only in that province.

Theoretically, you can insure anything, from tomorrow's weather to having to cancel a prepaid trip. But the three basic types of insurance are motor vehicle, property (which together is called "general insurance"), and life. Car insurance is handled provincially (the province itself insures cars in British Columbia, Manitoba, and Saskatchewan); the others can be federally or provincially regulated, depending on the insurer's licence.

The Insurance Policy

An insurance policy is a binding contract between the insurer and the policyholder that specifies what "perils" are covered, how, and to what extent; no policy covers "everything". A consumer-friendly policy clarifies what is and is not insured in plain, unambiguous language. The onus should not be on the policyholder to ask every question in advance, but on the insurer to predict and answer it, at least generally or by examples.

For instance, most home policies exclude damage from vermin, but if a squirrel or raccoon gets trapped in your house and damages it, you would need to know if your insurer deems all creatures that cause damage to be "vermin". Similarly, a life insurance policy should state what proof of death must accompany a claim, and within what time limit. (Imagine that the death occurs in a foreign country, and that various insurers would require any or all of a local or any newspaper obituary, a certificate from a provincially licensed or any funeral director, a specific or any medical certificate of death, or a costly and time-consuming document from the provincial registrar of records.)

One common factor among motor vehicle policies is that all provinces require cars to be insured for minimum amounts for certain perils; for instance, third-party liability coverage of at least $200,000 is usual. But each jurisdiction's is unique; for instance, Alberta uses a **tort-based insurance**

system whereas Ontario is **no-fault**, and you can sue for pain and suffering in some cases and not in others.

Within a province all car policies are identical, whereas non-car policies vary. That is, if 10 people in the same block have life or home policies from 10 insurers, probably no two policies would be the same. But the terms are identical in, for instance, Ontario's five million vehicle policies sold by about 150 competing firms.

As with all insurance, the **premium** relates to the risk as calculated by the insurer. Thus, the standard variables for car insurance rates are (apart from the insured's choices for optional extra coverage): where the principal driver lives, the amount driven and for what purposes, and the age and/ or driving record of the principal and other drivers. The last variable is the car's make and year as related to predicted cost of repair or replacement, likelihood of theft, and occupant injury protection; data on these variables are available from the Vehicle Information Centre of Canada, <www.vicc.com/>.

Private car insurers differ in other ways within a province, especially how much and on what basis they charge, whom they accept for a new policy and for a renewal, and the handling of claims. They also vary in billing and payment practices such as how far in advance they bill, whether they accept post-dated cheques or automatic fund withdrawal, and in the case of expiration due to non-payment, how they notify you, and how long any **grace period** is. Other differences include procedures for resolving disputes, the amount and duration of surcharges for what type of claims, and acceptance by telephone of temporary changes such as removing road coverage during periods of car storage.

Questions to Ask Insurers

All insurance tends to be complex and the language esoteric; for instance, the word "premium" has a different meaning to insurers than it does to others in other contexts. Moreover, most insurance buyers spend a few minutes deciding on coverage every few years whereas sellers ply their trade all day long, thus making for an unequal relationship.

Even though all policies within a province have the same terms, it seems that few vehicle owners have studied them. For instance, suppose you lend your Ontario-registered vehicle to a friend whose licence, unknown to either of you, had just expired. Following a collision, you would find that your car was not insured during the loan. Or, if the insurer discovers that you made inaccurate statements in your application, they could reject any claim.

Accordingly, questions that consumers might ask a private insurer are:

- If I have a full replacement coverage for property that becomes a write-off, how would you respond to my preference for a cash settlement rather than a replacement?

- If the property depreciates during my policy renewals, will you lower the premium for replacement coverage to reflect your decreased exposure?

- If I report minor damage in a telephone inquiry but decide not to file a claim, would my record be downgraded as if I had filed a claim on it?

- Will I be able to see my complete file on request?

- If I have complex questions, will I have access to your experienced experts as opposed to front-line office staffers?

- Have your terms been updated to cover modern needs such as home offices, satellite dishes, and laptop computers that are taken on trips?

- Will you make all your coverage options clear to me?

- Do you provide 24-hour claims service?

- How long after an incident do I have to make a claim?

- Assuming that your claims records differentiate between at-fault and not-at-fault claims, if you judged me to have been one per cent at fault in an incident, would you log it as an "at-fault" claim?

- Does your firm have an arbitration service for an *independent* review of disputes, such as The Co-operators and Royal have?

- If in my initial interview I answered "No" to the question "Do you deep fry?" would a claim for a fire caused by a visiting relative who left a deep fryer unattended be rejected?

- In 1999, an Ontario widow tried to collect on a life insurance policy her husband had bought to cover their $63,000 mortgage. After his sudden fatal heart attack, the insurer rejected the claim. He had indicated no intestinal illness, but his medical records showed mild colitis (which was unrelated to his death at age 45). A judge ruled that the application form was poorly worded and easily misunderstood, and that the husband had not intended to mislead. The insurer filed an appeal. How would your firm handle such a case?

In the case of agents and brokers, it might be useful to find out which insurers they represent (usually between one and eight), and how they are paid (for instance, whether some forms of optional coverage are particularly lucrative). You can also ask what services they offer, for instance, if you want help with an after-hours problem, or information on an insurer's underwriting guidelines.

The complete insurance statutes of at least five provinces (Alberta, British Columbia, New Brunswick, Ontario, and Quebec) can be accessed from <www.insurance-finance.com/canada.htm> and choosing Canadian Insurance Law Links. A comprehensive summary of provincial and territorial car policies is in the brochure "Facts" from the Insurance Bureau of Canada, 151 Yonge, Toronto M5C 2W7, or <www.ibc.ca>.

MOTOR VEHICLES

It often costs a year's income to buy a car; some are as expensive as an average house. Many owners think of the subsequent operating expenses in terms of fuel only, disregarding maintenance and repair costs. Additionally, the fixed expenses (insurance, licensing, and perhaps storage and periodic safety checks) continue throughout the ownership and can exceed the purchase price.

It's commonly believed that one's most expensive purchase is a house, with the car coming second. But real estate generally increases in value whereas cars depreciate, usually dropping half their value in three years and becoming near-worthless within a decade. Thus, over their lifetimes, many people have lost more money on their motor vehicles than on any other assets.

In addition, mechanically defective vehicles are troublesome to the owner and potentially dangerous to the public, and cosmetic imperfections that the dealer dismisses can destroy owner satisfaction. Automobiles do come with warranties, but they are not always the answer. Prior to the 1950s, most warranties lasted 30 to 90 days; today they range from one to four years. But this can be false security on modern, complex cars that are not designed to be fixed in the backyard as they once were. This is illustrated in the following composite example:

> When Ms. Buyer's new car does not start she has it towed to the dealer and later picks it up. Next day, it still won't start. After it has been in the shop for several days more, she is told the battery is bad, and as the manufacturer's warranty excludes tires and batteries she has to deal with the battery maker. A new battery is not a cure; the starter is serviced after two weeks at the dealer. The problem recurs; this time, after a month "waiting for parts" a computer chip is replaced. When it still hesitates she is accused of flooding the engine, using the wrong or dirty fuel, or leaving the lights on. When she insists that the car is defective, the dealer refers her to the manufacturer ("We only sold it to you; we did not make it"), who referred her back ("Your contract is with the dealer.") She has only paid for towing and taxis, but the car has been out of service for months, the problem persists, and when the warranty expires she will have to pay for work that she is not sure was performed competently or at all.

Those who purchase extended coverage may find that there are so many restrictions, which are always interpreted by the insurer (if it remains in business), that it is worthless. To seek redress through the court system generally requires time, expertise, funds, and the help of a mechanically adept lawyer to argue against the weight of an experienced dealer, service technician, and factory representative. The above are the reasons for the coverage of motor vehicles here. The next two sections are more on legal alternatives than entitlements.

Automobile Protection Association

The Automobile Protection Association (APA) is a Canadian non-profit association that publishes *Lemon-Aid*, which is both a quarterly magazine that is sent to members, and an annual paperback book series sold in bookstores. APA advises on vehicles, publishes information on "secret warranties" and dealer costs, lobbies for improved legislation on industry quality and sales practices, and recommends garages and products.

For instance, in early 1977, the Canadian car industry announced a plain language lease agreement designed to correct long-standing abuses. Subsequently, APA researchers posing as ordinary shoppers visited some 50 dealers. They found that meaningful disclosure of the lease details were still hard to find; for instance, "Not one Ford dealer outside Quebec accurately revealed the true cost of a two-year Red Carpet lease."

APA's head office is 292 St. Joseph Blvd. W., Montreal H2V 2N7, (514) APA-5555; the Toronto office is 2 Carlton St., M5B 1J3, (416) 204-1444; the Web site is <www.apa.ca>. Annual membership costs $52 plus tax.

CAMVAP

Lemon Laws

In the 1980s, some American states were passing **lemon laws** to protect car buyers from being stuck with a vehicle that proved to be unduly troublesome. Now, every state has such a law but there is none in Canada. Each state's law is unique, but a typical provision is that after three attempts or a total of 30 days in the shop to repair the same component or system on a non-commercial, low-mileage new car, the buyer is entitled to a refund of the purchase price. (Many states require that every "manufacturer buy-back" be so designated on the vehicle registration, so that the next buyer will be aware of serious problems.) Canadians wondering if their car would be considered a "lemon" elsewhere can review a summary of every state's definition at <www.carprices.com/insider_tips/lemon_law.html>.

To preclude lemon laws from entering Canada, the car manufacturers, in consultation with the MCCR, proposed an arbitration service for Ontario (where about half the country's cars are purchased), with a view to extending it nationally if successful. The Ontario Motor Vehicle Arbitration Plan (OMVAP) originated in 1986; in 1994 it became CAMVAP, the Canadian Motor Vehicle Arbitration Plan. Its Web site is <www.camvap.ca>.

Using CAMVAP

If your car has a defect that the dealer cannot or will not rectify, and you report this without success to the manufacturer's representative, you are entitled to invoke the plan. You will receive a list of three local arbitrators with their backgrounds and qualifications, and you choose any one to review the documentation and to schedule a hearing at which both sides present their case. The arbitrator, with the power to order full repayment of the purchase cost, is given the task of coming to a decision that is fair to both sides.

The arbitrator functions like a judge in a court of law, but there are no costs to you (the plan is funded by the car industry), and the hearings take place in a casual atmosphere in your home town; in a recent year, hearings occurred in 100 communities throughout the country, usually in a hotel room or Better Business Bureau office. Arbitrators are trained in CAMVAP issues and procedures; three-quarters are lawyers, sometimes retired. There are about 150 on call, one-third of whom are in Ontario. The plan pays $300 plus expenses and disbursements for the arbitrator's time and expertise in running the hearing and issuing a report and decision; for instance, the arbitrator can hire a technician (usually through the Canadian Automobile Association) to examine the case.

After invoking CAMVAP, you may receive an offer from the manufacturer or dealer to rectify the problem (or to compensate you) as an alternative to proceeding with a hearing. It is your option to accept this or to continue with the CAMVAP process. Once a hearing takes place, you waive the right to take further legal action if you are not satisfied with the outcome. After the repairs or replacements ordered by the arbitrator have been completed within the stipulated time but not to your satisfaction, you may request a further hearing; in one such case the follow-up result was a buy-back.

CAMVAP is universal with two exceptions. Every province and territory except Quebec is a signatory, and all Canadian manufacturers/importers participate other than BMW and its subsidiary Land Rover (and a few exotic, high-performance brands such as Aston Martin and Lamborghini). The plan covers the current model year and back four model years (the cut-off date being Sept 30) for the original and all successive owners.

In 1997, the most recent year for which full data is available at the time of this writing, of the 469 cases processed, 329 were arbitrated (over half of which were in Ontario). About 200 were decided in favour of the consumer; in 148 cases repairs were made or the consumer was reimbursed for those already paid for (averaging over $1,000 per case), 49 involved the car being bought back (with or without a price reduction, averaging over $18,000 per vehicle) or, in three cases, replaced; and 15 consumers were reimbursed for miscellaneous out-of-pocket expenses. The 659 problems involved, in order, the engine, transmission, exterior, steering/suspension, brakes, computer/electrical, interior temperature, and accessories.

Who appeared before the arbitrator? The consumer arrived alone in 182 of the hearings, accompanied by a relative in 129, with a witness in 14, and with a lawyer in four. On the other side, the manufacturer's representative attended alone in 223 cases, with a technician in 84, and accompanied by a dealer representative in 22 of the hearings.

All consumers who use the plan are surveyed for their satisfaction with various dimensions of their experience by an outside firm; the results are also posted on the Web and listed in the annual report. A major determinant of satisfaction is a speedy resolution of a usually long-standing problem; the average time to complete the arbitration was 60 days.

The plan is continually undergoing modification based on participant feedback. For instance, vehicles used for any commercial purpose were excluded, but as the distinction between business and personal use became blurred, this restriction was lifted in 1999. As another example, until 1999 all participants were bound by a confidentiality agreement, but as of October the Web site will report quarterly results by consumer complaint and arbitrator decision in terms of car year, make, and model.

CAMVAP is self-described as fast, fair, friendly, free, and final. Indeed, it is a well-run and powerful remedy serving the interests of Canadian car buyers, costing the Canadian car industry over $1-million per year. Nonetheless, there are two serious weaknesses. One is public awareness, which could be rectified if a CAMVAP brochure were placed in the glove compartment of every eligible vehicle sold by dealers. The other is what happens to vehicles that are bought back, over 250 so far. If the provincial licensing authorities agreed to note or "brand" on the registration that the vehicle was a CAMVAP-ordered buy-back, it would alert subsequent purchasers to the possibility of problems that were not fixable for the previous owner.

CAMVAP can be accessed throughout Canada at 1-800-207-0685; the Web site is <www.camvap.ca>. A consumer brochure is available in most car dealerships and in small claims and civil courts, or by mail, and contact information is provided in the owners or warranty manuals of most new cars currently sold in Canada. Services are available in French as PAVAC (Programme d'arbitrage pour les véhicules automobiles du Canada) at the same Web site. The head office is Suite 300, 595 Bay St., Toronto M5G 2C2; regional offices are Atlantic, Ontario, Manitoba, Saskatchewan, British Columbia & Yukon, and Alberta & Territories.

Buying/Selling a Used Vehicle in Ontario

Within living memory, transferring ownership of a used car was little harder than switching cat ownership; it is now more complex than buying/selling a house. The Ontario regulations are covered here because more used vehicles change ownership each year in this province than in any other (one million yearly), and because Ontario's car-transfer regulations date from the 1990s.

Legal and procedural aspects, and a few consumer pointers, are provided in this section. In it, the word "car" refers also to motorcycles, vans, and light trucks. Trucks over 3,000 kg are subject to different regulations, as are commercial dealers.

Obligations of the Seller

If you sell your car privately, you can expect to get more for it than a dealer would pay you, but less than the dealer would sell it for. If you plan to buy a replacement car, consider that by trading it in at a car dealership you would pay taxes amounting to 15 per cent only on the additional amount rather than on the total cost of the new car. But to sell it yourself, read on.

You must complete a Used Vehicle Information Package. Available for $20 from the MCCR or any of the 300 Driver and Vehicle Licence Issuing Offices, it addresses the vehicle's registration and lien record and retail sales tax. Fill out the Bill of Sale portion, and remind the buyer to take the package to a Driver and Vehicle Licence Issuing Office within six days. You also complete and sign the Application for Transfer on the back of the registration permit, and give it (but not the "plate portion") to the buyer.

If you sign any document attesting to the condition of the car, make sure there can be no question as to accuracy. Otherwise, preface your statements about the distance it has gone (odometers can be reset or replaced), accident history, mechanical condition, and so forth, with "As far as I know, ..."

Before surrendering the car, get the payment, total and secure, in hand. Also remove and keep your licence plates; otherwise, if the buyer has a collision or gets a speeding or parking ticket, you are responsible. You can attach them to another car after advising a Driver and Vehicle Licence Issuing Office of the change, or you can hand them in and apply for a refund for any full non-expired months that you had paid for.

Obligations of the Buyer

When you have found a prospective purchase, if it is claimed to come with the manufacturer's warranty still in effect, ask a dealership to verify this from the VIN and to tell you if any manufacturer recalls on this car have been performed. It is also prudent to ask the seller for a written statement that summarizes the condition and the accident and repair history of the car, and to read it carefully. As well, ask if the owner's manual and repair and service invoices are available for inspection (so you can see if it has been properly serviced) and included with the car.

The cost savings from buying a car used are such that most owners seldom ever buy a new one. But if the above tips are news to you, and if you are not savvy about cars and you do not get the help of someone who is, you are unwise to buy one from a private seller you do not know and trust. For instance, in suits for misrepresentation, breach of contract, or negligence, plaintiffs are at a disadvantage when the defendant is a private individual rather than a licensed business. But we will assume that you have come to an informed decision to make an offer to a private seller, and want to know the procedure.

Ask to see the Used Vehicle Information Package and check it for any outstanding liens registered against the car, anything untoward in the registration history (such as past ownership by Toronto Taxi or Peel Police), and whether the name and signature of the seller exactly match those on the registration. If the car has a safety certificate, check that the date is current and the VIN is accurate; if not, you can make your offer conditional on the seller providing the certificate (or you can buy it "as is"). In southern Ontario the car will also have to have a valid emission inspection certificate.

After purchase, you must register the car at a Driver and Vehicle Licence Issuing Office within six days. Bring the Used Vehicle Information Package, the Application for Transfer (the vehicle portion of the permit), your Ontario Driver's Licence or other identification, and (if you are using the existing licence plates) the plate portion of the permit. Then you pay for the new licence plates if required, and the registration fee.

You will also pay the retail sales tax, which is based on the larger of the declared purchase price or the "Canadian Red Book" wholesale value calculated at the time of the transaction. If you paid less than the Red Book figure and an accepted appraisal supports the low price, you pay tax on the higher of the declared amount paid or the appraised value; details on the procedures are available from the licensing office. No sales tax is paid when the car is gifted to a spouse, parent/step-parent, offspring, grandparent, grandchild, or in-law (son, daughter, father, mother). It is also exempt for Status Indians and most diplomats. The GST is also collected at this time.

Even if it's a gift from a relative, before you can drive the car (as opposed to storing it, using it off-road or on private property, or towing it on a public roadway), it will need a Safety Standards Certificate. This can be obtained at a licensed Motor Vehicle Inspection Station; there are over 10,000 across Ontario. The certificate, for which either you or the seller pays, is issued when a mechanical inspection indicates that the car meets the minimum safety standards required by the *Highway Traffic Act*.[16] It is valid for 36 days after the date recorded on the certificate, but it does not warrant that the car will not need repairs one day after that date. It ignores non-safety components; some, such as the engine or transmission, may be costly to fix, so you can ask to have them evaluated separately for an additional fee.

Another requirement before registering the car for use on the road system is a written declaration of insurance coverage. If convicted of giving false information, this is fraud for which you could be fined $2,500, and lose your car for three months and your driver's licence for a year. Your insurance must include third-party liability of $200,000 (throughout Canada except Quebec where it is $50,000), but prudent owners, especially if they own other property of value, pay the small extra premium to insure for $500,000 or $1-million.

The car's driver, whether or not the owner, must have at hand the insurer-supplied pink form (or a photocopy) showing that the required coverage is in force on that date; if you do not produce it when asked by a police officer you are subject to a $75 fine. An officer who believes you didn't produce it because you're not insured could repeatedly charge you if you drive off. Driving an uninsured car is a more serious offence; the fine is $5,000 to $25,000 on the first conviction and $10,000 to $50,000 on subsequent ones plus possible loss of your driver's licence. This includes producing a pink slip that is found to be invalid because, for instance, you cancelled it for a refund, or the coverage lapsed when you did not pay for a renewal (claiming you did not receive the bill will not protect you).

Having bought the car, read the owner's manual, ensure that your licence (and that of any borrower) is valid, drive carefully, and think of all the money you saved. More information about transferring ownership is available from the Ministry of Consumer and Commercial Relations at 1-800-267-8847 (325-8847 in Toronto).

CHAPTER SUMMARY

The unofficial terms "consumer" and "consumer law" refer to lay persons and the regulations that affect them in the marketplace. Most statutes could be "consumer legislation" for someone, so the introduction explains what was chosen for coverage. The history behind the lack of consumer protection until recently is explained. One basic and hidden aspect of consumer-protection law is the establishment of product standards; types and regulators are outlined. Types of laws are differentiated. The chapter focuses on rights, but also touches on responsibilities. The introduction ends with how to locate federal and provincial laws.

The next main section outlines federal consumer legislation. The prime agency is Industry Canada, which governs various aspects of marketing. Three of its statutes regulate the labelling of dry goods, textiles, and precious metals; the fourth is the *Competition Act*, which deals with deception and inac-

---

[16] R.S.O. 1990, c. H.8.

curacy in advertising as well as fair trade practices. Health Canada's *Food and Drugs Act* sets purity and labelling standards in products such as foods and medicines, and the *Hazardous Products Act* regulates potentially harmful items. The *Bank Act* regulates many aspects of the banking industry.

Ontario consumers are protected primarily by the MCCR. The *Business Practices Act* focuses on misrepresentation, and the *Consumer Protection Act* covers executory contracts. The *Consumer Reporting Act* regulates what are commonly termed credit bureaus. When someone does not pay for having goods repaired or stored, The *Repair and Storage Liens Act* establishes the rights and procedures for both sides. The *Motor Vehicle Repair Act* is a recent statute designed to protect car-owners from being overcharged by mechanics. The *Sale of Goods Act* protects you if you tell a presumably knowledgeable seller what you want an item for and it turns out to be unsuitable for that use. The Financial Services Commission regulates insurance and financial institutions.

Quebec was then examined; there the *Consumer Protection Act* is a 1994 statute designed to comprehensively protect consumers and regulate businesses. Except for the occasional weak spot, it is a set of regulations that could serve as a model for other jurisdictions.

The Commentary section made a number of minor suggestions for improvements. The main recommendation is for all equivalent jurisdictions to modify their legislation with the aim of achieving as much consistency as regional differences allow.

The section on insurance outlines the principles of this industry and the federal and provincial legislative control. It also provides some basic consumer advice and sources of further information. The following main section on motor vehicles is similar, providing general consumer information and legislative data, particularly around the private transfer of car ownership in Ontario.

GLOSSARY OF NEW TERMS AND KEY CONCEPTS

bait-and-switch	A behaviour that consists of luring a customer to a store for a bargain that the seller does not plan to honour, and switching the buyer to a more profitable item.
Bank Act	The federal statute that tightly regulates banks and bank-like institutions such as trust companies.
bid rigging	The collusion by competing firms to increase the size of the bid that will be accepted.
Business Practices Act	The Ontario statute that defines and prohibits abusive selling practices.
Canadian Standards Association (CSA)	This organization is the main developer and tester of standards for a vast range of products, from boxes to boxing gloves.
caselaw	Law made up of legal rules that have been established by past court judgments, as opposed to statute law.
caveat emptor	In Latin this phrase means "Let the buyer beware."
civil law	The law and legal procedures governing disputes between individuals or between individuals and businesses constitutes the civil law, in contrast to criminal law.
common law	The unwritten law established by custom and precedent, as opposed to statutory law; the phrase also describes the Anglo-Canadian judicial system.
Competition Act	A federal statute prohibiting misleading advertising and deceptive marketing practices.
compliance with description	The right to inspect delivered goods before accepting them and to reject them if they are not as ordered.

consumer	A common, general term referring to an average or ordinary person, as opposed to a corporation, business, or professional person.
consumer law	A phrase generally refers to regulations that affect lay people in the marketplace.
Consumer Packaging and Labelling Act	A federal statute regulating the label on dry goods.
Consumer Protection Act	A comprehensive recent set of statutes that protect consumers and regulate businesses in the Province of Quebec and is part of the *Quebec Civil Code*.
Consumer Reporting Act	An Ontario statute governing credit-reporting agencies.
credit-reporting agency	A commercial firm that collects, keeps, and sells to merchants records of writs and judgments, and credit transactions.
criminal law	The law based on the *Criminal Code of Canada*, and other federal criminal law, enforced by the government prosecuting an individual or firm. Contrast with civil law.
cross selling	Behaviour consists of discounting one product if the customer buys another.
discriminatory allowance	Behaviour consists of discounts or rebates that are offered to only certain purchasers.
executory contract	A contract in which delivery of goods, performance of a service, or payment in full, is not made at the time the contract is entered into.
Financial Services Commission of Ontario	The commission regulates financial and insurance institutions.
Food and Drugs Act	A federal statute regulating purity in and labelling of products such as foods, cosmetics, medicines, and contraceptives.
good title	Meaning what you bought is yours to control, use, or resell.
grace period	In insurance, this is a time that your coverage remains in effect (while awaiting the payment for renewal) even though the policy has expired.
Hazardous Products Act	A federal statute prohibiting or regulating products that can be harmful.
Industry Canada	The prime federal government consumer-protection agency, mainly governing marketing, including packaging and labelling, and advertising.
lemon laws	A popular term for U.S. state laws that provide recourse to owners of persistently defective cars.
lien	The right of someone to keep or to put a claim on another's property to secure an unpaid bill usually for repairs or storage.
MCCR	An abbreviation stands for the Ministry of Consumer and Commercial Relations, the largest Ontario governmental agency, the main source of consumer protection in the province.
merchantability	Products that are of good quality and that can properly serve their purpose.
multilevel marketing	*See* pyramid selling.
no-fault insurance	Insurance coverage that pays all or part of the policyholder's loss regardless of who was to blame. It reduces wrangling and litigation, although fault still determines police charges and insurance premiums.
non-possessory lien	A lien on property that the owed party does not have physical possession and control over.
personal information reporting agency	A commercial firm that collects, keeps, and sells data on individuals' lifestyles and credit history to merchants.
Precious Metals Marking Act	A federal statute regulating the claims for and symbols stamped on precious metals, primarily gold and silver.
predatory pricing	A behaviour of setting a price so low as to drive out competitors.
premium	The fee charged by insurers for coverage.

product standards	Rules or conventions that ensure the safety, quality, fit, or other aspects originally of products and increasingly of services, too.
pyramid selling	The distribution of products in which the first buyer recruits others, each of whom recruits still others, and so forth is called pyramid selling and is also termed multilevel marketing.
recission	This means cancellation.
referral selling	The behaviour of offering a benefit to a buyer for finding another customer for the seller. It is illegal in Ontario and some other provinces.
Repair and Storage Liens Act (**RSLA**)	An Ontario statute governing the rights and procedures for both sides when a bill for repairs or storage is not paid.
Sale of Goods Act	A statute derived from common law, found in many jurisdictions, generally specifying that goods must be suitable for the purpose for which you announced to the seller that you will use them.
statutory laws	Laws that are enacted, written down, and printed by some level of government, as opposed to common law that originates less formally.
Textile Labelling Act	A federal statute governing the labelling mainly of clothing.
tied selling	A scheme requiring a client to buy one product as a condition of buying another.
tort-based insurance	Insurance coverage in which the insurer of the at-fault driver pays more than the not-at-fault driver, fault possibly determined at trial.
Underwriters' Laboratories of Canada (ULC)	The main developer and verifier of product standards related to safety.
VIN	The acronym that means Vehicle Identification Number, a unique series of digits and letters on a plate attached under the front left window and elsewhere on every motor vehicle. A standardized code identifies the maker, date and plant of assembly, type of vehicle, and certain equipment. Used in registration, insurance, and usually for repair records.

REVIEW QUESTIONS

1. How would you define consumer and consumer law?

2. What products that you can see right now likely have no standards, voluntary standards, and required standards?

3. Why are there more consumer protection laws concerning your purchase of a T.V. set than there are for services offering to repair it?

4. What is meant by pyramid selling, and why should it be illegal?

5. If you wanted to offer a biodegradable product, how would you justify the use of the term?

6. How are consumers protected when buying a used car in Ontario?

7. How do banks differ from other businesses?

8. Hamilton door-to-door seller Sid E. Slikker pressures Vera E. Olde to buy a Mira-Vac for $1,000. She pays $300 in cash, is credited $400 for a trade-in on her Hoover, and promises to pay the balance the next day, whereupon Sid delivers the Mira-Vac and takes the Hoover. The moments he leaves, she changes her mind. What are their rights?

9. Give an example of how you would protect yourself under the *Sale of Goods Act* in making a purchase.

10. Why are many consumers uncertain or confused about insurance?

DISCUSSION QUESTIONS

1. Why would you not expect the phrase consumer law to appear in a dictionary of legal terms?

2. Why do many commercial buildings show outside banners stating "ISO 9000 Registered"?

3. Think of an example of how the *Competition Act* would not seem easily applicable to a consumer issue in the next generation.

4. You are a federal minister. A trade organization complains that the penalties for prohibited trade practices are unreasonably high. How would you respond?

5. If you were overhauling the regulations on interest rates, what changes would you make?

6. What aspects of the *Bank Act* would you tighten and what aspects would you loosen; why?

7. How does the consumer legislation in Quebec differ generally from that in other provinces?

8. How much might you pay for motor vehicles over your lifetime, and how does this contrast with other major expenses?

9. If the Quebec *Consumer Protection Act* were to serve as a model for other jurisdictions, what changes would you recommend?

SUGGESTED READINGS

Kenkel, Joseph H., & William S. Chalmers. *Small Claims and Simplified Procedure Litigation*, 3d ed. (Markham, Ont.: Butterworths, 1998).

Morin, Guy, & François Tôth. *Loi sur la protection du consommateur et règlement d'application. Consumer Protection Act and Regulation Respecting its Application* (Scarborough, Ont.: Carswell, 1998).

Olivo, Laurence M. *Debtor Creditor Law and Procedure* (Toronto, Ont.: Emond Montgomery Publications, 1999).

Smyth, J.E., & D.A. Soberman. *The Law and Business Administration in Canada*, 8th ed. (Toronto, Ont.: Prentice-Hall, 1998).

Stikeman, E. *Competition Act and Commentary — 2000* (Markham, Ont.: Butterworths, 1999).

Willes, John A. *Contemporary Canadian Business Law*. 4th ed. (Toronto, Ont.: McGraw-Hill Ryerson, 1994).

Zuher, Marvin A. *Ontario Small Claims Court Practice*. Annual editions (Toronto, Ont.: Carswell).

Human Rights in Ontario

Stanley Gershman
BARRISTER AND SOLICITOR

Learning Objectives

At the conclusion of this chapter, the reader should be able to:

➢ understand the history of human rights legislation and the reasons for its existence

➢ distinguish between international, federal, and provincial legislation relative to human rights

➢ comprehend the history and evolution of the *Ontario Human Rights Code*

➢ identify the grounds, social areas, and exceptions included in the Code

➢ appreciate the fluidity of human rights legislation and how it continues to evolve in response to changes in our concept of social justice

TABLE OF CONTENTS

THE HISTORY OF HUMAN RIGHTS

> Human Rights legislation ... is the skillful blending of educational and legal techniques *in the pursuit of social justice.* (Daniel Hill, former chair of the Ontario Human Rights Commission, italics added.)

The provincial and federal human rights laws and the *Canadian Charter of Rights and Freedoms* are relatively recent manifestations of a human rights revolution that can be traced through certain outstanding historical documents. The first was the proclamation of the Magna Carta ("The Great Charter") by King John of England in 1215 after the barons had rebelled against his disregard for the limits of his power. Later, in 1689, Parliament passed the Bill of Rights, confirming the rights of the people and further limiting the powers of the king. The demand by the English nobility for the sharing of political power by the monarchy was a demand for greater equality and a response to the tyranny of the monarchy. The revolution was broadened and carried forward in the American Declaration of Independence of 1776, which preceded the American Revolution; the French Declaration of the Rights of Man and Citizen of 1789, which inspired the French Revolution; and the American Bill of Rights of 1791, which was enacted as an amendment to the American Constitution. These latter proclamations were the response of peoples oppressed by the tyranny of both the monarchy and the nobility, and they were demands made by such people for greater equality. They helped provide the basis for the formation of modern democratic institutions and forms of government.

The Declaration of Independence stated that, "We hold these truths to be self-evident, that all men are created equal, that they are endowed by their Creator with certain inalienable Rights, that among these are Life, Liberty and the pursuit of Happiness — That to secure these rights, Governments are instituted among Men...." In fighting against the tyranny of the English monarchy and the English social system, the Americans wished to emphasize the equality of all men, in the sense that they wished to denounce the notion of special advantages being meted out to people on the basis of their accident of birth (i.e., the English class system and an aristocracy based on birthright). They stated that the very justification for the existence of government was the notion that it exists to promote and secure certain basic rights for all its citizens equally.[1]

Unfortunately, their concept of the equality of all men and their notion of social justice were grounded in a different social milieu and reality than what exists today. The early Americans were predominantly of white, European background, and they brought with them their prejudices towards others of different backgrounds. These "others" — such as Aboriginals and Blacks — being different, were conceived of as devoid of the same human attributes or qualities as they themselves possessed. The Americans also came from a monarchical society conceived of as a hierarchy of graded ranks and degrees. These influences persuaded the Americans to subjugate and exploit these others, and deny them the full rights of citizenship. The Americans also brought with them the accumulated prejudices of their culture towards women. These "others", then, did not, at first, appear to fit the definition of the "men" referred to in their stated ideal of equality. As a result, the members of the American power structure were not only victims but also per-

---

[1] Not only did the American Colonialists wish to create a different sort of social hierarchy, they were also concerned about the oppressive taxes and trade restrictions imposed by a British king and a British Parliament in which they had no representation. The Americans were influenced by the Lockean concept of liberty in their belief that political power could only be legitimately exercised with the consent of the governed.

petrators of oppression.[2] Nonetheless, according to one prominent American historian, by the time the American Revolution had run its course, American society had been radically and thoroughly transformed. Far from remaining monarchical, hierarchy-ridden subjects, Americans soon became the most liberal and democratic people in the world. The Revolution and its ideology were conducive to, and made possible, the anti-slavery and women's rights movements of the 19th century, as well as current egalitarian thinking. It made the interests and the prosperity of ordinary people — their "pursuit of happiness" — the goal of society and government. They substituted their own notion of a meritocracy for the European aristocracy, and they considered that a man's merit rested entirely with himself, without any regard to family, blood, or connection. But the achievement of higher office and position was not considered available to the existing poor and humble inhabitants, and was more likely to accrue to their sons, who could acquire the requisite education, skills and refinement. Black slavery became conspicuous in a way that it had not been in the older monarchical society, and many Americans began attacking it with a vehemence that had been inconceivable earlier. This change in attitude led inexorably to the Civil War and the eventual abolition of slavery in 1875 with the 13th amendment to the U.S. Constitution.[3]

Strangely, however, slavery as an institution had been abolished in England and Canada earlier than in the United States. The Kings Bench, in 1772, made its first anti-slavery decision. In 1833 Britain passed the *Abolition of Slavery Act*, and in 1838 it abolished slavery throughout the Empire. In 1793 Upper Canada prohibited slavery but did not free the existing slaves until 1819. A study was released in 2002 by Anti-Slavery International to coincide with the United Nations session on slavery, which reported that tens of millions of slaves continue to exist today in Africa, Asia, and Latin America.

Canada's founding ideal was never stated in terms of rights and equality, but was based on "peace, order, and good government". The British government was perceived relatively benignly by both the French Canadians, whose rights were guaranteed by the *Quebec Act* in 1774, and the United Empire Loyalists, who were given the right to settle in Ontario in 1791 and who felt more loyal and less rebellious towards the British government than the Americans did. Protection of individual liberty and equality was less of a priority to the Canadians of the time than it had been to the early Americans.[4]

World War II was a great catalyst for the continued evolution of human rights. It brought together groups whose differences faded before the common threat of the Axis powers (Germany, Italy and Japan). People of different nationalities, colour and ethnic and religious backgrounds fighting together against tyranny helped to break down the barriers created by such differences. The prominent role of women in maintaining industrial productivity while men were away fighting changed society's perception of their proper place. The Jewish Holocaust made obvious to the world community the need for united action to protect human rights. It led to the formation of the United Nations — the beginning of a world community — and to the proclamation and acceptance of the Universal Declaration of Human Rights. The later struggle

---

[2] Thomas Jefferson, who drafted the Declaration of Independence, apparently wished to condemn slavery (in an early draft of the Declaration) but was prevented from doing so by his fellow Virginian slaveholders. It was ironic that the United States would proclaim that all men were created equal and engage in a fight for freedom and liberty, and yet be a nation of slaveholders.

[3] Gordon S. Wood, "The War of Independence was a Social Revolution" in William Dudley, ed., *The American Revolution — Opposing Viewpoints* (San Diego, Calif.: Greenhaven Press Inc., 1992) at 264–67.

[4] Mr. Justice Mark McGuigan, "The Protection of Freedom and the Achievement of Equality in Canada" in G. Gall, ed., *Civil Liberties in Canada — Entering the 1980s*, 9th ed. (Toronto, Ont.: Butterworth's, 1982) at 225–26.

The "Persons" Case: *Edwards v. Attorney General for Canada* [1930] A.C. 124

EXHIBIT 21.1

> ... if in the past no women had acceded to such a position, it was because custom prevented it, and customs become traditions stronger than law and remain unchallenged long after having lost their raison d'être.
>
> — The British Privy Council

Canadian women received the legislative right to vote in their own name in 1918, and by 1921 the first woman was elected to the House of Commons.[†] Despite this progress towards equality between men and women, there remained the question of whether or not women could be appointed to the Senate of Canada. The issue was brought to the forefront in 1927 when Emily Murphy, an Edmonton judge and women's rights advocate, spearheaded a group of five women who put the constitutional question, based on the *British North America Act of 1867* ("BNA"), before the Supreme Court of Canada. Ingeniously, Murphy found a little-known section of the *Supreme Court Act* that allowed five persons to petition the government to obtain a legal interpretation of a provision in the BNA.

Section 24 of the *British North America Act* stipulated that properly qualified "persons" appointed by the Governor General "had to be at least 30 years old, hold property, be worth at least four thousand dollars and reside within the province for which they were appointed". While some women would have met the qualifications regarding age, property, finances, and residency set out in the Act, the issue soon boiled down to the pivotal question of whether or not women were considered "persons" under the BNA.

In 1928 the Supreme Court of Canada ruled that women were not "persons" under the BNA. The Court based this decision on a narrow and historical interpretation of the word "persons", stating that at the time the BNA was enacted, women were unable to serve in public office at common law and, thus, the word "persons" did not apply to women. Canada could be seen to be a patriarchical society at the time, and Ms. Murphy determined that the most efficient way to resolve the issue was to have it looked at from a "purely legal" aspect: that is, does "persons", under the BNA, include women? Therefore, it was decided to put the matter before the final court of appeal for Canadians — the Judicial Committee of the Privy Council in London, England.

The Privy Council heard the appeal in the summer of 1929 and rejected the Crown argument based on the narrow, historical interpretation of the word "persons". The court indicated that the word "persons" was an ambiguous term that did not provide clarity as to the intention of section 24. Therefore, their Lordships stated in the decision rendered that "[t]he Act should be on all occasions interpreted in a large, liberal and comprehensive spirit, considering the magnitude of the subjects with which it purports to deal in very few words". (Even today the courts favour this broad approach to the interpretation of constitutional rights, and this approach has facilitated the ongoing evolution of human rights.) The Privy Council went on to say that the fact that women had been given the right to vote under the BNA grew from an interpretation of "persons" that included both men and women. In addition, their Lordships had analyzed sections of the BNA in the hopes of illuminating the meaning of "persons". The BNA included the term "male persons" in other sections, and their Lordships concluded that where such term was "expressly used it is desired to confine the matter in issue to males". In other words, the Act was clear when it was speaking to only one sex and, therefore, the more general "persons" should be read to include both men and women.

Based on this analysis, their Lordships stated that they "have come to the conclusion that the word 'persons' in section 24 includes members both of the male and female sex and that, therefore, the question propounded by the Governor-General must be answered in the affirmative and ... women are eligible to be summoned to and become members of the Senate of Canada". Prime Minister Mackenzie King appointed Canada's first woman senator in 1930.

[†] Historical background sourced from "The 'Persons' Case", National Archives of Canada; and "Defining 'Persons' Under the BNA Act", Department of Justice Canada: <http://canada.justice.gc.ca/en/justice2000/30mile.html>.

EXHIBIT 21.2

Preamble to the *Ontario Human Rights Code*

"WHEREAS recognition of the inherent dignity and the equal and inalienable rights of all members of the human family is the foundation of freedom, justice and peace in the world and is in accord with the Universal Declaration of Human Rights as proclaimed by the United Nations;

AND WHEREAS it is public policy in Ontario to recognize the dignity and worth of every person and to provide for equal rights and opportunities without discrimination that is contrary to law, and having as its aim the creation of a climate of understanding and mutual respect for the dignity and worth of each person so that each person feels a part of the community and able to contribute fully to the development and well-being of the community and the Province;

AND WHEREAS these principles have been confirmed in Ontario by a number of enactments of the Legislature and it is desirable to revise and extend the protection of human rights in Ontario;

Therefore, Her Majesty, by and with the advice and consent of the Legislative Assembly of the Province of Ontario, Enacts as follows...."

---

for racial equality by the civil rights movement in the United States and the parallel movements promoting women's rights, gay rights, Aboriginal rights, children's rights, seniors' rights, language rights and the rights of the disabled have all put social justice at the top of our political and social agenda. These developments have led to an evolving concept of social justice and to the enactment and development of rights legislation.

It is the recognition of the equal worth and dignity of all men and women, of whatever race, colour, ethnicity, nationality, political or religious belief, gender, or any other characteristic that seemingly differentiates us, that underlies the equality provisions of our Charter and our human rights codes. These codes reflect a new morality and a new concept of social justice.

As with all conceptions of morality, a misunderstood, distorted, or misapplied idea of human rights can deteriorate into the dangerous absurdities and over-reactions sometimes referred to as a concern for the "politically correct".[5] Together with a disregard for due process, this mindset can lead to hearings akin to witch hunts. It is surprising how often in history an instrument created to achieve justice has, instead, been used as an instrument of oppression.[6]

---

[5] An example is the statement that a person's value is necessarily associated with a group identity rather than an individual character. It is illustrated by material distributed in a university orientation course that teaches that Blacks, not being in a dominant position in society, cannot be racist, and that white males in positions of power generally make racist decisions that consciously impact more favourably on white people than on minorities: Alan Charles Kors & Harvey Silverglate, *The Shadow University* (New York, N.Y.: The Free Press, 1998) at 220. Contrast this with Martin Luther King's famous plea for the day when a person would be judged by the content of the person's character rather than by the colour of the person's skin.

[6] A further example is provided by Ian Hunter in his *Globe and Mail* article, "What next? Anti-harassment training in the crib?" (December 29, 2006), where he refers to a decision by an administrator of the Washington County School Board who imposed a suspension on a five-year-old student in the State of Maryland for sexual harassment of a girl in his class. The boy had mischieviously pinched her bottom. Online: <http://www.iapm.ca/newsmanager/anmviewer.asp?a=511&z=13&print=yes>

THE NATURE OF HUMAN RIGHTS CODES

Human rights codes, including Ontario's, can be seen to be an effort to provide the citizens of our society, especially those identified with minority groups who have traditionally been discriminated against, with freedom from discrimination and to remove any unfair disadvantages that may have been imposed on them by the majority or by those who have exercised social and economic power. These Acts also seek to recognize and preserve the dignity and self-esteem of our citizens by protecting such persons against any harassment based on such discrimination. To that extent, our human rights legislation extends our democratic values. As we discuss later, it also paradoxically limits the freedom of others. People are restricted from interfering with equality rights, and these restrictions may interfere with such constitutionally recognized freedoms as freedom of speech, freedom of opinion, and freedom of religion, as well as certain economic freedoms, such as freedom of contract and freedom of commerce.[7]

It may seem contradictory that, in order to protect the rights of some, we must restrict the rights and freedoms of others; but our ultimate goal is not solely to protect individual rights or freedoms but, rather, to achieve social justice and a peaceful community free from oppression and abuse.

As has been stated, what is sought is equality of access and opportunity: that is, freedom from discrimination or differential treatment based on characteristics (e.g., gender, creed) that our sense of justice dictates should not be considered relevant to one's opportunity to obtain the services, goods, or advantages available in our community.[8] There are, and likely always will be, benefits, advantages, and opportunities that will accrue to some because of individual merit, personal characteristics, or good fortune. Thus, these codes do not purport to remedy all forms of differential treatment but only discrimination based on those characteristics considered to be irrelevant. Our sense of justice dictates that it is a person's character, not the person's skin colour, and the person's conduct, not the person's group identity, that should determine how we deal with that person.

There has been some criticism that the scope of human rights legislation is too narrow. It has become generally accepted that social justice requires that the distribution of wealth and income in society cannot be allowed to be determined solely by the natural distribution of abilities and talents.[9] In other words, he who has been given less in life may have to be given more by the law — the notion of distributive justice. But the degree of one's adherence to this notion depends on one's political orientation, and so is not crystallized as a human right in our Charter or our human rights codes. There is a concern that ensuring greater equality of benefits would lead to social stagnation. This type of social justice would lead to economic inefficiency. It would rob individuals of the incentive to work — to achieve results by utilizing their talents and abilities. Some say that society may even undermine the self-confidence of those at the bottom by telling them that the answer to poverty involves granting them more rights rather than any efforts they may make to improve themselves through their own hard work and self-denial. Our rights revolution

---

[7] Our later discussion of the provisions of the *Ontario Human Rights Code* will illustrate this point.

[8] It should be noted that the *Charter of Rights and Freedoms* does not appear to restrict illegal discrimination to specific grounds. The grounds are listed merely as examples of particular forms of discrimination. In effect, this allows the courts to find illegal grounds for discrimination beyond those listed in s. 15. In Ontario, any new grounds for discrimination under the *Human Rights Code* can be added only by the legislature. In these ways our human rights legislation can grow to keep pace with our evolving concept of social justice.

[9] Mr. Justice Mark MacGuigan, *supra* at 35.

and rights culture has created too much emphasis on social rights and not enough emphasis on individual responsibility and duty.

Although there is some truth in these criticisms of a broader human rights approach, ensuring equality of opportunity may require more than simply providing negative rights or protection from discrimination on what we perceive to be irrelevant grounds. It could be argued that if we value equality of opportunity for all our citizens as a measure of social justice, then perhaps we must institute positive rights that create the economic, social, and educational conditions for this to occur: certain government services, the maintenance of public institutions, some measure of income redistribution, and the definition of rights that will encompass such values. Most people cannot overcome the barriers that a lack of resources entails without a more even playing field. These measures would help accomplish the goal, stated in the preamble to the *Ontario Human Rights Code*, that each person should feel a part of the community and be able to contribute fully to its development and well-being. It would also give more citizens the opportunity to be engaged in what Thomas Jefferson proposed as their inalienable right to pursue happiness.

COMPARISON OF THE UNIVERSAL DECLARATION OF HUMAN RIGHTS, THE CHARTER AND HUMAN RIGHTS CODES

The UN Universal Declaration of Human Rights ("Universal Declaration") was, along with certain international covenants, an international statement of rights agreed to by many of the world's nations, and ultimately was a catalyst for the formulation of the human rights codes in many nations, including Canada and its provinces, as well as for the enactment of a charter of rights as part of our Constitution.[10] The Ontario *Human Rights Code*, the first such code enacted in Canada, was originally passed in 1962, and was followed by enactments by the other provinces and the federal government. The rights set out in the Universal Declaration went far beyond those subsequently set out in the Ontario Code because, in addition to equality rights and freedom from discrimination, the Universal Declaration purported to also guarantee economic and educational rights. In article 25 it declared that "everyone has the right to a standard of living adequate for the health and well being of himself and of his family, including food, clothing, receiving medical care, and necessary social services, and the right to security in the event of unemployment ..." and in article 23.3, "everyone who works has the right to a just and favourable remuneration ensuring ... an existence worthy of human dignity." In article 26, it proclaimed that everyone has the right to a free elementary education, and that higher education should be equally accessible to all on the basis of merit. Civil and political rights, as well as equality rights, were guaranteed in a subsequent *International Covenant on Civil and Political Rights* and in other covenants that the member nations agreed to. The inclusion of social and economic rights in the Universal Declaration reflected the broader interpretation of equality of opportunity described in the previous section.

The *Charter of Rights and Freedoms* ("Charter") forms part of our Constitution and applies to the actions and legislation of federal and provincial governments. The Charter protects various rights and freedoms, such as civil rights, political rights, legal rights, and equality rights, including freedom from discrimination, but does not protect economic or educational rights (other parts of the Constitution, however, do offer some protections for educational

---

[10] John Humphrey, a Canadian law professor at McGill University, played a prominent role in the drafting of the Universal Declaration and in shepherding it through the process of its adoption by the General Assembly in 1948.

rights), as such protection would appear to violate the prevailing North American political ethos. The Charter, in this sense, then, fails to fulfill all the goals of the Universal Declaration.

Human rights codes such as Ontario's ("Code") are even more limited than the Charter. The Code protects only those rights known as equality rights, or the freedom from discrimination that is found in section 15 of the Charter:

> (1) Every individual is equal before and under the law and has the right to the equal protection and equal benefit of the law without discrimination and, in particular, without discrimination based on race, national or ethnic origin, colour, religion, sex, age or mental or physical disability.

> (2) Subsection (1) does not preclude any law, program or activity that has as its object the amelioration of conditions of disadvantaged individuals or groups including those that are disadvantaged because of race, national or ethnic origin, colour, religion, sex, age, or mental or physical disability.

The Code carries over into the private sphere the constitutional restrictions imposed on government by section 15 of the Charter. The concept of human rights in Ontario's legislation also has a much more restrictive meaning than it does in the Universal Declaration because it is based on the more restrictive concept of social justice and equality of opportunity that does not extend to shared benefits or economic rights.

Neither does the Code deal directly with an individual's political and civil rights, as such rights are related to the relationship between government and the individual and so are dealt with in the Charter. The Code protects individuals against discrimination in private transactions with other individuals and private institutions or agencies.[11] The Code is not part of the Canadian Constitution but is only a statute passed by the provincial legislature. Because of the importance of its subject, however, it has been given a quasi-constitutional status by legislation[12] and by the courts[13] so that its provisions are generously and broadly interpreted and given primacy over other statutes within the same jurisdiction: that is, any provision in another Ontario statute that conflicts with a provision in the Code will be considered inoperative.

In fact, as discussed above, human rights codes can simply be looked at as the application of section 15 of the Charter — equality rights — to the private sphere. The courts have indicated that all human rights codes must be interpreted in a manner consistent with the interpretation of section 15 of the Charter.[14] And all provincial and federal human rights legislation is said to be relevant to the interpretation of any one human rights statute, regardless of mere differences in terminology, because their objectives are the same and, legally, must comply with section 15 in order to be valid.

The court will apply this notion in cases that come before it where a particular human rights code does not reflect the protections given against discrimination in the Charter. The court will strike out the Code's offensive provision.[15]

---

[11] It also protects individuals against the actions of government officials and programs that provide public services or benefits to such individuals (OHR Code, s. 47(1)): *Ontario Human Rights Commission v. Ontario Ministry of Health* (1994), 19 O.R. (3d) 387 (C.A.).

[12] In Ontario by s. 47(2) of the Code.

[13] *Winnipeg School Division No. 1 v. Craton*, [1985] 2 S.C.R. 150, 21 DLR (4th) 1.

[14] *Entrop v. Imperial Oil Ltd.* (2000), C.C.E.L. (3d) 19 (Ont. C.A.).

[15] In fact, the Supreme Court of Canada has even gone so far as to amend a provincial human rights statute to add a ground of discrimination (sexual orientation) that was absent from the statute. In the case, the employee of a college was terminated on the grounds of violating the college's policy against homosexuality. The Alberta Human

An example was the case of *Re Blainey v. Ontario Hockey Association, et al.*[16] Justine Blainey had qualified on the basis of her ability to play for a hockey team that belonged to the Ontario Hockey Association ("O.H.A."). The rules of the Association, however, prohibited females from playing on its hockey teams. Blainey then lodged a complaint with the Ontario Human Rights Commission ("O.H.R.C."), claiming the prohibition violated her right under section 1 of the Code to equal treatment with respect to services and facilities without discrimination because of sex. The O.H.R.C. dismissed her case because of section 19 of the Code (now s. 20(1)), which stated that section 1 was not infringed where participation in an athletic activity is restricted to persons of the same sex. The Ontario Court of Appeal allowed Blainey's appeal from this decision on the basis that section 19 violated section 15 of the Charter, since it was governmental legislation that denied equality of treatment based on sex. The court struck out this section of the Code so that Blainey could then re-apply under the Code without having to face section 19. The O.H.R.C. then allowed Blainey her new application, striking out the O.H.A.'s regulation as a violation of section 1 of the *Ontario Human Rights Code*.

The court pointed out, however, that section 15 equality rights are not absolute by virtue of section 1 of the Charter.[17] An enactment may deny equality of treatment based on a prohibited ground and, nonetheless, be constitutional if it is shown to be a reasonable limit on such rights that is justifiable in a free and democratic society. Section 19's allowing discrimination against females was too broad a prohibition to be justified. It was not limited to situations where it would be justified: that is, where it was necessary to promote public decency or for the physical protection of participants. Had section 19 stated these limitations, it likely would have been considered valid and enforceable and could have been applied in the Blainey case to test the enforceability of the O.H.A. regulation.[18]

The idea that human rights are not absolute is also reflected in the provisions of the human rights codes and the way they are interpreted. Part II of the Code reflects this concept, as does the reasonableness requirement in the definition of harassment in the Code and the interpretations of the Human Rights Code sections by Human Rights Boards of Inquiry.

THE HISTORY AND EVOLUTION OF HUMAN RIGHTS LAW IN ONTARIO

The courts used to consider acts of discrimination irrelevant on the basis of freedom of contract and freedom of commerce. Any person could conduct a business or execute a deal in the manner that would best advance that

---

Rights Commission refused to accept his complaint that the grounds for his dismissal were discriminatory because the Alberta Human Rights statute did not include sexual orientation as a prohibited ground of discrimination. The court found that the omission of this protection was an unjustified violation of s. 15 of the Charter, and ordered that the term "sexual orientation" be "read" into the statute as if it were part of the statute. (*Vriend v. Alberta* (1998), 156 DLR (4th) 385.)

[16] (1986), 54 O.R. (2d) 513, 26 DLR (4th) 728 (Ont. C.A.).

[17] The *Canadian Charter of Rights and Freedoms* (s. 1) guarantees the rights and freedoms set out in it subject only to such reasonable limits prescribed by law as can be demonstrably justified in a free and democratic society.

[18] The Ontario government subsequently introduced s. 20(1) of the *Ontario Human Rights Code*, which states that the right under s. 1 to equal treatment with respect to service and facilities without discrimination because of sex is not infringed where the use of the services or facilities is restricted to persons of the same sex on the ground of public decency.

person's own interests, even if that meant discriminating against others on the basis of their race or colour, so long as that person complied with any contractual obligations he or she had entered into.[19] This meant that while, in 1899, a theatre was found to be in breach of contract for refusing to seat a black couple who had purchased tickets in advance for a concert, in 1919 a theatre was able to refuse to enter into a contract to sell an orchestra seat to a black man and to offer to sell him only a balcony seat. In the 1899 example, a contract had been broken, and the fact that the couple were black was irrelevant. In the second case, the theatre's policy that prohibited the sale of orchestra seats to Blacks was considered lawful because it offended neither morality nor public order. In 1924 a court upheld the decision of a restaurant owner who refused to serve some patrons solely because of their race. A person had the freedom to decide with whom to enter into contracts. Even if public policy at the time would consider racial discrimination as offensive (which it didn't), there would be a problem prohibiting discrimination using the common law.

It is true that contracts that offended public policy (i.e., contracts that the courts considered by their terms to be prejudicial to the social or economic interest of the community) were forbidden. The difficulty is that public policy would allow the courts to strike out a term of a contract already entered into, but there was no contractual or common law concept that required a person to enter into a contract he or she did not wish to enter into in the first place. Contracts were by definition supposed to be voluntary arrangements. Human rights legislation, in effect, embodied the novel concept that persons would be required to *enter into contracts* they did not wish to enter into to provide goods or services, or, at least, they could not refuse to enter such contracts on the basis of any of the prohibited grounds.

In 1944 Ontario passed the *Racial Discrimination Act*. The Act prohibited the displaying of signs or other representations expressing racial or religious discrimination. For the first time, an Ontario legislature recognized that racial and religious discrimination was against public policy. This meant that human rights could no longer be subordinated to commercial, contractual or property rights. In 1945 Mr. Justice Mackay of the Ontario High Court, in the case *Re Drummond Wren*,[20] used the statutory recognition of this policy to strike down a property covenant that prohibited the sale of a property to "Jews or persons of objectionable nationality". The illegal covenant did not violate the actual provision of the Act, but it did violate the public policy expressed by the Act's provisions.[21]

In 1947 Saskatchewan passed a more comprehensive statute, the *Saskatchewan Bill of Rights*, which dealt with discrimination as well as political and civil liberties. The Ontario *Racial Discrimination Act* and the Saskatchewan *Bill of Rights* were both quasi-criminal in nature, so complainant victims had to resort to penal sanctions through the criminal courts to enforce the rights they had been given. There were many drawbacks. First, many victims were reluctant to take criminal action. There were also many obstacles to a successful prosecution. The victims had to substantiate their claim using the criminal burden of proof: that is, beyond a reasonable doubt, which was more onerous than the civil burden of proof. It was extremely difficult to prove that a person had not been denied access for a reason other than a discriminatory one. Criminal court judges were also reluctant to convict anyone for what they

---

[19] *Christie v. York Corporation* [1940], S.C.R. 140.

[20] (1945), O.R. 778.

[21] Ian Hunter, "Human Rights Legislation in Canada: Its Origin, Development and Interpretation" (1976) 15 U. Western Ontario. L. Rev. 21 at 25.

did not regard as a criminal act. The sanction of a fine did not really help the person discriminated against in obtaining a job or accommodation or service. Victims were discouraged from lodging complaints because of these difficulties and, often, the very existence of the anti-discriminatory legislation was not well publicized (or promoted) and, therefore, not well known.[22]

As a result, in 1951 Ontario passed the *Fair Employment Practices Act*[23] and, later, the *Fair Accommodation Practices Act*[24]. In the place of the victim having to lay an **information** to initiate a prosecution, provision was made for the filing of a complaint with the relevant government ministry. The process continued with an administrative investigation, then conciliation and possible settlement. However, the onus for bringing the matter forward was still placed on the individual victim, although the administrative machinery of the state was placed at his disposal. There were few or no ministry staff who were assigned this task on a full-time basis. As a result, few complaints were made or, if made, processed.

Finally, in 1962, Ontario enacted the *Ontario Human Rights Code*, which encompassed a broad range of human rights protections to be administered by the Ontario Human Rights Commission, which had been established a year earlier. The rationale behind the establishment of the Commission and of the procedural and substantive provisions of the Code was that the prevention of discrimination was important not only to the individual victim but also to the community as a whole. The Supreme Court of Canada pointed out in a 1986 decision that the Code's main approach is not to punish the perpetrator of discrimination but to provide relief for the victim of discrimination.[25]

THE ONTARIO HUMAN RIGHTS CODE

The 1962 version of the Code was a much simpler version of the present Code. There were only six recognized grounds of discrimination: race, creed, colour, nationality, ancestry, and place of origin. By 1980 there were 8 grounds, sex and marital status having been added. By 1990 there were 13 basic grounds, and a 14th ground was added in 1999. In the 1990s, new concepts, such as constructive discrimination, discrimination by association, harassment, and the validity of affirmative action programs were added. The continued addition of new grounds over time and the introduction of new concepts reflect the continuing evolution of our society's vision of social justice.

The Code is directed to eliminating discrimination in various social areas, yet does not define the concept of **discrimination**. A survey of early human rights decisions by Professor Ian Hunter led him to define the term as follows:

> Discrimination means treating people differently because of ... [one of the prohibited grounds] as result of which the complainant suffers adverse consequences, or a serious affront to dignity; the motive for the discriminatory treatment, ... is irrelevant, except possibly in mitigation of the penalty.[26]

The Basic Rights and Responsibilities

The *Ontario Human Rights Code* contains an introductory section (or preamble) and five parts. Part I sets out the basic rights and responsibilities, and

---

[22] See *R v. McKay* (1955), 113 CCC 56.
[23] S.O. 1951, c. 24.
[24] S.O. 1954, c. 28.
[25] *O'Malley v. Simpson-Sears Ltd.* (1986), 64 NR 161 (S.C.C.).
[26] Ian Hunter, *Human Rights Legislation in Canada* at 33–34.

consists of nine sections. These sections set out the right of every person to equal treatment with respect to what are called various "**social areas**", including services, goods and facilities (s. 1), and the occupancy of accommodation (s. 2(1)), the making of contracts (s. 3), employment (s. 5(1)), and membership in any trade union, occupational association or self-governing profession (s. 6). The protection directed against discrimination in these areas is based on 15 grounds, including the original 1962 grounds, except for nationality:

- race
- ancestry
- place of origin
- colour
- ethnic origin
- citizenship
- creed (religion)
- sex
- sexual orientation (heterosexuality or homosexuality)
- age
- marital status (single, married, divorced, separated, common law partnership)
- family status (parent, child relationship)
- disability
- the receipt of public assistance
- criminal record

Same-sex partnership status was added in 1999.[27] The right to equal accommodation now also includes discrimination against those in receipt of public assistance, which was added as a 14th prohibited ground of discrimination in 2005.[28] The right to equal treatment with regard to employment adds record of offences as a 15th prohibited ground as of 2005, but this ground is defined as meaning a provincial offence (as opposed to a criminal or federal offence) or a criminal offence in respect of which a pardon has been granted. Therefore, a criminal record can still be used as a basis for refusing employment without attracting a human rights complaint.

Part I also prohibits various forms of harassment based on the 15 grounds in accommodation (s. 2(2)) and employment (s. 5(2)). Harassment on the basis of sex in accommodation and the workplace is set out separately (s. 7(1) and (2)), and protects everyone from sexual solicitation by a person in a position to confer a benefit and from reprisal for turning down such a solicitation (s. 7(3)). Harassment is defined in Part II, section 10 as engaging in a course of vexatious comment or conduct that is known or ought reasonably to be known to be unwelcome. Boards of Inquiry have expanded the statutory definitions so that both the victim's reaction to the harassing conduct or words must be a reasonable reaction in the circumstances and, also, a reasonable respondent would be aware that the words or conduct were offensive. As stated by the Board in *Gnosh v. Douglas Inc. (No. 2)*[29] (a case involving harassment based on handicap), "[whether the comments in that case amounted to harassment] depends upon whether reasonable people similarly handicapped would find such conduct to be unwelcome, and if so, whether reasonable people in the respondent's position would know that to be the case."

---

[27] S.C. 1999, c. 6, s. 28.
[28] OHR Code, s. 2(1).
[29] 17 C.H.R.R. at D221–223

Indirect Discrimination

According to section 9, "No person shall ... do, directly or indirectly, anything that infringes a right under this part." This section prohibits **indirect discrimination** or harassment. For example, if a building manager directs her superintendent not to rent to people of a particular ethnicity, both the manager and the superintendent can be named in the human rights complaint because the manager indirectly caused the discrimination on the prohibited ground. The section can also be used to support a claim for the creation of a **poisoned environment** or indirect harassment. The complainant feels that her workplace or housing is hostile or unwelcoming to her because of insulting or degrading comments about others, similarly situated, in the context of a ground in the Code.

Constructive Discrimination

Finally, it should be noted that identical treatment is not necessarily synonymous with equal treatment and might amount to discrimination. In a B.C. case a mining company, after a complaint, made its campsite accommodations available to both male and female employees. The company, however, made no structural alterations to its bunkhouses, so female employees would have to share toilet and shower facilities with male residents. A female employee filed a complaint of sex discrimination, and the company stated that it had made its camp accommodation available to its female employees on the same terms and conditions as its male employees. The Board of Inquiry found discrimination, saying that discrimination can result from strict equality as well as inequality and that identical treatment does not necessarily mean equal treatment or the absence of discrimination.[30] The female employee would, in effect, have to endure embarrassment, and modesty would prevent her from continuing her employment. This situation is now covered by section 11(1) of the Ontario Code, which introduced the concept of constructive discrimination.

Constructive discrimination arises when the application of a nondiscriminatory requirement, qualification, or other factor results in discrimination (s. 11(1)).[31] The requirement (qualification or other factor) does not *expressly* exclude any group. However, when the particular requirement is met, the *result* is discriminatory. The section, however, exempts the respondent in such a situation from liability where the questioned requirement is reasonable and bona fide in the circumstances,[32] or the Act specifically indicates that to discriminate because of such ground is not an infringement of a right. Imposing a height or weight restriction as a requirement for a job that would effectively exclude women would amount to a violation of this section unless the respondent could show that the requirement or policy was reasonable and bone fide in the circumstances, or that the Code declares that such requirement is not an infringement.

The BFOR (Bona Fide Occupational Requirement) Defence

Section 11(1) allows an employer to refuse to employ a member of a "discriminated" group if the refusal is based on a BFOR, but the Board of Inquiry must first be satisfied that the needs of members of that group cannot be accommodated without undue hardship to the respondent (s. 11(2)). In the B.C. mining case discussed above, if the mining company had refused to hire the female complainant on the basis that she would have to share shower and

---

[30] Ian Hunter, *ibid.* at 32, referring to *Tharp v. Lornex Mining Corporation, Report of a Board of Inquiry under the B.C. Human Rights Code* dated 1975 at 13.

[31] This is why constructive discrimination is also referred to as adverse effect discrimination.

[32] This is known as a BFOR (i.e., a bona fide occupational requirement).

change room facilities with the men, then the company could argue that in the light of common conceptions of public decency, this factor for refusing employment was reasonable and bona fide. The employer, to be successful, however, would have to show that building a separate shower and change room facility was excessively expensive and would create an undue hardship.[33] = difficulty

The Balancing of Rights and Freedoms

Part II is called "Interpretation and Application" and clarifies definitions and the interpretation and application of the rights set out in Part I. Its provisions implicitly recognize that rights and freedoms are not absolute and, in any given situation, may be in conflict, requiring a balancing of such rights. This approach supports the idea that the remedying of a violation of a person's equality or group rights might conflict with another person's individual rights or freedoms or other values, and supports the Code's overriding philosophy that the proper resolution of a human rights complaint may often involve mediation or conciliation. As one Ontario Court of Appeal judge stated, "Most legislation that attempts to benefit one segment of society is [in a broad sense] discriminatory of those not the object of its beneficence."[34]

In order to understand the basis for such competing claims, we need to consider the section of the Charter in which many such claims or rights are set out. Section 2 states the following:

> Everyone has the following fundamental freedoms:
> (a) freedom of conscience and religion;
> (b) freedom of thought, belief, opinion and expression, including freedom of the press and other media of communication;
> (c) freedom of peaceful assembly; and
> (d) freedom of association.

These and other Charter rights must also be balanced against section 1 of the Charter as discussed on page 500 above. To illustrate the conflict between competing rights and values, the *National Post*, in an editorial, recently criticized a ruling of a one-woman Board of Inquiry of the Saskatchewan Human Rights Commission. The ruling dealt with a 1997 newspaper advertisement placed by the individual respondent, Mr. Owens, who is an evangelical Christian. The ad contained a drawing of two men holding hands surrounded by a circle with a slash through it. Accompanying the drawing were four passages from the Bible that support the view that homosexuality is a sin. The inquiry officer stated that this ad infringed the equivalent of the *Ontario Human Rights Code*, section 13, prohibiting a person "who publishes, displays or causes the publication or display of any ... representation" that is intended by the person to cause the infringement of a right under Part I. The officer stated the ad would "tend to expose homosexuals to hatred and ridicule." The officer said that "[t]here [was] no question that the respondent believed that he was publicly expressing his honestly held religious belief." Yet, since those beliefs could be interpreted to be "an affront to the complainants' dignity on the basis of their sexual orientation", the adjudicator ordered both respondents (Mr. Owens and the newspaper) to pay $4,500.00 to the complainants and forbade them from publishing similar messages in the future. The *National Post* editorial was concerned about the violation of the respondent's freedom of speech. The bedrock principle of free speech is that

---

[33] For an authoritative interpretation and application of this concept by the Supreme Court of Canada, see *British Columbia (Public Service Employee Relations Commission) v B.C. G.S.E.V.* (1999), 176 DLR (4th) 1.

[34] Finlayson J.A., *ibid.* at 37, *Re Blainey*.

society should not prohibit "the expression of ideas that we find offensive or disagreeable". Another author, commenting on a similar case in the same newspaper, stated that when it comes to the expression of any opinion that reflects the moral principles that Canadians have historically held, the principle of free speech tends to be cast aside in favour of the modern liberal notion that an individual has the right not to be offended by anything they see or hear. Thus, to maintain a non-offensive climate, unwelcome views are suppressed rather than debated.[35] Of course, this ruling might be said to also violate Mr. Owen's freedom of conscience and religion, or his right to act on or express his religious belief.

In another case in Ontario, the O.H.R.C. ruled in 2000 that Scott Brockie,[36] a professional printer with traditional Christian views on sexuality, could not decline job orders from a gay organization, as a violation of section 1 of the *Ontario Human Rights Code*. The Commission stated that while he was free to hold his religious beliefs and practise them in his home and in his Christian community, homosexual rights took precedence elsewhere. It appears that there is a hierarchy of values and freedoms, where certain rights and freedoms take precedence over others.

On the other hand, certain other rights and freedoms are specifically given precedence over the rights set out in Part I. For example, freedom of association is specifically protected in section 21(1), which allows for discrimination in the occupancy of residential accommodation where the owner of the premises, or his or her family, will be sharing a bathroom or kitchen facility with a prospective occupant in the house where they reside. The right to freedom of association is given further precedence in section 20(3), which allows a recreational club to discriminate in restricting access to its services and facilities, and section 24(1), which allows a person to discriminate in the hiring of an employee to look after the medical or personal needs of an ill child or aged or ill spouse or relative. Section 24(1)(a) allows a religious, philanthropic, educational, fraternal, or social institution or organization primarily engaged in serving the interests of persons identified by their race, place of origin, colour, ethnic origin, creed, sex, age, etc., to employ only persons similarly identified if the qualification is a reasonable and bona fide qualification because of the nature of the employment.

There are other values that are judicially recognized as justifiable limitations, such as biological limitations, social mores, public policy, academic freedom and economic freedom. Thus, while age is a prohibited ground of discrimination, the notion of the biological and human limitations of childhood (as well as economic rights and social mores) are recognized, since age as a prohibited ground is defined as meaning 18 years of age or more (s. 10(1)), which allows for children under 18 to be treated differently than adults and allows for limiting their freedoms and rights regarding employment as well as the other social areas. The Code also formerly recognized the biological limitations of age regarding seniors by stating in section 10 that age did not include persons 65 years of age or older so that such persons could be treated differently, and they could be "discriminated" against by, for example, imposing mandatory retirement of such persons in an employment contract. However, in 2006, section 10 was amended to omit the reference to the 65-year limitation in the age definition so that today a person 65 years of age or more cannot be discriminated against (as a general rule) by forced retirement. An

---

[35] *National Post* (June 23, 2001)
[36] *Brillinger v. Brockie* (September 29, 1999) Doc. 99-012 (Ont. Bd. of Inquiry) and (February 24, 2000) Doc. 000-003-R (Ont. Bd. of Inquiry).

employer can still refuse to employ an elderly person on the basis of age only if such disqualification can be justified as bona fide and reasonable because of the nature of the employment. Similarly, employment discrimination on the basis of sex, marital status, or record of offence (s. 24(1)(b)) is allowed if the qualification is bona fide and reasonable.

Social and economic realities may intercede to modify restrictions or exemptions. In certain circumstances, necessity may obviate the need to restrict a minor's rights. Accommodation cannot be denied to a person who is 16 or 17 years old if he or she has withdrawn from parental control (s. 4). Nor can a person under 65 years of age complain of discrimination on the basis of age where persons over 65 years of age, in recognition of their reduced earning power, are given a special advantage or preferential treatment, such as a lower rate charged for bus fares or for theatre tickets (s. 15). Similarly, section 14 allows for special programs to overcome barriers or disadvantages to traditionally disadvantaged groups recognized in the various grounds. An interesting illustration of the potential use of this section is the argument used in the *Blainey* case that if girls were allowed to play on boys' teams, then there would be nothing to stop a team in the girls' hockey league from gaining an unfair advantage by recruiting boys to play on its team. The Board of Inquiry stated that the women's league could prohibit its teams from recruiting boys. Women's hockey qualified as a special program under the auspices of section 14, to assist a disadvantaged group (women), and such a program could, therefore, be limited to such group. This limitation would not, therefore, be considered adverse discrimination.[37]

A handicapped person can be refused a job — i.e., "discriminated" against — in the area of employment on the basis of handicap where said person is incapable of performing the essential duties or requirements of such job because of such handicap (s. 17(1)); otherwise, the employer's economic right to earn a living or run the business efficiently would be seriously compromised. But the employer must be able to argue that the disability cannot be accommodated without undue hardship (s. 17(2)) so that there is a positive obligation to alleviate conditions that might constitute a barrier to a person with a particular handicap to be hired for or continue in a job so long as the burden on the employer is not excessive. This duty to accommodate handicapped persons is not restricted to employment. For example, section 17(1) by implication would also require accommodation for handicapped persons in the provision of services in the absence of undue hardship (e.g., special toilet facilities or space for wheelchair ramps to allow entrance to facilities open to the public, such as movie theatres or sports venues).

Allowing landlords to do credit checks and use income information and rental history without these practices being complained of as acts of discrimination or harassment implicitly recognizes landlords's economic right to conduct their business efficiently.

Discrimination on the basis of sex precludes depriving a woman of any services or opportunities because she is or may become pregnant (s. 10(2)). However, social mores or public policy are recognized when the use of services or facilities are restricted to persons of the same sex on the ground of public decency (s. 20(1)); or when persons under 19 years of age are denied entry to premises where liquor is served or prohibited from purchasing alcoholic beverages (s. 20(2)) or from purchasing tobacco or tobacco products (s. 20(4)); or when accommodation in a residence is restricted to persons of the same sex (s. 21(2)).

---

[37] Adverse discrimination involves giving an unfair advantage to a member of a group ordinarily discriminated against.

The definition of "harassment" in the Code as interpreted by Boards of Inquiry that is described above incorporates the use of objective or community standards as to whether the conduct in question is acceptable in the circumstances or infringes our sense of justice. The definition as interpreted invites us to judge the reasonableness of both the respondent's conduct or words and the reasonableness of the victim's response to such conduct. Without this dual reasonableness requirement, respondents could be subject to irrational or abusive complaints based solely on an alleged victim's alleged subjective response. This would make people in certain positions, such as teachers, landlords, employers, and employees extremely vulnerable if they have to deal with those who might be vengeful, paranoid, hypersensitive, ignorant, irrational, or manipulative, and those who can take advantage of the stated grounds of complaint. There is no definition of discrimination in the Code and also no statutory reasonableness requirement, but Boards of Inquiry appear to incorporate a reasonableness test where the context requires it.

Another potential defence could be the legitimate purpose defence. In the case of *Matthews v. Memorial University of Newfoundland, Faculty of Medicine*,[38] a medical student complained to the Newfoundland Human Rights Commission, alleging that he had been discriminated against and harassed by members of the Faculty of Medicine of Memorial University. The student complained because certain instructors and the dean placed evaluations and a letter in the student's academic file referring to the student's having a speech impediment (a stutter), which they stated was a serious communication problem and which, in the long run, would affect his ability to function with patients. These comments were considered to constitute harassment on the ground of disability. The comments had caused the complainant a great deal of stress and affected his ability to perform at his best capacity. The evidence showed that a majority of those doctors who had had an opportunity to come into contact with the complainant stated they had had no problem understanding him and felt that his speech impediment did not impact on his ability to function as a competent physician. Had the majority opinion been otherwise, the board implied, it would have dismissed the complaint. It stated that the fact that the subject comments were vexatious to the complainant does not necessarily mean that harassment exists. They may be excluded from the purview of the harassment section if they were legitimate comments regarding the complainant's performance as a medical student. This decision recognizes that comments that are vexatious to a complainant and that are related to a prohibited ground may nonetheless be protected from complaint because the person making these comments has a legitimate reason for doing so. The person made these comments in furtherance of a relationship with the complainant gave that person the obligation or licence to render such judgments or opinions. This approach could be used to assist teachers, employers, and other persons in mentor or supervisory positions.

Part III of the Code deals with the structure and function of the Commission. Part IV deals with how the rights given in Parts I and II are enforced.

These parts are discussed in another chapter. Part V defines certain terms, including the use of the term "person", and extends its meaning beyond that given in the *Interpretation Act* to include several types of organizations, associations, and municipalities (s. 46). It indicates that the Act binds the Crown (s. 47) and also, in section 48, sets out the type of regulations that can be made by the Lieutenant Governor in Council (i.e., the Ontario Cabinet).

---

[38] (1989) 15 C.H.R.R. D/399 (Nfld. Bd. of Inquiry).

THE FUTURE OF HUMAN RIGHTS CODES ———————————————

> At the end of the twentieth century, the liberal myth that humanity is progressing to an ever more enlightened and tolerant state looks as fantastic as any of the other millennial myths we have considered.[39]

Historically, human rights has appeared to be an evolving concept driven by an expanding notion of social justice: a movement towards bringing the right to dignity and equality to an ever larger segment of an increasingly diverse society. But in a volatile and unstable world beset by burgeoning poverty, cultural and religious clashes, environmental degradation, scarcity of resources, social instability, and economic crises, can we continue to look forward to the evolutionary expansion of human rights, or is such a process in danger of being halted or even reversed?

As already discussed,[40] the expansion of human rights can lead to conflict with other rights, freedoms and values, even those deeply held by certain increasingly influential constituencies within society. A balance must be found, allowing certain rights to predominate over others. The current balance seems to favour the equality rights[41] that underlie the human rights code, where these rights conflict with certain important individual freedoms, such as religious freedom, freedom of speech and opinion, and commercial and property rights associated with free enterprise economies.

The case of *Bruker v. Marcovitz*[42] serves to illustrate the degree of intrusion of equality rights into the realm of religious freedom in the sense of the right of the members of a particular religious group to follow their religion's rules and traditions. The Supreme Court of Canada decided to uphold a trial court's decision that a wife should receive a $47,000.00 damage award, compensating her for her husband's exercising his traditional religious right to refuse his consent to a Jewish religious divorce. The husband had agreed to grant the consent as part of a settlement agreement arrived at in the course of civil divorce proceedings but delayed honouring this agreement for 15 years until the wife was almost 47, effectively destroying her opportunity to validly remarry and bear children in accordance with her Jewish religion.

The majority of the Court (in a 7–2 decision) stated that the husband's claim to the freedom to practise his religion was outweighed by the harm to the wife personally and to the public's interest in protecting fundamental values, such as equality rights, autonomous choice in marriage and divorce and the enforcement of contractual obligations. The dissenting judges pointed out that in this case the wife's civil rights were not an issue. She had been granted a civil divorce and was free to remarry civilly. It was only her religious rights that were at issue as a result of religious rules, and the Court should not intrude in the religious sphere or in religious disputes.

So the Court here interfered in the realm of religion by sanctioning the husband for following a religious rule that would have had the effect of promoting gender inequality. By doing so, it would justify the Court's interfering with the traditional faiths and practices of not only Judaism but also of Islam, Catholicism, fundamentalist Protestantism and other religions whose rules and practices might offend the Court's notions of gender or other equality rights.[43]

---

[39] Karen Armstrong, *The Battle for God* (New York, N.Y.: Ballantine Books, 2001) at 367.

[40] See "The Balancing of Rights and Freedoms" on page 505.

[41] The right of members of certain groups or segments of society that have been traditionally discriminated against to be free from discrimination and harassment.

[42] (2007) S.C.C. 54

[43] Although this was not a case brought under any human rights code, it illustrates the Court's policy bias in favour of equality rights underlying such codes.

Other illustrations where the courts have promoted equality rights over religious freedom include a decision upholding a conviction under an Ontario law requiring the use of motorcycle helmets by all persons against a Sikh who claimed an exemption from such law because his religion required him to wear a turban as a head covering *(R. v. Badesha*, [2008] O.J. No. 854), as well as the illustrations given on pages 505 and 506 in the previous section ("The Balancing of Rights and Powers").

Many scholars and commentators, however, have pointed out the growing resurgence in number and political influence of religious fundamentalism, an ideology which stands in opposition to the secularist approach of human rights advocates. The fundamentalist religious approach promotes the notion of traditional absolute values and adamantly opposes secularist concepts of democracy, separation of church and state and tolerance. Kevin Phillips in *American Theocracy* points out that according to a *Newsweek* Poll of December 2004, 55 percent of the U.S. population believes that the Bible is literally accurate and inerrant.[44] In addition, there are those in other religions that hold the same belief about their holy books such as the Hebrew Bible and the *Koran*.[45] These books all promulgate patriarchal values that run counter to the equality rights that underlie human rights legislation. Those who hold such beliefs emphasize the dominating authority of the husband and father, oppose women's equality and gay rights and are intolerant of any dissent to their beliefs. They are antinomians — i.e., they believe the laws of God should trump the laws of man and that any religious beliefs and practices other than their own are satanical.

The fundamentalist Christian credo includes a belief that each person must find personal salvation by mastering his or her own soul and coming to an acceptance of and belief in Jesus as his or saviour. Fundamentalist Christians do not hold society (or government) responsible for man's failings and so are less concerned with social change as they are with personal change — another reason for them to challenge any government effort to effect social change through regulation — i.e., human rights codes.[46]

Another problem facing the maintenance and expansion of human rights legislation is the recent effort to expand the scope of such legislation in certain jurisdictions to interfere with freedom of speech and opinion. A complaint was made to the Canadian Human Rights Commission recently regarding an article written by Mark Steyn, alleging many Muslims who are sympathetic to terrorism are migrating to Western societies and are intending to take over these societies by exploiting their religion's high birth rate. A similar complaint was made to the Alberta Human Rights Commission regarding Ezra Levant's publishing controversial cartoons depicting the Prophet Mohammed in an unflattering light. Both of these commissions are operating under the auspices of human rights legislation (unlike Ontario's *Human Rights Code*) that allows for complaints against publication of material likely to expose a person

---

[44] Kevin Phillips, *American Theocracy: The Peril and Politics of Radical Religion, Oil and Borrowed Money in the 21st Century* (New York, N.Y.: Viking, 2006) at 184.

[45] Both the United States and Canada are governed federally by neo-conservative parties who are strongly influenced by fundamentalist religionists. Between the two chambers of Congress, 186 members of the U.S. House of Representatives and 45 Senators earned high approval ratings from fundamentalist Christian advocacy groups. The U.S. President and the Secretary of State profess their allegiance to fundamentalist Christian religions. See Lewis Lapham, "The Wrath of the Lamb", *Harper's Magazine* (May 2005) at 8–9; Chris Hedges, *American Fascists: The Christian Right and the War on America* (New York, N.Y.: Free Press, 2006) at 22–23.

[46] A leading Canadian pollster, Michael Adams, finds Canadians to be about half as religious as Americans, although as many as 61% to 69% hold religious beliefs (e.g., belief in heaven and God). See *The Globe and Mail*, "My Canada doesn't include religiosity" (January 10, 2005).

or class of persons to hatred or contempt. Neither of these publications incited violence or other injustices against Muslims. Both of these complaints are being seriously entertained. This so-called hate speech legislation constitutes a serious restriction on the right to freedom of speech and opinion and should likely be considered a violation of the Canadian *Charter of Rights and Freedoms*.[47]

This attack on freedom of speech is an example of overreaching by those in charge of protecting human rights. Other examples of absurd and insidious applications of human rights concepts include the illustration in note 6 on page 496 involving a five-year-old Maryland student. In the same article, Ian Hunter also referred to a four-year-old pre-kindergarten student in Texas, who was suspended for inappropriately hugging a female teacher's aide. Such overreaching can only have the effect of bringing human rights legislation and tribunals into disrepute.

A third line of attack on human rights legislation comes from the neo-conservative ideologues who oppose government regulation or control over the private economy. As they point out, human rights laws grant privileges to those who are relatively poor and powerless over those who are relatively rich and powerful (employers, owners of businesses and landlords). After all, these laws forbid those in such positions of power from discriminating against potential or actual employees, customers, or tenants on the basis of their gender, religion, race, disability, etc. Employers, for example, must go out of their way to accommodate employees belonging to disadvantaged groups "regardless of resulting hardship for their employer".[48] Employees, on the other hand, can refuse any job offer or quit their jobs even if their reason for doing so is the employer's gender, religion, colour, creed, etc. Similar unbalanced restrictions apply to business owners vis-à-vis consumers, and landlords vis-à-vis tenants.[49]

We see how our equality rights legislation can interfere with the honoured rights, such as freedom of contract and private property rights, freedom of religion and freedom of speech. Such legislation interferes with these rights and freedoms when those who attempt to exercise such rights hold certain rigid ideologies and exercise certain practices that favour imposing dominant hierarchical relationships among religions, groups and genders. There is a conflict between them and those who emphasize the need to acknowledge and respect the equality and inherent dignity of individuals regardless of their particular group, race or gender. The future of human rights may depend on which world view will gain the ascendancy. It may depend on which world view will help our western nations and perhaps civilization itself meet the coming challenges outlined at the beginning of this topic.

---

[47] The Supreme Court of Canada in the John Ross Taylor case (*Canada (Human Rights Commission) v. Taylor* [1990] 3 S.C.R. 892) indicated that the Canadian Human Rights Commission hate speech prohibition was constitutionally acceptable on certain conditions. Jeremy Waldron refers to hate speech legislation that might protect members of minority groups against religious or racial hatred while safeguarding freedom of speech and opinion in a constitutionally acceptable manner. The United Kingdom's 2006 *Racial and Religious Hatred Act*, which prohibits such hatred, provides that it shall not be interpreted "to prohibit or restrict discussion, criticism or expression of antipathy, dislike, ridicule or insult of particular religions or the beliefs or practices of their adherents, or urging such adherents to cease practising their religion or belief system." The purpose of this language is to distinguish between hatred of persons (forbidden) and opposition to institutions and doctrines (allowed). (See "What to Do About Hate Speech", *The New York Review of Books*, 55:12 (July 17, 2008) 52). But note also s. 319 of the Canadian *Criminal Code*, which prohibits public incitement of hatred towards identifiable groups, where such incitement is likely to lead to a breach of the peace.

[48] This notion is somewhat distorted as seen in my previous discussion regarding employee accommodation (page 504, "The BFOR Defence").

[49] See Karen Selick, "There are some rights we can do without" *The Globe and Mail* (August 24, 2007).

CHAPTER SUMMARY

This chapter provides the reader with a brief history of the evolution of human rights by tracing the topic back to its early roots in both Europe and North America. The impact of World War II entailed a more mature concept of equality and social justice, as illustrated by the adoption of the Universal Declaration of Human Rights that recognized the equal worth and dignity of all men and women.

The nature of human rights codes was discussed relative to their goal of providing equal opportunity and freedom from discrimination, along with how these negative rights may interfere with other rights. The preamble to the Ontario *Human Rights Code* ("Code") was investigated, as was the ongoing addition of new grounds by the legislature that exemplify how human rights are constantly evolving.

A comparison of the Universal Declaration of Human Rights (an international covenant between nations), the *Canadian Charter of Rights and Freedom* (which forms part of our Constitution), and the human rights codes (which protect equality rights in dealings between individuals in the private sphere) was conducted. The idea that human rights are not absolute was discussed.

The history and evolution of human rights law in Ontario was examined. Early legislation was based on contract law, and later legislation comprised separate Acts that had a narrow application. These former Acts were later codified into our present Code. The quasi-criminal focus of earlier legislation was examined, along with the associated drawbacks that led to our present administrative process.

The substantive parts of the Ontario *Human Rights Code*, along with the preamble, were reviewed. The social areas and grounds were defined, and the Code's relationship to the Charter regarding conflicting rights was discussed. It was noted that discrimination and justifiable limitations in certain circumstances were permitted under the Code.

GLOSSARY OF NEW TERMS AND KEY CONCEPTS

constructive discrimination	The treatment of members of a group that is identical to treatment of members of another group that, because of the characteristics of the members of the first group, results in unequal treatment or opportunities for the members of the first group.
discrimination	Treating a person in a different manner because of one of the prohibited grounds, as a result of which the person suffers some adverse consequence or a serious affront to dignity.
indirect discrimination	Another term used to describe a poisoned environment.
information	The equivalent, in the criminal context, of a statement of claim in the civil context — the name of an originating process.
poisoned environment	Comments or conduct directed towards others that create a hostile or unwelcoming environment for a person.
social areas	Relating to the areas of services, accommodation, employment, contracts, and membership in vocational associations and trade unions, which are covered by the Code.

REVIEW QUESTIONS

1. Describe the apparent difference in the concept of the "equality of all men" for the early Americans and for our society today.

2. How did World War II act as a catalyst in the evolution of human rights?

3. What are the main goals of human rights codes?

4. (a) In what major way do the rights set out in the United Nations Universal Declaration of Human Rights differ from the rights set out in our Charter and human rights codes?

   (b) In what ways does the *Charter of Rights and Freedoms* differ from the Ontario *Human Rights Code*?

5. What is the legal effect of section 15 of the *Canadian Charter of Rights and Freedoms* on the Ontario *Human Rights Code*?

6. Why is the concept of requiring a contract to satisfy public policy by itself inadequate to protect equality rights?

7. What difficulties were presented for effective enforcement of human rights by quasi-criminal legislation, such as the former Ontario *Racial Discrimination Act*?

8. What are the various social areas for which the Ontario Human Rights Commission requires equal treatment?

9. What are the basic 14 grounds that apply to every social area?

10. What are the statutory and Board of Inquiry requirements for a finding of harassment?

11. What is indirect discrimination?

12. What is constructive discrimination?

13. What is the BFOR defence, and how is it applied in an employment situation?

14. What freedoms often come into conflict with the Code's equality rights?

15. What values often provide justifiable limitations on equality rights?

16. The *Charter of Rights and Freedoms* applies to the actions and legislation of which level(s) of government?

17. How did the courts perceive acts of discrimination in contracts or the provision of services prior to the enactment of our human rights code?

DISCUSSION QUESTIONS

1. Is Ontario's *Human Rights Code* aimed at prohibiting all forms of differential or discriminatory treatment? Can you think of a type of discriminatory treatment that would not be prohibited?

2. Is there an argument for including social and economic rights in Ontario's *Human Rights Code*? Why might it not be a good idea?

3. Why have several additional grounds and concepts been introduced in Ontario since the introduction of its human rights code in 1962?

4. Robin is handicapped and has applied for a full-time job for which she meets the required qualifications. The potential employer doesn't hire Robin and says that the reason is that Robin cannot perform all the duties required in the job. Can the employer not hire Robin for this reason?

SUGGESTED READING

Bowland, Adelyn L. *The 2008 Annotated Ontario Human Rights Code* (Toronto, Ont.: Carswell, 2007).

Gall, G. *Civil Liberties in Canada — Entering the 1980s*, 9th Edition (Toronto, Ont.: Butterworths, 1982).

Hunter, Ian. "Human Rights Legislation in Canada: Its Origin, Development and Interpretation" (1976) 15 U.W.O. L. Rev. 21.

Ignatieff, Michael. *The Rights Revolution* (Toronto, Ont.: House of Anansi Press, 2000).

Kors, Cl., & H. Silverglate. *The Shadow University* (New York: The Free Press, 1998).

Ontario Human Rights Commission, *Report of the Ontario Human Rights Commission*, 2006–2007. Available online: <http://www.ohrc.on.ca/en/resources/annualreports/ar0607?page=eng-Contents.html>.

The Resolution of Human Rights Complaints in Ontario

Janet I. Mason
BARRISTER AND SOLICITOR

Learning Objectives

At the conclusion of this chapter, the reader should be able to:

➢ understand the various roles of the Human Rights Commission and the Human Rights Tribunal of Ontario in the human rights enforcement process

➢ comprehend the steps involved in the complaint process with the Human Rights Commission

➢ distinguish between mediation and conciliation

➢ describe how a decision is made by the Human Rights Commission

➢ comprehend the procedural steps at the Tribunal

➢ understand the types of evidence that are admissible at a hearing

➢ describe the types of orders that can be imposed

➢ identify pending charges to resolution process

TABLE OF CONTENTS

THE ROLE OF THE HUMAN RIGHTS COMMISSION

The Ontario Human Rights Commission ("Commission") was the first human rights enforcement agency to operate in Canada. It came into operation in 1962 with the proclamation of the Ontario *Human Rights Code*[1] ("Code"). The Commission's function is set out in Part III of the Code, with amendments pending:

> **29.** It is the function of the Commission,
> (a) to forward the policy that the dignity and worth of every person be recognized and that equal rights and opportunities be provided without discrimination that is contrary to law;
> (b) to promote an understanding and acceptance of and compliance with this Act;
> (c) to recommend for consideration a special plan or program designed to meet the requirements of subsection 14(1), subject to the right of a person aggrieved by the implementation of the plan or program to request the Commission to reconsider its recommendation and section 37 applies with necessary modifications;
> (d) to develop and conduct programs of public information and education and undertake, direct and encourage research designed to eliminate discriminatory practices that infringe rights under this Act;
> (e) to examine and review any statute or regulation, and any program or policy made by or under a statute and make recommendations on any provision, program or policy, that in its opinion is inconsistent with the intent of this Act;
> (f) to inquire into incidents of and conditions leading or tending to lead to tension or conflict based upon identification by a prohibited ground of discrimination and take appropriate action to eliminate the source of tension or conflict;
> (g) to initiate investigations into problems based upon identification by a prohibited ground of discrimination that may arise in a community, and encourage and co-ordinate plans, programs and activities to reduce or prevent such problems;
> (h) to promote, assist and encourage public, municipal or private agencies, organizations, groups or persons to engage in programs to alleviate tensions and conflicts based upon identification by a prohibited ground of discrimination;
> (i) to enforce this Act and orders of the Tribunal;
> (j) to perform the functions assigned to it by this or any other Act.

The Commission is made up of a chair and vice-chair who are designated by the Lieutenant Governor in Council — i.e., the provincial Cabinet. The Commission must provide an annual report by June of each year to the Attorney General, detailing the affairs of the Commission for the year ended March 31st of the year in which the report is submitted. The report details, among other things, the number of cases opened and closed, the average length of time until resolution, and whether project objectives for the relevant year were met.[2]

The Commission has the power to decide whether or not a complaint is carried forward at any stage of the process. As the Commission does not deal with complainants directly (in that a party does not meet with a commissioner), it relies on the recommendations of an employee of the Commission, the human rights officer, when making a decision, but it is not bound to fol-

---

[1]   R.S.O. 1990, c. H.19.

[2]   See Ontario Human Rights Commission, *Annual Report 2006–2007*, online: <http://www.ohrc.on.ca/en/resources/annualreports/ar0607/pdf> (September 17, 2007).

low the recommendation submitted. The Commission may initiate a complaint itself in the case of systemic discrimination, or if it feels that it would be in the public interest to bring the complaint forward, or at the request of any person whose right under Part I of the Code has been infringed. The Commission may decide to combine complaints where the same individual is involved or where there is a question of law or fact common to several complaints. It is important to note that the Commission has discretion as to whether or not to deal with any complaint. The limits of this discretion are set out in section 34 and regard the appropriateness of the involvement of the Commission in the matter, the validity of the complaint, jurisdiction, and the time limit for filing a complaint. Following are the limits of discretion set out in section 34:

1. Matters that can be more appropriately dealt with under another Act should be dealt with under that other Act: for example, the *Labour Relations Act* (in a unionized work environment), where there is a collective agreement and grievance procedure in place. This prevents and minimizes duplication of proceedings. The Commission retains the power to investigate any human rights complaint, notwithstanding the existence of alternative procedures under another Act when it appears that it is in the public interest to ensure the discrimination is eradicated.

2. Where the Commission considers the complaint to be trivial, frivolous, vexatious or made in bad faith, the Commission may exercise its discretion not to deal with the complaint (e.g., if the complaint has no basis in law or evidence to support it).

3. Where the complaint is not within the jurisdiction of the Commission (such as a complaint against a bank or post office, which would fall under federal jurisdiction and would therefore be handled by the Canadian Human Rights Commission), the Commission cannot consider the complaint.

4. If the facts on which the complaint is based occurred more than six months prior to the complaint being filed with the Commission, the Commission has the right not to proceed with the complaint.

If appropriate, the person will be referred to the proper jurisdiction or agency by the intake officer when the Commission is contacted. The referral of an unsettled complaint to the Human Rights Tribunal of Ontario ("Tribunal" or "the HRTO") for a hearing remains at the discretion of the Commission under section 36(1).[3]

Human rights officers employed by the Commission investigate and mediate between the parties to effect settlement of the complaint and to provide recommendations to the Commission. There is also a department exclusively dedicated to investigating systemic discrimination, and another comprising policy analysts responsible for the development and application of the Code, specially trained mediators and lawyers who argue on behalf of the Commission at the Tribunal.

---

[3] Note: many complaints are handled internally in a workplace or other institutional setting where such workplace or institution has its own human rights policy and enforcement process. If the Ontario Human Rights Commission feels the matter has been, or could have been, dealt with satisfactorily, it will dismiss or refuse to pursue the complaint.

The 2006–2007 statistics published in the Commission's *Annual Report* identified that the Commission began the year with a pre-existing caseload of 2,889 cases. The Commission received 42,937 inquiries and opened 2,337 formal complaints during the reporting year — i.e., only about 5 percent of inquiries resulted in a formal complaint being filed. There were 1,978 files "completed", with the average time to completion identified as 14.6 months. The Commission exercised its section 34 discretion to dismiss in 7.1 percent of cases completed or referred to the Tribunal. A total of 58.9 percent of cases (completed or referred) were resolved by mediation or settlement in an average timeframe of 13.7 months, and 18.5 percent were withdrawn. There are 762 backlogged cases — i.e., about 25 percent of active cases — and 169 cases are over three years old. The Commission ended the year with a 7.6 percent higher active caseload (3,099 cases) over the previous reporting year.

THE ROLE OF THE HUMAN RIGHTS TRIBUNAL OF ONTARIO

The Tribunal is independent of and functions separately from the Ontario Human Rights Commission. The Tribunal's members are appointed by the Lieutenant Governor in Council, who also appoints a chair and may appoint one or more vice-chairs. The chair can assign a **panel** of one or more members to act as adjudicators at a hearing. Therefore, it is not necessary that all members be present at each hearing, allowing for less delay and increased efficiency.

The Tribunal has the authority to make rules governing its own practice and procedure relevant to the conducting of its affairs.[4] Tribunal regulations are not legislative regulations under the *Regulations Act* but are, simply, a venue through which the Tribunal can establish procedural efficiency.

The Tribunal is an administrative body that hears human rights complaints that have been referred to it by the Commission. The proceedings are quasi-judicial and similar in format to a trial. At the hearing, evidence is transcribed and witnesses swear/affirm their testimony prior to delivering it. However, there are a few differences that the reader should be aware of. In criminal proceedings, the burden of proof must be beyond a reasonable doubt. In a tribunal hearing, the burden required is, as in a civil proceeding, on the balance of probabilities. To meet the balance of probabilities, it must be shown that it is more likely than not that the respondent infringed a right of the complainant. Civil remedies, such as compensation for losses suffered by the complainant (general and/or special damages), are available. The Commission can also request remedies in the public interest to prevent future occurrences of similar conduct. The Code is remedial in nature. Its purpose is to correct policy and/or educate a respondent who has deliberately or inadvertently infringed on a person's right. Hearings are generally open to the public and media, but this is at the discretion of the chair. Tribunal decisions are published in the *Canadian Human Rights Reporter* and can be appealed to Divisional Court by any party.

---

[4] The *Statutory Powers Procoedure Act*, R.S.O. 1980, c. S.22 ("SPPA"), empowers the Tribunal to make its rules (s. 25.1), deals with procedural matters and applies to hearings. In the event of a conflict between the rules and SPPA, the SPPA governs (r. 3).

THE COMPLAINT PROCESS AT
THE HUMAN RIGHTS COMMISSION

People can contact the Commission when they believe that one of their rights under the Code has been infringed. Ideally, prior to contacting the Commission, the person should document the instances of the alleged infringement(s), including dates, times, witnesses present, and any attempts that have been made to remedy the situation by any party. The inquiry services representative will generally be the first contact at the Commission. Information provided will assist the representative in determining whether or not the Code is involved. If the situation falls under one of the categories in section 34 of the Code listed earlier in this chapter, the person may be referred to an appropriate agency (e.g., a union) if that person is under a collective agreement or to the Ontario Rental Housing Tribunal where the matter concerns an illegal rent increase, for resolution.

If the matter appears to be one where it is suitable for the Commission to assure jurisdiction and there is possible infringement under the Code, a complaint form will be forwarded to the person making the complaint. The completed form is then returned to the Commission. An infringement must be based on an enumerated ground and have occurred in one of the **social areas**[5] covered by the Code. Alternatively, the Commission may decide to bring a complaint itself if it receives multiple complaints against the same alleged offender. This may, for example, include an employer who is repeatedly not hiring people from a particular ethnic background or a landlord who won't rent units to single women.

Upon the Commission's receiving a completed complaint form that reveals what it considers a potentially valid complaint under the Code that is within its jurisdiction, the complainant may be contacted for further information and/or documents. A remedy must be included in the complaint, and Commission staff may assist the complainant in determining the best remedy available. Once the complaint has been signed by the complainant and delivered to the Commission, it is considered "filed".

The complaint is regarded as a legal document and must follow a prescribed form. The complaint process is considered a legal proceeding, and the parties are referred to as the **complainant**, who is the person alleging the infringement of a right under the Code, and the **respondent**, who is the individual alleged to have infringed a right under the Code. The Commission does not formally represent the complainant in the proceeding; it represents the public interest. There may be more than one respondent in a complaint. For example, if the infringement occurred in the workplace, respondents can include the worker who committed the infringement, the supervisor who was informed of the infringement and did not make any attempt to remedy it, and the corporation itself that did not have an effective human rights policy in place. The Commission can add parties at any time during the proceeding when it appears that an additional party has also infringed a right. Legal or agent representation is an option available to all parties in a complaint. All named parties in the complaint must be served with a copy of the complaint, and the Commission generally sends the complaint out within 30 days of its completion.

---

[5] The Code identifies that a person has the right to equal treatment (freedom from discrimination) in the following social areas to which the Code applies: services, goods and facilities (s. 1); occupancy of accommodation (s. 2); contracts (ss. 3, 4); employment (s. 5); and vocational associations (s. 6).

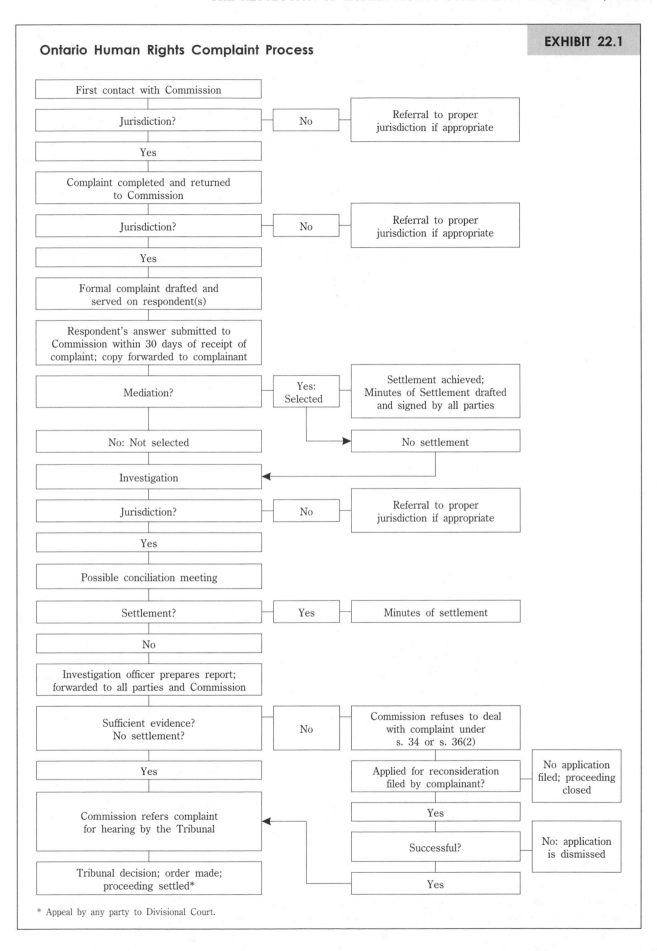

Ontario Human Rights Complaint Process

EXHIBIT 22.1

First contact with Commission

Jurisdiction? — No → Referral to proper jurisdiction if appropriate

Yes

Complaint completed and returned to Commission

Jurisdiction? — No → Referral to proper jurisdiction if appropriate

Yes

Formal complaint drafted and served on respondent(s)

Respondent's answer submitted to Commission within 30 days of receipt of complaint; copy forwarded to complainant

Mediation? — Yes: Selected → Settlement achieved; Minutes of Settlement drafted and signed by all parties

No: Not selected → No settlement

Investigation

Jurisdiction? — No → Referral to proper jurisdiction if appropriate

Yes

Possible conciliation meeting

Settlement? — Yes → Minutes of settlement

No

Investigation officer prepares report; forwarded to all parties and Commission

Sufficient evidence? No settlement? — No → Commission refuses to deal with complaint under s. 34 or s. 36(2)

Yes

Applied for reconsideration filed by complainant? → No application filed; proceeding closed

Commission refers complaint for hearing by the Tribunal

Yes

Successful? → No: application is dismissed

Tribunal decision; order made; proceeding settled*

Yes

* Appeal by any party to Divisional Court.

The respondent is required to answer the complaint within 30 days from the date of the covering letter that accompanied the complaint. The answer written generally contains a rebuttal to the alleged complaint and may argue that the complaint should be dismissed pursuant to section 34. The respondent will also include any relevant documents and names of witnesses. A copy of the written answer is forwarded to the complainant.

In the event that the Commission determines that the matter is not within its jurisdiction, a written response from the Commission will be sent to the complainant. The Commission's reason(s) for not dealing with the complaint will be stated, along with the applicable part of section 34 of the Code. If the complainant disagrees with the reasons given by the Commission for refusing to handle his or her complaint, the complainant may ask the Commission for **reconsideration** of the decision under section 37 within 15 days of the date of mailing of the reasons.

A complaint may be amended after filing, but generally only if the amendment will not result in prejudice to the respondent — for example, by adding elements that contradict the complaint as originally stated. If the complaint progresses to a tribunal hearing, the Tribunal has the power to amend the grounds of a complaint if the evidence demonstrates — for example, an additional ground for the complaint arises under the Code, or it appears that the complainant has been the object of retaliatory behaviour by the respondent since filing.

Where the Tribunal amends a ground in the complaint, the respondent is given notice and will likely be allowed an adjournment to prepare for the amended ground(s). Though the Tribunal's power in this matter may seem heavy-handed, it is important to appreciate how the complaint proceeding, with its originating complaint, differs from a criminal proceeding and its related indictment. A complaint simply serves as a *general notice* to the respondent regarding the nature of the complaint, whereas an indictment is a *specific* printed or written accusation of crime made against one or more people.[6] Moreover, the Code is remedial and in compliance with the overarching goal.

Case Management

In 2006 and 2007, the Commission began two case management initiatives in an attempt to clear up the backlog of cases and reduce delay. Case assessments were conducted in May 2006, and conciliation was emphasized. Files were reviewed for completeness and missing information and documents obtained. Some files were prepared for investigation and legal assessments of complaints obtained. There were 598 files reviewed and assessed in total; 301 files were prepared for investigation and the backlog reduced by 101 files. A similar pilot project commenced in February 2007 to provide for the early assessment of complaints and to institute "fact-finding meetings" as a pre-investigation tool that also imposed a fixed mediation date.[7]

Mediation

Mediation is voluntary within the scope of the Code and, in combination with conciliation, is successful in resolving over half of the complaints filed with the Commission.[8] It is offered to the parties where the respondent's answer is received. Specially trained mediators oversee and facilitate the process but

[6] *Cousens v. Nurses' Assn. (Canada)* (1981), 2 C.H.R.R. D/365 (Ont. Bd. of Inquiry).

[7] *Supra* note 2 at 33.

[8] Voluntariness may be vitiated with the application of the 2007 pilot project above. If so, "mediation" is really an early "conciliation". Mediation is arguably an inherently voluntary process.

| When Does Encouraging a Settlement become Coercing a Settlement? | EXHIBIT 22.2 |

In 1985, Ms. Johnson agreed to settlement of her human rights complaint, but later felt that she had been coerced by the Commission into accepting the settlement offer. In 1991 she submitted an application for judicial review of the Commission's decision not to appoint a Board of Inquiry (now the Tribunal) to hear and decide her complaint. Unfortunately for Ms. Johnson, the application was dismissed, as all members of the court agreed that too much time had elapsed since she had accepted the settlement to set aside the decision of the Commission.

However, Rosenberg J. noted in the written reasons for dismissal of the application that the Commission had, in fact, inappropriately coerced Ms. Johnson into agreeing to the settlement by stating that they would not refer the matter to the Board if she did not accept the settlement offer presented and would refuse to carry it forward. Furthermore, the Commission indicated that it would dismiss her complaint upon non-acceptance. Rosenberg J. found that the Commission did not consider whether the evidence warranted inquiry or whether inquiry was an appropriate procedure under the circumstances. The decision identified that the Commission is entitled to consider two primary matters after a failure to settle: (1) Is the procedure — e.g., referral to the Board of Inquiry — appropriate; and (2) does the evidence warrant an inquiry (i.e., does the evidence support the alleged complaint sufficiently to refer the matter for a hearing, as under section 36(1) of the Code?)

Source: *Johnson v. Hamilton (City)* (1992), 15 C.H.R.R. D/254 (Ont. Div. Ct.).

do not make any decision regarding potential outcomes. Rather, a mediation simply provides a neutral environment for discussion and resolution of the issue at hand. Mediation is not a "discovery" event where each party shares its evidence with the other, and all negotiations and statements made are confidential. Mediation allows those involved to work towards a settlement by clarifying misperceptions and checking facts to ensure that all parties are fully knowledgeable of the requirements of the Code and their proper application.

Although mediation is not technically mandatory, the Commission has a duty to endeavour to effect settlement of the complaint under s. 33(1) prior to referring the matter to the Tribunal. However, while the Commission has a duty to try to effect a settlement, as noted in Exhibit 22.2, it cannot coerce the parties into a settlement.

Settlement

When the parties reach a settlement during mediation, the mediation officer prepares Minutes of Settlement. The Minutes include the specifics agreed to by the complainant and respondent, along with releases, assurances, and any other document requiring the signature of the parties that is necessary for resolution. Settlement can also occur outside of mediation and will be similarly put in writing and signed by the parties. The Commission must approve settlements that include a term that will be implemented at a future date. The future term, for example, may relate to the design and implementation of a human rights policy. A Commission-approved settlement is the only settlement that can be enforced under s. 43.

Settlement may include requirements such as the complainant being granted housing, the reestablishment of a benefit, financial compensation, an apology, or human rights education for employees of a Corporation. A respondent does not usually admit to a human rights violation in a settlement, nor does the complainant retract an allegation. The Commission will no longer be involved in the complaint once settled, and the matter is considered closed.

Investigation

Where one or more of the parties do not wish to participate in mediation, or where no settlement is reached and s. 34 does not apply, a human rights investigation officer is assigned to investigate the complaint. This officer cannot be the same officer who was involved in mediation since the investigating officer should be a neutral party to the complaint. The officer will request evidence and information from all parties in order to establish an accurate view of the events of the complaint.

Section 33 of the Code empowers an investigation officer to enter into a place that is not a dwelling to review, examine, and obtain copies of relevant documents or things (e.g., computer files), or he/she can request that evidence be provided to them for analysis. If it is deemed necessary to enter a dwelling in order to obtain evidence or if a party refuses to disclose evidence, a search warrant can be obtained from a justice of the peace. Alternatively, the matter may be promptly referred to the Tribunal for a hearing. Parties and witnesses may be interviewed by the officer and are allowed to have a representative present should they so choose.

Effective February 2007, the investigation officer will review newly filed complaints. The officer will schedule a mediation meeting, if considered suitable, and a subsequent fact-finding meeting between the parties. If a respondent has not filed an answer to the complaint by the date of the scheduled mediation meeting, the officer will require the answer within 10 days. If the answer remains outstanding after that time, the officer may decide to cancel the fact-finding meeting and recommend that the complaint proceed directly to the Tribunal.

A letter will be sent to the parties requiring the production of certain documents, people or information prior to the fact-finding meeting. Pursuant to s. 33(6), if a respondent does not fulfill the production demand, the matter may proceed directly to the Tribunal. If a complainant does not produce what was requested, the matter may not be referred to the Tribunal.

Conciliation

Conciliation is a separate entity from mediation, and may not occur where unsuccessful mediation has taken place. It forms part of the Commission's mandate under s. 34 to effect settlement. Conciliation is usually scheduled by the investigating officer after the completion of the investigation. It would seem to be in a party's best interest to attend conciliation in order to assess the evidence gathered from investigation. There is a significant difference between mediation and conciliation: while mediation is confidential, conciliation is not. Statements made during a conciliation meeting may be introduced at a tribunal hearing via the case analysis that is prepared after investigation. Additionally, if a complainant refuses a reasonable offer of settlement at conciliation, the investigation officer will include this fact in the case analysis, which in turn may affect the Commission's decision as to whether or not to refer the matter for a hearing. Only "with prejudice" offers open for 30 days can be disclosed in the case analysis report. The parties will generally be asked to submit written settlement offers at conciliation.

At the conciliation meeting the investigation officer will present her/his findings concerning the evidence, which will indicate what the recommendation to the Commission would be in order to facilitate settlement between the parties. Remedies may also be presented and discussed. This is as close to a discovery process as the Commission gets, as there is no formal discovery in human rights proceedings at this stage.

Case Analysis

When conciliation fails to effect settlement or is not used, the investigation officer prepares a written report called a **case analysis**. The case analysis is forwarded to all parties and includes a summary of the evidence and may include a recommendation as to whether or not the matter warrants a tribunal hearing.[9] The case analysis is a thorough report that details the findings of the investigation, a summary of the evidence and conclusions regarding the complaint. Each party may make a written submission in response to the report and submit it to the Commission within 21 days from the date of mailing. This written response should bring to the attention of the Commission any evidence that the party feels has been overlooked in the analysis that should be brought to the Commission's attention. It could also raise issues not addressed in the summary. The Commission may ask the investigating officer to get clarification on an issue raised and may postpone its decision until the additional information is received.

The investigating officer does not have decision-making power regarding a referral of the matter to the Tribunal, but the commissioners do base their decision on the report submitted by the officer. The recommendation is not binding on the commissioners. The commissioners decide whether or not to send the matter to the Tribunal or discuss it under section 34 or 36(2) of the Code.

Commission jurisdiction is evaluated at virtually every step of the process. Where evidence is found that places the matter outside the jurisdiction of the Commission — e.g., it is discovered that the corporation has a union environment and collective agreement in place, but the complainant chose not to file a grievance — the Commission may refuse to deal with the matter under section 34. Reasons for the Commission refusing to deal with the complaint are in writing and sent to all parties.

Where the Commission does not effect settlement and the circumstance is appropriate and the evidence is sufficient to warrant a hearing, the Commission may refer the matter to the Tribunal under section 36. The Commission does not have to disclose the notes in its investigation file or evidence when referring the complaint to the Tribunal. The case analysis is considered sufficient.

Reconsideration

If the Commission decides to dismiss the complaint, the complainant has the right to ask the Commission to reconsider its decision under section 37 of the Code. No such right is available to the respondent. The Application for Reconsideration must be filed within 15 days of the decision's date of mailing (s. 37) with the Commission. The Application for Reconsideration must contain a concise statement of material facts supporting the complainant's position that the matter deserves reconsideration. This statement can raise a procedural or legal error, or involve new facts that have become available. Following is a list of material facts that can warrant reconsideration:

1. Where the original investigation missed relevant evidence, which may have some bearing on the Commission's original decision
2. Where changes in the factual circumstances have some bearing on the Commission's original decision
3. Where a witness recants on an earlier statement before the Commission made its original decision and/or provides new evidence, which has some bearing on the Commission's original decision
4. Where a witness who did not participate in the original investigation provides relevant and persuasive evidence in the application for reconsideration

---

[9] A disclosure letter may be completed instead of a case analysis. The phrase "case analysis" may be alternatively read as disclosure letter. Both documents disclose the substance of the case.

EXHIBIT 22.3

Jurisdiction Issue

On April 3, 1990, the complainant and respondent each received a letter from the Commission indicating its decision not to appoint a Board of Inquiry (now the Tribunal) regarding a complaint previously filed. The complainant's solicitor responded by sending a letter, dated April 12, 1990, requesting reconsideration and including an additional request for extra time to make a "meaningful and complete submission". The Commission acknowledged the receipt of the request for reconsideration and indicated that it had forwarded a copy of the request to the respondent. However, the respondent's solicitor did not receive any notification from the Commission until November 29, 1991, when a reconsideration request report was received. In early December the respondent replied to the letter, stating that the Commission could not allow reconsideration due to the non-compliance with section 37(1) (reconsideration must be filed within 15 days of receipt of the date of mailing of the Commission's decision), and that the application should be refused. Furthermore, it turned out that the complainant did not submit the required statement of material facts in support of reconsideration until April 1992 — a year after the original request for reconsideration.

In July 1992, the Commission informed all parties that it had granted the complainant's request for reconsideration and had requested a Board of Inquiry to settle the complaint but failed to give reasons for changing its decision. In October 1992, the parties were notified by letter that a Board of Inquiry had been appointed. The respondent appealed the appointment of the Board to the Divisional Court.

The Divisional Court judge decided the matter by stating that the decision made after reconsideration cannot stand because the Commission failed to comply with statutory requirements. Following is an outline of the list of statutory requirements that were not complied with:

i)   The Commission failed to give reasons for changing its decision, as required under section 37(3), and the judge indicated that this failure gave an appearance of unfairness to the respondent.

ii) Under section 37(1), the complainant has only 15 days from the date of mailing of the Commission's decision regarding the appointment of a Board of Inquiry in which to submit an application for reconsideration, and an extension of this time limit must be supported by written reasons that specify the "special reasons" that support the extension. The Commission had not properly given any time extension to the complainant, nor had the written statement in support of reconsideration been provided to the respondent.

iii) The complainant had failed to provide the necessary concise statement of the material facts in support of reconsideration, as required in section 37(1).

The judge went on to say that the Commission's conduct in the matter was obviously contrary to the provisions of its governing statute. As such, it was ordered that the decision of the Commission to appoint a Board of Inquiry be quashed. In addition, the Commission was ordered to pay the employer respondent its costs in the amount of $4,500.00.

Source: *Ontario (Ministry of Health) v. Ontario (Human Rights Commission)* (1993), 20 C.H.R.R. D/421, 48 C.C.E.L. 182 (Ont. Div. Ct.)

---

5.   Where authoritative case law, or applicable legislation, has some bearing on the Commission's original decision[10]

Upon receipt of the application, the Commission notifies the respondent(s) that reconsideration has been requested. The respondent has the opportunity to make a written submission to the application within 21 days, and a reconsideration officer will be assigned to the file. The officer will then

---

[10] Ontario Human Rights Commission, *Internal Guide for Processing Complaints* (March 2007).

review the file and determine whether the evidence warrants a reconsideration report. The parties will have 21 days to file additional submissions concerning the officer's reconsideration report if one is completed. The decision of the Commission regarding reconsideration is sent to all parties and is final. Judicial review of the Commission's decision is available and is generally based on an alleged breach of administrative duty or a lack of jurisdiction.

THE COMPLAINT PROCESS AT THE HUMAN RIGHTS TRIBUNAL OF ONTARIO

Once the Commission makes its decision to refer the matter to the Tribunal, a conference call will be scheduled within 30 days of the referral date. Then, once referred, the role of the Commission changes: it ceases to be an investigative body and becomes a party to the proceedings and has carriage of the complaint.

The Tribunal may add a party to the proceeding at any time if it feels that a new party has infringed a right under the Code. This may include someone who knew of the infringement, or ought to have known, and had authority to penalize or prevent the conduct regarding harassment in accommodation, harassment in employment, or harassment because of sex in accommodation or the workplace. For example, if the owner of a rental building knew that the property manager was discriminating against welfare recipients by refusing to offer them accommodation and did nothing to rectify the situation, the owner may be added to the proceeding as a party.

As in civil proceedings, motions, expert witnesses, summons to witnesses, requests for costs, and adjournments are available to a party in a tribunal hearing. Appropriate documents — e.g., a notice of motion — are filed with the Registrar. As proceedings are quasi-judicial, witnesses are required to swear or affirm their testimony. The Tribunal has its own rules of procedure, available online at its website <www.hrto.ca>. The rules identify service and filing requirements among other things.

The Mission of the Human Rights Tribunal of Ontario

EXHIBIT 22.4

¤ The Tribunal will play its role as a pillar in the human rights system by providing expeditious and accessible processes to assist the parties to resolve complaints brought before the Tribunal, and to determine complaints where the parties are unable to resolve them.

¤ The Tribunal will be activist to seek a fair, just and expeditious resolution of the merits of an application.

¤ The Tribunal will provide and promote meaningful and effective public interest remedies in appropriate cases. The Tribunal will not bar settlements where parties freely desire to resolve their dispute.

¤ The Tribunal will seek to maintain the highest standards of integrity and quality of work.

¤ The Tribunal will strive for consistency to enhance the parties' reasonable expectations of Tribunal policy and process, but will remain responsive to differing cases and party needs, and to an evolving understanding of human rights and discrimination.

¤ The Tribunal will strive to promote a clear understanding of the Tribunal's work among the general public. The Tribunal will work to be responsive to the needs of its stakeholder communities.

Source: Human Rights Tribunal of Ontario website <http://www.hrto.ca/NEW/about/mandate.asp>.

A party can request mediation through the Tribunal office at any time in the process, and mediation will be explored during the initial conference call. In the event that the Commission obtains a settlement with the respondent that satisfies its public interest mandate, it will withdraw from the proceeding. If the complainant does not similarly reach settlement with the respondent, a hearing may still take place. Upon the withdrawal of the Commission, the complainant assumes carriage of the proceeding. Settlement between the complainant, the Commission and the respondent is required in order to remove the proceeding from the hearing list.

A hearing can occur even when another court proceeding regarding the same facts but requesting a different remedy is underway. The Tribunal deals only with discrimination and harassment under the Code, and a civil suit — e.g., for lost wages as a result of being wrongfully dismissed due to ethnic origin — may be launched concurrently with the complaint. There is no apparent conflict with both proceedings running concurrently, provided the human rights claim is excluded from the civil action. Current case law supports a civil action that includes a corollary human rights claim. Legal advice should be obtained to determine the best forum under the particular circumstances.

A hearing is adjudicated by a panel, which usually consists of one person. The hearing is open to the public unless the chair decides otherwise, and Tribunal decisions are published in the *Canadian Human Rights Reporter*.

Intervenors: Persons Not a Party to the Proceeding

A person who is not a party to the proceeding but who wishes to participate in the proceeding must bring a motion to the Tribunal (r. 17). The motion sets out the person's interest in the matter and the degree of participation (intervention) being sought. The request must be served, along with proof of service, to all parties. The panel may decide to limit the right of intervention to a specific part of the proceeding and may further limit it to only a written submission.

The Tribunal applies a broad approach to its interpretation of the Code and its application to the complaints before it. The public interest is as important as the private interests of the complainant and the respondent. Therefore, other groups concerned with the public interest may be able to provide input and bring a broader perspective to the proceeding before the Tribunal.

It is also important for the Tribunal to ensure that everyone who may be affected by the remedy sought is given notice of the hearing. An example of this would be a human rights complaint on the grounds of disability in the social area of employment by a unionized employee, where the issue raised or remedy sought — e.g., the workplace must institute an accommodation policy, such as a building renovation to accommodate a wheelchair — has potential impact on the rights of other bargaining members (e.g., wheelchair access for additional entrances). Although they are not a party to the complaint, the hearing would be relevant to the entire bargaining unit and the Tribunal would ensure that the union received notice of the proceeding.

There are two types of intervenors, and status is determined by the Tribunal.[11] One is a person or persons who have a right or interest that may be affected by the decision (see example above) and who may be given the opportunity to submit evidence and lead witnesses. The other is referred to as **amicus curiae**, a Latin term indicating that the person is perceived as a "friend of the court" or, in this case, the Tribunal. A designation of amicus curiae indicates that the party is likely restricted to making written submis-

---

[11] *Sinclair v. Peel Non-Profit Housing Corp. (No. 2)* (1989), 11 C.H.R.R. D/342 (Ont. Bd. of Inquiry); *Leshner v. Ontario (No. 1)* (1991), 16 C.H.R.R. D/175 (Ont. Bd. of Inquiry).

The Tribunal Process

EXHIBIT 22.5

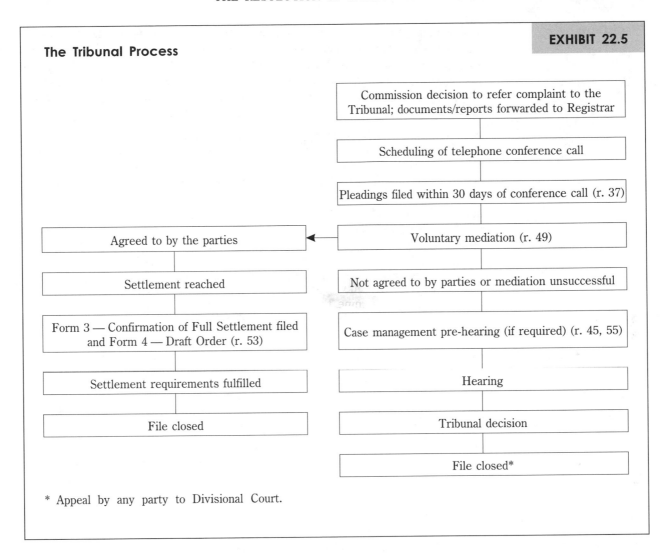

* Appeal by any party to Divisional Court.

sions for the purpose of assisting the panel in achieving a broader understanding of the facts or associated issues connected to the complaint. For example, a disability advocacy research group may request to intervene as an amicus curiae where the complaint involves accommodation for disabled people.

The Commencement of the Hearing

The hearing commences with the scheduling of the telephone conference call between the Tribunal and all parties and/or their representative within 30 days of the date of referral. The purpose of the conference call is to schedule relevant dates — e.g., for mediation — and to identify any preliminary and procedural matters that will need to be dealt with (r. 33). If there are such matters, then a case management pre-hearing will be scheduled, along with mediation agreed to. The conference call and/or pre-hearing will also identify any additional individuals who are not already named in the complaint and who require notice of the proceeding. This may happen where the Tribunal determines that the corporation that employs the respondent should be included as a party in the complaint. The Tribunal may also determine that additional sections of the Code are applicable to the complaint; the complaint would then need to be amended to include the additional section where an alleged infringement has occurred. The panel who oversees the conference call is not necessarily the same panel who will preside over the hearing.

Pleadings

The pleadings (r. 37 to 40) include a statement of the facts, the issue(s) in dispute, the desired remedy, and a notice of motion to amend the complaint if applicable. Pleadings are served on all the other parties in the proceeding and filed, with a statement of service (Form 1), with the Tribunal within 30 days of the conference call. In the event that the Commission has been permitted to withdraw from the hearing by the panel, the complainant must file the pleadings and assumes carriage of the proceeding.

The respondent must serve and file, along with a statement of service, a written response to the pleadings within 25 days of service of the statement of the facts, etc., noted above (r. 39). The response deals with issues raised in the complaint and the statement of facts that the respondent is relying on in his or her defence. The facts of the complaint that the respondent is willing to admit are listed along with the respondent's desired remedy and representation contact information. The respondent is also obligated to identify any person who is not named in the complaint but who may be affected by the proceeding, and must provide the person's contact information. The Commission and/or the complainant have five days from the date of service of the response in which to serve and file a reply (r. 40).

Mutual Disclosure

The Commission is required to give full disclosure of the results of its investigation to all parties within 30 days of the conference call (r. 41). Disclosure includes witness statements, documents, and evidence that relates to the complaint. The complainant is required to deliver witness statements and evidence by the same deadline (r. 42), while the respondent has 25 days after service of the Commission and complainant's disclosure to provide his or her material (r. 43). A failure to disclose by a party may mean that the party cannot refer to or enter the document or physical evidence at the hearing without the permission of the panel (r. 48).

Mediation and Settlement

With the consent of the parties, the matter can be referred to a mediator at any time during the tribunal process. Mediation is confidential, and statements made during the mediation cannot be admitted at the hearing without the agreement of the parties. Mediation usually takes place before a pre-hearing conference.

Settlement can also occur at any time and must be in writing and signed by the parties. Where settlement is reached, a Confirmation of Settlement (Form 3) is filed within 45 days of the date of settlement. The Confirmation of Settlement is signed by the parties and includes a draft order (Form 4).

Pre-hearing Conference

The pre-hearing conference takes place in the majority of cases before the Tribunal. The registrar will send notice to all parties identifying the date, time, place, and purpose of the case management pre-hearing. There may be more than one conference, depending on the complexity of the proceeding. The usual practice is for all parties and their representatives to attend. The Tribunal may issue notice requiring a party's attendance when the party's absence from the meeting results, or will result, in delay or is for the purpose of avoidance. A statement is also included in the notice, informing parties that whether they attend or not, binding orders may be made.

The Tribunal has the authority to compel a party to attend the pre-hearing conference to simplify or narrow down contentious issues and to allow for a more efficient use of the time scheduled for the hearing (r. 54, 55).

Evidence

A document submitted for evidence at the hearing must be filed in the Tribunal's record and marked as an exhibit with copies given to relevant witnesses, the panel, and each party. The panel may admit without proof or evidence any fact(s) agreed to by the parties. It is significant to note that the panel has discretion, through the SPPA, to admit any evidence, including hearsay and/or circumstantial evidence, that is relevant to the complaint. The weight and measure given to hearsay and/or circumstantial evidence at a hearing will turn on the particular facts and the body of other evidence presented.

Similar Act Evidence

Similar act evidence may be allowed at the hearing,[12] particularly in cases of alleged harassment. Harassment frequently occurs without witnesses. In some cases the matter may rest on the credibility of the parties involved. If so, the Tribunal may allow similar fact evidence where a pattern of behaviour is alleged. However, similar act evidence must relate to the complaint before the Tribunal. A complainant cannot submit similar act evidence of discrimination based on creed if the complaint only alleges sexual harassment. However, similar act evidence can be relevant, for example, in a complaint where a female employee is repeatedly told jokes of a sexual nature by her manager, which the employee finds offensive and sexually suggestive. Even though there are no witnesses to the alleged harassment, if other female employees have been told similar inappropriate jokes by the same manager named in the complaint, it is the evidence of these other female employees that may be admitted by the Tribunal as similar act evidence. Moreover, proving an intent to breach the Code is unnecessary, and similar act evidence, and/or circumstantial evidence, may be sufficient to meet the burden of proof.

Notice of Constitutional Question

If a party (a) plans to raise a question regarding the constitutional validity or applicability of an Act or of a regulation or by-law made under an Act or a rule of common law, or (b) intends to claim a remedy under section 24(1) of the *Canadian Charter of Rights and Freedoms* [*Charter*],[13] the party must file a Notice of Constitutional Question and serve it on all the other parties, along with the Attorney General of Canada and the Attorney General of Ontario, at least 15 days prior to the date the party plans to argue the question.[14] This notice is not a frequent occurrence at a tribunal hearing. If desired, the relevant attorney can intervene in the proceeding and make submissions to the panel regarding the question raised.

Orders

Once the hearing is concluded, the Tribunal is required to make its decision within 30 days (s. 41(5)). There are a number of remedies available, under section 41 of the Code, to the Tribunal, where discrimination or harassment is proven. As stated, the mandate of the Tribunal is to ensure that the Code is complied with, and it seeks to put complainants in the position they would otherwise have been in had the discrimination or harassment not occurred. This is accomplished through monetary and non-monetary orders or a combination of the two. An example of a non-monetary remedy could involve an employee who was denied a promotion on a discriminatory ground and the Tribunal orders a promotion equal to the one wrongly denied. That order may

---

[12] The Tribunal can admit and act on similar act evidence under SPPA, s. 15(1).

[13] Anyone whose rights or freedoms, as guaranteed by the Charter, have been infringed or denied may apply to a court of competent jurisdiction to obtain such remedy as the court considers appropriate and just in the circumstances: *Charter*, s. 24(1).

[14] Rule 70, *Ontario Board of Inquiry Rules of Practice*, 2004.

be accompanied by an order for back pay equal to the raise associated with the promotion, commencing on the date it was improperly denied (monetary damages). Section 41(1)(a) of the Code gives a broad power for orders to be made that require a respondent to perform a task — e.g., implement a human rights policy or conduct a human rights education seminar for management — that, in the Tribunal's opinion, is necessary to prevent a future breach. A letter of assurance regarding future compliance to the Code may also be required, and corporate respondents may be ordered to post the Tribunal decision in their office.[15] It is this type of non-money order that the Commission would seek in the public interest.

Monetary remedies are influenced by the particulars of each complaint, as illustrated in case law. They are used for compensating the complainant for an infringement of a right and may include compensation for losses suffered as a result of that infringement. An amount may also be ordered where a respondent is shown to have discriminated with intent, or where the harassment has been ongoing or particularly severe. A lesser amount may be ordered where the complainant has been shown to engage in retaliatory name-calling.[16] Monetary remedies available under section 41 of the Code are summarized below:

1. **General damages** are for mental anguish and/or damages for the loss of the right to be free from discrimination and breach of the Code. Mental anguish damages are capped at $10,000 (s. 41(1)(b)) and require a finding that the act(s) of the respondent was wilful (i.e., a deliberate act) or reckless (i.e., an act or practice engaged in with indifference as to its effect). Expert medical evidence is generally not required. Additional general damages may be awarded for infringing the complainant's right to be free from discrimination generally and/or for the specific breach of the Code as it relates to the complainant's injury to dignity and self-respect resulting from the act(s) of the respondent. While there is no statutory cap on this second category of general damages, some Tribunal decisions have applied the same $10,000 cap imposed on mental anguish damages.

2. **Special damages** may also be awarded — for example, in a situation where an employee has been denied a promotion on a discriminatory ground. The employer may be ordered to compensate, with interest, the employee for the difference between the employee's present salary and the salary of the higher position. Non-monetary relief may include an order entitling the complainant to the next available position.

3. **Pre-judgment interest** may apply to monetary remedies at the Tribunal's discretion.

4. **Costs** may be awarded, at the discretion of the Tribunal, to a respondent where the complaint has been shown to be trivial, frivolous, vexatious or made in bad faith by the complainant and would be paid by the Commission who initiated the claim (s. 41(4) and r. 71).

In the event that a respondent elects to disregard a Tribunal order, the respondent may be found guilty of an offence and be liable for a fine up to

---

[15] *Styres v. Paiken* (1982), 3 C.H.R.R. D/926 (Ont. Bd. of Inquiry) and *Abouchar v. Toronto (Metro School Board (No. 4)* (1999), 35 C.H.R.R. D/175 (Ont. Bd. of Inquiry).

[16] *Ahluwalia v. Metropolitan Toronto (Municipality) Commissioners of Police* (1983), 4 C.H.R.R. D/1757 (Ont. Bd. of Inquiry).

$25,000.00. It is prudent for a successful complainant to obtain a copy of the tribunal decision from the registrar and file it with the Ontario Superior Court of Justice. The filing ensures that the order can be enforced as an order of the court and post-judgment interest requested if necessary.

Appeals

Any party may appeal the decision of the Tribunal to the Divisional Court, and the appeal operates as a stay of the proceeding (s. 42(1) and r. 73). The court is free to make a decision on the appeal as it sees fit, and is not bound in any way by the decision of the Tribunal (s. 42(3)). An application for judicial review does not automatically stay the Tribunal's order (r. 74).

2007: ONTARIO'S NEW HUMAN RIGHTS REGIME

A variety of issues have plagued Ontario's human rights regime for decades, with delay being a frequently cited concern.[17] The current process can result in years passing before a complainant reaches the hearing stage. Criticism has also raised issues of the Commission and the Tribunal's independence, the conflicting role of the Commission in regard to its screening complaints while charged with promoting Code compliance and inadequate government funding. After reports from government-appointed task forces, along with consultation and discussion with various stakeholders, the legislature drafted extensive changes to Ontario's human rights regime.

On December 20, 2006, *An Act to Amend the Human Rights Code*[18] ("amendment") was **assented to** by the legislature. The amendment represents the most comprehensive changes to Ontario's human rights law since enactment in 1962. The changes address issues that include delay, education, accessibility and provision for greater transparency in the human rights process. The most significant procedural and structural changes are identified in this section.[19]

The amendment involves more than an overdue redesign of the existing system, which comprises the OHRC and HRTO. It includes the creation of an independent legal resource centre and the formation of two secretariats. As well, there will be choices for many applicants concerning the commencement of a proceeding and the provision of legal advice. A right to make oral submissions means that applicants will be guaranteed the opportunity to be heard. Remedies have been expanded and enforcement made easier.

The majority of the changes to Ontario's human rights regime came into force on June 30, 2008.[20] Transitional provisions permitted the Tribunal to make rules, appoint members, allow a complaint filed with the OHRC under the old regime to be transferred to the new regime and identify when the

---

[17] There have been many discussion papers and articles written about, and criticizing, the current regime. See, for example, The Cornish Task Force Report (1992), the La Forest Task Force (2000) and the Ontario Human Rights Commission, "Reviewing Ontario's Human Rights System", Discussion Paper (2005), online: <http://www.ohrc.on.ca/english/consultations/human-rights-review-discussion-paper.pdf> (August 29, 2007). The OHRC website provides a list of consultation and discussion documents at <http://www.ohrc.on.ca/english/publications/index.shtml#consultations> (August 29, 2007).

[18] S.O. 2006, c. 30.

[19] The amendment is available on <http://www.e-laws.gov.on.ca>; a review of the full procedure is beyond the scope of this chapter.

[20] The amendment provisions relating to the Ontario Human Rights Commission and Ontario Human Rights Tribunal came into force on June 30, 2008. The provisions relating to the Human Rights Legal Support Centre have not yet been given a proclamation date. The full list of proclamation dates is available online: <http://www.e-laws.gov.on.ca/html/tables/publicstatutesannotations/elaws_t_pu_st_an_t90h19.htm> (August 29, 2007).

OHRC retains carriage of preexisting proceedings (Part IV, ss. 49 to 57). Regulations may also be made to address additional transitional matters as they arise.

Highlights of Procedural Changes

Direct Access Model

A meaningful change is the restructuring of the resolution process from one of investigation, selection and carriage of a proceeding by the OHRC to a "direct access" model. Direct access means that people can commence a proceeding directly with the HRTO and obtain a hearing should the issue not be resolved beforehand. It is expected that this fundamental change will reduce delay, make the resolution of proceedings more accessible and eliminate any conflict of interest related to the current OHRC involvement.

A proceeding commences by way of application and not complaint, as it has been previously the case. A person (s. 34(1)), two or more people jointly (s. 34(1)(4)), a person or organization on behalf of another, where the person alleging discrimination consents (s. 34(5)), or the OHRC (s. 35) may file an application with the Tribunal. The ability of a group to file an application is new and permits entities, such as unions or special interest groups, to file claims directly with the HRTO and is discussed further below.

Limitation Period

The limitation period is one year from the date of the alleged infringement of a right or, where a series of infringements are alleged, one year from the date of the last incident (s. 34(1)). Section 34(2) permits the Tribunal to extend the one-year limitation period under certain circumstances. Previously, a six-month limitation period was in effect.

The Role of the Courts

Changes that involve the courts concern the authority to review a Tribunal decision and to hear and decide a Code infringement where it is part of a civil proceeding. Currently, a party has a statutory right to appeal the Tribunal's decision to the Divisional Court. A **privative clause** in the amendment expressly limits the ability of a reviewing court to change or substitute the Tribunal's decision with its own. Section 45.8 states that the Tribunal's decision is final, and only **patently unreasonable** decisions may be altered or set aside by judicial review. That would require, for example, that the decision under review be found to be unsupported by the facts. The court cannot substitute its own decision where it simply disagrees with the result of the Tribunal. The Tribunal can, when requested by a party, reconsider its own decision (s. 45.7). The failure of the Tribunal to follow its own rules is "not a ground for setting aside" a decision unless it results in a "substantial wrong which affected the final disposition of the matter" (s. 43(8)).

> **45.8** Subject to section 45.6 of this *Act*, section 221.1 of the *Statutory Powers Procedures Act* and the Tribunal rules, a decision of the Tribunal is final and not subject to appeal and shall not be altered or set aside in an application for judicial review or in any other proceeding unless the decision is patently unreasonable.

Counter-balances to the narrowed scope of judicial review include a new selection process for the Commission and the Tribunal appointments mandated under the Act (ss. 27 and 32, respectively), a party's right to an oral hearing, the HRTO's ability to intervene in the proceeding and the availability of legal advice or representation to applicants. These are discussed further in the next section of this chapter. In addition, the OHRC has authority under s. 45.6 to **state a case** to the Divisional Court, where it is a party to a proceeding and believes that a decision or order made by the Tribunal is inconsistent with Commission policy.

There have, in the past, been conflicting decisions regarding the court's ability to hear Code matters and award damages where the allegation arises within a civil proceeding. The amendment expressly permits the court to decide a Code infringement and award damages where the allegation is related to the main issue in the civil proceeding (s. 46.1(1)). Therefore a proceeding for wrongful dismissal, as an example, may include a separate but related allegation of discrimination, and the court can hear both grounds and award monetary compensation. Where a Code infringement is related to a civil action and included in the statement of claim, the person cannot file an application with the Tribunal (s. 34(11) and (12)). A party may want to consider the best forum in which to bring the human rights claim prior to pursuing it. A matter relating solely to an infringement of the Code must be heard by a tribunal with authority to hear the matter.

The Ontario Human Rights Commission

The amendment expands the OHRC, or Commission's, function regarding independence from government, education, policy development and research, and its ability to provide consistency in the application of the Code (s. 29). The changes facilitate independence by having members appointed by the Lieutenant Governor in Council (s. 27(2)), and the Commission will report to the legislature, not the Ministry of the Attorney General (s. 31.6(2)). Reports can be made directly to the public or to whomever the OHRC considers appropriate (s. 31.7) regarding the state of human rights, which facilitate independence, transparency and accountability. The Commission is not constrained by providing information only to government or at its request. The Commission will no longer receive and screen complaints for hearings, investigate all matters or mediate settlements. All adjudicative responsibilities are removed by the amendment.

The OHRC's goal is to ensure compliance with the Code and eliminate discriminatory practices (s. 29). The idea is that increased public awareness through general and specific educational initiatives will pro-actively increase Code compliance and reduce infringements. It is likely, however, that there will be an increase in applications initially. The Commission will provide guidelines on the interpretation and application of the Code. There is also a refocusing of the OHRC on systemic discrimination. Research into systemic discrimination will pinpoint areas, sectors or industries that require remediation, and information and education will then target those identified areas. Guidelines and policies can then be tailored to the problem area.

In addition to authorizing research, the amendment provides the OHRC with authority to request copies of applications and responses filed with the HRTO in order to review them and identify areas of systemic concern (s. 38). Whether research or a series of individual applications with similar facts suggest systemic discrimination, the OHRC has extensive power to make recommendations, co-ordinate remedial programs and activities, initiate reviews, commence proceedings, act as intervenor or conduct inquiries (s. 29). The only qualification is that the action taken must be in the **public interest**, but what constitutes public interest appears to be at the Commission's discretion.

The Commission has broad powers when conducting an inquiry or review similar to those before amendment (ss. 31 to 31.2). Those powers include entry without warrant and production of evidence (s. 31). They may be used, for example, for reviews, pro-active investigation of systemic discrimination or to gather evidence in support of an application. The powers appear broader in the sense that an inquiry can be undertaken on the Commission's own initiative and does not have to be tied to an application. Specifically, the OHRC has authority to promote, assist and encourage groups to participate in programs that will alleviate incidents of tension and conflict based on a prohibited ground (s. 29(e)). That provision expressly refers to the OHRC's initiating a review or inquiry where only conditions that *may* lead to tension or conflict based on the Code are present. This authority suggests that the Commission, for example, may thus insert itself in situations that involve an identified group. It would not require that an application be filed or that discrimination be demonstrated.

Ensuring consistency in the application of the Code relative to HRTO decisions and the drafting of legislation is also part of the Commission's mandate. While its policy guidelines regarding the application of the Code are not binding on the Tribunal, the HRTO may consider OHRC-approved policies when deciding a case (s. 45.5(1)). The Tribunal must consider the policy if requested by a party (s. 45.5(2)). If the Commission believes that a final HRTO decision it was involved in is inconsistent with its policies, it may request that the Tribunal state a case to the Divisional Court (s. 45.6), identified earlier. That procedure is unavailable where the OHRC has not been a party or has not acted as an intervenor. However, the Tribunal is obligated to state a case, in writing, on a question of law only where the Tribunal itself deems it "appropriate" (s. 45.6(2)). The Commission may also review a statute or regulation and make recommendations where any aspect of the law is inconsistent with the intent of the Code (s. 29).

The OHRC retains discretion to initiate an application (s. 35(1)) or intervene (s. 37(1)) in a proceeding where the issue is of public interest. The Commission's use of adjudication to advance its goal of compliance may arise from the performance of any of its functions: education, research, review or investigation. Where the applicant consents, the Commission may intervene as a party in the proceeding and fully participate in the proceeding and lead evidence (s. 37(2)). If the OHRC seeks to intervene under other circumstances, its degree of participation will be determined by the Tribunal (s. 37(1)). An intervenor generally cannot lead evidence or cross-examine as those rights attach only to a party. Alternatively, the Commission may bring its own application in the public interest, even if an individual has independently filed an application. The applications would likely be heard together (ss. 35(2) and (3)).

The Ontario Human Rights Tribunal

The amendment creates a more autonomous adjudicative body and enhances the HRTO, or Tribunal's, authority over the resolution process, procedure and available remedies. Its core values are to increase accessibility, fairness, transparency, timeliness and the opportunity to be heard.[21] It is anticipated that non-systemic applications will take less than one year to reach the hearing stage.[22]

The amendment facilitates autonomy by requiring that adjudicator appointments meet specified criteria, removing the OHRC from the selection process for hearings and limiting court interference in decisions (discussed above). Section 32 requires adjudicators to be appointed by the Lieutenant Governor in Council. The appointment process is to be competitive and requires candidates to be assessed on specified criteria, including the candidate's experience, knowledge or training in human rights law and issues, aptitude for both impartial adjudication, and alternative dispute resolution processes provided for in

---

[21] Online: <http://www.hrto.ca/NEW/about/mandate.asp> (July 8, 2008).

[22] Michael Gottheil, "An Approach to Proceedings Before the Human Rights Tribunal of Ontario — Draft for Discussion Purposes Only" (Paper presented to the Ontario Bar Association, 11 July 2007) at page 8.

the rules (s. 32(3)). By appointing a group of "experts" as adjudicators, the Tribunal's expertise in deciding human rights issues would be expected to surpass that of the courts and thus attract the court's deference to the decision made. Expertise is one of the factors that limits a court's review of tribunal decisions.

The Tribunal is to deal with applications by adopting practices and procedures that "offer the best opportunity for a fair, just and expeditious resolution of the merits of the applications" (s. 40). The HRTO is empowered to make its own rules of practice and procedure, including implementing forms of alternate dispute resolution, such as mediation (s. 43(1) and (3)(a)).[23] Mediation is expected to be available throughout the proceeding and may be recommended by the Tribunal, and a party is able to request, or decline, participation.

The Tribunal can, among other things, intervene in a proceeding to conduct examinations in chief or cross-examinations of a witness or require a party to produce evidence or a witness (s. 43(3)). Moreover, section 44(1) empowers the Tribunal to conduct an inquiry where requested by a party and where it is satisfied that an inquiry is necessary to obtain evidence, where the evidence may assist in a fair, just and expeditious resolution on the merits and where it is appropriate under the circumstances (s. 44). As well, the HRTO has broad power when conducting an inquiry (s. 44), which includes warrantless entry. People are legally obligated to comply with tribunal requests during inquiry (s. 44(10)).

The Tribunal can refer matters arising out of a proceeding to the Commission, where the Tribunal determines the issue may be of interest to the Commission (s. 45.4). The OHRC is not, however, obligated to deal with the matter. The amendment expressly entitles a party to the proceeding to an oral hearing and written reasons (s. 43(2)). Decisions of the Tribunal will be made public.[24]

Remedies under the current act distinguished between a monetary award, or damages, for breach of the Code and monetary compensation for "mental anguish", where the infringement was imposed wilfully or recklessly, to a maximum of $10,000. The amendment eliminates the distinction between those monetary awards, the precondition of wilful or reckless conduct and the "mental anguish" maximum (s. 45.2). It also permits the Tribunal to make an order with respect to a party's future practice, even where the order was not requested by the applicant (s. 45.2(1) and (2)):

> 45.2(1) On an application under section 34, the Tribunal may make one or more of the following orders ...
> 1. An order directing the party who infringed the right to pay monetary compensation to the party whose right was infringed for loss arising out of the infringement, including compensation for injury to dignity, feelings and self-respect.
> 2. An order directing the party who infringed the right to make restitution to the party whose right was infringed, other than through monetary compensation, for loss arising out of the infringement, including restitution for injury to dignity, feelings and self-respect.
> 3. An order directing any party to the application to do anything that, in the opinion of the Tribunal, the party ought to do to promote compliance with this Act.

---

[23] The Tribunal's *2004 Rules of Procedure* are available online: <http://www.hrto.ca/english/rules/2004rules.pdf> (August 29, 2007).

[24] For example, on <http://www.canlii.org>.

In a civil proceeding that includes an ancillary Code infringement, only the first two remedies directly above may be awarded (s. 46.1(1)). Therefore, the remedy sought will be an influencing factor in deciding the preferred forum in which to bring the application where **concurrent jurisdiction** exists.

A group (or person) may want to select the Tribunal where more than one has jurisdiction over the matter. This could arise in a civil proceeding, previously identified, or in a unionized workplace. The union might be seeking a systemic remedy. The union has recourse to the Ontario Labour Board, and arbitrators can hear Code applications. However, the arbitrator would be unable, for example, to amend a collective agreement, which may be the only way to address the systemic issue. Alternatively, a person may choose to file only with the HRTO because it has already decided a case on similar facts. Tribunal decisions are not expressly binding, but consistency would be expected.

Where two or more tribunals have concurrent jurisdiction to hear the application and an application has been filed with both, the HRTO retains jurisdiction over the matter. However, the HRTO would likely defer the application under its rules until the other tribunal has decided the matter. The HRTO will not, as is currently done by the OHRC, look to see whether the application "could or should" have proceeded under another act and dismiss on that basis. Section 45.1 permits the Tribunal to dismiss an application, on a case-by-case basis, only where the other proceeding has resolved the matter on the merits:

> The Tribunal may dismiss an application, in whole or in part, in accordance with its rules if the Tribunal is of the opinion that another proceeding has appropriately dealt with the substance of the application.

The Code currently permits only costs awards against the Commission, under particular circumstances, for the benefit of a respondent. There is no similar provision in the amendment. The Tribunal will be able to award costs against either party to the proceeding pursuant to the SPPA and its own rules. The SPPA permits costs only where the conduct of a party has been "unreasonable, frivolous or vexatious or a party has acted in bad faith" and a tribunal has made rules in respect of costs (SPPA s. 17.1(2) and (4)). In the event of a conflict between the Tribunal's rules, act or regulation and the SPPA, the SPPA is trumped (s. 42(2)).

The enforcement of awards is enhanced by s. 45.9(3), which permits an applicant to apply directly to the Tribunal if the written and signed settlement is breached within six months of the breach. Previously, an applicant seeking enforcement of a settlement had to reapply and, effectively, restart the OHRC process unless the settlement expressly permitted the Tribunal to deal with the issue.

The Human Rights Legal Support Centre ("HRLSC")

The creation of the HRLSC, or Centre, pursuant to the amendment is unique to Ontario's human rights regime. Its mandate is to "establish and administer a cost-effective and efficient system for providing support services, including legal services, respecting applications to the Tribunal under Part IV" (s. 45.12(a)). The purpose is to facilitate access to the HRTO. HRLSC is not an agency of the Crown and is independent of, but accountable to, the government of Ontario (s. 45.11). Information on procedure and process will be readily available to all who inquire and is expected to be available online. Applications may be prepared and submitted through the HRLSC but can be filed directly with the HRTO.

The Centre has authority to establish policies and priorities regarding its function that qualify its mandate. Services will be provided, province-wide

(s. 45.13(2)), "based on its financial resources" (s. 45.12(b)). Thus, financial resources will dictate the level of service available, and there is no right of specific entitlement. Legal assistance, however, will not be dependent on eligibility criteria, such as financial need.[25] While available for information and assistance, the Centre does not screen applications. An applicant is not obliged to use the HRLSC services, and an application can be filed directly with the HRTO.

The amendment, in s. 45.13, does specify particular services that will be provided:

(1) The Centre shall provide the following support services:
1. Advice and assistance, legal and otherwise, respecting the infringement of rights under Part I.
2. Legal services in relation to,
   (i) the making of applications to the Tribunal under Part IV,
   (ii) proceedings before the Tribunal under Part IV,
   (iii) applications for judicial review arising from Tribunal proceedings,
   (iv) stated case proceedings,
   (v) the enforcement of Tribunal orders,
3. Such other services as may be prescribed by regulation.

The delivery and range of availability of services will evolve once operation begins. Helena C. Birt, Transition Director, Human Rights Legal Support Centre, expects that there will be a staffed office located in Toronto and service networks across the province. Summary advice and assistance, substantive legal advice and support, legal representation and post-hearing services and support are anticipated.[26] Summary advice and assistance will include consideration of the merits of the claim, assistance in preparing applications, identifying issues and remedies, as well as preparing supporting documentation. It will also involve contact with the respondent to determine whether settlement is possible. Legal advice and assistance are potentially available at any stage in the proceeding. Partnerships between the HRLSC and existing community clinics and members of the private bar may evolve to augment service where needed. During the pre-hearing stage, representation may be provided by duty counsel or on a continuing solicitor/client basis.[27] Moreover, to assist with the enforcement of monetary awards, the Centre will offer information or advice regarding traditional methods, such as liens and garnishment.

While a respondent will be able to obtain general information or referrals from the HRLSC, legal representation is expected to be unavailable.[28]

Anti-Racism and Disability Rights Secretariats

The precise role of these two secretariats is not fully formed at present, but their function is identified under the act. Each secretariat is to conduct research and make recommendations to the OHRC, educate the public concerning discriminatory practices and other tasks as assigned by the Chief Commissioner, in order to eliminate these forms of discrimination (ss. 31.3(4) and 31.4(4)). Each secretariat will consist of a maximum of six people appointed by the Lieutenant Governor in Council on the advice of the Chief Commissioner (ss. 31.3(2) and 31.4(2)).

---

[25] Helena C. Birt, "The Ontario Human Rights Legal Support Centre: A Brief Introduction". Paper presented to the Ontario Bar Association, July 11, 2007, at p. 9.

[26] *Ibid.*

[27] *Ibid.* at p. 5.

[28] *Ibid.*

CHAPTER SUMMARY

This chapter identified the roles of the Human Rights Commission and the Human Rights Tribunal of Ontario in the human rights resolution process. The Commission has discretionary power to refer a complaint to the Tribunal, and the limits of this discretion are set out in sections 34 and 36 of the Code. The Tribunal is an administrative body and quasi-judicial in nature and may make monetary and non-monetary orders. The Code is remedial in nature.

The sequence of events in the complaint process at the Commission was discussed, including the powers of investigation under section 33 of the Code. The differences between mediation and conciliation were noted and related to confidentiality, appropriateness, and the potential for affecting the decision to refer the matter to the Tribunal or to dismiss under section 36(1). A complainant's right to reconsideration was also explored.

A description of the complaint process at the HRTO was presented. A discussion on intervenors, pleadings, and the pre-hearing conference followed. The type of evidence allowed at an administrative tribunal through the SPPA was briefly explained, and the types of orders available to an adjudicator and the relevant maximum were identified.

The chapter concluded with an overview of pending changes in the human rights resolution process.

GLOSSARY OF NEW TERMS AND KEY CONCEPTS

amicus curiae	A Latin term meaning "friend of the court", referring to an intervenor in a hearing, who may be allowed to make a written submission regarding the ramifications of a complaint.
assented to	When a bill is in its final form and accepted, or passed, by the legislature, it is assented to and becomes law.
case analysis	A report submitted by the investigation officer to the Commission summarizing the facts, issues, and evidence in a complaint. The case analysis will also include the officer's recommendation regarding the referral of the matter for a hearing.
complainant	The party in a human rights complaint who alleges that a right under the Code has been infringed.
concurrent jurisdiction	Where more than one adjudicative body has authority to decide the issue.
panel	One or more members of the Tribunal who adjudicate a hearing.
patently unreasonable	A standard of judicial review that shows the highest level of deference to the decision of an administrative adjudicative body; to set aside a decision, the decision being reviewed must be found to be without factual basis or legal authority.
privative clause	A clause in the enabling statute of an administrative adjudicative body that limits review of its decisions by the court.
public interest	Comprising the public concepts of justice and equality, which promote and advance the common good to the community within the social areas covered by the Code.
reconsideration	The process through which a complainant may request the Commission to reverse its decision regarding the non-referral of a complaint.
respondent	The party in a human rights complaint who is alleged to have infringed a right under the Code.
similar act evidence	A type of evidence allowed at the Tribunal to establish that a pattern of behaviour has occurred.
state a case	A written request to the court for a decision regarding a question of law.
social area	The Code only applies to specified social areas found in sections 1 to 6.

REVIEW QUESTIONS

1. What are the legislative functions of the Ontario Human Rights Commission under the Code?

2. By what criteria can the Commission make a decision to dismiss a complaint? Is the Commission bound to refer the complaint to the Tribunal if the complaint is outside of the dismissal criteria?

3. Distinguish between mediation and conciliation in the resolution process.

4. What types of evidence are admissible at the Tribunal?

5. Describe the two types of orders that can be made by an adjudicator, and give an example of each.

6. Identify the Commission's three objectives, which are included in its mandate.

7. The Commission has referred a complaint to the Tribunal for a hearing. Identify the three obligations the Board of Inquiry seeks to fulfill regarding the complaint.

8. A complainant wants to have a court reconsider the Commission's reconsideration decision. Should the complainant file an appeal or application for judicial review? Will the decision be stayed?

DISCUSSION QUESTIONS

1. In your view, what are the strengths and weaknesses of the present enforcement system?

2. Go to the Ontario Human Rights Commission website at <www.ohrc.on.ca>, and read some of the policies on human rights issues. Select one policy to investigate, and then contact an equality-seeking group that represents members relevant to the policy you have selected. Compose a summary of the group's perspective of the issue, along with any initiatives the Commission has undertaken regarding the matter. Present a discussion summary of your findings.

3. A friend has contacted you because a landlord has refused to rent her an available unit, saying that he doesn't rent to single mothers. What would you advise her to do? Explain the human rights resolution process to her.

4. You were denied a promotion at work that you felt should have been yours. Your supervisor has made questionable references in the past about your ethnic background, and you can't help but wonder if she discriminated against you regarding the promotion. You filed a grievance with the union of which you are a member. The union determined that there were no irregularities with the selection process used by your supervisor. You, however, want to file a human rights complaint. What are the chances of your phone call to the Commission resulting in a complaint being filed? Why?

5. A young woman has recently immigrated to Canada from a country where female genital mutilation, or "FGM" (also known as female circumcision, a procedure that removes part or all of a female's external sexual organs), is a cultural norm. The young woman's parents wish to continue this practice in Canada despite the fact that the young woman

does not consent. Does the young woman have a human rights complaint, and, if so, on what basis?

6. What is the most significant change in the function of the Human Rights Commission pursuant to the upcoming changes to the human rights process?

SUGGESTED READING

Cornish, Mary, et al. *Achieving Equality: A Report on Human Rights Reform* (Government of Ontario, 1992).

WEBSITES
Human Rights Legal Support Centre: <www.hrlsc.on.ca>
Ontario, Ministry of the Attorney General: Human Rights in Ontario, <www.attorney general.jus.gov.on.ca/english/ohrc>
Ontario Human Rights Commission: <www.ohrc.on.ca>
The Human Rights Tribunal of Ontario: <www.hrto.ca>

Aboriginal Rights

Janet I. Mason
BARRISTER AND SOLICITOR

Learning Objectives

After reading this chapter, the reader should be able to:

➢ understand why Aboriginal rights are considered *sui generis*

➢ understand elements of the historical treatment of First Nations by colonists and government and the effect of that treatment on their relationships

➢ appreciate why issues surrounding Aboriginal rights remain relevant today

➢ identify the various ways that an Indian band can acquire Aboriginal title to a tract of land

➢ comprehend the requirements for establishing Aboriginal title under the common law

➢ identify the requirements for establishing an Aboriginal right, other than title, under the common law

TABLE OF CONTENTS

INTRODUCTION

The fact that **Aboriginal** peoples occupied the land prior to the arrival of Europeans distinguishes them from other minority groups in Canada. It also provides the foundation from which Aboriginal rights arise and explains their unique treatment under the law.[1] When the first Europeans arrived in North America, the land was already occupied by tribes of Indians, or Aboriginals, who had been there for thousands of years.[2] When first contact was made between the two groups, the Aboriginal peoples were seen to be "liv[ing] in communities on the land ... participating in distinctive cultures, as they had done for centuries."[3] The Aboriginal population at that time has been estimated to be several million.[4] North American history clearly began long before the first European arrived on its shores.

Aboriginal communities have claimed, and some continue to claim, that they were sovereign nations prior to contact with Europeans and were treated as independent nations by early European colonists. As such, the Indians assert entitlement to certain rights that "encompass all aspects of their culture, including rights to land, traditions, and survival."[5] However, when the British Crown asserted **sovereignty** (i.e., supreme authority) over North America, it was not long before the "new" majority disempowered and marginalized the First Nations.[6] The Crown acquired sovereignty on the basis that it (like France, before ceding its claim) was the first to discover the "vacant" land of North America. It was an accepted practice in Europe at that time to consider land "vacant" where the inhabitants were "insufficiently Christian".[7]

The Canadian government has begun to acknowledge certain Aboriginal rights, but not the sovereignty (or more specifically, the right of self-government), of North America's indigenous population. "Since the *Constitution Act, 1982*,[8] does not explicitly acknowledge an aboriginal right of self-government, such a right does not exist as a matter of Canadian law."[9] Aboriginal rights issues remain unsettled as the federal government and First Nations seek to find a balance between two fundamentally different cultures. The goal is to try to reconcile the Aboriginal rights that flow from a prior occupation of the land with Crown sovereignty so that First Nations can maintain their culture.[10]

---

[1] Shin Imai, *Aboriginal Law Handbook*, 2d ed. (Toronto: Carswell, 1999) at 6 [Imai].

[2] The terms "Aboriginal", "First Nation", and "Indian" are respectfully used interchangeably throughout this chapter for the ease of the reader. These terms refer to the one group of founding peoples of Canada, the North American Indian, who was historically involved with the European colonists. The other two founding peoples, the Métis and Inuit, are identified separately. The words "band" and "tribe" are also used interchangeably to denote a particular Aboriginal community or group. All of these terms are open to debate or objection and may have a narrower, or broader, meaning in certain contexts. The usage in this introductory and general overview of Aboriginal history is as defined above.

[3] *R. v. Van der Peet*, [1996] 2 S.C.R. 507 at para. 30 [*Van der Peet*].

[4] Neal Salisbury, "The Indians' Old World: Native Americans and the coming of the Europeans" (1996) 53 William and Mary Quarterly 435 at 435.

[5] Imai, *supra* note 1 at 6.

[6] While it was originally the British Crown who dealt with Indian matters, it has been the responsibility of Canada's federal government since Confederation. The term "Crown" can be read as federal government.

[7] John Borrows, "Sovereignty's Alchemy: An Analysis of *Delgamuukw v. British Columbia*" (1997) 35 Osgoode Hall L.J. 125, at 132.

[8] Being Schedule B to the *Canada Act 1982* (U.K.), 1982, c. 11 [*Constitution Act, 1982*].

[9] The Constitutional Law Group, *Canadian Constitutional Law*, 3d ed. (Toronto: Emond Montgomery Publications Limited, 2003) at 522 [Law Group].

[10] Statistics Canada, 2001, reports an Aboriginal population of 976,305 comprising 608,850 North American Indians, 292,305 Métis and 45,070 Inuit. Canada's total population, according to the 2001 Census, is 29,630,030. This

All matters concerning Indians are under the power of the federal government as enunciated in s. 91(24) of the *Constitution Act, 1867*[11] and are considered to be ***sui generis*** (i.e., unique).[12] This *sui generis* nature emerged as a way to more fairly deal with issues arising from the prior occupation of North America by Aboriginal peoples and to allow courts to properly apply common law principles. An Aboriginal right is relevant only to a legislatively, or judicially, identified group within Canadian society who meet certain requirements. Existing Aboriginal rights, which are rights that existed and were not extinguished prior to the enactment of *Constitution Act, 1982*, are specifically protected in s. 35 of *The Canadian Charter of Rights and Freedoms*.[13] This *sui generis* nature also evolved as a way to reconcile disputes over rights. For example, the evidentiary standard in an Aboriginal rights claim is unique in that it permits oral evidence of historical facts, passed down through Aboriginal generations, to be admitted and relied upon in court.

Present-day Aboriginal rights cannot be properly understood without a consideration of the historical context through which they have evolved. A complete history is beyond the scope of this chapter, and only certain events have been selected to illustrate characteristics in a general way. More detailed information can be obtained by referencing the "Suggested Reading" section provided at the end of this chapter. The historical overview included here serves to provide the reader new to the subject with enough contextual background to understand the present law. The focus is on the relationship between Aboriginal peoples and government, whether that government was colonial or Canada's own. The overview also demonstrates that Aboriginal rights issues, generally viewed as consisting of land claims and a desire for Aboriginal self-government, remain unsettled. These issues have roots that can be traced back generations. The particular behaviours and incidents discussed are representative of the relationship between various European groups and First Nations. There was little difference, for example, in the relationship whether it concerned the French and the Huron or the British and the Iroquois. The focus is on the British and their Iroquois allies since the British eventually acquired sovereignty in North America. There were, and are, many tribes across Canada who have experienced similar treatment.

This chapter will begin with a discussion of some of the fundamental differences between the Aboriginal and European cultures. In addition to the First Nations' prior occupation of North America, a variety of factors have affected Aboriginal rights over time. These factors include the cultural differences between European settlers and Aboriginals, disease, the early relationship between settlers and First Nations, and a failure of government to fulfill contractual obligations contained in treaties. Once these issues have been examined, attention will then be given to legislation governing Indians, the content of an Aboriginal land title right, and the current requirements for establishing an existing, but unrecognized, Aboriginal right under the law.

---

means that the Aboriginal population comprises approximately 3% of the total population. Online: Statistics Canada <http://www12.statcan.ca/english/census01/home/Index.cfm> (August 2004). Statistics on Aboriginal peoples collected in the 2006 Census was released in January 2008 <http://www12.statcan.ca/english/census06/release/aboriginal.cfm>.

[11] (U.K.), 30 & 31 Vict., c. 3, reprinted in R.S.C. 1985, App. II, No. 5.

[12] Under this provision, the Inuit would also qualify as "Indian" under federal jurisdiction. However, the federal government does not consider the Métis to be under federal jurisdiction.

[13] Part I of the *Constitution Act, 1982*, being Schedule B to the *Canada Act 1982* (U.K.), 1982, c. 11 [the "Charter"]. For more information on the constitutional protection of Aboriginal rights, see the chapter titled "The Canadian Charter of Rights and Freedoms" in the complete edition of this book.

ABORIGINAL CULTURE

It was European colonists, consisting of the Dutch, French and British, who first formed relationships with the Aboriginal peoples they encountered. At the time of first contact between the groups, Aboriginal tribes lived in civilized and structured communities. Some of these communities were established on particular tracts of land, with hunting and fishing expeditions extending into the surrounding areas. Others enjoyed a nomadic existence that would, for example, follow the buffalo on seasonal hunts. Each Indian tribe was autonomous, although most shared common cultural attributes. The Cherokee and Iroquois, for example, were independent tribes who spoke different languages, but their cultural practices (such as annual celebrations and care of their poor) and spiritual beliefs were similarly based. Trade between bands was common and expanded to include trade with the Europeans when they arrived.

The First Nations people have enjoyed a highly developed social structure.[14] This early culture was generally grounded on a more evolved form of gender equality than that of the Europeans; certain personal attributes were culturally valued, and they embraced a spirituality that included an awareness of the fragility of the environment. Tribes commonly viewed women as having equal status to men. Words that differentiated between genders (e.g., *his* or *hers*) were absent from many Aboriginal languages. Women often sat on band councils and participated in the decision-making process. Band membership was sometimes established through maternal bloodlines, such as in the Gitksan or Wet'suwet'en tribes of British Columbia. The First Nations valued the attributes of self-discipline, adaptability, and humour. Self-discipline and adaptability were necessary for living off the land in a climate that could be harsh and unforgiving. Humour was particularly highly valued because it provided a source of comfort when life was hard.

Indian spirituality included a respect for, and relationship with, the land that they depended on for food and home. Bands regularly changed hunting grounds when the animal population became dangerously low. Many Indians were proficient farmers and knew to rotate crops so as not to deplete the soil. The "Great Spirit" or "Creator" (either term being the equivalent to the Europeans' concept of "God") existed in the land, people, and animals, and no single entity was considered to rank above the other. All entities constituted a temple of the Great Spirit and belonged to it.[15] Thus, a band had a relationship with the land but did not *own* it.

Leadership/Political Structure

The Indians had a political, or leadership, structure comprised of a band council and a community-based judicial system, and groups sometimes warred with neighbouring tribes. There was no central governmental authority for Indian tribes. Generally, each tribe had its own council made up of members of the community.[16] The band could be further divided into "houses" or "clans". Each **house or clan** may have had one or more hereditary chiefs — for example, the Wet'suwet'en band — with each chief being selected by a

---

[14] It is beyond the scope of this chapter, which focuses on the law, to discuss the cultural contributions of the three founding peoples to Canada's broader culture. International recognition of Indian and Inuit art is increasing, and other creative arts are also gaining attention as part of Canada's character.

[15] Ronald Wright, *Stolen Continents: Conquest and Resistance in the Americas*, 10th ed. (Toronto: Penguin, 2003) at 100 [Wright].

[16] *Ibid.*

group of elders. Band chiefs were sometimes replaced, or simply ignored, if they lacked the necessary leadership skills. Political decisions were made by council consensus and not by a simple majority (i.e., a 51% vote in favour of the decision). Since consensus was required, a chief had to be skilled in the art of persuasion. Dissenters could withdraw from the community. Council members that withdrew could leave the band with their supporters and establish a new community. In this way, a war between disagreeing band members could be avoided.

When a crime was committed, the Indians believed that it affected the whole community and not just the victim and offender. A **healing circle**, usually consisting of band elders, would be held where the members and the injured party would speak of the harm suffered. Offenders were expected to take responsibility for their behaviour. The council goal was to design a sentence that would rehabilitate and assist offenders so that they could remain as part of the community. When serious events such as murder occurred, the Indians generally believed in "an eye for an eye" and, historically, retribution was the standard response. Healing circles continue to be held today and are recognized by the courts.

Indian tribes did engage in wars with each other, and prisoners, including colonists, were often adopted by their captors. Inter-tribal wars were common in North America but rarely concerned a dispute over land. They were more likely to be started to effect retribution or achieve personal prestige, or for adoption.[17] Adoption was the most common reason since it was an efficient way to maintain or increase the band's population. Many of the colonists who were adopted were unwilling to return to colonial life even when given the opportunity. They acquired a preference for the Aboriginal way of life.

Written Language and Oral Evidence

The Indians did not have a written language when early treaties were entered into. Band history and important agreements were passed down orally from generation to generation. **Wampum belts** or strings were often used as an oral aid and were made of beads and coloured strings woven into symbolic designs. The Wampum belt's composition of beads and strings represented specific facts that were discussed more fully in the oral commentary that accompanied them. These belts were also used to record the terms of formal agreements the band entered into and then given to the other party to the negotiation. Oral commentary was always required as an accompaniment to the Wampum.

The importance of this oral tradition remains to the present day and is part of the *sui generis* nature of Aboriginal rights. An Aboriginal rights claim often involves evidence of the **oral history** passed on to each generation in order for the court to properly decide the matter. Under standard evidence rules, oral historical evidence is inadmissible. The Supreme Court of Canada decided in *Van der Peet*, however, that oral evidence is admissible in order to determine a land claim or other Aboriginal right: e.g., the right to hunt on a particular piece of land where title is not claimed. If the oral evidence was excluded, the claim would be likely to automatically fail because there would be insufficient evidence to support it. In *Van der Peet* the Aboriginal person had appealed a conviction for selling 10 fish caught under an Indian food fish licence. The accused asserted that the right to sell the fish for money was

---

[17] Olive Patricia Dickason, *Canada's First Nations: A History of Founding Peoples from Earliest Times*, 3d ed. (Toronto: Oxford University Press, 2002) at 63 [Dickason].

an Aboriginal right grounded in the band's history and culture.[18] While the Supreme Court upheld the conviction, it decided that the admissibility of the oral evidence was part of the *sui generis* nature of Aboriginal rights:

> [C]ourts should approach the rules of evidence, and interpret the evidence that exists, with a consciousness of the special nature of aboriginal claims, and of the evidentiary difficulties in proving a right which originates in times where there were no written records of the practices, customs and traditions engaged in. The courts must not undervalue the evidence presented by aboriginal claimants simply because that evidence does not conform precisely with the evidentiary standards that would be applied in, for example, a private law torts case.[19]

Prior to the Supreme Court's acceptance of oral evidence the Indians were unable to fully participate in a judicial system that gave greater consideration to written evidence, such as contracts or treaties. The written agreement, even where it did not reflect the Indians' understanding of the terms or their oral history, was seen to be more binding in court than Wampum belts and their accompanying commentary. This ignored the fact of the First Nations' existence in North America since "time immemorial" and any rights associated with their prior possession of the land.[20] Therefore, even where the terms of the agreement had been presented orally to the Indians in a way that differed from the written agreement, the written agreement superseded any verbal promise.

Status in the Aboriginal Community

Status in the Aboriginal community was commonly based on the distribution of wealth and not the acquisition of wealth. Status did not require that each Indian aspire to own an individual parcel of land. Rather, land was held communally by the band and could not be owned, sold, or given as a gift by an individual. The First Nations also believed in caring for widows and orphans, and ensuring that food and other necessaries were available for everyone in the community. A celebration would be held where the objective was to give away as much as possible to those in the band who were less fortunate. The Indians believed that becoming attached to material items would only lead to unhappiness when those items were lost or no longer of use. Giving wealth away prevented an attachment and also ensured that everyone had what was needed. The obligation of generosity was reciprocal. Often, the same items would be passed along to others each year. Ceremonies and the exchange of gifts with agreements were important cultural events. It was a highly evolved, and alien, social structure that the European colonists encountered upon their arrival. While the Aboriginals may not have had written language or European technology, they certainly were not the "savages" the Europeans called them. It could be said that the social structure of Aboriginal communities had, in fact, evolved beyond the class-based and exploitive European culture of that time.

---

[18] The specific requirements for making a successful Aboriginal title claim are discussed later in this chapter under "Land Claims".

[19] *Van der Peet, supra* note 3 at para. 68.

[20] Wright, *supra* note 15 at 129.

EUROPEAN CULTURE

The Europeans arrived in North America with political and cultural norms very different from those of the Aboriginal peoples they met. The Europeans had lived under a political and social hierarchy and assumed the same structure existed in the Indian communities. Therefore, the Europeans sought to deal with the *top* Aboriginal leader who could sign an agreement on behalf of the tribe. As identified, the Aboriginal population consisted of independent and autonomous bands and each was free to make its own decisions. The Europeans couldn't find a governing Indian tribe through which they could bind all tribes to an agreement.

However, some tribes would occasionally meet to make joint decisions on certain matters. For example, the Iroquois established a confederacy of eventually six separate tribes, later called the Six Nations. This confederacy had leaders from each band who would sit on a special council and come to a consensus regarding issues that affected the well-being of their communities: e.g., whether to side with the British or French or remain neutral during the war for control of the land. The confederacy could be viewed as a governing body over the participating tribes.

European life at the time was difficult for those not born into the privileged classes. Many settlers left for North America to acquire wealth and land — the two commodities denied them at home. The acquisition of wealth and ownership of land was their method of obtaining social status. North America offered a better standard of living and greater independence. The settlers arrived prepared to do whatever it took to ensure they received their share of the land. The Indian communities were soon viewed as the new peasant class, with the European settlers claiming status as the upper or ruling class.

Fundamental differences between Aboriginal and European-based cultures remain today. These differences present unique challenges for the Canadian government and Aboriginal peoples as they try to reconcile them. In June 2004, the Canadian Press reported that an Aboriginal band in British Columbia opposed the government's efforts to relocate an orca whale.[21] The Mowachaht-Muchalaht band believed that the orca contained the former chief's spirit, as his deathbed wish was that his spirit would inhabit an orca, and the orca appeared in the area shortly after the chief's death. The band wanted to act as steward to the orca and requested that the government provide money to support the whale and to conduct a "public education campaign for visitors using our title waters." The band also asked to be involved in the decision to relocate the whale at a "culturally appropriate time." The Department of Fisheries wanted to relocate the orca with its pod after conducting medical tests and believed this to be in the best interests of the whale. Reintegration with the pod would allow the whale to live normally and eliminate the public safety risk the orca presented by its presence at Mooya Bay and Gold River Harbour. While each position shared a concern for the orca, they were not easily reconciled because of fundamentally different perspectives: the government viewed the situation from a scientific standpoint, whereas the First Nations considered it a spiritual matter.

---

[21] Scott Sutherland, "Aboriginal band demands stop to plan to relocate Luna from their waters" *The [Vancouver] Province* (23 June 2004), online: Reunite Luna <http://www.reuniteluna.com/news_release.php?id=514>.

THE EPIDEMICS

Disease epidemics played an important role in the early relationship between the Indians and colonists and facilitated the marginalization of Aboriginal peoples. The isolation of North America's indigenous peoples from European and other populations meant that the Indians were susceptible to new diseases that the Europeans brought with them because the Indians had not acquired any natural resistance to these diseases. The resulting epidemics decimated the Aboriginal population. Eventually, the population of the First Nations became too low to repel the invaders by force. Many council leaders died of disease, leaving the Indians without experienced leadership at times when difficult decisions, such as treaty terms, needed to be made. The matter was further compounded by the fragmentation of Aboriginal peoples — the downside of band autonomy. The independent nature of Indian bands meant that they were vulnerable to the Europeans in the absence of competent leadership and collaboration with other bands.

There were two major epidemics that affected the Aboriginal population. The first occurred in the 16th century and originated in the southern United States. The second epidemic began in 1738 when a British slave ship arrived in South Carolina with a cargo that included smallpox. Half of the Cherokee Nation in the United States died of smallpox, including many of their leaders. The smallpox spread easily with trade between the Europeans and the Indians as well as inter-tribal trade, and it wasn't long before the epidemic had spread north to Montreal. The French colonists in Montreal suggested to the Indians that the smallpox was a deliberate attempt by the British to harm the Aboriginal people. The French hoped that this misinformation would increase support for their side and against the British as each group vied for dominance of the new land.

The French suggestion was indicative of what subsequently happened. The first recorded incident of modern germ warfare seems to have been between the British and the Iroquois. Lord Jeffrey Amherst, who deliberately ignored British obligations under treaties and failed to prevent illegal squatting on Indian land, wanted to be rid of the Indian population once the French were conquered. He was angry about the Indian uprising against settlers, even though the majority killed by the Indians had been illegal squatters. After France ceded its claim to North America, Amherst ordered his men to take the bed sheets used by smallpox victims and give them as gifts to the chiefs they met during parlays. In this way, smallpox spread quickly and further decimated the Iroquois population.

The effect of European diseases on the Indian population led to Britain's ultimate emergence as the ruling power in North America. The Indians lost many great leaders, and dissent within Aboriginal communities became common. Some felt that the Europeans should be resisted and ousted from the land, while others supported co-operation with the invaders. But, more important, the end result was that there were too few Indians left to force the Europeans to leave. The Iroquois leaders who survived the epidemics were left with no choice but to sue for peace with the British in order to survive.

THE EARLY RELATIONSHIP BETWEEN THE EUROPEANS AND INDIANS

The First Nations cautiously welcomed the newcomers and taught them how to survive in the new land. The colonists learned how to travel by toboggan, canoe and snowshoe and were introduced to new crops, such as corn and squash, which they sent home. In exchange, the Indians were able to obtain new technology, such as gunpowder. The British and French entered into trade agreements with the Indians and relied on them as military allies until the French ceded their claim to North America in favour of Britain. Without the help of the First Nations, the Europeans "would not have been able to survive the rigours of the climate, succeed in their business (fishing, whaling, fur trading), or dodge each other's bullets."[22] However, the relationship between the Europeans and the Aboriginal population was often uneasy.[23]

The Europeans were often unconcerned with fairness when trading with First Nations and were dependent on their Indian allies as they attempted to gain control of the land. In their drive to acquire wealth, some Europeans would ensure that the Indians they traded with were drunk before negotiations began. These traders exploited the Indians in their drunken state by obtaining furs at reduced prices. Military alliances between a First Nation and the French or British became common. These alliances were necessary as the Indians soon held the balance of power in North America because the military strength of each group (i.e., French, British and First Nations) was evenly matched. In addition, the native population knew the lay of the land and were adept at making quick military strikes and then fading into the forest. Both the French and British desired alliances with various bands to fight on their behalf in their quest for dominance of North America. In exchange, the First Nation received trade agreements and goods.

France, England and Spain signed the **Treaty of Paris** in 1763. The British emerged as the controlling European presence as France and Spain (who ceded Florida but retained other states) gave up their claims. The result was that Britain held the land east of the Mississippi and north to Canada. The Aboriginal tribes that had allowed Britain to gain power were not mentioned in this treaty. Concerned that more of their land would be taken over by settlers, a group of Ohio Indians led by Chief Pontiac began a war against the British to prevent further encroachment. The British won the war, with Amherst's help, but were aware that their resources for funding wars in North America were depleted. In order to prevent further Indian uprisings over land, two agreements specifically addressed the issue: the first was an agreement between the British and the Iroquois called the **Two Row Wampum** of the Iroquois (which included the terms that each group would not interfere with the other, and each would retain their own customs and law); and the second was the **Royal Proclamation** of 1763 issued by King George.[24]

The Royal Proclamation "portrays Indian nations as autonomous political entities, living under the protection of the Crown but retaining their own internal political authority" and states that the First Nations "were not to be 'molested or disturbed' on their lands."[25] It attempted to define the boundaries of the Indian's land and to prevent settlers from illegally establishing communities on identified land. The Royal Proclamation also stated that only the Crown, and not settlers, could purchase Indian land. This was to prevent the Indians from being exploited by unscrupulous settlers determined to own Indian land. However, the settlers refused to acknowledge the defined bound-

---

[22] Royal Commission on Aboriginal Peoples, *Looking Forward, Looking Back*, Volume 1 (Ottawa: Minister of Supply & Services, 1996); summary online: Indian and Northern Affairs Canada <http://www.ainc-inac.gc.ca/ch/rcap/rpt/lk_e.html> (August 2004) [cited to summary] at 7 [RCAP].

[23] It should be noted that the French, British and Dutch all had separate and independent dealings with First Nations.

[24] Imai, *supra* note 1 at 27. The Two Row Wampum "formed the basis of all ... treaties with other nations including the Dutch, the French, the British and the Americans." Online: Akwesasne <http://www.akwesasne.ca/tworowwampum.html> (August 2004) at 2.

[25] RCAP, *supra* note 22 at 9.

Cayuga Sachem Deskaheh's Last Public Address, 1925	**EXHIBIT 23.1**

My home is on the Grand River ... where, one hundred and forty winters ago, we had a little sea-shore of our own and a birch-bark navy.

You would call it Canada. We do not ...

We didn't think we would ever live long enough to find that a British promise was not good. An enemy's foot is on our country, and George the Fifth knows it for I told him so, but he will not lift his finger to protect us nor will any of his ministers ...

To punish us for trying to preserve our rights, the Canadian Government has now pretended to abolish our government [and] set up a Canadian-made government over us, composed of the few traitors among us who are willing to accept pay from Ottawa ...

One word more so that you will be sure to remember our people. If it had not been for them, you would not be here. If, one hundred and sixty-six winters ago, our warriors had not helped the British at Quebec ... it would have been a French-speaking people here today, not you. That part of your history cannot be blotted out by the stealing of our wampum belts in which that is recorded.

Source: Passage cited in Ronald Wright, *Stolen Continents: Conquest and Resistance in the Americas*, 10th ed. (Toronto: Penguin, 2003) at 345–46.

aries; they burned Indian towns and claimed the land as their own.[26] The British were unable, or unwilling, to enforce the boundaries on behalf of the Indians. After all, the French were no longer a threat to British power in North America, with the result that the Indians were no longer needed as military allies. The Indians were viewed as a barrier to large-scale, European settlement.

However, the British were still concerned about the lack of a dividing line between what are now Canada and the United States. In 1784 the British Crown transferred the Grand River tract of land, located along the western end of the Niagara Peninsula, to the Mohawk and Six Nations. It is interesting to note that this land transfer was made to "his majesty's faithful allies", indicating that the British viewed the Six Nations as an independent nation and not a conquered or dependent nation. The Indian presence on this land provided Britain with a buffer zone between them and the United States. The Iroquois maintained a military presence and would protect the north from southern invaders without putting any European at risk.[27]

As these events unfolded, the Indian bands again split into factions. Some groups believed that the British should be resisted and the land reclaimed. Others believed that they should acculturate to the emerging European economy. Some believed that if they didn't sell their land to the Crown, it would simply be taken from them by force. Joseph Brant was the leader of the Iroquois Confederacy located in Grand River. He advocated participation in the new economy and leased Grand River land, some of the finest agricultural land in Canada, to the white settlers in order to raise money for economic participation. The leases stipulated that the land remained the property of the

---

[26] Wright, *supra* note 15 at 221.

[27] As the border between Canada and the United States was being established, the Iroquois nation ended up being split, with some located on the Canadian side and some on the U.S. side. This, along with other reasons, resulted in two parallel Iroquois Confederacies. One was located on the Grand River, and the other in New York.

Iroquois Confederacy. This stipulation did not prevent the government from subsequently, and arbitrarily, declaring the leases to be irrevocable land concessions by the Iroquois to the British.

Towards the end of the 19th century it became clear that the United States would not invade its neighbour to the north. The Indian buffer states were no longer needed, and the Six Nations were viewed as an obstacle to the government's power over, and claim to, the land now called the Dominion of Canada. By 1867 the Six Nations were left with only 90 square miles of land on the Grand River. The Canadian government asserts that the Grand River is an Indian Reserve. The Iroquois maintain that the Grand River and other remaining lands are national territories similar to the state of Monaco. "Why, [the Indians ask], should a people who have never been conquered by Canada, and have never surrendered their independence, be colonized when other small nations are free? They add that if lands unjustly taken were returned to them, their countries might not be so small."[28]

By the middle of the 20th century, non-Aboriginals were being drawn to cities and no longer threatened Indian land. But the desire for Indian land was not diminished. Industrial growth created the need for electrical power, and dams were the least expensive way of generating that power. It was not unusual for Indian land to be expropriated to build a dam, which reduced construction costs. The result was that "[t]he Iroquois lost more land in fifteen years than they had lost in the preceding century."[29] The factories that sprang up around the dams often polluted the surrounding land and water, contaminating the Indians' traditional hunting and fishing grounds. Aboriginal rights to land remain unsettled to the present day.

THE *INDIAN ACT*

Once the military force of the First Nations was no longer required, the Canadian government decided that the most efficient way of dealing with the "Indian problem" was to assimilate the Indians into the broader Canadian culture. Assimilation could be seen as a way to avoid further land claims or the need for treaties — everyone would simply be Canadian. A variety of methods were used to achieve this goal, including special boarding schools for Aboriginal children, various legislation, and the offer of Canadian citizenship status. Students at Aboriginal residential schools were forbidden to speak their native language or practice their religion, which resulted in the breakdown of family and community bonds. The Canadian government could arbitrarily relocate Aboriginal communities. Registered Indians who volunteered for service in World Wars I and II returned home to find that they were denied the benefits available to non-Aboriginal veterans.[30] Until 1951, it was a criminal offence for Aboriginal peoples to hold feast ceremonies. As well, Quebec didn't allow Indians to vote until 1968, and between 1927 and 1951, it was illegal to raise money for Indian claims, effectively denying First Nations access to Canadian courts. Incentives, such as a small financial payment and ownership of a small piece of land, were held out to the Indians to encourage them to abandon their native roots to become voting members of Canada.[31] Few Indians took the government up on the offer. Today, the issue of self-

---

[28] Wright, *supra* note 15 at 221. Monaco is an independent country bordered by France on three sides and the Mediterranean Sea on the remaining side and covers only 195 hectares (1.95 square kilometres).

[29] *Ibid.* at 347.

[30] RCAP, *supra* note 22 at 14.

[31] Wright, *supra* note 15 at 335.

Duncan Campbell Scott, Head of Indian Affairs, 1920   EXHIBIT 23.2

I want to get rid of the Indian problem. Our objective is to continue until there is not a single Indian in Canada that has not been absorbed.

Source: Passage cited in Ronald Wright, *Stolen Continents: Conquest and Resistance in the Americas*, 10th ed. (Toronto: Penguin, 2003) at 340.

---

government is important as First Nations seek to protect and nurture their unique identity and culture.

The *Indian Act*[32] was an important piece of legislation that promoted the dissolution of Aboriginal culture. Many First Nations view the Act as paternalistic and controlling. In an attempt to legislate cultural assimilation, the Act tried to change Aboriginal concepts of land title, governance, inheritance, family law, economic activity, and community standards. The Act virtually ignored all Aboriginal traditions. Aboriginal women, because of the Act's discriminatory provisions, have voiced criticism. The women allege that the Act places men in leadership positions, imposing a patriarchal regime that perpetuates sexual discrimination and is unfair to women regarding property rights when marital breakdown occurs.

The legislation also governs band elections, the requirements for obtaining Indian status under the law, and the council's decision-making power. The *Indian Act* dictates rules for electing a chief and band council that reflect European culture and not Aboriginal culture. The Act further requires that a leader is chosen by a secret ballot (s. 74), which was not done in Aboriginal society. The Act also provides that the chief and council can be chosen by the band's custom: e.g., through hereditary lineage for the chief or, for the council, to serve for a period of time different from that stated in the Act (s. 2(1)). The Act does not, however, recognize traditional governing bodies, such as the Iroquois Confederacy.

Indian Status

The *Indian Act* defines who is classified as an Indian under the law (ss. 5 to 16) and, therefore, who is entitled to make claims and receive benefits. **Indian status** is assigned when the person shows that he or she is a descendant of a particular band for whom a reserve was established or where the band was a party to a treaty.[33] The person must register in order to obtain Indian status. The Act's classification scheme disregards the different ways by which certain Aboriginal groups established membership. The scheme provided that Indian status travelled exclusively down the patrilineal line (i.e., male descendant line). Some bands, such as the Mohawk and Iroquois, use the

---

[32] R.S.C. 1985, c. I-5; there is other legislation that also governs Indian matters: see, e.g., *First Nations Land Management Act*, S.C. 1999, c. 24; *Department of Indian Affairs and Northern Development Act*, R.S.C. 1985, c. I-6; and the *Indian Oil and Gas Act*, R.S.C. 1985, c. I-7. In 2005, the *First Nations Fiscal and Statistical Management Act*, S.C. 2005, c. 9 was enacted to facilitate economic development relating to taxation and to establish an institute to gather and analyze statistical data concerning First Nations and Aboriginal groups.

[33] Peter W. Hogg, *Constitutional Law of Canada*, Student ed. (Toronto: Thomson Canada Limited, 2002) at 579 [Hogg].

matrilineal line (i.e., female descendant line) for determining membership. An amendment to the *Indian Act* (Bill C-31 in 1985) allowed, among other things, women to regain Indian status where they had lost it by marriage to a non-Aboriginal and removed other discriminatory provisions from the Act. However, Indian status continues to require registration today and remains governed by the Act. Generally, new registrants are required to show that they have two grandparents, on either parent's line of ascent, who meet the descendant requirement (noted above) for registration.

The band also has the option of establishing a **membership or citizenship code** that identifies who can be a band member (s. 10). However, it does not automatically follow that these band members or citizens receive Indian status. Only those individuals who meet the registration requirements are entitled to status and the benefits contained in the *Indian Act*. These benefits include the right to vote in band elections, live on a reserve, and obtain Indian Affairs benefits and applicable tax exemptions. Entitlement to benefits may also be affected, based on whether or not the individual resides on the reserve.

Band Councils

The *Indian Act* allows the **band council** to pass by-laws concerning identified matters on the reserve. The council is required to pass a resolution, which contains the by-law, by a simple majority and the agreement of the chief. By-laws are usually created under the authority contained in section 86 of the Act. Such authority includes the ability to regulate who may reside on the reserve and the ability to enforce fishing and game regulations, taxation, alcohol, licensing and membership codes. However, all by-laws are subject to the approval of the Minister of Indian Affairs before being enacted, which limits the autonomy of the band. For many years, the government regularly withheld approval of submitted by-laws.

Aboriginal Taxation Exemption

Section 87 of the *Indian Act* exempts Aboriginal people's property from taxation but only where specific requirements are met. Exempt property is identified as being the "interest of an Indian or a band in reserve lands or surrendered lands" (s. 87(1)(a)) and the "personal property of an Indian or a band situated on a reserve" (s. 87(1)(b)). The purpose of the exemption is to "preserve the entitlements of Indian people to their reserve lands, and to ensure that the use of their property on their reserve lands is not eroded by taxation."[34] Since sub-section 87(1)(b) applies only to property situated on a reserve, the exemption will not apply to personal property acquired and held in the commercial mainstream. Section 87 is not a general ameliorative provision. "Personal property" is, however, broad enough to include employment income in relation to the payment of income tax.

The interpretation of "situated on a reserve" has been the primary source of litigation under section 87 in regard to income tax. In *Williams v. The Queen*,[35] the Supreme Court of Canada introduced a "connecting factors" test. The factors to be considered in determining whether the property is situated on a reserve concern the examination of the evidence that connects the property to the reserve. It is not necessary that the property be physically on the reserve under all circumstances. Factors will include, where relevant, the following:

---

[34] Indian and Northern Affairs Canada, *Status Indians and Taxes* <http://www.ainc-inac.gc.ca/pr/info/info113_e.html>.
[35] [1992] 1 S.C.R. 877.

1. The location or residence of the employer;
2. The location and surrounding circumstances of the work performed by the employee, including the nature of any benefit that accrued to the reserve from it;
3. The residence of the employee; and
4. The place where the employee is paid.

Each case is to be decided on its own facts, and structuring one's affairs for proper tax planning reasons is permissible.[36]

Shilling v. M.N.R.[37]

This case applied the connecting factors test in the context of income.

Ms. Shilling was a member of the Rama band, had resided in Toronto for a number of years after living on a reserve and was employed by a Native health centre in Toronto. Ms. Shilling's employment was under contract to an agency. The agency was a sole proprietorship owned by an Indian with its head office located on reserve but unrelated to the band Ms. Shilling belonged to. Ms. Shilling was not employed directly by the health centre itself. This was for tax planning reasons. It was believed that structuring the employment relationship in this way would permit Ms. Shilling to claim the s. 87(1)(b) exemption because all incidents related to employment were "on a reserve" and the health centre benefited the Aboriginal community. Ms. Shilling's salary was wired from the agency's reserve bank to her bank, located on another reserve. The lower court decided that the exemption applied.

The Federal Court of Appeal overturned the lower court's decision because the evidence did not meet the connecting factors test. There was no evidence that the reserve in which the employer-agency was located benefited from Shilling's employment. The appellate court found that there was a lack of evidence regarding where the agency had conducted business during the relevant time period, as there was a suggestion that business may have been conducted off-reserve. Ms. Shilling had not put the employment contract into evidence, making it impossible for the court to know the exact relationship between the agency and the health centre so as to determine against whom Ms. Shilling's legal rights could be enforced should the employment relationship break down. The court identified that the property being located on a reserve other than the one of which the person was a member likely precluded application of the exemption. The court decided that Ms. Shilling's provision of social services to off-reserve people in Toronto did not connect it to a reserve: "[M]erely because the nature of employment is to provide services to Indians does not connect that employment to an Indian reserve as a physical place."[38]

The residency of Ms. Shilling was relevant but not the decisive factor. The "location and nature of her employment" were the primary factors in the decision. The fact that the Aboriginal person resided off-reserve would therefore not, on its own, preclude the application of the exemption. Ms. Shilling's residency simply pointed in the same direction as the other evidence. Her employment was found to be in the commercial mainstream, and the exemption did not apply.[39]

---

[36] Structuring one's financial affairs to *avoid* paying tax(es) is legal; tax *evasion* is not.

[37] 2001 FCA 178 (CanLII) ["*Shilling*"].

[38] *Ibid.* para. 51.

[39] This proceeding asked the appellate court to answer a question of law — i.e., whether the exemption applied. In 2002, the Supreme Court of Canada dismissed Ms. Shilling's application for leave to appeal the court's answer to the question of law. The Crown's subsequent motion to dismiss Ms. Shilling's proceeding claiming exemption was

Creditor Enforcement Exemption

Section 89(1) of the *Indian Act* exempts the real and personal property of an Indian or a band situated on a reserve from "charge, pledge, mortgage, attachment, levy, seizure, distress or execution" in favour of a creditor other than an Indian or a band. Section 90(1) deems property to be on a reserve where it is (a) purchased by Her Majesty with Indian moneys or moneys appropriated by Parliament for the use and benefits of Indians or bands, or (b) given to the Indians or a band under a treaty or agreement between a band and Her majesty. This means that property located off-reserve can still be exempt where section 90(1) applies. Section 90 also applies to the tax exemption in section 87.

McDiarmid Lumber Ltd. v. God's Lake First Nation[40]

The facts concerned the building of a school on the reserve. God's Lake First Nation had engaged a contractor but later defaulted in payment. The creditor obtained default judgment. The creditor then moved to enforce the judgment by seizing the funds in the band's Winnipeg bank account. The band had entered into a treaty with the government in 1909 that included annual grants and funds to maintain schools. A lump sum was paid to the band and deposited into its bank account; the sum included funds for other reasons, such as improving the standard of living on reserve.

The Court decided that payments from the federal government to a First Nation that were deposited in an off-reserve bank in Winnipeg were not "situated on a reserve". The funds were not exempt from seizure by an unpaid creditor under section 89(1). The phrase was to be given its plain and ordinary meaning.

In this case, the band had alternatively submitted that section 90(1) would apply because the payment had been received from the government under an agreement. The issue for the Court was to define the content of "agreement" in the Act. Did it include any or all of a government payment under any agreement so as to deem the payment "on reserve" even if located elsewhere?

The Court began with a statement of the purpose underlying the exemption in the *Indian Act*, finding that its purpose was not to provide a general economic benefit to Indians:

> The Court confirmed in *Williams* that the purpose of the exemptions in ss. 87, 88 and 89 of the *Indian Act* "was to preserve the entitlements of Indians to their reserve lands and to ensure that the use of their property on their reserve lands was not eroded by the ability of governments to tax, or creditors to seize" (p. 885). The purpose is to protect what the Indian band was "given" in return for the surrender of Indian lands. The exemptions are tied to the reserve lands and the Indians' ability to preserve their lands against outside intrusion and diminishment. As Gonthier J. stated in *Williams*, "the purpose of the sections was not to confer a general economic benefit upon the Indians" (p. 885). For example, they do not exempt from seizure or taxation contractual arrangements in the commercial mainstream that amount to normal business transactions, but only "property that enures to Indians pursuant to treaties and their ancillary agreements": *Mitchell*, at p. 138. Only the latter is protected by s. 90(1)(*b*).[41]

---

granted and upheld on appeal: *Shilling v. Canada*, 2004 FCA 16. For cases where income was found to be situated on a reserve see *Williams v. The Queen*, [1992] 1 S.C.R. 877 and *Folster v. The Queen*, [1997] 3 F.C. 269 (C.A.).

[40] [2006] 2 S.C.R. 846, [2006] S.C.J. No. 58.

[41] *Ibid.* at para. 27.

The Court held that "agreement" was to be given a restricted meaning and that the agreement in question must be associated with a treaty.[42] Otherwise, the word "treaty" would not be needed in the provision as a qualifier, and any agreement between government and a band would suffice. The protection against exploitation underlying the exemption applied only to treaty entitlements that were often included in a more detailed, ancillary agreement. Policy reasons for this restricted meaning also favoured that finding. Obtaining credit in order for Aboriginal people to participate in economic pursuits and facilitate self-sufficiency and self-government is necessary as we all live in a credit-based market. The provincial credit regime is an important part of everyday life that applies equally to Indians save for the limited exemption.

The band failed in its claim for exemption because of a lack of evidence. The lump sum form of payment meant that neither the government nor the band could identify what portion of the total received was ancillary to the treaty and likely exempt. The payment was found to be a pool of money for a variety of purposes that included the enhancement of self-sufficiency and living standards in a wide range of areas. The judgment creditor was entitled to seize the funds.

The Métis and Inuit

There are two other quasi-founding Aboriginal groups, the **Métis** and **Inuit**, who do not qualify for Indian "status" and are, therefore, not governed by the *Indian Act*. The Métis are descendants from French colonist and Indian inter-marriages. The descendants from British colonist and Indian inter-marriages were referred to as half-breeds. Descendants from other Indian inter-marriages sometimes registered as non-status Indians. Today, there is little agreement concerning the requirements that identify a person as Métis. The identification of Métis peoples and their associated Aboriginal rights are issues separate from First Nation rights.[43] It is clear, however, that the Métis originated after contact with the Europeans. Therefore, the descendants of Indian inter-marriages did not have the same relationship with the Crown as the First Nations. The blending of the two cultures resulted in the creation of a distinct common culture and ethnic identity that also separates them from the First Nations. The result is that the Métis are treated differently by the government and are referred to as non-status Indians, despite their inclusion as "aboriginal" in the Constitution (s. 35).

A Métis governing council is not established in the same way as one for status Indians. The Métis council is created by the incorporation of a non-profit corporation and governed by the corporation's constitution and relevant legislation concerning not-for-profit organizations. The Métis are not recognized by the federal government as a people under federal jurisdiction and have been denied most federal benefits available to status Indians. The federal government does not include this Aboriginal group within the definition of "Indian" under s. 91(24) of the Constitution. It has been left to the provinces to deal with their particular Métis population and provide benefits.

---

[42] The Supreme Court also referred to one of its earlier decisions: "This Court has already considered the meaning of "agreement" in section 90(1)(b) and concluded that it should be restricted to agreements that flesh out commitments of the Crown to Indians in the treaty context of the surrender of their homelands": para. 26, referring to *Mitchell v. Peguis Indian Band*, [1990] 2 S.C.R. 85.

[43] For further discussion on Métis issues, see Imai, *supra* note 1 at 83–93. For more information concerning the identification of Métis, see *R. v. Powley* (1998), 58 C.R.R. (2d) 149, [1999] 1 C.N.L.R. 153 (Ont. Prov. Div.), as a starting point.

The Inuit, historically referred to as Eskimo, are the "indigenous peoples of the circumpolar north."[44] There is no formal Inuit registry and, therefore, a non-status/status distinction does not exist. The federal government considers the Inuit to be "Indian" under s. 91(24) of the Constitution. The Inuit population was also reduced by the epidemics. However, the arrival of a significant number of settlers did not occur until the middle of the twentieth century, and this differentiates them from the First Nations. Attempts were made to assimilate the Inuit culture, but recent developments show a willingness of government to establish agreements that respect this unique society.

The creation of the new territory of Nunavut (from part of the Northwest Territories) in 1999 was the result of a negotiated land claim agreement. This agreement allows the Inuit a formal role in making recommendations to the government concerning the land, environmental issues, land use planning, wildlife management, and establishing Inuit status. The territorial government of Nunavut follows the same structure as that of other provinces in Canada (i.e., an elected government leader and Cabinet). While Nunavut can be seen to provide a level of autonomy to the Inuit of that area, this autonomy does not amount to self-governance. In exchange for government protection of Inuit resources and land, the Aboriginal people were required to surrender all Aboriginal claims of any kind.

LAND CLAIMS

Aboriginal rights issues often arise regarding land. First Nations are able to claim a proprietary interest in land by **treaty** right, or because the land has been designated by the federal government as having **reserve** status, or by successfully having a **common law claim** affirmed by the court. A common law claim may assert a right to title of the land or be limited to using the land for a specific purpose. An Aboriginal interest in land is communally held and is a group right for the exclusive possession and use of an identified piece of land. There is no concept of private property within Aboriginal culture. Today, individual band members receive certificates of possession from the band. The certificate can be sold, but the purchaser must be another band member. The band, as a whole, can sell the land only to the federal government, who then transfers the title to the relevant province. This limited ability to sell land represents a fundamental difference between Aboriginal title and the usual form of land ownership in Canada (i.e., fee simple title) that allows the owner to sell the property to anyone. Aboriginal title to land is, however, considered a proprietary interest in the land and not just a licence to occupy the land.[45]

Aboriginal rights to land are not absolute, however, despite Constitutional protection. The government is permitted to infringe on a right where certain requirements for justification of the infringement are met. For example, conservation initiatives that limit an Aboriginal right to fish on an identified portion of land may justify an infringement on the band's fishing rights.[46] Con-

---

[44] Law Group, *supra* note 9 at 512. Most of the Inuit in Canada are located in the Northwest Territories, Quebec, Labrador, and Nunavut. Nunavut was formed in 1999 as a result of a land claim agreement between Canada and the Inuit of the eastern Arctic.

[45] *Delgamuukw v. British Columbia*, [1997] 3 S.C.R. 1010 at para. 113; (1997), 153 D.L.R. (4th) 193 [*Delgamuukw* cited to S.C.R.].

[46] See *R. v. Sparrow*, [1990] 1 S.C.R. 1075 where the Court outlines the test for government infringement on an Aboriginal right and holds that the extinguishment of an Aboriginal right by the Crown must be clear and unequivocal. The test in *Sparrow* was refined in *R. v. Gladstone*, [1996] 2 S.C.R. 723, where the Court enunciated

	EXHIBIT 23.3
The Report of the Royal Commission	

A careful reading of history shows that Canada was founded on a series of bargains with Aboriginal peoples — bargains this country has never fully honoured. Treaties between Aboriginal and non-Aboriginal governments were agreements to share the land. They were replaced by policies intended to ... remove Aboriginal people from their homelands ... suppress Aboriginal nations and their governments ... undermine Aboriginal cultures ... [and] stifle Aboriginal identity. It is now time to acknowledge the truth and begin to rebuild the relationship among peoples on the basis of honesty, mutual respect and fair sharing. The image of Canada in the world and at home demands no less.

Source: Royal Commission on Aboriginal Peoples, *Looking Forward, Looking Back*, Volume 1 (Ottawa: Minister of Supply & Services, 1996), Summary, online: <http://www.ainc-inac.gc.ca/ch/rcap/rpt/lk_e.html> (August 2004) [cited to summary] at 1–2.

servation issues would be considered a compelling objective that would be in the best interests of both the band and the broader community. Therefore, conservation would trump, at least temporarily, an Aboriginal right to fish. The government also has a **fiduciary duty**, which is to act in the best interests of Aboriginal peoples in all dealings with First Nations. This duty includes, or can be limited to, consulting with a band before infringing on its right.[47] The obligation to consult was recently expanded in *Mikisew Cree First Nation v. Canada (Minister of Canadian Heritage)*, [2005] 3 S.C.R. 388 where the Supreme Court held that the duty to consult extended to development of land adjacent to that belonging to First Nations, where development projects may affect treaty or land rights.

Treaties and Reserves

A treaty contains an exchange of promises entered into by both parties. The goal is to allow for peaceful coexistence between, and reconciliation of, First Nations and the Canadian community, of which they are a part. Historically, the First Nations entered treaties after being subjected to military force or when they had no way to refuse the government's demands.[48] Before the enactment of constitutional amendments, the government could unilaterally ignore or override a treaty right. The government could assert the belief that settlements did not require the consent of the First Nations and that Aboriginal rights existed only at the pleasure of the Crown. Therefore, a right could be extinguished or limited at the whim of the government. Once the amendments were proclaimed, it gave constitutional status to existing treaty and Aboriginal rights that had not been previously given up by First Nations. It also protects treaties and agreements entered into after 1982. This protec-

---

that "beyond conservation, there could be other 'compelling and substantial objectives'" by which the government could limit an Aboriginal right (para. 69). Other objectives include "pursuit of economic and regional fairness, and the recognition of the historical reliance upon, and participation in, the fishery by non-aboriginal groups, are the type of objectives which can ... satisfy this standard" (para. 75).

[47] The fiduciary duty of the Crown concerning Aboriginal title was held to exist in *Guerin v. The Queen*, [1984] 2 S.C.R. 335. The scope of the duty was enlarged in *Sparrow* to cover "all dealings" with Aboriginal peoples.

[48] Albert L. Hurtado and Peter Iverson, *Major Problems in American Indian History: Documents and Essays*, 2d ed. (Boston: Houghton Mifflin Company, 2000) at 184–85.

EXHIBIT 23.4   Section 18 of the *Indian Act*

18.(1) Reserves to be held for use and benefit of Indians — Subject to this Act, reserves are held by Her Majesty for the use and benefit of the respective bands for which they were set apart, and subject to this Act and to the terms of any treaty or surrender, the Governor in Council may determine whether any purpose for which lands in a reserve are used or are to be used is for the use and benefit of the band.

(2) **Use of reserves for schools, etc.** — The Minister may authorize the use of lands ... for the purpose of Indian schools, the administration of Indian Affairs, Indian burial grounds, Indian health projects or, with the consent of the council of the band, for any other purpose for the general welfare of the band, and may take any lands in a reserve required for those purposes, but ... compensation for that use shall be paid to the Indian ...

---

tion means that the government cannot override a treaty or other right by passing standard legislation.

Disputes often arise around the terms contained in early treaties. Land treaties generally involved terms that required the First Nations to give title of a large piece of land to the government in exchange for payment and the establishment of a reserve. The terms may also permit the band to hunt and fish on land adjacent to the reserve. First Nations believe that written treaties often do not reflect the terms agreed upon or their desire to retain independence. "Aboriginal people ... often say that their understanding, as transmitted through oral tradition, is that an agreement of peace and friendship was established in which they agreed to share the land with the Europeans, not sell it."[49] In practice, the government has generally treated surrendered land as its own, regardless of any Aboriginal right to use it, although such conduct would be limited today.

Treaties are not considered to be standard contracts or international agreements. A contract binds only the parties who sign it, whereas a treaty binds all band members regardless of whether their signature appears on the document. The treaty will also set out rights that apply to everyone in the band. An international treaty requires the legislature to adopt the agreement and proclaim it as a law in order for it to be binding. Indian treaties were not proclaimed. While there is evidence that early treaties contained terminology similar to that of a nation-to-nation agreement, Canada's First Nations are not domestically considered to be sovereign nation states. The Supreme Court of Canada views these treaties as unique documents, to be treated in a special way, which further reflects the *sui generis* nature of Aboriginal rights. For example, where a treaty dispute arises, the court may admit Aboriginal oral history evidence and consider the intentions of the First Nation and the government at the time the treaty was signed.[50]

---

[49] Imai, *supra* note 1 at 69.

[50] See *R. v. Marshall*, [1999] 3 S.C.R. 456, where the Court held that the interpretation of a treaty requires (i) a "generous" interpretation of the terms and, where a term is in doubt, it should be decided in favour of the Aboriginal band; and (ii) the written text is not determinative of the terms contained therein, and the court is required to consider the history and evidence surrounding the Aboriginal understanding of the term that conflicts with the written document. In this way the common intention of the parties at the time the treaty was entered into can be determined.

Reserve land is defined under the *Indian Act*, and the Act governs the land. Her Majesty or, more accurately, the government of Canada, holds title to the land. While designed to protect Aboriginal culture, reserves have had the effect of "isolat[ing] and impoverish[ing]" First Nations because the reserve land is usually too small and has inadequate resources by which to maintain the Aboriginal way of life.[51] The same restrictions on selling reserve land apply: that is, it can be sold only to the federal government. However, because the land is held communally, band consensus is required before any sale can be made. The First Nations' right of title to the land is extinguished when it is sold or given up and cannot be reclaimed.

Common Law Land Title Rights

Many tracts of land in Canada are occupied by Indians and have not been part of any land agreement or treaty. Aboriginal rights are often dealt with by negotiation or mediation between the government and the particular group of founding peoples. Alternatively, the First Nation may begin a proceeding that claims a common law right to title of identified land. British Columbia, for example, has large portions of land where Indian bands reside that have not been dealt with by a treaty or other agreement. The First Nation may seek to claim **Aboriginal title** through the courts. The Supreme Court of Canada in *Delgamuukw* dealt with a common law land title claim. While the Court decided that the matter required a new trial because of a defect in the pleadings and a failure of the trial judge to give proper weight to oral evidence, it did take the opportunity to clarify issues surrounding Aboriginal title under the common law.

Delgamuukw concerned a land claim that covered approximately 58,000 square kilometres in British Columbia. All of the Wet'suwet'en and most of the Gitksan First Nations made two communal claims for title to the land based on historical and present possession of the land and because of spiritual ceremonies that took place there. These ceremonies connected each band to the land. The Aboriginal claim failed at trial and on appeal. Justice McEachern held that there was insufficient evidence to support the inference that "the Indians possessed or controlled any part of the territory, other than for village sites and for aboriginal use in a way that would justify a declaration equivalent to ownership."[52] The Court also decided that any claim to the land had been extinguished by the government's intention to use the land for another purpose that was inconsistent with Aboriginal rights.[53] The majority of the Court of Appeal agreed that a claim for Aboriginal title had not been made out but disagreed with the assertion that Aboriginal rights had been extinguished. The necessary clear and plain intention by the Crown to extinguish such rights was absent from the evidence. However, this did not affect the trial decision concerning the Aboriginal title to the land.

The majority of the Supreme Court of Canada held that Aboriginal title was "the right to use land for a variety of activities, not all of which need be aspects of practices, customs and traditions which are integral to the distinctive cultures of aboriginal societies."[54] The right to title arises because of the band's occupation and possession of the land before the British asserted sovereignty over that land. The date of sovereignty in Canada varies by location. The band can use the land for any use, with one important limit: the land cannot be used in a way that violates the Aboriginal connection to it. For

---

[51] RCAP, *supra* note 22 at 11.

[52] *Delgamuukw*, *supra* note 45 at para. 18.

[53] *Ibid.* at para. 24.

[54] *Ibid.* at para. 111.

example, if the band asserts title because it has historically occupied and used the land for a special ceremony that forms the basis for obtaining Aboriginal title, the band cannot alter the land in a way that destroys this "physical and cultural" relationship with the land.[55] Therefore, building a shopping plaza on the ceremonial site could be seen to destroy the underlying connection with the land and would be irreconcilable with its historical use.

In order for a First Nation to establish a common law right to Aboriginal title, or joint title with another band, it must fulfill three requirements: "(i) the land must have been occupied prior to sovereignty; (ii) if present occupation is relied on as proof of occupation pre-sovereignty, there must be a continuity between the present and pre-sovereignty occupation; and (iii) at sovereignty, that occupation must have been exclusive."[56] In this case, British sovereignty over British Columbia occurred when the Oregon Boundary Treaty was signed in 1846. Under the common law, possession of the land before and since sovereignty is sufficient to ground Aboriginal title provided title has not been surrendered or extinguished. Evidence of the band's physical occupation of the land could be established in a variety of ways. The band could show that it had Aboriginal laws governing the land, constructed dwelling places on the land, enclosed fields, or cultivated the land, among other things.

Present occupation can be the more likely basis for asserting Aboriginal title because evidence of pre-sovereignty possession can be difficult to acquire. But continuity does not require that there is an unbroken chain of possession dating back to the pre-sovereignty period. The band is required to show a substantial maintenance of the connection between the people and the land even if the occupation and use of the land was disputed in the past or the nature of the occupation changed.[57] This is because the European colonists were unwilling to recognize Aboriginal title and simply took possession of the land they wanted. Applying this requirement too strictly (i.e., demanding an unbroken chain of occupation) would mean that most claims for Aboriginal title would fail for reasons that were beyond Aboriginal control.

Since Aboriginal title contains the right to *exclusive* use, as well as occupation of the land, the band must show that it had the ability to exclude others from the land. Otherwise, the Aboriginal title gained would be greater than that historically exercised. The court must determine exclusive use in the context of the Aboriginal society at the time of sovereignty. Requiring the band to show historical evidence of trespassing laws, for example, would impose a European standard on a society that was organized differently. Even where it is shown that other First Nations were located on the land or used it, exclusivity can be established where the band held the ability to exclude others. This could include evidence of other bands having to obtain permission before being granted access to the land.

OTHER ABORIGINAL RIGHTS TO LAND

Even where a First Nation cannot establish Aboriginal title to a tract of land, it may still have rights over that land in the absence of a land agreement. Other rights can arise "from the social organization and distinctive cultures of

---

[55] *Ibid.* at para. 132.
[56] *Ibid.* at para. 143.
[57] *Ibid.* at para. 154.

aboriginal peoples on that land."[58] These rights are considered inherent rights because they arise from the prior use of the land by the First Nations. The right can include the authority to engage in a particular activity, such as hunting or fishing, on an identified tract of land. The right must be seen necessary for the band's well-being and the continuation of their culture. The band must show that the Aboriginal right asserted is grounded in the "practices, customs and traditions that are integral to the distinctive cultures of aboriginal peoples." The practice, custom and tradition (hereinafter "Practice") must have existed prior to the first Aboriginal contact with the Europeans. This is a different point in time from the date used to determine a land title claim: i.e., the date of sovereignty. This limitation thus excludes cultural attributes that emerged as a result of European influences.

The requirements for establishing an Aboriginal right to use land for a specific purpose were outlined in *Sparrow* and *Van der Peet*. The general test enunciated by the Supreme Court of Canada is to be considered in the context of the particular band, the specific right being asserted, and whether the right is significant for maintaining the band's unique culture. The test has four components: (i) there must be sufficient evidence that the band lived as an organized society at the time the practice originated (e.g., the band had their own territory, name and resources); (ii) the Practice must be integral to the band's culture; (iii) the Practice must have originated prior to first contact with the Europeans; and (iv) while there must be evidence of sufficient continuity in the exercise of the Practice in the intervening time between pre-contact and the assertion of the right, an unbroken chain of continuity is not required. Exclusive possession of the land is not necessary.

While *Sparrow* provided the test to be met for establishing an Aboriginal right protected by section 35(1) of the Constitution, in *Van der Peet* the Supreme Court found that, as a preliminary step, the scope and nature of the Aboriginal right claimed may require definition. This is often relevant where an Aboriginal band or person is found in breach of legislation governing natural resources. The focus is less on identifying the right and more on determining the extent or scope of the right. The applicable test identified three factors that are used to characterize the scope and nature of the right:

1. The nature of the action that the applicant is claiming is done pursuant to an Aboriginal right
2. The nature of the conflict between governmental legislation and the right claimed
3. The ancestral traditions and practices that establish the right

In application, it seems that once the scope and nature of the protected right is identified using factors 1 and 3 above, consideration turns to whether the application of the legislation being challenged infringes the right or whether the right had been extinguished. There is some overlap in the evidence associated with the characterization of the right and the establishment of the right as both relate to pre-contact traditions and practice. In some cases, the establishment of the scope and nature of the right is determinative because the right claimed is not found to exist as framed, and the claim fails. Alternatively, where the claimed right is proved, it may be undisputed that the legislation would infringe the right and that a constitutional doctrine would apply to remedy the infringement; and where the right was previously extinguished, no infringement would be found. It will depend on the particular facts before the court.

---

[58] *Van der Peet, supra* note 3 at para. 74.

In *Van der Peet* the Aboriginal right being claimed was the right to sell fish for money. A band member had been convicted of selling the fish in violation of a fishing regulation. The accused asserted that commercial fishing was part of the distinctive culture of the Stó:lô band in British Columbia, of which she was a member. The Court held that the significance of the particular practice is a factor but will not, by itself, establish an Aboriginal right. The other requirements must also be met. The practice may be exercised in a modern form, such as using a motorboat rather than a canoe for fishing. The practice must be integral (i.e., a practice that makes the particular culture distinctively unique) to the culture of the Aboriginal band asserting the right. Therefore the right is relevant only to the particular band that *successfully* claims it and is not a general right that extends to all First Nations.

The claim failed in *Van der Peet* because the nature and scope of the right was not found to include commercial fishing. The Court held that the practice of exchanging fish for money or other goods was not an integral part of the distinctive Stó:lô culture that existed prior to contact. Prior to contact, the practice of selling fish in exchange for money or goods was only incidental to the main cultural activity of fishing for food.

The case of *R. v. Sappier; R. v. Gray*[59] similarly concerned the characterization of the scope and nature of the Aboriginal right claimed. It also answered the question of whether or not the pre-contact use of a natural resource for survival could give rise to an Aboriginal right.

R. v. Sappier; R. v. Gray

Two members of the Maliseet band and one member of the Mi'kmaq band were charged under provincial legislation with unlawful possession of, or cutting of, Crown timber from Crown land. The timber had been obtained from land traditionally harvested by the two First Nations. The timber was used for personal and not commercial use. The Maliseet had used the timber to construct a home and provide community firewood. The Mi'kmaq had used the timber to craft furniture. At trial, the First Nations members raised the defence of an Aboriginal and/or treaty right to harvest the timber and were acquitted. All of the acquittals were upheld by the provincial Court of Appeal, and the Supreme Court of Canada subsequently dismissed the appeal with reasons. The Supreme Court decided the case on the basis of the scope and nature of the Aboriginal right and found it unnecessary to deal with the treaty right submission.

The Court found that both First Nations had been migratory peoples before first contact with Europeans. They lived by travelling to where wildlife was available for hunting, and they used the waterways for transportation. The evidence demonstrated both bands had used timber for pre-contact domestic needs that included shelter, transportation, fuel and tools.

The Court identified that consideration was to focus on the importance of the actual Practice integral to the pre-contact culture of an Aboriginal people. To do so, the right had to be clearly defined first. A general right to a natural resource would be too broad and beyond the scope of historical practice. Moreover, "[A]n aboriginal right cannot be characterized as a right to a particular resource because to do so would be to treat it as akin to a common law property right." In characterizing Aboriginal rights as *sui generis*, the Supreme Court had, in *Sparrow*, rejected the application of traditional common law property concepts to such rights.

---

[59] 2006 SCC 54, [2006] 2 S.C.R. 686 [*Sappier*].

The Court considered the pre-contact Practice of the band in relation to the harvesting and use of timber as relevant to the definition of the content of the right. It is the pre-contact Practice that is central to the *Van der Peet* test for establishing an Aboriginal right to land. Pre-contact Practice required the Court to "grasp the importance of a resource to a particular aboriginal people ... to understand how that resource was harvested, extracted and utilized. These practices are the necessary 'aboriginal' component in aboriginal rights"[60] that are protected under section 35(1) of the Constitution. The Court then considered how the right might have evolved to its present-day form.

The Maliseet and Mi'kmaq's practice had been to use the timber "to fulfill the communities' domestic needs for things such as shelter, transportation, tools and fuel. [The Court defined the aboriginal right asserted as the right to] harvest wood for domestic uses as a member of the aboriginal community."[61] This definition delineated the right in accordance with its historical practice that reflected the way of life or distinctiveness of the particular Aboriginal community.

The use of the word "domestic" in the Supreme Court's decision means that the harvesting or possession of timber for commercial purposes is not included in the right. The phrase "as a member of the Aboriginal community" means that the right is a communal one that cannot be exercised independently by a band member. It was this particularized right that section 35 of the Constitution protected. The right did not provide *carte blanche* authority for the harvesting and use of timber by any band member, for any purpose, at any time and in any location.

Once the scope and nature of the right was defined, consideration turned to the historical exercise of the right and its integrality to the band's distinctive culture. The evidence demonstrated that the First Nations had practised the harvesting of wood for domestic purposes prior to European contact. The question was whether the practice was integral to the distinctive culture of the band. The Court had previously recognized an Aboriginal right based on evidence showing the importance of a resource to the pre-contact culture of an Aboriginal people. The Crown had also conceded in previous appeals that wood had been important to both bands for survival purposes in the pre-contact period and used in many facets of Aboriginal life.

The Court found that the fact that the activity was carried out for the purpose of survival did not automatically preclude it from being found integral to the band's distinctive culture. The notion that the pre-contact Practice upon which the right is based must go to the core of the society's identity — i.e., its single most important defining character — has never been the test for establishing an Aboriginal right. The claimant need only show that the Practice was integral to the Aboriginal society's pre-contact distinctive culture.

The protection afforded Aboriginal rights under section 35 of the Constitution arises from the simple fact of prior occupation of the lands now forming Canada. That underlying fact provides perspective for identifying whether a practice is part of a band's distinctive culture. While the right must be distinctive it is not required to be distinct.

> The focus of the Court should therefore be on the *nature* of this prior occupation. What is meant by "culture" is really an inquiry into the pre-contact way of life of a particular aboriginal community, including their means of survival, their socialization methods, their legal systems, and, potentially, their trading habits. The use of the word "distinctive" as a qualifier is meant to incorporate an element of aboriginal specificity. However, "distinctive"

---

[60] *Ibid.* at para. 22.
[61] *Ibid.* at para. 24.

does not mean "distinct", and the notion of aboriginality must not be reduced to "racialized stereotypes of Aboriginal peoples". ...

... [T]hese were migratory communities using the rivers and lakes of Eastern Canada for transportation and living essentially from hunting and fishing. The Court must therefore seek to understand how the particular pre-contact practice relied upon relates to that way of life. In the present cases, the practice of harvesting wood for domestic uses including shelter, transportation, fuel and tools is directly related to the way of life I have just described. I have already explained that we must discard the idea that the practice must go to the core of a people's culture. ...[62]

The Court held that "harvesting wood for domestic uses was undertaken for survival purposes is sufficient, given the evidence adduced at trial, to meet the integral to a distinctive culture threshold."[63] Based on the evidence provided, the Court decided that the practice of harvesting wood for domestic uses was integral to the pre-contact distinctive culture of both the Maliseet and Mi'kmaq peoples.

The inquiry did not end there. "The nature of the *right* had to be determined in light of present-day circumstances." The practice and uses associated with the right are permitted to evolve to reflect modern means. Otherwise, the right may be effectively vitiated or meaningless. An example would be where the right to harvest timber had to be done using the tools available in pre-contact times.

If aboriginal rights are not permitted to evolve and take modern forms, then they will become utterly useless. Surely the Crown cannot be suggesting that the respondents, all of whom live on a reserve, would be limited to building wigwams. If such were the case, the doctrine of aboriginal rights would truly be limited to recognizing and affirming a narrow subset of "anthropological curiosities", and our notion of aboriginality would be reduced to a small number of outdated stereotypes. The cultures of the aboriginal peoples who occupied the lands now forming Canada prior to the arrival of the Europeans, and who did so while living in organized societies with their own distinctive ways of life, cannot be reduced to wigwams, baskets and canoes.[64]

The right was found to be site-specific, limited to Crown land historically used for the practice and the timber's use limited as identified above. The existence of the specific Aboriginal right was exercisable only within its articulated scope and nature, and protected under section 35(1) of the Constitution.[65]

DISPUTES REGARDING ABORIGINAL LAND

The Indians express valid concerns over arbitrary decisions made regarding their land to the present day. Examples include the communities of Oka, Ipperwash, and Caledonia. Oka brought the land issue to the attention of the Canadian public and provided motivation to improve the land-dispute resolution process although confrontations dated back centuries.

---

[62] *Ibid.* at paras. 45 and 46.

[63] *Ibid.* at para. 46.

[64] *Ibid.* at para. 49.

[65] The Crown had not challenged the submission that legislation regulating the harvesting of timber infringed the Aboriginal right, if so found. The right was not shown to have been previously extinguished: *Ibid.*, para. 60. In this case, the nature and scope of the established right was determinative.

In 1990, the French Canadian resort town of Oka had a land crisis with its Mohawk community.[66] Earlier, in 1945, the Canadian government had set aside land the Mohawk claimed had belonged to it before the British asserted sovereignty. The government did not resolve the issue of the disputed land and the established reserve boundary did not include it. The government allowed the non-Aboriginal town council to take title to a portion of the disputed land in order to build a golf course. The Mohawks submitted a land claim to the government that replied (in 1977) that all claims dating from before the foundation of Canada in 1867 were not its problem.

The 1990 crisis arose when the town council wanted another portion of the disputed land, located beside an Indian cemetery, in order to expand the golf course. The Mohawk community built roadblocks and barricades, patrolled the area and protested the proposed expansion. In July of 1990, while negotiations were underway with the Mohawks, the Quebec police arrived at the request of the Oka mayor. The mayor was in favour of the golf course expansion.[67] The police later charged the roadblock, and gunfire was exchanged. After this exchange, one police officer was dead, but no conclusive evidence was provided as to which side was responsible for the death.[68]

Prime Minister Brian Mulroney subsequently made the army available to Quebec and appointed a mediator. Both Iroquois Confederacies expressed their concern over the government's handling of land claims and cited this as the major cause of the Oka crisis. The Confederacies suggested that negotiations begin between them and the federal and provincial governments in order to resolve the matter peacefully. The Mohawks broke off negotiations when the army moved up to the barricade. The army's relocation was criticized by human rights observers since it violated a prior agreement made by both levels of government.

The army advanced on the Oka Mohawks while other Indians and Canadians protested the government's handling of the crisis and its refusal to hear the First Nations' claim. The army attempted to prevent the reporters located inside the Mohawk stronghold from getting supplies, confiscated film, and otherwise tried to stop them from properly communicating details of the Oka crisis to the world. The Mohawks repeatedly made offers, indicating their willingness to begin a process of resolution and requested that "a joint commission from Quebec, Ottawa, the Iroquois Confederacy, and international human rights organizations [to] preside over the disengagement and judicial process."[69] Quebec declined to participate in a joint commission. Its primary interest seemed to be to use the army to force the Mohawks to surrender. At the beginning of September 1990, Canadian soldiers crept under a fence they had erected and clubbed a Mohawk warrior as he slept in his foxhole. At the end of the month, the 40 or so Mohawks remaining in their stronghold calmly walked out.

Since the Oka crisis, little progress has been made regarding Aboriginal land claims. With regard to Oka, Prime Minister Mulroney appointed a Royal Commission to explore the grievances of the First Nations and discontinued the policy of disqualifying land claims that were based on events prior to 1867. A portion of the disputed land was purchased by the government and transferred to the Mohawk community in 2000. However, "[M]any Mohawks

---

[66] For a more detailed analysis of the Oka crisis, see Wright, *supra* note 15 at 350–75 and Dickason, *supra* note 17 at 326.

[67] *Ibid.* at 353.

[68] *Ibid.*

[69] *Ibid.* at 362.

resented being 'given' what they regard as rightly theirs."[70] More recently, the creation of the new Inuit territory (discussed below) indicates a willingness of government to acknowledge Canada's First Nations to a greater degree. However, many Aboriginal peoples see self-government as necessary for maintaining their unique culture.[71]

The long-awaited report of the Ipperwash Inquiry was released in May 2007 and concerned the death of Mr. Dudley George, an Aboriginal protestor shot by an O.P.P. officer at Ipperwash Provincial Park in 1995. The inquiry concluded that government and the O.P.P. had improperly dealt with the matter and that both levels of government had not established a viable policy for the resolution of Aboriginal land claims. The protest concerned reserve land that had been temporarily appropriated during World War II as a military training site and not returned. Aboriginal people and supporters who were occupying the land in protest believed the appropriated land contained a sacred burial site. Despite persistent attempts to regain the Aboriginal land, 50 years had gone by and the federal government continued to refuse its return.

The Premier and the O.P.P. did not agree on the proper approach to the long-standing land claim protest and occupation, which was not conducive to a peaceful resolution. Members of government made racist comments, and the Premier wanted a speedy resolution to the occupation. The O.P.P.'s plan contained shortcomings, and both sides were wrong in their perceptions of the other's intentions. Cultural insensitivity and racism was evident in the conduct of some police officers. The inquiry concluded that these main factors, along with others, combined to lead to the death of Mr. George.

Since Ipperwash, no steps have been implemented to appropriately deal with the problem that caused the protest or to educate the Canadian public about the facts and delays underlying land claim tension:

> Unfortunately, the issues that were at the heart of the Ipperwash occupation remain to this day. This inexcusable delay and long neglect, by successive Federal governments, are at the heart of the Ipperwash story. … Research in the course of the inquiry showed that the flashpoints for aboriginal protests and occupations are very likely as intense today as they were at the time of Ipperwash. No one can predict where protests and occupations will occur, but the fundamental conditions and catalyst sparking such protests continue to exist in Ontario, more than a decade after Ipperwash.[72]

The report recommended, among other things, that the government create a Treaty Commission to deal with land claims in a fair and timely way. The standoff in Caledonia, which similarly dates back decades, is a recent example of ongoing conflict and government's failure to implement a regime for the effective and timely resolution of Aboriginal land claims. While inquiries are not binding on government and do not always impact government policies, Parliament has, since the release of the report, introduced a new land claims policy and is considering methods of reducing delay in the resolution of land claims.

---

[70] *Ibid.* at 371.

[71] Imai, *supra* note 1 at 115.

[72] The Ipperwash Inquiry, Press Release, "Commissioner's Statement" (May 31, 2007), online: <http://www.ipperwashinquiry.ca/li/pdf/Commissioner-s_Statement-May31_2007.pdf>; the full report is available online at <http://www.attorneygeneral.jus.gov.on.ca/inquiries/ipperwash/report/index.html>.

CHAPTER SUMMARY

This chapter identified that the prior occupation of North America by Aboriginal peoples is the underlying foundation for Aboriginal rights and their *sui generis* nature. All matters concerning Indians are under the jurisdiction of the federal government. Some factors that have affected the evolution of Aboriginal rights throughout history were discussed. These factors include fundamental cultural differences between the First Nations and European colonists, as well as the effects of epidemics on Aboriginal populations. In addition, the oral tradition of the Indians has become part of the *sui generis* nature of Aboriginal rights in that they are admissible in court when a claim is asserted.

The failure of colonial and Canadian governments to fulfill treaty and other obligations was examined. Aboriginal concern over the treatment of land claims remains relevant today, as illustrated by the discussion of the Oka crisis. The process of attempted assimilation of the First Nations into the Canadian culture was identified as including special schools, various pieces of legislation, and the holding out of incentives to encourage Aboriginal abandonment of cultural roots in exchange for Canadian citizenship. The requirements for status and band councils under the *Indian Act* were explained, and the non-status designation of the Métis and Inuit under the *Indian Act* was identified.

The methods by which a First Nation can ground an Aboriginal title claim were noted as being based on a treaty right or on the land having been designated as an Indian reserve, or by a successful common law claim. Land ownership in Aboriginal culture is a communally held right. Aboriginal title includes the right to exclusive possession and use of an identified piece of land. Such land can be sold only to the federal government and cannot be purchased by the public. The Supreme Court of Canada enunciated the necessary steps for establishing a common law claim to Aboriginal title, and these steps were identified. Where Aboriginal title is not established, the band may have rights to use the land for a particular purpose where certain requirements are met.

GLOSSARY OF NEW TERMS AND KEY CONCEPTS

Aboriginal (or Aboriginal peoples)	Referring to the indigenous peoples or original inhabitants of North America.
Aboriginal title	A communal right for the exclusive use and possession of an identified tract of land by an Indian band based on a history of exclusive occupation dating back to the time before British sovereignty.
band council	The governing body of a particular Indian tribe. The *Indian Act* contains the method for elections, or the tribe can choose a chief and council through custom; the council can pass by-laws that cover specific issues identified in the Act and that apply to their land subject to government approval.
Charter	Section 35 of the Charter specifically protects Aboriginal rights that were not extinguished or surrendered at the time the Charter came into force and prevents the government from unilaterally overriding or ignoring an established Aboriginal right.
common law claim	An Aboriginal rights claim without reference to a treaty or other land agreement. It requires that certain conditions be met but is not restricted to land title claims, and can be a claim for the specific use of an identified tract of land based on historical use.
fiduciary duty	A legal duty whereby a party must act or make a decision that is in the best interests of another party.

healing circle	Used for sentencing under an Aboriginal judiciary regime, the circle consists of a group of community members. The goal of the circle is to provide an opportunity to address the harm suffered by the victim and the community and to design a sentence that rehabilitates offenders and allows them to remain as part of the community.
house or clan	A band may be subdivided into houses or clans; each house or clan can have one or more hereditary chiefs, and each chief is selected by the elders.
Indian Act	Legislation designed to facilitate the assimilation of Aboriginal peoples into the larger Canadian culture. It governs Indian status, council elections, band governance, inheritance, family law, and economic activity.
Indian status	The requirements for acquiring Indian status are contained in the *Indian Act*; only status Indians are able to obtain benefits enunciated in the Act; registration is required before status is assigned.
Inuit	The indigenous peoples of the circumpolar north; they are not status Indians, and the *Indian Act* does not govern them.
membership or citizenship code	The *Indian Act* permits a band to design its own requirements for membership or citizenship in the band. For example, permitting a non-Aboriginal to be a member and live on a reserve is not the same as "status" under the Act and does not automatically entitle the member or citizen to any other benefit.
Métis	Generally speaking, the Métis are descendants from inter-marriages between Europeans and Indians; they are referred to as "non-status" Indians and are not governed by the *Indian Act*. The provincial government deals with Métis issues and benefits.
oral history	The spoken words of Aboriginal peoples concerning historical events and practices that have been passed down from generation to generation; it is admissible as evidence in court.
reserve	Land owned by the government but allocated for the use and benefit of an Indian band, which is subject to the *Indian Act* and any treaty terms. Reserve land can only be sold or surrendered to the federal government.
Royal Proclamation	Signed in 1763 by Britain's King George, this document attempted to establish boundaries around Indian land and also stipulated that this land could be sold only to the government.
sovereignty	The supreme or ultimate authority in a state.
sui generis	Unique or of its own kind. Aboriginal rights are *sui generis* because of the fact of prior occupation by Aboriginal peoples. The methods for establishing these rights and the content of the rights are also unique.
treaty	Generally considered to be a formal agreement made between two nations, but not in the context of the First Nations, since Canada does not recognize them as a nation; thus, it can include any Aboriginal right.
Treaty of Paris	Signed in 1763 by France, Spain and Britain, this document allowed Britain to gain control of North America when the other countries ceded their claims to the land.
Two Row Wampum	An agreement entered into by the Iroquois and British that included terms under which each group agreed not to interfere with the other.
Wampum belts	Used as an aid to oral commentary, they record historical facts and terms in agreements in lieu of written language.

REVIEW QUESTIONS

1. What is the basis for an Aboriginal right to land that does not concern a claim for Aboriginal title? Identify the requirements that must be satisfied for such a common law claim to succeed.

2. What was the purpose of the Royal Proclamation in relation to Aboriginal rights?

3. What facts must be established before a person can be designated as having Indian status?

4. Why are healing circles held in the Aboriginal culture? What is the purpose of an Aboriginal healing circle?

5. How did Indian tribes traditionally make political decisions? Describe the option historically available to a dissenter in the decision.

6. Identify how the Supreme Court of Canada defined "distinctive culture" for the purposes of establishing an Aboriginal right to the use of land, and provide an example that would form part of a band's distinctive culture.

DISCUSSION QUESTIONS

1. An Indian band has allowed the non-Aboriginal spouse of a member to obtain citizenship in the band. Will the spouse be able to obtain benefits under the *Indian Act*?

2. In 1895 a treaty was entered into between an Indian band and the government. The written treaty established an Indian reserve, included compensation for the purchase of other Indian land, and contained a clause that severely limited the band's right to hunt and fish on land adjacent to the reserve. However, the Indians expressed concern during negotiation about the maintenance of their hunting and fishing rights and were verbally assured that these rights would be respected. The hunting and fishing rights met the requirements for establishing a common law claim for an Aboriginal right to use the land for hunting and fishing. Can the band make a common law claim that will override the terms contained in the treaty?

3. An Aboriginal band has Aboriginal title, as of June 1985, to a tract of land located in British Columbia. The provincial government has decided, in 2004, to expropriate the land in order to build an industrial park. Discuss. What difference, if any, would it make if title had been established in 1975 and the provincial government attempted to expropriate the land in 1980?

4. An Indian band in Newfoundland does not have a land agreement that deals with the land it has occupied for generations. What evidence is the band required to produce in order to make a successful common law claim to title of the land? Would it make a difference if a portion of the identified land had been communally and exclusively shared with another independent band?

5. Identify and discuss some of the fundamental differences between Aboriginal and early European cultures.

6. A band had a pre-contact practice of obtaining water from a stream on land it does not have title to. It used the water for survival, cooking, washing and in construction of shelter. The band seeks to bottle and sell the water from the stream and an adjoining lake as a business enterprise. Discuss whether or not the band would be successful in its claim for an Aboriginal right to do so.

SUGGESTED READING

Borrows, John. "Sovereignty's Alchemy: An Analysis of *Delgamuukw v. British Columbia*" (1997) 35 Osgoode Hall L.J. 125.

Cairns, Alan C. *Citizens Plus: Aboriginal Peoples and the Canadian State* (Vancouver: UBC Press, 2000).

Carcone, Janet Mason, & Stanley Gershman. "The Charter of Rights and Freedoms" in Laurence M. Olivo, ed., *Introduction to Law in Canada* (Toronto: Captus Press, 2004).

Constitutional Law Group, The. *Canadian Constitutional Law*, 3d ed. (Toronto: Emond Montgomery Publications Limited, 2003).

Dickason, Olive Patricia. *Canada's First Nations: A History of Founding Peoples from Earliest Times*, 3d ed. (Toronto: Oxford University Press, 2002).

Eccles, W.J. *The Canadian Frontier, 1534–1760 (Histories of the American Frontier)* (New Mexico: University of New Mexico Press, 1965).

Hogg, Peter W. *Constitutional Law of Canada*, Student ed. (Toronto: Thomson Canada Limited, 2002).

Hurtado, Albert L., & Peter Iverson. *Major Problems in American Indian History: Documents and Essays*, 2d ed. (Boston: Houghton Mifflin Company, 2000).

Imai, Shin. *Aboriginal Law Handbook*, 2d ed. (Toronto: Carswell, 1999).

———. *Indian Act and Aboriginal Constitutional Provisions* (Toronto: Carswell, 2004).

Royal Commission on Aboriginal Peoples. *Looking Forward, Looking Back*, Volume 1 (Ottawa: Minister of Supply & Services, 1996).

Salisbury, Neal. "The Indians' Old World: Native Americans and the coming of the Europeans" (1996) 53 William and Mary Quarterly 435.

Wright, Ronald. *Stolen Continents: Conquest and Resistance in the Americas*, 10th ed. (Toronto: Penguin, 2003).

Administrative Law

Irv Ash
SENECA COLLEGE

Learning Objectives

After reading this chapter, the reader should be able to:

➢ define administrative law

➢ differentiate between the three branches or functions of government

➢ elaborate on various concepts of public policy

➢ explain the reasons for, the types of, and the functions of agencies

➢ compare and contrast agencies and courts

➢ identify specific rules and procedures for a specific agency

➢ assess the relevant provisions of the *Statutory Powers Procedure Act* as they relate to the rules and procedures of Ontario agencies

➢ document how various sections of the *Charter of Rights and Freedoms* have been applied to agency proceedings

➢ illustrate and discuss principles that flow from the duty to act fairly

➢ distinguish between the remedies of reconsideration, appeal and judicial review that may be available in respect of an agency proceeding

➢ outline various concerns in respect of appealing an agency proceeding

➢ summarize the various remedies available from an agency proceeding pursuant to judicial review

TABLE OF CONTENTS

INTRODUCTION

In the past 20 years, the number of cases involving administrative law have increased tremendously. The reason for the increase is tied to both the explosive growth of government and the definition of "administrative law". The definition involves government and governmental delegates, the legal restrictions imposed on the government when implementing public policy, and the remedies available to persons "harmed" by the misuse of governmental power. This chapter will attempt, in varying detail, to deal with each component of this definition.

The courts have been given the **jurisdiction**, both **inherent** and **statutory**, to oversee and remedy many governmental actions. This jurisdiction or power derives, in common law, from the *Magna Carta* in 1215 and has been strengthened over the years by various statutes and case law. Further, in Canada, greater jurisdiction has been given to the courts by the constitutional documents that instituted and regulate the country, and by the federal-provincial split of powers. Before delving into various aspects of administrative law, it is necessary to review some aspects of government and the Constitution and to further discuss the concept of public policy and how it is legislated and enforced in our system.

BRANCHES OF GOVERNMENT

Canada has three branches (or functions) of government. The legislative (or parliamentary) branch includes elected Members of Parliament, whether federal or provincial, and the appointed Senate. The major task of this branch is to introduce, debate, and institute new legislation, and amend and/or repeal existing legislation. Once the legislation is enacted and **proclaimed in force**, it is the main duty of the executive branch to ensure compliance with such legislation and subordinate governmental policy instruments that may be in force (regulations and orders-in-council). This is achieved through the work of government ministries, departments, and agencies, as well as through boards, commissions, and tribunals. The third branch of government, the judicial branch, has a basic obligation to interpret the legislation presented before it in specific cases in order to resolve disputes. If there is no specific relevant legislation, the judicial branch must also determine the law to be applied. In addition to this basic obligation to interpret the legislation put before them, there has developed a review component of the courts' powers. The courts oversee not only the appropriate exercise of substantive powers of government (constitutional law) but also the exercise of government's procedural powers (administrative law).

PUBLIC POLICY

In discussing the branches of government in Canada, reference was made to the legislative function, including legislation. It should be noted that almost all legislation is initiated by the governing party. By starting the legislative process and then shepherding it to its conclusion, the governing party is putting into law parts of its governmental or public policy. This is just one facet of public policy that can be defined as a "conscious choice [of government or governmental authority] that leads to deliberate action — the passage of a law, the spending of money, an official speech or gesture, or some observable act — or inaction."[1] If it is conceded that the function of government is to govern, then any action taken by government in governing is public policy.

MECHANICS OF PUBLIC POLICY

Many different paths can be taken in order to achieve what the government of the day perceives as its objectives. A lot of policy is developed internally in the caucus of the elected members of the governing party and through consultation with their advisors (sometimes their constituents) and the civil service. Policy also derives from the party platform prior to elections; it can originate in any number of ways as allowed by that party's internal constitution and is developed in answer to current issues. For example, policy actions can follow from senior ministers floating "trial balloons" at speaking engagements and in media interviews, from public hearings before standing committees of the legislature, or from reports from royal commissions appointed to investigate certain issues. Upon determining the substance of the proposed public policy in a specific area, the government makes it governmental policy or law in a variety of ways that include (a) legislation and (b) orders-in-council properly published in the **gazette**.

After the legislative function has been carried out, the next step is to enforce the legislation. If the legislation is regulatory — that is, it involves control of public and/or private sector operations in the "public interest" — mechanisms will be found to achieve the desired ends. This is also the case for legislation that is operational in nature, such as legislation in respect of delivery of goods and/or services, review and/or advice, the use and conservation of resources, or legislation for disciplinary or other purposes.

Governments continue to enact and enforce more and more regulatory legislation. The main function of the executive branch of government concerns enforcing these laws. That function is often achieved by civil servants working for various ministries in the government, usually in specialized regulatory bodies. It should be noted that under constitutional law, the government can delegate, to bodies it creates, its powers to legislate and enforce laws. Such bodies shall, for the purposes of this chapter, be called agencies (which also includes boards, commissions, authorities, committees, and tribunals). Although administrative law can and does deal with actions of Cabinet ministers and/or other elected members of government, it mostly involves judicial review and/or appeals (to be discussed later) from agencies.

AGENCIES

There are various reasons why a government would appoint an agency to deal with a specific area, including, but not limited to, the following:

1. Specific expertise can be developed and applied.

2. The magnitude and complexity of government and its attendant workload requires a shift in responsibilities from elected members to such experts.

---

[1] Stephen Brooks, *Public Policy in Canada, An Introduction* at 12.

3. It is more efficient in time and costs to use an agency to deal with recurrent matters.

4. It offers a more precise, yet flexible and timely, way to deal with specific situations than going through the more cumbersome elected bodies.

5. It is a way to distance the government from the public effect of certain decisions or actions.

6. It allows future unforeseen events to be dealt with more efficiently.

Because there are many and diverse reasons why agencies are created, there are many agencies in existence. In 1990, the number in Ontario totalled 485. By 1994, that number had grown to 716.[2]

There are three main types of agencies:

- Advisory — provide information to government that will assist in developing policy or the ongoing delivery of programs. Some examples of Ontario advisory agencies include the Ontario Advisory Council on Senior Citizens and the Ontario Advisory Council for Disabled Persons.

- Operational — main function is to deliver goods and/or services necessary to implement approved government policy or programs. Operational agencies in Ontario include the Workplace Safety and Insurance Board and Ontario Hydro.

- Regulatory — decision-making bodies that control public- or private-sector operations as authorized by their enabling legislation, or the exercise of a licence-review function or an appeal function, with respect to both government and third-party decisions. The Canadian Radio and Telecommunications Commission (CRTC) and the Ontario Human Rights Commission are examples of regulatory bodies.

Agencies may, if empowered, exercise legislative, executive, and judicial functions. As will be discussed, the legislative function includes the ability to make rules and regulations in respect of procedure to be followed before the agency. The executive function includes research and advice on, and administration and enforcement of, government policy. The judicial function allows for adjudication on specific situations and may determine individual rights, privileges and obligations. An agency may have any or all of the above-mentioned powers, which must be specifically delegated by the legislation that establishes the agency.

An agency is established by legislation enacted by the government. That **enabling legislation** will have provisions that may delegate power to the agency in order to carry out certain stated objectives. Such legislation will usually set out general procedures of the agency, such as who has the right to appear before such agency and the jurisdiction and powers of such agency. Further, the agency may be able to make rules and regulations regarding its own procedures. Finally, the legislation will authorize the staffing of the agency and determine who may be eligible to be employed there.

---

[2] Government of Ontario, *Guide to Agencies, Boards and Commissions of the Government of Ontario 1994* (Toronto, Ont.: Queen's Printer, 1995) at 3.

	EXHIBIT 24.1

The Differences between the Courts and the Agencies

COURTS	AGENCIES
¤ interpret and apply the law	¤ formulate (by regulation), interpret, and apply the law
¤ *stare decisis* applied (inflexible)	¤ no *stare decisis*, although attempts to be relatively consistent (flexible)
¤ formal — specific rules and procedures to be followed	¤ more informal — there may or may not be specific rules and procedures to be followed, but more procedural latitude is allowed
¤ make decisions based strictly on law; no policy or public interest concerns	¤ make many decisions based on public policy
¤ no relationship with parties before them either before or after hearing	¤ likely to have many relationships with parties both before and after adjudication
¤ unlikely to have expertise in area to be decided	¤ usually have expertise in area to be decided

AGENCIES COMPARED TO COURTS

One function of agencies is adjudicative. Agencies may determine rights, privileges, and/or obligations of persons in relation to another person or to a group or to society. An agency acting under such powers has been seen as having a **judicial or quasi-judicial function** that would seem to encroach on the judicial branch of government — that is, the court system.

There is considerable case law on the differences between the courts and agencies. Some agencies do have some similarities to courts, in that both interpret legislation and apply it to specific cases. However, there are differences in the two bodies (see Exhibit 24.1).

One of the most contentious issues in the court–agency comparison is how far the judiciary should go in recognizing agencies' obligations to make decisions based on public interest (or the collective good of society). Public interest is foreign to the courts, which have always looked to individual rights first and foremost. This tension can be observed in the greater or lesser control that the courts have exercised over agencies during the past 50 years, to be discussed later in this chapter.

STEPS TO DETERMINE RULES OF AGENCIES

We shall next examine the legal restrictions imposed on agencies. To determine the specific rules and procedures, or legal restrictions, followed by a specific agency, the following should be reviewed:

1. Enabling statute creating the agency.
2. Regulations pursuant to the enabling statute.
3. If applicable, general legislation that details rules and procedures that apply to certain agencies.

4. The *Charter of Rights and Freedoms*[3] (the Charter).
5. Rules, guidelines and/or directives formulated by the agency.
6. Rules set out in notices issued generally and/or for particular proceeding.
7. An overall common law requirement to "act fairly", and rules derived therefrom.

Each of these steps shall be discussed at some length to clarify how such rules and procedures are found.

Enabling Statute

As we saw above, agencies must be created by government statute that sets up an agency to advise on, operate in and/or regulate a legislated area. Usually, such an enabling statute will detail the composition of the agency, its powers and jurisdiction and, occasionally, some rules and procedures. An agency that is set up under a specific enabling Act may also be named as the relevant agency to hear appeals of issues under different legislation. For example, the Social Assistance Review Board (SARB) and its successor, the Social Benefits Tribunal (SBT), was created pursuant to the *Ministry of Community and Social Assistance Act*,[4] but it is also the appropriate board for the *Family Benefits Act*,[5] the *General Welfare Assistance Act*[6] and the *Vocational Rehabilitation Services Act*.[7] Any general information about rules or procedures for SARB and SBT would initially be found in its enabling Act, and usually not in the other Acts.

Regulations Pursuant to the Enabling Statute

Enabling Acts will have provisions that allow regulations to be made in respect of the rules and procedures to be applied by the agencies. Powers to develop and **promulgate** regulations are often granted to the Governor General in Council (federal Cabinet) or the Lieutenant Governor in Council (provincial Cabinet), depending on whether the enabling Act is federal or provincial. The procedures in respect of SARB and SBT, as an illustration, are prescribed in regulations by the Ontario Lieutenant Governor in Council. Such regulations will usually give details regarding documentation to be provided in a hearing, time limits with which there must be compliance, and other hearing procedures.

Legislation That Establishes Rules for Many Boards

Some provincial jurisdictions (currently Alberta and Ontario) have provisions that govern procedures of numerous agencies set out in one statute. In Ontario, the statute is entitled the *Statutory Powers Procedure Act*[8] (SPPA). Originally enacted in the 1970s to provide "minimum rules for proceedings of certain tribunals", the SPPA was an attempt by the Ontario government to codify the rules and procedures that the court system had developed for administrative agencies over the years, through the common law "duty to act fairly" and its predecessor concept, the "**rules of natural justice**". It was felt that there should be somewhat common rules and procedure for those agencies required to hold a hearing — that is, to exercise a "statutory power of decision".

---

[3] *Constitution Act 1982*, R.S.C. 1985, Appendix II, No. 44, Part 1.
[4] *Ministry of Community and Social Assistance Act*, R.S.O. 1990, c. M.20.
[5] *Family Benefits Act*, R.S.O. 1990, c. F.2.
[6] *General Welfare Assistance Act*, R.S.O. 1990, c. G.6.
[7] *Vocational Rehabilitation Services Act*, R.S.O. 1990, c. V.5.
[8] *Statutory Powers Procedure Act*, R.S.O. 1990, c. S.22.

It is important to note that the SPPA applies to all Ontario agencies unless they are explicitly excluded by the provisions of the SPPA or another statute.

As initially conceived and enacted, the SPPA dealt with such matters as the following:

1. Determining who are the parties to a proceeding.
2. Notice provisions to advise of the case to be met, and providing time to prepare.
3. Requiring public hearings unless there are reasons for private hearings.
4. Appropriate representation of parties at hearing, including examination and possibly cross-examination of witnesses.
5. Powers of agencies to compel evidence.
6. Rules regarding admissibility of evidence.
7. Written decisions to be provided to all participants after the hearing.
8. The need for the agency to compile a record of the proceedings.

All of those matters are part of the common law "duty to act fairly", to be discussed below.

Certain amendments were made in 1994 to the SPPA, under the *Statute Law Amendment Act (Government Management and Services)*,[9] that allow agencies that fall within the SPPA to have more cost-effective and efficient proceedings. Some of the amendments include the following: (a) a general provision allowing any agency under the SPPA to make its own rules and procedures, and to promulgate them in the form of regulations; (b) a recognition of the value, where appropriate, of both written hearings and, especially, electronic hearings by amending the previous rules to allow such hearings; and (c) a provision permitting agencies to have pre-hearing conferences, determine more questions about admissibility of evidence, make interim orders, and have the power to review and vary a decision. More recent amendments to the SPPA in 1999 made certain changes, especially, but not limited to, inserting provisions for the appointment, with the consent of all the parties, of mediators, conciliators and negotiators to facilitate resolution of a matter before a tribunal. This alternative dispute resolution mirrors similar programs instituted in the civil court system to try to resolve matters without going to the time, expense and hard feelings of a court hearing.

Charter of Rights and Freedoms

There are many general statements made in the Charter in terms of individual rights and freedoms. The judiciary has been given the power under the Charter to determine if a person's freedoms or rights have been infringed upon by some governmental law or action (including actions of agencies, as they are creations of governmental law). The judiciary has used various sections of the Charter to review the rules and procedures and, ultimately, the decisions of agencies.

Section 7 of the Charter states that, "Everyone has the *right to life, liberty and security of the person* and the right not to be deprived thereof, except in accordance with the *principles of fundamental justice*." Through a series of decisions, the Supreme Court of Canada (SCC) has read into those italicized words, principles of procedural fairness. Although such principles existed in the common law concept of the rules of natural justice, the Charter has entrenched those principles as part of the basic constitutional law of Canada.

---

[9] *Statute Law Amendment Act (Government Management and Services)*, S.O. 1994 c. 27.

Two leading authors on administrative law,[10] after analyzing the decisions of the Supreme Court of Canada, summarized the principles as follows:

> These [principles] include the rights to notice, and a hearing, and unbiased decision-making and all the other related, procedural rights. One must then ask whether any particular procedural right should be afforded in the specific case. Several limiting factors should be examined. First, the purpose of the impugned legislation should be considered and a balance should be struck between the demands of fairness and efficiency. The competing interests of the state and the individual must be balanced. Second, in extradition matters at least (and perhaps more generally), the Court may ask whether denying the remedy would "shock" the conscience of Canadians or violate the standards of the international community. Third, the nature of the decision-making function will be analyzed. Depending upon where the function resides on the continuum of administrative decision-making, a higher or lower degree of procedural fairness will be required. The closer the decision-maker is to the legislative (or policy) end of the spectrum, the lower the standard of procedural fundamental justice which is required. A higher degree of fairness is required as the decision-maker moves along the spectrum toward judicial or quasi-judicial deliberations.

Agencies have powers to force production of documents or evidence by summons and/or subpoena, or to permit entry of premises to conduct searches by search warrant. They must comply with section 8 of the Charter, which states that such seizures or searches must be reasonable. Various decisions in the courts have determined that individuals have some sort of sliding scale in their right to privacy. The reasonableness of privacy is dependent on the circumstances, such as the purposes of the search and other related factors. Further, certain procedural safeguards usually must be maintained, such as an impartial decision-maker authorizing such search or seizure on reasonable evidence supplied.

Section 13 of the Charter states, "A witness who testifies in any proceedings has the right not to have any incriminating evidence so given used to incriminate that witness in any other proceedings, except in a prosecution for perjury or for the giving of contradictory evidence." This section is not the same as the American Fifth Amendment, which allows a person to not give any evidence that would tend to incriminate oneself. Instead, evidence given by a person may not be used to incriminate that person in a subsequent proceeding.

Section 14 of the Charter states, "A party or witness in any proceeding who does not understand or speak the language in which the proceedings are conducted or who is deaf has the right to the assistance of an interpreter." Further, the interpreter must translate word for word and not summarize the information being translated. Notice that the Charter makes no reference as to who pays for the interpreter, making such issue open for discussion.

Rules, Guidelines, and Directives Formulated by the Agency

Some enabling statutes, such as the Ontario *Workplace Safety and Insurance Act, 1997*,[11] under subsection 159(1) for the Workplace Safety and Insurance Board (WSIB) and subsection 173(1) for the Workplace Safety and Insurance Appeals Tribunal (WSIAT), give specific power to agencies to determine their own practice and procedure. Depending on the statute, the rules the agency makes in respect of practice and procedure may have the force and effect of a regulation. The regulation, however, must be approved by the appropriate Cabinet, and the guidelines to promulgate such rules as regulations must be

---

[10] Jones & de Villars, *Principles of Administrative Law* at 57–58.
[11] *Workplace Safety and Insurance Act, 1997*, S.O. 1997 c. 16, Sch. A.

followed. If, however, the agency has made its rules in a non-statutory form, as described in the next paragraph, such rules must be followed if they are mandatory.

Rules Set Out in Notice Generally or for a Particular Proceeding

For reasons of flexibility, agencies usually have some latitude in determining which rules should apply generally and in a particular proceeding, provided that the overriding concern of fairness is met. This concern is also addressed when determining whether the specific rules are mandatory (must be followed) or directory (may be followed). Although consistency in rules is preferable, it is not necessary to follow all rules if there is a risk of unfair treatment. It is recognized that in these situations agencies have to broadly interpret, and even change, rules as long as no party is prejudiced. On the other hand, if some or all of the parties have acted in reliance upon a specific rule, it would not be correct to amend such rule.

Common Law Requirement to "Act Fairly" and the Rules Derived Therefrom

The six steps to determine the rules of any agency discussed above should be observed through the lens of the court-developed "duty to act fairly" and its predecessor concept, the "rules of natural justice". The rules of natural justice have largely been supplanted by the duty of fairness and, therefore, are not very relevant here. The courts have used the obligation to require anybody to act fairly, as a means to determine a person's rights and obligations. A successful attack, by way of judicial review as discussed later, has been decried by some opponents as interference with agencies' freedom to act in determining the public interest. The reply to this position notes that the courts will only interfere where a party is treated unfairly and where the decision has a sufficiently serious effect on the party. This suggests that the more adverse the effect on the party, the greater the duty to act fairly, as shown by an increase in the procedural protections. But in an emergency, an agency may be entitled to have more flexibility in its procedural protections, at least initially. Therefore, it can be argued that there is a sliding scale of procedural protections mandated on an agency, depending on certain factors that sometimes are recognized by the courts.

Notwithstanding any other requirements, before an agency can make a decision adverse to a person's interest, at a minimum the person should be:

- told of the case to be met; and
- given an opportunity to respond.

Both "notice of the case" and "right to respond" can range, depending on the circumstances, from verbal advice to written notice to provision of documentary evidence in the former situation, and from written to electronic or, most likely, oral hearing in the latter situation. These minimum requirements can be observed in rules adopted by most agencies to be fair to the parties because the courts would likely impose them anyway. However, even if no rules are prescribed for an agency to follow, the duty to act fairly will impose a number of rules on the agency, as outlined in the next paragraphs.

Status

One of the most important preliminary matters to be decided by an agency is who has the status to appear before it. A person who should appear before an agency but is denied an opportunity to appear would be considered unfairly treated. The most likely person to have status as a party to the proceeding is a person who may be seriously affected by the outcome of the proceeding. Factors used to determine whether a person is seriously affected include the subject matter of the proceeding, the person's interest in the subject matter, and the effect that the decision might have on that interest. Using the concept of "serious effect" allows not only persons directly affected, such as a named party or the complainant in a disciplinary proceeding, but members of the public who may have the status of an **intervenor**. This is especially important in an agency environment, where the public interest is so compelling and where the effect of a decision might be far reaching.

Notice

The general principle here states that, except for emergencies, advance notice advising of a proceeding where a decision may be made must be given to all persons who would be affected by the decision. Such notice should be explicit and state the time and place of the proceeding, in order that those persons affected may take action to protect their position. Whether service is verbal, written, or even by newspaper advertisement, it must be effective: the notice must reach the person and be timely enough to permit the person to adequately prepare.

Disclosure

In order for the person affected by the possible decision to have an opportunity to make appropriate submissions, the person should be informed of the case to be met. That includes disclosure of (a) all relevant information that the agency may take into account when rendering a decision, (b) the issues as presented to the agency, and (c) the penalties that could be imposed on the person. A party to a proceeding may very well be entitled to more disclosure than an intervenor. In some circumstances, only partial or even no disclosure is permissible when it involves confidential information or information that would cause harm if released. Disclosure of information must be timely and should be given as soon as reasonably possible in the circumstances.

Adjournments (or Stays)

Even where there is no provision in the enabling statute to allow it, agencies have inherent discretionary jurisdiction to adjourn proceedings to ensure fairness. An agency would likely grant a stay in the following situations: (a) a party received insufficient notice, (b) a party received late or improper disclosure, (c) a new issue is raised in the hearing, requiring time for a party to prepare, and (d) a related matter is being heard in another agency or in court. In determining whether to grant a discretionary adjournment, an agency will usually review factors such as complexity of the proceeding; previous stays, if any; interests of the persons affected; and costs of the stay. If a stay is granted, the agency will likely fix the time and place for the resumption of the proceedings.

Effective Participation (Especially the Right to Counsel)

In order for a party to properly deal with a hearing, such party must be present at the hearing. That means the agency should carry on with a hearing only if all parties are present, unless it is shown that such missing party or parties had effective notice of the hearing but decided not to attend. In almost all circumstances, any person who has a right to appear in a hearing has the right to be represented by counsel who can present the case for the person. An agency may have some discretion, under its enabling Act, to allow counsel. Concerns such as the ability of the parties involved to represent themselves, the nature and complexity of the proceeding (the more complex or serious the matter, the more likely that counsel will be allowed), and the possible consequences of the proceeding are taken into account. If an agency denies use of counsel, it must state its reasons for doing so. Unless the legislation requires it, the counsel does not have to be a lawyer and, in fact, almost all agencies will allow paralegals or laypersons with some specialized knowledge to represent parties in a hearing.

Public or Private (In Camera) Hearings

The general rule for most hearings, whether in court or before an agency, states that they should be public, for reasons of fairness and as a safeguard against covert actions. However, especially for hearings before an agency, there is discretion to have *in camera* hearings for national security reasons or if a person, such as a party or even a witness, could be harmed by a public hearing. In some situations, such as a hearing before the Workplace Safety and Insurance Appeals Tribunal, the hearing is private unless the parties to the proceedings unanimously agree to allow the public to be present. This situation likely has to do with a possibility of embarrassment if evidence as to a worker's physical condition and health became public knowledge.

Evidence

In order to reach a decision, an agency must base all findings of fact upon the relevant evidence. On the whole, the rules of evidence, which are formal and usually strictly applied in court, are much less formal when applied by an agency. Therefore, such uncertain types of evidence as hearsay and somewhat unqualified "expert" evidence will likely be admitted, although in determining whether to admit the evidence the agency must determine its relevance. Even if the evidence is admissible, the agency must also determine the evidence's weight (probative value) and its credibility. If the evidence does not have much value or is not believable, possibly because of contradictions, the agency will likely gloss over the evidence. An agency also has the right to take notice of commonly accepted facts without the need for evidence to prove those facts.

Witnesses

Witnesses before an agency can give evidence in written or oral form, depending on the circumstances and the provisions of relevant legislation. Oral evidence is usually adduced by questions of the party calling the witness, or by members of the agency itself, which often has a wide latitude to participate in an active way, unlike most court proceedings. The difficult issue for most agencies to determine is when a party has the right to cross-examine a witness, which can be done whether the initial submission is in a written or oral form. Although certain acts require cross-examination, an agency has discretionary power to grant it. The party must convince the agency that the party should be given the opportunity to correct or controvert any relevant and prejudicial statement made by the witness. More specifically, cross-examination will be allowed if it is the only means to reveal or test the evidence that goes to the heart of the hearing where there is conflicting and/or contradictory evidence, as if cross-examination provides the best way to assess the credibility of the witness.

Proof

Parties who bring an application to appear before an agency usually carry the burden of proving their case. However, the standard used to determine if the burden has been met is not the **"beyond a reasonable doubt" test** used in criminal court proceedings but, rather, the **"balance of probabilities" test** used in civil court proceedings. In making a finding of fact and the eventual decision, the agency should be reasonably satisfied that the fact occurred, which depends on such factors as the nature of the facts to be proven and the consequences that would flow from the finding of fact. Once the parties with the burden or onus to prove the case have finished their submissions, the other parties have the ability to make a motion for a non-suit (dismissal) without making any submissions. In determining whether to grant the motion, the agency must determine whether the first party made a *prima facie* case. The *prima facie* test, a test that has less of a burden than the balance of probability test the agency will use in making its final decision, requires looking at the evidence in the light most favourable to the parties who presented it. Even if the evidence is weak and not very credible, if there is any evidence at all to support the contentions of the parties presenting the case, the agency should not grant a motion of non-suit.

Evidence by Compulsion

Pursuant to legislation, many agencies are granted powers to obtain relevant evidence in the following ways:

1. exercise of search and/or seizure powers;
2. use of inspection powers; and
3. use of subpoena and/or summons powers, which are subject to section 8 of the Charter.

In respect of search and/or seizure, an authorized person is permitted to pay a surprise visit to search for and/or seize evidence. Prior authorization is given by a person, usually not a member of the agency, but not necessarily a judge. Such person should not have an interest in the proceeding and should be satisfied on reasonable and probable grounds, provided under oath, that it is reasonable to grant such search and/or seizure warrant. The search should not be a general search but should be a search in respect of a specific situation and anything relevant to it.

Inspection orders permit inspectors to view premises for spot audits and to regulate businesses as allowed under the enabling Act. The usual purpose of the inspection is to protect the public interest and is likely to be carried on during reasonable hours.

Documents and/or witnesses can be subpoenaed to require production and/or attendance, respectively. If there is non-compliance, contempt proceedings can be initiated before the appropriate court. If non-compliance is proven beyond reasonable doubt, the offender can be imprisoned unless there is compliance. Certain documents cannot be compelled, most commonly those that are privileged, such as solicitor–client communications for the purposes of obtaining legal advice, and Cabinet or ministerial communications where disclosure would prejudice the public interest. Summonses will be granted to compel a witness to appear if the party requesting it can show that such witness is reluctant to appear, the likely evidence obtained is relevant, and it is unlikely to be obtained in any other fashion than by a summons.

Orders and Decisions

Unless required by the appropriate legislation to be in writing, an oral final order or decision is acceptable. The decision should be given as expeditiously as possible, and some enabling Acts even have a specific time limit for a decision to be handed down. Although it may not be required, agencies usually give reasons for the decision, especially if the decision might be raised in court on appeal or by way of judicial review (to be discussed later). The following are some of the problems that can arise if the reasons for the decision are not included:

1. Lack of reasons may undermine confidence in the agency.
2. The court will disregard the agency's expertise if it is not demonstrated by stated reasons for the decision.
3. The court can derive adverse inferences if there are no reasons to review.
4. A disturbing impression of injustice may be left with those reading the decision.
5. The parties do not know why the decision was made, or if there are any grounds for appeal or judicial review.

Further, if the enabling Act requires reasons to be given, and there are none, the decision is likely null and void. The reasons, as given, should adequately explain how the agency reached its conclusions, whether based on fact, law, or public policy.

Over and above the rules or procedures to be followed by agencies in respect of the duty to act fairly, two other principles, derived originally from the rules of natural justice, are important: the decision-maker must be impartial (no bias), and the decision-maker must not fetter his or her discretion. Not following either principle will likely lead to a successful application for judicial review.

Bias

If, in the exercise of its powers, an agency is found to lack neutrality, has not been impartial and/or has had personal interests in mind, the decision of the agency will likely be null and void. If a member of an agency is found to be biased, that member will be disqualified from hearing the case. Indicators of bias of a member of the adjudicating agency body include the following:

- Pecuniary interest in the proceeding
- Having a friend, business associate, or relative as a party or a witness, unless it is a past and/or distant connection
- Improper conduct at the hearing, such as flippant or derogatory language, expressed feelings of hostility or antagonism, or repeated interference in the proceeding
- Private meetings with one party to the exclusion of others
- Social meetings with parties or witnesses prior to or during the hearing
- A Predetermined view of the issues (although a tentative prior view is acceptable as long as there is an opening for persuasion)

It is important to remember that an appearance of bias or a reasonable apprehension of bias (where a reasonable person would suspect that a member may be influenced by improper considerations to favour one party over another) will likely be sufficient for a court to find bias. Therefore, if a member of an agency board hearing a case believes there may be a possible bias situation, it is best if the member abstains from the decision or, possibly, disqualifies himself from the proceeding. Once that is done, an unbiased member or unbiased panel can be put in place. It should also be noted that certain agencies are, under statute, biased, such as labour arbitration boards with members drawn from management and labour.

Improperly Fettering Discretion

Agencies, in most circumstances, as previously noted, are given wide discretion in such areas as the responsibility to apply rules to each situation as it arises, as long as the agency is fair. Other areas of discretion include determining whether a specific situation is covered by the legislation, which action is warranted, and considerations of public policy applied to specific situations.

An agency must funnel all of its decisions through the obligation to promote the objects of its enabling legislation. If an agency exercises its discretion arbitrarily or dishonestly, the courts may rule that the agency is acting in bad faith and that, therefore, the actions of the agency are reviewable. Bad faith, however, must be proven. Indicators of bad faith, such as discriminating against a specific person for different treatment, or making a decision based on an improper purpose or irrelevant considerations, would go a long way in proving bad faith.

The most likely example of improper fettering of discretion is the application, by an agency, of *stare decisis*, or standing by precedent. Most agencies keep accessible copies of decisions, and it is quite common for appropriate and, sometimes, inappropriate decisions to be submitted to an agency. If the agency bases its decision solely or predominately on a prior decision without proper regard to the actual case before it, a court would likely determine that there has been improper fettering of its discretion. Although consistency is desirable, it is not an all-encompassing obligation for an agency as it is in the judicial branch of government. Further, there are ways to make a decision without making it obvious that *stare decisis* was used.

Not only is it inappropriate to improperly fetter discretion, it is also wrong to not exercise discretion that is conferred on an agency. In the right circumstances, to be discussed in the following section on judicial review, such agency can be compelled to exercise its discretion.

REMEDIES AVAILABLE IF A DECISION OF AN AGENCY IS NOT SATISFACTORY

Once an agency has made a decision, the parties should comply. There are legal mechanisms available to try to ensure compliance. However, depending on certain circumstances, especially when permitted to do so by legislation, a party may be able to have the decision

* reconsidered,
* appealed, or
* reviewed

by making an application of judicial review. Reconsideration involves an agency revisiting a case, after the agency made a decision to look at the case again because of a request to do so. An appeal is requested to allow an appellate body, either an appellate agency or a court, to reconsider the result on the merits of a case because the decision may be "wrong". An application for judicial review is made because there is some question not of the results but of the rules and procedures used to achieve such result. To better understand these options or alternatives that can be exercised, each shall be discussed in turn.

Reconsideration

Under either its enabling Act or some other general legislation, such as the *Statutory Powers Procedure Act*, some agencies are given the power to review or reconsider the decision made and to change it, if appropriate. An example of a reconsideration involving an agency would be the case of an applicant for some type of financial assistance benefits in respect of vocational rehabilitation, who has applied for a hearing with the Social Assistance Review Board. If SARB has made a decision to refuse benefits, the party who was denied has the option to request a reconsideration by SARB, to appeal the decision to court, or to apply for judicial review. In choosing the appropriate option, it is important for the party to assess the reasons for its attempt to have the decision reversed. If the party does not like the decision, but does not have any new evidence or cannot point to errors made by SARB, the party should not take any action. However, if the party has evidence of such errors as relevant evidence not considered, bias, unfair treatment by non-adherence to appropriate procedures, or mistakes of law or fact, the party should select the appropriate option. If a ground such as new evidence exists, it would be best for the party in this example to request a reconsideration. Factors making this the best option include the expeditiousness and the cost of a reconsideration being overwhelmingly more in favour of the party than either of the other options. In other words, it will happen much sooner and costs much less. The appropriate legislation will state the scope of a reconsideration, if any.

Appeal

The second option available to the party in the example would be to appeal the decision. In respect of a decision of SARB, the appeal goes to Ontario Divisional Court. In order to determine if any appeal rights exist against the decision of any agency, either the enabling Act or other appropriate legislation must be consulted. If there are no appeal rights explicitly granted, in respect of an agency's decision, in the legislation, no appeal can be made. Note that the legislation could designate a court, as in the example, or another agency to hear the appeal. For example, decisions from the Workplace Safety and Insurance Board are appealed to the Workplace Safety and Insurance Appeals Tribunal. The following matters in respect of appeals need to be discussed.

Status (Who May Appeal?)

As will be seen in most of the discussion of appeals, one must first and always look at the legislation to determine who can appeal. If the Act states that only a "party" may appeal, or is silent on the matter, then only a party to a proceeding can appeal. However, the legislation could be broader and give status to appeal to such persons as intervenors or, even, some members of the general public. This can be achieved by the use of such phrases as "adversely affected", "aggrieved person" or, even, "interested party". The appellate body has the right to determine if the "appellant" is allowed to appeal under the words of the legislation. Although somewhat unusual because of the possible appearance of bias, some Acts allow the agency to be an appellant.

Scope of Appeal

The scope of appeal, or the grounds upon which an appeal can be heard, is set out in the statute. Such grounds can be that the agency made errors on questions of jurisdiction, law or fact, or some combination of such grounds. In brief, the following points are raised:

- A question of jurisdiction relates to whether the agency did not have the power to hear the case or, if initially having such power, commits some act to lose or exceed such power. Actions taken outside jurisdiction are **ultra vires** (outside the power) and may be rendered null and void.

- A question of law relates to the interpretation and application of the law to the facts of a specific case. Although this appears to be a clear position, there has been much blurring of whether a suggested error is a question of law, fact, or jurisdiction.

- A Question of fact relates to the facts as found or determined by the adjudicator, usually after the perusal of the submissions of witnesses and physical and documentary evidence.

Some case law suggests it is an error of jurisdiction to make a decision where there is a total lack of evidence. Usually issues related to evidence are considered questions of fact. However, if necessary (where an appellate body wants to have the right to grant an appeal even though the Act limits appeals to questions of jurisdiction), it has been decided in some cases to call it an error of jurisdiction. The question of alleged errors and their categorization is even more important for judicial review and shall be discussed further below.

Type of Appeal

Depending on the statute, the appellate body could hear the appeal in a number of ways:

- A hearing *de novo* (a new hearing), where the appellate body would act as a new adjudicator and rehear the matter without any reference to the decision appealed. The parties would be able to submit any and all evidence to support their positions.

- A new hearing where the appellate body has the right to look at and, even, defer somewhat to the decision appealed from.

- Review of a record of the agency that arrived at the decision, without oral hearing of arguments by the party or parties, regarding errors made by the agency that appear on the record. This method is most often used in appeals from a court decision.

Further, the error must be appealable pursuant to the statute granting the appeal rights. In this way of appeal, the agency is required to produce a record that will usually include the following documents: (a) specific decision under appeal, (b) any interlocutory or interim orders, (c) the reasons for the decision, (d) the notice for the original adjudication from which the decision arose, (e) all documentary evidence and (f) the transcript of the proceedings. The first means of appeal is the broadest and, in effect, puts the appellate body in the position of a body hearing the matter for the first time.

The method of appeal will have a direct relationship to the powers of the appellate body to make a decision. If the first way is the type required by statute, the appellate body's decision will replace that of the original agency decision-maker. However, the other ways, especially the third one, will likely mean a return to the agency for a new hearing, although before a new adjudicator(s). To ensure that the new adjudicator does not make the same mistakes, the appellate body may be able to provide directions along with the order for a new hearing.

General Concerns Regarding Appeals

Items such as notice of appeal, leave to appeal (where required), and stay of an agency decision during the process of appeal are all detailed in the enabling Act or other relevant legislation. Normally, rules about the time to file and where to file an appeal are strictly enforced. There is, however, the ability in most circumstances to exercise discretion to extend the time where it would be fair to do so. If leave to appeal is required, a *prima facie* case must be made by the possible appellant of the substance of the arguments supporting the requested appeal. The general position on stays (or holding in abeyance) is that an application for a stay before the appellate body must be granted if the decision has been appealed. Normally, the agency's decision is effective immediately, even if an appeal has been launched; but the appellate body, if granted such power, can order a stay until the decision is made on the appeal.

Two further points should be made about appeals and how they relate to applications for judicial review. First, it is usually better, if the grounds allow it, to launch an appeal rather than make application for judicial review. The powers of the appellate body to possibly hear the case anew and consider the merits of the decision are almost always wider than the reviewing court's power. Second, if the application for judicial review is made while appeal rights exist but have not been explored, the court will almost invariably refuse to hear the application until all appeal rights have been exhausted.

Judicial Review

The third way that a decision of an agency can be challenged is by an application for judicial review. Such application was formerly by the mechanism of a prerogative writ. This method is still available, but other mechanisms now exist to provide similar review. This method shall be considered in detail, including (a) specific remedies available, (b) the grounds for the types of review, (c) statutory provisions to try to limit or even prevent review, and (d) other specific concerns.

Prerogative Writs

Prerogative writs were the mechanisms developed over the centuries by English common law to control arbitrary government action. Initially, they were orders issued by the Crown to oversee and direct the actions of its underlings. Over time, issuance of these writs was transferred to superior courts and became part of their inherent jurisdiction to supervise governmental decisions.

As these writs can be granted on a discretionary basis (similar to equitable remedies), there are certain situations where the court will usually refuse to grant such remedy. As previously discussed, if there is another valid remedy available, such as appeal, the court will likely not grant the application. Another reason to exercise the discretion not to grant a writ is that such grant would be ineffective because it was academic or useless. Other situations where the writ may be refused include where the party objecting and bringing the application has

1. waived or acquiesced knowingly in the agency's error;
2. taken too long to seek this remedy (*laches*); or
3. by his conduct, such as bad faith, become disentitled to review (**clean hands doctrine**).

Generally, the court requires that the applicant for a writ be a person who has a sufficient interest in the proceeding. The application is brought against an agency who, depending on circumstances, may be able to participate actively in the court review, or may only be a neutral friend of the court.

The five prerogative writs still in use, to varying degrees, are *certiorari*, prohibition, *mandamus*, *quo warranto* and *habeas corpus*. Following is a discussion of each of these writs:

□ *CERTIORARI*

This writ allows the court to quash (basically, stop or nullify) a final decision of an agency on certain grounds, usually errors of jurisdiction made by the agency. Originally part of the superior court's inherent jurisdiction to supervise inferior courts, it was extended over the years to include certain supervisory powers over agencies. It can only be applied once the agency has made the improper decision, and not before that time. Historically, *certiorari* was available if an agency acted judicially or quasi-judicially; however, recent cases have decided that it can also be used to quash decisions of agencies acting administratively. Limitations to the use of this writ include its non-applicability to legislative decisions or delegated legislation or the Crown itself (except for certain situations). However, the writ does apply to public bodies whose power is granted by legislation.

☐ PROHIBITION

Prohibition is essentially the same as *certiorari* in terms of history and its limitations, except that it can be applied for at any stage prior to the making of the final decision. It is used, therefore, to try to prevent something from being done outside the jurisdiction of the decision-maker before the ultimate order or award is made.

☐ MANDAMUS

An application for *mandamus*, if granted, will result in an order by the court to compel an agency to perform a statutorily required duty where the agency has refused to do its duty. If the power an agency is refusing to exercise is discretionary, *mandamus* would likely issue — but only to require such agency to exercise the discretion, not to dictate the way it must be exercised. In order to use this writ the following circumstances must exist:

- The applicant must have status to apply; in this situation, there must be a public duty to act owed by an agency to the applicant.
- An explicit demand has been made to such agency that it act, and there has been a refusal to do so.
- As with all prerogative writs, it does not apply against the Crown or its agents when not acting under a statutory duty.

☐ *QUO WARRANTO*

Rarely applied for, this writ, if granted, will state that a person has no right to hold a public office. It is of little relevance to agency proceedings.

☐ HABEAS CORPUS

This writ, which is centuries old, is used to quash an illegal detention of the applicant. Only the detained persons or someone acting on their behalf can make application. The grounds for granting the writ relate to errors of law or jurisdiction.

Statutory Applications in the Nature of Judicial Review

☐ PROVINCIAL (ONTARIO AND ALBERTA)

Most provinces have legislation to provide potential applicants with an alternative to requesting one of the prerogative writs against provincial agencies. In fact, some of the provinces, including Ontario, have, in effect, abolished some of the prerogative writs. The Ontario statute that accomplishes that task is the *Judicial Review Procedure Act*[12] (the JRPA), specifically section 7, which turns applications for *mandamus*, prohibition, and *certiorari* into an application under the JRPA. The intent of the legislation was to make such applications a summary proceeding with fairly consistent procedures that should be heard by the Ontario Divisional Court. Under section 2(1)(1), an application is made by way of an originating notice to request an order in the nature of *mandamus*, prohibition, and *certiorari*. That provision means that all the law developed under those three specified remedies is still important. The JRPA, in section 2(1)(2), also puts into summary form two kinds of private law remedies (to be discussed later) historically available to applicants. Under the clause, the applicant can request a declaration or an injunction, or both

---

[12] *Judicial Review Procedure Act*, R.S.O. 1990, c. J.1.

remedies, in relation to the exercise or purported exercise of a statutory power of decision. "Statutory power of decision" is defined as the power conferred on an agency by a statute to make a decision affecting the rights, duties or powers of any person, or the eligibility of a person to receive a licence or benefit. Note that the application in replacement of the three prerogative writs is not restricted to the exercise of statutory power. Detailed rules of procedure in respect of the JRPA are set out in the Ontario *Rules of Civil Procedure*. Also note that the definition of "party" includes some groups that are not persons at law and, therefore, likely did not previously have standing to bring an application for a prerogative writ. Alberta has very similar legislation to the Ontario legislation discussed in this paragraph.

□ FEDERAL

In making application in the nature of any of the prerogative writs against an agency under federal jurisdiction, the *Federal Court Act*[13] (the FCA) states that all such applications are in the exclusive jurisdiction of the Federal Court, Trial Division. An exception to this provision provides for applications in respect of 15 specified federal agencies to be in the exclusive jurisdiction of the Federal Court of Appeal. The application for judicial review, so called, is made pursuant to the rules and procedures of section 18.1 of the FCA. As in the JRPA, such applications are meant to be heard in a summary fashion. The section further gives extensive powers to the court to order all the types of relief that could be granted under the prerogative writs, if any of the enumerated errors exists. When the FCA was first enacted, certain wordings allowed for an application for judicial review only if the agency was acting in a judicial or quasi-judicial manner. This led to many cases where the issue was not whether there was an error that could be reviewed, but whether the agency was exercising a judicial or quasi-judicial jurisdiction. Recognizing this problem, the legislators amended the FCA, effective in 1992, to remove the distinction between judicial or quasi-judicial jurisdiction.

Remedies under Private Law

Relief may also exist pursuant to common law and/or equitable remedies awarded through an ordinary action. Specifically, one could simply sue the agency in tort, likely for some form of negligence, although some intentional torts could also support the action. In this situation the claimant alleges that an agency has either committed some intentionally improper action that interferes with that person (intentional tort), or is careless in performing some action that causes damage to the person to whom such agency owes a duty of care (negligence). In order for an action in tort to succeed, the action complained of must be illegal or **ultra vires**. A review of the case law indicates that the court will likely find agencies liable if the elements of the specific tort can be proven. However, the courts have also recognized the need for flexibility for agencies to effectively function. It should also be noted that, historically, there was a limit to which parties could be sued due to "Crown immunity", which basically prevented a person from bringing a tort action against the Crown in an official capacity. Federal and provincial legislation has effectively brought Crown immunity, in most circumstances in this instance, to an end — although strict time limits have been imposed to restrict somewhat the right of action. There is much more material to be discussed about tortious actions that can be brought against agencies, but that is outside the scope of this chapter; however, the relief that can be granted in consequence of a successful action in tort can include the following:

---

[13] *Federal Court Act*, R.S.C. 1985, c. F-7.

☐ DECLARATORY RELIEF

This discretionary relief (also known as declaratory judgment or declaration) is a non-coercive judgment of the court setting out the legal positions of the parties and/or the law applicable to them. Although not binding, since there is no legal way to enforce such a judgment, declarations have become an accepted way for a person to have a court determine if an agency had the power to take certain actions. It is also a very flexible remedy, with few technical requirements to be followed, and can be used in a number of ways. The courts have normally issued declarations against agencies as part of their supervisory function in respect of the legality of some governmental actions. Remember that a declaration can be obtained in summary fashion under the FCA and, with limitations in respect of an exercise of statutory power, under the JRPA.

☐ INJUNCTION

An injunction is a discretionary equitable remedy in which the court can order a party to act or refrain from acting in a certain way, and if there is non-compliance a party would be liable for contempt of court. There are two main types of injunctions, both of which have been used against agencies after a successful tortious action. One type is a mandatory injunction, somewhat similar to *mandamus*, to compel an agency to act in a lawful manner. The other type is a prohibitory injunction, somewhat similar to prohibition, to restrain an agency that acts, or even threatens to act, in an illegal fashion. Further, injunctions are available on an interim basis, without a full-blown trial and, possibly, without notice to the other side. An interim injunction will enjoin an agency until such time as the cause of action is tried and, possibly, a permanent injunction is granted. Standing to bring an action for an injunction, along with Crown immunity issues, must be addressed before an injunction can be successfully obtained. Also, in a similar way to declaratory relief, injunctive relief can be granted under both the FCA, for federal agencies, and under the JRPA, for Ontario agencies.

☐ DAMAGES

In any successful action for tort the court has the obligation to award the common law remedy of damages to compensate the victim for certain types of loss or injury suffered as result of the tort. Once the amount (or quantum) of damages is proven on the balance of probabilities to the court's satisfaction, the court will order the **tortfeasor** to pay such damages. Not only will the innocent party be compensated for losses suffered through no fault of such party, but liability for damages may act as a deterrence to the wrongdoer. The potential for deterrence can clearly be seen in the ability of the court to award punitive or exemplary damages in circumstances where an agency has acted maliciously. These principles in respect of damages have been accepted if a tort action has been successful against an agency. One issue still open for resolution is whether a purely economic loss is compensable. As in the other two private remedies examined above, items such as standing and Crown immunity may be relevant. There is no provision for a summary award of damages in either the FCA or the JRPA.

Although in some jurisdictions it is possible to apply for one or more prerogative writs, to apply for statutory judicial review, and to commence a private law action for one or more of the private law remedies, most persons will likely only make application under the appropriate statute. An application is made in a summary fashion and is, therefore, less costly and more expedient and provides grounds, in most circumstances, at least as broad as the other remedies. Although a discussion of grounds for judicial review can be overwhelming, the following are some concepts to remember.

Grounds for Judicial Review

As previously mentioned, the grounds for most appeals of agency decisions usually relate to the merits or the result of the decision by questioning the findings of fact by the adjudicator. Typically, the grounds for judicial review relate to how the result was achieved and are likely determined by looking for jurisdictional or legal errors made. It is possible that a resourceful court can make what appears to be a possible question of fact into a question of law; however, the grounds for judicial review tend to be very narrow. A vast amount of case law exists on the sole issue of whether an alleged error of an agency is reviewable, but an analysis of the law is beyond the scope of this chapter. However, certain principles can be canvassed.

The major focus of determining proper grounds for judicial review revolves around the statutory power of an agency to take a particular action. Usually the court must determine if the statutory power exists or, if it does exist, whether an agency has either exceeded or has somehow lost its statutory power. This is a search to discover the jurisdiction of the agency. It can also be classified as a question of law because if an agency took an action without the statutory power or the jurisdiction to do so, such action is declared illegal. Determining jurisdiction often requires the reviewing court to interpret appropriate legislation to determine exactly what is an agency's jurisdiction.

As an agency is a creation of its enabling Act and other relevant legislation, understanding the words of all of such legislation is usually the first step the court takes to determine whether an agency has acquired the appropriate jurisdiction. Other initial issues may include whether the agency is validly constituted — that is, has proper appointment and delegation — and whether there has been compliance with all preliminary matters, such as proper notice. Any or all of these issues may be examined in order for the court to determine if the agency has acquired jurisdiction.

If the jurisdiction is properly acquired, an agency's actions can still be reviewed if it exceeds or loses its jurisdiction. Broadly speaking, an agency can exceed or lose jurisdiction in three ways: (a) abuse of discretion, (b) noncompliance with the duty to be fair, and (c) bias. (Refer to material detailed earlier in this chapter for a more comprehensive discussion.) Certain concepts regarding each of the three ways jurisdiction can be lost now follow.

Abuse of discretion can include actions such as the following:

- Exercising a discretionary power in bad faith for improper or irrelevant considerations
- Making a decision with no evidence whatsoever or by ignoring relevant evidence
- Using discretion to obtain an improper result because it is discriminatory or unreasonable, or is made based on a misunderstanding of the law
- Improperly fettering or restricting the exercise of discretion

Notice how an evidentiary problem, which is normally a question of fact, can become an abuse of discretion issue. A reviewing court can find that because there is no evidence to support the exercise of discretion, an agency has lost its jurisdiction and, therefore, the decision is reviewable.

The origins of procedural fairness, or the duty of an agency to be fair to parties before it, derive from the rules of natural justice. These rules of natural justice, developed over the centuries to try to ensure that a party was treated fairly, were initially reserved for agencies acting in a judicial or quasi-judicial manner. The need to characterize the function of an agency was all-important because if an agency was acting in a legislative or executive manner, the rules of natural justice were likely not applicable. However, in most but not all situations, it is no longer relevant to characterize function, since an agency is required to act fairly in most of its functions. The determination of whether an agency has acted fairly is based upon whether the rules flowing from the duty to act fairly, as stated earlier in this chapter, have been followed. Such rules of natural justice are basically the same rules derived from the duty to be fair. Remember that how closely any such rule must be followed is dependent on fairness to the persons involved in the proceeding.

The loss of jurisdiction due to the bias of an agency also derives from the duty to be fair. Various types of bias in respect of agencies are discussed elsewhere in this chapter. It is important to note the problem of whether bias should be judged by the strict objective test used in courts, or by a more subjective standard for agencies that need to consider public policy in coming to decisions. Such public policy obligations may make the actions of an agency appear biased to a party. Many agency members have criticized the courts in going too far to make agency proceedings appear like court proceedings. Different considerations often apply between agencies and courts.

A further ground for review, specifically for an application for an order of, or in the nature of, *certiorari*, is an error on the face of the record. These are errors of law and not jurisdictional errors. The errors are clear and obvious when the record of the proceeding is read; such errors allow the court to quash a decision of an agency. An example of an error of law is an agency incorrectly interpreting and/or applying a statutory provision other than its own enabling legislation. Numerous recent cases have tried to place limitations on which errors of law on the face of the record are quashable by positing tests to be followed. These tests arose to try to deal with "privative clauses", discussed next. The most important test suggests that errors of law that are "patently unreasonable" are errors of jurisdiction and, therefore, reviewable even with a privative clause. This test has been used, and possibly misused, in numerous court decisions to try to determine the ambit of judicial review by way of *certiorari*. Such cases have made it difficult to state a consistent principle to be applied, other than that the test is important in this area, mostly as a way around a privative clause.

Privative Clauses

A privative clause is a statutory provision intended to prevent, or at least limit, the right of the judiciary to hear judicial review applications or even appeals. The legislature's intent in using such a clause derives from a concern that the courts have intervened too readily and in areas better left to an agency's expertise and streamlined procedure. No matter what the specific wording of a privative clause is, it will not prevent a court from reviewing an agency's action based on a jurisdictional error. Therefore, a privative clause will be of use only where there is an error of law on the face of the record. The three common general types of privative clauses in use are as follows:

1. A final and binding clause, or similar wording, that means there is no appeal from an agency's decision, but that still allows the court to determine whether any jurisdictional errors exist if the decision is patently unreasonable.

2. An exclusive jurisdiction clause to the effect that only an agency has exclusive jurisdiction to determine certain matters. This clause has the same basic effect as in item 1.

3. A clause that prevents any application for any prerogative writ or declaration. Again, this clause has the same basic effect as in item 1.

There has been much discussion about whether an agency's decision should be reviewable by the courts and, if so, what the appropriate limits are, if any, to such review. This is yet another issue that threatens to go totally unanswered in the near, and possibly distant, future. There are still other concerns that are usually considered under judicial review.

Other Concerns in Judicial Review

There are always time limits, invariably short, within which to apply for judicial review. Such time limits often are strictly enforced, although there is often some discretion, based on fairness, to extend the time. The time is usually found in the enabling legislation or any rules pursuant to it. A stay of an agency decision is not automatically in place upon making an application for judicial review. It must be specifically and separately applied for to the appropriate court, which must be convinced of the efficacy of granting a stay. The hearing is a review, and not a new hearing, which is why the record, as discussed previously, is so important. This is an absolute necessity where the review application is based on an error on the face of the record. Problems occur in this area when the agency does not have much in the way of transcripts. Usually the winner in an application for judicial review will have costs awarded in its favour.

POSSIBLE TRENDS IN ADMINISTRATIVE LAW IN CANADA

There is a fair amount of tension between those who believe that agencies should have comparative freedom from the courts and those who want agencies to follow many rules and procedures as overseen by courts. On one hand, there is the obligation on agencies to follow and, even, develop public policy, which is or may be foreign to the court's perspective of individual rights. On the other hand, there is the court's traditional role to ensure justice is done and seen to be done. There is a need for the expertise and cost-effectiveness of agencies, but should it be at the expense of fairness to a specific person? There have been relatively recent examples of methods to try to find new ways to resolve issues even before they get to an agency hearing, let alone to court. One example is the use of mediation in some situations before the WSIB. There have been attempts to have a different forum for review than the court, as in the use in a number of provinces of an ombudsperson. This governmental, yet independent, official has the power to scrutinize governmental abuses affecting members of the public. Such investigation includes not only how the result was achieved but the merits of the result. In England, a Council of Tribunals was created to review and approve all rules and procedures adopted by agencies. Such a comprehensive and considered approach to ensure fair rules may mean less need for parties to appear before the court suggesting an unfair rule. Even if some or all of the steps discussed in this paragraph are taken, the cases will still be forthcoming. There are just too many concerns still debated to foresee an early end to the tension.

CHAPTER SUMMARY

In this chapter, the reader discovered a definition of administrative law that led into a discussion of the three branches of government. After a summary review of public policy, the essential characteristics of agencies were introduced.

Specifically, agencies were seen as creations of government that, if empowered to do so, can exercise many of the same functions of any or all of the three branches of government. Various types of agencies and a comparison between agencies and courts followed.

After the concept and uses of agencies were explored, there was a lengthy discussion of the ways to determine what specific rules and procedures are applicable to a specific agency. This discussion included an exploration of such factors as the Ontario *Statutory Powers Procedure Act*; sections 7, 8, 13 and 14 of the *Charter of Rights and Freedoms*; and the "duty to act fairly". The duty to act fairly was first defined and then broken down into some of its component parts to allow the reader to discover how the common law provides at least some procedural protections to parties involved in an agency proceeding. Other common principles of no bias and not fettering the discretion of the decision-maker were also introduced.

The reader was then introduced to the remedies available if there is a complaint or concern regarding an agency proceeding. The remedies are (a) reconsideration by the same agency, (b) appeal to another agency or to court or both, or (c) judicial review to the courts. Substantial details regarding the requirements, procedure, scope, and type of appeal were discussed. Also reviewed were the remedies available under judicial review: (a) prerogative writs, (b) statutory applications, both federally and in Ontario, and (c) private law remedies of tort, declaratory relief, injunction, and damages.

Finally, there was a discussion of possible future trends in administrative law in Canada.

GLOSSARY OF NEW TERMS AND KEY CONCEPTS

balance of probabilities test	The standard used by the trier of fact in a civil proceeding (the judge or the jury, where appropriate) to determine whether the plaintiff or the defendant has won the case. If the evidence is more in favour of one party, even if just barely, then that party should be awarded the decision in the case.
beyond a reasonable doubt test	The standard used by the trier of fact in a criminal proceeding (judge or the jury, where appropriate) to determine whether the accused is found guilty or not guilty. If there is any reasonable doubt that the accused did not commit the offence charged, there must be a finding of not guilty.
clean hands doctrine	A principle of the law of equity that requires someone seeking to invoke an equitable rule to have conducted herself fairly and honourably in the events leading up to the proceeding, and in the proceeding itself.
enabling legislation (act, statute)	A law that permits a person (which for most purposes includes an individual, a corporation, and an agency) to do something that, prior to the law, the person was not permitted to do.
gazette	The name of a publication issued by both the federal and provincial governments in Canada on a regular basis, containing official notices and announcements and in which regulations made under the authority of a statute are first published.
judicial or quasi-judicial (function, manner, jurisdiction)	The authority or power of a court or a body similar to a court (that is, a body with the power to decide a person's rights) to decide matters before it. The rules of natural justice were historically applied to these bodies as well as to court proceedings. These bodies were different from agencies, whose decisions applying administrative jurisdiction were not subject to the rules of natural justice.
inherent jurisdiction (also statutory jurisdiction)	A power or right that is vested in an authority (agency or court) intrinsically, whereas statutory jurisdiction is a power or right that is vested in an authority derived from legislation.
intervenor	A person who is given status to participate in a proceeding even though the person is not a party to the proceeding.

proclaimed in force	A bill does not come into force (or become a statute) automatically when it is passed; it must first be proclaimed in force — that is, officially recognized as a statute.
promulgate	To publish a law.
rules of natural justice	The procedural standards imposed historically under common law in any proceeding where a party's rights may be affected by a decision-maker.
stare decisis	Latin, meaning "following precedent"; a legal doctrine that says that if a prior case is decided in a higher court in the same jurisdiction and on similar facts, then that prior case decision must be followed by subsequent courts.
tortfeasor	A person who commits a tort (a civil wrong excluding an action in contract).
ultra vires	Latin, meaning "outside (or beyond) the power"; an action or a statute that is determined by the courts to be outside the powers assigned to the legislature that enacted it.

REVIEW QUESTIONS

1. What are the three branches of government in Canada?

2. Describe how public policy becomes law in Canada.

3. Where would you find how an agency was created and the powers granted to it?

4. Discuss at least five reasons an agency may be created.

5. Detail the three types of agencies that can exist.

6. Set out five differences between an agency and a court.

7. What are the seven steps to determine which rules and procedures apply to a specific agency?

8. How does the *Statutory Powers Procedure Act* determine rules and procedures to be applied to an Ontario agency?

9. Discuss how four sections of the *Charter of Rights and Freedoms* are used to imply rules to be used in an agency proceeding.

10. What are the two main components or principles that are derived from the "duty to act fairly"?

11. List and explain the three remedies available if there is a problem or concern arising from an agency proceeding.

12. Set out three types of appeal and the scope of each type of appeal.

13. What are the remedies available when it is determined that judicial review will be allowed?

14. Discuss the grounds that must exist before judicial review may be awarded.

15. What is a privative clause, and how is it used to avoid judicial review?

16. List and discuss three methods in which public policy is derived or developed.

17. In order for notice to meet the requirement of the duty to act fairly, how may it be given in order to achieve its ends?

18. What is the usual burden of proof used by agencies to determine whether a case has been proven?

19. How does an agency deal with "hearsay" evidence before it at a hearing?

20. List three ways in which most agencies can obtain evidence by compulsion.

21. List three types of relief available if a person successfully sues an agency under tort law.

DISCUSSION QUESTIONS

1. Agencies are a better way to determine a person's rights than are the courts. Discuss.

2. If an agency is meant to deal with matters in an expeditious and cost-effective manner and with the expertise developed in the agency, is it worthwhile or even appropriate to allow a court to interfere with an agency's decision?

3. Have the various statutory and common law protections imposed on an agency's proceedings placed enough or too many rules on an agency's proceedings?

4. Should there be so many remedies available to a person who is concerned with an agency proceeding?

5. What changes would you make in Canadian administrative law? Why?

6. Why do the philosophies of some incoming governments lead to an expansion of the numbers and powers of agencies, and some lead to a contraction of the numbers and powers of agencies?

7. Discuss the current and future effects of the *Charter of Rights and Freedom* on agencies.

8. List four indicators of bias in an agency and/or an adjudicating member.

SUGGESTED READINGS

Blake, Sara. *Administrative Law in Canada*, 2d ed. (Toronto, Ont.: Butterworths, 1997).

Brooks, Stephen. *Public Policy in Canada: An Introduction*, 3d ed. (Toronto, Ont.: Oxford University Press, 1998).

Finkelstein, Neil, & Brian M. Rogers, eds. *Recent Developments in Administrative Law* (Toronto, Ont.: Carswell, 1987).

Jones, David, & Anne de Villars. *Principles of Administrative Law*, 2d ed. (Toronto, Ont.: Carswell, 1994).

Law Society of Upper Canada. *Administrative Law: Principles, Practice and Pluralism* (Scarborough, Ont.: Carswell, 1993).

———. *Recent Developments in Administrative Law* (Toronto, Ont.: Department of Continuing Legal Education, 1995).

Macaulay, Robert W., & James L.H. Sprague. *Practice and Procedure before Administrative Tribunals* (Toronto, Ont.: Carswell, 1994).

Moskoff, Franklin R., ed. *Administrative Tribunals: A Practice Handbook for Legal Counsel* (Aurora, Ont.: Canada Law Book Inc., 1989).

Swaigen, John. *Administrative Law: Principles and Advocacy* (Toronto, Ont.: Emond Montgomery Publications Limited, 2005).

WEBSITES

University of Toronto Law Library with Administrative Law links:
<http://www.law-lib.utoronto.ca/resources/topic/admin.htm>

York University Law Library with Administrative Law links:
<http://library.osgoode.yorku.ca/res_web_links_adm.html>

The Canadian Legal Network website, providing links to other sites:
<http://canlaw.net/administrative.htm>

University of Montreal Faculty of Law site with many links to statutes, cases etc.:
<http://www.lexum.umontreal.ca/index-en.html>

Almost every administrative agency has its own website, which usually include the rules and forms used by the agency, a link to its enabling legislation and past decisions made by the agency. Following are a sample of the websites:

Federal agencies
Canadian Radio-television and Telecommunications Commission: <www.crtc.gc.ca>
Immigration and Refugee Board: <www.irb-cisr.gc.ca>
Office of the Commissioner of Review Tribunals CPP/OAS: <www.ocrt-bctr.gc.ca>

Ontario agencies
Workplace Safety and Insurance Board: <www.wsib.on.ca>
Workplace Safety and Insurance Appeal Tribunal: <www.wsiat.on.ca>
Social Benefits Tribunal: <www.sbt.gov.on.ca>
Human Right Tribunal of Ontario: <www.hrto.ca>

Alternative Dispute Resolution

Michele Braniff
MEDIATOR

Learning Objectives

At the conclusion of this chapter, the reader should be able to:

➢ understand the meaning of the term "ADR" and appreciate the differences between the various processes of dispute resolution

➢ understand how ADR processes fit into the legal system

➢ understand the role of an arbitrator and appreciate how an arbitration process would work

➢ critically assess key approaches and strategies for interest-based negotiation

➢ distinguish mediation from arbitration and negotiation models, identify the various factors in the selection of an appropriate model for dispute resolution and the choice of the neutral third party

➢ discuss roles and responsibilities of parties, counsel, and the mediator

➢ prepare for a role-play to practise interest-based negotiation and a role-play of a mediation

TABLE OF CONTENTS

INTRODUCTION

During the mid- to late-1990s, Canadian legal systems for dispute resolution adapted rapidly from the traditions of the 19th century directly to the technologies and processes for the new millennium. New systems for electronic filing and tracking of court documents facilitated a shift from a court-centred system for dispute resolution to one that relies on a network of innovative and client-centred procedures for early resolution and settlement of disputes.

The acronym **ADR** is commonly applied in Canada and the United States to refer to a variety of methodologies and processes for dispute resolution outside of the courtroom. ADR, or alternative dispute resolution, is an inclusive description, referring to **negotiation**, **mediation**, **arbitration** and a wide variety of hybrid models for dispute resolution. The systems are described as "alternative" because they provide options other than court and litigation; however, these dispute resolution processes are increasingly incorporated into court systems and treated by litigants and their counsel as part of a litigation practice.

Historical Context

Negotiated settlements have historically been part of the litigation system. Over 90 percent of litigated cases would settle without a judicial decision. In the Canadian common law system, like the British system from which it developed, judicial decisions develop out of the consistent application of legal principles based on **precedent**. Canadian business, community, family, and government interaction unfolds in the shadow of a strong civil court system. By and large, often with the assistance of lawyers and other professionals, Canadians can govern their personal and business affairs with a fairly good idea of rights, rules, regulations, and laws. We have a system where people can make agreements that can be relied on and that will be enforced by the courts if necessary. Parties enter into agreements to avoid or to settle disputes.

For hundreds of years, the Canadian law developed through a system where a small proportion of cases would go to trial, but the vast majority would be resolved through a negotiated settlement based on the parties' and their lawyers' best approximation of a judicially determined outcome. Since World War II, the legal system has seen increasing volumes of cases taken to court. A variety of factors are at work, including demographic trends, such as population growth and migration to urban areas; increasingly complex and wider government intervention through statutes and regulations; and more complicated business, government, and social interaction. The litigation system has become more expensive, with longer trial lists.

Increased government intervention has resulted in a proliferation of administrative decision makers in the form of boards and tribunals. These boards are granted statutory powers to administer a wide variety of decisions with respect to labour and employment matters, human rights issues, municipal and land use matters, and insurance and workers' compensation issues. There are limited rights to appeal administrative decisions — usually on the grounds of major misapplication of legal principles or the denial of **natural justice**. Natural justice is the right to hear the other side's case and to cross-examine, defend, and call independent evidence. Administrative tribunals typically have a process much like court but, often, with more relaxed or informal rules of process and with hearings heard by one to three decision makers on the board.

Through the years, statutes have provided for referral of matters to arbitration, either as part of an administrative process or as an alternative to litigation. An arbitration is much like litigation, except that the decision maker, the arbitrator, is most commonly chosen by the parties.

Mediation has perhaps the shortest history as an option to a litigated outcome. Although there are some long-standing traditions of consensus-based and participatory decision making in some Canadian cultures, such as among the Quakers and the North American Indians, mediation began to be more widely available during the 1980s. Community-based mediation projects developed across Canada as a grass-roots response to crimes such as vandalism and neighbourhood scuffles. The first mediation case was a result of the vandalism of some homes in Elmira by a group of boys. This first community mediation was an attempt to provide **restorative justice** through a facilitated meeting between the accused young men and the homeowners who had been vandalized. The concept of restorative justice is one of community equilibrium, accountability, and reparation. Community mediation programs have spread through many cities in Canada, where they operate with trained volunteers to resolve some criminal matters and a wide variety of disputes between neighbours. These programs have helped to create an awareness of and educate the public about mediation and consensus-based processes.

In addition to the grass-roots development of community mediation programs, referral to mediation began to occur with respect to labour and trade union disputes and, also, for family law litigation. Mediation offered a forum for joint problem-solving in an informal setting that moved the parties away from adversarial positions.

Contemporaneously, management studies in business began to encourage more facilitative styles, with emphasis on team development and participatory decision-making processes in the workplace. Workplace decision making evolved from authoritarian, or top–down, models to encompass two-way communication for wider input by staff, consensus-based models for meetings and facilitated approaches to human resources.

Cultural changes were also reflected in advertising and marketing campaigns, which shifted from the hard sell method of buy-what-we-sell and began to embrace the "win/win" approach of listening to the consumer's needs in order to sell what the customer wants. Listening to the customer became a key component in sales and marketing strategies.

By the late 1980s and early 1990s, there was a proliferation, in Canada, of a wide range of models for decision making that included new approaches to negotiation, mediation, facilitative workplace management, and referral of disputes to arbitration and administrative tribunals. These approaches had originally developed on a sector-by-sector basis. The next stage was a consolidation and cross-germination of experience through the recognition of commonalities between the various methodologies and sectors. Practitioners and trainers founded networks and organizations and began to describe themselves as a multidisciplinary profession working in the common field of ADR. A growing backlog of cases in the court systems increased willingness of lawyers and litigators to resort to the more quickly available dispute resolution alternatives of mediation and arbitration. American experimentation with and development of ADR is probably 10 to 20 years ahead of the Canadian experience, and the availability of literature, professional training, and testimonials from the United States accelerated Canadian interest in ADR.

Professional organizations for mediators and arbitrators, at provincial, national, and international levels, have consolidated the interests and presence of ADR practitioners through the development and widespread adoption of codes of ethics and standards for practice and training. ADR is not regulated as a profession by the government or by any professional body; however, organizations such as the Arbitration and Mediation Institute of Ontario and the Ontario Association of Family Mediators have designations for recognition of training and experience that help to define a standard of qualification for their professional members. Many ADR practitioners are professionals

EXHIBIT 25.1

Conflict Resolution Network Canada

Conflict Resolution Network Canada is Canada's largest broad-based conflict resolution organization. It is a national organization and has been active for over 20 years in engaging people in peaceful processes to help build safe and healthy families, communities and workplaces. CR Network Canada describes its promotion of conflict resolution activities as focusing on five strategies: supporting conflict resolution education; encouraging innovation; promoting excellence in conflict resolution practice; influencing public policy; and supporting Canada's international role as a leader for peace and conflict resolution.

The Network has studied the evolution of training activities in Canada and reports tremendous growth in the number of trainers and training organizations in every province and territory in Canada, particularly British Columbia, Saskatchewan, New Brunswick, Newfoundland, and Ontario. In 1988, the Network studied ADR training opportunities and listed 10 to 15 trainers, 2 to 3 associations and organizations, and 4 or 5 academic institutions. In June 1999, the Network's database included over 75 sources of training. The Network estimates that in Ontario alone approximately 2,500 students and 1,500 professionals enrol each year in conflict resolution training. The CR Network Canada website lists 187 private and public institutions offering conflict resolution courses. Prior to 1992, universities and colleges were only marginally involved in ADR training but more recently are designing courses for certificate and both undergraduate and graduate degrees in conflict resolution through faculties of law, social work, education, and environmental studies. The Network reported that in 1999, it was dealing with 38 publishers who produce texts, instruction manuals or other resources in conflict resolution. Most recently, CR Network Canada has partnered with the National Film Board of Canada. The CR Network Canada online bookstore offers over 300 titles about conflict resolution.

The fastest growing fields for ADR training have been identified by the Network as follows: divorce and separation, landlord/tenant, small claims, public policy disputes, victim/offender, restorative justice, land use, environment, workplace, employment, community or neighbourhood disputes, consumer complaints, and insurance.

Source: *The Network: Interaction for Conflict Resolution*, unpublished file data, June 1999; Conflict Resolution Network Canada website: <www.crnetwork.ca>.

---

qualified and regulated as lawyers, social workers or accountants. For example, the Law Society of Upper Canada, the governing body for lawyers in Ontario, has amended its Code of Ethics to deal with issues facing lawyers in the role of mediator. Conferences and professional and trade publications about ADR have also had a role in developing understanding and innovation for ADR processes and strategies.

The most recent development in the ADR field has been its transition from an alternative to litigation to a part of the litigation system. The professionalization of the field has given ADR credibility. Attorney Generals in the various provinces have been faced with relatively little funding for civil litigation and growing dissatisfaction with inefficient court processes. The less formal, faster and more flexible processes of ADR promise a cost-effective way to deal with case volume through the early resolution of an increased number of court cases. Administrative boards and tribunals have systemized processes that send disputants to arbitration and mediation prior to scheduling of a board hearing. Technological case management and electronic filing and tracking provide an efficient way to incorporate the more client-centred processes of ADR into court and administrative systems. At the approach of the year 2000, a number of provinces have created pilot projects through which alternative dispute resolution has become a component in the court system.

THE DISPUTE RESOLUTION SPECTRUM

Exploring the Dispute Resolution Spectrum

Alternative dispute resolution is the categorization by process or procedure of a variety of methods for the resolution of disputes. Dispute resolution theory offers a systematic comparison of **dispute resolution** models along a **spectrum**. Factors that vary across the spectrum are formality, control of the process by participants rather than by a third party, and the extent of self-enforcement of the rules of process by the parties. Negotiation is participant-controlled without formal rules of practice; parties negotiate without third-party intervention. Mediation relies on a third party to facilitate communication and to provide some formality of process while parties retain the role of substantive decision making. Arbitration allows the parties to select a third party and to agree in advance with respect to the rules of process but delegates the substantive decision-making power to the neutral third party or arbitrator. Administrative boards and tribunals operate similarly to courts but usually follow less formal and more expedited rules of process and procedure. If parties go to court, the dispute will be resolved according to the court rules of procedure, and decisions will be made by a judge appointed by the court. The parties do not have control over the process or over the substantive decision making.

Each process may also be compared along its own spectrum. Parties may negotiate in a very informal setting or may set an agenda, retain legal counsel or defer aspects of their decisions to mutually agreed on experts, such as an accountant or an architect. Both mediation and arbitration involve intervention by a neutral third party, who is usually chosen by the parties. There is a great deal of flexibility with respect to process, and there are med-arb models for dispute resolution in which the parties agree to a process that begins as a mediation but assigns decision making to the mediator to become an arbitrator in the event of an impasse between the parties. Some parties agree to steps for dispute resolution commencing with referral to mediation and provide for appointment of a different party as arbitrator if the mediation is unsuccessful. Rules of practice in some Canadian jurisdictions include an informal pre-trial settlement conference with a judge that has many similarities to mediation.

The availability of a variety of options means that parties can select a process that is most appropriate to their needs. However, even more fundamentally important than selecting an appropriate process is the need for the parties to understand the process and to match expectations for dispute resolution with the model they have chosen. Selection of the appropriate process requires consideration of a number of aspects of the dispute.

Parties to a dispute often measure the outcome or resolution in terms of one of three dimensions: (1) the extent that each party has accomplished his or her substantive goals: that is, a *task-focused analysis*; (2) the effect or repercussions on the relationship, which is a *relationship-focused assessment* of the process; and (3) comfort of the participants with the cost, timeliness, and manner of resolution, which is an *experiential evaluation* of the process.

By way of illustration, picture a soccer or hockey team. If you measure the team's success by standings and number of wins, you are applying a task-focused analysis. A relationship-focused assessment would define a successful team as one with cohesiveness and a strong team spirit. The experiential evaluation looks at whether the team had fun.

In a negotiation, the parties maintain responsibility to manage the task, the relationship, and the experience. In a mediation, the neutral third party manages the process in a manner responsive to both the relationship and the experience in order to facilitate a comfortable setting for the parties to concentrate their efforts on the task. Increasing levels of formality in arbitration and in the courts put less emphasis on the relationship and increased focus on the task. The experience is subject to application of rules that offers predictability rather than responsiveness and may not facilitate timeliness or cost-efficiency.

The spectrum of dispute resolution can be studied in another context by looking at **power**, **rights**, and **interests** as the three bases for resolving conflict. Power is about using resources to influence or compel compliance by others. Sources of power include physical strength, social status, gender, race, financial status, voting strength, personal charisma, position in an organizational hierarchy. Abuse of power takes the form of physical confrontation or threats, economic sanctions, intimidation. Processes that are power-based include elections, legislation, strikes, and war, while rights are created and defined by laws, regulations, court decisions, policies, agreements, past practices, customs, or conventions. Rights are the subject of adjudicative tribunals, such as arbitration, administrative tribunals, and the courts. In a democratic process, individual rights are often balanced with democratically elected hierarchies of power. Interests are less tangible and measurable and are often explored by asking about needs, concerns, fears, expectations, priorities, assumptions, goals, hopes, and aspirations. The processes include interest-based negotiation and interest-based mediation. Rights-based processes do not usually explore or attempt to accommodate the interests of the parties.

To return to the game analogy, without any rules in a competitive setting, the game can degenerate into a contest of the biggest and strongest — a game about power. If the players agree to play by recognized rules, however, and perhaps choose a referee to arbitrate or enforce the rules, the game would be rights-based. The game can also be played just for fun, for exercise, or to learn skills rather than to compete with another team. Activity may be skills-focused on drills or a game without score keeping. The application and enforcement of rules can minimize risks of abuse of power and maximize the interests of the players, whether those interests are for a competitive contest, for fun, or for exercise or learning.

If there is potential for abuse of power or the perception of vulnerability to an abuse of power, a rights-based and very formal process is appropriate. Where the interests of the parties are significant, they need to be addressed in the dispute resolution process, and the parties should be wary of committing to a formal process that will largely ignore interests.

Negotiation

Negotiation is an interactive process between two or more parties in which they attempt to reach agreement about an exchange of rights, responsibilities, benefits, and obligations in the form of a sale, a settlement, or other bargain. A careful negotiation prior to a sale or at the beginning of a relationship will often result in agreed-on mechanisms that will prevent or de-escalate conflict in the event of a later dispute. It is important to keep in mind that negotiation occurs at the stages of conflict avoidance as well as in the context of dispute resolution.

Negotiation is the simplest and least formal process, and it is not surprising that its effectiveness and efficiency vary widely. Negotiation is a process that is most vulnerable to an abuse of power. Negotiators may focus on rights or interests or may discuss both, and they often have different negotiation styles based on whether the negotiator focuses on task, relationship, or experiential factors. A relationship-oriented individual may be very vulnerable to making too many substantive concessions when confronted with a task-focused negotiator. Negotiators may fail to appreciate experiential elements and end up making non-sustainable agreements because of pressures caused by time deadlines or by unpleasant interaction.

The effectiveness of negotiation can be improved tremendously when a negotiator develops skills and strategies and adopts evaluation criteria for self-

---

EXHIBIT 25.2	Negotiating Skills and Effectiveness of Lawyers

Gerald Williams, Associate Dean and Professor of Law at Brigham University in Utah, conducted an experiment to study the negotiating skills and effectiveness of lawyers. The experiment involved 40 experienced and practising lawyers from a midwestern city in the United States who were asked to prepare and conduct settlement negotiations with respect to a personal injury case. All lawyers were given identical facts; they were effected by the same insurance laws and provided the same data about comparable jury trials. They were given two weeks to prepare and told that the results of the negotiation exercise would be published. The lawyers were divided into pairs, with one half representing the injured plaintiff and the other half, the defendant insurance company. Tabulation of the results showed a wide range in opening demands and in settlement amounts, with 3 of 14 negotiating groups reporting an impasse or failure to reach settlement. Plaintiff opening demands varied from a low of $32,000 to a high of $675,000. Counsel for defendant made opening offers ranging from $3,000 to $50,000. Negotiated settlements ranged between $15,000 to $95,000, with little pattern or logic between the opening numbers and the final settlement.

Professor Williams takes the view that many lawyers rely on hard-line tactics for negotiation because they lack adequate training in collaborative models of negotiation. Legal practice and culture traditionally are developed out of an adversarial and aggressive style of negotiation. While many law schools now endorse collaborative and interest-based negotiation styles, the academic setting is more conducive to learning styles based on reading and lecture format with limited opportunity for experiential and practical learning. Williams advocates the adaptation of university classes to nurture the environment required to facilitate opportunities for students to practise skills in order to train and develop highly effective negotiators.

Source: Law Society of Upper Canada, *Alternative Dispute Resolution*, 42nd Bar Admission Course, 1999, Day 9–3; Larry C. Farmer & Gerald R. Williams, "The Rigorous Application of Deliberate Practice Methods in Skills Courses", UCLA/IALS Sixth International Clinical Conference Enriching Clinical Education, online: <http://www.law.ucla.edu/docs/farmer_williams-_deliberate_practice_methods.pdf>; Google.com — "Gerald Williams, University of Utah, negotiation".

---

assessment. A key element to successful use of negotiation is the ability to objectively determine when to continue negotiation until finalization of an agreement and when to abandon or adjourn the negotiation to pursue other alternatives, such as another process for dispute resolution.

Mediation

Mediation is a process in which a neutral third party assists two or more parties to reach a voluntary, negotiated settlement of issues in a dispute. Key elements are that participation of parties is voluntary and that the role of the mediator is to provide structure to the process. In practice, there are a variety of different styles, objectives, and mediation models that are applied to provide structure to the mediation process. Factors of influence are the participants' expectations, the nature of the dispute, and the objectives and style of the mediator. The role of the mediator can be very facilitative and client-centred. Alternatively, the mediator may take a less facilitative role. For example, the parties may select a mediator who has expertise in a particular area, and they may seek the mediator's expert opinion on issues in dispute. Retired judges who mediate usually offer a process in which their opinion is an integral element in the mediation.

An important variable is whether the mediation focuses upon rights or interests. Rights are the clearly defined rules, regulations, laws, and contracts that may be the determining factor in some disputes. Interests are the less tangible motivating elements, perhaps arising from the parties' relationship or the needs, goals, expectations, and assumptions of the individuals involved in the dispute.

Mediation may be described as **interest-based**. The mediator encourages the parties to explore interests, develop a large number of options, and assess the options jointly by objective and mutually acceptable criteria. The role of the mediator is to help the parties express to one another their needs and expectations, and to brainstorm for lots of options, searching for a win/win approach that gives each party as much as possible with as little sacrifice or cost to either side.

By way of contrast, **rights-based mediation** focuses on rules, contract interpretation or the law. It is also called **early neutral evaluation**, or **evaluative mediation**. The mediator evaluates the case in the context of rules, such as the law or generally accepted accounting principles. The expertise and credibility of the mediator are extremely important in this model. Labour mediations, for example, are usually rights-based. In Ontario the pretrial conference is an evaluative intervention in that the judge listens informally to the facts and legal aspects of a case and makes a preliminary assessment of his or her view of a likely court decision.

Collaborative Law

In recognition of the impact of process upon family relationships in matrimonial disputes, associations of lawyers, in various cities across Ontario and elsewhere, are working towards a less adversarial approach. Lawyers are forming associations for collaborative law based on a commitment to interest-based negotiations and win/win outcomes. Associations of collaborative lawyers agree to participate in training in interest-based negotiation and to establish a process for negotiation. Collaborative law is based on a four-way agreement between the lawyers and their clients to follow a non-adversarial practice. The website for collaborative law, <www.collaborativelaw.ca>, describes the process as "about cooperation not confrontation" and states that the spouses and the collaborative lawyers all work together as a team:

> The Collaborative Family Law Process uses informal discussions and conferences to settle all issues. In the Collaborative Family Law Process both clients will:
> - treat each other with respect;
> - listen to each others' perspectives, interests and concerns;
> - explore all possible choices;
> - let go of the past in order to focus on the future.

Members regard this collaborative style as very different from trial-based law. In fact, a usual term of agreement is that, if the dispute is not settled and clients subsequently decide to take the matter to court, both of the collaborative lawyers will refer the files to different lawyers for the trial preparation and process.

Arbitration

Arbitration involves the appointment or selection of an independent party to make a decision that will be binding and enforceable upon the parties to a dispute. Parties may agree, or may be required by legislation, to arbitrate with a chosen, or a prescribed, procedure and evidentiary requirements to be followed. In comparison to a mediation or negotiation, an arbitration is quite formal, with a rights-based application of rules and safeguards for natural justice and fairness. In addition to substantive decisions about the merits of the case, the arbitrator will interpret the rules for the arbitration process, including regarding admissibility of evidence, assessment of credibility of witnesses and the onus of proof and weight of evidence, and also the timing and order of the advocate's argument and submissions.

Usually, selection of the arbitrator is based on qualifications or expertise with respect to legal or technical aspects of the case. For example, parties in dispute about payment requirements prescribed by contract for architectural services may appoint a lawyer, an architect or, perhaps, an accountant as the arbitrator. The arbitrator may be appointed with instructions to consider expert evidence and render a decision based on that evidence in a process similar to the consideration of evidence by a judge in court. Alternatively, the parties may agree to a process that leaves more room for the arbitrator to apply his or her own expertise in addition to, or instead of, independent expert opinion from the parties' respective technical witnesses.

Arbitrated decisions are generally private and confidential among the parties, and the reasons of the arbitrator are rarely collected or published. Occasionally, one of the parties seeks judicial review of an arbitrated decision and then, because the facts and reasons of the arbitrator are considered by the court, there is a publication by the court-reporting services as part of the court case. Parties will refer matters to arbitration for a consideration of facts, credibility, an expert application of technical matters or for the application of clear legal principles or interpretation of an agreement. Where there is a new point of law to be determined, matters usually are referred to court.

Other Dispute Resolution Choices

There are also many hybrid and partial models that have developed for the resolution of disputes. Parties may refer certain issues to a fact-finder or to an arbitrator or may agree to a sequence of steps so that negotiation, mediation, and then arbitration are explored prior to taking a matter to court.

There is also legislation that appoints boards and tribunals with jurisdiction to make decisions and that may include referral to a mediator or arbitrator as part of a multi-step procedure.

Application of Process to the Legal System

Referral of matters to ADR takes place in one of four contexts:

1. contractual undertaking to use an ADR process;
2. private sector systems design;
3. systems design for public sector disputes; or
4. court-connected dispute resolution system.

The process, procedure, and expectations of the users vary from one context to another and are dependent on the sector in which the dispute occurs.

ADR by Contract

This is the simplest application of an ADR process. For example, a dispute develops, and the parties attempt to negotiate a settlement. Failing resolution, they may then consider process issues and agree to refer their dispute to mediation, **neutral fact-finding**, or arbitration. The referral to an ADR process will usually be confirmed in writing, and the choice of process, date, selection of mediator or arbitrator, and nature of proceedings will be established by agreement of the parties.

ADR by agreement also occurs as part of a conflict avoidance strategy at the formation of legal relationships during contract negotiations. Many business people and their lawyers are including dispute resolution clauses as a standard form in a commercial contract or as part of matrimonial or other settlements. The dispute resolution clause is a commitment to negotiate, mediate, arbitrate, or to use some combination of ADR process prior to taking the other party to court. The clause may specify the process, selection criteria, or method of selecting a mediator, or it may provide detailed procedures for resolution of any dispute. The purpose of such clauses is to create a mechanism for a speedy and cost-effective way to resolve disputes and to minimize negative impact upon the relationship.

Private Sector Systems Design

Business and non-profit organizations may create a policy for employees, staff, or clients that encompasses an ADR procedure in the event of disagreement. Unionized work environments often have legislative remedies available for collective agreement disagreements, negotiation breakdowns, or grievances. An in-house procedure must comply with, and may be complementary to, collective agreement and legislative requirements. Increasingly, workplaces are implementing systems on a voluntary basis. For example, most Canadian universities have harassment policies that map out informal avenues for involvement of specialized staff from a human resources or **ombudsman** office to investigate or interview complainants, witnesses, and respondents. Often there are tiers, with first-stage intervention featuring internal avenues, and a mediation model at an intermediary stage culminating in a more formal hearing process, often including some right of appeal.

As business, academic and non-profit organizations move into more decentralized and team-based structures, their needs increase for flexible, time-sensitive, and informal options for dispute resolution. In simpler and slower-paced times, many organizations coped well with de facto organizational response. Modern organizations, however, are dealing with re-organization, downsizing, dramatic and fast-paced changes and, perhaps, erosion of morale, trust, or employee loyalty. There is increasing workplace diversity with respect to gender, culture, and demographic differences.

Human resources staff increasingly take on a facilitative role within the workplace and, often, act in the capacity of an in-house mediator. A mediator who is on staff with an organization has knowledge of the culture and expectations of the organization but is usually not directly involved with the group or the department where the dispute or complaint began.

In contrast to an adjudicative model based on defined criteria of eligibility or limited areas of complaint, the new systems are designed to collect employee feedback and suggestions on a proactive basis before a situation escalates. The ADR process is often implemented in conjunction with training, team-building, and interest-based negotiation strategies, and as part of a general implementation of consensus-based decision making. ADR processes are also often implemented in response to concern about power imbalances or deadlocks with rights-based systems. Often the design is based on informal, interest-based processes at commencement with progression to rights-based procedures or adjudication.

Systems Design for Public Sector Disputes

Dispute resolution systems for conflict prevention and management are increasingly being implemented by government ministries, agencies, boards, and commissions for municipal, provincial, and federal matters. The system is implemented by statutes or regulations and may require use of arbitration or mediation or other ADR processes for specific types of disputes between non-government parties or with respect to disputes of private organizations or individuals with government ministries or other offices.

The use of mediation and arbitration for labour matters has been widespread across Canada for decades. Legislation stipulates the procedure for referral of collective agreement and grievance issues to mediation and/or arbitration by independent mediators and arbitrators who are not employed by or affiliated with the Labour Board.

In Ontario, in late 1998 and early 1999, the **Ministry of the Attorney General** created a **Dispute Resolution Office** as a resource for design of dispute resolutions systems; assistance to draft dispute resolution clauses in contracts, agreements, policies and legislation; negotiation and mediation training; and support of government groups committed to ADR. The mandate of the Dispute Resolution Office is to encourage the use of ADR by Ontario government offices and to promote dispute resolution processes as "a cost-effective and more responsive means of resolving disputes." The Ontario Dispute Resolution Office works with the Ministries of Agriculture, Education, Intergovernmental Affairs, Environment, and Attorney General and with the Human Rights Commission and the **Financial Services Commission of Ontario**.

Currently in Ontario, there are dispute resolution systems in a wide variety of government departments, ministries, and boards. For example, the Ontario Municipal Board has implemented a process using former and current Municipal Board members as board mediators who offer a rights-based assessment or opinion, encourage informal discussion and debate between the parties, and provide a mediation report and summary sheet that may formalize terms of settlement or refer the matter to a hearing before another board member. The **Workplace Safety and Insurance Board** has been including mediation as part of its return to work (RTW) solutions since February 4, 1999. Mediation is without charge to the worker. The WSIB website advises that mediations usually take about two to three hours with an appeal to the WSIB Appeals branch if dissatisfied with the resolution. The RTW mediator is on staff with the board and works with the workplace parties to help resolve disputes about the return to work of an injured worker using a rights-based model. If the mediation is not successful, the mediator becomes the decision maker and decides possible penalties or impact on benefits. A mediator's decision may be appealed by the parties to the Workplace Safety and Insurance Board.

These ministry initiatives for ADR are different from the client-centred and facilitative models used when parties voluntarily select an uninvolved third-party neutral because the staff mediator is mandated to follow ministry guidelines and, often, has significant power over the parties, including the right to order a settlement in the event of disagreement.

Court-Connected Dispute Resolution Systems

In the 1980s, rules for civil litigation introduced the **pre-trial conference**, which involved a mandatory meeting between counsel and a judge to discuss the merits of a case and to canvas reasonable terms for settlement. Pre-trials generally were scheduled after a case was on a trial list — that is, after examinations for discovery and completion of motions. The pre-trial judge is not the one who will try the case. The settlement discussions are very rights-based and centred on respect for the pre-trial judge's expertise. Cases settle at pre-trial where issues involve matters of law or rule interpretation rather than issues of fact or credibility. Effectiveness of a pre-trial is usually a product of the quality of preparation and expertise of counsel and of the pre-trial judge.

In contrast, various pilot projects and innovative court programs throughout Canada in the late 1990s began to explore earlier and more client-centred dispute resolution systems. The goal was to design a process that would mandate referral to a mediator early in the litigation; however, systems designers wanted to preserve the voluntary nature of mediation. Cost was also a factor,

ADR for Insurance Cases	EXHIBIT 25.3

The Financial Services Commission of Ontario was evaluated independently by the Honourable George W. Adams, QC, and described in his evaluation report as the largest and most comprehensive dispute resolution system of any Ontario administrative board or commission, and a "pioneer on the cutting edge of dispute resolution best practices". The Dispute Resolution Group (DRG) at the Financial Services Commission of Ontario (FSCO) mediates, arbitrates, and resolves personal injury disputes between consumers and no-fault car insurance companies. The process for dispute resolution is contained in the Ontario *Insurance Act* and in a *Dispute Resolution Practice Code* developed by the commission, which are available online at <http://www.fsco.gov.on.ca/english/insurance/auto/drs/resources.asp>.

Mediation

Mediations are conducted within 60 days of an application being registered with the commission. The mediation is the mandatory first step when a person disputes the insurance company's decision about accident benefits. Mediations are conducted by telephone conference or in person, and each mediator conducts about eight mediations per week. Eighty-one percent of claimants have legal counsel for the mediation. The mediator writes a written report at the conclusion of the mediation, indicating whether or not issues have been settled. In 1998, the FSCO reported that 78 percent of all claims settled some or all issues at the mediation stage.

Arbitration

Where the claim is not settled at mediation, the claimant (but not the insurance company) may go to private arbitration, arbitrate through the FSCO, or proceed to the court system. Once a claimant requests arbitration, the insurance company is permitted to raise its own new issues for arbitration. The first step for an FSCO arbitration hearing is the arbitration pre-hearing meeting, where issues are identified, preliminary matters may be resolved, exchange of productions is arranged, and another attempt is made to mediate a resolution. If the matter is not resolved at the pre-hearing, the arbitrator has discretion to set a future date to resume settlement discussions or may ask for a list of witnesses and set the hearing date. The arbitration is a formal hearing, and the arbitrator provides a written decision. In 1998, 87 percent of cases settled before a written decision was issued.

Neutral Evaluation

Where there has been an application for arbitration and the fee has been paid, on application, issues can be referred to an experienced evaluator. On such an application, arbitration is suspended until the evaluation has been completed. The FSCO provides a non-binding opinion of the likely outcome. If the case is not resolved after neutral evaluation, it is fast-tracked for arbitration. The FSCO arbitrator provides a review of the positions of the parties and assesses the probable range of outcomes. In 1998, FSCO received 142 applications for neutral evaluation, and 75 percent of cases that went to neutral evaluation were resolved at that stage in the proceedings.

Appeals

Either party may appeal the decision of the arbitrator, after the hearing. The appeal is to the Director of Arbitrations or her delegates. Appeals are allowed with respect to issues of law but are not allowed with respect to findings of fact.

Source: *Dispute Resolution at the Financial Services Commission of Ontario*, FSCO Brochure, May 1999; Financial Services Commission of Ontario website: <www.ontarioinsurance.com>.

with policy makers favouring user-pay systems rather than building mediation costs into the operational budget of the whole civil litigation system. Emphasis was upon enhancing interest-based settlement discussions and enhancing the preservation of relationships between parties and a speedy, cost-effective, and informal discussion structure.

There was institutional recognition of the essential differences arising in the context of separation, divorce, and family law disputes. Policy makers were concerned about universality and the need to offer funding subsidies where disputants had inadequate resources to pay the costs of mediation. Second, there was recognition of the impact of power imbalances in domestic settings where physical violence could be a significant factor in dispute resolution. Accordingly, mediation models for family law disputes have developed as part of newly designed family courts with heavy emphasis on mediator qualifications and screening for domestic violence. Mediators are trained to use sophisticated questionnaires and to interview spouses separately in order to more easily identify and screen out families where there is a risk of physical violence. Currently, the court system, often through a combination of civil and criminal remedies and sanctions, is the most effective way to deal with physical intimidation and violence.

In Ontario, the **Unified Family Court** in Hamilton operated for over 10 years as a pilot project with totally subsidized family mediation as an in-house program with staff mediators. There are now 17 family court locations where mediation is available. Government funding is available for mediations conducted at court locations, while funding is user-pay for off-site mediations.

The *Ontario Child and Family Services Act* was amended in 2006 to include a directive obliging Children Aid Societies to consider ADR at any stage in the proceedings. Under the legislation, a judge has power to adjourn a case in order to allow ADR to take place.

The Canadian Bar Association Systems of Justice Implementation Committee's Working Group on Dispute Resolution Standards has proposed *Draft Model Guidelines for Court-Connected Mediation Programs*. The study examines standards for selection of mediators both in the family and non-family sectors and recommends separate rosters and special standards for the family mediators to encompass safeguards and screening for domestic violence. The study also notes programs in British Columbia, Alberta, and Ontario that provide mandatory parent education sessions to give information about family and divorce mediation, and about the impact of separation and divorce on children. The sessions emphasize the importance of effective parental communication in facilitating successful transition by children during the separation and divorce process.

Non-family civil litigation is a different venue for the application of ADR to the mainstream court system. Saskatchewan was the first Canadian jurisdiction to introduce an initial mediation session for parties involved in non-family civil litigation. The program consisted of a short mediation session for orientation and public education. There were settlement discussions in the mandatory session, and parties were able to continue the mediation process through a voluntary referral on a per file basis. Amendments were made to the Saskatchewan *Queen's Bench Act* in March 1994 to introduce the pilot project in Regina and Swift Current. The pilot project was evaluated for Saskatchewan Justice by a private and independent corporation through a series of surveys and interviews. The evaluation report found a high level of client and lawyer satisfaction with the program, and an increased understanding of the case by litigants as a result of the session. Some cases settled at the initial session, and a significant proportion of clients whose cases did not settle reported changing their plans to proceed through ADR after an initial decision to use the court process. Fewer lawyers indicated a change in advice about appropriate venue.

Following small pilot projects in Toronto and Ottawa, Ontario introduced a **Mandatory Mediation** Program on January 4, 1999, in the City of Toronto and the Regional Municipality of Ottawa-Carleton. On December 31, 2002, the program was expanded to Windsor, Ontario. The goal of the program is to

Collaboration	EXHIBIT 25.4

One of the classic illustrations about collaboration is a fable about two mules tethered together and struggling as one pulls east and the other tugs to the west. Both animals are strong. They are prisoners of their resistance and have been locked in the same spot for hours. Finally, the mules stop in exhaustion. Like most of the animals from traditional fables, they are gifted with communication skills more acute than most humans.

The eastern mule exclaims in righteous frustration, "You stupid mule. We are prisoners here and we are starving to death. I want to be able to move! I am hungry!"

The western mule mocks him: "What do you think I am trying to do? Just lift your head and look to the west!"

The eastern mule is impatient: "I cannot imagine why I would want to look or go to the west when there is a huge stack of grain to the east!" But he turns his head and, looking to the west, realizes that there is also a stack of grain to the west!

The mules look silently to the east and to the west and then, nodding knowingly to one another, walk easterly together and eat contentedly and then, move in harmony towards the setting sun, to complete their repast.

provide an accessible and affordable alternative to court processes. The Ministry of the Attorney General website explains:

> Many parties negotiate during the course of litigation. Over 90 percent of all lawsuits settle before getting to the trial stage. Under the Ontario Mandatory Mediation Program, cases are referred to a mediation session early in the litigation process to give parties an opportunity to discuss the issues in dispute. With the assistance of a trained mediator, the parties explore settlement options and may be able to avoid the pretrial and trial process.

The Mandatory Mediation Program has been implemented in Ontario by a revision to the **Ontario Rules of Civil Procedure**, involving a co-operative venture between members of bench, bar, the public, and ministry staff. This collaboration has the potential to become a model for consensus-based government policy reform. It also represents a fundamental shift in the basic tenets of the civil justice system.

An evaluation of the mandatory mediation programs in Toronto and Ottawa submitted to the Civil Rules Committee on March 12, 2001, concluded that the program "demonstrated positive impact on the pace, costs and outcomes of litigation".[1]

The Evaluation of the Ontario Mandatory Mediation Program concluded that

> [m]andatory mediation under the Rule has resulted in significant reductions in the time taken to dispose of cases. Mandatory mediation has resulted in decreased costs to the litigants. Mandatory mediation has resulted in a high proportion of cases (roughly 40% overall) being completely settled earlier in the litigation process — with other benefits being noted in many of the other cases that do not completely settle. In general, litigants and lawyers have expressed considerable satisfaction with the mediation process under Rule 24.1.[2]

---

[1]   Robert G. Hann & Carl Baar, with Lee Axon, Susan Binnie and Fred Zemans, *Evaluation of the Ontario Mandatory Mediation Program (Rule 24.1): Executive Summary and Recommendations* (Toronto, Ont.: Queen's Printer, March 12, 2001), online: <http://www.attorneygeneral.jus.gov.on.ca/english/courts/manmed/execsummary.asp>.

[2]   *Ibid.*

Mandatory mediation has been implemented in the context of **case management**. Case management involves computerization and tracking of court files in order to impose judicial scrutiny with respect to time frames. Historically, the rules have imposed time frames for various stages of litigated proceedings; however, enforcement has been almost non-existent. High volumes of court cases, backlogs and waiting lists for trials, and a non-centralized system requiring one litigant to apply to court to enforce timeliness, plus a cultural expectation of long delays, have mitigated against any viable enforcement mechanisms to keep parties on track. New technologies and high consumer dissatisfaction with the costs and delays of the court provide method and incentive to streamline and fast-track cases for settlement or trial.

Litigants must schedule a mediation session within 90 days from the date when the first **Statement of Defence** is filed. Permission of a **Case Management Master** or judge is required for any extension of time. Parties select a mediator, or, if they fail to do so, a mediator is appointed from a roster of private-sector mediators. Fees are prescribed in the rules on a user-pay basis, with legal aid or other financial relief available through a financial eligibility test available for impecunious litigants. Cases that do not settle during mediation proceed through the traditional path to trial.

Mediators are selected by a **local mediation committee** comprising representatives from the judiciary, lawyers, mediators, members of the public, and the Ministry of the Attorney General. Mediators apply to be considered and will be selected for the roster upon satisfactory demonstration that they have appropriate mediation experience, training, educational or professional background and understanding of the civil justice system.

Case law has developed on procedural points after motions to decide where, when and how the mediation should proceed. Perhaps of greater practical significance than the body of case law is the impact that mediation has had on the legal culture. At the beginning of the pilot project, lawyers would behave in mediation in much the same way as at a trial — often taking charge of the process, orchestrating clients's involvement in the process and limiting input to matters of evidence and seeking to persuade the mediator of their case. As lawyers have worked with the mediation process through its first few years, they have begun to recognize the importance and difference of the role of the client in this informal process.

PROCESS AND PROCEDURE

The ADR options most commonly applied for dispute resolution are negotiation, mediation and arbitration. Each has its own key characteristics with respect to process and procedure, and a range of areas where there is flexibility for parties to modify or customize formalities and expectations.

Negotiation

Negotiation is a very informal process for dispute resolution. The parties retain responsibility and control over the substantive issues in dispute and also with respect to the interaction, agenda and process. Negotiation is as old as language and civilization itself, pre-dating the development of both currency and barter economies. However, in recent years, there has increasingly been a study and focus on effective strategies for negotiation. The concept of **principled negotiation** or **win/win negotiation**[3] has been analyzed and taught in

---

[3] Strategies developed and explored by Roger Fisher, William Ury & Bruce Patton in *Getting to Yes: Negotiating Agreement Without Giving In*, 2d ed. (New York: Penguin Books, 1991).

workshops and books in various forums, including primary schools, sales and marketing seminars, management training courses, and law schools.

The strategy of principled or interest-based negotiation is based on joint problem solving, brainstorming, and creativity. In contrast, **positional bargaining** occurs when parties deliberately take an opening position from which they intend to make marginal concessions. This is the bargaining of the flea market, where the buyer offers $100 for the antique chair ticketed with a price of $250. Positional bargaining can be confrontational or adversarial and is usually measured by attributing success to the party who makes the fewest or least expensive concessions.

In contrast, principled negotiation begins with an inquiry rather than a contest. It is based on listening to the other party rather than on dominating. The strategy is to find out about the underlying interests of each party: what are the assumptions, concerns, fears, hopes, priorities, expectations, values, beliefs? Interest-based negotiators attempt to transcend the task of dividing the pie by redefining it into a bigger pie.

For example, two sisters are fighting over an orange. The choice seems to be to give the orange to one or the other or to cut it in half. The interest-based strategy is to find out why. As it turns out, one sister wants to eat the fruit and the other wants the zest in order to bake a cake. Based on this information, each sister can have everything she wanted from the whole orange if one keeps the fruit and the other, the zest.[4]

Whereas the positional negotiator faces an adversary across a chasm of differences, the principled negotiator looks at the process as a journey rather than a destination. The view from the top of the mountain is very different and problematic when each party is standing at the peak of a different mountain. Building bridges from mountain top to mountain top can be expensive and impractical. The principled negotiator uses listening and active communication skills to travel with the other party from the base of the mountain. The analysis is often symbolically represented by a diagram of two overlapping triangles. (See Exhibit 25.5.) The interests of each party forms the base of the triangle. The party's position is like the peak of a triangle. Metaphorically, the new triangle formed by the overlapping areas is a new set of options for joint decision making — a new mountain to climb together.

The principled negotiator is one who shifts the process from one of persuasion or competition to an inquiry. The first step is to listen to the other person's perspective. The inquiry is most effectively launched with journalistic and **open questions** — Where? How? When? What happened? Parties should be cautious with "why" questions because they often generate a very defensive response. An alternative approach may be to ask what the person expected to happen or what assumptions had been made.

Active listening requires a concentrated response to another person — often through reading facial expression and body language and repeating back what the person has said. For example, in response to a loud and expressive description of the events leading up to a rear-end collision, the listener can acknowledge the emotional and substantive content of the story by words such as the following: "So you are quite angry that the car did not seem to slow down at all before it ran into the back of your vehicle!" Repeating back what has been heard gives the storyteller the opportunity to clarify and correct: "No, I was more stunned and shocked then angry. I did not get angry until I went over to the vehicle to talk to the driver and noticed the strong smell of alcohol."

---

4 *Ibid.* at 73.

| EXHIBIT 25.5 | Negotiation: A Process of Building Bridges |

The interests of the parties to a dispute can be represented by points on a page.

Position "A"

Position "B"

Upon inquiry, the parties discover the underlying interests that have motivated each party to take the positions. They explore hopes, aspirations, concerns, fears, values, priorities, assumptions, values, goals, needs. When parties move away from the black-and-white adversarial world of positions, they discover many shared interests. Interest-based negotiation works with the triangle of shared interests and acknowledges with respect areas of different interest.

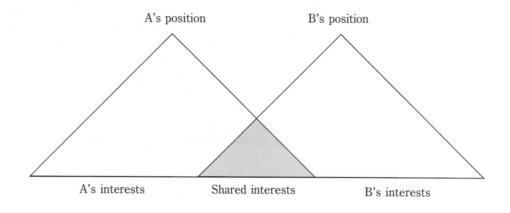

Acknowledgment is an extremely important part of listening. A listener who acknowledges that he or she has heard the other party can set an extremely respectful and courteous tone for interaction. The next step is to seek clarification. In order to minimize misunderstanding, the listener should make no assumptions. Questions of clarification emphasize the inquiring nature of the interaction.

Closed questions and leading questions are more appropriate for a debate or the cross-examination of a courtroom. **Closed questions** invite a "yes" or "no" answer, while leading questions attempt to undermine the other person's credibility or to identify logical weaknesses or inconsistencies in the story. These are techniques more suited to persuasion than to an objective inquiry.

The principled negotiator is hard on the problem but soft on the people.[5] He or she is committed to a process of joint problem solving, and interaction is based on mutual respect and a willingness to show flexibility and adaptability. The process begins with each person listening to the other's story. The next stage is to identify the goals, assumptions, expectations, fears, interests, values, and concerns of those involved. The investigative part of the inquiry provides a foundation of mutual understanding to develop an atmosphere for brainstorming.

---

[5] *Ibid.* at 11.

Brainstorming is non-judgmental and unstructured. Instead of finding *the* solution, parties look for numerous options, all of which are charted or written down. Sometimes a very impractical idea can be a jumping-off point for a simple and elegant option. Parties can emphasize the collaborative nature of the brainstorming idea by using a whiteboard or flip chart, or by sharing paper notes at a round table, or by sitting side by side rather than across from one another.

The next step is to evaluate the options using objective criteria. At this point, the parties can review the list of interests as criteria to measure the various options. For example, in a court environment, the parenting issues facing a separating couple can become a custody battle. Principled negotiation would begin with an inquiry about what the children and the adults need and prefer. The parents would confirm shared values and explore some of the differences in expectation, discipline styles, and work schedules. The list of interests may include the following:

- Quality time with both parents
- Consistency in key expectations for behaviour and responsibility of children
- Time with parents rather than a third party babysitter, where possible
- Assistance with math homework
- Time for creative play
- Getting the children to school on time

As the parties acknowledge shared values, the needs of the children, and the strengths of each parent, there is potential to develop solutions that allow a balance between the two parental households so that the influence and care of the respective parents are complementary. Where one parent bases the day on routine and schedule and the other is a free spirit, they could take positions and may be tempted to attack each other's personal qualities with labels such as "anal retentive" or "completely irresponsible". Alternatively, they could jointly inquire into a way to schedule time and agree on standards in both parents' homes that would encourage following and learning scheduling in one home with an expectation for the child to be self-regulating and responsible for timekeeping at the other home. With shared understanding and common goals, the parents can brainstorm for options and jointly select solutions that build a better nurturing environment. Collaboration makes available resources from both parents that collectively will give the children a richer learning and loving environment than either parent could provide alone.

Interest-based negotiation is a process in which parties commit to a respectful and listening interaction in order to jointly resolve the substantive problem. The principled negotiator recognizes that there is value in accommodating the other's interests. The process tends to happen naturally where parties have a strong and valued relationship. The adversarial process, on the other hand, tends to sweep people into the shadows of their differences. Interaction can be very unpleasant and counter-productive. In contrast, the principled negotiator respects and acknowledges the interests of the other party in the context of joint problem solving.

The essence of the positional bargainer is the caricature of the salesman who could (and would) "sell coal in Newcastle" or "blocks of ice on Baffin Island". Marketing strategies in the 1990s focused on listening to customers and offering ways to satisfy their needs. The market has become more sophisticated as it has evolved from "buy what I sell" to a customer-focused model.

The principled negotiator does not measure success as a contest to be won or lost. The Harvard Negotiation Project developed a measuring standard to plan and assess interest-based negotiated settlements.[6] **BATNA** is the Best Alternative to a Negotiated Agreement. While consumers are usually fairly sophisticated in comparison shopping before they negotiate the purchase of large-ticket items, parties to a dispute often fail to accurately assess their alternatives. For example, a person may want to buy a used vehicle and prefer the colour blue. If she knows that she can buy a grey used car of the same make, model, and relative conditions for $12,000 and have it painted blue at a cost of $2,500, this information can provide a relevant context to measure the success of her negotiation to buy the blue car of her dreams. The salesman may be nice or unpleasant, may make a ridiculous trade-in offer, or may offer to split the difference between his asking price and her best offer. Interaction can be distracting and may make the negotiation process look successful or unsuccessful. Unfortunately, negotiators often measure success by the interaction. However, if our car buyer knows her BATNA, she will not pay a whole lot more than $14,500 to buy the blue used car. She may prefer to buy blue than to arrange for a paint job, but she probably will not be willing to pay an extra $10,000 to buy the blue vehicle.

In the context of dispute resolution, parties often fail to appreciate the full measure of the BATNA. They may also need to look at the **WATNA** — the Worst Alternative to a Negotiated Agreement. The interaction may have costs in the form of timing, delay, legal fees, costs that are usually significant. There may be relationship costs. Before parties come to the negotiation table, they should make a thorough and accurate assessment of the best (and the worst) alternative to a negotiated agreement.

In order to ensure a final and binding settlement, negotiating parties must reach agreement on key points and document their agreement through a binding and enforceable contract.

Mediation

Mediation is a dispute resolution process in which the parties invite a mutually agreed upon third party or mediator to take responsibility for the interaction. The mediator looks after the process, often establishing and enforcing **ground rules** for courteous and respectful behaviour, taking charge of the agenda, and looking after scheduling of meetings. Typical ground rules include the following: each party will listen to the other without interrupting; there will be no name-calling; parties will try to be brief; parties will be courteous.

The mediator may

- confirm that each party has authority to settle the dispute on the day of the mediation session;
- ask the parties to address one another by first name;
- encourage parties to treat the process as a joint problem-solving session or inquiry
- suggest that parties try to persuade one another rather than present a case to the mediator.

The mediator may provide a written agenda, or **terms of mediation**, to set the tone of interaction and/or may verbally outline the intended steps or stages of the mediation session. A mediation may be scheduled to begin and end in one day or may be scheduled with shorter sessions over a period of time.

The agenda may include arrangements for exchange of documents or other disclosure at a set date prior to the mediation. Some mediators use fur-

---

[6] *Ibid.* at 100–1.

niture or room arrangements to set the tone of the interaction through use of a round table, a whiteboard or flip chart, or separate rooms. A **break-away room** can be used to facilitate discussion (if more than one person represents each side) or to allow separate discussion by each party with the mediator. Some mediators conduct a mediation session with all parties together for the entire session. Other mediations may involve joint sessions plus time out for discussion in separate rooms. There is also a **shuttle style of mediation** in which the mediator meets separately with each party.

The mediator will also provide guidance to ensure that all necessary persons attend, or are represented, at the mediation. In some contexts, parties will bring legal counsel or other expert advisors to the mediation session. Alternatively, lawyers may not attend the mediation session, but multiple mediation sessions may be scheduled to facilitate access to legal advice for each party in between sessions. It is part of the function of the mediator to ensure that all **stakeholders**, the key participants in a dispute, have a voice in the mediation process. For example, if two tenants in a shopping mall have a dispute, it may be necessary to include the landlord in the mediation process if options for resolution include matters that would require changes to the lease or location within the shopping mall. Stakeholders may attend the mediation session, or the process may utilize telephone access or arrangements to adjourn for input from the absent stakeholder. Ideally, questions about presence and voice of stakeholders are anticipated and discussed as part of the agenda on a proactive basis.

Before delegating responsibility for process and interaction, parties should be very clear in their expectations about the role of the mediator. Just as musicians celebrate their art in the sounds of classical, jazz, country, polka, rock and roll, or rap music, mediators can be compared across a range of roles, styles, and preferred processes.

Some mediation models are extremely client-centred processes in which the role of the mediator is to be responsive to the needs of the parties. Essentially, the mediator will identify choices at an experiential and relationship level and with respect to the tasks. The mediator will facilitate effective communication and better listening by each party and will help the parties to generate creative problem solving. The intervention of a third-party facilitator can improve the resolution experience and focus the parties on joint problem solving rather than on a contest or competition. This type of mediation is often called a **joint problem solving** or **facilitative mediation** and is often used in a family, community, or workplace setting where the parties have a strong and trusting relationship but are dealing with controversial task-focused issues and concerns about preserving the relationship and minimizing experiential unpleasantness.

The role of the mediator in the facilitative model is often to assist with data problems, such as lack of information, misinformation, or data collection or evaluation. The mediator can bring focus to elicit data, set up a structure for information exchange so that the parties can either resolve differences in value or look for areas of agreement that accommodate their differences in perspective. The facilitative or joint problem-solving mediation is typically used in an interest-based mediation.

The different approaches to mediation of the various models can be illustrated by looking at a simple fact situation. A horse rancher dies. There is a will, and it provides a scheme of division giving one-half of the horses to the eldest son, one-quarter to the middle son, and one-fifth to the youngest son. The estate consists of 19 horses.

The facilitative mediator would meet the sons at the ranch, riding in on her own horse and, removing the saddle and bridle, would lead her horse to pasture with the 19 estate horses. She would encourage discussion and

---

EXHIBIT 25.6

Narrative Mediation

Recognition of the role of story has been an important and recent development in the field of counselling and therapy and has been introduced as a style of mediation. This is a very client-centred process. The mediator goes beyond the stories of each party and searches for the areas of discrepancy between the different stories and for patterns that underlie the stories. The philosophy of narrative mediation is based on a model of human behaviour in which actions and interaction are driven by old stories that have been playing over and over again, with modifications, through various events and transactions. The narrative mediation is a forum where the parties are guided to find new stories and to re-write their expectations. People tend to base expectations of what others will do in the future on behaviours from the past. A new story offers a new explanation of past interactions and may inspire different and more functional expectations and interaction for the future.

---

negotiation among the three sons, and let them decide a method for choosing the horses. The mediator has facilitated the choosing process because now the sons are able to apply a formula to a herd of 20. The oldest son can take one-half or 10 horses; the second son would take one-quarter or 5 horses; and the youngest son would choose one-fifth or 4 horses. The mediator rides away on her own horse, which was the 20th in the pasture.

The *rights-based mediation* would encourage discussion about entitlement, laws, and rules and may look at birth order, and investment of time, effort, or money in the ranch by each of the sons. The task-focused application of legal criteria to assign horses among the three sons could take place either with or without consideration of the relationship or the experiential effects. The mediator could work with the 19-horse herd, or she could lend her horse to the herd to facilitate the division.

However, the dispute may involve issues beyond the legalities or rules of interpreting entitlement of the will or the challenge of fractioning a live herd of animals according to a formula. Sometimes there are emotional or psychological complications arising out of the relationship or history. There may be differences in values or disputes relating to social justice, fairness and concepts of right and wrong.

Therapeutic or healing mediation heavily emphasizes relationship and community. Examples include workplace facilitations to deal with transition, change, downsizing, or harassment programs. Community-based mediation programs may offer this kind of process for neighbourhood disputes. The mediator who applies a therapeutic or healing model may ask the sons about their relationship with their deceased father and with each other.

Transformative mediation strives to encourage the parties to appreciate positive aspects of the relationship and to offer recognition of one another's points of view. Studied and advocated by Bush and Folger in their book, *The Promise of Mediation*, this model strives to empower the parties and to afford opportunities for disputants to see themselves and each other differently. The mediator may inquire about how the sons each feel about horses and ranching, or ask whether there were daughters in the family. In a *transformative mediation*, the mediator sees her role as being to shift paradigms and question assumptions of the parties.

The **restorative justice model** is used in victim-offender mediation programs that provide an informal and healing dimension to the criminal justice system. This model can be complementary with a transformative approach. A restorative model could be used in a situation where the conflict between the brothers has escalated into a threatening confrontation, perhaps involving an assault or complaint to the police.

Historically, the setting of disputes was often determinative of the model so that healing or transformative approaches were applied in community mediation programs, and insurance disputes were often determined in a rights-based model. As mediation develops as a profession, there is a wider academic study of theory and growing cross-germination of ideas.

Selection of the mediator is a key element of the resolution process, and it should be appropriate for the nature of the dispute and meet the expectations of all stakeholders. Parties who are more knowledgeable and sophisticated will enhance their chances of the resolution of the dispute by working effectively together in choosing the mediator and providing input to the mediator with respect to process for interaction.

Mediator experience and competence can be assessed by evaluating the mediators' professional or academic background, training in mediation, and mediation experience. Mediation is a multidisciplinary field, and mediators may have education or credentials in a wide variety of fields, such as law, social work, labour relations, human resources, behavioural sciences, religious ministry, or teaching. Mediation training is offered privately by a number of well-respected practitioners and also through academic institutions, such as universities or colleges. Parties should also make sure that they are comfortable with the mediator to ensure a satisfactory interaction and an environment that is conducive to settlement discussions.

Participation or interaction of the parties will vary, depending on the role of the mediator and the model of mediation. Where the mediation is rights-based and the mediator is making recommendations or an assessment to be used to assist the parties in negotiation, the parties will participate through advocacy and models of persuasion. In contrast, other mediation models require participation through active listening and effective communication. It is the role of the mediator to set the tone of the parties' participation, often either by conducting an inquiry through open-ended questions, **reframing** and other strategies, or by helping the parties to engage in an inquiry.

By way of analogy, if we compare a settlement agreement to a fishing expedition, the mediator-centred models are ones in which the parties come along on the fishing expedition, but the mediator catches the fish. In the transformative, restorative justice, and therapeutic models, the mediator gives step-by-step instructions to bait the hook, to cast, when and how much to reel in the line, and where to hold the net. The parties and mediator have "gone fishing together" but may not have learned enough to be able to go fishing alone in the future. The most facilitative models are ones where the mediator teaches the parties how to fish.

Parties who have a strong relationship of mutual respect may work together most effectively with a very facilitative model. Where the parties wish to preserve a relationship but have areas of distrust or diffidence to one another, they need a facilitative mediator who has the skills and resources to intervene at key points and redirect the interaction. Disputes are often complex. One party may have an intricate understanding about how to navigate the eddies, currents, and bends of the river while the other party knows where to find the fish. They may have fishing skills but not be able to apply those skills together at this river. In life, as in rivers, the fish may not always be found in the most easily accessible waters. The role of the mediator is to take charge of the fishing expedition. Different mediators have different approaches to the teaching, guiding, and intervention components of the fishing expedition.

Some parties simply want a resolution; they may have no interest in the joys of the fishing trip, no need to scrutinize the healthiness of the live fish, or concern about whether the river is polluted. They will go to the market and buy some fish. Arbitration is the choice. Currently, there is no settlement equivalent to the ease and comfort of simply ordering fish from a restaurant menu.

There are some parties and some disputes for whom any mediator with a minimum amount of training and experience will be able to help reach a settlement. There are other parties and situations that could not be successfully mediated even by someone possessing the essence of divine or secular wisdom. However, most situations are between the two extremes.

The substantive outcome of a mediation is a settlement that is negotiated by the parties. Accordingly, the finality of a mediated agreement is achieved in the same way as a negotiated agreement: that is, by way of a valid and enforceable contract, signed by both parties.

Arbitration

Arbitration is a more formal process in which the parties select, or are bound by the appointment of, a neutral third party to make a substantive decision to resolve the dispute. The arbitrator also takes responsibility to ensure compliance with rules of evidence and procedure that may be imposed by statute or be agreed upon in advance by the parties.

Typically, rules of evidence and procedure are more relaxed but based on the court process. Provincial legislation generally provides a framework for the process but permits parties to contractually modify and amend.

Arbitration is a rights-based, adversarial model. It meets the fundamental criteria of natural justice: each party has the right to be heard, and the right to hear and to reply to the case against him. Decisions are based on evidence and on principles of law.

The arbitrator will give each party an opportunity to present evidence, usually through witnesses and by way of documents that are agreed upon as evidence by the parties or are identified by the witnesses. Witnesses usually swear or affirm, and, therefore, there is additional formality in the form of an oath or promise "to tell the whole truth and nothing but the truth." The decision maker will weigh evidence by its credibility. Evidence may be conclusive or may be sufficient to shift the onus of proof to the other party. For example, written contracts that are signed and witnessed provide more conclusive proof about the terms of a contract than oral evidence of each person's recollection of what was in agreement. One party may produce in evidence a dinner roll containing a nail that he swears came from the other party's bakery. Such evidence shifts the onus to the bakery to establish that the dinner roll came from some other baker or that the nail was inserted in the dinner roll after it left the bake shop.

An arbitrator will respond to objections of the party and make rulings or decisions about evidence or procedure. The arbitrator will hear submissions by the party on matters of process and, before completion of the arbitration, about the merits of the case. The arbitrator may make a decision immediately or may adjourn and provide a decision later. Usually, there will be written reasons for the decision.

An arbitrator will make findings of fact based on the weight and credibility of the evidence presented. The arbitrator does not purport to find the truth or to discover what happened. An arbitrated decision is an assessment of the evidence and the submissions presented at the arbitration. Accordingly, technicalities and presentation are very important. Parties often seek legal advice or representation for an arbitration. They may require experts to provide evidence as to the appropriate interpretation or assessment of the evidence. Experts provide written reports that are usually exchanged prior to the arbitration and, on consent of the parties, accepted as evidence at the arbitration.

Often the arbitration process is structured much like a civil trial, but parties may, by agreement, create or amend the process to best suit their needs. For example, they may jointly select an expert to conduct an inspection of a piece of technical equipment or a building, and to decide whether the equipment complies with design specifications. Often, accountants are selected to arbitrate matters involving forensic accounting issues and may be asked to apply generally accepted accounting principles to analyze financial statements. In a trial, a judge would hear expert evidence from accountant witnesses for both parties and make an assessment based on that evidence.

The finality of an arbitration is enforced by legislation and judicial cases that have significantly limited situations where a court will overrule or set aside arbitrated decisions. A party who does not like an arbitrated decision has limited recourse for appeal, and non-compliance or non-payment may result in application of the court remedies for collection. However, because there are additional costs to import an arbitrated decision into the court process, most disputants avoid arbitration if they anticipate the possibility of a collection or compliance problem.

Selecting the Appropriate ADR Model

The key factor for selection of an ADR model is that the parties have some insight about the nature of the dispute and the context of their interaction and relationship. The advantage of ADR models are that the spectrum offers a range of dispute resolution models and, therefore, parties can select the model that is most suitable to their needs. One of the key elements causing dissatisfaction with the civil justice system is that it fails to meet the expectations of litigators. People look forward to their "day in court" but fail to appreciate the time, resources, and energy consumed by the court system. Choice of ADR model should be based on meeting the expectation and needs of the parties with respect to interaction (timing, cost, comfort), the relationship, and the substantive matters.

APPLICATION OF THEORY

The communication strategies inherent in effective principled negotiation and mediation are life skills best explored through experiential learning models. People communicate and negotiate from a very young age and develop a preference for those methods and techniques that appear to be effective in the environment in which they function. The study of ADR is an examination of process issues that separately examines key elements such as interaction, relationship development, and substantive decision making. The relevance of interests, rights, and powers varies depending on circumstance and perspectives of participants.

Role-plays are an effective experiential learning device through which students can practise negotiation or mediation strategies with coaching and the opportunity to debrief. The fact situation is described in an instruction sheet, and each actor is provided with separate and confidential instructions as to interests, concerns, or challenges that will determine how his or her script will unfold in the role play. Students are asked to act out the role-play as realistically as possible with a view to exploring and assisting fellow students to explore the emotional and experiential elements of the role-play situation. The role-play attempts to provide a realistic and non-threatening simulation of a potential real-life negotiation or communication opportunity.

CHAPTER SUMMARY

In this chapter, the reader was introduced to Alternative Dispute Resolution as a field that focuses on the process of finding agreement between disputing parties. The chapter explored the history and development of ADR and the way it fits into the court process and into various other venues for resolving disputes.

The chapter then examined the process and design characteristics of negotiation, mediation, and arbitration and compared the venues and situations where each form of ADR may be used. The similarities and differences of the different forms of ADR were studied and compared.

Next, the chapter examined the forms of ADR in terms of process design in the context of selection of a form of ADR by private agreement and implementation in the public sector, through private process design and recent developments of ADR programs as part of the court process.

The chapter concluded with a practical application and examination of negotiation and mediation strategies. There are opportunities for practising these strategies through role-plays based on real-life negotiation and mediation situations.

GLOSSARY OF NEW TERMS AND KEY CONCEPTS

active listening   A strategy for responsive communication that involves attention to body language, facial expression, and questions of clarification. Active listening is accomplished through an empathetic acknowledgment of both the emotional and verbal content of the message.

ADR   An acronym of alternative dispute resolution, ADR refers to dispute resolution processes other than the civil court system. The term encompasses negotiation, mediation, arbitration, and other hybrid or similar processes for dispute resolution. The term "ADR" also refers to the multidisciplinary field of study about dispute resolution that focuses on the process, procedure and methodology of resolving disputes.

arbitration   A process for dispute resolution in which a neutral third party is selected or appointed to make a decision for parties to a dispute to resolve some or all of the issues in contention.

BATNA   An acronym for the Best Alternative to a Negotiated Agreement, BATNA is a measuring standard estimated by an inquiry into the costs, risks, and available resources for a negotiator's most attractive plan of action other than resolution through negotiation with this party. The negotiator measures the expected outcome of Plan B as a way to decide whether or not to continue with the negotiation of Plan A. (Compare WATNA.)

brainstorming   A collaborative and creative activity that is usually most effective in groups, to generate a wide choice of options in an open and non-judgmental environment.

break-away room   An additional and private room that is used in the mediation process to facilitate private communication between the mediator and a participant or participants, or among participants, where matters can be dealt with in confidence and without disclosure to others involved in the process.

case management   In the civil justice court system, this is a system of computerization and tracking of court files in order to provide supervision of time frames by a judge or other officer of the court.

Case Management Master   In the Ontario case management system, this is the judicial officer appointed by the court to deal with the procedural issues arising from non-compliance with time sanctions of the rules of practice.

closed questions   Queries that are phrased to elicit a yes or no, either/or response.

dispute resolution spectrum	A metaphor used in the study of ADR to describe the processes of dispute resolution in comparison to one another, like colours through a prism.
Dispute Resolution Office	A newly created department of the Ministry of the Attorney General in Ontario to encourage use of ADR by Ontario government offices.
early neutral evaluation	A dispute resolution process, or component of the process, in which a neutral third party provides an expert opinion as to the likely outcome of the issues in dispute. The process is similar to arbitration.
evaluative mediation	A dispute resolution process in which the neutral third party makes a substantive assessment of the issues in dispute in order to encourage the parties to reach settlement. This process is most effective where parties have high confidence in the expertise and competence of the neutral party.
facilitative mediation	A mediation model in which the neutral third party intervenes, predominantly with respect to communication and agenda, and takes a minimal role with respect to evaluation or involvement with the substantive matters in dispute.
Financial Services Commission of Ontario	The administrative body under the *Insurance Act* in Ontario that has responsibility to regulate insurance companies and provide a resolution process for insurance disputes.
ground rules	The basic agreements in a mediation about courtesy and respect to which the mediator asks the parties to agree in order to provide an environment conducive to effective communication and respectful negotiation.
healing mediation	Also referred to as **therapeutic mediation**, this is a mediation model in which the neutral third party intervenes at a level designed to improve the health or balance of the relationship or to change the perspectives or attitudes of one or more parties to the dispute.
interest-based mediation	A mediation model that includes or focuses on an inquiry into the interests of the parties.
interests	The intangible factors that motivate human behaviour, individually and in groups, such as concerns, values, hopes, assumptions, priorities, expectations, fears, needs.
joint problem solving	A mediation model that takes a very practical approach to the issues in dispute to encourage the parties to find mutually acceptable objective criteria and options for a resolution of their differences. Goals of the process are often equated with satisfaction of needs.
local mediation committee	Pursuant to the Mandatory Mediation Program in Ontario, a committee for a judicial district, with responsibility to select and monitor the mediators on the local roster. The committee consists of members of the community, lawyers, judges, mediators, and a representative of the Ministry of the Attorney General.
mandatory mediation	A court-connected process for dispute resolution that requires parties to attend a mediation session. There are significant sanctions for non-attendance. The process is voluntary in that, while attendance is mandatory, participation is not evaluated.
mediation	A process for dispute resolution through which a neutral third party facilitates communication between parties to a dispute in order to attempt to reconcile their differences and broker a settlement of some or all issues in dispute.
Ministry of the Attorney General	In provincial government, the office of the Cabinet minister in charge of the civil and criminal court systems.
natural justice	A principle of administrative law based on democratic notions of basic fairness that include the right to hear what is said against the person, the right to reply by way of evidence, and argument before a decision will be made in a hearing or quasi-hearing.
negotiation	An informal process for dispute resolution in which parties communicate for the purpose of bargaining with one another.
neutral fact-finding	A process in which a neutral third party is chosen by parties or appointed to investigate and make findings of fact as part of a resolution of issues in dispute.
neutral evaluation	A process introduced in 1996 as part of the arbitration process for insurance disputes dealt with by the Financial Services Commission of Ontario.

ombudsman	An office created in government or private organizations to provide a safe space or user-friendly environment for the investigation of complaints. Usually an ombudsman has responsibility to safeguard individual rights in the context of a real or perceived power imbalance between the potential complainant and the larger organization.
Ontario Rules of Civil Procedure	The very detailed rules for civil litigation passed by regulation that prescribe the forms, time requirements, rights, and responsibilities for the procedures involved in bringing a dispute through the civil court system in Ontario.
open questions	A strategy for communication that relies on journalistic questions that encourage story-telling response rather than simply yes or no answers.
positional bargaining	A competitive or adversarial bargaining process in which parties deliberately take an opening posture from which they intend to make concessions.
power	In the context of dispute resolution, the use of resources to influence or compel compliance by others. Sources of power include physical strength, charisma, social status, wealth, status, position. Abuse of power takes the form of physical confrontation, threats, economic sanction, or intimidation.
precedent	A legal decision. Canadian common law has developed historically from the judicial tradition of following earlier legal decisions so that cases that are similar are decided according to similar legal principles.
pre-trial conference	In civil court cases, an informal meeting between lawyers and a trial judge in which the judge makes a substantive assessment of the issues in dispute in order to encourage the parties to reach settlement. The judge who attends the pre-trial is usually not the same judge who would be hearing the case at trial.
principled negotiation	A process of bargaining and communication in which one or more parties listen to both sides of the dispute in order to attempt to reach a settlement based on mutually acceptable objective criteria. (Also referred to as **win/win negotiation.**)
reframing	A communication strategy for active listening in which the listener repeats back what he or she has heard. The technique may be used for clarification or to distill the message by verbalizing the emotional content. Sometimes, in the context of a mediation, the mediator will re-phrase a message by one party into a content that the other party will be willing or able to hear and acknowledge.
restorative justice	A concept of fairness based on notions of balance and healing that views relationships and social institutions in terms of an ecosystem; restorative justice does not seek revenge or punishment but, rather, reconciliation and assumption of responsibility.
restorative justice model	A mediation model often used in victim-offender reconciliation or neighbourhood disputes that seeks reconciliation, healing and the assumption of responsibility for rectification of hurt or damage.
rights	The fundamental freedoms and protections guaranteed in a democratic society. Rights are created by laws, regulations, agreements, court decisions, policies, past practices, customs, and conventions.
rights-based mediation	A mediation process that focuses on the legal issues between the parties as provided by law, contract, or convention.
shuttle style of mediation	A mediation process in which the parties to a dispute communicate indirectly through the mediator rather than speaking directly to one another. The mediator shuttles from party to party. This method is used where there are significant power imbalances or where the emotional overlay makes person-to-person contact untenable to one or both parties.
stakeholders	Those persons or organizations who may be affected by the resolution of a dispute, either by a potential benefit or risk.
statement of defence	The pleading, filed and served in response to the claim against the defendant, that summarizes the law and facts upon which the defendant will rely at trial.
terms of mediation	The process for a mediation as outlined verbally or in writing by the mediator.

therapeutic mediation	Also referred to as **healing mediation**, this is a mediation model in which the neutral third party challenges the parties to improve the health or balance of the relationship or to change the perspectives or attitudes of one or more parties to the dispute.
transformative mediation	A mediation model that acknowledges human capacity for growth and development in response to change. Transformative mediation casts the role of mediator to empower the parties by facilitating opportunities for participants in the mediation to see themselves and each other differently.
Unified Family Court	A court system for family disputes that has jurisdiction over all family matters. The traditional system limits jurisdiction of provincially appointed judges who cannot determine matters of property or divorce. The unified family court system provides streamlined and one-stop-shopping for family law matters.
WATNA	An acronym, the **Worst Alternative to a Negotiated Agreement**; a measuring standard estimated by an inquiry into the costs, risks, and available resources for a negotiator's least attractive plan of action other than resolution through negotiation with this party. The WATNA is often used to complete the cost/benefit analysis that begins by an inquiry into his or her **BATNA**.
win/win negotiation	A process of communication and bargaining in which one or more parties makes a commitment to look for settlement options that provide benefits and solve the problems to both sides to a dispute. The term is used to distinguish the process from the win/lose competitive bargaining of **positional negotiation**. (Win/win negotiation is also referred to as **principled bargaining**.)
Workplace Safety and Insurance Board	The administrative board in Ontario that was created by statute to administer issues of safe work environments, return to work, and compensation for injured workers. Formerly, these responsibilities were held by the Workers' Compensation Board. New legislation has changed the emphasis from compensation to that of safety and prevention.

REVIEW QUESTIONS

1. How is mediation different from arbitration?

2. Compare rights and interests in the context of ADR.

3. In what situations do parties typically negotiate?

4. What are the key characteristics of mediation?

5. Compare interest-based and rights-based mediation.

6. What happens if collaborative law negotiations break down and the matter goes to trial?

7. What is the role of an arbitrator?

8. Name and summarize the four contexts in which disputes are referred to an ADR process.

9. Compare interest-based negotiation to positional bargaining.

10. How can participants measure the settlement options when they are negotiating or mediating?

11. What is the basis for an arbitrator's decision?

DISCUSSION QUESTIONS

1. What considerations are relevant in selecting a dispute resolution process where there is a power imbalance or potential for an abuse of power?

2. What are some factors parties should consider in the selection of a mediator?

3. In what circumstances would parties choose arbitration rather than mediation?

4. Compare public sector mediation models to private mediations.

5. What are the challenges in assessing BATNA or WATNA when the alternative to a negotiated agreement is litigation?

SUGGESTED READINGS

Bush, Robert A.B., & Joseph P. Folger. *The Promise of Mediation* (San Francisco: Jossey-Bass Inc., 1994).

DeBono, Edward, *Conflicts: A Better Way to Resolve Them* (Toronto, Ont.: Penguin Books, 1991).

Fisher, R., & S. Brown. *Getting Together* (New York: Viking Penguin, 1989).

Fisher, R., & W. Ury. *Getting to Yes: Negotiating Agreement Without Giving In* (Boston: Houghton Mifflin, 1981).

Fisher, Roger, & Danny Ertel. *Getting Ready to Negotiate: The Getting to Yes Workbook* (New York: Penguin Books, 1995).

WEBSITES

Conflict Resolution Network: <www.crnetwork.ca>

Collaborative Family Lawyers of Canada: <www.collaborativelaw.ca>

Financial Services Commission of Ontario (FSCO): <www.ontarioinsurance.com>

Ontario Ministry of The Attorney General: <www.attorneygeneral.jus.gov.on.ca>

ServiceOntario e-Laws: <www.e-laws.gov.on.ca>

Workplace Safety and Insurance Board (WSIB): <www.wsib.on.ca>

Health Care Law in Canada

Sharon McCleave
SENECA COLLEGE

Learning Objectives

After reading this chapter, the reader should be able to:

➤ explain the legislative structure surrounding health care delivery at the federal and territorial/provincial levels

➤ summarize how precedent influences court proceedings in medical law

➤ classify various forms of legal consent found in the medical setting, including the use of the *emergency doctrine*

➤ predict situations where the disclosure of a patient's medical information would be required

➤ relate how the power of a medical health officer is similar to police power when dealing with the public and issues of communicable diseases

➤ identify the criteria that allow supervised injection facilities to be exempt from the laws regarding possession defined in the *Controlled Drugs and Substances Act*

➤ summarize the legal status of voluntary euthanasia, non-voluntary euthanasia, involuntary euthanasia, and assisted suicide

➤ compare and contrast the *living will* and the *advance directive*

➤ identify how common law has come to shape the status of abortion in Canada

TABLE OF CONTENTS

THE PROVISION OF HEALTH CARE AND HEALTH CARE LAW

Medical treatment for Canadians is largely covered by government funds, and medical care is therefore considered a publicly funded entity. Generally speaking, it means that any Canadian that is insurable has access to basic medical care that will be financially covered by a provincial or territorial health plan.

In actuality, roughly 70 percent of Canada's health care costs are publicly covered and the remaining 30 percent is paid for through the private sector. For example, the cost of services such as pharmacy, physiotherapy, dentistry, chiropractic, optometry, acupuncture and ambulance transportation are *generally* not assumed by provincial or territorial health care insurance plans.

The *Canada Health Act*

The *Canada Health Act* (CHA) is a federal Act that provides the legislative framework for public health care insurance throughout the country. It carefully outlines the parameters in which each province and territory determines its public health care policy. In return for adhering to the binding principles of the CHA, the federal government makes financial contributions to each provincial and territorial health care insurance plan. The binding principles of the CHA legislation are intended to make certain that all insurable Canadians have equal access to essential medical care without burdensome "out-of-pocket" costs. The core guiding principles of the CHA are *public administration, comprehensiveness, universality, portability*, and *accessibility*. (See Exhibit 26.1 for their definitions.)

Individuals in Canada are able to obtain provincial or territorial health insurance if they are Canadian citizens or permanent residents. In New Brunswick, Quebec, Ontario and British Columbia, a three-month "eligibility period" exists for permanent residents before coverage becomes active. Some people will decide to purchase private insurance during this time. For refugees arriving in these provinces, however, emergency and essential services will be provided to them at the expense of the province during the three-month

---

EXHIBIT 26.1	Program Criteria of the *Canada Health Act*

Public Administration: This refers to the management of public health care. Provinces and territories are obligated to provide insured medical services to all qualified citizens on a non-profit basis. All records of activity are publicly audited, and the provision of care must meet the guidelines of the individual provincial or territorial governments.

Comprehensiveness: Each province and territory must cover *all* medical services that have been determined to be publicly funded.

Universality: All insured persons of a province or territory are entitled to publicly funded health care on equal terms and conditions.

Portability: There are a few considerations regarding portability. If a person moves from one province to another, the home province is obligated to cover any medical costs until the new province assumes responsibility at a time not to exceed three months. Individuals who are absent from the province for a period of time are entitled to remain covered under the province's insurance plan during their absence.

Accessibility: This refers to the ability to receive care by insured individuals. All insured Canadians have a right to medical care that is reasonably available and without discrimination on the basis of socio-economic status, age, or state of health.

period. It is important to note that while most residents are provided for by their province or territory, some special populations in Canada receive funding for medical care *directly* from the federal government. These individuals include First Nations people, the Royal Canadian Mounted Police, inmates of federal prisons, and military personnel.

The *Canada Health Act* (CHA) was established in 1984 and was the result of a long evolution of health care policies and strategies in the country. By the beginning of the 20th century, organized medical initiatives were seen in a variety of settings: overcrowding in new urban centres generated public health Acts; unions created trust funds to cover the costs of work injuries; and hospital care was ensured by religious charities to those unable to afford private physicians. In 1947, the Saskatchewan government, under the leadership of Tommy Douglas, passed the *Saskatchewan Hospitalization Act* to ensure publicly funded hospital care to the province's residents. It was the initial step in Canada to ensure care for all, irrespective of financial means. Federal involvement in sharing medical costs was fully established 10 years later with the *Hospital Insurance and Diagnostic Services Act* (HIDS Act). By 1961, all provinces and territories had adopted a collaborative agreement with the federal government to share the costs of hospital care and diagnostic procedures.

Canada's health care system required more refining, however, because only the cost of hospital care was covered, and the cost of out-patient treatment was not. The *Medical Care Act*, introduced by Lester B. Pearson's federal government in 1966, changed that. The Act established cost-sharing between federal and provincial bodies to cover medical treatment in *and* out of the hospital. During the era of the *Medical Care Act*, however, user fees and extra billing by physicians were still permitted. User fees were extra costs imposed on the patient for the use of medical services. Extra billing, on the other hand, was a practice used by physicians to charge patients for care above and beyond what they were to receive from the government-run insurance plan. When the CHA evolved out of the *Medical Care Act*, it required the practices of user fees and extra billing to be eliminated.

Overall, the federal Act sets the legal boundaries within which provinces and territories deliver health care. If individual jurisdictions do not adhere to the five guiding principles of the CHA or do little to halt the use of extra-billing or user-fee practices, the federal government is obligated to intervene and impose penalties. Generally, the federal government is keeping a relatively close eye on the preservation of the five guiding principles of the CHA, but this is changing. As a result of increasingly escalating health costs, the federal government has been less likely to impose penalties on jurisdictions that do not discourage extra billing and user fees. Since the late 1990s, the federal government has also halted penalties placed on jurisdictions that have allowed private health care clinics to open. Another increasing trend is the **delisting** of health care services, leaving more medical treatments to be covered privately. While it means the jurisdictions that decide to delist forgo a certain amount of federal financial assistance, it is a decision that is still thought to be economically advantageous.

Health Care Law

The law as it pertains to health follows the common law tradition in which *stare decisis* or precedent governs court decisions. Within this framework the judge-made *law of torts* applies. Quebec offers an exception: health law in this province is governed by the *Civil Code of Quebec*, and tort law is replaced by the *law of obligations*.

CONSENT TO TREATMENT

According to common law in Canada, individuals have a right to self-determination and consent to medical treatment. In other words, they have the right to refuse unwanted physical interference. When a medical act is performed on someone without consent, it is considered a battery (or, in this situation, **medical battery**).

The issue of consent is particularly noteworthy in today's medical environment. At one point in time, the physician/patient relationship was one of paternalism and authority: the physician "knew what was best" and the patient complied without asking questions. Today, patients are expecting more control in the planning of their care. The physician/patient relationship is becoming more collaborative and egalitarian as patients become more informed of their health through mass media, the Internet, and consumer advertising for pharmaceutical drugs. The result is that consent, now more than ever, is a factor the health care professional cannot overlook before administering medical treatment.

The essence of consent is that it must be voluntary, informed (based on accurate knowledge), obtained without coercion or deceit, and related to a specific procedure. In the medical field, consent may be expressed or implied. Consent by a parent is also considered appropriate in the case of the treatment of minors. In *certain* circumstances, consent is not required at all.

It is important to note that even though most examples given in this chapter depict the interactions between patient and physician, in reality these laws are generally applicable to all in the health care field: nurses, nurse practitioners, medical technicians, rehabilitation specialists, and home-care providers, to name a few.

Express Consent

Express consent is considered given when a patient explicitly asks for a treatment or authorizes a procedure to be undertaken. Express consent may be *verbal*, where a patient may ask for the removal of a mole or an annual flu shot, or it may also be *written*, as in the case of signing documents for a surgical procedure.

Implied Consent

Implied consent is not a verbal or written consent but is determined by the physician according to patient behaviour. If the patient conducts him/herself in a way that allows the physician to proceed with treatment, the physician presumes consent is given. It is certainly the most common form of consent seen in daily interactions between physician and patient. Typical examples include a patient holding out his arm to have his blood pressure checked, or removing his shirt so the physician can listen to his heart. Implied consent is also seen when a patient takes a requisition form from a physician to a clinic to have his ankle X-rayed.

Although the implied consent is very common, whether it has actually been given is open to interpretation. In tort law, when a patient's implied consent *cannot* be determined to be reasonably affirmative, an action of medical battery may be successful. It is the physician's responsibility to understand and interpret the cues of implied consent with accuracy.

Informed Consent

Informed consent describes the patient's awareness about a procedure before it is undertaken. For example, if a patient is in need of a hip replacement, the physician is required to state what the surgery involves, the risks, and the expected outcomes.

In the case of a surgical procedure, the consent is for the specific operation indicated. If the surgeon performs the operation and decides to undertake a secondary procedure because it "might be useful", he or she is vulnerable to legal liability. For example, a physician, during a surgical procedure to remove a patient's adenoids (small lymph nodes in the sinuses), decided to also remove the tonsils. While the physician argues the intent was to simply prevent the possibility of tonsillar infections in the future, the patient did not consent to the latter surgery. The physician therefore committed the tort of medical battery. It is also technically possible to charge the physician with a criminal offence of having committed an assault, although this is rare.

Surgery, however, can uncover situations that the physician or patient might not have anticipated. Therefore, if a surgeon discovers an unexpected and potentially dangerous medical condition during an operation, he/she is allowed to perform an extended procedure (or the extra-required surgery) for the sake of the patient's life. For example, a surgeon performs an operation to remove a cancerous tumour. During the procedure, she notices the cancer has spread to nearby lymph nodes. Realising the cancer has spread (or *metastasized*), she removes the infected lymph nodes at the same time. By carefully determining that the removal was necessary for health and safety of the patient with metastatic cancer, the extended procedure would be defendable in the court of law.

The Treatment of Minors

Medical care to those under the age of majority (18 or 19 years old, depending on the province) is provided with consent being obtained in a variety of ways.

A child up to the approximate age of six is determined to be an *infant*, and consent to treatment is obtained from parents or guardians. Parents cannot *refuse* consent to medical intervention if the treatment is necessary for the health of an infant. If this should happen, the infant is put under the care of the state and the treatment is performed. The most common example is parents' refusal to a procedure that conflicts with their religious beliefs (see Exhibit 26.2). The law recognizes parents' right to practise their religion but

---

When Treatment Is in Conflict with Patient's Religious Beliefs   **EXHIBIT 26.2**

Sheena was a premature infant. At one month of age, and after a variety of medical treatments her parents had consented to, Sheena's hemoglobin level dropped. Fearing for the life of the infant, the physicians requested consent to perform a blood transfusion. The parents were Jehovah's Witnesses and refused consent. A hearing was subsequently granted on short notice, and the Provincial Court (Family Division) put the infant under the wardship of the Children's Aid Society for 72 hours. A blood transfusion was given and her condition improved to a degree, but her health care team determined she was also in need of surgery. The wardship was extended for a further 21 days, and the surgery, with the necessary blood transfusions, was completed. The infant was then returned to the care of her parents.

Sheena's parents appealed the decisions on the basis of section 2(*a*) of the *Charter* (everyone has the fundamental freedom of conscience and religion) and section 7 of the *Charter* (everyone has the right to life, liberty and security of the person). The appeal was dismissed by the trial judge on the grounds that "neither s. 2(*a*) nor the liberty interest of s. 7 permits parents to endanger the lives of their children."

Source: *B.(R.) v. Children's Aid Society of Metropolitan Toronto*, [1995] 1 S.C.R. 315.

does not allow them to impose their beliefs on the infant in need of medical care.

Minors are youth between the approximate age of six and the age of majority. While this group is loosely divided between "immature" and "mature" minors, the division is ambiguous and open to interpretation by the courts. It is generally assumed that in life-threatening situations, life-saving medical procedures will be implemented even though the youth does not wish it. In other situations, the needs of the minor will be recognized with the understanding that the youth is old enough to comprehend the repercussions of the decision he has made. For example, a minor would have grounds to refuse to take medication for hyperactivity in spite of her parents wanting her to. However, if she wanted to refuse chemotherapy for the treatment of cancer, her parents could "step in" and provide consent for the life-saving therapy.

The Emergency Doctrine

If the patient is unable to give consent to treatment for whatever reason, a health care provider may intervene and provide medical treatment if necessary for the preservation of life. Termed the **emergency doctrine**, it allows health care providers to perform a procedure in an attempt to save a patient's life when the patient is unable to communicate. An example of this might be when a patient is unconscious after a motor vehicle accident and a paramedic applies a brace to the victim's injured neck.

MEDICAL NEGLIGENCE

When a physician performs a medical act without consent, the physician is liable for the intentional tort of battery. The tort of **medical negligence** occurs when the practitioner, who is established as the caregiver in the patient/physician relationship, performs a medical act that causes undue harm to the patient.

Negligence can occur in various aspects of medical care, whether it be relating to the diagnosis, the proper referral to specialists, the recording of medical documents, communication with the patient, or the very treatment itself (see Exhibit 26.3).

EXHIBIT 26.3	Factors in the Consideration of Medical Negligence

¤ Did the physician perform in a way that is consistent with accepted standards of the profession?

¤ Was the physician reasonably informed about the most recent clinical procedures in his or her field?

¤ Did the physician decide to perform a procedure that was beyond his or her clinical competence?

¤ Did the physician adequately inform his or her patient about the risks and the possible outcomes of a procedure?

¤ Was the physician competent in referring the patient to an appropriate specialist or someone able to provide a second opinion when needed?

¤ Did the physician make a diagnosis that reasonably determined the type of disorder and urgency for emergency care?

Standard of Care

In a negligence action, the plaintiff (patient) must prove that the defendant (physician) failed to meet the standard of care expected of an ordinarily competent physician in a given situation. If the patient proves the failure to meet the standard of care, the physician is in **breach of the duty of care**. Generally, a physician must possess and use a degree of skill or care expected of physicians in any given medical situation. The standard of care test does not require the physician to be flawless in the exercise of his or her skills — or to put it another way, he or she does not have to be at the top of the medical school graduating class. At the same time, he or she should not be at the bottom, either. The physician is also not liable for an error of judgment if it was one that an ordinarily competent physician might have made.

The test used to determine the standard of care is objective: Did the physician meet the generally accepted standards of practice expected ordinarily of a practitioner in a similar community in similar cases? If he or she did, then the duty of care has not been breached and there can be no negligence. If the physician is a specialist, then the standard is that of the ordinary, prudent specialist. Again, the specialist does not have to be the best in the world, but he or she should be meeting the standards of an ordinarily competent and skilled specialist. If an ordinary physician is providing treatment that specialists normally provide, he or she is not expected to meet the standards imposed on a specialist.

Causation-in-Fact

When a physician is accused of negligence, the plaintiff has the burden of proof. In other words, if a patient has suffered illness or disability from the treatment provided by the physician in question, the patient must prove that it was the *direct* result of the physician's negligence. Physicians are not liable just because a patient does not respond well to treatment.

The patient can prove negligence through such means as medical documents, test results, and expert witnesses. If it is determined that the physician performed a negligent act, an award of monetary damages is made to the plaintiff. Some factors may affect the outcome of the claim; therefore, the plaintiff needs to be aware of them.

Limitation of Actions

Provincial law dictates how much time a plaintiff has to commence a lawsuit. Depending on the province or territory, this amount of time may be one or two years after the plaintiff begins to notice the negative health effects of the physician's negligent actions. If the claim is made too late, the action will not be allowed to proceed because the time limit for bringing a lawsuit has expired.

Mitigation of Loss

Patients who have received negligent treatment still have a responsibility to care for themselves. When a physician offers treatment to alleviate the illness due to negligence, it is in the best interest of the patient to consent and comply. If the patient refuses, the monetary award will be reduced as a result.

Contributory Negligence

In some cases, the patient's lifestyle behaviours are considered. If the court determines that the patient does not typically demonstrate good, healthy lifestyle behaviours, the award for negligent behaviour by the physician is reduced. An example of this might involve a patient whose arm, after being treated for a fracture, fails to heal properly or not heal at all. The physician might have been negligent in not setting the bone properly; but if the patient

| EXHIBIT 26.4 | Assessment of Causation-in-Fact |

Mrs. Snell, a 70-year-old woman who was "legally blind" in the right eye, consented to cataract surgery performed by Dr. Farrell. He injected a local anaesthetic into the eye and noticed retrobulbar bleeding, a condition that can progress to a hemorrhage and cause permanent damage to the eye. Dr. Farrell palpated the eye, waited 30 minutes, and determined it was safe to proceed with the surgery.

By the end of the procedure, there was more blood in the eye and Mrs. Snell was in considerable pain. The blood took approximately nine months to clear, and by this point, the optic nerve had atrophied, leaving Mrs. Snell completely blind in the right eye.

Expert witnesses could not state with certainty that the hemorrhage had occurred as a direct result of the surgery since Mrs. Snell was moderately hypertensive and a diabetic, two factors that also predisposed her to retrobulbal hemorrhage. However, they also stated that whenever a bleed occurs (other than the modest amount from administering the anaesthetic), surgery should not proceed. The judge accepted evidence from Mrs. Snell that during the procedure she heard Dr. Farrell tell another physician that he would have to hurry the operation (presumably to complete the procedure before the bleeding became too severe).

Mrs. Snell's claim was upheld and Dr. Farrell was found liable for negligence. The trial judge noted that although the expert witnesses could not determine when the actual hemorrhage might have occurred, the surgery should not have proceeded at all when there was blood in the eye. He found the doctor's decision to quickly complete the operation before the blood accumulated to be negligent. He concluded, on the basis of sound probabilities, that Mrs. Snell had proven her case.

Source: *Snell v. Farrell*, [1990] 2 S.C.R. 311.

chooses to play sports and attempt heavy labour with his cast on, these factors will *contribute* to the poor healing that originated with the physician's poor casting technique. Here, the patient will have his damage award reduced to the extent that his own acts made the situation created by the physician worse than it otherwise would have been.

Quantification of Damage Award

If a patient has been subject to medical negligence, how much should the damage award be? In the late 1970s, a series of cases in the Supreme Court of Canada laid the framework for determining or quantifying the monetary award to the plaintiff.[1]

In the case of a negligent act that creates a temporary illness or inconvenience, common law dictates a monetary amount consistent with previous settlements. Each case is unique, however; and so, considerations is given to the type of illness and the specific effects on the individual. For example, it is not likely that a temporary infection from a surgery will receive more compensation than the complete loss of limb function. In another situation, the loss of nerve function in a finger would be considered more debilitating to a musician than to a marathon runner.

When debilitating damage has been done that results in the patient needing ongoing medical care for the rest of his/her life, a lump sum payment may be made. Such an award is determined upon a complex series of consider-

[1] See the following: *Andrews v. Grand & Toy Alberta Ltd.*, [1978] 2 S.C.R. 229, 3 C.C.L.T. 225, [1978] 1 W.W.R. 577, 8 A.R. 182, 83 D.L.R. (3d) 452, 19 N.R. 50; *Teno v. Arnold*, [1978] 2 S.C.R. 287, 3 C.C.L.T. 272, 83 D.L.R. (3d) 609, 19 N.R.1; *Thornton v. Board of School Trustees of School District No. 57 (Prince George)*, [1978] 2 S.C.R. 267, 3 C.C.L.T.257, [1978] 1 W.W.R. 607, 83 D.L.R. (3d) 480, 19 N.R. 552.

ations (e.g., the estimated life expectancy of the patient, the type of care needed over the patient's remaining life span, etc.). The exception to this might occur if an out-of-court settlement is made. In this case, the award called a structured settlement would be paid in instalments over the course of the remaining life of the plaintiff. While this approach creates an assured, tax-exempt income, the overall amount of an out-of-court settlement is usually less than the lump sum agreement.

If a patient dies as a result of medical negligence, the dependants of the deceased are provided with the financial means to cover the immediate funeral and other associated expenses. Dependants may also receive a sum for the loss of care, guidance and companionship. As one lawyer quipped, if you injure someone, it is cheaper if the person dies than if the person lives and require treatment and care.

PATIENT CONFIDENTIALITY

Medical personnel are under strict ethical rules to maintain patient confidentiality. Put another way, physicians, nurses, pharmacists, paramedics, etc. *all* have a **duty of non-disclosure**. The patient/practitioner relationship is deeply compromised if the patient is unable to disclose personal information without fear of exposure. The **fiduciary relationship** that exists between patient and health care provider requires the health practitioners to act in good faith in the patient's interest and, thus, assures trust and confidence — key components to successful medical care. Patient confidentiality is also protected by provincial privacy legislation that protects patient charts in the medical setting. Federally, the *Personal Information Protection and Electronic Documents Act* (PIPEDA) has many similarities to provincial and territorial Acts, but it is limited to commercial medical practices only (e.g., physiotherapists, dentists, pharmacists, and physicians working outside of the hospital in private practice). Between PIPEDA at the federal level and comprehensive privacy Acts at the provincial level, patient confidentiality is protected by law *irrespective* of whether the setting is private or public.

When Disclosure Is Required

Although laws have been set up to protect patient confidentiality, there are situations when it would be appropriate (or required) for the health care provider to turn over medical files for scrutiny.

Public Health Authorities

Provinces have public health policies that require physicians to report certain communicable diseases or situations that can prove to be harmful to an individual when discovered (see Exhibit 26.5). The duty of disclosure in these circumstances is important for monitoring the spread of illness and overall public safety. The information is a vital component to containing an outbreak and providing data for medical research. Each province and territory has a register of reportable diseases; and while these registries are similar in many ways, there are also geographical variations according to epidemiologic trends. It varies across jurisdictions as to what type of information is provided to public health authorities. Most jurisdictions require identifiable information (like the name and address of the infected person). Occasionally, a patient with a communicable disease such as tuberculosis will have his or her occupation provided to the local public health authority.

In the three territories and in Prince Edward Island, Alberta, and British Columbia, members of the public are also required to report if they know someone with a communicable disease or who has died from one. There are

---

EXHIBIT 26.5

Reportable Diseases

The following are some examples of reportable diseases common to most jurisdictions in the country. The list is by no means exhaustive as there are many rare and tropical diseases not considered here.

COMMUNICABLE DISEASES	SEXUALLY TRANSMITTED DISEASES
¤ Anthrax	¤ Chlamydia
¤ Botulism	¤ Gonococcal infections (i.e., gonorrhea)
¤ Chicken pox (in population clusters)	¤ Genital herpes
¤ Foodborne illnesses (i.e., "food poisoning")	¤ HIV/AIDS
¤ Hepatitis (all forms)	¤ Syphilis
¤ Meningitis (all forms)	
¤ Pertussis (whooping cough)	
¤ Rabies	
¤ Rubella (German measles)	
¤ Toxoplasmosis	
¤ Tuberculosis	
¤ Waterborne illnesses	
¤ Yellow fever	

---

more jurisdictions (e.g., Alberta, Newfoundland, and Prince Edward Island) that are now requiring *contact notification* as well. For example, family members in contact with an individual newly diagnosed with tuberculosis would need to be notified of that person's condition.

Legal Authorities

In recent years there has been a growing concern regarding the number of stab wounds and gunshot injuries presenting in hospital emergency departments. This has created a conflict of interest between legal authorities and medical professions. While legal authorities would like to have the information on and from the victim in order to prosecute the perpetrator, medical personnel have different priorities. Physicians are primarily concerned with breaching patient confidentiality, but they are also concerned that victims would avoid treatment, knowing their identity would be disclosed to police by the attending practitioner.

In spite of these concerns by the medical profession, Ontario introduced the *Mandatory Gunshot Wounds Reporting Act* in September 2005, requiring health care professionals to report the name of the victim and the hospital providing the care. The Act calls for an oral disclosure of the incident as soon as it is possible without causing undue disruption of hospital activities. Disclosure of the patient's name is required irrespective of the circumstances: the wound may be from a criminal act or a hunting accident or may be self-inflicted. The Act also has a provision to protect reporting facilities from proceedings for damage after a disclosure has been made. It does not, however, require the hospital to detain a patient who has sought treatment for a gunshot wound. In September 2007, Saskatchewan introduced a similar *Gunshot and Stab Wounds Mandatory Reporting Act*. This Act requires, however, that the identity of any victim presenting at a hospital in Saskatchewan with a gunshot or stab wound be provided to the police.

Lastly, to ensure the health and safety of all Canadians, the physician is also obligated by law to report those who are considered unsafe drivers, who are committing acts of child abuse, or who are being sexually abused by another health care practitioner.

Patient Consent to Disclosure

Sometimes patients will request that information from their medical history be shared. Such a situation may arise when the patient needs documents to be sent to another physician, health care provider, or insurance company. The patient who expressly consents to the sharing of information also has the right to qualify what information gets released. However, if the patient selects what can be divulged in a way that will alter or misrepresent his or her condition, the physician is not required to comply with the instructions. For example, a patient may wish to apply for life insurance and asks for all of his records to be sent *except* for an abnormal test result he recently received. In this situation, the physician would be in no way obligated to fulfill the patient's request to selectively disclose his medical records.

In a Court of Law

The medical information about a patient, if needed in a court of law, must be supplied by the physician or the person who compiled the medical record. If the health practitioner refuses, the practitioner may be summonsed to give evidence orally, or to provide medical records, or to both. If the practitioner fails to answer the summons, he or she may be found in contempt and be fined or jailed.

Patient Access to Records

A patient's medical chart is the property of the physician in charge or of the clinic the patient visited. However, this does not mean the contents of the file are within the complete control of the health care provider (see Exhibit 26.6). In the modern medical context where patients have more control over decisions of their treatment protocol, it is also a patient's right to see what is contained in the file. The physician is, therefore, obligated to allow the patient to see what has been written about the diagnosis and treatment. Medical documents can be difficult to understand by those untrained in the field, however.

EXHIBIT 26.6

Patient's Right of Access to Records

Margaret MacDonald asked her physician for copies of the medical documents found in her file. Dr. Elizabeth McInerney complied by providing copies of the records she wrote herself but did not copy the documentation prepared by other physicians. The reasoning was that those particular documents were the property of the other physicians and that it would be unethical to copy them without their knowledge.

While the documents are the property of the physicians who prepared them, patients are entitled to access all information contained in their medical file. In upholding the fiduciary physician/patient relationship, it is the responsibility of the physician to not only maintain patient confidentiality but also patient trust. With this trust comes the obligation to reveal information about the patient's case.

Mrs. MacDonald had applied for an order to have her entire chart released, and the Court awarded her request.

Source: *McInerney v. MacDonald*, [1992] 2 S.C.R. 138

For this reason, physicians or hospitals usually incorporate procedures that allow the patient to view charts while a health care professional is present. In this way, the information can be shared in a way that is in proper context and understood by the patient.

In rare circumstances the physician may determine that the well-being of a patient might be jeopardized if the patient has access to the medical file. If this is the case, a patient has a right to seek a court order for the release of the documents. In this situation, the physician will be asked to defend the position of non-disclosure in the court of law.

The Rules of Professional Conduct for lawyers and for paralegals requires medical information received in respect of a client to be shown to the client, even where a medical practitioner directs that it not be revealed. The proper position for a lawyer or paralegal is to refuse to accept the medical report under those conditions. Where revelation of the information to the client might harm the client, the lawyer or paralegal should encourage the client to review the record first with the medical practitioner.

PUBLIC HEALTH AND THE LAW

Public health law is found in provincial and territorial statutes. Federally, there are two key public health Acts: the *Quarantine Act* and the *Department of Health Act*.

The new *Quarantine Act* was given Royal Assent in 2005. The change in the Act was in large part a result of the SARS outbreak in 2003; it provides the Government of Canada with enhanced power at entry points to check the spread of **communicable disease** entering the country. The new Act includes extended power to appoint appropriate health officers, divert transportation vehicles to other landing points, and establish detaining facilities to hold or quarantine individuals.

The *Department of Health Act* is in place for the preservation of health among Canadians. It provides the minister with such responsibilities as overseeing the safety of consumer products, health promotion, research, and the protection of health of those travelling by air, sea, or rail.

Within provinces and territories, medical health officers (MHOs) are afforded many rights and privileges to ensure the health of their communities. They are provided with these powers so that they can locate carriers of communicable disease and ultimately work to contain the spread of the illness. There are laws regarding the power to enter facilities, detain patients, examine patients, and isolate them if necessary.

Entering a Facility to Examine

Under public health law, a health officer can enter a private residence to examine those suspected (on reasonable grounds) of carrying a contagious illness or sexually transmitted disease. While jurisdictions across Canada have specific stipulations on the power to enter, generally a warrant or written authority provided by a chief health officer is required. In Ontario, a medical health officer entering a room *specifically* used as a dwelling place requires the consent of the occupant.

Those refused to be examined or to adhere to the directives of public health officials face fines and/or incarceration. Individuals who *knowingly* spread communicable diseases (i.e., with criminal intent) may be charged under the *Criminal Code* and dealt with accordingly:

180.(1) Every one who commits a common nuisance and thereby
  (a) endangers the lives, safety or health of the public, or
  (b) causes physical injury to any person,

is guilty of an indictable offence and liable to imprisonment for a term not exceeding two years.

221. Every one who by criminal negligence causes bodily harm to another person is guilty of an indictable offence and liable to imprisonment for a term not exceeding ten years.

273.(1) Every one commits an aggravated sexual assault who, in committing a sexual assault, wounds, maims, disfigures or endangers the life of the complainant.

Closing a Facility, Isolation, and Quarantine

The widespread authority of MHOs allows them to close buildings and gathering places in an attempt to contain a suspected or known illness that threatens to become an **epidemic**. Examples of facilities include public gathering places, entertainment venues, places of worship, schools, daycare centres, and campgrounds.

In all jurisdictions, MHOs also have the power to **isolate** and **quarantine**. Isolation may involve containment at a hospital or the prevention of movement in and out of residence. Isolation is enforced when a person or persons are known to be infected with a communicable disease. The MHO may quarantine an individual or group of people if they have been — or suspected to have been — exposed to a communicable disease but have not yet presented with signs and symptoms of illness. Detaining powers are often for the recalcitrant individual who does not wish to co-operate with the investigative process. The law allows for the MHO to detain an individual, if necessary, for medical examination, treatment, and the prevention of the spread of disease.

Supervised Injection Facilities

In 2003, Vancouver became the first Canadian city to open a supervised (or *safer*) injection facility (SIF) for injection drug users (IDUs). The centres provide safe areas, supervised by medical staff, for IDUs to inject using sterile equipment. The centres were created in an attempt to decrease public drug use, accidental overdose, and the spread of infectious illness, such as HIV/AIDS and hepatitis C, through needle-sharing. With medical staff present, the SIF also acts as an area for safe injection education and obtaining health information.

The facilities are legally sanctioned areas for the safe injection of pre-obtained illicit drugs *on the condition* that the IDUs participate in ongoing research and evaluation regarding SIF's effectiveness in reducing overdose-related deaths, blood-borne illness, and public drug use. Medical staff and "research subjects" (the IDUs) are exempt from the laws regarding possession defined in the *Controlled Drugs and Substances Act* (CDSA) *only* when they are within the interior borders of the SIF. Furthermore, the illicit drugs permitted at the centre may only be of the kinds that are injected.

Under current regulation, only the IDU can inject himself or herself when on the premises. Anyone requiring assistance cannot recruit injection from medical staff, nor have a friend assist with the injection if done within the parameters of the site.

EUTHANASIA AND REFUSING TREATMENT

The issue of terminating a life that is considered in some way futile is very complex. Common law in Canada offers concrete parameters in some situations but presents variable legal outcomes in other cases involving the termination of life. It is an area of moral and ethical concern that is likely to generate more debate in the future for many reasons. Individuals are living longer, leaving them more susceptible to incapacitating chronic illness that greatly affects their quality of life. Patients are also more informed about their care, and they expect to contribute to the medical decision-making of their own health. Finally, with the increasing technological advances in medicine, the prolongation of life is more feasible, albeit at a financial cost.

Euthanasia and Assisted Suicide

In health care and health care law, "euthanasia" and "assisted suicide" are two of the terms used to describe the cessation of life.

Euthanasia may be defined as voluntary or involuntary. **Voluntary euthanasia** is the act of one individual deliberately ending the life of another as a means to eliminate suffering. It is performed on the consent of a **competent** individual or as the result of a valid advance directive. A competent patient is one who is able to understand the current situation, the repercussions of any decision he or she makes regarding the state of his or her health, and who has the ability to communicate such a decision. When life support is withdrawn from a competent patient, it is voluntary euthanasia; when it is withdrawn from an **incompetent** patient or in the absence of consent, it is called **non-voluntary euthanasia**.

Involuntary euthanasia is also an act of terminating a life to end suffering, but it is performed *against* the wishes of a competent individual or contrary to the terms of a valid advance directive. This is considered the same as manslaughter or murder.

All situations of euthanasia involve an individual engaging in a method that *actively* terminates the life of another as a means to end suffering: an example would be the injection of a lethal dose of medication to the patient in question.

Assisted suicide, on the other hand, occurs when a health care professional or other person *provides* medical information or specific tools to an individual so that that individual obtains the capacity to end his or her own life. (See Exhibit 26.7.)

EXHIBIT 26.7

Right to Assisted Suicide

Sue Rodriguez was a 42-year-old woman who suffered from the progressively debilitating neurological disease, ALS (amyotrophic lateral sclerosis). By the end-stage of the disease she would be confined to bed on a respirator and nourished by way of gastrotomy. Rodriguez wanted the right to be able to take her own life when her condition became unbearable for her. She requested that a physician provide her with the technical means to commit suicide because in the last stage of her illness she would be too physically disabled to undertake the task unaided. Rodriguez took her case to the Supreme Court on the basis that section 241(*b*) of the *Criminal Code* breached her rights according to sections 7, 12, and 15 of the *Charter*. She argued that as a physically disabled person, she had lost the fundamental right to decide her life course because she did not have the physical ability to take her own life. Assisted suicide would return to her the physical means already afforded to able persons. In spite of her arguments, the Supreme Court upheld section 241(*b*) of the *Code* and dismissed her application. It was determined that section 241 had an important role in the preservation of the sanctity of life, and according to Justice Sopinka, its integrity was particularly necessary to protect vulnerable individuals "who might be induced in moments of weakness to commit suicide."

Sue Rodriguez took her life four months after the trial, apparently assisted by an anonymous physician.

Source: *Rodriguez v. British Columbia (Attorney General)*, [1993] 3 S.C.R. 519

Right to Refuse Treatment

EXHIBIT 26.8

Nancy B. was a 25-year-old woman with Guillain-Barré syndrome. The disease left her permanently paralyzed and on mechanical ventilation in order to remain alive. After living as a quadriplegic for four years, Nancy made a request to her physician to remove her ventilation. He refused her request on the basis that it would be unethical and unlawful for him to do so.

The court realized Nancy B. was mentally competent and her request for the removal of the ventilator was a conscientious refusal of treatment. Justice Jacques Dufour made the following statement (at p. 394):

> Sections 222 to 241 of the Criminal Code deal with different forms of homicide. What I have just reviewed is sufficient to conclude that the person who will have to stop Nancy B.'s respiratory support treatment in order to allow nature to take its course, will not in any manner commit the crimes prohibited by these sections. The same goes for s. 241, aiding suicide. I would however add that homicide and suicide are not natural deaths, whereas in the present case, if the plaintiff's death takes place after the respiratory support treatment is stopped at her request, it would be the result of nature taking its course.

Five weeks after the court's decision, the mechanical ventilation was removed and Nancy B. died peacefully.

Source: *Nancy B. v. Hôtel-Dieu de Quebec* (1992), 86 D.L.R. (4th) 385; 69 C.C.C. (3d) 450 (Que. Sup. Ct.).

As stated in section 241 of the *Criminal Code*, both euthanasia and assisted suicide are illegal in Canada:

> Every one who (a) counsels a person to commit suicide, or (b) aids or abets a person to commit suicide, whether suicide ensues or not, is guilty of an indictable offence and liable to imprisonment for a term not exceeding fourteen years.

Refusing Treatment by a Competent Individual

While euthanasia or the active administration of a procedure that would end life is illegal, the *refusal of treatment* by an individual is not only legal but also a fundamental right according to section 7 of the *Charter*. Because of this, a competent patient who decides he or she does not want life-prolonging procedures (without being influenced or coerced) is entitled to have the treatment *withheld* or *withdrawn*. The treatment in question might be the supply of hydration/nutrition, surgery, pharmaceutical intervention, or the sustaining of life by mechanical ventilation.

Life-Prolonging Treatment for the Incompetent Patient

Every day, physicians are faced with patients who are so severely ill that they remain alive only by medical life-support. Although they are incompetent and cannot consent (i.e., they remain in a **persistent vegetative state**), it is not too uncommon for the physician to withhold or withdraw life-supporting measures. In common law, there is no precedent that clearly defines a legal framework for the termination of life-support for an individual who will in no way benefit or recover from the treatment. However, there have been cases in other Commonwealth countries that have *shaped* common law in Canada to be tolerant of this current practice. The Law Reform Commission of Canada has also released a document entitled *Euthanasia, Aiding Suicide, and Cessation of Treatment*. The paper endorses the practice of withholding or withdrawing life-support from a patient whose outcome is futile and encourages a firm legal position to be created in which physicians can work. Since its release in 1982, there have been no changes in Canadian law, but the proposed recommendations have not been rejected. So, while the termination of life-support of incompetent patients is done in the course of current medical practice, it is done on the basis of sound medical and ethical reasoning — not in accordance with defined law.

The Living Will

Some individuals have drawn up a living will in anticipation of an illness that will render them incompetent to participate in medical decision making. A **living will** is a document that indicates the circumstances under which a patient would want life-prolonging measures to cease. In other words, the individual defines when life-support for him or her should terminate. The living will has been useful in some cases, but the nature of the document leaves itself open to interpretation. For example, the directive is applicable only when the *specific* condition for which life-support is provided is experienced: a directive to halt life-support after a heart attack will raise questions by medical staff if the person is on life-support after a motor vehicle accident. Another area of conflict arises when a family member or loved one challenges the will and wants to overturn it. Finally, living wills are not always made apparent to health care staff. No wishes can be adhered to if there is no knowledge that directives exist.

The Advance Directive

The **advance directive** is a document that received legal recognition in many jurisdictions as a result of the 1990 case *Malette v. Shulman*. Like the living will it is a document intended for the physician should the individual become incompetent. Unlike the living will, however, the advanced directive describes what *treatments* the individual prefers as well as when treatment should cease. The advance directive consists of two parts: (i) the *instruction directive* clarifies what treatments are preferred and what are not, and (ii) the *proxy directive* identifies a person designated to negotiate treatment options on behalf of the patient who has become incompetent.

EXHIBIT 26.9

When Treatment Becomes a Battery

Georgette Malette was unconscious and rushed to the hospital in Kirkland Lake after being involved in a car accident. The accident, which took the life of her husband, left Malette with serious injuries. Upon arrival at the hospital, a nurse discovered a card in Malette's possession. The card stated that Malette was a Jehovah's Witness and that under no circumstances should a blood transfusion be administered. Dr. Shulman was made aware of the document.

While in hospital, Malette's condition began to deteriorate due to the profuse bleeding she was suffering. In spite of the specific instructions indicated on the card, Shulman ordered and administered a blood transfusion himself on the basis that it was his responsibility to preserve the life and health of his patients.

Malette made a successful recovery and brought an action against the physician and hospital staff. It was decided that with the knowledge of the instruction card she was carrying, the *emergency doctrine* was not applicable. The court determined that the physician has committed the tort of battery, and the plaintiff was awarded $20,000.

Source: *Malette v. Shulman* (1990), 72 O.R. (2d) 417; [1990] O.J. No. 450 (C.A.).

In the best situation, the advance directive increases communication between the individual drawing it up and his or her loved ones. Furthermore, there is less ambiguity for the treating physician regarding the degree of intervention the patient wants should he or she become seriously ill. As can be expected, the more details the document provides, the more valuable it becomes. Generally, the advance directive allows for the individual to determine how much medical intervention to be provided (i.e., from "prolong life" to "provide comfort care *only*") to treatment options such as dialysis, mechanical breathing, pharmaceutical intervention and blood transfusions.

REPRODUCTIVE HEALTH AND THE LAW

Few areas of law feature as many "hot buttons" as the law relating to human reproduction. While the state has been removing itself from the bedrooms of the nation since the 1960s, issues concerning the right to reproduce, and the right not to, continue to be matters of dispute.

Sterilization

Common law contemplates a variety of situations regarding the sterilization of an individual. Considerations are made regarding competence of the individual, consent to the procedure, and the reasons for the surgery to be performed.

Consent to Sterilization by the Competent Individual

Sterilization for the purpose of contraception is certainly an option for the competent adult. If the individual is married, he or she has the right to opt for sterilization without the consent of his or her spouse, as confirmed by section 15 of the *Charter*. If a patient wishes to be sterilized and the physician does not feel it is in the patient's best interest, the physician is not compelled by law to perform the procedure. In keeping with standards of medical practice, however, the physician is obliged to refer the patient to another physician who will more likely meet the patient's needs.

Sterilization of the Incompetent Individual

Common law is not as definitive when sterilization involves an incompetent individual. If a mentally challenged individual is able to understand the connection between intercourse, pregnancy, and the consequences of sterilization, he or she is able to make decisions regarding his or her reproductive health and consent accordingly. However, if a patient is so mentally challenged that sterilization cannot be understood, the involuntary procedure must be done with great care.

To sterilize an incompetent patient simply to prevent the genetically damaged individual from having children is **eugenic sterilization** and is completely illegal. *Occasionally*, the Supreme Court of Canada will recognize the therapeutic sterilization for the physical or mental protection of the patient, and the Court uses the **parens patriae** jurisdiction solely to ensure the health and safety of a vulnerable individual. Unfortunately, therapeutic sterilization is not governed by a consistent set of guidelines in common law. It might be safe to say that sterilization would be warranted if a uterine tumour in the incompetent patient was threatening to metastasize (spread to nearby tissue), or the patient was *so* emotionally vulnerable and mentally compromised that a pregnancy would have detrimental psychological effects on her.[2]

---

[2] See *E. (Mrs.) v. Eve*, [1986] 2 S.C.R. 388.

Rights of the Fetus

When a fetus is *in utero* (unborn), it does not have rights nor is it considered — legally — a person.[3] This is confirmed by section 223(1) of the *Criminal Code* which states the following:

> A child becomes a human being within the meaning of this Act when it has completely proceeded, in a living state, from the body of its mother, whether or not (a) it has breathed; (b) it has an independent circulation; or (c) the navel string is severed.

On occasion section 223(1) has resulted in unfortunate consequences, particularly when a mother takes drugs or engages in harmful lifestyle behaviours during pregnancy that ultimately affect the health of the unborn child. In the case of *R. v. Drummond*,[4] the circumstances were particularly noteworthy. Brenda Drummond was acquitted of attempted murder after shooting a pellet gun into her vagina just before she came to term. The baby was fortunate to have survived the ordeal, being born alive a few days later with a pellet lodged in his head.

A certain amount of legal protection *does* exist for the neonate when it is being delivered. Section 242 of the *Criminal Code* states that a pregnant woman is guilty of an indictable offence if she fails to obtain assistance for a birth she wishes to conceal or with the intent that the child shall not live. Section 238(1) of the *Criminal Code* states that a person is guilty of murder and liable to imprisonment for life when causing the death of a newborn in the act of birth. However, as subsection (2) clarifies, the charge *does not* apply to an individual that causes the death of the newborn in order to save the life of the mother.

Abortion

Section 287 of the *Criminal Code* states that an individual who, by any means, procures a miscarriage in another woman is liable to imprisonment for life. A pregnant woman who, by any means, induces the miscarriage of her own fetus is liable to imprisonment for a maximum sentence of two years. The *Criminal Code* makes exceptions, however. It states that a hospital-based physician, under the guidance of a therapeutic abortion committee, may perform a therapeutic abortion if the pregnancy is likely to endanger the life or health of the mother. There is ambiguity here, however, as the term "health" is not clarified. The therapeutic abortion committee then, depending on ethical leanings, can wield considerable power over the decision to grant an abortion to the woman in need.

In 1988, the Supreme Court of Canada reduced the significance of section 287 in the case involving Henry Morgentaler, a Canadian physician wanting to perform legal and accessible abortions. The Supreme Court of Canada held section 287 impeded upon section 7 of the *Charter of Rights and Freedoms*. As Chief Justice Brian Dickson stated, "Forcing a woman, by threat of criminal sanction[,] to carry a foetus to term unless she meets certain criteria unrelated to her own priorities and aspirations, is a profound interference with a woman's body and thus a violation of her security of the person." Since then the federal government has failed to implement any legislative framework controlling abortion practices. In other words, there is no *criminal* regulation of the practice. Most jurisdictions today cover medical abortion by provincial and territorial health care insurance plans. Women have access to the procedure through hospitals, public health care clinics, and a few private centres. Unfor-

---

[3] See *Tremblay v. Daigle*, [1989] 2 S.C.R. 530. This case also addresses the lack of precedent that supports the rights of the father to veto a woman's decision to have an abortion.
[4] (1996) O.J. No. 4597.

tunately, even today, women who live in remote areas or who cannot afford quick access to a private clinic are subsequently unable to exercise the right to abortion.

Wrongful Birth

Wrongful birth is a tort that results from the negligence of a physician prior to delivery that results in the birth of a disabled child. Wrongful birth does not mean the physician performed a procedure that caused disability in the newborn. It pertains to a physician's knowing that a child is likely to be born disabled and failing to disclose this information to the parents. The parents are able to make the claim on the basis that they were uninformed of the situation and were therefore unable to consider therapeutic abortion as an option.

The increasing effectiveness of amniocentesis, ultrasound, and genetic testing are making the tort of wrongful birth a more common occurrence. The physician must also be continually aware of the medications prescribed to the pregnant woman and alert her to any chance that teratogenesis (birth defects) might result. Lastly, wrongful birth may be alleged if the physician does not carefully consider the chance of a newborn inheriting a condition that has been recognized in previous births by the mother.

In every wrongful birth case, when presented in the court of law, the prosecution must prove the physician had a reasonable degree of knowledge about the outcome of the birth and failed to disclose that to the parents.[5] The prosecution must also prove the birth was a direct result of the physician's failing to disclose the likely outcome of the newborn's health. In other words, the parents would need to demonstrate that, had they known about the disability of the child, they would have opted for therapeutic abortion. If the preventable birth of a disabled child is determined to inflict undue hardship on the parents and offspring, an award is made to the prosecution.

MENTAL HEALTH LAW

The law protecting the rights of patients with mental illness is different than the law for patients receiving general medical care. In the field of mental health, patients who are very ill are frequently unable to make decisions about their treatment that is in their own best interest or in the best interest of others around them. Therefore, the issues most frequently encountered in mental health law generally involve involuntary hospitalization and treatment without consent.

There are challenges in mental health law. While the *Charter of Rights and Freedoms* ensures Canadians the right to liberty and freedom from involuntary detainment, patients with severe mental illness are at risk to themselves and others if care is not implemented. Those who advocate for patients' rights claim that any sort of involuntary hospitalization is imposing and authoritarian. They suggest that uninvited treatment violates tenets of the *Charter* and removes the liberty and dignity of the patient. Sections 9 and 15 are considered when addressing the rights of those requiring involuntary committal:

> **9.** Everyone has the right not to be arbitrarily detained or imprisoned.

> **15.**(1) Every individual is equal before and under the law and has the right to the equal protection and equal benefit of the law without discrimination and, in particular, without discrimination based on race, national or ethnic origin, colour, religion, sex, age or mental or physical disability.

---

[5] See *Arndt v. Smith*, [1997] 2 S.C.R. 539.

Conversely, those who adhere to human needs principles suggest that a legal framework for involuntary care is necessary for the immediate safety of the patient *and* for the benefit of the patient's long-term rights and freedoms. Certainly, untreated mental illness contributes to homelessness, fills shelters, overtaxes supportive housing projects, and creates overwhelming challenges for the families of those who are ill.

While those with less severe psychiatric disorders can voluntarily enter into care and be protected by common law, those with severe illness (e.g., bipolar disorder, major depression with suicidal tendencies, schizophrenia) fall within the guidelines of *statutory law*. The management of mental health patients by statute creates a fine balance between acknowledging patients' rights according to the Charter, **lawful compulsion**, and issues regarding consent to treatment.[6]

Involuntary Admission to Hospital

For those whose judgment and reasoning are impaired by mental illness, *lawful compulsion* or committing a patient to psychiatric care is admissible. The patient can be committed for medical assessment and thereafter for treatment, but each of these steps requires a certificate of committal to be completed by one or more physicians. In cases of involuntary committal, the patient is given certain rights. A tribunal review is available to all psychiatric patients involuntarily committed for the purpose of evaluating the admission criteria and discharge plans. The review board is necessarily a neutral body, with the sole purpose of deciding whether the treatment of the patient was fair, ethical, and in the patient's best interest.

Criteria for Committal

While there are some differences between the provinces in determining if a patient should be involuntarily hospitalized, some criteria are consistent throughout the country. All jurisdictions require the patient to meet a *dangerousness standard*, which determines if the patient is to be a threat to the physical safety of himself or herself or others. In Ontario, Saskatchewan, Manitoba and British Columbia, the dangerousness criteria also include the patient's risk of impending mental or physical *deterioration*. Another basis for involuntary admission is *inappropriateness for voluntary treatment*. In this situation, the patient's reasoned thinking and judgment are so greatly impaired a conscientious decision for voluntary treatment is impossible. Finally, all jurisdictions require a *diagnosis of mental disorder* to be made.[7]

Variations between jurisdictions exist. In the Yukon Territory, British Columbia, Saskatchewan, Manitoba, Quebec, Prince Edward Island, New Brunswick, and Newfoundland, "dangerousness" has come to encompass *non-bodily* or *psychological* harm. In Saskatchewan, Manitoba, and British Columbia, criteria for admission also requires the patient *to be in need of treatment*.

The rights of those who are mentally ill, while for the most part protected, are monitored by advocacy groups throughout the country, who ensure section 15 of the *Charter* is upheld by medical authorities. Patients with severe mental illness *can* be committed involuntarily, but they have access to a tribunal board, ombudsmen or similar advocacy groups, legal council, or any designated representative to ensure that the rights *and* well-being of all involved are preserved.

---

[6] See *Fleming v. Reid* (1991), 4 O.R. (3d) 74 (C.A.).

[7] The actual definition of "mental disorder" varies across jurisdictions. The most serious mental disorders, however, are *all* included within this otherwise arbitrary definition.

Because it is generally the most serious disorders that demand involuntary committal, it is rare for those with mild disorders to be detained against their will.

MEDICAL MARIJUANA IN CANADA

The use of marijuana for medical purposes became legal in Canada in 2001. (The process of legalization began in the late 1990s after Terry Parker, who suffered from grand-mal epilepsy, was found not guilty of growing and using marijuana for medicinal reasons.) Health Canada's *Medical Marijuana Access Division* (MMAD) regulates the use of medical marijuana, and the legislation is described in the *Marijuana Medical Access Regulations*.

The Application Process

A patient can be prescribed medical marijuana by a family doctor or medical specialist. Both patient and physician complete application forms, and the patient supplies his or her photograph with the documents. The application provided by the physician includes the patient's diagnosis, the dosage required, and the predicted course of treatment. The forms are resubmitted annually in order to provide Health Canada ongoing information regarding the progression of the treatment.

The types of illness deemed manageable by marijuana are indicated by categories. "Category one" conditions are those that create extreme pain, seizures, or cachexia (weight loss, fatigue and nausea, seen with terminal illness). The conditions include spinal injury or spinal cord disease, multiple sclerosis, epilepsy, severe arthritis, HIV/AIDS, and cancer. "Category two" illnesses are not specifically identified but are conditions that have been debilitating to the patient and that have not responded to any traditional therapy.

Obtaining Medicinal Marijuana

During the application process, the patient selects how he or she will obtain the marijuana and provides the appropriate data to Health Canada. Medical marijuana can be sent out at monthly intervals by Health Canada, grown by the patient, or produced by a grower designated by the patient. For plants to be grown by the patient or designate, strict rules apply. The seeds must be obtained from Health Canada, and the applicant needs to declare where the plant will be grown, how many plants will be cultivated, how the product will be securely stored, and give assurance the plants will be away from daycare centres, schools, or playgrounds. If the patient designates a grower (who must be over 18 years of age), similar rules apply. Designate growers may grow plants at the patient's residence or their own, but in both cases the method of production and procedures regarding security are maintained. Patients using marijuana are provided with an authorization card that allows them to have in their possession one month's supply of dried product at any given time. Growers are also provided with authorization to possess, as well as with a licence to grow and process limited quantities of the plant for medicinal purposes.

CHAPTER SUMMARY

Most medical treatment for Canadians is publicly funded so that any Canadian that is insurable has access to basic medical care, which is financially covered by a governmental health plan. The *Canada Health Act* (CHA) is a federal Act that provides the legislative framework for public health care insurance throughout the country. The law as it pertains to health follows the common law tradition. In Quebec, the *Civil Code of Quebec* and the *law of obligations* provide the legislative framework for medical law.

Consent to treatment is necessary for medical care, or a charge of medical battery may be laid. In the case of negligence, the physician has failed to provide an adequate standard of care. One of the core functions of the health care practitioner is to maintain patient confidentiality; however, the physician is obligated to release certain medical information to public health authorities, legal authorities, and in the court of law.

Medical health officers are afforded the right to enter buildings and examine individuals who are thought to have a communicable disease. They also carry the power to detain, isolate, and quarantine an individual or individuals as a means to contain the spread of disease.

Euthanasia is illegal in Canada, but common law has been tolerant in the cessation of life-support to those who are in a persistent vegetative state or whose treatment outcome is futile. Individuals, however, have the right to refuse treatment.

Unborn fetuses do not hold legal rights, and they are not considered by law to be human beings until they are born alive. Abortion is covered by public health insurance, and it is within a woman's rights to opt for the procedure — with or without the consent of a spouse or partner. Wrongful birth is a tort that results when a physician, knowing that a child will likely be born disabled, fails to disclose this information to the parents.

Mental health law has specific stipulations for seriously ill patients. While those with less severe psychiatric disorders can voluntarily enter into care and be protected by common law, those with severe illness fall within the guidelines of *statutory law*. The criteria for involuntary admission to hospital vary from jurisdiction to jurisdiction.

The use of marijuana for medical purposes was legalized in Canada in 2001. The *Medical Marijuana Access Division* of Health Canada carefully regulates the application process, production, distribution, possession, and use of marijuana for therapeutic use.

GLOSSARY OF NEW TERMS AND KEY CONCEPTS

advance directive	A document prepared by an individual that outlines the type of treatment desired and when treatment efforts be terminated should the person become incompetent.
assisted suicide	The voluntary termination of one's life using the knowledge, means, or both of another individual.
breach of the duty of care	The failure to perform a professional obligation or act to an accepted level or standard of care.
communicable disease	An infectious agent or toxic product that can be transmitted from person to person or animal to person.
competent	A person who is of sound mind and is therefore able to make, act accordingly upon, and understand the consequences of decisions regarding his or her health and medical treatment.
delisting	The elimination of a medical service from a provincial or territorial health care insurance plan so that the patient must pay for the service out-of-pocket.
duty of non-disclosure	The professional obligation to hold a patient's medical information in confidence
emergency doctrine	A provision that allows a health care professional to perform treatment that is considered to be life-saving on an incompetent patient (and therefore without consent).
epidemic	An outbreak of an infectious illness in a community or population that is widespread or greater than what would normally be expected.

eugenic sterilization	A surgical procedure on an individual that eliminates reproductive capacity. In this situation it is done to eliminate the continuation of genetic traits or behaviours determined to be unwanted or "substandard".
fiduciary relationship	In medicine, a relationship between health care provider and patient in which the practitioner is responsible for ensuring the patient's trust and confidence in good faith.
incompetent	A person who is not of sound mind and is therefore unable to make, act upon, and understand the consequences of decisions regarding his or her health and medical treatment. Incompetence also applies if the individual has been threatened or coerced into a particular decision.
involuntary euthanasia	The act of ending a life by one person to eliminate suffering of a competent individual who does not wish the procedure to be carried out.
isolate	To separate and contain an individual or individuals known to have a communicable disease in order to prevent the spread of illness.
lawful compulsion	The compelling or inducement by legal authority to carry out a required act.
living will	A document made by a competent individual indicating when life-prolonging treatment be terminated in the event he or she becomes incompetent.
medical battery	The intentional violation of a patient's right for the purpose of delivering medical care.
medical negligence	A tort that resulted from a medical act performed by a physician that causes undue harm to the patient.
non-voluntary euthanasia	The termination of life by one person as a means to end the suffering of another who is incompetent, or when consent has not been obtained.
parens patriae	Latin, meaning "father of his country". It refers to the government's duty to act as the ultimate guardian for those who are unable to care for themselves as a means to ensure their health and safety.
persistent vegetative state	A condition that involves the absence of higher brain function. While the reflexes for breathing, heart rate, blood pressure, and digestion remain, the patient has no awareness of the external environment at all. In other words, the patient remains alive by the presence of basic neurological functioning only.
quarantine	To separate and contain an individual or individuals suspected or known to have been exposed to a communicable disease but are not yet showing signs and symptoms of the illness.
voluntary euthanasia	The termination of one's life by another as a means to end suffering. The individual wishing the act has provided consent to have it carried out.

REVIEW QUESTIONS

1. Identify ways the provincial and territorial management of health care has begun to deviate from the standards originally set out in the *Canada Health Act*.

2. At the scene of a motor vehicle accident, paramedics splint the broken leg and administer oxygen to an unconsciousness woman. What is the legal basis that allows them to do this without her consent?

3. Identify situations where a physician would be required to disclose the medical information of a patient.

4. A patient provides consent to have his medical history released. Under what circumstance can the physician refuse her patient's request?

5. A client seeks counsel, complaining about the actions of his physician. What criteria would a lawyer use to determine whether or not the physician was negligent in the case? How would a lawyer determine the physician's actions were that of negligence and not battery?

6. Explore situations where the *Quarantine Act* and the *Department of Health Act* would apply. How would public health legislation treat an outbreak of meningitis in Ontario differently from a group of infected individuals in a ship off the coast of Vancouver Island?

7. A drug addict who possesses and uses street drugs is not arrested for injecting drugs at an SIF. Outline why he is able to do this, and state what criteria he must follow to avoid arrest.

8. What criteria would a physician consider before admitting a patient to a psychiatric ward on an involuntary basis?

9. A patient is refusing treatment in the psychiatric ward of a hospital. Outline the course of action that would typically occur in such a situation. What rights does the patient have?

10. A client tells her lawyer she was charged with possession of marijuana but claims she needs it for a medical condition. What are the requirements to grow, possess, and use medicinal marijuana legally?

DISCUSSION QUESTIONS

1. List some common situations in which personal privacy and the obligation of confidentiality conflict with other private or public interests. Analyze and resolve legal issues that arise from such conflicts.

2. Assisted suicide and obtaining assistance for injecting drugs at SIFs are illegal. Discuss how the law is in conflict with the rights of disabled persons.

3. Explore Saskatchewan's and Ontario's mandatory reporting Acts for gunshot and stab wounds. What are the advantages and disadvantages of this Act according to the legal and medical professions?

4. Using web resources that support and oppose the practice of euthanasia, debate the ethical and legal dilemmas that arise with this issue. Discuss the advantages and disadvantages that have been seen with the practice in the Netherlands.

5. More and more medical services are being delisted from provincial and territorial health care insurance plans. Debate whether this trend is a benefit or liability to Canada's public health care system. Will privatization ensure health care by decreasing wait times for treatment, or does it jeopardize the core values in which the *Canada Health Act* is based?

SUGGESTED READING

Caulfield, Timothy A., & Barbara von Tigerstrom. (Eds.). *Health Care Reform and the Law in Canada: Meeting the Challenge* (Edmonton, Alta.: University of Alberta, 2002).

Downie, Jocelyn, Timothy Caulfield, & Colleen Flood. (Eds.). *Canadian Health Law and Policy*, 2d Ed. (Markham, Ont.: Butterworths, 2002).

Eaves, D., J.R.P. Ogloff, & R. Roesch. *Mental Disorders and the Criminal Code: Legal Background and Contemporary Perspectives*. (Burnaby, B.C.: Simon Fraser University, 2000).

Sneiderman, Barney, John C. Irvine, & Philip H. Osborne. *Canadian Medical Law: An Introduction for Physicians, Nurses, and other Health Care Professionals* (Scarborough, Ont.: Carswell, 2003).

Sport and the Law

Susan Haslip
ALGONQUIN COLLEGE

Learning Objectives

After reading this chapter, the reader should be able to:

➢ describe how sport is organized in Canada

➢ understand how the high performance sport system fits within the international sport movement

➢ explain how the organization of sport relates to the jurisdiction of sport in Canada

➢ identify the areas where sport and the law intersect in Canada

➢ identify some challenges arising with the funding of sport in Canada

➢ explain factors informing the under-representation of identified groups in sport

➢ describe how human rights instruments affect sport

➢ explain how sport is affected by policies and law on official languages

➢ explain how doping is dealt with in the Canadian sport system

➢ describe how disputes are dealt with in the Canadian sport system

TABLE OF CONTENTS

INTRODUCTION

Sport, while operating by its own set of rules and principles, does not exist in a vacuum. While there is no distinct "sports law"[1] *per se*, sport and the law do intersect. This chapter explores a number of these points of intersection in the Canadian amateur sport system. As such, it does not canvass "professional" sport (i.e., the National Hockey League, the Canadian Football League, the National Football League, motor sport racing). The chapter starts with an overview of the organization of sport in Canada and a consideration of how the domestic sport system fits within the international sport movement. Issues impacting the "high performance" sport system in the area of funding, including the adequacy of funding, the impact of the federal tobacco policy and the *Income Tax Act* are explored. Factors informing the **under-representation** of women, visible minorities, **Aboriginal peoples** and **athletes with a disability** (or disabilities) are explored. The intersection of other policies and laws, including instruments related to human rights, official languages, doping and dispute resolution are canvassed.

ORGANIZATION OF AMATEUR SPORT

"Sport" in Canada can best be understood when viewed as *a* component of a *physical activity spectrum*. The *Minister's Task Force on Federal Sport Policy*, for example, defines "sport" as "one part of a physical activity spectrum that includes play, fitness activities, recreational sport, organized competitive sport and high performance sport"[2] (see Exhibit 27.1). While terms such as "play" and "fitness activities" are commonly understood, distinctions between "recreational", "competitive" and "high performance" sport levels may not be as well-known and are outlined at Exhibit 27.2.

The entire sport structure is premised on the ideal of attaining Olympic status. If one envisions a pyramid, leisure-type activities are located at the bottom of the pyramid while international competition is located at the top. The higher one moves up the pyramid, the higher the level of performance. National Sport Organizations (NSOs) (and, by extension, their respective Provincial Sport Organizations (PSOs)) form part of the international sport movement — a "complex, multi-layered, interdependent entity" (see Exhibit 27.3). An appreciation of where domestic sport organizations fit within the international sport movement is important in order to appreciate not only where high performance sport fits within that structure but also to appreciate how the international sport federations impact domestic sport organizations.

The international sport movement comprises a number of bodies, including non-governmental organizations (NGOs). The Olympic Movement is one such NGO.[3] This movement consists of the International Olympic Committee (IOC) and the International Paralympic Committee (IPC), the National Olympic Committees (NOCs) and National Paralympic Committees (NPCs) of each country (i.e., the Canadian Olympic Committee, the Canadian Paralympic Committee), and international sport federation (ISF) bodies (i.e., the International Amateur Boxing Association). The IOC is *the* key player, responsible for delegating the control and development of a given sport to the appropriate interna-

---

[1] John Barnes, *Sports and the Law in Canada*, 3d ed. (Toronto: Butterworths, 1996) at 2, n4.

[2] Minister of State Fitness and Amateur Sport, *Sport: The Way Ahead — The Report of the Minister's Task Force on Federal Sport Policy* (Ottawa: Minister of Supply and Services Canada, 1992) at 22. (Task Force Report)

[3] *Ibid.* at 131.

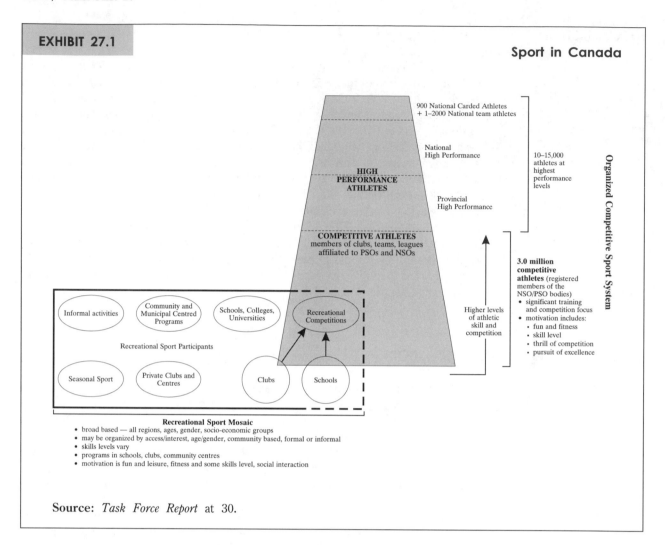

EXHIBIT 27.1

Sport in Canada

Source: *Task Force Report* at 30.

EXHIBIT 27.2

Description of Sport Levels

CHARACTERISTIC	LEVEL		
	RECREATION	COMPETITIVE	HIGH PERFORMANCE
Level of Play	informal (i.e., pickup game) to more organized (i.e., university, college, seasonal sport)	extensive involvement in organized sport (i.e., member of team affiliated with national sport organization)	high performance (i.e., at provincial, national and international levels)
Key Motivating Factor	fun, leisure, fitness, social interaction	fun, fitness, excitement of competition, desire to improve skills, pursuit of excellence	pursuit of excellence
Skill Level	some, usually obtained during participation	elevated athletic skill and competition	highest level acquired through extensive training, skill, competition

Source: *Task Force Report* at 30.

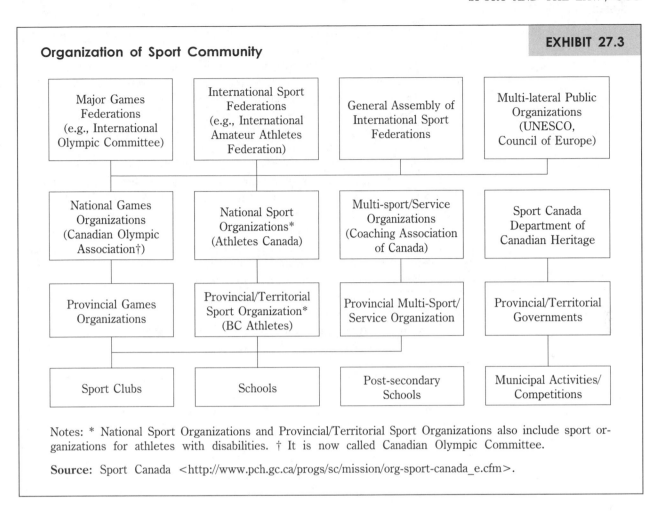

EXHIBIT 27.3

Organization of Sport Community

Major Games Federations (e.g., International Olympic Committee)	International Sport Federations (e.g., International Amateur Athletes Federation)	General Assembly of International Sport Federations	Multi-lateral Public Organizations (UNESCO, Council of Europe)
National Games Organizations (Canadian Olympic Association†)	National Sport Organizations* (Athletes Canada)	Multi-sport/Service Organizations (Coaching Association of Canada)	Sport Canada Department of Canadian Heritage
Provincial Games Organizations	Provincial/Territorial Sport Organization* (BC Athletes)	Provincial Multi-Sport/ Service Organization	Provincial/Territorial Governments
Sport Clubs	Schools	Post-secondary Schools	Municipal Activities/ Competitions

Notes: * National Sport Organizations and Provincial/Territorial Sport Organizations also include sport organizations for athletes with disabilities. † It is now called Canadian Olympic Committee.

Source: Sport Canada <http://www.pch.gc.ca/progs/sc/mission/org-sport-canada_e.cfm>.

tional sport federation and NOCs. International sport federations serve as a governing force for the control and development of their respective sports at an international level. An NSO, in turn, is required to comply with the rules of its ISF. The Canadian Amateur Boxing Association (a national sport organization or NSO), for example, is influenced by, and must comply with, the rules of its respective international federation, the International Amateur Boxing Association (or its more commonly known French acronym, the AIBA). Similarly, a provincial sport organization (or PSO), such as the Ontario Amateur Boxing Association, is influenced by and must comply with the rules of its NSO. Failure to comply with the rules of a governing body means that the governing body likely will not recognize the non-complying organization. In high performance sport, recognition is equated with existence. It follows, therefore, that non-recognition is typically fatal. An organization that is not recognized is ineligible for competition, as competitions are limited to recognized bodies. A competition that includes athletes from unrecognized bodies is considered "contaminated". Athletes from a recognized organization that compete with a "contaminated" athlete themselves become contaminated.

REGULATION OF SPORT

"Amateur" (i.e., "non-professional") sport in Canada is affected at a variety of levels by a variety of laws. The starting point when considering legislative regulation of any area is the *Constitution Act, 1867*. Sections 91 and 92 of this

Act set out the areas within federal and provincial jurisdiction, respectively. These sections are silent, however, when it comes to sport. Despite this silence, private and community organizations that fall within provincial jurisdiction have typically taken a lead in the area of sport development and participation. Constitutional authority for such involvement stems from the provinces having exclusive jurisdiction over areas such as education, property and civil rights, municipal institutions, public lands and general matters of a merely local or private nature (sections 93, 92(13), 92(8), 92(5) and 92(16), respectively).[4] Pursuant to this authority, for example, provincial legislation affecting the area of sport and recreation is enacted.[5] Federal government jurisdiction in the area of sport stems from one of a number of areas, including the exercise of federal "spending power" in order to complement provincial or private contribution[6] or where the matter in issue involves a matter of "national or international significance".[7] Other rationales include sections concerning Parliament's residual authority to enact laws for the peace, order and good government of Canada, trade and commerce, tax, military, criminal law, immigration and citizenship (*Constitution Act, 1867*, sections 91, 91(2), 91(3), 91(7), 91(27) and 91(25) and 95, respectively).

While these constitutional rationales for federal government involvement in sport have existed since 1867, the federal government's support of amateur sport dates from the early 1960s, with the enactment in 1961 of the *Fitness and Amateur Sport Act* (Bill C-131)[8] (FASA) and the creation of the Fitness and Amateur Sport Branch of what was then the Department of National Health and Welfare. (The FASA was subsequently repealed and replaced in 2003 by the *Physical Activity and Sport Act*.[9]) The Fitness and Amateur Sport Branch consisted of a sport unit and a recreation unit. The former unit funded "mainstream" high performance sport organizations (i.e., NSOs), while the recreation unit funded disability-based sport organizations. Federal involvement in sport at that time was fuelled by concerns with the general fitness levels of Canadians, stemming in large part from Canada's results in high performance international competition. An agreement reached between the provinces and territories resulted in a provision in the Act concerning a "federal–provincial agreement" whereby the federal government would contribute funding to sport at the provincial level.[10] A sport organization looking to avail itself of this funding needed to establish that it had a PSO responsible for its sport.[11] Further funding was available where it could be shown that a sport had a NSO responsible for it.[12] The effect of this was that the provinces and territories focused on sport development, from a community level of participation, which includes recreation, to a level of athletic excellence just below national team standards, while the federal government directed its energies to high performance sport at national and international levels.

---

[4]   *Supra* note 1 at 10.

[5]   Stephen Bird, for example, references a May 1985 publication of the Ontario Ministry of Tourism and Recreation that listed almost 100 Acts and Regulations that affect recreation in Ontario. See: Stephen Bird, *Recreation and the Law*, 2d ed. (Toronto: Thomson Canada, 1997) at 5.

[6]   *Supra* note 1 at 11.

[7]   *Ibid.*

[8]   R.S.C. 1985, c. F-25 (repealed by the *Physical Activity and Sport Act*, S.C. 2003, c. 2, s. 39).

[9]   S.C. 2003, c. 2 (Bill C-12). The Act received Royal Assent on 10 March 2003 and the majority of the Act came into force 15 June 2003 (P.C. 2003-941 12 June 2003). (Registration SI/2003-129, 2 July 2003.)

[10]   B. Schrodt, "Changes in the Governance of Amateur Sport in Canada" (May 1983) 14:1 *Canadian Journal of History of Sport* 1 at 6.

[11]   *Ibid.*

[12]   *Ibid.*

In 1993, responsibility for high performance sport was transferred from the Fitness and Amateur Sport Branch of the Department of National Health and Welfare to Sport Canada, a branch of the identity sector of the Department of Canadian Heritage. Paragraph 4(2)(f) of the *Department of Canadian Heritage Act* provided at that time that the Minister of Canadian Heritage had jurisdiction for, among other things, "the encouragement, promotion and development of amateur sport".[13] While the federal focus remains largely the same, the reference to "amateur" was deleted by way of an amendment provided for in the *Physical Activity and Sport Act*.[14] The position of Secretary of State (Amateur Sport), attached to the Department of Canadian Heritage, created in 1998, took on responsibility for high performance sport. The latter position has subsequently been replaced under Prime Minister Paul Martin's government by a Minister of State (Sport) (Stan Keyes). As at 2007, Sport Canada is listed as a branch of the International and Intergovernmental Affairs and Sport Sector within this same department.[15] The Honourable Helena Guergis is presently the Secretary of State (Foreign Affairs and International Trade) and (Sport).[16] Sport Canada's mission as at 2007 "is to enhance opportunities for all Canadians to participate and excel in sport. This is achieved by enhancing the capacity of the Canadian sport system, encouraging participation in sport and enabling Canadians with talent and dedication to achieve excellence in international sport."[17]

The Canadian Sport Policy, released by the federal government in May 2002, outlines four goals to be achieved by 2012:

1. *Enhanced Participation*, demonstrated by the involvement in quality sport activities at all levels and in all forms of participation of a "significantly higher proportion of Canadians from all segments of society";

2. *Enhanced Excellence*, demonstrated by an expanded pool of talented athletes and the systematic achievement of world class results "at the highest levels of international competition through fair and ethical means" by Canadian athletes and teams;

3. *Enhanced Capacity*, as illustrated by having "the essential components of an ethically based, athlete/participant-centred development system ... in place", which are "continually modernized and strengthened as required"; and

4. *Enhanced Interaction*, whereby "the components of the sport system are more connected and co-ordinated as a result of the committed collaboration and communication amongst the stakeholders".[18]

In an effort to achieve these four goals by 2012, Sport Canada provides financial support through three primary programs, two of which include separate sub-components:[19]

---

[13] S.C. 1995, c. 11.

[14] Online: Canada's Parliament <http://www.parl.gc.ca/37/1/parlbus/chambus/house/bills/government/C-54/C-54_3/90184 b-2E.html#20>.

[15] Online: Sport Canada <http://www.pch.gc.ca/progs/sc/index_e.cfm>.

[16] Online: Canadian Heritage <http://www.pch.gc.ca/pc-ch/min/guergis/portfolio_e.cfm>.

[17] Online: Canadian Heritage <http://www.pch.gc.ca/progs/sc/prog/index_e.cfm>.

[18] Online: Sport Canada, *The Canadian Sport Policy*, "Towards the Vision" <http://www.pch.gc.ca/progs/sc/pol/pcs-csp/ 2003/4_e.cfm>.

[19] Online: Sport Canada <http://www.pch.gc.ca/pgm/sc/pgm/index-eng.cfm>.

1. Sport Support Program
   * National Sport Organization (NSO) component;
   * Multisport Service Organization (MSO) component; and
   * Project Stream component.

2. Hosting Program
   * International Major Multi-Sport Games component;
   * International Single Sport Events component;
   * International Strategic Focus Events component; and
   * Canada Games component.

3. Athlete Assistance Program (AAP)

Sport Canada supports a number of initiatives, including mainstream and disability-based sport organizations at a national level (i.e., the Canadian Amateur Boxing Association, the Canadian Wheelchair Basketball Association); multi-sport/multi-service organizations (i.e., the Canadian Olympic Committee, the Canadian Paralympic Committee); and national sport centres. Sport Canada contributes some funding for "major Games" (i.e., the Olympic Games, Paralympic Games) and the hosting of major single-sport events. Some athletes receive funding through the "Athlete Assistance Program". The federal government has also injected monies to develop Olympic and Paralympic champions for upcoming Olympic Games into the Canadian Olympic Committee's "Excellence Fund".[20] The federal contribution is illustrative of the federal government's championing of partnerships and, in particular, the corporate sponsorship of national sport organizations, events and programs. Sport Canada also provides funding for a number of other initiatives, including for Aboriginal people. Initiatives in this area include the Aboriginal Sport Circle (Circle), a "national body" of Aboriginal persons that represents the interests of Aboriginal people in sport, the North American Indigenous Games (NAIG) and Aboriginal coaching initiatives.

Athletes with a Disability

Some persons with disabilities participate in the **mainstream sport** system, while others participate in a **parallel sport system** for athletes with a disability. There are three main global movements, and each movement is focused on a major Games: the Paralympics, the Special Olympics and the World Games for the Deaf. Each movement has an international body that is responsible for co-ordinating its major Games. Domestic development of **sport for athletes with a disability** has reflected the three-pronged international movement. In addition, disability-specific (i.e., amputee, blind) *multi*-sport organizations were created (i.e., the Canadian Amputee Sports Association, the Canadian Blind Sports Association). In some cases a sport organization developed around a specific sport — i.e., the Canadian Association for Disabled Skiing.

Since 1993, a number of sports for Paralympic athletes in Canada have been integrating with mainstream NSOs whereby sport for athletes with a disability becomes an integral part of either all or almost all aspects of the operation of the mainstream sport organization. In addition to the Paralympic movement, the Special Olympics are devoted to athletes with intellectual disabilities. Minimum disability requirements exist to participate in these Games. The Canadian Special Olympics organization has made a concerted effort to

---

[20] See, for example, Martin Cleary, "Project Delivers future Olympians $7.4 million in funding" *The [Ottawa] Citizen* (11 December 2003) B3; and Pierre LeBrun, "Potential medal winners in line for extra cash" *The [Ottawa] Citizen* (26 February 2003) C2.

forge partnerships with mainstream sport organizations in an effort to access more sport-specific technical expertise for training programs for athletes, as well as additional opportunities for competition. The Canadian Deaf Sports Association generally has supported the existence of the World Deaf Games — a parallel sport system for the deaf operated by the deaf. Sport Canada's long-awaited Policy on Sport for Persons with a Disability was made publicly available in June 2006.[21]

Aboriginal Sport

Aboriginal athletes may participate in the mainstream sport system, the disability sport system or an Aboriginal sport system. Another long-awaited policy, Sport Canada's Policy on Aboriginal Peoples' Participation in Sport (Aboriginal Sport Policy), was made publicly available in May 2005.[22] The North American Indigenous Games (NAIG), for example, a "segregated, developing high performance event for Aboriginal athletes"[23], are a component of that system. The NAIG provide

> a culturally appropriate competition venue for a large number of junior Aboriginal athletes to express and enhance their cultural heritage. For Aboriginal community sport leaders and athletes, the NAIG provides an incentive and focus for community sport development and leadership participation. For Aboriginal athletes with high performance potential, NAIG training and competition provide an opportunity to improve skills in readiness for Canada Games team selection trials.[24]

As at 2007, a total of six NAIG have been held: Edmonton, Alberta (1990); Prince Albert, Saskatchewan (1993); Duluth, Minnesota (1995); Victoria, British Columbia (1997); Winnipeg, Manitoba (2002); and Denver, Colorado (2006). The 2008 NAIG is to be held in the Cowichan Valley, British Columbia.

CONTROVERSIES

Adequacy of Support

Funding levels for amateur sport in Canada are a contentious issue among high performance athletes. The "See You In Athens" advertisement was illustrative of this concern. The advertisement depicted athletes living in poverty and carrying a sign that reads "hungry for gold":

> With nearly seventy percent living below the poverty line, what do our athletes have to do next? Beg? The harsh reality is, in the four years leading up to the games, most won't be able to afford proper nutrition, housing, equipment, or even basic essentials like a coach. What kind of country treats their athletes this way? Well, certainly not the Americans, Australians, or Germans. The See You In Athens Fund is a non-profit organization that puts money directly in the hands of athletes who need it.[25]

A further concern arises in light of the considerable funding differences between the mainstream sport system, the sport system for athletes with a disability and the Aboriginal sport system and the athletes participating in

---

[21] Online: Sport Canada, *Policy on Sport for Persons with a Disability,* HTML version <http://www.pch.gc.ca/progs/sc/pol/pwad/tdm_e.cfm> and pdf format <http://www.pch.gc.ca/progs/sc/pol/pwad/pwad_e.pdf>.

[22] Online: Sport Canada <http://www.pch.gc.ca/progs/sc/pol/aboriginal/index_e.cfm>.

[23] Aboriginal Sport Circle, *Aboriginal Sport Development: The Role of Coaching Development, the NAIG and Provincial/Territorial Aboriginal Sport Bodies* (October 1998) [unpublished] at 7.

[24] *Ibid.* The Canada Games are a biennial celebration of Canadian sport that targets youth under 20 years of age. Athletes from other provinces and territories compete.

[25] See, for example, the advertisement in the *Ottawa Citizen* (19 July 2003) at C5. See also Wayne Scanlan, "Athletes' advocates talking tough" *The [Ottawa] Citizen* (19 March 2003) D1, D7.

those respective systems. Differences are evident, for example, in the three systems with respect to the funding of sport organizations and sport programming and support for major Games and coaching initiatives.

Impact of Tobacco Policy and Legislation on Funding of Sport

Despite the federal government's recognition of, and emphasis on, corporate sponsorship of national sport organizations and events, Sport Canada proceeded to introduce its controversial *Federal Government Policy on Tobacco Sponsorship of National Sport Organizations* (Tobacco Policy) in March 1985.[26] The Tobacco Policy preceded the enactment of, and is entirely independent of, federal tobacco legislation. While the Tobacco Policy is concerned with the prohibition of tobacco sponsorship, the *Tobacco Act*[27] places restrictions on the size, placement and content of sponsorship advertisements by tobacco companies.

The Tobacco Policy provides that

> ... effective immediately, all national amateur sport bodies funded in part by the federal government will be required to desist from associating in any new or renewed sponsorship arrangements with the tobacco products industry. The federal government will withhold all funds from *national amateur sport organizations* associating in any sponsorship, promotional or other financial support arrangements (e.g., advertising) with the tobacco products industry *for events or programs **predominantly** involving amateur athletes*.[28] [emphases added]

The policy also provides that a sponsorship contract in existence at the time the policy went into effect would be permitted to run to completion; however, federal funding would be withheld from any sport organization that opted to continue such a contract beyond its expiry date.

While the Tobacco Policy may appear to be well-intentioned, it is clearly designed to make tobacco sponsorship unattractive and to have the effect of restricting the corporate sponsorship of national sport. The policy, however, may not be as limiting as it first seems as there appear to be several loopholes. For example, the policy purports to withhold funds from *national sport organizations*. Explicit reference in the policy to NSOs is significant, as it suggests that while those organizations and their respective programming would be caught by the policy, the policy would likely *not* apply to other bodies receiving federal funding (i.e., national sport centres, major games organizations and athletes receiving funds through the Athletes Assistance Program). The policy's explicit reference to *predominantly amateur* athletes is also relevant, as the policy presumably would not apply to a national sport organization whose membership consisted predominantly of *professional* athletes (provided the organization satisfied all other funding criteria). This policy would also likely not apply to an organization that does not use the word "amateur" to describe its athletes. The latter point, however, could be contested, given that there is relatively little distinction today between an "amateur" and a "professional" athlete.

---

[26] Online: Sport Canada <http://www.pch.gc.ca/progs/sc/pol/tabac-tobacco/index_e.cfm>.

[27] S.C. 1997, c. 13. Bill C-71 (the *Tobacco Act*, with the exception of two subsections, came into force on Royal Assent, 25 April 1997).

[28] *Supra* note 26.

Sport and Charitable Status under the Income Tax Act

"Charitable" status in law is dependent on the common law rather than statute law. The starting point is the preamble to the *Statute of Charitable Uses*.[29] The definition was then succinctly captured by Lord Macnaghten in an 1891 decision commonly referred to as the *Pemsel* decision:

> "Charity" in its legal sense comprises four principal divisions: trusts for the relief of poverty; trusts for the advancement of education; trusts for the advancement of religion; and trusts for other purposes beneficial to the community, not falling under any of the preceding heads.[30]

Sport is not specifically identified in any of these four categories and is, thus, not specifically recognized as having charitable status at common law. This is not to say that sport cannot be a means by which to achieve a recognized charitable purpose in law (i.e., as a part of a general program that promotes participation as a means by which to improve certain physical conditions or overall healthy recreation) or that it does not form part of an overall educational program (i.e., universities, schools).

From the government's perspective, sport for the sake of sport does not qualify for charitable status. As a result, a donation made to a sport organization is not tax exempt, and the recipient organization is unable to issue an official tax receipt. Thus, fundraising attempts by sport organizations have historically proven to be challenging.[31] The federal government, in recognition of the limits posed by this challenge and in an attempt to provide non-profit national organizations that promote amateur sport across Canada with some form of tax relief, amended the *Income Tax Act* in 1972 to provide an equivalent-to-charitable status for Canadian Amateur Athletic Associations (CAAA) (s. 248, s. 149(1)(l)). An organization seeking to qualify for charitable status must apply to be registered — and, if approved, receives the status of a Registered Canadian Amateur Athletic Association (RCAAA). Four types of organizations are eligible for RCAAA status: national sport organizations, multi-sport national and international events (i.e., the Olympics), legacy facilities and multi-sport training centres. In order to apply for RCAAA status, the organization in question completes the required form (T1189). In order to obtain the status of an RCAAA, the organization must satisfy the definition of a CAAA (i.e., it must be created under a law in force in Canada, be a resident in Canada and satisfy the definition of a non-profit organization at paragraph 149(1)(l) of the *Income Tax Act*). In addition, the CAAA's main purpose and function must be to promote amateur athletics in Canada on a "nation-wide basis".

Revocation of status as a *registered* Canadian Amateur Athlete Association is a cause for concern. An RCAAA's status may be revoked for a variety of reasons. While an RCAAA is able to channel its funds to another organization — i.e., a provincial organization — the decision to do so must be that of the RCAAA and not attached as a condition to the donation. An RCAAA that accepts a gift or donation made on the condition (either express or implied) that the recipient RCAAA make a gift or donation to another person or association may, therefore, lose its status (ss. 149(1)(l), 168(1)(f)). An RCAAA may also lose its status where it issues a tax receipt to someone for the payment for a service — i.e., a fee paid to a coach. The basis for this is that there exists a distinction in law between a "gift", for which a receipt may be issued,

---

[29] 1601, 43 Eliz. I, c. 4.

[30] *Com'rs for Special Purposes of Income Tax v. Pemsel*, [1891] A.C. 531 at 583.

[31] A charitable organization can issue an official donation receipt to the donor; the donation is exempt from income tax by the recipient, and the donor may claim tax relief (*Income Tax Act*, R.S.C. 1985 (5th Supp.), c. I-1, ss. 110.1, 149(1) and 118.1, respectively).

and payment for a service that does not qualify as a gift and would, therefore, be ineligible for a tax receipt.

The 2006 Federal Court of Appeal decision on *A.Y.S.A. Amateur Youth Soccer Association v. Canada Revenue Agency*[32] upheld the decision of the Minister of National Revenue to refuse to recognize a sport body, the Amateur Youth Soccer Association of Ontario, as a registered charity on the basis that the promotion of sport was not recognized as a charitable purpose.

A unanimous Federal Court of Appeal wrote the following:

> In formulating this status in 1972, Parliament must be taken to have been aware that no association which has, as its main purpose, the pursuit of amateur sport could qualify as a charity under the common law, and hence, under the Act. That is the background against which Parliament opted to provide a charity-like treatment for amateur athletic associations, but only with respect to those which met the requirements specified in paragraph 248(1).
>
> This brief legislative history shows that Parliament has put its mind to the tax treatment of amateur sports associations and that it was willing to forgo federal tax dollars to promote amateur sport in Canada, but only if the funds were to be expended on a country-wide basis. Parliament did not want to assist in the funding of these associations if the beneficiaries were to be limited to a province or region.
>
> In my view, this scheme precludes the possibility that an amateur sport association be treated as a charity under the Act. Parliament gave these associations a special status under the Act subject to specific terms and conditions. It follows that Parliament must be taken to have occupied the field respecting the tax treatment of amateur sports associations, regardless of their status in the law of charity. Indeed, as this case illustrates, to hold otherwise would frustrate Parliament's clearly expressed intent to limit the federal funding of amateur sports associations to those which operate nationally.
>
> I, therefore, conclude that regardless of the state of common law, the Act forecloses the possibility that an association such as the appellant, whose primary purpose is the pursuit of amateur sport, can be registered as a charity under the Act. ...[33]

The FCA's decision was appealed to the Supreme Court of Canada, which granted leave to appeal. The appeal was dismissed.[34]

Justice Rothstein, writing for eight judges, noted that the fact that an organization did not qualify as an RCAAA was not tantamount to a finding that the organization could not be characterized as a charity within the meaning of the *Income Tax Act*. Put another way, Justice Rothstein did not perceive section 248(1) of the *Income Tax Act* as setting out a complete code for determining whether or not a sport organization was eligible for charitable status. As a result, the fact that the A.Y.S.A.'s mandate was not nation-wide and thus rendered it ineligible for RCAAA status did not mean that it may not qualify as a charity. As a result, Justice Rothstein had occasion to examine the common law test of charity and whether or not the A.Y.S.A. qualified as a charity. Ultimately it was determined that the A.Y.S.A. did not qualify as a charity because its purposes and activities were not considered charitable.[35]

Justice Abella, on the other hand, considered the definition of RCAAA as evidence that Parliament had intentionally excluded other amateur athletic organizations from qualifying for such status and therefore was of the opinion

---

[32] 2006 FCA 136.

[33] 2006 FCA 136 at paras. 20–23.

[34] 2007 SCC 42; available online: <http://scc.lexum.umontreal.ca/en/2007/2007scc42/2007scc42.html>.

[35] 2007 SCC 42 at paras. 1–45.

that resort to the common law test of whether the A.Y.S.A. qualified as a charity was unnecessary.[36]

Commencing in 2007, the Government of Canada now allows a non-refundable tax credit on eligible amounts of up to $500 paid by parents to register a child in an eligible program of physical activity.[37]

UNDER-REPRESENTATION

Sport Canada's *Strategic Directions* established a series of goals in relation to its strategic objectives for the period 1998–2001. One of the goals identified was "to increase access and equity in sport for targeted under-represented groups."[38] The groups identified were women, Aboriginal peoples, visible minorities and athletes with a disability. This goal is reflected in the *Physical Activity and Sport Act* (PASA) (which, it will be recalled, repealed the *Fitness and Amateur Sport Act*). The PASA's objectives include to "encourage, promote and develop physical activity and sport in Canada" (s. 5). The Act's object also provides that "[t]he Minister may take any measures that the Minister considers appropriate to further those objects, and in particular may ... (m) facilitate the participation of under-represented groups in the Canadian sport system" (s. 5(m)).

Sport Canada's website in 2007 listed 10 strategic directions — none of which specifically referenced increasing access and equity in sport for these targeted under-represented groups:

- Strengthen Sport Leadership
- Provide Strategic Support for High Performance Programming
- Promote Technically Sound Sport Development
- Enhance Opportunities for Sport Participation
- Maximize the Benefits of Hosting
- Promote Linguistic Duality in the Canadian Sport System
- Strengthen the Ethical Foundation of Sport
- Expand the Body of Knowledge about Sport
- Strengthen Sport Canada Program and Policy Evaluation
- Harmonize the Canadian Sport System[39]

The fact that these 10 strategic directions do not make specific reference to increasing access and equity in sport for women, Aboriginal peoples, visible minorities and athletes with a disability, however, is not to suggest that one or more of these directions could not be employed to support such efforts. The strategic direction of enhancing opportunities for sports participation, for example, could be considered to support such ends.

Women

The *Sport Canada Policy on Women in Sport* dates to 1986. It provides that Sport Canada will work in co-operation with other levels of government and agencies to "increase participation opportunities for women in all forms of competitive sport."[40] In pursuit of its strategic objective to increase access and

---

[36] 2007 SCC 42 at paras. 46–59.

[37] See Canada Revenue Agency, *Children's Fitness Tax Credit* <http://www.cra-arc.gc.ca/whatsnew/fitness-e.html>.

[38] Sport Canada, *Strategic Directions (1998–2001)* (Ottawa: Sport Canada, 1998).

[39] Sport Canada, *Mission* <http://www.pch.gc.ca/progs/sc/mission/index_e.cfm>.

[40] Sport Canada, *Sport Canada Policy on Women and Sport* (Ottawa: Sport Fitness and Amateur Sport, 1986), online: <http://www.pch.gc.ca/progs/sc/pol/femmes-women/index_e.cfm>.

equity for women, Sport Canada identified as a strategic objective the provision of "leadership and support to achieve equitable opportunities for female athletes, coaches, officials and leaders."[41] While national sport organizations are required to satisfy national "gender equity standards", the "depth and expression" of that commitment varies considerably.[42] According to the Canadian Association for the Advancement of Women and Sport (CAAWS), for example, "inequities in funding and participation opportunities available for women in sport"[43] continue to exist.

The CAAWS seized the opportunity presented by debate surrounding the introduction of a new sport Act to address the issue of gender equity in sport. The CAAWS submitted a request to the House of Commons subcommittee on sport to amend Bill C-54 to include a provision requiring "universities and national sport programs to give equal opportunity and funding for women and men."[44] Following an agreement reached between the CAAWS and then Secretary of State (Amateur Sport) Paul DeVillers, CAAWS agreed to withdraw its demand for the inclusion of this provision. Bill C-54 was reintroduced as Bill C-12 and then enacted as the *Physical Activity and Sport Act*. The key factor informing this agreement was a written commitment from DeVillers that Sport Canada would create "an accountability framework that clearly articulates how existing national standards are to be applied in such areas as funding, coaching and staffing if national sport bodies are to continue to receive funding."[45] According to CAAWS Chair Shawnee Scatliff, "[t]he new accountability framework will smooth out those differences and nudge negligent sports organizations in the right direction."[46] The CAAWS will have a hand in the development and implementation of the accountability framework, including input into the consequences that flow to national sport bodies that fail to satisfy the terms of the accountability framework. DeVillers also promised CAAWS that the government will use the national women's sport strategy currently being developed by the CAAWS to develop a federal program to promote increased physical activity among girls.[47] This latter initiative is timely given that a February 2003 survey found that 67 percent of the women surveyed are too busy to play a sport, while the daughters of 46 percent of the women surveyed recently stopped playing a sport.[48]

The Sport Funding and Accountability Framework (SFAF) is the mechanism employed by the Department of Canadian Heritage to identify which National Sport Organizations and Multi-Sport and Service Organizations are eligible for various Sport Canada funding/contribution programs, in which areas, at which level and under which conditions. The SFAF III is the third edition of the SFAF and covers the funding cycle running from April 1, 2005, through to March 31, 2010.[49]

The SFAF consists of four steps: eligibility, assessment, funding and accountability. The eligibility criteria for NSOs and MSOs are set out in separate documents. The NSOs eligibility criteria are used to create a list of NSOs eligible for assessment by Sport Canada under the SFAF III. In order to

[41] Wayne Kondro, "Imposed sport equity 'not appropriate'" *The [Ottawa] Citizen* (24 May 2002).

[42] *Ibid.*

[43] *Ibid.*

[44] *Ibid.*

[45] Wayne Kondro, "Women withdraw gender equity demand" *The [Ottawa] Citizen* (6 June 2002).

[46] *Ibid.*

[47] *Ibid.*

[48] Joanne Laucius, "Many women too busy to play a sport: survey" *The [Ottawa] Citizen* (11 April 2003) A14.

[49] Online: Sport Canada, *Sport Funding and Accountability Framework III (SFAF III): 2005–2010* <http://www.patrimoinecanadien.gc.ca/progs/sc/prog/cfrs-sfaf/sfafelig2005_e.cfm>.

determine if an NSO is eligible for funding, the entity is assessed against a series of criteria. The criteria are designed to determine whether an NSO has "reached a requisite level of development and capacity enabling them to provide technically and ethically safe and sound sport programs and activities that are accessible to all Canadians."[50]

In order to enter the SFAF process and qualify for funding for the 2005–2010 funding cycle, an NSO must complete and submit an eligibility application. This requirement applies to all NSOs, even those that have previously received funding. It is important to note that a determination that an NSO satisfies the eligibility criteria is not tantamount to a finding that the organization will be funded but rather means that the NSO is able to access the next step in the SFAF process (assessment). The assessment stage entails an evaluation of an NSO's size, scope, performance and potential. NSOs are then ranked with respect to contribution of the organization to goals outlined in the Canadian Sport Policy in four areas — participation, excellence, capacity and interaction. Funding levels, in turn, are informed by the assessment scores and tied to the achievement of "National Accountability Standards" as well as compliance with contribution guidelines. A funding decision is made by the responsible minister once the SFAF process is complete.[51]

The first of the four steps, eligibility, consists of three sections: general criteria (Section A), national scope (Section B), and international scope (Section C). In order for an NSO to be considered "eligible", it must satisfy all of the Section A criteria and all criteria in either Section B or Section C. NSOs completing the Section C criteria are to complete it for both mainstream disciplines and disciplines for athletes with a disability. The onus is on the NSO to providing supporting documentation where required. One of the Section A (general) criteria, which must be satisfied by all NSOs in order to be considered for funding, is A13:

> The NSO has a formal policy or policies demonstrating commitment to equity and access, notably for women, persons with a disability and Aboriginal peoples as athletes, coaches, officials, volunteers and leaders.[52]

However, Annex A13 provides that where an NSO exceeds 40 percent female participation or representation in all areas (i.e., athletes, coaches, officials, volunteers and leaders), the NSO is not required to have a formal policy on women and sport.[53]

Aboriginal Peoples

It is undisputed that Aboriginal peoples are under-represented in the Canadian sport system. This is both ironic and troubling given that sport is "deeply rooted in the cultural history of [...] indigenous peoples"[54] and directly related to the cultural experience of indigenous peoples.[55]

While the reasons for Aboriginal under-representation in the Canadian sport system are complex, a few reasons will be briefly canvassed here. A key consideration when discussing such under-representation is a lack of sport programming, facilities and equipment. This absence is attributable, in

---

[50] *Ibid.*

[51] *Ibid.*

[52] *Ibid.*

[53] *Ibid.*

[54] *Supra* note 2 at 153.

[55] Alwyn Morris, "The Olympic Experience: An Aboriginal Perspective" 9–11 at 9 in T. Taylor, ed., *How You Play the Game: Papers from the First International Conference on Sports and Human Rights (September 1–3, 1999)* (Australia: Human Rights Council of Australia, 2000).

considerable part, to the absence of funding for such initiatives. The area of **Aboriginal sport** has virtually been ignored by all levels of government. While the federal government has "jurisdiction" over Indians pursuant to subsection 91(24) of the *Constitution Act, 1867*, it has, until relatively recently, taken very little interest in Aboriginal sport. The federal government, however, has generally adopted the position that Aboriginal sport initiatives did not qualify as "high performance" sport and, thus, were outside the jurisdiction of the federal government. Historically, most provinces have taken the position that Aboriginal sport fell within the federal government's exclusive jurisdiction and, thus, was not a provincial concern. This issue as to responsibility for Aboriginal sport remains unresolved.

"Pro-active" federal government involvement in the area of Aboriginal sport dates to the 1970s when the government, recognizing the absence of opportunities for sport and recreation in Aboriginal communities, initiated several projects designed to assimilate Aboriginal peoples into the mainstream sport system. In an effort to assist Aboriginal athletes to compete in the mainstream sport system, the federal government in 1970 introduced a two-year pilot project that provided funding to Aboriginal associations in five provinces (Alberta, Manitoba, Saskatchewan, British Columbia and Québec) through to 1972.[56] Sub-objectives included broadening the participation base of Aboriginal people, increasing both the quality and diversity of opportunities for Aboriginal people and raising the level of performance in Aboriginal communities.[57] Interest in the two-year initiative spread to Aboriginal groups in other provinces and, ultimately, resulted in the creation of a Native Sport and Recreation Program (NSRP) in 1972. The NSRP, a five-year program structured to aid Aboriginal organizations develop sport and recreation programs,[58] was extended for an additional year (1977–1978). A review conducted that year verified that "sport and recreation [were] integral components of indigenous culture and that the program had facilitated community development significantly."[59] A further two-year extension was granted (1978–1980), and funding was approved for 1980–1981. The funds for that year, however, were not advanced, and the NSRP program was eliminated without notice to, or consultation with, Aboriginal peoples.[60]

The unceremonial demise of the NSRP was apparently owing to a difference in vision. The federal government appears to have supported the development of a segregated sport system that would then be "integrated" into the mainstream system — in other words, Aboriginal athletes would train to attain a level of performance that would enable them to compete in competitive events in mainstream sport with, generally, non-Aboriginal Canadians. This vision, however, kept the sport programming focus on mainstream sport. Aboriginal sport organizations envisioned a model that allowed Aboriginal athletes to participate in the mainstream sport system, if they so desired, but also sought to provide a meaningful alternative — a segregated parallel sport system that included "sport" *and* more "traditional" elements, such as the powwow. The segregation aspect is significant: (i) it provides "for sufficient participation numbers to more equitably meet the needs of Aboriginal young people showing an interest and talent for sport[...]", and (ii) "Aboriginal

---

[56] *Supra* note 2 at 153.

[57] *Ibid.*

[58] *Ibid.*

[59] *Ibid.*

[60] V. Paraschak, "Knowing Ourselves Through the 'Other': Indigenous Peoples in Sport in Canada" in R. Jones & K. Armour, eds., *Sociology of Sport: Theory and Practice* (Essex: Longman, 2000) 153–66 (at 15). Copy of original from Paraschak on file with writer. All page references are to copy on file with writer.

athletes benefit most from early developmental experiences that occur in the supportive environment that retains an Aboriginal orientation."[61]

Following the demise of the NSRP program in 1981, with the exception of the Arctic Winter Games, there were no further attempts at a federal level to develop sport programming in Aboriginal communities until the early 1990s.[62] Renewed federal interest in the 1990s coincided with a series of reports acknowledging the importance of sport to Aboriginal peoples and the under-representation of Aboriginal people in the Canadian sport system: the May 1992 Minister's Task Force Report on Federal Sport Policy,[63] the 1996 report of the Royal Commission of Aboriginal Peoples[64] and a 1998 report of a Sub-Committee of the Standing Committee on Canadian Heritage tasked with studying sport in Canada.[65]

In addition to lack of funding for programming initiatives, remote geographic locations pose challenges for some communities. Aboriginal people living **off-territories** frequently face the challenge of insensitive programs and staff. Stereotypes and **racism**[66] also present barriers. A lack of qualified physical activity and recreation leaders for Aboriginal people and a dearth of Aboriginal coaches present further barriers to Aboriginal participation. Barriers to the development of Aboriginal coaches include difficulties accessing the National Certification Coaching Program, the location of Aboriginal communities, a curriculum that does not address the reality of Aboriginal peoples, and the under-representation of Aboriginal course conductors.[67]

Aboriginal people and their descendants have likened sport to "the strongest type of medicine" because of its "preventative nature",[68] and are championing sport as a mechanism to address "many of the social ills facing Aboriginal people"[69] and the "heightened health risks"[70] faced by Aboriginal youth. While the federal government does contribute funding to Aboriginal sport, it does so in conjunction with access and equity initiatives and not as a right. A contemporary interpretation of the "medicine chest" clause in Treaty No. 6 (and an oral clause in Treaties 7, 8, 10 and 11) may support the inclusion of sport and recreation opportunities.[71] In addition, existing Aboriginal and treaty rights, such as rights flowing from the medicine chest clause in the above-noted treaties, are entrenched in Canada's *Constitution Act, 1982*. If a contemporary interpretation of the medicine chest clause supports sport opportunities, this would mean that an Aboriginal right to sport exists — and is constitutionally entrenched in Canada's Constitution. This line of argument has

---

[61] Aboriginal Sport Circle, *Aboriginal Sport Development, supra* note 15 at 7.

[62] *Supra* note 2 at 154.

[63] *Ibid.*

[64] Royal Commission on Aboriginal Peoples, *Bridging the Cultural Divide: A Report on Aboriginal People and Criminal Justice in Canada* (Ottawa: Supply and Services Canada, 1996).

[65] Canada, *Sport — Leadership, Partnership and Accountability — Everybody's Business* (Ottawa: House of Commons, 1998) at 129.

[66] Saskatchewan Interagency Committee for the Elimination of Racism from Sport and Recreation, *Eliminating Racism from Sport and Recreation: A leader's resource* (Saskatoon: The Agency, 1995), online: The Leisure Information Network <www.lin.ca/resource/html/racism.htm>.

[67] Aboriginal Sport Circle, *Aboriginal Sport Development, supra* note 15 at 5–6.

[68] Alwyn Morris, *Aboriginal Sport Circle Presentation* (Corner Brook, Newfoundland, 1999) at 9.

[69] *Ibid.*

[70] *Ibid.* at 2.

[71] Susan Haslip, "A Treaty Right to Sport?" (June 2001) 8:2 Murdoch Univ. L. Rev., online: Murdoch University Electronic Journal of Law <http://www.murdoch.edu.au/elaw/issues/v8n2/haslip82.html>; and Susan Haslip & Victoria Edwards, "Does Sport Belong in the Medicine Chest?" in Vicky Paraschak & Janice Forsyth, eds., *Proceedings of the 2002 North American Indigenous Games Research Symposium* (Winnipeg: University of Manitoba, 2003).

interesting ramifications, given that case law supporting the existence of incidental rights may be used to support the existence of incidental rights to coaching and the existence of sport/recreational facilities.[72]

As noted earlier, the federal government released its long-awaited policy concerning sport and Aboriginal peoples in 2005: *Sport Canada's Policy on Aboriginal Peoples' Participation in Sport* [*Aboriginal Sport Policy*].[73]

The *Aboriginal Sport Policy* contains a number of strengths. A key starting point in a consideration on the strengths of the *Aboriginal Sport Policy* is the existence of the policy itself. The existence of the policy is illustrative of the ability of Aboriginal and non-Aboriginal Peoples working together to produce a document that confirms and clarifies Sport Canada's — read this as the federal government's — intentions concerning the increased participation of Aboriginal Peoples in sport, recreation and physical education.

The interrelationship between the *Aboriginal Sport Policy* and the *Canadian Sport Policy* (also published by Sport Canada, in 2002) is also an important strength as it illustrates that the *Aboriginal Sport Policy* does not exist in a vacuum. The *Aboriginal Sport Policy* states that it is guided by the principles in the *Canadian Sport Policy*.[74] One of these principles describes sport as based on equity and access.[75] The *Aboriginal Sport Policy*'s focus on increased participation opportunities for Aboriginal Peoples in sport, recreation and physical education provides an example of this commitment in process. To this end the *Aboriginal Sport Policy* provides that it "aims to ensure that the vision of the CSP [Canadian Sport Policy] is inclusive; that it has the power to enhance the experience of — and access to — sport for all, including Aboriginal Peoples living in Canada."[76] Reference in these policies to increased participation opportunities for Aboriginal Peoples is related to the goal of increasing access and equity in sport — a goal confirmed in the *Physical Activity and Sport Act* (citation omitted) enacted in 2003. Reference in both policies to the barriers faced by Aboriginal Peoples in relation to meaningful participation in sport,[77] including socio-economic barriers (the significance of which is discussed in further detail below), is important since it provides express recognition of these barriers.

The fact that this explicit recognition of barriers appears in a policy document (*Canadian Sport Policy*) endorsed by the federal/provincial/territorial ministers responsible for sport is significant since it provides a baseline from which to move forward rather than revisit whether such barriers exist.

An additional strength of the *Aboriginal Sport Policy* is its reference to diversity. This policy provides that while economies of scale dictate the need for having core organizations serving the "general population",

> *An inclusive sport system serving a diverse population will, by necessity, include organizations, programs and events that serve distinct populations.*[78] [emphasis added]

The strengths identified in the *Aboriginal Sport Policy* can be utilized to assist in dismantling the barriers faced by Aboriginal Peoples in relation to

---

[72] See Haslip, "A Treaty Right to Sport?", *ibid.*; and Haslip & Edwards, *ibid.*

[73] Sport Canada, *Sport Canada's Policy on Aboriginal Peoples' Participation in Sport*; online: <http://www.pch.gc.ca/progs/sc/pol/aboriginal/index_e.cfm>.

[74] Ibid., p. 2.

[75] Sport Canada, *The Canadian Sport Policy*, p. 13; online: <http://www.pch.gc.ca/progs/sc/pol/pcs-csp/2003/polsport_e.pdf>.

[76] *Supra* note 72, p. 1.

[77] *Supra* note 72, pp. 4–5; note 74, pp. 9–10.

[78] *Supra* note 72, p. 2.

participation in sport, recreation and physical education. This being said, however, the effective and meaningful operationalization of statements made by the Government of Canada in both its Aboriginal Sport Policy document and the Canada Sport Policy document concerning Aboriginal peoples require careful monitoring and assessment. By way of example, the *Aboriginal Sport Policy* document provides that "Sport Canada will develop and implement an Action Plan for the Policy on Aboriginal Peoples' Participation in Sport."[79] As of fall 2008, however, this document does not appear to be publicly available from Sport Canada.[80]

Visible Minorities

When this chapter was first written, it was observed that Sport Canada did not have a policy on visible minorities in the Canadian sport system. As of fall 2008, Sport Canada still has not made such a policy publicly available. In pursuit of its strategic objective to increase access and equity for visible minorities, however, Sport Canada indicated it would provide leadership and support to foster the inclusion of visible minorities in the Canadian sport system.[81] The reasons for the under-representation of visible minorities in the Canadian sport system are complex. One factor, however, is racism. An article in the *Ottawa Citizen* reported on a number of incidents in which racial slurs were alleged to have been advanced against athletes in the Ontario Hockey League (OHL). A Sault Ste. Marie Greyhounds player, for example, left his club after learning from teammates that a coach had used a racial slur when referring to him. The player returned following the coach's resignation. The same article also refers to an incident during the 2000–2001 season in which a member of the Barrie Colts received a two-game suspension for a racial slur directed at a Kingston Frontenacs player. A second Barrie Colts' player received a four-game suspension for a comment he reportedly directed at a Sault Ste. Marie Greyhounds goaltender.

The incidents in question are troubling — particularly in light of the fact that "a memo posted in every OHL team's dressing room details the league's policy on harassment, abuse, taunting and slurs based on race and national or ethnic origin."[82] While a policy document will clearly not in and of itself solve the problem of racism in the Canadian sport system, it would serve as an example of much-needed government leadership in this area. The absence of a policy on visible minorities and sport may itself be interpreted as sending a message. Given that slurs concerning sexual orientation are also commonplace in sport, *quare* why reference to sexual orientation is omitted from the policy?

Athletes with a Disability/Disabilities

According to a 1991 Health and Activity Limitation Survey conducted by Statistics Canada, 4.2 million Canadians were living with a disability. Of that 4.2 million, 65 percent (or 2.7 million) were under the age of 65. A 2001 Statistics Canada's Survey provides that 12.4 percent or 3.6 million Canadians have disabilities related to activity and functional limitations.[83] While the latter

---

[79] Supra note 72, "Implementation", online: <http://www.pch.gc.ca/progs/sc/pol/aboriginal/2005/4_e.cfm>.

[80] For further discussion concerning the Aboriginal Sport Policy and challenges related to its implementation, see Susan Haslip, "A Consideration of Sport Canada's Policy on Aboriginal Peoples' Participation in Sport", Aboriginal Sport Forum Presentation — Barriers to Aboriginal Sport Panel, November 2005, Ottawa.

[81] Kondro, *supra* note 28.

[82] Donna Spence, "Player returning, but Greyhounds' boss quits over racial slur" *The [Ottawa] Citizen* (11 March 2003) B1, B2.

[83] Statistics Canada, "Participation and Activity Limitation Survey: A profile of disability in Canada", *The Daily*, December 3, 2002.

statistic suggests that the number of Canadians with disabilities had declined in the previous decade, there is no reason to believe that the challenges experienced by persons with disabilities have declined. Despite advances made, persons living with a disability or disabilities continue to experience barriers to their full participation in community life. The sport universe is a microcosm of that community life. As such, the physical and attitudinal barriers faced by persons with disabilities in day-to-day life are also experienced by persons with disabilities in the sport world. Athletes with disabilities continue to be under-represented in the Canadian sport system. The federal government has acknowledged this under-representation and promised to "provide leadership and support to increase access and equity in sport for athletes with a disability."[84]

The area of sport for athletes with a disability is complex, and issues arising are multifaceted. One component of this complexity is that the sport community for athletes with a disability is somewhat fragmented. In addition to dealing with issues of gender and race, divisions exist within different disability groups and within the same disability group owing to the severity of the disability. In addition, the sport structure for athletes with a disability is in a state of flux. There is a movement, for example, towards the **integration** of some disability-based sport organizations into their mainstream counterpart. "**Reverse integration**" is also a challenge, where athletes from the mainstream sport system compete in a sport, such as wheelchair basketball, that was conceived for athletes with a disability. At a high performance level, eligibility and classification are key considerations. The three major Games movements (i.e., the Paralympics, Special Olympics and Deaf Sport) each have minimal disability requirements to determine eligibility. Classification systems for athletes based on the type and/or severity of disability exist at the Paralympics. These systems, however, are the subject of controversy. Possible manipulation of divisioning of Special Olympians is also open to dispute.

Sport Canada has made some contributions in the area of sport for athletes with a disability or with disabilities. Inequities in both representation and funding remain. As noted above, Sport Canada's Policy on Sport for Persons with a Disability was released in June 2006. The policy contains a number of strengths, not the least of which is the existence of the policy itself. As is the case with the policy on Aboriginal sport, the Policy on Sport for Persons with a Disability provides that "Sport Canada will develop and implement an Action Plan for its Policy on Sport for Persons with a Disability."[85] As at fall 2007, however, such a document does not appear to be publicly available from Sport Canada.

HUMAN RIGHTS LEGISLATION

Human rights legislation (i.e., provincial human rights codes and the *Canadian Charter of Rights and Freedoms*[86]) also impact the domestic sport system. An interesting case in point is that of Sikh boxer Pardeep Singh Nagra. Nagra was an Olympic hopeful vying for a place on Canada's national team for the 2000 Olympics in Sydney, Australia, in the light-flyweight division (48 kilogram weight class). Nagra is a practising Sikh and, pursuant to the

---

[84] Sport Canada, *Strategic Directions*, *supra* note 26.

[85] Sport Canada, *Policy on Sport for Persons with a Disability*, "6.0 Policy Implementation and Evaluation", online: <http://www.pch.gc.ca/progs/sc/pol/pwad/6_e.cfm>.

[86] *Canadian Charter of Rights and Freedoms*, Part I of the *Constitution Act, 1982*, being Sch. B to the *Canada Act 1982* (U.K.), 1982, c. 11.

requirements of that faith, is required to "maintain unshorn hair".[87] Nagra's beard, however, worn pursuant to this tenet of his faith, conflicts with the rules of his sport. However, the rules of the International Amateur Boxing Association (more commonly known as the Association Internationale de Boxe Amateur — AIBA), the international sport federation responsible for boxing, require boxers to be clean-shaven. A finding that a boxer is clean-shaven is a component of a successful medical examination at the "weigh in" stage prior to the start of the tournament. Failure to satisfy this threshold results in a boxer being declared ineligible to box. An exception is made for boxers who wear a thin moustache not extending beyond the upper lip. The rules of the Canadian Amateur Boxing Association (CABA), the National Sport Organization responsible for the sport of boxing in Canada, reflect those of its international sport federation, the AIBA. Similarly, the rules of the Ontario Amateur Boxing Association (OABA), the Provincial Sport Organization responsible for the sport of boxing in Ontario, reflect those of its national federation, the CABA.

The OABA, citing the CABA's rules, attempted to prevent Nagra from competing in a provincial qualifying tournament since he was not clean-shaven. Mr. Nagra filed a successful complaint with the Ontario Human Rights Tribunal, which decided that the no-beard rule was contrary to Nagra's rights, and that he could compete if he wore netting over his beard during the competition.[88] Success at this tournament qualified Nagra for the 1999 national championships hosted by the CABA in Campbell River, B.C. The national tournament was a qualifying tournament for membership on the Sydney 2000 Olympic team. This time the CABA took up the fight, arguing that since the CABA's and the AIBA's rules make no exceptions for persons wearing beards, Nagra was in breach of that rule and was ineligible to fight. Nagra sought and obtained an interim order from Justice Somers on December 1, 1999, permitting Nagra to fight at the B.C. tournament.[89]

Justice Somers' decision presented a problem for the CABA. Failure to comply with the court order meant that the CABA could be found in contempt of court. It also meant that Nagra would likely launch a claim for damages due to lost opportunity. Compliance with the court order, however, meant that the CABA would likely face sanctions and repercussions for breach of the rules of its international body. Further, otherwise eligible boxers competing against Nagra could find themselves declared ineligible under the so-called **contamination rule** for fighting with a boxer declared ineligible. The CABA opted to postpone the light-flyweight class in Campbell River until the national intermediate championships in January 2000 in St. Catharines, Ontario. In the interim, it sought and obtained the AIBA's reaction. The AIBA agreed that it if Nagra obtained a court order requiring him to box, the AIBA would not impose sanctions against the CABA to the extent that a court ordered that the CABA's rules be altered. A court order issued from Justice Low on January 12, 2000, declared the CABA's rule prohibiting the wearing of a beard where the boxer did so for "legitimate and bona fide religious reasons" to be "inconsistent with the principles and tenets of Canadian human rights law and

---

[87] Anne Lowthian, Executive Director, World Sikh Organization, *Ontario Today*, Canadian Broadcasting Corporation Radio (2 December 1999) from 12:31 p.m. to 12:41 p.m. reported by Bowdens Media Monitoring Ltd., Ottawa, Ontario.

[88] J. Christie, "Ministers offer support to boxer" *The Globe & Mail* (9 December 1999), online: *The Globe and Mail* <http://www.globeandmail.com/>. The Ontario *Human Rights Code*, for example, provides that

> Every person has a right to equal treatment with respect to services, goods and facilities, without discrimination because of race, ancestry, place of origin, colour, ethnic origin, citizenship, creed, sex, sexual orientation, age, marital status, same-sex partnership status, family status or disability (R.S.O. 1990, c. H.19, s. 1).

[89] *Nagra v. Canadian Amateur Boxing Assn.* (1 December 1999), Ottawa 99-CV-180990 (Ont. Sup. Ct.).

the Canadian Charter of Rights and Freedoms"[90] and ordered the CABA to permit Nagra to fight at the upcoming tournament in St. Catharines.[91] The CABA neither consented to nor opposed the court order, and no one from the CABA attended the hearing.[92] While the decision ensured that Nagra would be able to fight, he faced opposition outside the ring. Nagra reported that he felt unsafe while preparing for a fight in St. Catharines, Ontario, in January 2000 and that he was threatened by a man carrying a razor and scissors during the national championships.[93] Pursuant to an agreement reached between counsel for both parties, the CABA requested that the AIBA amend its rule concerning boxers and beards and encouraged its provincial organizations (branch members) to follow Justice Low's order. It also provided notice of an amendment to its impugned rule at its 2000 Annual General Meeting.

OFFICIAL LANGUAGES

The *Treasury Board Policy on Official Languages*[94] and the *Official Languages Act*[95] also impact upon the domestic sport system in Canada. Treasury Board policy, for example, provides that

> [i]t is government policy that federal institutions providing grants or contributions to voluntary non-governmental organizations for activities, projects or programs involving service to a public composed of members of both official language communities must take the necessary measures to ensure that the recipients of public funds respect the spirit and the intent of the Official Languages Act when serving the public.[96]

The objective behind this policy is

> [t]o ensure that when grants or contributions are made to voluntary non-governmental organizations serving the members of the public of both official language communities, communications with and services to the public are provided in both official languages in accordance with the spirit and intent of Part IV of the Official Languages Act.[97]

Sport Canada, a branch of the identity sector of the Department of Canadian Heritage, is subject to the *Official Languages Act* (Part IV of this Act, ss. 21–31).

> Where it is determined that an activity, project or program that receives financial assistance is national in scope and provides services to the general public of both linguistic communities, the relevant federal institution is required to ensure that the recipient organization will:
>
> (a) make any announcements to the public concerning the activity, project or program in both official languages;
>
> (b) actively offer services to members of the public in both official languages;

---

[90] *Nagra v. Canadian Amateur Boxing Assn*, [2000] O.J. No. 850 (Sup. Ct.) (QL).

[91] *Ibid.*

[92] *Ibid.*

[93] No author, "Bearded boxer faced threat at B.C. tourney" *The [Ottawa] Citizen* (3 February 2000) B5.

[94] Sport Canada's website references *Treasury Board Policy on Official Languages* at <http://www.patrimoine canadien.gc.ca/progs/sc/pol/lang/index_e.cfm>. The text of the policy as it appears on the Treasury Board website is available at <http://www.tbs-sct.gc.ca/pubs_pol/hrpubs/offlang/chap1_4-1_e.asp>.

[95] R.S.C. 1985 (4th Supp.), c. 31.

[96] *Supra* note 67.

[97] *Ibid.*

(c) make available in both official languages any documents for the general public relating to the activities, projects or programs;

(d) encourage members of both official language communities to participate in the activities, projects or programs; and

(e) organize activities, projects or programs, when appropriate, in such a manner as to meet the needs of the two linguistic communities.[98]

In light of these requirements, most organizations funded by Sport Canada are required to sign a contribution agreement that sets out the requirements the recipient organization must satisfy in order to receive funding. One such requirement concerns official languages whereby organizations agree to provide services in both of Canada's official languages.

The depth and expression of the commitment to official language requirements, however, varies. Several athletes from national sport organizations, for example, brought their language-related concerns to the attention of then Secretary of State (Amateur Sport) Denis Coderre. Coderre raised his concerns and, in response to these concerns, the Office of the Commissioner of Official Languages commenced an investigation into allegations that French-speaking athletes were unable to develop to their full potential within current sport programs. The Commissioner's first report, released in June 2000, found that these allegations could be readily supported.[99] As a result, 16 recommendations were advanced as part of a strategy to ensure that the Canadian sport system fully reflected Canada's two official languages. Fifteen of the sixteen recommendations were directed at Sport Canada, while the remaining recommendation was directed at the Treasury Board. The Commissioner's follow-up report, issued in June 2003, found that Sport Canada had complied with three of the fifteen recommendations and had partially implemented nine others. Sport Canada failed to address three of the recommendations. The recommendation made to the Treasury Board was partially implemented.[100]

A study funded by the Department of Canadian Heritage, *Linguistic Barriers to Access to High Performance Sport Study — 2005*, notes that Sport Canada's Canadian Sport Policy provides that "linguistic duality is an essential feature of the sports system and that all persons, regardless of language or culture, should be able to participate in this system." The funded report further provides that "the Canadian Sport Policy is aimed at eliminating language barriers imposed on Francophone athletes by providing them with essential services in their own language, such as coaching[...]" and notes that "Sport Canada consulted with the Office of the Commissioner of Official Languages in the course of formulating this policy."[101]

As noted above, the Sport Funding and Accountability Framework (SFAF) consists of four steps. The NSOs eligibility criteria is used to create a list of NSOs eligible for assessment by Sport Canada under the SFAF III. In order to determine if an NSO is eligible for funding, the entity is assessed against a series of criteria. In order to enter the SFAF process and qualify for funding

[98] *Ibid.*

[99] Office of the Commissioner of Official Languages, *Official Languages in the Canadian Sports System*, vol. 1 (Ottawa: Public Works and Government Services Canada. 2000), online: <http://www.ocol-clo.gc.ca/docs/e/sport1_e.pdf>.

[100] Office of the Commissioner of Official Languages, *Official Languages in the Canadian Sports System: Follow-Up — Getting a second wind!* (Ottawa: Public Works and Government Services Canada, 2003) at 1, online: <http://www.ocol-clo.gc.ca/docs/e/SportEng.pdf>; see also No Author, "Sport body still getting failing grade in French" *The [Ottawa] Citizen* (12 June 2003) B10.

[101] Mira Svoboda, Senior Consultant, EKOS Research Associates & Peter Donnelly, Ph.D., Director, Centre for Sport Policy Studies University of Toronto, 2006 <http://www.canadianheritage.gc.ca/progs/sc/pubs/obstacles_linguistiques-linguistic_barriers/index_e.cfm>.

for the 2005–2010 funding cycle, an NSO must complete and submit an eligibility application. This requirement applies to all NSOs, even those that have previously received funding. It is important to note that a determination that an NSO satisfies the eligibility criteria is not tantamount to a finding that the organization will be funded but rather means that the NSO is able to access the next step in the SFAF process (assessment).

The first of the four steps, eligibility, consists of three sections: general criteria (Section A), national scope (Section B) and international scope (Section C). In order for an NSO to be considered "eligible" it must satisfy all of the Section A criteria. One of the Section A (general) criteria that must be satisfied by all NSOs in order to be considered for funding is A12:

> The NSO has a formal policy on Official Languages that complies with Sport Canada contribution guidelines on Official Languages.[102]

Annex A12 clarifies that "[a] policy on Official Languages should include how the organization commits to promoting Canada's two official languages within its operations. This policy should extend to the delivery of services in both French and English to athletes within the sport system and to communications with the public."[103] Annex A12 further provides that those NSOs that did not receive funding in 2003–2004 are required to submit a copy of their policies or procedures demonstrating compliance with guidelines.[104]

DOPING

In 1991 Sport Canada introduced a policy on doping in sport. Following two further reviews of the policy in 1998 and 1999, the *Canadian Policy on Doping in Sport* (Doping Policy) came into effect on January 1, 2000.

The Canadian Policy Against Doping in Sport (2004) replaces all previous anti-doping policies (including the 1991 and 2000 versions).[105] This policy provides that doping "involves Prohibited Substances or Prohibited Methods that are designed to enhance sporting performance, pose a real or potential risk to the health and integrity of Athletes and/or are unethical."[106]

The 2004 anti-doping policy in sport is the basis for the Canadian Anti-Doping Program administered by the Canadian Centre for Ethics in Sport (CCES). This program, in turn, is comprised of "General Principles and Rules and Standards for Canadian Sport Organizations, their affiliated members and their Participants who are responsible for implementing it, and is intended to be the basis for any related or complementary policies of Governments."[107]

The policy "commits to the implementation of the mandatory and other portions of the World Anti-Doping Program, including the World Anti-Doping Code, the mandatory International Standards and the Models of Best Practice."[108]

As a condition of receiving federal government funding, NSOs and MSOs are required to adopt the Canadian Policy Against Doping in Sport and to

---

[102] Sport Canada, *Sport Funding and Accountability Framework III (SFAF III): 2005–2010*, online: <http://www.patrimoinecanadien.gc.ca/progs/sc/prog/cfrs-sfaf/sfafelig2005_e.cfm>.

[103] *Ibid.*

[104] *Ibid.*

[105] Sport Canada, *The Canadian Policy Against Doping in Sport*, online: <http://www.pch.gc.ca/progs/sc/pol/dop/index_e.cfm>.

[106] *Ibid.*

[107] *Ibid.*

[108] *Ibid.*

respect the designated authority of the CCES on all anti-doping matters. NSOs and their PSO/TSO affiliates are also obligated to implement anti-doping measures to the extent required by their respective international sport bodies.[109]

The policy applies not only to athletes but also to coaches, doctors and other support staff (i.e., Athlete Support Personnel) and to National Sport Organizations. The basis of the policy's application to individuals is "the contractual relationship which exists between Sport Organizations and their members or Participants through those individuals' agreement to participate in sport according to its rules. Sport Organizations committed to doping-free sport will adopt the POLICY and the General Principles and Rules and Standards of the Canadian Anti-Doping Program as part of their governing documents and thus as an important part of the rules of sport and the rights and obligations governing their members and Participants."[110] Additional information concerning the Canadian Anti-Doping Program may be obtained from the Canadian Centre for Ethics in Sport website (http://www.cces.ca).

The consequences of an athlete tested positive for doping include being stripped of his or her medal(s). Canadian athletes have seen their medal status change. Ben Johnson, for example, was stripped of his gold medal for the 100-metre final at the 1988 Summer Olympics in Seoul, for which he also set a world record, after reportedly tested positive for the anabolic steroid stanozolol.[111] Beckie Scott, a member of Cross Country Canada, saw her medal status change from bronze to gold after the gold and silver medalists were stripped of their medals after reportedly testing positive for a banned blood doping agent.[112]

While issues around performance enhancement in the mainstream sport system are relatively well-known, similar issues arising in the sport movement for athletes with a disability "[remain] unknown and [receive] little publicity".[113] Many Canadians, for example, while familiar with the Johnson situation, would likely be unfamiliar with the fact that, in 1995, "a high-profile Canadian wheelchair athlete was caught by Canadian sport officials using the banned substance stanozolol".[114] Yet it is arguably the case that athletes with a disability may have even more incentive to participate in doping practices:

> In able-bodied sport, centimeters and hundredths of a second can mean the difference between financial glory or no rewards at all. In comparison, athletes with a disability find few financial rewards and public adulation is sparse. Nevertheless, competing (and winning) provides strong personal rewards. Self esteem as an athlete, developing a renewed sense of independence and control, and coping with a disability, all appear to be linked to athletic excellence. These reasons may in fact be more powerful than any financial gain, and an athlete with a disability may be more willing to sacrifice a great deal simply for the opportunity to see [him]/herself as competitive and worthy, in an effort to claim or reclaim a stronger sense of self-esteem and self-worth.[115]

---

[109] *Ibid.*

[110] *Ibid.*

[111] See, for example, No author, "I'm still the best, Ben says" *The [Ottawa] Citizen* (25 September 2003) C7.

[112] See, for example, No author, "Skier Scott set to celebrate medal upgrade" *The [Ottawa] Citizen* (21 October 2003) B3; Dan Barnes, "Five hundred and one days later, a silver lining for Beckie Scott" *The [Ottawa] Citizen* (30 June 2003) D1, D2; Jim Morris, "Canadians find IOC stance on Scott gold mystifying" *The [Ottawa] Citizen* (20 December 2003) C5.

[113] See, for example, David Legg & Daniel S. Mason, "Autonomic Dysreflexia in Wheelchair Sport: A New Game in the Legal Arena?" (1998) 8 Marq. Sports L.J. 225 at 227.

[114] *Ibid.*

[115] *Ibid.* at 236.

There are also some unique doping issues that arise in the world of athletes with a disability. **Autonomic dysreflexia**, for example, entails the self-infliction of bodily harm by athletes to obtain "a naturally-occurring bodily response"[116] — a boost of adrenaline that permits athletes to enhance performance.[117] Self-infliction takes many forms, including distending the bladder by ingesting fluids, clamping or obstructing the catheter, excessively tight leg strapping or tightening, or deliberately inflicting trauma to the lower limb,[118] deliberately twisting or sitting on a scrotum or extended sitting in a race chair or race equipment to raise blood pressure.[119] A spinal cord injured athlete, for example, self-inflicts an injury in an area where he or she does not receive a pain sensation and receives the "benefit" of an adrenaline rush, without the pain.[120] The risks involved with this practice are significant due to elevated blood pressure associated with the desired adrenaline rush. Responses include "cerebral [hemorrhage], blindness, aphasia, seizure, cardiac dysrythmia, retinal [hemorrhage], apnea, cardiac arrest and death".[121]

A number of reports have noted that upwards of 90 percent of wheelchair quadriplegia athletes intentionally induced an autonomic dysreflexia response in order to enhance performance.[122] Despite increased vigilance, however, as at 1998, there were no documented cases of this activity in a sport setting.[123] Legg and Mason posit that, given the prevalence of this form of boosting and given the gain to be provided by boosting, the absence of detection is likely attributable to inadequate control mechanisms and judges concerned about falsely accusing an athlete.[124]

DISPUTE RESOLUTION

Conflict in sport is inevitable.[125] The inevitable nature of conflict is attributed to a variety of factors, including the "'enormous ambition' attached to participating in sport, the scarcity of available opportunities and resources and the great diversity of backgrounds and experiences among participants, nationalities and regions in Canada."[126] Conflicts arise, for example, between an athlete and his or her national sport organization, a coach and a national sport organization and/or an athlete and a coach over issues such as team selection criteria, disciplinary matters and linguistic rights. A conflict may also arise between a national sport organization and its respective international sport federation.

Given the inevitability of conflict in sport, it is surprising to find that little concern was given to the need for a dispute resolution system for sport in Canada until the early 1990s. In 1994, an Alternative Dispute Resolution (ADR) Committee recommended an independent dispute resolution system for sport. The Centre for Sport and the Law introduced such a program in Febru-

---

[116] *Ibid.* at 228.

[117] *Ibid.*

[118] *Ibid.* at 231.

[119] *Ibid.* at 233, n36.

[120] *Ibid.* at 228.

[121] *Ibid.* at 231.

[122] *Ibid.*

[123] *Ibid.* at 231, n29.

[124] *Ibid.* at 235, n43.

[125] Bruce Kidd, News Conference with the Secretary of State for Amateur Sport and Others at 4 (5 January 2000) (transcript available from Media Q Inc.).

[126] Susan Haslip, "A Consideration of the Need for a National Dispute Resolution System for National Sport Organizations in Canada" (2001) 11(2) Marq. Sports L.J. 245 at 247–48 citing Kidd, *supra* note 80.

ary of 1996, but this disbanded in 1997 as a result of federal government funding cutbacks. In January 2000, then Secretary of State (Amateur Sport) Denis Coderre expressed a desire to develop a national dispute resolution system for the high performance sport community. An ADR Work Group was formed and charged with drafting a report that outlined options for a national ADR system. The Work Group's Report, presented to Coderre in June 2000, identified the need for such a system to deal with "widely acknowledged" problems in Canada's high performance sport community.[127]

The *Physical Activity and Sport Act* provides for the creation of such a centre — the Sport Dispute Resolution Centre of Canada. The Centre's purpose is to provide an ADR service for sport disputes for the sport community (s. 10(1)(a)). The Centre has the jurisdiction to hear a variety of disputes, including those among sport organizations and between a sport organizations and those connected with it, including members of the organization (s. 10(2)). The Centre includes a dispute resolution secretariat and a resource centre (s. 9(1)).

CHAPTER SUMMARY

The intersection of sport and the law in Canada presents an interesting dynamic. As the overview of the Canadian sport system suggests, national sport organizations are affected by the rules of their respective international sport federations. Provincial sport organizations are, in turn, impacted by these rules and organizations. Domestic sport organizations are also impacted by a variety of policies and legislation. Sport Canada, the federal body responsible for high performance sport at a national level, has made considerable advances in addressing doping issues and providing for a national body with jurisdiction to hear sport-related disputes. Despite these advances, the federal government also appears to have dropped the ball in some areas, including addressing the under-representation of women, Aboriginal peoples, visible minorities and persons with disabilities in the Canadian sport system. Improvements are still required in the area of official languages. Additional challenges faced by the domestic sport system include concerns with the funding of sport — particularly as it relates to sport for Aboriginal peoples and for athletes with a disability(ies). The federal Tobacco Policy presents considerable obstacles to fundraising efforts by national sport organizations. While amendments to the *Income Tax Act* providing for Registered Canadian Amateur Athletic Associations are of some benefit to sport organizations, restrictions accompanying such status limit a National Sport Organization's flexibility. The intersection of human rights instruments and sport suggests that sport organizations need to be vigilant and take a leadership role in anticipating possible conflicts with their rules and in playing a pro-active role in ensuring that their rules reflect and respect human rights norms.

GLOSSARY OF NEW TERMS AND KEY CONCEPTS

Aboriginal sport   Sport delivered, where possible, at all levels (i.e., national, provincial/territorial, regional, local) by and for Aboriginal peoples.

Aboriginal peoples   Defined in the *Constitution Act, 1982*, as the Indian, Métis, and Inuit people of Canada.

---

[127] Haslip, *supra* note 91 at 263.

athletes with a disability	Athletes with a physical, sensory and/or intellectual disability. This phraseology is important since it places emphasis on the *athlete* and not the disability.
autonomic dysreflexia	The self-infliction of bodily harm by athletes to obtain an adrenaline boost to enhance performance.
contamination rule	A rule in high performance sport providing that where a competition is not formally recognized or sanctioned by its respective sport body, a participant in such a competition is considered "contaminated". As a result of this status, any athlete competing with a "contaminated athlete" is also considered "contaminated".
integration	A process of planning and providing for opportunities for athletes with a disability and/or sport for athletes with a disability to work together with non-disability-based (i.e., mainstream) sport organizations.
mainstream sport	The "traditional" sport system.
off-territory	A term used in reference to Aboriginal peoples in Canada living in urban and rural areas that are outside of reserves created by the federal government.
parallel sport system	A separate venue for sport that operates separately from the mainstream sport system. Examples include sport systems for Aboriginal peoples and athletes with a disability or disabilities.
racism	Prejudicial or stereotypical acts, attitudes, comments or institutional structures that lead to discrimination or harassment directed towards a group on the basis of its ethno-cultural background, perceived racial origin or colour.
reverse integration	Where athletes from the mainstream sport system compete in a sport conceived for athletes with a disability.
sport for athletes with a disability	Training and competition for athletes with a disability as well as related support systems.
under-representation	A situation where an identifiable group of persons in a sphere such as sport are not represented in proportion to their representation in the general population. Examples include women, Aboriginal peoples, visible minorities and athletes with a disability.

REVIEW QUESTIONS

1. Identify areas where sport and the law intersect in Canada.

2. Explain how sport is organized in Canada.

3. Describe how the organization of sport in Canada relates to jurisdictional responsibility for sport.

4. How does the Minister's Task Force on Federal Sport Policy define "sport"?

5. Describe the difference between recreational, competitive and high performance sport.

6. How does the high performance sport system fit within the international sport movement?

7. Identify government initiatives for Aboriginal sport.

8. Describe the importance of the North American Indigenous Games to Aboriginal peoples.

9. Identify challenges facing sport organizations seeking to raise funds in Canada.

10. Identify concerns arising with the funding of sport in Canada.

11. What is the Tobacco Policy? Explain how this policy impacts national sport organizations.

12. What benefits accrue to Registered Canadian Amateur Athletic Associations?

13. How can an RCAAA lose its status?

14. Identify groups currently under-represented in the Canadian sport system.

15. What general pronouncements has the federal government made concerning addressing the under-representation of these groups?

16. How did the Canadian Association for the Advancement of Women in Sport respond to the proposed *Physical Activity and Sport Act*? What was the basis for this response? How was the matter addressed?

17. Outline the history of the federal government's involvement in sport for Aboriginal peoples.

18. What is reverse integration?

19. How do human rights instruments impact on sport in Canada?

20. Explain the dilemma faced by a national sport organization where human rights law conflicts with the policies of its international sport federation.

21. How do federal initiatives, such as legislation and policy on official languages, impact the national sport system?

22. Which body is responsible for monitoring doping in the Canadian sport system?

23. Identify a concern with doping unique to athletes with a disability.

24. Identify the organization that has legislative jurisdiction to deal with disputes arising in sport in Canada. What sort of disputes can be heard through this organization?

25. Identify and describe a concern arising with the introduction of the Aboriginal Sport Policy.

DISCUSSION QUESTIONS

1. Does the law have a place in the Canadian sport system?

2. Is the expenditure of tax dollars to support a select group of high performance athletes justifiable?

3. Were advertisements promoting the "See You in Athens" effort appropriate?

4. Should a sport organization be able to circumvent the federal tobacco policy by not using the word "amateur" to describe its athletes?

5. Should concerns with access and equity be addressed by government at the level of high performance sport?

6. Can parallel sport systems be justified?

7. Justice Low declared the Canadian Amateur Boxing Association's (CABA) rule prohibiting the wearing of a beard where the boxer did so for bona fide religious reasons to be inconsistent with the principles of human rights instruments (i.e., human rights codes, the Charter) and

ordered the CABA to permit Mr. Nagra to fight at the upcoming tournament in St. Catharines. Explain how you would have decided that case.

8. Describe the significance of the judgment of Justice Rothstein in *A.Y.S.A. Amateur Youth Soccer Association v. Canada Revenue Agency*, 2007 SCC 42; online: <http://scc.lexum.umontreal.ca/en/2007/2007scc42/2007scc42.html>.

SUGGESTED READINGS

GENERAL

Barnes, John. *Sports and the Law in Canada*, 3d ed. (Toronto: Butterworths, 1997).

Bird, Stephen. *Recreation and the Law*, 2d ed. (Scarborough: Thomson, 1997).

Canada. *Canadian Sport Policy* (Hull, Québec: Sport Canada, 2002).

Canada. *The Canadian Sport Policy: Federal-Provincial/Territorial Priorities For Collaborative Action 2002–2005* (Hull, Québec: Sport Canada, 2002).

Canada. *Towards A Canadian Sport Policy: Report on the National Summit on Sport* (National Summit on Sport — Ottawa, April 27–28, 2001) (Ottawa: Public Works and Government Services Canada, 2001).

Canada, Sport Canada. *Strategic Directions (1998–2001)* (Ottawa: Sport Canada, 1998).

Canada, House of Commons. *Sport — Leadership, Partnership and Accountability — Everybody's Business* (Ottawa: Sub-Committee on the Study of Sport in Canada, 1998) (Chair: Clifford Lincoln).

Crossman, Jane, ed. *Canadian Sport Sociology* (Scarborough: Thomson, 2003).

Holman, Margery, Dick Moriarty & Janice Forsyth, eds. *Sports, Fitness and the Law: North American Perspectives*, 2d ed. (Toronto: Canadian Scholars' Press, 2001).

Minister of State Fitness and Amateur Sport. *Sport: The Way Ahead — The Report of the Minister's Task Force on Federal Sport Policy* (Ottawa: Minister of Supply and Services Canada, 1992).

Schrodt, B. "Changes in the Governance of Amateur Sport in Canada" (May 1983) 14:1 *Canadian Journal of History of Sport* 1.

Website

Sport Canada: Home, <http://www.pch.gc.ca/progs/sc/index_e.cfm>; Strategic Directions, <http://www.pch.gc.ca/progs/sc/mission/index_e.cfm>

ABORIGINAL SPORT

Canada. *Policy on Sport Canada's Policy on Aboriginal Peoples' Participation in Sport* (Hull, Quebec: Public Works and Government Services Canada, 2005).

Haslip, Susan. "A Consideration of Sport Canada's Policy on Aboriginal Peoples' Participation in Sport". Paper presented at 2005 Aboriginal Sport Forum — Ottawa 2005, in Vicky Paraschak & Janice Forsyth, eds., *Aboriginal Sport Forum Proceedings* (Ottawa: Sport Canada, 2006).

Haslip, Susan. "A Treaty Right to Sport?" (June 2001) 8:2 Murdoch Univ. L. Rev., online: Murdoch University Electronic Journal of Law <http://www.murdoch.edu.au/elaw/issues/v8n2/haslip82.html>.

Haslip, Susan, & Victoria Edwards. "Does Sport Belong in the Medicine Chest?" in Vicky Paraschak & Janice Forsyth, eds., *Proceedings of the 2002 North American Indigenous Games Research Symposium* (Winnipeg: University of Manitoba, 2003).

King, C. Richard, ed. *Native Americans and Sport* (Armonk, N.Y.: M.E. Sharpe, 2004).

Morris, Alwyn. "The Olympic Experience: An Aboriginal Perspective" 9–11 at 9 in T. Taylor, ed., *How You Play the Game: Papers from the First International Conference on Sports and Human Rights (September 1–3, 1999)* (Australia: Human Rights Council of Australia, 2000).

Paraschak, Vicky. "Knowing Ourselves Through the 'Other': Indigenous Peoples in Sport in Canada" in R. Jones & K. Armour, eds., *Sociology of Sport: Theory and Practice* (Essex: Longman, 2000) 153.

———. "The Native Sport and Recreation Program, 1972–1981: Patterns of Resistance, Patterns of Reproduction" (1995) 26:2 *Canadian Journal of History of Sport* 1.

Robinson, Laura. "Native runners honoured decades after relay" *The [Ottawa] Citizen* (3 November 2003) A2.

ATHLETES WITH A DISABILITY
Canada, Sport Canada. *Policy on Sport for Persons With A Disability* (Hull, Quebec: Public Works and Government Service Canada, 2006).
Canada (Statistics Canada). Participation and Activity Limitation Survey: A profile of disability in Canada, *The Daily*, December 3, 2002.
DePauw, Karen P., & Susan J. Gavron. *Disability and Sport* (Champaign, Illinois: Human Kinetics, 1995).
Gregson, Ian. *Irresistible Force: Disability Sport in Canada* (Victoria: Polestar, 1999).

DISPUTE RESOLUTION
Sport Canada. *A Win-Win Solution: Creating A National Alternate Dispute Resolution System For Amateur Sport in Canada* / Report of the Work Group to the Secretary of State (Amateur Sport) (Hull, Québec: Secretary of State (Amateur Sport) = secrétaire d'état au Sport amateur, 2000).
Corbett, R., H. Potter & H.A. Findlay. *Administrative Appeals — A Handbook for Sport Organizations* (Edmonton: Centre for Sport and Law, 1995).
Haslip, Susan. "A Consideration of the Need for a National Dispute Resolution System for National Sport Organizations in Canada" (2001) 11:2 Marq. Sports L.J. 245.
———. "Just Do It? A Consideration of Alternative Dispute Resolution and Amateur Sport" in *Proceedings of the Conflict Resolution Symposium: 2000* (Ottawa: Carleton University, 2001).
———. "Takin' my ball and goin' home: Amateur Sport and ADR" (Spring 2000) *Canadian International Institute of Applied Negotiations News* 12.
———. "Leveling the Playing Field: A Consideration of the Need for an Alternative Dispute Resolution System for High Performance Sport in Canada" (April/May 2000) 11:2 For the Record 3.
Haslip, Susan, & Victoria Edwards. "Parent Contracts — A Mechanism for Playing Nicely Together?" (Spring 2002) Canadian International Institute of Applied Negotiations News 8.
———. "Putting the Fun Back into Sport: Parent Contracts as a Mechanism for Managing Conflict — Are We There Yet?" in *Proceedings of the Conflict Resolution Symposium: 2001* (Ottawa: Carleton University, 2001).

Website
ADRsportRED: <http://www.adrsportred.ca/>.

DOPING
Canada. *Canadian Policy Against Doping in Sport* (2007), online: <http://www.pch.gc.ca/progs/sc/pol/dop/index_e.cfm>.
Canada, Sport Canada. "Canadian Policy on Doping in Sport", online: <http://www.pch.gc.ca/progs/sc/pol/dop/index_e.cfm>.
Canada, Sport Canada. *Canadian Strategy for Ethical Conduct in Sport: Policy Framework* (24 May 2002), online: <http://www.pch.gc.ca/progs/sc/pol/eth2002/StEthic.pdf>.
Hatch, Hilary Joy. "On Your Mark, Get Set, Stop! Drug-Testing Appeals in the International Amateur Athletic Federation" 16 Loyola L.A. Int'l & Comp. L.J. 537.
Legg, David, & Daniel S. Mason. "Autonomic Dysreflexia in Wheelchair Sport: A New Game in the Legal Arena?" (1998) 8 Marq. Sports L.J. 225.

Website
Canadian Centre for Ethics in Sport: <http://www.cces.ca>

OFFICIAL LANGUAGES
Canada, Sport Canada. "Treasury Board Policy on Official Languages", online: <http://www.patrimoinecanadien.gc.ca/progs/sc/pol/lang/index_e.cfm>.
Canada, Sport Canada. *Sport Funding and Accountability Framework III (SFAF III): 2005–2010*, online: <http://www.patrimoinecanadien.gc.ca/progs/sc/prog/cfrs-sfaf/sfafelig2005_e.cfm>.
Office of the Commissioner of Official Languages. *Official Languages in the Canadian Sports System*, vol. 1 (Ottawa: Public Works and Government Services Canada, 2000), online: <http://www.ocol-clo.gc.ca/docs/e/sport1_e.pdf>.
———. *Official Languages in the Canadian Sports System: Follow-Up — Getting a second wind!* (Ottawa: Public Works and Government Services Canada. 2003) at 1, online: <http://www.ocol-clo.gc.ca/docs/e/SportEng.pdf>.

Svoboda, Mira & Peter Donnelly. 2006. *Linguistic Barriers to Access to High Performance Sport Study — 2005*, online: Sport Canada <http://www.canadianheritage. gc.ca/progs/sc/pubs/obstacles_linguistiques-linguistic_barriers/index_e.cfm>.

Website
Department of Canadian Heritage: <http://www.patrimoinecanadien.gc.ca>

TOBACCO
Canada, Sport Canada. "Federal Government Policy on Tobacco Sponsorship of National Sport Organizations" (March 1985), online: <http://www.pch.gc.ca/progs/ sc/pol/tabac-tobacco/index_e.cfm>.

WOMEN
Canada, Sport Fitness and Amateur Sport. *Sport Canada Policy on Women and Sport* (Ottawa: Sport Fitness and Amateur Sport, 1986), online: Sport Canada <http:// www.pch.gc.ca/progs/sc/pol/femmes-women/index_e.cfm>.
Smith, Lissa, ed. *Nike is a Goddess: The History of Women in Sports* (New York: Atlantic Monthly Press, 1998).

Website
Canadian Association for the Advancement of Women and Sport and Physical Activity: <www.caaws.ca>

CASES OF SIGNIFICANCE
United Kingdom
Com'rs for Special Purposes of Income Tax v. Pemsel, [1891] A.C. 531.

Canada
A.Y.S.A. Amateur Youth Soccer Association v. Canada Revenue Agency, 2006 FCA 136.
A.Y.S.A. Amateur Youth Soccer Association v. Canada Revenue Agency, 2007 SCC 42.
Nagra v. Canadian Amateur Boxing Assn. (1 December 1999), Ottawa 99-CV-180990 (Ont. Sup. Ct.).
Nagra v. Canadian Amateur Boxing Assn., [2000] O.J. No. 850 (Sup. Ct.) (QL).

RELEVANT LEGISLATION
Domestic
Canadian Charter of Rights and Freedoms, Part I of the *Constitution Act, 1982*, being Sch. B to the *Canada Act 1982* (U.K.), 1982, c. 11.
Constitution Act, 1982, being Sch. B to the *Canada Act 1982* (U.K.), 1982, c. 11.
Department of Canadian Heritage Act, S.C. 1995, c. 11.
Fitness and Amateur Sport Act, R.S.C. 1985, c. F-25 [repealed].
Income Tax Act, R.S.C. 1985 (5th Supp.), c. I-1.
Official Languages Act, R.S.C. 1985 (4th Supp), c. 31.
Ontario *Human Rights Code*, R.S.O. 1990, c. H.19.
Physical Activity and Sport Act, S.C. 2003, c. 2.
Tobacco Act, S.C. 1997, c. 13.

International
Olympic Charter, online: Olympic Movement <http://multimedia.olympic.org/pdf/en_ report_122.pdf>

Family Law

Laurence M. Olivo
SENECA COLLEGE

Learning Objectives

After reading this chapter, the reader should be able to:

> ➢ understand what areas are generally considered part of family law in Canada

> ➢ appreciate the extent to which economic, social, and cultural factors shape family law

> ➢ appreciate the extent to which family law has evolved in the past few decades, and be aware of the forces that have led to that evolution

> ➢ understand the contractual nature of the engagement and of marriage

> ➢ know the requirements of a valid marriage

> ➢ know what constitutes a common law relationship and, generally, know what consequences flow from such a relationship

> ➢ know what the grounds for divorce are, and the consequences that flow from divorce in respect of custody, support, and property division

> ➢ be aware of situations where a marriage might be subject to annulment instead of divorce

> ➢ understand and apply concepts that determine custody, support, and property division

> ➢ trace the process whereby a child might proceed from being a child in need of protection to becoming a Crown ward being placed for adoption

> ➢ distinguish among the different routes to adoption

TABLE OF CONTENTS

INTRODUCTION: THE SCOPE OF FAMILY LAW

In Canada, most people consider "family law" to be basically about divorce, and of course, divorce *is* a big part of family law. However, family law can best be understood by thinking of families as going through a sort of life cycle. At various stages in the cycle, legal issues arise that are part of family law. Here is an overview.

Family Formation

At this stage, when a couple decides to form a permanent relationship, there are social and legal changes in their status that affect their rights and responsibilities. If they marry, certain legal rights and liabilities follow. If the couple intends to form a permanent relationship without the formalities of an engagement or marriage, there are still legal consequences that will flow from this arrangement, although they will differ in some respects from the consequences of marriage. Family formation rules will affect families that are composed of same-sex partners, with or without children. Further, while we usually assume that a family is based on a conjugal (sexual) relationship, that may not always be the case. Thus, we will often have to consider as a "family" other kinds of permanent relationships: for example, a single adult raising an adopted child or an unrelated child, or two siblings living together.

Family Dissolution

If the partnership between the couple does not work out and they decide to end it, then it becomes necessary to deal with the consequences of the termination. If the parties were formally married, then they will probably wish to have their union formally terminated by a divorce, although they need not do so unless one or the other wishes to remarry. However, even if they decide to live separately without divorcing, decisions will have to be made about the care and support of the couple's children, the support of a spouse who is not able to be self-supporting, and how the property acquired during the marriage is to be disposed of. In many respects the law dealing with the dissolution of a family resembles the law relating to the dissolution of a business partnership. As we will see later, the legal similarity between dissolutions of families and partnerships is not an accident.

Family dissolution, where a couple separates and each party goes his or her own way, is what most people understand "family law" to be about; indeed, most lawyers who practise in this area spend much of their time attending to separation, divorce, and its consequences. However, there are other ways in which destructive forces can cause families to become dysfunctional and to disintegrate. This situation gives rise to legal rights and remedies that are different from those that arise when spouses decide to dissolve their family unit.

Child Protection

While adults are presumed to be competent to protect their own interests, the law recognizes that children are not able to protect themselves when destructive forces begin to affect a family. Where the adults in a family, for whatever reason, are unable to properly care for a child, or they neglect or abuse a child, the law may step in to declare that child to be in need of protection. This usually happens when the parents or other adults responsible for the child's care are unable to provide proper care. The law's intervention here is independent of any decision by spouses to end their relationship. Intervention is entirely dependent on whether or not the child is in some danger that triggers the operation of the law. Child protection legislation is designed to protect the child, at first, within the family unit, which often means providing assistance to the family as well as to the child. If this approach does not work, then the state reserves the right to protect the child by removing it from a dysfunctional family, and placing it in a family, or in another social setting, where the child will be protected and cared for.[1]

There is another aspect of child protection that is relatively new and is not necessarily connected to family dissolution or dysfunction. While traditional child protection law is concerned with ensuring that children do not come to harm in the face of obvious situations of danger, new initiatives in this area focus on ensuring that children have equal access to benefits that all children should have. For example, recent developments have focused on the right of children to education and treatment that will meet their particular needs, rather than focusing on merely giving access to whatever education or treatment might be available.

Adoption

When a family has been dissolved by divorce, or is non-existent, or has become non-functional for other reasons, social and legal decisions have to be made so that children will continue to receive care and nurturing within a family setting, if possible. In divorce situations, this problem is often dealt with by giving one parent custody of the child, but having both parents remain involved with the child. Where neither parent is able, nor prepared, to care for a child, then the law allows for the child to be adopted into another family; at that point, the child ceases to be a member of its former family and becomes, legally, the child of the adopting family.

ORIGINS OF CANADIAN FAMILY LAW

So far, we have described some of the subjects and issues that are the concern of family law. We now turn to examine some of the historical, social, cultural, and legal forces that give rise to family law in Canada.

The Role of the Family in Society

To understand how family law developed, it helps to examine the role of the family in society in Britain and Europe from the end of the Middle Ages to the present, as this was the place and time in which family law as we know it developed. The family — often in its extended form, including more than one generation under one roof — was the basic unit of society. It performed many functions now performed in whole or in part elsewhere: e.g., education and the care of old, sick, and disabled members. Then as now, the family also functioned as an economic unit, organizing its resources and members to maximize wealth.

The family unit was rigidly structured. The oldest male member usually directed the family and controlled its female and more junior members. Both society and the law saw a husband and wife as one person — and that person was the husband. As head of the family, he could determine to whom, and in what trade, his son was to be apprenticed; he could determine what land should be bought or sold; he could decide the type and level of education his children would receive, and he was in charge of religious training and belief, as well. It is important that he could also decide whom his children could marry — it was his choice, not his wife's, and certainly not his children's.

His word was law within the family. Any opposition could be met with various forms of corporal punishment that might today be considered crimi-

---

[1] The idea that the child should not be taken from the family except as a last resort is beginning to give way to the idea that physical protection of the child should take precedence over the preservation of a poorly functioning family. This trend is observable in amendments to child protection legislation passed in Ontario in 1999.

nal assault. The ultimate penalty was expulsion from the family. In an age before social-welfare institutions, becoming disconnected from one's family had serious consequences, both economic and social. This was particularly so for women, whose economic needs, until the Industrial Revolution, were primarily met by performing domestic work within the family, not by working outside the home. There were not, prior to the 20th century, many jobs available for women outside the home: if we look at European literature from before the 20th century, we see few women described as working outside the home, unless they are unmarried — and even then, there was an expectation that marriage would put an end to such employment.[2]

In literature, the woman who was beyond marriageable age and still single was often seen as pitiful or laughable: occupying economically marginal positions, or reduced to the role of economic dependant of other family members. No one would argue that the role of "spinster" or "maiden aunt" was desirable or glamorous or that it conferred high social standing or economic clout.[3] An exception to this was the single woman who controlled wealth: a rich woman who did not marry actually had an advantage over a rich woman who did marry. Until the 1880s, in most North American jurisdictions, a married woman lost the right to own and control her property — her property rights passed to her husband on marriage. A single woman, on the other hand, had the same rights over property as a man. Generally, however, a woman acquired wealth and status as either a daughter or a wife, in a family setting, but rarely as a person in her own right.

A Marriageable Woman as a Form of Moveable Sexual Property

Prior to this century, a woman's economic value to the family resulted from her ability to maintain the family unit by providing domestic services and by providing heirs. Her skills and potential here determined, in part, her marriageability, as did whatever wealth she might bring with her in the form of a **dowry** (which made her an economically more attractive proposition over other competitors; after all, any marriageable woman could be expected to be able to bear children and run a house). A woman without a dowry had diminished opportunities for marriage. She could expect either not to marry or to marry someone relatively undesirable: someone of lower social or economic status than her own family's, or someone old or unpleasant, or both.

The importance of a dowry reflected the family's strategy in arranging a marriage for a daughter. What a father hoped to do was make an economically advantageous match for his daughter (i.e., that her economic needs, currently met by the father, would now be met by her husband) and for his own family by creating an economic alliance with another family. This was a common practice among European royalty, who married their children to the children of kings of other countries in order to reinforce diplomatic or other political alliances between nations. On a smaller scale, a farmer might make a match for his daughter with the son of an owner of adjacent land, with a view that the two farms might eventually be combined to form a more powerful economic unit.[4]

---

[2] Well into the 20th century in North America, women schoolteachers were required to resign their positions when they married.

[3] The role of widow, however, might indeed confer high status, which came not from widowhood but from the status of the widow's deceased husband and the wealth that he left her. Ultimately, it could be said that the widow's status came from the fact that she had been a married woman.

[4] This discussion of economic factors in marriage arrangements applies to the middle and upper classes. The poor did not have an economic surplus to provide dowries for daughters. Conversely, this gave more freedom to a woman from a poor family, as economic factors played a much smaller role in choosing a mate. Did poorer women then get to marry for love or have more control over choosing a mate? Perhaps, although unlike the middle and upper

In this environment, the senior male relative arranged the marriage and had to consent to the arrangement. Men and women did not choose their own mate; romantic love or magnetic attraction was not a factor to be considered, and certainly it was not the basis for the choice. It might well be the case that the bride and groom did not even meet until shortly before the marriage. Again, an examination of European literature reveals that love relationships often feature men and women who are unmarried and unlikely to marry each other, or who are married but not to each other. The relationship of Romeo and Juliet is a good example of the impossible relationship where love is front and centre, but marriage unlikely.

Physical attractiveness was a plus, but not a requirement. A woman's chastity and her ability to bear children, however, were extremely important, although verifying these qualities before marriage was difficult. Chastity had a symbolic and practical importance. A chaste woman was assumed to be obedient and controllable: good qualities in a wife. A woman chaste at the time of marriage might also be assumed to be chaste after marriage, providing exclusive sexual services for her husband. This was not just a question of loyalty and obedience. In a world where wealth was centred on the family and passed on to younger generations within a family by inheritance, it became important to know that the heirs were, biologically, the husband's heirs. We can think of wives, in this context, as the conduit through which family wealth could be transmitted over time and preserved within the family over time.

To conclude the overview of a woman's position in a traditional family, her value lay in domestic and breeding skills, which made her a marriageable commodity that her senior male relative could dispose of to his, and the family's, benefit as if she were a piece of moveable sexual property to be transferred to the highest bidder.

Sources of Canadian Family Law

English Family Law Underlying Family Law in Canada

Early Canadian family law, like much else legal, was inherited from England. What follows is a quick overview of English common law in the premodern period. The most significant thing about English family law was that there was not much of it. As the family structure was **patriarchal**, many of the decisions affecting its members were not legal matters at all but were left to the father as lawmaker and decision maker. The power, to be sure, was not unlimited: a father could not kill a disobedient family member without being punished by the state's legal system. Such law as there was often served to back and support the senior male decision maker and, generally, to preserve the structure of the family against forces that might subvert it.

A principal rule here was the common law doctrine referred to as the **unity of personality**. It defined a married couple as a unitary body. This meant that a husband and wife were one person for the purpose of the law in family-related matters and that control of the person was vested in the husband. In family matters, therefore, so long as her husband lived, the wife had no legal control over family property or over children. She could not sue or be sued in her own name, and she was bound by her husband's decisions in legal matters. This effectively allowed a husband to add legal powers over the family to the economic and other power that he already enjoyed.

classes, the poor did not leave evidence in the form of written records, such as marriage contracts, deeds, or correspondence.

The woman was in no better position as a daughter than she was as a wife. As noted earlier, her father had the right to dispose of her in marriage. While technically, as a matter of the law of marriage, she had to freely consent to the marriage, enormous economic and social pressures could be brought to obtain that consent. Once a woman was disposed of in marriage, control over her passed from her father to her husband, who then had legal control as a result of the unity of personality doctrine. This was reinforced by the fact that at law, his wife's property passed into his control during marriage. He could sell it, keep its profits and did not have to account to anyone. Similarly, the dowry the wife brought into the marriage became his property or the property of his family.

The family, once formed, could not be dissolved. As a basic social structure, the family could not be subjected to destruction without causing social chaos. Further, there were strong Christian religious rules that supported this view by prohibiting divorce. Prior to 1857 in England, it was not possible to obtain a divorce from any English court to terminate a marriage. In cases of serious abuse by a husband, a wife could apply to church courts (called **ecclesiastical courts**) for a *divorce mensa et thoro*. This decree permitted a wife to reside separately from her husband but only if he was abusive. She might also obtain an order for **alimony**, an allowance to be paid her by the husband, permitting her to live, as the case law said, "modestly and in retirement", often at a greatly reduced standard of living.

If a wife was difficult to control, the law offered no specific remedy, as the husband was expected to control and discipline her himself; indeed, the law countenanced this by granting him, among other things, the right of physical chastisement (now known as spousal assault) to control her. In this context, there was no need to apply for court orders. The husband had enough power and authority to do the job himself.

But there were other legal forces that gave a husband a good deal of control over his wife, and made it very difficult for her to find a better life without him. First of all, until 1857 there was no legal divorce. Only in rare instances and only where parties were wealthy and influential enough, could they terminate a marriage, and then only by an Act of Parliament.

If she chose to leave her husband where the law gave her no right to do so, she had to find some way to meet her economic needs. A deserting wife was not entitled to any support payments (unless she had the court's permission to separate and could meet the tests for alimony). Economics dictated that she find another man to support her. However, the law created great difficulty for any man prepared to do this: Any man who enticed her away or offered her shelter and support could be sued by her husband for damages for the tort of harbouring his wife or enticing his wife away. Any man who offered the wife a sexual relationship (whether she had left her husband or not) could be sued for the civil tort of **criminal conversation** for interfering with the husband's sexual monopoly over his wife. Lastly, even her children were not hers. Children, at common law, were seen as the property of the father, and decisions about them were not based on what was best for the child but on whose property the child was. Unless the father was clearly a physical danger to the children, he was presumed to have a right to custody and control over them; and the wife, in these circumstances, would have no rights at all.

Early Canadian Family Law

From the English common law described above, family law in Canada evolved. There were some immediate differences. First, the *Constitution Act, 1867* divided legislative power between the federal government and the provinces. One of the results of this was that the power over family law was split between the provinces and the federal government. The federal government has power to determine what is required for a valid marriage and may make divorce law, including law governing support and custody issues, when a couple is obtaining a divorce. The provinces have an independent and separate power to make laws to determine how family property issues are resolved, and they have a concurrent or shared power over custody and support where the marriage has broken down but the parties will not divorce. This division of power has been the source of much confusion: different provinces have made up different rules covering support, custody, and property issues that reflect local conditions or values within the particular province. Because there was a lack of agreement in the provinces about divorce, this resulted in a stalemate that prevented forming a consensus that would tolerate a federally enacted national divorce law.

In matters of divorce, in 1857, England abolished the ecclesiastical courts as a relic of the Middle Ages and established its first divorce court. This was never a big issue in Canada, however, as ecclesiastical courts were never established here; however, neither were divorce courts, at least initially, because of the opposition of Roman Catholic Quebec to divorce in any form. What happened instead was that individual provinces asked the federal government to pass a Divorce Act that would apply to that province alone. This was done, for example, in Ontario, in the early 20th century. The first Acts were cautious: allowing a husband a divorce for a wife's adultery; later, a wife was allowed a divorce on the husband's cruelty; still later, the grounds of cruelty and adultery were made grounds for either to divorce. It is important to note that while divorce was available in courts in some provinces, it was still necessary for Quebec residents, until 1968, to apply to Parliament to dissolve their marriage. Also, divorce was not available on no-fault grounds. One spouse had to prove that the other had committed some kind of legally recognized matrimonial offence, such as cruelty or adultery.

Support in family breakdown situations was still tied to fault. Blameworthy wives would not receive support on a divorce. Nor would they receive alimony if they separated, unless the husband was blameworthy and the wives were innocent of wrongdoing and were prepared to take the husband back in the marriage relationship.

For poorer women who were deserted by their husbands, provincial legislation provided for a simple court application to provide support; amounts awarded under this statute were generally lower than alimony awards, reflecting a differential application of the law dependent in part on the social class of the applicant.

Matters with respect to property improved for married women in the 1880s, both in England and Canada (except Quebec, where the reforms came in the early 20th century). An Act called *The Married Woman's Property Act* allowed married women to continue to own and control property free of their husband's control. This, of course, was only of use to the small minority of women who actually had property to own and control.

Under this Act, a couple deciding, on consent, to separate could do so without a court order. Also, they could enter into an agreement to deal with post-separation matters, including support, child custody, and property division.

The unity of personality theory was imported to Canada and, with modifications, survived until the mid-20th century. Wives had limited rights to sue or be sued. Spouses could not sue each other, except to dissolve marriages; nor could they give evidence against each other in criminal cases. The unity of personality doctrine also gave the husband control over children, and meant that a wife could not gain custody of children. However, by the beginning of the 20th century, the idea that children were more than miniature adults was gaining currency, and with it came the idea that custody should be determined in accordance with the best interest of the child, not the property rights of the father.

Current Trends in Canadian Family Law

As a consequence of the rise of the women's movement in the late 1960s, pressure began to be applied to change and modernize family law in Canada by making family law rules apply equally to men and women.

In the first wave of reform in the 1970s, the focus was on elimination of legal rules that discriminated on the basis of sex; in the later stages, there was an emphasis on discriminatory effects of law that might, on its face, be gender neutral. The elimination of the unity of personality doctrine and the abolition of the action for criminal conversation are examples of the first type of reform. Laws to make support enforcement easier and to set minimum child-support standards are examples of the later stages of the reform process.

While the actual laws vary from province to province, some clear trends have emerged that are reflected in the current law discussed in the rest of this chapter:

1. Since 1968, there has been a Canada-wide *Divorce Act*. The courts now recognize marriage breakdown as the basis for a divorce without anyone having to be at fault, although a fault basis for divorce is still available.

2. Support is generally based on need of the recipient and the ability of the payer to pay; who was, or was not, a "bad spouse" is not material. Men, as well as women, are eligible to receive support.

3. There is a growing concern with ensuring that support payments, once ordered, continue to be paid. Many provinces, and the federal government, have enacted legislation to assist recipients in enforcing support rights.

4. There is a consensus that child support amounts are often inadequate. There are now federal child-support guidelines that fix child support by use of a formula that takes into account expenses, the region of the country where the child lives, parental income, and other factors. This has resulted in standardized support awards, although there is some room for judicial discretion. The main purposes of the guidelines are to reduce the amount of litigation on this issue and raise the amount of money given in child support awards. It is likely that most provinces will adopt or adapt child support guidelines for provincial child support proceedings in the future.

5. Following the successful introduction of child support guidelines, a draft spousal support guideline is now circulating among family lawyers to be considered for use in spousal support claims under the *Divorce Act*. If adopted, it will likely also be used with support applications under provincial family law legislation. Some lawyers are beginning to use the guidelines in their practices, even though they are not binding. Once spousal support guidelines become part of the law, it is likely that spousal support, like child support, will cease to be a contentious issue in family breakdown cases.

6. Custody is determined according to what is best for a child. There is a growing movement to ensure that the non-custodial parent's access rights are respected and enforced. Safeguards are also available to make it easier to retake a child abducted by the non-custodial parent. Under proposed amendments to the federal *Divorce Act*, the distinction

between "custody" and "access" will be ended, and the law will then speak of "shared custody" or "parenting orders". It is believed that this change in language will help to eliminate the idea of winners and losers in custody cases, where the "winner" gets custody and the "loser" gets access. Instead, by using the term "shared custody", it is hoped that parents will see custody as a shared responsibility after, as well as before, divorce. However, it appears that in most cases one parent will have dominant responsibility, so the change may be no more than linguistic.

7. Property is no longer dealt with in terms of who owned or had title to it. Generally, if property was acquired or owned during the marriage, there is an assumption that each spouse contributed to its acquisition, and each should share in its value at the time of separation, no matter which of them actually owned the property.

8. While family law usually deals with rights and remedies for married couples ending their marriage, many of these rights are now available to same-sex couples, as well as men and women who are cohabiting in permanent relationships, though not married to each other.

9. Since about 1990, same-sex couples have been treated more and more like heterosexual couples, first in informal unions and later in marriage unions. Courts in seven provinces by 2004 had held that refusing gay and lesbian couples the right to marry violated their equality rights under s. 15 of the *Charter of Rights and Freedoms*. As a result, the federal government referred the matter to the Supreme Court of Canada, on a **reference**, asking if it would be valid for the federal government to change the law to permit gays and lesbians to marry. The Supreme Court, in December 2004, in *Reference Re Legal Capacity for Marriage*,[5] held that the federal government, which has the power to determine who may marry, could legislate to permit gay and lesbian marriages. In January 2005, the prime minister announced that the government would introduce amendments to the federal *Marriage Act* to permit same-sex unions. The legislation was introduced and became law in July 2005. Some provinces, notably Alberta, have said that they will use the power to issue licences and regulate the ceremony of marriage to refuse to issue licences to same-sex couples and refuse to sanction or recognize such marriages. This is unlikely to be successful, as once the federal government has determined that same-sex unions are valid, the provinces are unlikely to be able to prevent such marriages without violating the equality rights of same-sex couples.

10. Various attempts have been made to reduce the conflict in matrimonial disputes. Mandatory mediation is now a required part of the litigation process in many provinces. Increasingly, child custody cases require the use of neutral assessors to make recommendations to the court on custody, and the trend is to push for joint custody, rather than to reinforce the winner-take-all approach that characterized custody disputes in the past. More recently, some family lawyers have begun to develop an approach called collaborative family law. The lawyers and their clients agree to negotiate a settlement without going to court. As long as the negotiations continue, neither party can resort to the courts. It is only when the negotiations break down that the parties can move

---

[5] [2003] S.C.C.A. No. 329, December 9, 2004.

the dispute to court. The lawyers involved in the negotiations agree not to represent the parties in court. The cost of engaging new lawyers is perceived to strongly encourage the parties not to let the negotiations fail.

FAMILY FORMATION

Normally, the law does not pay much attention to family formation, as couples are expected to be able to do this without much assistance. The processes of courtship and marriage arrangements are seen as social and emotional, rather than legal. But there are legal rules that underlie the processes, and they usually emerge when the processes get into difficulty.

The Engagement

The **engagement** or **betrothal** is an exchange of promises by a man and a woman to marry. In earlier times, the promise could be made by parents on behalf of children, even when the children were minors; however, in the case of minors, the promises would have to be confirmed when the children reached the age of majority. In the absence of parents making formal arrangements, men and women come to an agreement on their own. The engagement is a formalization of the agreement, usually with the man giving a ring to the woman. The ring functions like a deposit on goods, requiring the recipient to hold the goods off the market until the time stipulated for making the final payment and taking delivery. In this case, a woman who accepts the ring is actually promising not to marry anyone else, removing herself, so to speak, from the market.

All of this is academic until one of the parties breaks off the engagement. Then the question arises, "Who gets to keep the ring?" It used to be the case that the person who wrongfully broke off the relationship forfeited the right to keep the ring or other engagement gift from the other party. However, modern legislation has eroded this rule[6] in many jurisdictions.

Marriage

Historically, the marriage ceremony was social, cultural, and religious in nature, although it has legal aspects as well. In a country like Canada, with a multicultural population, the ceremonial requirements are kept to a minimum. There must be someone to perform the ceremony or at least to supervise it. There must be formal witnesses (usually two), and the couple must publicly state that they are taking each other as spouses and that they freely consent to doing so.

The law requires, in most provinces, that persons seeking to marry obtain a licence, usually through their local municipal office. Alternatively, they may go through a religious process of having **banns** published. This requires that someone announce the intention of the parties to marry at a religious service. The exact procedure is not specified, to allow individual religions to publish banns in accordance with the custom of that religion. The purpose of both the licence and the banns is to permit objections to be made to the marriage, on the ground that one or both parties is not entitled to marry.

The question of entitlement turns on a number of factors. The persons marrying must be both over the age of majority, although minors may marry

---

[6] For example, see s. 33 of the Ontario *Marriage Act*, which says that the fact that the donor broke off the relationship is not a factor to be considered in determining the ownership of gifts given in contemplation of marriage.

in some circumstances with parental consent. The couple must have the mental capacity to understand what a marriage is, to know that the event they are attending is their marriage ceremony, and to give consent to marry. Any prior marriages for either must have been terminated by death or divorce. The couple also may not marry if they are too closely related.

At the time of marriage both parties must have the capacity for sexual intercourse, although consummation of the marriage by sexual intercourse is not a requirement, provided both parties do not insist on consummation.

Spouses who go through a marriage ceremony without having met all of the requirements for marriage may find that their marriage is void.

Marriage law in Canada does not seem to contemplate **polygynous** or **polyandrous** marriages, even though there are large numbers of residents who practise religions that permit such marriages. The law here is very complicated, but it would appear that a resident of Canada who was married polygamously in a country where **polygamous** marriages are permitted has made a valid marriage. If the same person sought to marry polygamously in Canada, that marriage would likely be void on the ground that such marriages are not legally permitted in Canada. The barrier to polygamous marriages may violate the *Charter of Rights and Freedoms* by interfering with the free exercise of religion, including the right to marry according to the rules of one's own faith.

As of July 2005, the amendments to the *Marriage Act* now permit gay and lesbian couples to marry anywhere within Canada. Accordingly, provinces will be required to issue marriage licences to gay and lesbian couples. However, the Act also permits the clergy of any faith that does not recognize the rights of gays and lesbians to marry to refuse to perform religious marriage ceremonies for gay and lesbian couples.

Common Law Relationships

What used to be called "living in sin" by your grandmother has now become an acceptable form of behaviour for many Canadians. While the majority of couples who form permanent relationships still marry, a large minority of men and women enter into long-term relationships, living together in a monogamous sexual relationship, raising children, buying houses — doing everything married spouses do, except go through a marriage ceremony.

We refer to this type of relationship as one of **cohabitation**, and the partners are referred to as **unmarried spouses**.

This type of relationship has sometimes been described as a common law relationship, although technically it is not that: a common law relationship is one where the couple represents to others that they are married, when in fact they are not. In these circumstances the "spouses" would acquire some spousal rights at common law. The breakthrough for unmarried spouses came with modern family law legislation, which, first of all, gave the children of such unions the same rights of support and inheritance[7] that children of marriages have. Second, the law recognized that unmarried spouses were obliged to support each other if the relationship ended, provided the parties had lived together for several years.[8] There are still some differences in legal remedies for married and unmarried spouses: in order to claim an interest in property

---

[7] The idea that the child of unmarried parents was, at law, the child of no one, with no right to inherit from his or her parents, has been superseded by provincial legislation. All children now have the rights that only legitimate children previously had. "Bastard" still remains a term of abuse, but it has no legal significance. See, for example, Ontario's *Children's Law Reform Act*, R.S.O. 1990, c. C.12, s. 1.

[8] For example, s. 29 of the Ontario *Family Law Act* requires that the parties cohabit for not less than three years to be eligible for support if cohabitation ends.

under family law rules in most jurisdictions, it is necessary to be married; for unmarried spouses, property rights must be determined under usual common law rules, as if the common law spouses were unrelated strangers.

It also appears that the rights of unmarried spouses are being extended to **same-sex couples**.

FAMILY DISSOLUTION

When spouses decide that their relationship has come to an end, it is necessary for them to deal with spousal and child support, child custody, and property division, and then terminate their relationship by divorce (if they were in a marriage relationship). They may deal with all these matters, except divorce, by voluntarily negotiating a **separation agreement**, or, if they cannot agree, they can apply to the courts for remedies or agree to have a private arbitrator decide the issues.

Domestic Agreements

In addition to using a separation agreement after a relationship ends, it is also possible to determine some matters before marriage if the spouses decide to enter into a **marriage contract**, or, if they are not intending to marry, a **cohabitation agreement**. The terms of all of these types of agreements are enforceable. However, there are some limits to the use of marriage contracts and cohabitation agreements: the spouses are not permitted to decide custody issues, although they may in a separation agreement. The reasoning behind this is that one cannot decide who will get custody of a child not yet born, as this would not be in a child's best interest. As well, most lawyers advise against setting down detailed rules about who does what in a marriage.

Marriage contracts and cohabitation agreements are unusual in most parts of Canada, at least for young couples starting their first marriage or cohabitation arrangement. The reason for this is that these agreements focus on what happens when the relationship breaks up. Most young couples, for reasons of sentiment, find this distasteful or even ominous. Further, most young couples do not have any money or assets to warrant drafting an agreement. However, for older couples, previously married and now entering into a second marriage or permanent relationship, marriage contracts are more common. Spouses here often have assets and children from earlier marriages, whose interests they would like to protect.

Divorce and Annulment

There are two ways to formally terminate a marriage — divorce or annulment. A marriage is terminated by annulment only when the marriage is not valid. Marriages can be invalid because the spouses did not freely consent to marry, they were too closely related, one of them was still married to someone else, or the ceremony was defective in some material way. In these examples, the marriages would be *void ab initio*: the defects were external and made the marriages void from the very beginning. They could not be subsequently validated.

There is another type of invalid marriage that is not *void ab initio* but merely voidable by one party or the other. This means that the marriage is considered valid as long as neither party complains of the defect. For example, if a couple chooses not to consummate the marriage, the marriage is valid if neither makes an issue of non-consummation. However, if one party is unwilling or unable to have sexual intercourse and the other spouse is not prepared to accept the situation, the dissatisfied spouse can ask to have the marriage annulled by the court. A court order, declaring a marriage annulled, results in a marriage that is a **nullity** — that is, it is deemed never to have been a marriage.

Annulment by a court is not the same as a religious annulment. Some religions that do not permit their members to divorce may consider religious annulments where there is some question that the marriage was not valid. These religious annulments may meet the internal requirements of a particular religion, and the spouse in an annulled marriage is free to remarry in his or her own religion, without violating religious rules about divorce. However, for the marriage to be legally annulled, the spouses must apply to a court for an order declaring the marriage to be a nullity. A marriage that is annulled by a court is deemed never to have been a marriage at all; in other words, the person is considered as having never been married and is, therefore, thought of as free to marry. A marriage annulled by a religious body has no legal significance. In the eyes of the state, the spouses are still legally married until they obtain a nullity or a divorce decree from a court.

In earlier times, when divorces were difficult to obtain, couples might engage in ingenious arguments in order to have a marriage declared a nullity. Nullity proceedings are much more unusual today because it is generally simpler to treat one's marriage as valid and to obtain a divorce.

Until 1968 in Canada, there were different divorce laws for each province that was prepared to allow divorce. Generally, the courts allowed for divorce when one spouse had committed a matrimonial offence. In 1968, a Canada-wide *Divorce Act* was passed that allowed for divorce on an additional ground: marriage breakdown where the spouses had been living separately for more than three years. Additionally, it was also possible to obtain custody and support along with a divorce.

In 1986, the federal divorce laws were again streamlined — the many grounds of divorce were reduced to one: marriage breakdown by reason of adultery, cruelty, or separation for more than one year. The current Act also contains provisions to encourage mediated settlements, and where there is a support or custody order as well, the Act permits the former spouses to vary a support order if circumstances change after the order was made. The next revisions to the *Divorce Act* will likely focus on new ways of dealing with custody and access to children to reduce conflict between divorcing parents over issues involving the children. It is also likely that the *Divorce Act* may require adjustments to dissolve same-sex marriages.

Support and Support Enforcement

Under current federal divorce law, divorcing spouses may obtain support for themselves or for their dependent children. Under the law of most provinces, spouses who separate because of marriage breakdown may also apply for support on the basis of marriage breakdown before they file for divorce, or without ever filing for divorce. In most provinces, who caused the breakdown is not relevant. What is relevant is whether a dependant has a need for support where the other spouse is able to meet the need. (Children receiving support are assumed to be in need and unable to meet the need themselves.)

There are some trends that have emerged in recent years. Dependent spouses, unless they are unemployable, are expected to become self-supporting. This has meant, in many cases, that a wife would be expected to become self-supporting within several years of the breakup of the marriage by obtaining job training so that support would be time limited and function as a training allowance. The fact that many women in this position also have the responsibility for children means that they have child care burdens on top of training for, finding, and keeping employment. A consequence of this pattern is that women have more responsibility and less income than was the case while they were married. Men, freed from day-to-day child care responsibilities, appear to have more options and room to manoeuvre economically than their ex-wives do, in part as a result of the fact that spousal support that they pay is often time limited.

Another trend emerging is concerned with guaranteeing that child support is adequate. American and Canadian data suggest that after marriage breakdown, children and their mothers often find themselves with a falling standard of living, while the former husband, after an initial drop in income, begins to recover his standard of living. This has resulted in two legal initiatives: support enforcement and child support guidelines.

Starting in the 1980s, a number of Canadian jurisdictions began to confront the problem of support orders in default. Data showed that in most cases support orders were honoured for the first few months but that, as time went on, payments were likely to become sporadic and then stop, resulting in billions of dollars in back support going uncollected because the recipients, being support dependants, did not have the resources to hire a lawyer to enforce the order. Support recipients in these circumstances often ended up on welfare, with the result that the support payer passed his obligations to the state. In answer to this, Manitoba, followed by other provinces, passed legislation establishing government offices that would monitor and enforce support obligations, using conventional judgment enforcement techniques, such as **garnisheeing** wages, seizing and selling property of the debtor, and jailing debtors for non-payment. The federal government, for its part, has enacted legislation that permits access to federal data banks so that enforcement agencies can more easily locate debtors and garnishee tax refunds, wages of federal civil servants, and other federal payments otherwise due to the support payer.[9]

The enforcement initiative has had some impact on defaulters, but determined non-payers continue to hinder collection of support debts. The "second generation" of support-enforcement legislation aims at increasing efficiency of collection by deducting support debts directly from wages before there is a default by the payer. This works in the same way as income tax withholding, where income tax is deducted from the taxpayer's wages without the taxpayer having any choice in the matter.[10]

With respect to child support, the federal government has implemented a formula-based method of determining child support that is intended to reduce judicial discretion to determine the amounts of support, and to result in higher and more realistic support awards for most families. It is still too early to tell whether the goals will be achieved in full.

Custody

The custody of children, determined on the basis of property rights in children until the mid-19th century, is now determined on the basis of a broad legal concept — "the best interest of the child". This development took hold in the late 19th century as part of social and cultural changes that began to recognize childhood as a distinct psycho-social stage in human development. Previously, children who survived infancy were often thought of as miniature adults and were assumed to be more resilient than they perhaps were.

---

[9] The two federal acts are the *Garnishment and Pension Diversion Act* and the *Family Orders and Agreements Enforcement Assistance Act (Canada)*.

[10] This approach has been incorporated into Ontario enforcement legislation, *The Family Support Plan Act*, ss. 3.1–3.13 (now *The Family Responsibility Act*).

In its early stages, "the best interest of the child" was interpreted to mean that the mother, as the family member responsible for raising and nurturing children, was most likely to obtain custody and child support. In later years, the courts have, at least in theory, become more gender neutral in awarding custody; however, most custody orders are still made in favour of women, reflecting the fact that women are still primarily responsible for child rearing in Canadian society. It is quite clear that the "best-interest" principle focuses on the psycho-social needs of the child, rather than on merely material needs. Whoever can give the child the most material things does not necessarily win custody.

Custody can be awarded by a court granting a divorce or, in the absence of divorce proceedings, the court may act under provincial legislation. In the latter case, many provinces permit anyone to apply for custody — the right of custody is really a child's right and, therefore, in appropriate cases the choice should not be restricted to competing parents.

The process of deciding custody has become more sophisticated. There is a growing movement towards the use of child-custody assessments by child psychologists and other "experts", on which the court relies in making its decisions. As well, the courts and legislation encourage the use of mediation and other forms of **alternative dispute resolution** for all family law matters, but especially for custody. To some extent, this protects the child from being involved directly in the conflict and anger that often results from court proceedings. The courts, experts in legal decision making, are not necessarily expert in making decisions about how a child's psycho-social needs are to be met. Many judges have embraced assessments willingly, though there has been some criticism that the courts have abandoned their duty to make legal decisions, which are now effectively being made by psychologists and social workers.

One area of reform in the custody area arose as a result of a serious problem in a small minority of cases: child abduction by the non-custodial parent. This can be a particular problem if the abducting parent has ties or connections outside Canada, in which case it is difficult to obtain the child's return, as the custodial parent often has to fight a long-distance court battle in a foreign jurisdiction. Part of the remedy for this has been that most Canadian provinces have, by legislation, agreed to enforce *The Convention on Civil Aspects of International Child Abduction* (also called the Hague Convention). Canada has signed the covenant and is a participating state, although provinces must agree to enforce the covenant within each province, as this is a provincial rather than federal jurisdictional matter. The result of this is that children wrongfully brought into a province from abroad will be quickly returned to the custodial parent as a result of the provincial Attorney General taking immediate action. Other nations that have signed the convention will return children wrongfully taken or retained in their country to Canada. Additionally, the definition of "kidnapping" in the *Criminal Code of Canada* has been expanded to include child abduction from a parent with lawful custody.

Property Settlement

At common law, marriage conferred no special property rights on spouses. The general rules prevailed: if a party could show that he or she owned or had title to an asset, then the asset belonged to the owning spouse. The law of equity, which softened the harsh effect of common law rules, recognized that a non-owner could acquire rights in an asset by contributing to the creation, improvement, or acquisition of the asset in a concrete way, usually by contributing money or money's worth. However, this rule did not recognize the indirect contribution a spouse might make, for example, by attending

---

Illustration of the Partnership Asset-Sharing Model **EXHIBIT 28.1**

- ¤   Wife enters marriage with $10 in assets, and leaves with $100 in assets.
- ¤   Husband enters marriage with $50 in assets, and leaves with $200 in assets.

> Her "profit" is $100 − $10 = $ 90
>
> His "profit" is $200 − $50 = $150

- ¤   For equalized sharing of the assets, the spouse with the lesser profit is entitled to one-half the difference between the profits of both of them:

> (the greater profit) minus (the smaller profit)
> = the difference between the two profits
> = $150 − $90 = $60

- ¤   The difference is then divided into two equal parts: $60 ÷ 2 = $30
- ¤   The difference is subtracted from the greater and added to the lesser profit, so that both leave the marriage with "equal profits":

> Greater profit: $150 − $30 = $120 (final equalized profit)
>
> Lesser profit: $90 + $30 = $120 (final equalized profit)

---

to domestic matters and freeing up the other spouse to make money and buy assets.

Opponents of the common law approach have argued that marriage is an economic partnership, where each partner carries out partnership activities that together result in the creation of partnership wealth that both partners should share, regardless of who legally owns the assets. The rationale for this approach is expressed in the Ontario *Family Law Act*, section 5(7):

> The purpose of this section is to recognize that child care, household management and financial provision are the joint responsibilities of the spouses and that inherent in the marital relationship there is equal contribution, whether financial or otherwise, by the spouses to the assumption of these responsibilities, entitling each spouse to the equalization of the net family properties (of both of them)....

The arguments for equal sharing of "partnership assets" on marriage breakdown have generally prevailed, and provinces generally have followed the approach illustrated in the passage noted above. The Ontario legislation illustrates how the scheme works: it requires each spouse to note the value of the assets each has on entering marriage and on leaving the marriage. (See Exhibit 28.1 for an application.) If the value has increased, then it is presumed that the increase, or profit, is due to joint efforts and is to be shared with the other spouse so that both spouses leave with equal partnership wealth.[11] Most of these legislative schemes have provisions to safeguard against equal distributions in circumstances where that would be unfair.

---

[11] The actual legislative scheme is somewhat more complicated; see the Ontario *Family Law Act*, R.S.O. 1990, ss. 4–16.

CHILD PROTECTION

While child-custody issues arise as a consequence of divorce or separation, there are other times where the welfare of children becomes the concern of the law — either because the child or the child's family has become so dysfunctional that society deems it necessary to interfere with the child and his or her family.

Generally speaking, the law recognizes the right of families to be free from state interference. Because of this, much of child protection law is concerned with striking a balance between the right of families to be free of the state, and the right of the state to step in where the situation warrants. When the children's rights movement arose in the 19th century (at the same time as, and as part of, movements to prevent cruelty to animals), its adherents tended to be paternalistic and interventionist, imposing middle-class, Anglo-Canadian standards on immigrant, native, and working-class families. Since that time, the balance has shifted, and principles underlying child protection are much more respectful of varying community standards and ways of doing things. The shift is illustrated by the principles set out in section 1 of Ontario's *Child and Family Services Act*:[12]

Paramount purpose

(1) The paramount purpose of this Act is to promote the best interests, protection and well being of children.

Other purposes

(2) The additional purposes of this Act, so long as they are consistent with the best interests, protection and well being of children, are:

1. To recognize that while parents may need help in caring for their children, that help should give support to the autonomy and integrity of the family unit and, wherever possible, be provided on the basis of mutual consent.
2. To recognize that the least disruptive course of action that is available and is appropriate in a particular case to help a child should be considered.
3. To recognize that children's services should be provided in a manner that,
    i. respects a child's need for continuity of care and for stable relationships within a family and cultural environment,
    ii. takes into account physical, cultural, emotional, spiritual, mental and developmental needs and differences among children,
    iii. provides early assessment, planning and decision-making to achieve permanent plans for children in accordance with their best interests, and
    iv. includes the participation of a child, his or her parents and relatives and the members of the child's extended family and community, where appropriate.
4. To recognize that, wherever possible, services to children and their families should be provided in a manner that respects cultural, religious and regional differences.
5. To recognize that Indian and native people should be entitled to provide, wherever possible, their own child and family services, and that all services to Indian and native children and families should be provided in a manner that recognizes their culture, heritage and traditions and the concept of the extended family.

---

[12] R.S.O. 1990, c. C.11, as am. by S.O. 2007, c. 9, s. 25.

As a result of some notorious cases of child abuse where the child had been left with the family and had died, a number of provinces are re-examining the point at which a child should be removed from home. Ontario, for example, in 1999 amended its child protection legislation to make physical protection of the child a higher priority.

"Child in Need of Protection"

This broad term describes a child who is at risk of serious mental or physical harm either caused by family members or that family members or caregivers are unable to prevent. The term also includes a child in need of medical or psychiatric care, where that care is not otherwise provided and where serious harm might result if it is not. The category also covers children who are uncontrollable and who have committed serious offences but who are not subject to the *Youth Criminal Justice Act* because they are under 12 years of age.

Where a child is believed to be in need of protection, child care workers or the police are required, in extreme cases, to take the child to a place of safety and to commence court proceedings to have the child declared in need of protection. In the first instance, if the child is found to be in need of protection, the court will make an order designed to treat the child in the family setting. Usually the supervision of this process is given to a **Children's Aid Society**.

Wardships and Adoptions

If the child is successfully treated, the child protection order is allowed to lapse, and the child is returned to his family. However, if the child has no family or other caregiver or if the court finds that the family is too damaging and harmful for the child, the child is made a ward of the state either as a Children's Aid Society ward or, if the matter is more serious, as a Crown ward. If a child has been made a Crown ward and cannot be returned to the family setting, the child is required to be put up for adoption. Often such children are beyond preschool age and cannot be adopted easily. Such children may go into a foster family or a group home prior to adoption: if, indeed, they are ever adopted.

Adoption of Crown wards is only one kind of adoption. There are also adoptions of newborns and "step-parent" adoptions. Newborn adoptions arise where a woman has given birth to a child and has decided not to keep the child. There are elaborate procedures to ensure that proper consent has been given so that the birth mother cannot try to reclaim the child after the child has gone to the adoptive home. In some provinces, Children's Aid supervises these adoptions. In others, the jurisdiction may be shared with private licensees who charge a fee for the adoption service (but not for the child, as we are not yet at the stage where we are willing to treat children as property for purchase).

Step-parent adoptions typically involve a person adopting the child of his or her spouse, where that child is the product of the spouse's former marriage or of an earlier relationship. These adoptions are typically privately arranged, and are minimally supervised by the state or the courts.

CHAPTER SUMMARY

In this chapter, the reader was given a general overview of family law in Canada. While focusing on divorce and family dissolution, we also examined child welfare and adoption. General principles and trends were identified, and the reader was cautioned that, aside from divorce law, most of family law is provincial. While there is much similarity, there is substantial variation in the law of the 10 provinces and the territories.

The chapter discussed family law in the context of social and cultural values and assumptions surrounding the family. The origins of family law in English common law were examined, including limits on divorce, and the requirement of bad behaviour by a husband as a prerequisite for very limited remedies for a wronged wife.

Current trends in family law were then identified, including family law remedies being available without having to prove who is at fault, a growing concern with the adequacy of child support both in terms of amount, and in terms of certainty that payments will be made over time. The law is also expanding remedies to include couples who are in a permanent relationship, though not married. There is also a trend towards defining "family" in a more inclusive way, to include, among other things, same-sex couples. Last, there is a trend towards treating spousal property as if it were partnership property, to be shared equally if the "partnership" dissolves.

Contemporary family law was then examined following the sequences in a family's "life cycle", from formation to dissolution. The legal aspects of betrothal and marriage were examined and compared to so-called common law relationships. This was followed by an examination of the law relating to divorce and annulment, support, and custody, both in the context of divorce and provincial legislation. Lastly, we examined developments in the law relating to property distribution on dissolution of a marriage.

The chapter then turned to child protection and child welfare, identifying the principles under which this law operates today and examining the child-protection process through several stages, culminating in adoption. This type of adoption was distinguished from newborn and "step-parent" adoptions.

GLOSSARY OF NEW TERMS AND KEY CONCEPTS

alimony	An award of support payable to a wife whose husband has engaged in matrimonial misconduct; as a condition of receiving alimony, the wife has to be prepared to forgive the husband and take him back, although the courts softened this requirement in later years. Alimony has been replaced as a remedy by statutory-support provisions in the *Divorce Act*, and in provincial legislation.
alternative dispute resolution (ADR)	The latest trend in settling disputes by negotiation, rather than by fighting it out in court. Many members of the bar and the public have jumped on the ADR bandwagon as a panacea. However, if the parties do not have equality of bargaining power (often the case in family breakdown), ADR can result in the weaker party doing far worse than it might do after a court fight.
banns	A public announcement of an intention to marry, made at a religious service.
betrothal	An agreement, contractual in nature, to marry at a later date. The social and cultural event we call an engagement is the outward sign of what has legally occurred.
Children's Aid Society	An organization, originally a private, voluntary, charitable group, that is given statutory powers and government funding to protect children in many Canadian jurisdictions.
cohabitation	A situation where a man and a woman live in a permanent, sexually monogamous, marriage-like relationship, without being formally married.
cohabitation agreement	A form of domestic agreement that permits those intending to cohabit to agree on issues relating to property and support if the relationship ends.
criminal conversation	Neither criminal, nor a conversation, this is a legal wrong done to a husband by another man who has sexual intercourse with his, the husband's, wife. This tort was abolished by statute in most jurisdictions by the 1970s.

dowry	A contractual payment, enforceable in law, to the parents of a groom by the parents of the bride. Dowries are no longer part of the arrangements in most European and North American marriages, particularly where the bride and groom choose each other rather than have their parents choose for them. The payment may be seen as a contractual inducement to purchase akin to the manufacturer's rebate offered by some car manufacturers on slow-moving models. In societies where women have a very high economic value, a groom's family might have to pay a "bride price" for the right to marry the bride.
divorce mensa et thoro	An order from the old ecclesiastical courts that would permit spouses to cease to live together, in circumstances of serious abuse or violence, where it was impossible for them to continue doing so. They were still legally married, however, and could not re-marry unless one spouse died.
ecclesiastical courts	A system of English courts that dealt with the affairs of the Church of England, the legal rights and liabilities of the clergy and, in a limited way, with some family law matters. These courts were abolished in 1857 in England, and were never introduced to Canada.
engagement	*See* **betrothal.**
garnisheeing, garnishment	A method of enforcing a judgment for the payment of money by requiring a third party who owes money to the judgment-debtor to pay that amount, or a part of it, to the court for the benefit of the judgment-creditor.
marriage contract	Also called an **ante nuptual** agreement. The same thing as a cohabitation agreement, except that the parties intend to marry. *See* **cohabitation agreement.**
nullity	Usually refers to a court order declaring a marriage to be null and void. Such a marriage is said to be a nullity.
patriarchal	Usually used to describe a pattern of authority in society in which males have the most power and authority. A patriarchal family, therefore, is one in which the father is the principal authority and decision maker.
polygamy	The union of one man with two or more women, or one woman with two or more men, to form a family unit.
polygynous/polyandrous	A polygynous marriage is one where a man may have more than one wife at a time. A polyandrous marriage is one where a wife may have more than one husband.
reference	a procedure by which the Government of Canada refers important legal or factual questions to the Supreme Court of Canada and asks the Court to give the government its opinion.
same-sex couple	Two homosexuals or lesbians who cohabit in a long-term conjugal relationship that resembles that of a heterosexual couple.
separation agreement	An agreement whereby spouses who are ending their marriage decide terms about issues related to support, custody, and division of property.
unity of personality	A common law doctrine that defined a married couple as one person in law, with the authority over that person vested in the husband. The effect of the doctrine was to deprive a married woman of most legal rights, including legal control of her property and children.
unmarried spouses	"Spouse" usually means a married person; but where a couple has formed a long-term relationship that looks like a marriage relationship without a formal marriage ceremony, the term "unmarried spouse" is used to describe the members of this relationship.
void ab initio	"Void from the very beginning."

REVIEW QUESTIONS

1. Explain how the law and customs relating to marriage and divorce in the premodern period supported the family as an economic unit.

2. What is alimony? How does it differ from modern law related to spousal support?

3. What are some of the requirements of a valid marriage?

4. When is a marriage dissolved by a divorce decree? When by a nullity decree?

5. What are some of the current problems with the laws of spousal and child support?

6. What is the general principle applied to determine custody disputes?

7. What is the rationale for equalizing the spouses' shares in family property when the marriage ends?

8. Describe the steps that might be taken with a child whose parents are alcoholic and physically abusive.

9. What are the different types of adoption, and how do they differ?

10. Describe new developments with respect to the following:

    (a) Ensuring that child support is paid regularly as ordered by the court
    (b) Making the determination of child support fairer and more equitable

11. Suppose Margaret, who is separated from Gary, does not want Gary to see the kids. They have not yet divorced, and there is no court order in respect of custody. She decides to move with the kids back to England without telling him. What rights does Gary have?

12. What is "collaborative divorce", and what is its purpose?

13. What is "shared custody"?

DISCUSSION QUESTIONS

1. How do the structure and operation of the traditional family explain the following legal rules?

    (a) The unitary personality doctrine
    (b) The tort of criminal conversation
    (c) The tort of harbouring and/or enticement
    (d) Divorce *mensa et thoro*
    (e) Alimony

2. An unrelated man and woman may form a family unit. Should an unrelated man and man or an unrelated woman and woman be allowed to form a family unit recognized by law? Should a brother and sister, or parent and child, form family units recognized by law? What criteria should we use to define a family? What kind of legal recognition should be given?

3. John and Mary are in a custody dispute regarding their child Henry, age 13. John is a workaholic, who travels a lot and earns a very good living. He will be able to give Henry lessons and summer camp and can afford a housekeeper to look after Henry when he is not there. He is a very

loving dad and shares an interest in sports and outdoor activities with Henry.

Mary will have to return to work and will not be earning as much as John. Until the marriage ended, she did almost all of the child rearing and has a strong, warm, and loving relationship with Henry. Henry confides in her and finds her easier to talk to than his dad. Mary will continue to live in the family home if she gets custody.

How would you apply the "best-interest" test to determine who should get custody?

4. Miranda is quite wealthy, in love with Mel, and wants to marry him. Mel is a musician, has no money, and doesn't earn very much. He is reluctant to marry because of the differences in wealth; however, he finally agrees. During the marriage, Mel stops working and lies around all the time watching soap operas on T.V. He also drinks and physically abuses Miranda. Miranda continues to work and brings in all the family income; she also has to look after the house as Mel feels that is "women's work". After six months, Miranda has had enough and ends the marriage. Mel is now asking to have their family property divided into equal shares.

Miranda objects to the equal division. What arguments can she make that might persuade a court not to make an equal division?

5. Jerrold, age 11, has been picked up by the police while wandering downtown at 2:00 a.m. His parents are drunk, as usual, and the police discover they are unaware of his absence. Jerrold is generally bedraggled and unkempt. When he shows up at school, which is not often, he is inattentive and disruptive. On physical examination, there is evidence of active tuberculosis, a highly infectious disease.

   (a) What criteria should apply to this case in considering whether Jerrold is a "child in need of protection"?

   (b) Bearing in mind the principles underlying child protection legislation, what would you put in the child protection order?

   (c) Assuming that Jerrold cannot, in his interests, be returned to his family, what happens?

6. If we permit same-sex marriages in Canada, should we also permit polygynous marriages (where a husband may marry more than one wife) or polygamous ones (where a wife may marry more than one husband)?

7. "An engagement ring is just a ring." Discuss.

SUGGESTED READINGS

Consolidate Ontario Family Law Statutes and Regulations, Annual ed. (Toronto, Ont.: Carswell).

Kronby, Malcolm. *Canadian Family Law*, 9th ed. (Toronto, Ont.: John Wiley & Sons Canada, 2006).

MacDonald, J., & L. Ferrier. *Canadian Divorce Law and Practice*, 2d ed. (Toronto, Ont.: Carswell, 2000).

WEBSITES

Ministry of the Attorney General Ontario: <http://www.attorneygeneral.jus.gov.on.ca/english/family/>

- "Family Arbitration": <http://www.attorneygeneral.jus.gov.on.ca/english/family/arbitration/>

Department of Justice: <http://canada.justice.gc.ca/eng/pi/sup-pen/grl/lawsr-loisr.html>

- *Federal Child Support Guidelines*
  <http://canada.justice.gc.ca/eng/pi/sup-pen/grl/fcsg-lfpae.html>
- *Spousal Support Advisory Guidelines: A Draft Proposal*
  <http://canada.justice.gc.ca/eng/dept-min/pub/ss-pae/proj/toc-tdm.html>

Women and the Law

T. Brettel Dawson
CARLETON UNIVERSITY

Jennifer Quaile
CARLETON UNIVERSITY

Learning Objectives

At reading this chapter, the reader should be able to

➢ explain the feminist critique of law as containing gender bias in rules, processes, and attitudes and the argument that law is socially constructed around categories such as gender and race

➢ cite actual instances of gender bias in the law on the part of judges and legislatures, as well as some of the historic breakthroughs made by women in relation to their legal status

➢ describe the range of the equality guarantees in Canadian law

➢ understand that different meanings have been suggested for "equality" in law and that different legal tests or principles are attached to them

➢ understand and identify processes of law and social change related to the positions of women in Canadian society and the contradictory and complex nature of legal reform as it affects women

TABLE OF CONTENTS

INTRODUCTION: THE GENDER ISSUE IN LAW

In her influential book, *Feminism Unmodified*, **feminist** legal theorist Catharine MacKinnon commented that "at the heart of every women's initiative for civil equality from suffrage to the [U.S.] equal rights amendment" has been the "simple notion that law respond to women as well as to men" and that women "participate in defining the terms that create the standards, and be a voice in drawing the lines."[1] As readers of this book will already be aware, law plays an important role in our society: it regulates conduct, provides benefits, or imposes restrictions, and provides an avenue for resolving disputes and obtaining remedies. Law is powerful in our society; it is also a place in which competing conceptions of social and legal relationships and ordering are articulated and contested. It is important, then, that law — its rules, its judges, and its processes — are not affected by bias. Australian legal academic Professor Margaret Thornton is not alone, however, in suggesting that "[s]o successful has been the prevailing ideology of law as a neutral arbiter of disputes and as a positive instrument of social change, rather than as a primary determinant of social relations, that little attention has been directed to the possibility that the form of law itself might be flawed."[2] Madam Justice Bertha Wilson, the first woman to be appointed as a judge of the Supreme Court of Canada, echoed this concern in a public lecture in 1990 in which she said:

> many studies have found overwhelming evidence that gender-based myths, biases and stereotypes are deeply imbedded in the attitudes of many male judges, as well as in the law itself ... in some areas of law ... a distinctly male perspective is clearly discernable [*sic*] and has resulted in legal principles that are not fundamentally sound, and should be revisited as and when the opportunity presents itself.[3]

These sorts of problems constitute the "gender issue in law". Identifying these problems and issues, and working creatively and persistently to change them, has defined the project of feminist legal scholarship. In a 1988 article in the *New York Times*, entitled "Feminist Scholars Spurring Rethinking of Law", Tamar Lewin observed that "in a flood of recent articles in legal journals, feminist scholars are proposing a basic rethinking of everything from the doctrine of negligence to the criminal laws about rape." She quoted Professor Martha Minow, of Harvard Law School, who commented, "In many cases, the legal framework doesn't allow us to do justice. Where that's true, we have to change the framework. That's what good lawyering is, feminist or not."

In this chapter, we explore the implications of the "gender issue in law", the idea that law has a gender dimension and can affect women and men differently and, indeed, that it can affect different groups of men and women differently depending on their class, race/ethnicity, and family status. Understanding the gender issue in law can assist us in examining and responding to legal and social issues involving women. In the next section, we examine some of the history of women's inequality in Canadian law; in identifying some important breakthroughs for women, we also explore the complexity of law and social change and ask some difficult questions about how positive these changes were and for whom. Our examples include the historic restrictions on married women's ability to own property, the exclusion of women from the right to vote, and the struggle for women to be permitted to become lawyers. A com-

---

[1] Catharine MacKinnon, *Feminism Unmodified* (Cambridge, Mass.: Harvard University Press, 1987) at 228.
[2] Margaret Thornton, "Feminist Jurisprudence: Illusion or Reality" (1986) 3 Aust. J.L. & Soc. 5 at 8.
[3] Madam Justice Bertha Wilson, "Will Women Judges Really Make a Difference?" (1990) Barbara Betcherman Lecture, Osgoode Hall Law School.

mon issue in these examples was whether women were "legal persons". For many years, women were considered "non-persons" in law and, as such, had no power, rights, or capacity in law. The struggle to change this situation was one of the defining features of the women's movement in the first 30 years of this century.

In the third section of the chapter, we examine the impact that gender-biased judicial attitudes and legal rules have had on women's efforts to be included in legal standards and to have law respond to them equally and fairly. We will see that profoundly sexist views of women have affected legal outcomes throughout the years and, sadly, continue to do so. In the fourth section of the chapter we explore the scope and meaning of sex equality guarantees in Canadian law. A case study on pay equity in the federal public service brings together many of the themes of the chapter, including the need to look at law in relation to social and economic dynamics and to place formal legal processes in the context of workplace and policy-based processes. We conclude the chapter by outlining several current equality issues and asking readers to identify the equality problems at stake and the ways in which differing approaches to equality affect how we respond to these problems, and to articulate and argue for what they believe are just and appropriate ways to resolve them.

THE STRUGGLE FOR WOMEN TO BECOME LEGAL PERSONS

We would like to think that we have gone a long way from the days when employed women had to leave their jobs when they married (or more recently, when employed married women had to leave their jobs when they became pregnant), or when married women could not own property, or obtain custody of their children. We would also like to think we are a long way away from the time when women were not considered to be "**legal persons**", could not vote, go to university, or become doctors, lawyers, or members of Parliament. The breakthrough case which established that women were "legal persons" was a 1929 decision of the Judicial Committee of the English Privy Council Court. The case involved the question of whether women were included in the term "persons" who were eligible to be called as senators. The Canadian Supreme Court had decided that women were not persons and that the framers of our Constitution could not possibly have meant to include women in the term. The Privy Council reversed this decision. This was the famous "persons case". The Lord Chancellor, Lord Sankey, echoed our hopes of progressive movement to a more equal society when he commented that the exclusion of women from public office was "a relic of times more barbarous than ours."[4] Interestingly, much before this, in 1917, an Alberta court had refused to accept the argument that women were not legal persons. A person convicted of vagrancy was appealing his conviction because it had been made by a woman magistrate. The Court expressed the view that it was "returning to the more liberal and enlightened view of the middle ages in England and passing over the narrower and more hardened view, which ... by the middle of the 19th century had gained ascendancy."[5] What the Alberta Court made clearer than the Privy Council was that the legal status of women is not "natural" or "inevitable" but reflects social choices and changes over time and according to social context. Nevertheless, such optimism aside, it

---

[4] *Edwards v. Attorney General for Canada*, [1930] A.C. 124.
[5] *R. v. Cyr*, [1917] 3 W.W.R. 849.

remains true that barriers to women's equality have not all been eliminated at the end of this century.

Of course, many formal barriers to women's legal capacity and full participation in our society have been removed. In this section we look at three examples of such change. We outline the changes and move on to examine a number of difficult questions that these breakthroughs also raise. It is clear that the gradual elimination of legal barriers affecting women was not only, or at all, the result of enlightened and progressive motivations. Moreover, the changes in women's legal status did not improve the social and economic position of all women equally and contemporaneously. These examples also suggest that the barriers and inequalities experienced by women were not individual problems or the result of irrational or atypical actions; rather, they were problems ingrained in systems of thought, rules, and legal processes. The examples in the next two sections of the chapter make clear what U.S. feminist legal scholar Deborah Rhode meant when she commented that the "three core assumptions of feminist critical theories are that gender is a central category for analysis, that equality between women and men is a crucial social objective and that equality for all women cannot be achieved without fundamental social transformation."[6]

Married Women and Property

Prior to the mid-19th century, married women could not own property. Marital property law was predicated on the concept of "legal unity", in which a woman lost her separate legal identity and capacity when she married. The legal rationale for this was explained by Sir William Blackstone, a leading law commentator in the 18th century, who regarded it as a self-evident principle of law that "by marriage the husband and wife are one person in law; that is, the very being or legal existence of the woman is suspended during marriage, or at least is incorporated into that of the husband, under whose wing, protection and *cover* she performs everything...."[7] In practice this meant that a married woman could not own property and that all property in the family unit belonged to her husband. The story is told of a prominent suffragist in England, Millicent Garrett Fawcett, who had her purse snatched on a London street. When the charge against the young thief was read out in court, it stated that he had stolen "from the person of Millicent Fawcett a purse containing [a sum of money], being the property of Henry Fawcett" who was her husband. Similarly, even after a marriage had broken down in fact (a divorce in law could only be obtained by private Act of Parliament at one time), an estranged husband could claim any assets or income earned by his wife because they legally belonged to him.

The *Married Women's Property Act*s in the 1880s in the United Kingdom and in Canada (although New Brunswick's initial legislation was much earlier in 1851) changed the law to permit married women to own property. The Acts also ensured that husbands no longer held claim to their wives' property upon marriage.

The struggle for the law to be changed had been long and hard fought. On its face it looked to be a victory for the women's movement. However, researchers have compellingly demonstrated that the legislative motivations for the enactment of the *Married Women's Property Act*s were not primarily to enhance the legal status of women. Rather, they were motivated by other

---

[6] Deborah Rhode, "Feminist Critical Theories" (1990) 42 Stanf. L. Rev. 617.

[7] W. Blackstone, *Commentaries on the Laws of England*, Book I (Chicago: University of Chicago Press, 1979), c. 15 at 442.

interests, particularly those of creditors.[8] Similarly, the state was motivated to introduce the legislation out of its own interests in limiting the costs of social assistance rather than in order to protect women or promote women's equality. Sociologist Jane Ursel has pointed out that the state needed to "minimize the number of dependents upon the public purse."[9] This happened to coincide with women's desire to own their own property. Thus, the state and women held only a shared interest in dismantling laws which had always been costly to women and had gradually become costly to the state. With the reform of marital property laws, women were given more power over family finances. These laws, however, were not intended to allow women to become more independent or equal, but only to provide them with "some economic security in case of their husbands' death or desertion."[10] It should be noted too that the concept of equal division of marital property on marriage breakdown did not occur until the Family Law Acts in the 1970s and 1980s.

This example makes it evident that assumptions regarding women's subordinate role in marriage were structured into legal rules. Changes to marital property rights for women were heavily influenced by economic and political factors, and indeed the changes were not motivated by an interest in achieving women's equality. They may well have led to greater economic security for some women of more advantageous class positions (who had always had some protection through the use of family trusts), yet it is questionable whether, for example, working class married women actually gained from the *Married Women's Property Act*s. Similarly, even today with laws providing for division of marital property on marriage breakdown and the so-called "clean break principle" of spousal independence upon divorce, women may receive an ambiguous benefit. In our society, income rather than property assets is the main source of economic wealth and security; however, income is not normally divided. Spousal support on marriage breakdown is very limited. Finally, provincial legislation providing for property division on marriage breakdown does not apply to property on Indian reserves and hence does not benefit aboriginal women living on such reserves.

Women and the Vote

In 1997, it seems amazing that Canadian women in this century could not vote in federal, provincial or local elections. In 1916, Manitoba, Alberta and Saskatchewan were the first provinces to extend the franchise to non-aboriginal women.[11] Ontario and British Columbia extended to non-aboriginal women the right to vote provincially in 1917.[12] The last province to award the franchise to women was Quebec in 1940.[13] The federal franchise was awarded

---

[8] See, e.g., Norma Basch, *In the Eyes of the Law: Women, Marriage and Property in Nineteenth Century New York* (Ithaca, New York: Cornell University Press, 1982).

[9] Jane Ursel, *Private Lives, Public Policy: 100 Years of State Intervention in the Family* (Toronto, Ont.: Women's Press, 1992) at 300.

[10] Sandra Burt, "Legislators, Women, and Public Policy", in Sandra Burt, Lorraine Code, and Lindsay Dorney, eds., *Changing Patterns: Women in Canada* (Toronto, Ont.: McClelland & Stewart, 1988) 126 at 130.

[11] Manitoba: *An Act to Amend the "Manitoba Election Act"*, 6 Geo. V, c. 36; Alberta: *The Equal Suffrage Statutory Law Amendment Act*, 6 Geo. V, c. 5; Saskatchewan: *An Act to Amend the Statute Law*, 6 Geo. V, c. 37, s. 1.

[12] Ontario: *The Ontario Franchise Act*, 1917, 7 Geo. V, c. 5. Women could not, however, be elected to the Legislative Assembly, nor could they hold office until 1919: *Women's Assembly Qualification Act, 1919*, 9 Geo. V, c. 8. British Columbia: *Provincial Elections Act Amendment Act, 1917*, 7–8 Geo. V, c. 23.

[13] *An Act Granting to Women the Right to Vote and be Eligible as Candidates*, 4 Geo. VI, c. 7. The right to vote in local elections was delayed until 1941: *An Act to Amend the Cities and Towns Act*, 5 Geo. VI, c. 41; and *An Act to Amend the Municipal Code*, 5 Geo. VI, c. 69.

to all non-aboriginal women in 1918,[14] but it was not until 1960 that aboriginal women were given an unrestricted right to the vote federally. Quebec was the last province to extend the provincial franchise to aboriginal men and women when it did so in 1969.[15]

Race was a major factor in restrictions on the vote in Canada. Federal suffrage legislation continued to discriminate after 1918 on the basis of race and ethnicity. Until 1948, Canadians of Chinese, Japanese, and East Indian ethnic origins were not allowed to vote unless they were war veterans.[16] Legislation also prevented "Eskimos" (as the Inuit had been called) from voting until 1950. The *Indian Act* (1876), 39 Vict., c. 18 provided in section 3(12) that "the term 'person' means an individual other than an Indian, unless the context clearly requires another construction." The *Electoral Franchise Act* (1885), although including (status) Indians within its definition of "person" went on to exclude from the right to vote a wide range of "Indians", a restriction repeated in the 1890 Act.

We are familiar with the suffrage movement and the efforts of the women's movement in advocating for the vote at the beginning of this century.[17] Gaining the right to vote was such an important issue for women because the right to vote is fundamental to full citizenship; participation in the political process is a basic political right of citizens in a democracy. What seems to us to be a straightforward matter of justice, however, is anything but in terms of the history of women and the vote. Today in equality struggles, we still often hear the refrains of arguments used against giving women the vote. In Quebec, Cardinal Villeneuve's views were influential. In March 1940, he listed four reasons that women should not vote: (1) suffrage would militate against the family unit; (2) women would be exposed to the passions of elections; (3) most women in Quebec did not want the vote; and (4) social reforms could be achieved by women's organizations outside of politics.[18] Nellie McClung, a prominent suffragist, mocked such views in her essay, "Hardy Perennials", commenting on one of these kinds of arguments in the following terms:

> There is [an argument against giving women the vote], that if women were ever given the chance to participate in outside affairs then family quarrels would result ... [but] father and son have been known to live under the same roof and vote differently, and yet live! If a husband and wife are going to find cause to quarrel they will find cause for dispute easily enough, and will not be compelled to wait until election day.[19]

The vote was won, albeit slowly and unevenly. Gaining the right to vote was a high-priority issue for middle-class women. The majority of women who

---

[14] *An Act to Confer the Electoral Franchise upon Women*, 8–9 Geo. V, c. 20 gave to non-aboriginal women the right to vote in federal elections.

[15] Some of the dates of provincial enfranchisement of aboriginal persons were: British Columbia (1949), Manitoba (1952), Ontario (1954), Saskatchewan (1960), New Brunswick and Prince Edward Island (1963).

[16] In 1924, the federal government had awarded the franchise to approximately 4,000 Native Indians who were war veterans (Joseph Krauter and Morris Davis, *Minority Canadians: Ethnic Groups* (Toronto, Ont.: Methuen, 1978) at 75). In 1917, the *Military Voters Act*, S.C. 1917, c. 35 extended the federal vote to all Canadian men and women on active duty, including Indians. The *Dominion Elections Act* S.C. 1920, c. 46, s. 29(1) gave the vote to "Indians who served in the World War (later extended to the Second World War as well) but excluded Indians ordinarily resident on an Indian reservation."

[17] A number of women played a leading role in the Canadian suffrage movement, most notably Nellie McClung, Emily Murphy, Alice Jamieson, Louise McKinney, Irene Parlby, and Emily Stowe.

[18] Catherine L. Cleverdon, *The Woman Suffrage Movement in Canada* (Toronto, Ont.: University of Toronto Press, 1974) at 257.

[19] Nellie McClung, *In Times Like These* (Toronto, Ont.: University of Toronto Press, 1972) at 5.

were active in the leading suffrage associations, and who led the suffrage movement, had relatively high social positions; many were professionals such as doctors and educators and 60 per cent of the female suffragists held jobs. Carol Bacchi has noted that this is a "rather exceptional number" given that in 1911, only 14 per cent of women in Canada were employed for wages.[20] Labour groups and organized farm women's groups in the Western provinces also actively worked towards the enfranchisement of women through their own organizations. However, few ever joined the ranks of the suffrage societies, perhaps because of political differences.[21] Yet their enduring struggle should not be under-emphasized — after all, the prairie provinces were the first to grant the franchise to non-aboriginal women.

As in the case of married women's property, however, a number of competing interests were in motion around allowing women to vote. One lucid exchange on the topic appears in the historical record of the parliamentary debates. In 1929, Agnes McPhail, who had been Canada's first woman M.P. when she was elected in 1921, rose in the House of Commons to challenge the government of the day, which was claiming credit for first granting women a partial right to the federal vote in the *War Times Election Act*, 1917, S.C. 1917, c. 39. She said,

> I am astounded that [credit should be claimed] for the Conservative party for giving the franchise to women. I do not know of anything more scandalous except the *War Time Elections Act*, of which it was a part, than the manner of granting the franchise to women in 1917. Does the hon. member ... and his party not know that it was the starvation and the fighting and the going to jail and the forcible feeding suffered by the suffragettes of Great Britain, and to a lesser extent of the United States, that gave the franchise to Canadian women? [At which point some hon. members laughed. Agnes McPhail continued:] Hon. members do not show good sense in laughing at that. It is true; it is not a thing to be laughed at. The Conservative government ... gave votes to women in 1917, but not to all women. That would be too risky ... they gave votes to women who they thought would vote for them at that particular time ... they gave votes to some women, not to all women, and not because they were intelligent, but because they had a husband or a brother or a son fighting at the front. Whether war time or not, it was a very stupid way of extending the franchise to women.[22]

This initial law had indeed not been in any way a victory for the suffrage movement; its intention was merely to allow men fighting the war overseas to have a sort of "proxy" vote through their female relatives. Of course, that such a matter was legislated provides a clear insight into just how important and fundamental the right to vote was regarded as being, albeit for men. Catherine Cleverdon has quoted the Secretary of State as noting that the soldiers' female relatives were "likely to vote in such a way ... as they themselves would do upon our shores."[23]

McPhail clearly pointed out the distinct reasons for granting some women the vote in 1917. Obviously, the state's reasons for granting suffrage to women were not predicated on a desire to ensure full citizenship rights for women. Legislative change regarding women and the vote took a slow and uneven path. As in changes regarding marital property, its inception was not

---

[20] Carol Bacchi, "Divided Allegiances: The Response of Farm and Labour Women to Suffrage", in Linda Kealy, ed., *A Not Unreasonable Claim, 1880–1920s* (Toronto: The Women's Press, 1974) 89 at 91.

[21] *Ibid.* at 90.

[22] Canada, House of Commons, *Debates & Proceedings* (Hansard) (19 March 1929).

[23] Catherine L. Cleverdon, *The Woman Suffrage Movement in Canada* (Toronto: University of Toronto Press, 1974) at 125.

Lawyer Firsts	**EXHIBIT 29.1**

¤ In 1897, Clara Brett Martin was called to the Bar in the Province of Ontario, and was simultaneously admitted to practise as a solicitor. She was the first woman in the entire British Empire to be admitted to the practice of law. Certainly, the path was opened for other women to enter the legal profession.

¤ In 1912, Mabel French was the first woman to gain the right to practise law in two provinces (New Brunswick and British Columbia).

¤ In 1924, Vera Parsons became the first woman criminal lawyer in Ontario, and the first woman lawyer to appear before judge and jury. She was also one of the first women lawyers with a disability; she had polio and used a cane. It was not until 1941 that Quebec granted women the right to be admitted to the practice of law. Access to the legal profession was delayed for women of racial minorities.

¤ In 1946, Greta Wong Grant was the first Chinese-Canadian lawyer in Canada.

¤ Delia Opekokew was the first Native woman to be admitted to the Bar in Saskatchewan (1979), and also the first in Ontario (1983).

¤ In 1984, Marva Jemmott was appointed as a Queen's Counsel, the first black woman to receive this honour.

¤ In 1992, Paule Gauthier became the first woman president of the Canadian Bar Association.

grounded in any desire to grant all women full and equal political participation. Assumptions about women's rightful place in society informed restrictive legislation, and impeded women's efforts to gain the vote. This is a recurrent theme in much of the history of women and the law.

Canada's First Woman Lawyer

In 1897, Clara Brett Martin was called to the Bar in the Province of Ontario, and was simultaneously admitted to practise as a solicitor. She was the first woman in the entire British Empire to be admitted to the practice of law. Her accomplishment did not come without a struggle and the support of senior politicians including the Premier, Oliver Mowatt. In 1891, she petitioned the Law Society of Upper Canada (the governing body for lawyers in the province) for permission to become a student member; such membership was a prerequisite to articling as a clerk, attending lectures, and sitting the exams required to receive a certificate of fitness to practise as a solicitor. The Law Society denied her petition, interpreting its governing statute as permitting only men to be admitted to the practice of law. Clara Brett Martin succeeded in having her case raised in the Ontario legislature and legislation was ultimately passed to permit women to become solicitors.[24] In order to implement this legislation, the Law Society was required to alter its regulations; initially it refused to do so, deeming it "inexpedient". However, in a narrow vote (12 for; 11 against) and after various machinations, rules for admitting women were eventually approved. Clara Brett Martin then registered as a **student-at-law**. Partway through her study, she decided that she wanted to be admitted as a barrister as well as a solicitor (at the time, the profession of law was divided into two branches) She was once again faced with a struggle with the Law Society. In 1895, legislation was passed to allow women to be called to the bar.[25] Once

---

[24] *An Act to Provide for the Admission of Women to the Study and Practice of Law*, 1892, 55 Vict., c. 32 (Ont.).

[25] *An Act to Amend the Act to Provide for the Admission of Women to the Study and Practice of Law*, 1895, 58 Vict., c. 27 (Ont.).

again, the Law Society resisted drawing up the necessary regulations; eventually it altered its regulations in 1896.

Throughout her studies, she was "dogged with various degrees of scrutiny, harassment and ridicule." The following quote demonstrates her motivation: "If it were not that I set out to open the way to the bar for others of my sex, I would have given up the effort long ago. You would not believe how many obstacles I have had to overcome single-handed."[26] She maintained an active interest in women's issues and in women's rights generally throughout her career as a lawyer. She remained single. Her health began to decline by 1920, and she died in 1923 at the relatively young age of 49.

Clara Brett Martin has been regarded as a pathbreaker and role model for women wishing to enter the legal profession. However, in 1989, a letter written by Martin in 1915 to the Attorney General was found in the archives of the Law Society of Upper Canada. In the letter, Martin made comments which were clearly and unequivocally anti-Semitic, casting aspersions on the real estate transactions of Jewish individuals and requesting that the Attorney General take legal action. These views show that although she was sensitive to aspects of sexism, Martin was clearly not so mindful of discrimination against Jews. The discovery of her letter led to a storm of controversy over Martin's stature in women's legal history. Law professor Constance Backhouse reminds us that Martin's anti-Semitism is a telling example of how we can perpetrate certain forms of discrimination while at the same we are struggling for the elimination of other forms.[27]

JUDGING AND GENDER

In this section of the chapter, we examine the impact that gender-biased judicial attitudes and legal rules have had on women as litigants or participants in the legal process. In the last section, we discussed examples which focused on the role of legislation and legislative change in influencing women's equality. The roles of politicians, leaders of the legal profession, and women's activists were touched upon. However, in understanding the scope of the gender issue in law, it is vital to include the role of judges. It is judges who articulate, interpret, and apply legal principles to fact situations brought before them by litigants unable to settle their disputes. It is judges who interpret legislation and provide remedies. It is judges who control the courtrooms. Their world views and assumptions — and their gender biases — play a very significant role in determining the scope and pace of legal change for women.

Of course, the "official" version of how judges do their jobs[28] is that they are objective, impartial, and neutral in reaching their decisions.[29] Many written judgments and transcripts of oral remarks suggest, however, that in practice judges have allowed gender bias to influence their decision making. Sometimes this can be seen as the product of individual bias; other times, the

---

[26] *Buffalo Express* (1896), undated clipping, archives of the Women's Law Association of Ontario as quoted in Constance Backhouse, "'To Open the Way for Others of My Sex': Clara Brett Martin's Career as Canada's First Woman Lawyer" (1985) 1 C.J.W.L. 1 at 22.

[27] Constance Backhouse, "Clara Brett Martin: Canadian Heroine or Not?" (1992) 5 C.J.W.L. 263–79.

[28] To further explore ideas about judging, refer to Hon. Bertha Wilson, "Will Women Judges Really Make a Difference?" (1990) 28 Osgoode Hall L.J. 507; J.A.G. Griffiths, *The Politics of the Judiciary*, 2d ed. (London: Fontana, 1981); Peter Russell, *The Judiciary in Canada: The Third Branch of Government* (Toronto, Ont.: McGraw-Hill Ryerson, 1987).

[29] See also Mary Jane Mossman, "Feminism and Legal Method: The Difference it Makes" (1987) 3 Wisconsin Women's L.J. 147, and (1986) 3 Aust. J. L. & Soc. 30.

Judicial Firsts

EXHIBIT 29.2

- ¤ In 1916, Emily Murphy was the first woman to be appointed as police magistrate in the British Empire. Her initial jurisdiction was the City of Edmonton. However, it was later extended throughout Alberta. She presided over a women's police court where cases were heard in the absence of men.
- ¤ In 1917, Helen Gregory McGill was appointed as Judge of the Juvenile Court in Vancouver, British Columbia.
- ¤ In 1934, Helen Kinnear became the first woman in the British Commonwealth to be appointed as King's Counsel — an honour granted to senior, respected members of the legal profession. In 1943, Kinnear was appointed as County Court Judge, and became the first woman lawyer in the British Empire to be appointed to a superior court judgeship.
- ¤ In 1971, Mabel Van Camp became the first woman appointed to the Ontario Supreme Court.
- ¤ In 1973, Jean Folster was the first Native woman to be appointed as a magistrate in Manitoba.
- ¤ In 1975, Agnes Sempler of the Northwest Territories was the first aboriginal woman to be appointed as Justice of Peace.
- ¤ In 1976, Rosalie Abella became the first Jewish woman to be appointed as judge in the Ontario Provincial Court.
- ¤ In 1982, Bertha Wilson was the first woman to be appointed to the Supreme Court of Canada.
- ¤ In 1987, Canada had its first black woman judge, when Corrine Sparks was appointed to the family court in Nova Scotia. In 1979, she had been the first black woman to graduate in law school in Dalhousie University, Nova Scotia.
- ¤ In 1991, Terry Vyse became the first aboriginal person, man or woman, to be appointed as judge in Ontario when she was appointed to the Provincial Court of Ontario;
- ¤ In 1993, Maryka Omatsu became the first woman of Japanese ancestry to be appointed as Judge of the Ontario Provincial Court.
- ¤ In 1994, Rose Boyko, a T'Sekani woman from British Columbia, became the first aboriginal woman appointed by the federal government to a superior court, when she was appointed to the Ontario High Court.

---

statements made by the various judges reflect the dominant thinking or views of the time. Also of concern is where a judge, without overt bias, applies a rule into which bias is already built. This section discusses a number of examples of problematic, even appalling, judicial comments; what may be most unsettling, though, is that while some comments are from long ago, some are very recent indeed. And, while some of these comments may seem absurd, quaint, or even ridiculous, we need to remember that they had an impact on individual outcomes and systemic responses to women.

Judicial Attitudes to Women: Gender Bias

In 1977, a 21-year-old man was convicted in Toronto of a criminal charge of unlawfully confining an 18-year-old woman. He had gone to a house with a knife in his hand, broken down a door, ripped the telephone off the wall, and forcibly seized the woman. He was on probation for similar offences at the time of these events. The trial judge, Judge Bewley, sentenced him to six months in prison. In so doing, he made the following comments about the young woman and her friends:

> There is a girl here, or a couple of girls, young nubile females, who've been around a bit, eh? They've travelled from Ontario to here, they're a free floating type of female, young for their age, very nubile, very attractive, surely, but, I suppose, basically I have to look at it this way, still impressionable,

still stupid ... you know women don't get much brains before they're thirty anyway ... but at the age of eighteen or so, they make some stupid mistakes, mostly because we males who know better, lead them into it....

I found him technically guilty of unlawful confinement, you know, but I'm not too sympathetic towards these stupid girls. There's no big deal, right? It isn't as if he held up ... an innocent driver, getting away from something or threatened a policeman with a knife or something. He's demonstrating his manhood to a little girl eighteen years of age, who's probably half inclined to think he's a man by showing a knife, so big deal, eh?

So, I could give him five years, but I don't think under the circumstances of this case, I'd be entitled to give him five years, because as we clearly have said before, he got mixed up with a silly, little bunch of girls who mean well, they got scared because he was proving himself a macho man, was going to haul one of them out and talk to her even if she got scared and ran into the bedroom, so we've got a bunch of clucking females running around, and they are all so scared that they have to call the Police.[30]

These comments show a very patronizing and disrespectful view of young women. They paint a very different picture of events from that recorded in the facts of this man's criminal conduct. They also display a distressing acceptance that, somehow, violent conduct by men towards women is not very serious. (Similarly, in 1982, Members of the House of Commons had to apologize for an outburst of disbelieving laughter when a parliamentary report on battered wives was tabled in Parliament.[31]) The direct impact of Judge Bewley's attitude in the cited case was more lenient sentencing than one might expect; the indirect impact on the young women hearing these comments was likely profound.

These comments were not unprecedented, nor were they the last of this kind. Remarks made in December 1989 by Judge Bourassa, a territorial court judge in the Northwest Territories, raised similar concerns. He was quoted by the *Edmonton Journal* as saying, "The majority of rapes in the Northwest Territories occur when the woman is drunk and passed out. A man comes along and sees a pair of hips and helps himself. That contrasts sharply to the cases I dealt with before (as a judge in southern Canada) of the dainty co-ed who gets jumped from behind."[32] The judge later said that he regretted his remarks and a Judicial Inquiry recommended against disciplinary action. In another Northwest Territories case, Mr. Justice Mark De Weerdt ruled in 1990 that "a man who beat his wife deserved a lighter sentence because she provoked him" by wearing a lewd T-shirt. The shirt, showing cartoon polar bears engaged in a sexual act, could be seen as "implying the possibility, if not the actual promise of sexual perversity and promiscuity." In his ruling, Judge De Weerdt said that the T-shirt's implication "could be understood by the other spouse as an imminent threat that she might commit adultery." Such a threat would be "calculated to arouse alarm, fear, and anger in that other spouse, with clearly foreseeable consequences," he said. Instead of a prison sentence, the judge imposed a fine of $1,000. Again, a ready tolerance of male violence against women found its way into a judicial outcome.

A remark made by Judge Denys Dionne during an assault and weapons trial in the Montreal suburb of Longueuil on 27 January 1989, which came to light early in 1990, is also instructive of gender bias on the part of judges. It was reported that Judge Dionne interjected during argument with the comment, "Rules are like women, they are made to be violated." A lawyer

---

[30] *R. v. Tourangeau* (25 August 1977), unreported (B.C. Provincial Court, Vancouver). See further, M.E. Atcheson, M. Eberts and B. Symes, *Women and Legal Action* (Ottawa: CACSW, 1984), at 40–42.

[31] House of Commons, *Debates*, 12 May 1982, 17334; 13 May 1982, 17368; 14 May 1982, 17423–424.

[32] *Edmonton Journal* (20 December 1989).

involved in the case responded, "Exactly." An official complaint was made against the judge by the Quebec Ministry of Justice to the Quebec Judicial Council. *The Globe and Mail* reported the proceedings of the hearing on 13 February 1990. In explanation, the judge argued that he had made the remark sarcastically to dismiss an argument advanced by a defence lawyer. An audio recording revealed that a lawyer was stressing how "all good principles of law have their exceptions" when Dionne interjected with the comment. He testified to the panel that he first heard the controversial remark about 30 years ago from a respected Quebec jurist. A witness, Crown prosecutor Michel Breton, who was in court when Dionne uttered the 1989 comment, said he considered the remark a "farce" or a "quip" made in impatience to the defence lawyer: "It was something I've heard before," he said. "I was not surprised and I didn't notice any surprise in the courtroom."[33] How deeply entrenched — and normalized — such comments may be is suggested by this comment and indeed by Judge Dionne's testimony that he had originally heard the remark from a "respected jurist". In June 1990, the disciplinary committee ruled that the comment by Judge Dionne was "sexist, in extremely bad taste and unacceptable coming from a judge." It also said that the comments tarnished the image of justice and could lead people to believe that some judges are prejudiced and incapable of rendering impartial decisions. Dionne was to be "severely reprimanded" but not removed from the bench; the goal of the reprimand would be to make sure that the judge realized such statements are wrong and will not be tolerated.

A similar inquiry was held in 1993 into comments made by Judge Frank Allen, a Manitoba provincial court judge. He received a reprimand from the Manitoba Judicial Council in relation to a range of remarks dating back to 1985 when he had commented, while sentencing a man who had threatened to kill his former girlfriend and himself, "I can tell you from 60-odd years of experience that there isn't any woman worth the trouble you got yourself into." In 1989, Judge Allen had reprimanded a female lawyer who was seeking an adjournment because her nursing infant was running an extremely high fever and throwing up antibiotics, and she herself was feeling unwell. The judge suggested that she find a replacement "who is not trying to be a mother and a lawyer at the same time." The Council concluded that judges do not have the right to make such sexist comments, but held that Judge Allen's remarks did not prove that he was incompetent. Of course, this raises the question of whether one can be a good judge (or a good lawyer) if one is profoundly sexist and antipathetic to women's rights to equality and respect. Certainly, Ontario Provincial Court Judge Walter Hryciuk crossed the line. He was ordered removed from the bench in 1993 for sexual misconduct following an inquiry which accepted allegations by two female Crown attorneys that he had sexually harassed and touched them, made lewd remarks, and had forced his tongue into one of the women's mouth during an unwanted kiss.

Very recently indeed, in March 1996, the Canadian **Judicial Council** held a hearing to investigate comments made by Judge Jean Bienvenue of the Quebec Superior Court, who had presided over the trial of a woman accused of murdering her husband. During the trial, he told the woman that by slashing her husband's throat, she made him suffer more than the victims of the Nazi gas chambers: "the Nazis did not eliminate millions of Jews in a painful and bloody manner," he said, "they died in gas chambers without suffering." Female violence to men appears to be judged by a different standard than male violence to women. The judge also said that women can "become more

---

[33] Eric Siblin, *Canadian Press Newswire*, 11 April 1990.

depraved than men" and referred (in French) to the woman as a "négresse" which, in French, is a pejorative term equivalent to describing Blacks as niggers.

These comments and actions by judges became public due to media reporting and when complaints were made to Judicial Councils which oversee the conduct of judges. In 1992, the Canadian Bar Association (CBA) initiated a Task Force to inquire into gender bias in the legal profession. This Task Force was chaired by now-retired Supreme Court Justice, Hon. Bertha Wilson. In its far-ranging report, the Task Force recommended, *inter alia*, parental leave policies for female and male lawyers, flexible work arrangements, workplace equity, sexual harassment policies, commissions to investigate gender-based complaints against judges, and mandatory courses on gender and racial bias for all newly appointed and sitting judges. Following the submission of the Task Force Report, the CBA passed a resolution at its meetings of February 1994, recognizing inequalities in the legal profession, and initiated a process directed towards establishing a similar inquiry into racism in the legal profession.

Public and Private Roles

Clara Brett Martin's struggle to become the first woman lawyer showed us that opposition to women having a public or professional role was legally and socially entrenched. In provinces other than Ontario, women went to court to argue that prohibitions on them becoming lawyers should be set aside. The responses by judges included outrage, incredulity, and implacable opposition. One telling example comes from the case of Annie MacDonald Langstaff, a resident of Quebec who petitioned the Quebec Superior Court in 1915, after her application to take the preliminary bar examination was refused because she was a woman. Mr. Justice Saint-Pierre rejected her petition and blustered:

> I would put within the range of possibilities though by no means a commendable one, the admission of a woman to the profession of solicitor or to that of *avoue*, but I hold that to admit a woman and more particularly, a married woman as a barrister, that is to say, as a person *who pleads cases at the bar before judges or juries in open court and in the presence of the public*, would be nothing short of a direct infringement upon public order and a manifest violation of the law of good morals and public decency.
>
> Let us for a moment picture to ourselves a woman appearing a defending or prosecuting counsel in a case of rapt (sic) [rape] and putting to the complainant the questions which must of all necessity be asked in order to make proof of the acts which are of the essence of the crime or which are equally necessary to meet and repeal the charge. No woman possessing the least sense of decency could possibly do so without throwing a blur upon her own dignity and without bringing into utter contempt the honour and respect due to her sex.

A classic statement in this genre was made in the United States by Justice Bradley in the 1879 case of *Bradwell v. Illinois*. His views were later cited and accepted in Canadian cases. In *Bradwell*, Myra Bradwell, who had legal education and published a successful legal newspaper in Chicago, was petitioning the court to be permitted to become a practising lawyer. She based her case on the U.S. Constitution which provided that no state should make laws abridging the "rights or immunities of citizens", which Bradwell took to include the economic right to practise a profession. Her case went all the way to the U.S. Supreme Court which dismissed her petition. In the words of Justice Bradley:

> Civil law as well as nature herself has always recognised a wide difference in the respective spheres and destinies of man and woman. Man is or should

be, woman's protector and defender. The natural and proper timidity and delicacy which belongs to the female sex evidently unfits it for many of the occupations of civil life. The constitution of the family organization, which is founded in the divine ordinance, as well as in the nature of things, indicates the domestic sphere as that which properly belongs to the domain and functions of womanhood.

Interestingly, 60 of the leading lawyers of Chicago petitioned the state governor to appoint her a Notary Public while her case was pending in the Supreme Court. And, three years after the decision, Bradwell did become an honorary member of the bar.[34]

A more contemporary example of women's aspirations to a public, professional role being rebuffed is the story of comments made to Bertha Wilson upon starting law school. The exchange took place in 1954 between Wilson and one of her male law professors. He sneered at her, "Why would someone like you, at age 31, with a husband to look after you, want to study law?" She replied that she wanted to study law "as part of a liberal education", to which the professor replied, "Look, my dear, we have no room here for dilettantes. Why don't you just go home and take up crocheting?"[35] We can be glad that she did not take this particular advice!

A romantic paternalism is also apparent in many of the cases which refused to allow women to vote or study at university. In an 1863 English case, *Chorlton v. Lings*, women's efforts to register to vote in a city election were challenged and rebuffed by the Court. One of the judges, Sir James Easte Willes, rationalized his refusal to permit women to vote in the following terms:

> What was the cause of the exclusion of women, it is not necessary to go into: but admitting that fickleness of judgment and liability to influence have sometimes been suggested as the ground of exclusion, I must protest against it being supposed to arise in this country from any under-rating of the sex either in point of intellect or worth. That would be quite inconsistent with one of the glories of our civilisation — the respect and honour in which women are held. This is not a mere fancy of my own but will be found in Seldon, in the discussion of the origin of the exclusion of women from judicial and like public functions, where the author gives preference for this reason, that the exemption was founded upon motives of decorum, and was a privilege of the sex.

Despite protestations of respect for women, a thread of case law exists in which women were clearly grouped together with children in assessing legal capacity. For example, in the 1873 case of *Daniels v. Clegg*, a United States court, when concerned with the standard of diligence required of a 20-year-old woman, decided that she should not be required to conform to the standards of the "reasonable man", the accepted standard in assessing conduct. Rather, concessions were to be made for her because of "the incompetency indicated by her age and sex ... which was less in degree, it is true than in the case of a mere child; but the difference is in degree only, and not in principle." Similarly in the 1867 Irish case of *The Queen v. Crosthwaite*, a case concerned with whether a woman was included in the term "persons" in a municipal voting Act, one of the judges, Baron Deasy, stated that:

> [T]he general policy of the law is to exclude [women] from any such intervention ... partly on the supposition that such subjects are beyond their cognizance, as requiring a judgment superior to that which they possess, and

---

[34] See, generally, Martha Minow, "Forming Under Everything That Grows" (1985) Wisconsin L.R. 819 at 846–50.

[35] David Vienneau, "Speaking Her Mind: Supreme Court Judge Bertha Wilson" *Toronto Star* (13 September 1990) D1, D3.

partly on the ground that it is inconsistent with the delicacy and modesty of their sex, that they should be mixed up in the strife and turmoil of a contested election. (at 472)

... That the law in recognising the distinction of the sexes assumes a greater worthiness in the male than in the female, is manifest in the law of descent; that it has regard to the infirmity of bodily strength and ability in the female, by rendering her incompetent for some offices and privileges, or incapacitating her from the discharge of duties thereto belonging, cannot be questioned. Again, that she is subject to incapacities from a presumed inferiority of discretion and judgment, seems also certain: a woman was not admitted as a witness in a case of villeinage against a man; and the reason assigned is, because of her "fragility."

In the same case, Baron Fitzgerald wholeheartedly agreed with his judicial brother, and added for himself that he could:

have no doubt that in substance the reason of the Common Law still applies; and that the course of education and mental training to which women, happily for us and themselves, are subject, does render them far less fit than men for the administration of public affairs. ... Having regard to every one of the reasons of Common Law, the subordination of sex, the inferiority of bodily ability, and the mental inferiority in the sense explained ... I am not sorry ... to come to the conclusion that this judgment ought to be reversed.

More blunt still were comments arising out of the effort made in 1869 by Sophia Jex-Blake and six other women, together known as the "Edinburgh Seven", to study at the Edinburgh Medical School. Their efforts were rebuffed by the University and the full weight of the law was used in support. Lord Neaves, a member of the full bench of the Scottish Court of Session which heard the women's appeal in 1873, had little apparent hesitation in supporting the expulsion of the women from the School. In his decision he stated:

It is a belief, widely entertained that there is great difference in the mental constitution of the two sexes, just as there is in their physical conformation. The powers and susceptibilities of women are as noble as those of men; but they are thought to be different, and, in particular, it is considered that they have not the same power of intense labour as men are endowed with. If this be so, it must form serious objection to uniting them under the same course of academic study. ... A disregard of such an inequality would be fatal to any scheme of public instruction, for, as it is certain that the general mass of an army cannot move more rapidly than its weakest and slowest portion, so a general course of study must be toned and tempered down to suit the average of all the classes of students for whom it is intended; and that average will always be lowered by the existence of any considerable numbers who cannot keep pace with the rest.

Add to this the special acquirements and accomplishments at which women must aim, but from which men may easily remain exempt. Much time must, or ought to be, given by women to the acquisition of a knowledge of household affairs and family duties, as well as to those ornamental parts of education which tend so much to social refinement and domestic happiness, and the study necessary for mastering these must always form a serious distraction from severer pursuits, while there is little doubt that, in public estimation, the want of these feminine arts and attractions in a woman would be ill supplied by such branches of knowledge as a University could bestow. ... [this] case certainly affords no ground from subverting the constitution of our universities, or affecting the dignity and weight which belong to the highest honour attending the medical profession....

Any change which would incur the risk of lowering the standard that now exists, and which we have seen exemplified in so many of our great physicians and professors, is infinitely to be deprecated, and such a danger, I think would be incurred by the revolution in the medical teaching of our universities that has here been attempted to be brought about; while at the same time it would otherwise affect and in my opinion, deteriorate our Universities in a way unknown to any period of their history.

These comments contain a disturbing set of assumptions about women, and clearly sought to assign women to a separate, private sphere. The assumptions made included that men were superior to women in mental and physical ability, that only men were (or should be) involved in public (important) matters, and that women were "less worthy" than men. Their inclusion in university study would lower presumptively rigorous standards and undermine the professions, to say nothing of injuring women's health and well-being. Ethel Benjamin, who was the second woman to become a lawyer in the British Empire (she was admitted in New Zealand in May 1897), placed at the top of her law school class and in reply to queries as to whether her health had been affected replied, "No, my health did not suffer in the least. Do I look like an invalid?" Suffragist Nellie McClung also reminded her readers in 1916 that the same men who recoiled from the idea of women leaving the "sacred precincts of home" had their offices "scrubbed by poor women who do their work while other people sleep." McClung suggested that it was "the thought of women getting into comfortable and well-paid positions which wrings their manly hearts."[36] Justice Brennan of the U.S. Supreme Court added another insight in a 1973 case which considered sex classifications involving dependents' benefits for servicemen and women. He commented in *Frontiero v. Richardson*, that "there can be no doubt that our nation has a long and unfortunate history of sex discrimination. Traditionally, such discrimination was rationalized by an attitude of 'romantic paternalism' which, in practical effect, put women, not on a pedestal, but in a cage."

The Scope of Legal Rules

Many of the comments included in this section of the chapter have identified the gender bias of individual judges. But what if the rules themselves are not neutral in their effect or formulation but are themselves gender biased? Of course, the legal rule that only "persons" could vote, be lawyers, go to university, or be called to the Senate of Canada, which underlay many of the cases discussed so far, is a prime example of a rule being the source of discrimination. What has obscured that point for us today is that it seems so clear that it was the judges' interpretation and application of the rule that led to discrimination against women in many cases. However, there is no shortage of other examples of rules which contain prejudice. A good example is found in the 1985 N.W.T. case of *R. v. Oquataq*. This was a sexual assault case. The accused was challenging restrictions contained in the *Criminal Code* which restricted his right to ask questions of the complainant about her sexual conduct with other people on other occasions. These restrictions related to the law of evidence (which determines what information can be admitted in a trial). The restrictions were designed to counteract the role of stereotype and myth in the trial process. However, Mr. Justice Marshall held that the restrictions were unconstitutional. In so finding he made the following extraordinary admission:

> Although relating chastity to likelihood of consent [to sexual activity] is unfair, it has comprised part of the carefully balanced evidentiary process. ... The question of the proper evaluation of such evidence is a difficult one. It is a question of logic — what is legally relevant, what is logically probative of the issues with which we are dealing. ... Now then, in logic, is willingness to consent to have intercourse outside of marriage or established relationships ... is [such] sexual indulgence logically probative of consent on a particular

---

[36] McClung, *supra* note 22 at 56.

occasion? ... Does it mean, the girl [sic] was more likely to have consented? [In my view] it is logically probative. The problem with this assumption is that it denies both autonomy and dignity to women ... [but] our test for judicial truth is based on probabilities ... it may show rank prejudice; but we use it.[37]

Similarly, judges may follow the logic of existing reasoning to reach a result — but fail to notice that the reasoning on which it is based excludes the experiences or understandings of women and, as a result, denies them an appropriate legal remedy. Four examples of this can be given. The Manitoba Court of Appeal held in 1986 that to consider sexual harassment to be sex discrimination was "amazing". Instead, the judges opined, if not all women in a workplace were harassed, the attention given to some women, must be because they are attractive, not because they are women.[38] The Supreme Court of Canada later reversed this ruling, holding that sexual harassment was indeed sex discrimination. The Manitoba Court of Appeal also rejected the defence of self-defence raised to a murder charge against a battered aboriginal woman, Lyn Lavallee, referring to it as "fanciful".[39] The decision met a similar fate in the Supreme Court of Canada, which accepted that evidence of the "battered woman syndrome" was admissible to support a defence to such a charge. A third example is the ruling of the New Brunswick Court of Appeal that touching a woman's breast should not be considered to be a sexual assault. The judges reasoned that breasts are "secondary sexual characteristics", in the same manner as a man's beard is a secondary sexual characteristic. They reasoned that only the touching of genitalia should be considered "sexual" assault in order to avoid "absurdity" and to preserve the ability of a man to "steal a goodnight kiss".[40] The Supreme Court of Canada reversed this ruling, accepting that breasts have a sexual meaning in our society. The final example is of a trial court judge in Ottawa, who acquitted a man charged with threatening serious bodily harm. He had written explicit letters to three cheerleaders of a football team in which he had made it clear that he knew where they lived and would have sexual intercourse with them even if he had to rape them. The trial judge held that this was not a threat to cause the women serious bodily harm.[41] This ruling too, was reversed on appeal.

Another aspect of the problem of gender bias in legal rules is when law, as a result of excluding women's experiences, has failed to develop appropriate legal frameworks. The prime areas in which this kind of problem exists is in the area of pregnancy. An example is provided by a case which involved the criminal prosecution of two midwives, who were alleged to have been negligent in their actions during a childbirth resulting in the death of the foetus prior to completed birth. In this 1991 case, the legal question was whether the foetus could be characterized as a "person" within the scope of the criminal offence. Legal reasoning built around the idea of the centrality and separateness of individuals forced the analysis to focus on whether the foetus was a legal person or not to the exclusion of the surrounding events — namely, childbirth and the intimate connectedness of the foetus with its mother.

---

[37] Marshall J in *R. v. Oquataq* (1985), 18 C.C.C. (3d) 440, at 450 (N.W.T.).

[38] *Janzen v. Platy Enterprises* (1986), 43 Man. R. (2d) 293.

[39] *R. v. Lavallee* (1988), 52 Man. R. (2d) 274.

[40] *R. v. Chase* (1984), 40 C.R. (3d) 282.

[41] *R. v. McGraw* (8 November 1988, Dist. Ct. of Ont., Flanagan, D.C.J.); also reproduced in (1989) 21 Ottawa L. Rev. 201.

The result of the case (an acquittal) is less important here than the insightful argument made to the Supreme Court by an intervenor in the case, the Women's Legal Education and Action Fund (LEAF). It argued:

> Traditionally legal method proceeds by analogy and distinction, making it tempting to compare the relationship between a pregnant woman and her fetus to relations already mapped by law. However, there are no adequate analogies to pregnancy and childbirth and attempts to find them distort reality. Had women not been excluded from participation in the legal system, the unique relationship between the woman and her fetus and the experience of pregnancy in the life of women — hardly new facts — might have engendered their own fundamental legal concepts and doctrines, as elaborate as doctrines dealing with commercial partnerships for example.

The point that LEAF was making — independently of the merits of the case — was that the legal principles and forms of reasoning simply didn't fit the situation and that appropriate principles, concepts, and doctrines to deal with it had not been developed within a legal system that took men and men's life cycles as the norm.

WORKING TOWARDS EQUALITY IN LAW AND LIFE

On 17 April 1985 the equality rights section of the 1982 *Canadian Charter of Rights and Freedoms* came into effect. The Charter sets the standard for all legislation and government action in Canada. The *Canadian Charter of Rights and Freedoms* sets out a range of guaranteed rights. If a piece of legislation or other government action is thought to be inconsistent with Charter rights, it can be challenged in the courts. If the judges agree, they can strike it down or give a remedy which removes the inconsistency and upholds the basic right.

Section 15(1) sets out the scope of equality rights in the following terms:

> Every individual is equal before and under the law and has the right to the equal protection and equal benefit of the law without discrimination, and in particular, without discrimination based on race, national or ethnic origin, colour, religion, sex, age or mental or physical disability.

Section 15(2) clarifies that "any law, program or activity which has as its objective the amelioration of conditions of disadvantaged individuals or groups" is not precluded by the main equality clause. This subsection is important for claims to equality because there is a recognition that special treatment is required to alleviate inequalities which stem from discrimination. It recognizes that differential treatment may be necessary given the "historical realities" of the position of individuals or groups in society. Section 28 of the Charter guarantees the rights and freedoms set out in the Charter equally to "male and female persons".

While the Charter covers government action in the form of legislation and the actions of government officials, the actions of private individuals and corporations in relation to employment, services, and accommodation are regulated by provincial human rights legislation. Federally regulated employers, including the federal government itself as employer, are governed by the *Canadian Human Rights Act* 1976–77, c. 33, s. 1. The purpose of this Act is to:

> extend the laws in Canada to give effect, within the purview of matters coming within the legislative authority of Parliament, to the principle that every individual should have an equal opportunity with other individuals to make for himself or herself the life that he or she is able and wishes to have, consistent with his or her duties and obligations as a member of society,

without being hindered in or prevented from doing so by discriminatory practices based on race, national or ethnic origin, colour, religion, age, sex, marital status, family status, disability or conviction for an offence for which a pardon has been granted.

In Ontario, the current *Human Rights Code*, which has its roots in legislation that came into effect in 1958 and 1961, has been extended over the years to protect people against discrimination based on race, ancestry, place of origin, colour, ethnic origin, citizenship, creed, sex (including sexual harassment and pregnancy), sexual orientation, age, marital status, family status, handicap, and the receipt of public assistance.

A wide range of more specific legislation addressing the legal situation of women (among other groups) also exists (e.g., pay equity laws, employment equity laws, family laws, and provisions in the *Criminal Code*). Often municipal by-laws and collective agreements prohibit certain forms of discrimination. The national bodies of trade unions in Canada have had a longstanding commitment to equality guarantees. At the international level, Canada is a signatory to several international conventions and treaties which commit the country to seeking to achieve certain standards. Of particular interest is the United Nations *Convention on the Elimination of All Forms of Discrimination Against Women* (which was adopted by the UN in 1979 and came into force in 1981). Thus, from the loftiest international levels to the most mundane of municipal regulation, a commitment to equality, including sex equality, has been steadily included in Canadian law. This may prove to be one of the most useful and enduring breakthroughs of the century; the prevalence of equality as a current legal concept certainly means that an understanding of the concept and an ability to use it are essential parts of the gender issue in law. That said, there are many different conceptions of what equality means and different approaches to achieving equality. At its minimum, of course, equality means the right to be free from discrimination and to be able to participate and contribute to society as a full citizen. Before we move to discuss these points theoretically, we include a case study which raises many issues related to equality legislation, approaches to equality and the processes involved in claiming equality in Canada.

Human Rights Legislation and Gender: Pay Equity

For many years, women in the labour force have been paid less than men. Data on wage differences by gender were first collected by Statistics Canada in 1967: the average earnings of women working on a full-time, full-year basis was 58 per cent of those of their male counterparts. In 1993, women earned 72 per cent of male earnings.[42] To what can we attribute the gendered wage gap? How is it that women are paid less than men? Different arguments exist on this point. Some argue that men earn wages which are sufficient to provide for the needs of their families. The so-called "family wage" allows women to stay home, raise children, and maintain the family. If women enter the paid labour force, they do so only to earn some extra money for the family; therefore, lower wages are justified. Others believe that pay inequities between men and women reflect the fact that women do work that is worth less. This would imply that secretarial work is worth less than janitorial work. A third position, human capital theory, posits that women have not invested in their own development in terms of education, training, and skills. According to this line of reasoning, women are paid less because they have not learned the skills nor obtained appropriate education which would lead to higher wages.

---

[42] Statistics Canada, Housing, Family and Social Statistics Division, Target Groups Project, *Women in Canada: A Statistical Report*, 3d ed. (Ottawa: Statistics Canada, 1995) at 86.

EXHIBIT 29.3

Legislature Firks

¤ In 1917, Louise McKinney and Roberta MacAdams became the first women elected to a provincial legislature (Alberta).

¤ In 1921, Mary Ellen Smith was the first woman in the British Empire to serve as a Cabinet minister. She was the "Minister without Portfolio" in the British Columbia legislature. In 1920, women were granted the right to hold political office and to sit in Parliament.

¤ In 1922, Agnes McPhail became the first woman member of parliament in the federal House of Commons.

¤ In 1928, the Supreme Court of Canada ruled that women were not among the "qualified persons" eligible to be called to sit as senators. This decision was reversed by the English Privy Council in 1929. Cairine Wilson was the first woman Senator in 1930.

¤ In 1949, Nancy Hodges became the first woman Parliamentary Speaker in the Commonwealth when she was appointed Speaker in the British Columbia legislature.

¤ In 1957, Ellen Fairclough was the first federal Cabinet minister; she was appointed as the Secretary of State.

¤ In 1971, Margaret Birch became the first woman Cabinet minister in Ontario.

¤ In 1972, Rosemary Brown became the first black woman to be elected to a Canadian legislature when she was elected as a New Democratic Party member in British Columbia.

¤ In 1973, Muriel Ferguson became the first woman Speaker of the Senate.

¤ In 1980, Jeanne Sauvé was appointed the first woman Speaker of the House of Commons. In 1984, she was the first woman appointed as Governor-General of Canada.

¤ In 1980, Alexa McDonough was the first woman to lead a provincial party when she was elected leader of the Nova Scotia New Democratic Party. The first woman leader of a political party was Thérèse Casgrain who led the Co-operative Commonwealth Federation in Quebec in 1951.

¤ In 1984, Anne Clare Cools was the first black woman to be appointed to the Senate of Canada.

¤ In 1988, Ethel Blondin was the first aboriginal woman to be elected to the federal Parliament; in 1993, she was the first to be appointed to the federal Cabinet when she became Minister of State for Youth and Training.

¤ In 1990, Audrey McLaughlin became the first woman in North America to lead a major political party (New Democratic Party).

¤ In 1990, Zanana Akande became the first black woman elected to the provincial legislature in Ontario.

¤ In 1993, Jean Augustine became the first black woman to be elected to the House of Commons, when she was elected Liberal Member of Parliament for a Toronto riding.

¤ In 1993, Catherine Callback became the first woman elected as provincial premier, when she led the Liberal Party to victory in Prince Edward Island.

There are several assumptions beneath these claims. Underlying the notion of the male family wage are the assumptions that male wages are indeed sufficient to provide for female dependents, and that women ought to be dependent on men to provide for them. These assumptions are contradicted by evidence which shows that most women work in the labour force out of economic necessity, and not because of the desire to earn pocket money. The dual-income family has become an economic necessity: to support a household, 60–80 hours of paid work per week are required.[43] The argument

---

[43] Canadian Advisory Council on the Status of Women, *Expanding Our Horizons: The Work of the Canadian Advisory Council on the Status of Women and its Context* (Ottawa: CACSW, 1993) at 73.

that women have invested less in their education is easily refuted. Women who are university graduates and are employed full-time earn only 75 per cent as much as their male counterparts.[44]

It becomes apparent, then, that wages are assigned by gender. Again, several explanations have been suggested for how this takes place. One argument is that the difference is a result of pure wage discrimination on the basis of gender, where women do comparable work to that of men yet are paid less. Another suggestion is that it is due to the occupational sex-segregation of the labour force whereby women are concentrated in a narrow range of low-paid occupations. Certainly, the segregated labour force is a crucial explanatory factor of the wage gap and female-dominated jobs remain under-valued and under-paid. In 1990, women's share of the 10 lowest-paying occupations was 73 per cent while their share of the 10 highest-paying occupations was only 20 per cent.[45] Women are held in female-dominated jobs by processes that "reproduce class and gender; processes deeply rooted in ideas about women's domesticity and women's employment."[46] Wage differences are explained as a function of the gender division of labour, and the division of labour is a function of wage differences.[47] Women, then, are caught up in a vicious circle.

The fact that women in the labour force earn less than men is a serious problem which has long-term impacts on women. Consider that the wage gap leads to a "pension gap" between women and men because pensions are based on earnings while in the paid labour force. Lower earnings increase the chance of living in poverty in old age. In 1993, women aged 65 and over had incomes which were only 63 per cent of their male counterparts.[48] Lower earnings also translate into lower unemployment insurance benefits when maternity or parental leave is taken or upon job loss. It is a matter of gross unfairness to women that they are paid less than men by virtue of their sex. As Wilson points out, "few women earn enough to support themselves or their dependents on their own."[49] Single-parent families headed by women are especially likely to have low incomes. In 1993, 60 per cent of these families had incomes which were below the Low Income Cut-offs established by Statistics Canada.[50] For example, in 1992 these families spent more than 55 per cent of their income on food, clothing, and shelter.[51]

Social policy, legislation, and economic practices combine to reproduce the gendered wage gap. Not surprisingly, then, the wage gap varies according to factors such as women's marital status, age, and education. Consider that, statistically, marriage weakens women's earning potential: in 1993, the average annual earnings of single women of all age groups was 96 per cent of their male counterparts while married women earned only 68 per cent of men's average earnings.[52] The wage gap also generally increases with age. While

---

[44] Statistics Canada, 1995 at 87.

[45] Canadian Advisory Council on the Status of Women, *Work in Progress: Tracking Women's Equality in Canada* (Ottawa: CACSW, 1994) at 8.

[46] S.J. Wilson, *Women, Families, and Work*, 3d ed. (Toronto, Ont.: McGraw-Hill Ryerson, 1991) at 95.

[47] Martha MacDonald, as cited in Pat Armstrong & Hugh Armstrong, *Theorizing Women's Work* (Toronto, Ont.: Garamond Press, 1990) at 59.

[48] Statistics Canada, 1995 at 92.

[49] Wilson, 1991 at 95.

[50] According to Statistics Canada, "families or individuals are classified as 'low income' if they spend, on average, at least 20 percentage points more of their pre-tax income than the Canadian average on food, shelter, and clothing" (Statistics Canada, 1995 at 86).

[51] *Ibid.* at 85.

[52] *Ibid.* at 87.

women aged 15 to 24 earn on average 91 per cent of male earnings, those aged 55 and over earn only 69 per cent of male wages.[53] As for the effect of education on the wage gap, at all levels of educational attainment, women's earnings are less than those of men. Women with less than a high school education earn only 65 per cent of their male counterparts, while those with a university degree earn 75 per cent.[54]

Given that a serious and pervasive wage gap exists, the problem shifts to finding principles and processes which would be effective to close the gap. The term "**pay equity**" has been coined to express the aspiration to remedy this problem. Although we are now familiar with the term, it is interesting to note that it did not even exist at the beginning of the 1980s. By the end of the decade, however, pay equity was being called "the working women's issue of the 1980s."[55] Various legislative initiatives concerning pay equity have been taken. Federal legislation covers employees of federal departments, agencies, and corporations under federal jurisdiction; all other workers are covered by provincial legislation. Pay equity legislation was first introduced in the 1950s and 1960s by both the federal government and by the provinces. Its principle was "equal pay for equal, or 'substantially similar' work."[56] This legislation proved to be ineffective because the concept of "substantially similar" work was narrowly interpreted by the courts — minor differences were sure to be found when comparing work. On the other hand, international standards for pay equity were first introduced in 1948 by a United Nations policy, the International Labour Organization's (ILO) Convention 100. This policy called for "equal remuneration for men and women workers for work of equal value." This principle was a broader interpretation of pay equity. But it was not until 1972, after the women's movement had re-emerged as a political force in the late 1960s, that the Canadian federal government endorsed this principle and committed itself to amending its legislation to conform to the ILO standards.

The first provincial jurisdiction to introduce equal pay for work of equal value was Quebec in 1975. Two years later, the federal government introduced its pay equity legislation for federal workers in the *Canadian Human Rights Act*, and Labour Canada became responsible for enforcing standards of pay equity. The amendment to the Act reads:

> 11.(1) It is a discriminatory practice for an employer to establish or maintain differences in wages between male and female employees employed in the same establishment who are performing work of equal value.

As a result of this amendment, it became possible for individuals or groups to initiate complaints to the Canadian Human Rights Commission to rectify pay inequities. This approach is a complaint-based process rather than a "proactive approach", like that contained in Ontario's *Pay Equity Act*, 1987 which established a system of job comparison and salary adjustment and required all employers in the public sector and all private sector employers of more than 100 employees to achieve pay equity in their workplaces.

However, even with federal, provincial, and international standards in place, progress has been very slow in achieving wage improvements for women. Indeed, it is estimated that if pay increases continue at the present rate it will take another 60 years before women can expect to earn as much

---

[53] *Ibid.* at 97.

[54] *Ibid.* at 95.

[55] Debra J. Lewis, *Just Give Us the Money: A Discussion of Wage Discrimination and Pay Equity* (Vancouver: Women's Research Centre, 1988) at 221.

[56] See e.g., *Female Employee Fair Remuneration Act*, S.O. 1951, c. 26.

as men.[57] This figure helps to us to see that, important as law is in establishing standards and removing barriers, it is not sufficient by itself to affect change in social and economic structures. A combination of social, political, and legal action is needed. In the area of "pay equity", we have a good example of law being joined by the women's movement and labour unions in a multi-pronged strategy. These groups have the resources, knowledge, and the mandate to struggle for effective change. They also represent the constituencies affected by the problem.

Unions and unionization are important for several reasons. Unions improve wages for their members, and through grievance procedures, and monitoring and communication functions are able to take collective action for individual workers who would otherwise have very little individual bargaining power.[58] The wage gap is less for unionized than for non-unionized workers.[59] However, unions represent only 31 per cent of all paid women workers while the unionization rate for men is higher at 38 per cent.[60]

The lengthy struggle for pay equity by federal government employees is one example of the specific role that both political and legal action have in addressing the issue of pay equity. Federal pay equity legislation was intended to address wage discrimination on the basis of gender; the basic principle is "equal pay for work of equal value", and it allows women's jobs to be compared to men's jobs. One of the first collective complaints to the Canadian Human Rights Commission (CHRC) was filed by the union representing federal government employees, the Public Service Alliance of Canada (PSAC). This complaint was made in 1979 on behalf of women librarians who earned 20 per cent less than their male counterparts. The Treasury Board, the employer of all federal government workers, was adamantly opposed to the principle of pay equity. Besides increasing the amount paid out for wages, it might undermine their control of job classification.[61] The employees had two alternatives: the political approach to strike over pay inequities or the legal approach of taking their case to the CHRC. They chose the latter approach, and two years after the initial demand was delivered to the Treasury Board, a negotiated settlement was reached in favour of the employees. With the assistance of the CHRC, librarians received wage adjustments amounting to $2.3-million. Although the librarians were successful, the Treasury Board refused to add clauses concerning equal value into the collective agreement with other groups of employees. Seventy-five per cent of all women in the public service are concentrated in four lower-echelon categories: secretarial, clerical, administrative, and program management. Almost half are in clerical jobs.

By 1984, the PSAC had filed complaints on behalf of the clerical group, of which 80 per cent were women. This time, however, Treasury Board was not about to risk losing the case before the CHRC and announced that a joint union-management committee would undertake a study to investigate pay inequity, and work towards achieving equal pay. This study took over five years to complete, and only with the PSAC's threat to reactivate its complaints before the CHRC did Treasury Board finally announce the results of

---

[57] Canadian Advisory Council on the Status of Women, 1993 at 75.

[58] Morley Gunderson & Leon Muszynski, *Women and Labour Market Poverty* (Ottawa: Canadian Advisory Council on the Status of Women, 1990) at 129.

[59] Wilson, 1991 at 102.

[60] Statistics Canada, 1995 at 77.

[61] See, generally, Rosemary Warskett, "Political Power, Technical Disputes, and Unequal Pay: A Federal Case" in Judy Fudge & Patricia McDermott, eds., *Just Wages: A Feminist Assessment of Pay Equity* (Toronto, Ont.: University of Toronto Press, 1991) at 172–92.

the study and the payments which would be made. The payments made in 1990, however, fell short of the results of the study and in 1992 the Treasury Board announced that it would not comply with the retroactive pay requirements of the *Canadian Human Rights Act*.

PSAC continued to pursue the issue through the CHRC. In 1996 the CHRC ruled that the original study results were valid and should be used as the basis for determining compensatory awards. The PSAC estimates that the federal government could owe up to $1.5 billion in back pay to 80,000 clerical workers, encompassing six job groups: clerks, secretaries and typists, data processors, librarians, hospital services staff, and educational support staff. Unless this matter is settled, a hearing before the Human Rights Tribunal is scheduled to determine how the wages of workers in female-dominated jobs are to be increased. The study guidelines suggest that a clerk earning $13 per hour doing comparable work to male-dominated jobs earning an average of $14 per hour should receive an increase in wages to $14. However, the Treasury Board is expected to argue that the adjustment would discriminate against men who earn below the average $14 pay rate.[62]

This issue and case example demonstrates the importance of legal standards, union-based action, and sheer persistence in the cause of justice and equality for women. It would be difficult to envision an individual worker having the resources to struggle for pay equity over a period of 11 years against the federal government. However, it also demonstrates the limitations of pay equity legislation. The Treasury Board took unilateral action to avoid compliance, and used its resources to extend the complaint process, causing delay and expense. Perhaps the final lesson of this example is that law does not operate in a vacuum, but is very much part of a wider social, political, and economic environment. Accordingly, just changing the law will not mean that the problem is solved.

Meanings of Equality

In the previous parts of this section, we have outlined the legislation which contains equality guarantees in Canadian law. We have also explored the operation of one of these guarantees in practice — the pay equity guarantee in the federal *Canadian Human Rights Act*. Readers should, then, have a good idea about what the law provides and a sense of the context in which it applies. In this section and the next, we turn to a more theoretical discussion, but a discussion which has very real and immediate application: what does "equality" mean in Canadian law — what is an equality problem? — and how can we achieve equality in life and law for women?

There are different conceptions of equality which in turn lead to differing approaches to *achieving* equality. Does it mean that no distinctions are to be made between groups of persons, or does equality require that some distinctions be made in some circumstances? If we take some differences into account, is that a form of "special treatment" or an exception to a general equality standard? Is it even possible to identify the ways in which women and men are different or the same in order to identify whether they are being treated similarly to each other? On the other hand, is it more meaningful to think of inequality as arising from being in a disadvantaged or oppressed social position — being a member of a group which receives fewer benefits or suffers harms or exclusion based on perceptions about the worth and social role of that group? If we think of equality in that way, equality would mean the removal of disadvantage and would lead us to focus on social structures rather than only individual circumstances.

---

[62] See, e.g., "PS hits new barrier in $1.5B pay-equity claim" *The Ottawa Citizen* (21 March 1996) A1.

Another set of debates about equality focuses on the objectives of equality-seeking. One school of thought advocates **"formal equality"** — where all overt or obvious distinctions or restrictions are removed from the law. In this approach, the key thing is to provide individual equality of opportunity and the removal of formal barriers. One example of formal equality is gender neutrality in the drafting of legislation or in the formulation of legal rules. Under this line of thinking, equality is satisfied by changing the legal standard of conduct from "reasonable man" to "reasonable person" and by assuming that the standard now includes women too. Similarly, the crime of "rape" was changed to "sexual assault" and phrased to include women as perpetrators. Obscured in the change, of course, is the fact that the overwhelming number of perpetrators are men and rape is a serious social problem involving the exercise of unequal power by men over women. Of course, formal equality can sometimes be very effective. An unequal rule that only men can administer wills, do certain jobs, access athletic facilities and so forth, can be equalized by allowing both men and women to do these things without distinction. This has been called a "liberal approach" to equality. It has three central features: it focuses on the individual rather than on social systems; it considers that the state should have the very limited role of responding to complaints; and thirdly, it places faith in the neutrality of the "rule of law".[63]

A different school of thought advocates **"substantive or result equality"** where the focus is on equality of outcome or equality of condition. This approach critiques formal equality, noting that "treating those who are unequal in terms of power and resources as though they are the same allows certain disparities to persist, while an illusion of fairness is created."[64] Under this approach, the focus shifts from only procedures and intentions, to institutions and structural forms of discrimination. Rules or standards which have a disparate impact on women are considered problematic, whether or not they are written in gender-neutral terms. The focus, then, is on whether a law, policy, or practice operates to the detriment of women or has a particular impact upon them that differs from the impact on men. Under this approach, "discrimination is interpreted as the subordination of an individual by virtue of her or his membership in a particular class of persons or the subordination of a social group."[65]

These two main approaches to equality have given rise to distinct legal principles of equality. The approach of "formal equality" has fostered two principles: the "similarly situated test" of equality and the differential or special treatment modification of this strict form of equality. The "similarly situated test" was at one time the most common perception of equality. It regards equality as meaning that everyone should be treated in the same way. Likes should be treated alike; those who are unalike should not be treated in the same manner. Of course, it is difficult to be sure of the ways in which people are the same or different and to ascribe importance to these characteristics. This approach also assumes a standard against which being the same or different can be assessed. The question here is, Who sets the initial standard? Experience in law with this approach suggests that the standard has been set based on existing norms; in law, as we have seen, these norms have tended to be defined from men's experiences. Feminist Diana Majury has commented that in an unequal world, dominant groups inevitably set the standards for

[63] See, generally, Colleen Sheppard, "Equality, Ideology and Oppression: Women and the Canadian Charter of Rights and Freedoms" in C. Boyle et al., *Charterwatch: Reflections on Equality* (Toronto, Ont.: Carswell, 1986) at 195.
[64] *Ibid.* at 204.
[65] *Ibid.* at 216.

"equality"[66] Women, then, must show that they are the same as men and ought to be treated in the same way. A variation on this approach is the so-called "differences" or "special treatment" principle, pursuant to which women can be provided with accommodation for their biological differences from men (e.g., pregnancy, childbirth, and lactation).

The "substantive equality" approach has fostered the principle of a contextual approach to equality or an anti-subordination approach to equality. The third principle of equality arising from the aspiration to achieve substantive equality is the "contextual" or "anti-subordination principle" of equality. Here the focus shifts away from assessing sameness and difference to seeking to identify the impacts of policies, procedures, or rules. In its more radical form, it focuses on experiences "that happen almost exclusively to women ... the most sex-differential abuses of women as a gender" and it poses equality questions as "questions of the distribution of power" in our society. Under this approach, women's "sex-segregation into poverty", "the range of issues known as violence against women", and "the difference sex makes" rather than the sex difference become the focal points for defining equality issues and what solutions are necessary.[67] In its less radical form, there is "some contextualized discussion and some focus on disadvantage and inequality."[68] The Supreme Court of Canada has moved in this direction, turning away from the "similarly situated" test as being inconsistent with the objectives of the Charter. In the case of *Andrews v. The Law Society of British Columbia*,[69] Mr. Justice McIntyre commented:

> The mere equality of application of similarly situated groups or individuals does not afford a realistic test for a violation of equality rights. For, as has been said, a bad law will not be saved merely because it operates equally upon those to whom it has application. Nor will a law necessarily be bad because it makes distinctions.... Consideration must be given to the content of the law, to its purpose, and its impact upon those to whom it applies and also upon those whom it excludes from its application.

In Canada, then, a substantive view of equality is being developed.

Current Equality Issues for Discussion

Child Support

Following marriage breakdown, the determination of child support is based on the principle that both parents have an equal responsibility towards their children and should contribute "in accordance with their own means to the needs of the children."[70] The onus is on the custodial parent (usually the mother) to ask for child support. Levels of child support are often a bargaining chip in divorce negotiations; they can easily be bargained away. Under the provisions of the *Income Tax Act* S.C. 1970-71-72, c. 63, any payments made to a custodial parent for the maintenance of her children are required to be included in her income. A corollary to this provision allows the non-custodial parent to deduct these same support payments from his income for income tax purposes.

---

[66] See, generally, Diana Majury, "Equality and Discrimination According to the Supreme Court of Canada" (1990–91) 4 C.J.W.L. at 407.

[67] See, generally, the work of Catharine MacKinnon, in particular, "Difference and Dominance: On Sex Discrimination" in *Feminism Unmodified* (Cambridge, Mass.: Harvard University Press, 1987) 32 at 40–42. See also Diana Majury, "Strategizing In Equality" (1987) 3 Wisconsin Women's L.J.

[68] See, generally, Diana Majury, "Equality and Discrimination According to the Supreme Court of Canada" *supra* note 66.

[69] [1989] 1 S.C.R. 143.

[70] Federal/Provincial/Territorial Family Law Committee, 1991: 5.

Suzanne Thibaudeau, a custodial mother of two children, stopped paying taxes on her child support payments in 1988. In 1992, she argued in the Tax Court of Canada that by imposing a tax burden on money which she was to use exclusively for the benefit of her children, the *Income Tax Act* infringed her right to equality guaranteed by section 15(1) of the Charter of Rights. At the trial level, she was unsuccessful. The judge ruled that the court which had awarded support payments to Thibaudeau had accounted for the effects of income tax when it determined the amount of the payments. Thus, the judge concluded that there was no violation of Thibaudeau's equality because the payments had been "grossed up" in the routine operation of the family law system. Her appeal to the Federal Court in 1994 was successful. Mr. Justice Hugessen pointed out that although adverse tax effects could and should have been corrected when determining support amounts, this is "not always, or even usually" the case. He concluded that the *Income Tax Act* violated the rights of custodial parents to equality before and under the law albeit on the basis of family status rather than sex.

The government appealed this decision to Canada's highest court, the Supreme Court of Canada. In May 1995 the Federal Court's ruling was reversed. The majority of the Supreme Court judges (which did not include the two woman judges) commented:

> The purpose of s. 15(1) is to protect human dignity by ensuring that all individuals are recognized at law as being equally deserving of concern, respect and consideration. Consequently, it is the effect that an impugned distinction has upon a claimant which is the prime concern under s. 15(1). Here, the group of single custodial parents receiving child support payments is not placed under a burden by the inclusion/deduction regime. Although there may be some cases in which the gross-up calculations shift a portion of the payer's tax liability upon the recipient spouse, one cannot necessarily extrapolate from this that a "burden" has been created, at least not for the purposes of s. 15(1).

The Court also ruled that the *Income Tax Act* operates at the "level of the couple" and was designed to minimize the tax consequences of support payments, thereby "promoting the best interests of the children" by ensuring that more money is available to provide for their care:

> If anything, the inclusion/deduction regime confers a benefit on the post-divorce "family unit." The fact that one member of the unit might derive a greater benefit from the legislation than the other does not, in and of itself, trigger a s. 15(1) violation, nor does it lead to a finding that the distinction in any way amounts to a denial of equal benefit or protection of the law.

In essence, the Court ruled that any unfair displacement of the tax liability between the custodial and non-custodial parents "lies in the family law system", not in the *Income Tax Act*. As such, the majority concluded that the *Income Tax Act* did not discriminate against custodial parents. As readers may be aware, the federal government responded to the public outcry at this decision with new rules for the taxation of child support in its 1996 Federal Budget.[71] Under these rules, child support paid under orders or agreements made after 1 May 1997 will no longer be taxed as income to the recipient, or be tax deductible for the payer. Guidelines accounting for the new tax rules will be introduced to aid in setting consistent and fair child support awards. New enforcement mechanisms, including suspension of passports and permitting

---

[71] "The New Child Support Package" (Ottawa: Government of Canada, 6 March 1996).

arrears for child support to be deducted from federal public service employee pension benefits are contained in legislation introduced in the House of Commons on 30 May 1996.

Sexual Assault and Therapy Records

Hubert Patrick O'Connor, a bishop of the Roman Catholic Church, was charged in 1991 with two counts of rape and two counts of indecent assault on four of his former students, as a result of incidents which occurred while he was the principal of a Native residential school in Williams Lake, B.C., in the 1960s. At his trial, O'Connor argued that his lawyers should have access to the entire medical, counselling, and school records of the four students. He justified this on "the need to test the complainants' credibility, as well as to determine issues such as recent complaint and corroboration." The court agreed and ordered the Crown prosecution to disclose all files from therapists, counsellors, psychologists, or psychiatrists with whom the women had sought treatment concerning sexual assault or sexual abuse. In 1992, the Crown applied to the British Columbia Supreme Court for directions regarding the disclosure order. The women who had brought the charges were not prepared to comply with the Court order. The judges expressed surprise at the fact that the Crown was not complying with the order.

One Crown counsel, Wendy Harvey, argued that disclosure of medical and therapeutic records would "revictimize the victims", and suggested that the order to disclose "exhibited gender bias".

The B.C. Supreme Court upheld the lower court order to disclose the records. The Crown appealed to the Supreme Court of Canada; LEAF intervened in this case, arguing that personal records should not be used in sexual violence cases to attack women's credibility. To allow records to be produced is a direct violation of women's right to equality. As Karen Busby notes, requests for personal records are made "almost exclusively in sexual violence cases."[72] Requests are made under the assumption that women frequently lie about sexual violence "out of vindictiveness, malice or delusion." Furthermore, a law requiring disclosure of personal records would have a disproportionate impact on women. For example, as Busby notes, counsellor-patient relationships would be undermined, attention would be distorted away from the incident at hand towards whether the "complainant is worthy of the law's protection", and women's reporting of sexual assault would likely be discouraged. The majority of the Supreme Court of Canada ruled in favour of records disclosure, holding that defendants in sexual assault cases need only establish that counselling records are "likely to have relevance" for a judge to order that they be produced. A process was established by which judges would review and assess records in the exercise of judicial discretion.

A spokesperson for a rape crisis centre in Ontario has remarked that since the Supreme Court decision, the percentage of women at her centre who decide to report their sexual assault to police has dropped from 36 per cent to 15.[73] In essence, women are forced to choose between laying criminal charges and seeking professional help for themselves.[74] Some rape crisis centres have resorted to keeping only minimal records. Other "more defiant groups" have shredded documents.[75]

---

[72] Karen Busby, "Supreme Court decisions on the use of personal records in sexual assault cases — what it means for women" *Leaf Lines* 7, 1996 at 4.

[73] "New bill restricts access to records" *The Globe and Mail* (31 May 1996) A1.

[74] *Ibid.* at A3.

[75] *Ibid.* at A1.

Regarding it as an "urgent" problem, the Minister of Justice announced on 31 May 1996 that he plans to introduce legislation that would restrict access to records. It would be impermissible for lawyers to launch "fishing expeditions" to see whether there is something in the records that would damage the credibility of the victim. Courts would be required to establish relevance of therapy records, and would restrict access to only those parts of the records that are deemed important to the case. In addition, defendants would be allowed to ask for counselling records at the trial stage only, not in the preliminary hearing. A provincial court judge rather than a justice of the peace would be able to issue subpoenas for such records. The Minister of Justice commented that it was important to "balance the rights of the accused with the equality and privacy rights given to victims by the Charter of Rights and Freedoms."[76]

The Legal Curriculum

Legal education is a critical space where ideas and attitudes about law are shaped. As Elizabeth Schneider has pointed out, "law schools transmit our first messages about what is permissible in law."[77] In 1988, the Faculty Council at a major Canadian law school passed an "Equality Resolution". It stated in regard to teaching and learning at the Law School that:

> The faculty and students, in order to continue and expand efforts to promote freedom from discrimination both within the Law School and in society at large, undertake to consider the following measures in relation to teaching and learning:
> (a) inclusion in teaching materials of works or references to works that demonstrate the impact of law on groups that are or have been subjected to discrimination, or inclusion in teaching materials of explanations for the omission of such works or references;
> (b) placement of teaching materials that support or exhibit discrimination within a context that identifies their discriminatory nature and that invites open and critical comment on it;
> (c) use of language in the classroom, in written materials, and in examinations that is free from discriminatory stereotypes and references;
> (d) use of other measures, such as holding seminars about non-discriminatory teaching materials and methods, which demonstrate continuing sensitivity to the problems faced by individuals and groups subject to discrimination; and
> (e) a heightening awareness of the existence of systematic discrimination.

CONCLUSION

In her CBC Massey Lectures in 1990, renowned Canadian scientist Ursula Franklin outlined a theory which she called "Franklin's earthworm theory of social change." She suggested that "social change will not come to us like an avalanche down a mountain. Social change will come through seeds growing in well-prepared soil — and it is we, like the earthworms, who prepare the soil." Being able to identify and analyse problems of gender bias in processes, rules, and personnel involved in the legal system is an important step in being able to work for change in that system. What is also important, however, is imagination — being able to envisage what an equal and just society and legal

---

[76] *Ibid.*
[77] Elizabeth Schneider, "Task Force Reports on Women and the Courts: The Challenge for Legal Education" (1988) J. Legal Educ. 38 at 88.

system would look like. The legal imagination is the seed for change; understanding is our preparation and consistent tending and work in the soil will help change to grow and bear fruit.

CHAPTER SUMMARY

This chapter has outlined and analysed legal breakthroughs for women, examined the problems of gender bias in judging and legal rules, and explored the meanings and applications of equality guarantees contained in Canadian law, most particularly as they affect women's equality. One of the themes of the chapter has been that law changes in complex and inconsistent ways; change is often slow and contested. Law does not by itself cause or cure complex social inequalities. In the end, law is a terrain of struggle in which contested meanings and visions of society are debated. Law, then, plays an important role in the struggles to eliminate gender bias and achieve women's equality. However, it is not the only — or even the most important — place to begin. Our questions have moved beyond "adding women" into law; the focus is much more on the structure and operation of law and the "simple notion that law respond to women as well as to men."[78] We hope that in reading this chapter, readers have developed historical and substantive knowledge of the gender issue in law. We hope, too, that they have been equipped with analytical and theoretical skills with which to identify, debate, and act on issues.

GLOSSARY OF NEW TERMS AND KEY CONCEPTS

feminist	"If we conceive of feminism as more than a frivolous label, if we conceive of it as an ethics, a methodology, a more complex way of thinking about, and thus more responsibly acting upon, the conditions of human life, we need a self-knowledge that can only develop through a steady, passionate attention to all female experience. I cannot imagine a feminist evolution leading to radical change in the public/private realm of gender that is not rooted in the conviction that all of women's lives are important; that the lives of men cannot be understood by burying the lives of women; and that to make visible the full meaning of women's experience, to reinterpret knowledge in terms of that experience, is now the most important task of thinking" Adrienne Rich, "Towards a Woman-Centred University", in *On Lies, Secrets and Silences* (New York: MacMillan, 1980).
legal person	"Legal personality refers to the particular device by which the law creates or recognizes units to which it ascribes certain powers and capacities. ... A legal system must be provided with a basic unit before full legal relationships can be devised which will fulfill the primary purpose of organizing social facts. The legal person is the unit or entity adopted." G. Paton, *Textbook on Jurisprudence*, 4th ed. (London: Oxford University Press, 1972) at 392.
Judicial Council	A panel of senior judges which oversees the conduct of judges.
pay equity	Term which refers to legislation and policies designed to implement the principle of equal pay for work of equal value and eliminate the wage gap between male and female workers.
formal equality	An approach to equality where the focus is on equality of opportunity and the removal of overt distinctions between men and women in legislation and policy. Associated with the "similarly situated" test of equality.

---

[78] MacKinnon, *supra* note 1.

student-at-law	Another term used to describe a law student who is completing his or her practical bar admission training and his or her articled clerkship. See also **articling clerk**, above.
substantive equality	An approach to equality where the focus is on equality of outcome or equality of condition. Associated with the contextual, disadvantage-focused test of equality.

REVIEW QUESTIONS

1. What are three examples of ways in which women have been discriminated against in Canadian law?

2. What was the "Persons Case", and what is its significance?

3. When did women in Canada receive the right to vote?

4. Who was Canada's first woman lawyer?

5. In what ways can "gender bias" be present in judicial opinions? Why does gender bias matter?

6. What action can be taken when a judge demonstrates gender bias?

7. What is the *Canadian Charter of Rights and Freedoms* and what equality guarantees are contained within it?

8. What other guarantees of equality exist in law?

9. What reasons can explain the wage gap between men and women in the Canadian workforce? What are some of the consequences of unequal pay for women?

10. What does the term "pay equity" refer to?

11. What different meanings can be given to the term "equality"? Explain the differences between "formal equality" and "substantive equality".

12. Which legal principle of equality has been adopted by the Supreme Court of Canada?

DISCUSSION QUESTIONS

1. How important do you think the *Married Women's Property Act*s were? How significant is it that interests other than women's equality influenced the legislation?

2. What arguments can be made to challenge the views of Cardinal Villeneuve against giving women the right to vote?

3. The example of Clara Brett Martin reminds us that struggles to gain equality for women have sometimes benefited "particular" women rather than all women. Do you think that these limited and partial breakthroughs nevertheless pave the way for all women to gain benefits? Or do you think that they maintain rather than challenge or change the *status quo*? Can you think of other examples or potential issues?

4. Should courses on gender and racial bias be mandatory for all judges, or might this requirement conflict with judicial independence?

5. What remedies are appropriate for judges who are found to have made sexist or racist comments?

6. In an English case in 1979, *Jeremiah v. Ministry of Defence*, the senior judge of the Court of Appeal, Lord Denning, dismissed a claim by a male worker that an exception made for women that relieved them from having to work overtime in a dirty area of a munitions factory constituted sex discrimination against him. One of the reasons for his decision was that Mr. Jeremiah had little regard for "chivalry or the women's hair-dos ... a woman's hair is her crowning glory, so it is said. She does not like to have it disturbed, especially when she has just had a 'hair-do'." What critique can you make of Lord Denning's comments in light of the discussion in this section?

7. What might a legal system that was structured around women's lives as well as men's lives look like? Can you think of examples?

8. There are two models of pay equity legislation. One is "complaint-based"; the other is "proactive". Which model do you think holds the most promise for remedying the inequality in wages faced by women in the labour force?

9. Use the various approaches to equality to identify whether the fact situation in the Thibaudeau case raises an equality problem. If it does, what kind of an equality problem is it?

10. Do you agree with the Supreme Court of Canada's conclusion that section 15 of the *Charter of Rights and Freedoms* had not been violated by the *Income Tax Act*? What factors did the Supreme Court take into account? What other factors might it have taken into account?

11. Use the various approaches to equality to identify whether the fact situation in the O'Connor case raises an equality problem. If it does, what kind of an equality problem is it?

12. The Charter also contains a right to "life, liberty and security of the person" (s. 7) and a right to a full and fair defence to a criminal charge (s. 11(d)). Does a case like O'Connor raise a problem of balancing equality rights with these rights? How should such a situation be approached?

13. Why might a commitment to "equality" in legal education be important? Are there any objections to this goal? In what areas might legal education be unequal?

14. How would you implement the "Equality Resolution"? What concrete changes do you think might need to be made in a law school or in a law course?

SUGGESTED READINGS

Boyd, Susan, & Elizabeth Sheehy. *Canadian Feminist Perspectives on Law: An Annotated Bibliography of interdisciplinary Writings* (Toronto, Ont.: Resources for Feminist Research, 1989). (Second edition in preparation)

Canadian Journal of Women and the Law (1985–current).

Chunn, Dorothy, & Joan Brockman, eds. *Investigating Gender Bias: Law, Courts and the Legal Profession* (Toronto, Ont.: Thompson Educational Publishers, 1993).

Dawson, T. Brettel, ed. *Women, Law and Social Change: Core Readings and Current Issues*, 3d ed. (North York, Ont.: Captus Press, 1998).

MacKinnon, Catharine. *Feminism Unmodified* (Cambridge, Mass: Harvard University Press, 1987).

Razack, Sherene. *Canadian Feminism and the Law* (Toronto, Ont.: Second Story Press, 1991).

Smart, Carol. *Feminism and the Power of Law* (London: Routledge, 1989).

Task Force on Gender Equality. *Touchstones for Change: Equality, Diversity and Accountability* (Ottawa, Ont.: Canadian Bar Association, 1993).

Williams, Patricia. *The Alchemy of Race and Rights* (Cambridge, Mass: Harvard University Press, 1991).

Children, Youth, and the Law

David Turner
UNIVERSITY OF VICTORIA

Learning Objectives

After reading this chapter, the reader should be able to:

➢ understand how and where the law treats children and youth differently than adults
➢ understand notions of children's rights
➢ identify key legal areas and processes affecting children and youth
➢ identify key legal issues for children and youth

TABLE OF CONTENTS

INTRODUCTION

The Victorian saying, "Children should be seen and not heard" is still used in Canada today by some traditional families. It illustrates the persistent relative powerlessness of many children in relation to their parents and other authorities. In principle, the law recognizes that children and youth should be accorded a voice and special rights. This chapter explores the law and rights applying to children and youth in contemporary Canada, and identifies key issues and legal gaps.

HISTORICAL OVERVIEW

Contemporary North American media prominently feature stories about child and youth issues: in particular, youth crime, child abuse, learning disabilities, child poverty, and adoption. It is easy to forget that the law, and society in general, essentially ignored children until the past century. Children were viewed as miniature adults, inheriting the social status and occupations of their families. If they were poor, their labour was usually required and, often, exploited on the farm or in the mine, factory, or workhouse; if wealthy, they were protected by guardians, nannies, and private tutors, and their estates (inherited lands and money) were held in trust.

The mid-19th century saw the beginnings of **special protection** in England (on whose law our common law is based), primarily to cushion the negative impacts of industrialization. For example, the *Factories Act* prohibited young child labour, and the *Schools Act* initiated public education on a limited basis. In the United States, the first juvenile justice system emerged in the 1890s, with special laws, courts, and correctional facilities. Shortly thereafter a juvenile justice system developed in Canada, along with private children's aid societies to protect orphaned, abandoned, or neglected children. The next two decades saw the development of the first "child welfare" laws across the provinces: Ontario's *Children's Protection Act*, the *School Act* of British Columbia and the first *Juvenile Delinquents Act* at the federal level.

Until the current era of State intervention, parents — especially fathers — had total control over the welfare, discipline, and religious education of their children. The prohibitions in the criminal law for killing or maiming a child, or depriving the child of the necessities of life, were often ignored, so children were at their parents' mercy. Even today this parental power, though tempered, is reflected in Canadian law. Section 43 of the *Criminal Code* allows, as a defence to what might otherwise be a charge of assault, for a parent or guardian or teacher (*in loco parentis*) to exercise reasonable force in correcting or disciplining a child. (Note, though, that in most provinces and territories, teachers are now prohibited from using corporal punishment in public schools.) Also, in family law, children in custody disputes are still "awarded" to either parent as if they are owned as property by them: the concept of parent rights still has priority.

The view gradually prevailed that when parents failed in their responsibility of caring for their children, the state (or its agencies) was entitled to intervene to protect them. It became accepted that children required different treatment than adults. Law in Canada has, since the mid-20th century, evolved to become an instrument of social policy and redistribution of social resources, rather than being simply a regulator of private commercial affairs. One result has been state powers to intervene to protect vulnerable children and youth. Social welfare legislation, such as the Canada Health and Social Transfer (formerly Canada Assistance Plan) allowed federal cost sharing for provincial child protection, child care, and education programs. Impetus was given to the expansion of comprehensive child welfare laws and social services for children in every province and territory.

More recently, legal and political questions have resurfaced about the changing roles of parent, child, and state. A backlash has emerged against some kinds of State intervention into what is viewed as the private sanctuary of the family. Traditional political ideologies have harnessed this resentment against "state interference". An effort to reassert parental (or state) rights over children and youth has also re-emerged in calls for harsher penalties under the *Youth Criminal Justice Act*.[1] Likewise, the credibility of statements of children when testifying to sexual or physical abuse by their parents in criminal or child welfare law has been challenged. Law is attempting to balance competing rights and interests.

JURISDICTION

As mentioned in an earlier chapter, the Canadian Constitution (ss. 91 and 92 of the *British North America Act, 1867*) lists how the powers to make laws are divided between the federal and provincial governments. Fairly random division has led to a patchwork of responsibility where child law is concerned. For instance, criminal law is the prerogative (that is, lies within the jurisdiction) of the federal government. So, criminal law dealing with youth over 12 and under 18 is the same across Canada. The *Juvenile Delinquents Act* was replaced in 1984 by the *Young Offenders Act* and, in April 2003, the *Youth Criminal Justice Act*, which is the current instrument of youth justice across the country. However, the administration of justice is provincial: youth justice courts and correctional services are administered by each province, so the actual justice that youths receive may vary.

Civil law is the prerogative of the provinces, which means that matters such as child welfare, education, health, mental health, and family law (except divorce, which is federal) may differ among the provinces. Later in this chapter we will summarize the main principles that are shared across the country.

Jurisdictional differences also arise through issues of age. For instance, in British Columbia a "child" under the *Family Relations Act*[2] is a young person under 19, but a child under the federal *Divorce Act*[3] is a person up to the age of 16. The duration of child maintenance (financial support by parents) after marriage breakdown might differ, depending on which statute is used. A "child" for child welfare purposes is under 18 in Quebec, but under 19 in British Columbia.

First Nations children on reserves are subject to another complication of jurisdiction. Aboriginal affairs are legally controlled by the federal government under the *Indian Act*, yet the child welfare law and services for those children remains a provincial responsibility. A serious gap has long existed, especially as bands have tried to gain local control of welfare services.

---

[1] S.C. 2002, c. 1 (assented to 19 February 2002, proclaimed in force April 1, 2003).
[2] R.S.B.C. 1996, c. 128.
[3] R.S.C. 1985, c. 3 (2nd Supp.).

HOW LAW TREATS CHILDREN DIFFERENTLY

The notions of limited **"capacity"** (the competency to make informed decisions) and **"dependency"** (that children are vulnerable and require guardians or the state to protect them) are historical concepts still in operation today. They account for the emergence of special laws, rights, and policies dealing with children and youth.

Many legal rules in Canada are age-related, on the assumption that maturity, and its accompanying responsibility or privilege, arrives (or is sufficiently consolidated) at a particular chronological time in a young person's development. Change from child **status** to legal status as an adult comes at the **age of majority**, which is 18 in most provinces. Voting, entering into binding contracts, and consenting to marriage are all examples of the privilege of majority. What is confusing is the variation in legal age for different activities:

- The age at which young people may drive is 16, but 19[4] is the legal age for the consumption of alcohol and buying cigarettes, and the age at which a young person ceases being a "child" under the protection legislation.[5]

- A fetus is not recognized as a "person" under the *Charter of Rights and Freedoms*, yet it can be a "child in need of protection" under the child welfare Acts of some provinces.

- Federally, consent in criminal law to sexual activity applies at the age of 14 — except in the case of anal intercourse, when a young person must be 18.

- A child must be over 12 to be held criminally responsible.[6] In most provinces, only a youth 14 or over can be assumed to understand the nature of the oath in testifying, without an inquiry being made as to the child's capacity.

- Within the *Criminal Code*, age requirements can be different for similar offences. For example, it is an offence to unlawfully abandon or expose a child under 10 so that "its [sic] life is or is likely to be endangered" — yet the necessaries of life must be provided to all under 16.[7]

- Civilly, minors (young people under the age of majority) cannot be held liable for breaches of contracts. The exceptions are for purchases of food, clothing, and necessaries, and beneficial services such as an apprenticeship contract.

These discrepancies within child laws of each province and across Canada can be explained by different historical developments, objectives, jurisdictions, and application of the public or politicians' values.

Another outcome of the notion that children are vulnerable and have special needs is the establishment of a separate court. In British Columbia, for example, this is the Family Division of the Provincial Courts (see Exhibit 30.1). This court deals with child protection, custody, maintenance and access in Family Court, and with young offenders matters in Youth Justice Court. Family Court and Youth Justice Court are still open and public in British Columbia, though they are often located apart from regular provincial courts. Cases may be held in a closed hearing if it is in the child's best interests. In

---

[4] Except in Alberta, Quebec and Manitoba, where legal drinking age is 18.
[5] *Child, Family and Community Service Act*, 1996, c. 46.
[6] *Youth Criminal Justice Act*, 2002, s. 2(1).
[7] *Criminal Code of Canada*, R.S.C. 1985, c. C-46, ss. 215 and 218.

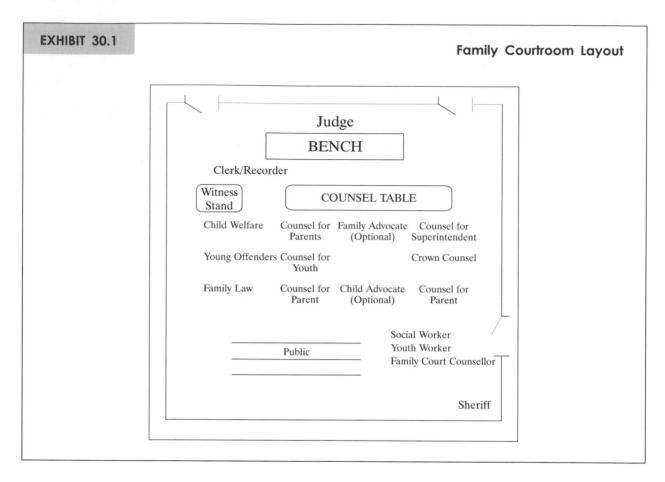

EXHIBIT 30.1   **Family Courtroom Layout**

Judge

BENCH

Clerk/Recorder

Witness Stand

COUNSEL TABLE

Child Welfare   Counsel for   Family Advocate   Counsel for
                   Parents   (Optional)   Superintendent

Young Offenders Counsel for   Crown Counsel
                 Youth

Family Law   Counsel for   Child Advocate   Counsel for
                  Parent   (Optional)   Parent

                                 Social Worker
                 Public   Youth Worker
                                 Family Court Counsellor

                                                    Sheriff

Ontario, all members of the public, except the parties, are excluded from Family Court, though media can attend with restrictions on publishing names and identifying information on the child or youth.

ISSUES OF CHILDREN'S RIGHTS

The concept of children's rights, as distinct from the rights of adults, has arisen in law in fairly recent times as the notion of vulnerability has gained acceptance. The major rights of children can be classified as follows:

Legal and Administrative Rights

In theory, children and youth enjoy many of the same rights as adults. These include those set out in the *Charter of Rights and Freedoms*: legal rights such as representation by counsel; anti-discrimination rights; and rights to fairness in court processes and bureaucratic decision making. In reality, at the federal level, the *Youth Criminal Justice Act* is one of the few statutes that clearly delineates legal rights for youth. It should be noted that several Human Rights Codes, including British Columbia's *Human Rights Code*, are limited in scope to adults over 19 in prohibiting discrimination in public facilities, tenancy, and employment. This may be seen as violating the Charter provision on age equality (s. 15) and could be open to future legal challenges. To date, few child cases have proceeded to the higher courts on Charter challenges, except in the case of young offenders appealing transfer of their criminal case to the ordinary courts.

In many provinces, an ombudsman has jurisdiction to review the **administrative fairness** of decisions by government ministries dealing with children. In British Columbia, this has recently been extended to cover two other authorities: school boards governing schools and municipalities responsible for parks, recreation, and public facilities, such as libraries and community centres. The creation of external **accountability mechanisms** for children's rights and services established by provincial statutes, such as the Office of the Children's Lawyer in Ontario, the Child Advocate in Alberta and the Office of the Representative for Children and Youth[8] in British Columbia, means that decisions that affect children by adults such as teachers, social workers, and foster parents are more open to public scrutiny.

Rights to Social Services

The provision of services for children and their families, such as social services, health care, child care, family support, and education, are found in distinct statutes, such as Ontario's *Child and Family Services Act*,[9] British Columbia's *Employment and Assistance Act*,[10] and Manitoba's *Public Schools Act*.[11] However, as will be discussed below, it is questionable whether children have rights to demand those services, other than the right to basic provision. Provision of preventative services, such as those provided by counsellors, homemakers, and child care workers, is at the discretion of bureaucrats[12] and is subject to funding as politicians in government choose.

Rights to Standards of Care

Ideally, children and youth should have the legal right to a particular standard of care in their own or relatives' homes, as well as in state facilities, such as foster homes, child care and treatment centres, schools, and correctional institutions. Minimal community standards of parental care are enforced through the child protection legislation of each province. Certain state facilities, such as daycare centres and hospitals, are licensed, and some schools are accredited, while foster homes are monitored by social workers. Correctional centres and care facilities are inspected by offices of government — such as the Deputy Ombudsman for Children and Correctional Inspectorate in British Columbia, or the Office of Child and Family Service Advocacy in Ontario — but usually only after receiving specific complaints.

More jurisdictions are considering incorporating principles of rights to services and standards for children in the care of the state. Ontario's *Child and Family Services Act*[13] includes a section on rights, ranging from the right to reasonable privacy and possession of personal goods to meals that are well-balanced and of good quality; from age-appropriate clothing to "the right to be consulted and heard whenever significant decisions are made respecting education, religion, medical treatment, and discharge, placement, and transfer plans." B.C.'s *Child, Family and Community Service Act*[14] reflects these rights

8   This replaced the combined offices of the former Children's Commissioner and Child and Youth Advocate.

9   R.S.O. 1990, c. 11.

10 S.B.C. 2002, c. 40.

11 R.S.M. 1987, c. P250.

12 See David Turner, "Children's Rights to Service in Canada", in David Turner and Max R. Uhlemann, *Holding Governments Accountable for Children's Rights: The Canadian Experience*, ch. 4, pp. 132–62 (Victoria, B.C.: Sedgewick Society for Consumer and Public Education, School of Social Work, University of Victoria, 1990).

13 R.S.O. 1990, c. 11, Part V.

14 R.S.B.C. 1996, c. 46.

for children but adds an additional right: "to receive guidance and encouragement to maintain their cultural heritage."

Children not in the care of the state may require similar protection, but no province has yet enacted a general Bill of Rights for *all* children.

Obstacles to Implementation of Child Rights

There are several ambiguities, contradictions, and obstacles to the implementation of child rights.

Competing Concepts of Child Rights

The concept of child rights is often viewed as competing with other rights, such as parental authority or the State's right to social control and law and order. In 1989, the United Nations passed a resolution on the Convention of the Rights of the Child,[15] which is intended to be morally binding on the nations that signed the document. It sets out a series of principles for states to adopt and to implement in all legislation and policies dealing with children. These principles include not discriminating against children and ensuring that all social welfare institutions, courts, and administrative and legislative bodies use the best interests of the child as the primary consideration in all their actions concerning children.[16]

Do Canada's laws and social policies conform to this principle? It remains to be seen whether the recent *Youth Criminal Justice Act* will continue to reinforce the pattern, established by the *Young Offenders Act*, of putting the protection interests of society over the needs and interests of young persons. Holding young offenders "responsible" by substantial imprisonment in youth and adult correctional facilities may not be in their "best interests". But youth are seen as threatening the law-and-order attitudes held by many members of the public, so the call for even tougher sentences is what is receiving attention. Likewise, most levels of family income assistance paid by law or regulation are well below the poverty line across Canada; this seems to violate Article 27.1 of the U.N. resolution, which reads, "States Parties recognize the right of every child to a standard of living adequate for the child's physical, mental, spiritual, moral and social development." The United Nations has recently condemned Canada's rates of child poverty. But many Canadians see this as purely a parental responsibility, in which government has no justification for interfering.

Child Rights versus Child Needs

The *Youth Criminal Justice Act* is one of the few laws specifying children's and youth's automatic right to counsel. Their legal rights are thus protected, but some argue it is at the expense of their interests. The right to due process may interfere with the need of young persons for swift and meaningful consequences for their illegal behaviour. Legal defences and technicalities may widen the gap between the "legal" and "moral" guilt of youngsters who are still developing a social value system.

Others, however, see these rights as a protection against the abuses of the earlier *Juvenile Delinquents Act*,[17] where children and youth were imprisoned as criminals (delinquents) for such *status offences* as being beyond the control of their parents or running away from foster homes.

---

[15] Resolution of the United Nations General Assembly: Convention on the Rights of the Child, December 1989.
[16] Idem, Article 3.
[17] R.S.C. 1970, c. J-3.

Enforceability

One person's rights necessarily impose duties on another person. In most cases, governments have great discretion in the provision of services to children, even where certain "rights" are mandated by law. For example, do children have a right to protection? They probably do but in a limited fashion: a government or private child welfare agency may have the obligation to investigate child abuse allegations, but the apprehension (removal) of the child or the provision of preventative services to the child and the child's family is purely discretionary, and rarely enforceable by the courts. Do children have a right to an education? Most laws compel parents to have their children attend school between certain ages, but children do not necessarily have the right to an individualized education. It is often at the discretion of the province, school board, or particular school as to what actually happens in the classroom.

Access to Rights

Cutbacks to public services directly affect children, yet, as non-voters, it is a challenge to have their voices echo in the legislative chambers of Canada. There is a great need for **advocacy** when new laws or changes to existing laws are being considered. Legal advocates are sometimes available on individual family matters affecting children, such as custody battles; but in British Columbia, their appointment has been at the discretion of judges or the Attorney General.[18] Now many jurisdictions are developing permanent advocacy and review mechanisms, such as an Ombudsman for Children, who monitors the ministries dealing with children, or the recent Office of the Representative for Children and Youth in British Columbia,[19] which deals with complaints on behalf of children in the child welfare system. Ontario has the Office of the Children's Lawyer employing social workers to investigate custody and access or education complaints. In Quebec, Youth Protection Committees monitor child welfare and corrections complaints — in particular, rights violations.

KEY SUBSTANTIVE AREAS

There are several areas of law that deal centrally with children and their interests. Although most areas are under provincial jurisdiction (with the prime exception of young offenders) and vary in detail, there are common principles and processes that are outlined here.

Child Welfare

This area of civil law is in the jurisdiction of the provinces, though certain programs for child care are cost-shared with the federal government through the Canada Assistance Plan (which is currently under political review). The principle is that families have the responsibility to care for and raise their children within certain limits. The state, as represented by a provincial authority (ministry, superintendent's or director's office or private children's aid society), is legally empowered to protect children who are at risk or whose standard of care fails to meet minimal community levels. The process is triggered by *a complaint or report* (see Exhibit 30.2), usually from a neighbour, teacher, or physician, who believes a child is in need of protection. This need is legally defined in each child welfare statute, and usually includes physical and sexual abuse, and neglect. But apart from statutes in Ontario, Alberta,

---

[18] *Family Relations Act*, R.S.B.C. 1996, c. 128.
[19] *Representative for Children and Youth Act*, S.B.C. 2006, c. 29.

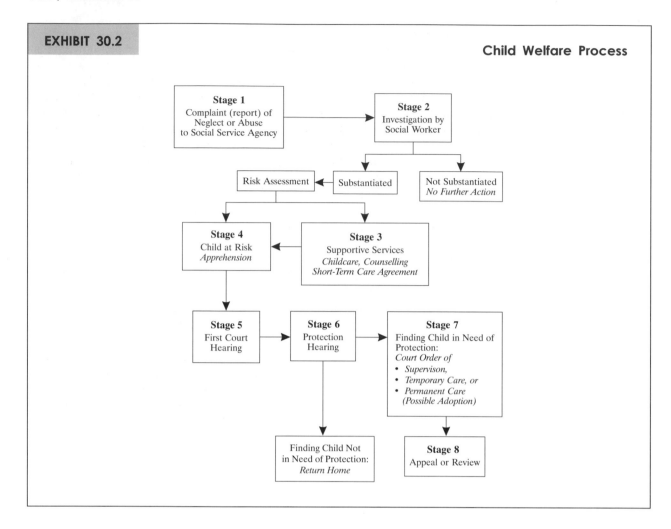

EXHIBIT 30.2

Child Welfare Process

and British Columbia, most are vague and interventionist.[20] For instance, New Brunswick's definition includes "living in unfit or improper circumstances",[21] which encompasses a variety of "evils" and lifestyles whose interpretation depends on the social worker's or judge's values. The three jurisdictions mentioned above, by contrast, have closely defined circumstances for intervention, including clarification of "emotional abuse or neglect".

The next stage[22] is the *investigation* of the veracity of the complaint by a social worker. If it is, in the social worker's judgment, substantiated, supportive services, such as a child care worker, counselling, or a voluntary care agreement with the parents may be offered. If the child is at risk, the social worker will usually protect by an "*apprehension*" or "*removal*": taking the child into care. In some jurisdictions, the "offending" parent can be ordered to leave the home and to refrain from contact with the child until the issue is reviewed by a court. The worker or police officer may remove the child without a warrant or court order if the child's safety or well-being is

[20] Dick Barnhorst & Bernd Walter, "Child Protection Legislation in Canada" in Nicholas Bala, Joseph Hornick & Robin Vogel, eds. *Canadian Child Welfare Law: Children, Families and the State* (Toronto, Ont.: Thompson Educational Publishing, 1991) at 21.

[21] *Family Services Act*, S.N.B. 1980, c. F-2.2, s. 31(1).

[22] For details on the various stages, see David Turner & Max R. Uhlemann, "Child Protection and the Legal Process" in *A Legal Handbook for the Helping Professional*, 3d ed. (Victoria, B.C., 2007), c. 3, or Bala, *supra* note 19.

in immediate danger,[23] and may enter any premises, vehicle, or vessel by force, if necessary. The child then is taken into *temporary care* and placed in a reception centre or foster home, and the situation is reviewed by the Family Court in a short time (within seven days in British Columbia). The state or agency presents the case for review through its counsel. Parents or relatives are notified by the social worker and may contest through their lawyer. The child is not usually separately represented except in exceptional circumstances. The court can order health and psychiatric assessments to assist in its deliberations. If the judge decides there is prima facie evidence that protection is required (in British Columbia, the requirement is reasonable grounds to believe the child is in need of protection), the case is set for a full *protection hearing*, a process that can be quite adversarial if contested. A child may be represented by a separate counsel, known as a *Family Advocate*, but budgets for this are very limited.

Child welfare is civil, so the standard of proof is on the balance of probabilities. This means the court decides whether the evidence shows the child is more likely to be in need of protection than not. Family Court can be less formal in its procedures than other courts. In fact, since abuse often happens in the privacy of families, without witnesses, the civil doctrine of *res ipsa loquitur* (let the matter speak for itself) can apply, which allows the circumstances to be taken into account in assessing causation of injury. For instance, where no witness saw the injury being inflicted, if, in the mind of a reasonable person, the bruising and other circumstances are consistent with non-accidental injury, then the court can assume the child was intentionally abused. If the child is found to be in need of protection, then the court can make a *court order* of supervision, or temporary or permanent custody (care or wardship) to the state or agency. Supervision allows the social worker to monitor the care of the child back at home. A custody (care) order suspends or terminates parental rights. Permanent wards can be adopted out, but if over 12 years old, they must consent.

Most child welfare legislation emphasizes "the best interests of the child", though many jurisdictions expand this to ensure that the safety and well-being of the child remain the paramount considerations. The interpretation of this depends largely on the judgment of the social worker, reviewable by the judge whenever an apprehension takes place. Any appeals are to the Supreme Court of the province.

British Columbia, along with some other provinces, such as Alberta, has recently been considering court orders of secure care for children who

(a) have an emotional or behavioural condition that presents a high risk of serious harm or injury to themselves, and
(b) are unable or unwilling to take steps to reduce that risk.[24]

Secure care controversially bridges the philosophies of child welfare and youth justice. This is a place where some child care professionals believe there is a treatment gap, especially since youth corrections and control under the *Youth Criminal Justice Act* are not available for children under the age of 12. Others reject this approach as unnecessarily stigmatizing children, arguing that secure care is similar in nature to imprisonment with enforced treatment. These critics view it as responding to the demand for greater social control by parents and the state over the non–criminal behaviour of children in politically conservative times.

---

[23] British Columbia's *Child, Family and Community Service Act*, R.S.B.C. 1996 c. 46, s. 30.
[24] *Secure Care Act of British Columbia*, Bill 25, 2000, s. 2.

Youth Justice[25]

Across Canada, the same law and process apply to youth (12 to 18 years old) in conflict with the criminal law. The reason is that both the *Criminal Code* and *Youth Criminal Justice Act* (YCJA), which replaced the *Young Offenders Act* in 2003, are federal. Each province has a separate provincial process for dealing with youth who violate provincial statutes (such as liquor offences) or municipal by-laws (such as skateboarding in prohibited areas). Children under 12 are not dealt with as criminals but are referred to the child welfare system.

The philosophy of the YCJA establishes the principles and tone that courts, police and correctional services are expected to follow in dealing with young offenders. It is a tricky balancing act between often competing principles[26] that address the goals of the justice system, the rights of young persons and of victims of their crimes.

The goals are outlined in section 3 of the YCJA as follows:

1. To prevent crime by addressing the circumstances underlying a young person's offending behaviour

2. To rehabilitate young persons who commit offences and reintegrate them into society

3. To ensure that a young person is subject to meaningful consequences for his or her offence in order to promote the long-term protection of the public

Furthermore, the YCJA states that the criminal justice system for young persons must be separate from that of adults and must emphasize the following:

1. Rehabilitation and reintegration

2. Fair and proportionate accountability that is consistent with the greater dependency of young persons and their reduced level of maturity

3. Enhanced procedural protection to ensure that young persons are treated fairly, and that their rights, including their right to privacy, are protected

4. Timely intervention that reinforces the link between the offending behaviour and its consequences

5. The promptness and speed with which persons responsible for enforcing this Act must act, given young people's perception of time

The YCJA goes on to state that within the limits of fair and proportionate accountability, the measures taken against young persons who commit offences should achieve the following:

1. Reinforce respect for societal values.

2. Encourage the repair of harm done to victims and the community.

3. Be meaningful for the individual young person, given his or her needs and level of development, and, where appropriate, involve the parents, the extended family, the community and social or other agencies in the young person's rehabilitation and reintegration.

---

[25] For details, see Jim Hackler, "Youth Justice and the Legal Process" in David Turner & Max R. Uhlemann, *supra* note 21 at 284–315; see also ch. 8.

[26] *Youth Criminal Justice Act*, S.C. 2002, c. 1, s. 3.

4. Respect gender, ethnic, cultural and linguistic differences and respond to the needs of Aboriginal young persons and of young persons with special requirements.

Young persons have rights and freedoms in their own right, such as a right to be heard in the course of and to participate in the processes, other than the decision to prosecute, that lead to decisions that affect them; and young persons have special guarantees of their rights and freedoms. Victims should be treated with courtesy, compassion and respect for their dignity and privacy and should suffer the minimum degree of inconvenience as a result of their involvement with the youth criminal justice system. Victims also should be provided with information about the proceedings and given an opportunity to participate and be heard, and parents should be informed of measures or proceedings involving their children and encouraged to support them in addressing their offending behaviour.

First and less serious offenders are to be dealt with by alternative (called extra-judicial) measures, including police cautions, pre-charge screening (diversion from court) or community-based programs, such as work service for the victim or community. Youth Justice Committees from the community can be used to recommend appropriate extra-judicial measures. However, the Youth Justice Court can now use adult measures in responding to violent or repeat young offenders over 14 (which usually means lengthier jail sentences that can end up in the adult correctional system). Institutional custody is possible if there is no reasonable alternative or combination of other measures available. It would be discussed in a pre-sentence report prepared by a youth worker (see below). The judge or youth worker may call a conference of professionals and community members involved with the young person to give advice on appropriate measures or sentences. This conference might recommend that **restorative justice** processes be utilized.

The needs of the youth and the responsibility of parents are counter-balanced by the need to protect society. Ideally, incarceration (imprisonment) is a last resort but has gained more prominence as community and preventative resources have been reduced by many provincial governments. Youth enjoy full legal rights, including Charter rights, in this justice model, apart from the right to trial by jury, which is not available at Youth Justice Court. The most used Charter rights are the following:

1. Being informed of the reasons for arrest
2. The right to remain silent
3. The right to consult a lawyer without delay

Youth are also entitled to consult a parent or appropriate adult in deciding whether or not to make a statement to police, and they cannot be coerced by the police's power or authority.

The young offender process begins in a fashion similar to that of the adult system (see Exhibit 30.3), with *a report of an alleged crime*. A police *investigation* follows, which may or may not lead to the arrest of a young person. If charged, the youth may be held in detention for the next Youth Justice Court hearing, released with a notice to appear in Youth Justice Court, or issued a summons and returned home. This decision is at the **discretion** of the police at this stage. Crown Counsel (the prosecutor) ultimately decides whether or not the youth will be prosecuted in court and the nature of the charges. Crown may decide, because of the circumstances of the offence and/ or the social history of the youth, to use alternative measures (diversion), such as community service, a warning, or victim-offender mediation. A youth

---

EXHIBIT 30.3

Young Offender Process

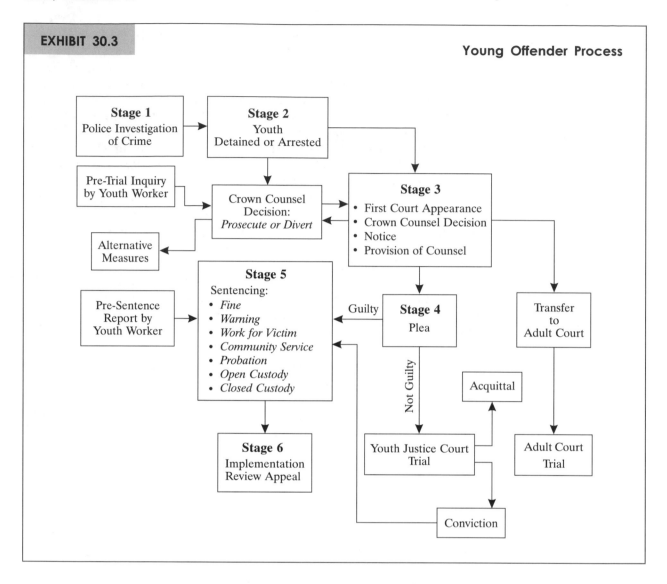

---

worker (probation officer) may provide a social study on the youth's background, called a *pre-trial inquiry*, to assist Crown Counsel in this decision.

If a youth has been arrested and held in a youth detention facility, the youth must appear before a court or justice of the peace within 24 hours for consideration of bail ("judicial interim release", in legal terminology) or continued detention (remand). At this *first appearance*, the youth's age is also at issue to determine that the court has jurisdiction. When the youth has had opportunity to fully instruct counsel, a *plea* of "guilty" or "not guilty" may be entered. A guilty plea leads to a sentencing hearing, and a youth worker may be asked to prepare a pre-disposition (sentence) report for the judge. A "not guilty" plea results in a trial date being set. The format of a *trial* is the same as in the adult criminal courts, apart from the prohibition on publishing identifying details.

The *Youth Criminal Justice Act* delineates a range of penalties, from warnings and fines through probation and compensation to the victim, to "open" and "closed" (secure) custody in a correctional facility, to a maximum of three years (six years for first-degree murder). Before incarceration is ordered, the court must consider the recommendations of a youth worker (probation officer) in a pre-disposition report, which is based on considerations that may include the impact of the offence on the victim; the youth's social history, including family, school and employment; and the Youth Justice Court record of the youth. Probation is a community alternative to imprisonment under the supervision of a youth worker. It may include conditions of social control, such as a curfew; reporting to the youth worker; a "red zone" (an area of the community that the youth can enter only with permission) or direction as to where the youth must live; and conditions of social support, such as counselling or alcohol treatment. Violation of conditions may result in a return to court for further sentencing. Secure custody is incarceration in a youth jail. Unlike the adult system, a reduction in sentence for good behaviour is not automatic. Open custody can be a camp setting, residential treatment, centre or closely supervised correctional group home. For serious crimes, a youth over 14 may be transferred, after a hearing initiated by the Crown, to the adult court for trial and/or sentencing. The youth cannot be publicly identified in Youth Justice Court. A conviction results in a Youth Justice Court record, which is removed after a period of time following completion of the disposition (sentence). Appeals on indictable offences are to the Court of Appeal or on summary offences to the Supreme Court of the province.

The YCJA introduced some innovations in direction, process, and intended outcomes. They include the following:

- A stated goal is to reduce the present over-reliance on incarceration for non-violent young persons. This remains to be seen.

- Youth aged 14–16 accused of serious or violent crimes (known as **presumptive offences**) will be dealt with in Youth Justice Court instead of being transferred to ordinary adult court. Such youth can be subject to preliminary hearings, and if the Crown successfully applies to the court, they will receive adult sentences upon conviction for indictable offences that an adult is liable to a sentence of imprisonment of more than two years. A maximum youth sentence for first-degree murder is six years in custody followed by four years of supervision. This compares with an adult sentence of life imprisonment.

- The YCJA and the system rely on communities, families, parents and others to adopt multi-disciplinary approaches to prevent youth crime by dealing with its underlying causes, responding to the needs of young persons, and providing guidance and support to those at risk of criminal offending. This goes against the current trend in many provinces to cut back social services.

- Youth Justice Courts will have powers of trial by jury presided over by specially appointed Superior Court Judges. Preliminary hearings, as in the adult system, will also be available.

- Provisions have been made in the YCJA for five new youth sentences: a reprimand; an intensive support and supervision program order; a program attendance order; a deferred custody and supervision order; and an intensive rehabilitative custody and supervision order. However, the availability of a number of these new sentences would be dependent on the establishment of programs by the provinces. Some critics argue that provincial funds would be drained away into expensive custodial facilities rather than creative community services.

Health Services

The right to life, liberty, and security of the person in the *Charter of Rights and Freedoms* reflects the right to life as stated in Article 6 of the U.N. Convention on the Rights of the Child and, in Article 24, to the "highest attainable standard of health and to facilities for the treatment of illness and the rehabilitation of health." Section 7 of the Charter was used in the highly publicized British Columbia case[27] of a seven-year-old hydrocephalic boy whose parents refused consent to replace a drain shunt in his skull. Medical opinion asserted that failure to do this would lead to physical deterioration and subsequent death. The British Columbia Superintendent intervened to protect the child and appealed to the Supreme Court of British Columbia. The court overturned the lower court decision and ordered the operation, finding that parents could not be allowed to determine the future quality of life for their son.

Concerning jurisdiction, the *Constitution Act* of 1867 does not specifically mention health. Life and health protection provisions under the federal *Criminal Code* have already been mentioned. The *Medical Care Act* of 1968 establishes programs that will be cost-shared with all the provinces. These include most health areas, such as hospitals, physician services, immunizations, health promotion, and mental treatment. Insured services for children depend on their parents being registered; but, again, the age definition of "child" varies among provinces: 18 in Saskatchewan, 19 in Manitoba, and 21 in Alberta.

Consent by children to medical and mental health treatment is a key issue. Only New Brunswick and British Columbia have clear legal provisions about this. The New Brunswick legislation[28] allows children of 16 and above to enjoy the same consent rights as adults; and rights of consent extend to those under 16 if, in the opinion of two physicians, the children understand the nature and consequences of the intended medical treatment and if allowing them to consent to it is in their best interests. British Columbia goes further by allowing a child (under 19) to give effective consent to health care, without the parent's knowledge or consent, under the following conditions: The health treatment provider (usually a physician) must have explained "the nature and consequences and the reasonable foreseeable benefits and risks"; he or she must be satisfied the child or youth understands and has concluded that the health care is in the child's best interests.[29] In other provinces, parental consent is required unless the child (under 18 in Saskatchewan, for instance) is in immediate danger. This authority can be overruled by the courts.

Unless clearly contrary to the child's best interests, Canadian courts and laws have been generally reluctant to interfere with parents' rights in this area, especially with consent to mental health treatment or admission to a facility. In Ontario, the *Mental Health Act*[30] presumes that children under 16 are not competent to consent, but they can apply for review. The age of medical consent in Quebec is 14. In British Columbia, children under 16 admitted voluntarily to a mental health facility by parents or relatives must, upon admission or as soon as they become capable of comprehension, be informed of reasons for their detention and be informed of rights to counsel, *habeas corpus* (the right to have their detention reviewed by a court), and rights to a board or tribunal review. Young people over 16 have the capacity to request admission in their own right.[31] Many other provinces are silent on these issues of age and consent, leaving physicians cautious about administering medical treatment, such as contraception, to children under 16.

---

[27] Re S.D. 1983, 34 R.F.L. (2nd) 34 B.C.S.C.
[28] *Medical Consent of Minors Act*, R.S.N.B. 1973, c. M-6.1, s. 2.
[29] *Infants Act*, R.S.B.C. 1996, c. 223, s. 17.
[30] R.S.O. 1990, c. M.7, s. 5.
[31] *Mental Health Act*, R.S.B.C. 1996, c. 288.

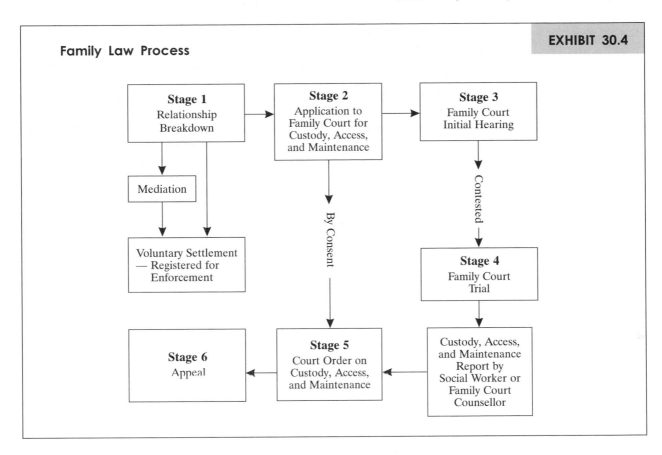

EXHIBIT 30.4

Family Law Process

Stage 1 — Relationship Breakdown

Stage 2 — Application to Family Court for Custody, Access, and Maintenance

Stage 3 — Family Court Initial Hearing

Mediation

Voluntary Settlement — Registered for Enforcement

By Consent

Contested

Stage 4 — Family Court Trial

Stage 6 — Appeal

Stage 5 — Court Order on Custody, Access, and Maintenance

Custody, Access, and Maintenance Report by Social Worker or Family Court Counsellor

Family Law

Family law is civil and under the jurisdiction of the provinces, apart from the granting of divorces. Brief comments will be made on those issues that affect children and youth, such as custody and access, guardianship, maintenance, and family violence. These issues can also arise as part of a *Divorce Act* action under federal law, or as part of a marriage or common-law separation under provincial family laws. *Custody* is the physical care and control of a child and normally includes the legal components of guardianship, such as the right to determine medical treatment, education, and religion. *Access* means the right to visit a child, usually exercised by the parent not having custody. Where parents are co-operative, courts can order joint or shared custody. (See Exhibit 30.4.)

Upon the breakdown of a marriage or common-law relationship, the parents can privately agree on the custody arrangements for the children, and this can be registered in the courts for enforcement. Disputes can be resolved by alternative methods, such as family mediation, where a neutral third person helps the parents to resolve the dispute in the interests of the children. Litigation (court action) involves an *application* to the Family Court at the provincial level or Divorce Court at the supreme level in each province. Both are civil hearings where the court is obligated by law to act in the child's best interests. The "best interest" criteria are similar and set out in provincial family law statutes or the *Divorce Act*. They usually include health and emotional well-being, special needs, love, affection, training and education, financial resources, stability and security, and the child's views, whenever appropriate.[32]

---

[32] *Family Relations Act*, R.S.B.C. 1996, c. 128, s. 24.

A *contested hearing* is much like a trial, with the parties bringing witnesses, such as psychiatrists or friends, to support their position. The court determines the capacity of each parent to provide for the child's best interests, often through a custody report prepared by a social worker or family court counsellor. The court will then make a *custody order*, which can be enforced. Violations can result in the police apprehending and returning a child to the lawful custodian, and interference with court-ordered custody rights may constitute a criminal offence.[33] Courts can also order civil restraining orders or criminal peace bonds to prevent parents and relatives without custody from interfering with or harassing children.

Courts can also order and enforce *maintenance* (financial support) for children. Child support guidelines on maintenance amounts were introduced in amendments to the *Divorce Act* in 1997. In some jurisdictions, children under 19 can apply for maintenance from their parents.[34] If parents are incapable of providing maintenance, it may constitute child welfare grounds or support an application for income assistance for independent youth aged 16 to 19 years old.

Violence: Child Physical and Sexual Abuse

Physical or sexual violence against children by their parents or caregivers may constitute grounds for criminal charges, child welfare apprehension or civil suits in the tort (civil wrong) of assault and battery. Recently, children (often after becoming adults) have been both suing their parents, caregivers or teachers in residential schools and treatment centres for damages, and reporting them to the police for criminal action. The *Criminal Code* contains a special section on such offences against children, including sexual exploitation by persons in a position of authority or trust.

There are special rules of evidence and process for criminal cases of child sexual abuse.[35] Child victims under 18 may be allowed to testify outside the courtroom, watched by the accused on closed circuit television or from behind a screen. Videotaped evidence of victims under 18 years old may be admitted under certain conditions, as long as it is verified in court and the child is open to cross-examination. Videotaped evidence can also be presented at the sentencing stage as part of a victim-impact statement (a report to the court from the victims as to the impact of the crime on their life). Crown counsel and victim services can be useful in preparing children to testify.

Adoption

Adoption law is of provincial jurisdiction and is civil in nature. An *adoption order* permanently transfers the relationship (including rights and responsibilities) of parent and child from the biological (birth) parents to the parents adopting the child. The adoptive parents gain full custody and guardianship. Birth mothers can *consent* to an adoption 11 days after the child's birth in British Columbia. The voluntary consent can then only be withdrawn if clearly within the best interests of the child. Other jurisdictions allow a period of grace for such revocations. Disclosure of information identifying the birth parents is prohibited without their consent, unless release is essential for the health and well-being of the adopted child or adult. Most provinces have developed Adoption Registries that allow birth parents and adult adopted children who seek identifying information to do so. If requests match, then

---

[33] *Criminal Code of Canada*, R.S.C. 1985, c. C-46, s. 282.

[34] See *Family Relations Act*, note 31, s. 88.

[35] See Nicholas Lang, Timothy Stokes, and Laurie J. Soloway, "Family Violence and the Criminal Court System", ch. 8 in David Turner & Max R. Uhlemann, *supra* note 21.

reunions can be arranged. This is the "passive" registry model. In several provinces, "active" registries will now conduct searches for adoptee applicants over 19, with a discreet attempt to contact the birth parents to see if they consent to disclosure for a reunion. British Columbia's proposed new Act, currently being debated in the legislature, would allow automatic disclosure at 19 unless a veto is filed.

A couple can adopt children privately, through the provincial government Ministry of Social Services or Children's Aid Society, or from a spouse's former relationship. In the first two instances, the Ministry in British Columbia will have a social worker conduct an *adoption study* after six months to determine whether the adopting parents are fit to adopt. Ontario prohibits private placement for adoption, except through approval of the Director of Child Welfare. Persons over 12 years old must consent to their adoption. Until recently, in British Columbia, a couple had to be married to adopt a healthy child. British Columbia's new Act[36] removes restrictions and allows gay and common-law couples and single people to adopt, and results in more open contact between child and birth parents. An Application to Adopt is made to the Supreme Court, usually in documentation form only, accompanied by the superintendent's (or director's) or society's report.

Education

Each province has its own *Education or School Act* that regulates the conduct of students and teachers, who follow a curriculum set by the provincial government. Common provisions include the following:

1. The compulsory attendance of students from 6 or 7 years old to 15 or 16, unless receiving approved home instruction.

2. A prohibition on corporal punishment.

3. Rules for the discipline and review of student behaviour, including the power of principals to suspend for a maximum fixed period, and of the school board to expel — usually after a hearing.

4. Parent rights to request an exemption to religious exercises. Note that some provinces have only denominational (religious) public school systems.

5. The rights of schools to maintain confidential student records. Some provinces give parents full rights of access to those records.

6. Processes for disciplining teachers for professional misconduct. Several provinces have established separate Colleges of Teachers for certification and professional discipline.

Issues of student rights to freedom of speech and expression and issues of access and integration are recently bringing Charter implications into school law. Section 23 allows parents of the French or (chiefly in Quebec) English linguistic minority the right of instruction for their children in that language, where the numbers of children warrant it. However, this does not include the right to French immersion for English-speaking students. Only a few provinces mention vaguely a child's right to an appropriate education. Saskatchewan states that children between 6 and 12 have a right to receive instruction appropriate to their grade. Ontario's *Education Act* provides for compulsory special education programs, directed by a placement committee and reviewed by a Special Education Tribunal.

---

[36] *Adoption Act,* R.S.B.C. 1996, c. 5.

LEGAL ISSUES FOR CHILDREN

Children's law is difficult to pull together, being dispersed as it is in numerous Acts. Past law reform commissions[37] have proposed a comprehensive Bill of Children's Rights, such as a Charter for Children, to reflect in more specific detail in Canada the spirit of the U.N. Convention. The proposed bill, which was not passed, included the power of courts to order that specific services to children and youth be provided by governments. This would have overcome the present problem of the inability of parents and children to legally demand appropriate services that remain at government discretion, for the most part.

Within each province there is often a complex web of ministries, services and agencies serving children and youth. Families and children find this bureaucracy difficult to navigate. Legislation is required to consolidate and rationalize this delivery, perhaps in a single, comprehensive government ministry.

While all children are unique and require equal treatment in law, several groups are seriously disadvantaged and need special consideration.

Aboriginal Children

The status of First Nations in Canada and their political goals of self-government demand that the law deal differently, and in culturally more appropriate ways, with Aboriginal children. It is recognized that native children are disproportionately represented in our state care and youth correctional systems. In order to change this, new legal and social mechanisms are required. Bands across Canada are taking over their own child welfare, youth justice, and education programs. Child welfare laws are recognizing the importance of preserving an Aboriginal child's cultural heritage and involving the child's Aboriginal community in the decision about her future. Youth justice is involving tribal circles for decision making, and experimenting with such traditional penalties as banishment. Native custom adoption is gaining recognition, and native schools are developing as part of, or separately from, public education.

Ethnic Minority Children

Like Aboriginal children, other racial minorities are over-represented in care and correctional systems in some provinces. Cultural sensitivity in the law and in the process and in the treatment of minority children is still lacking. Perhaps community cultural standards are not being considered, despite the provision in section 27 of the Charter, which urges that the Charter be interpreted in a way "consistent with the preservation and enhancement of the multicultural heritage of Canadians." Only children in care in some provinces — and those in court who are entitled to an interpreter — clearly have rights to maintain their cultural heritage. However, many school boards are finally developing race relations by-laws and policies.

Children in Poverty

According to many reports,[38] including the community panel on the new *Child Welfare Act* in British Columbia, poverty has been viewed as a crucial factor in child abuse, neglect, and ill-health. Yet human rights protections do not prohibit discrimination on the basis of socio-economic status. Nowhere

---

[37] For instance, the British Columbia Royal Commission on Family and Children's Rights (1975) chaired by Justice Berger.

[38] *Making Changes: A Place to Start* (Victoria, B.C.: Ministry of Social Services, 1994); and *Child Poverty in Canada, Report Card 1995: Campaign 2000* (Toronto, Ont.: Family Services Association, 1995).

in Canada are family welfare (income assistance) rates anywhere near the accepted poverty cutoffs. There are insufficient child care spaces for parents and children who require them. Some argue that Canada is contravening the spirit of the U.N. Convention.

Children with Special Needs

Where access of a child with a disability to a regular classroom is concerned, several cases challenging **segregation** (separate education) have occurred across Canada. In Nova Scotia, a student won a case against segregation to a special classroom for children with disabilities.[39] The Supreme Court of Canada ruled that integration was not automatic but that the decision between integration and segregation was to be made on the basis of the child's best interest.[40] The *Schools Act* of New Brunswick stands alone in insisting that exceptional students be placed with non-exceptional students within regular classroom settings to the extent considered practicable by the school board.

Because of jurisdictional differences, the laws for children across Canada remain inconsistent and patchy. Canadian society is experiencing a conflict of values in determining the degree to which children and youth should enjoy rights independent of their parents or guardians. As with all law, this incorporation of rights and principles into law for children is dynamic and tries to reflect current values and social demands.

LAWS PERTAINING TO PROFESSIONALS WORKING WITH CHILDREN

Professionals working with children and youth need to know about child rights and special laws so that they can act as fair and reasonable persons *in loco parentis*, and as advocates. Criminal record checks are now routinely required for persons employed to work with children, and many jurisdictions maintain registries of child abusers. The *Criminal Code* and professional codes of ethics for social workers, nurses, psychologists, teachers, and child care workers prohibit the exploitation of children.

CHAPTER SUMMARY

This chapter explored briefly the extent to which children and youth are provided, and have been provided in the past, with rights and protections in Canadian law. Key areas of law and process affecting the status of children and youth were discussed, and some common principles identified. Obstacles to rights and key issues were touched on, together with identified groups of children requiring special protection.

GLOSSARY OF NEW TERMS AND KEY CONCEPTS

accountability mechanisms	Processes in law that allow for the review or monitoring of decisions or services provided by an authority such as a government ministry. The Ombudsman Office is a major example.

---

[39] *Elwood v. Halifax County-Bedford District School Board* (1987), N.S.S.C. unreported.
[40] *Eaton v. Brant County Board of Education* (1997), 1 S.C.R. 241.

administrative fairness	Rules of fairness in the decision-making process, such as the right to receive reasons for a decision and to appeal it.
advocacy	Literally meaning "speaking to", the skill of assisting often disempowered persons, such as children, to put their case across to an authority or to speak on their behalf and represent their interests in partisan fashion. Lawyers are the most formal type of advocate.
age of majority	The age when the law assumes a child ("minor" or "infant") has attained the capacity and competency to act fully and legally as an independent adult.
capacity	The legal ability to be competent to understand the implications of one's decisions.
consent	Agreeing to a choice, an offer, or a proposed treatment in an informed way. Like "capacity", it is crucial for children and for persons suffering from mental disability.
dependency	The notion that children are vulnerable and require parents, guardians or the state to protect them.
discretion	The ability to make a choice without an obligation in law. It usually concerns the unrestricted ability of a government official to offer a service or not.
in loco parentis	Latin for "in the place of a parent", meaning a person who is legally acting as a parent or substitute, such as a teacher or foster parent. Section 43 of the *Criminal Code* gives special disciplinary powers to such persons.
presumptive offences	Serious offences (murder, attempted murder, manslaughter, and aggravated sexual assault) where youth aged between 14 and 16 are presumed to require an adult sentence upon conviction after a preliminary hearing has been successfully applied for by the Crown. The Youth Justice Court can now impose an adult sentence.
restorative justice	A process for resolution of criminal acts where offenders face the victims and hear of the impact of their crime. It may result in apology and compensation. The process might be mediated by community members assisted by police and justice personnel. Models include group conferencing, sentencing circles and First Nations healing circles.
secure care	A court order under child welfare legislation where children with identified problems, such as addictions, can be cared for and treated in a controlled, often closed, setting to protect them from harming themselves.
segregation	The practice of separating children with special needs into special classrooms or schools.
special protection	Special provisions and processes for children in law beyond what a competent adult might receive or be subject to, based on the notion of the vulnerability of children.
status	The legal position of a child in relation to parents or the state. Children in care have wardship status.

REVIEW QUESTIONS

1. Why are there different ages identified in laws for the various changes in status and services for children and youth?

2. Identify three categories of children's rights and the major differences between them.

3. What obstacles exist to the full implementation of independent rights for children and youth?

4. Where does the right to be provided with counsel exist?

5. Identify the key principles in child welfare and young offenders law.

6. Why do certain groups of children require special protection?

7. Identify where the principles of child welfare and youth justice overlap.

8. Under the provisions of the *Youth Criminal Justice Act*, identify the different ways young offenders accused of serious crime might be dealt with.

DISCUSSION QUESTIONS

1. Discuss how far the equality rights in section 15 of the Charter apply to children and youth in reality.

2. Discuss potential conflicts in society or family life if children were to have full rights independent of their parents.

3. What rights does the reader, as a student, have in college classes? How is this different from public education at a primary or secondary level?

4. Exercises

   (a) Imagine that you are a social worker investigating an allegation of child abuse. Identify and discuss some key facts you would want to know before apprehending a particular 10-year-old child. Explain to the child in understandable words the key steps in the process of coming into care. If you have time, you may wish to attend Family Court locally and interview a social worker.

   (b) Imagine that you are a youth worker preparing a pre-disposition report on a young offender. Identify and discuss what key information you would need in recommending a sentence to the court. Examine sections 41 and 42 of the *Youth Criminal Justice Act*, and explain the sentencing options to the youth. You may wish to visit Youth Justice Court and interview a youth worker.

   (c) Imagine that you are a family court counsellor or social worker preparing a custody and access report on an eight-year-old child. Identify and discuss the key factors that the court would take into account in its decision. Explain these to the child. You may wish to visit Family Court locally and interview a family court counsellor or social worker.

5. Exercise: In small groups, examine recent newspaper articles on young offender cases and the recent changes in the *Youth Criminal Justice Act*. Each group should explore how far these cases and reforms apply or change the existing balance of criteria and principles listed under the section "Youth Justice". Students should identify whether they agree or not, and why, with the proposed amendments.

6. Discuss how far children's rights might be compromised under the application of the secure care provisions.

7. Some Provinces have recently suggested that the principle of deterrence should be incorporated into the principles of the *Youth Criminal Justice Act*. Discuss whether you agree or not, exploring potential implications of incorporation.

8. Discuss how far the laws of your province that affect children and youth are in accordance with the following principles taken directly from the United Nations Declaration of the Rights of the Child:

Principle 1 The child shall enjoy all the rights set forth in this Declaration. Every child, without any exception whatsoever, shall be entitled to these rights, without distinction or discrimination on account of race, colour, sex, language, religion, political or other opinion, national or social origin, property, birth or other status, whether of himself or of his family.

Principle 2 The child shall enjoy special protection, and shall be given opportunities and facilities, by law and by other means, to enable him to develop physically, mentally, morally, spiritually and socially in a healthy and normal manner and in conditions of freedom and dignity. In the enactment of laws for this purpose, the best interests of the child shall be the paramount consideration.

Principle 3 The child shall be entitled from his birth to a name and a nationality.

Principle 4 The child shall enjoy the benefits of social security. He shall be entitled to grow and develop in health; to this end, special care and protection shall be provided both to him and to his mother, including adequate pre-natal and post-natal care. The child shall have the right to adequate nutrition, housing, recreation and medical services.

Principle 5 The child who is physically, mentally or socially handicapped shall be given the special treatment, education and care required by his particular condition.

Principle 6 The child, for the full and harmonious development of his personality, needs love and understanding. He shall, wherever possible, grow up in the care and under the responsibility of his parents, and, in any case, in an atmosphere of affection and of moral and material security; a child of tender years shall not, save in exceptional circumstances, be separated from his mother. Society and the public authorities shall have the duty to extend particular care to children without a family and to those without adequate means of support. Payment of state and other assistance towards the maintenance of children of large families is desirable.

Principle 7 The child is entitled to receive education, which shall be free and compulsory, at least in the elementary stages. He shall be given an education which will promote his general culture and enable him, on a basis of equal opportunity, to develop his abilities, his individual judgement, and his sense of moral and social responsibility, and to become a useful member of society.

The best interests of the child shall be the guiding principle of those responsible for his education and guidance; that responsibility lies in the first place with his parents.

The child shall have full opportunity for play and recreation, which should be directed to the same purposes as education; society and the public authorities shall endeavour to promote the enjoyment of this right.

Principle 8 The child shall in all circumstances be among the first to receive protection and relief.

Principle 9 The child shall be protected against all forms of neglect, cruelty and exploitation. He shall not be the subject of traffic, in any form.

The child shall not be admitted to employment before an appropriate minimum age; he shall in no case be caused or permitted to engage in any occupation or employment which would prejudice his health or education, or interfere with his physical, mental or moral development.

Principle 10 The child shall be protected from practices which may foster racial, religious and any other form of discrimination. He shall be brought up in a spirit of understanding, tolerance, friendship among peoples, peace and universal brotherhood, and in full consciousness that his energy and talents should be devoted to the service of his fellow men.

SUGGESTED READINGS

Bala, N. *Youth Criminal Justice Law* (Toronto, Ont.: Irwin Law, 2003).

Bala, N., J.P. Hornick, H.N. Snyder, & J.J. Paetsch, eds. *An International Comparison of Problems and Solutions* (Toronto, Ont.: Thompson Educational Publishing, 2002).

Bala, N., M.K. Zapf, R.J. Williams, R. Vogl, & J.P. Hornick, eds. *Canadian Child Welfare Law: Children, Families and the State*, 2d ed. (Toronto, Ont.: Thompson Educational, 2004).

British Columbia, Ministry for Children and Families. *Know Your Rights Under the Child, Family and Community Service Act: A Guide for Young People in Care* (Victoria, B.C.: Author, 1998).

Howe, R.B., & K. Covell. (eds.) *A Question of Commitment: Children's Rights in Canada* (Waterloo, Ont.: Wilfrid Laurier University Press, 2007).

Doyle, S., T. Farrell, & A. Sheppard. *For the Record: The Youth Criminal Justice Act: A New Law for Canadian Youth, A New Collaborative Approach*, 2d ed. (St. John's, Nfld.: Public Legal Information Association of Newfoundland, 2003).

Justice for Children and Youth. *Age Based Laws/Rights*, online: <www.jfcy.org/agebased.html>.

Payne, J., Q.C., & M. Payne. *Canadian Family Law*, 2d ed. (Toronto, Ont.: Irwin Law, 2006).

Turner, D., & M.R. Uhlemann. *A Legal Handbook for the Helping Professional*, 3d ed. (Victoria, B.C.: Sedgewick Society for Consumer and Public Education, School of Social Work, 2007). [Especially Chapter 3, "Child Protection and Legal Process"; Chapter 4, "Children's Rights to Services in Canada"; Chapter 5, "Aboriginal Self-Determination and Child Protection Law"; Chapter 6, "Adoptions"; Chapter 7, "Family Law"; Chapter 9, "Youth Justice and the Legal Process"; and Chapter 13, "Education and the Law"]

Umbreit, M.S. "Victim-Offender Mediation in Criminal Conflict: Toward Restorative Justice", in E. Kruk, ed., *Mediation and Conflict Resolution in Social Work and Human Services* (Chicago: Nelson-Hall Publishers, 2000).

Vogl, R., & N. Bala. *Testifying on Behalf of Children: A Handbook for Canadian Professionals* (Toronto, Ont.: Thompson Educational, 2001).

For information on child welfare legislation, see

British Columbia

British Columbia. *YCJA: British Columbia*, 2d ed. (Victoria, B.C.: BC Government, 2004). This pocket guide provides detailed information for practitioners in British Columbia. Based on *Moving Forward: Pocket Guide to the Youth Criminal Justice Act Canada* developed by the Nova Scotia Department of Justice, it applies across Canada, since criminal legislation is a national responsibility.

Ontario

Geigen-Miller, M. *It's Time to Break the Silence: Creating Meaningful Access to Rights and Advocacy Services for Young People in Care in Ontario* (Toronto, Ont.: Defence for Children International, 2003).

Zuker, M.A., R.C. Hammond, & R.C. Flynn. *Children's Law Handbook* (Toronto, Ont.: Carswell, 2006).

General

Canada. *Child Welfare in Canada 2000*, online: <http://www.hrsdc.gc.ca/en/cs/sp/sdc/ socpol/publications/reports/2000-000033/page00.shtml>

Nicholas Bala, Michael Kim Zapf, R. James Williams, Robin Vogl, & Joseph P. Hornick (eds.). *Canadian Child Welfare Law: Children, Families, and the State*, 2d ed. (Toronto, Ont.: Thompson Educational Publishing, 2004).

WEBSITE

Canadian Coalition for the Rights of Children: <www.rightsofchildren.ca>

Estate Planning

DeeAnn M. Gonsalves
SENECA COLLEGE

Learning Objectives

After reading this chapter, the reader should be able to:

➢ understand what a will is
➢ appreciate the advantages of making a will
➢ understand the legal and formal requirements for making a will
➢ identify the information required to prepare a will
➢ identify the key clauses in a will
➢ understand the execution requirements of a will
➢ understand how a will can be amended or revoked
➢ demonstrate an awareness of intestacy laws
➢ understand what a power of attorney for property is
➢ understand what a power of attorney for personal care is
➢ understand the legal and formal requirements for making powers of attorney
➢ appreciate the limitations of a power of attorney
➢ understand how a power of attorney can be revoked
➢ demonstrate an awareness of what may happen when someone becomes incapacitated without having made a power of attorney

TABLE OF CONTENTS

INTRODUCTION

It has been said that in life there are only two certainties: death and taxes.[1] The area of estates law, particularly that of estate planning, provides us with an opportunity to address these certainties. The act of estate planning can benefit everyone, from the smallest to the largest estate holder.

What Is an Estate?

An **estate** is all of the property, both real and personal, that someone has an interest in. Estate property may be in the possession of the owner or owed to him or her.

What Is Estate Planning?

Estate planning is the process of organizing one's affairs with respect to the preservation, management and distribution of his or her property during an incapacity or upon death. Estate planning includes the preparation of documents that may assist with the management of the estate of the deceased or incapacitated person. The estate planning process includes choosing someone to handle the estate. It also often includes structuring one's affairs to minimize taxes, probate fees, and other costs and to provide for loved ones.

Common Estate Documents

The most common estate documents are a **will** and powers of attorney for property and personal care. In some cases, additional documents are required for trusts, private corporations, or other entities.

WILLS

What Is a Will?

A will is a written document that sets out a person's directions for the management and distribution of his or her property upon death. A will may also appoint someone, commonly known as an **executor** in the case of a male appointee and an **executrix** in the case of a female appointee, to be in charge of the estate.[2]

The Advantages of Making a Will

Controlling the Disposition of Your Estate

A will allows its maker, known as the **testator** in the case of a male and the **testatrix** in the case of a female, to control the disposition of his or her estate to his or her beneficiaries following his or her demise. A will sets out a plan for the executor to follow with respect to the management and distribution of estate assets, the payment of debts, and other matters. A will specifies who shall receive estate assets. Without a will, government legislation dictates who the heirs are. If those heirs are of the age of majority, they will inherit at the time of the death. With a will, the payment of inheritances can be postponed, beyond the age of majority, through the use of trusts. Such **testamentary trusts** can also be used to benefit some disabled and spendthrift beneficiaries.

---

[1] Benjamin Franklin, 1789, in a letter to M. Leroy.

[2] Given that many estate terms are specifically masculine or feminine, the author has been unable to use gender-neutral terms in some parts of this text.

Choosing an Executor and Beneficiaries

In order to administer the estate, the will should appoint an executor or executrix. In some jurisdictions, terms such as **personal representative** or **estate trustee with a will** are used. One or more persons may be appointed as executor. Some testators appoint a trust company to act as their executor.

An executor obtains his authority to act directly from the will. With a will, an executor may commence his or her duties immediately following the testator's death.

Without a will in place, someone is said to die intestate. Intestacy laws in each province set out who should be appointed to manage the intestate estate. This person is commonly known as the **administrator** of the estate if they are a male and as the **administratrix** if they are a female. In some jurisdictions they are known as the personal representative or the **estate trustee without a will**. In an intestacy, administration of the estate cannot begin until a grant of **letters of administration**; or, in some provinces, such as Ontario, a **certificate of appointment of estate trustee without a will** is obtained from the court.

In his will the testator names the person or persons who are to receive his assets upon his death. These people are known as beneficiaries. Beneficiaries often include family members, friends, and charities.

A will allows the testator to specify which items of property each **beneficiary** shall receive. When drafting a will, care should be taken to name an alternate beneficiary to inherit in the event that the original beneficiary predeceases the testator.

Without a will, provincial legislation sets out how an estate will be divided. There is a commonly held misconception that legally married spouses will automatically inherit each other's estates, thereby dispensing with the need for a will. In most provinces and territories, this is not the case. Where the deceased is survived by a spouse and children, the estate or some portion of it is divided between the spouse and the children. For a more detailed look at provincial and territorial intestacy laws, please consult the table of provincial and territorial intestacy laws set out in Exhibit 31.1. Note that the table sets out legislation only for legally married spouses.

Intestacy and Matrimonial Property Legislation

A well-drafted will can circumvent provincial intestacy laws. Without a will or with a poorly drafted will, an estate or part of it must be distributed in accordance with provincial intestacy laws.

In some cases, a well-drafted will, in conjunction with a domestic contract, such as a marriage contract, can avoid the application of legislation regarding the division of matrimonial property upon the death of a spouse. Couples embarking upon a second marriage later in life may use a will, combined with a domestic contract, to preserve the bulk of their estate for their children from their first marriages while still providing for each other.

In most jurisdictions, couples in a common law relationship are not legally entitled to a share of their partner's property upon the partner's death.[3] However, a couple in a common law relationship may execute wills leaving property to each other.

---

[3] In British Columbia, the *Estates Administration Act* provides that after two years of residing together, common law spouses have the same rights on intestacy as married spouses.

In Manitoba and Nova Scotia, the provincial *Vital Statistics Act*s provide that common law spouses can register their domestic partnership to obtain the same rights as married spouses under intestacy laws.

EXHIBIT 31.1			Summary of Canadian Intestacy Legislation
PROVINCE/ TERRITORY	**LEGISLATION**	**SPOUSE & ONE CHILD**	**SPOUSE & TWO OR MORE CHILDREN**
Alberta	*Intestate Succession Act*	$40,000 to spouse with remainder divided equally between the spouse and child	$40,000 to spouse plus 1/3 of the remainder with the other 2/3 divided equally among children
British Columbia	*Estate Administration Act*	$65,000 to spouse with remainder divided equally between spouse and child	$65,000 to spouse plus 1/3 of the remainder with the other 2/3 divided equally among children
Manitoba	*Intestate Succession Act*	All to spouse[1]	All to spouse[1]
New Brunswick	*Devolution of Estates Act*	Marital property[2] to spouse with remainder of property divided equally between spouse and child	Marital property to spouse plus 1/3 of the remainder with the other 2/3 divided equally among children
Newfoundland	*Intestate Succession Act*	All property divided equally between spouse and child	1/3 of property to spouse with the other 2/3 divided equally among children
Northwest Territories	*Intestate Succession Act*	$50,000 to spouse with the remainder divided equally between spouse and child	$50,000 to spouse plus 1/3 of the remainder with the other 2/3 divided equally among children
Nova Scotia	*Intestate Succession Act*	$50,000 to spouse (or house and contents) with the remainder divided equally between spouse and child	$50,000 (or house and contents) to spouse plus 1/3 of the remainder with the other 2/3 divided equally among children
Nunavut	*Intestate Succession Act*	$50,000 to spouse with the remainder divided equally between spouse and child	$50,000 to spouse plus 1/3 of remainder with the other 2/3 divided equally among children
Ontario	*Succession Law Reform Act*	$200,000 to spouse with the remainder divided equally between spouse and child	$200,000 to spouse plus 1/3 of remainder with the other 2/3 divided equally among children
Prince Edward Island	*Probate Act*	All property divided equally between spouse and child	1/3 of property to spouse with the other 2/3 divided equally among children
Quebec	*Quebec Civil Code*	One-third to spouse and remaining two-thirds to child	1/3 of property to spouse with the other 2/3 divided equally among children
Saskatchewan	*The Intestate Succession Act, 1996*	$100,000 to spouse with the remainder divided equally between spouse and child	$100,000 to spouse plus 1/3 of remainder with the other 2/3 divided equally among children
Yukon Territory	*Estate Administration Act*	$75,000 to spouse with the remainder divided equally between spouse and child	$75,000 to spouse plus 1/3 of the remainder with the other 2/3 divided equally among children

[1] If the surviving spouse is not the biological parent of the child or children, then the spouse receives the greater of $50,000 or one-half of the estate; the spouse will also get one-half of the remainder while the other one-half goes to the child or is shared equally among the children, if there is more than one child: *Intestate Succession Act*, C.C.S.M. c. I85, s. 2(2).
[2] Marital property as defined in *Marital Property Act*, S.N.B., 1980, c. M-1.1.

Providing for a Common Disaster

Most wills contain a special provision known as a "**common disaster clause**". This clause is included in order to address the situation where both spouses die within a short time of each other. An example of a common disaster clause is contained in paragraph 8(e) of the sample will set out in Exhibit 31.2. The clause states that, in order to inherit under the will, the surviving spouse must outlive the deceased by 30 or more days. Thirty days is the figure that is usually used to reflect an assumption that if someone survives an accidental injury by more than 30 days, they are unlikely to die from their injuries. The will usually provides for an alternate beneficiary to inherit in the event that the surviving spouse dies before the 30-day period has concluded.

Without a will or with a will that does not contain a common disaster clause, the family of the spouse who first succumbed to his or her injuries would not inherit anything from their family member's estate. By way of an example, assume that a childless couple, who had not yet made their wills, was involved in a serious car accident. Unfortunately the accident resulted in the death of the husband at the scene of the accident. The wife died two hours later. As the wife outlived her husband, she inherited the husband's entire estate upon his death. As a result of her death, her next of kin — her parents or, if they had predeceased her, then her siblings — inherited her entire estate. The wife's estate also included the husband's estate. The husband's family did not receive any part of his estate as the wife had outlived him, albeit by only two hours. As well, in Ontario and in some other provinces, probate tax would have to be paid twice on the husband's assets. The tax would have to be paid to probate his estate over to his wife and again on her entire estate, which now includes his estate. If the couple had children surviving them, the children would inherit their parents' estates. There would still be an advantage to having a common disaster clause, as the estates could be directly probated to the children, resulting in probate tax being paid only once on each estate.

Some provinces have legislation in place to provide for a more equitable distribution of property where spouses die simultaneously. It should be noted, however, that simultaneous death is a rare occurrence. In Ontario, section 55 of the *Succession Law Reform Act*[4] provides that where the spouses die simultaneously or in circumstances rendering it uncertain which of them survived the other, each spouse's property shall be disposed of as if he or she had survived the other. In the example above, if the husband and wife had died at precisely the same time, the husband's estate would pass to his family, and the wife's estate would pass to her family, as each spouse would be deemed to have survived the other.

Family Law Provisions for Beneficiaries

If someone receives an inheritance, as a result of an intestacy or from a poorly drafted will, he or she may have to share the earnings on their inheritance with their estranged spouse. Matrimonial property legislation, such as Ontario's *Family Law Act*,[5] provides that inheritances are generally excluded from a spouse's net family property and, therefore, are not subject to division or equalization upon a marriage breakdown. However, any earnings generated by an inheritance, such as interest, dividends, or capital gains, constitute part of a spouse's net family property. These earnings are subject to division or

---

[4] *Succession Law Reform Act*, R.S.O. 1990, c. S.26.
[5] *Family Law Act*, R.S.O. 1990, c. F.3.

EXHIBIT 31.2

A Sample Will

LAST WILL AND TESTAMENT OF
ELIZABETH LOUISE COLLINS

THIS IS THE LAST WILL of me, Elizabeth Louise Collins, also known as Liz Collins, of the City of Brampton, in the Regional Municipality of Peel, and Province of Ontario.

Part I
Initial Matters

Interpretation

1. In interpreting this will it is my intention that the headings are intended only as guidelines and are not to be interpreted as being part of the text of this my will.
2. Children as referred to in this will shall mean my son, Jason Oliver Collins, and my daughter, Angela Louise Collins.

Revocation of Prior Wills

3. I REVOKE all wills, codicils, and other testamentary dispositions that I have made before the time of signing this will.

Appointment of Executor

4. I APPOINT my spouse, namely Robert Allen Collins, to be the Executor of my will. In this my will and in any codicil to it I refer to my Executor and my alternate Executor as my Estate Trustee.
5. If my Estate Trustee should:
   (a) predecease me, or
   (b) survive me but die without having proved this my will,
   (c) be unable or unwilling to act, or
   (d) cease to be a resident in Canada, or shall be absent from Canada in any calendar year for a period or periods, the aggregate of which is one hundred and eighty (180) days or more, then I APPOINT my brother, namely Austin Cory Reynolds, to be the alternate Executor of my Will, to act in his place.

Organ Donation

6. I direct my trustee to donate any organs that can be of any use for transplant purposes.

Cremation

7. It is my wish to have my remains cremated and scattered from the bow of my sailboat on Lake Ontario with Vivaldi's *The Four Seasons* playing in the background.

Part II
Disposition of Estate

8. I give all of my property, both real and personal wherever located, including all property over which I have a general power of appointment, to my Estate Trustee upon the following trusts:

   Payment of Debts
   (a) to pay:
       (i) my debts and cremation expenses, and
       (ii) the expenses of administering my estate and the trusts created by this will and any codicil to this will

   Legacy and Bequest
   (b) to transfer to my daughter, Angela, my diamond engagement and wedding rings.
   (c) to pay the sum of $1,500 to the Canadian Cancer Society.

   Memorandum
   (d) to distribute all personal and household items in accordance with a memorandum that I may leave among my personal papers or attached to a copy of this will

A Sample Will

EXHIBIT 31.2 (continued)

Residue

(e) to pay or transfer the residue of my estate to my spouse, namely, Robert Allen Collins, if he survives me by a period of at least thirty days.

(f) If my spouse should predecease me, or survive me but die within a period of thirty days after my death, to divide the residue of my estate equally among my children surviving me and to pay or transfer to each child who has attained the age of 25 years, as of the date of my death, his or her share of my estate.

(g) to pay to my spouse, should he survive me, an allowance to meet his basic needs during the thirty days following my death. During that time my spouse shall have full use of all of my household items, furnishings, and personal goods.

Trust for Children

(h) If any child of mine is entitled to a share of my estate but has not yet reached the age of 25 years as of the date of my death, I direct my Estate Trustee to do as follows:

   (i) to hold such child's share and invest it;

   (ii) to use the income and capital, or so much thereof as my Estate Trustee in his uncontrolled discretion considers advisable to or for the care, maintenance, education, support, or advancement of such child which may include payments to the custodians of the children for such purposes; and

   (iii) to pay or transfer the balance in such share to such child when the child attains the age of 25 years.

Any income not so used in any year and the income derived therefrom shall be accumulated (but only for a period not exceeding twenty-one years from the date of my death) by investing the same and the resulting income therefrom and such accumulations shall be added to the share or interest from which they arose and devolve therewith.

(i) If any of my children should predecease me, leaving issue alive at the date of my death, his or her share is to be equally divided among such issue by representation in equal shares per stirpes.

(j) If any of my children should predecease me, leaving no issue surviving him or her or the date of my death, the share of my Estate to which such deceased child would otherwise be entitled shall be divided equally among his or her other surviving siblings alive at the date of my death.

Share of Minors and Incapable Beneficiaries

(k) Except as set out in paragraphs 8(f) and (h) herein, if any person should become entitled to any share in my estate while he or she is incapable of executing a release or has not yet attained the age of 25, the share of such person shall be held and kept invested by my Estate Trustee and the income and capital or so much thereof as my Estate Trustee in his absolute discretion considers necessary or advisable shall be used for the benefit of such person until he or she attains the age of 25 or in the case of any incapacity on the part of my beneficiary, until the beneficiary is no longer incapable.

Custodians and Guardians for the Children and their Property

(l) If Robert Allen Collins predeceases me or at the time of my death has been found to be mentally incapable of caring for our children, and we have any children who have not yet attained the age of majority, I appoint my brother, Matthew Lawrence Reynolds, to have custody of my children and to the extent that I am capable of so doing, I also appoint Matthew Lawrence Reynolds to be the guardian of my children's present and future property during their infancy.

   It is my wish that my custodian and guardian make an application within 90 days from the date of my death, as provided for in the *Children's Law Reform Act*, or in any successor or similar legislation thereto, to have custody of my children and to be appointed as the guardian of any property that my children had at the time of my death or that they may acquire after my death.

EXHIBIT 31.2 (continued)

A Sample Will

(m) I direct my Estate Trustee, at his discretion, to pay, from the trust established in Paragraph 8(h) of this will, to my custodian, such amounts as my custodian may require from time to time for the maintenance of a home for my children and to pay the cost of clothing, feeding, and educating my children, it being my wish that the resources of my estate be made available to the custodian in order that there be no financial or physical burden placed upon him by reason of his undertaking to look after my children.

<u>Part III</u>
<u>Powers of Estate Trustee</u>

9. For all purposes contained in this my will I give to my Estate Trustee the following powers:

Power of Sale
(a) to sell any part of my estate not consisting of money at such time or times, in such manner, and at such time or times, in such manner, and upon such terms and either for cash or credit, or part cash and part credit as my Estate Trustee deems advisable;

Power not to Convert Estate
(b) to postpone the conversion of my estate, or any part or parts thereof for such length of time as my Estate Trustee may think best;

Retain Investments
(c) to retain any portion of my estate in the form in which it may be at the time of my death (notwithstanding that it may not be a form of an investment in which trustees are authorized to invest trust funds, and whether or not there is a liability attached to any such portion of my estate) for such length of time as my Estate Trustee deems advisable, and my Estate Trustee shall not be held responsible for any loss that may happen to my estate by reason of so doing;

Division of Assets in Specie
(d) upon any distribution of my estate or any part thereof or the setting up of any trust or fund established under this my will or any codicil hereto to distribute or set aside assets in specie; for the purpose of any such distribution or setting aside, to place such value on all assets from time to time forming part of my estate as shall seem just and proper to my Estate Trustee in his uncontrolled discretion and any such valuation shall be absolutely final and binding and conclusive on all beneficiaries hereunder; and upon any distribution or setting aside to determine to whom or to what trust specific assets shall be given or allocated and to distribute or set aside the same subject to the payment of such amounts as shall be necessary to adjust the share of the various beneficiaries;

Power to Borrow
(e) at any time and from time to time to borrow money upon the security of all or any assets of my estate in such manner, on such terms, and conditions, for such length of time and for such purposes connected with my estate as my Estate Trustee deems advisable, and such borrowing may be from any person or corporation notwithstanding that such person or corporation may be a member of my family or a beneficiary or trustee under my will, and the person or corporation from whom my Estate Trustee borrows shall be entitled to receive and be paid for his, her or its own benefit such interest as my Estate Trustee has decided upon; and

Elections Under the Income Tax Act
(f) to make any elections, determinations and designations under the *Income Tax Act* which in his discretion or on the advice of a professional tax advisor he deems advisable.

A Sample Will

EXHIBIT 31.2 (continued)

Family Law Act

10. I hereby expressly state that all property and income, including but not limited to interest, dividends, and capital gains, from property given under the terms of this my will to any beneficiary at the time of my death shall be excluded from the net family property of such beneficiary for all purposes of the *Family Law Act* as amended from time to time or any similar or successor legislation.

IN TESTIMONY WHEREOF I have to this my last will and testament, written upon this and the three preceding pages of paper, subscribed my name this _____ day of _____ , 200___ .

SIGNED, PUBLISHED AND DECLARED	)
By the said testatrix,	)
Elizabeth Louise Collins,	)
as and for her last will and	)
testament, in the presence of	) _____
us, both present at the same	) Elizabeth Louise Collins
time, who at her request,	)
in her presence and in the	)
presence of each other, have	)
hereunto subscribed our names	)
as witnesses.	)

WITNESS: WITNESS:
_____   _____

Name: _____   Name: _____

Address: _____   Address: _____

_____   _____

Occupation: _____   Occupation: _____

equalization upon a marriage breakdown, unless the will in which the gift was made contains a clause excluding such earnings from a division of matrimonial property. An example of such a clause can be found in paragraph 10 of the sample will contained in Exhibit 31.2. In most cases a family law clause should be included in a will.

Provisions for Minors and Special Beneficiaries

A will can be used to appoint a temporary custodian and guardian for a minor child. The child, following the death of his or her custodial parents, usually resides with the temporary custodian named in the will. The custodian must apply to the local family court for an order granting him or her permanent custody. A will can suggest permanent custodians but cannot make the final appointment as custody of a child must always be determined in regard to what is in the child's best interests. A suggestion made in a will years ago may or may not be what would be in the child's best interests upon the deaths of his or her custodial parents. A court makes that determination following the loss. The parent's suggestions, as set out in his or her will, are, however, strongly considered by the court in making its decision.

A will can also be used to suggest a guardian for a minor child's property. Children generally do not have a great deal of property, although many children do have their own bank accounts from funds given to them on birthdays and other special occasions. Some children have an income from modelling, acting or other part-time jobs. Upon the death of a parent, a child may be entitled to Canada Pension Plan survivor benefits. Minor children often require a guardian to collect these benefits on their behalf. The suggested guardian must apply to the local family court for an order granting him or her guardianship of the child's property. Many people appoint the same person(s) to be their children's custodians and guardians. In some cases, however, it may be desirable to appoint different people to handle each responsibility.

Without a will, children receive their inheritances when they reach the age of majority. With a will parents can raise the age of inheritance to a higher age, such as 21, 25, or 30, or have the money paid out in stages. In paragraph 8(f) of the sample will contained in Exhibit 31.2, the age of inheritance has been raised to age 25. However, in paragraph 8(h)(ii) of the sample will, the trustee of the children's inheritance has been given the power to encroach upon, meaning to use, some of the funds for the children's education and other purposes deemed worthy by the trustee.

A will can be used to set up a trust fund to assist a beneficiary with special needs. For example, a parent of a child with a severe mental impairment could use his or her will to set up a trust to permit funds to be available for the child's needs. In some situations a trust can be set up to provide funds that may be used for the child's needs while still preserving the child's access to government programs and benefits.[6] In other cases, trusts could be established for beneficiaries with substance abuse or gambling problems. In these circumstances the trust could be structured to pay the beneficiary's rent or provide them with a monthly income in place of a one-time inheritance payment.

Cost and Time Savings

A will speaks from the moment of death. It contains instructions for the executor to follow. In some cases, an entire estate can be administered using the will alone, without having to get a grant from the court.

Without a will someone must, in most cases, apply to the court for a grant permitting him or her to administer the estate. In some jurisdictions, it can take weeks to obtain a court grant. As well, in order to obtain a grant from the court, probate tax must be paid on the value of most estate assets. Dying with a will in place can save the estate and the beneficiaries time and money.

Financial and Tax Planning

A will provides the testator with an opportunity to do some tax planning. Spousal trusts and **rollovers** can be used in a will to defer the payment of taxes. A will can also be used to make special provisions for any business that the testator owns.

With a will, the testator leaves behind a plan for the management of his or her estate. Instructions can be given as to the types of investments to be

---

[6] In Ontario, an absolute discretionary trust, known as a Henson trust, preserves the right of a disabled person to continue receiving benefits despite being a beneficiary under a discretionary trust. The trust is named after Leonard Henson, who made such trust provisions for his disabled daughter. When the Ontario Ministry of Social Services revoked Miss Henson's benefits as a result of the trust, the Henson family successfully challenged the ministry's actions and had Ms. Henson's benefits reinstated.

made. If there is no will or if the will does not set out the estate trustee's powers regarding investments, the estate trustee must adhere to provincial trustee legislation. In a will the testator can instruct the executor as to whether assets should be sold immediately or held until a later time. Without a will, property may have to be sold, under less than favourable market conditions, in order to liquidate estate assets to satisfy provincial intestacy laws. With a will, the property could be rented out and sold later on when the market is more favourable.

DRAFTING A WILL

Legal Requirements for Making a Will

There are three legal requirements for making a will. The testator must, subject to a few exceptions, be of the age of majority. He or she must also possess **testamentary capacity** and have knowledge of and approve the contents of the will.

Age Restrictions and Exceptions

Most legislation concerning wills provides that you cannot make a will unless you have reached the age of majority. There are some exceptions to the rule. For example, in Ontario, the *Succession Law Reform Act* permits persons under 18 to make a will if they are married or have been married or if the will is made in contemplation of marriage.[7] Someone under 18 who is a member of the regular Canadian Forces or on active service or is a sailor at sea or in the course of a voyage may also make a will.[8]

Testamentary Capacity

In order to make a valid will the testator must be mentally capable of doing so. The courts have set out four characteristics that demonstrate capacity.[9] These four characteristics are as follows:

1. The testator understands the nature of the activity that he is engaged in. At a minimum he should understand that he is making a will to dispose of his property following his death.

2. The testator understands the extent of his property.

3. The testator is aware of his "moral obligations". The term "moral obligations" refers to those persons that society would normally expect someone to leave their estate to, such as spouse and children. The testator may not be required to leave his estate to such persons; however, he should have turned his mind to those "obligations" when making his will.[10]

4. The testator understands the consequences of his will. For example, if he has four adult children and if his will instructs the executor to divide the estate among three of the children, the testator must understand

---

[7] *Succession Law Reform Act*, R.S.O. 1990, c. S.26, ss. 8(1)(a) and (b).
[8] *Succession Law Reform Act*, R.S.O. 1990, c. S.26, ss. 8(1)(c) and (d).
[9] *Banks v. Goodfellow* (1870), L.R. 5 Q.B. 549.
[10] Unless a marriage contract is in place, in most jurisdictions if the will does not provide for a spouse, the spouse can elect in place of the will to claim an equalization of net family property. A testator is not usually required to name his adult children in his will. A child in those circumstances will have a claim against the estate only if the deceased was supporting him or her.

that one of his children will not receive anything from the estate. In such a case it is recommended that the testator include in his will the reason for excluding one of the adult children.

Knowledge and Approval of the Contents of the Will

The testator must know what is in his will and must approve such contents. The testator should read his will prior to signing it. The testator's signature at the end of his will should confirm his knowledge and approval of the contents of the will. Many lawyers have testators initial the bottom of each page of the will to indicate that they have reviewed the will and to prevent the unscrupulous insertion of supplementary pages into the will in which gifts are made that the testator did not authorize.

Information Required to Draft the Will

Executors and Trustees

The appointment in a will of an executor, sometimes known as an estate trustee with a will or a personal representative, is not legally required. However, it is standard practice to appoint at least one executor in a will to manage the estate upon the testator's death. The testator may name more than one executor to act. It is recommended that an alternate executor or executrix be named in the will so that he or she can be replaced in the event that he or she predeceases the testator, is unable or unwilling to act, or moves outside the province.

The executor, unless the will states otherwise, is the trustee of the entire estate. The testator should also provide the names of any additional trustees to be named in the will. For example, there may be a trust established in the will for the testator's minor children. The testator may appoint the executor as trustee of this trust fund or may appoint another trustee to manage the children's trust. If a trust is to remain in place for a number of years, some testators appoint a trust company to act as the trustee.

Care should be taken in choosing an executor. Testators should choose someone that they trust to follow their instructions and manage their property and financial affairs. It is advantageous to choose someone with knowledge of the testator's affairs. Age and ability to deal with others should also be considered. Someone likely to remain in Ontario is a factor to consider to avoid the possibility of any trust in the will becoming a foreign trust. To deal with this possibility an alternate executor should always be named.

Assets

The testator should provide instructions concerning the disposal of his assets upon death. There may be gifts of specific items of property to specific persons; these are known as **bequests.** There may be gifts of money to specific persons; these are known as **legacies.** Instructions should be given as to the transfer of any assets into trusts. The testator may also leave instructions as to how his assets should be invested or sold.

Memorandum

Quite often a testator has collectible items that he wishes to leave to various friends and family members. Instead of putting these instructions in a will, the testator may draft a legal or a **precatory memorandum** dealing with such gifts. Only a legal memorandum is legally binding on the executor and the estate. A legal memorandum must be prepared before the will and be referred to and incorporated into the will. A legal memorandum can be changed only if the will is changed.

A precatory memorandum, on the other hand, is not legally binding; however, it does provide the executor with a statement of the testator's wishes in regard to the division of his property. A precatory memorandum can be prepared and changed at any time and does not need to be mentioned in the will.

Children

If a testator has minor children, he should provide the names of suggested custodians and guardians. He should also specify at what age children should inherit property. If a testator does not have any children of his own, he may still want to specify an age of inheritance in his will if he wants to postpone the payment of a minor's inheritance beyond the age of majority. This might be necessary if there is a possibility that a minor might inherit property from the testator through a parent who is a direct beneficiary of the testator.

Trusts

The testator should give instructions for any trusts that are to be set up in his will. Trusts may be established for minor children, charities, some disabled beneficiaries or for other purposes. The name of the trustee will be required, along with the names of any alternate trustees. The beneficiaries and alternate beneficiaries of the trust should be specified. The terms of the trust will need to be known, including the duration of the trust and any investment and encroachment instructions concerning the trust.

Funeral Instructions

Some testators wish to provide funeral, burial, cremation, or organ donation instructions in their wills. Although such instructions may be set out in a will, they are strictly advisory in nature and are not legally binding on the executor. The executor has the final word as to the disposal of the deceased's remains. If a testator desires a certain type of funeral, burial or cremation, he should consider prearranging it and should make his wishes known to his family. In regard to organ donation or the donation of one's body for scientific research, many provinces permit their residents to register their intentions in this regard, in some cases, through the renewal of their driver's licence. On a practical note, a will is not the best place in which to leave such instructions as the will is often not located or read until after burial or cremation has taken place.

Standard Powers

Most wills provide the executor with a set of standard powers, such as the power to hold assets, to sell assets, to convert assets, and to borrow and lend estate funds, and to place a value upon estate assets at their discretion. Examples of such standard powers are found in paragraph 9 of the sample will set out at Exhibit 31.2.

TYPES OF WILLS

Formally Attested Wills

The most common form of a will is the **formally attested will**. Such a will is generally typewritten and is signed by the testator in the presence of at least two witnesses who attest to its execution. Attestation is defined as signing one's name, as a witness, to the execution of a document. **Execution** refers to signing — in this case, the signing of the will.

As with all wills, a formally attested will must meet the legal requirements for a valid will, noted earlier. In addition, there are four formal requirements that a formally attested will must meet in order to be valid. These requirements are as follows:

1. The will must be in writing. Wills cannot be made by recording instructions on videotape, CD, cassette tape, DVD or by e-mail. Electronic signatures are not valid for the purposes of a will.

2. The will must be signed by the testator at the end of the will. In Ontario there are provisions in place for someone to sign a will for the testator as long as it is signed in the testator's presence and under his direction.[11] There are also special provisions for the signing of a will by someone who signs with an "X" and for blind or illiterate persons.

3. A formally attested will must be witnessed by two or more persons. The testator signs the will in the presence of the witnesses, who each sign in the presence of each other and the testator. Witnesses must be of the age of majority and should not be a beneficiary or the spouse of a beneficiary.[12] It is *always* prudent to have an **affidavit of execution** sworn by one of the witnesses following the execution of the will. An affidavit of execution confirms that the proper witnessing procedures were followed. The affidavit should be stored with the will as it must be given to the court when the will is submitted for a grant of probate following the testator's death. A sample affidavit of execution form is contained in Exhibit 31.3.

4. The last formal requirement of a will is that it have a disposing intention. This means that the testator's intention, in regard to his will, was that it would be used upon his death to dispose of his property. In some cases, courts have been asked to declare letters from testators to their lawyers, in which they suggest instructions for the disposal of their estate, to be wills. The courts, in such cases, must decide if the letter simply gave instructions for the lawyer's consideration or was intended to actually dispose of the property as a will.

Holograph Wills

In many jurisdictions, a testator may make a legally binding **holograph will**. A holograph will is a will that has been made entirely in the testator's own handwriting and signed by him. Such a will does not require any witnesses.

As with all wills, a holograph will must meet the legal requirements, noted earlier, for a valid will. In regard to formal requirements, the holograph will must be made in the testator's own handwriting and signed by him. The holograph will must also have a disposing intention. Although it is not a legal requirement to do so, it is a good idea to date a holograph will.

Military Wills

Some legislation, such as Ontario's *Succession Law Reform Act*, relaxes the usual formal requirements of a will for members of the Canadian Forces on active service or for a sailor at sea or in the course of a voyage.[13]

Such wills, even if typewritten, do not require any witnesses. At the time of death, in order to validate such a will, a certificate of active service must be obtained from the appropriate forces.

---

[11] *Succession Law Reform Act*, R.S.O. 1990, c. S.26, s. 4(1)(a).

[12] In Ontario, s. 12(3) of the *Succession Law Reform Act*, R.S.O. 1990, c. S.26, may be used to validate a gift made to a beneficiary or spouse who witnessed the will if said person can show the court that he or she did not exercise any improper or undue influence.

[13] *Succession Law Reform Act*, R.S.O. 1990, c. S.26, s. 5(1).

Affidavit of Execution of Will or Codicil   **EXHIBIT 31.3**

ONTARIO
SUPERIOR COURT OF JUSTICE

IN THE MATTER OF THE EXECUTION OF A WILL OR CODICIL OF *(insert name)*

AFFIDAVIT

    I, *(insert name)*, of *(insert city or town and county or district, metropolitan or regional municipality or residence)* make oath and say/affirm:

1. On *(date)*, I was present and saw the document marked as Exhibit "A" to this my affidavit executed by *(insert name)*.

2. *(Insert name)* executed the document in the presence of myself and *(insert name of other witness and city or town, county or district, metropolitan or regional municipality of residence)*. We were both present at the same time, and signed the document in the testator's presence as attesting witnesses.

SWORN/AFFIRMED BEFORE   )
me at the   of   )
in the   of   )
this   day of   , 20   .   )
)
)
)
)

_____

A Commissioner for Taking Affidavits *(or as may be)*

NOTE: If the testator was blind or signed by making his or her mark, add the following paragraph:

3. Before its execution, the document was read over to the testator, who (was blind) signed by making his or her mark. The testator appeared to understand the contents.

WARNING: A beneficiary or the spouse of a beneficiary should not be a witness.

Indian Act Wills

Under the federal *Indian Act*,[14] the federal government may accept any written instrument signed by an Indian, indicating his or her wishes regarding the disposition of his or her property, as a will. Such a will has to be approved by the Minister of Indian Affairs following the testator's death.

Split Wills

In some cases, where permitted by law, a testator may choose to prepare two wills, only one of which will be submitted to the court for a grant of probate. The will prepared for submission to the court deals only with those assets for which a grant of probate, known in Ontario as a **certificate of appointment of estate trustee with a will**, is required for disposal of the asset.[15] For example, real estate held solely in the testator's name would be included in this will.

---

[14] *Indian Act*, R.S.C. 1985, c. I-5, s. 45.

[15] In Ontario, Form 74.4.1 under the Rules of Civil Procedure entitled an Application for a Certificate of Appointment of Estate Trustee with a Will (Individual Applicant), limited to assets referred to in the will, should be used.

The other will would cover assets for which a court grant is not required. Such assets might include household furnishings or shares in a privately held corporation. By the use of **split wills**, probate tax can be reduced. Caution must be exercised when drafting split wills in order to ensure that one will does not revoke the other will. The use of standard will clauses that revoke all previous wills must be avoided in split wills; otherwise, the last will executed may revoke the first will made in the pair of split wills.

Foreign and International Wills

If someone has property outside of Canada, it may be necessary to have, in addition to a will made in Canada, a will made in a foreign jurisdiction to cover the assets in that country. Care must be taken in drafting such wills in order to ensure that they can co-exist. The standard revocation clause should not be included in co-existing wills. In some cases a single will, called an international will, can be used to cover all of the testator's assets in different countries. There is a United Nations Convention, of which Canada is a signatory, that provides a Uniform Law on the Form of an International Will. Unfortunately, the list of signatories to the convention is short. To ensure that an international will made under the convention will suffice, the list of countries that have signed the convention must be reviewed.

EXECUTION OF A WILL

Formal and Legal Requirements

As set out earlier, in order for a will to be legally valid, all of the applicable legal and formal requirements must be met.

Witnessing Requirements and Restrictions

A formally attested will must be attested to by at least two witnesses, who must be of the age of majority. The witnesses should be of sound mind, and they should not be beneficiaries under the will or spouses of a beneficiary. Executors, provided that they are not a beneficiary, may witness a will.

Affidavit of Execution

Following the execution of the will, one of the witnesses should swear an affidavit confirming that the proper procedure for witnessing the will was followed. In most cases, it is prudent to have the affidavit of execution prepared as close in time to the signing of the will as possible as it may be difficult to track down witnesses in the future. (See Exhibit 31.3 for a sample affidavit of execution form.)

Safekeeping of the Will

The lawyer who drafts the will usually stores the original will in a fireproof file cabinet in her office. The lawyer has a duty to keep the client's property, including the client's will, safe. In some jurisdictions, wills may also be stored with the local Estates Court for a small fee.[16]

AMENDING A WILL

Alterations

If a will must be altered prior to its execution and if the production of an amended will is impossible, then the alteration should be neatly printed on the will and the testator and the witnesses should write their initials next to the change. If part of the will is to be deleted prior to its execution, the part of

---

[16] In Ontario, the *Estates Act*, R.S.O. 1990, c. E.21, s. 2, establishes a wills depository with the courts.

the will to be deleted should be neatly crossed out and the testator and the witnesses should write their initials next to the deletions.

If the will is altered after its execution, then the alteration should be neatly printed on the will and the testator and at least two witnesses should sign their full signatures at or near the changes. Any part of the will that is to be deleted should be neatly crossed out, with the testator and at least two witnesses signing their full signatures at or near the deletions. These methods of alteration should be used for minor changes only.

Codicils and New Wills

A **codicil** is a document made after a will that alters part of the will. Codicils are usually made for minor changes to the will, such as the substitution of an executor when the original executor has died. The codicil may be made on a holograph or a formally attested basis. The codicil should be dated and should specify the change in the will and then confirm all other terms of the will. Caution should be exercised in using codicils as the original will and the codicil will become public record if a court grant is sought. If, for example, you are replacing one beneficiary with another beneficiary, you may not want the original beneficiary to know that they were named in the will at one time. When changes of this nature are required the testator should consider making a new will.

REVOKING A WILL

Intentional Revocation

A will may be revoked by making a new will provided that the testator has the mental capacity to make a valid will. A will can also be revoked by a written declaration to revoke the will. In some jurisdictions, a will can also be revoked if the testator burns, tears, or otherwise destroys the will with the intention to do so. The testator may destroy the will himself, or instruct another person under his direction and in his presence to destroy it.[17]

Automatic Revocation and Exceptions

In many jurisdictions, including Ontario, marriage automatically revokes a will subject to some exceptions. If the will was made in contemplation of the marriage, states this fact and names the testator's fiancée, the will remains valid after marriage. As well, a surviving spouse may, within the one-year period following the deceased's death, elect to have a will remain valid that was executed prior to the marriage.[18]

Effect of Divorce on the Will

If someone divorces after the execution of his will, the will is still valid. However, the appointment of his former spouse as his executor is no longer valid unless the will sets out a contrary intention. In regard to gifts made to the former spouse in the will, the former spouse is treated as if she had predeceased the testator, effectively removing her from the will, unless a contrary intention appears in the will.

---

[17] *Succession Law Reform Act*, R.S.O. 1990, c. S.26, s. 15(d).

[18] *Succession Law Reform Act*, R.S.O. 1990, c. S.26, s. 16. In one case when the husband died, the wife was able to elect in favour of a will made prior to the marriage when the couple had been in a common-law relationship. This was of benefit to the wife as her share under the will was larger than what she would have received under intestacy provisions, which would have had a greater share going to his children from his first marriage.

INTESTACY

Intestacy Defined

Intestacy refers to the situation where someone has died without a valid will in place. An intestacy results when someone never made a will or when someone made a will, but the will is not valid. For example, there may have been an error in the execution of the will, or the testator may have lacked testamentary capacity when he made the will.

Legislation Concerning Intestacy

Every province and territory has legislation setting out how an estate will be divided in the event of an intestacy. In most cases, such legislation provides that, where there is a surviving spouse, that spouse in entitled to the bulk of the estate. Where there is a surviving spouse and children, most legislation provides that some portion of the estate is to be divided between the surviving spouse and the deceased's children. In Ontario, for example, *Part II* of the *Succession Law Reform Act* provides that where the deceased's estate is valued at more than $200,000, the surviving spouse (the term "spouse" in that part of the legislation referring only to legally married spouses[19]) receives the first $200,000 of the estate. This is referred to as the preferential share. If there is one child, then the child and the spouse equally share the portion of the estate over $200,000. This portion of the estate is known as the distributive share. Where there are two or more children, the spouse receives one-third of the distributive share and the children equally share the remaining two-thirds. If a child predeceases his parents, that child's **issue** (or descendants) stand in their parent's place with respect to the division of the estate. The term "issue" refers to one's direct descendants. A summary of the provisions for spouses and children regarding an intestacy is provided in Exhibit 31.1. In some cases a surviving spouse may fare better financially by making an election for an equalization of net family property instead of accepting the inheritance under the intestacy provisions. The surviving spouse should consult a lawyer to discuss his or her options.

Intestate Distribution Where There Is No Surviving Spouse

Where the deceased does not have a surviving spouse, legislation sets out the division of his or her estate. In Ontario, for example, when the deceased does not have a surviving spouse, his or her estate is divided equally among his or her children. If the deceased does not have any children or other descendants, such as grandchildren or other issue, and his or he r parents are still alive, then the parents inherit the estate. If the parents predeceased the **intestate**, then his or her siblings share the estate. If any of the siblings predeceased the intestate, leaving issue, then their issue share the sibling's share by representation **per stirpes**, meaning that such issue take their parent's share, divided equally among themselves. If there are no surviving siblings, the next in line to share in the estate are the deceased's nieces and nephews. They share the deceased's estate equally without representation for their issue. In summary, the following persons are those in line to inherit where the deceased did not have a surviving spouse:

1. The deceased's children
2. The deceased's other issue, such as grandchildren or great grandchildren
3. If there are no issue, the deceased's parents

---

[19] In some provinces, a person other than a legally married spouse may qualify to receive a preferential share of the estate.

Table of Consanguinity — Showing Degrees of Relationship by Blood

EXHIBIT 31.4

INSTRUCTIONS

Place the subject/decedent for whom you need to establish relationships in the blank box. The labelled boxes will then list the relationship by title to the subject and the degree of distance from the subject.

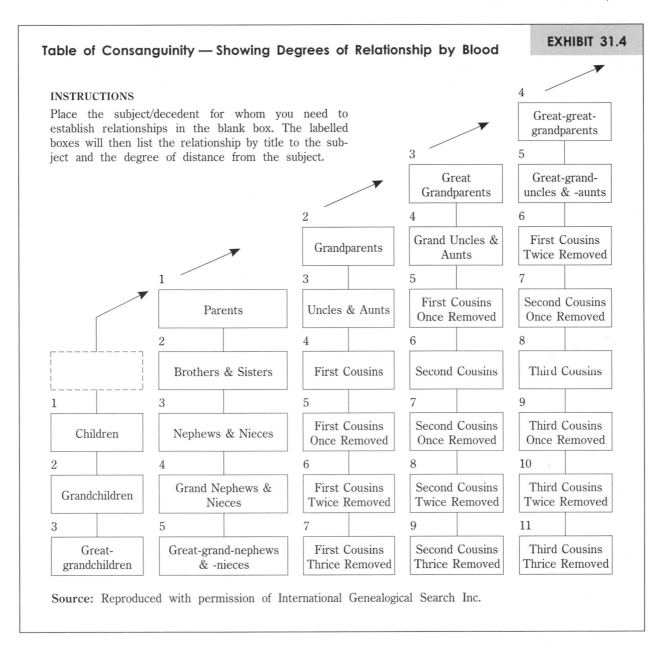

Source: Reproduced with permission of International Genealogical Search Inc.

4. If there are no issue or surviving parents, the deceased's siblings
5. If there are no surviving siblings, the deceased's nieces and nephews

If none of the aforementioned relatives survived the intestate, then the estate is divided equally among the deceased's closest next of kin. A table of **consanguinity** may be used in order to determine the degree of closeness of the surviving next of kin to the deceased. A table of consanguinity is contained in Exhibit 31.4. The table is to be used only where there are no surviving nieces or nephews; it can be used to determine the degree of closeness of a particular relative. Relatives of the same degree of closeness to the deceased share equally in the estate. For example, assume that the deceased was survived by a first cousin, a grand uncle, and a second cousin. Using the table of consanguinity you would find that the first cousin and the grand uncle are both four degrees of distance from the deceased. Being the closest living relatives, they would equally share the estate. The second cousin, at six degrees of distance, would be excluded. If the intestate has no living next of kin, in most cases, his or her estate becomes the property of the provincial government. In such cases the deceased's estate **escheats** to the provincial government.

POWERS OF ATTORNEY

What Is a Power of Attorney?

A power of attorney is a legal document in which one person, known as the **grantor**, appoints another person, known as the **attorney**, to have power to act on his or her behalf concerning his or her property and/or personal care decisions.

Types of Powers of Attorney

There are three main types of powers of attorney: a general power of attorney for property, a continuing power of attorney for property, and a continuing power of attorney for personal care. The rules, terminology, and forms for powers of attorney vary from jurisdiction to jurisdiction. For a summary of names of Canadian powers of attorney for property legislation, see Exhibit

EXHIBIT 31.5	**Summary of Canadian Powers of Attorney for Property Legislation**

PROVINCE/TERRITORY	LEGISLATION	DOCUMENT NAME
Alberta	*Powers of Attorney Act*	Enduring Power of Attorney
British Columbia	*Representation Agreement Act*	Representation Agreement for Property or Finances
Manitoba	*Powers of Attorney Act*	Springing or Enduring Power of Attorney
New Brunswick	*Property Act*	Power of Attorney
Newfoundland	*Enduring Powers of Attorney Act*	Enduring Power of Attorney
Northwest Territories	*Powers of Attorney Act*	Springing or Enduring Power of Attorney
Nova Scotia	*Powers of Attorney Act*	Enduring Power of Attorney
Nunavut	*Powers of Attorney Act*	Springing or Enduring Power of Attorney
Ontario	*Substitute Decisions Act*	Power of Attorney for Property
Prince Edward Island	*Powers of Attorney Act*	Power of Attorney
Quebec	*Quebec Civil Code*	Mandate given in anticipation of Incapacity[1]
Saskatchewan	*The Powers of Attorney Act, 2002*	Enduring Power of Attorney
Yukon	*Enduring Power of Attorney Act*	Enduring Power of Attorney

[1] The mandatary must apply to the court for certification of the grantor's incapacity.

Summary of Canadian Powers of Attorney for Personal Care Legislation

EXHIBIT 31.6

PROVINCE/TERRITORY	LEGISLATION	DOCUMENT NAME
Alberta	*Personal Directives Act*	Personal Directive
British Columbia	*Representation Agreement Act*	Representation Agreement for Health Care
Manitoba	*Health Care Directives Act*	Health Care Directive
New Brunswick	*Infirm Persons Act*	Power of Attorney for Personal Care
Newfoundland	*Advanced Health Care Directives Act*	Advance Health Care Directive
Northwest Territories	None	None
Nova Scotia	*Medical Consent Act*	Authorization to give medical consent
Nunavut	None	None
Ontario	*Substitute Decisions Act, 1992*	Power of Attorney for Personal Care
Prince Edward Island	*Consent to Treatment and Health Care Directives Act*	Health Care Directive
Quebec	*Quebec Civil Code*	Mandate given in anticipation of Incapacity
Saskatchewan	*The Health Care Directives and Substitute Decision Makers Act*	Health Care Directive
Yukon	None	None

31.5; for a summary of the names of Canadian powers of attorney for personal care legislation, see Exhibit 31.6. In some cases multiple powers of attorney, in different jurisdictions, may be required.

General Power of Attorney for Property

A general **power of attorney for property** is a legal document wherein someone gives another person or persons, known as the attorney or attorneys, power over all of his or her property and authorizes them to make decisions concerning such property. The attorney can act on the grantor's behalf concerning his or her property and can do almost anything in regard to such property that the grantor could do. The attorney, for example, can make decisions for the grantor in regard to his or her bank accounts, other investments, real estate, and most other types of property.

A general power of attorney for property is effective upon execution and is often used for one specific transaction. Such a power of attorney cannot be used during a subsequent incapacity. An example of a situation where a general power of attorney would be of assistance is where the owner of a property will be outside of the country at the time of the closing of the sale of the property. The owner can give a general power of attorney for property to someone to sign the sale-closing documents on his or her behalf.

A general power of attorney for property ends when a grantor terminates it or upon any termination date set out in the document itself. The general power of attorney for property will also terminate upon the death of the attorney or the grantor or upon the incapacity of the grantor or of the attorney (where an alternate attorney has not been named).

Continuing or Enduring Power of Attorney for Property

Most powers of attorney for property are continuing powers of attorney for property. They may also be known as enduring powers of attorney. These powers of attorney state that the attorney may continue to act for the grantor if he or she subsequently becomes mentally incapacitated. The advantage of having a continuing power of attorney for property is that it permits the attorney to continue to act if the grantor becomes mentally incapable of managing his or her property after the power of attorney has been made.[20]

Power of Attorney for Personal Care

A **power of attorney for personal care**, where recognized by law, is a legal document in which someone, called the grantor, gives someone else, namely, the attorney, the power to make personal care, health, and treatment decisions for her if she becomes mentally incapable of making such decisions on her own. An attorney using a power of attorney for personal care can make health care, diet, medical treatment, grooming, safety, and other personal care decisions for the grantor. A power of attorney for personal care is sometimes referred to as an advanced health care directive. The power of attorney for personal care may include a **living will**.

DRAFTING A CONTINUING POWER OF ATTORNEY FOR PROPERTY

Formats and forms for use as a power of attorney for property vary from jurisdiction to jurisdiction. Legislation for a particular jurisdiction should be consulted. In Ontario, for example, there is no prescribed form to use. Exhibit 31.7 shows a format that is routinely used to make a Continuing Power of Attorney for Property.

The Grantor

The grantor is the person making the power of attorney for property.

Age Restrictions Concerning the Grantor

The grantor of a power of attorney for property must be of the age of majority. In Ontario he or she must be 18 years of age or older.

Mental Capacity of the Grantor

In Ontario, the *Substitute Decisions Act, 1992*,[21] sets out the factors to be considered in order to determine if a person is capable of giving a continuing power of attorney for property. Under section 8(1) of the *Substitute Decisions*

---

[20] Note that in Newfoundland a power of attorney automatically terminates if the donor becomes incompetent. In Quebec the power of attorney document must be homologated by the court in order to come into effect.
[21] *Substitute Decisions Act, 1992*, S.O. 1992, c. 30.

	EXHIBIT 31.7
Continuing Power of Attorney for Property	

THIS CONTINUING POWER OF ATTORNEY FOR PROPERTY is given by Elizabeth Louise Collins, of the City of Brampton, in the Regional Municipality of Peel.

Appointment and Authorization

1. I APPOINT my spouse, Robert Allen Collins, to be my attorney for property. I authorize my attorney to do, on my behalf, anything that I could do if capable, except make a will, subject to any conditions and restrictions contained herein. I also authorize my attorney to exercise his powers under this power of attorney for the benefit of any person that I am under a legal obligation to provide for.

Substitution

2. If the above appointed attorney refuses to act, or is unable to act by reason of death, court removal, resignation, or incapacity, then I SUBSTITUTE AND APPOINT my brother, namely Austin Cory Reynolds, to act as my attorney in place of my attorney appointed in paragraph one herein and I authorize him, if required to act as my attorney, to do, on my behalf, anything which I could do if capable, except make a will, subject to any conditions and restrictions contained herein.

Continuing Power

3. It is my intention that this document be a continuing power of attorney for property under the *Substitute Decisions Act, 1992*, as amended, and any successor or similar legislation and it is my intention that this continuing power of attorney be used during any subsequent incapacity.

Authorization

4. I appoint my attorney as my legal representative for all purposes of the *Income Tax Act* (Canada) and I authorize my attorney to examine, settle, liquidate and adjust all or any accounts pending between me and any person including any accounts and income tax matters with the Canada Revenue Agency.

Litigation Guardian

5. I direct that my attorney shall be authorized to act as my litigation guardian if one is required to commence, defend or represent me in any court proceedings.

Family Law Act Consent

6. If my spouse seeks to dispose of or encumber any interest in a matrimonial home in which I have a right to possession under Part II of the *Family Law Act*, or any successor or similar legislation, I authorize my attorney for me and in my name to consent to the transaction, if it would be in my best interests to do so.

Conditions and Restrictions

7. I direct my attorney to utilize my financial resources to allow me to remain in my house as long as possible despite any incapacity on my part.

Gifts and Donations

8. I authorize my attorney to make reasonable gifts to my family and very close friends and to make charitable donations in my name, from my property, subject to the guiding principles set out in the *Substitute Decisions Act, 1992*.

Effective Date

9. This continuing power of attorney for property shall come into effect at the time of execution.

Revocation

10. I revoke any prior Continuing Power of Attorney for Property given by me.

EXHIBIT 31.7 (continued) **Continuing Power of Attorney for Property**

Compensation

11. I authorize my attorney to take annual compensation from my property in accordance with the fee scale prescribed by regulation for the compensation of attorneys pursuant to the provision of the *Substitute Decisions Act, 1992* as amended and its regulations or any succeeding or similar legislation.

EXECUTED at   this   day of   , 20   , in the presence of both witnesses, each present at the same time.

We, the witnesses to this power of attorney, have signed this power of attorney in the presence of the grantor and in the presence of each other on the date shown herein. Neither one of us has any reason to believe that the grantor is incapable of giving a continuing power of attorney for property.

_____
Elizabeth Louise Collins

WITNESS: WITNESS:

_____   )   _____

Name: _____   )   Name: _____

Address: _____   )   Address: _____

_____   )   _____

Occupation: _____   )   Occupation: _____

Act, 1992, a person is capable of giving a continuing power of attorney for property if he or she

(a) knows what kind of property he or she has and its approximate value;
(b) is aware of obligations owed to his or her dependants;
(c) knows that the attorney will be able to do on the person's behalf anything in respect of property that the person could do if capable, except make a will, subject to the conditions and restrictions set out in the power of attorney;
(d) knows that the attorney must account for his or her dealings with the person's property;
(e) knows that he or she may, if capable, revoke the continuing power of attorney;
(f) appreciates that unless the attorney manages the property prudently, its value may decline; and
(g) appreciates the possibility that the attorney could misuse the authority given to him or her.

The Attorney

The grantor can appoint one or more persons of the age of majority to be their attorney(s). Although the appointee is called an attorney, he or she does not have to be a lawyer. If two or more attorneys are named, they are to act jointly, unless the power of attorney provides otherwise. An alternate attorney or attorneys may be named to act as attorney in the event that the original attorney has died, resigned, or is unable to act. The attorney named should be someone who is capable of acting in that capacity. As the attorney will be entrusted with overseeing and managing all of the grantor's property, someone who is responsible, trustworthy, and able to manage money should be chosen. The attorney must keep an account of the grantor's property and financial dealings. The power of attorney may provide that an attorney is to be compensated or may state that the attorney has agreed not to be compensated for his or her efforts.

Commencement Date

Unless it stated otherwise, the power of attorney is effective from the date that it is signed even though the grantor may be capable of managing his or her affairs. If the attorney uses the power of attorney while the grantor is still capable, he or she does so as agent of the grantor and should obtain input from the grantor as to all decisions made.

A continuing power of attorney stipulates that in the event that the grantor subsequently becomes incapacitated, the power of attorney will continue to be effective. A grantor may execute a power of attorney and store it in a safe place, intending it to be used only if she becomes incapable of managing her own affairs. In some cases the grantor will store the power of attorney with a third party, such as a lawyer, and leave written instructions with the document indicating when it should be used. For example, the grantor might direct that the power of attorney should be used only if the grantor directs so in writing or her doctor certifies that she is incapable of managing her own property. The power of attorney document itself may include a condition that it will only come into effect upon any incapacity of the grantor as certified by his or her doctor. The document may set out the definition of "incapacity" or remain silent as to the definition, in which case the definition of "incapacity" contained in the legislation that governs powers of attorney would be used. In Ontario, the *Substitute Decisions Act, 1992* defines incapacity in section 6 of the act as the situation whereby "[a] person is incapable of managing property if the person is not able to understand information that is relevant to making a decision in the management of his or her property, or is not able to appreciate the reasonably foreseeable consequences of a decision or lack of decision."[22]

Limitations, Conditions, and Restrictions in the Continuing Power of Attorney for Property

An attorney under a continuing power of attorney for property can act on behalf of the incapable person for all matters in respect of property that the incapable person could do if capable, except make a will. The attorney should obtain a copy of the grantor's will to ensure that the grantor does not dispose of property that has been bequeathed in the will unless the disposition of such property is necessary to meet the needs of the grantor. An attorney cannot use a power of attorney to carry out any of the grantor's functions of an office, such as sitting as a director or replacing the grantor as estate trustee on someone's estate.

The attorney is bound by any conditions and restrictions set out in the power of attorney itself. A condition is a requirement that must be met before the power of attorney can be used. For example, the power of attorney might say that an assessment of incapacity must be made before the power of attorney can be used. The power of attorney may also contain restrictions. A restriction is a limitation placed on the attorney's authority. For example, the grantor may state in the power of attorney that his or her cottage should not be sold unless it is absolutely necessary to do so in order to meet the grantor's financial needs.

---

[22] *Substitute Decisions Act, 1992*, S.O. 1992, c. 30.

In all cases, attorneys are fiduciaries and must utilize their powers diligently, with honesty and integrity and in good faith for the grantor's benefit.

DRAFTING A POWER OF ATTORNEY FOR PERSONAL CARE

Formats and forms for use as a power of attorney for personal care vary from jurisdiction to jurisdiction. Legislation for your jurisdiction should be consulted. In Ontario, for example, there is no prescribed form to use. Exhibit 31.8 shows a format that is routinely used to make a Power of Attorney for Personal Care.

The Grantor

The grantor is the person making the power of attorney for personal care.

Age Restrictions Concerning the Grantor
Legislation concerning powers of attorney for personal care establishes the minimum age of the grantor. In some cases an actual age is stipulated, whereas in other jurisdictions a test of maturity is used to determine the age at which someone can make a personal care power of attorney. In Ontario, the grantor of the power of attorney for personal care must be 16 years of age or older.

Mental Capacity of the Grantor
The grantor must be mentally capable of making a power of attorney for personal care. There is a lower threshold of capacity to meet than that required for the granting of a power of attorney for property. In the case of a power of attorney for personal care, the *Substitute Decisions Act, 1992*, in section 47(1), provides that the grantor will be considered capable of making a power of attorney for personal care if he or she has the ability to understand whether or not the proposed attorney has a genuine concern for his or her welfare and appreciates that the attorney may need to make decisions for him or her.

The Attorney

A grantor can appoint one or more persons to be his or her attorney under a power of attorney for personal care. Although named as attorney, the appointee does not need to be a lawyer. In different jurisdictions the attorney may be known by a different term, such as proxy, representative, agent, deemed guardian, or substitute decision maker.

Legislation concerning powers of attorney for personal care sets out the minimum age of an attorney. In Ontario, the attorney acting on a power of attorney for personal care must be at least 16 years of age or older. Section 46(3) of the *Substitute Decisions Act, 1992* states that the attorney cannot be someone who provides health care, residential, social, training or support services to the grantor for compensation, unless the attorney is also the spouse, partner or relative of the grantor. The grantor can appoint one or more attorneys. If two or more attorneys are appointed, they shall act jointly unless the power of attorney provides otherwise. The grantor may also name an alternate attorney to act in the event that the original attorney dies, resigns or becomes incapable of acting as the attorney. The attorney must keep a record of the decisions made by him or her.

Attorneys acting on a power of attorney for personal care are not compensated, although the power of attorney may provide for the reimbursement of out-of-pocket expenses.

Power of Attorney for Personal Care	**EXHIBIT 31.8**

THIS POWER OF ATTORNEY FOR PERSONAL CARE is given by Elizabeth Louise Collins, of the City of Brampton, in the Regional Municipality of Peel.

Appointment

1. I APPOINT my spouse, Robert Allen Collins, to be my attorney for personal care pursuant to the *Substitute Decisions Act, 1992* and any succeeding or similar legislation.

Authority

2. In accordance with the *Substitute Decisions Act, 1992*, I authorize my attorney to make decisions, on my behalf, concerning my personal care, and to give or refuse consent on my behalf to any treatment to which the *Health Care Consent Act, 1996* applies.

Substitution

3. If my attorney refuses to act, or is unable to act by reason of death, court removal, incapacity or he has resigned or he is not available to act when there is the necessity for a decision to be made to which the *Health Care Consent Act, 1996* applies concerning my personal care or treatment then I SUBSTITUTE AND APPOINT my brother, Austin Cory Reynolds, to act as my attorney for personal care.

Reimbursement for Expenses

4. All expenses incurred by my attorney for personal care in carrying out his duties, including obtaining any assessment of my capacity, shall be payable by me or my attorney for property out of my assets.

Living Will Clause

5. My attorney should be guided by my desire that if I have a terminal condition from which there is no possibility whatsoever of recovery, I direct that lifesaving procedures be withheld or withdrawn and that I be permitted to die with dignity. I do, however, direct that I be given medication and/or treatment to alleviate pain. I indemnify my attorney from any liability he may incur in reliance upon my directions contained in this clause of my power of attorney.

Conditions or Restrictions

6. None

Revocation

7. I revoke any prior power of attorney for personal care given by me.

EXECUTED at   this   day of   , 20   in the presence of both witnesses, each present at the same time.

We are the subscribing witnesses to this power of attorney for personal care. We were both present and saw it executed by the grantor on the above noted date. Neither one of us has any reason to believe that the grantor is incapable of giving a power of attorney for personal care. We have both attained the age of majority and neither of us is a spouse or child of the grantor or considered in law as her spouse or child and neither of us is a person whose property is under guardianship or who has a guardian of the person.

_____
Elizabeth Louise Collins

WITNESS: WITNESS:

_____)   _____

Name: _____)   Name: _____

Address: _____)   Address: _____

_____)   _____

Occupation: _____)   Occupation: _____

Commencement Date

A power of attorney for personal care cannot be used unless the grantor is incapable. In some cases, due to illness or side effects of medication, the grantor may alternate between capacity and incapacity. The grantor may be capable of making some decisions but not others. Section 45 of the *Substitute Decisions Act, 1992* provides that a person is incapable of his or her own personal care "if the person is not able to understand information that is relevant to making a decision concerning his or her own health care, nutrition, shelter, clothing, hygiene or safety, or is not able to appreciate the reasonably foreseeable consequences of a decision or lack of a decision."

Limitations, Conditions, and Restrictions in the Power of Attorney for Personal Care

As mentioned above, the attorney can act under a power of attorney for personal care only in the event of incapacity on the part of the grantor to make personal care decisions. The power of attorney itself may stipulate conditions. For example, the grantor may set out some instructions in regard to certain types of treatment or the withholding of treatment. For example, a grantor may state that, in the event that there is no chance for her recovery, she does not wish to be resuscitated. On the other hand, the grantor may direct that all means for treatment, including experimental treatments, should be used to allow her to live as long as possible. As lawyers are not medical professionals, to ensure that the grantor's instructions in this regard are correct, the grantor should be advised to consult with his or her doctor or with an expert in bioethics.

EXECUTION OF POWERS OF ATTORNEY

In the case of both types of powers of attorney the document must be in writing, signed by the grantor and witnessed by at least two witnesses.

Witnessing Requirements

Legislation concerning the execution of a power of attorney varies from province to province and territory. In some provinces one witness to the execution of the power of attorney is permitted, while in other provinces, such as Ontario, both types of powers of attorney require two witnesses, who must be 18 years of age or older. The grantor must sign the power of attorney in the presence of the two witnesses, who both sign in the presence of each other and the grantor. In Ontario, the following people cannot act as witnesses:[23]

(a) The attorney or the attorney's spouse or partner[24]
(b) The grantor's spouse, partner, child, or someone the grantor treats as his or her child
(c) Someone under 18
(d) Someone who has a guardian of the grantor's property (which means that someone has been appointed by a court to represent the grantor due to his or her own mental incapacity)

---

[23] *Substitute Decisions Act, 1992*, S.O. 1992, c. 30, s. 10(2) for property and s. 48(2) for personal care (which refers back to s. 10(2)).

[24] The *Substitute Decisions Act* defines "spouse" as a person of the opposite sex to whom the person is married or has lived common law with for at least a year, or with whom the person has a child or has entered into a cohabitation agreement. "Partner" is defined as a person of the same sex if the two have lived common law for at least a year or have a child together or have entered into a cohabitation agreement or have lived together for at least one year and have a close personal relationship that is of primary importance in both person's lives.

(e) Someone who has a guardian of the person (which means that someone has been appointed by a court to make personal care decisions for the grantor due to his or her own mental incapacity)

In Ontario, the legislation provides that a court may declare a power of attorney to be effective in some cases, even though a non-permitted witness has acted.

TERMINATION AND REVOCATION OF POWERS OF ATTORNEY

A power of attorney may be revoked by the making of a new power of attorney provided that the grantor is mentally capable of doing so. The grantor, if mentally capable of doing so, may also revoke an existing power of attorney using a signed written revocation, which has been witnessed by two or more people. The death, resignation, or mental incapacity of the attorney may also terminate a power of attorney if there is not a joint or an alternate attorney named to act. The death of the grantor also terminates a power of attorney. If a court order is made appointing a guardian for the grantor, the power of attorney is terminated. A power of attorney cannot be revoked by destruction.

INCAPACITY WITHOUT A POWER OF ATTORNEY

In the event that someone has not made a power of attorney and becomes incapacitated, depending upon which decisions need to be made, there may be legislation in place to address such person's need for assistance. Under Ontario's *Health Care Consent Act*,[25] anyone who is hospitalized or is receiving care or undergoing treatment at a facility covered by the Act must consent to any procedure or treatment. If the patient is incapable of giving consent, the Act sets out who can give consent on the patient's behalf. Section 20 of the Act establishes a hierarchy of persons who are given the authority to make health care and treatment decisions for individuals incapable of doing so. A person appointed by the court as the person's guardian is first in line to give consent on that person's behalf, followed by the person's attorney appointed under a power of attorney for personal care. If the person does not have a guardian or an attorney, then the person's spouse or partner (including a common law partner of one year) is first in line to consent on the person's behalf, followed by the person's child or parent.

If someone becomes incapacitated without having a power of attorney in place, one or more persons can apply to the court to become the guardian of the person and the guardian of his or her property. The guardian of the person makes personal and health care decisions while the guardian of the property makes decisions in regard to his or her property.

In some cases, under legislation in some jurisdictions, a court application may not be required in order to become the guardian of someone's property. In Ontario, if a person is assessed as being incapable of managing his or her own affairs (for example, when the person enters a psychiatric hospital), a copy of the assessment is forwarded to the Office of the Public Guardian and Trustee, who becomes the Statutory Guardian of the person's property. A close family member or friend may apply to the Office of the Public Guardian

---

[25] *Health Care Consent Act, 1996*, S.O. 1996, c. 2, Sched. A.

and Trustee to take over as statutory guardian of the person's property. A management plan as to how the proposed guardian would manage the incapable person's affairs must be filed. In some cases, security may have to be posted in order for someone to be permitted to act as the person's guardian. There is no equivalent procedure for substitute personal care decision-makers. For personal care decisions, a power of attorney for personal care or a court order or use of the *Health Care Consent Act* is required. Note that, in some cases, a person deemed to be incapable of managing his or her own affairs may appeal that decision to the Consent and Capacity Board unless her or she has included special provisions in a power of attorney for personal care waiving the right to appeal.[26]

In a situation where someone poses a threat to his or her own life or health, there may be mental health legislation in place that could be used to have a doctor order to commit the person to a hospital for an assessment. Where the person does not have a doctor, someone may be able to appear before a justice of the peace for a warrant for the person's committal for an assessment.

CHAPTER SUMMARY

In this chapter the reader was introduced to estates law and the concept of estate planning. The key documents of an estate plan, particularly a will and powers of attorney, were examined. The advantages of making a will were explored. The process of making a will, including the legal and formal requirements and information required to make a will, were also covered. There was an examination of the different types of wills, and special attention was given to the requirements for execution of a valid will. The process of amending and revoking wills was also covered. Intestacy, the state of dying without a valid will in place, followed the will provisions in the chapter. A table was given setting out intestacy provisions across the country.

Powers of attorney for property and powers of attorney for personal care were defined. The factors to be considered in drafting powers of attorney were considered for each type of power of attorney; the requirements for execution of powers of attorney were also explored. The process of terminating and revoking powers of attorney was also covered. Some attention was given to the situation wherein someone without a valid power of attorney becomes incapacitated and unable to manage his or her affairs and is unable to make personal care decisions. In this context, statutory and court appointed guardians were discussed.

The chapter contained examples of some key estate planning documents, including a will, an affidavit of execution of a will, a continuing power of attorney for property and a power of attorney for personal care.

---

[26] Special provisions are not routinely included in a power of attorney. However, if a person suffers from a condition that could progress to a state where they are in denial of their condition, they might choose to include special provisions that permit the use of reasonable force to have them assessed and set out a waiver of any appeals of a capacity assessment.

GLOSSARY OF NEW TERMS AND KEY CONCEPTS

administrator	A male person appointed by a grant of the court to administer an intestate estate.
administratrix	A female person appointed by a grant of the court to administer an intestate estate.
affidavit of execution	A document sworn by a witness to a will that states that the proper witnessing procedure was followed. The affidavit also states that the witness believes that the testator is over 18 years of age.
attorney	A person named by the grantor in a power of attorney to act for the grantor by managing his or her property and/or making personal care decisions.
beneficiary	The recipient of a gift made in a will or a person for whom trust property is held.
bequest	A gift of a specific item of personal property made in a will.
certificate of appointment of estate trustee with a will	A document issued by the court that certifies that the will is the last valid will of the deceased and confirming the appointment of the estate trustee.
certificate of appointment of estate trustee without a will	A document issued by the court appointing someone to administer the intestate estate.
codicil	A document made after a will that alters a will.
common disaster clause	A provision in a will to deal with the situation wherein two people die within a short time of each other.
consanguinity	The degree of relationship between persons descended from a common ancestor.
escheat	The situation where ownership of the deceased's property passes to the provincial government.
estate	All of the property, both real and personal, that someone has an interest in.
estate planning	The process of arranging one's affairs for his or her death or incapacity and setting out instructions regarding the management of his or her property upon incapacity or after death.
estate trustee with a will	The executor or executrix named in a will.
estate trustee without a will	The person appointed by the court to manage an intestate estate.
execution	The proper signing of a legal document, usually in the presence of witness(es).
executor	A male person appointed in a will to manage the estate following the testator's death.
executrix	A female person appointed in a will to manage the estate following the testator's death.
formally attested will	A will that has been executed in the presence of at least two witnesses.
grantor	A person who is making a power of attorney.
holograph will	A will, valid in certain jurisdictions, that has been made entirely in the testator's own handwriting and signed by him or her.
intestacy	The situation where someone dies without having a valid will.
intestate	A person who has died without a valid will, or condition of having died without a valid will.
issue	Those persons who have all descended from a common ancestor.
legacies	Gifts of money set out in a will.
letters of administration	A court grant appointing someone to administer an intestate estate.
living will	A document containing instructions for medical treatment and health care or the withholding of such treatment or care. Usually part of a power of attorney for personal care.

military wills	Wills made by members of the Canadian Forces on active service or by sailors at sea.
per stirpes	The process whereby a deceased beneficiary's direct lineal descendants are entitled, by representation, to equally share the original gift that the beneficiary was entitled to.
personal representative	In some jurisdictions, the executor or executrix is termed the personal representative.
power of attorney for personal care	A legal document in which the grantor names someone to be his or her attorney to make health and personal care decisions for him or her in the event that he or she is incapable of doing so.
power of attorney for property	A legal document in which the grantor gives someone, namely the attorney, the power to make financial decisions for the grantor.
precatory memorandum	A memorandum containing the testator's wishes regarding the disposition of assets, or giving funeral, burial or other instructions. It is not legally binding.
rollover	A term used in estate and income tax law to describe the transfer of property from one person to another without the property being taxed as it normally would be when it is transferred. Spouses are permitted to roll over property from one to the other without it being taxed until the recipient spouse sells the property or dies.
split wills	The situation where someone makes two valid, co-existing wills, only one of which will be submitted to the court for probate.
testamentary capacity	The state of being mentally capable of making a will.
testamentary trust	A trust set up in a will to take effect upon death.
testator	A male person who makes his will.
testatrix	A female person who makes her will.
trustee	A person appointed in a trust instrument to manage trust assets on behalf of the beneficiaries of the trust.
will	A written document that sets out the directions for the management and distribution of a person's property following that person's death.

REVIEW QUESTIONS

1. Explain three advantages of making a will.

2. Why might a testator make more than one will?

3. Describe three situations where someone under the age of majority may be legally permitted to make a will.

4. List three factors that a testator should consider when choosing an executor.

5. Set out the four characteristics that illustrate whether someone has testamentary capacity to make a will.

6. Explain the witnessing procedure for a formally attested will.

7. What are the legal requirements for a valid holograph will?

8. How does a legal memorandum differ from a precatory one?

9. Describe two ways in which a will can be amended.

10. What are some ways in which a will can be revoked?

11. What is a continuing power of attorney for property?

12. What is a power of attorney for personal care?

13. Explain two ways in which a power of attorney can be revoked.

14. What happens to an intestate estate if there are no living next of kin?

DISCUSSION QUESTIONS

1. Ingrid, an Ontario resident, would like to make a will. She has a common law spouse named Oscar. Ingrid and Oscar have been together for 10 years. They do not have any children together. Ingrid has a son, Michael, from her previous marriage. She is divorced. Her eldest son, Angelo, predeceased her. Angelo is survived by two daughters: Karen, who is 12, and Kendra, who is 10. The net value of Ingrid's estate is $400,000.

    (a) Describe how Ingrid's estate would be divided if she died intestate.

    (b) Ingrid calls her lawyer on a Friday afternoon. She is leaving for a vacation in Tahiti the next day and is worried that she does not have a will. Is there anything that Ingrid can do about a will before she goes on vacation?

    (c) Michael is 15 years of age. Ingrid is worried as to what would happen to him if she died. What should she put in her will to deal with her concerns?

    (d) Ingrid would like to state in her will that her body may be donated for scientific research and that her organs may be used for transplant purposes. Discuss whether or not it is a good idea to put such clauses in a will.

    (e) Assume that Ingrid made a will leaving Oscar $100,000. Two years later, she and Oscar separate. Does Ingrid need to do anything with her will?

2. Marvin is divorced. He has two children, aged 7 and 8. He wants to make a will, but he has a number concerns, set out below, which must first be addressed.

    (a) Marvin plans to name his best friend, Roger, as his estate trustee. He is, however, worried that Roger may move to Argentina to be with his family. In that case, he would not want him acting as estate trustee. What should be done in the will to cover this possibility?

    (b) Marvin has sole custody of the children. He has heard that he needs both a custodian and a guardian. Explain the difference.

    (c) Marvin has heard that children inherit money at 18 unless other provisions are made for them. What can he do in his will to postpone the children's age of inheritance?

    (d) If Marvin is able to tie up the children's money until they are older, he is afraid that they would not be able to attend college or university. How could he ensure in his will that the money would be available for such purposes?

    (e) Marvin is worried that the children might end up in unhappy marriages and be required to share their inheritances and any earnings on such inheritances with their estranged spouses. Is there anything that can be put into Marvin's will to avoid this possibility?

3. Norman has heard that he should have powers of attorney to protect his assets and to have someone make decisions for him if he is incapable of doing so.

(a) What are two types of powers of attorney that Norman should consider making?

(b) Describe some of the advantages of each type of power of attorney.

(c) Explain the difference between conditions and restrictions, and give an example of each.

(d) What might happen if Norman becomes incapable without having made powers of attorney?

SUGGESTED READINGS

Best, Jeanne, & Dawn Dudley Oosterhoff. *Willing and Able. A Practical Guide to Powers of Attorney in Ontario*, 2d Ed. (Belleville, Ont.: Essence Publishing, 2004).

Botnick, David. *Wills for Ontario*, 15th Ed. (North Vancouver, B.C.: Self-Counsel Press, 2001).

Carter, Tom. *Wills Guide for Canada* (North Vancouver, B.C.: Self-Counsel Press, 2001).

Fazakas, Derek. *Wills and Estates*, 2d Ed. (Toronto, Ont.: Emond-Montgomery, 2004).

MacGregor, Mary L. *Preparation of Wills and Powers of Attorney, First Interview to Final Report*, 3d Ed. (Toronto, Ont.: Canada Law Book Inc., 2004).

Sweatman, Jasmine. *Guide to Powers of Attorney* (Toronto, Ont.: Canada Law Book Inc., 2002).

VIDEO

Advocacy Centre for the Elderly. *The Issues Behind Signing a Power of Attorney* (Toronto: Advocacy Centre for the Elderly, video, October 2000).

Estate Administration

DeeAnn M. Gonsalves
SENECA COLLEGE

Learning Objectives

After reading this chapter, the reader should be able to:

➢ identify the estate trustee
➢ understand the responsibilities of the estate trustee
➢ appreciate some of the potential difficulties that the estate trustee may face
➢ understand how to obtain a court certificate
➢ understand how to calculate estate administration tax
➢ identify the tasks involved with the distribution of the estate
➢ appreciate how to deal with some key creditors
➢ demonstrate an awareness of dependants' relief legislation
➢ demonstrate an awareness of matrimonial property legislation
➢ appreciate the possible challenges to a will

TABLE OF CONTENTS

INTRODUCTION

It has been said that "death pays all debts".[1] Many an estate executor has wished that this proverb were true. The reality is that our debts outlive us. The executor of an estate must deal with the deceased's debts as part of the administration of an estate. Dealing with a deceased's creditors is but one of the many tasks that an executor must attend to as part of the administration of an estate.

What Is Estate Administration?

Estate administration refers to the steps that must be taken following a death in order to deal with the deceased's remains, assets, and liabilities.

THE ESTATE TRUSTEE

Estate Trustee With a Will

If the deceased left a valid will, the document should be reviewed to determine if one or more estate trustees are named. The estate trustee with a will is the person named in the will to administer the estate. It is not a requirement of a valid will that an estate trustee be named. In most cases, however, one or more estate trustees are named in a will. The estate trustee with a will is more commonly known as the **executor**, for a male appointee, and the **executrix**, for a female appointee. In Ontario, however, legislation has changed the terminology to be used from executor or executrix to **estate trustee with a will**. Many financial institutions, however, still commonly use the term *executor*.[2]

Where there is an executor or executrix named in the will, that person receives his or her authority to act from the will itself immediately upon the death of the testator. If more than one executor is named in the will, they must be unanimous in their decisions, unless the will contains a majority clause.

If the executor has predeceased the deceased, any co-executors may act alone, although they will have to provide proof of the death of the other executor to the institutions that they deal with. If there is only one executor named in the will and he predeceases the deceased, the will should be reviewed to determine if an alternate executor has been named to act in his or her place. If an alternate executor has not been named, then by the process of **devolution**, the executor named in the deceased executor's will becomes the executor of both estates.

Estate Trustee Without a Will

If a will does not name an executor or if the deceased died intestate, meaning that he or she did not leave behind a valid will, then someone must apply to the court to be appointed as the estate trustee without a will. The estate trustee without a will is more commonly known as the **administrator**, in the case of a male appointee, and the **administratrix**, in the case of a female appointee. In order to be appointed as the estate trustee, the applicant must apply to the court for a **certificate of appointment of estate trustee without a will**, known in some jurisdictions as **letters of administration**.

---

[1] From a 17th century proverb first included in T. Fuller, *Gnomologia*, 1732.

[2] Given that many estate terms are specifically masculine or feminine, the author has been unable to use gender neutral terms in some parts of the text.

INITIAL RESPONSIBILITIES OF THE ESTATE TRUSTEE

Dealing with the Deceased's Remains

The estate trustee should review the deceased's will, driver's licence, and any organ donor card in order to determine if the deceased left any instructions regarding body donation for science or organ or tissues donation. If no instructions were left in this regard, the deceased's spouse or, if there is no spouse, the deceased's next of kin will be asked to make any decisions in this regard.

The estate trustee is responsible for the disposal of the deceased's remains. If the deceased died intestate or the will does not name an estate trustee, then the deceased's next of kin becomes responsible for the disposal of the remains. The decision must be made as to whether the deceased should be cremated, interred in the ground or entombed in a **mausoleum**. The estate trustee or next of kin will also make any funeral or memorial service arrangements. The deceased may have left instructions concerning such matters, but such instructions are only **precatory** in nature, meaning that they are simply an expression of the deceased's wishes and are not legally binding on the executor. As there are laws concerning the disposal of human remains, the deceased's final instructions in this regard cannot be legally binding. For example, if the deceased wanted to be interred in his favourite car, this would not be legally possible in most jurisdictions.

The estate trustee in planning the funeral should bear in mind the lifestyle to which the deceased was accustomed. If the executor spends an excessive amount on funeral expenses, he or she may become personally liable for such costs.

Minor Children and Dependants

The estate trustee must make arrangements for the deceased's minor children and dependants. If the deceased was the child's remaining custodial parent, the will, if there is one, should be reviewed to determine whether the deceased appointed a temporary **custodian**. In Ontario, such appointments are valid for 90 days following the death of the custodial parents. During that time, the temporary custodian should apply to the local family court in order to be appointed the permanent custodian of the child.[3] The courts will make an order based on what is in the child's best interests, taking into consideration the deceased's wishes as expressed in the will. Whether or not there is a will in place, any person can apply to the court for custody of the children.

A minor child also requires a **guardian of property**. If there is a will, it should be reviewed to determine if the deceased named someone to be the temporary guardian of the child's property. Quite often, the will names the same person as custodian and guardian. The proposed guardian must apply to the local family court for an order appointing him or her as the guardian of the child's property.[4] The guardian may have to post a bond with the court in order to secure his or her actions. Once appointed, the guardian can take control of the child's property, which may include bank accounts and other investments. The guardian should also arrange for the payment of any benefits the child may be entitled to, such as Canada Pension Plan survivor benefits.

The estate trustee must consider the financial needs of any dependants following the testator's death. She should review the will to determine what provisions have been made for dependants. The estate is responsible for the support of the deceased's dependants. In some cases the deceased's will

---

[3] *Children's Law Reform Act*, R.S.O. 1990, c. C.12, s. 61.
[4] *Children's Law Reform Act*, R.S.O. 1990, c. C.12, s. 47.

directs that a testamentary trust be set up for minor children or other dependants. The trust must hold and invest the beneficiaries' inheritances until they are a stipulated age. However, it is common for the trustee to be given the authority to use some of the trust funds to pay for a child's education or for other worthy expenses.

Locating and Reviewing the Will

As soon as possible following the death of the deceased, his or her last will should be located. The deceased's papers can be reviewed to determine if a will is among them. If a copy of a will is found, it will probably say on the copy where the original will is stored. A will prepared by a lawyer is usually stored in the lawyer's office. If a will is not found, it is wise to contact all of the lawyers that the deceased dealt with over his or her lifetime in order to determine if they are in possession of a will. In some jurisdictions, such as Ontario, a will may also be held on deposit at the deceased's local Estates Court. The estate trustee can ask the court to check its registry to determine if they are holding a will made by the deceased. In many cases where a will cannot be found, an advertisement looking for anyone with knowledge of a will of the deceased is published. In Ontario such advertisements routinely appear in the Law Society of Upper Canada's weekly *Ontario Reports* bulletin.

If a will is found, it may or may not have an affidavit of execution with it. If it does not have an affidavit of execution, the lawyer who prepared the will should be asked to prepare one as soon as possible as it will be required for an application for probate from the court.

Locating and Reviewing any Relevant Contracts

The deceased's papers should be reviewed to determine if he or she entered into any contracts that may affect the disposition of the estate. Such contracts could include a domestic contract, such as a marriage contract, cohabitation agreement, or separation agreement. If the deceased owned a business, he or she may be a party to a partnership or shareholder agreement that could affect the estate.

Locating and Securing the Assets

The estate trustee is responsible for locating and securing the deceased's assets. He or she must investigate the deceased's affairs to ensure that all assets are found. The executor or administrator is responsible for the safe-keeping of the assets. The executor may have to arrange to have locks changed, a safety deposit box rented, insurance limits reviewed and ownership documents updated. The estate trustee will also have to call in any loans made by the deceased, as receivables form part of the estate. An inventory of all assets should be made. Some estate trustees find it helpful to take photos or make a video of the deceased's assets.

Keeping Accounts

The estate trustee must document all estate transactions, particularly in regard to financial matters. All incoming and outgoing monies must be strictly accounted for. The estate trustee should retain receipts for all estate transactions. The estate trustee could be called upon at any time to provide **accounts** to beneficiaries, creditors, and the court.

COURT CERTIFICATES

Determining Whether a Certificate Is Required

If there is a valid will that appoints an estate trustee, the estate trustee should consider whether the will itself is sufficient to administer the estate. In such cases a certificate from the court will not be required. This could result in substantial savings to the estate as **estate administration tax** would not have to be paid. Some financial institutions accept a will, along with a death certificate and a signed agreement to indemnify the institution if the funds are wrongly paid out, in place of a court certificate. The executor should check with the financial institutions holding the deceased's assets to determine their policy in this regard. Some institutions will accept such documentation in place of a certificate if the estate is valued at under $20,000.

Without a will most financial institutions require a court certificate in order to transfer the deceased's assets to the estate. However, if the estate was fairly small, and the sole beneficiary is the deceased's spouse, the financial institution may permit a transfer to the spouse without a will upon receipt of a death certificate and an indemnification from the surviving spouse.

Obtaining Court Certificates

Certificate of Appointment of Estate Trustee With a Will

A **certificate of appointment of estate trustee with a will** is a document granted by the court. The certificate confirms that the will submitted to the court is the last valid will of the deceased. It also validates the appointment of the estate trustee. The certificate is referred to in some jurisdictions as a grant of probate or **letters probate**.

A certificate of appointment of estate trustee with a will provides proof to anyone relying on the certificate that this is the deceased's last will and that the person acting as executor has been approved by the court. Once a certificate is granted, if a later will is found, the estate trustee is not liable for having acted under the earlier will as long as he or she diligently searched for a later will.

The procedure for obtaining a certificate of appointment of estate trustee with a will varies from jurisdiction to jurisdiction. In Ontario there is a prescribed application form that must be completed. A sample application form is found in Exhibit 32.1. The application form solicits information regarding the name, address, and marital status of the deceased. Questions are also asked about the will, any codicils, and whether any witnesses to the will are beneficiaries of the estate. The value of the estate must be set out. The person applying to be the estate trustee must swear that he or she is of the age of majority and that he or she does not know of any later will. The person must also swear that he or she will faithfully administer the estate and render a complete and true account of the administration of the estate. A Notice of Application must also be completed. A sample Notice of Application is found in Exhibit 32.2. The Notice of Application must be served on all of the beneficiaries and contingent beneficiaries named in the will. The beneficiaries and contingent beneficiaries must also receive a copy of the portion of the will dealing with their gift. Residuary beneficiaries, being those beneficiaries named to receive the residue of the estate, must receive a copy of the entire will. If any of the beneficiaries are minors, the application must be served upon their parent or guardian and, also, upon the Office of the Children's Lawyer. If there are beneficiaries who are mentally incapacitated, the application must be served upon their attorney or guardian. If the mentally incapable person does not have an attorney or a guardian, then service should be made upon the Office of the Public Guardian and Trustee. If a charity is named as a beneficiary the charity and the Office of the Public Guardian and Trustee must be served.

Once the application has been made to the court, the court registrar reviews its registry to determine if the court is in possession of a more recent will. The court also searches to see if an application has been commenced in another jurisdiction. If the court does not find a more recent will and there are no other applications pending and no one has filed a notice of

EXHIBIT 32.1	Application Form for a Certificate of Appointment of Estate Trustee With a Will

FORM 74.4
Courts of Justice Act
APPLICATION FOR CERTIFICATE OF APPOINTMENT OF ESTATE TRUSTEE
WITH A WILL (INDIVIDUAL APPLICANT)

ONTARIO

SUPERIOR COURT OF JUSTICE

at Brampton

APPLICATION FOR CERTIFICATE OF APPOINTMENT OF ESTATE TRUSTEE WITH A WILL (INDIVIDUAL APPLICANT)

(Form 74.4 Under the Rules)

This application is filed by *(insert name and address)*

Brown & Hudson, Barristers & Solicitors, 6 Apple Avenue, Brampton, Ontario, L6X 3L4, Telephone: 905-453-2222

DETAILS ABOUT THE DECEASED PERSON

Complete in full as applicable

First given name	Second given name	Third given name	Surname
Elizabeth	Louise		Collins

And if the deceased was known by any other name(s), state below the full name(s) used including surname.

First given name	Second given name	Third given name	Surname
Liz			Collins

Address of fixed place of abode *(street or postal address)* *(city or town)*	*(county or district)*
17 Queen Street, Brampton, Ontario, L6X 7T4	Peel

If the deceased person had no fixed place of abode in Ontario, did he or she have property in Ontario? ☐ No ☐ Yes	**Last occupation of deceased person** Teacher

Place of death *(city or town; county or district)*	Date of Death *(day, month, year)*	Date of last will *(marked as Exhibit "A")* *(day, month, year)*
City of Brampton; Regional Municipality of Peel	31/07/2008	03/12/2007

Was the deceased person 18 years of age or older at the date of the will (or 21 years of age or older if the will is dated earlier than September 1, 1971)? If not, explain why certificate is being sought. Give details in an attached schedule.	☐ No ☒ Yes

Date of codicil (marked as Exhibit "B") *(day, month year)*	**Date of codicil** (marked as Exhibit "C") *(day, month, year)*
N/A	N/A

Marital status	☐ Unmarried	☒ Married	☐ Widowed	☐ Divorced

Did the deceased person marry after the date of the will? If yes, explain why certificate is being sought. Give details in an attached schedule.	☒ No ☐ Yes

Was a marriage of the deceased person terminated by a judgment absolute of divorce, or declared a nullity, after the date of the will? If yes, give details in an attached schedule.	☒ No ☐ Yes

Is any person who signed the will or a codicil as witness or for the testator, or the spouse of such person, a beneficiary under the will? If yes, give details in an attached schedule.	☒ No ☐ Yes

Application Form for a Certificate of Appointment of Estate Trustee With a Will

EXHIBIT 32.1 (continued)

VALUE OF ASSETS OF ESTATE

Do not include in the total amount: insurance payable to a named beneficiary or assigned for value, property held jointly and passing by survivorship, or real estate outside Ontario.

Personal Property	Real estate, net of encumbrances	Total
$ 200,000	$ 100,000	$ 300,000

Is there any person entitled to an interest in the estate who is not an applicant?	☐ No	☒ Yes

If a person named in the will or a codicil as estate trustee is not an applicant, explain.

If a person not named in the will or a codicil as estate trustee is an applicant, explain why that person is entitled to apply.

If the spouse of the deceased is an applicant, has the spouse elected to receive the entitlement under section 5 of the *Family Law Act*? If yes, explain why the spouse is entitled to apply.	☒ No	☐ Yes

AFFIDAVIT(S) OF APPLICANT(S)
(Attach a separate sheet for additional affidavits, if necessary)

I, an applicant named in this application, make oath and say/affirm:

1. I am 18 years of age or older.
2. The exhibit(s) referred to in this application are the last will and each codicil (where applicable) of the deceased person and I do not know of any later will or codicil.
3. I will faithfully administer the deceased person's property according to law and render a complete and true account of my administration when lawfully required.
4. If I am not named as estate trustee in the will or codicil, consents of persons who together have a majority interest in the value of the assets of the estate at the date of death are attached.
5. The information contained in this application and in any attached schedules is true, to the best of my knowledge and belief.

Name *(surname and forename(s))*	Occupation
Collins, Robert Allen	Firefighter

Address *(street or postal address)*	*(city or town)*	*(province)*	*(postal code)*
17 Queen Street	Brampton	Ontario	L6X 7T4

Sworn/Affirmed before me at the   City

of   Brampton

in the   Regional Municipality

of   Peel

this _____ day of _____ , 20 _____

_____
Signature of applicant

_____
A Commissioner for taking Affidavits *(or as may be)*

Name *(surname and forename(s))*	Occupation

Address *(street or postal address)*	*(city or town)*	*(province)*	*(postal code)*

Sworn/Affirmed before me at the _____

of _____

in the _____

of _____

this _____ day of _____ , 20 _____

_____
Signature of applicant

_____
A Commissioner for taking Affidavits *(or as may be)*

Source: Ontario Court Services Website, <http://www.ontariocourtforms.on.ca/english/civil/>.

EXHIBIT 32.2

FORM 74.7
Courts of Justice Act
NOTICE OF AN APPLICATION FOR A CERTIFICATE OF APPOINTMENT OF ESTATE TRUSTEE
WITH A WILL

ONTARIO

SUPERIOR COURT OF JUSTICE

IN THE ESTATE OF ELIZABETH LOUISE COLLINS, also known as LIZ COLLINS, deceased.
(insert name)

**NOTICE OF AN APPLICATION FOR A
CERTIFICATE OF APPOINTMENT OF ESTATE
TRUSTEE WITH A WILL**

1. The deceased died on July 31, 2008.

2. Attached to this notice are:

    (A) If the notice is sent to or in respect of a person entitled only to a specified item of property or stated amount of money, an extract of the part or parts of the will or codicil relating to the gift, or a copy of the will (and codicil(s), if any).

    (B) If the notice is sent to or in respect of any other beneficiary, a copy of the will (and codicil(s), if any).

    (C) If the notice is sent to the Children's Lawyer or the Public Guardian and Trustee, a copy of the will (and codicil(s), if any), and if it is not included in the notice, a statement of the estimated value of the interest of the person represented.

3. The applicant named in this notice is applying for a certificate of appointment of estate trustee with a will.

APPLICANT

Name	Address
Robert Allen Collins	17 Queen St., Brampton, Ontario L6X 7T4

4. The following persons who are less than 18 years of age are entitled, whether their interest is contingent or vested, to share in the distribution of the estate:

Name	Date of Birth *(day, month, year)*	Name and Address of Parent or Guardian	Estimated Value of Interest in Estate*
Angela Collins	18/01/1998	Robert Allen Collins 17 Queen Street Brampton, Ontario L6X 7T4	Beneficiary of $3,000 jewellery

* Note: *The Estimated Value of Interest in Estate may be omitted in the form if it is included in a separate schedule attached to the notice sent to the Children's Lawyer.*

5. The following persons who are mentally incapable within the meaning of section 6 of the *Substitute Decisions Act, 1992* in respect of an issue in the proceeding, and who have guardians or attorneys acting under powers of attorney with authority to act in the proceeding, are entitled, whether their interest is contingent or vested, to share in the distribution of the estate:

Name and Address of Person	Name and Address of Guardian or Attorney*
N/A	

* *Specify whether guardian or attorney*

6. The following persons who are mentally incapable within the meaning of section 6 of the *Substitute Decisions Act, 1992* in respect of an issue in the proceeding, and who do not have guardians or attorneys acting under powers of attorney with authority to act in the proceeding, are entitled, whether their interest is contingent or vested, to share in the distribution of the estate:

Name and Address of Person	Estimated Value of Interest in Estate*
N/A	

* Note: *The Estimated Value of Interest in Estate may be omitted in the form if it is included in a separate schedule attached to the notice sent to the Public Guardian and Trustee.*

7. Unborn or unascertained persons may be entitled to share in the distribution of the estate. *(Delete if not applicable)*

8. All other persons and charities entitled, whether their interest is contingent or vested, to share in the distribution of the estate are as follows:

Name	Address
Robert Allen Collins	17 Queen Street, Brampton, ON L6X 7T4
Canadian Cancer Society	2 Main Street, Brampton, ON, L6X 8W1

Notice of Application

EXHIBIT 32.2 (continued)

9. This notice is being sent, by regular lettermail, to all adult persons and charities named above in this notice (except to an applicant who is entitled to share in the distribution of the estate), to the Public Guardian and Trustee if paragraph 6 applies, to a parent or guardian of the minor and to the Children's Lawyer if paragraph 4 applies, to the guardian or attorney if paragraph 5 applies, and to the Children's Lawyer if paragraph 7 applies.

10. The following persons named in the Will or being a member of a class of beneficiaries under the Will may be entitled to be served but have not been served for the reasons shown below:

Name of person (as it appears in will, if applicable)   **Reasons not served**

If paragraph 10 does not apply insert "Not Applicable."

DATE:

. . . . .

Source: Ontario Court Services Website, <http://www.ontariocourtforms.on.ca/english/civil/>.

---

objection to the issuance of a certificate of estate trustee, the court will go ahead and issue a certificate of estate trustee with a will. It may take four to six weeks to obtain a certificate from the court. A copy of a certificate of appointment of estate trustee with a will is included in Exhibit 32.3. The original will is an exhibit to the certificate. Notarial copies of the certificate should be made as they will be required by most of the financial institutions that the estate will be dealing with.

Other Certificates

If the deceased obtained a certificate of estate trustee with a will or probate of a will from another Canadian province or territory or the United Kingdom or any British possession, that certificate and the will, if there is one, may be submitted to an Ontario court for **resealing**. The resealed certificate may be used to deal with the deceased's Ontario assets.

If the deceased obtained a certificate of estate trustee with a will or probate of a will from a jurisdiction outside of Canada, the United Kingdom or a British possession, that certificate and the will may be submitted to an Ontario court to facilitate the granting of an ancillary certificate. The ancillary certificate, also known as an **ancillary grant**, may be used to deal with the deceased's Ontario assets.

If the estate is involved in litigation, a **certificate of appointment of estate trustee during litigation** may be obtained. A court order is required for such a certificate. The estate trustee during litigation may perform routine estate administration tasks but cannot distribute the estate without a court order.

If the sole estate trustee dies intestate or becomes incapable of administering the estate, then someone will have to apply for a certificate of appointment of succeeding estate trustee with a will in order for the estate administration to be completed.

Certificate of Appointment of Estate Trustee Without a Will

Where the deceased did not leave a valid will, someone must apply to the court in order to be appointed as administrator of the estate. In Ontario

---

Certificate of Appointment of Estate Trustee With a Will

FORM 74.13

Courts of Justice Act

CERTIFICATE OF APPOINTMENT OF ESTATE TRUSTEE WITH A WILL

ONTARIO

SUPERIOR COURT OF JUSTICE

IN THE ESTATE OF   ELIZABETH   LOUISE   COLLINS   ,

deceased,

late of   the City of Brampton, Regional Municipality of Peel

occupation   Teacher

who died on   July 31, 2008

certificate of appointment
of estate trustee with a will

Applicant	Address	Occupation
Robert Allen Collins	17 Queen St., Brampton, ON L6X 7T4	Firefighter

     This CERTIFICATE OF APPOINTMENT OF ESTATE TRUSTEE WITH A WILL is hereby issued under the seal of the court to the applicant named above. A copy of the deceased's last will (and codicil(s), if any) is attached.

Date _____

                                      _____

                                      Registrar

                                      Address of court office

                                      7755 Hurontario Street, Brampton, ON L6V 2M7

Source: Ontario Court Services Website, <http://www.ontariocourtforms.on.ca/english/civil/>.

---

this person is known as the **estate trustee without a will**. The **certificate of appointment of estate trustee without a will** is required in order to provide someone with the authority to administer the estate. Legislation prescribes who should apply to be the estate trustee without a will. In Ontario the deceased's surviving spouse, including a common law spouse, and the deceased's next of kin have the first right to apply to be the estate trustee.[5] More than one person may be appointed to act.

     If the original estate trustee without a will dies or becomes incapable of completing the administration of the estate, a certificate of appointment of succeeding estate trustee without a will may be required.

     If the estate trustee without a will obtained the court certificate, also known as letters of administration, from another Canadian province or territory, or from the United Kingdom or a British possession, the estate trustee

---

[5] *Estates Act*, R.S.O. 1990, c. E.21, as amended, s. 29(1).

can ask an Ontario court to reseal the original certificate so that it can be used to administer the deceased's Ontario assets.

If the estate trustee without a will obtained the certificate from somewhere other than Canada, the United Kingdom, or a British possession, he or she must apply for a certificate of appointment of a foreign estate trustee's nominee as estate trustee without a will in order to deal with the deceased's Ontario assets. As there is no will, the nominee for estate trustee must be an Ontario resident.

Estate Administration Tax

In order to obtain a certificate from the court, probate tax must be paid in all Canadian jurisdictions. Such fees vary greatly across the country and are known in some places as **probate fees**, probate taxes, court fees or, in the case of Ontario, as an **estate administration tax**. The tax is based on the value of the deceased's estate subject to a few exclusions and deductions. If the value of the estate is unknown, an estimate may be made and tax paid to the court on that basis. If an estimate is given, an undertaking must be made to the court to provide the true value of the estate within six months, and to pay any additional tax or to apply for a refund of tax if the value of the estate given was too low or too high. (See Exhibit 32.4 for Canadian estate administration/probate tax rates.)

Estate Administration Tax Inclusions, Exclusions, and Deductions

☐ INCLUSIONS

Each jurisdiction varies as to which items must be included in the value of the estate for estate administration tax purposes. In Ontario, for example, most of the deceased's Ontario assets must be included in the value of the estate. There are very few exclusions and deductions. The only permitted deduction is an encumbrance, such as a mortgage, on any real property that is included in the estate for estate administration tax purposes.[6]

☐ EXCLUSIONS

There are some items that are excluded from the value of an estate for estate administration tax purposes. Insurance, such as life insurance, that is payable to a named beneficiary or assigned for value is excluded. This exception also applies to RRSPs, RRIFs, and pension plans with a named beneficiary. Any assets held in **joint tenancy**, such as real estate or joint bank accounts, are excluded as they pass to the joint owner by right of survivorship and do not form part of the estate. Property located outside of Ontario is also excluded. Such property will be dealt with in its own jurisdiction. A *donatio mortis causa*, being a gift made in contemplation of death and conditional upon death, is also excluded as it is, technically, property given away while the deceased, albeit close to death, was still alive. Real property cannot be the subject of a *donatio mortis causa*.

☐ DEDUCTIONS

Each jurisdiction has its own laws as to what can be deducted from the value of the estate for estate administration tax purposes. In Alberta, for example, all of the deceased's debts can be deducted from the value of his or her property at the time of his or her death. Other provinces permit some deductions, such as funeral expenses. In Ontario, there is only one allowable

---

6 *Estate Administration Tax Act, 1998*, S.O. 1998, c. 34, Sch., s. 1.

EXHIBIT 32.4		Canadian Estate Administration/Probate Tax Rates
PROVINCE / TERRITORY	**ESTATE VALUE**	**PROBATE TAX RATE**[1]
Alberta	Up to $10,000 $10,001 – $25,000 $25,001 – $125,000 $125,001 – $250,000 Over $250,000	$25 $100 $200 $300 $400
British Columbia	Up to $25,000 Over $25,000 $25,001 – $50,000 On value over $50,000	$0 $208 (administration fee) $6 per $1,000 (or 0.6%) $14 per $1,000 (or 1.4%)
Manitoba	Up to $10,000 On value over $10,000	$70 $7 per $1,000 (or 0.7%)
New Brunswick	Up to $5,000 $5,001 – $10,000 $10,001 – $15,000 $15,001 – $20,000 On value over $20,000	$25 $50 $75 $100 $5 per $1,000 (or 0.5%)
Newfoundland & Labrador	Up to $1,000 On value over $1,000	$60 $5 per $1,000 (or 0.5%)
Northwest Territories	Up to $10,000 $10,001 – $25,000 $25,001 – $125,000 $125,001 – $250,000 Over $250,000	$25 $100 $200 $300 $400
Nova Scotia	Up to $10,000 $10,001 – $25,000 $25,001 – $50,000 $50,001 – $100,000 On value over $100,000	$74.76 $187.97 $312.92 $875.76 $14.79 per $1,000 (or 1.479%)
Nunavut	Up to $10,000 $10,001 – $25,000 $25,001 – $125,000 $125,001 – $250,000 On value over $250,000	$25 $100 $200 $300 $400
Ontario	Up to $1,000 If estate is over $1,000, on the first $50,000 On value over $50,000	0 $ 5 per $1,000 (or 0.5%) $15 per $1,000 (or 1.5%)
Prince Edward Island	Up to $10,000 $10,001 – $25,000 $25,001 – $50,000 $50,001 – $100,000 On value over $100,000	$50 $100 $200 $400 $4 per $1,000 (or 0.4%)
Quebec	Notarial wills Non-notarial wills: natural person/corporation	0 $93/$104
Saskatchewan	For all amounts	$7 per $1,000 (or 0.7%)
Yukon Territory	Up to $25,000 Over 25,000	0 $140

[1] Fees are subject to change at any time. Check current legislation to ensure accuracy.

deduction. Only an encumbrance against any real property that is included in the value of the estate can be deducted. Other debts cannot be deducted. Assume that an Ontario resident died owning a car worth $15,000, with a car loan outstanding in the amount of $12,000. The estate trustee would have to include the full $15,000 value of the car in the estate's value even though there is a $12,000 debt associated with the vehicle. Credit card debt, in Ontario, also cannot be deducted from the value of the estate. In Ontario, therefore, the value of the estate for estate administration tax purposes is the value of the estate at the date of death less the outstanding balance on any encumbrance on real property that is included in the value of the estate. In some instances, if an Ontario resident has a number of consumer debts, he or she might consider replacing them with a mortgage that would be deductible from the value of the estate for estate administration tax purposes.

Posting Security

In most cases, if a certificate of estate trustee without a will is required, the court will demand that security be posted. The court wants to ensure that any beneficiaries or creditors who suffer losses as a result of any wrongdoing by the estate trustee can be compensated. In Ontario, section 35 of the *Estates Act* states that "every person to whom a grant of administration, including administration with the will annexed, is committed shall give a bond to the judge of the court..."[7]

☐ ESTATE ADMINISTRATION BONDS

Where there is not a will there is a presumption that security is required.[8] Such security is usually posted in the form of an **estate administration bond**. An estate administration bond is a promise by the estate trustee to fulfill his or her estate obligations and a promise by the estate trustee and a third party to compensate beneficiaries and creditors who suffer a loss if the estate trustee does not fulfill those obligations. Administration bonds can be purchased from some insurance, fidelity, or guarantee companies. The bond must be maintained in place until the estate is wound up. There is an annual premium for the bond, and the bond must be made payable to the court. In the event that a claim is made against a bond, the bond funds will be paid into court. The beneficiaries and creditors who have suffered a loss are then able to make a claim to the court for compensation. When an administration bond is purchased, it only needs to be in the amount of the estate.

☐ SURETIES

Instead of purchasing an estate administration bond, the estate trustee may post security with the court by providing sureties. A **surety** is a person who promises to pay money in the event that the principal, in this case the estate trustee, fails to perform his or her duties. If the estate is worth more than $100,000, two sureties must each pledge an amount equal to the value of the estate, thereby providing security equal to two times the value of the estate. In the case of an estate worth less than $100,000, one surety is sufficient.[9] If necessary, application can be made to the court to reduce the

---

[7] R.S.O. 1990, c. E.21, s. 35. Note that administration in this context of this section refers to the situation where there is an intestacy.

[8] In some circumstances where there is a will, security must still be posted: for example, if the estate trustee is not named in the will, or he or she is not a Canadian resident. However, in many cases the court may make an order reducing or dispensing with a bond.

[9] *Estates Act*, R.S.O. 1990, c. E.21, ss. 35 and 37, and Rule 74.11 of the Ontario *Rules of Civil Procedure*, R.R.O. 1990, Reg. 194.

amount of security required if posting all of the security required would cause hardships.

In some cases the court does not require security. If the estate trustee is a government body, such as the Office of the Public Guardian and Trustee, a bond is not required.[10] If the estate trustee is a trust company, the practice of the court is to waive the bond requirement.

In some cases, the court will not require a bond, or an application can be made to dispense with a bond. Where the deceased died intestate leaving behind a spouse and an estate worth less than the $200,000 preferential share, a bond will not be required if a satisfactory affidavit regarding the deceased's debts is filed with the court.[11] Where all of the beneficiaries are of the age of majority, are mentally capable, and they all consent to dispense with a bond, the court may dispense with the bond. The court, however, must be satisfied that the deceased's debts have been or will be paid from the estate.

CREDITORS OF THE ESTATE

The estate cannot be distributed to the beneficiaries until all of the outstanding debts of the deceased and the estate have been paid.

Locating Creditors

The estate trustee must ascertain the deceased's debts. All debts should be verified. Valid debts must be paid, and any questionable debts should be challenged. The estate trustee will need to review the deceased's records and incoming mail, including e-mail, in order to ascertain what the debts are. Inquiries should also be made at the deceased's banks and other financial institutions to determine if there are any outstanding loans, credit cards, or lines of credit. The estate trustee should also inquire as to whether there is credit life insurance on any of the outstanding debts.

Advertising for Creditors

In many cases, the estate trustee will advertise in a newspaper in the area where the deceased resided for creditors of the estate to come forward. If the deceased died intestate, it is common practice to advertise for creditors. In Ontario, if an advertisement for creditors has not been placed in regard to an intestate estate, the estate trustee must wait at least a full year before distributing the estate. If an advertisement is placed, the estate trustee can distribute the estate before the year is up. In some cases, even where there is a will, it is wise to advertise for creditors. An advertisement should be placed if the estate trustee is uncertain as to whether all of the deceased's creditors have been identified. In the case of the death of a business owner, it would be wise to advertise because the estate trustee, unless he or she was involved in the day-to-day activity of the business, may not be aware of all of the creditors. In all cases, advertising relieves the estate trustee from liability for debts that were not identified because the advertisement itself gave notice to all creditors to come forward and make their claims. If, however, the estate trustee is the sole beneficiary of the estate, the estate trustee may not advertise for creditors, as such creditors can trace their debt to gifts made to beneficiaries.

Advertisements for creditors are made in accordance with the local practice in the jurisdiction where the deceased resided and/or worked. In Toronto,

---

[10] *Estates Act*, R.S.O. 1990, c. E.21, s. 36(1).

[11] *Estates Act*, R.S.O. 1990, c. E.21, s. 36(2).

Ontario, for example, the practice is to insert an advertisement for creditors, on at least two separate occasions, in a major daily newspaper, at least one week apart. Creditors are given at least one month from the date of the first publication to come forward with their claims.

Canada Revenue Agency

A creditor common to most estates is the Canada Revenue Agency, once known as Revenue Canada. Everyone who dies has at least one income tax return that must be completed.

Final Income Tax Returns

In every estate, there is at least one income tax return to be completed for the deceased. The most common tax return to be done upon death is the terminal income tax return. This is the final income tax return for the deceased. This return is used to report the deceased's income from January 1st of the year of death up to and including the date of death. A regular T1 income tax form is used. The usual income tax deductions and personal tax credits may be claimed. There are, however, some differences from the usual income tax return. For example, medical expenses may be claimed for a 24-month period that includes the date of death. While alive, someone can claim medical expenses only for a 12-month period. As well, any capital losses can be deducted from the deceased's income. This practice is not permitted during a person's lifetime. During one's lifetime, he or she may deduct capital losses only from capital gains. Personal tax credits can be claimed for the full year even if the deceased passed away on January 1st.

The due date for the filing of the terminal income tax return is the later of April 30th of the year following the date of death or six months after the date of death. Thus, if the deceased died in November or December, the return would be due six months from the date of death. In all other cases the terminal income tax return would be due no later than April 30th of the year following the date of death. For example, if the deceased died on February 15th, Year 0, the terminal income tax return must be filed no later than April 30th, Year 1.

In some cases, certain types of income may be reported on an alternate income tax return, such as a rights or things return. An example of a right or thing would be income or dividends that have been declared or earned but not paid as of the date of death. If, for example, a worker who was paid only at the end of each month died on February 15th, his February pay would be a right or thing that could be included on a separate tax return. There are situations where other optional tax returns could be filed: for example, if the deceased was receiving income from a **trust** or he or she was a partner or a sole proprietor of a business. It is to a taxpayer's advantage, where possible, to file multiple income tax returns. By doing so, income can be spread out into smaller amounts over various returns and taxed at the lower rates used for lower incomes. As a result, the overall tax bill should be lower. As well, personal tax credits can be claimed on every income tax return filed. In some cases foreign tax returns or corporate tax returns must also be filed. The estate itself must file a T3 trust income tax return each year until it is wound up.

Deemed Disposition Upon Death

In addition to including income from the deceased's employment, investments, and other sources on the deceased's terminal income tax return, any capital gains that would arise from a disposition of all capital property upon death must be included. When someone dies, all the property that person owned at the time of death are deemed to be sold. This is called a **deemed**

disposition of property. In the case of capital property, this may result in a capital gain or a capital loss. Capital property is, in a general sense, property that is not used up during the deceased's lifetime. Examples of capital property include real estate, shares in a corporation, some jewellery, and antiques. The estate trustee calculates the gain in the value of the deceased's property by subtracting the net cost of the asset from its fair market value as of the date of death. The resulting figure is called the **capital gain** or, in the event of a negative figure, the capital loss. A capital gain must be reported for income tax purposes. A capital loss may be reported. Capital losses may be deducted from capital gains, or on the terminal income tax return they may be deducted from the deceased's income.

Where a person's assets are left to the surviving spouse or to a true **spousal trust**, there is an exemption from the deemed disposition upon death rule. In such cases, the assets are rolled over from the deceased's estate to the spouse or to a true spousal trust on a tax-deferred basis. Capital gains will not be realized on these assets until the spouse disposes of them or dies. In most cases taxes deferred are taxes saved as the surviving spouse will likely be in a lower tax bracket at the time of his or her death.

Capital Gains

When an item of capital property appreciates in value, if it is sold (or, in the case of death, is deemed to be sold) there is a resulting capital gain. Assume, for example, that someone purchased shares in Canadian Ore Company for $500 five years before her death. When the shareholder died the shares were worth $1,000. At the time of death, the deceased is deemed to have sold all of her property, including the shares in Canadian Ore Company. The deemed sale price is the fair market value of the shares as of the date of death. Accordingly, if the shares were worth $1,000 at the time of death, the estate trustee would subtract the share's cost price of $500 (no adjustments have been made for fees, commissions, or other costs), resulting in a capital gain of $500. In Canada at this time, only 50 percent of a capital gain has to be included in someone's income for income tax purposes. Therefore, from the $500 capital gain, the sum of $250 (50% of the capital gain) would be reported as income on the terminal income tax return.

For certain types of property, including qualified family farm property and certain Canadian small businesses, there is a $750,000 enhanced lifetime exemption from capital gains in certain situations.

Clearance Certificates

After the final income tax return(s) for the deceased and the estate have been submitted, the estate trustee should apply to the Canada Revenue Agency for a **clearance certificate**. This certificate provides proof that the required tax returns were submitted and that any outstanding taxes, penalties or interest have been paid. Once the certificate has been received, the estate trustee is absolved of any liability for unpaid income taxes. If the estate trustee is the sole beneficiary, a clearance certificate is not usually required since creditors, including the Canada Revenue Agency, can trace assets to the beneficiaries.

Other Creditors

The estate trustee must deal with all of the deceased's creditors. Such creditors could include banks, credit card companies, landlords, car leasing companies and others. If someone claims that the deceased owed him or her money at the time of death, the estate trustee must demand corroborating evidence before considering any payment to such a creditor. The estate trustee should always verify amounts owed, obtain receipts for payment, and request the return of any deposits paid by the deceased. In some cases, a deposit for services will have been required. As the deceased no longer needs the services, the deposit should be paid to the estate. Inquiries as to credit insurance should also be made. For example, many mortgagors purchase mortgage insurance. The proceeds of such insurance will usually pay the outstanding balance of the mortgage in the event of death. There may also be credit insurance on some of the deceased's credit cards.

INSURANCE AND OTHER BENEFITS

Life Insurance Policies

The deceased may have a life insurance policy through his or her place of employment. He or she may also have purchased insurance privately. If there is a designated beneficiary on such policies, the policy death benefit does not become part of the estate and need not be dealt with by the estate trustee. However, as the estate trustee possesses information concerning the deceased and the death, the estate trustee usually assists with the redemption of life insurance policies and other benefits. The insurance company should be contacted in order to determine what is required to pay out the death benefit. At a minimum the insurer usually requires the original insurance policy, a funeral director's statement of death, and the completion of its own claimant's statement.

Canada Pension Plan Benefits

There may be employee and government death benefits to which the estate is entitled. If the deceased contributed to the Canadian Pension Plan, an application should be made for the death benefit. If the deceased left behind a spouse and/or dependent children, an application should be made on their behalf for survivor benefits.

Other Death Benefits

Depending on the deceased's circumstances and the circumstances surrounding the deceased's death, there may be other death benefits available to the estate and/or the survivors. If the deceased died as a result of a motor vehicle accident, there may be automobile insurance benefits available. If the deceased died as a result of a workplace accident, there may be worker's compensation benefits available.[12] Some employee health and pension plans also provide death and survivor benefits. The estate trustee should contact the deceased's employer and/or benefit provider to determine whether there are any such benefits available.

IDENTIFYING AND LOCATING BENEFICIARIES

The estate trustee must determine who the beneficiaries of the estate are. If there is a will, the will should be reviewed as a starting point to determining beneficiaries. Without a will, inquiries must be made as to possible beneficiaries. In some cases birth, death, and marriage records may need to be searched.

---

[12] In Ontario, in the event of death resulting from a workplace accident, there may be benefits available to the estate and the surviving family from the Workplace Safety and Insurance Board.

Recognition of illegitimate children

The estate trustee has a duty to identify and locate all beneficiaries. Inquiries should be made by the estate trustee to determine if there are any children born outside of the deceased's or any beneficiary's marriage. Illegitimate children are fully recognized at law. There is no distinction, in estate legislation, as to whether children were born within or outside the confines of marriage. The deceased's will, however, may contain a clause excluding any children born out of wedlock. The will could also exclude illegitimate adult children by defining children to include only those named in the definitions or interpretations sections of their will. An example of such a clause might be as follows:

> Children as referred to in this will shall mean my son, Jason Oliver Collins, and my daughter, Angela Louise Collins.

Half-siblings

Half-siblings who share one parent are considered at law to be full-blooded relatives. If the will or intestacy laws provide for a share of the estate to go to a sibling, half-siblings would be included to the same extent as full-blooded siblings.

Alternate Beneficiaries

For every gift made in a will, an alternate beneficiary should be named. The alternate beneficiary would replace the original beneficiary if that beneficiary predeceased the testator. One or more alternate beneficiaries may be named.

Lapses

If an alternate beneficiary has not been named in a will and the beneficiary has predeceased the testator, the gift is said to **lapse**. The property that is the subject of the lapse becomes part of the **residue** of the estate. The residue will be distributed to the residuary beneficiaries.

Anti-lapse Provisions

In some cases, where the beneficiary is a child, grandchild, or sibling of the deceased, the law provides, through **anti-lapse provisions**, that the gift will not lapse but will pass to the deceased beneficiary's heirs, usually meaning the beneficiary's spouse and/or children.[13]

Gifts made to a charity do not lapse. If the charity no longer exists at the time of death, the estate trustee can apply to the court using the **cy-prés doctrine** to have the court make an order permitting the gift to be given to a charity with a similar purpose. The Office of the Public Guardian and Trustee must be served with such an application.

DISTRIBUTING THE ESTATE

Once an estate trustee has attended to the deceased's debts and other estate matters, he or she can arrange for the distribution of the estate.

According to the Will

The estate trustee, in distributing the estate, must follow the provisions of the deceased's will unless there is a court order authorizing him or her to do otherwise. Gifts given outright in the will to beneficiaries who have reached the age of majority should be given. The estate trustee should always secure a written release from a beneficiary before paying out an inheritance. If

[13] *Succession Law Reform Act*, R.S.O. 1990, c. S.26, s. 31.

a beneficiary is under the age of majority, there may be a trust set out in the will into which the minor's inheritance should be paid. In the event that the will does not contain instructions for a testamentary trust and the beneficiary is a minor, the share will have to be paid by the estate trustee into court until the minor is of the age of majority. The public accountant of the court will arrange for interest to be accumulated on such funds.

Ademption and Abatement

If the subject of a gift no longer exists at the date of death, the gift is said to have adeemed. When **ademption** has occurred, the gift cannot be made. The estate trustee cannot substitute other property for the lost item. For example, Marie stated in her will that her niece, Sylvia, was to receive her emerald ring. However, Marie lost the ring three years before her death. The gift would adeem and Sylvia would not receive the ring or anything in its place.

Sometimes there is not enough money in the estate to pay the creditors and the beneficiaries. If this situation occurs, the estate trustee must abate some of the beneficiaries' legacies in order to obtain the necessary funds to pay the creditors. The beneficiaries' legacies will be reduced. Gifts of residue are the first in line to be reduced or used entirely to pay creditors. If the residue is insufficient to pay the creditors, then general legacies, followed by **demonstrative legacies** and **specific legacies**, are reduced or taken to pay creditors. The last gift to abate is a gift of real property, also known as a devise.

The order of **abatement** of gifts is as follows:

1. Residue is the first part of the estate to be abated in order to pay creditors.
2. General legacies then abate.
3. Demonstrative legacies abate next.
4. Specific legacies abate last, with real estate devises being the final specific legacy to be abated.

An example of a situation where abatement would occur would be a case where the estate consisted of a car, a bank account containing $10,000 and cash of $10,000. The estate's creditors in this case are owed $14,000. The deceased's will left the car to her brother and $10,000 from her bank account to a friend. As the creditors must be paid first, the friend's demonstrative legacy of $10,000 would have to be reduced by $4,000 to pay the creditors. As there was no residue in the estate and no general legacies, the demonstrative legacy had to be abated. As the abatement of the gift of the bank account was sufficient to pay creditors, the specific legacy was passed on intact. The deceased's brother received the car, and the friend received the balance of $6,000 from the account.

Trusts and Life Interests

The executor must establish any testamentary trusts set out in the will. Assets may need to be liquidated to obtain the funds required for such trusts. There may also be life interests granted that will have to be respected. For example, the deceased's will may give the surviving spouse a **life interest** in her late husband's house. She then has the right to use the property until her death. If she does not live there, she may rent out the property.

Investing

The will itself may contain instructions or suggestions as to how to invest the assets of the estate. If the will is silent in this regard or the deceased died intestate, the *Trustee Act* for the deceased's jurisdiction sets out the standard to be followed by the estate trustee. In Ontario, for example, a trustee, including an estate trustee, must invest funds as a prudent investor would.[14]

Intestate Distribution

If a will cannot be found, the law presumes that the deceased never made a will or that he or she had a will but destroyed it. Where the deceased died without a valid will in place, the provincial or territorial intestacy laws must be adhered to. On occasion, even with a will, there may be a partial intestacy. This situation could occur where a will does not contain a residue clause. The executor would have to follow provincial or territorial intestacy laws to distribute the residue of the estate in such a case.

DISTRIBUTION OF PARTICULAR ASSETS

Bank Deposits

In most cases, the deceased will have been the owner of one or more bank accounts at the time of death. If the deceased had a joint bank account, the surviving owner of the account, in most cases, automatically becomes the sole owner of the account by right of survivorship.[15] The surviving owner should provide the bank with proof of death of the deceased and request that the account be put into the surviving owner's name alone.

The estate trustee should contact the deceased's banks to determine if they require a certificate of estate trustee in order to transfer the deceased's funds. In most cases, the estate trustee will set up an estate bank account. The deceased's accounts should be closed and the funds transferred to the estate bank account. If there is a certificate of appointment of estate trustee, the bank will generally require the certificate, proof of death and a letter requesting the closure of the account and the transfer of funds to the estate bank account. Without a certificate the bank will need a notarized copy of the will, proof of death, and an indemnity in favour of the bank, signed by the estate trustee, promising that if the funds are wrongly paid out the estate trustee will be liable for their repayment. Some banks also require a declaration of transmission. A declaration of transmission is a document from the estate trustee that sets out information about the deceased, the deceased's death, and the deceased's debts. A letter should be sent to the bank inquiring whether the deceased held any other accounts or investments, including Guaranteed Investment Certificates (GICs), other investments certificates, RRSPS, RRIFS or locked in pension funds with the bank. The letter should also request information as to whether there are any outstanding loans, credit cards, lines of credit or other debts with the bank. The estate trustee should also ask if the deceased has a safety deposit box at the bank.

Real Property

Real property, including land, houses, cottages, and condominiums, is one of the most complex estate assets to deal with. If the deceased owned any real property, the estate trustee must make inquiries as to various matters concerning the property. There are searches to be done, consents to be obtained

---

[14] *Trustee Act*, R.S.O. 1990, c. T.23.

[15] In some cases, even though the account is joint in the sense that it has two or more owners, it may not be a true joint account. For example, an elderly parent may put an adult child on as a signatory to the account to help with banking, but the child never deposits funds to, or uses, the account otherwise. The estate trustee in such a situation will have to determine if it was a true joint account passing solely to the child named on the account, or whether the account funds should become part of the estate.

and special documents to be prepared. The assistance of a lawyer regarding transfers of real property to and from an estate is recommended.

If there is a mortgage on the property the estate trustee should make inquiries to determine if there is insurance on the mortgage that would pay the outstanding balance on the mortgage. If a person inherits a property with a mortgage on it, that person receives the property subject to the mortgage.[16]

A subsearch of the title of the property should also be arranged to determine the names of the owners on title. The subsearch will also reveal whether there are any mortgages or other encumbrances on title. The manner in which title to the property is held should also be noted. If, for example, the property is owned in joint tenancy, in most cases, title to the property automatically passes to the remaining owner(s) upon the death of the other owner. Property held in joint tenancy usually does not become part of the deceased's estate. However, if the property is a matrimonial home held in joint tenancy with someone other than the surviving spouse, the joint tenancy is severed at the time of death and the deceased's share of the property becomes part of the estate.

Real property laws vary from province to province and territory in Canada. Accordingly, the law that must be utilized is that of the province or territory where the property is located. In Ontario, for example, there are currently two systems of land registration: the registry system and the land titles system. The laws for each system differ. For example, in the registry system, if the deceased left a valid will, the will itself may be used for the transfer of the property. A certificate of appointment of estate trustee with a will is not required. However, in the land titles system, in most circumstances, even where there is a will, a certificate of estate trustee is required to transfer the property.[17]

Corporate Shares and Bonds

The deceased may have owned shares in a public or a private corporation at the time of his or her death. The estate trustee may require the assistance of a transfer agent or stockbroker to assist with the transfer of shares. The estate trustee should ask what is required for the transfer of the shares to the estate trustee or, in some cases, directly to a beneficiary. The estate trustee will also need to determine the value of the shares as of their date of purchase and as of the date of death for estate administration and income tax purposes. A stockbroker can assist with the valuation. The documentation required to transfer shares usually includes the share certificates endorsed by the estate trustee, a notarized copy of the certificate of appointment of estate trustee, a declaration of transmission from the estate trustee setting out information about the deceased and the deceased's debts in order to permit the transfer, a letter of direction from the estate trustees to the agent confirming their agreement to the transfer, and a guaranty of the estate trustee's signature proving that it is indeed the signature of the estate trustee. The estate trustees can have their signatures guaranteed by their banks. In some cases, particularly if the estate trustee is not in possession of the share certificates, a power of attorney to transfer the shares may be required. If there is a will, in some instances, the transfer agent may be able to transfer the shares without a certificate of estate trustee. However, not all transfer agents will do so. Without a will, a certificate of estate trustee is

---

[16] Forms of property other than real property are usually inherited on a debt-free basis. For example, if someone inherits a car with a loan outstanding on it, the estate pays off the loan.

[17] Under the Ontario *Land Titles Act*, R.S.O. 1990, c. L.5, a certificate of estate trustee is not required in the land titles system where the land registrar waives the certificate and the value of the estate is under $50,000.

almost always required in order to transfer shares due to the fact that, in the absence of a will or a certificate of estate trustee, there is no one authorized to represent the estate.

The deceased at the time of death may have owned corporate bonds. The bond itself generally sets out the face value, the interest rate, and when the interest is to be paid. The documentation required to transfer corporate bonds is the same as the documentation set out above for shares, with the exception of the shares themselves. For bonds, the bonds endorsed by the estate trustee or a power of attorney to transfer the bonds is required.

Canada Savings Bonds

The estate trustee should search for any Canada Savings Bonds that the deceased may own. The deceased's pay stubs may indicate that he or she had been purchasing Canada Savings Bonds through payroll deductions. The Bank of Canada can provide information as to any bonds owned by the deceased. If the deceased had Canada Savings Bonds worth $200,000 or less and the recipient of the bonds or their proceeds will be the deceased's spouse, a certificate of estate trustee is not required. If the recipient is not the deceased's spouse, a certificate is not required if the bonds are worth under $20,000. In order to transfer or pay out the bonds, the Bank of Canada will require a notarized copy of the will, if there is one; the bonds; proof of death; a letter of direction from the estate trustee(s) indicating their consent to the redemption or transfer of the bonds; and the bank's completed Form 534C.

Registered Retirement Savings Plans

The deceased may have a Registered Retirement Savings Plan (RRSP) or a Registered Retirement Income Fund (RRIF). The estate trustee should review the plan documents and statements to determine if there is a named beneficiary. The deceased's will should also be reviewed to determine if a beneficiary has been named in the will. The latest named beneficiary is the beneficiary. The beneficiary will receive the full proceeds of the RRSP, although, in most cases, the proceeds of the RRSP will be taxable on the deceased's final income tax return as a result of the deemed disposition of assets upon death. The estate has to pay the income tax on the RRSP proceeds from other assets.

The income tax consequences of RRSPs should be taken into consideration during the estate planning process. If, for example, the deceased had two children and she left a GIC worth $50,000 to one child and named her other child as the beneficiary of her $50,000 RRSP, assuming that there were no other assets, the child receiving the RRSP would receive $50,000. The child receiving the GIC, however, would receive less than the full $50,000 because some of the GIC funds would have to be used to pay the income taxes that were incurred as a result of the inclusion of the value of the RRSP funds on the deceased's final income tax return.

The RRSP funds must be included in the deceased's income as a result of the deemed disposition of assets upon death. As income tax has yet to be paid on such funds, the accumulated funds must now be reported and income tax be paid on them. During one's lifetime, RRSP contributions are deducted from income for income tax purposes, and the funds accumulate on a tax-deferred basis. RRSP funds are taxed only when they are withdrawn from the fund or upon the death of the fund owner. Depending on the deceased's tax bracket, the child receiving the GIC might, for example, receive only $30,000 because the sum of $20,000 would have to be used to pay income taxes. The deceased could have named the estate as beneficiary of the RRSP. If the children were named as equal beneficiaries of the estate, the funds to pay the income tax on the RRSP would be taken out of the estate itself, and the remaining funds from both the GIC and the RRSP would be divided equally between the two children. The only disadvantage of this course of action is that the value of the RRSP would have to be included in the estate, thereby increasing the amount of estate administration tax payable.

There is an advantage, in some circumstances, to naming the estate as the beneficiary on an RRSP, as the beneficiaries under the will would not have to share any income generated by their inheritance with their spouse upon any marriage breakdown if the deceased's will contained the standard family law clause.

If the beneficiary of the RRSP or RRIF is the deceased's spouse, including most common law spouses, a rollover of the deceased's RRSP/RRIF funds into the surviving spouse's RRSP is permitted. This rollover has the advantage of postponing income tax payable on the RRSP until the surviving spouse removes funds from the plan or dies. Taxes deferred are usually taxes saved. By the time the surviving spouse cashes in the RRSP or dies, he or she will usually have retired and may be in a lower tax bracket than the deceased may have been in at the time of the deceased's death.

In order to cash out or transfer the RRSP, the holder of the plan will require proof of death, a completed claimant's statement, and a copy of the certificate of appointment of estate trustee, if there is one. If there is no certificate but there is a will, a copy of the will is required.

Other Assets

The deceased likely owned other property at the time of his or her death. He or she likely owned some clothing, jewellery, furniture, household appliances and other items. The deceased's will should be consulted to determine how these assets should be distributed. Some wills give the estate trustee discretion to dispose of clothing and other items of nominal value as he or she sees fit, including making a donation of same to a charitable organization. Without a will, such items often have to be sold by estate auction or otherwise, with the proceeds going into the estate to be distributed in accordance with intestacy laws. For special items of value, such as jewellery, collectibles or antiques, the estate trustee may have to obtain valuations from qualified appraisers. If the deceased owned a motor vehicle at the time of death, the local Ministry of Transportation should be consulted in order to determine what documentation will be required for the sale or transfer of the vehicle. The insurer of the vehicle should be advised of the death.

ESTATE TRUSTEE COMPENSATION

On Consent

An estate trustee is entitled to compensation for his or her efforts in administering the estate. Some jurisdictions have legislation setting out the rates of compensation. Other jurisdictions rely on the common law principles of compensation. In Ontario, the *Trustee Act*[18] states that a trustee, guardian or personal representative is entitled to such fair and reasonable allowance for the care, pains and trouble, and the time expended in and about the estate, as may be allowed by a judge of the Superior Court of Justice. The *Trustee Act* also provides that the amount of compensation may be settled, although the estate is not before the court in an action.[19] In some cases this permits the estate trustee and the beneficiaries of the estate to reach an agreement, outside of the courts, as to estate trustee compensation. Such an agree-

[18] R.S.O. 1990, c. T.23, s. 61(1).
[19] *Trustee Act*, R.S.O. 1990, c. T.23, s. 61(2).

ment would not be possible if the deceased died without a will and there were minor children involved because the Office of the Children's Lawyer usually requires the court to approve such compensation.

Where the quantum of estate trustee compensation can be agreed upon by the parties, the estate trustee should provide the beneficiaries with a summary of the funds entering and leaving the estate along with a list of estate expenditures. A statement of proposed compensation should also be included. The estate trustee should include a breakdown of the proposed distribution of the estate. The estate trustee also sends each beneficiary a release form with the statements. If the beneficiary agrees with the estate summary, proposed estate trustee compensation, and proposed distribution of the estate, he or she signs the release and returns it to the estate trustee. An estate trustee should never pay out estate funds to beneficiaries without first obtaining a signed release. Minor and incompetent beneficiaries cannot give a valid release. In those cases, a passing of accounts before the court may be necessary.

In some cases an estate trustee does not take any compensation for his or her work. If the estate trustee is the sole beneficiary of the estate, it would not be in the estate trustee's best interests to take executor's compensation, which is considered to be taxable income. Such income must be reported on the executor's annual personal income tax return. Inheritances, on the other hand, are not taxable income. If the estate trustee is a close family member and does not wish to take funds out of the estate, he or she may waive compensation, preferring to act out of natural love and affection.

If an estate trustee is also a beneficiary, unless the will says otherwise, there is a presumption, albeit a rebuttable one, that the estate trustee will not take compensation because the inheritance is compensation enough.

Passing of Accounts

Although it is easier, quicker, and less expensive to have the estate trustee's accounts and compensation approved by the beneficiaries, such a procedure cannot always take place. On occasion, a formal **passing of accounts** is required through the courts to approve the executor's accounts and compensation and permit the estate to be closed. If a beneficiary, for example, refuses to approve the executor's accounts, the executor will have no choice but to have the courts pass the accounts.

The passing of accounts in court is a process whereby the estate trustee submits his or her accounts, estate statements, and request for compensation to the court for scrutiny by a judge. Original receipts and statements, collectively known as "vouchers", must be available for review by the judge. Any trustee, including an estate trustee, can apply to the court to pass their accounts. As well, anyone who appears to have a financial interest in the estate can ask the court for an order that an estate trustee pass his or her accounts.[20] Such an order could be sought by beneficiaries, contingent beneficiaries, creditors or other parties who appear to have a financial interest in the estate.

The estate trustee's accounts should include a statement of the original assets in the estate, along with statements of **capital receipts** and disbursements, and revenue receipts and disbursements. Capital receipts include property that came into the estate, such as real estate. **Capital disbursements** relate to the payment of property out of the estate, such as the payment of estate administration taxes or the payment of legacies to beneficiaries. The accounts must also include a statement of revenue receipts and one of reve-

---

[20] Rule 74.15(1)(h) of The Ontario *Rules of Civil Procedure*, R.R.O. 1990, Reg. 194.

nue disbursements. **Revenue receipts** relate to monies earned by the estate on its assets, such as bank account interest. **Revenue disbursements** relate to funds spent to maintain income-generating property. An example of a revenue disbursement would be the payment of a bank service charge. The accounts should include a summary page of capital and revenue receipts and disbursements, along with a statement of investments, a statement of unrealized assets left in the estate, and statements of the proposed distribution of the estate, as well as the estate trustee's proposed compensation. If there are any liabilities to the estate that remain to be dealt with, they should be set out on a statement as well. The accounts are accompanied by a Notice of Application setting out the court date and an affidavit verifying the accounts. The application and the affidavit must be served on everyone who appears to have an interest in the estate, along with a blank notice of objection form inviting the recipient to object to the accounts. The judge at the passing of accounts will scrutinize the statements and determine if items have been properly appropriated between capital and revenue. The judge will determine if the compensation claimed by the estate trustee is reasonable and will make an order regarding the accounts and the executor's compensation. Although the court determines each case on its own merits, there are five factors that the court considers in determining executor's compensation:[21]

1. The size of the trust
2. The care, responsibility and risks assumed by the trustee
3. The time spent by the trustee carrying out his or her responsibilities
4. The skill and ability displayed by the trustee
5. The results obtained and the degree of success associated with the trustee's efforts

Over the years the courts have developed an informal tariff that they apply to compensation for estate trustees. This tariff is used in Ontario and other jurisdictions where compensation has not been fixed by legislation. The estate trustee is generally awarded compensation comprising the following:

1. The sum of 2.5% of the capital receipts of the estate
2. The sum of 2.5% of the capital disbursements of the estate
3. The sum of 2.5% of the revenue receipts of the estate
4. The sum of 2.5% of the revenue disbursements of the estate

Many people equate executor fees with the sum of 5 percent of the value of the estate. While not strictly accurate, in a straightforward estate that is administered in a very timely fashion, the executor may only have capital receipts and disbursements to deal with as revenue receipts and disbursements generally accrue in a more drawn out estate. If capital property entered the estate at the time of death and was distributed soon thereafter, the estate trustee would claim 2.5 percent of capital receipts plus 2.5 percent of capital disbursements for a total of 5 percent. If the estate is a particularly complex one, the estate trustee can also ask the court to award a care and management fee totalling two-fifths of 1 percent of the value of the estate. In some cases, the executor and the testator sign a compensation agreement predetermining the amount of estate trustee compensation. Trust companies that have been asked to act as estate trustee have the testator sign a compensa-

---

[21] *Laing Estate v. Laing Estate*, (sub nom. *Logan v. Laing Estate*) 11 E.T.R. (2d) 268 (Ont. Div. Ct) which was affirmed by the Ontario Court of Appeal at 41 OR (3d) 571.

tion agreement, with the rate of compensation usually being more than the usual tariff applied by the court. If there is more than one estate trustee, the trustees themselves must decide how the fee will be shared.

Unless there is an accusation of fraud, accounts passed by the court should not be re-examined at a later date.

Releases

Once the accounts have been approved by the court, the estate trustee can distribute the estate in accordance with the distribution statement presented to the court and in accordance with the deceased's will or the intestacy laws. Prior to paying the beneficiaries their inheritances, the estate trustee should have each beneficiary sign a release acknowledging that the beneficiary accepts the proposed distribution as his or her inheritance and absolves the estate trustee from liability. If the court has approved the proposed distribution, releases are not required.

ESTATE LITIGATION

The three most common types of estate litigation involve claims for support by dependants of the deceased, matrimonial property claims against the estate, and challenges to the will.

Dependants' Relief Claims

Who Are the Dependants?

Dependants are those persons when the deceased was supporting or was obligated by law to support at the time of his or her death. Support is given a broad interpretation. It includes not only the payment of financial support but other situations where support is less visible, such as the situation where a couple resided together and both purchased groceries and other household items. When one dies, the other loses the support of the deceased towards family purchases. Each jurisdiction has its own legislation setting out provisions for dependants to seek support from the estate. In Ontario, Part V of the *Succession Law Reform Act*[22] governs dependant's relief. Such legislation generally includes spouses, both married and common law, and same-sex spouses. Under Ontario legislation spouses are considered common law if they cohabited continuously for three or more years or were in a relationship of some permanence and had a child together. Under Ontario legislation other potential dependants include children, both natural and adopted, and those the deceased had a settled intention to treat as his or her own child. Children conceived as of the date of death but not yet born may be dependants upon their birth. Parents of the deceased, or grandparents and someone who demonstrated a settled intention to treat the deceased as their child, may also be dependants. Siblings may be dependants as well.

The person claiming dependant's relief from the estate must be a member of one of the categories of dependants set out above. As well, the deceased must have been supporting the alleged dependant at the time of death or have been under a legal obligation to support the dependant. Spouses have a legal obligation to support each other unless they have signed a domestic contract relieving each other from such an obligation. Parents are obligated to support their children, and adult children are obligated to support their parents under the Ontario *Family Law Act*.[23] There is no obligation at law to support one's siblings. However, if the deceased was supporting his or

---

[22] R.S.O. 1990, c. S.26.

her sibling, there may be a continuing obligation to do so. In some instances there may a court order or agreement that obligated the deceased to pay support. Whether or not such support was being paid, there is an obligation to the dependants in whose favour the order was made. The order can be enforced against the estate.

Making the Claim

The dependant claims support from the estate by commencing an application in the Superior Court of Justice in the county where the deceased lived. The application can be brought by the dependant or, in the case of a minor, by the dependant's parent. In some cases the Ministry of Community and Social Services brings an application on behalf of someone who is receiving social assistance benefits. The applicant must file an affidavit that sets out the grounds for the claim. The application must be made within six months from the date that the certificate of estate trustee was granted.[23] The court considers the claimant's assets, income, present and future needs, health, and other factors when setting the quantum of support. The court may grant temporary and/or permanent relief. Support may be ordered to be paid in a lump sum or by ongoing payments, which may be limited to a certain time period or may be ordered to be paid indefinitely. If support is ordered to be paid indefinitely and the dependant's circumstances change — for example, the dependant remarries — the estate can apply for a variation of the original order to reduce or end the support payments.

Matrimonial Property Legislation Claims

Every jurisdiction has family law legislation stipulating how assets should be divided upon a marriage breakdown. Marriage breakdown generally includes separation, divorce, and death. Some legislation, such as Ontario's *Family Law Act*,[24] contains property division provisions that apply only to legally married spouses. Legislation in some other jurisdictions also applies to common law spouses.[25]

Notifying the Surviving Spouse

If the deceased was married at the time of death, the estate trustee should advise the surviving spouse, in writing, that he or she should seek independent legal advice in regard to any claims that he or she might have against the estate. The estate trustee should not distribute any part of the estate in the six months following the deceased's death without obtaining the consent of the surviving spouse.

Election by the Surviving Spouse

A surviving spouse should consult with a lawyer to determine whether it would be in his or her best interests to elect an **equalization of net family property**. If the deceased's will provides that the surviving spouse is to share the estate with other beneficiaries, it may be financially advantageous for the spouse to decline his or her share under the will and elect an equalization payment. If, for example, the deceased had children and died intestate, and the estate is worth more than the preferential share ($200,000

---

[23] *Succession Law Reform Act*, R.S.O. 1990, c. S.26, s. 61.

[24] R.S.O. 1990, c. F.3, Part II covers the division of property.

[25] In Manitoba and Nova Scotia, common-law partners can register their partnership under the provincial *Vital Statistics Act*s to obtain the same property rights as legally married spouses. In British Columbia, the *Estates Administration Act* provides that after two years of residing together common law, spouses have the same rights on intestacy as legally married spouses.

in Ontario), it may be to the surviving spouse's advantage to elect an equalization of family property. Generally speaking, the surviving spouse is entitled to one-half of the difference in the net family property of the deceased and the surviving spouse's. For example, if the deceased's net family property was $400,000 and the surviving spouse's net family property was $100,000, the surviving spouse would be entitled to an equalization payment of $150,000. If the spouse were left only $100,000 under a will, then an equalization would be more favourable. However, in these circumstances, if the deceased died intestate, then the spouse would be better off financially to take the preferential share of $200,000 plus a portion of the distributive share of the estate, such share varying depending on whether there is one child, or two or more children.

There are certain items that each spouse can deduct or exclude from their net family property, such as property (other than the matrimonial home) owned on the date of marriage, damages received for personal injuries, and inheritances. A spouse's property is valued as of the day before the date of death in order to include assets such as the cash value of life insurance policies and property held in joint tenancy.

The surviving spouse, under Ontario's *Family Law Act*, has six months from the date of death to elect to make an equalization of net family property.[26] An election form is filed with the Ontario Estate Registrar, and a court application is commenced. The spouse will also have to file an affidavit and a financial statement with the court. The estate trustee will have to file a financial statement for the estate.

Challenges to the Will

Improper Execution

In order to be valid a will must be signed by the testator. If it is a holograph will, it must also be entirely handwritten by the testator. If it is a formally attested will, it must have been signed by the testator in the presence of two or more witnesses, who both sign in the presence of each other and the testator. An affidavit of execution sworn by one of the witnesses is generally sufficient evidence of proper execution. On occasion, however, solemn proof of the will's execution is required. Such proof is provided by having one of the witnesses testify under oath in court as to the will's proper execution. Sometimes a will is invalid because it was witnessed by only one person. On other occasions it is discovered that both witnesses were not present when the testator signed the will. A will that has not been properly executed may be set aside. The burden of proving proper execution of the will is placed upon the **propounder** of the will. The propounder is the person trying to uphold the will's validity.

Lack of Testamentary Capacity

At the time of giving instructions for the will and at the time of signing the will, the testator must possess the testamentary capacity to make a will. This generally means that the testator must be aware that he or she is making a will; the testator knows the extent of his or her property; and the testator understands the consequences of his or her will and his or her moral obligations.[27]

If a person who appears to have an interest in the estate believes that the testator did not have the requisite testamentary capacity to make a will, that person can ask the court to set aside the will. The testator's prior will

---

[26] *Family Law Act*, R.S.O. 1990, c. F.3, s. 7(1).
[27] *Banks v. Goodfellow*, (1870) L.R. 5 Q.B. 549.

would then become the binding will. If there was no prior will, the estate would then be distributed in accordance with intestacy laws.

Lack of Knowledge and Approval of the Will's Contents

In order for a will to be valid, the testator must have had knowledge of, and have approved, the will's contents. Lawyers generally ensure that this is done by mailing a draft of the will to the client along with written instructions to the testator to read over the will to ensure that it meets with their approval. At the signing of the will the lawyer also reviews the will with the testator and has the testator initial the bottom of each page before signing the will.

In some cases there is both a lack of testamentary capacity and a lack of knowledge and approval of the will's contents.

Undue Influence

If a testator was subjected to **undue influence** by someone to make and execute a will, the will is invalid. The undue influence may be physical or emotional. Undue influence occurs when the testator is pressured or coerced by someone to sign a will that does not reflect his or her true wishes. In order to set aside the will on the grounds of undue influence, the person impugning the will must prove on a balance of probabilities that the testator was unduly influenced to sign the will. The **impugner** is the party that is trying to strike down the will. Undue influence may be suspected, for example, where the testator makes a new will, leaving the bulk of his or her estate to his or her new caregiver. The caregiver may have arranged the appointment with the lawyer and attended with the testator to ensure that he or she was included in the will. In these circumstances, the testator may have been unduly influenced to make the new will. The testator may have believed that he or she would be mistreated or abandoned by the caregiver if he or she did not change the will or make a new will.

CHAPTER SUMMARY

In this chapter the reader was introduced to the main elements of estate administration. There was a discussion of the roles and responsibilities of estate trustees with or without a will. Some attention was given to the responsibilities of the estate trustee, including dealing with the deceased's remains and dependants. The importance of locating and reviewing the deceased's will, contracts, and assets was covered. The process of obtaining court certificates, including the calculation of estate administration tax and the provision of administration bonds, was also examined. Finding and paying estate creditors, including the Canada Revenue Agency, is discussed. Insurance, particularly life insurance and other benefits such as Canada Pension Plan benefits and allowances, were examined. The steps in identifying and locating beneficiaries were given. Difficulties with the distribution of the estate, including lapses, ademption, and abatement, were also covered. Other areas of responsibility, such as investing and intestate distribution, were briefly examined. Some instruction was given as to the distribution of particular assets, such as real property, shares, bonds, bank deposits, and RRSPS. The process of passing accounts on consent and in court were discussed. The chapter concluded with a look at three common areas of estate litigation: dependant's relief claims, matrimonial property legislation claims, and challenges to the will.

GLOSSARY OF NEW TERMS AND KEY CONCEPTS

abatement	The process whereby residue and gifts made under a will are reduced in order to pay estate creditors.
accounts	Records of the property entering and leaving the estate.
ademption	The situation where the subject of a gift made in a will no longer exists at the date of death. For example, a testator leaves a car to his nephew in his will, but the car is sold before the testator's death.
administrator	A male appointed by the court to administer an intestate estate.
administratrix	A female appointed by the court to administer an intestate estate.
ancillary grant	The court grant given where the estate trustee has a will and a court certificate from outside of Canada, the United Kingdom and any British possession.
anti-lapse provisions	Legislation that permits a deceased beneficiary's heirs to take their inheritance where the beneficiary has predeceased the testator. In Ontario the anti-lapse provisions apply to a beneficiary's child, grandchild, or sibling.
capital disbursements	Property leaving the estate.
capital gain	The increase in the value of property from the date of purchase to the date of disposition.
capital receipts	Property coming into the estate.
certificate of appointment of estate trustee with a will	A document granted by the court that certifies that the will is the last valid will of the deceased and that confirms the appointment of the estate trustee.
certificate of appointment of estate trustee without a will	A document granted by the court appointing someone to administer the intestate estate.
certificate of estate trustee during litigation	A document appointing an estate trustee, by court order, to act for the estate during estate litigation. This trustee cannot distribute the estate without a court order.
clearance certificate	A certificate from the Canada Revenue Agency that confirms that all of the deceased's income tax returns have been filed and that any taxes, interest, or penalties have been paid.
custodian	The person appointed to have custody and care of minor children.
cy-prés doctrine	Provision whereby a gift made in a will to a charity may be redirected by the court to another charity with similar purposes to the original charity where the original charity no longer exists.
donatio mortis causa	A gift made in contemplation of death and conditional upon the donor's death occurring.
deemed disposition	The situation where the deceased is considered to have disposed of all of his or her property at the time of his or her death for income tax purposes.
demonstrative legacy	A gift to be paid from a specific source. For example, "I leave to my niece $5,000 from my investment account at ABC Bank Ltd."
devolution	The situation where an executor dies, and his or her executor takes over the administration of an estate.
equalization of net family property	The process whereby spouses determine the net value of their property as of the date of marriage and the valuation date (in estate situations, the day before the date of death). If the value of the deceased's net family property is greater than the surviving spouse's, the surviving spouse may elect an equalization of net family property in place of a gift under a will or the application of intestacy distribution laws.
estate administration bond	A promise by the estate trustee to fulfill the estate obligations, and a promise by the estate trustee and a third party to indemnify any beneficiaries and creditors who have

suffered a loss as a result of any failure by the estate trustee to carry out his or her duties.

estate administration tax	A tax that must be paid to the court based on the value of the deceased's estate when obtaining a certificate of estate trustee from the court.
estate trustee with a will	The person named in the will to administer the estate.
estate trustee without a will	The person appointed by the court to administer an intestate estate.
executor	A male person appointed in a will to administer the estate.
executrix	A female person appointed in a will to administer the estate.
guardian of property	The person appointed to manage someone else's person or property. For example, a minor child requires a guardian of property.
impugner	The person trying to strike down the will.
joint tenancy	A method of holding title to property whereby if one owner dies the remaining joint owners automatically become the owner(s) of the property by right of survivorship.
lapse	The situation that occurs where a beneficiary has predeceased the testator and an alternate beneficiary has not been named in the will.
letters of administration	A court grant appointing someone to administer an intestate estate.
letters probate	A court grant confirming the appointment of an executor named in a will to act and confirming the validity of the will as the last valid will.
life interest	The situation where someone is granted the use of a property for the remainder of his or her life.
mausoleum	An above ground tomb.
passing of accounts	The process whereby a trustee submits his or her records, statements, accounts, and receipts to the court for approval.
precatory	Precatory requests or directions are an expression of the testator's wishes regarding his or her estate. These requests or directions are not legally binding.
probate fees	A tax charged by the court on the value of the estate when obtaining a certificate of estate trustee from the court.
propounder	The person trying to uphold the will.
resealing	The application of the Ontario court seal to a certificate of estate trustee with or without a will made in another province, the United Kingdom, or a British possession.
residue	The part of the estate remaining after all legacies have been paid.
revenue disbursements	Money spent to maintain an income-generating property.
revenue receipts	Income generated by estate assets.
specific legacy	A gift of a particular item: for example, my Rolex watch to my son.
spousal trust	A trust in favour of a spouse where all of the income must be paid only to the spouse during the spouse's lifetime, and no one else is entitled to any of the capital during the spouse's lifetime.
surety	Someone who promises to pay money if the estate trustee fails to carry out his or her duties properly.
trust	A relationship wherein property is transferred from one person, the settlor or testator, to another person, the trustee, to be held by the trustee for the benefit of a third party, namely the beneficiary. The relationship is governed by the instrument that establishes the trust and by the legislation and case law governing trusts.
undue influence	The situation wherein a testator was emotionally or physically coerced by someone to make or change his or her will such that it no longer reflects the testator's wishes.

REVIEW QUESTIONS

1. How does an estate trustee with a will differ from an estate trustee without a will?

2. What type of funeral arrangements should an estate trustee make?

3. How can you find someone's will?

4. Describe a situation where an estate asset could be transferred without a court certificate.

5. Calculate the estate administration tax that would have to be paid in your jurisdiction on an estate with a net value of $500,000.

6. What is the purpose of an estate administration bond, and how can the estate trustee post security for the administration of the estate?

7. Describe two situations in which the court might dispense with an administration bond.

8. Why would an estate trustee advertise for creditors?

9. Describe two income tax returns that the estate trustee may file.

10. Provide an example of ademption.

11. Why might it be necessary for the estate trustee to pass his or her accounts in court?

12. When should a spouse consider electing an equalization of net family property?

13. Who could be eligible to make a claim for dependant's relief?

14. What is undue influence?

15. What is abatement?

16. Explain estate trustee compensation.

DISCUSSION QUESTIONS

1. Rachel died intestate on October 15, Year 1. She was survived by her spouse, James, and three children: Carol, age 22; Jeremy, age 19; and Ellen, age 15. Rachel had the following assets at the time of her death:

   - a house worth $200,000 held in joint tenancy with James
   - a condominium in New York, New York, U.S.A., worth $200,000
   - life insurance of $100,000 payable to her estate
   - RRSP worth $50,000 payable to James
   - a sole bank account with $20,000 in it
   - Canada Savings Bonds worth $10,000
   - a car worth $10,000
   - household items valued at $10,000

   Her only debt is a $5,000 car loan.

   Answer the following questions:

   (a) Calculate the value of the estate for estate administration tax purposes.

   (b) Explain what has been excluded from the estate for estate administration tax purposes.

(c) Explain what has been deducted from the estate for estate administration tax purposes.

(d) Calculate the estate administration tax to be paid, assuming that she died in Ontario.

(e) Who will be the beneficiaries of the estate, and what proportion of the estate will each beneficiary receive?

(f) Who can be appointed as estate trustee?

(g) What matters should be considered for Ellen?

(h) Will a court certificate be required for the transfer of all of the assets? If not, explain.

(i) If Rachel owned an antique desk that she purchased for $1,000 a few years ago, and at the time of her death it was worth $5,000, what would be the income tax treatment of that asset?

2. Allen, an Ontario resident, died on March 2nd, Year 0. He was survived by his spouse, Kelly. They did not have any children. In his will, Allen left Kelly $100,000. At the time of his death, the net value of his estate was $500,000. Answer the following questions:

(a) Should Kelly consider electing an equalization of net family property? Why or why not?

(b) If Kelly decides to make an election, how long does she have to act?

(c) If Kelly decides to make an election, what date will be used as the property valuation date?

(d) What effect would an election by Kelly have on the gift left to her in the will?

(e) What effect would an equalization by Kelly have on the gifts made in the will to other beneficiaries?

3. Frank recently passed away. He was single without dependants. His will leaves his car to his friend Joe. It also leaves $5,000 from his ING Investment Account to his friend Gretchen and $3,000 to his friend Helen. He leaves the residue to his friend William. At death Frank's car is worth $5,000, his ING Investment account has $5,000, and he has $2,000 in loose cash. He owes a credit card debt of $3,000. Describe how the estate will be paid out.

SUGGESTED READINGS

Fazakas, Derek. *Wills and Estates*, 2d Ed. (Toronto, Ont.: Emond-Montgomery, 2004).

Gibbs, Karen M., et al. *The Practical Guide to Ontario Estate Administration*, 4th Ed. (Toronto, Ont.: Carswell, 2001).

Spenceley, Robert. *Estate Administration In Ontario: A Practical Guide* (North York, Ont.: CCH Canadian Limited, 1996).

Intellectual Property Law

Teresa Cheung
BARRISTER AND SOLICITOR

Alex Wellington
RYERSON UNIVERSITY

Learning Objectives

After reading this chapter, the reader should be able to:

➢ define intellectual property, and differentiate the main types of intellectual property

➢ appreciate the importance of intellectual property in contemporary society

➢ recognize the main sources of intellectual property law in Canada

➢ understand the importance of international treaty obligations

➢ know the crucial aspects of patent protection

➢ know the crucial aspects of copyright protection

➢ appreciate the differences between copyright and neighbouring rights

➢ know the crucial aspects of trademark protection

➢ understand the differences between registered marks (statutory) and unregistered trademarks (common law), and the benefits of registration

➢ identify the kind of activities that constitute infringement of intellectual property rights

➢ appreciate the significance of legal protection for trade secrets and confidential information

➢ recognize the range of remedies available in the context of intellectual property litigation

➢ summarize the various remedies that can be granted in intellectual property cases

TABLE OF CONTENTS

INTRODUCTION

The Meaning of Intellectual Property

The phrase "intellectual property" (IP) refers to creations or products of the mind, intangible and incorporeal items, which can be created, owned, and exploited exclusively by an owner (or someone authorized by an owner) for commercial advantage. Such proprietary creations can be inventions; methods; processes; compounds; compositions; literary, artistic, and musical works and performances; and compilations. Intellectual property protection can apply to an almost bewildering array of entities, as can be seen from selective examples: radios, cameras, televisions, exercise machines, mechanical pencils, computer programs, recipes, periwinkle extract, vaccines, antibiotics, and cell lines generated from spleen tissue. Symbols, names, images, and designs used in association with goods and services in trade and commerce are also forms of intellectual property in that they are intangible elements that hold commercial value for the owner.

Intellectual property generates "property rights" that are legally protectable, yet differ in important ways from other property rights, such as those for real property (land and what is attached to land, e.g., houses) or personal property (everything else). The most familiar items that have long attracted intellectual property protection are books, which are protected under copyright law, and mechanical devices (such as a mousetrap), which are protected under patent law. When an author takes pen to paper (or clicks on a keypad to open up a screen) and produces an original work that is then published (or fixed in tangible form), she is legally entitled to prevent others from copying her work without her authorization. The book itself is the carrier of intellectual property, but the book as an object can be bought and sold by many persons without infringing the author's intellectual property rights. Someone who steals the book itself will be committing a theft of property but will not be committing an intellectual property infringement. However, if someone takes the book and photocopies it, or a substantial portion of it, and then sells the photocopy, that person will be infringing the author's copyright. Thus, the book as a literary work subject to copyright protection is distinct from the book as a physical object, or a piece of personal property.

With tangible property, one person's exclusive possession prevents others from making use of the item of property, and the consumption by one person typically prevents simultaneous consumption by others. In terms used by economists, property is both excludable and rival. Most intellectual property, in contrast, is non-rival, since ideas and information can be consumed by many simultaneously. Without legal protection, intellectual property would not naturally be excludable, either. There is normally an inherent "scarcity" with physical property, but not so with intellectual property. Legal protection, in effect, creates an artificial "scarcity" by building legal fences around creations and inventions that provide their creators and inventors with control over how, by whom, and when, the creations and inventions are to be used, or merely accessed. The presumption is that creators and inventors would be reluctant to invest their time, energy, and expertise if others could simply "copy" their creations and inventions without a comparable investment.

Society's rationales for legal measures to protect intellectual property include the following: (i) to appropriately reward creators and inventors for their labour; (ii) to induce potential creators and inventors to produce a social benefit, by providing an incentive; and (iii) the determination, following a calculation of social benefits, that, overall, society will be better off with intellectual property protection than without. Among the benefits society is expected to realize are those arising from technological advancement and innovation and from the transfer and dissemination of technology. There are many public policy debates over where the boundaries are to be drawn between what is legally protected as privately ownable intellectual property and what falls into the "public domain" or the "common heritage of humanity".

The Evolution of Intellectual Property

Intellectual property was formerly thought to be a dry, dense, and overly technical subject in the domain of lawyers or the legally trained. In today's society, intellectual property has become the subject of intense public scrutiny, a *cause célèbre* hotly debated on the editorial pages of newspapers and on blogs, even generating extensive lobbying campaigns on Facebook, the social networking site.[1]

Intellectual property has become a pervasive feature of market economies in the information age and a prominent source of wealth in the knowledge society. International intellectual property agreements have expanded the reach of fundamental intellectual property norms and harmonized substantive legal rules across different countries and legal traditions. The earliest multilateral treaties concerned with intellectual property protection date from the late 1880s — the *Paris Convention for the Protection of Industrial Property* (1883) and the *Berne Convention for the Protection of Literary and Artistic Works* (1886). Canada is a signatory to both those conventions, as well as to the more recent *Rome Convention on the Protection of Performers, Producers of Phonograms and Broadcasting Organizations* (1961). Adherents to international agreements commit themselves to the principle of **"national treatment"**, or non-discrimination, ensuring that each country grants the same rights to foreign citizens, residents, and corporations as it grants to its own citizens, residents, and corporations. By becoming a signatory to an international agreement, member countries such as Canada commit themselves to adopt domestic legislation that implements those international commitments.

Canada has signed one of the most high-profile contemporary global agreements, the *Trade-Related Aspects of Intellectual Property, Including Trade in Counterfeit Goods* (TRIPs), administered by the World Trade Organization (Annex 1C to the *World Trade Agreement* of 1994). TRIPs was negotiated at the Uruguay Round of the General Agreement on Tariffs and Trade (GATT). It sets minimum standards for levels of intellectual property protections, as well as enforcement procedures, remedies, and processes for dispute resolution. In addition, the North American Free Trade Agreement (NAFTA), signed by Canada, Mexico, and the United States, includes provisions governing intellectual property protection. See Exhibit 33.1, which shows selected international agreements dealing with intellectual property protection.

Most forms of intellectual property in Canada and around the world are protected under the legal regimes of copyright, patents, and trademarks. Other intellectual property statutes less frequently encountered in Canada are the *Industrial Design Act*, the *Integrated Circuit Topography Act*, and the *Plant Breeders' Rights Act*[2] (See Exhibit 33.2). The common law also protects trade secrets. This chapter focuses predominantly on the legal regimes protecting copyright, patents, and trademarks. Trade secrets are briefly discussed as well.

---

[1] The advocacy coalition, Fair Copyright for Canada, launched an innovative Facebook campaign, spearheaded by legal scholar Michael Geist, in response to Bill C-61, which included amendments to the *Copyright Act*. The bill was initially scheduled to be introduced by the minority Conservative government in December 2007, but was withheld until June 2008. The campaign generated a remarkable response (attracting about 40,000 supporters) and attracted substantial media coverage: <http://www.facebook.com/group.php?gid=6315846683>.

[2] *Industrial Design Act*, R.S.C. 1985, c. I-9; *Integrated Circuit Topography Act*, S.C. 1990, c. 37; *Plant Breeders' Rights Act*, S.C. 1990, c. 20.

EXHIBIT 33.1   International Agreements on Intellectual Property

INTELLECTUAL PROPERTY AGREEMENTS

¤ World Intellectual Property Organization (WIPO) Internet Treaties (1996)
  • WIPO Copyright Treaty
  • WIPO Performances and Phonograms Treaty

¤ Rome Convention/International Convention for the Protection of Performers, Producers of Phonograms and Broadcasting Organizations (Neighbouring Rights) (1961)

¤ Madrid Agreement/Madrid System for the International Registration of Marks (1891)

¤ Berne Convention for the Protection of Literary and Artistic Works (1886)

¤ Paris Convention for the Protection of Industrial Property (1883)

- -

INTELLECTUAL PROPERTY-RELATED TRADE AGREEMENTS

¤ Security and Prosperity Partnership (SSP) Negotiations: North American Free Trade Agreement (NAFTA) + (ongoing)

¤ NAFTA (1994)

¤ Canada–U.S. Free Trade Agreement (1989)

¤ General Agreement on Tariffs and Trade (1947/1994)
  • Uruguay Round (1986–1994)
    • Word Trade Organization Agreement (1995)
    • Trade-Related Aspects of Intellectual Property Rights (TRIPs) — Annex 1C to Marakesh Agreement Establishing the World Trade Organization (GATT 1994)

Canada has had domestic laws dedicated to intellectual property protection for a very long time. The first British intellectual property laws were the *Statute of Monopolies* of 1624 (dealing with patents) and the *Statute of Anne* of 1790 (dealing with copyright). Lower Canada enacted an initial patent law in 1824, followed by one in Upper Canada two years later.[3] The first *Patent Act* proper was passed in 1869.[4] As for copyright law, Lower Canada enacted an initial law in 1832, replaced subsequently by very different laws and culminating in the most recent *Copyright Act*, which may soon be amended further.[5] The Province of Canada passed a trademark law in 1860 that was soon repealed and replaced with the *Trade Marks and Designs Act* of 1861, which underwent several crucial transformations before the current *Trademarks Act* was passed.[6]

---

[3] W.L. Hayhurst, "Intellectual Property Laws in Canada: The British Tradition, the American Influence and the French Factor" (May 1996) 10 *Intellectual Property Journal* 265.

[4] Current patent legislation: *Patent Act*, R.S.C. 1985, c. P-4.

[5] Current copyright legislation: *Copyright Act*, R.S.C. 1985, c. C-42.

[6] Current trademark legislation: *Trade-marks Act*, R.S.C. 1985, c. T-13. The official name of the existing Canadian law includes a hyphen in the word "trade-mark".

		EXHIBIT 33.2
Protection Provided by Intellectual Property Legislation in Canada		

COPYRIGHT ACT	INDUSTRIAL DESIGN ACT	INTEGRATED CIRCUIT TOPOGRAPHY ACT	PATENT ACT	PLANT BREEDERS' RIGHTS ACT	TRADE-MARKS ACT
Originality, not copied, results from author's skill and judgment; ideas not protected (expression only)	Originality, not copied, novel design *or* new use for old design	Creator is typically owner (unless employee)	Utility	New variety of plant	Distinctive mark
Fixation in material form necessary	Functional articles mass produced	Application within 2 years of design's use	Novelty	Distinct	Use in Association with wares or services
Design for mass-produced items (more than 50 functional items) not protected	Functional features or principles of construction not protected	Complementary to patent protection for circuit itself	Non-obviousness	Uniform	Mark — Common law and registered
Author usually first owner of copyright	Ideas not protected; colour not protected	N/A	Patentable subject matter	Stable	Certification mark
Registration not required	Registration required		Scientific theorems or principles not protected		Distinguishing guise
Term of protection: Life of Author plus 50 years.	Term of protection: 10 years	Term of protection: 10 years	Term of protection: 20 years	Term of protection: 18 years	Registration valid for 15 years (Registered Trademark)

SOURCES OF INTELLECTUAL PROPERTY LAW

The Constitution   For patent and copyright law, there is an explicit constitutional basis; for trademark law, the constitutional basis is mostly inferred. Sections 91(22) and (23) of the *Constitution Act, 1867* expressly stipulate that the legal regimes for patents and copyright fall under federal jurisdiction. Jurisdiction over trademarks is shared between the federal and provincial governments. The overlap in federal and provincial jurisdictions can be inferred from the exclusive provincial power over property and civil rights in section 92(13) of the Constitution, and from the federal power to regulate (international and inter-provincial) trade and commerce found in section 91(2). The sources of law governing trademarks derive from both the federal *Trade-marks Act* and at common law. The *Trade-marks Act* covers matters pertaining to the registration of trademarks, infringement of registered trademarks, and passing-off of unregistered trademarks.

Common Law Basis for Trademark Law and Trade Secrets Law

Trademark owners can enforce common law rights associated with their trademarks or trade names by bringing a passing-off action in the superior courts at the provincial level. Owners of trade secrets, or of confidential information, can rely upon the common law in cases of misappropriation. These topics are discussed in more detail below.

COPYRIGHT LAW

Defining "Copyright"

In Canada, copyright protection is derived exclusively from the *Copyright Act*. A copyright owner is given the exclusive right to produce or reproduce, to perform, or to publish a work or any substantial part of a work in "any material form". The aspect of "any material form" conveys the concept of media neutrality, which enables copyright protection to adapt to future technological advancements. Copyright includes the following economic rights:

- To translate the work
- To convert a dramatic work into a novel or other non-dramatic work
- To convert a work into a performance
- To make a sound recording or film by which the work may be mechanically reproduced or performed
- To communicate the work to the public by telecommunications
- To reproduce, adapt, and publicly present the work as a cinematographic work
- To rent out a computer program or sound recording

Purposes of Copyright Protection

The Supreme Court of Canada has interpreted the purpose of the *Copyright Act* as twofold: to encourage the production and dissemination of artistic and intellectual works as a matter of public interest, and to justly reward the creators of works as an incentive for the creation of artistic and intellectual works.[7] Given that continual technological advancements generates new methods of access to and reproduction of creative works in mass quantities, these dual purposes are often at odds, as is illustrated by the cases summarized in Exhibits 33.3, 33.4, 33.5, and 33.6.

Who Is an Author and Who Is an Owner?

Interestingly, the concept of "author" is not specifically defined in the *Copyright Act*, although the term is understood to refer to the maker of a creative work. The general rule is that the first copyright owner of a work is the author of the work. Ownership can then be transferred by the author through written assignment. An exception to the general rule is where the work was produced in the course of employment, in which case, the copyright is owned by the employer (as per s. 13(2) of the Act). The exception does not apply to freelancers; simply paying a freelancer to produce a work does not entitle the

---

[7] *Théberge v. Galerie d'Art du Petit Champlain Inc.*, 2002 SCC 34, [2002] 2 S.C.R. 336.

	EXHIBIT 33.3

Impact of Technology Copyright

The *Robertson v. Thomson Corp.* case illustrates the impact of technological advances on the competing rights of copyright owners. The case explores the extent of copyright ownership in freelance articles acquired by *The Globe and Mail* for publication in its newspapers, and whether that copyright interest extends to reproduction of those articles in another medium.

Journalist Heather Robertson discovered that several articles she had authored for *The Globe and Mail* were available through online databases that could be searched by title, author, or keyword. The articles were also accessible through a *Globe and Mail* CD-ROM that archived the paper's daily editions by date of publication. Robertson's contract had not addressed these uses of her work. The lawsuit was certified as a class action on behalf of all freelance authors for *The Globe and Mail* since 1944.

The central issue was whether the newspaper could republish those individual articles in electronic databases such as Info Globe Online without further compensation to the freelance authors. The republication in the databases was distinct from the republication of the newspaper as a collective work.

The majority decision of the Supreme Court ruled that the *Copyright Act* did not permit the newspaper to reproduce individual freelance articles as part of an electronic database without the author's consent. The Court found that the electronic databases were not simply conversions of the newspaper from the "print realm to the electronic world"; they were instead a new collective work. The newspaper's copyright is in the newspaper as a compilation of articles, and is thus limited to the right to reproduce the newspaper in its entirety or a substantial part of the newspaper (as long as the "essence" is preserved). Thus, the newspaper could offer users a daily compendium of daily newspaper editions, in the CD-ROM format; that format retained the originality of the original work. The newspaper's copyright, however, does not extend to the republication of freelance articles as part of a different compilation of works. The freelance writers, as owners of their freelance works, hold the exclusive right to reproduce their articles. The Court confirmed that the *Copyright Act* expressly protects the writers' copyright in their articles, even if the article is part of a compiled work, by restating section 2.1(2): "[t]he mere fact that a work is included in a compilation does not increase, decrease or otherwise affect the protection conferred by this *Act* in respect of the copyright in the work."

The dissenting opinion focused on the concept of media neutrality in the copyright of the newspaper. The minority judges were critical of the way that the majority applied the notion of technological neutrality in the context of the case.

Source: *Robertson v. Thomson Corp.*, 2006 SCC 43, [2006] 2 S.C.R. 363.

---

customer to the rights in the work.[8] Another exception is where an engraving, photograph, or portrait is ordered by a customer and there was no agreement concerning ownership. In this case, the first owner of copyright is the person who ordered the engraving, photograph, or portrait. Thus, under current Canadian copyright law, a corporation can be an "author" of a photograph, but not of other traditional works. Proposed reforms to the *Copyright Act* introduced during the summer of 2008 would provide photographers with the same right to be, as authors, the first owner of a work. Corporations can be, and often are, the owners of copyright works. As noted by David Vaver, "worldwide, the vast majority of copyrights of both traditional and non-traditional material are owned by corporations".[9]

---

[8] For industrial designs or integrated circuit topographies (ICTs), by contrast, the person who orders the work to be done, under contract, will be the first owner of the design or the ICT, whether the maker of the design or the ICT is a freelancer or an employee.

[9] David Vaver, *Intellectual Property Law* (Toronto: Irwin Law, 1997) at 73.

What Works Are Protected by Copyright?

The *Copyright Act* (s. 5(1)), provides that copyright subsists in Canada for every "original literary, dramatic, musical and artistic work". A "literary work" includes "tables, computer programs, and compilations of literary works" (s. 2). Copyright law protects the expression of ideas in these works. It does *not* protect the ideas themselves, but only the expression of those ideas. The ideas are public property, and it is the expression of the ideas that belongs to the author. This means that a work must be fixed in material form to attract copyright protection. Copyright does not protect methods or principles of manufacture or construction. The *Copyright Act* (s. 64) will remove copyright protection from design elements of finished "useful" articles, such as boats, kettles, dresses, and so on (but not ornamental sculptures) *if* more than 50 copies of the article are made. Note that photographs, or sketches or patterns for those useful items, are not covered by this stipulation (and thus stay within the *Copyright Act*), since they are merely carriers of artistic or literary matter, rather than useful articles.

Industrial Design Protection Distinct from Copyright

Industrial designs are defined by the Canadian Intellectual Property Office (CIPO) as the features of shape, configuration, pattern, or ornament (or combinations of those) which are applied to finished articles. An article is defined as any thing that is made by hand, tool, or machine. Examples of industrial designs include the shape of a table or ornamentation on a spoon handle. Industrial designs give an article "eye appeal". Legal protection will not cover the following: functional features, the principles of construction, ideas, or colour *per se*.

To obtain protection, a design must be original, which means that it must be either novel in itself (distinct from previously registered designs) or applied to a different article (i.e., new use for an old design) and it must be registered. To register a design under the *Industrial Design Act*, it is necessary to submit an application to the Industrial Design Branch of the CIPO. Industrial design protection provides an absolute right to exclude, not just a right to prevent copying. Protection lasts for 10 years.

Industrial designs can qualify for protection under *both* the *Industrial Design Act* and under the *Copyright Act*, as long as the articles concerned do *not* have a utilitarian function and are *not* mass produced (i.e., less than 50 copies are to be made), as noted just above.

Copyright Works Must Be Original

"Originality" is the defining feature of a copyrighted work. For a work to be original, the work must be an expression of the author's "skill and judgment" and must not be copied. The standard of whether a work is "original" is an oft-litigated issue. The case law has seen two competing doctrines concerning the standard of originality in order for copyright to subsist. One approach requires there to be "creativity", which is the prevailing standard in U.S. case law. The other approach, adopted by the United Kinggdom and Australia, is the "sweat of brow" or "industriousness" standard in which copyright subsists where there is an investment of labour.

Canada adopts a middle-ground approach in requiring an exercise of skill and judgment in the creation of a work. For example, copyright exists where discernment and ability are used in the arrangement of a database and the compilation of data. Hence, under Canadian law, it is necessary for the work to be more than a mere copy of another work, but it need not be creative in the sense of being novel or unique. At minimum, there must be sufficient intellectual effort to go beyond a merely mechanical exercise. For example, changing a font in the publication would be considered a mechanical exercise. However, originality is found in a newspaper in that it is a compilation of articles arising out of the arrangement of content brought about by the exercise of skill, judgment, and labour.

The Supreme Court has emphasized that the adoption of the *skill and judgment* standard of originality serves to balance the public interest in promoting the creation and dissemination of works of arts and intellect and in obtaining a just reward for the creator. Requiring the exercise of skill and judgment encourages innovative enhancements to works already in the public domain and, thus, the creation of new works.

Term of Copyright Protection

The term of copyright protection is the life of the author plus 50 years following the remainder of the calendar year in which the author dies (s. 6). In a case of joint authorship, the term of copyright continues for 50 years following the end of the calendar year of the death of the last author to die (s. 9). In other jurisdictions, such as the United States and the European Union, the term of copyright protection is 70 years plus the life of the author.

Moral Rights

The author of a work has the right to the "integrity of the work" and "to be associated with the work as its author by name or under pseudonym and the right to remain anonymous" (s. 14.1). The "integrity of the work" refers to being protected from acts that "prejudice the honour or reputation of the author". **Moral rights** are infringed if the work is "distorted, mutilated or modified" or "used in association with a product, service, cause or institution" in such a way that it injures the author's reputation. For example, the *Copyright Act* presumes that there is prejudice where a painting, sculpture, or engraving is distorted, mutilated, or modified without the artist's consent. The term of moral rights is the same as the term of copyright. Moral rights may not be assigned, but can be waived in part or in whole. Thus, an author can waive, or decline to exercise, his or her moral rights, but he or she cannot enter into a contract to assign them to another (i.e., they are not "for sale").

A leading Canadian moral rights case involved the prominent artist Michael Snow, whose public art work, *Flight stop*, is a familiar site to visitors of Toronto's Eaton Centre shopping mall. The shopping centre's management decided to bedeck the installation of life-sized Canadian geese in flight with red ribbons as Christmas decorations in 1981. Michael Snow pursued legal action against the Eaton Centre, requesting an injunction to have the ribbons removed, arguing that they distorted, and offended the integrity of, his work. The then-Ontario High Court of Justice granted the injunction, thereby upholding Snow's moral rights.[10]

Neighbouring Rights

Neighbouring rights are generally those rights that are not related to the right of the author who created the work, but are the rights related to the performance or broadcast of a work, or to the making of a sound recording. In 1997, the *Copyright Act* was amended to include three categories of neighbouring rights: (i) rights of performers in performances; (ii) rights of makers of sound recording (producers of phonograms), and (iii) rights of broadcasters in their communication signals (e.g., radio and television programs). These amendments fulfilled Canada's obligations under the *Rome Convention*. Neighbouring rights are rationalized as legal protection designed to benefit those persons who assist intellectual creators to communicate their messages and to disseminate their works to the public at large.

---

[10] *Snow v. Eaton Centre Ltd.* (1982), 70 C.P.R. (2d) 105. A photo of the sculpture can be found online: <http://www.deathbycopyright.ca/index.php?/archives/56-Michael-Snows-geese-sculpture-at-the-Eaton-Centre.html>.

Copyright Board and Copyright Collectives The administration of copyright and remuneration for copyright holders are set out in Part VII of the *Copyright Act*. In Canada, administration is generally carried out by a cluster of collective societies, and the determination of tariffs and royalties for copyright holders is regulated by the Copyright Board of Canada. A "collective society" is defined in the *Copyright Act* as a society, association, or corporation that carries on the business of collective administration of copyright for the benefit of those who authorize the collective to act to their behalf. The *Copyright Act* recognizes the collective societies under the four regimes: (i) music performing rights and certain neighbouring rights, (ii) general or hybrid regime, (iii) re-transmission regime, and (iv) private copying regime.

The collective applies to the Copyright Board for a tariff to be certified. The tariff is the price for a particular use of a copyrighted work. Examples include the applications for tariffs submitted to the Copyright Board by the Neighbouring Rights Collective of Canada to cover the following:

- Royalties for payments to performers (i.e., recording artists and musicians) and makers (i.e., record labels) for the public performance of their sound recordings in movies played by movie theatres, drive-ins or similar establishments (Tariff No. 7)

- Royalties for performers and makers for the communication of their sound recordings over the Internet by simulcasting and non-interactive webcasting services (Tariff No. 8)

- Royalties for performers and makers for the use of sound recordings in programming provided by commercial television stations, as well as cable and satellite companies (Tariff No. 9)[11]

The Copyright Board of Canada has jurisdiction over copyright collective societies representing film and television producers and broadcasters, authors of works and dramatic works, musicians and performers, owners of re-transmission, broadcasters, screenwriters, and visual artists. The mandates of the Copyright Board, as authorized in the *Copyright Act*, are to establish royalties for the use of copyrighted works that a collective society has been mandated to administer for the benefit of those owners of works, and to supervise agreements between users and licensing bodies. It can also issue licences when copyright owners cannot be located. The Copyright Board is essentially an economic regulatory body created and authorized by the *Copyright Act* to carry out its functions in the form of a quasi-judicial tribunal.

Collectives predominate in Canada, so a large proportion of copyright-enforcement activity relating to tariffs (i.e., royalties) is handled by collectives. Copyright matters not within the jurisdiction of the collective are handled by the right holder.

Fair Dealing Defence Distinct from Fair Use As a matter of public policy, "fair dealing" defences are carved out in section 29 of the *Copyright Act*. The permitted activities are enumerated, and specified. The fair dealing defence permits use of copyrighted works where the work is used: (i) for research or private study, (ii) criticism or review, or (iii) news reporting, without any "motive of gain". In the cases of criticism or review and news reporting, it is not an infringement if the source of the work is given, or if acknowledgment is given of the author, performer, maker of the

---

[11] Neighbouring Rights Collective of Canada, Information Sheets for Tariff No. 7, Tariff No. 8, and Tariff No. 9 <http://www.nrdv.ca/english/docs/Info%20Sheets%20on%20NRCC%202008%20Tariff%20Filings.pdf>

Fair Dealing? EXHIBIT 33.4

The *CCH* case illustrates the "fair dealing" defence in the case of "research and private study". The case is about the balance between the rights of an author and the rights of access for users. The Law Society is the statutory body that regulates the legal profession in Ontario in the public interest. The legal publisher, CCH Canadian Ltd., sued the Law Society for copyright infringement. The issue was whether the Law Society breaches copyright when it provides a custom photocopy service and self-serve photocopiers for copying summaries of case law produced by CCH. The patrons of the service include lawyers, judges, students, and researchers.

The case has attracted considerable attention due to the judicial language, which emphasizes the need for a "proper balance" between the rights of copyright owners to exploit works, and the rights of the public, often characterized as "users' rights", to access copies for purposes of legal research. To benefit from the fair dealing defence, a user needs to prove: (i) that the purpose of dealing with the work (i.e., copying) was for research or private study, and (ii) that the dealing was fair in the circumstances.

The Supreme Court unanimously held that the Law Society did not infringe copyright by providing single copies of the publisher's works to its members through the custom photocopy service. The Law Society's dealings with the case summaries were for research and thus are considered fair dealing under section 29 of the *Copyright Act*. The Court clarified that "research" must be given a large and liberal interpretation to ensure that user's rights are not unduly constrained. Research is not limited to non-commercial or private contexts. Research for the purpose of advising clients in legal cases, including preparing legal briefs and arguments, is considered research under the *Copyright Act*. The determination of "fair dealing" is a question of degree and impression. Consideration is made of the number and extent of quotations and extracts, the use of the extracts, and the proportion of extracts to commentary.

Source: *CCH Canadian Ltd. v. Law Society of Upper Canada*, 2004 SCC 13, [2004] 1 S.C.R. 339.

---

sound recording, or broadcaster of the communication signal. In the *Law Society of Upper Canada v. CCH Canadian Ltd.* case, the Supreme Court had occasion to elaborate on the substance of the fair dealing defence, in particular as it pertains to research (Exhibit 33.4).

It is important to emphasize that the **fair dealing** defence is different, in important ways, from the **fair use** defence that is provided under the United States *Copyright Act*. Under the U.S. *Copyright Act*, making use of copyrighted work for purposes such as criticism, comment, news reporting, teaching (including multiple copies for classroom use), scholarship, or research, is *not* an infringement of copyright. The fair use provision is considered to be much broader than the fair dealing provision found in Canadian law, and includes uses such as parody, which are not found in the Canadian *Copyright Act*.

Factors for Fair Dealing

The Supreme Court set out the following factors for applying the fair dealing exception in the context of private study or research in the *CCH Canadian Ltd. v. Law Society of Upper Canada* case:

1. **Purpose of the Dealing**
   Elaboration: There must be an allowable purpose, one that is mentioned expressly in the Act. Moreover, within allowable purposes there is variability, such that philanthropic research is more likely to be fair than commercial research.

2. **Character of the Dealing**
   Elaboration: This refers to the way that the allegedly infringed work was dealt with. For example, reproducing a single copy for a single requester is more likely to be considered fair than providing for widespread dissemination. Destroying a copy after use will favour a finding of fairness.

3. **Amount of the Dealing**
   Elaboration: Here, it is important to consider the number and types of activities undertaken. As to what would be unfair, the court suggested this example: one patron requesting copies of multiple reported judicial decisions from the same series or volume over a short period of time. In such a case, the patron would be expected to purchase the works from the publisher.

4. **Alternatives to the Dealing**
   Elaboration: Can the dealing be carried out with equivalent and non-copyright protected material instead? Circumstances to be considered include "whether the material is reasonably available elsewhere, or whether the publishers have an effective monopoly". The more alternatives available, the less fair copying would be, and *vice versa*. Consider whether the source work was available within a reasonable time at an ordinary commercial price.

5. **Nature of the Work**
   Elaboration: If the work has not yet been published, its reproduction could lead to wider dissemination and, thus, could potentially be fair in accordance with the goals of copyright law. If a work was confidential, however, that could tip the scales towards a finding that the dealing was not fair. Some of the jurisprudence suggests that for works which are factual in nature, fair dealing may be more readily found than for works which are creative or imaginative.

6. **Effect of the Dealing on the Work**
   Elaboration: Under this heading, courts consider the degree to which the use may prejudice the sale, or diminish the profits, or supersede the objects, of the original work. If the copying was done in order to be incorporated into a competing work, it is less likely to be considered fair.

Copyright Infringement

In determining whether a substantial part of a work has been reproduced, one has to consider the qualitative nature of the reproduction rather than simply the quantitative amount. Independent creation is allowable under copyright law, whereas independent creation can be an infringement of a patent, an industrial design or a trademark.

COPYRIGHT CONTROVERSIES

Music Downloading and Peer-to-Peer File Sharing

There is a general pattern that new technologies (such as the photocopier and the videocassette recorder) create opportunities for widespread and inexpensive copying of works. The advent of computer programs to facilitate peer-to-peer (P2P) file sharing has led to the mushrooming of unauthorized reproduction of recorded music and, more recently, movies distributed through the Internet. Various economic studies have been done to try to quantify the amounts of revenue the music industry is losing out on owing to the popular-

	EXHIBIT 33.5

Copyright Infringement over the Internet

The case originated in an attempt by the Canadian Recording Industry Association (CRIA), representing BMG Canada Inc. and other record companies, to discover the identities of 29 Internet users who had downloaded music through the use of peer-to-peer (P2P) file sharing programs (KaZaA), thereby allegedly infringing copyright. The CRIA asked the Federal Court to order five Internet Service Providers (ISPs) — Bell Canada/Sympatico, Rogers Cable, Shaw, Telus, and Videotron Ltée. — to disclose names and contact information of clients (identified by their Internet Protocol or IP addresses), so as to facilitate CRIA suing them. The trial judge, Mr. Justice Von Finckenstein of the Federal Court, refused to order the release of that information, holding that CRIA had not made a strong enough case, and that it was not clear that the acts the 29 users were accused of were actually acts of copyright infringement. Justice Von Finckenstein held that users engaging in P2P music file sharing were not necessarily infringing copyright, nor "distributing" or "authorizing" reproduction of sound recordings contrary to Canadian copyright law. The trial judge set out a multi-part test for identification of "John Does", which included the following particulars:

(i) a *prima facie* case of copyright infringement being made by the applicants against the alleged wrongdoers;

(ii) determination that the ISPs in question were the only practical sources to identify the peer-to-peer users; and

(iii) finding that legitimate privacy concerns evidenced in the case were outweighed by the applicants' interest in an order for disclosure.

The trial judge highlighted the potential for an innocent account holder to be wrongly identified, given the complications of ascertaining the actual identities of alleged infringers in the light of the practices of ISPs. An example was provided by Shaw of the same IP address being assigned to many users in situations involving local area networks and network routers. Not finding the conditions set out just above to have been satisfied, the trial judge declined to issue an order for disclosure.

The trial decision was appealed to the Federal Court of Appeal, which unanimously dismissed the appeal. The FCA held that CRIA needed to adduce additional evidence before proceeding with the 29 actions filed to date. The Court of Appeal did call into question some of the statements made by the trial judge in the lower court, such as the statement that downloading a song for personal use did not amount to infringement under the *Copyright Act*. The Court of Appeal noted that the trial judge had not considered whether all requirements for application of the "personal use" exemption (copy for private use) had been met. Furthermore, the Court of Appeal held that where an Internet user invites other persons with Internet access to have copyright music transferred to them, and then copied, authorization may be established. Moreover, placing a copy on a shared directory linked to a P2P file-sharing program may amount to distribution for the purposes of the *Copyright Act*. Sexton J.A. emphasized that while privacy concerns have to be taken into account, those concerns must yield to public concerns for protecting intellectual property "in situations where infringement threatens to erode those rights". Ultimately, the Federal Court of Appeal did not find in favour of CRIA.

Source: *BMG Canada Inc. v. John Doe (F.C.A.),* 2005 FCA 193, [2005] 4 F.C.R. 81.

ity of the new technologies; the music industry insists that it is in the billions, with significant declines in CD sales as the proof. In the United States, the Recording Industry Association of America (RIAA), a trade group representing the major record labels, has pursued a strategy of aggressive litigation. RIAA took legal action for copyright infringement against the Napster online centralized file-sharing service created by an American university student (Shawn Fanning), leading to it being shut down (it was started up again in a different form by others). Then, the RIAA started taking legal action against consumers who have engaged in unauthorized downloading of

---

EXHIBIT 33.6

Should ISPs Pay for Their Customers' Copyright Infringement?

The issues in this case concerned the extent to which music communicated through the medium of the Internet is protected under Canadian copyright law and whether caching constitutes infringement. The Society of Composers, Authors and Music Publishers of Canada (SOCAN) made the claim that Canadian Internet providers should pay royalties because some of their customers download copyrighted works. The case also looked at whether or not the creation of "cache" copies of copyrighted works constitutes infringement. (Cache refers to a means of temporarily storing files used to house documents being transferred across the Internet.)

The Supreme Court found that communication occurs between the host and the recipient, and that ISPs merely facilitate that communication (they are the "means of telecommunication"). The Court held that neither Internet Service providers (ISPs) nor host server operators "communicate" or "authorize the communication" of musical works in violation of SOCAN's rights under the *Copyright Act*. Authorization requires that a defendant give approval to, sanction, permit, favour, or encourage infringing conduct.

When ISPs limit their activities to providing the means for others to use their service to communicate by telecommunication, they are in effect shielded from liability. The use of a cache server was included in the rubric of acceptable practices since it was deemed by the Court to be merely a way to deliver faster and more economical service, undertaken only for technical reasons. The Court noted that it would be impracticable to require ISPs to monitor the content posted on their servers in order to determine whether that content is in compliance with copyright and other laws.

Nonetheless, where an ISP acts as a content provider, or is otherwise associated with the provision of content, it may become liable for effecting or authorizing the communication of music, if the circumstances so warrant. If it can be shown that a certain relationship, or degree of control, exists between the ISP and the provider of infringing content, or the ISP's activities cease to be "content neutral", then the ISP could potentially become liable for authorizing infringing communications. An ISP will be especially vulnerable to liability if it neglects to remove material upon being notified of infringing content on its system, in a timely manner. The practice recommended to avoid potential liability is known as "notice and takedown".

The Court commented on the importance of ISPs in the Canadian context as follows: "It is clear that Parliament did not want copyright disputes between creators and users to be visited on the heads of the Internet intermediaries, whose continued expansion and development is considered to be vital to national economic growth".

Source: *Society of Composers, Authors and Music Publishers of Canada v. Canadian Assn. of Internet Providers*, 2004 SCC 45, [2004] 2 S.C.R. 427.

---

music through a variety of other decentralized file-sharing programs (including kaZaA). Some of the alleged infringers sued have been college students and parents of file-sharing children. News reports have estimated that about 20,000 lawsuits have been initiated; the vast majority of those have ended in settlements.

In Canada, the CRIA (Canadian Recording Industry Association), which is the Canadian equivalent to the RIAA, attempted to sue peer-to-peer file-sharing Internet users in the case of *BMG Canada Inc. v. John Doe*. The plaintiffs were unable to convince the courts (both the Federal Court and the Federal Court of Appeal) to order the release of the identities of the Internet service providers' customers in order to proceed with litigation (Exhibit 33.5). In another case on related issues, *SOCAN v. Canadian Association of Internet Providers*, the collective copyright society SOCAN was unable to convince the Supreme Court that Internet service providers should be required to pay royalties because some of their customers download copyrighted works (Exhibit 33.6).

Digital Copyright Reform

Canada is a signatory to what are known as the World Intellectual Property Organization's Internet treaties. One deals with Copyright (WIPO Copyright Treaty, or WCT) and the other deals with Neighbouring Rights (WIPO Performances and Phonograms Treaty, or WPPT). The previous Liberal government had promised to implement reforms to the *Copyright Act*, in accordance with those treaty obligations, but Bill C-60 died on the order table when the government fell. The minority Conservative government indicated in its Throne Speech that copyright reform was on their agenda, and they have subsequently brought forth Bill C-61. The bill went through first reading in June of 2008, and it is too soon to tell whether the Conservatives will ultimately be successful in getting it passed through Parliament.

The main purposes of the proposed amendments of the *Copyright Act* are to

(a) update the rights and protections of copyright owners to better address the Internet, in line with international standards
(b) clarify the liability of Internet service providers
(c) permit certain uses for educational and research purposes of Internet and other digital technologies to facilitate technology-enhanced learning, inter-library loans, the delivery of educational material and access to publicly available material on the Internet
(d) permit certain uses of copyright material for private purposes, and
(e) amend provisions of the Act relating to photographs to give photographers the same rights as other creators.[12]

The new law is designed to ban peer-to-peer file sharing, and to make it illegal for consumers to get around digital locks, in provisions known as anti-circumvention rules, which echo those found in the *Digital Millennium Copyright Act* (*DMCA*) in the United States. Copyright owners have come to rely increasingly upon technological protection measures (TPMs) and digital rights management (DRM) to block access to digital content, except with the authorization of the owner. CDs and DVDs thus often come with encryption to prevent copying. The new bill would make it contrary to law to circumvent the encryption, as does the *DMCA*, and potentially even to possess devices or software capable of doing so. The daily newspapers and countless information technology-related blog entries evidence the negative consumer reaction those particular features of the legal reforms have provoked. Other aspects of the new law, which should be less contentious, include provisions allowing consumers to legally time shift (i.e., to record a television show for later viewing), format shift (e.g., to convert a purchased VCR tape into a DVD format), and to make private copies of music (e.g., by transferring songs from a purchased CD to an iPod for personal use).

Another, related legal reform has already been implemented. In 2007, the federal government passed an amendment to the *Criminal Code* (s. 432), making it an offence to (i) record a movie in a theatre without the consent of the theatre manager, and/or (ii) to do so for the purpose of selling, renting, or other commercial distribution. The court can now order the forfeiture of any equipment used in the commission of those offences. Although the *Copyright Act* already contained a provision (s. 42) making the camcording of a movie a part of copyright infringement (i.e., making a copy of work for sale or rental), the Canadian Motion Picture Distributors Association (CMPDA) and the Motion Picture Association of America (MPAA) aggressively advocated for the

---

12 Canada, Bill C-61, *An Act to amend the Copyright Act*, 2nd Sess., 39th Parl., 2007–2008, Summary (first reading, June 12, 2008). Available online: <www.parl.gc.ca>. A series of Fact Sheets are also available on the Industry Canada website: "Copyright Reform Process", <www.ic.gc.ca/epic/site/crp-prda.nsf/en/h_rp01157e.html> (accessed: August 31, 2008).

much stronger criminal sanctions to provide a more effective deterrent. Previously, people were simply ejected but not charged for camcording in a movie theatre (claiming it was for personal use), and they kept their equipment. Now, charges could be laid and recording equipment confiscated.

There are international trade implications to these legal developments. Section 301 of the U.S. *Trade Act* enables the U.S. government to impose trade sanctions on countries that it deems to be lacking adequate protection for American intellectual property. The 2008 report of the Office of the U.S. Trade Representative (USTR) indicated that Canada was singled out for "serious concern", although it was left on a "watch list" (along with 35 other countries meriting bilateral attention) rather than elevated to the "priority watch list" as had been recommended by the International Intellectual Property Alliance (IIPA), a private sector coalition representing U.S. copyright-based industries. The USTR emphasizes Canada's failure to implement the WIPO Internet treaties. Having been "put on notice" by USTR in this way, Canada is expected to address the U.S. industry's concerns, or face the risk of possible trade sanctions in the future.

The federal government has recently announced that it will work with other international trading partners towards a possible Anti-Counterfeiting Trade Agreement (ACTA).

PATENT LAW

What Is a Patent?

A patent is a government-issued document granting an inventor or an owner of a patented invention a monopoly to exclude others from making, using, and selling the invention for a limited period of time. This exclusive right of exploitation is intended to protect business interests. The right to exclude others from using the invention gives the patent owner a head start to commercially exploit the patent. In exchange for this monopoly, the inventor provides disclosure of the invention to the public, so that the public may gain the benefit of the disclosure. Otherwise, the inventor could simply keep the invention secret. This exchange is often referred to as the *quid pro quo* of the patent right, or the bargain theory of patent law. The bargain between the inventor and the public serves the public policy of encouraging research and development, innovation, and economic activity. Hence, fulfilling the requirements of disclosure is crucial.

Whereas copyright protection applies from the moment of creation, patent protection will apply only once a patent has been granted by the Canadian Intellectual Property Office. The person who is "first to file" a patent application is entitled to patent protection in Canada and in most other jurisdictions. Some inventions, such as computer programs, may be eligible for both copyright and patent protection.

Defining "Invention": Criteria for Patentability

The "invention" must meet several conditions in order for a patent to be granted. First, "invention" is defined in the *Patent Act* (s. 2) as "any new and useful art, process, machine, manufacture or composition of matter". Hence, the invention must be patentable "subject matter", meaning that it must fall within one of the categories of "useful art, process, machine, manufacture or composition of matter". The invention must also meet the conditions of being "new", "useful", and "non-obvious". The disclosure in the patent application must meet the requirements for specification of an invention set out in section 27(3) of the *Patent Act*. The specification can include drawings, illustrations, and so on. The disclosure must fully describe the invention and how it operates or is used so that a "person skilled in the art" can make or use the invention. It must set out the steps in a process or the method of making or using a machine, manufacture, or composition of matter in a clear and concise way.

The first condition of patentability is that the invention must fall within one of the classes of patentable *subject matter*, that being "any new and useful art, process, machine, manufacture or composition of matter". The case of *Harvard College v. Canada (Commissioner of Patents)* addresses the issue of whether a transgenic non-human organism can be an invention (Exhibit 33.7).

What Is an Invention?

EXHIBIT 33.7

Dupont licensed the invention of a mouse ("oncomouse") that was bred to be susceptible to cancer for the purpose of biomedical research. The genetically altered gene is incorporated into a plasmid and injected into a fertilized mouse egg, which is then implanted into a host mouse. That implanted egg, when born, becomes a "founder mouse", used to produce offspring containing the oncogene. The commercial value and utility of the invention is in the alteration of the genetic code of the oncomouse.

Harvard College had filed for a patent on the invention in Canada. Harvard's patent application covered three claims: (i) a method for creating the mouse using a modified gene, (ii) the cellular material making up the mouse, and (iii) a transgenic mammal containing the modified gene. The Patent Commissioner rejected the third claim to the end product of the mouse itself, and Harvard appealed that decision. The Commissioner's decision emphasized that the inventors did not have full control over all the characteristics of the founder mouse.

The case went to the Federal Court Trial Division (upholding the Patent Commissioner's decision), and then to the Federal Court of Appeal (overturning the lower court's decision and finding in favour of Harvard), ending up in the Supreme Court of Canada. The issue was whether the oncomouse, as a higher life form produced by genetic engineering and natural gestation, is patentable under section 2 of the *Patent Act*. Several public interest advocacy groups, including the Canadian Council of Churches, the Canadian Environmental Law Association, and Animal Alliance, were granted intervenor status in the case. There was significant media coverage of the case by the time it reached the final stage.

Both the majority and dissenting decisions of the Supreme Court found the fertilized, genetically altered oncomouse *egg* to be patentable. However, the Court differed by a margin of five to four as to whether the mouse produced by natural gestation (but wholly composed of altered cells not found in nature) is as itself an "invention" defined in the *Patent Act*.

The majority decision (authored by Mr. Justice Michel Bastarache) held that a transgenic non-human mammal does not qualify as a "manufacture" or "composition of matter" and hence is not patentable. The body of the genetically altered mouse does not consist of substances or ingredients that have been mixed together by a person. It was the majority opinion that the issue of patenting higher life forms should be left to Parliament to legislate, as it is beyond the institutional competence of the Supreme Court to rule on the related policy issues concerning the research and experimental use, exemption, and value issues concerning the commodification of human life.

The minority opinion (authored by Mr. Justice Ian Binnie) concluded that patenting of higher life forms should be patentable, and insisted that doing so would not involve a radical departure from the traditional patent regime. The mouse should be deemed a "composition of matter", according to the dissenting judges.

The implication of the *Harvard Mouse* case is that patent applications for higher-life-form patents will be denied in Canada. Canada is now the only developed country to disallow higher life forms as patentable subject matter. However, both majority and dissenting decisions found the fertilized genetically altered oncomouse egg to be patentable subject matter, even though the mammal is not patentable. Thus, Harvard was granted patent protection for the method of creating the mouse and the cells that make up the mouse.

Source: *Harvard College v. Canada (Commissioner of Patents)*, 2002 SCC 76, [2002] 4 S.C.R. 45.

The *Patent Act* is not meant to protect mere ideas in the abstract. Mere scientific principle or abstract theorem is set out in the statute (s. 27(8)) as a non-patentable exception. Mathematical formulae and calculations made by a computer are not considered patentable subject matter. The rationale for this exception is that the purpose of the *Patent Act* is to protect ideas that produce tangible results that are reproducible and have practical application.

Devices or drugs for treating illness in humans or animals are patentable. But professional skills or methods of medical treatment such as a method for cleaning teeth (to make them bacteria free) or for using adhesives in post surgical suturing have been held to be excluded from patentability in Canada. In contrast, American patent law does allow for claims relating to methods of medical treatment or invasive surgical methods. For example, a patent claim to "A method of treating rhinitis [inflammation of nasal passages] comprising administering X" would potentially be allowable in the United States but not accepted in Canada.[13] The reasoning for this exclusion in Canadian patent law is that professional skills such as medical treatment fall outside industry, trade, and commerce, which are the fields that the patent system was designed to serve. Secondly, the exercise of discretion and judgment in carrying out the professional skill leads to uncontrollable or irreproducible outcomes. There is also a public policy rationale for the exclusion from patentability of medical or surgical treatments, since otherwise operating surgeons or prescribing physicians could be vulnerable to patent-infringement actions. Some claims pertaining to cosmetic methods and methods of treating animals for economic benefit are allowed in Canadian patent applications.

The other criteria for patentability are **novelty**, **non-obviousness**, and **utility**. An invention is "new" or "novel" if it is not anticipated by "prior art". **"Prior art"** is the body of knowledge existing prior to the date of the filing of the patent. The invention must also be "non-obvious" in the sense that it must not be obvious to a "person skilled in the art" (s. 28(3)), who is a fictitious person deemed to have reached an average level of skill in the field of the invention in a patent application. This notional person is used as a standard by which to judge the novelty and especially the non-obviousness of the invention. An invention must also be "useful" or have "utility" in the sense that it can be applied towards a practical purpose, as opposed to being purely theoretical. Unpatentable inventions include perpetual motion machines, or Mr. X's "death ray".[14] Systems for doing things that do not result in a tangible product have been found to be unpatentable in Canada. Examples include systems for becoming rich, efficient conduct of a business, securing payment of a discount, and for better government.

Term of Patent Protection

For patents based on applications filed on or after October 1, 1989, the term of protection is 20 years from the filing date (as per s. 44 of the *Patent Act*). For patents based on applications filed before October 1, 1989, that had not expired as of July 12, 2001, the term of protection is the later of 17 years from the date on which the patent is issued, or 20 years from the filing date (as per s. 45(2) of the Act). As a point of interest, the provisions of the *Patent Act* relating to the term of protection were amended in 2001 to bring the Act into conformity with TRIPs, after the World Trade Organization ruled in 2000 that Canada's term of protection for certain patents (those filed before October 1, 1989) was inconsistent with TRIPs.

---

[13] Euan Taylor, "Patenting Methods of Medical Treatment", Davis and Company, *Intelligence*, 10 (February 2007).

[14] *X v. Canada (Commissioner of Patents)* (1981), 59 C.P.R. (2d) 134 (F.C.A.).

Infringement of Patent Rights

The test for patent infringement is whether the acts or conduct in question deprive the inventor, in whole or in part, directly or indirectly, of the advantage of the patented invention.

PATENT CONTROVERSIES

There have been several flashpoints for public debates over the desirability of patent protection; one concerns essential medicines and another concerns patents on genes and life forms.

Essential Medicines

Researchers and activists who focus on the global health crisis surrounding HIV/AIDS have targeted patent protection for essential, life-saving medicines, as a crucial barrier to dealing with the problems faced by developing countries. There is currently a global campaign to advocate for legal and policy reforms in both developed and developing countries to try to ameliorate the impact of the high costs of existing medicines to treat HIV/AIDS.[15]

The Government of South Africa was faced with litigation from pharmaceutical companies owning patents on drugs to treat HIV/AIDS during the late 1990s. The government had passed a law which sought to do two things to bring down drug prices: (i) take advantage of a "grey market", or parallel importation (from unlicensed but cheaper sources of the drugs), and (ii) use compulsory licensing, which would enable local manufacturers to be licensed to produce generic versions of patented medicines. The brand-name pharmaceutical companies objected to the undermining of their intellectual property rights and pushed for trade sanctions against South Africa. Forty drug companies joined together and threatened to pursue lengthy and costly litigation against the South African government. After global protests, and considerable pressure from the international non-government organization (NGO) community, the drug companies backed off from the lawsuits.

The World Trade Organization negotiations for the Doha Declaration resulted in a separate declaration on TRIPS (the *Trade-Related Aspects of Intellectual Property Rights*) and public health, which was designed to respond to concerns about the possible implications of the TRIPS Agreement for access to essential, life-saving medicines. That special declaration emphasizes that "[the] TRIPS Agreement does not and should not prevent member governments from acting to protect public health. It affirms governments' right to use the agreement's flexibilities in order to avoid any reticence the governments may feel."[16]

In 2005, Canada passed Bill C-9, known as the *Jean Chretien Pledge to Africa Act*, which amended the *Patent Act* and the *Food and Drugs Act*. The legislation was a response to a 2005 decision of the World Trade Organization (WTO) to waive certain obligations in TRIPs (relating to s. 31(f)). The result of that WTO decision is that developed countries such as Canada are now able to authorize someone other than a patent holder to manufacture and export essential medicines under compulsory licences to countries with no, or insufficient, pharmaceutical manufacturing capacity. The legislation contains

---

[15] Campaign for Access to Essential Medicines, <http://www.accessmed-msf.org/>. In addition to focusing on the high cost of prescription drugs, the campaign emphasizes the need to stimulate research into new medicines for neglected diseases such as tuberculosis, sleeping sickness, and malaria.

[16] World Trade Organization, Doha Declaration Explained: <http://www.wto.org/english/tratop_e/dda_e/dohaexplained_e.htm#trips>.

a list of eligible medicines, and aims to provide greater access to pharmaceutical products for addressing public health problems, especially those arising from HIV/AIDS.

Gene Patents and Lifeform Patents

Considerable public debate and discussion has been devoted to the issues of genetic patents and life-form patents, in Canada and abroad. One debate concerns whether higher life forms should be patentable. In Canada, the Supreme Court was asked to rule on the patentability of a mammalian life form, a genetically altered mouse used in cancer research. The Supreme Court ruled, in *Harvard College v. Canada (Commissioner of Patents)*, that while patents could be granted on lower life forms and genes (including micro-organisms, seeds) and human genes, cells, and DNA sequences, higher lifeforms will not be patentable in Canada (Exhibit 33.7). In another case involving patents on genetically altered plants, *Monsanto Canada v. Schmeiser*, issues concerning patent infringement were the focus. See Exhibit 33.8.

The genetic patent on breast cancer genes (BRCA1 and BRCA2) held by the Utah-based firm Myriad Genetics has stimulated controversy in Ontario and throughout Europe. The provincial government in Ontario performs predictive genetic testing for hereditary breast and ovarian cancers, testing which involves the specific breast cancer genes that are the subject matter of Myriad's patents (obtained during the mid-1990s). The Ontario government has not entered into a licensing arrangement with Myriad Genetics. The company sent a "cease and desist" letter to the Government of Ontario in mid-2001, alleging that the government was violating Myriad's patents.[17]

The company demanded that the provincial government send the samples to Myriad's operations in Utah, where the tests would cost on average about US$3,850 (rather than $1,150).[18]

The Ontario government declined to agree to Myriad's request, citing the problematic legal, ethical, and financial implications of doing so. The government insisted that paying Ontario hospitals to carry out the testing did not constitute infringement of "any valid claim" of Myriad's patents. As a point of interest, a similar request by Myriad for payment sent to European governments resulted in the launch of a public campaign in opposition, and the use of an "opposition challenge", which is an administrative proceeding available under European Union patent law. After that administrative intervention, Myriad lost protection for one breast cancer gene patent entirely and the other patent was significantly narrowed.

TRADEMARK LAW

What Are Trademarks, Trade Names, Certification Marks, and Distinguishing Guise?

A trademark is a mark used to distinguish goods or services from other goods and services. The following, while not an exhaustive list, can each be a trademark: a word, a coined word (such as ESSO, then EXXON), numbers, or a combination of numbers and letters, a design (such as Macdonald's Golden Arches), colour combinations, signs and symbols, and sound marks. In contrast, a trade name signifies the entire business entity under which the business is conducted, whether that name is the corporate name, or the name of the partnership or sole proprietorship. A trade name must be registered under

---

[17] Similar letters were sent to the governments of Alberta, British Columbia, and Quebec. Quebec agreed to Myriad's request, while British Columbia temporarily suspended the testing.

[18] Laura Eggertson, "Ontario Defies US Firm's Genetic Patent, Continues Cancer Screening" (2002) 166:4 *Canadian Medical Association Journal* 494.

EXHIBIT 33.8

Gene Patent Infringer or Innocent Infringer?

Percy Schmeiser was a farmer in Saskatchewan whose farm was found to have very substantial amounts of a genetically modified crop invented by Monsanto called Monsanto's Roundup Ready Canola. Monsanto's patent covers the modified gene which, when inserted into the DNA of canola plants, gives the ensuing plants tolerance to glyphosate, which kills weeds, and is marketed under the trademark "Roundup". Hence, the plants are known as "Roundup Ready" canola. Monsanto claimed patent protection not for the genetically modified plant itself, but rather for the genes that make up the plant.

Mr. Schmeiser did not have a licence for the use of Monsanto's Canola. When the GM plants were discovered on his property, Mr. Schmeiser claimed that contamination had occurred in one or more of the following ways: (i) either wind or insect activities had lead to crossfield breeding; or (ii) seeds were blown from passing trucks or dropped from passing farm equipment; or (iii) plants were blown from neighbours' fields. At the initial trial, expert evidence adduced led to the Federal Court finding that none of the alleged sources could explain the concentration or extent of "Roundup Ready" canola found on Mr. Schmeiser's farm. The trial judge found that Mr. Schmeiser knew or ought to have known that the plants from which he had saved seeds for planting were glyphosate tolerant. The case ultimately ended up in the Supreme Court, after Mr. Schmeiser appealed the finding of liability by the Federal Court of Appeal. Both the appeal courts upheld an injunction against using the plants containing the patented gene.

The issue was whether Schmeiser infringed Monsanto's patent through the use of Monsanto's patented gene by collecting, saving and planting the seeds.

The majority of the Supreme Court found that Mr. Schmeiser infringed Monsanto's patent because he used the patented invention within the context of commercial farming without paying a licence fee and, hence, deprived Monsanto of the full extent of its monopoly right. The Court emphasized that the function of the statutory patent monopoly is to protect business interests.

The test articulated for infringement is whether the defendant's conduct deprives the inventor, in whole or in part, directly or indirectly, of the advantage of the patented invention. Infringement can occur where the patented invention (i.e., in this case, the gene) is part of a broader unpatented structure or process (i.e., a plant) if the patented invention is a significant part of, or important to, the defendant's activities that involve the unpatented structure. Even possession of a patented object or an object incorporating a patented feature may be infringement if the infringer derives a "stand-by" or "insurance" utility from the object.

Several court rulings of the case noted that how an invention comes into possession of an infringer is an issue which has especial salience in the context of gene patents. What if somehow plants containing modified genes end up on a person's property unbeknownst to that person (an innocent infringer)? Could the company which owned the patent still obtain a remedy for infringement? The majority of the Court noted that an alleged defendant may be found not to infringe by proving that its possession is "innocent of any actual use or intention to use" the patented invention.

This case, as did the Harvard Mouse case, generated very significant amounts of publicity; it even has its own website developed and maintained by Mr. Schmeiser (The *Monsanto v Schmeiser* website: <http://www.percyschmeiser.com/>).

Source: *Monsanto Canada Inc. v. Schmeiser*, 2004 SCC 34, [2004] 1 S.C.R. 902.

the applicable provincial statute governing business names. A trade name could potentially be registered as a trademark under the *Trade-marks Act*, if it is also used as a trademark. The Canadian Intellectual Property Office gives the following example to distinguish a trademark and a trade name: A company called A.B.C. Ltd. (trade name) sells ice cream under the name A.B.C. in association with that ice cream. In that case, A.B.C. Ltd. could also apply for trademark protection for "A.B.C." However, if A.B.C. Ltd. instead promotes its ice cream in association with the word "Northpole", "A.B.C." would not then be considered a trademark.

Under Canadian law, certification marks and distinguishing guises are trademarks. A certification mark is a mark used to distinguish goods and services that meet a defined standard. That standard can be with respect to character, quality, or working conditions under which the good was produced or the service was performed. The wool symbol on clothing tags and the logo of the Association of Professional Engineers are examples of certification marks.

A distinguishing guise refers to a shape of goods or their containers or a mode of packaging goods such that the appearance of the good distinguishes the good from others. The shape of the Toblerone chocolate bar and of the classic Coca-Cola bottles, and the grill on a Rolls Royce car are all examples of distinguishing guises. The *Trade-marks Act* (s. 13) prohibits the registration of a distinguishing guise where the feature would "limit the development of any art or industry". Utilitarian features are also disclaimed from the registration of distinguishing guises.

Registered Trademarks

A trademark can be registered in the Trade-marks Registry with the Canadian Intellectual Property Office (CIPO), or it can be unregistered, in which case it is called a trademark at common law.

The registration is a lengthy process that begins with filing an application setting out the trademark and a description of the goods and services associated with the mark. Next, an examination of the mark is conducted by a trademarks examiner at CIPO to determine if the trademark is registrable, taking into account the indicia of non-registrability pursuant to section 12 of the *Trade-marks Act*. If the examiner finds the trademark registrable, the trademark is advertised in the *Trade-marks Journal* for interested persons to oppose the registration within a two-month period. The opposition may be pursuant to one of the grounds in the Act (s. 38(2)). If there is no opposition to the application or the opposition is unsuccessful, the trademark is then registered.

Although use of an unregistered mark is protected by common law rights, there are benefits to registering a trademark. The owner of a registered trademark has the exclusive right to use the mark in association with the goods and services described in the registration throughout Canada. Registration confers a presumption at law that the owner is entitled to exclusive use of the mark. Subject to certain enumerated exceptions, the use of a mark that is confusing with the registered trademark is deemed to be an infringement under the Act (s. 20).

Unregistered Common Law Trademarks

In order for an unregistered mark to acquire rights at common law, it must be used such that it becomes a distinguishing mark pointing to the source of a good or service. The mark should have garnered goodwill for the business using it. Use of the trademark is broadly defined to encompass all forms of advertising and verbal usage. In this sense, the mark acquires "reputation" and "distinctiveness". The reputation of the mark may be local or widespread, spanning the country, the continent, or the world. For an unregistered trademark, the scope of legal protection will be limited to the geographical area in which "distinctiveness" is shown for the mark.

The regulation of trademarks has its roots in the prevention of misrepresentation to the public as to source of a good or service. Unregistered trademarks that have acquired a reputation indicating a source of a product or service attracted rights under the common law. Hence, the common law recognition of unregistered trademarks is concerned with preventing misrepresentation.

	EXHIBIT 33.9
The Difference between Trademark Protection and Patent Protection	

The patent for the Lego blocks had expired in Canada and in other countries. After expiry of the last Lego patent in Canada, Ritvik, the makers of Mega Bloks, brought to market a line of small blocks identical in size to the Lego blocks and featuring the same Lego design of interlocking bricks using the geometrical pattern of stubs on top with tubes underneath. Ritvik sold the bricks in Canada and in other countries under the name "Micro Mega Bloks". Mega Bloks had become a significant global competitor to Lego. Lego attempted to protect its market share and goodwill against its competitor by bringing a passing-off claim pursuant to section 7(b) of the *Trade-marks Act*. Lego asserted that the geometric pattern of raised studs on the top of the Lego bricks is a distinguishing guise. Lego sought to compel its competitor to sell Mega Bloks with a disclaimer that Mega Bloks are not Lego bricks and are not supplied by Kirkbi. Kirkbi argued that consumers would be confused if such a disclaimer is not made, and that would constitute passing-off.

The Supreme Court of Canada unanimously dismissed Kirkbi's claim, stating that a purely functional design may not be the basis of a trademark, whether registered or unregistered. The law of passing-off cannot be used to perpetuate monopoly rights enjoyed under expired patents.

This case also illustrates the distinction between patents and trademark protection. Patents protect new products and processes and are premised on the concept of a bargain between the inventor and the public. In exchange for the disclosure of the invention, the patent confers a time-limited monopoly to the patent owner, giving the owner the exclusive right to use and market the subject matter of the patent.

Trademark protection is concerned not with the product itself but with the distinctiveness of the product's marketing. Trademarks identify for the consumer the source of a product or service in a distinctive manner so that consumers know what they are buying and from whom. Because the consumer market relies on brand marketing, the identity of a product holds great economic value for the trademark owners.

The Kirkbi case asks whether the distinguishing guise can be the product itself. The resulting Court decision says that despite the connection between the mark and its product, a mark must not be confused with the product itself.

Source: *Kirkbi AG v. Ritvik Holdings Inc.*, 2005 SCC 65, [2005] 3 S.C.R. 302.

Trademarks and Overlap with Other Types of Intellectual Property

Trademark protection can potentially apply to the same subject matter as copyright protection. The cartoon character Mickey Mouse, for instance, is subject to copyright protection, and Mickey Mouse is also a trademark of the Disney company. Other companies are legally restricted from using the Mickey Mouse logo in connection with their goods and products without permission from Disney, because doing so would risk confusing consumers.

If an industrial design is associated by the public with a single source of the product, then an industrial design could attract trademark protection as well. The design could be protected under common law trademark rights, or potentially registered as a "distinguishing guise".

See Exhibit 33.9 for a summary of a case involving the LEGO blocks, in which the Supreme Court of Canada elaborated on the distinctions between patent protection and trademark protection.

Term of Protection

The registration period for a trademark is 15 years and is renewable for successive 15-year periods. It is essential that a trademark be in use in order for the owner to maintain its rights. If, three years after registration, a trademark is not used, an interested party may apply to the Federal Court to have the trademark expunged for non-use. A trademark may also be expunged without

> **EXHIBIT 33.10**
>
> **When Trademark Protection Doesn't Apply**
>
> A restaurateur applied to register its trademark "Barbie" and related design in association with restaurant, take-out, catering, and banquet services. Mattel opposed the application on grounds that its own "Barbie" mark used in association with dolls and doll accessories is so famous that the average consumer would be misled into making a trade connection between Barbie, the restaurant, and Mattel's doll. The Trade-marks Opposition Board ("Board") found in favour of the restaurant and allowed the application for reason that the use of "Barbie" for a small chain of restaurants in Montreal would not likely create confusion with Mattel's trademark. The Board's decision was upheld on appeal and by the Supreme Court of Canada.
>
> The issue in this case is whether the owner of a famous trademark can use trademark law to prevent the use of a common name such as "Barbie" in relation to other goods and services that are not related to the goods and services associated with the fame of the famous trademark. The fame of the "Barbie" mark was in association with dolls and did not extend to restaurant services as there was no evidence that Mattel used "Barbie" for restaurant services.
>
> The Court found the fame of the "Barbie" brand is a surrounding circumstance of importance, but it is not the overriding factor that would eclipse the other factors listed in section 6(5) of the *Trade-marks Act*. The Court reasoned that no person should be permitted to "fence in the common of the English or French languages and words of a general nature cannot be appropriated over a wide area" (*Mattel, Inc. v. 3894207 Canada Inc.*, para. 75).
>
> The Supreme Court reiterated the purpose and public benefit of trademark law is to assure consumers of the source and quality of the product and services that they are buying. The Court called trademark law a form of "consumer protection legislation" and regulation to encourage "fair competition". Hence, trademark law seeks to balance the competing interests of consumer protection, fair or open competition between merchants, and protecting the investment of the trademark owner in the mark. In seeking this balance, the Court must not grant exclusivity that exceeds the purpose of trademark law.
>
> **Source:** *Mattel, Inc. v. 3894207 Canada Inc.*, [2006] 1 S.C.R. 772, 2006 SCC 22.

the three-year requirement if an interested party applies on the grounds that the trademark has been abandoned, was not registratable, was not distinctive, or the applicant was not entitled to registration (s. 45 and s. 57 of the Act).

Infringement Actions Trademark owners can take legal action to prevent competitors from using the same, or a "confusingly similar", mark in such a way that there is a reasonable likelihood that the public would think the competitor's products or services are being made by the real trademark holder. The trademark owner needs to show that the use by the competitor has done damage to the goodwill or reputation of the owner's business. With respect to a registered trademark, an infringement action is generally commenced in Federal Court pursuant to sections 7 and 20 of the *Trade-marks Act*.

An action to stop the infringement of an unregistered trademark is recognized as a "passing-off" action in common law and can be commenced in Federal Court pursuant to s. 7(c) and (e) of the *Trade-marks Act*. Or, a common law passing-off action may be commenced in a superior court at the provincial court.

Determining Trademark Confusion The *Trade-marks Act* (s. 6) requires that "all surrounding circumstances" be taken into consideration in the determination of confusion. The Act lists five factors to be taken into account:

- The degree of distinctiveness and the extent of the reputation of the trademark
- The length of time the mark has been in use
- The nature of the goods and services or business
- The nature of trade
- The degree of resemblance between the trademarks in the appearance or sound or in the ideas suggested by them

This list is not exhaustive, and the courts have emphasized that all surrounding circumstances be taken into account and that no one factor trumps another factor.

The question of whether two trademarks are confusing is asked from "the point of view of the average hurried consumer having an imperfect recollection of the opponent's mark who might have encountered the trade mark of the applicant in association with the applicant's wares in the market-place" (*Mattel, Inc. v. 3894207 Canada Inc.*, as discussed in Exhibit 33.10). The law recognizes that the consumer's decision-making process will depend on the type of purchase. A person buying a car or appliance will pay more attention to the brand than when buying a mid-price meal. In some contexts, the purchaser will be bilingual. In determining confusion, the intent of the competitor using the similar trademark is not a relevant factor. What needs to be proved is "likelihood" of confusion and not "actual confusion". Evidence of actual confusion is persuasive, although not necessary.

Passing-Off Tort Action

The passing-off action has a long history in the common law, dating back to the seventeenth century. Originally, its roots are the law of deceit, which was concerned with honesty and fairness in trade and competition. The aims of the passing-off action were to ensure that buyers knew what they were purchasing and from whom. It was also to protect the economic interest that traders held in their reputation and name. The modern doctrine of passing-off that evolved from these principles is now enshrined in the federal *Trade-marks Act* while existing concurrently in common law.

Passing-off of a common law trademark is the use of a mark in such a way that it is a misrepresentation of the source of the product or service. The passing-off can take the form of use of the *same mark* to fraudulently pass off a good or service for the legitimate good or service, or it could be the use of a *confusingly similar mark* for products and services of the same type. Passing-off can arise where the mark is used in one locale, and the same or similar mark is used by another business in another location such that it is confusing to those who see the marks. The owner of the mark in the original locale can assert that its advertising and marketing has a spillover effect into other geographic locations and that it has plans to expand its business in those locations and needs to protect the goodwill it has invested in its trademark. In a 1990 English Court of Appeal decision, a test with three criteria was established to determine whether a product or service is passing-off:

1. The common law trademark has acquired reputation or goodwill through the use of the mark in association with the goods or service.
2. The infringing party has made a misrepresentation that is deceptive or is confusing to those who see the mark.
3. The owner of the trademark has suffered damages from the infringing party's benefit of the mark's goodwill and reputation.[19]

---

[19] *Reckitt & Coleman Products Limited v. Borden Inc. and Ors*, [1990] 1 All E.R. 873.

Famous Trademarks and the Depreciation of Goodwill

Famous marks were recognized in trademarks legislation in 1953 when the "depreciation of goodwill" cause of action was added to the *Trade-marks Act.* Section 22 states that "[n]o person shall use a trademark registered by another person in a manner that is likely to have the effect of depreciating the value of the goodwill attaching thereto." The depreciation of goodwill cause of action is similar the "anti-dilution" remedy in the United States. The U.S. concept of "dilution" is not concerned with confusion but with the diminishment of a mark's uniqueness and distinctiveness in the public's perception caused by the unauthorized use of the mark.

In 2006, the Supreme Court of Canada adjudicated two cases involving famous trademarks known worldwide versus lesser-known but registered trademarks used in Canada. The first case involved the trademark "Barbie" used in association with a doll. The second case involved "Veuve Clicquot", the famous mark for champagne and other luxury goods. In both cases, the Supreme Court recognized the existence of famous marks, and of the importance of protecting the goodwill associated with famous marks. However, despite acknowledging the importance of the fame of the marks, the lower courts and the Supreme Court found in favour of the lesser-known marks in both cases.

What is common between both cases is that the fame of the trademark is an important factor but is only one of several factors in determining whether there is confusion when taking into consideration the surrounding circumstances. The *Veuve Clicquot* case is important in that it also clarifies the test for proving deprecation of goodwill under the *Trade-marks Act.*

TRADE SECRETS AND CONFIDENTIAL INFORMATION

The terms "trade secret" and "confidential information" are applied to information (i) that has commercial value, (ii) that is not commonly known, and (iii) for which efforts have been made to maintain confidentiality. Another term lawyers will use is "proprietary information". Such information is said to give the owner an opportunity to obtain an advantage over competitors who lack it. Trade secrets can include any of the following: code, compound, device, drawing, formula, mechanism, pattern, plan, process, program, recipe, tool, technique, provided that it is not generally known or readily ascertainable by the public. The terms **trade secret** and **confidential information** are normally used interchangeably, but they can be distinguished. Trade secrets are often said to relate to know-how, while confidential information may include proposed trade names or compilations of information such as customer lists, for instance. The most familiar example of a trade secret is the recipe for Coca-Cola.

Trade secrets can be sold, licensed, or otherwise exploited for pecuniary gain. Trade-secrecy protection lasts for as long as the object of protection remains secret, which means there is an indefinite term of protection. If a firm X acquires a trade secret owned by Y through industrial espionage or unauthorized disclosure by an employee, then Y could sue X to prevent use of the secret or to require X to pay Y a licensing fee. But if the information becomes publicly known, by independent discovery or examination of the product, it can no longer be protected as a trade secret. For some assets, such as a computer program or a database, which are protected by copyright or patent law, reverse engineering could potentially lead to copyright or patent infringement. If something is a trade secret, then it cannot be patented, because inventions must be disclosed to the public to get patent protection. Inventors must choose whether to keep the invention a secret or to apply for patent protection.

| A Case of Depreciation of Goodwill | EXHIBIT 33.11 |

Veuve Clicquot brought an action against the defendant, a mid-priced women's clothing boutique for confusion in the marketplace under section 20 and for depreciation of goodwill under section 22 of the *Trade-marks Act*. This case is significant for the Supreme Court analysis of the depreciation of goodwill cause of action.

It was established at trial and affirmed on appeal that Veuve Clicquot is indeed a famous trademark representing the very best champagne and extending to other luxury products. The Court affirmed that fame or strength of a trademark is a very important factor but is only one in a number of other circumstances to be weighted. Despite its fame, Veuve Clicquot was not able to prove that the clothing boutique's use of a similar mark was confusing or that it would depreciate the goodwill of the senior mark.

Veuve Clicquot did not give evidence of actual confusion. Nor did the expert evidence given by Veuve Clicquot establish the likelihood of confusion. The evidence merely provided a conjecture of possible confusion. Hence, the claim for confusion was rejected by the lower courts and upheld on appeal to the Supreme Court.

The next stage of analysis concerned the depreciation of goodwill. Goodwill is not defined in the *Trade-marks Act*. Its ordinary meaning connotes "the positive association that attracts customers towards its owner's wares and services rather than its competitors" (*Veuve Clicquot*, para 50). The depreciation of goodwill does not require proof of confusion, but rather, whether the use of the mark creates an association in minds of the relevant group of consumers such that there is likely depreciation in the value of the goodwill attaching to the mark. A mental association does not automatically result in depreciation of goodwill.

There are four elements to prove depreciation of goodwill:

1. The registered trademark was used by the offending party in connection with goods or services regardless of whether the goods or services are in competition.
2. The registered trademark must have acquired goodwill through being sufficiently well known, although the mark need not be famous.
3. There must be a link between the offending use (although not necessarily confusing use) that would likely have an effect on goodwill.
4. The likely effect of the offending use is the depreciation of the value of goodwill.

The plaintiff was unable to prove that the defendant's use of "Cliquot" in its store would cause a consumer to make a link or connection between the plaintiff's mark and mid-priced women's clothing. And, where there is no such mental association, there can be no depreciation of goodwill.

The standard of proof is "likelihood" that the defendant's use would depreciate the plaintiff's mark. It is not sufficient to prove that depreciation "could" occur. Nor is it necessary to prove that depreciation "did" occur. It is essential that the offending use in question caused damage to the goodwill. It is not necessary that the use be confusing. In determining the existence of goodwill, the relevant factors to consider are recognition of the mark, volume of sales, market share of the products carrying the mark, reach and duration of advertising and marketing using the mark, geographic reach of the mark, inherent and acquired distinctiveness of the mark, whether the mark is confined to a narrow or specialized trade, and whether the mark identifies quality.

Source: *Veuve Clicquot Ponsardin v. Boutiques Cliquot Ltée*, 2006 SCC 23, [2006] 1 S.C.R. 824.

Trade secrets can be revealed to particular persons under specified conditions, for instance, with the signing of a confidentiality agreement that forbids disclosure. A business may wish to disclose a trade secret for reasons of marketing, evaluation, or to obtain financial backing. Some contracts of employment contain a confidentiality agreement binding the employee. A non-competition agreement prevents an employee from using contacts or information gained during the course of employment for the benefit of a competitor, or from setting up a competing establishment once that person leaves the original place of employment. Such agreements typically set out a specific period of time and geographic area for the non-competition obligation to apply. Otherwise, if the terms are too restrictive, the agreements are at risk of being found to be in restraint of trade by a court, if challenged.

Confidentiality agreements are also referred to as "non-disclosure agreements". Although such agreements usually take the form of a written contract, an obligation of confidentiality, or non-disclosure, can be implied or inferred in the context of business relationships. As an example, a business that conducts patent searches for inventors would be expected to keep any information about the invention secret, even if no written agreement had been signed, because of the nature of the business.

Significantly, the Supreme Court of Canada has ruled, in *R. v. Stewart*,[20] that misappropriation of confidential information cannot constitute "theft" as that term appears within the context of the *Criminal Code*. So, although confidential information is protected with intellectual property-like measures, it is not considered a fully fledged property right.

To pursue an action for "breach of confidence", a plaintiff needs to show that the information at issue had the "necessary quality of confidence". Numerous factors can be of assistance for determining whether specific information has the requisite "quality of confidence" in a particular case, including the following: (i) the extent to which the information is publicly available; (ii) the extent to which the information is known within the proprietor's business or known by employees and others involved in the owner's business; (iii) measures taken by the owner to guard the secrecy of the information; (iv) the value of the information to the owner and its competitors; (v) the amount of money or effort expended by the owner in developing the information; and (vi) the ease or difficulty with which the information could be properly acquired or duplicated by others through their own independent endeavours.[21]

Other factors considered by courts include (i) the degree to which the owner regards and treats the information as confidential, and (ii) the degree to which the recipient regards and treats the information as confidential.

A plaintiff also needs to establish that information was disclosed to a recipient in circumstances under which the recipient ought to have known that it was confidential, and that the defendant misused the information. A plaintiff can sue for copyright infringement as well as for breach of confidence, if copyright applies.

In the case of *Cadbury Schweppes Inc. v. FBI Foods Ltd.*,[22] the Supreme Court elaborated on the cause of action referred to as "breach of confidence" and on issues relating to remedies. The plaintiff Cadbury Schweppes' subsidiary, Duffy-Mott, had licensed the formula for making "Clamato" to Caesar Canning, the predecessor of FBI Foods. Clamato consisted of a confection of tomato juice and clam broth. The licence agreement had prohibited the recipient of the formula from manufacturing or distributing products, other than "Clamato", which contained tomato juice and clam broth. Duffy-Mott communicated confidential information to Caesar Canning about the recipe before the licensing relationship was terminated. Subsequently, Caesar Canning began to manufacture and distribute its own tomato juice product, "Caesar Cocktail", consisting of the Clamato recipe without the clam broth. After FBI Foods pur-

---

[20] [1988] 1 S.C.R. 963.
[21] *Pharand Ski Corp. v. The Queen in Right of Alberta* (1991), 37 C.P.R. (3d) 288 (Alta. Q.B.).
[22] [1999] 1 S.C.R. 142.

chased the assets of Caesar Canning, upon the bankruptcy of the latter, it continued to put out the Caesar Cocktail product. Cadbury Schweppes eventually commenced an action for breach of confidence against FBI Foods.

Courts at the trial and appeal levels found that FBI Foods was liable for breach of confidence, by virtue of its use of the Clamato recipe to formulate Caesar Cocktail. FBI Foods was enjoined from using the technical information and advice which had been provided by Cadbury Schweppes under the licence. The Supreme Court set aside the permanent injunction, holding that it was unduly prejudicial to the defendant, particularly in light of the plaintiff's delay in pursuing legal action (five years after termination of the licence). The Supreme Court found that the recipe was "not very special information"; it was not "rocket science", as Mr. Justice Ian Binnie, author of the decision, put it. If FBI Foods had wanted to, it could have produced a sufficiently close "copy-cat" product within about a year of the termination of the licence agreement. Thus, FBI Foods effectively got a "head-start" of a year by continuing to use the Clamato recipe. The Supreme Court found that Cadbury was entitled to lost profits for the year following the termination.

REMEDIES

Plaintiffs who pursue civil litigation, for example, intellectual property owners who sue alleged infringers, normally ask the court to provide them with a remedy. The remedies available to intellectual property rights-holders include damages, injunctions, and accounting of profits. Damages consist of monetary compensation for the harm, injury, or loss suffered by the plaintiff through the unlawful acts of the defendant. An **injunction** is an order or decree by which a party to an action is required to do, or refrain from doing, a particular thing. A mandatory, or positive, injunction requires the party so ordered to do something, whereas a restrictive, or prohibitory injunction prohibits the party so ordered from doing something. A mandatory injunction must define precisely what it is that the defendant is ordered to do. Likewise, a prohibitory injunction needs to specify just what wrongful action the defendant is to refrain from committing or continuing. As regards time, injunctions are either interlocutory (interim or temporary) or perpetual (also known as permanent). Temporary, or interim injunctions, are granted pending the final outcome of the dispute at trial and they cease at the end of the trial. Permanent injunctions are granted at the outcome of a trial. A further remedy available to intellectual property rights-holders is delivery of infringing goods (or offending labels) in the possession of the defendant, an ancillary order that can accompany an injunction against infringement. Normally, such an order will provide infringers with the option of destroying the infringing goods on oath.

Another remedy that plays an important role in intellectual property cases is an **account of profits**. If an infringer profits more by its wrongdoing than the right-holder loses, the court can order an account of profit to prevent unjust enrichment and provide a deterrent to infringement. This remedy can be available even when a right-holder has suffered no actual loss (and thus there is nothing to compensate for by way of damages). The infringing party is required to "lay open" its books (to determine the amount of net after-tax profits), and moreover the claimant can usually recover, compound prejudgment interest at prime rate on the profits. The account of profit is typically awarded as an alternative to damages, except in the case of copyright, where a plaintiff may have both. A qualification in those situations is that double counting on the same unit has to be avoided, so that only the amount of the defendant's profits that were not accounted for in the calculation of the plaintiff's damages can be added in.

CHAPTER SUMMARY

Intellectual property law covers three main types of intellectual property in Canada: copyright, patents, and trademarks, each of which is represented by a federal statute. In addition, there is common law protection available for unregistered trademarks, and for trade secrets and confidential information. The point is emphasized in this chapter that many features of intellectual property protection in the domestic context reflect the globalization of norms through international agreements.

This chapter has provided a definition of intellectual property and a discussion of the public policy rationales for legal protection of inventions and creations. The chapter surveys the crucial aspects of the three main types of intellectual property, defining each and setting out the main criteria for protection, the term of protection, and the basis for infringement. We have highlighted several prominent controversies surrounding copyright law and patent law in the modern age. Significant Canadian intellectual property cases are summarized that deal with music downloading (through peer-to-peer file sharing), gene patents, and famous trademarks. The protection of trade secrets and confidential information, very important in the everyday business context, is also briefly surveyed. The types of remedies available to intellectual property rights-holders are explained and differentiated.

GLOSSARY OF NEW TERMS AND KEY CONCEPTS

account of profits
A remedy that can be available to plaintiffs in intellectual property litigation, requiring the infringing defendant to detail the profits made from infringing activities and to pay those monies to the claimant.

assignment
Voluntary transfer of the ownership of an intellectual property right. The person transferring is the assignor and the recipient is the assignee.

breach of confidence
Legally actionable wrong of disclosing or using commercially valuable, confidential information, which a person received in confidence, or took improperly for a purpose not authorized by the confider.

class action
A civil lawsuit in which a representative plaintiff acts on behalf of a defined class of plaintiffs (e.g., all consumers injured by a particular faulty product, or all investors induced to invest in a particular fraudulent business scheme). A class action allows the issues common to a large number of separate potential cases to be heard in one trial.

common law
Judge-made law, arising from cases as distinct from statutory law.

compilation
A copyrighted work comprising of a selection or arrangement of literary, dramatic, musical, or artistic work, or an arrangement of data such as a directory or database.

confidential information
Commercial information that is valuable to a business if it remains secret, and that can be protected through contracts, and also through the "breach of confidence" cause of action at common law.

confusion
The misleading inference that goods and services derive from a particular source, when those goods and services actually derive from another source. The likelihood of confusion must be proven in order for trademark infringement to be found.

copyright
The legal protection given to original artistic, dramatic, literary, and musical works for the term of the author's life plus 50 years in Canada. The French term is "droit d'auteur".

Copyright Board
Tribunal established under the *Copyright Act*, which has authority over rate approvals (tariffs) for cable re-transmission, broadcasting, and blank audio-recording media levies. Appeals of the decisions of the Copyright Board go directly to the Federal Court of Appeal.

copyright collective	A society, association, or corporation that carries on the business of collective administration of copyright for the benefit of those who authorize the collective to act on their behalf.
digital rights management	Technology used to protect the interests of those who own content (such as copyright owners), and which is intended to prevent illegal distribution of content over the Internet. Typically, authorized recipients or users of copyrighted materials — files, music, movies, etc. — must acquire a licence in order to consume the protected material in accordance with rules set by the content owner.
distinctiveness	The quality of a trademark that distinguishes the goods and services from other goods and services. Distinctiveness is acquired through use of the trademark.
distinguishing guise	The shape of goods or their containers or a mode of packaging goods such that the appearance of the good distinguishes the good from others.
expungement	In trademark law, the striking of a trademark from the registry on the basis of non-use after three years of registration, or on grounds that the trademark has been abandoned, was not registrable, was not distinctive, or that the applicant was not entitled to registration. In patent law, a declaration that a patent is void, and is to be struck or deleted from the registry.
fair dealing	In Canadian law, a defence to copyright infringement.
fair use	In American law, a defence to copyright infringement.
famous trademark	A trademark whose "aura" transcends the goods and services with which it is normally associated.
goodwill	The positive association that attracts owners towards its owner's goods and services rather than to those of its competitors.
impeachment	Proceedings concerning the invalidation of a patent under Canadian law.
industrial design	The features of shape, ornamentation, or pattern that are applied to mass-produced finished articles can be protected under the *Industrial Design Act* in Canada. Limited protection for the first fifty copies of such articles can be obtained under the *Copyright Act*.
infringement	Violation or breach of an intellectual property right for which the rights-holder could go to court to recover civil remedies against the infringer. Some specified copyright infringements are also criminal offences.
injunction	A court order that can require a positive act (a mandatory injunction) or the cessation of an activity (a negative, or restrictive injunction). Such court orders can be granted pre-trial (interim or interlocutory injunction) or after the completion of a trial (final injunction). Failure to comply with an injunction can lead to proceedings for contempt of court. Injunctions are an important remedy in intellectual property cases.
integrated circuit topography	The three-dimensional configurations of the materials that form integrated circuits, which are protected under the *ICT Act* in Canada. The equivalent to what is known in the United States as "semiconductor chip protection".
intellectual property	Creations or products of the mind, intangible and incorporeal items that can be created, owned, and exploited exclusively by an owner, or by someone authorized by the owner (as under a licence), for commercial advantage.
licence	An intellectual property rights-holder can "licence" others to do what only the rights-holder (licensor) is legally entitled to do, thereby giving permission for the licencee to exercise those rights. An exclusive licence gives the exploitation right to a licencee to the exclusion of the right-holder, whereas a sole licence enables the right-holder to continue to exercise the intellectual property right. A non-exclusive licence allows the licensor to contract with several licencees in the same area.
moral rights	An author's right in the integrity of the work, the right to be associated with the work as its author by name or under a pseudonym, and the right to remain anonymous. Authors of copyrighted works are entitled to have their work properly attributed and for their work not to be prejudicially modified or associated with other products. Moral rights are legally enforceable. The French phrase is "droits moraux".

national treatment	Principle of non-discrimination in matters of trade. International intellectual property agreements oblige member countries, such as Canada, to extend to all other member countries the same rights that accrue to Canadians.
neighbouring rights	Rights that are related to or "neighbour" on copyright.
non-competition agreement	An agreement under which one party agrees not to compete with the other party for a specified period of time or within a particular area. Non-competition terms are generally included in an employment contract (and intended to continue in force after the cessation of the employment) or a contract for the sale of a business.
non-disclosure agreement	A legally binding contract in which a person or business promises to keep confidential certain information or trade secrets imparted by the owner, and agrees not to disclose the confidential information or trade secret to others without proper authorization by the owner.
non-obviousness	One of the statutory criteria for patentability. An invention needs to be non-obvious to those who are skilled in the relevant field of expertise.
novelty	One of the statutory criteria for patentability which requires the invention to be new and not anticipated by prior art (see *prior art*, below).
originality	The threshold requirement for a work to by protected by copyright law in Canada. In Canada, originality arises when the work is not copied, and when the work is, at a minimum, the expression of the author's skill and judgment. Works that are not original cannot be protected by copyright.
parallel import	Importation of a product legally made abroad into Canada without the authorization of the Canadian intellectual property owner. Also known as "grey marketing".
passing-off	The legally actionable wrong of misrepresenting one's business, goods, or services as another's business, goods, or services, to the detriment of the rights-holder.
patent	Intellectual property protection for inventions that meet the statutory criteria (utility, novelty, and non-obviousness) and are patentable subject matter.
piracy	The term commonly used by intellectual property owners to refer to those who infringe their intellectual property rights.
plant breeders' rights	Rights pertaining to new varieties of plants that are new, distinct, uniform, and stable, and are protected under the *Plant Breeders' Rights Act* in Canada.
prior art	The body of knowledge in the area of the invention that exists prior to the filing date of the patent. The patent examiner surveys the prior art of an invention to determine whether the invention meets the criteria of novelty and non-obviousness.
prosecution	Term used in the context of pursuing an action for intellectual property infringement, as in patent prosecution or trademark prosecution, and distinct from prosecution under criminal law.
registered trademark	A trademark registered with the Canadian Intellectual Property Office. A registered trademark confers the exclusive right to use the mark throughout Canada.
rival/non-rival	Goods for which possession by one person reduces the amount available for consumption by another have the feature of "rivalry". Non-rivalry refers to goods for which consumption by one consumer can occur without preventing simultaneous consumption by others.
royalty	Money which is payable for the authorized use of an intellectual property right.
technological protection measures	Devices, mechanisms, or systems designed to protect against, or restrict, unauthorized use of material stored in digital formats. These can include encryption technologies, access-protection codes, and other software and hardware measures.
trademark	A mark used to distinguish the products, goods, or services of one trader from others.
trade name	The name under which a corporation, firm, or individual carries on a business. Trade names are registrable under the *Trade-marks Act*.

trade secret

Commercially valuable information, such as formulas, recipes, plans, or technical know-how. Protection under common law is available for companies who develop trade secrets and make efforts to maintain their secrecy.

treaty

An international agreement, which can also be referred to as a convention. Upon signing onto a treaty, Canada and other member countries are committed to implementing domestic legislation to give effect to the treaty obligations.

unfair competition

A synonym for misappropriation of business interests to the injury of their owner. A term that covers a range of legally actionable wrongs under common law, including passing-off, injurious falsehood, interference with economic relations.

utility

In patent law, one of the fundamental requirements that must be met for an invention to be patentable. Utility requires the invention to apply towards a practical purpose, as opposed to being purely theoretical. In European law, the phrase "industrial application" is used instead.

waiver

Giving up a right to which one is entitled.

WIPO

World Intellectual Property Organization. An agency of the United Nations, headquartered in Geneva, Switzerland. WIPO administers many crucial intellectual property treaties. Established by the WIPO Convention from 1967 with a mandate to promote the protection of intellectual property across the globe.

REVIEW QUESTIONS

1. What is intellectual property? Compare and contrast the purposes of each of the main types of intellectual property protection (i.e., copyright, patents, and trademarks).

2. What are the sources of intellectual property law? Under which jurisdiction(s) do copyright, patents, and trademarks fall in Canada?

3. Who is an author and who is an owner, under copyright law? What is a work and what kinds of works are protectable?

4. What are neighbouring rights? Name three different kinds. How are they connected to copyright?

5. What are moral rights? What is an example of a Canadian case dealing with moral rights?

6. What is the fair-dealing defence and when does it apply? List and describe the six factors for applying the fair-dealing defence.

7. How have technological advancements posed particular challenges for copyright law? How have copyright owners responded to those challenges?

8. What is a patent? What is an invention?

9. What are the main criteria for patentability? What kinds of subject matter are excluded from patentability, and why?

10. Compare and contrast trademarks, trade names, certification marks, and distinguishing guises. Provide examples of each.

11. Describe the process of registering a trademark. How, by contrast, do trademarks get protection under common law?

12. What are the factors that courts take into consideration in infringement actions based on "confusion" under the *Trade-marks Act*? What are the factors that are considered in "passing off" actions?

13. What is a trade secret? Provide examples. Is there a difference between trade secrets and confidential information?

14. What factors are considered when determining whether a particular piece of information has the necessary "quality of confidence" to merit legal protection?

15. How long does legal protection for a trade secret last? When can the information in a trade secret no longer be protected? Can a trade secret be patented?

16. Compare the term of protection for each of copyright, industrial design, integrated circuit topography, patents, plant breeders' rights, trademarks, and trade secrets.

DISCUSSION QUESTIONS

1. What are the rationales for intellectual property protection? How does intellectual property differ from other types of property? Why do some critics object to the expansion of intellectual property as a "privatization of the commons"?

2. The federal government's proposed new amendments to the *Copyright Act* may make it illegal for a consumer to transfer music from a copy-protected CD to his or her iPod (through circumvention of the encryption). What are some of the main purposes of the proposed amendments, and how might consumers respond to them?

3. What are the copyright issues concerning the role of Internet Service Providers that have arisen in Canada, and what have the courts said about their potential liability? Do you agree with the courts' rulings?

4. What are the connections between patent law and access to essential medicines? How has Canadian law been reformed as a result of a World Trade Organization decision dealing with the issue of access to essential medicines? Do you agree with the reform?

5. Should higher life forms be patentable subject matter? What has the Supreme Court of Canada ruled about the patentability of a genetically modified mammal in the case involving the Harvard Mouse?

6. What are famous marks? Give some examples. What is the rationale for giving them special protection? What did the Supreme Court of Canada say about protecting famous marks under Canadian law in recent cases? Do you agree?

7. John Henry has discovered that his intellectual property rights in a computer program have been infringed, and he would like to pursue litigation. What types of remedies are available to him? Compare and contrast these remedies.

SUGGESTED READING

Henderson, Gordon F. (ed.), *Patent Law of Canada* (Toronto, Ont.: Carswell, 1994).
——, *Trade-marks Law of Canada* (Toronto, Ont.: Carswell, 1994).

Judge, Elizabeth, and Daniel Gervais. *Intellectual Property: The Law in Canada* (Toronto, Ont.: Thomson/Carswell, 2005).

Murray, Laura, and Samuel Trosow. *Canadian Copyright: A Citizen's Guide* (Toronto, Ont.: Between The Lines, 2007).

Vaver, David. *Copyright Law* (Toronto, Ont.: Irwin Law, 2000).

———. *Intellectual Property Law* (Toronto, Ont.: Irwin Law, 1997).

WEBSITES

Canadian Heritage, Copyright Policy Branch: <http://www.canadianheritage.gc.ca/progs/ac-ca/progs/pda-cpb/index_e.cfm>

Canadian Intellectual Property Office: <http://www.cipo.ic.gc.ca/epic/site/cipointernet-internetopic.nsf/en/Home>

CIPO Patents: <http://www.cipo.ic.gc.ca/epic/site/cipointernet-internetopic.nsf/en/h_wr00001e.html>

CIPO Trademarks: <http://www.cipo.ic.gc.ca/epic/site/cipointernet-internetopic.nsf/en/h_wr00002e.html>

CIPO Copyrights: <http://www.cipo.ic.gc.ca/epic/site/cipointernet-internetopic.nsf/en/h_wr00003e.html>

Canadian Internet Policy and Public Interest Clinic: <http://www.cippic.ca/en/>

Copyright Board of Canada: <http://www.cb-cda.gc.ca/new-e.html>

World Intellectual Property Organization: <http://www.wipo.int/portal/index.html.en>

Environmental Law

Allan Greenbaum
YORK UNIVERSITY

Alex Wellington
RYERSON UNIVERSITY

Learning Objectives

After reading this chapter, the reader should be able to:

➤ understand where "environmental law" fits in the Canadian legal system and Constitution

➤ understand how pollution is regulated under environmental statute law

➤ explain the difference between regulatory or "quasi-criminal" offences typical of environmental law and "true crimes", with particular reference to the "due diligence" defence

➤ identify, distinguish, and compare the enforcement options available to environmental officials in dealing with infractions of pollution-control laws and regulations

➤ appreciate the significance of liability of directors and officers for pollution offences

➤ understand the basic elements of the environmental assessment process

➤ appreciate the challenges of regulating toxic substances and recognize the complexities of risk assessment

➤ identify and distinguish the main common law causes of action that can be used in lawsuits over environmental harm

➤ understand the advantages and disadvantages of civil litigation as a way of addressing environmental problems

➤ identify and describe some legal tools available to governments to help protect natural areas and rare species

TABLE OF CONTENTS

INTRODUCTION

What Is Environmental Law?

Environmental law is a remarkably broad category, given that the notion of the environment is so all-encompassing. *Webster's Dictionary* defines "environment" as the "circumstances, objects or conditions by which one is surrounded", and, more usefully for our purposes, as "the complex of physical, chemical, and biotic factors (as climate, soil and living things) that act upon an organism or an ecological community and ultimately determine its form and survival". Specifically, "environmental law" refers to laws concerning the discharge of harmful substances into the air, water, or soil; nature preservation laws; and legal procedures for screening projects and substances that might have a harmful impact on human health or the natural environment.

The following examples could all be considered instances of environmental law:

- A lawsuit taken by a property owner against a vendor upon discovery that a newly purchased piece of land is contaminated from previous uses
- A class action lawsuit, on behalf of residents of a neighbourhood contaminated by cancer-causing chemicals, against the company that released the chemicals
- A certificate of approval allowing a pulp and paper mill to emit effluent into a river subject to terms and condition specifying the maximum amounts of which kinds of pollutants allowed to be present in the effluent
- Regulations requiring cars to have emission-control devices in working order
- Rules requiring that in order to be sold, pesticides must undergo a risk assessment to show that they do not pose an unacceptable risk to human health, if properly used
- Laws against killing members of designated endangered species of plants or animals

Environmental law came to be recognized as a distinct field in the late 1960s and early 1970s, when much of the legislative framework of modern environmental law was created. Environmental issues such as climate change and toxic chemical exposure continue to make headlines, however, and environmental law continues to evolve accordingly.

Types and Sources of Environmental Law

Environmental law includes both private (civil) and public (criminal, regulatory and administrative) law. *Private* environmental law mostly falls under the law of torts. Environmental harm caused by a specific identifiable party that threatens the health or property (or interferes with the property rights) of some other specific party may become the subject of a civil lawsuit should the injured party choose to sue. The main *source* of private environmental law is common law (judge-made law, based on precedent).

Public environmental law includes pollution regulation, nature-protection laws, and assessment and approval processes for projects like dams and highways or for potentially hazardous substances like pesticides. Here the state is understood as acting to protect the environment in the public interest (in contrast to **private law**, in which individuals go to court to protect their private rights). The main *sources* of public environmental law are statutes and regulations. *Statutes* are laws passed by Parliament or by provincial legislatures. Important federal environmental statutes include the *Fisheries Act*, the *Canadian Environmental Protection Act*, and the *Canadian Environmental Assessment Act*. Similar legislation exists at the provincial level; examples in Ontario include the *Environmental Assessment Act*, the *Environmental Protection Act*, and the *Ontario Water Resources Act*. Environmental statutes typically do not contain detailed rules about what is or is not allowed. Those rules are found in regulations. *Regulations* are detailed rules created by officials empowered by statutes to do so. The authority for making environmental regulations is usually delegated to Cabinet, although the actual work of drafting regulations falls to civil servants in the relevant department (for instance, the federal Department or provincial Ministry of the Environment). *Judges* play an important role in making public law because it is their job to *interpret* and apply statutes and to rule on their constitutionality. In addition, judges have been especially important in defining the burden of proof and the defences available in environmental cases.

Another source of law are principles enshrined in international agreements, which may then become incorporated into Canadian law through federal or provincial legislation, or judicial interpretation. A particularly influential example in the environmental context is the **precautionary principle**, which holds that actions should be taken to reduce or eliminate likely environmental hazards even if the causal link between a particular, suspected hazard has not yet been proven or fully understood scientifically. It is thus of especial relevance to environmental risk assessment.

The 1992 *Rio Declaration* defines the precautionary principle as follows:

> In order to protect the environment, the precautionary approach shall be widely applied by States according to their capabilities. Where there are threats of serious or irreversible damage, lack of full scientific certainty shall not be used as a reason for postponing cost-effective measures to prevent environmental degradation. [*Rio Declaration*, Principle 15][1]

That definition has been incorporated into the *Canadian Environmental Protection Act, 1999* [CEPA], S.C. 1999, c. 33. Other Canadian federal laws that have incorporated the precautionary principle include the *Canadian Environmental Assessment Act*, S.C. 1992, c. 37; *Pest Control Products Act*, S.C. 2002, c. 28; and the *Species At Risk Act*, S.C. 2002, c. 29. The Nova Scotia *Endangered Species Act*, S.N.S. 1998, c. 11, and the Ontario *Endangered Species Act*, S.O. 2007, c. 6, are examples of provincial laws. The precautionary principle was also cited by the Supreme Court of Canada in the *Spraytech v. Hudson* decision (discussed in Exhibit 34.2 later).

Constitutional Issues: Which Level of Government Is Responsible for the Environment?

The division of powers between the federal and provincial governments is set out in sections 91 and 92 of the *Constitution Act, 1867*. The "environment" is not a matter listed under either the federal or provincial heads of power. This ambiguity, unfortunately, has led to much litigation and intergovernmental wrangling. Exhibit 34.1 discusses a few significant cases that have concerned jurisdiction over the environment.

Provincial environmental jurisdiction is based on provincial jurisdiction over public lands and forests, natural resources, property and civil rights, local works and undertakings, and "all matters of a merely local" nature. *Federal* environmental jurisdiction is based on federal jurisdiction over fisheries, navigation, and shipping; criminal law; international and interprovincial affairs; and the "peace, order and good government" (POGG) power.

As interpreted by the courts, the peace, order and good government (POGG) clause gives the federal government jurisdiction over matters of "national concern", which cannot, by their nature, be adequately addressed by

---

[1] United Nations Conference on Environment and Development, Rio Declaration on Environment and Development, 1992: <http://www.un.org/documents/ga/conf151/aconf15126-1annex1.htm>

<table>
<tr><td>**EXHIBIT 34.1**</td><td>**Jurisdiction and Environmental Assessment**</td></tr>
</table>

During the late 1980s and early 1990s, the issue of the scope of federal jurisdiction over the environment was examined by the courts in two cases involving dams. One case involved construction of a dam on the Oldman River in Alberta and the other concerned plans by the Saskatchewan Water Corporation to build dams on the Rafferty and Alameda rivers. Project proponents insisted that the projects required approval only from the relevant provincial government. Opponents of the projects challenged them on the basis that the projects impacted on matters of federal government responsibility (including migratory birds and lands owned or administered by the federal government), and thus provincial environmental impact statements were not sufficient for the projects to proceed. Courts in both cases sided with environmentalists in upholding concurrent federal and provincial jurisdiction over environmental matters, even though both federal and provincial governments wanted to see the exercise of federal environmental responsibilities delegated or "downloaded" to provincial governments. The combined effect of these cases forced the federal government to acknowledge and exercise jurisdiction over the environment in matters concerning environmental assessment. As a result, the federal government passed the *Canadian Environmental Assessment Act* in 1992.

The *Friends of the Oldman River* case is also significant because it contains judicial language about the importance of approaching environmental management in an integrated manner. In it, Justice LaForest specifically states: "I cannot accept that the concept of environmental quality is confined to the biophysical environment alone; such an interpretation is unduly myopic and contrary to the generally held view that the 'environment' is a diffuse subject matter" (*Friends of the Oldman River Society v. Minister of Transport*, at 37). In connection with these issues, the Supreme Court of Canada took the view that so long as the subject matter about which a federal department (or provincial ministry) is deciding falls clearly within the (statutory and constitutional) purview of that department or ministry, it may take into account an indefinite range of relevant social, economic and environmental criteria or considerations in making that decision. Commentators emphasize that the passage in question represents the Court's first reference to the Brundtland Report, *Our Common Future*, produced by the World Commission on Environment and Development (WCED).

Sources: *Friends of the Oldman River Society v. Minister of Transport*, [1992] 1 S.C.R. 3; *Canadian Wildlife Federation v. Canada (Minister of the Environment)*, [1989] 3 F.C. 309 (T.D.), aff'd (1989), 99 N.R. 72 (F.C.A.).

---

provincial governments acting separately. The Supreme Court, in *R. v. Crown Zellerbach*,[2] found that the federal *Ocean Dumping Control Act* met that criterion because its purpose had a "singleness, distinctiveness and indivisibility that clearly distinguishes it from matters of provincial concern". In *R. v. Hydro-Quebec*,[3] however, the Supreme Court declined to use the POGG clause to uphold the constitutionality of provisions of the *Canadian Environmental Protection Act* (*CEPA*), because the latter legislation's broader concern with substances harmful to the environment was more diffuse. Rather, a slim 5 to 4 majority found provisions of *CEPA* regulating toxic substances constitutional under the federal criminal law power.

In practice, federal and provincial governments exercise shared or concurrent jurisdiction over environmental law. This arrangement suits both provincial and federal governments, since it allows governments either to take credit

---

[2] [1981] 1 S.C.R. 401.
[3] [1997] 3 S.C.R. 213.

	EXHIBIT 34.2

Courts Rule on Municipal Pesticide By-Laws

The courts (up to and including the Supreme Court of Canada) have upheld the power of municipalities to ban or restrict the "cosmetic" use of pesticides, although the pesticides have been approved for use under federal and provincial law. "Cosmetic use" means using insecticides and herbicides (weed killers) to protect lawns and flowers, etc., rather than crops, dwellings, or human health. These bans are based on the argument that the possible (if unproven) health risks associated with these chemicals outweigh merely cosmetic benefits. The first such ban was enacted in 1991 by Hudson, Quebec, a suburb of Montreal.

When Spraytech, a lawn-care company, was charged with violating the Hudson bylaw, it argued that the bylaw was beyond the authority of the municipality to enact. It made two arguments. First, it argued that according to the Quebec *Cities and Towns Act*, municipalities cannot regulate hazardous substances without provincial government approval. Second, it argued that the federal and provincial governments had approved the products in question, and that these laws trump municipal bylaws in case of conflict.

The Hudson case made its way all the way up to the Supreme Court of Canada. In *114957 Canada Ltée (Spraytech, Société d'arrosage) v. Hudson (Town)*, the Supreme Court upheld the bylaw. It ruled that the bylaw was within the general power conferred on municipalities by the *Cities and Towns Act* to make bylaws to secure public health. It also ruled that there was no conflict between the bylaw and federal and provincial pesticides laws, since the latter *permit* people to use the pesticides, but don't *require* them to do so. Municipalities thus have the power to restrict the purposes for which the pesticides are used.

Since the 2001 Supreme Court decision in the Hudson case, hundreds of other cities and towns across Canada have enacted similar by-laws. Toronto passed a cosmetic pesticide ban similar to Hudson's in 2003. Toronto's bylaw was also challenged in court, this time by Croplife Canada, a pesticide industry group, in the case of *Croplife v. City of Toronto*. Again, the courts upheld the bylaw. In both the Hudson and Toronto cases, many environmental, health, and municipal organizations appeared before the courts as *intervenors* arguing in support of the bylaws.

In June 2008, the Ontario government passed legislation (the *Cosmetic Pesticides Ban Act*) prohibiting the cosmetic use of pesticides across the province, but this legislation also nullified the municipal pesticide bylaws.

Sources: *114957 Canada Ltée (Spraytech, Société d'arrosage) v. Hudson (Town)*, [2001] 2 S.C.R. 241; *Croplife Canada v. Toronto (City)* (2003), 68 O.R. (3d) 520 (Ont. Sup. Ct.) (Motions Court), 2003 CanLII 24713 (ON S.C.); *Croplife Canada v. Toronto (City)* (2005), 75 O.R. (3d) 357 (C.A.), (2005), 2005 CanLII 15709 (ON C.A.), leave to appeal to S.C.C. refused, [2005] S.C.C.A. No. 329.

for action or to avoid blame for inaction by "passing the buck", depending on which course seems most politically expedient. In recent years, the different levels of government have taken steps to co-ordinate their environmental responsibilities and to avoid duplication.

Municipalities are a third level of government. Their environmental responsibilities include local land-use planning (which was originally devised as a way to avert environmental tort litigation), urban form, and other matters related to local health and well-being. Unlike the provincial and federal governments, municipalities have no independent constitutional basis of authority, but have only those legal powers given to them by provincial legislation. Courts used to interpret this legislation narrowly, but have lately moved in a more liberal direction when it comes to interpreting the scope of municipal jurisdiction. This means that municipalities can "try out" at the local level policy initiatives that might then be adopted by senior levels of government. See Exhibit 34.2 for discussion of a much-publicized Supreme Court case dealing with municipal environmental jurisdiction.

POLLUTION-CONTROL LAW: THE REGULATORY SYSTEM

To remedy the deficiencies of the common law (to be discussed later on in this chapter), Canadian governments have set up a statute-based public law system for the regulation of pollution and other threats to the environment. This regulatory system is the main focus of environmental law.

The Legal Structure of the Regulatory System

Both federal and provincial regulatory systems derive from legislation. A typical environmental statute will define a number of *offences* and delegate rule-making, decision-making, and administrative authority to various *officials*. Roughly speaking, there are three levels of rules in pollution-control laws:

1. *Statutory prohibitions* against emitting harmful pollution. The statute will generally make it an offence to violate the statutory prohibition unless the polluter is in compliance with regulations or the terms of a permit or approval.

2. *Regulations*, which are much more specific, detailed, and technical than are the statutory prohibitions. The statute will also typically make it (at least potentially) an offence to be out of compliance with a regulation or approval.

3. In many cases, statutes require that certain kinds of polluters must have a *permit*, *licence*, or **certificate of approval**. To operate a specified kind of polluting enterprise without the appropriate permit or approval would be an offence, as would violating the terms and conditions of the permit. These terms and conditions are often based on regulations but are also tailored to specific circumstances. *Control orders* or *compliance orders* are also rules at this level.

All three levels of rules refer explicitly or implicitly to *standards*. Standards define what is and is not allowed by the rule, such as what exactly constitutes unlawful pollution in a given situation.

Standards and Standard-Setting

A variety of different kinds of standards are used in environmental law. We will describe a few of the major types of environmental standards and then say a bit about how standards are set — in theory and in practice.

Types of Standards

Ambient standards are standards for acceptable or unacceptable environmental quality. They are typically expressed in terms of concentrations of some pollutant such as coliform bacteria in water or particulate matter in air. Ambient standards usually function as guidelines, objectives, or targets used in setting regulatory standards rather than as standards that play a role in rules directly affecting polluters. An exception would be rules that require certain large emitters to stop operations on days when the air pollution index exceeds a certain threshold (the ambient standard).

Prescriptive standards stipulate processes, technologies, or materials. For example, a prescriptive standard might stipulate that a flue-gas scrubber of a particular design must be installed in a smelter or coal-fired power station. Voluntary industry standards and codes of "best practices" are also often prescriptive in form.

Performance standards stipulate a particular outcome but do not say how that outcome is to be achieved. They provide less guidance to polluters than prescriptive standards do, but more flexibility for innovation. Environmental

	EXHIBIT 34.3
Types of Quantitative Effluent Standards	

TYPE	DESCRIPTION
Absolute	x units of pollutant per unit time (e.g., kg. of pollutant per day)
Concentration	x units of pollutant per unit of effluent (e.g., kg. of pollutant per cubic metre of effluent)
Rate/Intensity	x units of pollutant per unit production (e.g., kg. of pollutant per tonne of product)
Relative	percent reduction relative to baseline-level emissions (e.g., 6 percent below 1990 emissions)

performance standards include effluent standards stipulating maximum allowable pollution emissions, energy efficiency standards, and so on.

Effluent standards (discharge standards) are performance standards related to pollution emissions. There are two kinds. *Impact standards* refer directly to the impact of the effluent, such as the toxicity of the effluent to fish or other aquatic organisms (as evidenced by the **fish toxicity test**). *Quantitative standards* stipulate an allowable quantity of a given pollutant in the effluent. Types of quantitative effluent standards are summarized in Exhibit 34.3.

Standard-setting

Regulatory standard-setting, in practice, takes into account both environmental quality objectives and the cost to business of meeting those objectives. Regulations may require polluters to use "best available technology economically achievable" ("BATEA"), or for effluent standards to be set "as low as reasonably achievable" (the "ALARA" principle). This balancing act is illustrated by the practice of the Ontario Ministry of the Environment in relation to hazardous air pollutants. The basic regulatory standard is set on the basis of health criteria (e.g., pollutant concentration that will cause less than a one-in-a-million increase in the risk of cancer to those exposed). Polluters who have trouble meeting the standard may, however, apply for an altered (relaxed) standard, citing technology and cost constraints. The altered standard must, however, meet the ALARA criterion and may not exceed an upper threshold defined (depending on the pollutant) as 10 or 100 times the basic standard.

Traditionally in Canada, environmental regulatory standard-setting has involved much negotiation between government and business. More recently, federal and provincial legislation (most particularly the Ontario *Environmental Bill of Rights*) has given the public the opportunity to review, to comment on, and in some circumstances to appeal the standard-setting and approval-granting decisions of government officials.

Statutory Prohibitions Environmental statutes typically include prohibitions on pollution and other kinds of environmentally damaging activities phrased in very broad language. For example, section 36(3) of the federal *Fisheries Act* makes it an offence to deposit a "deleterious substance" in water "frequented by fish" and outlines conditions under which this will be permitted. Similarly, section 14(1) of the

Ontario *Environmental Protection Act* prohibits "the discharge of a contaminant into the natural environment, if the discharge causes or may cause an adverse effect". Because of the broad and vague language in such provisions, the actual meaning of the prohibition depends on *statutory interpretation* on the part of officials and, ultimately, judges.

In the case of the *Fisheries Act* provision, "deleterious" has been interpreted in terms of an impact standard, namely the fish toxicity test. It has, moreover, been interpreted as an effluent standard, applied to the "substance" itself. If a substance fails the fish toxicity test, then it is deemed "deleterious", and you are prohibited from putting it where it will get into water inhabited by fish, even if it will enter the water in such small quantities as to be harmless. The Ontario *EPA* provision, in contrast, refers to an "adverse effect" on the environment. In interpreting that provision, courts will also use an impact standard, but they will apply it to the receiving medium (e.g., water or air) rather than to the "contaminant" itself. In our example, you would not be in violation of the Ontario *EPA* prohibition if only harmless quantities of the contaminant could reach the water.

Another feature of statutory prohibitions is that they make exceptions for activities authorized by regulations or permits. The extent of these exceptions again depends on the precise wording of the statute, as interpreted by the courts.

Regulations

Regulations, unlike statutory prohibitions, generally contain explicit and detailed standards, as well as detailed rules about how the regulated party is to monitor and report on emissions. Regulations may incorporate either prescriptive or performance standards, or some combination of both. Ontario's Local Air Quality regulation (O. Reg. 419/2005) is an example of a regulation that incorporates ambient standards. It requires designated air polluters to model (with computers) the dispersion of their effluent in the air to ensure that the concentration of regulated pollutants does not exceed concentration standards at specified "points of impingement".

Regulations that legally impose prescriptive standards are sometimes referred to as "command and control" regulations. The term "command and control" (or "command-penalty") regulation is also used more generally to refer to regulations that impose mandatory standards. Under command and control regulations in this sense, polluters are liable to be punished if they violate the standards written into the regulation. Such regulations are contrasted with "economic instruments" such as financial incentives, pollution taxes, or tradable pollution credits, which allow a given polluter to emit more than the standard if they pay more or buy additional credits from polluters who pollute less than the standard (thus rewarding those who pollute less and costing — but not punishing — those who pollute more). Economic instruments are sometimes criticized as creating a "licence to pollute", but it is important to realize that except in rare instances where pollution is banned altogether, command and control regulations *also* create a *free* licence to pollute so long as the regulatory standards are not violated or exceeded. Command and control regulations (especially those with prescriptive standards) are frequently criticized as being rigid, inefficient, and discouraging innovation. They have often proved effective in reducing pollution, however, and compliance costs usually turn out to be lower than predicted (especially as predicted by affected businesses).

Permits and Approvals

Pollution-control statutes typically require those who wish to undertake an enterprise or activity that will release wastes or contaminants into the environment to get official permission to do so. Depending on the jurisdiction, the permission document legally required is called a "permit", "licence", "consent", or "certificate of approval". The process for obtaining a permit, and some of the required terms and conditions, will be set out in the statute and regulations. Although the terms of permits will usually be based on standards in regulations, regulations may also give officials the discretion to vary those standards — for example, to impose stricter standards than those in the regulation to take into account the sensitivity of the environment into which the pollution is being discharged or the cumulative effects of multiple pollution sources.

Polluters generally have the right to appeal official decisions regarding whether and on what conditions to grant approvals. These appeals are heard by an administrative tribunal. Members of the public may also have standing to appeal environmental permit decisions. In some jurisdictions, only those who can show that they are personally affected will have the right to appeal. In Ontario, the *Environmental Bill of Rights* requires all such permits (called "instruments") to be posted on a website for public review and comment, and gives any member of the public the right to apply for leave (permission) to appeal the permit. To be granted leave, the appellant must show they have some grounds to claim that the decision was unreasonable. Approvals granted under the federal *Canadian Environmental Protection Act 1999* are also posted in an online registry for public review and comment, but are not subject to a public right of appeal.

ENFORCEMENT OF POLLUTION REGULATIONS

The Spectrum of Responses to Non-compliance	What happens if a polluter subject to pollution-control laws is detected violating a statutory prohibition, a regulation, or the terms of a permit or approval? Enforcement officials have a range of options, displayed in Exhibit 34.4. We summarize them briefly here and provide more detail below. A notable feature of environmental enforcement is the role of *negotiation* between polluters and enforcement officials. In Canada, polluters have often had the opportunity both to negotiate what the rules will be, and to negotiate what will happen when they have broken those rules.
Forbearance	The first option, which involves the least use of law, is to exercise **forbearance**. That is, the officials in question may decline to impose legal sanctions. Officials are likely to choose forbearance if they are persuaded that (i) the violation poses no serious risk; (ii) the costs of compliance would be too great for the polluter (or society as a whole); (iii) more time is required for the polluter to come into compliance (and that additional time would be reasonable); and/or (iv) the polluter has already made good faith efforts to comply with the law. In some cases, government enforcement agencies will exercise forbearance simply because they lack the resources — in terms of money and personnel — to go after every polluter who is in violation of the law.
Prosecution	At the other end of the enforcement spectrum is *prosecution* — that is, *charging* the polluter with an *offence*. A successful prosecution results in a finding of *guilt*, i.e., in the *conviction* of the *accused*. In environmental cases, the accused is usually a corporation, but individual officers (executives, managers, or directors) may also be held personally liable.

Most environmental offences are what judges call "public welfare", "regulatory", or "quasi-criminal" offences. The prosecution of these offences, in

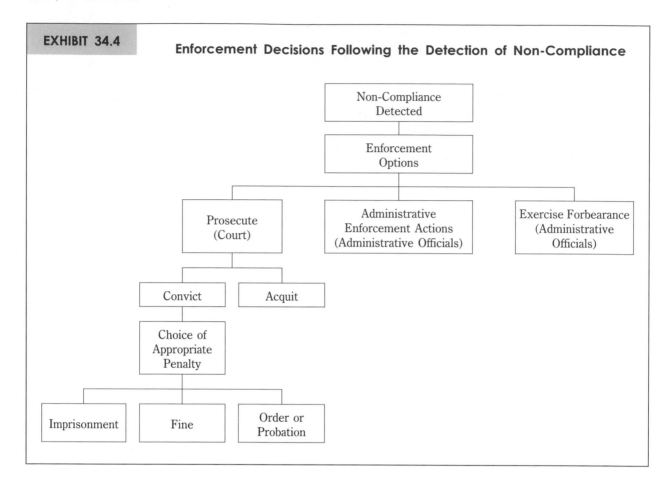

EXHIBIT 34.4

Enforcement Decisions Following the Detection of Non-Compliance

accordance with the *Provincial Offences Act* in Ontario, is procedurally the same as the prosecution of summary conviction criminal offences. The process begins with the laying of an "information". If the accused pleads "not guilty", there is a trial. As in a criminal trial, the prosecutor must prove beyond a reasonable doubt all the relevant facts establishing the *actus reus* (guilty act). For example, in a *Fisheries Act* prosecution, the prosecutor might have to prove — beyond a reasonable doubt and in conformity with the laws of admissible evidence — that effluent emitted from the accused's pulp mill at such and such a place and time in such and such a quantity was toxic to fish (meeting the impact standard used to interpret the statutory prohibition) and that the mill was at that time out of compliance with performance and prescriptive standards found in the relevant regulations and permits. This can be quite a burden for the prosecution to bear.

Strict Liability and the Due Diligence Defence

Where quasi-criminal regulatory offences differ from "true crimes" is with respect to the "mental element". Criminal liability normally requires proof not only of the *actus reus* but of the *mens rea* (guilty mind). That is, the accused must not only have done the illegal act, but to have *intended* it (or at least to have been reckless). Because in most cases it would be almost impossible to *prove* that a company *intended* to violate pollution standards or other "public welfare" rules, courts have been reluctant to hold the prosecution to the "true crime" standard in such cases. At the same time, courts have also been very reluctant to interpret these offences (which can be punishable by heavy fines or imprisonment) as imposing "absolute liability". An **absolute**

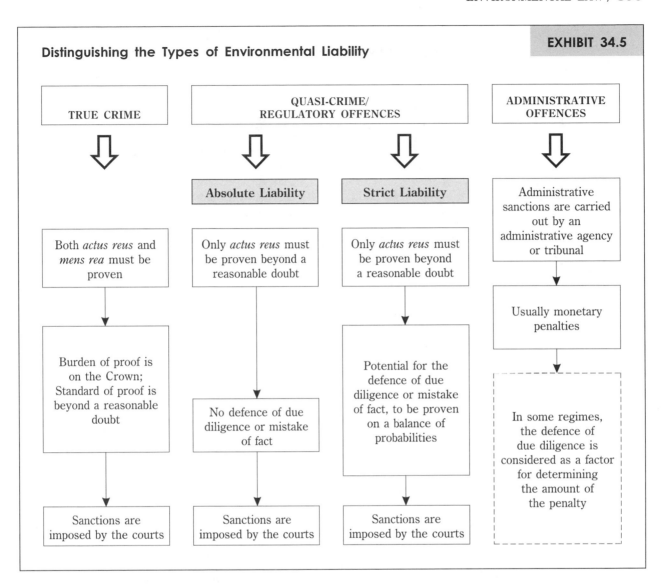

EXHIBIT 34.5

Distinguishing the Types of Environmental Liability

liability offence is one where only *actus reus* need be proven, and there is no potential for a due diligence defence. See Exhibit 34.5 for an illustration of the distinctions between true criminal liability, strict liability, and absolute liability.

The Canadian courts (most notably the Supreme Court in *R. v. Sault Ste. Marie*[4]) have articulated a concept of "strict liability" as appropriate for the vast majority of environmental and other "quasi-criminal" offences. **Strict liability** in this sense is intermediate between true criminal liability (where intent must be proven) and absolute liability (where one may be found guilty for entirely unintended, unavoidable acts). (Strict liability in this context needs to be distinguished from the *tort* of strict liability, discussed below.) For strict liability offences, the prosecution need only prove the *actus reus*; at that point, the onus shifts to the accused to prove (on a balance of probabilities) that they had exercised **due diligence** (reasonable care) to avoid the offence. If the accused persuades the court that the violation had occurred

---

[4] [1978] 2 S.C.R. 1299.

EXHIBIT 34.6 　　　　　**A Case about Pollution, Directors' Liability, and Due Diligence**

The *R. v. Bata Industries Ltd.* case illustrates several points about strict liability/due diligence, officers' personal liability, and sentencing options.

Bata Industries Limited operated a shoe factory in Batawa, Ontario. Improperly stored toxic wastes leaked into the soil and contaminated the groundwater. The Ministry of the Environment prosecuted the corporation, and also the corporation's Chief Executive Officer, its President and the on-site General Manager, for violations of the *Ontario Water Resources Act* and the Ontario *Environmental Protection Act*.

The trial judge found that the corporation, the General Manager, and the President had failed to exercise due diligence and convicted them. He found that the CEO had acted reasonably in relying on information from the General Manager and so acquitted him.

Judge Ormston articulated the following influential set of criteria for due diligence:

¤ Did the Board of Directors establish a pollution-prevention "system"? Was there supervision or inspection? Was there improvement in business methods? Did he exhort those he controlled or influenced?

¤ Did each Director ensure that the Corporate officers have been instructed to set up with a system sufficient within the terms and practices of its industry of ensuring compliance with environmental laws, to ensure that the officers report back periodically to the Board of the operations of the system, and to ensure that the officers are instructed to report any substantial non-compliance to the Board in a timely manner?

¤ The Directors are responsible for reviewing the environmental compliance reports provided by the officers of the corporation but are justified in placing reasonable reliance on reports provided to them by corporate officers, consultants, counsel, or other informed parties.

¤ The Directors should substantiate that the officers are promptly addressing environmental concerns brought to their attention by government agencies or other concerned parties, including shareholders.

¤ The Directors should be aware of the standards of their industry and other industries that deal with similar environmental pollutants or risks.

¤ The Directors should immediately and personally react when they have notice the system has failed.

The trial judge also noted: "Within this general profile and dependent upon the nature and structure of the corporate activity, one would hope to find remedial and contingency plans for spills, a system of ongoing environmental audit, training programs, sufficient authority to act and other indices of a proactive environmental policy."

Bata Ltd. was fined $60,000 and ordered to pay that money (subsequently reduced to $30,000 on appeal) into a local toxic waste disposal program. The General Manager and the President were each ordered to pay $12,000 (this was reduced to $6,000 each on appeal). The trial judge found that the CEO had acted reasonably in relying on information from the General Manager and so acquitted him. The probation order required Bata Ltd. to publish information about the conviction and sentences on the front page of its newsletter and prohibited it from indemnifying the President and General Manager for their personal fines (this latter probation condition was struck down on appeal).

Source: *R. v. Bata Industries Ltd.* (1992), 9 O.R. (3d) 329 (Prov. Ct.).

---

despite reasonable precautions to avoid it, then the accused will be acquitted. A well-known statement of due diligence criteria is found in the trial level decision in *R. v. Bata*[5] (see Exhibit 34.6).

---

[5] (1992), 9 O.R. (3d) 329 (Prov. Ct.).

Directors' Liability

When companies pollute, liability might be incurred by both the corporation itself and by the individual flesh-and-blood people who are responsible for the actions of corporations. Thus, there is also the prospect of personal liability for directors, officers, and others for environmental and other offences (see Exhibit 34.6). That liability can be civil or quasi-criminal, or even true criminal liability (as with recent amendments to the *Criminal Code* providing for true criminal liability for some workplace health and safety offences).

Sentencing

Conviction will result in a *sentence*. The commonest sentencing options for environmental offences are *fines* and *probation orders* (which may include publicizing the conviction and taking steps to remedy the environmental harm done and to prevent future infractions). In rare cases, individual officers may be sentenced to prison, usually in cases where they have wilfully and persistently defied court orders or obstructed enforcement efforts. Maximum (and sometimes minimum) sentences (fines and prison terms) are stipulated in the statute under which the accused is charged, but judges have quite a lot of discretion in sentencing. Conviction under federal (but not provincial) statutes may also result in a criminal record.

The stigma of conviction makes prosecution (especially if individual officers as well as companies are charged) a powerful deterrent. For this reason, many environmental advocates and legal scholars would like to see greater use of prosecution. Prosecution is, however, more difficult, costly, and time-consuming for enforcement officials than most other enforcement options.

Private Prosecution

If a polluter is in violation of the law and authorities are declining to enforce the law, a private individual can lay charges. This is called a private prosecution. In a private prosecution, a private party is taking the role usually taken by the Crown. It remains an action to enforce public law, however, and needs to be distinguished from civil litigation to enforce the plaintiff's private rights. The federal *Fisheries Act* provides that private prosecutors receive a share of a fine resulting from a successful prosecution. Even with this provision, private prosecution is difficult and expensive, especially if the prosecutors do not enjoy the active co-operation of government enforcement officials (which they sometimes do).

Administrative Enforcement Measures

Between prosecution and forbearance lie a range of *administrative enforcement measures*. These measures can be divided up in various ways. One way is to distinguish between *administrative compliance measures* (such as orders), which require the violator to do or cease to do something, and **administrative monetary penalties** (AMPs) and tickets, which impose a fine. In Ontario, environmental AMPs are calculated on the basis of a formula that takes into account the type, seriousness, and duration of the offence, the amount of money the polluter saved by polluting, and any mitigating circumstances. Environmental tickets, which are used by both provincial and federal authorities, are like traffic tickets and impose a small fine for minor infractions. Another way to divide up this middle ground between prosecution and forbearance is to draw a distinction between purely administrative actions (such as orders and AMPs), which are imposed by officials or administrative tribunals entirely apart from the court system, and alternative enforcement measures such as tickets and federal "environmental protection alternative measures" (EPAMs), which are technically within the jurisdiction of the courts. With these latter measures, violators have the option of avoiding or suspending prosecution by paying a set fine or agreeing to other terms and conditions.

Administrative measures are an attractive enforcement option because they are usually faster and less expensive than prosecution.

ENVIRONMENTAL IMPACT AND SUBSTANCE RISK ASSESSMENT

Canadian law prescribes assessment processes for both projects ("environmental assessment") and potentially hazardous substances.

Environmental Assessment

Environmental impact assessment (EIA), or **environmental assessment (EA)**, as it is more often called in Canadian law, is a process by which the environmental effects of a proposed project are examined and a decision made about whether the project should be allowed to go ahead. There are both provincial and federal EA statutes. The cases discussed in Exhibit 34.1 concern environmental assessment and issues of jurisdiction between the two levels of government. EA is mainly required of public sector projects, and (depending on the province) designated categories of private projects (such as waste disposal facilities). Provincial projects are subject to provincial EA. Federal projects, or provincial projects that also require federal approval (such as dams on navigable rivers) or that otherwise impinge on matters of federal jurisdiction, also require federal EA. Federal and provincial EA processes may be combined in a single joint EA, and an EA may also be joined with an approval process required under other legislation.

The project being assessed (e.g., a highway) is called the "undertaking", and the body (usually a public agency, e.g., the Ministry of Transportation) that seeks to carry out the project is called the "proponent" or (in the federal *Canadian Environmental Assessment Act*) the "responsible authority" (RA). It is the responsibility of the proponent to conduct physical, biological, ecological, and social impact studies and to prepare a document describing the impacts of the undertaking as proposed. In cases of major undertakings, there should also be a comparison of expected impacts with the impacts of "alternatives to the undertaking" and with "alternative means of carrying out the undertaking", as well as suggestions for ways of mitigating the expected negative impacts. Since the number of issues and topics that could potentially be addressed in an EA is practically infinite, the proponent will first conduct a preliminary process called "scoping". In that process, the proponent will consult with affected parties (including other government departments and members of the public) to determine which issues and concerns ought to be addressed. Once the EA document is prepared it is again subject to review by other government officials and interested members of the public.

Since the EA document is prepared on behalf of the proponent, it will typically conclude that an undertaking is unlikely to cause undue environmental harm and should be approved. Environmentalists or others concerned about the undertaking may disagree. They may think that the EA report should not be accepted (because it is based on insufficient or faulty research) and/or that, on the basis of information in the report itself, the undertaking should not be approved. In such cases, they may request that the EA be subject to a hearing. At the hearing, the proponent and the opposing parties, often represented by lawyers, will submit evidence, call expert witnesses, and cross-examine other parties' witnesses. Then the EA tribunal will make a decision about whether to accept the report and/or approve the undertaking, and under what conditions.

Because some small undertakings (such as stream crossings) are frequent and routine, they may be assessed as a class (a class EA) rather than on an individual basis. If a particular instance of an undertaking in that class might have significant distinctive impacts not addressed in the class EA, it can be "bumped up" and be subject to its own EA as a separate undertaking.

Substance Assessment and Approval

Potentially hazardous substances, as well as undertakings, may have to go through a **risk assessment** and approval process under Canadian law. For example, under the federal *Pest Control Products Act*, all pesticides must undergo a risk assessment to be approved for use in Canada. Those found to pose an unacceptable risk will not be approved. More generally, all new substances produced in or imported into Canada must be assessed under the *Canadian Environmental Protection Act*. Substances listed as being in use as of 1986 (some 23,000 of them) may continue in use without being assessed but are gradually being assessed on a priority basis by Health Canada and Environment Canada. Substances that are found to be hazardous in some respect are placed on a Toxics List and are subject to a range of regulatory controls, guidelines, and voluntary measures. The definition of "toxic" is very broad and is relative to the quantity being emitted (so, for example, carbon dioxide — which you exhale with every breath and which plants need to survive — is listed because it is being generated in such quantities as to promote dangerous global warming). The nastiest and most persistent of these toxins are placed on the Virtual Elimination List and are effectively banned.

As with EA, the data and analysis upon which the risk assessment is based are provided by the proponents. Whereas EA requirements are open-ended, new substances regulations are long and complex, and stipulate in precise detail the kinds of data that must be submitted and the kinds of studies and tests that must be conducted to obtain those data. Producers do not, however, have to prove the substance is safe to be allowed to produce it under *CEPA*; rather, they must submit data which the government will use to regulate.

CIVIL LIABILITY FOR ENVIRONMENTAL HARM

If you or your property are harmed or threatened by pollution, noise, vibration, contamination, or changes in water level caused by the actions of another party, you may be able to sue that party. This would be an instance of private (civil) law, specifically tort law. If you (the plaintiff) are successful, the defendant will be found *civilly liable*. If the defendant is found liable, the plaintiff is entitled to a *remedy*. There are two main kinds of remedy: monetary compensation paid by the defendant (*damages*), and a court order requiring the defendant to stop (or not to commence) the harmful activity in question (an *injunction*). A plaintiff can be awarded both types of remedies, if the court so decides.

Although civil litigation is not a major aspect of environmental law, it is one of the best known. A number of high-profile cases (mainly in the United States, but also in Canada) have been based on the alleged contamination of a community by toxic substances from local industry, which is often claimed to result in elevated rates of cancer and other diseases. Such cases are referred to as *toxic torts*. Real-life toxic tort cases were dramatized in the 1998 film *A Civil Action* and the 2000 film *Erin Brockovich*.

In order to succeed, the plaintiff must prove, on a balance of probabilities, that the defendant in fact caused the harm alleged. In environmental cases, this is often no simple matter. For example, if you are claiming that the defendant's pollution caused you to get cancer, it is not enough to show that the defendant has emitted pollutants that have been linked to cancer. You must show that it was the defendant's pollution that probably caused *your* cancer. This usually raises complex technical issues of fact that are fraught with scientific uncertainty. The plaintiff must also show that the defendant's activity falls within a legally recognized **cause of action**.

Common Law Causes of Action

For the most part, civil liability still rests on causes of action derived from common law. Negligence is the most common form of tort liability in general, and it also plays a role in environmental litigation. There are three tort causes of action that arise from the plaintiff's property rights: trespass to land, breach of riparian rights, and private nuisance. Two other causes of action found in environmental tort cases are public nuisance and strict liability.

Negligence

The elements of a **negligence** action are the following:

1. *Duty of care.* The defendant must owe a legal duty to the victim. A duty is a legally enforceable obligation to conform to a particular standard of conduct. Except in malpractice and strict liability cases, the duty is set by what a "reasonable man of ordinary prudence" would have done. There is a general duty to prevent foreseeable injury to a victim.

2. *Breach of the duty.* The defendant breached that duty by failure to conform to the expected standard of care.

3. *Causation.* The breach was the cause of an injury to the victim. The causation does not need to be direct: defendant's act (or failure to act) could begin a continuous sequence of events that ended in plaintiff's injury, a so-called "proximate cause". The breach cannot be too remote a cause of the injury.

4. *Injury.* There must be an injury. In most cases, there must be a physical or financial injury to the victim, but sometimes emotional distress, embarrassment, or dignitary harms are adequate for recovery.

To proceed in a negligence action, a plaintiff does not have to be a landowner. Nor does the defendant have to have caused the environmental hazard in question; the defendant may, for example, have negligently failed to fulfill a duty to inform the plaintiff of the hazard or to remedy the situation. However, the plaintiff must show that the defendant had a duty of care and failed to fulfill that duty.

Trespass to Land

Trespass to land involves the defendant, without authorization, directly and intentionally entering on to the plaintiff's land or placing a foreign object or substance on it. Unlike most other torts, this may result in liability without proof of harm or loss. This means, for example, that you could get an injunction to stop someone from dumping debris on your property even if you could not show that the dumping interfered with your use of the land or diminished its value. This cause of action is of limited use in environmental cases because pollution is seldom introduced directly and intentionally onto the property of those affected. In one New Brunswick case, a company spraying forests with insecticide to control spruce budworm was found liable in trespass for directly and without permission spraying the plaintiffs' property.[6]

---

[6] *Friesen et. al. v. Forest Protection Ltd.* (1978), 22 N.B.R. (2d) 146 (QB).

	EXHIBIT 34.7
McKie v. K.V.P: A Classic Water Pollution Lawsuit and its Aftermath	

In 1946, Kalamazoo Vegetable Parchment (K.V.P.) acquired a pulp and paper mill in Espanola, Ontario, that had closed 15 years earlier in the Depression. The re-opened mill released several tonnes of effluent a day into the Spanish River. The pollution killed fish, destroyed wild rice beds that provided duck habitat, and made the water smell like rotting cabbage — undrinkable by people or farm animals.

In 1948, a group of downstream riparian landowners — including farmers, tourist operators, and a commercial fisher — sued KVP for private nuisance and violation of riparian rights. At the time, the company employed 1,500 people in town and had an agreement with the government that it would put no waste in the river "beyond that reasonably necessary for the operation". The company argued that the agreement gave it permission to pollute the river. It also argued that the pollutants were so diluted by the river as to be harmless, and that the court should take into account the mill's economic importance to the region.

The trial judge, Chief Justice McRuer, found in favour of the plaintiffs. He awarded the plaintiffs $5,600 in damages and an injunction giving the company six months to stop polluting the river. He reasoned that to allow the company to pollute would, in effect, be to expropriate the plaintiffs' riparian rights. This, he ruled, would be unlawful regardless of the economic impact of the injunction and regardless of whether the plaintiffs were actually harmed by the pollution.

K.V.P. appealed the decision and, meanwhile, successfully lobbied the provincial government to amend the *Lakes and Rivers Improvement Act* to include a provision allowing judges to refuse to grant an injunction in riparian rights cases if "having regard for all the circumstances" it is "proper and expedient" not to. By this time the case had reached the Supreme Court, which refused to quash the injunction because the legislation had been passed after the decision was appealed and could not be used retroactively. The Supreme Court also held that in this case damages alone could not provide a "complete and adequate remedy".

Finally, in 1950, the provincial government under Premier Leslie Frost passed special legislation (*An Act respecting the KVP Company Limited*) dissolving the injunction, so as to ensure the economic viability of the mill and the community dependent on it. After retiring from politics, former Premier Frost was appointed to K.V.P.'s board of directors.

Sources: *McKie et. al. v. The K.V.P. Co. Ltd.*, [1948] O.R. 398; *The K.V.P. Co. Ltd. v. Earl McKie et al.*, [1949] S.C.R. 698.

Breach of Riparian Rights

"Riparian" means having to do with a river bank. **Riparian rights** go along with ownership of land that adjoins a watercourse. Riparian owners have a right to use the water flowing through or situated next to their land, so long as they don't unreasonably affect the quantity or quality of water for other riparian owners. This means that if someone pollutes or diverts a stream flowing through or by your property, they have violated your riparian rights and you may sue them. Like trespass to land, breach of riparian rights is a tort in itself even if it does not result in harm or loss to the plaintiff, and the successful plaintiff may obtain an injunction to stop or forestall the pollution. Breach of riparian rights is one of the most important common law causes of action in Canadian environmental law. A famous Canadian riparian rights case is discussed in Exhibit 34.7.

Private Nuisance

Private nuisance arises when the defendant's activities unreasonably interfere with the plaintiff's use and enjoyment of their property. In contrast to the tort of negligence, "unreasonable" here refers to the effect on the plaintiff, not to the carelessness of the defendant. That is, the effect is a nuisance if it is more than what a "reasonable" (i.e., not unusually sensitive) person could be expected to put up with, even if the defendant took reasonable care to avoid causing it. In contrast to trespass to land or breach of riparian rights, the defendant will only be found liable if their activity harms the plaintiff's person or property in some way or substantially interferes with the plaintiff's comfort or convenience.

Any kind of pollution, including noise, vibration, smell, light, or dust, can constitute a nuisance. Many nuisance cases have involved backed-up sewers and flooded basements. One case involved damage to fruit trees in an orchard caused by road salt from a highway.[7] Nuisance is the most important common law cause of action in environmental law.

Public Nuisance

The tort of public nuisance is an odd hybrid of public and private law. **Public nuisance** involves the interference with public, not private, rights. Unfortunately, unless the harm in question *also* infringes the plaintiff's private rights, a private party does not have automatic standing to sue under common law and would require the permission of the Attorney General to be able to bring an action in court. For example, in *Hickey v. Electric Reduction Co.*,[8] commercial fishers of Placentia Bay, Newfoundland, were denied standing to sue a polluter who destroyed the fishery on which their livelihoods depended. The court held that right to fish in the ocean was not exclusive to the plaintiffs but was shared by the general public. In Ontario, the 1994 *Environmental Bill of Rights* eliminated this common law restriction on standing to sue in public nuisance. Public nuisance is still used rarely in Ontario and mainly comes up in conjunction with private nuisance and negligence in the context of class action suits.

Strict Liability (Rylands v. Fletcher Rule)

According to this rule, those who store hazardous substances on their land are liable for damage done should the substances escape, regardless of whether they have taken reasonable care to avoid this mishap. The elements to this cause of action are as follows:

1. The Defendant is in lawful occupation of property.
2. The stored property is a dangerous agent or thing constituting a non-natural use of land.
3. The agent or potential mischief-causing thing escapes from the defendant's property.
4. The escaped agent or potential mischief-causing thing ends up causing damage to the plaintiff.

There may be a fifth element, one which has been added more recently by some British and Canadian courts:

5. Damage should be reasonably foreseeable.

In the original 1868 case, *Rylands v. Fletcher*,[9] the defendant had created a water reservoir on land with improperly sealed abandoned mine shafts. Water drained down the shafts and then made its way into the plaintiff's mine nearby. Recent Canadian cases involving this cause of action include one

---

[7] *Schenk v. Ontario*, [1987] 2 S.C.R. 289.

[8] (1971), 2 Nfld. & P.E.I.R. 246.

[9] (1868), LR 3 HL 330, 339.

where the plaintiff's fishing gear was damaged by a surge of water from the defendant's hydro dam[10] and another where the plaintiff's crops were damaged by herbicides drifting from the defendant's neighbouring farm.[11]

Contract Issues

Common law doctrine concerning contract cases sets out circumstances in which vendors would have a duty to disclose information regarding the contaminated state of a property. *Caveat emptor*, a Latin term, which means "let the buyer beware", articulates "a legal maxim stating that the buyer takes the risk regarding the quality or condition of the property purchased, unless protected by warranty".[12] *Caveat emptor* applies specifically to situations with patent defects, which a prudent and diligent purchaser would be expected to discover upon inspection, exercising ordinary care prior to finalizing a purchase. Yet, for situations where there are latent defects, the purchaser is not expected to make the discovery beforehand.

It is important to note that the doctrine of *caveat emptor* will not apply to situations where there has been fraudulent representations or conduct. If a defect is latent, and if it could pose a risk of danger to life, health or the environment, then failure on the part of a vendor to disclose that information may constitute fraud. The deceived purchaser would then have legal grounds to sue for deceit.

There have been several cases from Ontario addressing these issues and holding that what constitutes a defect must be determined in the context of the intended use of the land. One is a real estate case, *801438 Ont. Inc. v. Badurina*,[13] which exemplifies the *caveat emptor* doctrine. The purchaser's action against the defendant vendor was dismissed because the Ontario Superior Court of Justice found that the vendor had made no representations as to the environmental condition of the land or to its potential for development. The court held that the purchaser could have ascertained for itself what would be the likely impact of adjacent contaminated land upon development potential.

Class Action Suits

A **class action** proceeding is a civil lawsuit in which a representative plaintiff acts on behalf of a defined class of plaintiffs (e.g., all consumers injured by a particular faulty product, or all investors induced to invest in a particular fraudulent business scheme). A class action allows the issues common to a large number of separate potential cases to be heard in one trial. Class actions thus avoid costs and duplication for the court system and the defendants. They also allow justice to be done in cases where one party inflicts a relatively small amount of harm on each of a large number of people for whom an individual lawsuit would not be worth while or would be unaffordable. For this reason they are obviously useful for pollution cases.

It is important to keep in mind that class actions differ from ordinary lawsuits only in respect of procedure, not substance. Class action is not a cause of action. All class action tort suits have to be based on one or more of the causes of action discussed above, just like individual tort actions (for instance, negligence).

---

[10] *Croft v. Nova Scotia Power Inc.* (2003), 125 *All Canada Weekly Summaries* (3d) 740.

[11] *Morassutti v. Lanoue* (2000), 96 *All Canada Weekly Summaries* (3d) 1084.

[12] National Association of Realtors — Real Estate Auction Committee, the National Auctioneers Association and the Auction Marketing Institute, Real Estate Glossary: <http://www.aaauctionservice.com/glossery_files/glossery.htm>.

[13] (2000), 34 RPR (3d) 306 (Ont. S.C.J.).

EXHIBIT 34.8   **A Canadian Toxic Tort Class Action**

From 1918 to 1984, Inco operated a nickel refinery in Port Colborne, Ontario. Over the years, the Inco refinery had released some 20,000 tonnes of nickel into the environment, mostly in the form of nickel oxide, a potent carcinogen. In 2001, Wilfred Pearson, a homeowner in the most contaminated part of town, launched a class action lawsuit against Inco on behalf of owners of contaminated property. The causes of action are the common law torts of negligence and private nuisance. At the time of writing (spring 2008), the case has yet to come to trial. All the legal decisions discussed here relate to pre-trial motions; they are about whether the case would be allowed to proceed as a class action.

The motions court judge refused to certify the class action. He found the definition of the class (all who resided in a defined area of Port Colborne after 1995) arbitrary and irrational, since it would include some people who had not been harmed and exclude some others who had been. He found that despite a number of valid common issues, so many complex individual issues would remain outstanding that no advantage would be gained by proceeding via a class action. The motions judge also found that Pearson would not make a good representative plaintiff because he lacked the necessary financial resources, his plan of litigation was vague, and, as one of the most seriously affected members of the class, he might have a conflict of interest with those who suffered minor loss and would prefer to settle the case quickly. Pearson was ordered to pay Inco's legal expenses. Pearson appealed the decision to Divisional Court and lost again. He appealed further to the Ontario Court of Appeal.

The Court of Appeal overturned the previous decisions and certified the class. The different outcome was partly due to Pearson having simplified the claim in the meantime, dropping the health issues and focusing on the effect of contamination on property values (which would be similar for all members of the class). It was also due to a shift by the courts to a more liberal interpretation of class action rules. The Court of Appeal recognized that in environmental cases, the definition of the plaintiff class would always have to be somewhat arbitrary, since pollution effects don't have clearly defined boundaries. It also acknowledged that only through class actions could many affected persons unable to afford litigation on their own have a chance seek justice in the courts.

Sources: *Pearson v. Inco et al.*, [2002] O.J. No. 2764, 33 C.P.C. (5th) 264 (Motions Court), *Pearson v. Inco et al.*, 2004 CanLII 34446 [re issues of substance] and 2004 CanLII 4038 [re issue of costs] (ON S.C.D.C.) (Divisional Court), *Pearson v. Inco et al.*, 2006 CanLII 913 (Ont. Court of Appeal).

A class action involves three main stages. First, the representative plaintiff must persuade the court to certify the class — i.e., to allow the case to go ahead as a class action with the plaintiff as its representative. The court will only do so if it is convinced that the members of the class were affected in ways that raise enough common issues of fact and law that it would be advantageous to address those common issues in a single trial. Next there is a trial on the common issues — the class action proper. Finally, there are individual proceedings in which members of the class are awarded damages based on their specific circumstances, in light of the outcome of the common trial.

Class action suits have long been a prominent part of American law. Canadian rules of civil procedure made large class actions impractical until class action legislation was passed, first in Quebec in 1978 and then in Ontario in 1993. Since then, most Canadian provinces have passed class action legislation. Perhaps surprisingly, few recent Canadian class action cases have involved environmental issues, and Canadian courts have been reluctant to certify class actions in environmental cases. Exhibit 34.8 describes an Ontario toxic tort class action currently before the courts.

Shortcomings of Civil Litigation

Civil litigation has major shortcomings as an approach to protecting the environment. It works best in cases where a single pollution source is affecting one or a few people (or, where class actions are available, a clearly definable class of people), and where the causal connection between the pollution and injury to those affected can be clearly demonstrated. Few environmental problems have this character. Imagine if we tried to deal with the problem of pollution from automobile exhaust by having all those affected (i.e., just about everybody) sue those responsible (also just about everybody)! Civil litigation is ill-suited to addressing diffuse environmental harms which affect people indirectly through effects on ecosystems (e.g., the effects of acid precipitation on forests and aquatic life) or on global physical systems (e.g., the effects of greenhouse gases on climate), and it does not take into account harms to nature itself that do not affect humans or their property. Finally, even if all the conditions for a successful environmental lawsuit were met, the economic costs of upholding the plaintiffs' rights might prove politically unacceptable, and the government might undo the ruling of the court through legislation — as happened in the famous case discussed in Exhibit 34.7.

The Walkerton Tragedy

Walkerton is a town of approximately 4,800 people, situated northwest of Toronto. Water for Walkerton's water supply comes from the groundwater of a number of wells, and it is meant to be treated with chlorine before entering the distribution system. Torrential rains falling over several days during the long weekend in May of 2000 washed bacteria from cattle manure into one of the town's water supply wells. The water supply became contaminated with a virulent strain of *Escherichia coli* [*E.coli*] and *Campylobacter jejuni*. As a result, 2,321 people became ill, of whom 65 were hospitalized, 25 were diagnosed with Hemolytic Uremic Syndrome (HUS) a serious and potentially fatal kidney condition, and 7 died.

Mike Harris, the Premier of Ontario at the time, ordered an inquiry into the Walkerton incident. The Walkerton Inquiry, conducted by Mr. Justice Dennis O'Connor,[14] had a broad mandate, including whether budgetary cuts to the Ministry of the Environment and privatization of water testing contributed to the outcome. The provincial government implemented substantial changes to the regulation of drinking water in Ontario, including the passage of the *Nutrient Management Act*, S.O. 2002, c. 4; the *Safe Drinking Water Act*, S.O. 2002, c. 32; and the *Clean Water Act*, S.O. 2006, c. 22. Associated regulations passed pursuant to the new laws provide enforceable prescriptive standards for water treatment and testing.

After the public inquiry and its own extensive criminal investigation, the Ontario Provincial Police charged Stan Koebel, General Manager of the Walkerton Public Utilities Commmssion (PUC), and his brother Frank Koebel, the PUC foreman, with public endangerment, fraud, and breach of trust. The brothers subsequently pled guilty to "committing a common nuisance"[15] by failing to discharge a legal duty. Witness testimony and other evidence pro-

---

[14] Dennis R. O'Connor [The Honorable Dennis R. O'Connor], *Part One Report of the Walkerton Inquiry: The Events of May 2000 and Related Issues* and *Part Two Report of the Walkerton Inquiry: A Strategy for Safe Drinking Water* (Toronto, Ont.: Queen's Printer for Ontario, 2002). <http://www.attorneygeneral.jus.gov.on.ca/english/about/pubs/walkerton/>.

[15] The offence is formally called common nuisance, and it is distinct from the common law (civil litigation) cause of action known as nuisance. The *Criminal Code of Canada*, R.S.C. 1985, c. C-46, section 180 provides as follows:

    180.(1) Every one who commits a common nuisance and thereby
    (a) endangers the lives, safety or health of the public, or
    (b) causes physical injury to any person,
        is guilty of an indictable offence and liable to imprisonment for a term not exceeding two years.

vided to the court revealed that the Koebels had failed to properly monitor, sample, test, and treat the water in the water distribution system, and that they had failed to accurately record required information. The court found that "Stan Koebel had put the lives, safety and health of the public at risk in general ... [and crucially] [w]hen the crisis hit, he did not provide complete information ... He contributed at least in part, to the delay in issuing the Boil Water Advisory, which caused some undeterminable number of people to become ill. Finally, he tried to cover up his wrongdoing with an inaccurate document."[16] Frank Koebel had helped his brother try to cover up what was going on when the crisis occurred, but his actions did not contribute to the delay in issuing the Boil Water advisory. Frank's practice of mislabeling samples defeated the purpose of the tests, and then hindered the quest to find the source of the problem.

Stan Koebel (then 51) received a one-year prison sentence. Justice Durno rejected a conditional discharge and probation for Stan as inconsistent with the purposes and principles of sentencing. Frank (then 46) received a conditional sentence, consisting of six months house arrest followed by three months of night curfew. Justice Durno rejected a probation and/or fine as inappropriate for Frank.

Another development arising out of the Walkerton tragedy was a class action lawsuit, *Smith v. Brockton (Municipality)*.[17] The class action was launched on June 14, 2000, in the Ontario Superior Court of Justice by four representative plaintiffs. The original defendants named were the municipality, the local health unit, the Walkerton PUC, and the PUC's general manager, Stan Koebel. On September 14, 2000, the Government of Ontario was added as a named defendant. The cause of action in the lawsuit was negligence (breach of duty of care). The plaintiffs claimed that the defendants were negligent in the design, management, maintenance, and operation of the Water Works system which led to the Class Members being exposed to infection. The lawsuit asked for approximately $300,000,000 in total, with one-third of that amount for general damages, and another third for aggravated and exemplary damages.

Between the launch of the class action and the commencement of the Walkerton Inquiry, the Ontario government set up a Walkerton Compensation plan. That plan was "designed to provide financial support and compensation to individuals and businesses affected by the water contamination in Walkerton Ontario from April to December 2000."[18]

In early 2001, Justice Winkler accepted the certification motion for the class action, and the parties began settlement discussions overseen by Justice Winkler. After an extensive negotiation period, involving 6 law firms and many lawyers, Chief Justice Le Sage accepted the settlement agreement that had been reached by the parties.[19]

---

(2) For the purposes of this section, every one commits a common nuisance who does an unlawful act or fails to discharge a legal duty and thereby

  (a) endangers the lives, safety, health, property or comfort of the public; or

  (b) obstructs the public in the exercise or enjoyment of any right that is common to all the subjects of Her Majesty in Canada.

[16] Court File No. 04-584 (20041220); 2004 CanLII 48879 (ON S.C.) at 51. [*R. v. Koebel and Koebel*] <http://www.canlii.org/en/on/onsc/doc/2004/2004canlii48879/2004canlii48879.html>

[17] *Smith v. Brockton (Municipality)* (2001), 106 A.C.W.S. (3d) 55.

[18] Website for Walkerton Compensation Plan: <http://www.walkertoncompensationplan.ca/>

[19] Settlement Approval Motion before Chief Justice LeSage at Walkerton, March 19, 2001, Court File 00-CV-192173CP, at p. 1: <http://www.strosbergco.com/walkerton/documents/web-walkerton-justice-lesage-reasons.pdf>. See also Walkerton Class Action Settlement: <http://www.ontla.on.ca/library/repository/mon/1000/10293853.pdf>.

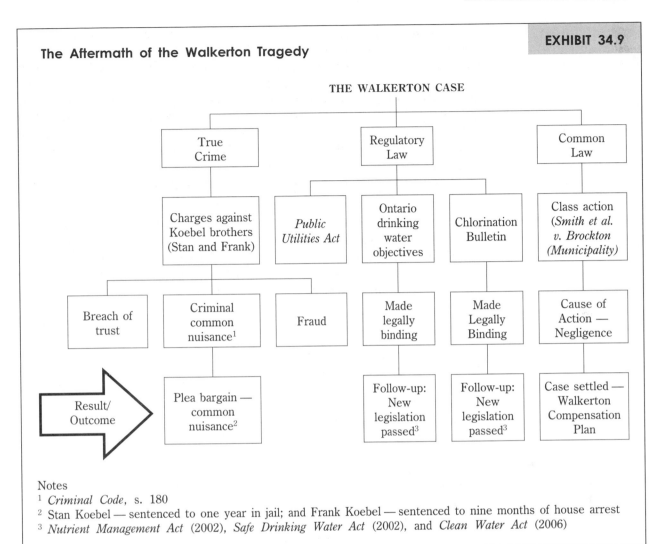

The Aftermath of the Walkerton Tragedy

EXHIBIT 34.9

THE WALKERTON CASE

True Crime / Regulatory Law / Common Law

Charges against Koebel brothers (Stan and Frank) — *Public Utilities Act* — Ontario drinking water objectives — Chlorination Bulletin — Class action (*Smith et al. v. Brockton (Municipality)*)

Breach of trust — Criminal common nuisance[1] — Fraud — Made legally binding — Made Legally Binding — Cause of Action — Negligence

Result/Outcome → Plea bargain — common nuisance[2] — Follow-up: New legislation passed[3] — Follow-up: New legislation passed[3] — Case settled — Walkerton Compensation Plan

Notes
[1] *Criminal Code*, s. 180
[2] Stan Koebel — sentenced to one year in jail; and Frank Koebel — sentenced to nine months of house arrest
[3] *Nutrient Management Act* (2002), *Safe Drinking Water Act* (2002), and *Clean Water Act* (2006)

The Walkerton class action settled without a legal judgment being issued. Plaintiffs got the compensation they sought without having to go to trial. In this respect the case was typical, since an estimated 90 to 97 percent of civil cases settle prior to adjudication. The publicity around the Walkerton tragedy and the class action likely moved the provincial government to act decisively in compensating the victims, launching the inquiry, and tightening up the regulations. The Walkerton class action case illustrates how common law litigation can proceed in response to failures of the regulatory system.

Exhibit 34.9 illustrates the intersection of true criminal law, regulatory law, and class action civil litigation in the aftermath of the Walkerton tragedy.

PROTECTION OF SPACES AND SPECIES

In this section we discuss various legal tools for protecting biodiversity and ecological function. These goals overlap, since both require the conservation of green spaces, both as habitat for non-humans and as providers of "ecological services" for humans. Green spaces are also conserved for the sake of their aesthetic, recreational, and amenity values.

Federal and Provincial Parks and Nature Reserves

National Parks

Section 4(1) *Canada National Parks Act* (*CNPA*) sets out the mandate for park management as follows: "The national parks of Canada are hereby dedicated to the people of Canada for their benefit, education and enjoyment, subject to this Act and regulations, and the parks shall be maintained and made use of so as to leave them unimpaired for the enjoyment of future generations." The *CNPA* s. 8(2) further requires *ecological integrity* to be "the first priority ... when considering all aspects" of park management. This somewhat contradictory set of objectives has given rise to litigation by environmentalists claiming that parks managers acted outside their mandate in approving facilities such as new roads or ski resorts in sensitive park areas.

National parks typically do not allow mining, logging, hydroelectric development, or sport hunting (in some cases aboriginal subsistence hunting is allowed). Only a minority of national parks, however, have designated wilderness zones that have only minimal visitor facilities and where no motorized access is permitted. Because resource extraction is excluded from national parks and ecological integrity is a priority consideration in their management, environmentalists and nature preservationists seek the expansion of the parks system as the most reliable way to ensure that a sufficient representation of the country's natural ecosystems and landscapes is protected. By the same token, park expansion is opposed by resource development advocates. Expansion of the system is thus a matter of political controversy.

Provincial Parks

All the Canadian provinces also have parks legislation. Provincial parks and nature reserves have similar objectives to national parks, but provincial parks systems do not necessarily exclude resource extraction activities, though parks may be zoned to exclude such activities from certain areas. For example, logging in Ontario's Algonquin Provincial Park is a perennial topic of controversy.

Municipal Land-Use Planning

Municipal governments (along with regional Conservation Authorities), in their planning and land-use regulation powers, can have tremendous direct and indirect effects (good or bad) on the environment. Municipalities can encourage or discourage urban development on environmentally sensitive lands such as ravines, floodplains, slopes, wetlands, headwaters, prime farmland, wildlife corridors and habitat for species intolerant of urban encroachment. They can encourage sprawling, automobile-dependent urban form or compact form friendly to walking, bicycling, and public transit. Urban planning law is a big topic in itself and beyond the scope of this chapter. In Canada, municipalities have a fair bit of power to restrict what owners can do with their land without having to compensate them, so long as their actions are not discriminatory, in bad faith, or factually baseless.

Endangered Species Legislation

The Committee on the Status of Endangered Wildlife in Canada (COSEWIC) is a body comprised of experts representing federal and provincial governments and agencies and national non-governmental conservation organizations, as well as independent scientists. It designates species of animals and plants as "endangered" (facing imminent extinction or extirpation from Canada) or "threatened" (likely to become endangered if their numbers continue to decline). There are parallel provincial bodies such as the Committee on the Status of Species at Risk in Ontario (COSSARO).

Endangered and threatened species are protected by both federal and provincial legislation. Federal legislation applies to marine species, migratory birds, and species on federal Crown land; provincial legislation applies otherwise. Both federal and provincial legislation prohibits killing, harming, harassing, or trading in members of endangered and threatened species, and contains measures to protect critical habitat. They differ in some respects, however.

Under the federal *Species at Risk Act* (*SARA*), the COSEWIC endangered species list has only an advisory function. *SARA* only actually protects those species on an official list of "species at risk", which Cabinet establishes by regulation, and Cabinet is not required to include all species on the COSEWIC list. Cabinet also takes the economic impact of putting a species or population on the protected list into account. By contrast, Ontario's *Endangered Species Act 2007* requires the province's official species at risk regulation to include all species designated by COSSARO. Once a species is listed, however, both federal and Ontario legislation require that the government prepare a species recovery strategy within a stipulated time frame and that this strategy protect critical habitat. *SARA* requires this strategy to be based on "the best available information", and this provision has been used by environmental groups to challenge recovery strategies in court as being inadequate and protecting insufficient habitat, contrary to the legislation. *SARA* also gives the federal government the power to protect federally protected endangered species on provincial lands if provincial governments fail to do so, but the federal government is reluctant to use this power.

CHAPTER SUMMARY

Environmental law refers to a broad umbrella of mixed, legal tools for protecting ecosystems and human well-being from pollution and other human-caused impacts on the environment. A focus of this chapter has been on pollution control. In some cases, pollution can be the grounds for private tort lawsuits, sometimes in class action proceedings. This chapter has surveyed the most important causes of action for civil litigation over environmental harm. More often, pollution is now addressed through public regulatory law at the federal, provincial, and municipal levels. Environmental statutes enable officials to draft regulations and permits that include legally enforceable standards. Non-compliance with these regulations and permits may result in quasi-criminal prosecution or the imposition of various kinds of administrative sanctions. In the prosecution of quasi-criminal (regulatory or public-welfare) offences, the Crown need not prove criminal intent, but the accused may resort to a defence of due diligence. Environmental law also provides processes for the assessment, approval, and regulation of potentially hazardous substances, and the assessment and approval of projects such as dams, landfills, and highways that may have a negative impact on the environment. Finally, laws relating to parks, nature reserves, and endangered species are used to protect biodiversity and natural heritage.

GLOSSARY OF NEW TERMS AND KEY CONCEPTS

absolute liability	A form of liability for which the prosecution need only show that the *actus reus* was committed (there is no mental element to the offence), and for which the defendant cannot raise the defence of due diligence.
administrative monetary penalty (AMP)	A fine for a regulatory violation imposed by an official or administrative tribunal empowered by legislation to do so.

administrative tribunal	A quasi-judicial body (i.e., something like, but not actually, a court) established by legislation to decide in disputes that arise in connection with the administration of legislative schemes. Administrative tribunals are common in areas of regulatory law.
ambient standard	An ambient standard defines an acceptable or allowable level or concentration of pollutant in the environment.
cause of action	A legal rule or doctrine that defines a basis for a valid lawsuit; in the case of a particular lawsuit, the set of relevant facts that falls under that rule.
certificate of approval	The term used in Ontario law for a licence or permit to pollute, issued in accordance with the *Ontario Environmental Protection Act* or the *Ontario Water Resources Act*. The terms and conditions in a certificate of approval are binding on the company concerned, and are directly enforceable by prosecution.
class action	A procedure whereby a person may sue on behalf of a large number of other people sharing a common interest in the matter without having to name them all individually as parties to the lawsuit.
due diligence defence	A defence available to persons or companies charged with regulatory offences. A person or firm wishing to rely upon this defence must be able to provide evidence that they have undertaken reasonable measures to comply with the requirements of the law and to prevent the prohibited act from occurring.
effluent standard	Defines how much of a given pollutant is allowed to be discharged from a given source over a given period of time, or the maximum concentration of the pollutant allowed in the outflow from that source.
environmental assessment (EA)	EA is an evaluation of the effects of a proposed project on natural and human environments. Its purpose is to predict how a project may damage or harm the environment, and whether unacceptable environmental impacts can be avoided or reduced before significant environmental changes occur. The term "environmental assessment" is used for both a process and a document resulting from that process.
fish toxicity test	Rainbow trout are placed in a tank containing a solution of a pollutant (e.g., pulp mill effluent) that has been diluted by 35 percent. If after four days more than 20 percent of the trout die, the solution is lethal and an offence has been committed under the *Fisheries Act*. Similar toxicity tests for water pollution use *Daphnia*, a tiny freshwater crustacean.
forbearance	The decision on the part of law enforcement officials to refrain from charging or penalizing a party who is found to be in violation of the law or in non-compliance with regulations.
jurisdiction	The power of a government or level of government to make laws concerning a given matter; the territory over which a government has power; a matter over which a court has power.
negligence	A common cause of action under tort law, in which a defendant can be found liable for breach of a duty of care, which results in injury occurring to a plaintiff. There is also a criminal offence of criminal negligence.
performance standard	Stipulates what must be accomplished (e.g., by how much a pollution source must reduce its emissions), but not how.
precautionary principle	A principle that requires actions to be taken to reduce or eliminate likely environmental hazards even if the causal link between a particular, suspected hazard has not yet been proven or fully understood scientifically.
prescriptive standard	Stipulates the technology, materials, etc. that must be used in order to abate pollution.
private law	Concerned with the rights and responsibilities of private parties in respect of one another (e.g., tort law, contract law, real estate transactions).
private nuisance	The tort of carrying on an activity that interferes with other people's reasonable use and enjoyment of their property (through noise, pollution, flooding, etc.)
public law	Concerned with relationships between individuals and the state, and with the operations of government (e.g., administrative law, constitutional law, criminal law).

public nuisance	A tort and a criminal offence covering an activity that harms the general public or interferes with rights common to the public (e.g., that obstructs a public road or damages public property).
riparian rights	The common law rights connected with the ownership of land abutting a body of water, specifically the right to undiminished quality and quantity of water in that body of water. Breach of those rights constitutes a tort.
risk assessment	The scientific analysis of the degree of risk posed to human and/or environmental health by a particular activity, for example, exposure to a given substance. Risk assessment may be legally required as part of the process of approving the activity or substance.
strict liability	In quasi-criminal, or regulatory law: liability for a violation committed without criminal intent, subject to the defence of due diligence. In tort law: liability for damage done by the escape of a dangerous substance stored on one's property, even if the escape was not due to negligence. Also known as the *Rylands v. Fletcher* rule.

REVIEW QUESTIONS

1. What are the differences between private law and public law? Describe and provide examples of each. Where does environmental law fit?

2. What are the three main sources of law? In what ways are they connected or interrelated?

3. Under which constitutional heads of power do federal and provincial governments have power and responsibility to enact environmental legislation?

4. How might municipal governments play a role in environmental protection? Name one other constitutionally relevant jurisdiction in Canada (besides the federal, provincial and municipal levels).

5. What are the differences between a statutory prohibition, a regulation, and a certificate of approval? How are each related to statute law?

6. What are the major kinds of standards that are found in environmental law, and how do they differ from each other?

7. What are the significant distinctions between absolute liability, strict liability, and true criminal liability?

8. What is forbearance and why does it happen?

9. Ministry officials discover that a company is violating pollution-control laws. What options, other than forbearance, do the enforcement officials have to address the issue?

10. What are the main stages in an environmental assessment process?

11. What must you do if you want to use a newly invented chemical in an industrial process?

12. What are the main common law causes of action found in environmental cases? Elaborate on the factors that courts take into consideration with each of those causes of action. Which common law causes of action require the plaintiff to show actual harm or loss in order to sue successfully? Which common law causes of action require that the plaintiff be a landowner?

13. What is a class action lawsuit? What are the three stages of such a lawsuit? What must a would-be representative plaintiff show in order to

certify a class? List some examples of environmental class action lawsuits in Canada.

14. How do the federal *Species at Risk Act* and the Ontario *Endangered Species Act, 2007* differ in the ways that they protect endangered species?

DISCUSSION QUESTIONS

1. Why do you think courts have been reluctant to interpret environmental offences as absolute liability offences? Do you agree with this approach? Why or why not?

2. Do you think that individual directors and officers within a company (as opposed to the company as a whole) should be held liable for environmental offences? Why or why not? What are some examples of personal liability for directors and officers, under regulatory law (quasi-criminal) and under true criminal law?

3. Of all the options that enforcement officials have to punish polluters, which do you think is the most effective and when? Why?

4. What are the relative advantages and disadvantages of civil litigation (private law) and the regulation of pollution through statutory law (public law)?

5. What are "toxic torts"? Which popular Hollywood movies have focused on class action litigation concerning toxic torts? How are toxic torts relevant in the Canadian context?

6. Joe (the defendant) has been found to be civilly liable for infringement of Danielle's (the plaintiff's) rights. What are the two main types of remedy that the court may award to Danielle and what are the variations between the two?

7. Should landowners and businesses be compensated for having to avoid disturbing the habitats of rare or endangered species? Why or why not? What problems could arise in either case?

SUGGESTED READINGS

Benidickson, Jamie. *Environmental Law*, 2d ed. (Toronto, Ont.: Irwin Law, 2002).

Boyd, David R. *Unnatural Law: Rethinking Canadian Environmental Law and Policy* (Vancouver, B.C.: UBC Press, 2003).

Greenbaum, Allan, & Alex Wellington. *Environmental Law and Policy in the Canadian Context* (Concord, Ont.: Captus Press, 2008).

Greenbaum, Allan, Alex Wellington, & Ron Pushchak, eds., *Canadian Issues in Environmental Law and Policy* (Concord, Ont.: Captus Press, 2008).

Hughes, Elaine, Alastair Lucas, & William Tilleman. *Environmental Law and Policy*, 3d ed. (Toronto, Ont.: Emond Montgomery, 2003).

WEBSITES

Canadian Environmental Law Association: <http://www.cela.ca/>

Canadian Institute for Environmental Law and Policy: <http://www.cielap.org/>

EcoJustice: <http://www.ecojustice.ca/>

Environmental Commissioner of Ontario: <http://www.eco.on.ca/eng/>

Environmental Defence: <http://www.environmentaldefence.ca/>

Ministry of Environment (MoE), Province of Ontario: <http://www.ene.gov.on.ca/en/index.php>

Immigration and Refugee Law

Sasha Baglay
UNIVERSITY OF ONTARIO INSTITUTE OF TECHNOLOGY

Learning Objectives

After reading this chapter, the reader should be able to:

➢ Become familiar with the legislative and institutional framework of Canadian immigration and refugee system

➢ Know the difference between the statuses of Canadian citizens, permanent residents, and foreign nationals

➢ Understand basic principles of immigrant selection under economic and family class

➢ Understand key concepts of refugee law and stages of the Canadian refugee determination process

➢ Know the basic principles of inadmissibility, immigration detention, and removal

➢ Appreciate the complexity of competing interests involved in immigration and refugee policy- and decision-making

TABLE OF CONTENTS

INTRODUCTION

Immigration and refugee protection are considered an inalienable part of Canada's history and identity. Since 1867, more than 17 million people have immigrated to Canada, including close to one million refugees and other humanitarian cases since World War II.[1] During the past decade, Canada admitted, on average, close to a quarter of a million permanent residents annually.[2]

While Canada is viewed as a nation welcoming immigrants and refugees, it is important to keep in mind that immigration law is inherently selective and exclusionary. It draws a line between citizens and non-citizens; it embodies the country's idea about "desirable" and "undesirable" candidates for admission often to the exclusion of persons with limited financial resources, low skill and education levels or individuals with certain medical conditions that might impose a burden on domestic healthcare or social service systems. This selectivity and differential treatment is based on the long-standing principle that non-citizens do not have an unqualified right to enter or remain in the country[3] and that the state has a sovereign right to control their admission and conditions of stay.

Immigration law applies to non-citizens only. Thus, many of those who have acquired Canadian citizenship at birth will hardly ever face the direct effect of Canadian immigration law (except perhaps for the inevitable border control at Canada's ports of entry). At the same time, those who are most affected by immigration law usually have no voice in the political system and/ or are in a too vulnerable or precarious position to speak up. For this reason, the work of human rights lawyers and organizations representing immigrants and refugees plays an important role in advocating for and protecting rights of non-citizens.

Thus, any reading of immigration law should be critical, considering not only who is admitted and how Canada benefits from that admission, but also who remains excluded and what are the gender, social class, and race impacts of such exclusion. Immigration law is not only about immigrant selection. It often engages some of the most fundamental individual rights such as the right to life and liberty, the right to be free from torture and other maltreatment. For example, is it permissible to deport a person to a country where he/she might face a risk of torture or persecution? What if that person represents a security threat to Canada? Is it permissible to detain non-citizens suspected of terrorist links for prolonged periods of time without an opportunity for detention review or release? Can a state refuse entry to persons who are fleeing their home countries in search of refugee protection?

Although the chapter discusses a number of cases that have touched on the above questions, it merely outlines the current state of law leaving it up to the reader to further critically engage with and question legal rules and judicial decisions.

---

[1]   Citizenship and Immigration Canada, "Facts and Figures 2009", online: <http://www.cic.gc.ca/english/resources/statistics/facts2009/index.asp> [CIC, "Facts and Figures 2009"]. However, in 2010, Canada admitted 280,636 individuals as permanent residents — the highest number in the past 50 years. Citizenship and Immigration Canada, "Preliminary tables — Permanent and temporary residents, 2010", online: <http://www.cic.gc.ca/english/resources/statistics/facts2010-preliminary/01.asp> [CIC, "Preliminary tables — Permanent and temporary residents, 2010"].

[2]   *Ibid.*

[3]   *Chiarelli v. Canada (Minister of Citizenship and Immigration)*, [1992] 1 S.C.R. 711 at 733–34.

HISTORY OF IMMIGRATION AND REFUGEE LAW IN CANADA

During the first decades after Confederation, immigration was viewed as a key element in industrial growth and nation-building. Therefore, it was actively promoted and there were relatively few restrictions on admission. However, by the turn of the 20th century, the arrival of immigrants with different culture, traditions, and religion started to raise concerns about the demographic composition of the country and stimulated introduction of restrictions aimed at preserving Canada as a white, predominantly British society. The policy focus shifted from attracting immigrants to selecting those that were viewed as the most desirable,[4] while also actively deterring unwanted immigration. Over the years, the Chinese head tax;[5] "continuous journey" rule;[6] and multiple exclusions targeting the poor, persons with disabilities, and persons of certain ethnic or racial background were introduced. Several economic downturns during the first decades of the 20th century created additional incentives for limiting immigration. The restrictive admission policies, accompanied by increased deportations and exclusions, were largely maintained until the mid-1940s.[7]

The post-World War II period was marked by gradual liberalization of admissions. Between 1947 and 1962, Canada admitted close to 250,000 displaced persons from Europe.[8] Many of them came under arranged labour schemes to remedy labour shortages in certain industries and agriculture or were selected on the basis of general economic potential, ethnic origin, and other characteristics.[9] However, after a period of time, Canada's labour force demands could no longer be satisfied by traditional sources from Europe, and the country had to re-evaluate and expand its selection criteria.[10] In 1962, Canada became the first major immigrant-receiving country to abolish most of its discriminatory admission policies. In 1967, the government introduced a skills-based points system for the selection of immigrants.

In 1969, Canada acceded to the 1951 *UN Convention Relating to the Status of Refugees* (*Refugee Convention*) and the 1967 *Protocol relating to the Status of Refugees* (*Refugee Protocol*). During the 1960s and 1970s, various groups of refugees were admitted to Canada, including Czechs uprooted by the Soviet invasion, Chileans escaping from the Pinochet regime, and Asians expelled by the Amin regime in Uganda. However, there was little evidence of a consistent long-term approach to assisting people in need. Rather, refugee admissions were carried out on an ad hoc basis in response to particular crises.

In 1973, the government announced a review of immigration policy in order to better reflect the ideas of multiculturalism and provide for a more systematic approach to immigrant and refugee admission. The 1976 *Immigra-*

---

[4] Ninette Kelley and Michael Trebilcock, *The Making of the Mosaic* (Toronto: University of Toronto Press, 1998) at 248.

[5] All Chinese immigrants were required to pay a prescribed tax in order to be allowed into Canada.

[6] This rule prevented admission of immigrants who had not travelled directly from their country of origin to Canada. At the time, travel routes from Asia were structured in a way that entailed a stopover, thereby making immigrants using them inadmissible to Canada. One of the famous cases is that of *Komagata Maru*, which arrived from China with 376 persons aboard. None of the passengers was allowed ashore and the ship had to sail back.

[7] Kelley & Trebilcock, *supra* note 4 at 165, 217, 229, 251.

[8] Valerie Knowles, "Forging Our Legacy: Canadian Citizenship and Immigration, 1900–1977" (2000), online: <www.cic.gc.ca>.

[9] Valerie Knowles, *Strangers at Our Gates: Canadian Immigration and Immigration Policy, 1540–1992* (Toronto: Dundurn Press, 1992) at 127.

[10] Jock Collins & Francis Henry, "Racism, Ethnicity and Immigration" in Howard Adelman et al. (eds.), *Immigration and Refugee Policy: Australia and Canada Compared*, (Toronto: University of Toronto Press, 1994) 515 at 530.

tion Act established many of the principles and procedures of contemporary Canadian immigration law, including classes of immigrants, refugee protection mechanisms, family reunification, and federal–provincial consultations and agreements on immigration.

In 2002, the *Immigration Act* was replaced with the *Immigration and Refugee Protection Act* (*IRPA*). The post-2002 period is characterized by several key trends:

- Increased focus on security and border control
- Optimization of selection of economic immigrants to facilitate their better labour market integration and to increase Canada's competitiveness in a global market for labour force (as demonstrated, for example, by the changes to the skilled worker class described below)
- Increasing admissions of temporary residents (particularly international students and temporary foreign workers) and introduction of the Canadian Experience Class, which allows some of these temporary residents to transition to permanent residence
- Restrictions on refugee protection, which are evident in the changes brought about by the 2010 *Balanced Refugee Reform Act*

LEGAL FRAMEWORK

Constitution Act, 1867: Division of Powers over Immigration

Two provisions — sections 91(25) and 95 — in the *Constitution Act, 1867* are of direct relevance to immigration and citizenship. Section 91(25) confers on the federal Parliament exclusive jurisdiction in the areas of naturalization and aliens. Section 95 establishes concurrent federal–provincial jurisdiction over immigration: the federal government may regulate immigration "into all or any of the Provinces" and each province may regulate immigration "in and for the Province". In case of a conflict between a federal and a provincial law, the former prevails.[11]

The role of the provinces in immigration regulation has fluctuated over time. Prior to Confederation and during the first decades afterwards, the provinces maintained a certain role in admission screening and immigrant recruitment. However, by the early 20th century, their interest in immigration regulation has decreased, and immigration became *de facto* an almost exclusively federal matter. The gradual revival of provincial involvement in immigration took place only in the late 1970s. First, Quebec negotiated progressively more powers over immigrant selection and settlement. From the 1990s onwards, other provinces and territories also started to seek roles in immigrant selection by negotiating Provincial/Territorial Nominee Agreements with the federal government. These agreements allow provinces and territories to select immigrants who have the potential to benefit a given province or territory and nominate them for immigration. Federal programs, however, currently remain the main avenues of admission and will be the main focus of discussion in this chapter.

The *Charter of Rights and Freedoms*

Immigration law traditionally and strictly distinguishes between citizens and non-citizens. However, the *Charter of Rights and Freedoms*, which enshrines a number of rights that are guaranteed to everyone, to a certain extent allows such a rigid distinction to be overcome. Four *Charter* rights have been most frequently invoked in the immigration context: section 7 (right to life, liberty

---

[11] *The British North America Act, 1867* 30 & 31 Victoria, c. 3 [*BNA*] subsequently entitled the *Constitution Act*, 1867 by Item 1 of the Schedule to the *Constitution Act, 1982*, (U.K.) 1982, c. 11, s. 95.

and security of person); section 10 (right to counsel); section 12 (prohibition of cruel and unusual treatment or punishment); section 15 (equality).

The *Charter* litigation has had an impact on the treatment of non-citizens in a number of areas and in some instances has also led to marked institutional changes. Two cases below are illustrative of this impact (see also the *Charkaoui* case in the section on security certificates).

Singh v. Minister of Employment and Immigration[12]

Are refugee claimants (that is, persons who are alleging a risk of persecution in their home countries and who have made a claim for protection in Canada) entitled to an oral hearing to determine whether they should be given protection?

Decisions on refugee protection have a crucial impact on the life and security of refugee claimants: if a person who fears persecution is denied protection, he/she may be returned to a country where his/her life would be at risk. Given the seriousness of the consequences of a negative decision, refugee claimants are entitled to fundamental justice under section 7 of the *Charter*, which at a minimum, requires that a refugee claimant is provided with an adequate opportunity to state his case and to know the case he/she has to meet.[13]

In the 1980s, a refugee determination process consisted of two main stages: first, a claimant was interviewed by an immigration officer; then, the transcript of the interview was sent to the Refugee Status Advisory Committee (RSAC), which decided whether to recommend acceptance of the claim. This procedure did not allow claimants an opportunity to be heard before the RSAC or to know and effectively challenge the information on the basis of which the decision on the claim was made. Thus, the Supreme Court found that the procedure violated principles of procedural fairness under section 7 of the *Charter* and that it could not be saved under section 1. The decision led to an overhaul of the inland refugee determination system with a view to provide for an oral hearing for all refugee claimants. To this end, the Immigration and Refugee Board was established in 1989 and since then has become an integral part of the institutional framework of immigration and refugee decision-making.

Suresh v. Canada (Minister of Citizenship and Immigration)[14]

May Canada deport a suspected terrorist to a country where he might face torture?

Mr. Suresh came to Canada from Sri Lanka in 1990 and was recognized as a **Convention refugee** in 1991. However, in 1995, the Canadian authorities detained him and commenced deportation proceedings on security grounds: the Canadian Security Intelligence Service was of the opinion that Mr. Suresh was a member and fundraiser of the Liberation Tigers of Tamil Eelam (LTTE), an alleged terrorist organization. Mr. Suresh fought the deportation, claiming that he would face torture in Sri Lanka. The Supreme Court emphasized that both Canadian and international law reject deportation to torture. Accordingly, the Court concluded that deportation to face torture is generally unconstitutional and that Canada should generally decline to deport persons to torture.

[12] *Singh v. Minister of Employment and Immigration*, [1985] 1 S.C.R. 177 [*Singh*].
[13] *Singh* at paras. 52–61.
[14] *Suresh v. Canada (Minister of Citizenship and Immigration)*, [2002] 1 S.C.R. 3.

However, the Court has failed to endorse an absolute prohibition on removal to torture and left open a possibility that in extraordinary circumstances such removal may be justified.

Legislation

The *Immigration and Refugee Protection Act (IRPA)* sets out the objectives of immigration and refugee policies, immigration classes, principles of non-citizens' admission to and stay in Canada, principles of refugee protection, as well as the authorities of the Minister of Citizenship and Immigration and of the Immigration and Refugee Board (IRB).

As framework legislation, the *IRPA* is concise and necessarily presupposes the broad delegation of legislative power to elaborate on the implementation of its core principles through regulations. The *Immigration and Refugee Protection Regulations* outline the details of various immigration categories and requirements, including selection criteria for each immigration class. For example, the *IRPA* stipulates that applicants in the economic class are selected on the basis of their ability to become economically established in Canada,[15] but it is the *Regulations* that spell out how this ability is to be evaluated (for example, they specify that applicants under the skilled worker class must demonstrate at least one year of work experience, availability of settlement funds and detail how the applicant's education, language proficiency, and other relevant credentials are to be assessed under the points system[16]).

Under the current legislative scheme, there are two major sets of conditions that an applicant must satisfy in order to be admitted for permanent residence:

1. Meet criteria of a particular immigration/refugee class. The Canadian immigration program is divided into three broad streams: economic, family, and refugee. The criteria under each stream reflect its underlying rationale: (a) economic stream — to satisfy Canada's objectives of economic, social, and cultural development; (b) family stream — to allow for family reunification; (c) refugee stream — to implement Canada's commitment to humanitarianism and international obligations. The economic class makes approximately 60 percent of the annual immigrant intake, while the family and refugee classes account for approximately 22 percent and 10–12 percent respectively.[17]

2. Not be inadmissible. In contrast to selection criteria, which reflect qualities considered desirable in potential applicants, **inadmissibility** describes individuals who are "undesirable" for admission. As a rule, persons found inadmissible will not be allowed to enter Canada or, if they are already in Canada, will be ordered removed.

INSTITUTIONAL FRAMEWORK

The institutional framework of Canadian immigration and refugee protection system is comprised of three key bodies: Citizenship and Immigration Canada (CIC), Immigration and Refugee Board (IRB) and Canada Border Services Agency (CBSA).

---

[15] *Immigration and Refugee Protection Act*, 2001, c. 27, s. 12(2) [*IRPA*].

[16] *Immigration and Refugee Protection Regulations*, SOR/2002-227 [*Regulations*], ss. 75–83.

[17] The rest is comprised of "other immigrants" such as those admitted under Humanitarian and Compassionate consideration and for reasons related to the person's need of protection in Canada. CIC, "Facts and Figures 2009", *supra* note 1.

Citizenship and Immigration Canada (CIC)

CIC is the government department with overall responsibility for immigration and refugee matters. It processes applications for permanent residence and for temporary admission of visitors, workers, and students; issues travel documents; decides on citizenship applications; determines eligibility of refugee claims made in Canada (see section on refugee law, below); and administers the resettlement of refugees from abroad.

Immigration and Refugee Board (IRB)

The Immigration and Refugee Board (IRB) is an independent administrative tribunal responsible for making decisions on a number of immigration and refugee matters. According to the *IRPA*, the IRB consists of four divisions:

- The Refugee Protection Division (RPD), which decides on refugee claims made in Canada
- The Immigration Division (ID), which holds admissibility hearings and detention reviews
- The Immigration Appeal Division (IAD), which hears appeals from refused family sponsorship applications and from removal orders
- The Refugee Appeal Division (RAD)

The RAD was intended to hear appeals on RPD decisions, but the provisions on the RAD have never been implemented and it currently does not exist. However, the recently passed *Balanced Refugee Reform Act* provides for the establishment of the RAD within one to one-and-a-half years.

Cases before the IRB are usually decided by one-member panels. Each division usually holds an in-person hearing; a hearing may also be conducted by phone or by videoconference. The person concerned has a right to be represented by counsel. Proceedings are usually conducted in public, except in refugee protection cases or where confidentiality may be required for other reasons. The hearings proceed in a less formal manner than before courts and are not limited by strict rules of evidence. Each division has its own rules of procedure, which outline applicable deadlines, disclosure requirements, and other issues. In addition, the IRB has developed "soft law" instruments (guidelines, jurisprudential guides, policies, instructions) which provide guidance on substantive or procedural issues and seek to ensure consistency of decision-making.

Canada Border Services Agency (CBSA)

The CBSA is responsible for border services related to the admission of persons, goods, animals, and plants into Canada. In the area of immigration, it conducts screening of individuals at ports of entry, carries out enforcement such as immigration detention and removal, and determines the eligibility of refugee claims made at the border.

CATEGORIES OF INDIVIDUALS IN CANADIAN IMMIGRATION LAW

Canada's immigration law distinguishes three types of status: foreign national, permanent resident, and Canadian citizen. Each of them demonstrates a different level of connection to Canada and provides for different scopes of rights for its holders.

Most of the rights under the *Charter* are guaranteed to "everyone" or "anyone" (for example, freedom of conscience and assembly, right to counsel, protection against arbitrary detention). Therefore, these rights will be available equally to Canadian citizens, permanent residents, and foreign nationals. However, the extent of other rights, especially in social and economic areas, often depends on the individual's immigration/citizenship status.

Citizens of Canada   Citizenship gives its holders full-fledged rights in Canada and creates certain expectations about Canada's consular assistance and diplomatic protection while abroad. For example, such *Charter* rights as the right to vote and stand in elections as well as the unconditional right to enter, remain in, and leave Canada are reserved exclusively for citizens. In addition, Canadian citizenship may be required in order to hold certain public offices[18] or perform certain public duties.[19]

Canadian citizenship may be acquired in one of the following ways:

- *Jus soli*: by birth in Canada's territory, except for children of foreign diplomats, consular, or other similarly situated officials

- *Jus sanguinis* (by descent): by birth outside of Canada to a Canadian citizen.

  Previously, Canadian citizens residing overseas were able to pass citizenship down to their children from generation to generation.[20] However, in 2008, the *Citizenship Act* was amended to limit citizenship by descent to the first generation born outside Canada. This means that a child born overseas will obtain Canadian citizenship only if at least one of his/her parents was born in Canada or became a Canadian citizen by naturalization. There are some exceptions to this rule, which apply to Canadian parents working abroad for the Canadian armed forces, the federal public administration or the public service of a province. Children who do not have access to automatic citizenship by *jus sanguinis* may be sponsored by their parents for permanent residence in Canada under the family class and subsequently apply for citizenship.

  > *Example:* Mary is born abroad to Canadian parents. Both of her parents were born in Canada, and Mary is the first generation born overseas. Thus, she will obtain Canadian citizenship by descent. However, if Mary gives birth outside of Canada, her child (second generation born overseas) will not automatically acquire Canadian citizenship by descent.

- By naturalization: this process allows immigrants to obtain Canadian citizenship. A person needs to first become a permanent resident and then, after a period of time, may apply for citizenship. To gain citizenship, a permanent resident must (a) make an application; (b) be at least 18 years of age; (c) demonstrate that he/she has resided as a permanent resident in Canada for at least three years in a four-year period immediately preceding the application; (d) have adequate knowledge of Canada, of citizens' rights and responsibilities, and of one of the official languages; (e) not be under a removal order or the subject of a declaration that he/she is a threat to the security of Canada or is a part of organized crime.

---

[18] For example, ombudsman and provincial court judges in Alberta. *Ombudsman Act*, R.S.A. 2000, c. O-8, s. 3(3); *Provincial Court Act*, R.S.A. 2000, c. P-31, s. 9.1.

[19] For example, to serve as a juror. *Jury Act*, 1998, S.S. 1998, c. J-4.2, s. 5; *Jury Act*, R.S.P.E.I. 1988, c. J-5.1, s. 4; *Juries Act*, R.S.O. 1990, c. J.3, s. 2; *Jury Act*, S.N.B. 1980, c. J-3.1, s. 2; *Jury Act*, R.S.A. 2000, c. J-3, s. 3.

[20] However, in order to retain that citizenship, the child needed to take the following steps by the age of 28: apply for retention of citizenship and either reside in Canada for at least a year before the application or demonstrate a substantial connection to Canada. Failing to do so would result in automatic loss of citizenship.

Permanent Residents In order to become a permanent resident, an individual needs to apply under one of Canada's immigration streams and meet the prescribed requirements. Permanent residents enjoy many of the same rights as citizens: they may freely work and study, access provincial healthcare and various types of programs such as social assistance, Child Tax Benefit, and student loans. However, permanent residents do not have a *Charter*-protected right to vote or run for office. Neither do they have an unqualified right to enter and remain in Canada, but they enjoy the right to inter-provincial mobility.

The central peculiarity of permanent resident status is its conditional nature. A permanent resident may lose his/her status in one of the following circumstances:

1. Failure to comply with the residency obligation. In order to maintain their status, permanent residents must be physically present in Canada for at least 730 days in each five-year period.

2. An individual is determined to be inadmissible and a removal order against him/her comes into force. For example, a permanent resident who has committed certain crimes may become inadmissible and, as a result, be subject to removal. The Supreme Court has confirmed that the deportation of a long-term resident who has committed a serious criminal offence does not infringe the *Charter*.[21]

3. Failure to comply with immigration class requirements. While the two above scenarios are applicable to any permanent resident, certain categories of immigrants may be subject to additional conditions. For example, persons under the entrepreneur class are required to demonstrate within the three-year period following their admission that they have established a qualifying business in Canada, control at least a third of the equity of the business, provide active and ongoing management of the business, and have created at least one full-time job for a Canadian citizen or a permanent resident (other than the entrepreneur's family members).

Foreign Nationals A "foreign national" is a person who is not a Canadian citizen or a permanent resident.[22] Foreign nationals may be admitted to Canada on a temporary basis as students, workers or visitors. They have a limited scope of rights largely determined by the intended purpose of their stay in Canada (see section on temporary residents, below); and they must depart at the end of their authorized stay. Foreign nationals who have applied for refugee protection in Canada as well as those who have been granted protection enjoy more extensive rights than other foreign nationals. This is done in recognition of Canada's international obligations as well as on an understanding that those who have fled violence, persecution, torture, and other risks need additional support and exemptions from certain immigration requirements (see the section on refugee protection for further details).

---

[21] *Chiarelli, supra* note 3.

[22] *IRPA, supra* note 15, s. 2(1).

IMMIGRATION LAW

Economic Immigration

By definition, immigrants in the economic class are selected on the basis of their ability to become economically established in Canada.[23] Thus, the selection criteria focus on characteristics that are considered indicative of this ability, namely education, work or business experience, language proficiency, financial resources, and other factors facilitating successful integration.

The economic class encompasses six categories, each governed by a distinct set of selection criteria:

* Skilled workers
* Canadian Experience Class (CEC)
* Business immigrants (investors, entrepreneurs, self-employed)
* Provincial and territorial nominees
* Quebec-selected immigrants
* Live-in caregivers

By way of illustration, this section will outline requirements under two of the above classes: skilled worker and the Canadian Experience Class. In addition, it will provide a brief overview of provincial/territorial nominee programs.

Skilled Worker Class

The skilled worker class is currently the major source of admissions in the economic stream, amounting to over 40,000 principal applicants and approximately 50,000 to 60,000 accompanying dependents (spouses and children) annually.[24]

In order to be approved for permanent residence under the skilled worker class, applicants must meet the following basic requirements: (a) have at least one year of full-time work experience in a skilled occupation in the past 10 years; (b) have adequate settlement funds;[25] and (c) accumulate at least 67 points on six selection factors.

The points system was designed to predict applicants' prospective employability in Canada. However, it was criticized as poorly linked to actual labour market needs.[26] Furthermore, due to the high volume of applications, applicants often had to wait for a decision for a number of years. In 2008, the CIC had a backlog of over 900,000 applications (two-thirds of them in the federal skilled worker class), and wait times could be as long as six years.[27]

In 2008 and 2010, the Minister of Citizenship and Immigration responded to the above concerns by introducing eligibility requirements, which sought to make the system more efficient. Before 2008, applicants in all skilled occupations could apply: as long as the application was complete and the required fees were paid, it was put into the processing queue to be assessed under the

---

[23] *Ibid.*, s. 12(2)

[24] CIC, "Facts and Figures 2009", *supra* note 1.

[25] The amount of settlement funds is determined according to the applicant's family size. Currently, the requirements are as follows: 1 family member — $11,115; 2 — $13,837; 3 — $17,011; 4 — $20,654; 5 — $23,425; 6 — $26,419; 7 or more — $29,414. Applicants who have arranged employment in Canada do not need to demonstrate availability of such funds. Citizenship and Immigration Canada, "Skilled workers and professionals: Who can apply — Proof of funds", online: <http://www.cic.gc.ca/english/immigrate/skilled/funds.asp>.

[26] L. Hawthorn, *Labour Market Outcomes for Migrant Professionals: Canada and Australia Compared* (2006), online: <http://cic.gc.ca/english/resources/research/2006-canada-australia.asp>; Jeffrey Reitz, "Tapping Immigrants' Skills: New Direction for Canadian Immigration Policy in the Knowledge Economy" (2005) 11 *IRPP Choices* 1.

[27] Citizenship and Immigration Canada, "Action Plan for Faster Immigration: Ministerial Instructions." (2008), online: <http://www.cic.gc.ca/english/DEPARTMENT/media/backgrounders/2008/2008-11-28.asp>.

points system and other requirements. In 2008, the application process under the skilled worker class changed and currently includes two stages:

1. Eligibility — to determine whether an application can be put into processing.

2. Assessment of eligible applications under the points system and other requirements of the skilled worker class.

Currently, eligibility is limited to persons with (a) an offer of employment in Canada or (b) one year of full-time work experience in one of 29 listed occupations[28] (these occupations were identified on the basis of labour market demands and stakeholder consultations). In addition, all applicants must supply results of an official language test confirming their proficiency in English and/ or French. Applications that do not meet these eligibility requirements will not be put into processing. Further, only a total of 20,000 applications will be considered annually under the category of 29 occupations in demand; within the 20,000 cap, only 1,000 applications can be considered per occupation. Thus, eligibility requirements effectively limit the range of applicants who will be considered under the skilled worker class.

Eligible applications are further assessed under the six selection factors of the points system:

- Education (maximum of 25 points)
- Language proficiency (maximum of 20 points)
- Work experience (maximum of 21 points)
- Arranged employment (maximum of 10 points)
- Age (maximum of 10 points)
- Adaptability (maximum of 10 points)

Exhibit 35.1 demonstrates how points are assigned under each factor, and Exhibit 35.2 illustrates how the point system applies on a skill worker application.

Canadian Experience Class

The Canadian Experience Class (CEC) was introduced in 2008 to allow foreign students and skilled temporary foreign workers who are already in Canada to apply for permanent residence. Accordingly, there are two streams within the CEC:

1. Temporary foreign workers — applicants must demonstrate at least two years of full-time skilled work experience in Canada within a three-year period preceding the application

2. Foreign students — applicants must have been enrolled in a full-time program of study of at least two years' duration in Canada; have completed the program and obtained a Canadian educational credential (e.g., degree, diploma, or certificate); and acquired at least one year of full-time skilled work experience in Canada within the two years preceding the application.

Applicants under both streams must demonstrate proficiency in English and/or French by providing results of an official language test. The CEC is a pass/fail system and does not rely on the points assessment. Currently, the CEC is a small program (only close to 4,000 principal applicants and their

---

[28] For the list of occupations, see Citizenship and Immigration Canada: <http://www.cic.gc.ca/english/immigrate/skilled/apply-who-instructions.asp#list>.

EXHIBIT 35.1	Assessment under the Points System

Education	Points
¤ You have a master's degree or PhD and at least 17 years of full-time or full-time equivalent study	25
¤ You have two or more university degrees at the Bachelor's level and at least 15 years of full-time or full-time equivalent study	22
¤ You have a three-year diploma, trade certificate or apprenticeship and at least 15 years of full-time or full-time equivalent study.	22
¤ You have a university degree of two years or more at the Bachelor's level and at least 14 years of full-time or full-time equivalent study.	20
¤ You have a two-year diploma, trade certificate or apprenticeship and at least 14 years of full-time or full-time equivalent study.	20
¤ You have a one-year university degree at the Bachelor's level and at least 13 years of full-time or full-time equivalent study.	15
¤ You have a one-year diploma, trade certificate or apprenticeship and at least 13 years of full-time or full-time equivalent study.	15
¤ You have a one-year diploma, trade certificate or apprenticeship and at least 12 years of full-time or full-time equivalent study.	12
¤ You completed high school.	5

Language Proficiency	Points for Each Ability (write, speak, listen, read)
First official language	
High proficiency	4
Moderate proficiency	2
Basic proficiency	1
Second official language	
High proficiency	2
Moderate proficiency	2
Basic proficiency	1

Work experience	Points
1 year	15
2 years	17
3 years	19
4 or more	21

Arranged Employment in Canada	Points
¤ You currently work in Canada on a temporary work permit and your employer has made an offer to employ you on an indeterminate basis.	10
¤ You currently work in Canada in a job that is exempt from confirmation by Human Resources and Social Development Canada (HRSDC) under an international agreement or a significant benefit category; your employer has made an offer to employ you on an indeterminate basis.	10
¤ You do not currently have a work permit and you do not intend to work in Canada before you have been issued a permanent resident visa; you have a full-time job offer that has been approved by HRSDC; your employer has made an offer to give you a permanent job if your permanent resident visa is issued.	10

Assessment under the Points System

EXHIBIT 35.1 (continued)

Age	Points
21–49	10
(2 points deducted for each year that the applicant is below 21 or over 49)	

Adaptability

		Points
Your spouse or common-law partner's level of education		3–5
¤ Secondary school (high school) diploma or less	0	
¤ A one-year diploma, trade certificate, apprenticeship or university degree, and at least 12 years of full-time or full-time equivalent studies	3	
¤ A two- or three-year diploma, trade certificate, apprenticeship or university degree, and at least 14 years of full-time or full-time equivalent studies	4	
¤ A master's degree or PhD and at least 17 years of full-time or full-time equivalent studies	5	

Previous Work in Canada

¤ You or your accompanying spouse or common-law partner have completed a minimum of one year of full-time work in Canada on a valid work permit. — 5

Previous Study in Canada

¤ You or your accompanying spouse or common-law partner have completed a program of full-time study of at least two years' duration at a post-secondary institution in Canada. You must have done this after you were 17 years old and with a valid study permit. — 5

Arranged Employment in Canada

¤ You can claim five additional points if you have arranged employment as described in the Arranged Employment selection factor. — 5

Relatives in Canada

¤ You or your accompanying spouse or common-law partner have a relative (parent, grandparent, child, grandchild, child of a parent, sibling, child of a grandparent, aunt or uncle, or grandchild of a parent, niece or nephew) who is residing in Canada and is a Canadian citizen or permanent resident. — 5

Source: Citizenship and Immigration Canada, "Skilled workers and professionals: Who can apply — Six selection factors and pass mark", online: <http://www.cic.gc.ca/english/immigrate/skilled/apply-factors.asp>.

EXHIBIT 35.2   **The Immigration Points System: A Skilled Worker Example**

Eduardo is a citizen of Mexico who wishes to apply for immigration to Canada under the skilled worker class. He is 32 years old, married with no children. Eduardo is a social worker with 2 years of work experience; he has a Bachelor's and a Master's degree in Social Work (and a combined 17 years of full-time study). His high proficiency in English (writing, speaking, reading, and oral comprehension) is confirmed by results of an official language test. His wife, Maria, is also a social worker and has a Master's degree and 17 years of study. Eduardo and Maria have approximately $17,000 saved in their bank account. Is Eduardo likely to be approved for immigration under the skilled worker class?

Eligibility

Social workers are on the list of 29 occupations in demand, and the number of applications received in this category has not yet reached the 1,000 cap (see <http://www.cic.gc.ca/english/immigrate/skilled/complete-applications.asp>). Eduardo also has results of an official language test ready. Thus, Eduardo's application is eligible for processing.

Assessment under the Points System

On the six selection factors, Eduardo is likely to score as follows:

Education	25 points	(a Master's degree and 17 years of study)
Language proficiency	16 points	(4 for each ability)
Work experience	17 points	(2 years of experience in social work)
Arranged employment	0 points	(Eduardo does not have arranged employment in Canada)
Age	10 points	(Eduardo is between 21 and 49)
Adaptability	5 points	(for the educational credentials of Eduardo's wife)
Total	73 points	(above the pass mark of 67)

Given that Eduardo does not have arranged employment, he will have to demonstrate at least $13,837 in settlement funds (for himself and Maria). Eduardo and Maria currently have $17,000 saved and, thus, would meet the requirement. In addition, both Eduardo and Maria must not be inadmissible.

When Eduardo applies for permanent residence, he will include his wife, Maria, in the application. Eduardo will be considered the principal applicant and Maria his accompanying family member. If Eduardo meets all the selection criteria and his application is approved, he and Maria will be issued permanent resident visas. Once admitted to Canada, they will become permanent residents and may subsequently apply for citizenship.

---

dependents admitted for permanent residence in 2010[29]), but it is projected to become a significant source of economic immigrants with a target of 26,000 by 2012.[30]

Provincial/Territorial Nominee Programs (PTNPs)

The skilled worker class and the CEC are federal programs. Their selection criteria are prescribed by the federal legislation; applications are processed by the federal department of CIC, and all applicants must meet the same criteria, regardless of their intended destination in Canada (except for Quebec). For the most part of the 20th century, admission to Canada was carried out overwhelmingly through federal streams. While such centralization of

---

[29] CIC, "Preliminary tables — Permanent and temporary residents, 2010", *supra* note 1.
[30] Auditor General of Canada, "Selecting Foreign Workers Under the Immigration Program" (2009), s. 2.27, online: <http://www.oag-bvg.gc.ca/internet/English/parl_oag_200911_02_e_33203.html#hd4c>.

selection criteria and processing offers many advantages, it may not always be effective in responding to regional diversity and specific provincial labour needs. Neither does it contain mechanisms to address the challenges associated with uneven distribution of newcomers across Canada (during 1999–2009, approximately 80 percent of newcomers settled in British Columbia, Ontario, and Quebec (mostly in Toronto, Montreal, and Vancouver[31])). In part due to these concerns, provinces and territories started to seek greater role in immigration regulation. This has been achieved, among other things, through the development of PTNPs, which allow provinces and territories to select immigrants who have the potential to benefit a given province or territory and nominate them for immigration.

All provinces (except for Quebec) and two territories (Yukon and Northwest Territories) have established nominee programs. Each province/territory is free to develop its own selection streams and criteria that best respond to its particular needs. Given significant regional diversity and distinct provincial/territorial objectives, there are currently over 50 selection streams under different PTNPs. Most provinces merely establish a minimum set of requirements that applicants must meet on a pass/fail basis, but some provinces (e.g., Manitoba) also use a provincially developed points system. All PTNPs have at least two streams: (skilled) worker and business stream. All provinces allow nomination of skilled workers, but some also provide opportunities for low skilled and semi-skilled workers in certain occupations (e.g., trucking, hotel and lodging, food processing, and food services industries in Alberta). In addition, some provinces allow nomination on the basis of family or community support. Thus, some PTNPs may provide a path to permanent residence for individuals who would not qualify under federal programs (e.g., a low-skilled worker who is ineligible under the skilled worker class or the CEC may qualify under Manitoba Provincial Nominee Program (PNP), which allows nomination of workers of all occupation levels).

The immigration process under PTNPs involves two steps:

1. Potential immigrants submit PTNP applications to a given province; those who meet the provincial selection criteria are nominated for immigration.

2. The nominated applicants submit applications for permanent residence to the CIC; security, criminality, and health checks are conducted and the CIC makes a decision on the permanent residence applications.

Thus, under the PTNP stream, both levels of government are involved in immigration processing: provinces are in charge of immigrant selection, while the federal CIC remains responsible for inadmissibility screening and final decision-making.

Over the past decade, PTNPs have grown significantly, from some 500 admissions in 1999 to over 36,000 in 2010.[32] This growth is likely to continue in the future and it is important to be aware of PTNPs as an emerging feature of the Canadian immigration system. Each PTNP has a website with detailed information about the selection and application process;[33] students are encouraged to check these websites and compare provincial/territorial programs to the federal skilled worker class and the CEC.

---

[31] CIC, "Facts and Figures, 2009", *supra* note 1.

[32] CIC, "Preliminary tables — Permanent and Temporary Residents, 2010", *supra* note 1.

[33] For example, Ontario PNP: <http://www.ontarioimmigration.ca/en/pnp/index.htm>; Manitoba PNP: <http://www2.immigratemanitoba.com/browse/howtoimmigrate/pnp/>; Alberta PNP: <http://www.albertacanada.com/immigration/immigrating/ainp.html>; Nova Scotia PNP: <http://novascotiaimmigration.com/nova-scotia-nominee-program>.

Family Immigration

Family reunification is one of the objectives of Canada's immigration policy.[34] Unlike the economic class, members of the family class are selected not on the basis of their ability to become economically established in Canada, but based on their relationship to a Canadian citizen or a permanent resident. In order to obtain permanent residence under the family class, two basic requirements must be met: (i) existence of an eligible Canadian sponsor and (ii) a qualifying familial relationship between the sponsor and the sponsored. The sponsor and the sponsored must meet a number of criteria and, correspondingly, the application process consists of two parts: (i) approval of a Canadian citizen or permanent resident as a sponsor; (ii) approval of the sponsored individual for permanent residence.

The following individuals may qualify to be sponsored under the family class:

- Sponsor's spouse, common-law partner, or conjugal partner

- Sponsor's dependent children, including adopted children

- Children under 18 years of age whom the sponsor intends to adopt in Canada

- Sponsor's parents

- Sponsor's grandparents

- Sponsor's orphaned brothers, sisters, nieces, nephews, and grandchildren who are under 18 years of age and who are not married and are not in a common-law relationship

- Any sponsor's relative, regardless of age, if the sponsor does not have a family member from the list above or an aunt or an uncle who could be sponsored or who is already a Canadian citizen, Indian, or permanent resident[35]

The above definition of family is notably different from our everyday understanding of family. For example, non-orphaned siblings and cousins are not on the list of persons who can be sponsored. Thus, immigration law not only imposes a certain definition of family but also, by virtue of that definition, controls the ability of Canadians to reunite with their relatives. Further, the *Regulations* outline in detail the meaning of each sponsored category. By way of illustration, we will briefly review the definitions of spouse, common-law partner, conjugal partner, and dependent child. Canada draws some distinctions between the "core" family members, such as a sponsor's spouse, partner, and children, and other family members. "Core" family enjoys more favourable treatment in the form of certain exemptions,[36] as well as expedited processing under the CIC policy.

Spouse

A marriage must be valid under the laws of the jurisdiction where it took place as well as under Canadian law. Following the redefinition of marriage as a "union of two persons",[37] same-sex marriages performed in Canada as

---

[34] *IRPA, supra* note 15, s. 3(1)(d).

[35] *Regulations, supra* note 16, s. 117(1).

[36] For example, spouses, partners and dependent children are exempt from medical inadmissibility on the grounds of excessive demand on health or social services. A Canadian sponsor who is seeking to sponsor his or her spouse, partner or dependent child is exempt from sponsorship ineligibility for lack of minimum income.

[37] *Civil Marriage Act*, S.C. 2005, c. 33, s. 2 (as amended by Bill C-38).

well as marriages performed in some foreign jurisdictions are valid for the purposes of immigration. In addition to requiring formal validity, immigration law takes into consideration the genuineness of a relationship (whether married or unmarried). A marriage, a common-law, or conjugal relationship will not be recognized if it was entered into primarily for immigration purposes or is not genuine. Further, some relationships are excluded from the family class and thus cannot be sponsored:

- Where a sponsor's spouse, common-law, or conjugal partner is under 16

- Where a sponsor or a sponsored individual is already married to someone else

- If the sponsored has lived apart from the sponsor for at least one year and either the sponsor or the sponsored are the common-law or conjugal partner of another person

- Where a sponsored individual was a sponsor's non-accompanying family member, but was not examined at the time when the sponsor applied to immigrate to Canada[38]

- Where a sponsor previously sponsored another spouse, common-law partner, or conjugal partner and a sponsorship undertaking (see explanation below) with respect to that spouse or partner is still in effect

Common-Law and Conjugal Partner

The *Regulations* define a common-law partner as an individual who is cohabiting with the sponsor in a conjugal relationship and who has cohabited with him/her for a period of at least one year.[39] A conjugal partner is "a foreign national residing outside Canada who is in a conjugal relationship with the sponsor and has been in that relationship for a period of at least one year."[40] The notion of conjugal partner was created to encompass couples who are prevented from marrying or living together due to circumstances beyond their control (e.g., immigration barriers; marital status — one of the persons is married to someone else and is living in a country where divorce is not possible; sexual orientation — same-sex relationships are not permitted in the country of person's residence).[41] Similarly to marriage, common-law and conjugal partnerships are defined in gender-neutral terms and therefore include same-sex and heterosexual relationships alike.

Unlike in a marriage, where a couple publicly declares its commitment to shared life at a specific point in time through a marriage ceremony, in a common-law or conjugal relationship there is no single point in time or a legal document (such as, for example, a marriage certificate) that attests to

---

[38] Applicants for immigration are required to list all their family members (spouse, common-law or conjugal partner and dependent children) in an immigration application, whether those family members will or will not accompany them to Canada. Further, all those family members (even if they do not accompany the applicant to Canada) must undergo medical examination and submit police clearances. For example, Eduardo (in Exhibit 35.2) is applying to immigrate to Canada under the economic class. He is married to Maria. Maria does not want to accompany Eduardo to Canada, but Eduardo nevertheless must list her on his application for permanent residence. If he fails to do so and Maria does not undergo the required examination, Eduardo will be precluded from sponsoring her under the family class at a later point. Section 117(9)(d) of the *Immigration and Refugee Protection Regulations* excludes from the family class a non-accompanying family member (in our case, Maria) who had not been examined at the time when the sponsor (Eduardo) applied for immigration to Canada.

[39] *Regulations, supra* note 16, s. 1.

[40] Ibid., s. 2.

[41] Citizenship and Immigration Canada, Overseas Processing Manual "Processing Members of the Family Class" at 31, online: <http://www.cic.gc.ca/english/resources/manuals/op/index.asp>

the couple's commitment. Thus, a determination of whether a common-law or a conjugal partnership exists is fact-based and is focused on examining a couple's attachment and interdependence — financial, social, emotional, and physical — over the passage of time. The CIC has identified a number of characteristics that usually have to be present in common-law, conjugal, and marital relationships:

- Mutual commitment to a shared life
- Exclusive — cannot be in more than one conjugal relationship at a time
- Intimate — commitment to sexual exclusivity
- Interdependent — physically, emotionally, financially, socially
- Permanent — long-term, genuine, and continuing relationship
- Present themselves as a couple
- Regarded by others as a couple
- Caring for children (if there are children)[42]

Dependent Child

The definition covers both biological and adopted children, who are in one of the following situations of dependency:

1. The child is under the age of 22 and is not married and not in a common-law relationships.

2. The child is a full-time student and has depended substantially on the parent's financial support since before the age of 22 or before getting married or forming a common-law relationship (if this happened before the age of 22).

3. The child is 22 or older and has depended substantially on the parent's financial support since before the age of 22 and is unable to be financially self-supporting due to a physical or mental condition.[43]

Requirements for Sponsors

In order to be eligible to sponsor relatives under the family class, an individual must meet three basic requirements: (i) be a Canadian citizen or permanent resident; (ii) be at least 18 years of age; and (iii) reside in Canada. Canadian citizens living abroad are eligible to apply for sponsorship of their spouse, common-law partner, conjugal partner or a dependent child as long as they demonstrate that they will return to reside in Canada once the sponsored individual becomes a permanent resident.

Even if the above requirements are met, an individual is ineligible as a sponsor if any of the following situations occurs:

- He/she is subject to a removal order.

- He/she is detained in a correctional institution.

- He/she has been convicted in or outside Canada of (a) an offence of a sexual nature, or an attempt or a threat to commit such an offence; or (b) a family violence offence that results in bodily harm, or an attempt or a threat to commit such an offence. Persons convicted in Canada become eligible for sponsorship five years after the completion of the imposed sentence. Persons convicted outside Canada become eligible for sponsorship if at least five years have elapsed since the completion of

---

[42] *Ibid.* at 19–20.

[43] *Regulations, supra* note 16, s. 2.

the imposed sentence and the person demonstrates that he/she has been rehabilitated.

- He/she is in default of any undertaking or any support payment ordered by a court.

- He/she is in undischarged bankruptcy.

- He/she has lower than the minimum necessary income. This requirement ensures that the sponsor is able to support his/her family and all sponsored persons. The minimum necessary income is based on the Low Income Cut-Off levels (LICO) for urban areas calculated by Statistics Canada. The required amounts of minimum necessary income are updated on a yearly basis and are based on the size of the sponsor's family unit.[44] Individuals sponsoring their spouse, partner or a dependent child are exempt from the requirement of minimum necessary income.

- He/she is in receipt of social assistance for a reason other than disability. The sponsor becomes eligible once he or she discontinues reliance on social assistance.

In addition, prospective sponsors must sign an undertaking to the Minister of Citizenship and Immigration, which ensures that the responsibility for supporting the sponsored individual(s) lies with the sponsor rather than the host society. The sponsor takes an obligation to provide for the basic needs of the sponsored during a prescribed period (see below). If during that period, the sponsored person(s) applies for social assistance, the sponsor undertakes to reimburse the government for the amounts received.

The length of a sponsorship undertaking is as follows:

1. For sponsor's spouse, common-law partner, or conjugal partner: 3 years.

2. For a dependent child who is under 22 when he or she becomes a permanent resident: 10 years or the day when the child reaches the age of 25 — whichever is shorter.

3. For a dependent child who is 22 or older when he or she becomes a permanent resident: 3 years.

4. For any other member of the family class: 10 years.

If family sponsorship is refused, a sponsor may appeal (with some exceptions[45]) to the Immigration Appeal Division of the IRB. If the appeal is allowed, CIC will resume processing the sponsorship application.

Temporary Residents There are three main categories of temporary residents: visitors, students, and temporary workers. During the past three years, Canada has been admitting, on average, over 180,000 foreign workers and over 80,000 foreign students annually.[46] There has been a steady increase in the admission of students and

---

[44] The 2011 LICO are as follows: a 2-person family unit — $27,674; 3 people — $34,022; 4 persons — $41,307; 5 persons — $46,850; 6 persons — $52,838; 7 persons — $58,827; more than 7 persons — for each additional person, add $5,989. Citizenship and Immigration Canada," Sponsorship of parents, grandparents, adopted children and other relatives — The sponsor's guide", online: <http://www.cic.gc.ca/english/information/applications/guides/5196E10.asp>.

[45] An appeal is not allowed for persons found inadmissible on the following grounds: serious criminality punished by a sentence of two years or more of imprisonment; organized criminality; security; violations of human or international rights; misrepresentation (unless the sponsored family member is the sponsor's spouse, common-law partner, or child).

[46] CIC, "Preliminary Tables — Permanent and Temporary Residents, 2010", *supra* note 1.

temporary foreign workers: a growth of over 40 percent between 2005 and 2010.[47] The increase is particularly noticeable in the category of low-skilled workers — largely due to the introduction of the Low-Skilled Project in 2002 in response to employer demands, particularly in the oil, gas, and construction industries. This is a change from the past when the emphasis in temporary admissions was on skilled workers and on two specific lower-skilled sectors (live-in caregivers and agricultural workers).[48]

As a general rule, foreign nationals need to apply for a visa prior to travelling to Canada, but nationals of some countries are exempt from this requirement.[49] In addition, individuals wishing to work or study in Canada usually need to apply for a work or a study permit, respectively. All applicants must satisfy Canadian immigration officers that they will comply with the conditions of stay and will leave Canada by the end of their authorized stay. In addition, there are specific requirements attached to applications for a work or a study permit.

As a rule, an applicant for a work permit needs to have a job offer from a Canadian employer that has been confirmed by Human Resources and Social Development Canada (HRSDC). The system of work permits seeks not only to regulate and track foreign nationals employed in Canada, but more importantly, to protect the Canadian labour market and in particular ensure that the employment of a foreign national is likely to have a neutral or positive effect on it. The latter objective is achieved through the process of HRSDC confirmation. It is usually an employer that seeks a job confirmation by demonstrating that it was not able to find a qualified Canadian citizen or permanent resident to fill the position. In addition, the work permit authorization process seeks to ensure that the foreign worker will be paid the prevailing wage rate in his/her occupation and that the recruitment of a foreign worker does not affect any labour dispute. Some types of jobs are exempt either from a requirement of a work permit or from a requirement of an HRSDC approval.

On April 1, 2011, new rules that seek to strengthen protection of temporary foreign workers from potential abuse and exploitation have come into effect. They include (i) more rigorous scrutiny of the genuineness of the job offer; (ii) a two-year prohibition from hiring temporary foreign workers for employers who fail to meet their commitments to workers with respect to wages and working conditions; and (iii) a limit on the length of time a temporary foreign worker may work in Canada: after working in Canada for four years, many workers will be required to wait for four years before becoming eligible to again temporarily work in Canada.

As a rule, foreign students must possess a study permit. As part of the application process, prospective students must produce an acceptance letter from an educational institution and demonstrate financial ability to pay tuition and subsistence expenses. Although the primary purpose of applicants' stay is study, Canadian immigration law provides for three scenarios in which foreign students are allowed to work:

1. On campus: full-time students with a valid study permit may work on campus without a work permit.

---

[47] CIC, "Facts and Figures, 2009", supra note 1; CIC, "Preliminary Tables — Permanent and Temporary Residents, 2010', *supra* note 1.

[48] Naomi Alboim, "Adjusting the Balance: Fixing Canada's Economic Immigration Policies" (2009), online: <www.maytree.com>.

[49] For a list of visa-exempt countries, see Citizenship and Immigration Canada at <http://www.cic.gc.ca/english/visit/visas.asp#exemptions>.

2. Off campus: full-time students enrolled at an educational institution that participates in the Off-Campus Work Permit Program may apply for a work permit to work off campus; students need to demonstrate that they have studied at the institution and maintained satisfactory academic standing for at least 6 months in the 12 months preceding the application;

3. After graduation: a post-graduation work permit allows students who have completed their studies to obtain Canadian work experience. They may accept employment in any field and are not required to obtain an HRSDC confirmation of a job offer. In order to be eligible for a post-graduation work permit, a student must have studied full-time at a Canadian institution in Canada, have completed a full-time program lasting at least eight months, and hold a valid study permit at the time of application. The application must be made within 90 days of formal notification that they have met the requirements of the program. A work permit can be up to three years, but not longer than the period of the student's studies.

The value of temporary work or study in Canada has increased with the introduction of the Canadian Experience Class (CEC), which provides foreign students and temporary skilled workers with an opportunity to apply for permanent residence. It is likely that more foreign nationals will consider choosing Canada as a destination for study or temporary work with a view to subsequently transitioning to permanent residence. However, the CEC provides a path to permanent residence to workers in skilled occupations only; it does not create similar opportunities for increasing numbers of low-skilled foreign workers in Canada.

Inadmissibility, Detention, and Removal

Immigration law outlines not only the positive characteristics that are sought in potential immigrants (for example, selection criteria in the economic class), but also features that make an applicant "undesirable." The latter are reflected in the grounds of inadmissibility, which either preclude an applicant's admission to Canada or if he/she is already in Canada may trigger enforcement action such as immigration arrest, detention and, ultimately, removal. The powers of removal, immigration arrest, and detention are quintessential exercises of state power to control admission of non-citizens as well as to contain and expel those who have violated immigration law or are otherwise considered to pose a risk to Canada or Canadians.

Grounds of Inadmissibility
The *IRPA* contains 10 grounds of inadmissibility:

1. **Health.** An individual's health condition is likely to be a danger to public health or safety or might be reasonably expected to cause excessive demand on health or social services; spouses, common-law partners, and dependent children of Canadian sponsors under the family class as well as resettled refugees and protected persons are exempt from inadmissibility on the basis of "excessive demand".

2. **Financial.** An individual is or will be unable or unwilling to support himself/herself or his/her dependents in Canada.

3. **Inadmissible family member.** An individual may be inadmissible if his or her accompanying family member and, in some circumstances, non-accompanying family member is inadmissible (for example, if the

applicant's dependent child is inadmissible on health grounds, the applicant may be inadmissible, too).

4. **Criminality.** This ground covers the following situations:
   (a) Conviction in Canada of an offence under an Act of Parliament punishable by way of indictment, or of two offences under any Act of Parliament not arising out of a single occurrence.
   (b) Conviction outside Canada of an offence that, if committed in Canada, would constitute an indictable offence under an Act of Parliament, or of two offences not arising out of a single occurrence that, if committed in Canada, would constitute offences under an Act of Parliament.
   (c) Committing an act outside Canada that is an offence in the place where it was committed and that, if committed in Canada, would constitute an indictable offence under an Act of Parliament.
   (d) Committing, on entering Canada, an offence under the *Criminal Code*, the *Immigration and Refugee Protection Act*, the *Firearms Act*, the *Customs Act*, or the *Controlled Drugs and Substances Act*.

5. **Serious criminality.** This ground covers the following situations:
   (a) Conviction in Canada of an offence under an Act of Parliament punishable by a maximum term of imprisonment of at least 10 years, or of an offence under an Act of Parliament for which a term of imprisonment of more than six months has been imposed.
   (b) Conviction outside Canada of an offence that, if committed in Canada, would constitute an offence under an Act of Parliament punishable by a maximum term of imprisonment of at least 10 years.
   (c) Committing an act outside Canada that is an offence in the place where it was committed and that, if committed in Canada, would constitute an offence under an Act of Parliament punishable by a maximum term of imprisonment of at least 10 years.

6. **Organized criminality.** An individual may be inadmissible on this ground for being a member of a criminal organization or for engaging, in the context of transnational crime, in activities such as people smuggling, trafficking in persons or money laundering.

7. **Security.** This ground encompasses such situations as engaging in espionage, in subversion of force of any government, in terrorism or in acts of violence that would or might endanger the lives or safety of persons in Canada; being a danger to the security of Canada or being a member of an organization that there are reasonable grounds to believe engages, has engaged or will engage in espionage, terrorism or subversion of any government by force.

8. **International and human rights violations.** An individual may be inadmissible on this ground for committing acts of genocide, war crimes or crimes against humanity outside Canada or for being a senior official in a government that engages or has engaged in terrorism, systematic or gross human rights violations, genocide, war crimes or crimes against humanity; this ground also applies to foreign nationals subject to travel sanctions by an international organization, of which Canada is a member.

9. **Misrepresentation.** This ground captures situations where an individual directly or indirectly misrepresented or withheld material facts that

induce or could induce an error in the administration of the *IRPA*; this ground does not apply to protected persons.

10. **Non-compliance with the *IRPA*** (e.g., failing to leave Canada once a person's authorized stay has expired; working without authorization).

The first four grounds apply only to foreign nationals; the rest apply to both foreign nationals and permanent residents.

Persons seeking to enter Canada, permanently or temporarily, must satisfy immigration officers that they are not inadmissible. For example, for this purpose, applicants for permanent residence are required to undergo a medical examination (to determine health admissibility) and provide police clearances from each country where they have resided for at least six consecutive months since reaching the age of 18 (to determine criminality admissibility). In addition, the CIC conducts background checks on applicants and their family members to find out if they may be inadmissible on other grounds.

If inadmissibility is discovered prior to entry, the person may not be issued a visa to enter Canada. If inadmissibility arises at the point of entry or after entry to Canada, an inadmissibility proceeding is started, which may ultimately lead to removal. First, an immigration officer prepares a report and submits it to the Minister's delegate (a senior official empowered to review inadmissibility reports). In some cases, the Minister's delegate can issue a removal order on the basis of the report. However, in most cases, the case is referred to the Immigration Division of the IRB for a hearing to determine whether the person concerned is inadmissible. If the person is inadmissible, the Division may issue a removal order.

Permanent residents and, in limited circumstances, foreign nationals can appeal a removal order to the Immigration Appeal Division. However, the right to appeal is removed from individuals who are inadmissible on the grounds of security, violating human or international rights, serious criminality, or organized criminality. If the appeal is allowed, a person is permitted to remain in Canada.

Health Inadmissibility: Excessive Demand on Health or Social Services

To illustrate the interpretation and application of inadmissibility grounds, this section discusses medical inadmissibility based on excessive demand on health or social services. Section 1 of the *Regulations* defines "excessive demand" in the following way:

> (*a*) a demand on health services or social services for which the anticipated costs would likely exceed average Canadian per capita health services and social services costs over a period of five consecutive years immediately following the most recent medical examination required by these Regulations, unless there is evidence that significant costs are likely to be incurred beyond that period, in which case the period is no more than 10 consecutive years; or
>
> (*b*) a demand on health services or social services that would add to existing waiting lists and would increase the rate of mortality and morbidity in Canada as a result of an inability to provide timely services to Canadian citizens or permanent residents.

The above definition, however, does not fully answer how excessive demand is to be established. For example, if a person has a health condition that is known to require services and supports that are expensive or in high demand, does this automatically lead to inadmissibility? What if an applicant is willing to attenuate public expenses and pay himself/herself for the necessary services? Is the applicant's financial ability and willingness to cover health or social service expenses relevant to the evaluation of "excessive demand"? Two important cases — *Hilewitz*[50] and *Deol*[51] — provided useful clarification of these issues.

The Hilewitz family applied to immigrate to Canada under the investor class (this class required applicants to have at least $800,000 net worth and make a $400,000 investment in Canada[52]) and has met the necessary financial requirements. However, one of the family's children, Gavin, had an intellectual disability, which was deemed to impose excessive demand on Canadian social services (such as special education and vocational training). As a result, he was inadmissible. The family indicated that it was able and willing to send Gavin to a private school and, thus, he would impose no demand on social services. Nevertheless, the family's application for permanent residence was refused. The Hilewitzes challenged the refusal, and their case reached all the way to the Supreme Court of Canada. The Supreme Court held that the family's ability and willingness to pay for social services was a relevant consideration in assessing "excessive demand". The Court emphasized that assessments need to be individualized. It is impossible to realistically determine the nature and extent of demands on services without considering medical as well as non-medical factors, including the applicant's ability and intention to pay for social services. If the need for services is determined only by the classification of a health condition, it becomes generic rather than individual and leads to an automatic exclusion of individuals with particular disabilities. Although *Hilewitz* was decided in the context of the investor class, as subsequently suggested by the Federal Court of Appeal, the holding applies to other categories of immigrants.[53]

Although ability and willingness to pay are relevant in the context of social services, this is not so in relation to health services. This is explained by the different funding and delivery schemes of health and social services. The social services scheme contemplates the contribution of families to the costs of providing certain services. As noted by the Supreme Court in *Hilewitz*, even if the intentions of the Hilewitz family regarding Gavin's education and training did not materialize, under the provincial social services scheme, the family would likely be required to contribute a substantial portion, if not the entire, cost of services. In contrast, healthcare is publicly funded and services are available without payment. Thus, it is not possible to enforce a personal undertaking to pay for health services after a person is admitted for permanent residence. Hence, in *Deol*, the Federal Court of Appeal found that the decision-maker made no error in not giving regard to the financial ability of the applicant to pay for health services.[54]

Immigration Detention

Like other aspects of immigration law, immigration detention applies to non-citizens only. It is considered to be of preventative and not penal nature. This is reflected in the three major grounds for arrest and detention:

---

[50] *Hilewitz v. Canada (Minister of Citizenship and Immigration); De Jong v. Canada (Minister of Citizenship and Immigration)*, [2005] 2 S.C.R. 706.

[51] *Deol v. Canada (Minister of Citizenship and Immigration)*, [2003] 1 F.C. 301 (C.A.).

[52] In 2010, these requirements were changed. Now an investor needs to have at least $1.6 million net worth and make an $800,000 investment in Canada. *Regulations, supra* note 16, s. 88(1).

[53] *Colaco v. Canada (Minister of Citizenship and Immigration)*, [2007] F.C.J. No. 1172 (C.A.).

[54] Ms. Deol applied to sponsor her father, mother and siblings to immigrate to Canada. The application was refused because the father had degenerative osteoarthritis, which was considered to cause excessive demand on health services in Canada (his condition would likely require knee replacement surgery at a cost of approximately $40,000).

- Inadmissibility and danger to the public (there are reasonable grounds to believe that a person is inadmissible and is a danger to the public)

- Flight risk (there are reasonable grounds to believe that a person is unlikely to appear for a future examination, inadmissibility hearing or removal from Canada)

- Identity (where an officer is not satisfied about a person's identity; for example, an individual has no identity documents or the documents are fraudulent)

Immigration arrest and detention is used to contain individuals, often in order to enable further enforcement action such as removal. Depending on the circumstances, arrest and detention may be carried out with or without a warrant, on entry into Canada or after admission to Canada. A person's right to counsel arises at the moment when he/she is ordered detained.[55]

Neither the *IRPA* nor the *Regulations* prescribe a temporal limit on detention. The *IRPA*, however, provides for regular detention reviews, and the *Regulations* establish safeguards against indefinite detention.[56] Detention reviews are conducted by the Immigration Division of the IRB, which has the power to order continued detention or release. Detention reviews are conducted with the following regularity:

1. First detention review — within 48 hours after the person was taken into detention or "without delay afterwards".
2. Second detention review — at least once during the seven days following the first review.
3. Each subsequent review — at least once during each 30-day period after each review.

Security Certificates

Security certificates are a special procedure that allows for detention and removal of foreign nationals and permanent residents who are inadmissible on grounds of security, violating human or international rights, serious criminality or organized criminality.[57] As seen from the grounds of inadmissibility, the procedure is intended for cases that are considered particularly serious and seeks to ensure containment and speedy removal of the persons concerned.

The procedure works in the following way:

1. The Minister of Citizenship and Immigration and the Minister of Public Safety and Emergency Preparedness sign a certificate stating that a given individual is inadmissible on one of the above-mentioned grounds; the Ministers may also issue a warrant for the arrest and detention of the person named in the certificate.

2. The certificate is referred to the Federal Court, which determines whether the certificate is reasonable.

3. If the certificate is upheld by the Court, it serves as conclusive proof that the person named in the certificate is inadmissible and clears the path for the person's removal from Canada.

---

[55] *Dragosin v. Canada*, [2003] F.C.J. No. 110.
[56] *IRPA, supra* note 15, s. 57; *Regulations, supra* note 16, s. 248.
[57] *IRPA, supra* note 15, s. 77(1).

Between 1991 and 2007, 28 security certificates were issued; 19 of them resulted in deportations.[58] The procedure proved highly problematic, particularly in relation to the five recent cases of Hassan Almrei, Adil Charkaoui, Mohammad Harkat, Mahmoud Jaballah, and Mohammad Mahjoub. All five persons have been subject to certificates for suspected links to terrorist organizations and, as a result, have spent anywhere between 2 and 7.25 years in detention.

Some of the major concerns as highlighted by the five cases were as follows:

1. *Inability to know the case to be met and effectively challenge government evidence.* The security certificate procedure provides for limitations on disclosure of information to the person concerned where such disclosure may be injurious to national security. Thus, the person named in the certificate may not be allowed to see all the evidence on which the government is building its case. The confidential information will be heard by the Federal Court in the absence of the person concerned and his/her counsel; they will be given only a summary of such evidence.

2. *Prolonged detention with limited opportunity for detention review and release.* Under the 2002 provisions of the *IRPA*, permanent residents subject to security certificates could be detained, but they had access to periodic detention reviews from the very start of detention. In contrast, foreign nationals had to be automatically detained, but they did not have similar access to detention review. They could apply for release only after the certificate was determined reasonable and if they had not been removed from Canada within 120 days after the certificate was upheld. Given the complicated process of collecting intelligence in national security cases and the lengthiness of its examination, in some cases, it took years until the decision on the certificate's reasonableness could be made. As a result, at least two of the five named persons have spent anywhere between three and five years in detention without even the possibility of applying for release (for example, a certificate against Mr. Jaballah was issued in August 2001, but it was determined reasonable only in 2006).

3. *Potential removal to face torture, risk to life or other ill-treatment.* All five named persons allege that they would face torture or persecution in the countries of intended destination. Hassan Almrei, Mohammad Harkat, and Mohammad Mahjoub have been granted Convention refugee status in Canada; that is, Canadian authorities have recognized that these three individuals would face persecution in their countries of origin. Adil Charkaoui and Mahmoud Jaballah, while not refugees, allege risk of torture if removed to Morocco and Egypt, respectively. Given that the Supreme Court decision in *Suresh* did not impose an absolute prohibition on removal to torture, it is possible that security certificates may become those "extraordinary circumstances" when removal may be justified.[59] However, given that the Supreme Court did not provide any

---

[58] Special Senate Committee on the *Anti-terrorism Act*, Fundamental Justice in Extraordinary Times: Main Report of the Special Senate Committee on the Anti-Terrorism Act (February 2007), <http://www.parl.gc.ca/39/1/parlbus/commbus/senate/Com-e/anti-e/rep-e/rep02feb07-e.htm#PROCEDURAL_FAIRNESS:__THE_NEED_FOR_A_SPECIAL_ADVOCATE>.

[59] It should be noted that in *Jaballah (Re)*, [2006] F.C.J. No. 1706, the Federal Court determined that the case did not create an exceptional circumstance warranting deportation to torture. The Court, however, also remarked that

indication as to what these extraordinary circumstances might be, it is likely that another Supreme Court decision will be necessary to ultimately resolve the issue.

In February 2007, the Supreme Court found that the security certificate procedure violated sections 7, 9, and 10 of the *Charter* and could not be saved under section 1.[60] Due to the lack of disclosure, the persons concerned were not able to know the case to be met and effectively respond to the allegations made by the government. This, in turn, undermined the ability of a judge to make a decision based on all available facts and the law and violated the right to a fair hearing under section 7. Further, the lack of regular detention reviews for foreign nationals violated the right not to be subject to arbitrary detention and the right to a prompt detention review.

As a result of the *Charkaoui* decision, the *IRPA* was amended to provide for a single regime of regular detention reviews for both permanent residents and foreign nationals as well as to establish a position of special advocate in order to mitigate concerns associated with the lack of disclosure. The function of the special advocate is to protect the interests of a person named in a security certificate during proceedings where confidential information is heard in his/her absence. The special advocate is given access to all information that is not disclosed to the person concerned and his/her counsel. The special advocate can challenge the relevance, reliability, and sufficiency of confidential information; make oral and written submissions; and cross-examine witnesses. Although the special advocate model partially compensates for non-disclosure, it is far from an optimal solution. Most notably, once the special advocate receives confidential information, he/she is prohibited from communicating with the person concerned, unless authorized by a judge. This significantly undermines the ability of special advocates to challenge or counter the information relied upon by the government.

The Minister of Justice established a list of lawyers who may act as special advocates. They are selected by an advisory committee which reviews applications and makes recommendations to the Minister. There are currently 23 lawyers on the list.[61]

In 2009, the Federal Court found that there was not sufficient information to conclude that Mr. Almrei was a member of Al Qaeda or an affiliated organization and quashed a certificate against him.[62] The same year, a certificate against Mr. Charkaoui was determined void as there was not sufficient evidence to justify it.[63] Both men have launched lawsuits seeking damages from the federal government for negligence and false imprisonment. The certificate against Mr. Harkat was upheld in December 2010,[64] but the decision is currently on appeal before the Federal Court of Appeal. The certificates against Mr. Jaballah and Mr. Mahjoub still await examination before the Federal Court.

---

this conclusion did not mean that Mr. Jaballah could not be deported. Rather, the Minister was not to exercise discretion in a manner that would violate the respondent's rights under the *Charter*.

[60] *Charkaoui v. Canada (Citizenship and Immigration)*, [2007] 1 S.C.R. 350.

[61] Justice Canada, online: <http://canada.justice.gc.ca/eng/news-nouv/nr-cp/2007/doc_32198.html>.

[62] *Almrei (Re)*, [2009] F.C.J. No. 1579.

[63] *Charkaoui (Re)*, [2009] F.C.J. No. 1208. The government was ordered to disclose a portion of confidential information on which it relied, but the authorities decided to withdraw that information instead of disclosing it to Charkaoui. As a result, the remaining evidence was not sufficient to justify the certificate.

[64] *Harkat (Re)*, [2010] F.C.J. No. 1428.

Removal Orders

There are three types of removal orders, which produce different consequences for persons subject to them:

- **Exclusion orders:** As a general rule, an exclusion order obliges a foreign national to obtain a written authorization in order to return to Canada during the one-year period after the exclusion order was enforced. A harsher regime applies to foreign nationals who are issued exclusion orders as a result of misrepresentation: they are subject to the requirement of obtaining a written authorization to return to Canada for a period of two years after the exclusion order was enforced.

- **Deportation orders:** A deportation order requires a person concerned to obtain a written authorization in order to return to Canada at any time after the deportation order was enforced.

- **Departure orders:** The departure order regime seeks to encourage speedy voluntary compliance with removal orders. Unlike exclusion or deportation orders, departure orders do not require an individual to obtain a written authorization to return to Canada. In order to benefit from this regime, a person must leave Canada within 30 days after the order became enforceable and verify the departure with immigration authorities. Failure to depart will lead to a departure order automatically becoming a deportation order.

REFUGEE LAW

Unlike immigrants, who are considered to move voluntarily in pursuit of better opportunities, refugees are involuntary migrants who are fleeing for their lives. To account for this reality, admission of refugees is based on principles that are different from immigrant selection. While immigrants are admitted on the basis of their potential contribution to Canada or relationship to a Canadian, the defining consideration in case of refugees is their need for protection.

The *Refugee Convention*

The 1951 *UN Convention Relating to the Status of Refugees (Refugee Convention)* and the 1967 *Protocol* create an international framework for refugee protection. Including Canada, 141 countries are parties to the *Convention* and the *Protocol*[65] and are consequently guided by their provisions in decision-making on refugee claims. At the international level, refugee protection efforts are led and coordinated by a specialized agency — the United Nations High Commissioner for Refugees (UNHCR). The UNHCR performs a variety of tasks, including assistance to refugees and other persons in need of protection, advocacy, response to emergency situations, refugee determination in certain countries, and promotion of durable solutions for the displaced.

According to the UNHCR, there were 43.3 million forcibly displaced people worldwide at the end of 2009.[66] The largest numbers of refugees originated from Afghanistan, Iraq, and Somalia, and the top three refugee-hosting

---

[65] United Nations High Commissioner for Refugees (UNHCR), "States Parties to the Convention and the Protocol", online: <http://www.unhcr.org/pages/49da0e466.html>.

[66] United Nations High Commissioner for Refugees (UNHCR), "2009 Global Trends: Refugees, Asylum-seekers, Returnees, Internally Displaced and Stateless Persons", online: <http://www.unhcr.org/4c11f0be9.html> [UNHCR, "2009 Global Trends"].

countries were Pakistan, Iran, and Syria.[67] Overall, approximately four-fifths of refugees are located in developing countries.[68] Thus, refugee burdens are distributed unequally: countries with fewer resources are also usually the ones bearing a significant refugee burden. These patterns are essential to understanding the global dynamics of refugee protection and the positioning of industrialized countries such as Canada in this context.

The regime of the *Refugee Convention* rests on three core concepts:

1. Definition of a refugee
2. *Non-refoulement* (means "no return")
3. Standards of treatment of refugees

The refugee definition forms the basis for determining whether a person concerned should be granted protection. It is discussed in detail in the section below.

The *non-refoulement* principle (Art. 33 of the *Refugee Convention*) prohibits expulsion of a refugee to a country where he/she may face persecution, unless that refugee constitutes a danger to security or poses a threat to the public of a host state. As a result of this principle, states' ability to remove refugees is more constrained than their ability to remove other categories of migrants.

Refugee protection can be considered meaningful and effective only if it allows for the inclusion of refugees in a host society. To this end, the *Refugee Convention* imposes an obligation on States Parties to ensure certain standards of treatment of refugees in a number of areas, including access to courts, freedom of religion and association, freedom of movement, elementary education, access to employment, housing, and social assistance. In Canada, these obligations have led to refugee claimants and refugees enjoying certain benefits that are not normally available to other foreign nationals. For example, refugee claimants and refugees have access to social assistance and the Interim Federal Health program; they are not required to have an HRSDC approval in order to be issued a work permit.

A refugee claim may be made inside or outside Canada. These two avenues correspond to the two streams of Canada's refugee protection system: inland refugee determination and refugee resettlement. A person who has made a claim for protection from within Canada and who is awaiting a decision on it is called a **refugee claimant** (often also referred to as an "asylum-seeker"). Since 2005, Canada has received between 20,000 and 37,000 refugee claims a year (the lowest was close to 20,000 in 2005 and the highest was approximately 37,000 in 2008).[69] Internationally, it ranked as the fourth largest recipient of asylum applications among industrialized countries in 2009.[70]

Grounds for Protection

In Canada, refugee protection may be granted on one of three grounds: (i) the *Refugee Convention*; (ii) risk of torture; and (iii) risk to life or risk of cruel and unusual treatment or punishment. The refugee determination procedure and the benefits of protection under all three grounds are the same.

---

[67] *Ibid.* at 6–8.

[68] *Ibid.*

[69] United Nations High Commissioner for Refugees (UNHCR), "Asylum Levels and Trends in Industrialized Countries: 2009" at 13, online: <http://www.unhcr.org/4ba7341a9.html> [UNHCR, "Asylum Levels in Industrialized Countries: 2009"].

[70] Close to 800,000 applications for asylum were made in 159 countries around the world in 2009. Out of these, over 222,000 were registered in South Africa — almost as many as were lodged in the 27 member states of the European Union combined. The United States ranked second, with 47,900 applications; France — third, with 42,100 claims, and Canada — fourth, with 34,000 applications. *Ibid.* at 16–17.

Definition of a Refugee
Article 1A(2) of the *Refugee Convention* defines a refugee as a person who

... owing to well-founded fear of being persecuted for reasons of race, religion, nationality, membership of a particular social group or political opinion, is outside the country of his nationality and is unable or, owing to such fear, is unwilling to avail himself of the protection of that country; or who, not having a nationality and being outside the country of his former habitual residence as a result of such events, is unable or, owing to such fear, is unwilling to return to it.

The UNHCR and national decision-making bodies have developed extensive jurisprudence and guidelines on the interpretation of key aspects of the definition:

1. **Persecution.** The *Convention* does not define the term "persecution", but it has been understood as serious human rights violations — systemic and sustained denial of core human rights.[71] The claimant must show that there is a "reasonable chance" or a "serious possibility" that he/she will be persecuted if returned to his/her **country of origin**.[72]

2. **Well-founded fear of persecution.** In order for fear to be considered well-founded, a subjective and objective element must be present: fear has to exist not only subjectively in the claimant's mind, but also be supported by the situation in the claimant's country of origin.[73] The objective element is established on the basis of information about the country of origin. To this end, the Canadian IRB has developed national documentation packages on individual countries, which contain a selection of documents on human rights, security conditions, and other issues relevant to refugee determination. The packages usually include such sources as reports of human rights organizations (e.g., Amnesty International, Human Rights Watch), media articles, and information collected by the IRB research directorate on specific issues.

3. **State protection.** The refugee definition reflects the surrogate nature of refugee protection: only where the claimant is unable or unwilling to obtain protection from his/her own state, can he/she turn to another state for protection. Such unwillingness or inability may arise in a variety of situations. For example, where the claimant's state itself is the persecutor (for example, government persecution of members of political opposition) protection is generally considered unavailable. Protection may also be unavailable where war, internal strife or other grave disturbance has led to the breakdown of the state apparatus. Claimants may also be unable or unwilling to obtain state protection where persecution is inflicted by private individuals and groups, but is tolerated by the authorities or where state authorities refuse to provide protection (for instance, a claimant suffers from domestic violence at the hand of her husband, but when she repeatedly complains to police, they take no action).

---

[71] *Canada (Attorney General) v. Ward*, [1993] 2 S.C.R. 689 at paras. 64–69. See also United Nations High Commissioner for Refugees (UNHCR), *Handbook on Procedures and Criteria for Determining Refugee Status under the 1951 Convention and the 1967 Protocol relating to the Status of Refugees*, HCR/IP/4/Eng/REV.1, 1979 (re-edited January 1992) at para 51 [UNHCR, Handbook on Determining Refugee Status].

[72] *Adjei v. Canada (Minister of Employment and Immigration)*, [1989] 2 F.C. 680 (C.A.).

[73] *UNHCR, Handbook on Determining Refugee Status, supra* note 72 at para. 38.

4. **Protection grounds.** The *Convention* makes protection available only in cases where persecution is inflicted on one or a combination of the five grounds: race, religion, nationality, political opinion, or membership of a particular social group. While the first four grounds are relatively self-explanatory, membership of a particular social group requires some elaboration. Internationally, there developed two major approaches to the definition of a "particular social group": the social perception approach and the protected characteristics approach. The **social perception approach** is focused on the external perception of the group by others, including persecutors. It asks whether a certain group is viewed as a distinct social group by reason of some characteristic, activity or goal that unites them.[74] The **protected characteristics approach** focuses on internal characteristics that unite persons in a group. In Canada, the foundations of this approach were laid by the Supreme Court in *Ward*,[75] which identified the following categories of particular social groups:

(1) groups defined by an innate, unchangeable characteristic;
(2) groups whose members voluntarily associate for reasons so fundamental to their human dignity that they should not be forced to forsake the association; and (3) groups associated by a former voluntary status, unalterable due to its historical permanence.

The examples of recognized particular social groups are women suffering from domestic violence, homosexuals, persons subject to forced sterilization, the poor, and trade unionists.

Exclusion from Refugee Protection

The issues of refugee definition go hand in hand with the issue of exclusion, i.e., who is not entitled to protection. The *Convention* envisions two scenarios in which a claimant who meets the refugee definition is nevertheless excluded from protection: (i) an individual is considered undeserving of protection or (ii) an individual is considered not to be in need of protection.

The first group is outlined in Art. 1 F of the *Refugee Convention* and includes situations where there are "serious reasons" to believe that the claimant (a) committed a crime against peace, a war crime, or a crime against humanity; (b) committed a serious non-political crime outside the country of refuge; or (c) is guilty of acts contrary to the purposes and principles of the United Nations.

The second set of grounds is found in Article 1E and applies in situations where a claimant has established residence outside the country where he/she fears persecution and has been granted most of the rights normally enjoyed by citizens in the new country of residence. This usually implies that the person, while not having citizenship, can safely live in the new country of residence and is protected against expulsion.[76] As a result, such a person is considered not to be in need of refugee protection elsewhere. For example, Miriam faces persecution in her **home country**, but then flees to country A where he/she is safe and is granted most of the rights enjoyed by citizens. If subsequently Miriam moves to a country B and makes a refugee claim there, she may be excluded from protection on the basis of Art. 1E.

---

[74] James C. Hathaway & Michelle Foster, "Membership of a Particular Social Group" (2003) 15:3 Int'l J. Ref. L. 477 at 483.

[75] *Ward, supra* note 72.

[76] UNHCR, *Handbook on Determining Refugee Status, supra* note 72 at para. 145.

Cessation of Protection

Cessation of protection refers to situations where refugee protection is no longer necessary. It may occur in the following situations:

- Where a refugee has voluntarily re-availed himself/herself of the protection of the country of his/her nationality
- Where a refugee has voluntarily reacquired his/her previous nationality
- Where a refugee has acquired a new nationality
- Where a refugee has voluntarily re-established himself/herself in the country which he/she left, owing to fear of persecution
- Where the circumstances that led to the individual's recognition as a refugee have ceased to exist[77]

Definition of Person in Need of Protection

The category of **person in need of protection** encompasses two grounds: (i) risk of torture, and (ii) risk to life or risk of cruel and unusual treatment or punishment. These two grounds give effect to Canada's obligations under the *Convention against Torture* (prohibition of torture and of removal to torture) and the *International Covenant on Civil and Political Rights* (ICCPR) (prohibition of torture, cruel, inhuman or degrading treatment or punishment and prohibition on removal to face such maltreatment). Unlike the *Refugee Convention*, neither of the two grounds requires that risk be connected to race, religion, nationality, political opinion or membership of a particular social group. Thus, they expand protection opportunities for persons who do not meet the Convention definition, but are nevertheless at risk.

The first ground is determined in reference to the definition of torture under the *Convention against Torture*:

> ... any act by which severe pain or suffering, whether physical or mental, is intentionally inflicted on a person for such purposes as obtaining from him or a third person information or a confession, punishing him for an act he or a third person has committed or is suspected of having committed, or intimidating or coercing him or a third person, or for any reason based on discrimination of any kind, when such pain or suffering is inflicted by or at the instigation of or with the consent or acquiescence of a public official or other person acting in an official capacity. It does not include pain or suffering arising only from, inherent in or incidental to lawful sanctions.[78]

As seen from the above definition, "torture" has distinct characteristics: (i) it causes severe pain or suffering; (2) it is inflicted for a certain purpose; (iii) it is carried out by or with the acquiescence of the state. Persons claiming protection on this ground must demonstrate that there are substantial grounds to believe that they would be subjected personally to a danger of torture.

The second ground within the notion of "person in need of protection" is risk to life or risk of cruel and unusual treatment or punishment. According to the *IRPA*, a claimant relying on this ground must demonstrate that he/she would face risk in every part of his/her country of origin; that the risk is not faced generally by other individuals in the country and that he/she is unable or unwilling to avail himself/herself of the protection of that country.[79]

Neither the *Convention against Torture* nor the ICCPR define "inhuman or degrading treatment or punishment". The distinction between torture and

---

[77] *Refugee Convention*, Art. 1C.

[78] *Convention against Torture and Other Cruel, Inhuman or Degrading Treatment or Punishment*, Adopted by General Assembly resolution 39/46 of 10 December 1984, Art. 1(1).

[79] *IRPA, supra* note 15, s. 97(1)(b).

inhuman or degrading treatment or punishment is often based on the difference in the kind, purpose, and severity of treatment, torture being considered an aggravated form of cruel, inhuman, or degrading treatment or punishment. Section 97(1)(b) of the *IRPA* excludes two types of risk from consideration under the risk to life or the risk of cruel and unusual treatment or punishment:

1. Risk inherent or incidental to lawful sanctions, unless they are imposed in disregard of accepted international standards
2. Risks caused by the inability of the claimant's home country to provide adequate health or medical care

Inland Refugees

Access to Inland Protection

The *Refugee Convention* does not compel States Parties to admit asylum-seekers or refugees. In fact, obligations under the *Convention* arise only once a person finds himself/herself in the territory of a State Party. Access to territory therefore becomes a determinative factor in the ability of asylum-seekers to access refugee protection; at the same time, states are using regulation of access to their territories to manage (often contrary to the spirit of the *Convention*) asylum flows and the extent of their refugee protection obligations. The measures that seek to prevent asylum-seekers or other migrants from arriving in a state territory are commonly known as **interdiction**. Interdiction includes, for example, visa requirements, carrier sanctions, stationing of immigration officers overseas, interception of boats at sea, and safe third country agreements.

Imposition of visa requirements on refugee-producing countries has been frequently utilized to reduce asylum flows. For example, high volumes of refugee claims from Mexico and the Czech Republic have been expressly cited as the reason for Canada's imposition of visa requirements on those countries in 2009.[80]

Carrier sanctions include imposition of fines on transportation companies that bring unauthorized migrants into a country as well as making carriers responsible for costs of removing those unauthorized migrants. Such sanctions create strong incentives for carriers to co-operate with immigration officials in pre-boarding checks and other screening in countries of origin.

The **safe third country** principle is usually used to preclude refugee claimants who have travelled through "safe" countries from being considered for protection in the state of final destination. So far, Canada has designated only one country — the United States — as "safe" and to this end has concluded a *Safe Third Country Agreement*[81] with the United States. According to the *Agreement*, which came into force in 2004, the state in which a refugee claimant arrived first should be responsible for determining his/her claim. This means that, for example, a claimant who travelled to Canada through the United States will not be given access to the Canadian refugee determination system, but instead will be directed to have his/her claim processed in the United States. The application of the *Agreement* is, however, limited in two respects. First, it applies only to claims made at the Canada–U.S. land border;

---

[80] CIC, News Release, "Canada imposes a visa on Mexico" <http://www.cic.gc.ca/english/department/media/releases/2009/2009-07-13.asp>. During 2008–2009, Mexico ranked as the top country of origin of refugee claimants in Canada; the Czech Republic was among the top ten countries of origin. UNHCR, "Asylum Levels in Industrialized Countries: 2009", *supra* note 70 at 33–34.

[81] *Agreement between the Government of Canada and the Government of the United States of America for Cooperation in the Examination of Refugee Status Claims from Nationals of Third Countries*, 5 December 2002, online: <http://www.cic.gc.ca/english/policy/safe-third.html>

if an individual has managed to enter Canadian territory, he/she will not be precluded from having a claim considered in Canada. Second, there are four main exceptions, which allow a claim to be considered in a state where an asylum-seeker wishes to seek protection and not in the state of first arrival. The following groups benefit from the exceptions:

- Unaccompanied minors
- Claimants who have a family member whose refugee claim was granted or who has lawful status (other than a visitor) in a receiving state
- Claimants who have a family member who is at least 18 years old and has a refugee claim pending in a receiving state
- Claimants who arrived in the receiving state's territory on a valid visa or who do not require a visa

In addition to the four exceptions outlined above, the *Agreement* allows Canada and the United States to make additional exceptions on public interest grounds. Canada has chosen to provide a public interest exception for individuals who have been charged with or convicted of an offence that could subject them to the death penalty in the United States or in any other country.

The *Agreement* has been criticized on a number of grounds, including for exposing many claimants to less favourable treatment in the United States than that accorded to refugee claimants in Canada. For example, the United States is more likely to detain asylum-seekers and to provide less sensitive consideration to gender-based claims. More claimants travel through the United States to Canada than the other way around. Thus, the *Agreement* has a disproportionate impact on the claimant's access to Canada's refugee system. In fact, the number of refugee claims made at the land border decreased by approximately 55 percent in 2005 compared with 2004 — a development that can be largely attributed to the *Agreement*.[82]

In 2005, the Canadian Council for Refugees (CCR), Amnesty International, and the Canadian Council of Churches, along with a Colombian asylum-seeker in the United States, challenged the *Agreement* in the Federal Court. They argued that the designation of the United States as a "safe third country" was invalid because the United States does not respect its obligations under the *Convention against Torture* and the *Refugee Convention* and that by returning refugee claimants to the United States, Canada is violating its international obligations and the claimants' *Charter* rights to life, liberty and security and to equality. The Federal Court upheld those arguments.[83] However, the decision was overturned by the Federal Court of Appeal[84] (leave to appeal to the Supreme Court denied) and, consequently, the Agreement remains in force.

Refugee Determination Process

The *Refugee Convention* sets out the key principles of refugee protection, but leaves it open to the states to decide on the specific design of their refugee determination systems. For this reason, one observes significant variation in refugee determination processes around the globe.

The Canadian refugee determination process consists of the following stages:

---

[82] CIC, "A Partnership for Protection: One-Year Review" (November 2006), online; CIC <http://www.cic.gc.ca/english/policy/partnership/index.html>

[83] *Canadian Council for Refugees v. Canada*, [2007] F.C.J. No. 1583.

[84] *Canadian Council for Refugees v. Canada*, [2008] F.C.J. No. 1002 (C.A.).

1. **Eligibility determination.** The first step after a refugee claim is made is to determine whether it should be referred to the IRB for a hearing. Claims are ineligible for a IRB hearing in the following situations:

   (a) Protection has already been conferred under the *IRPA*.

   (b) A person has been recognized as a *Convention* refugee in another country and may be returned there.

   (c) A claim has been previously rejected by the IRB or declared ineligible, withdrawn or abandoned.

   (d) A person came from a safe third country (currently, the United States).

   (e) A person was determined to be inadmissible on grounds of security, violating human or international rights, serious criminality or organized criminality.

   While the eligibility of claims made at the Canadian border is determined by the CBSA, eligibility of claims made from within Canada's territory is determined by the CIC. A decision that a claim is ineligible does not mean that a person is removed immediately. As a rule, he/she will be streamlined to the PRRA stage described below.

2. **Referral of the claim to the IRB.** Individuals with eligible claims are given a **Personal Information Form (PIF)**, which they must complete and submit to the IRB within 28 days. The PIF asks claimants to provide detailed information about themselves, including their education and employment history, travel route to Canada, and most importantly, their story and reasons for requesting protection. On the basis of the PIF, the IRB determines the most appropriate way to handle the claim (whether it will go through an expedited process or a regular hearing), identifies relevant issues to be considered at a hearing, and collects information on the claimant's country of origin.

3. **Hearing before a Refugee Protection Division** (RPD) of the IRB (see detailed description below).

4. **Claim accepted.** If a claim is accepted, the claimant receives protected status and may apply for permanent residence.

5. **Claim rejected.** If a claim is rejected, the claimant may pursue the following options:

   (a) Judicial review of the RPD decision before the Federal Court.

   (b) Pre-Removal Risk Assessment (**PRRA**). If no application for judicial review is filed or if the application for leave or for judicial review is rejected, a claimant will be getting closer to the removal stage and will usually be invited to submit a PRRA. As a rule, a successful PRRA leads to conferral of refugee protection and enables a person to apply for permanent residence.

6. **Removal.** If the PRRA is unsuccessful, arrangements are made by the CBSA to effectuate the person's removal.

Hearing before the RPD

Depending on the strength and complexity of a claim, it is scheduled for an expedited process or a hearing process.[85] In an expedited process, a

---

[85] Immigration and Refugee Board, "Process for Making a Claim for Refugee Protection", online: <http://www.irb.gc.ca/Eng/brdcom/references/procedures/proc/rpdspr/Pages/rpdp.aspx>.

claimant is interviewed by an IRB employee, a Refugee Protection Officer, who makes a recommendation about the claim. If the recommendation is positive, it may lead to acceptance of a claim without a hearing. However, if a positive determination cannot be made on the basis of the interview, the case is sent for a full hearing.

Most cases are decided through a hearing. The refugee determination process presupposes certain participatory rights for refugee claimants, namely the right to counsel, the right to submit documentary evidence in support of a claim, and the right to an interpreter.

A hearing typically includes the following participants:

- Refugee claimant
- Claimant's counsel
- Interpreter (if required)
- RPD Member
- Refugee Protection Officer (RPO) (not present in fast-tracked hearings if a case is relatively simple and has only one or two issues in question)

An RPD Member is in charge of the overall conduct of the hearing. He/she has the power to inquire into any matter that he/she considers relevant to establishing whether a claim is well-founded. The RPD Member determines whether the claim will be accepted or rejected. Currently, RPD Members are independent decision-makers appointed by the Governor in Council; they are selected through a multi-stage process, including screening and assessment by a Selection Advisory Board, a written test, an interview and a reference/validation check.

An **RPO** is an employee of the Board charged with assisting the Board in the handling of refugee claims. His/her task is to ensure that all relevant information is brought forward before the RPD Member. At a hearing, the RPO will typically question the claimant and make observations regarding the merits of the claim at the end of a hearing. However, unlike counsel for the claimant, the RPO is formally disinterested in the outcome of the claim and is not bound to take a particular side.

A hearing typically involves an RPO, Board Member, and claimant's counsel asking questions of a claimant. IRB Guideline 7 prescribes a particular order of questioning: first by the RPO, then by the Board Member, and finally by the claimant's counsel. This order of questioning may be varied (to allow the claimant's counsel to ask questions first) in cases where vulnerable claimants (such as survivors of torture, minors, elderly) are involved. The purpose of questioning is to obtain clarification on various aspects of the claim that are relevant to establishing the individual's need for protection. For the most part, they centre on the definitions of *Convention* refugee and person in need of protection and usually include such questions as the following: Can a claimant obtain protection from his/her country of origin? What is the nature of the risk feared? Who is persecuting the claimant (e.g., state agents or private groups/individuals)? Is the Board satisfied about the identity of the claimant? In addition, the RPD considers whether the claimant is generally credible. Refugee hearings are supposed to be non-adversarial. However, given that some questions may draw attention to inconsistencies or other issues that potentially undermine the claim, the hearing may become contentious.

A decision on a claim may be announced at the end of the hearing or may be reserved and communicated to the claimant at a later date. A person who receives protection on the basis of the *Refugee Convention* receives the status of a *Convention* refugee; a person who is granted protection on the basis of risk to life or risk of torture receives the status of a person in need of protection.

Canada's Inland Refugee Determination System

EXHIBIT 35.3

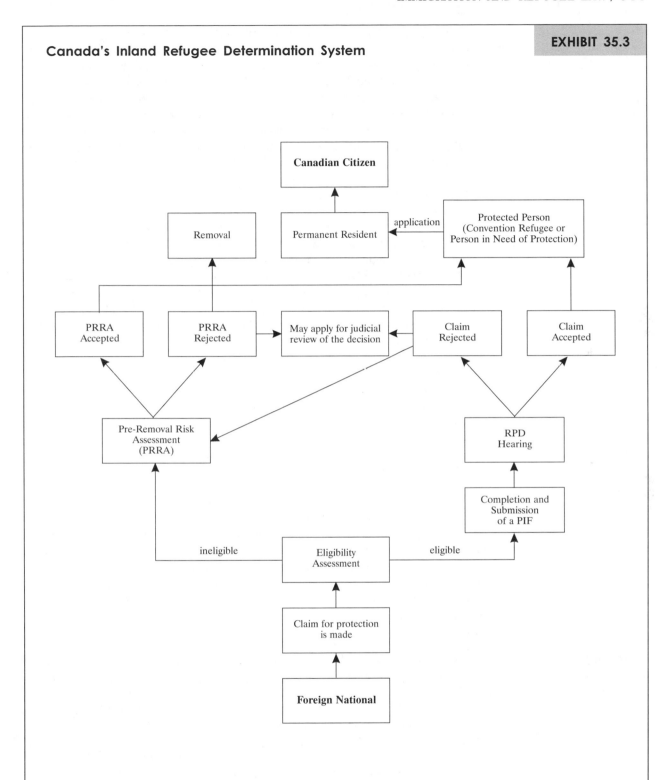

PIF = Personal Information Form
RPD = Refugee Protection Division
PRRA= Pre-Removal Risk Assessment

Note: This chart is valid until the changes under the *Balanced Refugee Reform Act,* S.C. 2010, c. 8, are implemented.

Pre-Removal Risk Assessment (PRRA)

As a rule, foreign nationals are presumed to be able to safely return to their countries of origin. However, there may be situations where the person concerned alleges that he or she would face risk in the country of destination. A Pre-Removal Risk Assessment (PRRA) is intended specifically for these types of situations to ensure that Canada does not return persons to danger. As a rule, PRRA applications consider the same protection grounds as the RPD, namely the risk of persecution, risk of torture, risk to life or risk of cruel and unusual treatment or punishment.[86] However, PRRA applications are usually decided without a hearing and are instead based on the written submissions of the applicant. In some cases, an interview may be held.

PRRA considers only new circumstances that have developed since the completion of previous proceedings (e.g., a refugee hearing). In cases of rejected refugee claimants, the main rationale behind a PRRA is to examine new risks that might have arisen between the date of a refugee hearing and the date when the claimant became ready for removal. Months often pass between these two events, especially if an application for judicial review of an RPD decision was made. During this period, new evidence might have become available or the applicant's circumstances or the situation in his/her country of origin might have changed to such an extent that they give rise to new or heightened risks to the applicant. However, an applicant may present only new evidence that arose after the IRB rejection, evidence that was not reasonably available, or evidence that the applicant could not reasonably have been expected to have presented at the time of the rejection.[87]

Judicial Review

As a rule, when an applicant for immigration or a refugee claimant receives a negative decision, he/she may apply for judicial review of that decision in the Federal Court. However, there is no automatic right to judicial review. First, an individual must seek leave (permission) to appeal. If leave is granted, then the case will proceed to the actual review. If an application for judicial review is successful, the case is returned to the original decision-making agency for re-determination. For example, if a judicial review of an RPD decision is successful, the case is sent back for another hearing before a different RPD panel. A decision of the Federal Court may be further appealed to the Federal Court of Appeal, but only if the judge of the Federal Court has certified that a serious question of general importance is involved.

Resettlement of Refugees from Overseas

Resettlement is one of the durable solutions, which is used in cases where a refugee can neither return to his/her country of origin nor integrate in the country of first asylum. The numbers of refugees who benefit from resettlement are small: in 2009, only one percent of the world's refugees were resettled.[88] A total of 112,400 refugees were admitted by 19 resettlement countries, including the United States (79,900), Canada (12,500), and Australia (11,100).[89] On average, Canada resettles around 12,000 refugees annually and consistently ranks among the top three countries of resettlement in the world.

---

[86] *IRPA, supra* note 15, s. 113(c).

[87] *IRPA, supra* note 15, s. 113(a).

[88] UNCHR, "2009 Global Trends", *supra* note 67 at 10.

[89] *Ibid.* at 12.

Although the resettlement process is governed by the same principles and basic definitions[90] as the inland refugee determination, it has some peculiarities. First, unlike spontaneous arrivals of refugee claimants, resettled refugees are processed overseas and are admitted to Canada only after having been determined to meet the criteria for protection and other applicable requirements. The more controlled nature of resettlement makes it possible to manage admissions and establish annual targets acceptable to the Canadian government. Second, the pre-planned nature of resettlement makes possible (and in fact requires) the presence of a Canadian sponsor who would support a resettled refugee both financially and emotionally upon arrival in Canada. Unlike in the inland process, where claimants may submit their claim directly to the authorities and do not need to have a Canadian sponsor, an application for resettlement usually must be accompanied by an undertaking or a referral. A referral is made by the UNHCR who identifies an individual for resettlement and transmits his/her file to Canadian authorities for consideration. Persons referred by the UNHCR are usually streamlined into government sponsorship. An "undertaking" is used in the context of refugee sponsorship by private groups or organizations; it is a written commitment to the Minister of Citizenship and Immigration that a group of persons or an organization will provide resettlement assistance, lodging, and other basic necessities in Canada for a resettled refugee and his/her family members.

The resettlement process entails two major components:

1. A decision on an individual's application for resettlement
2. An approval of a Canadian sponsor for that individual

Refugee sponsorship can take one of three main forms:

1. By the Canadian or Quebec government
2. By private entities (for example, an incorporated or an unincorporated organization; a group of five Canadian citizens or permanent residents)
3. Joint private–government initiatives

All groups or organizations who wish to sponsor refugees must complete an application and be approved by the CIC. They must meet a set of prescribed criteria, including proof of financial resources and a settlement plan for the refugee's arrival.

As a rule, resettled refugees are provided with assistance (such as income support, housing, settlement services) for up to 12 months after their arrival.[91] Persons with particular vulnerabilities (for example, survivors of torture, persons with disabilities) usually need extended support and may benefit from up to 36 months of assistance. Such cases are usually assigned to a joint government–private sponsorship, with government providing income support and private sponsors ensuring emotional support, guidance, and resettlement services.[92]

---

[90] Canadian legislation allows for resettlement of two categories of individuals: (i) persons who meet the *Convention* refugee definition; and (ii) persons in circumstances similar to those of *Convention* refugees. The latter category encompasses individuals who are at risk, but who do not fully meet the *Convention* refugee definition (for example, persons who have not left their countries of origin). For detailed definition of the second category, see Regulations, *supra* note 16, ss. 146–48.

[91] Citizenship and Immigration Canada, Overseas Processing Manual 5 "Overseas Selection and Processing of Convention Refugees Abroad Class and Members of the Humanitarian-protected Persons Abroad Classes" at 72.

[92] *Ibid.* at 20–21.

BALANCED REFUGEE REFORM ACT, 2010: CHANGES TO THE INLAND REFUGEE DETERMINATION PROCESS

In June 2010, Parliament passed the *Balanced Refugee Reform Act*, which was designed to bring significant changes to the refugee protection system. Given the extent of the changes, the implementation is to occur in several stages over the course of 12 to 18 months. Certain changes have already come into effect, but those requiring alteration of the current refugee determination process and its institutional structure will take several months to be implemented. Exhibit 35.4 summarizes the changes to the refugee determination process brought by this Act.

Some of the other major changes are as follows:

1. The Minister of Citizenship and Immigration will obtain power to designate countries of origin, which are considered normally non-refugee producing. While claims from designated countries will still be considered

---

EXHIBIT 35.4

Changes to the Refugee Determination Process

CURRENT SYSTEM	NEW SYSTEM
1. Eligibility determination.	1. No change.
2. Completion of a Personal Information Form (PIF) within 28 days.	2. The PIF will no longer exist. Instead, information on a claim will be gathered through an interview with an IRB employee; the interview will take place no sooner than 15 days after referral.
3. Hearing before an independent decision-maker (RPD Member) currently within about 19 months.	3. Hearing by a permanent public servant (RPD) within a timeframe to be established in the *Regulations*.
4. No appeal to the Refugee Appeal Division (RAD).	4. The RAD will be established where claimants rejected by the RPD can appeal their cases.
5. Access to multiple recourses for rejected claimants, including judicial review by the Federal Court after each, rejection — estimated 3 years.	5. Following the last negative IRB decision, access only to the Federal Court with a leave decision anticipated within 4 months.
6. Pre-Removal Risk Assessment (PRRA) application may be submitted once an individual is ready for removal, regardless of when the decision on refugee status was made. The PRRA is currently conducted by the CIC.	6. One-year bar on PRRA applications after the last decision at the IRB. The PRRA will be decided by the IRB.
7. Removed approximately three years after the last IRB decision.	7. Removed within one year after the last IRB decision without any access to a PRRA.

Source: Citizenship and Immigration Canada, "Operational Bulletin 222 — September 3, 2010", online: <http://www.cic.gc.ca/english/resources/manuals/bulletins/2010/ob222.asp>.

by the IRB, they will be fast-tracked with shorter timelines than other claims (for example, the RPD hearing will take place within 60 days as opposed to 90 days for other claimants; a RAD decision will be expected within 30 days as opposed to 120 days for the other claimants).

2. The RPD will have the authority to identify "manifestly unfounded claims", that is, claims considered by the decision-maker to be clearly fraudulent. These claims will be treated similarly to those from designated countries of origin and fast-tracked before the RAD.

3. Access to Pre-removal Risk Assessments (PRRA) will be limited. Rejected claimants will be precluded from making a PRRA for one year following the final IRB decision. However, persons who have not been removed within one year will be allowed to make a PRRA application.

4. Imposition of restriction on the factors that may be considered in applications for humanitarian and compassionate consideration (H&C). Currently, rejected claimants may make an H&C application to remain in Canada. In deciding on those applications, immigration officers may consider various factors, including risks that the applicant would face in his/her country of origin. Under the new amendments, the risk factors will no longer be considered. This amendment has already come into effect.

5. An Assisted Voluntary Returns program will be introduced to encourage rejected claimants to voluntarily depart Canada. Persons eligible to participate in the program will be given a plane ticket home and up to $2,000 in reintegration assistance. The assistance could be used for education, vocational training, job placements, or business pursuits. The money usually will not be given directly to the rejected claimant; instead, program funds would be managed and distributed by an independent service provider on behalf of the Government of Canada.

CHAPTER SUMMARY

The chapter has introduced the reader to the key concepts of immigration and refugee law. In Canada, individuals may be admitted for permanent residence under one of three streams: economic, family or refugee. Each stream has specifically tailored criteria to reflect the underlying rationale for admission. Economic immigrants are selected on the basis of their ability to become established in Canada and to contribute to the country's economic and social growth. With the development of PTNPs, selection of immigrants under the economic stream is exercised through (i) federal programs such as the CEC and skilled worker class and (ii) various provincial/territorial programs. Some applicants, particularly those in skilled occupations, may now have an opportunity of choosing between CEC, skilled worker class or various PTNPs, depending on which program offers faster processing and a higher likelihood of approval.

The family stream reflects the value of family reunification and provides for admission of foreign nationals on the basis of their relationship to a Canadian citizen or permanent resident. However, the opportunity for reunification is to an extent limited by immigration law's particular definition of family as well as sponsor eligibility requirements. Finally, refugee admissions are carried out in recognition of Canada's international obligations and are based on the individuals' need for protection as determined on the basis of the *Convention* refugee definition and the definition of a person in need of protection.

In addition to prescribing characteristics that warrant applicants' admission to Canada, immigration law sets out screening and enforcement mechanisms through inadmissibility, detention, and removal provisions.

GLOSSARY OF NEW TERMS AND KEY CONCEPTS

Convention refugee	A person who meets the definition of refugee in the 1951 *UN Convention relating to the Status of Refugees*. In general, it is someone who has left his or her home country and has a well-founded fear of persecution based on race, religion, nationality, political opinion, or membership of a particular social group and is unable or, by reason of his or her fear, unwilling to seek the protection of the home country.
eligibility determination	The first step in the refugee claim process to determine whether a claim is eligible for a hearing before the Immigration and Refugee Board.
home country (or country of origin)	The country of which an individual is a citizen, permanent resident or if an individual is stateless, the country in which he/she has regularly lived.
inadmissibility	A category in law meaning that a person cannot enter or remain in Canada or cannot become a permanent resident.
interdiction	measures designed to prevent non-citizens, including asylum-seekers, from entering state territory.
person in need of protection	A person in Canada whose removal to his/her home country would expose him/her to personal risk of torture or a risk to life or a risk of cruel and unusual treatment or punishment.
PIF	Personal Information Form — a form that contains a series of questions about the claimant's identity, family, work history, military service, and other aspects of his/her life, including citizenship and immigration matters; currently, every claimant must complete a PIF before his/her IRB hearing.
protected characteristics approach	An approach to identification of "particular social groups" for the purposes of the *Refugee Convention* definition; it focuses on internal characteristics that unite persons in a group. In Canada, the following categories of particular social groups have been identified: (i) groups defined by an innate, unchangeable characteristic; (ii) groups whose members voluntarily associate for reasons so fundamental to their human dignity that they should not be forced to forsake the association; and (iii) groups associated by a former voluntary status, unalterable due to its historical permanence.
protected person	A person who has received refugee protection from Canada either as a *Convention* refugee or as a person in need of protection.
PRRA	Pre-Removal Risk Assessment — a procedure conducted before removal to ensure that a person is not removed to face torture, risk to life or persecution in his/her country of origin; if the PRRA is successful, a person will usually receive refugee protection.
refugee claimant (or asylum seeker)	A person who has made a refugee claim in Canada, but whose case has not been decided yet.
refugee protection officer (RPO)	An IRB employee who is present at the refugee hearing and who helps to ensure that all relevant questions and information are put before the decision-maker.
safe third country	A country designated by the *Regulations* as a safe country of transit or residence in which an individual could have found protection as a refugee before arriving in the country where the person is now claiming refugee protection. For the purposes of Canadian refugee determination, the United States is currently the only country considered "safe".
social perception approach	An approach to identification of "particular social groups" for the purposes of the *Refugee Convention* definition; it is focuses on the external perception of the group by others, including persecutors.
Visa	An authorization to enter a country on a temporary or permanent basis.

REVIEW QUESTIONS

1. What is the difference between a citizen and a permanent resident of Canada?
2. Can a permanent resident lose his/her status? If yes, in what circumstances?
3. Are foreign students allowed to work in Canada? If yes, in what circumstances?
4. What is the role of the Immigration and Refugee Board in the Canadian immigration and refugee system?
5. Who is a refugee?
6. What does "non-*refoulement*" mean?
7. What are the stages of the current inland refugee determination process?
8. What is the "points system", and what are its main selection factors?
9. When can a person be subject to immigration detention?
10. What is a security certificate and what are some of the concerns associated with this procedure?
11. Who can be sponsored under the family class?
12. How can Canadian citizenship be acquired?

DISCUSSION QUESTIONS

1. Dan wants to sponsor his nephew to come to Canada under the family class. Dan is a 40-year-old Canadian citizen, but has lived outside Canada for the past three years and is not planning on returning to Canada in the near future. Is Dan likely to be approved as a sponsor? Is his nephew considered a member of the family class under Canadian immigration law?

2. Is it acceptable to deport non-citizens who pose a security risk to Canada to countries where they might face a risk of torture? Discuss in light of the Supreme Court decision in *Suresh* as well as Canada's obligations under the *Convention against Torture* (for the text of the *Convention*, see <http://www2.ohchr.org/english/law/cat.htm>).

3. Discuss the following scenario:

   Alex came to Canada from Zimbabwe in 2003. He asked for refugee protection in Canada as he was afraid to return to his own country. Alex claimed that he was persecuted by the police and ZANU-PF supporters because of his membership in the opposition party Movement for Democratic Change (MDC). He is claiming that if he goes back, he would be arbitrarily detained and possibly killed. Research the human rights situation in Zimbabwe (look for human rights reports, articles that document situation in the country). In your opinion, is Alex likely to obtain refugee protection in Canada?

   (Make sure to refer to the *Refugee Convention* definition.)

4. Ram is a 55-year-old biologist from Singapore. He has a Bachelor's and a Master's degree in biology from the National University of Singapore and a combined 17 years of study. He has 10 years of work experience as a biologist. He has high proficiency in English on all four abilities (speaking, writing, listening, and comprehension). Ram has no relatives in Canada and has never been to Canada. His wife has only secondary

school education and is a homemaker, but she hopes to get a part-time job when she settles in Canada. Ram and his wife have some $100,000 in savings. Is Ram eligible to apply under the skilled worker class? (For the list of in-demand occupations, see Citizenship and Immigration Canada: <http://www.cic.gc.ca/english/immigrate/skilled/apply-who-instructions.asp#list>.) If yes, what are his chances of getting approved for immigration? Is he likely to score above the pass mark on the points system?

SUGGESTED READINGS

Carasco, Emily, et al., *Immigration and Refugee Law: Cases, Materials, and Commentary* (Toronto: Emond Montgomery, 2007).

Castles, Stephen. "The Factors That Make and Unmake Migration Policies" (2004) 38 *International Migration Review* 852.

Kelley, Ninette, & Jean-François Durieux. "UNHCR and Current Challenges in International Refugee Protection" (2004) 1 *Refuge* 22.

WEBSITES

Citizenship and Immigration Canada: <www.cic.gc.ca>

Immigration and Refugee Board: <http://www.cisr-irb.gc.ca/index.htm>

Canada Border Services Agency: <http://www.cbsa-asfc.gc.ca/menu-e.html>

Canadian Council for Refugees: <http://www.ccrweb.ca/eng/engfront/frontpage.htm>

UN High Commissioner for Refugees: <http://www.unhcr.org>

Law and Policy in Theory and Practice

Sasha Baglay
UNIVERSITY OF ONTARIO INSTITUTE OF TECHNOLOGY

Alberto Salazar Valle
YORK UNIVERSITY

Learning Objectives

After reading this chapter, the reader should be able to:

➢ Appreciate the complexity and diversity of factors involved in the law- and policy-making process

➢ Appreciate the impact of the media and interest groups on the law- and policy-making process

➢ Understand with various strategies used by interest groups to influence public policy

➢ Understand the interaction of the legislative and judicial branches in developing regulatory frameworks

TABLE OF CONTENTS

INTRODUCTION

In the eyes of the general public, the law appears to be made on the basis of reason, knowledge, scientific evidence, and in pursuit of the general social good. As a result, it is often assumed that courts and legislators strike a reasonable balance among multiple values and interests involved in the making and enforcement of laws. While the public good is the underlying consideration of legal regulation, there are multiple factors affecting the content and design of laws. The process of law making is not necessarily unbiased and objective; in order to understand why and how a certain law has come about, it is important to be aware of the complexity of the law-making process and the various factors that influence it, directly or indirectly. By way of illustration, this chapter will discuss three such factors: interest groups, the media, and the judicial–legislative dialogue. It will also highlight the importance of critically examining whose interests are represented in or excluded from the law-making process; what perspective a given law reflects; and what is its impact on various groups in society.

INTEREST GROUPS, PUBLIC CHOICE, AND POWER

Definition and Types of Interest Groups

Interest groups can be defined as groups of individuals or organizations that share a common set of goals and have joined together to persuade the legislative, executive, or judicial branch to adopt a policy, law, or decision that will help protect or advance the interest of a given group.[1] These groups seek to influence legislators, government agencies, and courts so that the enactment, interpretation or enforcement of the law reflects their interests. This may result in giving a new content, direction or meaning to the law, which in turn may assign rights and obligations differently than originally intended.[2]

Almost any law or legal policy is likely to attract the attention of an **interest group**. A statute, regulation or court decision normally assigns rights and obligations that permit or prohibit certain behaviours or courses of action, affecting the social, economic or political positions of individuals and groups in society. Some groups may see this as a threat or an advantage to preserving or enhancing their interests. This perception of a threat or an opportunity may ignite individuals or groups with similar interest or those similarly affected by a law to collaborate and collectively communicate their views to legislators, regulators or courts. For example, Canada's Parliament enacted the *Tobacco Act* and the *Tobacco Products Information Regulations*, which permit information and brand-preference advertising, but forbid lifestyle advertising and promotion, advertising appealing to young persons, and false or misleading advertising or promotion. In addition, the size of mandatory and attributed

---

[1] Theodore J. Lowi & Benjamin Ginsberg, *American Government: Freedom and Power* 6th ed. (New York: W.W. Norton, 2000) 307; Anthony Champagne, *Interest Groups and Judicial Elections* (2001) 34 Loy. L.A. L. Rev. 1391 at 1392. Others have defined interest groups as non-political party, non-governmental organizations with members. See Michael T. Heaney, "Brokering Health Policy: Coalitions, Parties, and Interest Group Influence" (2006) 31 J. Health Pol. Pol'y & L. 887 at 930; Robert H. Salisbury, "Interest Representation: The Dominance of Institutions" (1984) 78 American Political Science Review 64–76.

[2] For instance, the regulation of interest-rate ceilings for consumer credit varies among the United Kingdom (no ceilings), France (ceilings), and Japan (lowered ceilings), and the explanation to these differences should be sought in the dynamics of the influence of interest groups and the institutional settings in each country. See Iain Ramsay " 'To heap distress upon distress?': Comparative Reflections on Interest-Rate Ceilings" (Spring 2010) 60:2 UTLJ 707–30. See also Iain Ramsay, "Interest Groups and the Politics of Consumer Bankruptcy Reform in Canada" (2003) 53:4 UTLJ 379–423.

health warnings on packaging was increased from 33 percent to 50 percent of the principal display surfaces. Several big tobacco manufacturers felt that this new legislation harmed their business interests and collectively decided to bring a legal action to challenge it, alleging that some provisions limited their right to freedom of expression under s. 2(*b*) of the *Charter* and that those limits were not justified under s. 1 of the *Charter*. In *Canada (Attorney General) v. JTI-Macdonald Corp.*,[3] the Supreme Court of Canada ruled that the requirement in the *Tobacco Products Information Regulations* that the government's health warnings occupy at least 50 percent of the principal display surfaces of packages infringes s. 2(b) of the *Charter*, but the infringement is justified under s. 1. Thus, the introduced increase in the size of tobacco warnings was deemed to be constitutional.

Multiple interest groups exist across almost any area of the social, economic, legal, political, and cultural life of society. As the law increasingly regulates most areas of life, diverse interest groups will form around multiple areas of law. These groups may range from business groups, minority groups, labour unions to professional associations. Generally, interest groups can be classified as self-interest groups (advance interests of members), public interest (advance the public good), and sectoral groups (represent specific sectors of society).[4] Often, these groups with diverging interests may compete in a single legal conflict. For instance, a legislation requiring the labelling of food products is likely to attract the interest of individual consumers, farmers, producers, retailers, advertisers, food scientists, food corporations, and consumer associations The Canadian Federation of Agriculture, for example, has said that the industry would face huge losses if mandatory labelling of genetically modified food (GM food) were implemented. "The fear is that consumers will see the labels as a warning and avoid these foods, and that food processors will reformulate their products to avoid GM foods rather than place labels."[5] It has also claimed that labels will increase the price of foods produced and processed in Canada. On the other hand, the Canadian public appears to appreciate the value of GM food labelling. According to a 1999 Environics poll, 80 percent of Canadians want GM foods to be labelled. Greenpeace Canada believes that number is closer to 95 per cent. Furthermore, consumer groups have noted that people just want to know what they are putting in their mouths, and any labelling would at least provide them with information so that they are in a better position to make an informed eating decision.[6]

These diverse interest groups often have multiple and conflicting expectations about how a given issue should be regulated. It is not surprising, then, that these groups engage in fierce competition to protect and promote their interests and values before legislators, regulators or courts. In order to penetrate the legal system, these groups are required to translate their interests into legal discourses, and for this purpose employ multiple strategies to influence law making.

Strategies Employed by Interest Groups

Among the strategies most commonly used by interest groups are (i) lobbying law- and policy-makers and (ii) litigation before courts.

---

[3] 2007 SCC 30, [2007] 2 S.C.R. 610.

[4] Eric Mintz, Livianna Tossutti, and Christopher Dunn, *Democracy, Diversity, and Good Government: An Introduction to Politics in Canada* (Toronto: Pearson Canada, 2011).

[5] "Genetically Modified Foods: A Primer" (CBC News Online, May 11, 2004) online: <http://www.cbc.ca/news/background/genetics_modification/>.

[6] *Ibid.*

Lobbying

The first strategy involves such activities as interaction with various political actors, advocacy and action campaigns to mobilize public opinion, letters and submissions to government bodies. As a rule, interest groups focus their efforts on one or more of the three target groups: politicians, government bureaucrats and political parties.[7] Ideally, interest groups would like to be involved at early stages of law- and policy-making, since this allows them to influence the very formulation of issues and policy agendas. Given that most legislation is usually initiated by the government in power, interest groups may target the cabinet and individual ministers in an attempt to attract attention to issues in need of a legislative response, as well as civil servants who are involved in research and drafting of law and policy proposals. However, the initial stages of law and policy formation are often not easily accessible. Instead, there may be more opportunities for providing input once a bill has been introduced in Parliament. One of the most common avenues for interest groups to influence a bill is at the committee stage (which usually happens after the second reading of a bill). As a part of their task of analyzing the bill, parliamentary committees often hear testimony and receive submissions from individuals and groups, which may, in turn, influence the committee's recommendations on the bill. In addition to directly pressuring policy-makers and bureaucrats, interest groups may use indirect strategies such as media and awareness campaigns to create a critical mass of public opinion on a given matter and thereby force politicians to act. For example, in the fall of 2010, the Canadian Council for Refugees (CCR), an umbrella organization committed to advocating on behalf of refugees in Canada, conducted a "take action" campaign against Bill C-49, which proposed measures that would negatively affect persons seeking asylum in Canada (e.g., in some cases provide for mandatory 1-year detention, impose restrictions on their access to permanent residence or permanent protection in Canada). The campaign sought to raise public awareness as well as encourage concerned individuals to write or speak to their members of Parliament to persuade them to vote against the bill. As of December 1, 2010, all opposition parties (Liberal Party, New Democratic Party, and Bloc Québécois) stated that they could not support Bill C-49 — a stance that in part may be attributed to the active advocacy campaign.[8]

Litigation

Unlike political lobbying, which is concentrated on either placing a certain issue on a legislative agenda or on influencing proposed legislation during the statutory enactment process, litigation usually seeks to challenge laws already in force. History demonstrates multiple instances where litigation was used to challenge the status quo, advance individual rights, or expose issues of discrimination and inequality. For example, in *Halpern v. Canada*[9], seven same-sex couples and Metropolitan Community Church of Toronto challenged the definition of marriage as a union between a man and a woman. Because the definition excluded same-sex couples, opposite-sex couples were able to marry, while same-sex couples were not. The Court found that such exclusion violated s. 15 (equality) under the *Charter* and could not be saved under s. 1. Effective immediately, the Court declared the existing definition invalid, and

---

[7] Robert K. Jackson & Doreen Jackson, *Canadian Government in Transition*, 5th ed. (Toronto: Pearson Canada, 2010) at 229.

[8] Canadian Council for Refugees, "C-49 — Anti-smuggling or anti-refugee?", online: <http://ccrweb.ca/en/c49>.

[9] [2003] O.J. No. 2268.

reformulated it as "the voluntary union for life of two persons to the exclusion of all others".

Interest groups can participate in court cases in one of two ways: (i) launch a case by either sponsoring it or filing a lawsuit in their own name; (ii) seek intervenor status in a pending case. As a rule, a legal action has to be brought by an individual or an entity affected by the legislation or government action in question. However, in some cases an interest group may be granted public interest standing to advance a case on behalf of affected individuals.

While launching a case allows an interest group control over the scope and formulation of issues, it is a very expensive, complex, and lengthy undertaking. Not every interest group will have the resources to support ongoing litigation. Furthermore, if the group loses a case, it may be ordered to pay a substantial portion of the costs of the winning side.[10]

Partially due to the financial constraints as well as procedural barriers associated with obtaining standing, some interest groups may choose to seek intervenor status in an already pending action launched by someone else. While intervenors do not have much control over the formulation of issues, they are able to advance legal arguments that reflect the group's position as well as bring to light additional information on the impact of the law in question on the segments of population whose interests the group represents. By introducing these additional perspectives, intervenors help mitigate one of the limitations of the adversarial process — its narrow focus on the positions of the two parties to the case. In fact, interest groups have been parties or intervenors in many of the Supreme Court's landmark cases where the Court was called to decide on important public interest issues such as abortion, aboriginal rights and land claims, equality of voters, euthanasia, capital punishment, gay rights, hate speech, judicial salaries, language rights, pornography, prisoner voting rights, sexual assault, Sunday closing, and tobacco advertising.[11] For example, in *Halpern v. Canada*, discussed above, the public importance of the definition of marriage attracted several interest groups and organizations as intervenors. The Canadian Human Rights Commission, Canadian Coalition of Liberal Rabbis for Same-Sex Marriage, Egale Canada (a national organization committed to advancing equality and justice for lesbian, gay, bisexual and trans-identified people, and their families) supported the position of the same-sex couples who challenged the definition of marriage. Two other intervenors — the Association for Marriage and the Family in Ontario and the Interfaith Coalition on Marriage and Family — made arguments against the redefinition of marriage.

Similarly, the case of Sue Rodriguez[12] on the issue of assisted suicide has had a number of intervenors, representing different points of view. Sue Rodriguez was suffering from amyotrophic lateral sclerosis — an illness due to which she would soon lose the ability to swallow, speak, move or breathe without assistance. She did not wish to die as long as she had the capacity to enjoy life, but, once she lost that capacity, she wanted to be able to terminate her life, at the time of her choosing, with the assistance of a physician. Given that s. 241(b) of the *Criminal Code* prohibits the giving of assistance to commit suicide, Sue Rodriguez brought a challenge to this section arguing that it violated s. 7 (right to life, liberty and security of person), s. 12 (prohibition of

---

[10] Kent Roach, "The Role of Litigation and the Charter in Interest Advocacy" in F. Leslie Seidle (ed.), *Equity and Community: The Charter, Interest Advocacy and Representation* (Montreal, Que.: Institute for Research on Public Policy, 1993) 159 at 173.

[11] Frederick Morton, *Law, Politics, and the Judicial Process in Canada*, 3d ed. (Calgary, AB: University of Calgary Press, 2002) at 302.

[12] *Rodriguez v. British Columbia (A.G.)*, [1993] 3 S.C.R. 519.

cruel and unusual treatment or punishment), and s. 15 (equality) of the *Charter*. The list of intervenors in her case included the British Columbia Coalition of People with Disabilities, Dying with Dignity, the Right to Die Society of Canada, the Coalition of Provincial Organizations of the Handicapped, the Pro-Life Society of British Columbia, the Pacific Physicians for Life Society, the Canadian Conference of Catholic Bishops, the Evangelical Fellowship of Canada, and People in Equal Participation Inc. Organizations such as the Coalition of Provincial Organizations of the Handicapped (COPOH) (a national, not-for-profit, umbrella organization which represents people with disabilities), Dying with Dignity (a national non-profit organization that provides education, information, and confidential support for individuals faced with making end-of-life decisions) and the Right to Die Society of Canada (an organization providing lobbying and education on the right-to-die options) supported Sue Rodriguez's arguments with respect to autonomy and self-determination in making decisions on life and death. COPOH also brought attention to the concerns of people with disabilities. It argued that the criminal prohibition of assisted suicide discriminated against people with disabilities who could not commit suicide without someone else's assistance. In addition, COPOH emphasized the importance of having safeguards in place to ensure that assisted suicides are a result of informed, mentally competent decision-making, free from coercion or undue influence. Five groups — the Conference of Catholic Bishops of Canada, the Evangelical Fellowship of Canada (a national association of Protestant faiths), People for Equal Participation (PEP) (an advocacy organization for disabled persons), Pro-Life Society of British Columbia, and Pacific Physicians for Life Society (a professional association of physicians) — made arguments that opposed Sue Rodriguez's motion. Most of these groups emphasized the value of protecting human life and promoting a life ethics. PEP largely focused on the vulnerability of persons with disabilities and the concerns about assisted suicide exacerbating such vulnerability.

Lobbying vs. Litigation

The relative advantages of lobbying versus litigation depend on a variety of factors, including the nature of the issue and the resources and status of a given interest group. The political disadvantage theory suggests that groups usually choose to litigate if other avenues of law or policy change, such as legislatures, are foreclosed.[13] However, this theory offers only a partial explanation of interest group behaviour. For example, it does not explain why more advantaged groups choose to litigate. Further studies have suggested that advantaged groups may opt to litigate in order to protect the gains achieved through legislatures or previous litigation.[14] It has also been noted that more advantaged groups may litigate more frequently because they have the resources to do so.[15] This is, for example, the case with business interest groups, which may resort to litigation to counter increasing government regulation in areas key to their activity.[16] For instance, tobacco corporations have

---

[13] Christopher Manfredi, "Constitutional Rights and Internet Advocacy: Litigating Educational Reform in Canada and the United States" in F. Leslie Seidle (ed.), *Equity and Community: The Charter, Interest Advocacy and Representation* (Montreal, Que.: Institute for Research on Public Policy, 1993) 91 at 93.

[14] Manfredi, *ibid.* at 94; Kim Lane Scheppele & Jack L. Walker, "The Litigation Strategies of Interest Groups" in Jack L. Walker (ed.), *Mobilizing Interest Groups in America* (Ann Arbor: Michigan University Press, 1991); Lee Epstein, *Conservatives in Court* (Knoxville: University of Tennessee Press, 1985).

[15] Manfredi, *ibid.*

[16] See generally, Gregory Hein, "Interest Group Litigation and Canadian Democracy" in Paul Howe & Peter H. Russell (eds.), *Judicial Power and Canadian Democracy* (Montreal and Kingston: McGill-Queen's University Press, 2001).

| EXHIBIT 36.1 | Litigation vs Lobbying: Action of Canadian Bar Association on Legal Aid |

The Canadian Bar Association (CBA) is a professional association whose primary purpose is to serve its members (legal professionals, judges, law students). However, it is also concerned with issues that have implications for the public at large, such as access to justice, law reform, and a fair justice system. One of the issues on its agenda is legal aid. Due to decades of financial cutbacks, legal aid, which is intended to provide access to legal services to low-income individuals, is inaccessible to many people in need and the scope of services is too limited. This, in turn, results in a cascading negative impact on people's lives.

For a number of years, the CBA has focused on lobbying and political advocacy on the issue. However, failing to achieve a desired result through lobbying, it turned to litigation. In 2005, it launched a court challenge, arguing that the inadequacies in the provision of legal aid amounted to breaches of the *Charter*, written and unwritten provisions of the Constitution, and international human rights instruments. The CBA sought a series of declarations and an order directing the government to maintain an effective and meaningful legal aid system. The lawsuit was dismissed, since the Court determined that the CBA lacked public interest standing and that it failed to meet the threshold requirements for establishing a reasonable cause of action. The CBA was also ordered to pay the defendant's costs (the government was the defendant). Despite the dismissal of the lawsuit, the CBA has not abandoned the idea of litigation and is working on identifying appropriate cases for further court challenges. It also continues lobbying and engaging in national education and awareness campaigns, as well as research, analysis, and policy development for legal aid reform.

This example is illustrative of several issues. First, advocacy on a given issue may require the use of a combination of strategies; it is not merely about choosing between litigation or lobbying. Second, although often viewed as an alternative to reform when lobbying is unsuccessful, litigation does not guarantee success either. Third, lack of success in pursuing traditional avenues of lobbying and litigation may lead to re-evaluation of these strategies as well as new emphasis on other means, such as public education and awareness. Fourth, as a public interest litigant, the CBA did not have a direct interest in the action. If the lawsuit had been successful, it would have improved legal aid to members of the community at large and only indirectly advance the interests of the Association's members by likely providing for an increase in the legal fees paid to lawyers.

Note

As a rule, claims with respect to *Charter* breaches have to be advanced in the context of individual cases (i.e., there has to be a specific situation involving an individual or an organization where a *Charter* breach has occurred). The CBA, however, took the position that its claim was of a systemic nature and did not advance it in the context of a specific case. The Court of Appeal upheld the decision of the lower court and concluded that (i) the statement of claim did not involve the particulars of individuals or their cases, and (ii) the breaches they suffered were too general to allow the courts to adjudicate such a claim. Similar reasoning applied to the CBA's arguments with respect to unwritten constitutional principles.

Sources
1. *Canadian Bar Assn. v. British Columbia*, [2006] B.C.J. No. 2015.
2. *Canadian Bar Assn. v. British Columbia*, [2008] B.C.J. No. 350.
3. Melina Buckley, *Moving Forward on Legal Aid: Research on Needs and Innovative Approaches*. Report for the Canadian Bar Association (July 2010), online: <http://www.cba.org/CBA/Advocacy/legalaid/default.aspx>.
4. CBA Considering Options for Phase II — Litigation Strategy to Improve Civil Legal Aid, <http://www.cba.org/CBA/Advocacy/legalaid/Litigation.aspx>.
5. CBA Position on Legal Aid, <http://www.cba.org/CBA/Advocacy/legalaid/position.aspx>.

sued the government of Canada several times seeking court decisions to strike down tobacco regulations. In 1995, in *RJR-MacDonald Inc. v. Canada (Attorney General)*,[17] the Supreme Court of Canada struck down provisions of the *Tobacco Products Control Act* that broadly prohibited all advertising and promotion of tobacco products, subject to specific exceptions, and required that unattributed warning labels be affixed on tobacco product packaging. In response to the Court's decision, Parliament enacted the *Tobacco Act* and the *Tobacco Products Information Regulations*, which among other things increased the size of warnings. Once again, tobacco manufacturers challenged the new legislation (see *Canada (Attorney General) v. JTI-Macdonald Corp.* discussed above), although in this case, the Supreme Court upheld the *Tobacco Products Information Regulations*.

The Challenge of Governing Interest Groups

While a sound expression of the views of various groups helps lawmakers to acquaint themselves with the values, interests, and social impact at stake, the reality is that interest groups do not necessarily compete on a level playing field and the influence of some interest groups may distort, rather than aid, the process of making and enforcing laws. Some groups may be better organized, greatly informed, more resourceful, more financially and political powerful, and more active than others. Often the difference in influence and power among interest groups reflects the social, political, economic, and legal inequalities in society. For instance, an interest group composed of ordinary citizens is likely to be less influential and powerful than a business group. Groups with greater social, political, economic or legal power will be in a better position to promote their interests and influence the making and enforcement of the law. For example, a study of over 2,500 Supreme Court and Federal Court decisions for the 1988–98 period found that, among the multiple organizations involved as litigants or intervenors coming from across the political spectrum, the most frequent participants were corporate interest groups, representing 56 percent of the total.[18] They brought 468 legal actions, far more than the other interests. Companies engaged in civil litigation against private parties and challenged regulations governing banking, federal elections, international trade, environmental protection, and the pharmaceutical industry.[19] Unlike other groups, corporations and business groups had the financial and organizational resources to bring numerous legal actions and to sustain prolonged and expensive litigation, which enabled them to defend or promote their interests before the courts. Thus, judges, legislators, and regulators may find themselves under significant pressure, particularly from the groups that have greater resources to advance their causes, and will have to make a serious effort to make independent decisions seeking to advance the best interest of society.

Yet, a search for independence and unbiased law making and enforcement involves more than having the determination to decide with impartiality and on the basis of reason, legal knowledge, and socially accepted values while balancing multiple competing interests. It requires that lawmakers are both familiar with the multiple strategies and methods that interest groups use and committed to containing excessive or distortive pressures from some interest groups. If courts, legislators. or regulators are to deal with strategic litigation

[17] 1995 CanLII 64 (S.C.C.), [1995] 3 S.C.R. 199.

[18] Gregory Hein, "Interest Group Litigation and Canadian Democracy" (March 2000) 6:2 Choices. Institute for Research on Public Policy, online: <http://www.irpp.org/choices/archive/vol6no2.pdf>.

[19] *Ibid.*

or the threat thereof, lobbying, participation in public consultations, media pressure, social networking, public protest, or public elections, they ought to do so in a manner that is democratic and effective in protecting the integrity of the process of making and enforcing the law.

The challenge for courts, legislators, and regulators is not only to channel and control the over-influence of powerful interest groups, but also to create real and effective opportunities for powerless groups to communicate their interests. It is ideal that lawmakers seek a democratic and fair engagement of all relevant groups so the law does not evolve solely on the basis of the input of influential groups. On the one hand, lawmakers should be receptive and open to the multiple ways of expressing the interests of relevant groups and must also create effective mechanisms to facilitate the communication of such interests. Governments should, for instance, expand the practice of conducting public consultations about proposed legislation as a way of reaching relevant unorganized groups or should provide financial and administrative support to less powerful groups. On the other hand, lawmakers should seek to enhance the transparency of any law-making process so that the general public and all interest groups know the content, procedure, and participants of a legal development, and, as a result, can hold lawmakers accountable. For example, while disclosing the number and names of interest groups that have participated in a law-making process, the government should release detailed information about the extent to which the concerns of multiple groups have been incorporated. This should also include a list of lobbyists and the groups that have been absent from such a process. These measures can help ensure that the law-making process is both reflective of multiple interests and more democratic in nature.

MEDIA, PUBLIC PRESSURE, AND LAW MAKING

The Media and the Legal System

The mass media is another factor that influences the making and enforcement of the law. While the media is often perceived as a provider of general information and evolving independently from the legal system, it may be instrumental in shaping the development of the law in society. The media gathers and disseminates information on new legal developments, communicates the opinions of various stakeholders on those developments, creates a forum for discussion and draws attention to pressing social and legal issues. In particular, this section examines the role of the mass media in improving the social acceptance and public accountability of the legal system.[20]

The gathering and mass communication of new court decisions, legislative changes, or various government policies through media such as radio, TV, or newspapers contribute to the dissemination of legal information and public awareness of the law. The public may be better informed and prepared to understand, accept, and abide by the new laws as the media selects, translates, synthesizes and spreads increasingly abundant and complex legal information. This helps improve social acceptance of the law and aids in creating a facilitative environment for respect and for enforcement of the law. The media may thus help the law gain greater acceptance and legitimacy in society.

---

[20] Jessica Feinstein, "The Hybrid's Handmaiden: Media Coverage of the Special Court for Sierra Leone, 7 Lyuchiilr 131" (Spring/Summer 2010) Loy. U. Chicago Int'l L. Rev. at 134 (discussing two general roles of the media in the context of criminal cases: "1) as facilitator of public awareness and distributor of information; and 2) as 'watchdog,' a critical check on abuse of power." For a discussion of an example, see John King Gamble and Nicole Lee Dirling, "Mass Media Coverage of International Law: (Benign) Neglect?, Distortion?" (2006) 18 Fla. J. Int'l L. 211.

On the other hand, the media may report on the performance of courts, legislatures, and regulators and as such play a role in holding them accountable to the public.[21] The mass media coverage and public reporting of legal developments may ignite public debate and critical awareness and mobilize individuals and interest groups. These groups and individuals will quickly learn about important legal changes, develop an opinion, and may organize to support or oppose a court decision, a legislative change, or a new regulatory policy. While the media often provides only brief versions of legal developments so that interested individuals and groups need to gather more information about the specifics and legal technicalities, the contribution of the media to such public accountability lies in its ability to rapidly and massively disseminate plain legal information among the general public, often exposing wrongs in the legal system.[22] This may trigger public action and public pressure on courts, legislators, regulators, and other actors and force them to eventually respond to it. For example, TV news and newspapers, covering the political and legal battles for the rights of various marginalized groups such as women, Aboriginal peoples and gays and lesbians, have helped people mobilize around such rights movements.[23] The media thus becomes not only a source of legal information and a factor in raising public awareness, but also an instrument for interested individuals and groups to communicate their dissent or support. The role of the media in improving the social acceptance or the public accountability of the legal system is unique in that it elevates a dissent or support to a massive phenomenon, namely a potentially widespread public pressure that lawmakers and other actors may find difficult to ignore.

Limits on the Role of the Media

A number of problems may, however, hinder the ability of the mass media to enhance the social acceptance and public accountability of the legal system and to facilitate legal change. Such a role for the media requires the presence of a significant number of independent, competent, and well-funded journalists and media corporations or organizations. Journalists should ideally be capable and committed to gathering, examining and reporting legal news on issues that are important to society and present the information with accuracy and independence and without fear of affecting the interests of powerful individuals and groups. Yet, journalists may misread laws, and judicial decisions are sometimes misinterpreted, sensationalized, and even lampooned[24] in the media, giving the public an inaccurate impression of the law and thus eroding confidence in the legal system.

Moreover, journalists may not necessarily be committed to such independence or can be under great pressure from those who manage and own media corporations. Media owners and managers may specify a particular role

---

[21] Feinstein, *ibid.* at 136 ("...the media may also play the role of watchdog over the judiciary or court. ...media coverage of court proceedings allows the public to monitor the judiciary's performance of its allotted duties, insuring that it is doing so without economic, jurisdictional, or political mismanagement"); M.A. "Mike" Kautsch, "Press Freedom and Fair Trials in Kansas: How Media and the Courts Have Struggled to Resolve Competing Claims of Constitutional Rights" (2009) 57 U. Kan. L. Rev. 1075 at 1140 (concluding "... Openness leads to public confidence in the judicial system. It enables the media to illuminate how the justice system works and to perform a checking function, holding judges and law enforcement accountable for their exercise of power and authority"); Lieve Gies, *Law and the Media: The Future of Uneasy Relationship* (New York: Routledge-Cavendish, 2008) at 93 (referring to the belief that the media contributes to the monitoring of the three branches of government as the Liberal media doctrine).

[22] Gies, *ibid.* at 91 (noting the self-chosen role of the media in exposing wrongs and problems in the legal system).

[23] Florian Sauvageau, David Schneiderman & David Taras, *The Last Word: Media Coverage of the Supreme Court of Canada* (Vancouver, BC: UBC Press, 2006) at 15.

[24] *Ibid.* at 9.

that a TV or radio program or newspaper should play in relation to the legal system. They may select journalists who are more willing to follow their views and values rather than being committed to independent journalism and the public interest. Managers and owners of media organizations may also set strict instructions as to how their journalists and, more generally, how a newspaper, TV or radio program should cover some legal news, including the desirable position to be adopted. This lack of independence often manifests itself through bias in the selection, gathering, reporting, timing, and examination of legal news as well as the direction of an opinion developed by journalists or editors. For instance, from 1998 to 2000, the *National Post*, owned by Conrad Black, waged a fierce ideological crusade against the activism of Canadian judges, attacking their judgments with relish and questioning the assumptions upon which the authority of the court rests.[25] Thus, the mass media may become an instrument for media owners and managers to set their own agenda or attempt to streamline the opinion of the public and lawmakers in a particular direction. These problems may be more severe when corporate groups or wealthy individuals control a large share of media ownership.[26]

Even if the traditional mass media is fairly independent, not all groups and individuals in society are equally able to use the mass media to communicate their views and thereby attempt to influence the making and enforcement of the law. Due to their financial resources and business and political connections, wealthy and powerful individuals and business or political groups are more likely to have access to the media to, for instance, promote a legal reform, launch a public campaign against a court decision or proposed law, or simply be in a better position to pressure journalists, media owners, and managers to serve a particular interest.[27] In contrast, ordinary citizens, consumers, and small civil society groups may have little or no access to the traditional mass media. While these groups may have their legal agenda and a message to communicate to lawmakers, they hardly have the power, finances, and organizational resources to use the media for such purposes. Not only may they be unable to engage in massive campaigns to promote their views, but they may also be exposed to the influence of biased legal news that is often produced and spread by non-independent journalists and influential individuals and groups. For example, the media coverage of tobacco litigation frequently neglects to discuss the significant resource imbalance between tobacco corporations and individual plaintiffs. Tobacco corporations hire the most powerful law firms and spend millions of dollars on producing documents to substantiate their interests in court. Yet, these factors of radically unequal wealth and disproportionate power among corporate defendants and individual plaintiffs are notably absent from most news coverage.[28] Individual plaintiffs rarely have access to the media to raise concerns about such power disparities, and the general public may ignore the extent to which such imbalances distort the decisions on tobacco litigation cases.

---

[25] *Ibid.* at 16.

[26] Enrique Armijo, "Media Ownership Regulation: A Comparative Perspective" (2009) 37 GAJICL 421 at 423–25 (noting that most Western democracies have adopted some form of restriction on media ownership concentration on the presumption that preventing excessive media ownership by a few powerful individuals or entities is desirable because "if allowed, [it] grants them the ability to shape opinion or exploit the market for personal gain by overrepresenting their own biases, interests, and viewpoints in public debate").

[27] Slavko Splichal, *Principles of Publicity and Press Freedom* 9 (Lanham, MD: Rowman & Littlefield Publishers, 2002) at 194 (noting that the "traditional media often block[s] innovation, particularly when they are heralds of particularistic interests of powerful interest groups behind them").

[28] See William Haltom & Michael J. McCann, *Distorting the Law: Politics, Media, and the Litigation Crisis* (Chicago: University of Chicago Press, 2004) at 287.

Furthermore, the ability of the media to help disseminate legal knowledge and improve the accountability of the legal system is limited by the pressures of consumer society. While the media may provide important legal information and seek to attract the attention of the public to critical social issues, ordinary citizens do not necessarily read or engage with them due to, for example, time constraints or the difficulties in processing overwhelming amounts of information. Moreover, reading and following legal news may be less attractive when compared with sport and business news. If this problem generally exists, it should not be surprising that legal news does not necessarily attract the interest of the general public, particularly when referring to complex legal information. In times of busy lifestyles, limited income, consumerism, and easy entertainment, reading legal news may not be appealing to a large section of the population. So, the so-called advantages of the media for enhancing the legitimacy and accountability of the legal system may only make sense for highly educated, legally minded or affluent citizens, and organized interest groups.

All of the above disparities obviously create unequal opportunities for different groups to use the media. This in turn affects the degree of influence that groups may exert on lawmakers and enforcers. It should thus not be a surprise that powerful and organized individuals and groups more frequently make effective use of the media to shape public knowledge of the law; develop and campaign for potentially leading legal opinions; and seek to alter the views of courts, legislators, regulators, and enforcers in a manner that serves their interests. Whether these individuals and groups succeed depends on the independence of courts, legislatures, and regulators as well as the presence of active, independent journalists and media corporations committed to promoting the public interest.[29]

The Growing Role of Social Media

These limitations on the traditional mass media have, in part, given rise to alternative media organizations and various forms of public activism through the Internet.[30] The public is increasingly posting information outside the traditional mass media and using not only the Internet but also signs, physical postings, and local radios. News, stories, and views otherwise not covered or under-reported by the traditional mass media are beginning to surface and gain public exposure. While it is unclear whether this informal media is having a significant direct impact on the legislature, courts or regulators, it is conceivable that at least it is helping to raise awareness and build public opinion on legal matters that may put some pressure on lawmakers.[31] As this informal media grows in influence and the limits of traditional media worsen, it is becoming hard for courts, legislatures, and regulators to completely ignore it. For example, since 2007, a Facebook group led by University of Ottawa law professor Michael Geist has been raising criticisms of Bill C-61, *An Act to*

---

[29] The ability of the media to influence the legal system is obviously an empirical matter and will also depend on the approach that one may adopt about the relationship between the media and the legal system. See Gies, *supra* note 21 at 92 (claiming that "[i]n common with the Liberal watchdog model, autopoietic theory envisages a strong degree of independence and friction between the media and the legal system but, unlike the liberal narrative, it arrives at the rather different conclusion that media discourse is necessarily and systematically at variance with the truth claims validated by the legal system").

[30] See e.g., L. Bennett, "New Media Power: The Internet and Global Activism" in N. Couldry & J. Curran (eds.), *Contesting Media Power: Alternative Media in a Networked World* (Oxford: Rowman and Littlefield, 2003).

[31] See e.g., Kautsch, *supra* note 21 at 1142 (noting that "judges face an expanding media, ranging from bloggers who seek courtroom seats during high-profile cases, and who may well be packing cell-phone cameras, to citizen-operated websites that are devoted to disseminating public but sensitive court information, such as the identities of undercover agents").

amend the Copyright Act, tabled in the second session of the 39th Parliament.[32] The Facebook group has almost 90,000 members and it is claimed that this online campaign contributed to the government's decision to conduct public consultations on copyright legislation in 2009.[33] It is thus desirable to both welcome the growth of the informal or social media and promote greater independent journalism for a vibrant democratic society and a solid legitimacy and accountability of the legal system.

INTERACTION BETWEEN THE LEGISLATURE AND THE JUDICIARY

The interaction between the legislature and the judiciary is the third and final factor of the law-making process to be discussed in this chapter. While the discussion of interest groups and the media exemplifies external pressures on government actors (e.g., legislators and regulators) forcing them to change the law or introduce a new one, judicial–legislative interaction deals with the relationship between branches of government. Two aspects of this interaction are of importance for a better understanding of the law-making process. First, a judicial decision that declares a certain law unconstitutional may force Parliament to re-examine the issue and amend the law or enact a new one. Thus, judicial decisions may be viewed as one of the factors that forces an issue on a legislative agenda. Second, the notion of the law-making process needs to appreciate that both legislatures and courts are involved in developing the law; knowledge of the roles played by each branch can help observers to better understand how a given law has emerged and whose perspective it reflects. In this respect, a number of questions need to be considered. For example, can each branch have a different perspective on how a given issue should be regulated? If the courts and legislature differ on a given issue, which of the two institutions has the final word on the regulation of that issue? Is it appropriate for courts to decide on issues of public policy or are these matters better suited for the legislature?

Academics are not unanimous in their assessment of the interaction between the two branches. Some emphasize the importance of Parliament's leading role in law making and express concerns about courts making decisions that profoundly affect public policy. Others suggest that the two branches work collaboratively in developing a shared constitutional interpretation.[34] Yet others suggest that the nature of interaction varies, depending on the issue at stake.[35] In some cases, courts and legislature may engage in a constructive "dialogue" where the perspectives of both branches are considered in developing a regulatory regime. In other cases, a dialogue does not occur in a productive way, but rather turns into a strong tension between diverging perspectives of the judiciary and the legislature.

While the legislature has the power to pass laws, courts possess the power of judicial review, whereby they can determine, among other things,

---

[32] Amanda Clarke, "Social Media: 4. Political Uses and Implications for Representative Democracy" Library of Parliament Background Paper (Publication No 2010-10-E, 22 March 2010, Ottawa, Canada, Library of Parliament) at 3, online: <http://dsp-psd.pwgsc.gc.ca/collections/collection_2010/bdp-lop/bp/2010-10-eng.pdf>.

[33] *Ibid.*; Michael Geist, "Critics Misjudged the Power of Digital advocacy" *Toronto Star*, January 18, 2010.

[34] Michael C. Dorf & Barry Friedman, "Shared Constitutional Interpretation" (2000) 2000 Sup. Ct. Rev. 61. See also similar position in Heather MacIvor, *Canadian Politics and Government in the Charter Era* (Toronto: Thomson Nelson Canada, 2006) at 148–49.

[35] See generally Kent Roach, *The Supreme Court on Trial: Judicial Activism or Democratic Dialogue* (Toronto: Irwin Law, 2001).

	EXHIBIT 36.2
The Interaction between the Supreme Court and Parliament in Creating a Regulatory Framework: Canada's Abortion Laws	

Until 1969, abortions in Canada were effectively prohibited. In 1969, Parliament amended the Criminal Code to allow abortions in certain circumstances, namely when performed in a hospital with the approval of a Therapeutic Abortion Committee (s. 251 of the Criminal Code); in the absence of such approval, obtaining or performing an abortion constituted a criminal offence. In 1983, Dr. Morgentaler, who provided abortions to women who had not obtained an approval from a committee, was charged under s. 251; in 1988, his appeal was heard by the Supreme Court. The majority of the Court concluded that s. 251 of the Criminal Code violated s. 7 of the *Charter* (right to life, liberty and security of person) and, thus, was of no force and effect. Section 251 was deemed to interfere with a woman's physical and bodily integrity; it also denied her the fundamental liberty of making decisions about her life and pregnancy. Although the legislative objective of protecting the fetus was pressing and substantial, the means chosen to achieve it (s. 251) were not reasonable and demonstrably justified under s. 1 of the *Charter*.

This decision demonstrates the different roles and perspectives of Parliament and the Supreme Court in developing abortion laws. Parliament has established a regulatory regime that allowed abortions in limited and controlled circumstances. The Supreme Court, exercising its power of judicial review, questioned the means that Parliament has chosen and the balance that it has struck between respect for women's rights and public interest in protecting the fetus. The effect of the Supreme Court's decision was that abortion was no longer criminalized. Yet, this did not mean that the Court had the last word on the issue. It was open to Parliament to respond to the judicial ruling by passing new legislation. In particular, it could pass a law that would still limit abortion rights, but in a less stringent manner than s. 251. In fact, in 1989, the government introduced a new abortion law — Bill C-43. However, due to the controversial nature of the issue it was never passed. Thus, the Supreme Court's decision effectively remained the last word on abortion practice in Canada, but it is still open to Parliament to revisit the issue in the future.

the constitutionality of acts passed by the legislative branch. When legislation or a part of it is struck down, this not only leads to a change in the regulatory regime concerning the matter at hand, but also provides a judicial assessment of the choices that the legislature made in passing the law. For example, a court may find that a legislative objective was not compelling enough to justify limitations on certain rights or that the legislature did not strike a reasonable balance between individual rights and social objectives. Given that such judicial decisions may alter public policy set out by the legislature, much debate has arisen about this so-called **judicial activism** and about whether it is appropriate for courts to engage in policy-making.

Judicial Activism

There is no single definition of judicial activism, but it usually refers to judicial decision-making that has the potential to re-evaluate and change public policy or regulatory regime set out by other branches of government. Roach has identified four components that help determine whether a court is acting in an activist manner:

1. The degree to which judges are free to introduce their own preferences into constitutional interpretation

2. The degree to which judges are eager to make and impose law

3. The degree to which judges are likely to recognize that constitutional rights would trump other rights or social interests

4. The extent to which courts displace decisions of other branches of government.[36]

The indicators of judicial activism include judicial willingness to make law, to dismiss reasons of other branches for restrictions on constitutional rights (a tendency to conclude that constitutional rights trump social interests) and to render decisions that are likely to leave limited options for legislative response or to force significant change to the preferred government policy.[37]

Judicial activism has been subjected to a number of criticisms. It is contended that activist courts engage in law making as opposed to their intended role of discovering and applying pre-existing law. The activist judiciary is seen as hijacking the role of Parliament. As Greene points out, the controversy over the law-making role of judges is rooted in part in a concept of democracy as government by a majority of elected legislators.[38] Then, judicial activism is viewed as undemocratic, since it leads to unelected and unaccountable courts making public policy decisions.[39] It is also feared that interest groups use litigation to bypass the traditional democratic process of elected legislatures and that activist courts may make decisions that unduly favour certain interest groups.[40] Some of these concerns are rooted in the nature of the adversarial process and in a misunderstanding of the capacity of courts to make policy decisions. When a legislature creates a law, it needs to consider the multiple competing interests that are involved and find a compromise that both respects those various interests and permits the achievement of necessary social objectives. To this end, government and legislative committees may conduct public consultations, hearings, and other activities intended to solicit the perspectives of multiple stakeholders. In contrast, courts make decisions based on legal arguments presented by the parties to a case (and intervenors, if present). These legal arguments may not necessarily represent the wider views of multiple groups that are not participating in the court case but may be affected by the decision. Further, litigation is an adversarial process and is not intended to find a compromise solution in the interests of society as a whole. While litigation can and has produced judgments supporting the rights of various groups, it is poorly equipped to address systemic causes of inequalities and, thus, in itself does not necessarily lead to more social justice.[41] In light of these limitations, it is argued that the parliamentary process may provide a better setting for not only considering the multiple perspectives and interests at stake, but also for developing a solution that strikes a better bal-

---

[36] *Ibid.* at 106–10.

[37] *Ibid.*

[38] Ian Greene, *The Courts* (Vancouver. BC: UBC Press, 2006) at 17.

[39] Kim Campbell, "Parliament's Role in Protecting the Rights and Freedoms of Canadians" in Philip Bryden, Steven Davis & John Russell (eds.), *Protecting Rights and Freedoms: Essays on the Charter's Place in Canada's Political, Legal, and Intellectual Life* (Toronto: University of Toronto Press, 1994) 23 at 31.

[40] See e.g., Greene, *supra* note 38 at 146. For example, left-wing critics claim the *Charter* litigation has legitimized neo-conservative policies and exacerbated societal inequalities (Andrew Petter, *The Politics of the Charter: The Illusive Promise of Constitutional Rights* (Toronto: University of Toronto Press, 2010)). In contrast, right-wing critics contend that *Charter* litigation has been used primarily by the so-called "court party" — social-reform–minded, left-leaning interest groups, professionals, and activists (Frederick Lee Morton and Reiner Knopff, *The Charter Revolution and the Court Party* (Toronto: Broadview Press, 2000)).

[41] Harry Arthurs, "More Litigation, More Justice? The Limits of Litigation as a Social Justice Strategy" in Julia Bass, W.A. Bogart & Frederick Zemans (eds.), *Access to Justice for a New Century* (Toronto: Irwin Law, 2005) 249 at 253–54. See also similar ideas by Petter, *ibid.*

ance among those interests.[42] Thus, it is argued that courts need to exercise restraint in adjudicating such matters and not replace the decision of the legislature with their own.

The Canadian Supreme Court: Activist or Not?

In Canada, the debate about judicial–legislative interaction became particularly lively following the adoption of the *Charter*. The *Charter* created preconditions for greater judicial involvement in social policy and expanded opportunities for interest groups to use litigation as a tool for reform.[43] Much of this debate has focused on the Supreme Court, since its decisions are likely to have the greatest policy implications. In fact, some argue that with the adoption of the *Charter*, the Supreme Court was transformed from a primarily adjudicative body to a policy-making body.

Why and how often do courts and particularly the Supreme Court, act in an activist manner? There is no agreement among scholars on several issues, such as whether the Supreme Court has been highly activist or not; what is the proper extent of such activism; and whether judicial activism has had a negative or positive impact on public policy. Some suggest that in certain instances the Supreme Court may be inclined to step in as a response to the failure of the legislative branch to address the matter.[44] Others suggest that the use of litigation by disadvantaged groups has compelled the Court to intervene to correct the disadvantage and at the same time has been used to legitimize the Court's activist role in certain types of cases.[45] For example, s. 15 litigation has been used by groups representing immigrants, sexual minorities, the poor, and ethnic groups to attain equality rights status.[46] Yet, others contend that the Supreme Court's willingness to act in a more or less activist manner depends on its perception of the issue at hand. Where the Court believes that the legislation in question involves issues that are more appropriately left to the legislature, the Court takes a hands-off approach and is more likely to uphold legislation. At the same time, where the Court considers itself to have a degree of first-hand expertise in the matter and where the legislature is not seen as possessing any comparative advantage, the Court is willing to be more activist.[47]

Parliament's Response to a Judicial Ruling: What Options Are Available?

As mentioned above, a judicial decision that strikes down a law or part of a law, may force Parliament to react. In Canada, Parliament can react to a judicial ruling in several ways:

1. It may pass a new law or modify existing law, keeping judicial guidance in mind; a new law may still contain restrictions on certain rights, but Parliament will need to consider the reasoning of the Court and the permissible limits outlined by the Court to ensure that the new law strikes a reasonable balance within the meaning of s. 1 of the *Charter*.

2. Parliament may take no action.

---

[42] Campbell, *supra* note 39 at 26.

[43] Manfredi, *supra* note 13 at 91.

[44] Roach, *supra* note 10 at 178; see also Greene, *supra* note 38 at 150.

[45] Ian Brodie, *Friends of the Court: The Privileging of Interest Group Litigants in Canada* (New York: State University of New York Press, 2002) at xiv.

[46] See useful discussion in Brodie, *ibid.*

[47] Patrick Monahan, "The Charter Then and Now" in Philip Bryden, Steven Davis & John Russell (eds.), *Protecting Rights and Freedoms: Essays on the Charter's Place in Canada's Political, Legal, and Intellectual Life* (Toronto: University of Toronto Press, 1994) 105 at 116.

3. Parliament may choose to pass new legislation that overrides a judicial decision; in its most forceful form, Parliament may use the s. 33 notwithstanding clause in order to immunize the new law from judicial scrutiny.

According to Hogg and Bushell,[48] a judicial–legislative dialogue occurs when Parliament responds to a judicial ruling. However, the nature of this dialogue will greatly depend on the nature of Parliament's response. The first option suggests a respectful and productive collaboration where each institution can learn from the other and appreciate different perspectives.[49] A judicial decision may bring to light interests and rights that have been neglected; at the same time, a legislative response may allow Parliament to educate the public and the Court about compelling objectives that justify reasonable limitations on certain rights.[50] This kind of interaction may lead to a better understanding of the issues and a more nuanced approach to their regulation. However, when Parliament chooses to override a judicial decision, the dialogue is transformed into a confrontation between the two branches. Parliament's response may suggest that the court's decision was unacceptable or that the court wrongly interpreted the law.[51] Such a scenario is well illustrated by Parliament's response to the Supreme Court's *Daviault* decision, described below. Another frequently invoked example of a legislature using the s. 33 notwithstanding clause to override a judicial decision is found in relation to Quebec language laws. Quebec courts and subsequently the Supreme Court have ruled that Bill 101, which required all commercial signs to be in French only, violated freedom of expression and could not be saved under s. 1 of the *Charter*. Within a week of the decision, the Quebec legislature used the notwithstanding clause and enacted a law that overrode the judicial decision (although in respect to outdoor signs only; other languages could be used in indoor advertising).[52]

The nature of judicial–legislative interaction is likely to remain a topic of lively debate for years to come. Regardless of one's position on the issue, it is important to acknowledge that both branches have a role to play in law- and policy-making. A robust democratic system requires a combination of both judicial and legislative activism as well as a constructive dialogue between the two in discovering a reasonable balance among competing interests.[53] While the parliamentary process offers opportunities for hearing views of multiple stakeholders and for developing a solution that is in the interests of society as a whole, in reality, this process may be tarnished by the effects of lobbying, media, and other pressures on legislators. In certain respects, judicial activism

[48] Peter W. Hogg & Allison A. Bushell, "The Charter Dialogue between Courts and Legislatures (or Perhaps the Charter of Rights Isn't Such a Bad Thing After All)" (1997) 35 Osgoode Hall L.J. 75; Peter W. Hogg, Allison A. Bushell Thornton & Wade K. Wright, "Charter Dialogue Revisited — Or "Much Ado about Metaphors" (2007) 45 Osgoode Hall L.J. 1. It should be noted that although the idea of dialogue has become rather influential in characterizing the interaction between Parliament and the Supreme Court, it has also been criticized on a number of grounds — see, for example, F.L. Morton, "Dialogue or Monologue?" in Paul Howe & Peter H. Russell (eds.), *Judicial Power and Canadian Democracy* (Montreal and Kingston: McGill-Queen's University Press, 2001) 111; Christopher P. Manfredi & James B. Kelly, "Six Degrees of Dialogue: A Response to Hogg and Bushell" (1999) 37 Osgoode Hall L. J. 153.

[49] Roach, *supra* note 35 at 264.

[50] Roach, *supra* note 35 at 264; also see Janet L Hiebert, *Charter Conflicts: What Is Parliament's role?* (Montreal: McGill-Queen's University Press, 2002).

[51] Roach, *supra* note 35 at 265.

[52] Roach, *supra* note 35 at 190.

[53] Roach, *supra* note 35 at 250–51.

may help to correct a structural defect of democracy, in that decisions made in response to political majorities may ignore or be insensitive to minorities.[54] It is thus important to look at the courts and legislature holistically, as parts of a larger political system and judicial–legislative interaction as one of the dynamics of that system.

The following two case studies illustrate the impact of the three factors — interest groups, the media, and judicial–legislative dialogue — on the development of regulatory regimes in two specific areas: defence of intoxication under criminal law and labelling of genetically modified foods.

Case Study: *R. v. Daviault*, [1994] 3 S.C.R. 63

Should extreme intoxication to the point of automatism or insanity be available as a defence to a charge of a general intent offence such as sexual assault? This question was at the centre of the *Daviault* case, and the Supreme Court's answer to it has produced an unprecedented amount of public and legislative debate. The case is thus a useful illustration of the role of the media, interest groups and judicial–legislative interaction in the crafting of the legal regime pertaining to the **defence of intoxication**.

Facts of the Case

The accused, Mr. Daviault, arrived at the complainant's house bringing her a bottle of brandy at her request. The complainant, a 65-year-old partially paralyzed woman in a wheelchair, drank some brandy and fell asleep. When she awoke during the night, Mr. Daviault grabbed and sexually assaulted her.

Prior to arriving at the complainant's house, Mr. Daviault consumed seven or eight bottles of beer and then some 35 ounces of brandy at her house. He claimed to have no recollection of what happened and denied sexually assaulting the complainant.

At trial, an expert witness estimated that Mr. Daviault's blood-alcohol content on the night in question would have been between 400 and 600 milligrams per 100 millilitres of blood — concentration that would cause death or a coma in an ordinary person. Given that Mr. Daviault was a chronic alcoholic, he was less susceptible to the effect of alcohol and, in his case, such extreme intoxication led to a blackout. The trial judge found that the accused committed the offence as described by the complainant, but nevertheless entered an acquittal as he had a reasonable doubt as to whether Mr. Daviault, due to extreme intoxication, possessed the intent necessary to commit the sexual assault. The Quebec Court of Appeal overturned the decision. Mr. Daviault appealed to the Supreme Court.

Background on the Defence of Intoxication

Prior to discussing the Supreme Court decision, it is worth providing some background on the applicable principles of criminal law and the defence of intoxication. Criminal offences consist of two elements: prohibited conduct (*actus reus*) and a mental element (*mens rea*). In order to obtain a conviction with respect to the so-called "true crimes",[55] the Crown has to prove both *actus reus* and *mens rea* beyond a reasonable doubt. The requirement of a mental element in particular, serves to ensure that morally innocent individuals — those who do not understand or intend the consequences of their acts —

---

[54] Brodie, *supra* note 45 at 123.

[55] Criminal law distinguishes between the so-called true crimes (acts or omissions that are considered inherently wrong and that require proof of both *mens rea* and *actus reus*; sexual assault is considered a true crime); strict liability offences (only *actus reus* needs to be proven, but the accused may raise the defence of due diligence) and absolute liability (only *actus reus* needs to be proven).

are not convicted. In the *Daviault* case, the trial judge has accepted that the *actus reus* of sexual assault had been committed, but he was not satisfied that the accused possessed the necessary *mens rea*; hence, acquittal was entered.

The defence of intoxication has developed as a common law rule (in other words, it was shaped by courts rather than by the legislature). Initially, courts have treated intoxication as an aggravating circumstance, but over time, it has been recognized that alcohol may impair individuals' ability to form the necessary *mens rea*. The key rules of intoxication have been authoritatively summarized in the 1920 UK House of Lords' decision on *Beard*.[56] According to that decision, intoxication could be a defence to a charge of specific intent offence, but never to a charge of general intent offence.[57] It is reasoned that the mental element in general intent offences is so minimal that no amount of alcohol or drugs would prevent one's capacity to form such intent.

Supreme Court Decision in R. v. Daviault

Until 1994, Canadian courts largely followed the *Beard* rules. Indeed, in overturning the trial judge's decision, the Quebec Court of Appeal essentially adhered to the *Beard* rules. However, on further appeal, the majority of the Supreme Court departed from the *Beard* rules by holding that where intoxication was so extreme as to lead to a state akin to automatism[58] or insanity, it could be a complete defence to a charge of a general intent offence[59]. The majority of the Supreme Court reasoned that extreme intoxication akin to automatism could render the accused incapable of either performing a voluntary act or of forming the minimal intent required for a general intent offence. If no defence were allowed in such circumstances, an accused would have to be found guilty even though there was a reasonable doubt regarding the voluntariness of his/her actions — this would go against one of the most fundamental principles of criminal law. The majority concluded that the rule that intoxication could never be a defence to crimes of general intent violated principles of fundamental justice under s. 7[60] and the presumption of innocence under s. 11(d) of the *Charter*.[61]

Reaction to the Supreme Court Decision

Although the extreme intoxication defence was likely to be successful only in rare situations — where an accused established on the balance of probabilities that he/she was in a state of intoxication akin to automatism or insanity — the decision provoked strong public reaction and extensive media coverage. The decision was criticized, *inter alia*, for ignoring the issue of violence against women and victims' rights generally. The decision of the majority of the Supreme Court was heavily focused on the due process rights of the accused, but it failed to consider the victim's perspective, particularly the gendered nature of sexual assaults and the link between intoxication and

[56] *Director of Public Prosecutions v. Beard*, [1920] A.C. 479 (H.L.).

[57] A general intent offence is an offence that seeks to achieve a certain immediate objective and requires only a conscious doing of a given prohibited act (e.g., a basic intent to apply force in the offence of assault). In contrast, special intent offences possess a further ulterior intent that goes beyond performance of an immediate act at hand (e.g., murder contains not only a general intent to, for example, fire a gun, but also an ulterior intent to do so in order to cause another person's death).

[58] Automatism refers to a situation where an accused has no control over his or her actions.

[59] *R. v. Daviault*, [1994] 3 S.C.R. 63.

[60] Section 7 reads: "Everyone has the right to life, liberty and security of the person and the right not to be deprived thereof except in accordance with the principles of fundamental justice."

[61] Section 11(d) reads: "Any person charged with an offence has the right ... (d) to be presumed innocent until proven guilty according to law in a fair and public hearing by an independent and impartial tribunal."

increased risk of violence.[62] Concerns have also been raised about the implications of the decision for women's trust in the criminal justice system. It was feared that *Daviault* would have a chilling effect on the willingness of victims to report abuse and press charges.[63]

Media Coverage of R. v. Daviault

The mass media was key in attracting the attention of the public to the decision and in keeping the debate alive for a prolonged period. On the one hand, it provided information on the decision, helped promote public awareness of various concerns associated with the decision, and provided a forum for debate. On the other hand, the style of reporting (in particular, how the gist of the decision was presented and whose commentaries of the decision were more widely cited) shaped public opinion of and reaction to the *Daviault* decision.[64] Given that most people do not have the time or interest to monitor and read Supreme Court decisions, media reports became one of the main sources of information and, consequently, the basis for forming an opinion on the issue.

Much of the media coverage focused on the immediate implication of the decision — that the defence of intoxication could be used with respect to all offences, including sexual assault — but the reasoning of the Court was not explained. The media has depicted the decision as allowing a person to become extremely intoxicated and then to use such extreme intoxication as a shield from criminal responsibility.[65] For example, some headlines read: "A License to Rape?"; "Drinking Ruled a Rape Defence"; "Has the Highest Court Lost Touch with Reality?"[66] As noted by some, public opinion was 'poisoned' by these representations.[67] Absent the explanation of the limits of the intoxication defence and the reasoning of the Court, media messages made it easy for the public to jump to conclusions and dismiss it as not making sense rather than seek to understand the multiple considerations involved in the judicial decision. This highlights not only the tremendous influence that the media may have on public opinion, but also the responsibility that comes with it: it is important that cases are reported in a way that not only presents the ultimate conclusion, but also the reasoning behind it.

While many articles acknowledged that the extreme intoxication defence was likely to succeed only in the rarest cases, this caveat was immediately overshadowed by the reporting on five acquittals based on the *Daviault* principles.[68] In fact, it was suggested that part of the problem was the way in

---

[62] Kent Roach, *Due Process and Victims' Rights: The New Law and Politics of Criminal Justice* (Toronto: University of Toronto Press, 1999) at 177–78.

[63] Elizabeth Sheeny, "A Brief on Bill C-72" (Ottawa: National Association of Women and the Law, 1995); Randha Jhappan, "The Equality Pit or the Rehabilitation of Justice?" in Randha Jhappan (ed.), *Women's Legal Strategies in Canada* (Toronto: University of Toronto Press, 2002) 175 at 212; Elizabeth Grant — invisibility of victims, gendered nature of sexual assault; Tu Thanh Ha, "Men's Defence of Drunkenness Sparks Plans to Change Law" *The Globe and Mail* (November 2, 1994); Debra Black, "A Licence to Rape? Women Fear That a Supreme Court Ruling Tells Men Sexual Assault Is Okay as Long as They're Drunk" *Toronto Star* (October 27, 1994) E1.

[64] See, for example, Black, *ibid.*; David Vienneau, "Drinking Ruled a Rape defence Feminists Outraged at Supreme Court Decision" *Toronto Star* (October 1, 1994) SA2; David Vienneau, "Drunkenness Ruling Said Based on Error: Intoxication Doesn't Cause 'Automatism,' Researcher Says", *Toronto Star* (April 12, 1995) A2; Sean Fine, "Has the Highest Court Lost Touch with Reality?" *The Globe and Mail* (October 8, 1994) D2; Clyde Farnsworth, "Women in Canada Upset by Court Rulings on Drunkenness" *New York Times* (November 10, 1994) 7; Ha, *ibid.*

[65] Professor Alan Young (Osgoode Hall Law School) quoted in Stephen Bindman, "Licence to Rape Outraged Many" *Southam News* (December 27, 1994).

[66] Black, *supra* note 63; Vienneau, "Drinking Ruled a Rape Defence", *supra* note 64; Fine, *supra* note 64.

[67] David Vienneau, "Judges under Fire for Drunkenness Defence" *Toronto Star* (November 9, 1994).

[68] Roach, *supra* note 62 at 178.

which lower courts have applied the decision.[69] While the reported acquittals have ignited further fears and opposition to *Daviault*, no similar attention was paid to the reversal of two of the acquittals on appeal and six unsuccessful cases that used the *Daviault* defence.[70]

Some sources reported that the *Daviault* decision has put under fire not only the Supreme Court, but also the judiciary generally. In a survey conducted by the *Toronto Star*, lower court justices have almost unanimously supported the Supreme Court decision, but they acknowledged the particular difficulty that the decision created, given the repulsive character of its factual circumstances.[71]

The media's continuing attention to the *Daviault* has likely contributed to the mobilization of public opinion on the issue and created indirect pressure on the government to promptly consider a legislative response. In fact, it was suggested that under this pressure, the Justice Minister's initial "go-slow" response to *Daviault* eventually turned into a promise to table legislation in February 1995 — only some five months after the release of the decision.[72] In the *Daviault* instance, the media acted not as a facilitator helping to promote public acceptance of a judicial decision, but, to the contrary, as a force igniting opposition to it and pushing for change.

Parliament's Response to the Daviault Decision

Several options for responding to the *Daviault* decision were considered, including the creation of a new offence of "criminal intoxication." According to this approach, even if someone was acquitted of assault on the basis of *Daviault* principles, he or she could still be found guilty of an offence of "criminal intoxication." Eventually, the government did not proceed with the criminal intoxication offence. Instead, it introduced s. 33.1 into the *Criminal Code* (Bill C-72), which provided that self-induced intoxication, no matter how extreme, cannot be a defence to a charge of any general intent offence that "includes as an element an assault or any other interference or threat of interference by a person with the bodily integrity of another person." The preamble to the bill provided extensive justification for the amendment that was strongly rooted in concerns about violence in Canadian society and particularly violence against women and children. Politically, the bill was presented as both a response to violence against women and as part of measures to get tougher on crime.[73]

As a result, the defence of intoxication is currently governed by a combination of common law and statutory rules:

1. With respect to general intent offences involving violence or the threat of violence, self-induced intoxication can never be a defence (s. 33.1 of the *Criminal Code*).

2. With respect to general intent offences that do not involve violence or threat of violence (e.g., a property offence), an accused may benefit from the intoxication defence if he/she proves on the balance of probabilities that the intoxication was so extreme as to lead to a state akin to automatism or insanity (as per *Daviault*).

---

[69] Professor Allan Hutchison (Osgoode Hall Law School) quoted in Stephen Bindman, "Licence to Rape Outraged Many", *Southam News* (December 27, 1994).

[70] Roach, *supra* note 62 at 178.

[71] Vienneau, *supra* note 67.

[72] Stephen Bindman, "Drunkenness Ruling Provoked Outrage" *Hamilton Spectator* (December 24, 1994).

[73] Roach, *supra* note 62 at 180.

3. With respect to specific intent offences, intoxication may be a defence where it prevents an accused from forming a specific intent (*Beard* rules).[74]

Judicial–Legislative Dialogue on the Defence of Intoxication and the Role of Interest Groups

The *Daviault* case is a good illustration of the factors involved in the law-making process discussed in the first half of the chapter. First, it demonstrates the role of both courts and the legislature in shaping legal rules: the defence of intoxication is governed by a combination of common law and statutory rules. Second, *Daviault* is a vivid example of judicial–legislative dialogue.[75] Bill C-72 was a direct response to the Supreme Court decision. Both the Supreme Court and Parliament have engaged with the issue of the defence of intoxication. In choosing to exercise its power to effectively override the judicial decision, Parliament not only conveyed its reaction to the *Daviault* decision, but also expressed its opinion on the proper balance that should be struck between protecting the rights of the accused and the interests of the public. Roach has characterized Bill C-72 as Parliament's "in-your-face" response to the Supreme Court, which essentially said that the Court decision's was unacceptable.[76] Notably, the judicial and legislative response represent different perspectives on the issue of criminal responsibility: the Court focused on the rights of the accused whereas Parliament framed Bill C-72 in the context of protecting the victim from violence.

Third, Parliament's response and the very choice of the amending language was shaped by public pressure and the input from various advocacy and interest groups obtained during the examination of Bill C-72 at the committee stage. The House of Commons Standing Committee on Justice and Legal Affairs received submissions and heard testimony from a number of organizations, including the National Association of Women and the Law, the Metro Action Committee on Public Violence Against Women and Children (METRAC), the Canadian Bar Association (CBA), the Canadian Psychiatric Association, and the Addiction Research Foundation.[77] Most of these groups are well known for engaging in advocacy to advance the causes of their members and other affected populations. It is of note that there were no intervenors in the *Daviault* appeal, but active advocacy campaigns have been undertaken by a number of organizations, particularly those concerned with women's rights, following the decision. Most likely, interest groups did not see the need to intervene in the case because it was not anticipated that the Supreme Court would make a new rule affecting women's interests and other public policy issues.[78]

Prior to the committee hearings on Bill C-72, a number of interest groups had been vocal in the media and awareness campaigns raising their concerns about the *Daviault* decision. A group of women's organizations formed a coalition that called for a national Day of Action against the *Daviault*

---

[74] Simon N. Verdun-Jones, *Criminal Law in Canada: Cases, Questions and the Code*, 5th ed. (Toronto: Nelson Education Limited, 2011) at 266–67.

[75] Hogg & Bushell, *supra* note 48 at paras. 49–50.

[76] Roach, *supra* note 35 at 274–77.

[77] House of Commons Standing Committee on Justice and Legal Affairs, Evidence — Meetings 158–163 (June 1995), online: <http://www.parl.gc.ca/35/Archives/committees351/jula/english_committee.html>.

[78] Christopher Manfredi, *Feminist Activism in the Supreme Court: Legal Mobilization and the Women's Legal Education and Action Fund* (Vancouver, BC: UBC Press, 2004) at 32.

decision on February 25, 1995.[79] Bill C-72 was tabled on February 24, the day before the national day of action.

At the committee stage, various interest groups contributed different perspectives on the proposed legislation to help the legislators make a more informed choice about the defence of intoxication. For example, the National Association of Women and the Law and METRAC represented women's organizations and provided critical assessment of the bill in the context of violence against women. In particular, they were concerned that the intoxication defence works to reinforce and excuse male violence against women by attributing the blame to alcohol and minimizing the significance of the violence.[80] The CBA, which represented the interests of lawyers across Canada, concentrated mostly on the clarifications of the bill's language and broader issues of criminal law reform.[81] For example, the testimony of CBA representatives provided some explanation on the distinction between general and specific intent offences, commentary on the usefulness of having a statement of purpose in Bill C-72, alternative ways to address *Daviault* such as introducing an offence of criminal intoxication and other legal issues. While the CBA provided legal analysis of Bill C-72, the Canadian Psychiatric Association and the Addiction Research Foundation supplied insights into the issues of intoxication, automatism, and amnesia from a medical perspective.[82] In particular, the briefs and testimony from the Canadian Psychiatric Association and the Addition Research Foundation pointed out that, in scientific terms, alcohol in and of itself cannot induce a state akin to automatism. They were concerned that the *Daviault* decision seemed to have created the legal defence of alcohol-induced intoxication akin to automatism, which is indefensible in scientific terms.

Case Study: Regulating Labelling of Genetically Modified (GM) Food in Canada

The Debate about GM Food Regulation

For centuries, people have consumed food largely produced from nature. Not any more. In recent decades, most foods we consume are genetically modified. Everything from bread to tomatoes, corn and soya oil are produced from altered food organisms. As people consume more and more genetically modified food (GM food), the controversy grows over the risk to public health and the environment associated with the consumption of GM food. Increasingly, the general public wonders if GM food poses a risk to human health and whether greater public awareness and further scientific research are needed. A central response to these concerns has been the strengthening of the regulation of food safety so that GM foods are scientifically examined before they are approved for human consumption. Nevertheless, GM food science is not sufficiently developed, and the regulatory framework for food safety is not necessarily fully reliable. Thus, concerns over the risk that GM food poses remain on the agendas of consumers, regulators, and the food industry.

---

[79] Testimony of Susan Bazilli (METRAC) before the House of Commons Standing Committee on Justice and Legal Affairs (June 6, 1995), online: <http://www.parl.gc.ca/35/Archives/committees351/jula/evidence/158_95-06-06/jula158_blk101.html>.

[80] Testimony of Liz Sheehy (National Association of Women and the Law) before the House of Commons Standing Committee on Justice and Legal Affairs (June 6, 1995), online: <http://www.parl.gc.ca/35/Archives/committees351/jula/evidence/158_95-06-06/jula158_blk101.html>.

[81] Testimony of Sheldon Pinx, Michelle K. Fuerst, Joan Bercovitch (CBA) before the House of Commons Standing Committee on Justice and Legal Affairs (June 6, 1995), online: <http://www.parl.gc.ca/35/Archives/committees351/jula/evidence/159_95-06-06/jula159_blk101.html>.

[82] Testimony of John Bradford (Canadian Psychiatric Association), Harold Kalant and Perry Kendall (Addiction Research Foundation) before the House of Commons Standing Committee on Justice and Legal Affairs (June 13, 1995), online: <http://www.parl.gc.ca/35/Archives/committees351/jula/evidence/161_95-06-13/jula161_blk101.html>.

An important regulatory solution to the controversy over the risk of consuming GM food has been labelling, which may indicate whether any food product is genetically modified. This information may enable consumers to freely choose or reject GM food and to decide the risk they can tolerate. However, food companies often question the necessity of GM food labelling because it imposes a significant cost on food production and marketing and creates an unnecessary disincentive for GM food consumption, thereby hindering the competitiveness of the agro-sector. Similarly, regulators are not necessarily persuaded of the need for GM food labelling, since they tend to believe that a strict pre-marketing regulation of GM food safety should be sufficient and serve the purpose of balancing consumers' interest in safety, on the one hand, and food companies' concern over the competitiveness of the food industry, on the other. These diverging views about GM food labelling have given rise to an ongoing debate over whether labelling is necessary and, if so, whether it should be voluntary or mandatory.

In the midst of public controversy, the Government of Canada decided to officially adopt voluntary labelling for GM food in 2004. That is to say, companies may voluntarily label GM food, but they are not legally required to indicate that the food is a product of genetic engineering. In order to regulate this regime, a Canadian standard for voluntary labelling of genetically engineered (GE) foods entitled *Voluntary Labelling and Advertising of Foods That Are and Are Not Products of Genetic Engineering* [the Standard] was developed.[83] This Standard addresses "non health and safety labelling (rather, labelling for method of production, for example, whether a food has or has not been produced through genetic engineering".[84] It was adopted by the Standards Council of Canada and seeks "to provide meaningful criteria for labelling, understandable messages for consumers, and a consistent policy to verify the truthfulness of labels."[85]

It is important to note that GM food labelling is concerned with information about the genetic modification of a food product and must be distinguished from the current mandatory labelling that is required for any food that poses a risk due to general health and safety concerns other than genetic modification.[86] For example, if the nutritional value or composition of the food has been changed, or if there is an allergen present in the food, genetically modified or not, the food must be labelled as such.[87] While there are several regulatory solutions, labelling may mitigate such a risk by informing or alerting consumers about the risk. This required labelling applies to all foods, including GM foods.[88]

The Role of Interest Groups and the Media in the Development of GM Food Labelling

The adoption of voluntary labelling of GM food in Canada may be seen by the public as a purely technical legal process of making food laws. The Standard passed after some consultation and was apparently developed on the basis of advice from regulators and scientists. However, in reality, the adoption of voluntary labelling of GM food was the culmination of a long process of public consultation and pressures from multiple interest groups. Biotechnology

---

83 Health Canada, <http://www.hc-sc.gc.ca/sr-sr/pubs/biotech/reg_gen_mod-eng.php>.

84 *Ibid.*

85 *Ibid.*

86 *Ibid.*

87 *Ibid.*

88 *Ibid.*

companies, the food industry, government agencies, political and business elites, consumer groups, and the media played an important role in the debate over GM food labelling and influenced the ultimate decision to make this labelling voluntary and not mandatory in Canada.

The public debate over GM food regulation has brought to light the diverging views that the government and multiple groups hold, as well as the pressures they have exerted to influence public policies in this area. Although there has not been a wide public debate over GM food in Canada, the government has sought the views of the general public. The government held a multi-stakeholder workshop in 1993 that included industry representatives and consumer, environmental, and health groups.[89] In 1994, the government also organized a workshop devoted to the issue of GM food labelling.[90] In March 1999, a consensus conference on genetically modified foods was held in Calgary, Alberta. The conference was organized by researchers at the University of Calgary, using funding from a federal research grant and the provincial government of Alberta. Many citizens were recruited to participate in this conference. The government eventually created a Canadian Biotechnology Advisory Committee, including a citizen representative from the Calgary conference, thus recognizing that more participatory legitimation for policy might be desirable.[91] The Canadian citizens' report resulting from the 1999 conference nevertheless reached substantially precautionary conclusions in contrast to the optimistic outlook more common among governing elites.[92] For example, raising concerns about biased information and the lack of public participation, the participating citizens noted that "[w]hile food biotechnology offers potential benefits, its long-term effects on the environment are unknown."[93]

The Canadian Biotechnology Advisory Committee (CBAC) attempted to provide Canadians with opportunities to discuss the social and ethical concerns associated with plant biotechnology until May 2007, when the Conservative government disbanded it.[94] In addition to advising the Government of Canada on the multiple aspects of biotechnology policy, the Committee had the mandate of enhancing public awareness of the technology and facilitating an open, transparent national conversation on key issues.[95] These forums for public participation created by the CBAC quickly revealed the tension between the views of the government and the public. In 2001, CBAC launched a public consultation on GM food, but the majority of environmental and public interest non-governmental organizations boycotted it, claiming that the remit of the CBAC was too narrow and lacked independence from the government.[96] In 2003, CBAC issued a "dialogue tool on genetically modified foods and feeds", the premise of which was that the different biotechnology products were acceptable and which reiterated that GM crops and food should be approved

---

[89] Grace Skogstad, *Internationalization and Canadian Agriculture: Policy and Governing Paradigms* (Toronto: University of Toronto Press, 2008) at 215.

[90] *Ibid.*

[91] Alberto R. Salazar V., "NAFTA Chapter 11, Regulatory Expropriation and Domestic Counter-Advertising Law" (2010) 27 Ariz. J. Int'l & Comp. L. 31 at 79–80.

[92] John Dryzek, Robert Goodin, Aviezer Tucker & Bernard Reber, "Promethean Elites Encounter Precautionary Publics: The Case of GM Foods" (2009) 34 Sci. Tech. & Human Values 263 at 274–75.

[93] Canadian Citizens' Conference on Food Biotechnology. Citizens' Final Report presented March 7, 1999, available at <http://www.ucalgary.ca/~pubconf/report.html>.

[94] Skogstad, *supra* note 89 at 224.

[95] *Ibid.*

[96] *Ibid.*

solely on the basis of scientific assessments.[97] This probably heightened the controversy over CBAC's independence and further revealed its discrepancy with the views of non-governmental interest groups.

The media also played a role in raising concerns about the controversial ties between the government and the biotechnology industry and the excessive influence of the food industry on the development of GM food policies in Canada. In an article published in the *Ottawa Citizen*, it was reported that the CBAC office was located in a government department, Industry Canada, and was a paid member of BIOTECanada, an advocacy group for biotechnology companies.[98] Furthermore, the close ties between the government and the biotechnology industry became evident as the media revealed the financial support that the government gives to that industry. Mark Abley, writing in the *Montreal Gazette*, reported that BIOTECanada received annual grants of $1.1 million under Industry Canada's Technology Outreach Program, some of which went directly to changing public perceptions of the biotechnology industry.[99] Angela Rickman, deputy director of the Sierra Club of Canada, a nongovernmental organization dedicated to the protection of the environment, complained that "[t]he government is acting as both the protector and the regulator of this industry".[100] The fact that biotechnology companies and the government appear to have been working toward improving the social acceptance of GM food becomes even more controversial in light of the opposite view held by the Canadian public. The polls reported by the media suggested that the Canadian public wants GM food labelled, and the majority are willing to pay more to identify genetically modified products.[101]

Given the prevailing ideas about the acceptability of GM food and the focus on the competitive advantage, productivity, and profitability of the Canadian agro-sector, it is conceivable that biotechnology companies have found GM food mandatory labelling too costly and contrary to their desire to expand GM food consumption and exports. There is some evidence that local business groups have in the past opposed the labelling of genetically modified products in Canada. This happened with the Biosafety Protocol. The United Nations' Protocol on Biosafety, in effect since September 2003, seeks to protect biodiversity by managing the environmental risks of the transboundary movement of living modified organisms (LMOs).[102] Among other things, exporters of commodities are required to label them as "may contain LMOs".[103] Canada has signed but has not yet ratified the Protocol.[104] "Its delay can be attributed to pressure brought by the Canadian farm community and export traders who fear the Protocol will raise their cost of exporting food products by requiring them to implement identity preservation systems".[105] This seems to have been the outcome of the organized efforts of the biotechnology industry. Indeed, as reported by the media, a number of companies and associations banded together in 1998 to form the Biosafety Protocol Consortia, which

---

[97] *Ibid.*

[98] See James Baxter, "Government paying to Lobby Itself: Industry Canada Is a Member — and a Client — of Group Organized to Influence Biotech Policy", *Ottawa Citizen* (April 10, 2000) A1.

[99] Mark Abley, "Biotech Lobby Got Millions from Ottawa: Public Cash Used to Alter Image", *Montreal Gazette* (February 28, 2000), also available at <http://healthcoalition.ca/archive/Biotech-IC.pdf>.

[100] Quoted in Abley, ibid.

[101] Sarah Staples, "Public Wants GM Food Labelled: Poll Finds Majority Willing to Pay More to Clearly Identify Modified Products" *Ottawa Citizen* (June 12, 2002) A1.

[102] Skogstad, *supra* note 89 at 221.

[103] Ibid.

[104] Skogstad, *supra* note 89 at 222.

[105] Ibid.

included Monsanto, BIOTECanada and CanGene (which, in 1999, received a loan of $700,000 from the Western Economic Diversification program, a government initiative).[106] This group hired Rick Walter (president of Biotech Consulting Group Inc.) to act as a lobbyist in Ottawa.[107]

The influence of the food industry on the regulation of food consumption and particularly genetically modified food should not be surprising. Marion Nestle has documented this problem in the United States,[108] and several pieces of evidence suggest that it may also be a serious problem in Canada. To further add to the above evidence, consider the following. A Canadian dietitian, commenting on Marion Nestle's book *Food Politics*, reveals some of the strategies that food corporations use in Canada to influence food regulations:

> In the [United States] and Canada, food is political for the simple reason that there is a lot of money, and profits, at stake . . . . While the details of the book are all American, in this era of free trade, its fundamental concepts and the issues it raises are also applicable in Canada. Indeed, I was told by a representative of a multinational food corporation at an industry-sponsored dietitians' event that his company loves to sponsor such events, because they know that when it comes time to change government regulations, they will have the support of dietitians.[109]

It should not come as a surprise that non-governmental groups have protested the expansion of GM crops and food and the over-influence of biotechnology companies on the development of GM food policies in Canada, including the lack of GM food labelling. For instance, in 2001, a coalition of farm, consumer, health, environmental, and industry organizations opposed Monsanto's attempts to commercialize genetically modified wheat in Canada. These groups raised serious concerns about market acceptance, environmental risk, and the lack of a democratic and transparent process in biotech regulation and policy.[110] Consumer groups, environmentalists, and social activists have been concerned about the fact that genetically modified food may provide abundant and cheap food at the expense of negatively affecting the environment and human health.[111]

Nevertheless, the attempts to make GM food labelling mandatory in Canada failed. A free vote in Parliament on October 17, 2001, defeated a bill by Liberal MP Charles Caccia. His private member's bill, C-287, would have required mandatory labelling of genetically altered foods. Interestingly, a year later, in August 2002, the Canadian Biotechnology Advisory Committee, often criticized for its close ties to the biotechnology companies, issued a report recommending the adoption of voluntary labelling of GM food, which in fact was officially adopted in 2004:

> We note that the mandatory labelling of GM foods is already required for health and safety reasons. CBAC recommends that the federal government adopt a voluntary system for labelling GM foods for matters other than health and safety. The majority of CBAC members believe that Canada

[106] Abley, *supra* note 99.

[107] *Ibid.*

[108] Marion Nestle, *Food Politics: How the Food Industry Influences Nutrition and Health* (Berkeley, CA: 2002); *Safe Food: Bacteria, Biotechnology, and Bioterrorism* (Berkeley, CA: 2003).

[109] Elaine Power, "Resource Review — Food Politics: How the Food Industry Influences Nutrition and Health", *Members Online Newsletter* (Dietitians of Canada, Toronto, Ontario), May 2003, available at <http://web.archive.org/web/20060630034213/http://foodpolitics.com/pdf/resrevfoodpoli.pdf>.

[110] Emily Eaton, "Getting Behind the Grain: The Politics of Genetic Modification on the Canadian Prairies" (2009) 41 Antipode 256.

[111] Skogstad, *supra* note 89 at 210.

should begin with a voluntary labelling system for GM foods to allow time for testing the system's adequacy and efficiency and to develop an accepted international standard; to provide consumers who wish to purchase GM-free products with the ability to identify them; to limit costs; and to avoid trade action where a mandatory labelling scheme would contravene trade agreements. ...

...

We recommend:

...

7.3 That the voluntary system be widely promulgated and promoted. ... [112]

Canada chose a lenient approach to GM food regulation in spite of the fact that the old international consensus that there were no fundamental differences between GM and non-GM products evaporated after 1997.[113] In fact, disparate regulatory frameworks of GM food developed in North America and Europe after 1997,[114] evidencing the existence of regulatory options and lack of consensus over the risks associated with GM food and the importance of consumer choice. Unlike in Canada, for instance, GM food labelling is mandatory in Europe. It should not be surprising, then, that public criticism of Canadian GM policies continues to increase and that the government has been forced to improve the legitimacy and effectiveness of its controversial policies in this area. In sum, "the Canadian institutional framework has been sensitive to the preferences of biotechnology plant developers and users, and less hospitable to critics of the technology and the Canadian regulatory approach".[115] This is despite the growing support of the Canadian public for GM food labelling.[116]

GM food policies, including labelling, have clearly developed in the midst of competing interest groups seeking to advance their discourses about risk and its regulation. On the one hand, the government, political elites, and the food industry have emphasized the focus on science-based food safety and the contribution of GM food and crops to improving the competitiveness and profitability of the Canadian agro-export sector.[117] On the other hand, consumer, environmental, and health groups have often raised concerns about the public health and environmental impact of GM food. Yet, it appears that the views of the biotechnology industry against mandatory GM food labelling have prevailed in the end. The views of the government and the biotechnology companies have been dominant in the decision on whether to require GM labelling despite significant public opposition and have overshadowed the views of consumers and even GM food scientists.

Clearly, there is a democratic deficit in the making of GM food laws, particularly in deciding the voluntary or mandatory nature of GM food labelling in Canada.

A critical factor in improving the democratic governance of GM food may be the role that independent food scientists can play. This is impor-

---

[112] The Canadian Biotechnology Advisory Committee, *Improving the Regulation of Genetically Modified Foods and Other Novel Foods in Canada* (Report to the Government of Canada, Biotechnology Ministerial Coordinating Committee, Ottawa, August 2002), xi and xviii, online: <http://dsp-psd.pwgsc.gc.ca/Collection/C2-589-2001-1E.pdf>.

[113] Skogstad, *supra* note 89 at 210.

[114] *Ibid.*

[115] Skogstad, *supra* note 89 at 211.

[116] Staples, *supra* note 101. See also The Canadian Biotechnology Advisory Committee, *supra* note 112, xi (noting that "[t]he dissenting member, Anne Mitchell, is strongly in favour of proceeding directly to mandatory labelling, and notes that a majority of respondents to our Interim Report urged a mandatory system.")

[117] Skogstad, *supra* note 89.

tant because knowledge of the risks associated with GM crops and food continues to be uncertain, and more solid and independent scientific research is needed.[118] Yet, private corporate interests increasingly dominate the research agenda, challenging the impartiality of food scientists and ultimately compromising the integrity of the regulatory system.[119] There are also concerns about the lack of public funding for independent research, which deprives scientists of a real opportunity to make independent research in this area. While regulation of GM food, particularly GM labelling, requires an advanced and reliable knowledge of the risks involved, that information is not necessarily available and, when progress is made, it is not necessarily widely discussed. Thus, there is a need to promote greater impartial research in this area and to make the views of independent food scientists more prominent in public debate to the extent of influencing regulatory policies and balancing corporate views.

It thus appears desirable to encourage some form of *independent scientist activism*. Independent food scientists, as another important interest group, should conduct intensive research on the risk of GM food for human health and the environment. Their findings should not only inform lawmakers and help review existing risk assessments and regulatory decisions,[120] but also provide key information for consumer education programs funded by the government and carried out independently from biotechnology companies.[121] In this respect, the media may also aid in promoting the independence of food scientists as well as disseminating research findings and greater information about the risks associated with GM food. The ensuing public awareness and the wider public debate based on independent scientific information will likely improve the democratic deliberation on the issue of GM food labelling. Rather than politicians or corporations deciding in boardrooms, the public in dialogue with scientists and other interest groups is to decide the level of risk it may want to tolerate and whether it needs GM food labels to make such a risk decision. Citizens, not business or political elites, should freely decide the degree of risk they wish to bear. This active participation of the public helps to democratize regulatory capitalism, since regulatory power is delegated not only to the government, the food industry, corporate agents, and professional

---

[118] See, e.g., The Canadian Biotechnology Advisory Committee, *supra* note 112, ix–xii ("...it is prudent to establish programs to determine whether there are any long-term adverse or beneficial effects attributable to these foods that are not revealed in pre-market assessments. ... The current approach to the assessment of environmental risk and ecosystem impacts of GM plants could be improved. ... We conclude that no scientific evidence exists to suggest that GM plants and foods currently in the market pose any greater health or environmental risk than other foods.... There is a need not only to develop methods for long-term surveillance of health and environmental impacts, but also to ensure that regulatory processes are able to deal effectively with the more complex products on the horizon."), online: <http://dsp-psd.pwgsc.gc.ca/Collection/C2-589-2001-1E.pdf>.

[119] Royal Society of Canada, Expert Panel on the Future of Food Biotechnology, *Elements of Precaution: Recommendations for the Regulation of Food Biotechnology in Canada*. Prepared for Health Canada, Canadian Food Inspection Agency, and Environment Canada, Ottawa, 2001, at ix and 212, online: <http://www.rsc.ca/files/publications/expert_panels/foodbiotechnolgoy/GMexsummaryEN.pdf>.

[120] In the past, the Royal Society of Canada's Expert Panel on the Future of Food Biotechnology, among several solutions, proposed an independent panel of experts to review the data and rationales upon which risk assessments and regulatory decisions were based. This recommendation was rejected by the Government of Canada. See Skogstad, *supra* note 89 at 228.

[121] Similar recommendations for greater information disclosure and public involvement in regulating GM food were made by CBAC in the past. See Canadian Biotechnology Advisory Committee, *supra* note 112 at ix, online: <http://dsp-psd.pwgsc.gc.ca/Collection/C2-589-2001-1E.pdf>.

It is important to note, however, that CBAC was criticized for its close ties to biotechnology companies. See Baxter, *supra* note 98. Its recommendations may then be taken with caution.

associations, but also to ordinary consumers and citizens, particularly when their health is at stake.

CHAPTER SUMMARY

Law making is a complex process influenced, directly and indirectly, by a variety of factors. This chapter has examined only three such factors: interest groups, the media, and judicial–legislative interaction. Each of the three has its own peculiar dynamics and is unique in how it may impact the law-making process. Interest groups may attempt to influence the nature and content of legal rules throughout the legislative process (e.g., by lobbying politicians to introduce a certain bill, making submissions at the committee stage) as well as after a law is passed (e.g., by challenging it in the courts). In contrast, the media plays a less direct role in the legal system: while not challenging a certain law or a government decision before the courts, it can subject an issue to the court of public opinion, thereby creating pressure for change. As a disseminator of mass information, it is able to influence public perception of laws, specific judicial decisions, and the legal system as a whole, as well as draw attention to and mobilize public opinion on certain issues. For example, the media scrutiny of the *Daviault* decision can be seen as one of the factors that not only moulded public opinion, but also pressured the government to react more quickly by introducing Bill C-72. Finally, judicial–legislative interaction refers to the dynamics between the two branches of government. The nature of such interaction varies: in some cases, it becomes a struggle between two opposing views on an issue; in others, it has been characterized as a productive dialogue seeking to find a reasonable balance among competing perspectives. The impact of these three factors — interest groups, the media, and judicial–legislative dialogue — should always be kept in mind in order to understand why and how a certain law came about as well as to be able to critically assess its underlying rationales.

GLOSSARY OF NEW TERMS AND KEY CONCEPTS

actus reus	A concept in criminal law denoting an act or omission that forms a part of an offence.
mens rea	A concept in criminal law that denotes the mental element of an offence.
defence of intoxication	A set of criminal law rules that outline in what circumstances intoxication may be a defence to a criminal charge.
interest group	A group of individuals or organizations that share a common set of goals and have joined together to persuade the legislative, executive or judicial branch to adopt a policy, law or decision that will help them protect or advance their interest.
judicial activism	A concept that refers to judicial decision-making that has the potential to re-evaluate and change public policy or a regulatory regime set out by other branches of government.

REVIEW QUESTIONS

1. What is an interest group?
2. What are the two main strategies used by interest groups to influence law and policy?
3. Why are powerful interest groups in a better position to influence law making?

4. How does the mass media influence the law-making process?
5. What are some of the problems that may prevent the mass media from having a positive impact on the legal system?
6. What are the advantages and disadvantages of pursuing litigation as a tool for social reform?
7. What is "judicial–legislative dialogue'?
8. Why can the case of *R. v. Daviault* be viewed as an example of legislative–judicial dialogue?
9. To what extent does the influence of interest groups explain the adoption of voluntary labelling of GM food in Canada?
10. What role did the mass media play in the regulation of GM food labelling?

DISCUSSION QUESTIONS

1. Using the concept of judicial–legislative dialogue, analyze the development of prisoners' right to vote in Canada. For the purpose of your discussion, examine the following sources: *Canada Elections Act*, R.S.C. 1985, c. E-2, s. 51(e) (prior to amendments in 1993), *Sauvé v. Canada (Attorney General)*, [1993] 2 S.C.R. 438; *Canada Elections Act*, R.S.C. 1985, c. E-2, s. 51(e) (as amended in 1993); and *Sauvé v. Canada (Chief Electoral Officer)*, [2002] 3 S.C.R. 519.
2. Research the Internet and find a Canadian-based interest group. Identify whose interests it represents and what techniques it uses to advance its cause.
3. What should be the interrelationship between the judiciary and the legislature in the law-making process? Should the perspective of one or the other prevail?
4. Explore potential solutions to the problem of the distortion of the ideal role of the media in law making by the over-influence of powerful interest groups.
5. Is the social media capable of engaging an increasing number of ordinary citizens so that they actively participate in the process of making and enforcing the law?

SUGGESTED READINGS

David Schneiderman & Kate Sutherland (eds.), *Charting the Consequences: The Impact of the Charter Rights on Canadian Law and Politics* (Toronto: University of Toronto Press, 1997).

Ian Greene, *The Courts* (Vancouver, BC: UBC Press, 2006).

Lori Hausegger et al., *Canadian Courts: Law, Politics, and Process* (Don Mills: Oxford University Press, 2009).

Heather MacIvor, *Canadian Politics and Government in the Charter Era* (Toronto: Thomson Nelson Canada, 2006).

Florian Sauvageau, David Schneiderman & David Taras, *The Last Word: Media Coverage of the Supreme Court of Canada* (Vancouver, BC: UBC Press, 2006).

Enrique Armijo, "Media Ownership Regulation: A Comparative Perspective" (2009) 37 Ga. J. Int'l & Comp. L. 421.

Residential Landlord and Tenant Law

Arlene Blatt
SENECA COLLEGE

Learning Objectives

After reading this chapter, the reader should be able to:

➢ Understand the basic rights and responsibilities of residential landlords and tenants in Ontario

➢ Explain how tenancy agreements are created

➢ Identify the different types of tenancies

➢ Explain the rules regarding rent and rent increases

➢ Describe how landlords and tenants can terminate a tenancy

➢ Understand sublets and assignments

➢ Describe proceedings at the Landlord and Tenant Board

➢ Understand mediation and other settlements between landlords and tenants

➢ Explain how to enforce orders from the Landlord and Tenant Board

TABLE OF CONTENTS

INTRODUCTION

Imagine that you are living in a house or apartment that you rent from the owner, your landlord. One of your main concerns as a tenant is likely about the rent. You want to know, for example, whether your rent will increase and, if so, by how much. You probably assume that your landlord will fix any repair or maintenance problems in your home, but that otherwise he or she will leave you alone and respect your privacy. You may have also have concerns about whether your landlord can ever force you to move out.

Now picture yourself as the owner and landlord of that house or apartment. You want a tenant who will pay the rent, not cause any damage to your property, and not disturb you or any other tenants living there. You certainly want the right to force a tenant to leave, if necessary.

As you can see, the interests of a landlord and tenant are quite different. The nature of the residential landlord–tenant relationship requires that a balance be struck between the interests of the landlord as owner of the rental property on the one hand, and the interests of the tenant as the person living there, on the other hand. The *Residential Tenancies Act, 2006* ("Act"),[1] the law that governs residential landlords and tenants in Ontario, attempts to achieve this balance. The Act defines the rights and responsibilities of both landlords and tenants, and sets out the procedures that must be followed when enforcing these rights and responsibilities. Since the Act governs most residential rental properties in Ontario, landlords and tenants must know what it says so that they can fully understand the extent of their legal rights and responsibilities.

This chapter examines the relationship between residential landlords and tenants in Ontario. It discusses how tenancies begin, how they end, the rights and responsibilities of both landlords and tenants, and rules about rent. This chapter talks about **eviction** and explains when and how a landlord can end a tenancy and evict the tenant. It also talks about how tenants can end their tenancy. Finally, it describes proceedings at the Landlord and Tenant Board (the "Board"), the administrative tribunal that administers the Act and resolves disputes between residential landlords and tenants. This chapter focuses only on the most common type of residential rental property — an apartment, duplex, house, or condominium unit. Other types of residential properties such as care homes, boarding houses, and mobile homes will not be discussed. While this chapter does address many of the main issues concerning residential landlords and tenants in Ontario, it is not a complete discussion of this area of law.

THE *RESIDENTIAL TENANCIES ACT*

The *Residential Tenancies Act* is the law that governs residential landlords and tenants in Ontario. The Act covers most types of rental residential properties and provides full and partial exemptions for some types of housing. For example, the Act does not apply at all to people who are in jail or who live in a hospital, hotel or motel, or an emergency shelter. It also does not apply at all to any type of living accommodation that requires the occupant to share a kitchen or bathroom with the owner, or a close family member of the owner. For certain other types of rental residential properties, the Act may provide only a partial exemption. For example, some of the rules about rent do not

---

[1] S.O. 2006, c. 17.

EXHIBIT 37.1

The *Residential Tenancies Act*

Purposes of the Act — Section 1

The purposes of this Act are to provide protection for residential tenants from unlawful rent increases and unlawful evictions, to establish a framework for the regulation of residential rents, to balance the rights and responsibilities of residential landlords and tenants and to provide for the adjudication of disputes and for other processes to informally resolve disputes.

Definition of "landlord" and "tenant" for the purposes of the Act

"landlord" includes,

    (a)   the owner of a rental unit or any other person who permits occupancy of a rental unit, other than a tenant who occupies a rental unit in a residential complex and who permits another person to also occupy the unit or any part of the unit,

    (b)   the heirs, assigns, personal representatives and successors in title of a person referred to in clause (a), and

    (c)   a person, other than a tenant occupying a rental unit in a residential complex, who is entitled to possession of the residential complex and who attempts to enforce any of the rights of a landlord under a tenancy agreement or this Act, including the right to collect rent.

"tenant" includes a person who pays rent in return for the right to occupy a rental unit and includes the tenant's heirs, assigns and personal representatives, but "tenant" does not include a person who has the right to occupy a rental unit by virtue of being,

    (a)   a co-owner of the residential complex in which the rental unit is located, or

    (b)   a shareholder of a corporation that owns the residential complex.

---

apply to people who live in subsidized housing. All of the full and partial exemptions are set out in the Act.

The Act defines the meaning of some of the terms that are used in its provisions. For example, s. 2 defines a "rental unit" as follows:

> [A]ny living accommodation used or intended for use as rented residential premises, and "rental unit" includes,
> (a) a site for a mobile home or site on which there is a land lease home used or intended for use as rented residential premises, and
> (b) a room in a boarding house, rooming house or lodging house and a unit in a care home.

You should refer to this section to see if a term has a defined meaning for the purposes of the Act.

The Act provides that it applies with respect to rental residential units in Ontario despite any agreement or waiver to the contrary. This means that landlords and tenants cannot agree, for example, that some or all of the provisions of the Act will not apply to them. The Act also provides that any provision in a **tenancy agreement** that is inconsistent with the Act is void and will not be enforced by the Board. The practical effect of these provisions is that the tenancy agreement is essentially irrelevant except as it specifies the amount of rent and the date when rent is due, whether utilities, parking and/or other services are included in the rent, and the term of the tenancy agreement. This is because the Act covers all the matters governing the landlord and tenant relationship, including the rights and responsibilities of both landlords and tenants.

THE TENANCY AGREEMENT

A tenancy begins with a written or oral agreement between a landlord and tenant for possession of a rental unit. A tenancy can also start with an implied agreement if, for example, the landlord accepts rent from a person who is living in the rental unit after acquiring it from a former tenant, but without entering into an oral or written tenancy agreement with the landlord. If there is a written tenancy agreement, no particular form of agreement is required. However, as noted above, any terms that are inconsistent with the Act are void and will not be enforced by the Board.

When considering a prospective tenant, a landlord may perform credit checks and can ask for banking information and other information about income, employment history, rental history, and personal and/or credit references. While a landlord may refuse a prospective tenant based on this information, a landlord cannot refuse to rent to someone based on any of the prohibited grounds of discrimination set out in Ontario's *Human Rights Code*.[2] This statute provides that "every person has a right to equal treatment with respect to the occupancy of accommodation, without discrimination because of race, ancestry, place of origin, colour, ethnic origin, citizenship, creed, sex, sexual orientation, age, marital status, family status, disability or the receipt of public assistance".[3] A landlord should not, for example, ask a prospective tenant about his or her ethnic background or whether he or she is gay, married, divorced, or plans on having children.

When a tenancy agreement is entered into, the landlord must provide the tenant with the landlord's legal name and address so that the tenant can contact the landlord if necessary and give the landlord any notices or other documents. If the tenancy agreement is not in writing, the landlord must provide the tenant with the landlord's contact information, in writing, within 21 days after the tenancy starts. If the tenancy agreement is in writing, the landlord must give the tenant a copy of the signed agreement within 21 days after the tenant signs it. The tenant is not required to pay rent until the landlord complies with this obligation. However, as soon as the landlord complies, the tenant must pay any withheld rent. Landlords must also provide all new tenants with information about the rights and responsibilities of landlords and tenants, the role of the Board, and how to contact the Board.[4] The landlord must give this information to the tenant on or before the date the tenancy begins. The Board has an information brochure available on its website that landlords can download and use for this purpose.

A tenancy starts on the day the tenant is entitled to possession of the rental unit, whether or not the tenant actually moves in on that date, regardless of the reason. For example, if a tenancy agreement says the tenant can move in on March 1, then the tenant will be responsible for March's rent, even if the tenant is unable to move in until the following month.

---

[2] R.S.O. 1990, c. H.19.

[3] *Ibid.*, s. 2(1).

[4] General information about the rights and responsibilities of landlords and tenants can be found on the Landlord and Tenant Board website: "Information for New Tenants", <http://www.ltb.gov.on.ca/en/Key_Information/STEL02_111600.html>.

TYPES OF TENANCIES: PERIODIC AND FIXED-TERM TENANCIES

Tenancies are either fixed-term or periodic. A **fixed-term tenancy** has a specified start date and end date, and can be for any length of time. Most new tenancy agreements provide for a fixed term of one year. A tenancy does not end when the fixed term expires. Instead, the tenancy automatically continues as a **periodic tenancy**, with all the same terms and conditions of the original tenancy, unless of course it has been renewed for another fixed term. A tenant does not have to agree to a landlord's request to renew a fixed-term tenancy that is coming to an end.

When a tenancy agreement does not specify an end date, the tenancy is deemed to be a periodic tenancy. The period involved is determined by the frequency with which the tenant pays rent. For example, if the tenant pays rent weekly, it is a weekly periodic tenancy. If the tenant pays rent monthly, it is a monthly periodic tenancy. Most tenants pay their rent monthly and therefore have a monthly periodic tenancy, also known simply as a monthly tenancy.

A periodic tenancy renews automatically at the end of each relevant period and continues this way until the tenancy is terminated by either the landlord or tenant. For example, a monthly periodic tenancy starts on the first day of the month and ends on the last day of that month, and then automatically renews for another month.

RIGHTS AND RESPONSIBILITIES OF RESIDENTIAL LANDLORDS AND TENANTS

Security of Tenure

The Act balances the right of tenants to **exclusive possession** of the rental unit for as long as they want against the right of landlords to evict tenants when the circumstances justify it. Tenants in Ontario have **security of tenure**, which means that they are protected against unjustified and unlawful evictions by their landlords. A landlord can evict a tenant only for the reasons specified in the Act and only after the landlord obtains an order from the Board terminating the tenancy and evicting the tenant. For example, even when a landlord has a reason specified in the Act to evict a tenant, the landlord is not allowed to lock the tenant out of the rental unit or otherwise force the tenant to move out. The only person who is allowed to evict a tenant is the **Sheriff**.

Privacy

The law recognizes that while tenants should have the right to privacy while living in a rental unit, landlords, as owners of the rental property, should have the right to enter a tenant's unit in certain circumstances.

The Act protects these rights by specifying when and how a landlord is allowed to enter a tenant's rental unit. In most cases, a landlord can enter only after giving the tenant 24 hours' prior written notice, and only for one of the permitted reasons set out in the Act. These reasons all deal with situations where a landlord will reasonably need to enter the rental unit, such as to fix something, inspect the unit for maintenance problems, or show the unit to a purchaser, mortgage lender, or insurer. As long as the landlord has a reason permitted under the Act, and gives the tenant the required written notice, the landlord is allowed to enter the rental unit anytime between the hours of 8 a.m. and 8 p.m., even if the tenant is not home.

The only times a landlord can legally enter a tenant's unit at any time of the day or night, and without telling the tenant ahead of time, are either when there is an emergency or when the tenant agrees to let the landlord enter, at the time of entry.

A landlord can also enter a tenant's unit without telling the tenant ahead of time, but only between the hours of 8 a.m. and 8 p.m., if the tenancy agreement requires the landlord to clean the rental unit, or if the tenancy agreement is ending and the landlord is showing the rental unit to a potential new tenant.

It is illegal for a landlord to enter a tenant's unit without complying with the provisions of the Act.

Maintenance and Repairs

Landlords are responsible for providing and maintaining a tenant's rental unit in a good state of repair, and for complying with all health, safety, housing, and maintenance standards set out in applicable bylaws. The rental unit includes whatever comes with it, such as appliances, as well as all the common areas of the **residential complex**, such as the lobby, hallways, elevators, stairwells, and parking areas. Even if a tenant was aware of a problem or maintenance issue before agreeing to rent the unit, the landlord must still take care of it. A landlord cannot, for example, refuse to fix a broken appliance just because the tenant knew it was broken before the tenant moved in. The landlord must provide the tenant with working appliances, not new or improved ones. This means that a landlord can replace a broken appliance that is beyond repair with a used appliance, as long as it works, and the tenant cannot insist on a new or better model.

If a tenant has a repair or maintenance problem in the rental unit, the tenant should notify the landlord of the problem, in writing, and ask the landlord to look after it. If the landlord does not fix the problem within a reasonable amount of time, the tenant may start an application at the Board for an order determining that the landlord has breached his or her repair and maintenance obligations under the Act. There are a number of different remedies the Board can order in this situation, the most common being an **abatement of rent** and/or an order requiring the landlord to repair or replace something in the rental unit by a certain date.

Many tenants who need repairs in their rental unit are tempted to withhold rent until the landlord completes the repairs. Tenants should not do this because the landlord will likely treat it as non-payment of rent and start eviction proceedings.

Tenants are responsible for any damage to the rental unit or the residential complex that is caused by them or their guests, whether intentionally or by accident. If a tenant fails to repair or pay for any such damage, the landlord may start an application at the Board not only for an order requiring the tenant to pay the cost of repairing the damage but also for an order to terminate the tenancy and evict the tenant.

Tenants are also responsible for keeping their rental unit reasonably clean. This does not mean they must be tidy, but rather that their place cannot be so filthy that it poses a health or safety risk to others.

Rent and Rent Control

There is no rent control on an empty rental unit, and a landlord is therefore free to charge a new tenant whatever amount of rent the landlord wants. The only exception to this rule is if the Board has ordered the landlord to complete certain repairs or maintenance in the rental unit. In this case, the landlord must charge a new tenant the same amount of rent as the previous tenant, but may increase the rent once the landlord completes the required work and removes the order.

The tenancy agreement will specify the amount of rent and when rent payments are due. It should also specify whether the rent includes any services, such as parking, electricity, heat, or cable.

Once a tenant moves into the rental unit, rent control takes effect and, in most cases, the landlord can increase the rent only once every 12 months by the rent increase **guideline**, which is set by the Ontario government every year. The guideline is expressed as a percentage and is the maximum percentage by which a landlord can raise the tenant's rent without obtaining approval from the Board. For example, assume the guideline for year 0 is 1.3 percent. During year 0, a landlord can increase a tenant's rent by 1.3 percent, assuming it has been 12 months since the tenant moved in or since the tenant's rent was last increased. For a tenant paying $1,000.00 per month, the increased rent will be $1,013.00. Even though landlords do not need approval for a guideline rent increase, they do have to provide the tenant with written notice of the rent increase at least 90 days before the date on which the increase is to take effect. If a tenant does not receive the required notice from his or her landlord, the tenant does not have to pay the increased rent.

In limited circumstances, the landlord and tenant can agree to increase the rent if, for example, the landlord offers to make major repairs or renovations in the rental unit, buy new equipment for the rental unit, or provide the tenant with a parking space or a new service or item such as satellite television, an air conditioner or a locker.

If the landlord wants to increase the rent above the guideline and cannot do so by agreement with the tenant, the landlord must start an application at the Board for an order approving the increase above the guideline. A landlord can apply for an increase above the guideline if his property taxes or utility costs have significantly increased, if he has completed necessary major repairs or renovations, or if he has incurred costs related to security services carried out by persons who are not employed by him. The landlord cannot increase a tenant's rent above the guideline amount without an order from the Board.

Payment of Rent

Rent is due on the date set out in the tenancy agreement, which is usually the first day of each month. Tenants pay their rent in advance, which means that the September 1st rent payment, for example, represents rent for the month of September, not August. If the tenant does not pay the rent in full, on or before the date it is due, the landlord is entitled to start proceedings to terminate the tenancy and evict the tenant for non-payment of rent. As you will see later, however, the tenant is given an opportunity to pay the rent owing and stop further proceedings.

Residential landlords do not have the right to seize any of the tenant's personal property in the rental unit as security for the payment of **arrears of rent**. This is known as **distraint** and is available only for commercial landlords. Residential landlords also do not have the right to charge the tenant **accelerated rent** under any circumstances.

Tenants usually pay their rent by cheque or cash. Tenants can choose to pay their rent by post-dated cheques or automatic payments (credit card or bank account debits) but landlords cannot insist that tenants pay by either of these methods. Landlords can request it, but tenants are entitled to refuse. If a tenant (or former tenant) asks the landlord for a receipt for any rent payments, the landlord must provide it, free of charge.

Last Month's Rent Deposit

On or before the date the tenancy starts, the tenant must give the landlord the first month's rent as well as a **last month's rent deposit**. The landlord can use the last month's rent deposit only as the rent payment for the last month of the tenancy, and for no other reason. For example, the landlord cannot use a tenant's last month's rent deposit to pay for damage caused by the tenant. When a tenant's rent increases, the landlord can ask the tenant to increase the amount of the last month's rent deposit to bring it up to the same amount as the new rent. Landlords are required to pay tenants interest on the rent deposit once a year. The interest rate is the same as the rent increase guideline. The practical effect of this is that in most cases, the amount owing to a tenant for interest on the last month's rent deposit will be offset by the amount owing to the landlord for increasing the deposit to the same amount as the new rent.

The last month's rent deposit is the only type of **security deposit** the landlord can require from a new tenant. A landlord is not allowed to charge the tenant a damage deposit or any other type of charge or fee as a condition of entering the tenancy agreement. However, the regulations made under the Act permit a landlord to ask a tenant for a key or remote entry card deposit, which cannot be more that it would cost to replace them and which must be refunded when the key or card is returned. The landlord can also charge the tenant the bank charges and an administrative charge not exceeding $20 for any NSF cheque.

Vital Services; Reasonable Enjoyment; Locking System

Landlords are not allowed to withhold or interfere with the reasonable supply of any **vital service** that they are obligated to provide under the tenancy agreement. Vital services include heat (from September 1 to June 15), electricity, gas, and water. Landlords are also not allowed to harass, obstruct, coerce or threaten tenants, or to interfere with the reasonable enjoyment of the rental unit or residential complex by a tenant or members of his or her household. Finally, a landlord is not allowed to change the locks on any doors in the rental unit or residential complex without giving the tenant replacement keys. If the landlord breaches any of these obligations, the tenant can apply to the Board for relief.

ASSIGNMENT AND SUBLETTING

Assignment and subletting are different and are treated differently under the Act. A **sublet** occurs when a tenant moves out of the rental unit temporarily and plans to move back into the unit before the end of the tenancy. The tenant finds someone else, called a **subtenant**, to live in the unit and pay rent during the tenant's absence. An **assignment** occurs when the tenant moves out of the rental unit permanently and transfers the tenancy to someone else, called an **assignee**. For example, assume that Lianisse, a tenant in Toronto with a fixed-term tenancy for one year that expires on March 31, accepts a part-time employment contract in Nova Scotia, commencing July 1. Assuming that Lianisse plans to move back into her rental unit when her contract ends, she will need to sublet her tenancy. If, on the other hand, her contract becomes permanent and she decides not to move back to Toronto at all, she will need to assign her tenancy. A tenant can sublet or assign the rental unit to someone else with the landlord's consent. The law protects the landlord's right to control who lives in his or her rental property and gives the landlord the right to withhold consent to a sublet or assignment of the unit to a potential subtenant or assignee, but only on reasonable grounds.

In an assignment, the landlord is also given the right to refuse consent to any assignment at all, regardless of who the potential assignee is, and the reason doesn't matter. This is because the law recognizes that a landlord can increase the rent charged only for a new tenant, but not for an assignee. Therefore, the provisions dealing with assignment protect the landlord's right to decide, based on **market rent**, whether or not to consent to the assignment, even before the tenant proposes a potential assignee. However, if the landlord refuses to consent to any assignment at all, the tenant is given the right to terminate the tenancy. For example, assume that Lucy is a landlord and one of her tenants, Jose, asks if he can assign his rental unit. If Jose's rent is well below market rent, and Lucy says no, Jose will terminate the tenancy, and Lucy will then be able to enter in to a new tenancy agreement and charge market rent. If, on the other hand, Jose's rent is well above market rent and **vacancy rates** in the area are high, Lucy will want Jose to assign the tenancy agreement to someone else. In this case, even if Lucy agrees to the idea of an assignment, she still has the right to refuse a potential assignee, but only on reasonable grounds.

If a tenant asks the landlord to consent to an assignment of the tenancy and the landlord does not respond within 7 days, the tenant has the right to terminate the tenancy on 30 days' notice to the landlord.

After an assignment, the assignee is responsible to the landlord for any breach of the tenancy agreement from the date of the assignment and may enforce against the landlord any of the landlord's obligations under the tenancy agreement or the Act. The original tenant is released from all future obligations but remains responsible to the landlord for any breaches that occurred before the assignment took place.

After a sublet, the subtenant is responsible to the tenant for the subtenant's obligations under the subletting agreement, and the original tenant continues to be responsible to the landlord for the payment of rent and for the tenant's other obligations under the tenancy agreement or the Act. A tenant cannot charge a subtenant a higher rent, or collect any kind of fee or deposit from the subtenant.

Sometimes a tenant will assign or sublet the tenancy without telling the landlord. The Act provides that any assignment or sublet that takes place without the landlord's consent is an unauthorized sublet or assignment. A landlord who finds out about an unauthorized sublet or assignment may apply to the Board to have the subtenant or assignee evicted. Alternatively, the landlord may negotiate a new tenancy agreement with the subtenant or assignee.

TERMINATING A TENANCY

Termination by the Tenant

Tenants can move out of the rental unit whenever they want but must give proper notice to the landlord, in accordance with the Act. The amount of notice a tenant must give is determined by the type of tenancy the tenant has. If the tenant has a fixed-term tenancy, the tenant must give the landlord at least 60 days' notice to terminate the tenancy effective the last day of the fixed-term tenancy. Even if the tenant gives more than 60 days' notice, the tenant cannot terminate the tenancy earlier than the date the fixed-term tenancy ends.

For example, assume that Carlos is a tenant with a fixed-term tenancy that expires on June 30. If Carlos wants to terminate his tenancy, he must give notice to his landlord by no later than May 1, for the tenancy to terminate effective the last day of his tenancy, or June 30. Even if Carlos gives notice to his landlord well before May 1, for example on January 1, his tenancy will still terminate effective June 30, because it is the last day of his fixed-term tenancy.

If a tenant with a monthly periodic tenancy wants to move out, the tenant must give the landlord at least 60 days' notice to terminate the tenancy effective the last day of the relevant month. In other words, the tenant counts 60 days from the date notice is given, and the earliest day the tenancy can be terminated is the last day of that month. For example, assume that Juanita is a tenant with a monthly periodic tenancy. If she gives her landlord notice on May 14, the earliest date she can terminate her tenancy is July 31. If on the other hand Juanita knows that she wants to terminate her tenancy effective the last day of a particular month, she must count backwards 60 days to determine the latest date by which she must give her landlord notice. For example, if she wants to move out on July 31, she must give her landlord notice by no later than June 1. Because February has only 28 days, the Act provides an exception to the 60-day notice period when the month of February is involved. It basically treats February as if it has 30 days.

If a tenant moves out without giving proper notice, the tenancy ends on the date the landlord rents the unit to a new tenant, or the earliest date the tenant can terminate the tenancy pursuant to the Act, whichever is earlier, and the tenant will be responsible to pay the rent owing up to this date. For instance, assume that Juanita (from the above example) forgot to give her landlord notice on or before June 1 and does not give notice until June 10. Unless Juanita's landlord finds a new tenant who can move in on August 1, Juanita's tenancy will end on August 31, which is the earliest date she can terminate her tenancy if she gives notice June 10. Juanita will be responsible for the rent owing for the month of August, even if she moves out at the end of July. The only way Juanita can avoid responsibility for the additional month's rent is if her landlord agrees to let her out of the tenancy agreement early, which the landlord may be willing to do if the tenant's rent is below market rent.

A tenant who gives notice to terminate the tenancy, or who reaches an agreement with the landlord to terminate the tenancy, cannot change his or her mind and must move out of the rental unit on or before the date the tenancy terminates. If the tenant does not move out of the rental unit on or before the date the tenancy ends by notice or agreement, the landlord can start an application at the Board for an order terminating the tenancy and evicting the tenant.

A tenant may also be able to terminate his or her tenancy by starting an application at the Board for an order ending the tenancy agreement because the landlord breached his/her obligations under the Act. If, for example, a landlord harasses a tenant, fails to maintain the rental property, alters the locking system, enters a tenant's unit illegally, withholds vital services, or interferes with a tenant's reasonable enjoyment of the rental property, one of the possible orders the Board can make is an order terminating the tenancy. The tenant will have to convince the Board that termination is a reasonable remedy in the circumstances.

Termination by the Landlord

Introduction

As discussed earlier, tenants have security of tenure, which means that the landlord can terminate a tenancy only in accordance with the Act. While the law protects tenants against unlawful evictions, it also recognizes that, in certain circumstances, termination of a tenancy by a landlord is necessary or justified. Therefore, the Act provides landlords with the right to terminate tenancies, but only for the reasons specified in the Act. Some of the reasons are based on the behaviour of the tenant, and are referred to as "fault" or "for cause" reasons. These reasons include such behaviour as causing damage or committing an illegal act in the rental property. If a landlord has a "for cause" reason, the landlord is allowed to terminate the tenancy early, in other words, before the end of a fixed term or period of the tenancy agreement.

Other reasons set out in the Act allow the landlord to terminate a tenancy even though the tenant has not done anything wrong. The Act recognizes that termination is justified in some circumstances, not because of the tenant's behaviour, but because of a legitimate need or interest of the landlord, such as if the rental property is going to be demolished or converted to a non-residential use. These reasons are often referred to as "no fault" reasons and allow the landlord to terminate the tenancy but, in this case, not before the end of a fixed term or period of the tenancy agreement. For both "no fault" and "for cause" reasons, the landlord must give the tenant proper notice of termination, in accordance with the Act.

Early Termination by the Landlord

A landlord may terminate a tenancy early (before the end of a fixed term or period of the tenancy agreement) only for a "for cause" reason specified in the Act. The Act permits early termination by the landlord if the tenant

- does not pay the rent in full,
- commits an illegal act in the rental unit or residential complex,
- does something in the rental unit or residential complex that impairs the safety of other tenants or the landlord,
- misrepresents his/her income (applies to subsidized or public housing only),
- causes damage to the rental unit or residential complex,
- substantially interferes with the reasonable enjoyment of other tenants or the landlord, or
- lets too many people live in the rental unit,

Having an animal in the rental unit is not, by itself, a ground for early termination. Tenants are allowed to have pets, even if they signed a tenancy agreement with a no-pet clause. Any clause that prohibits the presence of animals in the rental unit is deemed to be void under the Act.

The Act does, however, recognize that a "for cause" reason for terminating a tenancy early may be grounded on the presence or behaviour of an animal in the residential complex. It deals with applications based on animals in a separate provision, which is very complicated and confusing, but seems to suggest that a tenant can be evicted for owning a pet only if the pet is damaging the rental property, disturbing the landlord or other tenants, or causing the landlord or other tenants to suffer a serious allergic reaction. The provision also suggests that a tenant can be evicted if the breed or species of the tenant's pet is inherently dangerous.

If a landlord has a "for cause" reason to terminate the tenancy early, the landlord cannot attempt to evict the tenant him/herself by, for example, changing the tenant's locks or telling the tenant to move out. Instead, the landlord must start proceedings to terminate the tenancy and evict the tenant, following the specific procedures set out in the Act.

The first thing the landlord must do is to give the tenant a form called the **notice of termination**. There are different notice forms, depending on the reason for terminating the tenancy. For example, when a tenant has not paid rent, the landlord must use the "Notice to End a Tenancy Early for Non-payment of Rent" (also known as the form "N4"). All the notice forms can be downloaded from the Board's website. The notice of termination must set out the reasons why the landlord is terminating the tenancy and must specify the date the tenancy is being terminated. This date is called the termination date. Each "for cause" reason defined in the Act will set out how to determine the earliest possible termination date to insert in the notice of termination. For example, the earliest termination date that can be inserted in the form N4 is

EXHIBIT 37.2

Reasons for Early Termination by the Landlord

REASON FOR EARLY TERMINATION	RELEVANT SECTION OF ACT	EARLIEST TERMINATION DATE TO INSERT IN NOTICE OF TERMINATION*	AVAILABLE REMEDY PERIOD (AFTER RECEIVING NOTICE)
Non-Payment of Rent	59(1)	14th day after notice is given to tenant	14 days
Misrepresentation of Income	60(1)	20th day after notice is given to tenant	None
Illegal Act	61(1)	20th day after notice is given to tenant (10th day if illegal drugs are involved)	None
Damage	62(1)	20th day after notice is given to tenant	7 days
Extreme/ Wilful Damage	63(1)	10th day after notice is given to tenant	None
Substantial Interference with Reasonable Enjoyment	64(1)	20th day after notice is given to tenant	7 days
Substantial Interference with Reasonable Enjoyment (Landlord resides in building AND building contains not more than 3 units.)	65(1)	10th day after notice is given to tenant	None
Impairs Safety	66(1)	10th day after notice is given to tenant	None
Too Many Persons	67(1)	20th day after notice is given to tenant	7 days
Further Contravention (previous notice of termination under s. 62, 64, or 67 became void and within 6 months new ground arises under sections 60, 61, 62, 64, or 67)	68(1)	14th day after notice is given to tenant	None

* Add 5 days if the notice is going to be mailed to the tenant

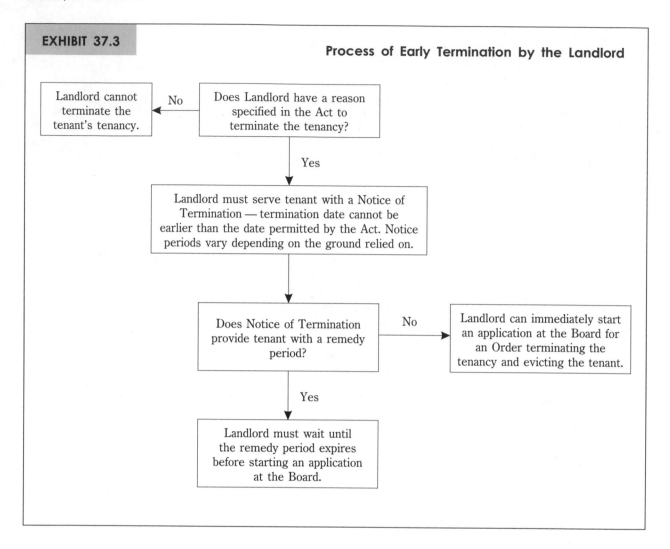

EXHIBIT 37.3

Process of Early Termination by the Landlord

Does Landlord have a reason specified in the Act to terminate the tenancy?

No → Landlord cannot terminate the tenant's tenancy.

Yes ↓

Landlord must serve tenant with a Notice of Termination — termination date cannot be earlier than the date permitted by the Act. Notice periods vary depending on the ground relied on.

↓

Does Notice of Termination provide tenant with a remedy period?

No → Landlord can immediately start an application at the Board for an Order terminating the tenancy and evicting the tenant.

Yes ↓

Landlord must wait until the remedy period expires before starting an application at the Board.

the 14th day after the date notice is given to the tenant (unless it's a daily or weekly tenancy, in which case it's the 7th day). In other words, if the landlord is giving a form N4 to a monthly tenant on September 5, the earliest termination date that the landlord can insert in the form N4 is September 19. (When counting days, do not include the day the notice is given, but do include the termination date. Add 5 days if the notice is going to be mailed to the tenant.)

Some "for cause" reasons allow the tenant to avoid further proceedings by doing something that is set out in the notice by a specific date. For example, the form N4 tells the tenant to either move out of the rental unit, or pay all the rent owing to the landlord, on or before the termination date set out in the notice. For each "for cause" reason that allows a tenant to do something to remedy the problem and stop further proceedings, the Act sets out what the tenant must do, and by when he/she must do it. The notice of termination form given to the tenant also contains this information.

If a tenant does not comply with the notice of termination, the landlord can start an application at the Board for an order terminating the tenancy and evicting the tenant. The application can be started as soon as the deadline for doing what is required to remedy the problem has expired.

If there is nothing the tenant can do to remedy the problem, for instance, if the tenant has committed an illegal act, then the tenant will be unable to avoid further proceedings. In this situation, the landlord can start an applica-

Notice to End a Tenancy Early for Non-Payment of Rent (Form N4): An Example

EXHIBIT 37.4

Louis Lopez is the owner of a duplex located at 123 Majestic Road West, Toronto, ON, M5N 3Z9. Trina Thompson is the tenant in unit #2. Trina's monthly rent is $1,000, due on the first of each month. Trina did not pay the rent due on September 1, year 0. Louis gives Trina the notice of termination on September 5, year 0.

Louis lives in unit #1. His phone number is 416-222-2222 and his e-mail address is <louis.lopez@hotmail.com>.

Notice To End a Tenancy Early For Non-payment of Rent

Form N4

To: (Tenant's name)	**From:** (Landlord's name)
Trina Thompson	Louis Lopez

This is a legal notice that could lead to you being evicted from your home.

Address of the Rental Unit

Street Number: 1 2 3   Street Name: M A J E S T I C

Street Type (e.g. Street, Avenue, Road): R O A D   Direction (e.g. East): W E S T   Unit/Apt./Suite: 2

Municipality (city, town, etc.): T O R O N T O   Province: O N   Postal Code: M 5 N 3 Z 9

This information is from your landlord:

I am giving you this notice because I believe you owe me $ 1,000.00 in rent.

See the table on the next page for the details about how I calculated this amount.

I can apply to the Landlord and Tenant Board to have you evicted if you do not:

- **pay this amount* by** 1 9 / 0 9 / 0 0 0 0 (dd / mm / yyyy) This date is called the **termination date**.

or

- **move out by the termination date**

* If another rent payment comes due on or before the date you make the above payment to your landlord, you must also pay this extra amount.

WHAT YOU NEED TO KNOW

The following information is provided by the Landlord and Tenant Board

The termination date

The date that the landlord gives you in this notice to pay or move out must be at least:
- 14 days after the landlord gives you the notice, if you rent by the month or year, or
- 7 days after the landlord gives you the notice, if you rent by the day or week.

What if you agree with the notice

If you agree that you owe the amount that the landlord is claiming, you should pay this amount by the termination date in this notice. If you do so, this notice becomes void and the landlord cannot apply to the Board to evict you. If you do not pay the amount owing, and the landlord applies to the Board to evict you, you will likely have to pay the landlord's filing fee of $170.00, plus what you owe.

If you move out by the date in this notice, your tenancy will end on the termination date. However, you may still owe money to your landlord. Your landlord will not be able to apply to the Board but they may still take you to Court for this money.

What if you disagree with the notice

If you disagree with what the landlord has put in this notice, you do not have to move out. You could talk to your landlord. You may also want to get legal advice. If you cannot work things out, and the landlord applies to the Board, you will be able to go to a hearing and explain why you disagree.

EXHIBIT 37.4 (continued)

Notice to End a Tenancy Early for Non-Payment of Rent (Form N4): An Example

How you will know if the landlord applies to the Board	The earliest date that the landlord can apply to the Board is the day after the termination date in this notice. If the landlord does apply, the Board will schedule a hearing and send you a letter. The landlord must also give you a copy of the Notice of Hearing and the application.
What you can do if the landlord applies to the Board	• Get legal advice immediately; you may be eligible for legal aid services. • Talk to your landlord about working out a payment plan. • Go to the hearing where you can respond to your landlord's claims; in most cases, before the hearing starts you can also talk to a Board mediator about mediating a payment plan.
How to get more information	For more information about this notice or about your rights, you can contact the Landlord and Tenant Board. You can reach the Board by phone at **416-645-8080** or toll-free at **1-888-332-3234**. You can also visit the Board's website at **www.LTB.gov.on.ca**.

This table is completed by the landlord to show how they calculated the total amount of rent claimed on page 1:

Rent Period		Rent Charged $	Rent Paid $	Rent Owing $
From: (dd/mm/yyyy)	To: (dd/mm/yyyy)			
01/09/0000	30/09/0000	1,000.00	,0.00	1,000.00
//	//	,.	,.	,.
//	//	,.	,.	,.
			Total Rent Owing $	1,000.00

Signature   ☒ Landlord   ☐ Agent

Signature	Date (dd/mm/yyyy)
Louis Lopez	05/09/0000

First Name: L O U I S

Last Name: L O P E Z

Company Name (if applicable):

Mailing Address: 1 2 3 M A J E S T I C R O A D W E S T

Unit/Apt./Suite: 1   Municipality (city, town, etc.): T O R O N T O   Province: O N

Postal Code: M 5 N 3 Z 9   Phone Number: (4 1 6) 2 2 2 2 2 2 2   Fax Number: ( )

E-mail Address: l o u i s . l o p e z @ h o t m a i l . c o m

10101

tion at the Board for an order terminating the tenancy and evicting the tenant immediately after giving the notice of termination to the tenant.

Termination by the Landlord at the End of a Fixed Term or Period

The Act provides additional grounds for a landlord to terminate the tenancy, but for these grounds, termination cannot be effective before the end of a fixed term or period of the tenancy. These grounds deal with situations where the landlord requires possession of the rental unit for reasons that, with one exception, have nothing to do with the tenant's behaviour. They are referred to as "no fault" grounds and include the following reasons:

- The landlord personally requires possession of the property (for him/herself, a member of his/her immediate family, or their caregiver).

- The landlord has agreed to sell the property and the purchaser, a member of his/her immediate family, or their caregiver want to move into the rental unit (this only applies if the residential complex contains three or fewer rental units).

- The landlord plans to demolish, carry out extensive repairs or renovations, or convert the rental property to a non-residential use.

The landlord can also terminate the tenancy at the end of the fixed term or period if the tenant is persistently late in paying the rent. Even though this reason *is* related to the tenant's behaviour, the Act includes it with the other "no fault" reasons for termination. Presumably this is because the rent is being paid, albeit late.

To proceed with termination for any of these reasons, the landlord must follow the specific procedures set out in the Act, which are generally the same as those discussed above for terminating a tenancy early. The "no fault" reasons provide quite lengthy notice periods (the longest being 120 days), and the termination date will always be at the end of a fixed term or period of the tenancy. For example, assume that Luisa is a landlord who wants to terminate a tenant's monthly tenancy because she intends to move into the rental unit. Luisa must give the tenant at least 60 days' notice, and the termination date will be on the last day of the month. If Luisa gives notice to her tenant on September 10, the earliest possible termination date is November 30. For all of the "no fault" reasons, the landlord can start an application at the Board immediately after giving the notice of termination to the tenant. However, the tenancy will not be terminated any earlier than the termination date set out in the notice. For instance, assume that the hearing for Luisa's application is in early October. Even if the Board allows her application, the Board will not order the termination date to be any earlier than November 30.

The End of the Tenancy

Even though the notice of termination tells the tenant that he or she must move out of the rental unit by the termination date, the tenant does not in fact have to move out. However, if the tenant does not move out and has not complied with any available remedy within the prescribed period of time, then the landlord can start an application at the Board for an order terminating the tenancy and evicting the tenant.

A tenant must be in possession of the rental unit at the time the landlord starts the application. If a tenant is no longer living in the rental unit, the Board has no jurisdiction over the matter.

To start an application, a Landlord must file a document, called the **application,** with the Board, together with a copy of the Notice of Termination the landlord previously gave to the tenant. While the Notice of Termination explains to the tenant the reasons for terminating the tenancy, the application explains to the Board what order the landlord is asking the Board to make. There are different types of applications about eviction depending on the reason for eviction, which are all available on the Board's website. When a landlord files an application, the Board schedules a hearing so that the landlord and tenant can present their case to an **adjudicator** who will make a decision about the application. The Landlord must give the tenant a copy of the application together with a **Notice of Hearing**, setting out the time and location of the Board hearing. As mentioned above, if the adjudicator decides to terminate the tenancy and evict the tenant, the tenancy will end on the termination date specified in the notice of termination.

PROCEEDINGS AT THE LANDLORD AND TENANT BOARD

Overview of the Board

The Board is the **administrative tribunal** that administers the Act and resolves disputes between residential landlords and tenants. It has exclusive jurisdiction over all landlord and tenant applications under the Act that come within the Board's monetary jurisdiction, which currently is $25,000. The Board also controls rent increases for most residential tenancies in Ontario. The Board maintains a website (www.ltb.gov.on.ca) that provides a great deal of information for both landlords and tenants about their rights and responsibilities under the Act. The website also provides a link to the Act and regulations, as well as to the Board's **Rules of Practice**, **Interpretation Guidelines** and selected decisions.

Types of Applications

Most applications that are started at the Board are landlord applications. In the Board's most recent fiscal year, 91 percent of applications filed were by landlords and only 9 percent were by tenants.[5] The majority of landlord applications are for termination of the tenancy and eviction. Of these, close to 80 percent involve arrears of rent.[6] If an application involves arrears of rent, a tenant is allowed to raise issues the tenant could have raised had the tenant started his or her own application, such as maintenance and repair issues, harassment, or illegal entry by the landlord.

The most common types of tenant applications are applications about maintenance, or about tenant rights such as the landlord interfering with the tenant's reasonable enjoyment of the rental unit.

The parties to an application are referred to as the **applicant** and the **respondent**.

The Hearing

Hearings at the Board are resolved by a government-appointed adjudicator, known as a Member of the Board. At the hearing, the Member listens to what each party has to say about the application. The applicant tries to convince the Member that the application should be granted, while the respondent tries to persuade the Member that it should not. This is done by presenting evidence that supports a party's case, such as documents, pictures, or the testimony of a witness. Parties to an application can represent themselves or have an agent act on their behalf. An agent can be a paralegal, lawyer or even a party's friend or relative. After both parties have presented

---

[5] Landlord and Tenant Board Annual Report 2009–2010, p. 16
[6] *Ibid.*, p. 18

their case, the Member will make a final decision about the application. A written copy of the decision, called an order, will be mailed to both the applicant and respondent.

Mediation and Other Settlements

The Board strongly encourages parties to try and resolve their dispute through mediation with a Board Mediator and employs mediators who are readily available to help parties reach an agreement. An important benefit of resolving an application through mediation as opposed to adjudication is that only an agreement mediated with a Board Mediator may override the provisions of the Act. For example, if the parties choose to meet with a Board Mediator, their mediated agreement can provide that the tenant will pay rent by post-dated cheques, or that the tenant will not have a pet in the rental unit. At a hearing, the Board Member cannot make an order containing these terms. The Board Member's decision must be within the limits of the Act.

If the parties resolve the entire application through mediation, the hearing is cancelled.

Otherwise, the hearing goes ahead and the member makes a final decision about the application. The mediation process is confidential meaning that the Board Member cannot be told anything that was said by the parties during their session with the mediator. All the Board Member will know is that the parties attempted mediation but were unable to resolve their dispute.

Parties to an application can also try to resolve their dispute themselves, without the assistance of a Board Mediator. If the parties reach an agreement, they can ask the Board Member to incorporate the terms of their agreement into an order, called a consent order.

If a party breaches any term of a mediated agreement or other settlement, the other party can pursue the remedies available under the Act. In most cases, either party can ask the Board to re-open the application and schedule a new hearing. In addition, landlords usually have the right to bring an **ex-parte application** to terminate the tenancy and evict the tenant when the tenant breaches a term of the mediated agreement or consent order.

Reviews, Amendments, and Appeals

Generally speaking, an order of the Board is final and binding on the parties to an application. However, the Act does allow a party to request an amendment, review or appeal of an order, in limited circumstances. For instance, if a party thinks the order contains a clerical error such as a misspelled name or incorrect calculation, the party can ask the Board to amend the order. The Board Member who prepared the order will correct any errors and replace the order with an amended order, which will be mailed to both parties. If a party thinks the order contains a more serious error, such as an error in how the member interpreted the law, then the party can ask the Board to review the Member's order. The order will be reviewed by a different member and, if he/she agrees that a serious error may have occurred, a new hearing will be scheduled to allow the parties to participate. Finally, a party can appeal an order of the Board to the Divisional Court (of the Superior Court of Justice) but only on a **question of law.**

Enforcing Board Orders

If a tenant does not move out as ordered by the Board, the landlord must file the Board order with the Sheriff's office. Only the Sheriff can enforce orders for eviction.

A tenant can stop the eviction only by paying all amounts owing to the landlord, including the Sheriff's fees, any time before the Sheriff enforces the

Board order. Once the Sheriff enforces the eviction order by changing the locks, the landlord regains possession of the rental unit.

A landlord must give a tenant who has been evicted the opportunity to collect his or her personal belongings that were left in the rental unit. The tenant has the right to come and pick them up any time between 8 a.m. and 8 p.m. during the 72 hours after the Sheriff has changed the locks.

If the Board order provides for the payment of money, the order is enforced using the enforcement mechanisms of the Small Claims Court, assuming the amount is not more than $25,000. The order is treated as if it were an order of the Small Claims Court. In other words, you do not need to get another order from the Small Claims Court to be able to enforce the Board order.

CHAPTER SUMMARY

This chapter provided an overview of the residential landlord and tenant relationship in Ontario. It examined the rights and responsibilities of both landlords and tenants under the Act, and included a discussion about how those rights and responsibilities are enforced. This chapter looked at how the law protects tenants against illegal evictions and rent increases, and guarantees their rights to privacy and exclusive possession of the rental unit. It also looked at how the law protects a landlord's interest in the rental property and explained under what circumstances landlords can enter a tenant's rental unit during the tenancy. It also explained when landlords can terminate a tenant's tenancy and evict the tenant. This chapter examined how landlords and tenants resolve disputes and familiarized you with Board procedures, including starting an application, mediation and other settlements, and the hearing. Finally, this chapter talked about Board orders and explained how they are enforced.

GLOSSARY OF NEW TERMS AND KEY CONCEPTS

abatement of rent	A reduction in the amount of the tenant's rent.
accelerated rent	The full amount of rent payable for the entire fixed term of a tenancy.
adjudication	At the Board, the dispute resolution process that gives a government-appointed member the power to preside over a hearing and make a final decision or order about an application.
administrative tribunal	A quasi-judicial (almost like a court) independent agency established under federal or provincial legislation.
applicant	The person who starts an application at the Board.
application	The form that starts proceedings at the Board and explains what the applicant is asking the Board for.
arrears of rent	Unpaid rent owing to the landlord.
assignee	The person to whom a tenant transfers the rental unit when the tenant moves out permanently.
assignment	Occurs when a tenant moves out of the rental unit permanently, and transfers the tenancy to someone else.
distraint	A landlord's right to seize the tenant's property in the rental unit, as security for the payment of arrears of rent.
eviction	Lawful removal of a tenant from the rental unit.

exclusive possession	The right to live in the rental unit to the exclusion of everyone else, including the owner.
ex-parte application	An application that is started at the Board without notice to the respondent.
fixed-term tenancy	A tenancy with a specified start date and end date.
guideline	The maximum percentage by which a landlord can annually increase the tenant's rent, without obtaining approval from the Board.
interpretation guidelines	The Board's policy statements that explain how members interpret the Act and deal with issues that arise in applications.
last month's rent deposit	A one-month rental payment, which is to be applied to the last month of the tenancy.
market rent	The amount of rent a landlord can reasonably expect to get for a rental unit.
notice of hearing	The notice that sets out the time and place of a Board hearing.
notice of termination	The form a landlord uses to give notice to the tenant that the landlord intends to end the tenancy for the reasons set out in the notice.
NSF cheque	A cheque that is returned because there are not sufficient funds in the account.
periodic tenancy	A tenancy without a specific end date, which renews automatically on a weekly, monthly or yearly periodic basis.
question of law	A question that is answered by interpreting and applying the relevant law.
residential complex	A building or house in which one or more rental units are located, including all the common areas, services, and facilities.
respondent	The person against whom an application has been started.
Rules of Practice	Procedural rules that must be followed under the Act.
security deposit	Defined in the Act to mean "money, property or a right paid or given by, or on behalf of, a tenant of a rental unit to a landlord or to anyone on the landlord's behalf to be held by or for the account of the landlord as security for the performance of an obligation or the payment of a liability of the tenant or to be returned to the tenant upon the happening of a condition".
security of tenure	Translated means: Security of the right to possess the property; provides tenants with legal protection against unlawful evictions.
sheriff	An officer of the superior court who is in charge of enforcing orders for eviction.
sublet	Occurs when a tenant moves out of the rental unit temporarily and gives someone else the right to live there for a prescribed amount of time.
subtenant	The person to whom a tenant gives the right to occupy the tenant's rental unit for a prescribed amount of time.
tenancy agreement	An oral, written or implied contract between a landlord and tenant for occupancy of a rental unit in exchange for the payment of rent; also known as a "lease agreement" or "lease".
vacancy rates	The percentage of rental units that are not occupied or rented at a given time.
vital service	Water, fuel, electricity, gas and, from September 1 to June 15, heat.

REVIEW QUESTIONS

1. What happens if there is a conflict between the terms of a tenancy agreement and the provisions of the *Residential Tenancies Act*?

2. How are disputes between residential landlords and tenants resolved?

3. A tenant pays $1,000.00 a month. When the tenant moves out, what will the rent be for a new tenant?

4. Can a landlord enter a tenant's rental unit to carry out a repair?

5. Does a tenant have to move out of the rental unit when the tenant's fixed term expires?

6. Does a landlord need a reason to refuse consent to an assignment of the rental unit?

7. What does a landlord have to do if a tenant's oven stops working?

8. Can a landlord change the locks and evict a tenant who is running an illegal drug trafficking operation in the rental unit?

9. What types of deposit can a landlord charge a new tenant?

10. How can a landlord enforce an order for the payment of arrears of rent?

11. In a sublet, who is responsible for the payment of rent to the landlord, the original tenant or the subtenant?

12. Can a landlord ever terminate a tenancy when the tenant has not done anything wrong?

13. Can a mediated agreement contain terms that are inconsistent with the *Residential Tenancies Act*?

14. What should you do if you receive an order from the Board and see that your name has not been spelled correctly?

DISCUSSION QUESTIONS

1. What is the earliest date a tenant can terminate a fixed-term tenancy that expires November 30, Year 0, assuming notice to terminate is given to the landlord on April 15, Year 0?

2. What is the earliest date a tenant can terminate a monthly periodic tenancy, assuming notice to terminate is given to the landlord on April 15, Year 0?

3. Tony Tenant entered into a one-year lease with Lucy Landlord on July 1, 2007. Tony bought a house and wants to terminate his tenancy. His house will be ready to move into at the end of June, so Tony hopes to be able to end his tenancy and move out of the rental unit on June 30. What is the latest date by which Tony must give notice to Lucy?

4. Lucinda is the landlord of an apartment building and is having a problem with three of her tenants. The first tenant has not paid the rent that was due two weeks ago, the second tenant is selling illegal drugs from the rental unit, and the third tenant just got a puppy, even though the tenancy agreement prohibits tenants from having pets. Discuss what Lucinda can do regarding the problem with each of these three tenants.

5. Telusa Tenant lives in an apartment building owned by Lorenzo Landlord. Before Telusa entered into the tenancy agreement, she noticed that the ceiling in the living room was damaged. She showed Lorenzo this damage and assumed it would be repaired by the time she moved in. Lorenzo will not repair the damage because he says Telusa knew it was there when she agreed to rent the unit. Discuss Telusa's rights in this situation, explaining whether or not it matters that the damage existed before she entered into the tenancy agreement.

6. Olivia entered into a tenancy agreement that provided she could move in to the rental unit on September 1. At the end of August, Olivia was in a serious car accident and was hospitalized for almost 8 weeks. She was unable to move into the rental unit until November 1. Who is responsible for the rent for the months of September and October?

7. Mohammed and Lucerne are tenants living in a three-bedroom house owned by Lionice. The rent is $1,000 per month, and they each give Lionice $500 per month. Lionice wants to rent the third bedroom in the house to another tenant so that Lionice can collect more rent. Explain whether or not Lionice can do this.

8. Sanjaya moved into an apartment in Toronto on September 1, Year 0 under a written lease for a fixed term of one year. While vacationing in Cuba at Christmas, Sanjaya met the love of his life and wants to return to Cuba as soon as possible. Discuss what Sanjaya can do if he wants to end his tenancy and move permanently to Cuba.

SUGGESTED READINGS

Butkus, Mavis J. *The 2011 Annotated Ontario Landlord and Tenant Statutes* (Toronto, Ontario: Carswell, 2010).

WEBSITES
Residential Tenancies Act: <http://www.canlii.ca/en/on/laws/stat/so-2006-c-17/latest/so-2006-c-17.html>
Landlord and Tenant Board: <http://www.ltb.gov.on.ca>
Community Legal Education Ontario (CLEO): <http://www.cleo.on.ca/english/index.htm>
Ontario Ministry of Municipal Affairs and Housing: <http://www.mah.gov.on.ca/>
Centre for Equality Rights in Accommodation (CERA): <http://www.equalityrights.org/cera/>
Landlord's Self Help-Centre: <http://www.landlordselfhelp.com/frontpage.asp>
Canada Mortgage and Housing Corporation: <http://www.cmhc.ca/>
Advocacy Centre for Tenants Ontario (ACTO): <http://www.acto.ca>
Federation of Metro Tenants' Associations: <http://www.torontotenants.org/>
Ontario Tenants Rights: <http://www.ontariotenants.ca/>

Index